ISBN 978-0-260-31456-7
PIBN 10981486

• DEPARTMENT OF THE AIR FORCE MANUAL — AFM 88-29
• DEPARTMENT OF THE ARMY TECHNICAL MANUAL — TM 5-785
• DEPARTMENT OF THE NAVY MANUAL — NAVFAC P-89

Facility Design and Planning

ENGINEERING WEATHER DATA

DEPARTMENTS OF THE AIR FORCE, THE ARMY, AND THE NAVY

1 JULY 1978

DEPARTMENTS OF THE AIR FORCE, THE ARMY,
AND THE NAVY
Washington DC 20330

AFM 88-29
TM 5-785
NAVFAC P-89
1 July 1978

Facility Design and Planning

ENGINEERING WEATHER DATA

This manual gives uniform engineering weather data for winter heating design, heating degree days, summer air conditioning design and criteria, for calculating energy consumption estimates, and cooling degree days.

Supersedes AFM 88-8, Chapter 6; TM 5-785; and NAFVAC P-89, 15 June 1967.
(See signature page for summary of changes.)
No of Printed Pages: 699
OPR: PREE (Oscar E. Richard, USAFETAC)
Approved by: Maj Gen W. D. Gilbert
Editor: Betty J. Nicholson
Distribution: (See page 6–10)

Chapter 6—Cooling Degree Day Data for Sites Outside the United States

The data in this manual were compiled by the Engineering Meteorology Section (ENE) of the USAF Environmental Technical Applications Center (USAFETAC), at the request of the Department of Defense (DOD). Air Force Directorate of Civil Engineering, U.S. Army Corps of Engineers and the Naval Facilities Engineering Command assisted in identifying the sites of interest to the Air Force, Army, and Navy respectively. The majority of sites listed are located at military installations. Data for locations other than those specifically listed in Chapters 1 through 4 may be obtained by written request, giving the coordinates and elevation of the desired site, to USAFETAC/ENE, Scott AFB IL 62225. USAFETAC, however, has the authority to provide such data only to DOD or its subordinate organizations and civilian contractors with military contracts. Requests for data for sites of nonmilitary governmental interest should be forwarded for processing to the National Climatic Center, Federal Building, Asheville NC 28801. Requests for data for sites of a nongovernmental interest should be obtained from a private consulting meteorologist. A list of their names and addresses may be obtained from the American Meteorological Society, 45 Beacon Street, Boston MA 02108.

Location. Stations are listed alphabetically—Chapter 1, 3, and 5 by state; Chapters 2, 4, and 6 by area and country. The latitude, longitude, and elevation for each station or site are given. In listing the stations in Chapter 3, it was attempted to list stations representative of the various climatic regimes experienced throughout the United States. In Chapter 4 an attempt was made to select stations representative of the various climatic regimes of major military interest outside the United States.

CHAPTER 1–WINTER DESIGN DATA FOR HEATING, AND SUMMER DESIGN AND CRITERIA DATA FOR AIR CONDITIONING FOR SITES IN THE UNITED STATES; AND CHAPTER 2–FOR SITES OUTSIDE THE UNITED STATES

Winter Design Data–Heating. These data are the dry bulb temperatures (°F) that are equalled or exceeded 99% and 97½% of the time, on the average, during the coldest 3 consecutive months. For the contiguous United States, these months have been standardized as December, January, and February, even through at a few sites, March was colder than December. The prevailing (Pvlg) wind direction is the wind direction occurring most frequently with the 97½% dry bulb winter design temperature. The mean wind speed (knots) is the average of those wind speed values which occur coincidently with the 97½% dry bulb winter design temperature.

Degree Days–Heating. Heating degree days are the mean annual number of degree days using a base of 65°F and a 30-year normal period of record when available.

Summer Design Data–Air Conditioning. These data are the dry bulb and wet bulb temperatures (°F) that are equalled or exceeded 1%, 2½% and 5% of the time, on the average, during the warmest 4 consecutive months, as determined from the monthly mean wet bulb temperature. For the contiguous United States, these months have been standardized as June, July, August, and September, even though at a few sites October was warmer than June. The mean coincident wet bulb temperatures (MCWB) listed with the 1%, 2½%, and 5% dry bulb summer design temperatures are the average of those wet bulb temperatures which occur coincidently with the respective dry bulb summer design temperatures. The mean daily range (difference between daily maximum and daily minimum temperature) is the average of all daily dry bulb temperature ranges for days on which the 2½% dry bulb summer design temperature is reached or exceeded. The prevailing (Pvlg) wind direction is the wind direction occurring most frequently with the 2½% dry bulb summer design temperature.

Summer Criteria Data–Air Conditioning. These data are the number of hours, on the average, that the dry bulb temperatures of 93°F and 80°F and the wet bulb temperatures of 73°F and 67°F are equalled or exceeded during the warmest 6 consecutive months as determined from the monthly mean wet bulb temperature. For the contiguous United States, these months have been standardized as May through October, even though at a few sites November was warmer than May.

CHAPTER 3–DATA FOR USE IN CALCULATING ENERGY CONSUMPTION ESTIMATES FOR SITES IN THE UNITED STATES; AND CHAPTER 4–FOR SITES OUTSIDE THE UNITED STATES

Any station listed in Chapter 3 or 4 had to have recorded 24 hourly observations per day for a period of at least 5 years. Due to rounding, the observation counts in the columns are not necessarily an exact count of the hours in an 8-hour period or for the month.

Dry Bulb Temperature Data. Temperature distributions are listed by 5 degree temperature intervals, by month, and annual. The distribution is further divided into 3 periods of the day, which define the major activity use of the installation; sleep (01–08 hrs), work (09–16 hrs), and recreation (17–00 hrs). Total observation columns list the distribution of temperature based on 24 hours per day.

Mean Coincident Wet Bulb Temperature Data. The mean coincident wet bulb

(MCWB) temperature value is the mean value of all those wet bulb temperatures which occur coincidently with the dry bulb temperatures in the particular 5 degree temperature interval. At the upper or warmer end of the mean coincident wet bulb distribution, the values occasionally reverse their trend because the highest wet bulb temperatures do not necessarily occur with the highest dry bulb temperatures.

CHAPTER 5—COOLING DEGREE DAY DATA FOR SITES IN THE UNITED STATES; AND CHAPTER 6—FOR SITES OUTSIDE THE UNITED STATES

Degree Day—Cooling. Cooling degree days are the mean annual number of cooling degree days using a base of 65°F and a 30-year normal period of record when available. Cooling degree days are the departure of the mean daily temperature above 65°F.

ABBREVIATIONS

'ing abbreviations, acronyms, and contractions are those used more than once in the station listing for chapters 1 through 6:

	Army Airfield
	Auxiliary Air Force Base
	Army Ammunition Plant
	Air Base
	Air Force
	Air Force Base
	Airfield
	Air Force Station
	Army Hospital
	Alberta
	Air National Guard
	Air National Guard Base
	Airport
	Air Station
	Auxiliary
	British Columbia
	Beach
	Center
	Coast Guard Air Station
	Coast Guard Station
	Chemical
	Complex
	County
	Communication
	Development
	Engineering
	Field
	Fort
	Fleet Weather Center
	Greater
	Hospital
	International Airport
	Island
	Manitoba
	Municipal Airport
'CRUITDEP	Marine Corps Recruiting Depot
	Material
	Marine Corps Air Station
	Mobile Construction Battalion
	Marine Corps Station
Mech	Mechanical
Med	Medical
Mem	Memorial
Mil	Military
Mod	Modification
Msl	Missile
Mt	Mountain
NAD	Naval Ammunition Depot
NAF	Naval Air Facility
NALF	Naval Auxiliary Landing Facility
NAS	Naval Air Station
NAVHOSP	Naval Hospital
NAVNATMEDCEN	Naval National Medical Center
NAVPHIBASE	Naval Amphibious Base
NAVSHIPYD	Naval Shipyard
NAVSTA	Naval Station
NAVSURFWPNCEN	Naval Surface Weapons Center
NB	Naval Base
NF	Naval Facility
Nfld	Newfoundland
No.	Number
NOP	Naval Ordnance Plant
NOS	Naval Ordnance Supply
NS	Nova Scotia
NSA	Naval Supply Annex
NSC	Naval Supply Center
NSGA	Naval Security Group Activity Office
NSRDC	Naval Ship Research and Development Center
NTC	Naval Training Center
NWT	Northwest Territories
Obsy	Observatory
Ont	Ontario
PG	Proving Ground
Pt	Point
Que	Quebec
RAF	Royal Air Force
Rec	Recreation
Res	Research
Rgnl	Regional
Rsvn	Reservation

. . . . Saskatchewan
. . . . Saint
. . . . Station
. . . . Terminal

USMA . . . . United States Military Academy
USNA . . . . United States Naval Academy
YT . . . . Yukon Territory

CHAPTER 1

WINTER DESIGN DATA FOR HEATING AND SUMMER DESIGN AND CRITERIA DATA FOR AIR CONDITIONING FOR SITES IN THE UNITED STATES

STATE	LOCATION			WINTER DESIGN DATA HEATING				DEGREE DAYS	SUMMER DESIGN DATA AIR CONDITIONING											SUMMER CRITERIA DATA AIR CONDITIONING			
				Dry Bulb					Dry Bulb								Wet Bulb			Dry Bulb		Wet Bulb	
Station	Lat	Long	Elev	99%	97.5%	Pvlg Wind	Mean Speed	Heating	1%	MCWB	2.5%	MCWB	Mean Daily Range	Pvlg Wind	5%	MCWB	1%	2.5%	5%	≥ 93°F	≥ 80°F	≥ 73°F	≥ 67°F
	° '	° '	feet	°F	°F	dir	knots	annual	°F	°F	°F	°F	°F	dir	°F	°F	°F	°F	°F	hrs	hrs	hrs	hrs
ALABAMA	N	W																					
Alabama Ordnance Works	33 20	86 21	430	19	23	SW	5	2806	97	77	94	76	25	SW	92	76	79	78	78	140	1251	1145	2620
Anniston Army Depot	33 37	85 58	765	18	22	SW	5	2806	97	77	94	76	25	SW	92	76	79	78	78	140	1251	1145	2620
Birmingham MAP	33 34	86 45	620	17	21	NNW	8	2844	96	74	94	75	23	WNW	92	74	78	77	76	116	1380	1033	2696
Brookley AFB/Mobile	30 38	88 04	26	26	29	N	8	1750	94	77	92	78	18	S	90	77	81	80	79	61	1697	2249	3505
Craig AFB/Selma	32 20	86 59	166	22	26	NNW	7	2155	97	78	95	77	21	WNW	93	77	81	80	79	196	1657	1821	3229
Dauphin Island AFS	30 15	88 06	5	31	35	N	9	1396	92	78	91	78	15	S	89	78	81	80	80	29	1833	2487	3600
Florence	34 48	87 40	581	17	21	NW	7	3199	97	74	94	74	23	NW	92	74	78	77	76	116	1380	1033	2696
Fort McClellan/Reilly AAF	33 43	85 47	790	18	22	SW	5	2806	97	77	94	76	25	SW	92	76	79	78	78	140	1251	1145	2620
Fort Rucker/Cairns AAF	31 16	85 43	305	23	27	NW	6	1968	94	76	92	76	20	W	91	76	80	79	78	75	1406	1591	3180
Gadsden	34 01	86 00	554	16	20	NNW	8	3059	96	75	94	75	23	WNW	92	74	78	77	76	116	1380	1033	2696
Gunter AFS	32 24	86 15	221	21	25	WNW	7	2153	95	77	94	77	21	W	92	76	80	79	78	126	1522	1485	3079
Hall ANG Station	31 19	85 27	400	23	27	NW	6	1968	94	76	92	76	20	W	91	76	80	79	78	75	1406	1591	3180
Hunter Loop Comm Facility	32 23	86 24	160	21	25	WNW	7	2153	95	77	94	77	21	W	92	76	80	79	78	126	1522	1485	3079
Huntsville	34 42	86 35	606	11	16	N	9	3302	95	75	93	74	23	SW	91	74	78	77	76	100	1288	846	2541
Maxwell AFB/Montgomery	32 23	86 22	169	21	25	WNW	7	2153	95	77	94	77	21	W	92	76	80	79	78	126	1522	1485	3079
Mobile/Bates Field	30 41	88 15	211	25	29	N	10	1684	95	77	93	77	20	N	91	76	80	79	78	93	1514	2086	3441
Montgomery/Dannelly Field	32 18	86 24	183	22	25	NW	7	2269	96	76	95	76	22	W	93	76	79	79	78	175	1579	1622	3128
Muscle Shoals	34 45	87 37	550	17	21	NW	7	3199	97	73	94	74	23	NW	92	74	78	77	76	116	1380	1033	2696
Redstone Arsenal	34 39	86 41	602	11	16	N	9	3302	95	75	93	74	23	SW	91	74	78	77	76	100	1288	846	2541
Selma use Craig AFB																							
Sheffield	34 46	87 42	480	17	21	NW	7	3199	97	74	94	74	23	NW	92	74	78	77	76	116	1380	1033	2696
Tuscaloosa MAP	33 13	87 37	169	20	23	N	5	2626	98	75	96	76	25	WNW	94	76	79	78	77	215	1436	1103	2549
ALASKA	N	W																					
Adak NAVSTA/Mitchell Field	51 53	176 39	19	20	23	W	7	8825	61	58	59	56	11	W	56	54	59	57	54	0	0	0	1
Anchorage IAP	61 10	150 01	114	-23	-18	SE	3	10911	71	59	68	58	18	WNW	66	56	60	59	57	0	0	0	0
Aniak	61 35	159 32	86	-44	-39	E	3	13412	76	61	71	59	25	NNW	68	57	62	60	58	0	10	0	1
Annette	55 02	131 34	110	13	17	NE	12	7053	74	61	70	59	17	NW	66	58	62	60	59	0	6	0	1
Anvil Mt	64 34	165 22	1100	-29	-27	N	8	14555	64	56	60	54	18	W	57	53	57	55	54	0	0	0	0
Attu/Casco Cove CGS	52 50	173E10	39	20	22	NW	12	8339	60	55	57	54	10	W	55	52	57	54	52	0	0	0	0
Aurora	62 24	145 02	1900	-41	-37	NNW	3	13593	76	59	73	57	31	SE	67	56	61	59	57	0	17	0	0
Barrow	71 18	156 47	31	-45	-41	SW	8	20265	57	53	53	50	16	SE	49	47	54	50	47	0	0	0	0
Barter Island	70 08	143 38	39	-45	-41	SW	7	19994	56	52	52	49	14	E	49	47	52	50	47	0	0	0	0
Bear Creek	65 15	151 55	1650	-40	-35	W	10	13861	77	60	73	59	22	WSW	70	57	63	60	59	0	6	0	0

ation	LOCATION					WINTER DESIGN DATA HEATING Dry Bulb				DEGREE DAYS	SUMMER DESIGN DATA AIR CONDITIONING Dry Bulb								Wet Bulb			SUMMER CRITERIA DATA AIR CONDITIONING Dry Bulb		Wet Bulb	
	Lat		Long		Elev	99%	97.5%	Pvlg Wind	Mean Speed	Heating	1%	MCWB	2.5%	MCWB	Mean Daily Range	Pvlg Wind	5%	MCWB	1%	2.5%	5%	≥ 93°F	≥ 80°F	≥ 73°F	≥ 67°F
	°	'	°	'	feet	°F	°F	dir	knots	annual	°F	°F	°F	°F	°F	dir	°F	°F	°F	°F	°F	hrs	hrs	hrs	hrs
CONT)	N		W																						
er Creek	63	03	141	49	2433	-51	-47	SW	2	14770	77	59	74	57	27	NW	71	56	61	59	57	0	12	0	1
el AFS	60	47	161	53	160	-32	-28	NNE	10	13203	74	60	69	58	20	N	66	57	62	59	57	0	4	0	2
el Aprt	60	47	161	48	125	-32	-28	NNE	10	13203	74	60	69	58	20	N	66	57	62	59	57		4		2
ies	66	55	151	31	644	-51	-45	NNW	4	15925	78	62	75	61	23	S	72	59	63	61	60		20		5
Delta/Allen AAF	64	00	145	44	1268	-48	-43	S	4	13698	80	61	76	60	24	N	73	58	62	60	59		30		1
Mountain	59	23	155	13	2150	-18	-13	N	10	12144	64	55	61	54	20	NW	57	52	57	54	53	0	0	0	0
k Rapids	63	29	145	50	2703	-35	-30	S	4	12553	77	59	73	58	20	N	70	56	60	58	57	0	11	0	0
r Lake AF Range	64	23	147	41	725	-50	-46	S	2	14068	80	61	77	59	27	N	74	59	63	61	60		38		4
ell Bay AFS	60	25	146	09	800	-5	0	NE	5	9765	67	57	63	57	22	SW	60	55	59	57	56		0		0
ion AFS	64	42	156	44	363	-47	-44	NW	3	14780	78	62	75	60	23	N	71	58	64	62	60		24		12
on Creek	64	18	146	32	1779	-42	-37	S	4	13298	79	60	75	59	24	N	72	57	61	59	58	0	22	0	1
Lisburne AFS	68	53	166	07	12	-34	-31	ESE	7	17063	60	53	56	51	13	SW	53	50	54	51	49	0	0	0	0
Newenham AFS	58	39	162	04	541	-14	-11	N	11	11481	60	54	58	53	10	SSE	56	52	55	54	53		0		0
Romanzof AFS	61	47	166	02	457	-17	-14	NE	18	13130	62	56	59	54	10	NE	57	52	57	54	52		0		0
Sarichef	54	36	164	55	560	9	12	NNW	14	9985	61	56	58	53	10	SSE	56	52	57	55	53		0		0
edral	63	23	143	47	2010	-55	-51	SW	2	15275	78	60	75	58	27	NW	72	57	62	60	58	0	17	0	1
Gulch	60	13	151	25	350	-27	-21	NNE	4	11375	68	59	64	57	18	SW	62	56	60	58	56	0	1	0	1
r AFS	64	20	149	10	600	-50	-47	E	4	14060	80	63	77	62	31	NE	73	60	65	63	61		32		10
Bay AFS	55	12	162	43	98	4	9	NNW	14	9865	60	56	57	53	10	SSE	55	52	57	55	53		0		0
ova	60	30	145	29	42	-7	-2	E	5	9765	70	58	66	58	22	SW	63	56	60	58	57		0		0
ond Ridge	59	41	151	37	1100	-1	2	NE	6	10394	63	56	61	55	19	S	58	54	57	56	54	0	0	0	0
elly	63	47	145	51	2954	-35	-30	S	4	12683	76	58	72	57	20	N	69	55	59	57	56	0	0	0	0
twood Bay	53	58	166	51	24	13	16	N	12	9197	68	62	63	59	12	N	59	56	62	59	56				4
twood Bay AFS	53	58	166	53	1250	8	11	N	15	10637	64	60	59	57	12		55	54	60	57	54				0
Harbor	53	53	166	32	13	13	16	N	12	9197	68	62	63	59	12		59	56	62	59	56				4
son AFB/Fairbanks	64	40	147	06	545	-52	-48	S	2	14498	80	61	77	59	27	SW	74	59	63	61	60	0	38	0	4
ndorf AFB/Anchorage	61	15	149	48	212	-22	-16	NE	4	10722	71	58	68	57	17	W	66	56	60	58	57	0	2	0	0
banks IAP	64	49	147	52	436	-51	-47	N	3	14345	82	62	78	60	27	W	75	59	64	62	60		53		5
Greely	63	58	145	44	1314	-48	-43	S	4	13698	80	61	76	60	24		73	58	62	60	59		30		1
Richardson/Bryant AAF	61	16	149	39	342	-22	-16	NE	4	10722	71	58	68	57	17		66	56	60	58	57		2		0
Wainwright	64	50	147	37	448	-51	-47	N	4	14345	82	62	78	60	27	WSW	75	59	64	62	60	0	50	0	5
Yukon AFS	66	34	145	15	431	-60	-57	NW		16084	80	62	77	60	24	N	73	59	66	63	61	1	2	1	23
na	64	44	156	56	152	-49	-46	W		15087	78	62	75	60	23		71	58	64	62	60	0	2	0	12
tle River	63	48	145	00	1512	-46	-41	S		13398	80	61	76	60	24		73	58	62	60	59	0	3	0	1

	LOCATION					WINTER DESIGN DATA HEATING				DEGREE DAYS	SUMMER DESIGN DATA AIR CONDITIONING											SUMMER CRITERIA DATA AIR CONDITIONING			
						Dry Bulb					Dry Bulb								Wet Bulb			Dry Bulb		Wet Bulb	
	Lat		Long		Elev	99%	97.5%	Pvlg Wind	Mean Speed	Heating	1%	MCWB	2.5%	MCWB	Mean Daily Range	Pvlg Wind	5%	MCWB	1%	2.5%	5%	≥ 93°F	≥ 80°F	≥ 73°F	≥ 67°F
	°	'	°	'	feet	°F	°F	dir	knots	annual	°F	°F	°F	°F	°F	dir	°F	°F	°F	°F	°F	hrs	hrs	hrs	hrs
	N		W																						
'eek	64	12	149	55	1722	-38	-35	E	10	13364	77	61	74	60	24	NE	70	58	63	61	59	0	13	0	2
ıtain	65	26	161	14	2835	-36	-32	N	9	14986	64	56	60	55	17	NW	58	53	58	56	54		0		0
	62	09	145	27	1572	-44	-40	NNW	3	13938	79	60	75	58	31	SE	71	57	62	60	58		22		0
e	64	24	146	57	1445	-46	-41	S	4	13398	80	61	76	60	24	N	73	58	62	60	59		30		1
	59	38	151	30	63	-5	-2	NE	6	10364	65	57	63	56	19	SW	61	55	58	57	55	0	0	0	0
	58	07	135	25	1538	-5	0	N	7	9552	72	59	68	57	24	W	65	56	60	58	57	0	0	0	0
	59	45	154	55	190	-24	-19	NNW	8	12144	71	59	68	58	20	WSW	64	56	61	58	57		11		1
tain AFS	66	00	153	42	1220	-44	-40	NW	3	15169	76	59	72	58	22	E	68	56	61	59	57		2		3
	58	22	134	35	12	-4	1	N	7	9007	74	60	70	58	24	W	67	57	61	59	58		4		0
'eek	64	26	156	50	1598	-35	-32	NW	3	13942	75	60	72	58	20	N	68	56	62	60	58	0	8	0	8
	60	34	151	15	92	-29	-23	NNE	4	11615	68	59	64	57	18	SW	62	56	60	58	56	0	1	0	1
	58	42	156	40	65	-26	-22	N	7	11582	74	61	69	58	25	W	66	57	62	59	57		16		4
	63	38	144	03	2170	-53	-49	SW	2	15080	78	60	75	58	27	NW	72	57	62	60	58		7		1
	57	45	152	29	73	10	13	WNW	14	8860	69	58	65	56	15	NW	62	55	60	58	56		1		1
	66	52	162	38	10	-43	-37	NE	6	16039	67	60	64	58	13	ESE	61	56	61	58	57	0	1	0	1
s	66	53	162	36	11	-43	-37	NE	6	16039	67	60	64	58	13	ESE	61	56	61	58	57	0	1	0	1
	61	10	149	59	96	-23	-18	SE	3	10911	71	59	68	58	18	WNW	66	56	60	59	57		0		0
	70	55	153	15	23	-45	-41	SW	8	20265	57	53	53	50	16	SE	49	47	54	50	47		0		0
	63	14	145	38	3600	-30	-26	NNW	3	13343	74	57	70	55	25	SE	66	54	59	57	55		0		0
	62	58	155	37	344	-52	-47	NW	2	14487	78	61	74	59	26	N	71	58	63	60	59	0	22	0	1
sland	59	27	146	18	79	18	21	NNE	15	8188	61	57	60	56	9	SW	58	55	58	57	56	0	0	0	0
	64	42	162	03	16	-39	-35	N	5	14505	70	60	66	59	17	SSW	64	57	62	60	58		3		3
AFS	64	57	148	21	2914	-36	-32	N	3	13795	75	57	71	55	27	WSW	68	54	59	57	55		6		0
	58	45	157	00	70	-18	-12	N	7	11133	73	61	69	58	16	W	66	57	62	59	57		3		4
	60	32	150	35	450	-32	-26	NNE	4	12054	76	59	72	57	21	SW	69	56	60	58	56	0	8	0	1
ke	61	37	149	15	460	-27	-22	NE	4	11220	78	59	75	58	23	W	72	57	61	59	58	0	24	0	0
	64	33	149	05	356	-53	-50	E	4	14539	80	63	77	62	31	NE	73	60	65	63	61		32		10
s	52	58	168	51	712	18	21	N	15	9555	58	57	56	55	6	SE	54	53	57	55	53		0		0
	64	30	165	26	13	-31	-27	N	4	14325	66	57	62	55	15	W	59	54	58	56	55		0		0
	63	53	160	31	490	-38	-33	ESE	6	14027	68	60	64	58	17	NW	62	57	61	59	57	0	0	0	1
rt	62	57	141	56	1713	-57	-53	SW	2	15634	78	60	75	58	27	NW	72	57	62	60	58	0	17	0	1
	59	32	139	51	84	0	5	E	6	9533	67	57	63	56	17	WSW	61	55	58	57	56	0	1	0	0
	70	31	149	53	10	-45	-41	SW	8	20265	57	53	53	50	16	SE	49	47	54	50	47	0	0	0	0

Station	Lat °	Lat '	Long °	Long '	Elev feet	Winter Dry Bulb 99% °F	97.5% °F	Pvlg Wind dir	Mean Speed knots	Degree Days Heating annual	Summer Dry Bulb 1% °F	MCWB °F	2.5% °F	MCWB °F	Mean Daily Range °F	Pvlg Wind dir	5% °F	MCWB °F	Wet Bulb 1% °F	2.5% °F	5% °F	Criteria Dry Bulb ≥ 93°F hrs	≥ 80°F hrs	Criteria Wet Bulb ≥ 73°F hrs	≥ 67°F hrs
NT)	N		W																						
ɩ Lake	62	58	145	28	3786	-29	-25	NNW	3	13483	73	56	69	54	25	SE	65	53	58	56	54	0	0	0	0
Dome	65	02	147	30	2588	-37	-33	N	10	13600	76	58	72	56	27	WSW	69	55	60	58	56	0	10	0	1
r Mountain	57	47	152	26	1390	7	10	WNW	14	[illegible]	[illegible]	[illegible]	[illegible]	[illegible]	16	NW	[illegible]	[illegible]	[illegible]	[illegible]	[illegible]				0
Barrow	71	19	156	38	8	-45	-41	SW	8	20265	57	53	53	50	16	SE	49	47	54	50	47	0	0	0	0
Lay	69	44	163	01	20	-41	-37	ESE	7	19194	59	53	55	51	13	SW	52	50	54	52	50	0	0	0	0
ɬeiden	56	59	158	38	105	-10	-6	NNW	11	10441	65	59	62	56	13	SSE	59	55	60	57	55				2
Moller	55	59	160	30	1050	-5	-1	NNE	12	10290	60	56	57	54	10	S	55	53	58	55	53				0
ː Creek	61	05	149	44	1250	-19	-13	NE	5	10814	68	57	65	56	17	W	63	55	59	57	56				0
ɪl Island	57	09	170	13	22	0	4	N	16	11119	52	49	50	48	7	S	50	48	50	49	48	0	0	0	0
ɪl	61	48	148	19	2573	-22	-18	NE	4	13531	72	57	69	54	18	W	65	52	58	55	53	0	0	0	0
ɖ Rec Annex	60	07	149	24	15	3	7	NE	6	9242	71	58	68	58	22	SW	65	56	60	58	57		3		0
ɑ AFB	52	43	174E	05	97	22	24	NW	16	9573	53	51	52	50	5	WSW	51	49	52	51	50		0		0
	57	03	135	20	67	14	17	E	8	8132	68	58	65	57	14	NW	63	56	60	58	57		1		0
ɩer Cove	55	05	131	35	123	13	17	NE	12	7053	74	61	70	59	17	NW	66	58	62	60	59	0	6	0	1
ɩna	60	32	151	05	212	-29	-23	NNE	4	11615	68	59	64	57	18	SW	62	56	60	58	56	0	1	0	0
evohn AFS	61	06	155	35	1573	-29	-26	N	9	12982	72	59	67	56	17	NW	63	54	60	57	55		2		0
sky Creek	59	53	151	47	300	-26	-20	NNE	4	10885	69	59	65	57	18	SW	63	56	60	58	56		0		
ta Pass	61	50	149	19	3443	-22	-18	N	12	14361	69	56	66	53	18	NW	62	51	57	54	52		0		
a	65	10	152	06	232	-53	-48	W	4	15116	80	62	76	61	29	WSW	73	59	65	62	61	0	31	0	11
ɩna AFS	62	54	155	58	964	-33	-28	E	4	13453	76	58	71	58	19	NE	68	56	60	58	56	0	17	0	0
ɩty AFS	65	34	167	55	269	-31	-27	N	20	16192	58	53	55	52	14	N	52	50	54	52	50		1		0
ɩa	62	06	146	10	2974	-31	-27	N	8	12763	76	58	72	56	26	SE	68	55	60	58	56		7		0
ɩleet	63	53	160	48	15	-39	-34	ESE	6	14027	69	60	65	58	17	NW	63	57	61	59	57		1		
ɩight	70	36	159	53	80	-45	-41	SW	8	19991	57	53	53	50	16	SE	49	47	54	50	47	0	0	0	0
ɩer	60	47	148	41	31	0	5	NE	4	9444	73	58	70	57	17	W	67	56	60	58	57	0	3	0	0
ɩga	60	04	142	25	39	6	10	E	6	9222	65	57	63	56	11	WSW	61	55	58	57	56		0		
ɩt	59	31	139	40	28	0	5	E	6	9533	67	57	63	56	17	WSW	61	55	58	57	56		1		
	N		W																						
ɩer use Williams AFB																									
-Monthan AFB/Tucson	32	11	110	54	2654	29	33	SE	5	1574	103	68	101	67	26	NW	99	67	74	72	72	595	2243	69	1268
ɩaff	35	08	111	40	7006	-2	4	NE	5	7322	84	55	82	55	32	SW	80	54	61	60	59	0	184	0	0
ɬuachuca/Libby AAF	31	35	110	20	4664	24	28	SW	5	2551	95	62	92	62	25	W	90	62	69	68	67	68	1154	0	209
Bend	32	54	112	43	859	29	32	SSE	5	1348	111	71	109	70	28	WSW	107	70	76	75	74	1524	3096	438	1568

STATE / Station	LOCATION Lat °	Lat '	Long °	Long '	Elev feet	WINTER DESIGN DATA HEATING Dry Bulb 99% °F	97.5% °F	Pvlg Wind dir	Mean Speed knots	DEGREE DAYS Heating annual	SUMMER DESIGN DATA AIR CONDITIONING Dry Bulb 1% °F	MCWB °F	2.5% °F	MCWB °F	Mean Daily Range °F	Pvlg Wind dir	5% °F	MCWB °F	Wet Bulb 1% °F	2.5% °F	5% °F	SUMMER CRITERIA DATA AIR CONDITIONING Dry Bulb ≥ 93°F hrs	≥ 80°F hrs	Wet Bulb ≥ 73°F hrs	≥ 67°F hrs
ARIZONA (CONT)	N		W																						
Holbrook	34	56	110	09	5264	4	9	SW	6	4826	96	61	94	60	33	WSW	92	60	66	65	64	120	1050	0	15
Luke AFB/Glendale	33	33	112	22	1101	32	34	N	5	1410	110	71	108	71	28	SSW	105	71	76	75	75	1189	2815	492	1727
Navajo Army Depot	35	14	111	50	7125	-2	4	NE	5	7322	84	55	82	55	32	SW	80	54	61	60	59	0	184	0	0
Nogales	31	21	110	55	3800	28	32	SW	5	2150	99	64	96	64	26	W	94	64	71	70	69	220	1786	4	732
Phoenix/Sky Harbor IAP	33	26	112	01	1112	31	34	E	4	1552	109	71	107	71	29	W	105	71	76	75	75	1192	2819	506	1758
Tucson IAP	32	07	110	56	2558	28	32	SE	6	1707	104	66	102	66	28	WNW	100	66	72	71	71	694	2297	18	1171
Williams AFB/Chandler	33	18	111	40	1385	29	32	ESE	4	1535	108	71	105	70	27	WNW	104	70	76	75	74	1211	2915	426	1762
Winslow MAP	35	01	110	44	4895	5	10	SW	6	4733	97	61	95	60	33	WSW	93	60	66	65	64	172	1165	0	15
Yuma MCAS/IAP	32	39	114	37	213	36	39	NNE	6	1005	111	72	109	72	28	WSW	107	71	79	78	77	1394	3136	949	1891
Yuma Test Station	32	52	114	26	225	37	39	SE	4	968	111	71	109	71	27	W	107	71	79	78	77	1493	3185	848	1838
ARKANSAS	N		W																						
Blytheville AFB	35	57	89	57	264	10	15	N	8	3760	96	78	94	77	22	SSW	91	76	81	80	78	109	1242	1113	2423
El Dorado/Goodwin Field	33	13	92	49	277	18	23	S	6	2645	98	76	96	76	26	SE	94	76	80	79	78	214	1405	1502	2908
Fayetteville/Drake Field	36	00	94	10	1251	7	12	NE	9	3839	97	72	94	73	27	SSW	92	73	77	76	75	126	966	527	1845
Fort Chaffee	35	18	94	17	440	12	17	NW	8	3336	101	76	98	76	27	SW	95	76	80	79	78	291	1505	1265	2656
Fort Smith MAP	35	20	94	22	463	12	17	NW	8	3336	101	75	98	76	27	SW	95	76	80	79	78	291	1505	1265	2656
Harrison	36	14	93	07	1105	7	12	N	6	3884	97	73	94	73	27	SSW	92	73	77	76	75	126	966	527	1845
Hot Springs/Memorial Field	34	29	93	06	535	17	23	N	8	2729	101	77	97	77	23	SW	94	77	80	79	78	231	1643	1408	2751
Little Rock/Adams Field	34	44	92	14	257	15	20	N	9	3354	99	76	96	77	23	SSW	94	77	80	79	78	206	1519	1408	2751
Little Rock AFB	34	55	92	09	311	14	18	N	7	3241	96	77	94	77	20	S	92	76	80	79	78	130	1402	1231	2619
Pine Bluff Arsenal	34	18	92	05	241	16	22	N	7	2588	100	78	97	77	24	SW	95	78	81	80	80	285	1524	1630	2814
Texarkana/Webb Field MAP	33	27	93	59	389	18	23	WNW	9	2531	98	76	96	77	22	SSW	93	76	80	79	78	198	1639	1715	3097
Walnut Ridge MAP	36	08	90	56	275	12	17	NNE	8	3352	98	74	95	74	24	SSW	93	74	79	77	76	155	1376	615	1991
CALIFORNIA	N		W																						
Alameda NAS/Nimitz Field	37	47	122	19	15	38	40	N	6	2507	84	66	79	63	21	W	75	63	66	65	63	3	90	0	24
Almaden AFS	37	10	121	54	3470	25	29	N	7	4468	91	61	88	61	20	S	86	60	63	62	61	14	542	0	0
Arcata	40	59	124	06	218	31	33	E	5	5029	68	60	65	59	15	NW	63	58	62	60	59	0	3	0	1
Bakersfield/Meadows Field	35	25	119	03	475	30	32	ENE	5	2185	104	70	101	69	28	WNW	98	68	73	71	70	483	1691	33	607
Barstow-Daggett Aprt	34	51	116	47	1927	26	29	WNW	7	2203	106	68	104	68	30	W	102	67	73	71	70	809	2133	32	461
Beale AFB/Marysville	39	07	121	26	113	28	30	N		2835	102	70	100	69	34	S	97	68	72	71	69	329	1294	24	456
Berkeley	37	52	122	15	345	34	36	NE		2973	83	64	79	63	20	NW	75	62	66	64	63	2	91	0	14
Bishop	37	22	118	22	4108	11	15	NW		4313	102	61	100	61	34	S	98	60	65	64	63	394	1196	0	4
Blue Canyon Aprt	39	17	120	42	5280	5	9	ENE	14	5704	85	58	83	57	18	SW	80	57	62	60	59	0	189	0	1
Boron AFS	35	05	117	35	3015	23	25	WNW	8	3000	104	67	102	67	35	WSW	99	66	70	69	67	504	1505	6	216

Station	Lat	Long	Elev	Winter Design Data Heating – Dry Bulb 99%	97.5%	Pvlg Wind	Mean Speed	Degree Days Heating	Summer Design Data Air Conditioning – Dry Bulb 1%	MCWB	2.5%	MCWB	Mean Daily Range	Pvlg Wind	5%	MCWB	Wet Bulb 1%	2.5%	5%	Summer Criteria Data Air Conditioning – Dry Bulb ≥ 93°F	≥ 80°F	Wet Bulb ≥ 73°F	≥ 67°F
	° '	° '	feet	°F	°F	dir	knots	annual	°F	°F	°F	°F	°F	dir	°F	°F	°F	°F	°F	hrs	hrs	hrs	hrs
ORNIA (CONT)	N	W																					
rbank	34 12	118 21	775	37	39	NW	3	1701	95	68	91	68	28	S	88	67	71	70	69	67	711	10	392
mbria AFS	35 32	121 04	690	35	38	ESE	5	3646	75	61	70	61	16	NW	67	60	63	61	60	2	28	0	3
mp Parks Comm Annex	37 44	121 53	684	24	27	WNW	5	3035	100	69	97	68	35	NW	93	67	71	70	68	169	863	8	318
mp Roberts	35 48	120 45	765	24	27	ESE	4	2890	103	69	100	69	45	NW	96	68	72	70	69	275	928	29	296
stle AFB/Merced	37 23	120 34	188	29	31	ESE	4	2590	102	70	99	69	33	NW	96	68	7	71	70	320	1294	22	505
nterville Beach	40 34	124 21	280	31	33	E	5	5029	68	60	65	59	15	NW	63	58	62	60	59	0	3	0	1
ico MAP	39 48	121 51	238	28	30	NW	5	2835	103	69	101	68	33	SSE	98	67	71	70	68	404	1410	15	385
ina Lake NAF/Armitage Fld	35 41	117 41	2283	22	25	SW	5	2560	107	68	105	67	33	S	102	66	72	70	68	806	2116	20	301
ula Vista	32 36	117 05	25	40	41	E	6	1839	78	70	76	69	10	W	74	68	71	70	69	4	34	6	426
mpton	33 53	118 13	65	38	40	NW	4	1606	91	69	87	69	21	NW	84	68	71	70	69	26	486	12	438
ncord NAD	38 01	122 00	23	24	27	WNW	5	3035	100	69	97	68	34	NW	94	67	71	70	68	188	921	8	318
rona	33 54	117 28	550	28	31	E	3	1875	102	70	98	69	34	W	95	68	74	72	71	214	1134	60	648
ronado	32 40	117 10	10	40	41	E	6	1839	78	70	76	69	10	W	74	68	71	70	69	4	34	6	426
sta Mesa ANG Station	33 40	117 53	49	37	39	NE	4	1482	89	69	85	68	23	SW	82	68	71	70	69	20	288	13	475
ows Landing	37 25	121 06	140	29	31	ESE	4	2767	102	70	99	69	33	NW	96	68	72	71	70	320	1294	22	505
ddeback Dry Lake Range	35 18	117 28	2300	20	22	WNW	3	3203	104	67	102	67	35	WSW	99	66	70	69	67	504	1505	6	216
ggett use Barstow-Daggett																							
xon	38 26	121 51	100	30	32	NNW	6	2826	100	69	96	68	36	WSW	92	67	71	69	68	165	815	15	327
nner Summit	39 19	120 20	7195	-1	3	NE	18	8290	78	54	75	54	19	WSW	73	53	58	56	55	0	13	0	3
wards AFB	34 54	117 52	2302	20	22	WNW	3	3077	104	67	102	67	35	WSW	99	66	70	69	67	504	1505	6	216
Centro NAF	32 49	115 40	-43	35	38	W	6	925	112	74	110	74	30	SE	108	74	81	80	78	1413	3067	904	1832
Toro MCAS/Santa Ana	33 40	117 44	383	39	41	E	4	1573	92	69	88	70	26	W	85	69	73	71	70	38	502	37	609
llbrook Annex	33 21	117 15	703	32	34	E	5	2077	97	70	94	70	29	W	91	69	73	71	70	112	846	37	609
rt Baker	37 50	122 28	15	38	40	W	5	3080	74	63	71	62	12	W	69	61	64	62	61	0	12	0	8
rt Barry	37 49	122 32	267	38	40	W	5	3080	74	63	71	62	12	W	69	61	64	62	61	0	12	0	8
rt Irwin	35 16	116 41	2500	26	29	WNW	7	2547	106	68	104	68	30	W	102	67	73	71	70	809	2133	32	461
rt MacArthur	33 43	118 18	200	40	42	E	4	1819	83	68	80	68	13	WSW	78	67	70	69	68	3	109	3	291
rt Mason	37 48	122 26	50	38	40	W	5	3080	74	63	71	62	12	W	69	61	64	62	61	0	12	0	8
rt Ord/Fritzsche AAF	36 41	121 46	134	30	32	E	5	3818	74	61	70	60	18	W	67	59	62	61	59	1	23	0	2
esno/Air Terminal	36 46	119 43	328	28	30	E	4	2650	102	70	100	69	34	WNW	97	68	72	71	70	374	1399	27	524
orge AFB/Victorville	34 35	117 23	2875	23	26	S	5	2885	102	66	100	65	31	S	98	64	69	68	67	433	1495	1	160
milton AFB/San Rafael	38 04	122 30	3	30	32	N	4	3311	89	68	84	66	33	SE	80	65	72	69	67	10	184	22	171
yward	37 39	122 07	47	32	34	E	5	2909	87	64	83	63	24	WNW	79	62	66	64	63	10	230	0	14
nter Liggett Mil Rsvn	36 01	121 14	1090	24	26	N	2	3332	102	71	99	69	46	E	97	67	74	72	70	358	1153	53	440

LOCATION	Lat	Long	Elev	WINTER DESIGN DATA HEATING Dry Bulb 99%	97.5%	Pvlg Wind	Mean Speed	DEGREE DAYS Heating	SUMMER DESIGN DATA AIR CONDITIONING Dry Bulb 1%	MCWB	2.5%	MCWB	Mean Daily Range	Pvlg Wind	5%	MCWB	Wet Bulb 1%	2.5%	5%	SUMMER CRITERIA DATA AIR CONDITIONING Dry Bulb ≥ 93°F	≥ 80°F	Wet Bulb ≥ 73°F	≥ 67°F
	° '	° '	feet	°F	°F	dir	knots	annual	°F	°F	°F	°F	°F	dir	°F	°F	°F	°F	°F	hrs	hrs	hrs	hrs
ONT)	N	W																					
. Beach NF/Ream Fld	32 34	117 07	23	40	41	E	6	1839	78	70	76	69	10	W	74	68	71	70	69	4	34	6	426
AFS	41 34	124 05	804	31	33	E		4445	68	60	65	59	15	NW	63	58	62	60	59	0	3	0	1
	34 55	117 55	2315	20	22	WNW		3077	104	67	102	67	35	WSW	99	66	70	69	67	504	1505	6	216
NAS/Reeves Field	36 20	119 57	237	25	28	W		2579	105	71	102	70	37	NNE	100	69	73	71	70	519	1577	40	555
n Army Hospital	37 48	122 27	20	38	40	W		3080	74	63	71	62	12	W	69	61	64	62	61	0	12	0	8
'e	37 42	121 57	500	24	27	WNW	5	3035	100	69	97	68	35	NW	93	67	71	70	68	169	863	8	318
ich	33 45	118 14	12	41	43	E	4	1819	83	68	80	68	15	WSW	77	67	70	69	68	7	99		291
ich/Daugherty Field	33 49	118 09	30	38	40	NW	4	1606	89	69	85	69	23	WNW	82	68	71	70	69	19	299	12	438
iitos NAS	33 47	118 03	35	37	39	NE	4	1482	89	69	85	68	23	SW	82	68	71	70	69	20	288	1	475
iles City Office	34 03	118 14	270	37	40	NW	4	1245	93	70	89	70	19	NW	86	69	72	71	70	38	581	2	586
iles IAP	33 56	118 24	97	41	43	E	4	1819	83	68	80	68	15	WSW	77	67	70	69	68	7	99	3	291
'B/Riverside	33 53	117 15	1533	29	32	N	4	2162	100	68	98	68	34	NW	95	67	72	71	70	269	1132	23	431
.and NAVSHIPYD	38 05	122 16	25	30	32	N	4	3311	89	68	84	66	33	SE	80	65	72	69	67	10	184	22	171
\FB/Sacramento	38 34	121 18	96	29	31	ESE	4	2600	101	69	98	69	35	W	96	68	71	70	69	259	1052	12	376
in AFB/Sacramento	38 40	121 24	76	29	31	NNW	4	2566	102	70	99	69	35	SW	96	68	72	70	69	299	1124	16	413
n Peak	34 53	119 48	5763	19	22	N	18	5200	89	59	86	59	18	S	84	58	63	61	60	3	345	0	0
ise Castle AFB																							
.ley AFS	37 55	122 35	2600	26	28	N	5	3400	97	65	94	65	40	W	91	64	68	67	65	107	701	13	72
NAS/Mitscher Field	32 52	117 08	477	39	41	E	5	1532	89	68	85	68	22	W	82	68	71	70	69	18	340	3	472
Field NAS	37 25	122 03	34	34	36	SE	4	2511	85	66	81	65	23	NNW	77	64	68	67	65	3	117	1	85
	35 02	118 11	2735	22	26	WNW	5	3012	105	67	102	67	35	WSW	100	66	70	69	67	499	1649	6	216
:/Siskiyou Co Aprt	41 46	22 28	2648	11	16	N	6	5474	97	65	94	65	40	NW	91	64	68	67	65	107	701		72
' FWC	36 36	21 52	162	35	38	SE	4	3556	75	63	71	61	17	NW	68	61	64	62	61	1	18		6
'/Presidio	36 36	121 54	100	35	38	SE	4	3556	75	63	71	61	17	NW	68	61	64	62	61	1	18		6
.o	37 53	121 55	3849	24	28	N	10	4600	90	60	87	60	18	S	85	59	62	61	60	8	454		0
)pointment	34 18	118 02	5900	19	21	NW	15	5200	86	62	84	60	18	SE	82	59	65	63	62	0	293	0	0
ia AFS	32 53	116 25	6199	18	20	NW	17	5445	84	62	82	60	18	SE	80	59	65	63	62	0	163	2	1
:ll ANG	37 49	122 04	2022	30	33	N	5	2809	96	68	92	67	26	WSW	89	66	69	68	67	74	676	0	160
;	34 48	119 08	8831	5	8	NW	20	7800	80	52	77	51	20	W	75	50	55	53	52	0	32	0	0
\S use Edwards AFB																							
ighlands ANGB	38 38	121 25	76	29	31	NNW	4	2566	102	70	99	69	35	SW	96	68	72	70	69	299	1124	16	413
\FB/San Bernardino	34 06	117 14	1156	31	33	E		1978	102	70	99	69	37	W	96	68	74	72	71	345	1206	60	648
Army Base	37 49	122 19	5	34	36	E	3	2909	85	64	80	63	24	WNW	75	62	66	64	63	5	92	0	14

ation	LOCATION			WINTER DESIGN DATA HEATING				DEGREE DAYS	SUMMER DESIGN DATA AIR CONDITIONING											SUMMER CRITERIA DATA AIR CONDITIONING			
				Dry Bulb					Dry Bulb								Wet Bulb			Dry Bulb		Wet Bulb	
	Lat	Long	Elev	99%	97.5%	Pvlg Wind	Mean Speed	Heating	1%	MCWB	2.5%	MCWB	Mean Daily Range	Pvlg Wind	5%	MCWB	1%	2.5%	5%	≥ 93°F	≥ 80°F	≥ 73°F	≥ 67°F
	° '	° '	feet	°F	°F	dir	knots	annual	°F	°F	°F	°F	°F	dir	°F	°F	°F	°F	°F	hrs	hrs	hrs	hrs
A (CONT)	N	W																					
and IAP	37 44	122 12	6	34	36	E	5	2909	85	64	80	63	24	WNW	75	62	66	64	63	5	92	0	14
and Navy Hospital	37 46	122 09	500	29	32	NW	5	2962	92	66	88	65	30	NW	84	64	68	67	66	29	360	0	129
Mountain	34 19	118 36	3000	22	25	NW	10	3200	98	66	96	65	28	SW	93	64	69	68	67	108	1016	1	160
rio IAP	34 03	117 36	952	31	33	E	4	2009	102	70	99	69	34	WSW	96	67	74	72	71	345	1200	60	648
dale	34 38	118 06	2542	18	22	SW	5	2929	103	65	101	65	35	WSW	98	64	69	67	66	449	1486	2	114
dena	34 09	118 09	864	32	35	E	3	1694	98	69	95	68	28	W	92	67	73	71	70	133	935	41	498
leton MCB	33 18	117 18	63	39	41	E	5	1532	89	68	85	68	22	W	82	68	71	70	69	18	340	13	472
leton MCB Coast	33 13	117 24	24	44	46	E	4	1782	81	70	78	70	10	NW	76	69	72	71	70	3	62	20	535
ar Point AFS	37 30	122 30	200	34	36	SE	4	3859	76	63	72	61	15	NW	70	61	64	62	61	0	13	0	6
n Peak	36 05	117 28	7400	10	13	NW	18	6800	83	57	80	56	18	W	78	55	60	58	57	0	75	0	0
rena AFS	38 57	123 44	200	32	34	E	5	4747	79	64	76	63	19	SW	73	62	65	64	62	0	30	0	13
rguello	34 34	120 40	76	32	35	ESE	6	3826	72	62	69	61	17	WNW	66	59	63	61	60	1	15	0	2
ugu NAS/Port Hueneme	34 07	119 07	13	37	39	NNE	5	2334	78	67	75	67	15	W	73	66	69	67	66	3	45	1	129
ur NF	36 20	121 54	361	35	38	SE	4	3556	75	63	71	61	17	NW	68	61	64	62	61	1	18	0	6
na	34 03	117 45	934	28	30	E	4	2166	102	70	99	69	35	W	95	68	74	72	71	267	1138	60	648
Hueneme	34 09	119 12	16	37	39	NNE	5	2334	78	67	75	67	15	W	73	66	69	67	66	3	45	1	129
Bluff MAP	40 09	122 15	342	29	31	NW	6	2688	105	68	102	67	32	SSE	100	66	71	69	68	478	1515	6	314
Mountain Flight Annex	35 22	117 38	3551	23	27	WNW	5	2946	104	67	101	67	30	WSW	99	66	70	69	67	425	1479	6	216
rbank AAP	37 43	120 55	135	29	31	ESE	4	2767	102	70	99	69	33	NW	96	68	72	71	70	320	1294	22	505
amento	38 31	121 30	17	30	32	NNW	6	2843	101	70	98	70	37	SW	94	69	72	71	70	208	955	25	452
amento Army Depot	38 31	121 24	42	29	31	ESE	4	2843	101	69	98	69	35	W	96	68	71	70	69	259	1052	12	376
Bernardino	34 07	117 19	1125	31	33	E	3	1891	102	70	99	69	37	W	96	68	74	72	71	345	1206	60	648
Bruno	37 37	122 25	20	35	38	S	5	3042	82	64	77	63	23	NW	73	62	65	64	62	2	63	0	13
Clemente Is NALF	33 01	118 35	181	47	48	WNW	6	1645	75	65	73	65	11	W	71	65	68	66	65	1	22	0	59
berg	34 45	118 44	4523	22	25	N	16	4427	93	61	90	61	19	S	88	60	65	63	62	32	631	0	5
Diego FWF	32 43	117 09	48	44	46	E	4	1782	81	70	78	70	10	NW	76	69	72	71	70	3	62	20	535
Diego IAP	32 44	117 10	13	42	44	NE	3	1507	83	69	80	69	14	WNW	78	68	71	70	68	6	110	4	435
Francisco IAP	37 37	122 23	8	35	38	S	5	3042	82	64	77	63	23	NW	73	62	65	64	62	2	63	0	13
Francisco/Presidio	37 48	122 28	20	38	40	W	5	3080	74	63	71	62	12	W	69	61	64	62	61	0	12	0	8
Jose MAP	37 22	121 56	56	34	36	SE	4	2416	85	66	81	65	23	NNW	77	64	68	67	65	3	117	1	85
Luis Obispo	35 20	120 43	250	33	35	E	4	2472	92	69	88	70	26	W	84	69	73	71	70	34	420	37	609
Nicolas Island	33 14	119 28	504	43	45	W	7	2454	80	63	75	63	19	NW	71	63	66	65	63	3	92	2	59
Pedro	33 43	118 16	10	40	42	E	4	1819	83	68	80	68	13	WSW	78	67	70	69	68	3	109	3	291

STATE / Station	LOCATION					WINTER DESIGN DATA HEATING				DEGREE DAYS	SUMMER DESIGN DATA AIR CONDITIONING											SUMMER CRITERIA DATA AIR CONDITIONING			
						Dry Bulb					Dry Bulb								Wet Bulb			Dry Bulb		Wet Bulb	
	Lat		Long		Elev	99%	97.5%	Pvlg Wind	Mean Speed	Heating	1%	MCWB	2.5%	MCWB	Mean Daily Range	Pvlg Wind	5%	MCWB	1%	2.5%	5%	≥ 93°F	≥ 80°F	≥ 73°F	≥ 67°F
	°	'	°	'	feet	°F	°F	dir	knots	annual	°F	°F	°F	°F	°F	dir	°F	°F	°F	°F	°F	hrs	hrs	hrs	hrs
CALIFORNIA (CONT)	N		W																						
San Rafael	37	58	122	33	31	30	32	N	4	3077	89	68	84	66	33	SE	80	65	72	69	67	10	184	22	171
Santa Ana MCAS	33	42	117	50	54	37	39	E	3	1675	89	69	85	68	23	SW	82	68	71	70	69	20	288	13	475
Santa Barbara MAP	34	26	119	50	10	34	36	NE	3	2470	81	67	77	66	19	SW	75	65	68	67	66	3	59	1	95
Santa Catalina	33	24	118	25	1568	39	42	W	10	2652	87	63	84	62	15	WSW	81	62	67	66	65	7	244	0	59
Santa Maria	34	54	120	27	236	31	33	E	4	3053	81	64	76	63	22	WNW	73	62	65	64	63	4	57	0	12
Santa Rosa/Sonoma Co Aprt	38	31	122	49	125	27	29	N	5	3065	99	68	95	67	34	SE	91	66	70	68	67	132	770	4	203
Seal Beach NAD	33	44	118	05	20	40	42	E	4	1819	83	68	80	68	15	WSW	78	67	70	69	68	3	109	3	291
Shafter AFS	35	30	119	10	425	30	32	ENE	5	2185	104	70	101	69	28	WNW	98	68	73	71	70	483	1691	33	607
Sharpe Army Depot	37	51	121	17	16	28	30	WNW	4	2806	100	69	97	68	35	NW	94	67	71	70	68	204	955	8	318
Sierra Army Depot	40	09	120	07	4110	6	11	N	4	5822	96	62	93	61	40	WNW	91	60	65	63	62	97	805	0	8
Skaggs Is NSGA	38	12	122	23	2	30	32	N	4	3311	89	68	84	66	33	SE	80	65	72	69	67	10	184	22	171
Stockton	37	54	121	15	22	28	30	WNW	4	2806	100	69	97	68	35	NW	94	67	71	70	68	204	955	8	318
Sunnyvale	37	23	122	02	30	34	36	SE	4	2511	85	66	81	65	23	NNW	77	64	68	67	65	3	117	1	85
Travis AFB/Fairfield	38	16	121	56	62	29	32	N	5	2725	99	68	95	67	35	WSW	91	66	70	68	67	121	686	4	203
Treasure Is NAVSTA	37	49	122	22	10	38	40	N	6	2507	84	66	79	63	21	W	75	63	66	65	63	3	90	0	24
Twentynine Palms MCB	34	14	116	03	1781	27	29	WNW	5	2006	107	68	105	68	30	W	103	67	73	71	70	952	2240	32	461
Two Rock Ranch Station	38	15	122	48	200	27	30	N	4	2966	98	68	94	66	32	SE	90	65	72	69	67	95	681	22	171
Vandenberg AFB/Lompoc	34	43	120	34	368	35	38	ESE	5	3451	75	61	70	61	16	NW	67	60	63	61	60	2	28	0	3
Van Nuys/Los Angeles	34	13	118	29	800	37	39	NW	3	1701	95	68	91	68	28	S	88	67	71	70	69	67	711	10	392
West Coast Radio Station	38	47	122	30	1380	22	24	N	7	3716	104	70	101	70	38	SE	98	69	72	71	70	342	1122	26	513
COLORADO	N		W																						
Buckley ANGB/Denver	39	42	104	45	5663	-6	1	S	6	6239	92	60	90	60	29	NE	87	59	65	64	62	23	540	0	9
Colorado Springs/Peterson	38	49	104	43	6145	-3	2	NE	7	6473	91	58	88	57	31	SSE	86	57	63	62	61	12	496	0	1
Denver/Stapleton IAP	39	45	104	52	5283	-5	1	S	8	6016	93	59	91	59	32	SE	89	59	64	63	62	35	667		3
Ent AFB/Colorado Springs	38	50	104	47	5980	-2	3	NE	7	6373	92	58	89	57	31	SSE	87	57	63	62	61	21	644	0	1
Fitzsimons AH/Denver	39	45	104	50	5375	-5	1	S	8	6016	93	59	91	59	32	SE	89	59	64	63	62	35	667	0	3
Fort Carson/Butts AAF	38	41	104	46	5840	-2	3	N	7	6373	92	59	89	58	31	SSE	87	58	64	63	62	31	722	0	11
Grand Junction/Walker Field	39	07	108	32	4843	2	7	ESE	5	5605	96	59	94	59	28	WNW	92	59	64	63	62	113	975	0	1
La Junta	38	03	103	30	4160	-3	3	W	8	5132	100	68	98	68	32	S	95	67	72	70	69	258	1139	22	415
Lamar	38	12	102	41	3703	-1	5	W	8	5402	102	69	100	69	32	S	97	68	73	71	70	389	1435	41	586
Lowry AFB/Denver	39	43	104	53	5396	-5	1	S	7	5978	93	61	90	60	30	N	88	60	65	64	63	29	639	0	13
Pueblo Army Depot	38	17	104	21	4700	-7	0	W	5	5394	97	61	95	61	34	SE	92	61	67	66	65	140	954		29
Pueblo Memorial Aprt	38	17	104	31	4684	-7	0	W	5	5394	97	61	95	61	34	SE	92	61	67	66	65	140	954	0	29
Rocky Mountain Arsenal	39	50	104	53	5184	-5	1	S	8	6016	93	59	91	59	32	SE	89	59	64	63	62	35	667	0	3

tion	LOCATION			WINTER DESIGN DATA HEATING				DEGREE DAYS	SUMMER DESIGN DATA AIR CONDITIONING											SUMMER CRITERIA DATA AIR CONDITIONING			
				Dry Bulb					Dry Bulb								Wet Bulb			Dry Bulb		Wet Bulb	
	Lat	Long	Elev	99%	97.5%	Pvlg Wind	Mean Speed	Heating	1%	MCWB	2.5%	MCWB	Mean Daily Range	Pvlg Wind	5%	MCWB	1%	2.5%	5%	≥ 93°F	≥ 80°F	≥ 73°F	≥ 67°F
	° ′	° ′	feet	°F	°F	dir	knots	annual	°F	°F	°F	°F	°F	dir	°F	°F	°F	°F	°F	hrs	hrs	hrs	hrs
(CONT)	N	W																					
dad	37 16	104 20	5761	-2	3	W	7	5642	93	61	91	61	32	WSW	89	61	66	65	64	38	737	1	17
Academy/Colorado Springs	39 00	104 53	7166	-8	-3	NE	7	6973	86	56	83	55	28	SSE	81	55	61	60	59	0	193	0	0
CUT	N	W																					
ley IAP/Windsor Locks	41 56	72 41	169	0	4	N	8	6350	91	74	88	72	25	SW	85	71	76	75	73	16	456	194	920
eport	41 11	73 11	25	6	9	NNW	13	5461	86	73	84	71	17	WSW	81	70	75	74	73	1	235	148	947
n	41 24	72 05	14	5	9	NW	10	6150	88	73	85	72	12	SW	83	71	76	75	74	0	338	254	1171
ord/Brainard Aprt	41 44	72 39	19	3	7	N	5	6105	91	74	88	73	24	SSW	85	72	77	75	74	18	476	253	1107
aven	41 19	72 55	6	3	7	NNE	7	5793	88	75	84	73	16	SW	82	72	76	75	74	3	245	237	1186
ord	41 03	73 32	109	6	9	NNW	13	5461	86	73	84	71	17	WSW	81	70	75	74	73	1	235	148	947
bury	41 35	73 04	843	-4	2	N	8	6672	88	73	85	71	25	SW	82	70	75	74	72	4	295	129	843
	N	W																					
AFB	39 08	75 28	28	11	15	W	9	4756	92	75	90	75	20	SW	87	74	79	77	76	23	658	585	1689
s	38 46	75 05	10	11	16	W	9	4333	90	75	88	75	18	SW	85	74	79	77	76	11	477	585	1689
ngton	39 45	75 33	79	10	14	WNW	9	4940	92	74	89	74	21	WSW	87	73	77	76	75	26	643	458	1475
ngton Airport	39 40	75 36	78	10	14	WNW	9	4940	92	74	89	74	21	WSW	87	73	77	76	75	26	643	458	1475
OF COLUMBIA	N	W																					
Map Service	38 57	77 07	250	11	15	WNW	11	4290	94	75	91	74	19	S	88	74	78	77	76	47	849	580	1744
ng-Anacostia Mil Cmplx	38 50	77 01	29	14	17	WNW	12	4153	94	75	92	75	19	S	90	74	78	77	76	59	967	620	1773
McNair	38 52	77 01	15	14	17	WNW	12	4153	94	75	92	75	19	S	90	74	78	77	76	59	967	620	1773
r Reed Army Med Cen	38 58	77 02	285	12	15	NW	10	4483	93	75	90	74	20	SSW	87	73	78	76	75	32	701	445	1573
ngton National Aprt	38 51	77 02	14	14	17	WNW	11	4211	93	75	91	74	19	S	89	74	78	77	76	41	910	580	1744
ngton Navy Yard	38 52	77 00	40	14	17	WNW	12	4153	94	75	92	75	19	S	90	74	78	77	76	59	967	620	1773
	N	W																					
chicola	29 43	85 01	20	29	33	N	8	1361	92	78	90	77	14	WSW	89	77	81	80	79	13	1908	2378	3630
Park	27 38	81 20	65	38	41	N	4	493	94	78	92	77	19	E	91	77	80	79	79	86	2021	2679	3980
oppitt Key	24 35	81 39	2	52	55	N	11	102	90	79	90	79	10	ESE	89	78	81	80	79	3	3360	3731	4327
n Bayou	30 23	86 11	10	27	31	N	8	1535	92	78	90	77	14	WSW	89	77	81	80	79	13	1908	2378	3630
on	27 54	82 18	40	39	41	NNW	9	678	93	76	91	76	19	SSW	89	76	79	78	78	20	1778	2555	3946
Canaveral AFS	28 29	80 34	16	35	38	NW	8	711	90	78	88	78	15	SE	87	78	80	79	79	4	1626	2777	4046
San Blas	29 41	85 21	10	30	34	N	8	1361	91	78	89	77	12	WSW	88	77	81	80	79	1	1908	2378	3630
en	30 23	86 27	12	26	28	N	6	1782	92	78	90	78	16	S	89	78	81	80	79	16	1760	2151	3466
Beach use Patrick AFB																							
na Beach	29 11	81 03	31	32	35	NW	8	897	92	78	90	77	18	E	88	77	80	79	78	23	1553	2355	3877

Station	Lat ° '	Long ° '	Elev feet	Winter Design Data Heating, Dry Bulb 99% °F	97.5% °F	Pvlg Wind dir	Mean Speed knots	Degree Days Heating annual	Summer Design Data Air Conditioning, Dry Bulb 1% °F	MCWB °F	2.5% °F	MCWB °F	Mean Daily Range °F	Pvlg Wind dir	5% °F	MCWB °F	Wet Bulb 1% °F	2.5% °F	5% °F	Summer Criteria Data Air Conditioning, Dry Bulb ≥ 93°F hrs	≥ 80°F hrs	Wet Bulb ≥ 73°F hrs	≥ 67°F hrs
(CONT)	N	W																					
n AFB/Valparaiso	30 29	86 31	85	25	29	N	7	1658	93	77	91	77	17	S	90	77	81	80	79	30	1788	2209	3472
Lauderdale	26 04	80 09	10	42	46	NW	9	244	92	78	91	78	15	ESE	90	78	80	79	79	13	2342	3292	4207
Myers/Page Fld	26 35	1 52	15	41	44	NNE	7	457	93	78	92	78	18	W	91	77	80	79	79	142	1890	3072	4131
esville MAP	29 41	2 16	152	28	31	W	6	1081	95	77	93	77	21	W	92	77	80	79	78	112	1504	1916	3587
stead AFB	25 29	80 24	7	43	47	N	7	218	90	78	89	78	12	E	88	78	80	79	79	2	2290	3162	4212
burt Field/Eglin No 9	30 26	6 41	35	26	28	N	6	1782	92	78	90	7	16	S	89	78	81	80	79	16	1760	2151	3466
sonville AFS	30 17	1 41	110	30	34	WSW	6	1212	94	79	92	78	17	ESE	90	78	81	80	79	61	1708	2220	3685
sonville/Cecil Fld NAS	30 13	1 53	80	28	31	W	6	1379	95	77	93	77	21	W	92	77	80	79	78	112	1504	1916	3587
sonville IAP	30 30	1 42	26	29	32	NW	7	1327	96	77	94	77	9	SW	92	76	79	79	78	126	1693	2269	3693
sonville NAS/Towers Fld	30 14	81 41	22	30	34	WSW	6	1212	94	79	92	78	7	ESE	90	78	81	80	79	61	1708	2220	3685
ter	26 57	0 04	26	41	45	NW	9	299	92	78	91	78	1	ESE	90	78	80	79	79	17	2276	3272	4194
West IAP	24 33	1 45	4	55	57	NNE	12	64	90	78	90	78		SE	89	78	80	79	79	1	3433	3778	4355
West NAS	24 34	1 41	6	52	55	N	11	102	90	79	90	79	1	ESE	89	78	81	80	79	3	3360	3731	4327
land	28 02	1 57	214	39	41	NNW	9	678	93	76	91	76	1	SSW	89	76	79	78	78	20	1778	2555	3946
Haven	30 15	85 37	69	29	33	N	8	1388	92	78	90	77	16	WSW	89	77	81	80	79	13	1908	2378	3630
ill AFB/Tampa	27 51	2 30	13	37	40	N	7	560	92	77	91	77	15	E	90	77	80	79	79	27	2031	2588	3976
ort NAVSTA	30 24	1 25	19	31	35	NW	7	1322	92	78	89	78	15	W	87	78	80	79	79	20	1492	2502	3850
y AFB/Orlando	28 27	81 20	96	34	38	N	7	709	92	76	91	76	18	E	90	76	79	78	78	28	1596	2195	3843
ourne Beach	28 03	0 33	15	36	39	NW	12	611	90	78	88	78	11	E	87	78	80	80	79	5	2088	2886	4135
i IAP	25 48	80 16	7	44	47	NNW	8	206	91	77	90	77	14	SE	89	77	79	79	78	8	2408	3313	4221
on/Whiting Field NAS	30 43	7 01	200	25	29	N	8	1743	95	76	93	76	21	S	91	76	79	79	78	99	1562	1718	3317
ndo	28 33	1 23	100	35	38	NNW	9	704	94	76	93	76	9	SSW	91	76	79	78	78	81	1675	2555	3946
ma City/Bay County	30 13	5 41	20	29	33	N	8	1388	92	78	90	77	14	WSW	89	77	81	80	79	13	1908	2378	3630
ick AFB/Cocoa Beach	28 14	0 36	9	39	43	NW	12	452	90	78	88	78	1	E	87	78	80	80	79	5	2088	2886	4135
acola/Ellyson Field NAS	30 31	87 12	115	25	29	NNE	7	1513	94	77	93	77	18	SW	91	77	80	79	79	91	2030	2344	3583
acola NAS/F Sherman Fld	30 21	7 19	30	26	30	N	9	1654	92	78	91	78	15	S	89	78	81	80	80	18	1923	2487	3600
acola/Saufley Field NAS	30 28	7 21	85	25	29	NNE	7	1513	94	77	93	77	18	SW	91	77	80	79	79	91	2030	2344	3583
e de Leon	29 04	80 55	10	32	35	NW	8	897	92	78	90	77	18	E	88	77	80	79	78	23	1553	2355	3877
mond AFS	25 37	0 24	83	43	47	N	7	218	90	78	89	78	12	E	88	78	80	79	79	2	2290	3162	4212
ra Beach	26 45	80 04	10	41	45	NW	9	299	92	78	91	78	15	ESE	90	78	80	79	79	17	2276	3272	4194
ugustine	29 58	1 20	10	31	35	NW	7	1051	92	78	89	78	15	W	87	78	80	79	79	2	1492	2502	3850
etersburg/Clearwater IAP	27 55	2 41	11	36	40	N	8	665	92	77	91	77	17	W	90	76	79	79	78	3	1881	2669	3930
ahassee MAP	30 23	4 22	55	27	30	NW	6	1563	94	77	92	76	20	NW	90	76	79	78	78	60	1460	1925	3465
a IAP	27 58	82 32	19	36	40	N	8	718	92	77	91	77	17	W	90	76	79	79	78	38	1881	2669	3930

TE Station	Lat °	Lat '	Long °	Long '	Elev feet	Winter Design Data Heating Dry Bulb 99% °F	97.5% °F	Pvlg Wind dir	Mean Speed knots	Degree Days Heating annual	Summer Design Data Air Conditioning Dry Bulb 1% °F	MCWB °F	2.5% °F	MCWB °F	Mean Daily Range °F	Pvlg Wind dir	5% °F	MCWB °F	Wet Bulb 1% °F	2.5% °F	5% °F	Summer Criteria Data Air Conditioning Dry Bulb ≥ 93°F hrs	≥ 80°F hrs	Wet Bulb ≥ 73°F hrs	≥ 67°F hrs
RIDA (CONT)	N		W																						
yndall AFB/Panama City	30	04	85	35	18	29	33	N	8	1413	92	78	90	77	14	WSW	89	77	81	80	79	13	1908	2378	3630
alkaria	27	57	80	33	15	36	40	NW	8	598	92	78	91	78	16	E	89	78	80	79	78	20	1915	2813	4035
ero Beach	27	40	80	20	1	37	41	NW	9	503	92	78	91	78	15	ESE	90	78	80	79	79	17	2276	3272	4194
est Palm Beach	26	41	80	06	1	41	45	NW	9	299	92	78	91	78	15	ESE	90	78	80	79	79	17	2276	3272	4194
RGIA	N		W																						
lbany NAS/Turner AFB	31	36	84	05	223	25	29	N	7	1793	97	77	95	76	22	W	93	76	80	79	78	216	1644	1695	3249
thens MAP	33	57	83	19	802	18	22	NW	9	2975	94	74	92	74	23	WNW	90	74	78	77	76	62	1122	820	2547
tlanta Army Depot	33	37	84	19	950	17	22	NW	11	3095	94	74	92	74	21	NW	90	73	77	76	75	52	1109	703	2454
tlanta/Hartsfield IAP	33	39	84	26	1010	17	22	NW	11	3095	94	74	92	74	21	NW	90	73	77	76	75	52	1109	703	2454
tlanta NAS/Dobbins AFB	33	55	84	31	1068	17	21	NNW	12	3273	94	74	92	74	23	NW	90	74	78	77	76	64	1129	732	2430
ugusta/Bush Field	33	22	81	58	136	20	23	W	4	2547	97	77	95	76	24	WSW	93	76	80	79	78	169	1422	1403	2889
ugusta/Daniel Field	33	28	82	03	424	20	23	W	4	2547	97	77	95	76	24	WSW	93	76	80	79	78	169	1422	1403	2889
olumbus Metro Aprt	32	31	84	56	385	21	25	NW	8	2378	95	76	94	76	24	W	92	75	79	78	77	140	1736	1472	3040
obbins AFB/Marietta	33	55	84	31	1068	17	21	NNW	12	3273	94	74	92	74	23	NW	90	74	78	77	76	64	1129	732	2430
ort Benning/Lawson AAF	32	21	85	00	232	21	24	NNW	6	2406	95	76	93	76	23	W	91	75	79	78	77	76	1296	1154	2843
ort Gordon	33	26	82	11	465	20	23	W	4	2547	97	77	95	76	24	WSW	93	76	80	79	78	169	1422	1403	2889
ort McPherson/Atlanta	33	42	84	26	1053	17	22	NW	11	3095	94	74	92	74	21	NW	90	73	77	76	75	52	1109	7 3	2454
ort Stewart/Wright AAF	31	52	81	37	88	23	26	WNW	7	1713	95	77	93	77	20	SW	91	77	80	79	78	83	1352	1702	3283
lynco NAS/Brunswick	31	15	81	29	25	26	29	NW	6	1765	93	79	91	78	19	SW	89	78	81	80	79	39	1365	2110	3559
unter AAF/Savannah	32	01	81	08	42	24	27	W	6	2029	93	78	91	77	19	W	90	77	80	79	78	50	1308	1691	3295
acon/L B Wilson Aprt ANG	32	42	83	39	354	22	26	NW	8	2240	98	75	96	75	23	WNW	94	75	79	78	77	224	1536	1295	2961
cCollum Aprt ANG/Marietta	34	01	84	36	1030	17	21	NNW	12	3273	94	74	92	74	23	NW	90	74	78	77	76	64	1129	732	2430
cKinnon Aprt ANG/Brunswick	31	08	81	23	20	29	32	NW	7	1331	92	78	89	78	15	[illegible]	87	78	80	79	79	20	1492	2502	3850
oody AFB/Valdosta	30	58	83	12	233	28	31	WNW	6	1549	96	77	94	77	21		92	76	80	79	78	133	1544	1895	3448
oultrie/Spence AF Aux Fld.	31	08	83	42	292	27	30	NW	8	1640	97	77	95	77	21		92	76	80	79	78	157	1627	2143	3479
obins AFB/Macon	32	38	83	36	294	21	25	NW	6	2244	96	77	93	76	22	W	91	75	79	78	77	113	1365	1213	2884
ome/Russell Field	34	21	85	10	637	17	22	N	7	3342	94	76	93	76	26	N	91	76	79	78	77	78	1086	922	2443
avannah AFS	32	01	81	10	68	24	27	W	6	2029	93	78	91	77	19	W	90	77	80	79	78	50	1308	1691	3295
avannah ANG Sta	32	00	81	06	42	24	27	W	6	2029	93	78	91	77	19	W	90	77	80	79	78	50	1308	1691	3295
avannah MAP ANG	32	08	81	12	50	24	27	WNW	7	1952	96	77	93	77	20	SW	91	77	80	79	78	109	1398	1772	3283
tatesboro Radar Bomb Site	32	29	81	45	180	24	27	WNW	7	1952	96	77	93	77	20	SW	91	77	80	79	78	109	1398	1772	3283
urner AFB/Albany NAS	31	36	84	05	223	25	29	N	7	1793	97	77	95	76	22	W	93	76	80	79	78	216	1644	1695	3249

LOCATION	Lat	Long	Elev	WINTER DESIGN DATA HEATING Dry Bulb 99%	97.5%	Pvlg Wind	Mean Speed	DEGREE DAYS Heating	SUMMER DESIGN DATA AIR CONDITIONING Dry Bulb 1%	MCWB	2.5%	MCWB	Mean Daily Range	Pvlg Wind	5%	MCWB	Wet Bulb 1%	2.5%	5%	SUMMER CRITERIA DATA AIR CONDITIONING Dry Bulb ≥ 93°F	≥ 80°F	Wet Bulb ≥ 73°F	≥ 67°F
	° ′	° ′	feet	°F	°F	dir	knots	annual	°F	°F	°F	°F	°F	dir	°F	°F	°F	°F	°F	hrs	hrs	hrs	hrs
	N	W																					
Point NAS	21 19	158 05	34	60	62	NE	4	1	87	74	86	74	13	ENE	85	74	77	76	75	0	1562	874	4192
Sands	22 01	1 9 47	14	58	59	NE	5		89	74	88	74	17	NE	87	74	77	76	75	1	1471	874	4192
AFB	21 22	1 7 43	15	58	60	W	6		85	74	84	74	10	NE	83	73	76	75	75		1091	954	4246
and	21 22	1 7 58	15	62	63	NW	5	0	87	73	86	73	11	ENE	85	72	76	75	74		1540	493	4136
sy	21 17	157 50	5	62	63	NW	5	0	87	73	86	73	11	ENE	85	72	76	75	74	0	1540	493	4136
	2 16	1 7 49	300	61	62	N	6		86	73	85	73	11	ENE	84	72	76	75	74		1414	493	4136
er	2 21	1 7 53	80	62	63	NW	5		87	73	86	73	11	ENE	85	72	76	75	74		1540	493	4136
	2 32	1 8 02	1100	53	55	NW	5	10	85	73	83	72	16	E	81	72	75	74	73		314	352	3835
FB/Honolulu IAP	21 20	1 7 55	13	62	63	NW	5	0	87	73	86	73	11	ENE	85	72	76	75	74	0	1540	493	4136
	19 43	155 05	36	61	62	SW	6	0	84	73	83	72	14	NE	82	72	75	74	74	0	728	468	3667
s	21 30	1 8 08	4000	47	49	W	13	1709	79	66	78	66	16	ENE	77	66	69	68	67		22	1	264
int	21 34	1 8 15	1120	55	57	W	10	190	83	72	82	72	10	NE	81	71	74	73	73		322	161	2255
	20 54	1 6 26	56	57	59	NE	5	0	90	75	89	74	21	N	88	74	77	75	75		1414	741	3590
Bay MCAS	21 27	1 7 46	18	65	66	NNE	9	0	85	75	84	74	8	NE	83	74	76	76	75	0	1186	1269	4370
S	22 09	159 38	4185	45	46	NE	14	979	81	66	80	66	13	ENE	78	65	68	67	67	0	88	0	243
mm Annex	21 28	1 8 03	800	58	59	NW		8	86	73	85	72	16	E	84	72	75	74	73		854	352	3835
	21 59	1 9 21	148	58	60	W		2	85	74	84	74	10	NE	83	73	76	75	75		1091	954	4246
AF Solar Obsy	21 23	1 8 06	1700	55	56	WNW		170	84	71	83	70	15	ENE	82	70	73	72	71		331	41	1493
rbor	21 20	1 7 57	15	62	63	NW		0	87	73	86	73	11	ENE	85	72	76	75	74	0	1540	493	4136
AFS	21 42	157 59	100	58	60	W	8	0	85	74	84	74	10	NE	83	73	76	75	75	0	1091	954	4246
d Barracks	21 30	1 8 02	850	58	59	WNW			86	73	85	72	16	E	84	72	75	74	73		854	352	3835
int AFS	18 56	1 5 41	310	56	57	N	1		87	73	85	72	14	NE	83	72	75	74	74		615	468	3667
Army Hospital	21 22	1 7 54	220	62	63	NW			87	73	86	73	11	ENE	85	72	76	75	74		1540	493	4136
	21 31	1 8 00	900	58	59	WNW		1	86	73	85	72	16	E	84	72	75	74	73	0	854	352	3835
AFB	21 29	158 02	840	58	59	WNW	8	8	86	73	85	72	16	E	84	72	75	74	73	0	854	352	3835
	N	W																					
	43 34	116 13	2838	3	10	SE	6	5833	96	65	94	64	32	NW	91	64	68	66	65	93	728	0	60
lls/Fanning Fld	43 31	112 4	4741	-11	-6	N	9	7888	89	61	87	61	37	S	84	59	65	63	61	6	357	0	7
	46 23	117 1	1413	-1	6	W	3	5464	96	65	93	64	33	WNW	90	63	67	66	64	78	631	1	52
Home AFB	43 02	115 4	2996	0	8	ESE	7	5732	99	64	97	63	35	NW	94	62	66	65	63	185	889	1	20
o	42 55	112 06	4454	-8	-1	NE	5	7063	94	61	91	60	35	W	89	59	64	63	61	48	609	0	4
reek	42 40	1 5 35	4000	-1	4	ESE	7	6353	100	62	97	61	35	NW	93	60	64	63	61	168	807		10
ls	42 29	1 4 29	4150	-3	2	SE	6	6731	99	62	95	61	35	NW	92	60	64	63	61	133	682	0	10
	43 40	116 58	2449	4	9	SE	6	5709	96	65	93	64	31	NW	90	64	68	66	65	94	685	0	60

Station	LOCATION Lat	Long	Elev	WINTER DESIGN DATA HEATING Dry Bulb 99%	97.5%	Pvlg Wind	Mean Speed	DEGREE DAYS Heating	SUMMER DESIGN DATA AIR CONDITIONING Dry Bulb 1%	MCWB	2.5%	MCWB	Mean Daily Range	Pvlg Wind	5%	MCWB	Wet Bulb 1%	2.5%	5%	SUMMER CRITERIA DATA AIR CONDITIONING Dry Bulb ≥ 93°F	≥ 80°F	Wet Bulb ≥ 73°F	≥ 67°F
	° ′	° ′	feet	°F	°F	dir	knots	annual	°F	°F	°F	°F	°F	dir	°F	°F	°F	°F	°F	hrs	hrs	hrs	hrs
IS	N	W																					
anute AFB	40 18	88 08	753	-4	1	W	10	5966	94	75	91	74	25	SSW	89	73	78	77	75	45	764	421	1386
icago/Midway Aprt	41 47	87 45	607	-5	0	NW	11	6127	94	74	91	73	23	SW	88	72	77	75	74	46	700	275	1111
icago/O Hare IAP	41 59	87 54	658	-8	-4	WNW	9	6497	91	74	89	74	24	SW	86	72	77	76	74	18	549	265	1028
nville/Vermilion Co	40 12	87 36	695	-4	1	W	10	5538	93	75	90	74	24	SSW	88	73	78	77	75	36	714	421	1386
catur	39 50	88 52	679	-3	2	NW	10	5344	94	75	91	74	24	SW	88	73	78	77	75	46	793	421	1386
rest Park NOP	41 53	87 50	650	-5	0	NW	11	6127	94	74	91	73	23	SW	88	72	77	75	74	46	700	275	1111
rt Sheridan/Haley AAF	42 13	87 49	690	-4	0	W	9	6068	92	76	89	74	15	SW	86	73	78	76	75	18	549	290	1064
lesburg MAP	40 56	90 26	764	-7	-2	WNW	8	6005	93	75	91	75	22	SW	88	74	78	77	75	41	714	394	1306
enview NAS	42 05	87 49	659	-6	-3	W	8	6582	92	76	89	74	22	SW	87	73	78	76	75	21	543	290	1064
anite City Army Depot	38 41	90 11	415	3	8	NW	9	4486	98	75	94	75	22	S	91	74	78	77	76	119	1223	645	1802
eat Lakes NTC	42 18	87 50	650	-4	0	W	9	6068	92	76	89	74	15	SW	86	73	78	76	75	18	549	290	1064
liet MAP	41 31	88 10	582	-5	0	NW	11	6180	93	75	90	74	26	SW	88	73	78	77	75	35	632	335	1131
line/Quad City Aprt	41 27	90 31	582	-9	-4	WNW	8	6395	93	75	91	75	24	SW	88	74	78	77	75	41	714	394	1306
oria	40 40	89 41	652	-8	-4	WNW	8	6098	91	75	89	74	23	SW	87	73	78	76	75	13	669	384	1349
incy MAP	39 57	91 12	769	-2	3	NW	11	5267	96	76	93	76	24	SSW	90	76	80	78	77	75	829	608	1607
ck Island Arsenal	41 31	90 33	575	-7	-3	W	8	5961	92	75	90	75	19	SW	88	74	78	77	75	20	867	394	1306
vanna Army Depot	42 11	90 15	640	-11	-7	NW	9	6694	90	74	87	74	22	SSE	85	73	77	76	75	8	457	323	1181
ott AFB/Belleville	38 33	89 51	453	1	6	WNW	8	4855	94	76	92	76	22	S	89	75	79	78	76	50	941	619	1764
ringfield/Capital	39 50	89 40	588	-3	2	NW	10	5558	94	75	92	74	24	SW	89	74	79	77	76	60	904	539	1579
IA	N	W																					
derson MAP	40 06	85 37	919	0	6	[illegible]	9	5580	95	76	92	75	25	SW	89	74	79	78	76	73	786	580	1687
kalar AFB/Columbus	39 16	85 54	651	3	7		9	5132	95	76	92	75	25	SW	90	74	79	78	76	65	872	580	1687
oomington/Monroe County	39 08	86 37	847	0	5		9	4905	95	76	92	75	25	SW	89	74	79	78	76	59	879	580	1687
mp Atterbury	39 22	86 03	757	3	7		9	5132	95	76	92	75	25	SW	90	74	79	78	76	65	872	580	1687
ane	38 49	86 52	734	3	9		9	4637	95	76	92	75	25	SW	89	74	79	78	76	62	925	580	1687
ansville/Dress Rgnl Aprt	38 03	87 32	381	4	9	NW	9	4624	95	76	93	75	25	SW	91	75	79	78	77	86	1084	777	1942
rt Benjamin Harrison	39 51	86 00	864	-2	2	WNW	10	5577	92	74	90	74	23	SW	87	73	78	76	75	24	682	400	1437
rt Wayne/Baer Fld	41 00	85 12	791	-4	1	WSW	10	6209	92	73	89	72	23	SW	87	72	77	75	74	24	618	245	1120
ry MAP	41 37	87 25	591	-4	2	SW	11	6165	91	73	88	73	24	SSW	85	72	77	75	74	18	519	234	1031
issom AFB/Bunker Hill	40 39	86 09	813	-6	-1	W	10	6278	90	74	88	73	22	SW	86	73	77	75	74	12	563	261	1117
diana AAP	38 25	85 39	600	5	10	NW	8	4640	95	74	93	74	24	SW	90	74	79	77	76	80	1022	668	1886
dianapolis/Weir Cook MAP	39 44	86 17	792	-2	2	WNW	10	5577	92	74	90	74	23	SW	87	73	78	76	75	24	682	400	1437
fferson Proving Ground	38 50	85 25	860	2	7	NW	8	5132	96	74	93	74	26	SW	90	74	79	77	76	90	932	668	1886
wport AAP	39 52	87 26	640	-1	4	NNW	7	5346	95	75	92	74	23	SSW	89	73	79	77	76	59	619	529	1576

	LOCATION			WINTER DESIGN DATA HEATING				DEGREE DAYS	SUMMER DESIGN DATA AIR CONDITIONING											SUMMER CRITERIA DATA AIR CONDITIONING			
STATE				Dry Bulb					Dry Bulb								Wet Bulb			Dry Bulb		Wet Bulb	
Station	Lat	Long	Elev	99%	97.5%	Pvlg Wind	Mean Speed	Heating	1%	MCWB	2.5%	MCWB	Mean Daily Range	Pvlg Wind	5%	MCWB	1%	2.5%	5%	≥ 93°F	≥ 80°F	≥ 73°F	≥ 67°F
	° '	° '	feet	°F	°F	dir	knots	annual	°F	°F	°F	°F	°F	dir	°F	°F	°F	°F	°F	hrs	hrs	hrs	hrs
INDIANA (CONT)	N	W																					
South Bend/St Joseph Aprt	41 42	86 19	773	-3	1	SW	11	6462	91	73	89	73	24	SSW	86	72	77	75	74	15	534	234	1031
Terre Haute/Hulman Fld	39 27	87 18	585	-2	4	NNW	7	5351	95	75	92	74	23	SSW	89	73	79	77	76	55	862	529	1576
IOWA	N	W																					
Burlington MAP	40 47	91 07	692	-7	-3	NW	9	6149	94	75	91	75	22	SSW	88	73	78	77	75	42	708	423	1370
Cedar Rapids MAP	41 53	91 42	863	-10	-5	NW	9	6601	91	76	88	75	23	S	86	74	78	77	75	17	532	364	1248
Des Moines MAP	41 32	93 39	938	-10	-5	NW	11	6710	94	75	91	74	23	S	88	73	78	77	75	43	691	400	1283
Dubuque MAP	42 24	90 42	1056	-12	-7	N	10	7277	90	74	88	73	21	SSW	86	72	77	75	74	11	605	252	1055
Fort Dodge MAP	42 33	94 11	1162	-12	-7	NW	11	7072	91	74	88	74	23	S	86	72	77	75	74	16	524	233	891
Iowa Army Ammunition Plant	40 49	91 15	730	-7	-3	NW	9	6149	94	75	91	75	22	SSW	88	73	78	77	75	42	708	423	1370
Iowa City MAP	41 38	91 33	661	-11	-6	NW	9	6404	92	76	89	76	26	SSW	87	74	80	78	76	17	612	400	1251
Mason City MAP	43 09	93 20	1213	-15	-11	NW	11	7901	90	74	88	74	23	S	85	72	77	75	74	11	444	233	891
Sioux City MAP	42 24	96 23	1095	-11	-7	NNW	9	6953	95	74	92	74	26	S	89	73	78	77	75	61	746	365	1188
Waterloo MAP	42 33	92 24	868	-15	-10	NW	9	7415	91	76	89	75	24	S	86	74	78	77	75	18	580	364	1248
KANSAS	N	W																					
Chanute	37 40	95 29	981	3	7	NNW	11	4566	100	74	97	74	25	SSW	94	74	78	77	76	210	1234	746	2069
Dodge City	37 46	99 58	2582	0	5	N	12	5046	100	69	97	69	27	SSW	95	69	74	73	71	239	1144	72	1081
Forbes ANGB/Topeka	38 57	95 40	1064	-1	4	N	8	5309	96	76	93	76	22	S	90	75	79	78	76	85	909	588	1674
Fort Leavenworth/Sherman AAF	39 22	94 55	770	-1	3	NNW	10	4822	96	77	93	76	25	S	91	76	81	79	77	93	990	678	1749
Fort Riley/Marshall AAF	39 03	96 46	1065	-1	3	NNE	8	5306	99	75	95	75	22	S	92	74	78	77	76	144	1094	510	1641
Goodland/Renner Fld	39 22	101 42	3654	-5	0	WSW	10	6119	99	66	96	65	33	S	93	66	71	70	68	176	893	6	369
Hutchinson MAP	38 04	97 52	1542	4	8	N	14	4671	102	72	99	72	26	S	97	72	77	75	74	311	1301	412	1758
Kansas City/Fairfax MAP	39 09	94 36	745	2	6	NW	9	4846	99	75	96	74	21	S	93	74	78	77	76	164	1278	654	1828
Kansas Ordnance Plant	37 20	95 13	925	5	9	NNW	10	4005	100	74	97	74	25	SSW	94	74	78	77	76	210	1234	746	2069
McConnell AFB/Wichita	37 38	97 16	1371	4	8	N	11	4695	100	74	96	74	24	S	93	73	78	76	75	168	1141	505	1840
Olathe NAS	38 50	94 53	1076	-1	3	NNW	9	4483	97	75	94	75	23	SSW	91	74	79	77	76	110	1069	557	1711
Parsons/Tri City	37 20	95 31	899	5	9	NNW	11	4158	100	74	97	74	25	SSW	94	74	79	77	76	210	1234	746	2069
Salina MAP	38 48	97 39	1272	0	5	N	8	4992	103	74	100	74	27	SSW	97	73	78	77	75	311	1367	606	1873
Schilling Manor	38 48	97 39	1272	0	5	N	8	4992	103	74	100	74	27	SSW	97	73	78	77	75	311	1367	606	1873
Smoky Hill AF Range	38 42	97 50	1440	1	6	N	11	4841	102	74	99	74	27	SSW	96	73	78	77	75	311	1301	606	1873
Sunflower Ordnance Works	38 56	95 00	925	-1	3	NNW	9	5030	98	75	95	75	23	SSW	92	74	79	77	76	137	1174	557	1711
Topeka/Philip Billard	39 04	95 38	877	0	4	NNW	10	5243	99	75	96	75	27	S	93	74	79	78	76	157	1100	668	1825
Wichita	37 39	97 25	1321	3	7	NNW	12	4687	101	72	98	73	25	SSW	96	73	77	76	75	270	1332	543	2005

KY	N	W																					
hland	38 33	82 44	546	5	10	W	6	4555	94	76	91	74	27	SW	89	73	78	77	75	47	797	470	1671
ue Grass Army Depot	37 41	84 14	1035	3	8	WNW	9	4729	93	73	91	73	24	SW	88	72	77	76	75	37	822	401	1641
vington	39 03	84 40	869	1	6	W	9	5070	92	73	90	72	23	SW	88	72	77	75	74	24	748	316	1423
rt Campbell/Campbell AAF	36 40	87 29	571	4	10	N	6	4290	94	77	92	75	22	W	89	74	79	77	76	56	998	664	1975
rt Knox/Godman AAF	37 54	85 58	753	1	7	W	7	4616	92	76	90	75	22	WSW	88	74	79	77	76	20	847	543	1740
xington/Blue Grass Field	38 02	84 36	966	3	8	WNW	9	4729	93	73	91	73	24	SW	88	72	77	76	75	37	822	401	1641
uisville/Standiford Field	38 11	85 44	477	5	10	NW	8	4640	95	74	93	74	24	SW	90	74	79	77	76	80	1022	668	1886
ensboro	37 45	87 10	407	5	10	NW	9	4220	97	76	94	75	25	SW	91	75	79	78	77	113	1106	777	1942
chmond	37 40	84 15	1043	3	8	WNW	9	4729	93	73	91	73	24	SW	88	72	77	76	75	37	822	401	1641
NA	N	W																					
exandria/Esler Field	31 24	92 18	92	23	27	N	7	2200	95	77	94	77	20	S	92	77	80	79	78	133	1599	1797	3264
rksdale AFB/Shreveport	32 30	93 40	167	19	24	N	6	2337	96	77	94	77	22	S	93	77	80	79	78	156	1518	1558	2996
ton Rouge/Ryan Aprt	30 32	91 09	64	25	29	ENE	8	1670	95	77	93	77	20	W	92	77	80	80	79	116	1667	2150	3482
aibourne	31 07	92 35	200	23	27	N	7	1964	95	77	94	77	20	S	92	77	80	79	79	133	1599	1797	3264
gland AFB/Alexandria	31 20	92 33	89	23	27	N	7	1964	95	77	94	77	20	S	92	77	80	79	79	133	1599	1797	3264
rt Polk/Polk AAF	31 03	93 11	330	23	27	N	7	1889	95	77	94	77	20	S	92	77	80	79	79	133	1599	1797	3264
mond ANG Comm Sta	30 31	90 24	40	26	30	ENE	8	1591	95	77	93	77	20	W	92	77	80	80	79	116	1667	2150	3482
fayette	30 12	92 00	42	26	30	N	8	1551	95	78	94	78	22	SW	92	78	81	80	79	142	1678	2476	3577
ke Charles AFS	30 10	93 10	15	27	31	N	9	1498	95	77	93	77	18	SSW	92	77	80	79	79	92	1766	2475	3589
ke Charles MAP	30 07	93 13	9	27	31	N	9	1498	95	77	93	77	18	SSW	92	77	80	79	79	92	1766	2475	3589
uisiana Ordnance Plant	32 34	93 34	195	19	24	N	6	2337	96	77	94	77	22	S	93	77	80	79	78	156	1518	1558	2996
nroe MAP	32 31	92 02	79	20	25	N	9	2311	99	77	96	76	22	S	94	76	79	79	78	244	1774	1853	3194
w Orleans Army Terminal	29 58	90 02	5	29	33	NNE	9	1465	93	78	92	78	18	SSW	90	77	81	80	79	44	1727	2572	3670
w Orleans/Moisant IAP	29 59	90 15	4	29	33	NNE	9	1465	93	78	92	78	18	SSW	90	77	81	80	79	44	1727	2572	3670
w Orleans NAS	29 50	90 01	3	28	31	NNE	8	1617	93	78	91	78	16	W	90	78	82	81	80	33	1639	2479	3618
reveport	32 28	93 49	254	20	25	N	9	2167	99	77	96	76	22	S	94	76	79	79	78	244	1774	1853	3194
	N	W																					
gusta	44 19	69 48	353	-7	-3	NNE	10	7826	88	73	85	70	25	WNW	82	68	74	72	70	5	246	63	442
ngor IAP/Dow AFB	44 48	68 50	192	-11	-6	WNW	7	8034	86	70	83	68	24	S	80	67	73	71	69	2	181	34	321
Harbor	44 27	68 22	84	-7	-3	NW	8	7240	86	70	83	68	22	W	80	67	73	71	69	1	170	34	321
unswick NAS	43 54	69 56	75	-6	-2	NW	8	7552	85	70	81	68	21	S	79	67	72	70	68	1	121	20	289
ks Harbor AFS	44 38	67 24	221	-11	-5	WNW	7	8056	86	70	83	69	22	WSW	80	67	73	71	69	1	171	34	321
ribou MAP	46 52	68 01	624	-18	-13	WSW	10	9632	84	69	81	67	25	SW	78	66	71	69	67	0	103	13	195

	WINTER DESIGN DATA HEATING							DEGREE DAYS	SUMMER DESIGN DATA AIR CONDITIONING											SUMMER CRITERIA DATA AIR CONDITIONING			
	LOCATION			Dry Bulb					Dry Bulb								Wet Bulb			Dry Bulb		Wet Bulb	
	Lat	Long	Elev	99%	97.5%	Pvlg Wind	Mean Speed	Heating	1%	MCWB	2.5%	MCWB	Mean Daily Range	Pvlg Wind	5%	MCWB	1%	2.5%	5%	≥ 93°F	≥ 80°F	≥ 73°F	≥ 67°F
	° ′	° ′	feet	°F	°F	dir	knots	annual	°F	°F	°F	°F	°F	dir	°F	°F	°F	°F	°F	hrs	hrs	hrs	hrs
	N	W																					
AFS	46 58	67 50	843	-16	-12	NW	8	9500	83	68	80	66	23	S	77	65	71	69	67	0	85	9	155
on AFS	45 05	69 05	930	-16	-10	WNW	7	9008	86	70	82	68	26	WSW	79	66	72	70	69	2	138	23	280
FB	46 57	67 53	746	-16	-12	NW	8	9500	83	68	80	66	23	S	77	65	71	69	67	0	85	9	155
ket	45 39	68 42	413	-13	-9	WNW	11	8533	87	69	83	68	27	WNW	80	66	72	70	68	5	188	23	279
	43 39	70 19	43	-6	-1	W	7	7498	87	72	84	71	25	S	81	69	74	72	70	3	206	68	458
t	44 27	68 55	7	-11	-6	NW	8	7467	86	70	83	68	24	W	80	67	73	71	69	2	181	34	321
arbor	44 20	68 04	11	-7	-3	NW	8	7240	86	70	83	68	22	W	80	67	73	71	69	1	170	34	32[illegible]
	N	W																					
PG/Phillips AAF	39 28	76 10	57	11	15	NW	8	5184	94	77	90	75	21	SSW	88	75	80	78	76	42	713	601	30
AFB	38 49	76 52	279	10	14	NW	10	4551	92	75	90	74	20	SSW	87	73	78	76	75	16	729	445	73
s USNA	38 59	76 29	40	15	18	WNW	9	4548	91	77	89	77	16	S	86	75	80	79	77	13	742	879	90
ge NTC	39 37	76 04	50	11	15	NW	8	5184	94	77	90	75	21	SSW	88	75	80	78	76	42	713	601	1 30
e/Martin Aprt	39 20	76 25	24	14	17	WNW	9	4866	92	77	89	76	18	S	87	75	80	78	76	27	727	740	1610
e/Washington IAP	39 11	76 40	148	10	1	W	9	4729	94	75	91	75	22	WSW	89	74	78	77	76	43	790	533	1613
NAVNATMEDCEN	39 00	77 06	310	12	1	NW	0	4645	94	75	92	74	20	SSW	89	73	78	76	75	47	726	445	1573
NSRDC	38 59	77 12	130	11	1	WNW	11	4290	94	75	91	74	19	S	88	74	78	77	76	41	809	580	1744
nd MAP	39 37	78 46	790	16	1	WNW	10	5012	92	75	89	74	26	W	87	74	77	76	75	20	596	314	1254
Arsenal	39 24	76 18	22	3	1[illegible]	WNW	9	4866	92	77	89	76	18	SSW	87	75	80	78	76	28	713	700	1761
rick	39 26	77 26	355		12	N		5059	93	76	91	75	26	WNW	88	74	79	77	76	35	647	472	1492
abird	39 16	76 32	32	1	19	WNW		4101	92	77	90	76	15	SW	87	75	80	78	77	23	813	800	1892
de/Tipton AAF	39 05	76 46	150		11	NW		4733	92	75	90	74	24	W	88	73	78	77	75	22	767	398	1393
hie	39 40	77 28	1320		12	WNW	1	5897	91	74	88	73	26	W	86	73	76	75	74	16	416	221	1078
k	39 27	77 25	313	[illegible]	12	N	[illegible]	5059	94	76	91	75	26	WNW	88	74	78	77	76	41	693	469	1466
wn	39 42	77 44	704		12	WNW	10	5152	94	75	91	74	26	W	89	74	77	76	75	44	702	384	1383
ead NOS	38 36	77 10	15		14	NW	6	4498	93	77	91	76	21	S	89	75	80	78	77	37	892	710	1884
River NAS	38 17	76 26	38		18	NW	11	4307	92	75	89	75	17	SW	87	74	79	77	76	20	772	682	1850
k NAVSURFWPNCEN	39 02	76 59	200	1[illegible]	15	NW	10	4483	93	75	90	74	20	SSW	87	73	78	76	75	27	670	445	1573
S	N	W																					
/Mech Res Cen	42 21	71 10	40			WNW	16	5621	91	73	88	71	21	SW	85	70	75	74	72	16	394	125	762
ogan IAP	42 22	71 02	15			WNW	16	5621	91	73	88	71	21	SW	85	70	75	74	72	16	394	125	762
lavy Base	42 21	71 03	15			WNW	16	5621	91	73	88	71	21	SW	85	70	75	74	72	16	394	125	762
er	41 43	71 08	190			NW	10	5774	87	72	84	71	20	SW	81	69	74	73	72	5	230	90	780
ens/Devens AAF	42 34	71 36	268	-[illegible]	[illegible]	NW	8	6475	92	73	89	72	24	WSW	86	70	76	74	73	26	466	154	770

Station	LOCATION Lat N (° ′)	Long W (° ′)	Elev (feet)	WINTER DESIGN DATA HEATING Dry Bulb 99% (°F)	97.5% (°F)	Pvlg Wind (dir)	Mean Speed (knots)	DEGREE DAYS Heating (annual)	SUMMER DESIGN DATA AIR CONDITIONING Dry Bulb 1% (°F)	MCWB (°F)	2.5% (°F)	MCWB (°F)	Mean Daily Range (°F)	Pvlg Wind (dir)	5% (°F)	MCWB (°F)	Wet Bulb 1% (°F)	2.5% (°F)	5% (°F)	SUMMER CRITERIA DATA AIR CONDITIONING Dry Bulb ≥ 93°F (hrs)	≥ 80°F (hrs)	Wet Bulb ≥ 73°F (hrs)	≥ 67°F (hrs)
HUSETTS (CONT)																							
scom AFB/Bedford	42 28	71 17	133	-2	3	NW	8	6474	90	73	87	72	24	WSW	84	70	76	74	73	10	394	154	770
rence MAP	42 43	71 07	147	-6	0	NW	8	6195	90	73	87	72	24	WSW	84	70	76	74	73	15	358	154	770
n	42 28	70 55	50	6	9	WNW	16	5621	91	73	88	71	21	SW	85	70	75	74	72	16	394	125	762
nard	42 25	71 29	205	-2	3	N	5	6539	90	73	87	72	26	W	84	71	76	74	73	10	394	165	803
tucket	41 15	70 10	12	14	17	NW	14	5929	79	70	77	70	13	SW	75	68	73	71	70	0	28	35	697
ick Laboratories	42 17	71 22	160	-3	2	NW	8	6144	93	73	90	72	24	WSW	87	70	76	74	73	35	539	154	770
Bedford MAP	41 41	70 58	79	5	9	NW	10	5395	85	72	82	71	17	SW	80	69	74	73	72	1	173	90	780
th Truro AFS	42 02	70 04	160	10	15	NW	10	5393	85	72	83	71	17	SW	80	69	74	73	72	1	142	90	780
s AFB/Falmouth	41 39	70 31	132	5	9	NW	10	6132	84	72	82	71	17	SW	79	69	74	73	72	1	137	90	780
tsfield MAP	42 26	73 18	1194	-8	-3	NW	12	7580	87	71	84	70	24	SW	81	68	73	72	70	1	185	38	451
ncy	42 14	71 00	20	6	9	WNW	16	5621	91	73	88	71	21	SW	85	70	75	74	72	16	394	125	762
em	42 32	70 52	40	3	8	WNW	16	5975	87	73	83	71	21	SW	80	70	75	74	72	4	152	125	762
th Weymouth NAS	42 09	70 57	156	2	6	NNW	8	6332	90	73	87	72	23	W	85	71	76	75	73	9	433	177	840
ingfield	42 06	72 35	195	1	6	N	8	5844	92	72	89	71	26	SSW	86	69	75	73	72	23	500	123	743
esly ANG Station	42 19	71 14	65	-3	2	NW	8	6144	93	73	90	72	24	WSW	87	70	76	74	73	35	539	154	770
tfield/Barnes MAP	42 10	72 43	270	-5	0	N	8	6794	90	72	87	71	26	SSW	84	69	75	73	72	9	402	123	743
tover AFB	42 12	72 32	245	-5	0	N	8	6794	90	72	87	71	26	SSW	84	69	75	73	72	9	402	123	743
cester	42 16	71 52	986	0	4	W	14	6848	87	71	84	70	21	W	81	68	73	72	70	2	212	40	476
N																							
ena/Phelps Collins Field	45 04	83 34	689	-11	-6	W	5	8518	89	70	85	70	21	SW	83	69	73	72	70	5	321	47	450
Arbor	42 17	83 45	926	1	5	SW	10	6306	92	72	89	71	24	SW	86	70	75	74	72	19	522	147	843
tle Creek Aprt	42 19	85 15	941	1	5	SW	8	6720	92	74	88	72	23	SW	85	70	76	74	73	21	477	168	833
shore	45 21	85 06	678	-3	2	NW	8	7669	88	72	85	71	23	WSW	81	69	75	73	71	4	221	80	548
ton Harbor/Ross Field	42 08	86 26	643	1	5	SSW	8	6296	91	72	88	72	23	WSW	85	70	75	74	72	14	465	142	800
umet AFS	47 22	88 10	1520	-11	-6	NW	9	9700	82	70	79	68	25	W	76	66	72	69	67	0	62	20	173
roit Arsenal	42 30	83 02	618	3	6	W	11	6228	91	73	88	72	21	SW	86	71	76	74	73	16	504	167	896
roit/City Aprt	42 25	83 01	619	3	6	W	11	6228	91	73	88	72	21	SW	86	71	76	74	73	16	504	167	896
re AFS	44 48	86 03	1000	-3	3	SSW	9	7617	85	72	82	71	25	SW	80	69	75	73	71	1	156	80	548
nt/Bishop Aprt	42 58	83 44	771	-4	1	SW	8	7041	90	73	87	72	24	SW	85	71	76	74	72	9	407	137	763
nd Rapids/Kent County	42 53	85 31	784	1	5	WNW	8	6801	91	72	88	72	23	WSW	85	70	75	74	72	12	467	142	800
cock/Houghton Co Mem	47 10	88 29	1091	-9	-4	NW	9	9499	84	71	81	69	25	W	78	67	73	70	68	0	104	29	237
ghton	47 10	88 30	1082	-9	-4	NW	9	9499	84	71	81	69	25	W	78	67	73	70	68	0	104	29	237
cheloe AFB	46 15	84 28	799	-14	-10	E	6	9234	84	70	81	68	25	SW	78	66	72	70	68	0	107	21	235
Sawyer AFB	46 21	87 24	1220	-16	-11	W	7	9498	86	70	82	68	27	SSW	79	66	72	70	68	3	151	25	250

STATE / Station	Location: Lat N (° ′)	Location: Long W (° ′)	Location: Elev (feet)	Winter Design Data, Heating, Dry Bulb: 99% (°F)	97.5% (°F)	Pvlg Wind (dir)	Mean Speed (knots)	Degree Days: Heating (annual)	Summer Design Data, Air Conditioning, Dry Bulb: 1% (°F)	MCWB (°F)	2.5% (°F)	MCWB (°F)	Mean Daily Range (°F)	Pvlg Wind (dir)	5% (°F)	MCWB (°F)	Wet Bulb: 1% (°F)	2.5% (°F)	5% (°F)	Summer Criteria Data, Air Conditioning, Dry Bulb: ≥ 93°F (hrs)	≥ 80°F (hrs)	Wet Bulb: ≥ 73°F (hrs)	≥ 67°F (hrs)
MICHIGAN (CONT)	N	W																					
Lansing/Capital City Aprt	42 47	84 36	841	-3	1	SW	1	6904	90	73	87	72	24	W	84	70	75	74	72	7	409	123	738
Michigan Army Missile Plant	42 34	83 01	615	2	5	W	1	6228	91	73	88	72	21	SW	86	71	76	74	73	16	504	167	896
Mount Clemens NAF	42 36	82 50	583	-1	3	W		6665	89	73	86	72	22	S	84	71	76	74	73	5	387	168	869
Muskegon/Muskegon Co Aprt	43 10	86 14	625	2	6	E		6890	86	72	84	70	22	SW	82	70	75	73	72	2	262	105	712
Port Austin AFS	44 02	83 00	670	-5	0	SW	2	7638	88	72	85	70	25	S	82	68	74	72	70	4	240	65	465
Port Huron	42 59	82 25	586	0			8	6564	90	73	87	72	22	S	83	71	76	74	73	11	348	168	869
Saginaw/Tri City Aprt	43 32	84 05	667	0		WS	7	7143	91	73	87	72	24	SW	84	71	76	74	72	15	365	131	642
Sault Sainte Marie AFS	46 28	84 22	721	-12	-4	W	7	9193	84	70	81	69	24	SW	77	66	72	70	68	0	96	25	243
Selfridge ANGB/Mt Clemens	42 36	82 50	583	-1	[illegible]	W	8	6665	89	73	86	72	22	S	84	71	76	74	73	15	387	168	869
Traverse City Aprt	44 45	85 35	624	-3	1	SSW	9	7698	89	72	86	71	25	SW	83	69	75	73	71	0	305	80	548
Wurtsmith AFB/Oscoda	44 27	83 24	634	-7	-3	SW	1	7929	88	72	85	70	25	S	81	68	74	72	70	1	227	65	465
Ypsilanti	42 14	83 32	716	1	3	SW	8	6424	92	72	89	71	24	SW	86	70	75	74	72	6	522	147	843
MINNESOTA	N	W																					
Baudette AFS	48 40	94 37	1100	-31	-26	W	7	10098	87	68	83	68	26	S	80	66	71	70	68	1	153	16	226
Bemidji MAP	47 31	94 56	1389	-31	-26	N	8	10203	88	69	85	69	27	S	81	67	73	71	69	6	213	4	314
Duluth IAP	46 50	92 11	1428	-21	-16	WNW	12	9757	85	70	82	68	23	WSW	79	66	72	70	68	0	131	2	226
Finland AFS	47 27	91 14	1950	-23	-18	WNW	12	10407	83	69	80	67	23	WSW	77	65	71	69	67	0	76	1	177
International Falls IAP	48 34	93 23	1179	-29	-25	W	7	10547	85	68	83	68	26	S	80	66	71	70	68	2	168	18	226
Minneapolis-St Paul IAP	44 53	93 13	834	-16	-12	NW		8310	92	75	89	73	23	S	86	71	77	75	73	19	475	17	772
Rochester MAP	43 55	92 30	1297	-17	-12	NW		8227	90	74	87	72	23	SSW	84	71	77	75	73	11	389	16	749
Twin Cities Ordnance Plant	45 05	93 10	970	-16	-12	NW	8	8310	92	75	89	73	23	S	86	71	77	75	73	19	475	178	772
MISSISSIPPI	N	W																					
Biloxi use Keesler AFB																							
Columbus AFB	33 39	88 27	219	15	20	N	7	2890	95	77	93	77	22	W	91	76	80	79	78	102	1333	1288	2825
Gulfport	30 22	89 06	33	28	31	N	8	1496	94	79	92	79	15	S	90	78	82	81	80	56	2096	2574	3644
Jackson/Allen Thompson Fld	32 19	90 05	310	21	25	NNW	6	2300	97	76	95	76	22	NW	93	76	79	78	78	185	1576	1561	3091
Keesler AFB/Biloxi	30 25	88 55	26	28	31	N	8	1549	94	79	92	79	15	S	90	78	82	81	80	56	2096	2574	3644
Meridian/Key Field ANG	32 20	88 45	290	19	23	N		2388	97	77	95	76	24	WSW	93	76	80	79	78	188	1568	1120	2649
Meridian NAS/McCain Field	32 33	88 34	317	16	21	N	6	2712	95	77	93	76	24	WSW	92	76	80	79	78	105	1331	1120	2649

Station	LOCATION Lat	Long	Elev	WINTER DESIGN DATA HEATING Dry Bulb 99%	97.5%	Pvlg Wind	Mean Speed	DEGREE DAYS Heating	SUMMER DESIGN DATA AIR CONDITIONING Dry Bulb 1%	MCWB	2.5%	MCWB	Mean Daily Range	Pvlg Wind	5%	MCWB	Wet Bulb 1%	2.5%	5%	SUMMER CRITERIA DATA AIR CONDITIONING Dry Bulb ≥ 93°F	≥ 80°F	Wet Bulb ≥ 73°F	≥ 67°F
	° '	° '	feet	°F	°F	dir	knots	annual	°F	°F	°F	°F	°F	dir	°F	°F	°F	°F	°F	hrs	hrs	hrs	hrs
.I (CONT)	N	W																					
]ibal	39 43	91 22	712	-2	3	NNW	11	5512	96	76	93	76	24	SSW	90	76	80	78	77	75	829	608	1607
'erson Barracks ANG	38 30	90 17	770	3	8	NW	9	4486	98	75	94	75	22	S	91	74	78	77	76	119	1223	645	1802
.in MAP	37 09	94 30	980	6	10	NNW	12	4188	100	73	97	73	24	SSW	94	73	78	77	76	214	1171	699	2058
sas City MAP	39 07	94 35	791	2	6	NW	9	4711	99	75	96	74	21	S	93	74	78	77	76	164	1278	654	1828
City Arsenal	39 06	94 15	810	-2	3	N	8	5218	93	76	91	76	21	S	88	74	78	77	76	37	796	490	1588
den MAP	36 36	89 59	295	11	16	NNE	9	3908	98	78	95	76	25	SSW	92	76	81	79	78	120	1375	1054	2310
]ards-Gebaur AFB/Grandview	38 51	94 [illegible]	1000	0	0	N	0	5218	93	76	91	76	21	S	88	74	78	77	76	37	796	490	1588
Joseph/Rosecrans Aprt	39 46	94 55	825	-3	2	NNW	9	5440	96	77	93	76	25	S	91	76	81	79	77	93	990	678	1749
.ouis AFS	38 45	90 22	570	2	6	NW	9	4750	97	75	94	75	22	WSW	91	74	78	77	76	103	1123	645	1802
.ouis/Lambert IAP	38 45	90 23	535	2	6	NW	9	4750	97	75	94	75	22	WSW	91	74	78	77	76	103	1123	645	1802
.ouis Ordnance Depot	38 41	90 16	580	3	8	NW	6	4486	98	75	94	75	22	S	91	74	78	77	76	119	1223	645	1802
ingfield MAP	37 14	93 23	1268	3	9	NNW	10	4570	96	73	93	74	23	S	91	74	78	77	75	92	975	566	1888
eman AFB/Knob Noster	38 43	93 33	869	-1	4	NNW	7	5012	95	76	92	76	22	SSW	90	75	79	78	76	58	913	601	1738
	N	W																					
ings/Logan IAP	45 48	108 32	3567	-15	-10	NE	9	7265	94	64	91	64	31	SW	88	63	67	66	64	50	537	1	42
te	45 57	112 30	5553	-24	-17	S	5	9719	86	58	83	56	37	NW	80	56	60	58	57	1	177	0	0
Bank	48 37	112 22	3838	-25	-20	NNW	9	9033	88	61	85	61	32	WSW	82	60	64	62	61	6	219	0	7
.on	45 15	112 33	5224	-18	-10	NE	8	8354	90	61	87	60	36	SW	84	59	63	62	60	7	310	0	4
sgow AFB	48 25	106 32	2760	-22	-18	E	8	9251	92	64	89	63	28	S	85	62	68	66	64	23	370	1	51
at Falls IAP	47 29	111 22	3662	-21	-15	SW	7	7652	91	60	88	60	30	WSW	85	59	64	62	60	18	364	0	6
re AFS	48 52	109 56	3200	-22	-15	NW	8	9058	93	63	89	62	30	SW	85	61	66	64	63	32	351	0	18
ena	46 36	112 00	3828	-21	-16	WNW	5	8190	91	60	88	60	35	WNW	85	59	64	62	61	15	326	0	4
ispell AFS	48 01	114 22	6780	-31	-24	NW	15	11024	89	55	86	55	35	W	82	54	58	56	55	0	205	0	0
istown	47 04	109 27	4122	-22	-16	NW	9	8586	90	62	87	61	33	NW	83	60	65	63	62	10	288	0	13
nstrom AFB	47 30	111 11	3525	-21	-15	WSW	5	7671	92	61	89	61	32	W	86	60	64	62	61	26	403	0	3
es City	46 26	105 52	2634	-20	-15	NW	7	7889	98	76	95	66	33	SE	92	65	70	68	67	123	691	6	154
soula	46 55	114 05	3190	-13	-6	ESE	7	7931	92	62	88	61	38	NW	85	60	65	63	62	20	346	0	8
eim AFS	48 52	106 28	3290	-27	-23	NW	8	9251	91	63	88	62	30	SW	84	61	67	65	63	21	278	0	32
A	N	W																					
hhusker AAP	40 55	98 29	1915	-8	-3	NNW	10	6420	97	72	94	71	27	S	91	71	75	74	73	113	818	193	1037
nd Island	40 58	98 19	1841	-8	-3	NNW	10	6420	97	72	94	71	27	S	91	72	75	74	73	113	818	193	1037
tings MAP	40 36	98 26	1954	-7	-3	NNW	10	6070	97	72	94	71	28	S	91	71	75	74	73	113	818	193	1037
coln MAP	40 51	96 45	1180	-5	-2	N	8	6218	99	75	95	74	26	S	92	74	78	77	76	143	991	508	1548

				WINTER DESIGN DATA HEATING				DEGREE DAYS	SUMMER DESIGN DATA AIR CONDITIONING											SUMMER CRITERIA DATA AIR CONDITIONING			
	LOCATION			Dry Bulb					Dry Bulb								Wet Bulb			Dry Bulb		Wet Bulb	
	Lat	Long	Elev	99%	97.5%	Pvlg Wind	Mean Speed	Heating	1%	MCWB	2.5%	MCWB	Mean Daily Range	Pvlg Wind	5%	MCWB	1%	2.5%	5%	≥ 93°F	≥ 80°F	≥ 73°F	≥ 67°F
	° ′	° ′	feet	°F	°F	dir	knots	annual	°F	°F	°F	°F	°F	dir	°F	°F	°F	°F	°F	hrs	hrs	hrs	hrs
ㄇ)	N	W																					
atte/Lee Bird Fld	41 08	100 41	2775	-8	-4	NW	9	6743	97	69	94	69	30	SSE	90	69	74	72	71	94	733	58	704
FB	41 07	95 55	1048	-8	-3	NW	8	6213	94	76	91	75	22	S	88	74	78	77	75	42	732	381	1292
pley Airfield	41 18	95 54	977	-8	-3	NW	8	6049	94	76	91	75	22	S	88	74	78	77	75	42	732	381	1292
uff	41 52	103 36	3958	-8	-3	NW	9	6774	95	65	92	65	32	SE	90	64	70	68	67	69	673	1	176
	N	W																					
ntain	37 32	115 45	7200	-13	-7	N	10	8264	84	55	82	54	36	SSW	80	53	58	57	56	0	146	0	0
	37 05	116 49	4959	8	12	N	8	5383	96	62	93	62	36	S	90	61	67	65	64	82	594	0	29
ity	39 10	119 46	4675	4	9	SSW	3	5753	94	60	91	59	40	WNW	89	58	63	61	60	59	644	0	1
reek	39 55	114 55	8250	-17	-11	S	12	8864	79	53	77	52	35	SSW	75	51	56	55	54	0	28	0	0
ock Camp	36 37	116 01	3315	14	17	N	5	3978	105	65	102	65	38	SW	100	64	70	68	67	556	1991	2	185
ge	38 41	115 02	5800	-9	-3	S	9	7614	91	58	89	57	36	SSW	87	56	61	60	59	10	586	0	0
	40 50	115 47	5050	-8	-2	E	4	7483	94	59	92	59	42	SW	90	58	63	62	60	55	687	0	1
	39 17	114 51	6253	-10	-4	S	9	7814	89	57	87	56	38	SSW	85	55	60	59	58	2	464	0	0
FS	39 24	118 43	4053	8	12	SSE	3	5229	98	63	96	63	36	WNW	93	62	66	65	64	181	1006	0	20
AS/Van Voorhis Fld	39 25	118 42	3934	8	12	SSE	3	5229	98	63	96	63	36	WNW	93	62	66	65	64	181	1006	0	20
	40 14	114 14	7053	-13	-7	S	10	8264	85	55	83	54	36	SSW	81	53	58	57	56	0	190	0	0
e NAD	38 32	118 40	4186	7	11	SSE	3	5508	97	62	95	62	36	WNW	92	61	65	64	63	132	878	0	9
prings AF Aux Fld	36 35	115 40	3123	16	19	N	4	3778	106	66	103	66	38	SW	101	65	71	69	68	659	2152	7	293
s/McCarran IAP	36 05	115 10	2162	25	28	W	7	2601	108	66	106	65	29	SW	104	65	71	70	69	943	2427	7	425
FB/Las Vegas	36 15	115 02	1868	24	27	NE	4	2377	110	68	107	68	31	SW	105	67	73	71	70	1063	2516	29	672
	39 30	119 47	4404	5	10	SSW	3	6022	95	61	92	60	43	WNW	90	59	64	62	61	67	704	0	3
B/Reno	39 40	119 52	5023	3	8	N	4	6398	91	59	89	58	37	W	87	58	62	60	59	15	542	0	0
AFS	38 03	117 14	7100	0	5	N	10	6650	88	57	86	56	34	S	84	55	61	59	58	0	372	0	0
MAP	38 04	117 05	5426	5	10	N	8	5900	94	60	92	59	34	S	90	58	64	62	61	62	865	0	4
ca AFS	41 00	117 46	6750	-13	-9	SE	10	8100	88	55	86	55	40	W	84	55	59	57	56	0	299	0	0
ca MAP	40 54	117 48	4301	-1	3	SE	5	6629	96	60	94	60	42	W	92	60	64	62	61	128	771	0	2
ton Mountain	37 58	115 30	6093	-9	-3	S	9	7614	90	57	88	56	38	SSW	86	55	60	59	58	4	542	0	0
E	N	W																					
MAP	43 12	71 30	342	-8	-3	NW	7	7360	90	72	87	70	26	SW	84	69	74	73	71	14	388	85	597
Fld/Manchester	42 56	71 26	233	-8	-3	N	11	7101	91	72	88	71	25	SW	85	70	75	74	72	15	538	127	764
	43 40	72 16	800	-16	-10	NNW	9	7680	90	72	87	71	27	SW	83	69	74	73	71	9	312	76	501
er use Grenier	43 00	71 28	170																				
lite Tracking	42 56	71 38	700	-10	-5	NW	7	7831	88	71	85	69	26	SW	82	68	73	72	70	5	249	41	483

ion	LOCATION			WINTER DESIGN DATA HEATING Dry Bulb				DEGREE DAYS	SUMMER DESIGN DATA AIR CONDITIONING Dry Bulb								Wet Bulb			SUMMER CRITERIA DATA AIR CONDITIONING Dry Bulb		Wet Bulb	
	Lat	Long	Elev	99%	97.5%	Pvlg Wind	Mean Speed	Heating	1%	MCWB	2.5%	MCWB	Mean Daily Range	Pvlg Wind	5%	MCWB	1%	2.5%	5%	≥ 93°F	≥ 80°F	≥ 73°F	≥ 67°F
	° '	° '	feet	°F	°F	dir	knots	annual	°F	°F	°F	°F	°F	dir	°F	°F	°F	°F	°F	hrs	hrs	hrs	hrs
SHIRE (CONT)	N	W																					
AFB/Portsmouth	43 04	70 49	101	-2	2	W	8	6846	89	73	85	71	23	W	83	70	75	74	72	6	295	114	609
mouth	43 05	70 44	100	-2	2	W	8	6846	88	73	84	71	23	W	82	70	75	74	72	3	220	114	609
Y	N	W																					
tic City	39 27	74 34	64	10	13	NW	11	4946	92	74	89	74	18	WSW	86	72	78	77	75	19	508	491	1543
ne NSC	40 40	74 06	10	10	14	WNW	11	5004	94	74	91	73	22	WSW	88	72	77	76	75	42	663	337	1259
ngton Ordnance Plant	40 05	74 52	10	8	11	W	9	4699	91	75	89	74	21	SW	86	73	78	76	75	14	600	373	1306
n	39 55	75 04	20	10	14	WNW	10	4865	93	75	90	74	20	WSW	87	72	77	76	75	31	687	417	1424
on	40 52	74 10	175	6	10	WNW	11	5231	94	74	91	73	22	WSW	88	72	77	76	75	42	663	337	1259
ANG	39 48	74 26	175	8	11	W	9	5139	91	75	89	74	21	SW	86	73	78	76	75	14	600	373	1306
	40 55	74 35	570	1	6	WNW	11	6245	92	73	89	72	22	WSW	86	71	76	75	74	23	508	309	1060
NAD	40 20	74 03	100	9	12	W	7	5128	91	75	88	74	22	W	85	73	77	76	75	16	430	398	1398
beth	40 40	74 14	33	10	14	WNW	11	5017	94	74	91	73	22	WSW	88	72	77	76	75	42	663	337	1259
Dix	40 01	74 38	172	8	11	W	9	5139	91	75	89	74	21	SW	86	73	78	76	75	14	600	373	1306
Hancock	40 28	74 00	19	13	16	NW	14	4737	90	73	87	72	17	SW	84	71	76	75	74	12	388	275	1222
Monmouth	40 19	74 02	15	9	12	W	7	5128	91	75	88	74	22	W	85	73	77	76	75	16	430	398	1398
boro AFS	39 50	74 58	200	8	11	W	9	5121	91	75	89	74	21	SW	86	73	78	76	75	14	600	373	1306
y City	40 44	74 03	135	10	14	WNW	11	5238	94	74	91	73	22	WSW	88	72	77	76	75	42	663	337	1259
urst NAS	40 02	74 21	103	7	10	WNW	7	5377	91	74	89	74	22	W	87	73	77	76	75	17	586	344	1313
re AFB	40 01	74 36	133	8	11	W	9	5139	91	75	89	74	21	SW	86	73	78	76	75	14	600	373	1306
k IAP	40 42	74 10	7	10	14	WNW	11	5034	94	74	91	73	22	WSW	88	72	77	76	75	42	663	337	1259
Amboy	40 31	74 17	20	10	14	WNW	11	5034	94	74	91	73	22	WSW	88	72	77	76	75	42	663	337	1259
inny Arsenal	40 56	74 34	706	1	6	WNW	11	6304	92	73	89	72	22	WSW	86	71	76	75	74	23	508	309	1060
on	40 13	74 46	56	11	14	W	9	4947	91	75	88	74	21	SW	85	73	78	76	75	14	526	373	1306
CO	N	W																					
uerque IAP/Kirtland AFB	35 03	106 37	5311	12	16	N	7	4337	96	61	94	61	27	W	92	61	66	65	64	119	1118	0	11
n AFB/Clovis	34 23	103 19	4283	8	13	W	8	4046	95	65	93	65	28	S	91	65	69	68	67	84	982	2	235
bad	32 20	104 16	3293	13	19	N	6	2835	103	67	100	67	29	SSE	97	67	72	71	70	414	1864	19	878
croft	32 57	105 44	9060	-1	3	N	15	7619	83	54	81	54	28	S	79	54	59	58	57	0	126	0	0
ngton MAP	36 44	108 14	5503	1	6	ENE	5	5713	95	63	93	62	31	SW	91	61	67	65	64	81	943	0	30
man AFB/Alamogordo	32 51	106 06	4093	14	19	N	4	3223	98	64	96	64	28	S	94	64	69	68	67	227	1473	2	176
and AFB/Albuquerque IAP	35 03	106 37	5311	12	16	N	7	4337	96	61	94	61	27	W	92	61	66	65	64	119	1118	0	11
ruces	32 18	106 55	4544	15	20	SE	5	3194	99	64	96	64	24	SE	94	64	69	68	67	215	1157	10	198
se Range	34 14	103 48	4500	7	12	W	8	3976	94	65	92	65	28	S	90	65	69	68	67	62	893	2	235
ll	33 18	104 32	3649	13	18	N	6	3697	100	66	98	66	29	SSE	96	66	71	70	69	350	1560	5	583

				WINTER DESIGN DATA HEATING				DEGREE DAYS	SUMMER DESIGN DATA AIR CONDITIONING											SUMMER CRITERIA DATA AIR CONDITIONING			
	LOCATION			Dry Bulb					Dry Bulb								Wet Bulb			Dry Bulb		Wet Bulb	
tion	Lat	Long	Elev	99%	97.5%	Pvlg Wind	Mean Speed	Heating	1%	MCWB	2.5%	MCWB	Mean Daily Range	Pvlg Wind	5%	MCWB	1%	2.5%	5%	≥ 93°F	≥ 80°F	≥ 73°F	≥ 67°F
	° '	° '	feet	°F	°F	dir	knots	annual	°F	°F	°F	°F	°F	dir	°F	°F	°F	°F	°F	hrs	hrs	hrs	hrs
CO (CONT)	N	W																					
mento Peak	32 47	105 49	9240	-1	3	NW	15	7968	81	54	79	54	21	SW	76	54	59	58	57	0	59	0	0
or Consequences	33 14	107 16	4858	14	18	NNW	8	3392	97	63	95	62	28	S	93	62	67	66	66	185	1374		65
cari	35 11	103 36	4039	8	13	NE	8	4047	99	66	97	66	30	SW	95	65	70	69	68	248	1232	1	418
r AFB/Roswell	33 18	104 32	3676	13	18	N	6	3697	100	66	98	66	29	SSE	96	66	71	70	69	350	1560	5	583
Sands Missile Range	32 23	106 29	4330	21	25	SE	5	2526	99	64	97	64	24	SE	95	64	69	68	67	278	1781	10	198
te Army Depot	35 31	108 35	6680	-1	4	ENE	10	5915	89	59	88	58	34	WSW	85	57	64	62	61	4	512	0	1
	35 06	108 47	6440	0	5	ENE	11	5815	90	59	89	58	34	WSW	86	58	64	62	61	8	616	0	1
K	N	W																					
y	42 45	73 48	275	-6	-1	WNW	8	6888	91	73	88	72	25	S	85	70	75	74	72	16	417	132	775
Procurement Center	40 45	74 00	40	11	15	WNW	15	4909	92	74	89	73	18	SW	87	72	76	75	74	25	602	309	1243
ampton/Broome Co Aprt	42 13	75 59	1590	-2	1	WSW	10	7285	86	71	83	69	21	WSW	81	68	73	72	70	2	205	41	518
lyn Navy Shipyard	40 42	73 58	15	11	15	WNW	15	4909	92	74	89	73	18	SW	87	72	76	75	74	25	602	309	1243
lo IAP	42 56	78 44	705	2	6	W	10	6927	88	71	85	70	21	SW	83	69	74	73	72	2	346	92	731
Drum	44 02	75 46	655	-14	-7	NW	5	7601	86	71	83	70	26	W	80	69	75	73	71	2	168	77	552
rk MAP	42 29	79 16	692	4	9	SSW	10	6851	88	73	85	72	20	WSW	83	71	75	74	72	2	317	141	814
Hamilton	40 36	74 02	21	12	15	WNW	14	5184	90	73	87	72	17	SSW	84	71	76	75	74	8	383	275	1222
Tilden	40 34	73 54	10	12	15	WNW	14	5184	90	73	87	72	17	SSW	84	71	76	75	74	8	383	275	1222
Totten	40 48	73 47	35	11	15	WNW	15	4812	92	74	89	73	18	SW	87	72	76	75	74	25	602	309	1243
Wadsworth	40 36	74 03	135	12	15	WNW	14	5184	90	73	87	72	17	SSW	84	71	76	75	74	8	383	275	1222
ort	40 38	73 35	15	12	15	WNW	14	5184	90	73	87	72	17	SSW	84	71	76	75	74	8	383	275	1222
Falls/Warren Co Aprt	43 20	73 37	328	-11	-5	NNW	6	7270	88	72	85	71	25	S	82	69	74	73	71	6	277	80	591
iss AFB/Rome	43 14	75 25	514	-11	-5	NW	5	7331	88	71	85	70	26	W	83	69	75	73	71	3	306	84	611
ngton	40 52	73 24	100	12	15	NNW	13	5084	91	74	88	73	19	SSW	85	72	77	76	74	21	476	331	1284
a/Tompkins Co Aprt	42 29	76 28	1099	-5	0	W	6	7052	88	71	85	71	31	SW	82	70	74	73	71	5	252	73	625
stown/Chautauqua Co	42 09	79 15	1723	-1	3	WSW	9	6849	88	70	86	70	29	WSW	83	69	74	72	71	1	305	50	627
pool	43 07	76 13	400	-3	2	N	7	6678	90	73	87	71	24	WNW	84	70	75	73	72	8	412	107	745
ort AFS	43 08	78 50	638	4	7	W	9	6724	89	74	86	72	23	SW	84	71	76	74	73	4	350	162	814
uk AFS	41 04	71 52	110	12	16	NW	9	5771	82	70	79	70	14	SW	77	69	74	73	72	0	52	93	873
ochelle	40 50	73 47	70	11	15	WNW	15	5161	92	74	89	73	18	SW	87	72	76	75	74	25	602	309	1243
ork/JFK IAP	40 39	73 47	13	12	15	WNW	14	5184	90	73	87	72	17	SSW	84	71	76	75	74	8	383	275	1222
ork/La Guardia Aprt	40 46	73 54	11	11	15	WNW	15	4909	92	74	89	73	18	SW	87	72	76	75	74	25	602	309	1243
ork NB	40 45	74 00	40	11	15	WNW	15	4909	92	74	89	73	18	SW	87	72	76	75	74	25	602	309	1243
rgh/Stewart Aprt	41 30	74 06	471	-1	4	W	10	6336	90	73	88	72	23	W	85	70	76	74	73	14	460	175	886

YORK (CONT)	N	W																				
agara Falls IAP	43 06	78 57	590	4	7	W	9	6688	89	74	86	72	23	SW	84	71	76	74	73	4	350	162	814
gdensburg	44 41	75 28	297	-13	-8	W	8	7777	88	73	85	71	25	SW	83	69	75	73	71	2	266	89	550
swego	43 28	76 33	300	1	7	E	7	6792	86	73	83	71	20	WSW	80	70	75	73	72	1	141	100	665
lattsburg AFB	44 39	73 28	235	-13	-8	NW	6	8044	86	70	83	69	22	SE	80	68	73	72	70	3	171	43	432
oughkeepsie/Dutchess Co	41 38	73 53	165	0	6	NNE	6	5824	92	74	89	74	27	SSW	86	72	77	75	74	26	490	249	1035
ochester/Monroe Co Aprt	43 07	77 40	547	1	5	WSW	11	6719	91	73	88	71	26	WSW	85	70	75	73	72	15	414	112	738
oslyn	40 47	73 36	100	12	15	NNW	13	5084	91	74	88	73	19	SSW	85	72	77	76	74	21	476	331	1301
aint Albans NAVHOSP	40 41	73 46	50	12	15	WNW	14	5184	90	73	87	72	17	SSW	84	71	76	75	74	8	383	275	1222
aratoga AFS	43 01	73 41	617	-12	-6	WNW	8	7180	91	72	89	71	25	S	86	69	74	73	71	18	470	88	662
chenectady	42 51	73 56	378	-4	1	WNW	8	6817	90	73	87	72	25	S	84	70	75	74	72	12	368	132	775
eneca Army Depot	42 45	76 50	750	0	5	NW	11	6359	92	73	88	71	24	SSW	85	70	75	73	72	20	463	107	745
uffolk Co/Westhampton Bch	40 51	72 38	67	7	10	NW	9	5951	86	72	83	71	18	SW	80	70	76	74	73	2	174	172	991
yracuse/Hancock IAP	43 07	76 07	410	-3	2	N	7	6772	90	73	87	71	24	WNW	84	70	75	73	72	8	412	107	745
roy	42 46	73 39	330	-6	-1	WNW	8	6888	91	73	88	72	25	S	85	70	75	74	72	16	417	132	775
tica/Oneida Co Aprt	43 09	75 23	742	-12	-6	NW	12	7299	88	73	85	71	22	W	82	70	75	73	71	7	251	87	604
atertown IAP	43 59	76 01	325	-11	-6	E	7	7376	86	73	83	71	20	WSW	81	70	75	73	72	1	222	100	665
atervliet Arsenal	42 43	73 42	35	1	5	WNW	8	6393	91	73	88	72	25	S	84	70	75	74	72	17	387	132	775
estchester Co/White Plains	41 04	73 43	439	5	9	NW	9	5802	90	75	87	73	23	W	84	73	77	75	74	13	376	265	1092
est Point USMA	41 23	73 57	160	2	6	NNE	6	5753	93	74	90	74	27	SSW	87	72	77	75	74	41	578	249	1035
hitestone	40 47	73 50	10	11	15	WNW	15	4909	92	74	89	73	18	SW	87	72	76	75	74	25	602	309	1243
onkers	40 56	73 53	50	11	15	WNW	15	5109	92	74	89	73	18	SW	87	72	76	75	74	25	602	309	1243
oungstown	43 14	79 02	300	4	7	W	9	6688	89	74	86	72	23	SW	84	71	76	74	73	4	350	162	814
H CAROLINA	N	W																				
sheville MAP	35 26	82 32	2140	10	14	NNW	12	4237	89	73	87	72	27	NNW	85	71	75	74	72	6	536	139	1143
adin ANG	35 22	80 08	455	18	22	NNW	6	3218	95	74	93	74	23	SW	91	74	77	76	76	87	1116	699	2288
amp Lejeune MCS	34 40	77 21	25	20	23	NNW	7	2901	93	80	90	79	18	S	88	77	81	80	79	30	1020	1481	2870
ape Hatteras	35 16	75 33	7	25	27	NNW	11	2731	87	78	86	77	12	SSW	85	77	80	79	78	0	832	1521	2771
harlotte/Douglas MAP	35 13	80 56	736	18	22	NNW	6	3218	95	74	93	74	23	SW	91	74	77	76	76	87	1116	699	2288
herry Point MCAS	34 54	76 53	29	20	24	N	8	2832	92	78	90	78	17	SSW	88	77	80	79	78	23	1055	1342	2760
are County	35 45	76 10	15	19	22	NW	8	3207	93	78	91	77	19	SW	89	76	80	78	78	30	957	1158	2461
denton Recovery Site	36 02	76 34	19	19	22	NW	8	3082	93	78	91	77	19	SW	89	76	80	78	78	30	957	1158	2461
lizabeth City CGAS/MAP	36 16	76 11	12	19	22	NW	8	3207	93	78	91	77	19	SW	89	76	80	78	78	30	957	1158	2461
ort Bragg/Simmons AAF	35 08	78 56	242	18	21	N	7	3105	94	76	92	76	21	WSW	89	75	78	77	76	60	1080	846	2376

ition	LOCATION Lat	Long	Elev	WINTER DESIGN DATA HEATING Dry Bulb 99%	97.5%	Pvlg Wind	Mean Speed	DEGREE DAYS Heating	SUMMER DESIGN DATA AIR CONDITIONING Dry Bulb 1%	MCWB	2.5%	MCWB	Mean Daily Range	Pvlg Wind	5%	MCWB	Wet Bulb 1%	2.5%	5%	SUMMER CRITERIA DATA AIR CONDITIONING Dry Bulb ≥ 93°F	≥ 80°F	Wet Bulb ≥ 73°F	≥ 67°F
	° '	° '	feet	°F	°F	dir	knots	annual	°F	°F	°F	°F	°F	dir	°F	°F	°F	°F	°F	hrs	hrs	hrs	hrs
ROLINA (CONT)	N	W																					
Fisher AFS	33 59	77 55	13	25	29	NNW	11	2353	89	78	87	77	13	SSW	85	77	80	79	78	2	823	1521	2771
ısboro	36 05	79 57	897	14	18	NE	7	3825	93	74	91	73	23	SW	89	73	77	76	75	37	878	488	1944
River MCAS	34 43	77 26	24	20	23	NNW	7	2901	93	80	90	79	18	S	88	77	81	80	79	30	1020	1481	2870
AFB/Fayetteville	35 10	79 01	218	17	20	N	6	3122	95	76	92	76	21	SSW	90	75	79	78	77	65	1131	931	2389
igh/Raleigh-Durham Aprt	35 52	78 47	434	16	20	N	7	3514	94	75	92	75	23	SW	90	75	78	77	76	57	977	748	2188
oke Rapids AFS	36 26	77 43	294	13	16	NW	6	3850	96	77	93	76	22	SW	91	76	79	78	77	96	1066	804	2086
our Johnson AFB	35 20	77 58	109	18	21	N	8	3124	94	77	91	76	20	SW	89	75	79	78	77	47	1069	1044	2478
/point Mil Ocean Trml	34 00	78 00	25	25	29	N	8	2353	89	79	87	78	13	SW	85	77	81	80	79	2	823	1557	2915
sboro ANG	34 57	80 04	455	18	22	NNW	6	3058	95	74	93	74	23	SW	91	74	77	76	76	87	1116	699	2288
ington/New Hanover Co	34 16	77 55	28	23	26	N	8	2433	93	79	91	78	18	SW	89	77	81	80	79	42	1149	1557	2915
ton-Salem	36 08	80 13	969	16	20	NW	8	3679	94	74	91	73	22	WSW	89	73	76	75	74	44	917	417	1897
KOTA	N	W																					
arck MAP	46 46	100 45	1647	-23	-19	WNW	7	9044	95	68	91	68	33	S	88	67	73	71	70	50	504	45	347
inson MAP	46 48	102 48	2585	-21	-17	WNW	12	8942	94	68	90	66	31	SSE	87	65	71	69	68	40	423	15	207
o/Hector Field	46 54	96 48	896	-22	-18	NNW	9	9271	92	73	89	71	26	S	85	69	76	74	72	25	439	115	572
ey AFS	47 30	97 52	1560	-25	-21	NNW	9	9752	90	69	87	69	27	S	83	67	73	71	69	10	296	41	284
una AFS	48 55	103 53	2380	-31	-26	W	10	9573	92	67	89	66	31	S	85	64	71	69	67	29	360	9	144
d Forks AFB	47 57	97 24	911	-26	-22	N	8	9963	91	70	87	70	27	S	84	68	74	72	70	15	338	68	389
t AFB	48 25	101 21	1668	-24	-20	WNW	10	9625	92	68	89	67	31	S	86	65	72	70	68	28	377	22	220
	N	W																					
n/Akron-Canton Aprt	40 55	81 26	1208	1	6	SW	9	6224	89	72	86	71	22	SW	84	70	75	73	72	6	395	112	871
Ash ANGB/Cincinnati	39 16	84 24	846	1	6	W	9	5070	92	73	90	72	23	SW	88	72	77	75	74	24	748	316	1423
Perry ANG	41 32	83 01	570	3	8	WSW	8	5857	90	73	87	72	21	SW	84	71	76	74	73	11	438	176	997
licothe	39 21	83 00	640	0	6	W	8	5075	95	75	92	74	22	WSW	90	73	78	76	74	68	884	272	1318
innati Aprt/Covington	39 03	84 40	869	1	6	W	9	5070	92	73	90	72	23	SW	88	72	77	75	74	24	748	316	1423
eland/Hopkins IAP	41 24	81 51	777	1	5	SW	12	6154	91	73	88	72	24	N	86	71	76	74	73	13	488	176	997
ton County AFB/Wilmington	39 26	83 48	1065	1	6	W	10	5073	91	73	88	72	22	SW	86	72	76	75	74	11	600	252	1288
mbus IAP	40 00	82 53	812	0	5	W	8	5702	92	73	90	73	24	SSW	87	72	77	75	74	28	690	282	1301
on MAP	39 54	84 13	1002	-1	4	WNW	11	5641	91	73	89	72	22	SW	86	71	76	75	73	16	627	222	1210
Hayes	39 58	82 59	800	0	5	W	8	5702	92	73	90	73	24	SSW	87	72	77	75	74	28	690	282	1301
ile AFS	39 43	84 09	750	-1	3	W	7	5455	91	74	89	73	22	W	87	72	77	76	74	12	686	297	1293
/Allen Co Aprt	40 42	84 02	975	-1	4	WNW	11	5838	94	74	91	73	23	SW	88	72	77	76	74	44	660	381	1523
Ordnance Mod Center	40 41	84 05	915	-1	4	WNW	11	5838	94	74	91	73	23	SW	88	72	77	76	74	44	660	381	1523

NT)	N	W																					
in Co Rgnl Aprt	41 21	82 11	794	1	6	SW	8	6094	93	73	91	72	24	SW	88	71	76	74	73	38	681	176	997
field/Lahm MAP	40 49	82 31	1295	0	5	W	8	5818	90	73	87	72	21	SW	85	72	76	74	73	9	431	183	989
rk	40 01	82 28	880	-1	5	W	8	5655	94	73	92	73	24	SSW	89	72	77	75	74	56	745	282	1301
smouth	38 45	82 55	540	5	10	W	8	4547	95	76	92	74	22	SW	89	73	78	77	75	66	942	470	1671
nna AAP	41 11	81 06	1130	-2	4	SW	9	6262	93	73	90	72	22	SW	87	71	76	74	73	38	563	176	1054
enbacker AFB/Columbus	39 49	82 56	744	-1	3	W	8	5567	90	74	88	73	22	WSW	86	72	77	75	73	11	575	223	1147
ewood AAP	39 15	84 40	670	1	6	W	9	5070	92	73	90	72	23	SW	88	72	77	76	74	34	748	316	1133
ngfield MAP	39 50	83 50	1052	-1	3	W	7	5284	91	74	89	73	22	W	87	72	77	76	74	12	686	297	1293
do/Toledo Express Aprt	41 36	83 48	669	-3	1	WSW	8	6381	90	73	88	73	25	SW	85	71	76	75	73	11	506	197	997
ht-Patterson AFB/Dayton	39 49	84 03	824	-1	3	W	7	5455	91	74	89	73	22	W	87	72	77	76	74	12	686	297	1293
gstown MAP	41 16	80 40	1178	-1	4	SW	10	6426	88	71	86	71	23	SW	84	70	74	73	71	4	371	82	729
sville MAP	39 57	81 54	900	1	7	W	6	5738	93	75	90	74	27	WSW	87	73	78	76	75	28	627	339	1314
A	N	W																					
s AFB	34 39	99 16	1378	11	16	N	10	3346	102	73	100	73	26	S	98	73	77	76	75	422	1684	633	2292
ton-Sherman AFB	35 20	99 12	1928	6	12	N	12	3931	100	73	97	72	25	S	95	71	75	74	74	243	1339	283	1821
Sill/Post AAF	34 39	98 24	1187	12	16	N	12	3367	101	74	99	74	25	S	96	74	78	77	76	346	1601	797	2412
ester NAD	34 50	95 55	776	14	19	N	10	3255	99	74	96	74	24	S	93	74	77	76	75	181	1505	618	2211
an	35 15	97 29	1181	9	13	N	10	3247	99	74	96	74	22	S	94	74	77	76	75	193	1331	618	2211
homa City AFS	35 24	97 22	1262	9	13	N	10	3588	99	74	96	74	22	S	94	74	77	76	75	193	1331	618	2211
homa City Aprt	35 24	97 36	1285	9	13	N	14	3695	100	74	97	74	24	SSW	95	73	78	77	76	240	1392	799	2357
lwater/Searcy Field	36 10	97 05	984	8	13	N	12	3631	100	74	96	74	25	SSW	93	74	77	76	75	145	1410	618	2211
er AFB/Oklahoma City	35 25	97 23	1291	9	13	N	10	3588	99	74	96	74	22	S	94	74	77	76	75	193	1331	618	2211
a IAP	36 12	95 54	650	8	13	N	11	3680	101	74	98	75	24	SSW	95	75	79	78	77	270	1543	1089	2478
e AFB/Enid	36 21	97 55	1307	9	13	NNE	13	3971	103	74	100	74	26	SSW	97	74	79	77	76	373	1521	836	2234
	N	W																					
ria	46 09	123 53	8	25	29	ESE	7	5295	75	65	71	62	20	NNW	68	61	65	63	62	1	16	0	14
s	43 35	119 03	4151	0	6	WNW	6	7212	91	61	89	59	35	NNW	86	58	63	61	60	19	462	0	1
allis MAP	44 30	123 17	246	18	22	N	6	4854	92	67	89	66	33	N	86	65	69	67	66	27	372	4	100
ne	44 07	123 13	359	17	22	N	7	4739	92	67	89	66	33	N	86	65	69	67	66	28	393	4	100
ts Pass	42 26	123 19	925	20	24	N	5	4375	99	69	96	68	38	N	93	67	71	69	68	160	700	9	255
AFS	42 04	121 58	6400	-3	2	N	7	7687	83	57	80	56	28	W	77	55	59	57	56	0	70	0	0
sley Field	42 09	121 44	4092	4	9	N	4	6987	90	61	87	60	37	W	84	59	63	61	60	6	354	0	1
ath Falls	42 09	121 44	4092	4	9	N	4	6987	90	61	87	60	37	W	84	59	63	61	60	6	354	0	1

STATE / Station	LOCATION: Lat (N)	LOCATION: Long (W)	LOCATION: Elev	WINTER DESIGN DATA HEATING, Dry Bulb: 99%	97.5%	Pvlg Wind	Mean Speed	DEGREE DAYS: Heating	SUMMER DESIGN DATA AIR CONDITIONING, Dry Bulb: 1%	MCWB	2.5%	MCWB	Mean Daily Range	Pvlg Wind	5%	MCWB	Wet Bulb: 1%	2.5%	5%	SUMMER CRITERIA DATA AIR CONDITIONING, Dry Bulb: ≥ 93°F	≥ 80°F	Wet Bulb: ≥ 73°F	≥ 67°F
	° '	° '	feet	°F	°F	dir	knots	annual	°F	°F	°F	°F	°F	dir	°F	°F	°F	°F	°F	hrs	hrs	hrs	hrs
OREGON (CONT)																							
Medford	42 22	122 52	1298	19	23	S	4	4930	98	68	94	67	39	WNW	91	66	70	68	67	111	673	3	156
MT Hebo AFS	45 13	123 45	3155	11	15	NNW	8	6293	84	62	81	60	30	NNW	77	58	63	61	59	0	94	0	3
North Bend AFS	43 32	124 10	748	29	32	SE	7	4688	69	60	67	60	14	NNW	66	59	62	61	60	0	2	0	1
Pendleton	45 41	118 51	1482	-2	5	NNW	6	5240	97	65	93	64	31	WNW	90	62	66	65	63	88	620	0	28
Portland IAP	45 36	122 36	21	17	23	ESE	12	4792	89	68	85	67	29	NW	81	65	69	67	66	11	210	4	101
Redmond	44 16	121 08	3084	-1	6	WNW	6	6643	92	63	89	61	38	NNW	86	60	65	63	61	25	404	0	7
Salem/McNary Field	44 55	123 01	196	18	23	N	6	4852	92	68	88	66	37	N	84	65	69	68	66	27	295	4	113
Umatilla Army Depot	45 48	119 25	590	1	8	NNW	6	5123	100	67	96	66	32	WNW	93	64	68	67	65	155	849	1	85
PENNSYLVANIA																							
Allentown	40 39	75 26	387	4	9	W	11	5827	92	73	88	72	23	SW	86	72	76	75	73	21	523	227	1091
Altoona/Blair Co Aprt	40 18	78 19	1504	0	5	WNW	11	6192	90	72	87	71	27	WSW	84	70	74	73	72	8	353	88	763
Benton AFS	41 20	76 17	2389	-8	-4	SW	8	8257	83	69	80	68	24	WSW	76	67	71	70	69	2	80	20	336
Brookville	41 09	79 06	1422	-2	4	WSW	9	6870	89	71	86	71	29	SW	83	70	74	73	72	4	333	87	731
Carlisle Barracks	40 12	77 11	475	4	9	W	9	5269	95	73	92	72	22	WSW	89	72	76	75	73	61	758	235	1191
Columbia	40 02	76 30	300	7	11	NW	11	5315	94	75	91	74	24	WSW	88	73	77	76	75	40	700	366	1326
Connellsville	39 57	79 39	1258	5	9	SW	7	5305	91	74	88	73	26	SW	85	72	76	75	74	18	488	258	1221
Erie IAP	42 05	80 11	731	4	9	SSW	10	6851	88	73	85	72	20	WSW	83	71	75	74	72	2	317	141	814
Folsom	39 54	75 19	100	10	14	WNW	10	4865	93	75	90	74	20	WSW	87	72	77	76	75	31	687	417	1424
Fort Indiantown Gap	40 26	76 34	475	4	8	NW	11	5609	93	75	90	74	24	WSW	87	73	77	76	75	36	627	366	1326
Frankford Arsenal	40 00	75 04	10	10	14	WNW	10	4865	93	75	90	74	20	WSW	87	72	77	76	75	31	687	417	1424
Freemansburg	40 37	75 20	225	5	10	W	11	5597	93	73	89	72	23	SW	87	72	76	75	73	28	609	227	1091
Harrisburg IAP/Olmsted	40 12	76 46	308	7	11	NW	11	5315	94	75	91	74	24	WSW	88	73	77	76	75	40	700	366	1326
Hazleton MAP	40 59	76 00	1604	0	4	SW	8	6471	89	71	86	70	24	WSW	83	69	73	72	71	7	302	71	720
Johnstown/Cambria Co Aprt	40 19	78 50	2284	-3	2	WNW	8	7804	86	70	83	70	27	WSW	80	68	72	71	70	0	170	32	515
Lancaster	40 07	76 18	403	4	8	NW	11	5583	93	75	90	74	24	WSW	87	73	77	76	75	36	631	366	1326
Letterkenny Army Depot	40 00	77 39	670	4	8	NW	11	5519	93	75	90	74	24	WSW	87	73	77	76	75	37	674	366	1326
Mechanicsburg	40 13	77 01	400	8	11	W	9	5224	92	73	89	72	22	WSW	87	72	76	75	73	26	628	235	1191
New Castle	41 01	80 22	825	2	7	WSW	10	5800	91	73	88	72	23	WSW	86	71	75	74	73	15	419	198	1065
New Cumberland Chem Plant	40 13	76 50	385	8	11	W	9	5224	92	73	89	72	22	WSW	87	72	76	75	73	26	628	235	1191
Philadelphia IAP	39 53	75 15	5	10	14	WNW	10	4865	93	75	90	74	20	WSW	87	72	77	76	75	31	687	417	1424
Philipsburg	40 53	78 05	1923	-2	3	WNW	8	7469	87	71	84	71	27	WSW	81	69	73	72	71	1	213	54	578
Pittsburgh IAP	40 30	80 13	1137	1	5	WSW	10	5930	89	72	86	71	23	WSW	84	70	74	73	72	5	461	105	886
Reading MAP	40 20	75 58	266	9	13	W	11	4931	92	73	89	72	23	SW	86	72	76	75	73	28	629	227	1091

ᴵVANIA (CONT)	N	W																				
anton AAP	41 24	75 40	730	3	7	SW	8	6114	90	72	87	71	24	WSW	84	70	74	73	72	13	431	105	798
te College ANG Station	40 48	77 52	1175	3	7	WNW	8	6132	90	72	87	71	26	WSW	84	70	74	73	72	12	390	117	773
yhanna Army Depot	41 11	75 25	1990	-2	2	WNW	8	6816	87	71	84	71	20	WSW	81	69	73	72	71	3	219	54	578
ley Forge General Hosp	40 07	75 33	245	3	8	WNW	10	5114	95	75	92	74	26	WSW	89	72	77	76	75	74	861	417	1424
kes-Barre-Scranton Aprt	41 20	75 44	930	1	5	SW	8	6277	90	72	87	71	24	WSW	84	70	74	73	72	10	406	105	798
liamsport	41 15	76 55	524	2	7	W	9	5981	92	73	89	72	25	WSW	86	70	75	74	73	28	555	180	968
low Grove NAS	40 12	75 09	361	7	11	WNW	10	5368	92	75	89	74	20	SW	86	73	77	76	75	30	859	479	1536
ming	41 17	75 51	550	3	7	SW	8	5817	92	73	89	72	24	WSW	86	71	75	74	73	23	583	176	987
ISLAND	N	W																				
sville	41 36	71 27	25	5	9	WNW	10	5840	88	73	85	72	19	SW	82	70	76	75	73	5	290	182	909
port NB	41 30	71 20	10	5	9	WNW	10	5840	88	73	85	72	19	SW	82	70	76	75	73	5	290	182	909
th Kingston ANG Sta	41 37	71 26	27	5	9	WNW	10	5840	88	73	85	72	19	SW	82	70	76	75	73	5	290	182	909
th Smithfield ANG Sta	41 58	71 35	465	1	5	WNW	11	6207	91	73	87	72	21	SW	84	70	75	74	73	13	330	162	864
vidence/Theo T Green MAP	41 44	71 26	51	5	9	WNW	11	5972	89	73	86	72	21	SW	83	70	75	74	73	6	321	162	864
nset Point NAS	41 36	71 25	30	5	9	WNW	10	5840	88	73	85	72	19	SW	82	70	76	75	73	5	290	182	909
CAROLINA	N	W																				
en AFS	33 39	81 41	525	21	25	W	6	2348	94	76	92	75	24	SW	90	75	79	78	77	89	1203	1186	2766
ufort MCAS	32 29	80 43	38	24	27	NW	7	2126	94	79	92	78	18	W	90	78	81	80	79	53	1378	1934	3326
rleston AFB/MAP	32 54	80 02	45	24	27	NNE	8	2146	93	78	91	78	19	SW	89	77	81	80	79	49	1252	1716	3161
rleston Army Depot	32 54	79 58	3	24	27	NNE	8	2146	93	78	91	78	19	SW	89	77	81	80	79	49	1252	1716	3161
umbia	33 57	81 07	213	20	24	W	6	2598	97	76	95	75	24	SW	93	75	79	78	77	165	1416	1186	2766
aldson AFB/Greenville	34 46	82 23	978	19	23	W	5	3089	95	75	93	74	23	W	90	73	78	76	75	78	1094	618	2259
rence MAP	34 11	79 43	147	22	25	N	7	2566	94	77	92	77	21	SW	90	76	80	79	78	70	1210	1272	2738
t Jackson	34 01	80 56	250	20	24	W	6	2598	97	76	95	75	24	SW	93	75	79	78	77	165	1416	1186	2766
rgetown	33 23	79 17	14	23	26	N	7	2228	92	79	90	78	18	SSW	88	77	81	80	79	33	1206	1649	3075
enville-Spartanburg Aprt	34 54	82 13	957	18	22	NW	8	3163	93	74	91	74	22	SW	89	74	77	76	75	37	1035	661	2301
ntire ANGB/Columbia	33 55	80 48	237	20	23	NNW	6	2828	95	76	92	76	21	W	90	75	79	78	77	72	1086	806	2381
tle Beach AFB	33 41	78 56	25	22	24	N	6	2696	91	79	89	78	16	S	87	78	81	80	79	18	1160	1582	2989
th Charleston AFS	32 53	80 01	41	24	27	NNE	8	2146	93	78	91	78	19	SW	89	77	81	80	79	49	1252	1716	3161
th Field	33 37	81 05	290	20	24	W	6	2598	97	76	95	75	24	SW	93	75	79	78	77	165	1416	1186	2766
ris Island MARCORPCRUITDEP	32 21	80 41	33	24	27	NW	7	2126	94	79	92	78	18	W	90	78	81	80	79	53	1378	1934	3326
ntsett	33 49	80 28	200	22	25	NNE	6	2453	95	77	92	76	20	W	90	75	79	78	77	75	1262	1131	2727

STATE / Station	LOCATION Lat ° '	LOCATION Long ° '	Elev feet	WINTER DESIGN DATA HEATING Dry Bulb 99% °F	97.5% °F	Pvlg Wind dir	Mean Speed knots	DEGREE DAYS Heating annual	SUMMER DESIGN DATA AIR CONDITIONING Dry Bulb 1% °F	MCWB °F	2.5% °F	MCWB °F	Mean Daily Range °F	Pvlg Wind dir	5% °F	MCWB °F	Wet Bulb 1% °F	2.5% °F	5% °F	SUMMER CRITERIA DATA AIR CONDITIONING Dry Bulb ≥ 93°F hrs	≥ 80°F hrs	Wet Bulb ≥ 73°F hrs	≥ 67°F hrs
SOUTH CAROLINA (CONT)	N	W																					
Shaw AFB/Sumter	33 58	80 28	252	22	25	NNE	6	2453	95	77	92	76	20	W	90	75	79	78	77	75	1262	1131	2727
Sumter	33 54	80 22	169	22	25	NNE	6	2482	95	77	92	76	20	W	90	75	79	78	77	75	1262	1131	2727
SOUTH DAKOTA	N	W																					
Aberdeen MAP	45 27	98 26	1296	-19	-15	NNW	8	8617	94	73	91	72	27	S	88	70	77	75	73	47	562	202	837
Ellsworth AFB/Rapid City	44 08	103 06	3276	-11	-7	N	11	7049	95	66	92	65	30	S	89	65	71	69	67	60	571	10	218
Huron	44 23	98 13	1281	-18	-14	NNW	8	8055	96	73	93	72	29	S	90	71	77	75	73	82	656	202	837
Pierre MAP	44 23	100 17	1742	-15	-10	NW	11	7677	99	71	95	71	30	SSE	92	69	75	74	72	124	757	115	665
Rapid City	44 03	103 04	3162	-11	-6	NNW	10	7324	97	66	93	65	33	SSE	90	65	71	70	68	89	630	11	233
Sioux Falls/Foss Fld	43 34	96 44	1418	-15	-11	NW	8	7838	94	73	91	72	26	S	88	71	76	75	73	48	599	170	796
TENNESSEE	N	W																					
Alcoa ANG Sta use Knoxville																							
Arnold Eng Dev Cen	35 23	86 05	1067	11	1	NW	8	3883	91	74	89	73	23	WSW	87	73	77	76	75	7	750	420	1721
Bristol/Tri City Aprt	36 29	82 24	1507	9	1	WNW	6	4306	91	72	89	72	24	SW	87	71	75	75	73	16	851	253	1606
Chattanooga/Lovell Field	35 02	85 12	665	13	1	NNW	8	3505	96	75	93	74	26	WSW	91	74	78	77	76	99	1158	790	2401
Holston Ordnance Works	36 31	82 40	1200	11	16	WNW	6	3695	93	73	91	73	24	SW	89	72	76	76	74	35	908	384	1943
Kingsport	36 31	82 30	1284	1	16	WNW	6	3695	93	73	91	73	24	SW	89	72	76	76	74	35	908	384	1943
Knoxville/Alcoa ANG Sta	35 49	83 59	980	1	19	NE	8	3478	94	74	92	73	23	W	90	73	77	76	75	52	1053	520	2150
Memphis Army Depot	35 05	89 59	295	1	18	N	10	3227	98	77	95	76	22	SW	93	76	80	79	78	166	1487	1327	2664
Memphis IAP	35 03	90 00	258	1	18	N	10	3227	98	77	95	76	22	SW	93	76	80	79	78	166	1487	1327	2664
Memphis NAS/Millington	35 20	89 53	322	12	17	N	8	3445	95	77	93	77	20	SW	91	76	80	79	78	73	1355	1222	2599
Milan Ordnance Plant	35 54	88 42	490	11	16	NNW	8	3685	99	76	96	76	25	SSW	93	76	80	79	78	170	1370	1220	2513
Nashville	36 07	86 41	590	9	14	NW	8	3696	97	75	94	74	23	WSW	91	74	78	77	76	104	1221	875	2328
Sewart AFB/Smyrna Aprt	36 00	86 32	543	8	13	NW	7	3949	95	75	92	74	23	WSW	90	74	78	77	76	72	1098	711	2103
Tullahoma Aprt	35 22	86 12	1072	8	13	NW	8	3577	96	74	93	73	23	WSW	91	73	77	76	75	94	1056	420	1721
Tullahoma/Arnold AFS	35 23	86 05	1067	11	16	NW	8	3883	91	74	89	73	23	WSW	87	73	77	76	75	7	750	420	1721
Volunteer Ordnance Works	35 05	85 08	750	13	18	NNW	8	3505	96	75	93	74	26	WSW	91	74	78	77	76	99	1158	790	2401
TEXAS	N	W																					
Abilene MAP	32 25	99 41	1784	15	20		12	2610	101	71	99	71	24	SSE	97	71	75	74	74	433	1922	340	2403
Aero Maintenance Center	27 46	97 26	40	32	36		12	930	95	78	94	78	17	SSE	92	78	80	80	79	134	2507	3238	3989
Amarillo	35 14	101 42	3604	6	11		11	4183	98	67	95	67	28	S	93	67	71	70	70	180	1181	9	739
Austin/Robert Mueller MAP	30 18	97 42	597	24	28	N	11	1737	100	74	98	74	23	S	97	74	78	77	77	430	2041	1959	3400
Beaumont/Jefferson Co	29 57	94 01	16	27	31	N	9	1518	95	79	93	78	18	S	91	78	81	80	80	88	1863	2787	3708

S (CONT)

	N		W																							
eaumont Army Hospital	31	49	106	28	4185	20	24	N	[illegible]	2678	100	64	98	64	25	S	96	64	69	68	68	370	1917	0	376
eeville/Chase Field NAS	28	22	97	40	190	30	33	N	0	1189	99	78	97	77	21	SSE	95	77	82	81	79	301	2144	2776	3786
ergstrom AFB/Austin	30	12	97	40	541	24	28	N	1	1712	99	74	97	75	22	S	96	75	79	78	77	363	1966	1844	3384
rooke Army Medical Center	29	28	98	27	785	25	30	N		1570	99	72	97	73	22	SSE	96	73	77	76	76	397	2049	1699	3426
rooks AFB	29	21	98	27	598	28	32	N	1	1272	100	74	98	74	22	SSE	97	74	78	77	77	460	2189	2185	3551
rownsville IAP	25	54	97	26	19	35	39	NNW	13	650	94	77	93	77	16	E	92	77	80	79	79	103	2456	3391	4090
rownwood	31	48	98	57	1386	18	22	N	9	2437	101	73	[illegible]	[illegible]	[illegible]	[illegible]	[illegible]	[illegible]	[illegible]	[illegible]	[illegible]	[illegible]	[illegible]	1045	3043
amp Bullis	[illegible]	41	98	45	1400	23	28	N	8	1952	100	74	97	74	23	S	94	74	78	77	76	220	1626	1481	3348
arswell AFB/Fort Worth	32	47	97	26	650	18	23	N	10	2301	101	75	99	75	22	S	97	74	78	77	76	415	1969	1182	2928
orpus Christi IAP	27	46	97	30	41	31	35	N	12	930	95	78	94	78	17	SSE	92	78	80	80	79	134	2507	3238	3989
orpus Christi NAS	27	42	97	17	19	34	38	N	12	899	92	79	91	79	12	SE	90	79	82	81	80	15	2845	3329	4036
allas/Love Field	32	51	96	51	481	18	22	N	19	2290	102	75	100	75	21	S	97	75	78	78	77	474	2208	1675	3103
allas NAS/Hensley Field	32	44	96	58	495	20	25	NNW		2308	102	76	100	76	22	S	98	76	79	78	77	497	2229	1764	3092
el Rio IAP	29	22	100	55	1026	26	31	NNW		1523	100	73	98	73	23	SE	97	73	79	77	76	509	2349	1260	3367
yess AFB/Abilene	32	25	99	51	1789	15	19	N		2682	100	71	98	71	23	S	96	71	75	74	73	342	1700	209	2089
agle Pass AFS	28	52	100	32	884	27	32	NNW	9	1423	101	73	99	73	24	ESE	98	73	78	78	77	605	2517	1426	3515
llington AFB/Houston	29	37	95	10	40	28	31	N	8	1384	95	78	94	78	19	S	92	78	81	80	80	114	1763	2373	3616
l Paso IAP	31	48	106	24	3918	20	24		7	2678	100	64	98	64	25	S	96	64	69	68	68	370	1917	0	376
ort Bliss/Biggs AAF	31	51	106	23	3947	19	23		5	2432	100	65	97	65	25	W	95	65	70	69	68	325	1813	5	373
ort Hood/Hood AAF	31	09	97	43	923	20	25		9	1959	99	73	97	73	23	S	95	73	77	76	75	295	1791	1045	3043
ort Hood/Robert Gray AAF	31	04	97	50	1015	20	25	N	9	1959	99	73	97	73	23	S	95	73	77	76	75	295	1791	1045	3043
ort Sam Houston	29	27	98	26	760	25	30	N	8	1570	99	73	97	73	22	SSE	96	73	77	76	76	397	2049	1699	3426
ort Wolters	32	50	98	04	900	17	21	NW	6	2432	102	75	100	74	24	S	98	74	78	77	76	489	1921	1136	2880
ort Worth IAP	32	50	97	03	537	17	22	N	1	2382	101	74	99	74	22	S	97	74	78	77	76	469	2095	1415	3087
alveston	29	18	94	48	7	31	36		15	1224	90	79	89	79	9	S	88	78	81	80	80	4	2603	2998	3932
arland ANG Station	32	54	96	39	558	18	22	NNW	10	2290	102	75	100	75	21	S	97	75	78	78	77	474	2208	1675	3103
oodfellow AFB/San Angelo	31	26	100	24	1877	18	22	NNE	10	2240	101	71	99	71	24	SSE	97	70	75	74	73	465	1978	245	2424
arlingen	26	14	97	39	35	35	39	NNW	10	693	96	77	94	77	18	SSE	93	77	80	79	79	223	2442	3294	4059
ondo MAP	29	21	99	11	901	26	29	N	8	1596	99	74	97	74	22	SSE	95	74	77	77	76	480	2159	1703	3374
ouston IAP	29	58	95	21	96	27	32	NNW	11	1434	96	77	94	77	19	S	92	77	80	79	79	132	1888	2694	3695
elly AFB/San Antonio	29	23	98	35	690	26	29	N	9	1520	99	74	97	74	22	SSE	96	74	78	77	76	352	1920	1774	3444
ingsville NAS	27	29	97	49	50	32	35	N		970	97	78	95	78	18	SE	94	78	81	80	80	258	2422	3154	3935
ackland AFB	29	23	98	37	670	26	29			1520	99	74	97	74	22	SSE	96	74	78	77	76	352	1920	1774	3444
a Porte ANG Station	29	40	95	04	24	29	32			1284	94	78	93	78	18	S	91	78	81	80	80	66	1568	2347	3782

TATE Station	LOCATION Lat		Long		Elev	WINTER DESIGN DATA HEATING Dry Bulb 99%	97.5%	Pvlg Wind	Mean Speed	DEGREE DAYS Heating	SUMMER DESIGN DATA AIR CONDITIONING Dry Bulb 1%	MCWB	2.5%	MCWB	Mean Daily Range	Pvlg Wind	5%	MCWB	Wet Bulb 1%	2.5%	5%	SUMMER CRITERIA DATA AIR CONDITIONING Dry Bulb ≥ 93°F	≥ 80°F	Wet Bulb ≥ 73°F	≥ 67°F
	°	'	°	'	feet	°F	°F	dir	knots	annual	°F	°F	°F	°F	°F	dir	°F	°F	°F	°F	°F	hrs	hrs	hrs	hrs
TEXAS (CONT)	N		W																						
Laredo AFB	27	32	99	27	512	32	36	N	8	986	102	73	101	73	24	SE	99	74	78	78	77	756	2653	2347	3782
Laredo IAP	27	37	99	31	539	32	36	N		986	102	74	101	74	24	SE	99	74	78	78	77	756	2653	2347	3782
Laughlin AFB	29	22	100	47	1081	26	31	NNW		1542	100	73	98	73	23	SE	97	73	79	77	76	509	2349	1260	3367
Lone Star Ordnance Plant	33	27	94	14	360	18	23	WNW		2531	98	77	96	77	22	SSW	93	76	80	79	78	198	1639	1715	3097
Longhorn Ordnance Works	32	40	94	09	295	19	24	N		2370	96	77	94	77	22	S	93	77	80	79	78	156	1518	1558	2996
Lubbock	33	39	101	49	3254	10	15	N	18	3545	98	69	96	69	27	S	94	69	73	72	71	225	1371	41	1266
Lufkin AFS	31	25	94	48	277	25	29	NNW	12	1940	99	76	97	76	22	S	94	76	80	79	78	239	186	1948	3129
Midland	31	57	102	11	2851	16	21	NE	9	2621	100	69	98	69	25	SSE	96	69	73	72	71	382	1793	54	1591
Nederland ANG Station	29	57	94	02	16	27	31	N	9	1518	95	79	93	78	18	S	91	78	81	80	80	88	1863	2787	3708
Oilton Msl Tracking Site	27	30	98	58	880	32	36	N	8	986	101	73	100	73	24	SE	98	73	78	77	77	649	2570	2204	3701
Orange	30	06	93	44	10	27	31	N	9	1498	95	77	93	77	18	SSW	92	77	80	79	79	92	1766	2475	3589
Paris/Cox Field	33	38	95	27	547	15	20	N	10	2903	100	75	98	75	22	S	95	74	78	77	76	292	171	1019	2689
Perrin AFB/Sherman	33	43	96	40	763	15	20	N	10	2837	100	75	98	75	22	S	95	74	78	77	76	292	171	1019	2689
Port Arthur	29	57	94	01	16	27	31	N	9	1518	95	79	93	78	18	S	91	78	81	80	80	88	186	2787	3708
Randolph AFB/San Antonio	29	32	98	17	761	25	29	N	8	1713	98	74	97	74	23	S	95	74	78	77	76	298	1779	1481	3348
Red River Army Depot	33	27	94	20	385	18	23	WNW	9	2531	98	77	96	77	22	SSW	93	76	80	79	78	198	1639	1715	3097
Reese AFB/Lubbock	33	36	102	03	3338	13	17	NNE	10	3453	98	68	96	68	28	SSE	94	68	73	72	70	224	1337	37	965
San Angelo/Mathis Field	31	22	100	30	1903	18	22	NNE	10	2240	101	71	99	71	24	SSE	97	70	75	74	73	465	1978	245	2424
San Antonio AFS	29	27	98	27	700	25	30	N	8	1570	99	73	97	73	22	SSE	96	73	77	76	76	397	2049	1699	3426
San Antonio IAP	29	32	98	28	788	25	30	N	8	1570	99	72	97	73	22	SSE	96	73	77	76	76	397	2049	1699	3426
Sheppard AFB/Wichita Falls	33	59	98	30	1015	14	18	N	11	2904	103	73	101	73	25	S	98	73	77	76	75	517	1999	826	2611
Tyler/Pounds Field	32	21	95	24	544	19	24	NNW	12	2553	99	76	97	76	22	S	95	76	80	79	78	248	1825	1948	3129
Waco/James Connally Aprt	31	38	97	04	475	20	25	N	11	2081	101	75	99	75	23	S	97	75	79	78	77	480	2089	1636	3180
Waco/Madison Cooper	31	37	97	13	501	21	26	NNW	12	2058	101	75	99	75	23	S	97	75	78	78	77	458	2134	1849	3245
Webb AFB/Big Spring	32	13	101	31	2561	16	20	NE	11	2678	100	69	97	69	24	S	95	69	74	73	72	331	1662	101	1485
Wichita Falls MAP	33	58	98	29	994	14	18	N	11	2904	103	73	101	73	25	S	98	73	77	76	75	517	1999	826	2611
UTAH	N		W																						
Bryce Canyon	37	42	112	09	7585	-11	-6	W		9133	84	57	81	56	37		80	56	63	60	58	0	149		4
Cedar City	37	42	113	06	5617	-2	5	SE		6137	93	60	91	60	32	S	89	59	65	63	62	42	766		9
Deseret Test Center	40	19	112	17	5200	-4	1	SE		6277	95	61	92	60	34		90	59	64	63	62	79	717		2
Dugway PG/Michales AAF	40	12	112	56	4340	0	5	SE	6	5877	99	63	96	62	34	W	94	61	66	65	64	224	1131	0	28
Hill AFB/Ogden	41	07	111	58	4785	6	10	ESE	9	6081	94	62	92	62	26	W	90	61	65	64	63	51	746	0	8
Hill AF Range	41	03	112	55	4422	4	8	N	4	5840	97	62	95	61	30	W	93	60	66	65	63	174	1069	0	19

(...NT)

Station	Lat N	Long W	Elev																			
...n MAP	41 12	112 01	4455	1	5	S	6	6012	93	63	91	61	26	SW	88	61	66	65	64	37	727	0	19
...o	40 13	111 43	4448	1	6	SE	5	5720	98	62	96	62	32	SW	94	61	66	65	64	185	989	0	26
... Lake City IAP	40 46	111 58	4220	3	8	SSE	6	5983	97	62	95	62	32	N	92	61	66	65	64	139	932		26
...e Army Depot	40 31	112 25	4700	4	7	SE	4	5941	93	61	91	61	24	N	88	60	65	64	63	41	704		5
... Army Depot	41 15	112 00	4270	2	6	S	6	6012	94	63	92	61	26	SW	89	61	66	65	64	59	849	0	19
...over AF Range	40 44	114 02	4237	8	12	ENE	4	5673	97	60	95	59	25	E	93	59	65	64	62	158	1144	0	4
	N	W																					
...ington IAP	44 28	73 09	332	-12	-7	E	7	7876	88	72	85	70	24	SSW	82	69	74	72	71	4	263	67	546
...lbans AFS	44 46	73 03	1310	-17	-11	E	9	8790	85	70	82	68	24	SSW	79	67	72	70	69	1	119	21	307
	N	W																					
...ngton Hall	38 52	77 06	200	13	17	WNW	11	4211	94	75	91	74	21	S	89	74	78	77	76	55	815	580	1744
...ord AFS	37 31	79 30	4220	-3	1	NW	9	7382	82	66	80	66	22	SW	77	65	69	68	67	0	87	0	216
...ron Station	38 48	77 07	60	13	17	WNW	11	4211	94	75	91	74	21	S	89	74	78	77	76	56	815	580	1744
... A P Hill	38 08	77 21	230	10	14	NW	6	4398	96	77	93	76	21	S	90	75	80	78	77	9	897	710	1884
... Pickett/Blackstone AAF	37 05	77 57	390	15	19	NW	6	3841	95	77	92	76	22	SW	90	76	79	78	77	6	905	804	2086
... Charles AFS	37 08	75 57	13	20	23	N	1	3474	90	77	88	76	17	SW	86	75	79	78	77	0	596	856	2184
...lottesville	38 02	78 31	870	14	18	NE	7	4162	94	74	91	74	23	SW	88	73	77	76	75	54	964	376	1544
...gren NAVSURFWPNCEN	38 20	77 02	21	10	14	NW	6	4498	93	77	91	76	21	S	89	75	80	78	77	39	892	710	1884
...Neck	36 47	75 57	10	19	22	N	11	3639	91	77	89	76	17	SW	87	75	79	78	77	12	708	856	2184
...es IAP	38 57	77 27	313	7	11	NW	9	5010	93	74	90	73	23	S	88	73	77	76	75	28	749	386	1417
... Belvoir/Davison AAF	38 43	77 11	69	8	12	NW	9	4891	92	76	90	75	23	S	88	74	78	77	76	23	781	551	1668
... Eustis/Felker AAF	37 08	76 37	12	17	20	N	0	3752	92	77	90	76	17	SSW	88	75	80	78	77	26	875	807	2065
... Lee	37 14	77 21	145	14	17	N	6	3939	95	76	92	76	22	SW	90	75	79	78	77	70	932	765	1973
... Lee AFS	37 14	77 20	75	14	17	N	6	3939	95	76	92	76	22	SW	90	75	79	78	77	70	932	765	1973
... Monroe	37 00	76 19	15	17	20	NW	9	3623	92	78	90	77	17	SW	87	76	79	78	77	21	809	1010	2290
... Myer	38 53	77 05	220	14	17	WNW	11	4211	93	75	91	74	19	S	89	74	78	77	76	41	910	580	1744
... Story	36 56	76 00	13	19	22	N	11	3639	91	77	89	76	17	SW	87	75	79	78	77	12	708	856	2184
...ley AFB/Hampton	37 05	76 21	10	17	20	NW	9	3623	92	78	90	77	17	SW	87	76	79	78	77	21	809	1010	2290
...le Creek NAVPHIBASE	36 54	76 09	15	20	22	NW	10	3488	93	77	91	76	19	SW	89	76	79	78	77	41	874	961	2238
...nburg MAP	37 20	79 12	916	12	16	NE	7	4233	93	74	90	74	23	SW	88	73	77	76	75	31	696	376	1544
...ssas/Davis Field	38 43	77 31	186	10	14	NW	6	4398	96	76	93	75	22	S	90	74	78	77	76	90	897	548	1650
...ort News/Patrick Henry	37 08	76 30	41	17	20	NW	9	3549	92	78	90	77	17	SW	87	76	79	78	77	21	809	1010	2290
...olk	36 54	76 12	22	20	22	NW	10	3488	93	77	91	76	19	SW	89	76	79	78	77	41	874	961	2238

LOCATION	Lat (° ')	Long (° ')	Elev (feet)	WINTER DESIGN DATA HEATING: Dry Bulb 99% (°F)	97.5% (°F)	Pvlg Wind (dir)	Mean Speed (knots)	DEGREE DAYS: Heating (annual)	SUMMER DESIGN DATA AIR CONDITIONING: Dry Bulb 1% (°F)	MCWB (°F)	2.5% (°F)	MCWB (°F)	Mean Daily Range (°F)	Pvlg Wind (dir)	5% (°F)	MCWB (°F)	Wet Bulb 1% (°F)	2.5% (°F)	5% (°F)	SUMMER CRITERIA DATA AIR CONDITIONING: Dry Bulb ≥ 93°F (hrs)	≥ 80°F (hrs)	Wet Bulb ≥ 73°F (hrs)	≥ 67°F (hrs)
)	N	W																					
NAS/Chambers Field	36 56	76 18	13	20	23	NNW	11	3451	93	77	91	76	17	SSW	89	76	80	78	77	39	930	932	2212
AS	36 49	76 02	22	19	22	N	11	3639	91	77	89	76	17	SW	87	75	79	78	77	12	708	856	2184
th	36 51	76 18	10	20	22	NW	10	3488	93	77	91	76	19	SW	89	76	79	78	77	41	874	961	2238
MCAS	38 30	77 18	12	10	14	NW	6	4349	93	77	91	76	21	S	89	75	80	78	77	37	892	710	1884
Ordnance Works	37 11	80 33	1750	9	14	NW	9	4680	91	71	89	71	24	SW	86	70	74	73	72	14	609	124	1213
/Byrd IAP	37 30	77 20	164	14	17	N	6	3939	95	76	92	76	22	SW	90	75	79	78	77	70	932	765	1973
Quartermaster Depot	37 26	77 27	122	14	17	N	6	3939	95	76	92	76	22	SW	90	75	79	78	77	70	932	765	1973
Woodrum Aprt	37 19	79 58	1193	12	16	NW	9	4307	93	72	91	72	24	SW	88	71	75	74	73	38	810	223	1468
/Shenandoah Valley	38 16	78 54	1201	12	16	NW	9	4307	93	72	91	72	24	SW	88	71	75	74	73	38	810	223	1468
1 Farms Station	38 45	77 41	425	7	11	NW	9	5010	93	74	90	73	23	S	88	73	77	76	75	28	749	386	1417
burg	37 16	76 42	70	17	20	N	10	3671	93	77	91	76	17	SSW	88	75	80	78	77	42	905	807	2065
	37 14	76 31	25	17	20	NW	9	3623	92	78	90	77	17	SW	87	76	79	78	77	21	809	1010	2290
	N	W																					
	46 59	123 49	12	25	28	ESE	6	5316	80	65	77	62	20	NNW	73	61	65	63	62	1	38	0	14
	47 43	122 43	15	21	25	E	8	5432	82	65	78	64	24	N	75	62	66	64	63	2	64	0	26
am IAP	48 48	122 32	158	10	15	NNE	15	5738	81	67	77	65	26	WSW	74	63	68	65	63	0	45	1	46
FS	48 55	122 44	65	10	15	NNE	15	5738	81	67	77	65	26	WSW	74	63	68	65	63	0	45	1	46
n NAVSHIPYD	47 34	122 39	7	21	25	E	8	5432	82	65	78	64	24	N	75	62	66	64	63	2	64	0	26
MAP	47 18	119 31	1272	4	8	N	8	5603	96	66	93	65	31	SSW	89	63	67	66	64	81	655	1	52
use Paine AFB																							
d AFB/Spokane	47 37	117 38	2462	1	7	NNE	7	6790	93	63	90	62	29	SSW	86	61	65	63	62	32	415	0	5
ton	47 39	122 25	225	21	25	ESE	6	5678	81	65	77	64	22	NNW	74	62	67	64	63	2	47	1	30
is/Gray AAF	47 05	122 35	301	19	24	S	6	5339	86	65	82	64	30	NNE	78	62	67	65	63	2	130	2	29
e Comm Sta ANG	47 33	117 33	2642	1	7	NNE	7	6806	93	63	90	62	29	SSW	86	61	65	63	62	32	415	0	5
	47 42	122 37	17	21	25	E	8	5432	82	65	78	64	24	N	75	62	66	64	63	2	64	0	26
	46 10	122 56	12	19	24	ESE	9	5064	88	68	85	67	26	NW	81	65	69	67	66	9	200	4	101
Army Hospital	47 06	122 32	275	19	24	S	5	5328	86	66	82	65	32	NNE	79	63	68	66	64	4	131	0	49
S	48 23	124 41	1430	26	29	E	24	5774	64	58	62	58	9	SW	60	57	60	59	58	0	0	0	0
	48 50	122 36	20	10	15	NNE	15	5738	81	67	77	65	26	WSW	74	63	68	65	63	0	45	1	46
AFB/Tacoma	47 09	122 29	322	19	24	S	5	5287	86	66	82	65	32	NNE	79	63	68	66	64	4	131	0	49
k AFS	47 34	117 05	5198	-1	4	SW	17	8840	77	58	74	57	20	SW	71	56	59	58	56	0	2	0	0
ke/Grant Co	47 12	119 19	1185	1	7	N	8	5809	97	66	94	65	31	SSW	90	63	67	66	64	97	675	1	52
	46 58	122 54	215	16	22	NE	4	5530	87	66	83	65	33	NE	79	64	67	66	64	5	139	0	46

TON (CONT)	N		W																					
ello AFS	46	50	119	10	1280	1	7	N	8	5809	97	66	94	65	31	SSW	90	63	67	66	64	97	675	1	52
ne AFB/Everett	47	55	122	07	596	21	25	ENE	6	5678	80	65	76	64	22	NNW	73	62	67	64	63	1	40	1	30
co/Tri-Cities Aprt	46	16	119	7	406	5	11	W W	5	4892	99	68	96	67	30	SW	92	66	70	68	67	145	844	5	220
ttle NSA	47	41	122	15	47	22	27	N	7	4650	85	68	82	66	24	N	78	65	69	67	65	3	120	5	93
ttle-Tacoma IAP	47	27	122	18	400	21	26	E	9	5185	84	65	80	64	26	N	76	62	66	64	63	3	87	0	22
kane IAP	47	38	117	31	2366	-6	2	NE	6	6835	93	64	90	63	30	SW	87	62	65	64	62	2	428	0	12
oma	47	15	122	30	100	19	24	S	5	4835	86	66	83	66	22	NNE	70	63	60	66	64	04	101	0	49
oosh Island	48	23	124	44	115	26	29	E	24	5774	64	58	62	58	9	SW	60	57	60	59	58	0	0	0	0
la Walla Aprt	46	06	118	17	1206	0	7	W	5	5187	97	67	94	66	29	W	90	65	69	67	66	98	632	3	109
dbey Island/Ault Fld	48	21	122	40	47	19	24	E	4	5520	79	65	76	64	20	W	71	62	67	64	63	1	26	1	30
dbey Is/Oak Harbor	48	17	122	39	55	20	24	E	4	5609	82	65	78	64	22	W	74	62	67	64	63	1	53	1	30
ima Firing Center	46	41	120	28	1262	-3	4	W	5	6109	95	65	92	65	37	NW	88	63	68	66	65	59	504	1	63
ima MAP	46	34	120	32	1052	-2	5	W		6009	96	65	93	65	37	NW	89	63	68	66	65	73	566	1	63
RGINIA	N		W																					
kley/Raleigh Co Aprt	37	47	81	07	2504	-2	4	WNW	9	5615	83	71	81	69	26	WNW	79	69	73	71	70	0	126	41	515
rleston/Kanawha Aprt	38	22	81	36	939	7	11	SW	8	4590	92	74	90	73	25	SW	87	72	76	75	74	25	744	315	1521
ins/Randolph Co Aprt	38	53	79	51	1948	1	6	WNW	9	5975	86	72	84	70	26	WNW	82	70	74	72	71	1	305	64	715
rmont	39	28	80	08	1298	4	10	SW	7	5208	94	74	90	73	26	SW	87	72	76	75	74	40	662	258	1221
tington	38	25	82	30	565	5	10	W	6	4374	94	76	91	74	27	SW	89	73	78	77	75	47	797	470	1671
tinsburg MAP	39	24	77	59	556	6	10	WNW	10	5231	93	75	90	74	26	W	88	74	77	76	75	35	684	384	1383
kersburg	39	16	81	34	615	7	11	WSW	7	4817	93	75	90	74	23	WSW	88	73	77	76	75	33	736	401	1528
eling/Ohio Co Aprt	40	11	80	39	1196	1	5	WSW	10	5930	89	72	86	71	23	WSW	84	70	74	73	72	5	461	105	886
SIN	N		W																					
igo AFS	45	03	89	14	1530	-22	-15	NNE	7	8460	88	71	84	70	23	SSW	81	68	74	72	70	8	234	44	387
ger Ordnance Works	43	22	89	45	880	-11	-7	WNW	0	7382	91	74	88	73	24	SSW	85	71	77	75	73	1	466	187	868
McCoy	44	01	90	41	870	-15	-12	NW		7558	91	75	88	72	22	SW	85	70	76	74	72	1	482	128	721
en Bay/Austin-Straubel	44	29	88	08	682	-13	-9	W		8098	88	74	85	72	23	SW	83	71	76	74	72		286	128	648
Crosse MAP	43	52	91	15	651	-13	-9	NW	1	7417	91	75	88	73	22	S	85	72	77	75	74	1	469	206	896
ison/Truax Field	43	08	89	20	858	-11	-7	NW	8	7730	91	74	88	73	24	SW	85	71	77	75	73	16	466	187	868
waukee/Gen Mitchell Fld	42	57	87	54	672	-8	-4	WNW	1	7444	90	74	87	73	23	SSW	84	71	76	74	73	10	346	161	791
kosh/Wittman Field	43	59	88	33	805	-14	-9	WNW		7602	89	74	86	72	21	SSW	83	71	76	74	72		309	128	648
k Field ANG/Camp Douglas	43	56	90	16	915	-15	-12	WNW		7773	91	75	88	72	22	SSW	85	70	76	74	72	1	482	128	721

STATE / Station	LOCATION			WINTER DESIGN DATA HEATING				DEGREE DAYS	SUMMER DESIGN DATA AIR CONDITIONING											SUMMER CRITERIA DATA AIR CONDITIONING			
				Dry Bulb					Dry Bulb								Wet Bulb			Dry Bulb		Wet Bulb	
	Lat	Long	Elev	99%	97.5%	Pvlg Wind	Mean Speed	Heating	1%	MCWB	2.5%	MCWB	Mean Daily Range	Pvlg Wind	5%	MCWB	1%	2.5%	5%	≧ 93°F	≧ 80°F	≧ 73°F	≧ 67°F
	° '	° '	feet	°F	°F	dir	knots	annual	°F	°F	°F	°F	°F	dir	°F	°F	°F	°F	°F	hrs	hrs	hrs	hrs
WYOMING	N	W																					
Casper IAP	42 55	106 28	5338	-11	-5	NE	10	7555	92	58	90	57	31	SW	87	57	63	61	60	20	559	0	1
Cheyenne MAP	41 09	104 49	6126	-9	-1	N	11	7255	89	58	86	58	31	WNW	84	57	63	62	60	2	355	0	0
F E Warren AFB/Cheyenne	41 09	104 50	6155	-9	-1	N	11	7255	89	58	86	58	31	WNW	84	57	63	62	60	2	355	0	0
Lander/Hunt Field	42 49	108 44	5563	-16	-11	E	5	7869	91	60	88	59	29	NW	85	59	64	62	60	1	428	0	1
Rock Springs	41 36	109 04	6745	-9	-3	WSW	10	8410	86	55	84	55	28	W	82	54	59	58	57	1	261	0	0
Sheridan	44 46	106 58	3964	-14	-8	NW	7	7708	94	62	91	62	33	N	88	61	66	65	63	54	561	0	24

CHAPTER 2

WINTER DESIGN DATA FOR HEATING AND SUMMER DESIGN AND CRITERIA DATA FOR AIR CONDITIONING FOR SITES OUTSIDE THE UNITED STATES

	LOCATION			WINTER DESIGN DATA HEATING				DEGREE DAYS	SUMMER DESIGN DATA AIR CONDITIONING											SUMMER CRITERIA DATA AIR CONDITIONING			
				Dry Bulb					Dry Bulb								Wet Bulb			Dry Bulb		Wet Bulb	
	Lat	Long	Elev	99%	97.5%	Pvlg Wind	Mean Speed	Heating	1%	MCWB	2.5%	MCWB	Mean Daily Range	Pvlg Wind	5%	MCWB	1%	2.5%	5%	≧ 93°F	≧ 80°F	≧ 73°F	≧ 67°F
	° '	° '	feet	°F	°F	dir	knots	annual	°F	°F	°F	°F	°F	dir	°F	°F	°F	°F	°F	hrs	hrs	hrs	hrs
	N 36 43	E 3 15	75	36	39	SW	5	1803	95	73	91	72	24	NE	88	72	77	75	74	50	774	265	1497
	N 3 50	E 11 31	2464	64	66	W	6	0	90	72	88	72	17	ENE	86	72	76	75	75	1	1104	828	4011
	N 8 59	E 38 48	7684	33	36	E	10	2148	83	63	80	62	22	S	78	61	66	65	64	3	264	0	13
	15 17	38 55	7628	36	38	E	9	1732	83	63	82	62	21	WNW	79	61	66	65	64	0	169	0	22
	15 37	39 27	33	64	66	W	6	0	106	81	104	80	16	N	102	79	86	85	84	1760	4235	4290	4416
	N 5 36	W 0 10	230	70	72	WSW	5	0	88	80	88	80	9	SW	88	80	82	81	81	2	2973	4180	4377
	N 5 15	W 3 56	20	70	72	WSW	5	0	88	80	88	80	9	SW	88	80	82	81	81	2	2973	4180	4377
	N 3 56	E 41 51	801	68	69	NE	7	0	99	78	97	78	17	SW	96	77	82	81	80	394	3184	2380	4065
	N 6 15	W 10 21	26	70	72	W	3	0	91	78	91	78	15	SSW	90	78	81	81	80	22	1900	3812	4383
	N 32 05	E 20 16	427	43	45	SSE	8	113	102	72	97	72	24	S	93	72	78	76	75	210	1535	648	2471
	32 41	13 10	262	37	39	S	5	136	108	72	104	71	29	N	100	71	77	76	75	491	1724	424	2102
	32 54	13 17	13	42	44	SSW	7	1116	98	71	94	71	21	E	90	72	79	78	77	114	1396	805	2492
Lyautey	N 34 18	W 6 36	20	38	41	E	4	1230	93	70	86	71	20	NW	82	71	74	73	72	32	338	106	1720
	34 03	6 46	276	40	42	SSE	6	1646	91	70	84	71	19	NNW	81	71	75	74	73	24	208	147	1504
half	35 43	5 54	46	41	43	E	6	1541	90	73	86	72	18	ENE	85	72	74	74	72	9	412	123	1370
	N 6 35	E 3 20	131	70	72	WSW	5	0	88	80	88	80	9	SW	88	80	82	81	81	2	2973	4180	4377

AFRICA (CONT)																							
SOUTH AFRICA	S	E																					
Pretoria	25 39	28 13	4094	30	33	E	8	1632	91	66	88	65	21	E	86	64	69	68	67	22	844	1	366
SUDAN	N	E																					
Khartoum	15 36	32 33	1257	54	57	N	8	0	108	70	105	70	24	SW	103	70	82	81	80	1678	3823	1465	2989
TUNISIA	N	W																					
Tunis	36 50	10 14	16	41	42	W	10	1697	97	75	93	75	80	E	90	73	70	77	73	87	1008	540	2078
UNITED ARAB REPUBLIC/EGYPT	N	E																					
Alexandria/Nouzha	31 10	29 57	-10	44	46	S	4	841	90	73	88	74	14	NNW	86	74	77	76	76	23	1217	872	2963
Cairo IAP	30 08	31 24	367	44	46	SSW	6	689	100	70	97	70	25	NNW	94	71	76	74	74	295	1892	308	2497
ZAIRE	S	E																					
Kinshasa	4 19	15 19	925	61	63	S	4	0	92	74	90	74	17	S	89	74	78	78	77	7	1454	2138	4358
ANTARCTIC CIRCLE																							
ANTARCTICA	S	E																					
Hallett Station	72 19	170 19	16	-38	-35	SW	4	22245	37	31	35	30	9	N	34	30	32	31	30	0	0	0	0
McMurdo Sound	77 51	166 40	80	-39	-36	ENE	15	23363	36	31	35	30	9	E	33	29	32	31	30	0	0	0	0
ASIA																							
ADEN	N	E																					
Aden IAP	12 50	45 02	10	68	70	E	12	0	99	81	98	80	14	SW	97	79	86	85	84	698	4261	4155	4413
AFGHANISTAN	N	E																					
Kabul IAP	34 33	69 13	5876	3	9	W	3	5273	97	68	95	66	33	N	93	64	72	70	68	155	1515	18	190
BAHRAIN	N	E																					
Bahrain IAP/Muharraq	26 16	50 37	6	52	54	WNW	14	172	102	80	100	80	12	NW	99	81	88	87	86	1298	4174	3984	4388
BANGLADESH	N	E																					
Dacca	23 46	90 23	23	52	54	N	5	79	92	82	91	80	9	SW	90	81	84	83	82	85	3590	4214	4367
BURMA	N	E																					
Rangoon	16 54	96 08	108	57	59	W	4	0	94	82	92	82	14	W	89	81	83	82	82	51	1979	4395	4416

	LOCATION			WINTER DESIGN DATA HEATING				DEGREE DAYS	SUMMER DESIGN DATA AIR CONDITIONING												SUMMER CRITERIA DATA AIR CONDITIONING			
				Dry Bulb					Dry Bulb								Wet Bulb			Dry Bulb		Wet Bulb	
	Lat	Long	Elev	99%	97.5%	Pvlg Wind	Mean Speed	Heating	1%	MCWB	2.5%	MCWB	Mean Daily Range	Pvlg Wind	5%	MCWB	1%	2.5%	5%	≥ 93°F	≥ 80°F	≥ 73°F	≥ 67°F
	° ′	° ′	feet	°F	°F	dir	knots	annual	°F	°F	°F	°F	°F	dir	°F	°F	°F	°F	°F	hrs	hrs	hrs	hrs
	N 11 33	E 104 51	33	64	66	N	4	0	95	80	93	80	15	W	91	80	81	81	81	182	2845	4342	4392
	N 6 49	E 79 53	16	68	70	NE	5	11	88	79	87	79	13	W	87	78	81	80	79	1	3274	4201	4411
	N 39 48	E 116 28	105	4	8	NNE		5580	95	74	91	73	18	WSW	88	72	77	76	75	56	922	374	1374
	31 10	121 26	16	23	25	WNW	6	3435	95	82	93	82	14	S	90	81	83	82	81	74	1255	1805	2750
P	N 22 19	E 114 12	16	46	49	N	9	543	92	80	90	80	10	W	89	79	82	81	81	11	2973	3647	4183
	N 19 05	E 72 51	36	61	63	N		0	95	81	92	80		W	90	79	82	81	81	95	2346	4345	4392
	22 39	88 27	13	51	53			108	99	81	96	82	1	S	93	82	86	85	84	365	3412	4248	4398
	17 27	78 28	1742	51	54			80	102	74	99	73	1	SW	96	73	78	77	76	305	1956	1574	4345
	13 00	80 11	49	62	64			0	101	81	99	81	19	W	97	81	86	85	84	590	3644	4376	4392
	28 35	77 12	705	38	40	[illegible]	[illegible]	456	106	77	104	77	18	NW	100	77	83	82	81	1078	3414	2565	3429
	S 6 09	E 106 51	16	70	71	WSW	6	0	90	79	89	79	12	E	88	79	81	80	80	0	2006	4114	4344
	N 30 22	E 48 15	10	36	39	W		784	113	74	111	74	31	WNW	109	73	81	79	77	1745	3510	529	2314
	32 37	51 40	5243	18	21	W		3545	99	63	97	63	25	E	95	62	68	65	63	250	1407	9	36
	30 16	56 57	5735	15	21	WNW		2819	100	68	98	64	26	W	96	63	70	66	64	378	2091	16	66
	36 16	59 38	3245	1	9	S	6	4279	97	64	95	63	29	E	93	63	68	66	65	188	1270	6	60
	29 32	52 35	4911	23	25	WNW	8	2778	102	66	100	64	26	W	99	64	68	66	65	654	1911	5	73
	38 08	46 15	4482	3	7	E	9	5194	95	62	93	62	21	W	90	61	66	64	63	70	866	0	23
bad IAP	35 41	51 19	3949	18	21	N	4	3428	101	62	99	61	23	SSE	97	61	66	65	64	496	2007	0	19
	N 33 14	E 44 14	112	30	32	WNW	5	1389	113	72	111	72	30	WNW	109	71	75	74	73	1554	3043	174	1485
	N 31 47	E 35 13	2654	35	37	W	12	2313	92	63	89	62	17	NW	86	62	70	69	68	24	748	0	383
	32 00	34 54	131	37	39	SE	5	1251	96	71	94	73	22	WNW	91	73	78	77	76	130	1390	651	2277

	LOCATION			WINTER DESIGN DATA HEATING				DEGREE DAYS	SUMMER DESIGN DATA AIR CONDITIONING											SUMMER CRITERIA DATA AIR CONDITIONING			
				Dry Bulb					Dry Bulb								Wet Bulb			Dry Bulb		Wet Bulb	
ion	Lat	Long	Elev	99%	97.5%	Pvlg Wind	Mean Speed	Heating	1%	MCWB	2.5%	MCWB	Mean Daily Range	Pvlg Wind	5%	MCWB	1%	2.5%	5%	≥ 93°F	≥ 80°F	≥ 73°F	≥ 67°F
	° '	° '	feet	°F	°F	dir	knots	annual	°F	°F	°F	°F	°F	dir	°F	°F	°F	°F	°F	hrs	hrs	hrs	hrs
)	N	E																					
ki	34 11	132 33	262	29	30	WNW	5	3025	91	78	89	78	13	SSE	87	78	80	79	78	11	995	1471	2368
a	33 52	130 38	105	30	32	SSE	10	3176	91	79	89	78	14	E	87	78	81	80	79	12	844	1380	2336
NAS	35 27	139 28	200	22	24	N	3	3225	90	79	88	78	15	S	86	77	81	79	78	6	655	1067	2175
Range/Okinawa	26 25	127 44	131	48	49	NNW	9	452	90	80	89	80	10	SE	88	79	82	81	80	1	2193	3023	3914
Asaka	35 48	139 36	115	22	24	NW	4	3588	93	78	91	78	17	S	89	77	80	79	78	35	786	965	2035
Chinen/Okinawa	26 09	127 47	476	51	52	N	14	372	88	78	87	78	9	E	86	78	80	79	79	0	1700	2560	3222
Hardy/Okinawa	26 28	128 00	49	49	50	NNW	9	352	89	79	88	79	10	SE	87	78	81	80	79	0	1860	2815	3895
Kubasaki/Okinawa	26 17	127 49	16	48	49	NNW	9	507	90	80	88	80	9	ESE	88	80	82	81	80	2	2164	3181	3992
Kue/Okinawa	26 18	127 46	16	48	49	NNW	9	452	90	80	89	80	10	SE	88	79	82	81	80	1	2193	3023	3914
Sansone/Okinawa	26 21	127 45	33	48	49	NNW	9	452	90	80	89	80	10	SE	88	79	82	81	80	1	2193	3023	3914
Sukiran/Okinawa	26 17	127 46	164	48	49	NNW	9	507	90	80	88	80	9	ESE	88	80	82	81	80	2	2164	3181	3992
Zama/Rankin Fld	35 30	139 24	359	22	24	N	3	3225	90	79	88	78	15	S	86	77	81	79	78	6	655	1067	2175
se AS	42 50	141 43	73	1	5	N	4	7542	83	75	80	73	17	SSE	78	71	76	74	73	0	93	158	677
AS	35 40	139 30	173	21	23	NW	4	3826	92	78	90	78	17	S	88	77	80	79	78	23	671	965	2035
MCAS/Okinawa	26 16	127 45	245	48	49	NNW	9	507	90	80	88	80	9	ESE	88	80	82	81	80	2	2164	3181	3992
AS	33 40	130 22	20	30	32	SSE	10	3176	91	79	89	78	14	E	87	78	81	80	79	12	844	1380	2336
te	41 49	140 45	116	10	14	WNW	7	7008	82	75	81	74	13	SSE	77	72	75	74	73	0	84	159	760
AB	35 51	139 25	295	24	26	W	4	3791	93	79	90	78	18	S	88	78	81	79	78	30	614	1029	2084
e Aux Airfield	33 35	130 27	22	29	30	SSE	6	3253	92	79	90	78	14	NNW	89	78	80	79	79	22	1055	1454	2362
i MCAS	34 09	132 14	8	29	30	WNW	5	3025	91	78	89	78	13	SSE	87	78	80	79	78	11	995	1471	2368
AB/Okinawa	26 21	127 46	140	48	49	NNW	9	452	90	80	89	80	10	SE	88	79	82	81	80	1	2193	3023	3914
eya	35 29	139 29	229	22	24	N	3	3225	90	79	88	78	15	S	86	77	81	79	78	6	655	1067	2175
zu	35 24	139 55	12	26	28	E	4	2895	88	79	86	78	12	SW	85	78	80	79	78	2	594	1220	2229
AB	40 42	141 22	118	17	19	W	9	5942	86	75	83	73	16	SW	81	72	76	75	73	3	190	190	872
a	39 42	141 10	512	12	16	SE	4	6311	88	74	86	75	16	S	82	73	77	76	74	1	290	355	1121
ki	32 44	129 51	87	30	32	N	6	2734	91	79	90	79	12	SW	88	78	81	80	79	9	1103	1579	2499
/Komaki AB	35 15	136 56	52	26	28	N	4	3501	94	79	92	79	18	SW	89	78	81	80	79	47	878	1227	2251
B/Okinawa	26 12	127 39	13	51	52	N	14	372	90	80	89	80	9	E	88	80	82	81	81	0	2456	3222	4037
IAP	34 47	135 27	49	27	28	NNW	5	3449	93	78	91	78	17	SW	89	78	80	79	79	33	906	1176	2204
	35 35	139 25	328	21	23	NW	4	3826	92	78	90	78	17	S	88	77	80	79	78	23	671	965	2035
o	43 03	141 20	50	1	5	SE	3	7360	86	75	82	73	15	SE	79	71	76	74	73	0	143	145	650
NB	33 09	129 43	50	30	32	N	6	2909	91	79	90	79	12	SW	88	78	81	80	79	9	1103	1579	2499
yama	33 26	130 22	3460	13	15	SSE	10	5814	80	71	78	70	11	NNW	76	69	72	71	70	0	21	7	586

	N		E																						
	35	42	139	24	305	21	23	NW	4	3826	92	78	90	78	17	S	88	77	80	79	78	23	671	965	2035
	35	33	139	46	9	30	32	NNW	7	3281	89	77	87	77	12	S	86	77	79	78	77	1	723	1099	2048
	35	26	139	38	33	30	32	NNW	7	3281	89	77	87	77	12	S	86	77	79	78	77	1	723	1099	2048
	35	17	139	40	174	32	33	N	9	2782	88	79	86	78	12	S	85	78	80	79	78	1	574	1278	2315
	35	44	139	20	456	23	25	W	4	3818	91	79	89	78	16	S	87	77	80	79	78	12	582	912	1961
	N		E																						
	31	58	35	59	2543	28	31	SW	8	2273	99	68	97	68	26	W	94	67	73	72	70	206	1363	53	525
	N		E																						
	37	23	26	55	131	3	6	N	5	5555	91	78	88	77	17	W	86	76	80	79	78	1	650	894	1800
	37	30	26	42	59	6	10	NNW	7	5276	90	78	88	78	15	WSW	87	77	81	80	79	5	797	1019	1913
	35	08	28	40	16	19	21	NW	12	4007	91	80	89	79	12	S	87	78	82	80	79	3	788	1207	2138
	37	28	126	38	33	6	10	NNW	7	5276	90	78	88	78	15	WSW	87	77	81	80	79	15	797	1019	1913
	37	45	128	57	20	11	15	W	11	4862	91	79	89	78	18	E	86	76	80	79	77	19	491	600	1543
	37	37	2	44	33	4	7	NW	17	5681	90	78	87	77	16	W	85	76	80	79	78	7	567	925	1875
ange	37	02	2	45	40	4	7	NW	10	5068	90	80	88	79	12	WNW	86	79	82	81	79	4	834	183	2062
	36	07	2	07	328	1	14	NW	8	4750	95	80	92	79	20	W	90	78	82	81	79	70	973	120	1994
	35	54	12	37	36	13	16	E	7	4802	90	80	87	79	11	W	85	78	81	80	79	4	755	1212	2090
	35	07	126	49	52	14	17	NNE	6	4445	93	80	91	79	18	SW	89	79	83	81	80	44	1052	1340	2277
	36	56	26	27	991	11	14	NW	10	5510	84	77	82	76	12	WNW	80	76	79	77	76	0	168	555	1557
	33	12	26	16	43	29	30	N	16	3230	89	81	87	80	11	SE	86	80	82	81	80	1	787	1481	2375
	37	51	26	49	167	0	4	N	5	5640	91	77	89	76	19	S	87	75	80	79	77	19	699	867	1773
	37	05	127	02	35	3	6	N	5	5555	91	78	88	77	17	W	86	76	80	79	78	11	650	894	1800
	35	09	129	03	112	20	22	NW	12	3841	89	80	87	79	12	S	85	78	81	80	79	1	608	1029	2023
	35	10	29	08	7	20	22	NW	12	3841	89	80	87	79	12	S	85	78	81	80	79	1	608	1029	2023
	36	57	127	02	62	6	9	N	6	5264	91	78	89	77	17	SW	87	77	82	80	79	23	874	1099	2024
	37	26	127	06	75	3	6	N	5	5555	91	78	88	77	17	W	86	76	80	79	78	11	650	894	1800
AP	37	33	126	48	59	4	7	NW	7	5681	90	78	87	77	16	W	85	76	80	79	78	7	567	925	1875
	35	53	128	40	98	12	15	NW	8	4622	96	80	93	79	20	W	91	78	82	81	79	95	1018	1120	1994
	36	20	127	23	226	8	11	N	8	5363	92	80	90	79	18	W	88	78	82	80	79	23	814	1109	2066
	37	54	127	04	263	-2	4	N	5	5334	93	79	91	78	21	N	88	77	81	80	79	67	1105	1013	1968
	37	44	127	03	184	0	4	N	5	5640	91	77	89	76	19	S	87	75	80	79	77	19	699	867	1773
	35	59	128	24	33	12	15	NW	8	4622	96	80	93	79	20	W	91	78	82	81	79	95	1018	1120	1994

AREA Country Station	LOCATION Lat	Long	Elev	WINTER DESIGN DATA HEATING Dry Bulb 99%	97.5%	Pvlg Wind	Mean Speed	DEGREE DAYS Heating	SUMMER DESIGN DATA AIR CONDITIONING Dry Bulb 1%	MCWB	2.5%	MCWB	Mean Daily Range	Pvlg Wind	5%	MCWB	Wet Bulb 1%	2.5%	5%	SUMMER CRITERIA DATA AIR CONDITIONING Dry Bulb ≥ 93°F	≥ 80°F	Wet Bulb ≥ 73°F	≥ 67°F
	° '	° '	feet	°F	°F	dir	knots	annual	°F	°F	°F	°F	°F	dir	°F	°F	°F	°F	°F	hrs	hrs	hrs	hrs
ASIA (CONT)																							
KOREA (CONT)	N	E																					
Yonchon	35 59	128 59	295	11	14	NW	8	4750	95	80	92	79	20	W	90	78	82	81	79	70	973	1120	1994
KUWAIT	N	E																					
Kuwait IAP	29 13	47 58	184	38	41	WNW	7	768	114	71	113	71	28	NNW	112	70	82	79	77	2235	3820	517	2173
LAOS	N	E																					
Saravane	15 43	106 25	574	55	57	E	3	6	94	80	92	80	18	W	90	80	82	81	80	172	2679	4168	4388
Vientiane	17 59	102 04	561	55	55	E	3	17	94	80	92	80	18	W	90	80	82	81	80	171	2121	4090	4388
LEBANON	N	E																					
Beirut IAP	33 49	35 29	85	43	45	E	3	944	89	76	88	76	14	WSW	86	76	79	78	77	2	1058	1132	2927
MALAYSIA	N	E																					
Butterworth	5 28	100 24	10	71	72	NNE	5	0	90	80	90	80	14	SSW	89	79	82	81	81	9	2830	4306	4398
Kuala Lumpur	3 07	101 33	89	70	72	N	4	0	93	79	92	79	18	W	91	78	81	80	80	45	2009	4004	4406
NEPAL	N	E																					
Katmandu IAP	27 42	85 22	4422	30	31	W	4	1663	89	73	87	72	16	NW	86	72	78	77	76	22	843	995	3020
PAKISTAN	N	E																					
Karachi Aprt	24 54	67 09	102	48	50	N	4	222	102	75	99	77	14	SSW	95	80	84	83	82	416	3951	3870	4240
Lahore	31 33	74 20	702	34	36	NW	3	939	107	76	104	77	23	SE	102	77	84	84	83	1106	3485	2742	3678
Peshawar	34 00	71 31	1181	31	34	W	5	1284	106	76	104	76	25	NE	101	75	82	82	81	913	3272	1895	2920
SAUDI ARABIA	N	E																					
Dhahran AB	26 16	50 10	75	46	48	WNW	11	282	111	74	109	74	24	N	107	74	86	85	84	1800	3904	2055	3674
Riyadh IAP	24 42	46 44	2047	37	41	N	8	506	111	68	110	67	23	N	109	66	74	73	71	1813	3392	82	710
SINGAPORE	N	E																					
Singapore Aprt	1 21	103 55	59	72	73	N	4	0	90	79	89	78	13	SE	88	79	81	80	80	4	2075	4349	4404
TAIWAN	N	E																					
Chiai	23 28	120 27	98	45	47	N	6	337	92	81	91	81	14	WSW	90	81	83	83	82	27	2207	3654	4218
Chiai AB	23 28	120 23	82	45	47	N	6	337	92	81	91	81	14	WSW	90	81	83	83	82	27	2207	3654	4218
Ching Chuan Kang AB	24 16	120 37	666	43	45	NNE	13	607	92	81	91	80	15	WSW	90	79	82	81	80	8	1675	3183	4067
Gold Mountain	25 08	121 33	1378	39	42	E	10	1020	90	79	88	78	16	E	87	78	81	81	80	2	1138	2684	3887
Grass Mountain	25 08	121 33	1302	39	42	E	10	1020	90	79	88	78	16	E	87	78	81	81	80	2	1138	2684	3887
San Yi	24 08	120 39	164	45	47	N	9	394	94	81	92	80	15	W	92	80	82	82	81	88	2164	3306	4076

LOCATION						WINTER DESIGN DATA HEATING				DEGREE DAYS	SUMMER DESIGN DATA AIR CONDITIONING											SUMMER CRITERIA DATA AIR CONDITIONING			
						Dry Bulb					Dry Bulb								Wet Bulb			Dry Bulb		Wet Bulb	
	Lat		Long		Elev	99%	97.5%	Pvlg Wind	Mean Speed	Heating	1%	MCWB	2.5%	MCWB	Mean Daily Range	Pvlg Wind	5%	MCWB	1%	2.5%	5%	≥ 93°F	≥ 80°F	≥ 73°F	≥ 67°F
	°	'	°	'	feet	°F	°F	dir	knots	annual	°F	°F	°F	°F	°F	dir	°F	°F	°F	°F	°F	hrs	hrs	hrs	hrs
)	N		E																						
Kou AS	25	05	121	23	820	40	43		7	869	91	79	89	79	16	E	88	79	82	82	1	6	1400	2976	3981
	24	11	120	39	364	44	46		19	475	93	81	91	80	15	W	91	80	82	82	1	40	1954	3306	4076
B	22	57	120	12	56	45	48		0	214	91	81	91	81	13	W	90	81	83	82	1	10	2478	3825	4285
AP	25	04	121	33	20	43	46	N	7	556	94	81	92	80	16	E	91	80	84	83	82	74	1932	3266	4094
	N		E																						
Don Muang IAP	3	55	100	37	12	62	64	NNE	4	0	97	81	96	80	19	S	94	80	83	82	81	353	3144	4368	4391
endship	5	04	102	08	591	60	62	ENE	5	0	97	76	95	77	17	W	94	77	80	79	78	373	2723	3791	4402
Pung	6	38	102	58	686	55	57	E	3	12	97	79	94	79	16	N	92	79	81	81	80	151	2730	3875	4375
ae San	12	34	100	57	200	65	67	NNW	7	0	91	80	90	80	9	S	88	80	82	81	81	4	2951	4355	4392
ama	3	42	100	52	6	62	64	NNE	4	0	97	81	96	80	19	S	94	80	83	82	81	353	3144	4368	4391
i	8	46	98	58	1063	50	52	N	2	18	93	78	91	78	17		90	76	80	80	78	141	2123	3898	4392
	4	56	102	04	797	59	61	ENE	5	4	96	76	94	77	17		93	77	80	79	78	250	2685	3791	4402
hanom	7	23	104	39	577	51	54	SE	3	27	95	81	93	80	17		91	80	83	82	81	188	2489	3939	4360
	15	14	104	52	443	58	60	NNE	6	1	95	79	92	79	15		91	79	81	80	80	170	2598	4070	4388
	7	23	102	47	574	55	57	E	3	12	97	79	94	79	16	N	92	79	81	81	80	151	2730	3875	4375
	12	40	101	00	33	66	68	NNW	7	0	92	80	91	80	9	S	89	80	82	81	81	12	3868	4355	4392
	N		E																						
S	39	57	32	53	2960	8	13	N	2	5148	96	65	93	65	31		90	64	67	66	65	80	747		50
senboga	40	07	32	59	3127	7	12	N	2	5513	95	65	92	65	31		89	64	67	66	65	60	663	0	50
urted	40	05	32	34	2750	9	14	N	2	4833	97	65	94	65	31		91	64	67	66	65	101	833	0	50
r	39	37	27	56	348	21	25	NNE	7	3411	97	69	93	69	31	W	90	69	73	72	70	92	829	37	767
/Izmir	38	31	27	01	17	27	30	NNE	8	2463	97	71	95	69	26	W	92	68	74	72	70	145	1237	45	648
Sta	42	02	35	11	164	29	32	SW	5	3522	84	72	82	72	11	NE	80	71	75	74	72	1	166	117	1044
ir AB	37	54	40	12	2251	11	16	WNW	4	3754	107	70	104	69	32	N	102	68	72	71	70	647	2124	29	472
r	39	47	30	34	2575	6	11	E	5	5487	95	67	92	66	31	NW	89	66	69	68	67	65	634	4	149
AB/Adana	37	00	35	26	239	32	34	NNE	19	1728	100	71	97	72	27	SW	94	73	78	78	77	263	1772	960	2278
/Yesilkoy	40	58	28	49	92	26	28	N	0	3604	88	69	86	69	18	NE	83	68	73	72	71	4	348	48	856
	38	27	27	15	92	27	30	NNE	8	2463	97	71	95	69	26	N	92	68	74	72	70	145	1237	45	648
	40	46	29	54	249	25	28	N	10	3401	93	70	90	70	18	NE	86	69	74	73	72	35	536	88	844
el AS	40	43	29	31	18	26	29	N	10	3433	90	70	87	70	18	NE	84	69	74	73	72	20	422	88	844
	38	21	38	18	3274	9	14	SW	4	4798	98	65	95	64	32	E	92	63	67	66	65	147	1187	0	47
Cyprus	35	09	33	17	735	35	37	SW	6	1880	99	69	97	68	26	W	95	68	75	74	73	278	1496	235	1568

T)																							
(CONT)	N	E																					
n	41 17	36 20	144	27	30	SW	5	3648	85	72	82	72	11	NE	80	71	75	74	72	3	182	117	1044
lar	38 32	27 07	3202	16	20	NNE	11	5041	93	66	90	65	20	N	87	65	69	68	67	70	514	1	173
	N	E																					
Ranh Bay	12 00	109 13	47	66	68	NW	7	13	95	80	94	78	16	E	92	78	82	81	80	183	3324	4063	4416
ng	16 03	108 12	30	60	62	NW	5	5	99	80	97	80	18	N	95	79	83	82	82	359	3039	4188	4373
Trang	12 14	109 12	16	66	68	WNW	5	0	95	79	94	80	15	ESE	93	79	82	82	81	162	3284	4213	4415
ku	14 00	108 01	2435	51	53	E	4	29	88	75	86	74	16	W	84	74	77	76	75	4	797	1024	4095
on/Tan Son Nhut	10 49	106 39	33	66	68	N	4	0	94	80	93	79	15	W	91	78	81	80	79	146	2704	4351	4391
OCEAN																							
ON ISLAND	S	W																					
nsion AAFB	7 58	14 24	282	69	69	ESE	13	0	86	75	85	75	9	ESE	84	74	76	76	75	0	1541	1689	4371
	N	W																					
s Field	38 46	27 06	180	46	48	W	9	1332	79	71	78	70	11	NW	76	69	72	71	70	0	24	17	889
A	N	W																					
da NAS/Kindley AFB	32 22	64 41	10	53	54	NW	16	325	86	76	85	76	7	S	84	76	78	77	77	0	1272	2014	3626
	N	W																					
fjordur	64 24	21 28	20	15	18	E	12	9016	63	53	61	53	10	E	59	52	55	55	54	0	0	0	0
vik NAS	63 59	22 36	169	14	17	NNE	14	8838	59	52	57	52	8	N	56	51	54	54	53	0	0	0	0
avik	64 08	21 56	59	15	18	E	12	9016	63	53	61	53	10	E	59	52	55	55	54	0	0	0	0
STATION VESSELS	N	W																					
	56 30	51 00	0	12	15	W	26	9473	52	50	52	50	4	S	51	49	51	50	49	0	0	0	0
	52 45	35 30	0	31	33	W	29	6509	61	60	60	58	4	S	58	56	60	58	57	0	0	0	0
	44 00	41 00	0	38	40	NW	31	2612	76	73	75	72	4	SW	74	71	73	72	71	0	0	49	958
	35 00	48 00	0	54	55	N	23	322	82	75	81	75	4	SW	80	74	77	76	75	0	391	1377	3406
AN CAPITAL TERRITORY	S	E																					
rra	35 19	149 11	1873	24	26	NE	1	4027	91	64	87	63	32	NW	84	63	69	68	66	15	315	1	113
TH WALES	S	E																					
y IAP	33 57	151 11	10	40	42	NW	4	1586	88	71	83	70	17	NE	80	70	74	73	72	16	201	73	1207

	LOCATION			WINTER DESIGN DATA HEATING				DEGREE DAYS	SUMMER DESIGN DATA AIR CONDITIONING											SUMMER CRITERIA DATA AIR CONDITIONING			
				Dry Bulb					Dry Bulb								Wet Bulb			Dry Bulb		Wet Bulb	
	Lat	Long	Elev	99%	97.5%	Pvlg Wind	Mean Speed	Heating	1%	MCWB	2.5%	MCWB	Mean Daily Range	Pvlg Wind	5%	MCWB	1%	2.5%	5%	≥ 93°F	≥ 80°F	≥ 73°F	≥ 67°F
	° ′	° ′	feet	°F	°F	dir	knots	annual	°F	°F	°F	°F	°F	dir	°F	°F	°F	°F	°F	hrs	hrs	hrs	hrs
IT)																							
RRITORY	S	E																					
rings	23 48	133 54	1781	34	36	W	2	1186	103	68	102	68	26	E	100	67	75	74	72	705	2332	122	894
	12 26	130 52	95	64	66	SE	6	0	92	80	91	80	11	NW	90	79	82	82	81	23	3186	4115	4322
	S	E																					
	27 26	153 05	7	45	47	SW	5	529	88	74	86	73	14	NE	85	73	77	76	75	5	841	554	2760
le	19 15	146 46	10	49	52	S	4	46	91	78	90	78	11	NE	88	78	81	80	79	10	2120	2820	4187
ILIA	S	E																					
	34 56	138 35	141	38	41	NE	5	2001	97	68	93	66	20	NW	89	65	72	69	68	94	664	24	210
	31 09	136 48	538	39	41	SW	7	1590	103	70	101	68	28	NW	98	67	74	72	70	427	1531	49	475
	S	E																					
e IAP	37 40	144 50	423	35	37	N	4	3187	94	69	89	68	30	N	85	67	71	70	68	39	299	4	212
TRALIA	S	E																					
t Cape	22 20	114 03	126	47	50	NE	5	132	107	78	105	77	15	NW	102	76	82	81	80	753	2483	1462	3145
P	31 56	115 58	56	38	40	ENE	4	1415	100	72	97	71	26	SW	93	70	76	75	73	151	822	146	908
	N	W																					
	17 06	61 46	75	69	71	E	7	3	88	79	87	78	8	E	87	78	80	80	79	0	3579	4292	4416
/Coolidge Field	17 08	61 47	62	69	71	E	7	3	88	79	87	78	8	E	87	78	80	80	79	0	3579	4292	4416
IDS	N	W																					
ay	26 59	77 40	12	47	50	NE	3	150	89	79	88	79	12	S	87	78	80	80	79	0	2356	3364	4215
a AAFB	25 16	76 19	45	61	63	E	8	9	89	78	88	78	11	E	88	78	80	80	79	0	2939	3807	4349
hama AAFB	26 37	78 22	7	47	50	NE	3	150	89	79	88	79	12	S	87	78	80	80	79	0	2356	3364	4215
rk AAFB	21 27	71 09	26	69	70	E	11	0	89	79	88	78	8	E	88	78	80	80	79	0	3850	4208	4404
arter Cay	27 05	78 00	21	47	50	NE	3	150	89	79	88	79	12	S	87	78	80	80	79	0	2356	3364	4215
a AAFB	22 22	73 01	80	66	67	E	9	0	89	79	88	78	10	E	88	78	80	80	79	0	3350	4017	4383
eek	21 30	71 10	80	69	70	E	11	0	89	79	88	78	8	E	88	78	80	80	79	0	3850	4208	4404
ador Island	24 04	74 32	10	63	64	E	8	0	90	78	89	78	11	E	89	78	80	80	79	0	2843	3827	4361
	N	W																					
mo Bay NAS	19 54	75 09	51	64	66	N	6	0	94	80	93	80	17	ESE	92	80	82	81	80	131	2790	3935	4411
ose Marti	22 59	82 24	246	52	55	N	11	46	91	77	90	77	17	E	89	77	81	79	78	3	1653	2966	4272

				WINTER DESIGN DATA HEATING				DEGREE DAYS	SUMMER DESIGN DATA AIR CONDITIONING											SUMMER CRITERIA DATA AIR CONDITIONING			
	LOCATION			Dry Bulb					Dry Bulb								Wet Bulb			Dry Bulb		Wet Bulb	
ion	Lat	Long	Elev	99%	97.5%	Pvlg Wind	Mean Speed	Heating	1%	MCWB	2.5%	MCWB	Mean Daily Range	Pvlg Wind	5%	MCWB	1%	2.5%	5%	≥ 93°F	≥ 80°F	≥ 73°F	≥ 67°F
	° '	° '	feet	°F	°F	dir	knots	annual	°F	°F	°F	°F	°F	dir	°F	°F	°F	°F	°F	hrs	hrs	hrs	hrs
SEA (CONT)																							
REPUBLIC	N	W																					
Domingo/Cauce	18 26	69 40	46	64	65	NNE	6	0	90	80	90	80	16	SE	88	79	81	81	80	3	1972	3689	4404
	N	W																					
Au prince	18 35	72 18	108	64	65	N	6	0	97	80	95	80	17	ESE	93	80	82	81	80	187	2455	2575	4406
	N	W																					
ton	17 56	76 47	10	63	65	N	8	0	94	79	92	79	17	ESE	91	79	81	80	79	75	2144	3233	4406
ICO	N	W																					
Buchanan	10 25	00 08	16	65	66	S	4	0	89	77	88	77	13	ENE	87	77	79	79	78	1	2227	3655	4413
AFB/Aguadilla	18 30	67 08	236	66	67	ESE	4	13	88	78	87	78	12	ENE	86	77	80	79	78	0	2087	3230	4392
velt Roads NAS	18 15	65 38	39	68	69	N	6	0	90	79	89	79	10	E	88	78	81	80	79	1	3154	4103	4415
Seca	18 26	66 11	200	65	66	S	4	0	89	77	88	77	13	ENE	87	77	79	79	78	1	2227	3655	4413
Jan/Isle Verde	18 26	66 00	10	65	66	S	4	0	89	77	88	77	13	ENE	87	77	79	79	78	1	2227	3655	4413
LANDS	N	W																					
omas/Truman Field	18 20	64 58	7	70	71	ENE	6	2	89	78	88	78	10	ENE	88	78	79	79	78	0	3126	4153	4416
MERICA																							
NE	N	W																					
ok AFB	8 58	79 33	30	72	73	NW		0	91	80	90	80	15	NW	89	79	81	80	80	9	1871	4260	4416
Amador	8 57	79 33	16	72	73	NW	3	16	91	80	90	80	15	NW	89	79	81	80	80	9	1871	4260	4416
Clayton	8 59	79 35	33	72	73	NW			91	80	90	80	15	NW	89	79	81	80	80	9	1871	4260	4416
Gulick	9 19	79 53	16	72	73	ENE			88	80	87	80	15	ESE	87	79	82	81	80	0	2331	4293	4392
Kobbe	8 55	79 36	98	72	73	N			89	79	88	79	12	NNW	87	79	81	80	79	4	1963	3832	4390
AFB/Balboa	8 55	79 36	51	72	73	N		10	89	79	88	79	12	NNW	87	79	81	80	79	4	1963	3832	4390
Heights	8 57	79 33	175	72	73	NW			91	80	90	80	15	NW	89	79	81	80	80	9	1871	4260	4416
Naval Station	8 57	79 34	15	72	73	NW			91	80	90	80	15	NW	89	79	81	80	80	9	1871	4260	4416
A	N	W																					
se	9 56	84 05	3845	51	53	NNE	10	49	85	69	83	69	17	NE	82	68	72	72	71	0	434	38	2197
OR	N	W																					
alvador	13 42	89 07	2021	56	57	N	11	0	92	75	90	75	15	S	89	75	78	77	77	56	1337	2060	4315
A	N	W																					
ala City	14 35	90 31	4885	48	50	NNE	12	185	79	65	77	65	18	NNE	76	65	68	67	66	0	48	1	206

(NT)																							
	N	W																					
	14 03	87 13	3305	51	53	NNW	6	76	88	72	87	71	20	NE	86	70	74	73	72	5	892	96	2556
	N	W																					
	12 07	86 11	174	66	67	SE	3	0	91	77	90	78	12	E	89	78	81	80	79	45	2085	3508	4410
	N	E																					
	47 16	11 24	1909	1	6	W	2	6408	86	67	83	66	21	E	80	65	69	67	66	1	164	1	117
chat	48 07	16 34	600	10	14	SE	10	5845	86	68	84	68	22	SSE	81	67	70	68	67	2	180	4	194
	N	E																					
	50 54	4 28	178	18	21	NE	8	5721	82	68	79	67	22	ENE	75	64	70	68	66		53	18	113
	50 34	3 49	223	17	21	N	7	6147	82	70	78	68	26	NNE	75	66	71	69	67		48	4	1 8
	51 12	2 52	13	21	25	ENE	9	5912	77	67	73	64	18	E	70	64	67	66	64	0	14	13	151
	50 48	4 21	328	19	21	NNE	8	5871	82	68	79	67	19	NE	75	65	70	68	66	0.	52	0	143
	N	E																					
astrup	55 38	12 40	16	16	19	NE	11	6630	75	65	73	64	14	N	71	62	66	65	64	0	2	0	28
	N	E																					
tula	60 19	24 58	167	-15	-10	E	4	9100	81	65	77	63	20	S	75	62	67	65	63	0	37	0	38
	N	E																					
ignac	44 50	0W42	161	24	27	NNE	6	4033	88	73	85	71	26	ENE	81	69	75	72	70	4	199	67	510
	48 57	4 21	262	16	20	E	4	5588	86	71	82	68	20	SW	79	66	72	69	67	4	135	20	213
	45 44	4 57	656	13	17	N	7	4900	88	70	85	69	25	S	82	67	72	70	68	2	218	23	322
rignane	43 27	5 13	66	26	28	N	9	3121	90	72	87	71	21	W	85	71	75	73	72	5	445	108	875
	47 10	1W36	89	24	27	NNE	6	4578	86	71	81	68	23	E	79	67	72	70	68	2	107	23	271
	48 44	2 24	292	21	23	NE	7	4986	84	69	81	68	22	E	78	66	70	69	67	0	98	6	180
	N	E																					
	49 25	11 50	1312	-5	3	NNW	3	7313	85	66	81	65	29	N	78	64	68	66	64	1	107	2	57
	49 18	10 35	1676	4	17	SSW	8	6655	84	67	80	65	23	SSW	77	64	69	67	65	0	87	6	85
g AAF	49 58	9 08	380	11	15	N	6	5730	87	68	83	68	26	N	80	66	71	69	67	4	171	14	193
	48 22	10 52	1588	13	17	NE	5	6569	86	68	82	67	28	ENE	80	66	69	68	66	1	158	1	139
	49 57	8 58	430	1	15	N	6	5730	87	68	83	68	26	N	80	66	71	69	67	4	171	14	193

(CONT)

Y (CONT)

	N		E																						
Aibling	47	52	11	59	1591	3	7	S	4	6500	86	67	82	66	24	N	78	65	68	67	65	8	146	0	77
Hersfeld/Johannesberg	50	51	9	43	787	8	13	S	6	6404	84	66	81	64	27	N	77	63	69	67	66	0	99	1	105
Kissingen	50	11	10	07	984	7	12	S	6	6702	83	66	80	65	27	N	76	63	68	66	64	0	81	1	72
Kreuznach	49	50	7	52	377	10	14	NE	4	5508	88	70	85	68	23	N	81	67	71	69	68		218	11	212
Tolz/Greiling AAF	47	45	11	35	2572	-1	5	SSW	4	6999	81	66	78	65	24	E	75	64	67	66	65		55	0	53
erg AAF	49	55	10	54	797	6	13	N	4	5995	86	66	83	66	24	S	80	65	69	68	66	1	152	4	118
holder AAF	49	39	7	18	1444	10	13	N	6	6513	82	67	80	66	27	N	76	64	60	67	66	1	91		
euth	49	30	1	34	1148	-4	4	NW	3	6950	85	66	81	65	29	S	78	64	68	66	64	1	107	2	57
htesgaden	47	38	3	0	1778	2	6	S	4	6813	85	67	81	66	24	N	77	65	68	67	65	1	103	0	77
in/Tempelhof AB	52	29	3	24	164	7	10	E	6	6154	85	68	81	65	20	E	78	64	69	67	65	3	101	1	81
urg AB	49	57	6	34	1228	12	15	E	8	6541	81	66	78	64	22	E	75	63	67	66	64	0	47	0	46
en	53	02	8	47	16	10	15	SE	6	6301	84	68	81	67	22	ESE	77	65	70	68	67	0	94	12	166
erhaven	53	33	8	33	7	14	18	ESE	8	6278	81	67	77	65	18	ENE	73	64	69	67	66	0	35	5	107
ingen	50	18	9	07	951	7	12	NNE	6	6702	83	66	80	65	27	SE	76	63	68	66	64	0	81	1	72
bach	50	26	8	4	591	9	14	N	4	6300	84	67	81	65	23	S	78	64	69	67	65	0	109	4	91
rg	50	17	10	59	1024	8	11	E	5	6734	84	66	82	65	21	W	79	64	69	67	66	1	144	3	104
lsheim	49	08	10	02	1404	4	7	SSW	8	6655	84	67	80	65	23	SSW	77	64	69	67	65	0	87	6	85
stadt	49	52	8	32	384	8	11	S	7	5971	86	68	82	67	18	E	79	66	70	68	67	5	134	5	156
ng AB	48	19	11	57	1514	3	8	NE	6	6749	87	68	83	68	26	E	80	66	71	69	67	4	160	1	155
ngen	49	34	11	07	919	1	7	ESE	4	6723	86	68	82	66	28	W	79	65	69	67	66	3	134	1	109
wege	51	12	9	50	525	8	13	E	8	6474	84	69	80	67	25	E	76	65	70	68	67	1	87	1	158
ht AAF	49	23	11	11	1265	1	7	NNW	5	6675	85	68	82	66	25	N	78	65	69	67	66	0	157	4	119
hen AAF	49	58	8	08	922	10	13	E	6	6038	85	67	81	66	23	N	77	65	70	67	66	2	137	1	178
kfurt/Rhein Main AB	50	02	8	44	368	8	11	NE	8	5971	86	68	82	67	25	SW	79	66	70	68	67	5	134	5	156
dberg/Ockstadt AAF	50	20	8	4	525	9	14	N	4	6300	84	67	81	65	23	S	78	64	69	67	65	0	109	4	91
a/Sickels AAF	50	32	9	38	1093	7	12	S	6	6702	83	66	80	65	27	N	76	63	68	66	64	0	81	1	72
ingen	48	27	10	52	1542	3	7	N	5	6569	86	68	82	67	27	E	80	66	69	68	66	1	158	1	139
isch	47	29	11	03	2470	1	5	WSW	2	7405	82	66	79	65	22	ENE	77	64	68	66	65	0	71	0	58
hausen	50	12	9	11	518	11	15	N	6	5730	87	68	83	68	26	N	80	66	71	69	67	4	171	14	193
ersheim	49	13	8	22	328	10	14	N	5	5375	88	69	84	68	25	N	80	66	71	69	67	6	229	19	262
elstadt AAF	49	40	9	56	984	1	7	ESE	4	6723	86	68	82	66	28	W	79	65	69	67	66	3	134	1	109
sen	50	35	8	42	591	9	14	N	4	6300	84	67	81	65	23	S	78	64	69	67	65	0	109	4	91
ingen	48	42	9	42	1083	5	10	N	5	6133	85	67	82	66	23	E	78	64	69	67	65	2	121	2	85

	LOCATION			WINTER DESIGN DATA HEATING				DEGREE DAYS	SUMMER DESIGN DATA AIR CONDITIONING											SUMMER CRITERIA DATA AIR CONDITIONING			
				Dry Bulb					Dry Bulb								Wet Bulb			Dry Bulb		Wet Bulb	
	Lat	Long	Elev	99%	97.5%	Pvlg Wind	Mean Speed	Heating	1%	MCWB	2.5%	MCWB	Mean Daily Range	Pvlg Wind	5%	MCWB	1%	2.5%	5%	≥ 93°F	≥ 80°F	≥ 73°F	≥ 67°F
	° ′	° ′	feet	°F	°F	dir	knots	annual	°F	°F	°F	°F	°F	dir	°F	°F	°F	°F	°F	hrs	hrs	hrs	hrs
NT)	N	E																					
hr AAF	49 41	11 56	1362	-5	13	NW		7313	85	66	81	65	29	N	78	64	68	66	64	1	107	2	57
m	50 04	8 35	368	8	11	NE	3	5971	86	68	82	67	25	SW	79	66	70	68	67	5	134	5	156
Hunsruck	49 57	7 16	1650	18	12	SE		7069	80	65	76	64	18	N	73	62	67	65	63		28	0	31
F	50 10	8 57	390	1	15	N		5730	87	68	83	68	26	N	80	66	71	69	67	0	171	14	193
	52 28	9 41	183	7	12	E		6398	84	69	81	67	25	E	77	65	70	68	67	4	91	11	158
rg AAF	49 23	8 39	359	12	16	N		5459	88	70	86	69	24	N	81	67	72	70	68		219	20	260
n	49 08	9 13	558	11	15	NE	8	5750	87	69	84	68	24	N	80	66	71	69	67	0	200	13	180
aurach	49 34	10 54	968	1	7	ESE	4	6723	86	68	82	66	28	W	79	65	69	67	66	3	34	1	109
ten AAF	49 36	7 11	1188	8	12	ENE	6	6423	85	67	81	66	28	WSW	78	64	69	67	65	2	111	4	97
m AAF	49 28	10 23	1168	2	6	E	7	6520	84	68	81	67	23	N	78	66	69	67	65	1	180	3	153
autern	49 26	7 50	853	8	12	ENE	6	6423	85	67	81	66	28	WSW	78	64	69	67	65	2	111	14	97
e AAF	49 01	8 22	410	7	2	NE	6	5295	88	69	84	68	26	WSW	80	66	71	69	67	6	239	8	265
	49 26	7 36	781		2	ENE	6	6423	85	67	81	66	28	WSW	78	64	69	67	65	2	11	4	97
ens	50 28	8 39	771		14	N	4	6300	84	67	81	65	23	S	78	64	69	67	65	0	09	4	91
n AAF	49 45	10 2	689		10	NNE	4	6035	88	69	85	67	28	E	81	65	70	68	66	6	89	15	158
	48 32	12 11	1509		8	NE	6	6749	87	69	83	68	26	E	80	66	71	69	67	4	160	1	155
l	49 24	7 32	787	8	12	ENE	6	6423	85	67	81	66	28	WSW	78	64	69	67	65	2	11	4	97
s	47 41	11 34	2264	0		SSW		6800	82	67	79	65	24	E	76	64	68	66	65		9	0	53
AS	50 02	8 15	450	3	1	E		5759	85	67	2	66	24	N	78	65	69	67	66		11	2	114
	49 59	8 16	397	3	1	E		5759	85	67	2	66	24	N	78	65	69	67	66		11	2	114
/Colman Barracks	49 30	8 29	295	11	1	N	4	5133	88	69	4	68	25	S	81	67	71	70	67	0	326	21	310
	51 59	7 44	164	2	16	N	4	6048	85	67	81	66	20	ESE	78	65	69	68	66	8	107	9	118
	48 05	11 36	1860	2	6	S	4	6813	85	67	81	66	24	N	77	65	68	67	65	1	103	0	77
n	48 33	9 47	2264	1	6	N	7	7313	81	65	78	64	25	E	74	62	67	65	63	0	44	0	32
	48 23	0 02	1509	4	9	N	5	6813	84	67	80	66	23	E	77	64	69	67	65	1	82	2	85
/Furth AAF	49 30	11 04	1030	1	7	ESE	4	6723	86	68	82	66	28	W	79	65	69	67	66	3	134	1	109
rgau	47 35	11 05	3937	-2	3	SW	7	7400	77	63	74	62	21	N	71	61	64	63	62	0	10	0	1
g	53 09	8 14	33	10		SE	6	6301	84	68	81	67	22	ESE	77	65	70	68	67		94	12	166
s	49 13	7 36	1411	10	5	NE	8	6415	82	67	79	65	22	WSW	76	64	69	67	65		60	1	79
AB/Landstuhl	49 26	7 36	780	8	12	ENE	6	6423	85	67	81	66	28	WSW	78	64	69	67	65		111	4	197
in AB	50 02	8 34	368	8	11	NE	8	5971	86	68	82	67	25	SW	79	66	70	68	67	0	134	15	156
heim	48 15	11 33	1575	3	8	NE	6	6749	87	69	83	68	26	E	80	66	71	69	67	0	160	1	155

ONT)

(CONT)

Station	Lat	Long																					
	N	E																					
ch AB	49 30	7 52	1052	10	13	ENE	7	6453	83	66	80	65	23	SW	77	64	68	66	65	0	84	1	72
nburg Range	48 45	11 48	1325	3	8	NE	6	6749	87	69	83	68	26	E	80	66	71	69	67	4	160	11	155
Dahlem AB	49 59	6 42	1197	0	14	E	8	6587	81	66	78	65	21	N	75	63	68	66	64	0	49	1	60
gart/Echterdingen AB	48 41	9 13	1300	4	9	N	5	6283	84	67	81	66	23	E	77	64	69	67	65	1	92	2	85
hof AB/Berlin	52 29	13 24	164	7	10	E	6	6154	85	68	81	65	20	E	78	64	69	67	65	3	101	1	81
dorf	54 22	10 33	10	15	20	SW	10	6468	79	67	76	65	18	S	73	64	69	67	66	0	30	5	107
den AB	50 03	8 20	460	13	16	E	5	[illegible]	[illegible]	[illegible]	[illegible]	[illegible]	24	N	78	65	69	67	66	3	116	2	114
rg	49 49	9 33	577	7	12	E	4	5952	87	68	83	66	22	W	80	64	70	68	66	4	179	3	116
ucken AB	49 13	7 24	1133	11	15	NE	8	6215	83	67	80	65	22	WSW	77	64	69	67	65	0	78	1	79
	N	E																					
s/Patrai	38 10	21 25	50	36	39	E	10	2033	93	72	91	70	21	N	89	71	75	74	73	38	869	198	1694
s/Hellinikon Aprt	37 54	23 44	33	34	37	N	9	1779	93	71	91	71	15	NNE	90	71	78	77	75	60	1343	412	1768
s	38 04	23 33	144	35	37	N	17	2126	95	71	93	70	20	S	91	69	76	73	72	106	1347	105	1142
on AS/Crete	35 20	25 11	125	43	45	N	13	1441	91	69	88	71	15	NW	84	70	75	74	72	20	737	138	1528
	39 39	22 27	240	22	26	N	9	3537	97	71	94	70	26	E	91	69	75	73	72	104	977	101	975
	38 50	20 43	7	33	35	E	10	2004	91	73	88	72	21	N	86	71	76	75	73	15	663	229	1503
kri	38 06	23 59	10	34	37	N	9	1779	93	71	91	71	15	NNE	90	71	78	77	75	60	1343	412	1768
	38 10	23 45	4544	19	22	N	10	5869	81	67	78	65	25	NE	75	64	69	67	66	0	38	2	94
s	37 59	23 34	7	34	37	N	9	1779	93	71	91	71	15	NNE	90	71	78	77	75	60	1343	412	1768
Bay/Crete	35 32	24 09	479	39	41	N	16	1907	93	69	90	69	20	WNW	88	68	73	71	70	53	836	36	1008
a	38 19	23 32	456	32	34	W	10	2671	95	72	92	72	23	N	90	71	75	73	71	71	961	108	963
	N	E																					
st/Ferihegy	47 26	19 14	443	8	13	N	5	5802	87	72	85	70	26	S	82	68	74	72	70	2	241	62	438
	N	W																					
IAP	53 26	6 15	223	28	30	W	9	5683	70	62	68	61	13	SW	66	60	64	62	61	0	1	0	1
n IAP	52 41	8 55	46	27	29	SE	4	5455	73	63	70	62	15	W	68	61	65	63	62	0	2	0	10
	N	E																					
AB	46 02	12 36	413	18	21	NNE	4	4386	88	72	86	71	21	N	83	69	74	72	71	4	340	69	670
si	40 39	17 57	49	36	39	W	13	2410	90	72	86	72	16	E	84	72	78	76	74	12	486	313	1608
ri/Elmas/Sardinia	39 15	9 03	13	37	39	NNW	5	2334	88	70	86	69	18		84	69	76	75	74	5	418	261	1411
arby/Leghorn	43 39	10 19	16	26	28	E	5	3286	90	71	86	71	23	WN	84	71	76	74	73	11	417	175	1082
derle/Vicenza	45 33	11 33	115	20	23	SW	3	4585	90	74	88	73	23		86	72	75	74	73	9	500	191	1103

LOCATION	Lat °	Lat ′	Long °	Long ′	Elev feet	WINTER DESIGN DATA HEATING Dry Bulb 99% °F	97.5% °F	Pvlg Wind dir	Mean Speed knots	DEGREE DAYS Heating annual	SUMMER DESIGN DATA AIR CONDITIONING Dry Bulb 1% °F	MCWB °F	2.5% °F	MCWB °F	Mean Daily Range °F	Pvlg Wind dir	5% °F	MCWB °F	Wet Bulb 1% °F	2.5% °F	5% °F	SUMMER CRITERIA DATA AIR CONDITIONING Dry Bulb ≥ 93°F hrs	≥ 80°F hrs	Wet Bulb ≥ 73°F hrs	≥ 67°F hrs
	N		E																						
	45	41	12	38	7	20	23	NNE	4	4286	89	73	87	72	19	SSE	84	70	75	73	72	1	469	59	644
lina	46	56	11	30	8790	-8	-4	NNW	30	12500	58	49	56	48	10	WSW	54	46	50	49	47		0	0	0
egure	44	14	8	11	1640	20	22	NNW	10	5937	82	68	80	67	13	WSW	77	65	69	68	66		79	13	103
	43	48	11	12	131	25	27	ENE	4	3308	95	72	92	70	26	W	89	70	74	73	72	6	658	95	935
escia	45	25	10	17	335	18	21	WNW	4	4951	89	74	86	73	21	WNW	85	73	76	74	73	0	433	201	1005
lena/Sardinia	41	13	9	25	30	35	38	SW	5	2472	88	72	86	71	11	WSW	84	70	77	75	73	1	312	192	1114
Leghorn	43	33	10	19	49	34	36	E	5	2538	84	70	82	70	11	WNW	80	70	74	73	72	1	178	88	1333
Franca	40	40	17	16	1190	28	30	S	10	4004	93	70	89	69	21	N	86	67	72	71	69	32	463	29	413
inate	45	26	9	17	351	17	20	W	4	4802	88	74	86	72	21	SW	85	72	76	74	73	1	429	173	987
lvarina	45	31	11	16	2221	20	23	NNW	10	5200	81	67	78	66	12	S	76	65	68	67	65	0	44	0	59
mone	44	12	10	42	7103	3	7	NNW	26	10664	66	55	63	52	10	WSW	60	52	57	55	54		0	0	0
rna	45	22	10	31	645	18	21	WNW	5	4723	89	74	86	73	21	S	85	72	76	74	73		450	190	980
ganella	46	09	11	02	6972	-1	3	NNW	26	10577	65	51	63	50	10	WSW	61	48	53	52	50		0	0	0
nda	45	19	11	41	1886	21	24	NNW	10	5116	82	68	79	67	13	S	77	65	69	68	66	0	59	13	103
rgine	40	56	14	43	4880	15	18	NW	15	6781	79	60	76	59	15	S	74	58	63	61	60	0	15	0	1
AF	40	53	14	18	289	32	35	N		2671	88	70	86	70	20	SSW	84	70	75	74	72	4	472	132	1061
Guisto	43	40	10	23	7	26	28	E		3286	90	71	86	71	23	WNW	84	71	76	74	73	11	417	175	1082
	44	01	12	38	39	26	29	WNW		4033	86	74	84	73	19	E	82	72	77	75	73	1	342	223	1042
mpino	41	48	12	35	423	27	30	E		2882	93	74	91	73	22	WSW	88	72	78	76	74	35	729	255	1286
Dei Normanni AS	40	39	17	42	361	34	37	W	16	2674	90	72	86	72	21	S	84	72	78	76	74	12	486	313	1608
a NAF/Sicily	37	24	14	55	72	32	35	W		2240	98	72	94	71	28	E	91	71	76	75	74	10	1124	243	1532
Tessera	45	30	12	20	7	23	26	NNE		4357	87	72	85	73	17	SSE	83	72	78	76	74		374	269	1176
illafranca	45	23	10	52	220	18	21	WNW		4723	90	73	87	72	21	S	85	71	75	73	72		468	120	1026
	45	34	11	31	128	20	23	SW	6	4585	90	74	88	73	23	E	86	72	75	74	73	0	500	191	1103
	N		E																						
m/Schiphol	52	18	4	46	-13	18	19	S		5880	81	69	77	67	19	E	73	65	70	68	66	0	31	1	126
e Schinnen	50	55	5	57	230	18	22	N		5734	82	67	78	66	21	N	75	65	69	68	66	1	60		126
Holland	51	59	4	09	26	23	26	NE		5667	79	67	76	66	15	E	72	64	68	67	65	0	27		100
erg AB	52	08		16	66	14	18	NE	8	6126	82	67	79	65	23	E	75	64	70	67	66	0	56	0	106
kerwold	52	46	6	11	33	17	20	N	5	6335	80	69	77	67	20	E	74	65	70	68	66	0	37	18	126
	52	24		53	49	18	20			5880	81	69	77	67	19	E	73	65	70	68	66	1	26	1	126
e	52	02		21	-7	18	19	N	4	5880	81	69	77	67	19	E	73	65	70	68	66	0	31	10	126
	51	39	5	42	72	14	18	N	6	6207	82	67	79	66	23	N	76	65	69	68	66	0	65	0	126

Station	Lat	Long	Elev	99%	97.5%	Pvlg Wind	Mean Speed	Heating	1%	MCWB	2.5%	MCWB	Mean Daily Range	Pvlg Wind	5%	MCWB	1%	2.5%	5%	≥ 93°F	≥ 80°F	≥ 73°F	≥ 67°F
	LOCATION			WINTER DESIGN DATA HEATING Dry Bulb				DEGREE DAYS	SUMMER DESIGN DATA AIR CONDITIONING Dry Bulb								Wet Bulb			SUMMER CRITERIA DATA AIR CONDITIONING Dry Bulb		Wet Bulb	
	° '	° '	feet	°F	°F	dir	knots	annual	°F	°F	°F	°F	°F	dir	°F	°F	°F	°F	°F	hrs	hrs	hrs	hrs
NT)																							
	N	E																					
Fornebu	59 54	10 37	56	-8	-4	NNW	2	8292	82	64	80	62	25	S	77	62	66	65	63	0	72	0	24
	N	E																					
/Okećie	52 11	20 59	361	-4	1	E	7	7166	84	68	81	66	22	SE	78	64	70	68	67	0	105	3	160
	N	W																					
/Portela	38 46	9 08	374	37	40	ENE	5	1972	91	70	88	69	23	N	84	68	72	71	69	19	332	27	493
	N	W3																					
te/Santa Pola	38 17	0 3	141	37	39	NW	9	1825	89	70	86	71	17	S	85	72	76	75	74	11	679	361	1809
ona/Montadas	41 17	2E04	13	31	34	N	11	2898	84	71	82	71	14	SW	81	71	75	74	72	0	236	141	1204
a	37 51	4 50	295	30	32	E	8	2285	102	73	100	72	33	W	97	71	75	74	73	415	1522	190	1297
	40 30	3 15	2900	19	21	N	5	4603	92	63	89	62	33	SW	87	62	67	65	64	21	528	1	40
	40 25	3 41	2149	25	28	NNE	5	3895	96	68	94	68	35	W	91	67	71	69	68	106	804	8	317
	36 40	4 29	36	39	41	NW	10	1896	94	69	90	68	20	NW	86	68	75	74	73	38	647	155	1351
a/Mahon	39 52	4E14	289	40	42	NNE	14	2216	87	73	85	73	14	SSW	83	72	76	75	74	3	454	258	1621
AB	37 10	5 37	287	31	33	ESE	3	2069	101	70	98	69	32	W	95	69	73	72	70	281	1236	43	781
Naval Station	36 39	6 21	86	36	38	NNE	6	1715	93	70	90	69	24	SE	87	69	75	73	72	35	674	113	1269
a/San Pablo	37 25	5 54	112	32	34	NE	7	2240	100	73	97	73	31	SW	95	72	77	75	74	265	1207	236	1411
on AB/Madrid	40 29	3 27	1991	23	25	N	3	3905	96	65	93	64	31	SW	91	64	69	67	66	94	833	5	101
ia	39 30	0 28	213	32	34	W	7	2469	90	70	86	71	18	ESE	85	72	76	74	74	13	637	250	1554
za AB	41 40	1 02	863	25	28	W	7	3339	96	68	93	67	27	E	90	67	72	70	69	78	705	10	389
	N	E																					
rg/Torslanda	57 43	11 47	26	3	8	N	8	7145	79	63	76	61	19	NW	73	61	66	64	63	0	22	0	14
olm/Bromma	59 21	17 57	49	-4	0	W	4	7832	81	64	79	64	22	S	76	61	66	65	63	0	48	0	28
ND	N	E																					
	46 55	7 30	1673	10	14	N	10	6450	83	66	80	64	18	E	77	63	68	66	64	1	84	0	41
/Cointrin	46 15	6 08	1411	16	19	N	8	5663	86	67	82	66	24	E	80	65	69	68	66	0	149	0	135
NGDOM	N	W																					
en/Dyce/Scotland	57 12	2 12	236	19	25	W	11	6901	72	63	68	61	17	S	66	59	63	61	60	0	0	0	1
ury RAF Sta	52 22	0 13	161	22	25	W	6	5732	78	65	75	63	21	N	72	61	66	64	63	0	17	1	23
ters RAF Sta	52 08	1E26	85	23	26	WNW	7	5685	76	65	73	63	18	S	70	61	66	64	63	0	5	0	20
Hill	51 17	0E00	870	19	23	N	8	6395	75	65	73	64	22	ENE	70	62	67	65	64	0	1	1	30
ton	51 43	0 32	515	21	24	N	9	5852	78	65	74	63	19	N	71	61	67	64	63	0	15	1	30

LOCATION				WINTER DESIGN DATA HEATING				DEGREE DAYS	SUMMER DESIGN DATA AIR CONDITIONING											SUMMER CRITERIA DATA AIR CONDITIONING			
				Dry Bulb					Dry Bulb								Wet Bulb			Dry Bulb		Wet Bulb	
	Lat	Long	Elev	99%	97.5%	Pvlg Wind	Mean Speed	Heating	1%	MCWB	2.5%	MCWB	Mean Daily Range	Pvlg Wind	5%	MCWB	1%	2.5%	5%	≥ 93°F	≥ 80°F	≥ 73°F	≥ 67°F
	° '	° '	feet	°F	°F	dir	knots	annual	°F	°F	°F	°F	°F	dir	°F	°F	°F	°F	°F	hrs	hrs	hrs	hrs
OM (CONT)	N	W																					
od Army Depot	53 24	2 39	75	23	26	E	7	5915	77	65	74	64	19	E	70	62	67	65	63	0	12	0	30
ds RAF Sta	52 18	0 32	299	22	25	W	6	5732	78	65	75	63	21	N	72	61	66	64	63	0	17	1	23
s Commons	51 38	0 58	794	20	23	N	10	6050	77	64	73	62	20	N	70	60	66	63	62	0	8	0	23
w	51 18	0E37	630	19	23	N	8	6345	75	65	73	64	22	ENE	70	62	67	65	63	0	1 1	1	30
n RAF Sta	51 59	1 12	400	21	24	N	9	5852	78	65	74	63	19	N	71	61	67	64	63	0	5	1	30
	52 12	1 05	500	21	24	N	9	5852	78	65	74	63	19	N	71	61	67	64	63	0	1 5	1	30
	51 18	0E59	250	27	29	WNW	7	5582	76	66	73	65	18	S	70	63	68	66	64	0	9	1	50
n/Scotland	55 57	3 21	135	21	25	WSW	6	6518	72	62	70	61	18	WSW	66	59	64	62	60	0	1	0	3
cotland	56 49	2 36	155	21	25	WSW	6	6222	76	62	73	61	16	WSW	71	59	64	62	60	0	9	0	3
we	51 58	1E28	101	23	26	NW	8	5672	76	65	73	63	19	S	71	62	66	64	63	0	8	0	22
les	54 22	0 40	761	24	26	SSW	12	6800	72	66	69	63	15	SSW	66	60	67	64	61	0	0	0	38
Hill	54 00	0 46	777	24	26	SSW	12	6800	72	66	69	63	15	SSW	66	60	67	64	61	0	0	0	38
Common	51 23	1 17	397	21	24	N	6	5707	78	64	74	62	21	E	71	61	66	64	62	0	17	1	23
ombe	51 38	0 46	500	21	24	N	9	5852	78	65	74	63	19	N	71	61	67	64	63	0	15	1	30
th RAF Sta	52 24	0E34	33	18	22	NNE	6	5798	79	66	76	64	23	N	72	62	67	65	63	0	24	0	36
/Scotland	56 23	2 52	39	23	27	WSW	9	6651	72	63	68	61	17	WSW	66	60	63	62	60	0		0	3
l Aprt	53 20	2 51	85	25	28	SE	7	5646	77	67	73	64	21	S	70	62	67	65	63	0		0	31
atwick Aprt	51 09	0 11	204	21	25		6	5945	77	66	75	65	23	ENE	72	63	68	66	64	0	1	1	50
eathrow Aprt	51 29	0 27	79	25	28	N	7	5188	79	65	77	64	20	E	73	62	67	65	64	0	20	0	43
rry/N Ireland	55 00	7 17	50	26	29	W	5	5825	71	62	69	61	13	SW	67	60	64	62	61	0	0	0	1
am Heath	52 03	1E14	22	23	26	NW	7	5790	77	65	74	63	19	S	71	61	66	64	63	0	12	0	24
Hill Sta	53 59	1 42	492	22	25	W	5	6251	76	65	73	64	15	E	70	62	67	65	63	0	12	0	30
ll RAF Sta	52 22	0E29	33	20	24	W	5	5602	79	66	76	64	21	N	73	62	67	65	63	0	26	1	37
th	52 23	25	244	22	25	W	6	5732	78	65	75	63	21	N	72	61	66	64	63	0	17	1	23
Hill	57 36	2 02	745	17	23	W	12	7300	70	62	66	60	16	S	64	58	62	60	59	0	0	0	0
rize Norton	51 45	1 35	285	20	23	E E	9	5938	78	65	75	63	21	E	71	61	66	64	63	0	18	1	28
k Aprt/Scotland	55 30	4 35	66	23	25	NE	5	6404	73	63	70	62	19	W	66	60	64	62	61	0	1	0	5
pe RAF Sta	52 50	0E45	217	23	26	E	9	5898	77	66	73	63	17	SW	70	62	67	65	63	0	15	1	32
islip	51 34	0 25	211	25	28	W	7	5188	79	65	77	64	20	E	73	62	67	65	64	0	26	0	43
	51 08	1E20	250	27	29	WSW	7	5304	72	66	70	65	16	W	68	63	68	66	64	0	2	3	59
yford RAF Sta	51 56	1 15	436	2 1	24		9	5852	78	65	74	63	19		71	61	67	64	63	0	1	1	30
ield RAF Sta	51 58	0E30	331	22	25	NN	7	5894	78	65	74	63	20		71	61	66	64	63	0	1	1	26
ge RAF Sta	52 05	1E24	95	23	26	NW	8	5672	76	65	73	63	19	N N	71	62	66	64	63	0	5	0	22

Country Station	Lat ° ′	Long ° ′	Elev feet	Winter Design Data Heating Dry Bulb 99% °F	97.5% °F	Pvlg Wind dir	Mean Speed knots	Degree Days Heating annual	Summer Design Data Air Conditioning Dry Bulb 1% °F	MCWB °F	2.5% °F	MCWB °F	Mean Daily Range °F	Pvlg Wind dir	5% °F	MCWB °F	Wet Bulb 1% °F	2.5% °F	5% °F	Summer Criteria Data Air Conditioning Dry Bulb ≥ 93°F hrs	≥ 80°F hrs	Wet Bulb ≥ 73°F hrs	≥ 67°F hrs
(CONT)																							
cow/Sheremetievo	N 55 58	E 37 25	623	-16	-13	N	4	9583	86	67	81	66	23	E	78	64	69	67	66	4	98	3	110
LAVIA																							
grade IAP	N 44 49	E 20 17	325	10	14	ESE	9	6067	89	70	86	69	24	SE	84	68	73	71	70	9	368	31	510
OCEAN																							
S ARCHIPELAGO																							
go Garcia NB	S 7 20	E 72 25	8	71	72	ENE	11	0	90	79	89	79	9	ENE	88	79	81	81	80	0	3532	4335	4416
ELLES																							
e/Anse La Rue	S 4 40	E 55 31	10	70	71	ENE	11	0	86	78	85	78	9	ENE	84	77	79	79	78	0	1361	4017	4392
AMERICA																							
A	N	W																					
entia NAS/Placentia Nfld	47 19	53 59	51	9	12	WNW	17	7754	68	65	66	63	11	SSW	64	61	65	64	62	0	0	0	17
strong Ont	50 17	88 54	1056	-41	-35	W	4	12719	83	68	79	65	29	SW	76	64	70	68	66	1	72	8	107
voort Island NWT	63 21	64 10	1207	-29	-26	W	10	17780	57	50	52	46	9	W	48	43	50	47	44	0	0	0	0
ughton Island NWT	67 33	63 47	1900	-33	-29	N	7	19351	55	48	54	46	7	S	50	44	49	47	45	0	0	0	0
on Bay NWT	68 45	109 04	358	-49	-45	NNW	11	21004	61	54	57	51	12	ESE	54	48	54	51	49	0	0	0	0
gary Aprt Alta	51 06	114 01	3540	-23	-19	NNW	8	9703	83	60	80	59	28	SE	77	59	63	61	60	0	93	0	2
bridge Bay Aprt NWT	69 06	105 07	82	-51	-48	W	6	22022	61	54	57	51	16	SE	54	48	54	51	49	0	0	0	0
e Dyer NWT	66 35	61 37	1289	-37	-34	E	5	18354	56	48	53	47	12	WNW	50	44	49	47	45		0	0	0
e Harrison Nfld	54 46	58 27	33	-20	-18	NW	19	10807	76	63	71	60	20	SSW	67	58	65	62	60		19	0	10
e Hooper NWT	68 26	66 47	1299	-35	-31	N	13	19417	57	50	54	47	8	W	50	45	51	48	45		0	0	0
e Parry NWT	70 10	124 41	56	-42	-39	WSW	6	19854	57	54	53	50	12	E	50	47	54	50	47	0	0	0	0
e Young NWT	68 56	116 55	59	-42	-39	SW	8	19854	57	54	53	50	12	SE	50	47	54	50	47	0	0	0	0
rchill Man	58 45	94 04	98	-38	-36	WNW	13	16728	78	63	73	61	25	SW	68	59	65	62	60		18	1	18
nton Point NWT	69 35	120 45	321	-42	-38	WNW	8	19854	57	54	53	50	14	SW	50	47	54	50	47		0	0	0
ar Lakes NWT	68 39	71 14	1690	-44	-42	NNW	10	20524	57	51	54	47	10	E	50	45	51	48	46		0	0	0
onton/Namao Aprt Alta	53 40	113 28	2256	-27	-22	E	9	10363	83	64	80	63	25	SE	76	61	66	64	62	0	79	0	23
t Nelson BC	58 50	122 35	1230	-39	-35	SSW	3	13164	82	62	78	60	27	SE	76	60	64	63	61	0	57	0	7
t Smith Aprt NWT	60 01	111 58	665	-46	-42	NW	4	14176	81	64	78	63	27	S	75	61	66	64	62		52	0	22
bisher Bay NWT	63 45	68 33	68	-40	-38	NNW	9	17876	62	51	58	49	15	NW	54	48	52	50	48		0	0	0
der IAP Nfld	48 57	54 34	482	-4	0	WNW	11	9254	80	67	77	66	21	SW	73	63	69	67	66		30	2	101

AREA Country Station	LOCATION Lat ° N	Lat '	Long ° W	Long '	Elev feet	WINTER DESIGN DATA HEATING Dry Bulb 99% °F	97.5% °F	Pvlg Wind dir	Mean Speed knots	DEGREE DAYS Heating annual	SUMMER DESIGN DATA AIR CONDITIONING Dry Bulb 1% °F	MCWB °F	2.5% °F	MCWB °F	Mean Daily Range °F	Pvlg Wind dir	5% °F	MCWB °F	Wet Bulb 1% °F	2.5% °F	5% °F	SUMMER CRITERIA DATA AIR CONDITIONING Dry Bulb ≥ 93°F hrs	≥ 80°F hrs	Wet Bulb ≥ 73°F hrs	≥ 67°F hrs
NORTH AMERICA (CONT)																									
CANADA (CONT)																									
Gladman Point NWT	68	40	97	48	75	-53	-49	NW	1	21873	61	55	59	53	13	SE	55	50	56	53	51	0	0	0	0
Goose Bay AB Nfld	53	19	60	25	144	-23	-20	WSW	9	11887	82	63	77	62	24	SW	73	60	66	64	62	2	49	1	23
Grande Prairie Alta	55	11	118	53	2190	-36	-31	NNW	6	11129	81	62	77	60	26	W	74	59	65	62	60	0	50	1	12
Halifax IAP NS	44	53	63	31	477	-4	0	WNW	11	8327	80	66	77	66	20	SSW	75	64	70	68	67	0	36	5	166
Hall Beach NWT	68	47	81	15	26	-49	-45	NW	10	21083	56	49	52	47	12	N	49	44	51	48	45	0	0	0	0
Hopedale AS Nfld	55	27	60	14	33	-23	-20	WSW	10	11680	72	59	66	57	15	SSW	63	56	61	59	57	0	2	0	2
Inuvik NWT	68	18	133	29	200	-54	-50	E	3	18200	77	60	74	58	24	SW	71	57	61	59	58	0	9	0	1
Jenny Lind NWT	68	39	101	44	59	-50	-47	W	6	22022	61	54	57	51	16	W	54	48	54	51	49	0	0	0	0
Kamloops BC	50	43	120	25	1133	-17	-9	ESE	10	6799	93	66	90	65	32	W	86	63	68	66	64	40	390	1	6
Kapuskasing Aprt Ont	49	25	82	28	752	-30	-26	W	5	11560	84	68	81	68	27	SW	77	65	71	69	67	1	100	14	153
Komakuk Beach YT	69	35	140	11	3	-45	-41	SW	7	19994	56	52	52	49	14	E	49	47	52	50	47	0	0		
Lady Franklin Point NWT	68	30	113	13	69	-46	-43	NE	6	20938	59	54	55	51	14	E	52	48	54	51	48	0	0		
Longstaff Bluff NWT	68	57	75	18	522	-42	-40	E	2	19444	57	51	53	48	7	NW	51	46	52	49	46	0	0		
Mackar Inlet NWT	68	18	85	41	1309	-49	-45	SSW	10	21466	58	50	54	48	8	WSW	51	46	52	50	47	0	0	0	0
Melville AS Nfld	53	18	60	32	934	-23	-20	WSW	10	12091	79	61	74	60	22	SW	70	58	64	62	60	0	26		0
Montreal IAP Que	45	28	73	45	98	-13	-9	WSW	9	8157	86	73	83	71	19	SW	81	70	75	73	71	2	205	79	54
Nicholson Peninsula NWT	69	54	128	58	321	-42	-39	WSW	6	19854	57	54	53	50	12	E	50	47	54	50	47	0	0	0	
North Bay Ont	46	22	79	25	1210	-18	-15	N	7	9654	82	68	79	67	19	SW	76	65	71	69	67	0	72	8	20
Ottawa IAP Ont	45	19	75	40	413	-15	-11	WNW	8	8693	86	71	83	69	21	SW	81	68	74	72	70	3	210	56	44
Padloping Island NWT	67	06	62	21	130	-40	-37	NW	6	16648	56	49	53	47	14	SSW	50	44	49	47	45	0	0	0	0
Pelly Bay NWT	68	26	89	43	1060	-51	-47	W	1	21426	63	54	59	52	10	SE	55	50	55	53	50	0	0		1
Porquis Junction Ont	48	44	80	48	100	-30	-25	W		11400	85	68	81	66	25	SW	78	64	70	68	66	2	115		133
Port Hardy BC	50	41	127	22	75	23	26	ESE	1	6677	68	60	65	58	15	NNW	63	57	61	60	58	0	1		1
Prince George BC	53	53	122	41	2218	-26	-20	N		9755	82	62	79	60	31	N	75	59	63	61	60	0	60	0	1
Resolute Aprt NWT	74	43	94	59	209	-48	-45	NW	3	22673	53	46	49	44	9	SE	47	43	47	45	43	0	0	0	0
Resolution Island NWT	61	35	64	39	1201	-29	-26	W	20	17111	57	48	52	46	13	W	50	45	50	47	45	0			0
Saglek AS Nfld	58	28	62	39	269	-22	-20	W	13	11822	68	57	65	56	17	W	60	52	59	55	53	0			2
St Anthony Nfld	51	22	55	38	344	-14	-10	W	15	10639	73	64	70	62	20	WSW	66	60	66	63	62	0			18
St Johns/Torbay Aprt Nfld	47	37	52	45	463	3	7	WNW	15	8991	76	67	73	65	18	WSW	70	63	70	67	65	0	0	0	95
Sandspit BC	53	15	131	49	20	17	20	NW	17	7182	69	61	66	60	11	W	64	59	62	61	60	0	0	0	1
Saskatoon Sask	52	10	106	41	1645	-31	-27	WSW	8	10856	88	65	85	64	30	S	81	62	68	66	64	6	21	1	52
Shepherd Bay NWT	68	49	93	26	167	-53	-49	NW	11	21873	61	55	59	53	13	SE	55	50	56	53	51	0		0	0
Shingle Point YT	68	57	137	13	174	-45	-41	SW	7	19994	56	52	52	49	14	E	49	47	52	50	47	0	0	0	0

Location	Lat	Long	Elev	Winter Design Data, Heating, Dry Bulb: 99%	97.5%	Pvlg Wind	Mean Speed	Degree Days: Heating	Summer Design Data, Air Conditioning, Dry Bulb: 1%	MCWB	2.5%	MCWB	Mean Daily Range	Pvlg Wind	5%	MCWB	Wet Bulb: 1%	2.5%	5%	Summer Criteria Data, Air Conditioning, Dry Bulb: ≥ 93°F	≥ 80°F	Wet Bulb: ≥ 73°F	≥ 67°F
	° '	° '	feet	°F	°F	dir	knots	annual	°F	°F	°F	°F	°F	dir	°F	°F	°F	°F	°F	hrs	hrs	hrs	hrs
ERICA (CONT)																							
(CONT)	N	W																					
Lookout Ont	50 07	91 54	1280	-33	-27	W	6	11156	82	66	79	65	21	W	76	64	69	67	66	0	77	4	114
nenville Aprt Nfld	48 32	58 33	44	-2	3	WNW	10	8717	75	65	72	64	16		69	62	67	65	64	0	5	1	35
Pas Man	53 58	101 06	894	-35	-30	WNW	8	12476	83	68	79	65	22	W	76	64	70	67	65	1	75	8	95
der Bay/Lakehead Ont	48 22	89 19	644	-25	-21	W	8	10568	84	68	80	66	28		77	64	70	68	66	0	87	10	127
nto IAP Ont	43 41	79 38	578	-4	0	N	10	7468	89	72	86	71	24	S	83	70	75	73	71	7	306	95	571
oyaktuk NWT	69 27	133 00	59	-42	-39	E	6	19854	57	54	53	50	17	E	50	47	54	50	47	0	0	0	0
ouver IAP BC	49 11	123 10	16	18	24	E	6	5606	77	66	75	64	18	[illegible]	72	67	67	66	64	0	9	1	29
ehorse YT	60 43	135 04	2289	-43	-38	NW	5	12475	78	57	74	56	26	E	71	54	58	57	55	0	18	0	0
peg IAP Man	49 54	97 14	786	-30	-25	W	8	10679	88	69	85	68	26	S	82	67	73	71	68	4	230	36	257
outh NS	43 50	66 05	136	6	9	NW	11	7340	73	65	70	64	16	S	68	62	67	66	64	0	1	1	35
owknife NWT	62 28	114 27	682	-46	-42	NE	5	15634	77	61	74	59	19	C	71	57	62	60	59	0	6	0	1
ND	N	W																					
erly Ice Cap	65 11	43 50	7998	-45	-42	W	13	23226	42	38	39	35	22	W	36	33	39	36	33	0	0	0	0
sak	65 32	37 11	118	-3	-1	W	11	13140	57	47	54	45	10	E	51	44	48	46	45	0	0	0	0
oqaqa	66 38	52 52	4721	-30	-24	SW	12	17547	51	45	49	44	10	S	47	42	46	44	42	0	0	0	
restrom AB	67 01	50 48	165	-36	-32	NE	6	15278	67	52	65	51	22	ENE	63	50	54	52	51	0	0	0	
AB	76 32	68 42	253	-36	-34	E	6	19613	54	45	51	44	10	E	49	42	46	44	43	0	0	0	
erly Ice Cap	66 29	46 17	7000	-43	-39	S	12	22104	44	38	41	36	22	S	38	35	39	37	35	0	0	0	0
	N	W																					
o City/Tacubaya	19 24	99 11	7575	30	33	NW	5	2572	84	60	82	59	22	N	79	58	62	61	60	2	245	0	1
CEAN																							
ISLANDS	N	E																					
/Central Babelthuap	7 22	134 33	186	74	75	NE	6	0	89	80	88	80	11	E	87	80	81	80	80	0	2588	4384	4392
Is Aprt	7 20	134 29	95	74	75	NE	6	0	89	80	88	80	11	E	87	80	81	80	80	0	2588	4384	4392
e	6 58	158 13	123	73	74	ESE	3		88	79	88	79	12	NE	87	79	81	80	80	0	2388	4313	4416
	7 28	151 51	6	76	77	ESE	5		88	81	87	80	9	NNE	86	79	82	81	80	2	3058	4404	4416
	9 29	138 05	51	75	76	SW	7		89	81	88	80	9	E	87	80	82	81	80	0	2667	4376	4392
NDS	S	E																					
	17 45	177 27	62	60	62	ESE	5	0	90	79	89	79	15	N	88	78	81	80	80	2	1896	3253	4331

on	Lat	Long	Elev	Winter Design Data Heating: Dry Bulb 99%	97.5%	Pvlg Wind	Mean Speed	Degree Days: Heating	Summer Design Data Air Conditioning: Dry Bulb 1%	MCWB	2.5%	MCWB	Mean Daily Range	Pvlg Wind	5%	MCWB	Wet Bulb 1%	2.5%	5%	Summer Criteria Data Air Conditioning: Dry Bulb ≥ 93°F	≥ 80°F	Wet Bulb ≥ 73°F	≥ 67°F
	° ′	° ′	feet	°F	°F	dir	knots	annual	°F	°F	°F	°F	°F	dir	°F	°F	°F	°F	°F	hrs	hrs	hrs	hrs
EAN (CONT)																							
ISLAND	N	W																					
:on AFB	16 44	169 32	7	71	72	ENE	14	0	87	77	86	76	7	E	85	75	79	78	77	0	2766	3926	4388
IDS	N	W																					
:mas Is Aprt	1 59	157 22	5	74	75	ENE	11	0	89	79	88	79	9	ENE	87	79	80	80	79	0	2425	4188	4344
SLANDS	N	E																					
\gana NAS	29	144 48	298	72	73	ENE	6		89	78	88	78	11	E	87	78	80	80	79		2487	4305	4416
\ndersen AFB	35	144 55	624	73	74	ENE	11		86	78	85	78	8	E	84	78	79	79	78	0	2301	4223	4416
ı/Kobler Fld	07	145 43	108	72	73	ENE	6		89	79	88	78	1	E	87	78	81	80	80	0	3533	4383	4392
ı/North Aux Afld	04	145 38	85	72	73	ENE	6	0	89	79	88	78	11	E	87	78	81	80	80	0	3533	4383	4392
ı/West Aux Afld	13 00	145 38	252	72	73	ENE	6	0	89	79	88	78	11	E	87	78	81	80	80	0	3538	4383	4392
ISLANDS	N	E																					
:ok	11 21	162 20	13	76	77	NE	17		89	80	88	80	8	E	87	79	82	82	81	0	4098	4389	4392
.ein/Bucholz AAF	8 43	167 44	9	76	77	ENE	15	0	90	80	89	79	7	E	88	79	82	81	81	2	3727	4410	4416
)	7 06	171 24	10	76	77	E	10	0	87	79	86	79	7	ENE	86	78	80	80	79	0	3634	4385	4392
:LAND	N	W																					
' Island NAVSTA	28 12	177 23	12	58	59	N	12	119	84	75	83	75	7	E	82	74	77	76	76	0	901	1823	3729
AND	S	E																					
:church	43 29	172 32	123	28	29	W	4	4623	82	64	79	63	25	NNW	75	62	66	65	63		63	1	24
John	43 59	170 28	3300	8	9	NW	15	8828	73	58	70	56	34	NW	66	55	60	59	57		2	0	0
ı	44 18	171 14	89	28	29	W	4	4623	82	64	79	63	25	NNW	75	62	66	65	63	0	63	1	24
ıgton Aprt	41 20	174 48	40	37	39	NE	6	3298	75	64	73	63	11	NNE	71	62	66	65	63	0	1	0	17
ATION VESSELS	N	W																					
	30 00	140 00	0	55	56	NE	15	410	75	69	74	68	4	ENE	73	67	70	69	68	0	0	0	619
	34 00	164 00	0	49	50	NW	24	788	82	77	81	76	4	SW	81	76	78	78	77	0	413	1724	3189
ISLANDS	N	E																					
)	16 25	120 36	4921	49	51	SE	5	157	79	66	78	66	13	SE	77	67	70	69	68	0	64	1	1077
AB	15 11	120 33	478	66	68	NW	5	0	94	76	92	76	16	S	91	77	80	79	78	69	1955	3671	4411
ᵖoint NAS	14 47	120 17	55	69	70	ENE	6	0	95	78	93	79	15	ENE	91	79	81	80	80	85	2590	4189	4416
ıay AB	16 24	120 37	4951	49	51	SE	5	157	79	66	78	66	13	SE	77	67	70	69	68	0	64	1	1077
ı	14 31	121 01	74	65	67	N	3	0	95	79	94	79	16	ESE	93	78	82	81	80	122	2148	4258	4413
ɜy Pt FWC	14 30	120 54	8	71	73	N	6	0	93	79	92	79	11	ESE	90	79	81	81	80	42	3329	4343	4416
ɩguel	14 58	120 04	13	69	70	ENE	6	0	95	79	93	79	15	ENE	91	79	81	80	80	85	2590	4189	4416

AREA / Country / Station	LOCATION Lat	LOCATION Long	LOCATION Elev	WINTER DESIGN DATA HEATING Dry Bulb 99%	97.5%	Pvlg Wind	Mean Speed	DEGREE DAYS Heating	SUMMER DESIGN DATA AIR CONDITIONING Dry Bulb 1%	MCWB	2.5%	MCWB	Mean Daily Range	Pvlg Wind	5%	MCWB	Wet Bulb 1%	2.5%	5%	SUMMER CRITERIA DATA AIR CONDITIONING Dry Bulb ≥ 93°F	≥ 80°F	Wet Bulb ≥ 73°F	≥ 67°F
	° '	° '	feet	°F	°F	dir	knots	annual	°F	°F	°F	°F	°F	dir	°F	°F	°F	°F	°F	hrs	hrs	hrs	hrs
PACIFIC OCEAN (CONT)																							
PHILIPPINE ISLANDS (CONT)	N	E																					
Subic Bay NB	14 49	120 17	12	69	70	ENE	6	0	95	79	93	79	15	ENE	91	79	81	80	80	85	2590	4189	4416
Wallace AS	16 35	120 19	10	69	70	ENE	6	0	95	79	93	79	15	ENE	91	79	81	80	80	85	2590	4189	4416
PHOENIX ISLANDS	S	W																					
Birnie Is	3 35	171 31	8	77	78	ENE	11	0	90	79	89	79	9	ENE	88	79	80	80	79	3	3843	4346	4416
Canton Aux Afld	2 46	171 43	10	77	78	ENE	11	0	90	79	89	79	9	ENE	88	79	80	80	79	3	3843	4346	4416
Enderbury Is	3 09	171 05	8	77	78	ENE	11	0	90	79	89	79	9	ENE	88	79	80	80	79	3	3843	4346	4416
Hull Is	4 30	172 14	5	77	78	ENE	11	0	90	79	89	79	9	ENE	88	79	80	80	79	3	3843	4346	4416
SOCIETY ISLANDS	S	W																					
Tahiti Is/FAAA Aprt	17 33	149 37	7	64	65	ESE	5	0	89	79	88	78	15	N	87	77	81	80	79	0	1574	2843	4329
WAKE ISLAND	N	E																					
Wake Island AFB	19 17	166 38	14	70	71	NE	14	0	88	79	87	78	8	ENE	87	78	80	79	79	0	3558	4325	4389
SOUTH AMERICA																							
ARGENTINA	S	W																					
Buenos Aires/Ezeiza	34 50	58 32	65	28	31	SW	9	2196	93	73	90	71	22	NNE	87	70	76	74	73	38	519	162	1127
La Quiaca	22 06	65 36	11348	15	17	N	8	5916	74	51	72	50	25	NE	70	49	54	53	52	0	1	0	0
BRAZIL	S	W																					
Belem/Valdecas	1 23	48 29	52	71	72	SE	5	0	90	79	90	79	16	E	88	78	81	79	79	2	1526	4049	4391
Rio de Janeiro Aprt	22 54	43 10	10	63	63	N	5	4	93	79	91	77	14	S	90	78	80	79	78	51	1792	2852	4144
CHILE	S	W																					
Santiago/Pupahuel	33 23	70 47	1575	28	32	NE	3	2627	90	67	88	66	31	WSW	86	66	69	68	67	7	720	5	206
COLUMBIA	N	W																					
Bogota/Eldorado	4 42	74 08	8356	40	42	NNW	3	3706	70	57	69	57	22	E	67	57	60	59	58	0	0	0	1
EQUADOR	S	W																					
Quito/Mariscal Sucre	0 08	78 29	9222	35	38	N	3	3465	71	55	70	54	22	N	69	53	57	56	55	0	0	0	0
FRENCH GUIANA	N	W																					
Cayenne	4 49	52 22	30	70	71	ENE	5	0	89	80	88	79	14	E	86	79	82	81	80	2	1780	4122	4416
PARAGUAY	S	W																					
Asuncion/Stroessner	25 14	57 31	292	31	35	NE	7	276	101	77	99	76	24	NE	96	75	80	79	78	352	1679	1521	3758

	LOCATION			WINTER DESIGN DATA HEATING				DEGREE DAYS	SUMMER DESIGN DATA AIR CONDITIONING												SUMMER CRITERIA DATA AIR CONDITIONING			
				Dry Bulb					Dry Bulb								Wet Bulb				Dry Bulb		Wet Bulb	
	Lat	Long	Elev	99%	97.5%	Pvlg Wind	Mean Speed	Heating	1%	MCWB	2.5%	MCWB	Mean Daily Range	Pvlg Wind	5%	MCWB	1%	2.5%	5%	≥ 93°F	≥ 80°F	≥ 73°F	≥ 67°F
	° ′	° ′	feet	°F	°F	dir	knots	annual	°F	°F	°F	°F	°F	dir	°F	°F	°F	°F	°F	hrs	hrs	hrs	hrs
...NT)																							
	S 12 01	W 77 07	112	55	56	S	6	262	82	73	80	72	12	S	79	72	74	73	72	0	113	104	2546
...amaribo	N 5 27	W 55 12	54	67	69	NE	7	0	95	81	94	81	18	E	92	80	83	82	81	154	1918	4085	4392
...arrasco	S 34 50	W 56 02	75	35	38	N	11	1942	90	72	87	70	20	NNE	83	68	75	73	71	16	359	88	885
...arlota	N 10 30	W 66 53	2740	54	56	S	5	36	86	72	84	71	11	E	83	70	74	73	72	0	684	177	3444

CHAPTER 3

DATA FOR USE IN CALCULATING ENERGY CONSUMPTION ESTIMATES FOR SITES IN THE UNITED STATES

BIRMINGHAM MAP ALABAMA

LAT 33 34N LONG 86 45W ELEV 620 FT

MEAN FREQUENCY OF OCCURRENCE OF DRY BULB TEMPERATURE (DEGREES F) WITH MEAN COINCIDENT WET BULB TEMPERATURE (DEGREES F) FOR EACH DRY BULB TEMPERATURE RANGE

Temperature Range	MAY Obsn Hour Gp 01 to 08	MAY Obsn Hour Gp 09 to 16	MAY Obsn Hour Gp 17 to 24	MAY Total Obsn	MAY MCWB	JUNE Obsn Hour Gp 01 to 08	JUNE Obsn Hour Gp 09 to 16	JUNE Obsn Hour Gp 17 to 24	JUNE Total Obsn	JUNE MCWB	JULY Obsn Hour Gp 01 to 08	JULY Obsn Hour Gp 09 to 16	JULY Obsn Hour Gp 17 to 24	JULY Total Obsn	JULY MCWB
105/109												0		0	74
100/104							1	0	1	75		3	0	3	74
95/99		2	0	2	71		10	1	11	74		12	2	14	75
90/94		16	3	19	70	0	45	9	54	74		56	13	69	75
85/89	0	49	12	61	69	3	68	24	95	72	3	86	29	118	74
80/84	4	62	26	92	68	15	62	43	120	71	22	56	52	130	73
75/79	15	50	41	106	67	51	36	66	153	70	75	28	86	189	72
70/74	47	34	58	139	65	93	14	66	173	68	121	8	59	188	70
65/69	75	22	58	155	63	51	5	22	78	64	22	1	6	29	66
60/64	49	9	27	85	58	18	1	6	25	59	5		1	6	60
55/59	30	3	14	47	54	6		2	8	56	1			1	57
50/54	14	1	6	21	49	2		0	2	50					
45/49	9	0	4	13	45	0			0	45					
40/44	5		0	5	41										
35/39	0			0	38										
30/34															
25/29															

Temperature Range	AUGUST Obsn Hour Gp 01 to 08	AUGUST Obsn Hour Gp 09 to 16	AUGUST Obsn Hour Gp 17 to 24	AUGUST Total Obsn	AUGUST MCWB	SEPTEMBER Obsn Hour Gp 01 to 08	SEPTEMBER Obsn Hour Gp 09 to 16	SEPTEMBER Obsn Hour Gp 17 to 24	SEPTEMBER Total Obsn	SEPTEMBER MCWB	OCTOBER Obsn Hour Gp 01 to 08	OCTOBER Obsn Hour Gp 09 to 16	OCTOBER Obsn Hour Gp 17 to 24	OCTOBER Total Obsn	OCTOBER MCWB
105/109															
100/104		0		0	76										
95/99		15	1	16	75		6	0	6	71					
90/94		64	11	75	75		28	3	31	72		2		2	73
85/89	3	86	29	118	74	1	53	13	67	71		13	1	14	68
80/84	19	54	55	128	73	4	64	28	96	70	0	37	4	41	66
75/79	65	23	88	176	72	29	46	52	127	69	2	52	13	67	65
70/74	118	5	52	175	69	74	27	70	171	67	19	49	33	101	64
65/69	32	1	10	43	65	64	12	44	120	63	35	38	46	119	61
60/64	9		2	11	61	38	3	21	62	59	41	30	48	119	57
55/59	2		0	2	57	22	1	8	31	54	44	17	40	101	53
50/54	0			0	53	8	0	2	10	50	45	8	33	86	49
45/49						1			1	46	26	3	18	47	44
40/44											22	1	9	32	40
35/39											9	0	3	12	35
30/34											3		1	4	31
25/29															27

BIRMINGHAM MAP ALABAMA

Temperature Range	NOVEMBER Obsn Hour Gp 01 to 08	NOVEMBER Obsn Hour Gp 09 to 16	NOVEMBER Obsn Hour Gp 17 to 24	NOVEMBER Total Obsn	NOVEMBER MCWB	DECEMBER Obsn Hour Gp 01 to 08	DECEMBER Obsn Hour Gp 09 to 16	DECEMBER Obsn Hour Gp 17 to 24	DECEMBER Total Obsn	DECEMBER MCWB	JANUARY Obsn Hour Gp 01 to 08	JANUARY Obsn Hour Gp 09 to 16	JANUARY Obsn Hour Gp 17 to 24	JANUARY Total Obsn	JANUARY MCWB
105/109															
100/104															
95/99															
90/94															
85/89															
80/84		1		1	67										
75/79		11	1	12	64		1		1	67		2		2	65
70/74	4	32	9	45	62	0	8	2	10	62		8	2	10	64
65/69	11	38	19	68	59	6	17	8	31	60	7	19	13	39	61
60/64	20	41	31	92	55	14	29	17	60	57	17	24	18	59	57
55/59	26	34	30	90	51	20	35	25	80	52	17	30	25	72	52
50/54	32	33	36	101	47	25	40	31	96	47	22	37	28	87	47
45/49	36	24	37	97	43	25	42	36	103	42	27	42	36	105	43
40/44	32	16	32	80	38	32	35	39	106	38	32	33	36	101	38
35/39	34	8	25	67	34	35	23	41	99	34	38	28	39	105	34
30/34	27	3	13	43	30	42	13	29	84	30	34	13	26	73	30
25/29	12	1	4	17	26	29	4	15	48	25	26	6	15	47	25
20/24	6	1	1	8	21	14	1	5	20	21	18	3	6	27	21
15/19	0	0	0	0	16	5	0	1	6	16	4	1	3	8	16
10/14	0	0		0	10	1	0	0	1	11	3	1	1	5	12
5/9	0			0	5	1	0	0	1	5	0	0	1	1	5
0/4						0		0	0	2	1	0	0	1	1
-5/-1											0			0	-2

Temperature Range	FEBRUARY Obsn Hour Gp 01 to 08	FEBRUARY Obsn Hour Gp 09 to 16	FEBRUARY Obsn Hour Gp 17 to 24	FEBRUARY Total Obsn	FEBRUARY MCWB	MARCH Obsn Hour Gp 01 to 08	MARCH Obsn Hour Gp 09 to 16	MARCH Obsn Hour Gp 17 to 24	MARCH Total Obsn	MARCH MCWB	APRIL Obsn Hour Gp 01 to 08	APRIL Obsn Hour Gp 09 to 16	APRIL Obsn Hour Gp 17 to 24	APRIL Total Obsn	APRIL MCWB
105/109															
100/104															
95/99															
90/94												0		0	65
85/89							0		0	61		6	0	6	67
80/84		0	0	0	66		6	1	7	65		37	7	44	65
75/79		4	1	5	65		13	5	18	63	1	43	21	65	63
70/74	0	15	5	20	61	2	28	13	43	61	13	46	38	97	62
65/69	6	24	14	44	59	16	37	28	81	58	37	41	51	129	59
60/64	14	35	26	75	55	21	41	36	98	54	54	30	39	123	56
55/59	26	36	31	93	51	34	38	42	114	51	36	20	32	88	51
50/54	26	29	29	84	46	36	34	36	106	46	33	12	24	69	47
45/49	30	30	35	95	42	30	24	31	85	42	27	5	18	50	43
40/44	32	21	33	86	38	39	16	30	85	38	21	1	8	30	39
35/39	32	15	23	70	34	35	6	17	58	34	14		2	16	35
30/34	26	8	14	48	30	26	3	7	36	30	4		0	4	31
25/29	15	4	8	27	25	7	0	2	9	26	0			0	28
20/24	9	1	3	13	20	1	0	1	2	20					
15/19	3	1	1	5	16	1			1	16					
10/14	1	0	1	2	11	0			0	13					
5/9	2		0	2	7										
0/4															
-5/-1															

Temperature Range	ANNUAL TOTAL Obsn Hour Gp 01 to 08	ANNUAL TOTAL Obsn Hour Gp 09 to 16	ANNUAL TOTAL Obsn Hour Gp 17 to 24	ANNUAL TOTAL Total Obsn	ANNUAL TOTAL MCWB
105/109		0		0	74
100/104		4	0	4	74
95/99		45	4	49	74
90/94	0	211	39	250	74
85/89	10	361	108	479	72
80/84	64	379	216	659	71
75/79	238	309	374	921	69
70/74	491	274	407	1172	67
65/69	362	255	319	936	61
60/64	300	243	272	815	57
55/59	264	214	249	727	52
50/54	243	194	225	662	47
45/49	211	170	215	596	43
40/44	215	123	187	525	38
35/39	197	80	150	427	34
30/34	162	40	90	292	30
25/29	90	15	44	149	25
20/24	48	6	16	70	21
15/19	13	2	5	20	16
10/14	5	1	2	8	11
5/9	3	0	1	4	6
0/4	1	0	0	1	1
-5/-1	0			0	-2

FORT RUCKER/CAIRNS AAF ALABAMA

LAT 31 16N LONG 85 43W ELEV 305 FT

MEAN FREQUENCY OF OCCURRENCE OF DRY BULB TEMPERATURE (DEGREES F) WITH MEAN COINCIDENT WET BULB TEMPERATURE (DEGREES F) FOR EACH DRY BULB TEMPERATURE RANGE

Temperature Range	MAY Obsn Hour Gp 01 to 08	MAY 09 to 16	MAY 17 to 24	MAY Total Obsn	MAY MCWB	JUNE Obsn Hour Gp 01 to 08	JUNE 09 to 16	JUNE 17 to 24	JUNE Total Obsn	JUNE MCWB	JULY Obsn Hour Gp 01 to 08	JULY 09 to 16	JULY 17 to 24	JULY Total Obsn	JULY MCWB
100/104							0		0	77		0		0	78
95/99		3		3	72		6	1	7	76		8	1	9	77
90/94		22	3	25	71		50	9	59	75		55	9	64	77
85/89		58	15	73	70	1	82	23	106	74	2	93	21	116	76
80/84	3	67	29	99	69	15	62	45	122	73	17	59	50	126	75
75/79	15	50	51	116	68	53	28	83	164	72	79	25	107	211	74
70/74	61	28	72	161	67	117	9	68	194	70	136	7	59	202	71
65/69	84	14	49	147	64	45	2	10	57	65	12	0	2	14	65
60/64	45	5	21	71	58	9	1	1	11	60	1		0	1	59
55/59	27	1	7	35	54	1			1	53	0			0	55
50/54	11		1	12	49	0			0	48					
45/49	2		0	2	45										
40/44	0			0	40										
35/39															
30/34															

Temperature Range	AUGUST Obsn Hour Gp 01 to 08	AUGUST 09 to 16	AUGUST 17 to 24	AUGUST Total Obsn	AUGUST MCWB	SEPTEMBER Obsn Hour Gp 01 to 08	SEPTEMBER 09 to 16	SEPTEMBER 17 to 24	SEPTEMBER Total Obsn	SEPTEMBER MCWB	OCTOBER Obsn Hour Gp 01 to 08	OCTOBER 09 to 16	OCTOBER 17 to 24	OCTOBER Total Obsn	OCTOBER MCWB
100/104		0		0	80										
95/99		5		5	78		1		1	75					
90/94		53	6	59	76		30	2	32	75		2		2	73
85/89	0	88	22	110	76		78	12	90	74		17	1	18	70
80/84	12	62	48	122	75	4	65	33	102	72		54	6	60	68
75/79	72	31	104	207	73	29	36	79	144	71	3	60	23	86	67
70/74	136	8	63	207	71	116	20	79	215	69	26	49	58	133	65
65/69	24	0	3	27	65	58	8	23	89	64	57	37	62	156	62
60/64	3		0	3	59	22	3	9	34	59	55	19	45	119	58
55/59	0			0	55	8	0	2	10	54	45	7	29	81	53
50/54						2		1	3	50	31	1	16	48	48
45/49						0		0	0	44	19	0	5	24	44
40/44						1			1	41	9	0	2	11	39
35/39						0			0	37	3		0	3	35
30/34											0			0	32

Temperature Range	NOVEMBER Obsn Hour Gp 01 to 08	NOVEMBER Obsn Hour Gp 09 to 16	NOVEMBER Obsn Hour Gp 17 to 24	NOVEMBER Total Obsn	NOVEMBER MCWB	DECEMBER Obsn Hour Gp 01 to 08	DECEMBER Obsn Hour Gp 09 to 16	DECEMBER Obsn Hour Gp 17 to 24	DECEMBER Total Obsn	DECEMBER MCWB	JANUARY Obsn Hour Gp 01 to 08	JANUARY Obsn Hour Gp 09 to 16	JANUARY Obsn Hour Gp 17 to 24	JANUARY Total Obsn	JANUARY MCWB	FEBRUARY Obsn Hour Gp 01 to 08	FEBRUARY Obsn Hour Gp 09 to 16	FEBRUARY Obsn Hour Gp 17 to 24	FEBRUARY Total Obsn	FEBRUARY MCWB	MARCH Obsn Hour Gp 01 to 08	MARCH Obsn Hour Gp 09 to 16	MARCH Obsn Hour Gp 17 to 24	MARCH Total Obsn	MARCH MCWB	APRIL Obsn Hour Gp 01 to 08	APRIL Obsn Hour Gp 09 to 16	APRIL Obsn Hour Gp 17 to 24	APRIL Total Obsn	APRIL MCWB	ANNUAL TOTAL Obsn Hour Gp 01 to 08	ANNUAL TOTAL Obsn Hour Gp 09 to 16	ANNUAL TOTAL Obsn Hour Gp 17 to 24	ANNUAL TOTAL Total Obsn	ANNUAL TOTAL MCWB
100/104																																0		0	78
95/99																																23	2	25	77
90/94			0	0	63																						0		0	72		212	29	241	75
85/89		1		1	72												0		0	71		1		1	67		15	1	16	70	3	433	95	531	74
80/84		7	0	7	70		1		1	71		0		0	69		3		3	67		7	1	8	65		53	11	64	67	51	440	223	714	72
75/79		33	2	35	65		11	0	11	67		6	0	6	67		11	1	12	66		28	6	34	64	2	59	26	87	65	253	378	482	1113	70
70/74	4	42	15	61	63	3	22	7	32	65	0	15	3	18	63	1	19	8	28	63	5	41	21	67	62	22	51	52	125	64	627	311	505	1443	68
65/69	16	44	34	94	60	12	33	17	62	61	7	23	13	43	61	9	24	17	50	60	15	42	33	90	59	52	34	60	146	61	391	261	323	975	62
60/64	31	43	44	118	56	12	38	26	76	56	17	33	26	76	57	17	33	26	76	56	27	41	51	119	56	55	18	47	120	58	294	234	296	824	57
55/59	35	28	44	107	52	21	42	37	100	52	21	38	32	91	52	22	34	32	88	51	11	[illegible]	44	110	51	44	7	25	76	53	265	190	250	705	52
50/54	44	22	41	107	48	33	37	44	114	47	27	39	39	105	47	24	35	39	98	46	39	27	39	105	46	32	2	13	47	48	243	163	233	639	47
45/49	40	11	29	80	43	40	31	42	113	43	27	36	36	99	42	30	28	36	94	42	48	18	28	94	42	21	0	4	25	43	227	124	180	531	43
40/44	34	6	19	59	38	39	21	36	96	38	41	28	40	109	38	37	20	31	88	38	34	8	18	60	38	9	0	1	10	39	204	83	147	434	38
35/39	22	1	7	30	34	36	9	21	66	34	37	16	30	83	33	37	11	19	67	34	24	2	8	34	33	2		0	2	34	161	39	85	285	34
30/34	11	0	3	14	29	30	3	13	46	29	40	10	17	67	29	27	4	10	41	29	11	0	2	13	29	0			0	30	119	17	45	181	29
25/29	2	0	1	3	25	18	1	3	22	25	18	4	8	30	24	14	1	3	18	24	3			3	25						55	6	15	76	25
20/24	1		0	1	19	3	1	1	5	20	8	1	3	12	20	5	0	0	5	20	0			0	23						17	2	4	23	20
15/19	0			0	18	1	0	0	1	16	3	0	1	4	16	1			1	16											5	0	1	6	16
10/14						0		0	0	10	1	0		1	11																1	0	0	1	11
5/9						0			0	7	1			1	7																1			1	7

HUNTSVILLE ALABAMA

LAT 34 42N LONG 86 35W ELEV 606 FT

MEAN FREQUENCY OF OCCURRENCE OF DRY BULB TEMPERATURE (DEGREES F) WITH MEAN COINCIDENT WET BULB TEMPERATURE (DEGREES F) FOR EACH DRY BULB TEMPERATURE RANGE

Temperature Range	MAY Obsn Hour Gp 01 to 08	MAY 09 to 16	MAY 17 to 24	MAY Total Obsn	MAY M C W B	JUNE Obsn Hour Gp 01 to 08	JUNE 09 to 16	JUNE 17 to 24	JUNE Total Obsn	JUNE M C W B	JULY Obsn Hour Gp 01 to 08	JULY 09 to 16	JULY 17 to 24	JULY Total Obsn	JULY M C W B
100/104												0		0	72
95/99		2		2	71		7	2	9	75		9	2	11	75
90/94		22	4	26	70		34	10	44	74		55	12	67	74
85/89		43	13	56	69	1	63	23	87	72	1	83	29	113	74
80/84	1	57	24	82	68	8	65	38	111	70	10	66	54	130	73
75/79	13	45	41	99	66	36	50	60	146	69	62	28	82	172	71
70/74	41	33	60	134	65	91	16	74	181	68	132	6	58	196	69
65/69	74	23	49	146	62	68	5	28	101	64	34	1	9	44	65
60/64	52	15	29	96	58	27	1	7	35	60	9		1	10	59
55/59	30	6	17	53	53	9	0	1	10	57	1			1	57
50/54	17	2	8	27	49	0			0	54					
45/49	13	0	4	17	44										
40/44	7		0	7	41										
35/39	1			1	38										
30/34															
25/29															

Temperature Range	AUGUST Obsn Hour Gp 01 to 08	AUGUST 09 to 16	AUGUST 17 to 24	AUGUST Total Obsn	AUGUST M C W B	SEPTEMBER Obsn Hour Gp 01 to 08	SEPTEMBER 09 to 16	SEPTEMBER 17 to 24	SEPTEMBER Total Obsn	SEPTEMBER M C W B	OCTOBER Obsn Hour Gp 01 to 08	OCTOBER 09 to 16	OCTOBER 17 to 24	OCTOBER Total Obsn	OCTOBER M C W B
100/104															
95/99		10	2	12	76		4	0	4	75					
90/94		58	12	70	74		23	4	27	73		1		1	71
85/89	1	77	28	106	74		55	13	68	72		12	1	13	68
80/84	9	62	51	122	73	3	54	28	85	70		44	6	50	65
75/79	56	28	85	169	71	25	45	50	120	69	2	44	16	62	65
70/74	127	11	58	196	70	73	34	69	176	67	16	41	33	90	64
65/69	44	2	11	57	65	59	21	46	126	63	30	37	48	115	61
60/64	12		2	14	61	48	4	21	73	59	41	34	46	121	56
55/59	1			1	55	20	1	8	29	53	42	21	39	102	53
50/54	1			1	53	11		2	13	50	46	10	33	89	48
45/49						3			3	46	32	4	16	52	44
40/44						0			0	43	23	0	8	31	40
35/39											13		3	16	35
30/34											4			4	31
25/29											0			0	28

Temperature Range	NOVEMBER Obsn Hour Gp 01 to 08	NOV 09 to 16	NOV 17 to 24	NOV Total Obsn	NOV MCWB	DECEMBER Obsn Hour Gp 01 to 08	DEC 09 to 16	DEC 17 to 24	DEC Total Obsn	DEC MCWB
100/104										
95/99										
90/94										
85/89										
80/84		1		1	65					
75/79		6	1	7	64					
70/74	2	23	3	28	61		3	0	3	60
65/69	9	39	23	71	59	2	8	3	13	57
60/64	23	39	27	89	55	6	19	10	35	56
55/59	22	43	33	98	51	14	28	20	62	52
50/54	31	29	43	103	47	24	36	24	84	47
45/49	41	26	40	107	43	20	36	32	88	42
40/44	35	18	28	81	39	30	40	40	110	38
35/39	29	11	23	63	34	40	31	42	113	34
30/34	28	4	14	46	30	39	26	35	100	29
25/29	14	3	3	20	26	35	13	24	72	25
20/24	6	1	3	10	20	22	6	11	39	20
15/19	2			2	18	12	1	4	17	16
10/14						3	1	1	5	11
5/9						1	1	1	3	6
0/4						1		0	1	2
-5/-1										

Temperature Range	JANUARY Obsn Hour Gp 01 to 08	JAN 09 to 16	JAN 17 to 24	JAN Total Obsn	JAN MCWB	FEBRUARY Obsn Hour Gp 01 to 08	FEB 09 to 16	FEB 17 to 24	FEB Total Obsn	FEB MCWB
100/104										
95/99										
90/94										
85/89										
80/84							0		0	60
75/79							2	0	2	65
70/74		2		2	63		9	2	11	60
65/69	1	9	2	12	60	3	13	6	22	59
60/64	7	13	9	29	56	7	22	14	43	55
55/59	8	22	15	45	51	11	[illegible]	24	[illegible]	51
50/54	19	34	21	74	47	18	27	21	66	46
45/49	22	37	34	93	43	29	33	36	98	42
40/44	31	40	37	108	38	32	38	41	111	38
35/39	34	33	44	111	34	39	27	36	102	34
30/34	34	23	36	93	30	34	16	24	74	29
25/29	38	14	22	74	25	26	8	14	48	25
20/24	25	12	13	50	20	14	2	4	20	20
15/19	13	6	9	28	16	5	0	1	6	17
10/14	10	2	6	18	11	2	0	0	2	11
5/9	4	2	1	7	7	1			1	6
0/4	2	1	1	4	1					
-5/-1	2		0	2	-3					

Temperature Range	MARCH Obsn Hour Gp 01 to 08	MAR 09 to 16	MAR 17 to 24	MAR Total Obsn	MAR MCWB	APRIL Obsn Hour Gp 01 to 08	APR 09 to 16	APR 17 to 24	APR Total Obsn	APR MCWB
100/104										
95/99										
90/94							0		0	69
85/89		1		1	59		10	1	11	67
80/84		4	1	5	59		27	8	35	64
75/79		10	3	13	61	0	34	16	50	63
70/74	1	20	9	30	60	9	44	35	88	61
65/69	10	27	21	58	58	38	38	49	125	58
60/64	14	39	31	84	54	52	34	40	126	[illegible]
55/59	29	38	38	105	50	36	26	33	95	50
50/54	34	34	33	101	46	32	16	28	76	47
45/49	28	32	37	97	42	30	8	18	56	43
40/44	37	22	39	98	38	23	3	9	35	39
35/39	44	11	21	76	34	15		3	18	35
30/34	35	8	10	53	30	5			5	31
25/29	13	3	4	20	25					
20/24	4	1	1	6	21					
15/19	0	0	0	0	15					
10/14	1			1	12					
5/9										
0/4										
-5/-1										

Temperature Range	ANNUAL TOTAL Obsn Hour Gp 01 to 08	09 to 16	17 to 24	Total Obsn	MCWB
100/104		0		0	72
95/99		32	6	38	75
90/94		193	42	235	74
85/89	3	344	108	455	72
80/84	31	380	210	621	70
75/79	194	292	354	840	69
70/74	492	242	401	1135	67
65/69	372	223	295	890	61
60/64	[illegible]	[illegible]	[illegible]	[illegible]	[illegible]
55/59	226	212	228	666	51
50/54	233	188	213	634	47
45/49	218	176	217	611	43
40/44	218	161	202	581	38
35/39	215	113	172	500	34
30/34	179	77	119	375	30
25/29	126	41	67	234	25
20/24	71	22	32	125	20
15/19	32	7	14	53	16
10/14	16	3	7	26	11
5/9	6	3	2	11	6
0/4	3	1	1	5	1
-5/-1	2		0	2	-3

MAXWELL AFB/MONTGOMERY ALABAMA

LAT 32 23N LONG 86 22W ELEV 169 FT

MEAN FREQUENCY OF OCCURRENCE OF DRY BULB TEMPERATURE (DEGREES F) WITH MEAN COINCIDENT WET BULB TEMPERATURE (DEGREES F) FOR EACH DRY BULB TEMPERATURE RANGE

Temperature Range	MAY Obsn Hour Gp 01 to 08	MAY 09 to 16	MAY 17 to 24	MAY Total Obsn	MAY MCWB	JUNE Obsn Hour Gp 01 to 08	JUNE 09 to 16	JUNE 17 to 24	JUNE Total Obsn	JUNE MCWB	JULY Obsn Hour Gp 01 to 08	JULY 09 to 16	JULY 17 to 24	JULY Total Obsn	JULY MCWB
105/109												0		0	82
100/104							1	0	1	80		2	0	2	78
95/99		2	0	2	73		9	2	11	76		16	3	19	77
90/94		21	5	26	72		54	15	69	75	0	64	16	80	76
85/89	0	59	19	78	70	1	77	31	109	74	2	82	34	118	76
80/84	1	65	32	98	69	12	58	52	122	72	20	56	63	139	75
75/79	17	48	52	117	68	63	29	75	167	71	101	22	88	211	73
70/74	65	31	70	166	66	109	10	51	170	69	116	6	42	164	70
65/69	78	14	40	132	63	41	2	11	54	65	8		1	9	65
60/64	45	4	18	67	58	11	0	3	14	60	1			1	60
55/59	24	2	9	35	54	2		0	2	55					
50/54	14	0	2	16	49	0			0	49					
45/49	3		0	3	44										
40/44	0			0	44										
35/39															
30/34															

Temperature Range	AUGUST Obsn Hour Gp 01 to 08	AUGUST 09 to 16	AUGUST 17 to 24	AUGUST Total Obsn	AUGUST MCWB	SEPTEMBER Obsn Hour Gp 01 to 08	SEPTEMBER 09 to 16	SEPTEMBER 17 to 24	SEPTEMBER Total Obsn	SEPTEMBER MCWB	OCTOBER Obsn Hour Gp 01 to 08	OCTOBER 09 to 16	OCTOBER 17 to 24	OCTOBER Total Obsn	OCTOBER MCWB
105/109															
100/104		0		0	78										
95/99		10	1	11	77		3	0	3	75		0		0	75
90/94		66	15	81	76		36	5	41	75		1	0	1	73
85/89	1	88	33	122	75		69	19	88	73		15	1	16	71
80/84	15	57	65	137	74	3	60	38	101	72	0	44	8	52	69
75/79	107	23	94	224	73	48	40	75	163	71	3	57	24	84	66
70/74	105	4	36	145	70	94	19	60	173	68	22	53	47	122	65
65/69	17	0	3	20	65	53	10	28	91	64	47	38	56	141	61
60/64	3		0	3	59	28	3	11	42	59	54	27	50	131	58
55/59						10	1	3	14	54	49	10	33	92	53
50/54						2	0	1	3	50	34	3	19	56	48
45/49						0		0	0	44	23	1	7	31	44
40/44						1			1	42	10		2	12	40
35/39											5		0	5	35
30/34											0			0	31

MAXWELL AFB/MONTGOMERY ALABAMA

Temperature Range	NOVEMBER Obsn Hour Gp 01 to 08	NOVEMBER Obsn Hour Gp 09 to 16	NOVEMBER Obsn Hour Gp 17 to 24	NOVEMBER Total Obsn	NOVEMBER MCWB	DECEMBER Obsn Hour Gp 01 to 08	DECEMBER Obsn Hour Gp 09 to 16	DECEMBER Obsn Hour Gp 17 to 24	DECEMBER Total Obsn	DECEMBER MCWB	JANUARY Obsn Hour Gp 01 to 08	JANUARY Obsn Hour Gp 09 to 16	JANUARY Obsn Hour Gp 17 to 24	JANUARY Total Obsn	JANUARY MCWB
105/109															
100/104															
95/99															
90/94															
85/89		0		0	73										
80/84		6	0	6	68		1		1	71		1		1	70
75/79		22	3	25	65		5	1	6	68		2	0	2	67
70/74	5	35	14	54	63	1	14	4	19	64	0	11	3	14	63
65/69	13	43	29	85	59	8	24	15	47	61	5	16	10	31	61
60/64	25	42	38	105	56	14	31	23	68	56	11	22	21	54	57
55/59	31	36	46	113	52	19	41	32	92	52	17	32	24	73	52
50/54	42	27	41	110	48	29	40	42	111	47	26	42	36	104	47
45/49	39	17	31	87	43	34	39	47	120	42	28	40	43	111	42
40/44	39	8	24	71	38	42	29	39	110	38	36	35	41	112	38
35/39	30	3	10	43	34	43	16	27	86	34	41	24	34	99	33
30/34	12	1	3	16	30	32	6	14	52	30	44	12	21	77	29
25/29	3	0	1	4	25	20	2	5	27	25	23	7	9	39	25
20/24	1	0	0	1	20	5	1	0	6	20	10	3	4	17	20
15/19	0			0	17	1	0	0	1	15	5	1	1	7	16
10/14							0	0	0	10	1	0	0	1	10
5/9						1			1	7	1	0		1	6
0/4											0			0	3

Temperature Range	FEBRUARY Obsn Hour Gp 01 to 08	FEBRUARY Obsn Hour Gp 09 to 16	FEBRUARY Obsn Hour Gp 17 to 24	FEBRUARY Total Obsn	FEBRUARY MCWB	MARCH Obsn Hour Gp 01 to 08	MARCH Obsn Hour Gp 09 to 16	MARCH Obsn Hour Gp 17 to 24	MARCH Total Obsn	MARCH MCWB	APRIL Obsn Hour Gp 01 to 08	APRIL Obsn Hour Gp 09 to 16	APRIL Obsn Hour Gp 17 to 24	APRIL Total Obsn	APRIL MCWB	ANNUAL TOTAL Obsn Hour Gp 01 to 08	ANNUAL TOTAL Obsn Hour Gp 09 to 16	ANNUAL TOTAL Obsn Hour Gp 17 to 24	ANNUAL TOTAL Total Obsn	ANNUAL TOTAL MCWB
105/109																	0		0	82
100/104																	3	0	3	78
95/99																	40	6	46	77
90/94												0		0	75	0	242	56	298	75
85/89		0		0	74		1		1	68		16	3	19	70	4	407	140	551	74
80/84		2	0	2	67		7	1	8	66		50	16	66	67	51	407	275	733	72
75/79		8	2	10	66	0	24	6	30	63	3	49	30	82	65	342	329	450	1121	70
70/74	1	16	8	25	62	3	31	19	53	61	21	48	53	122	63	542	278	407	1227	67
65/69	7	22	17	46	60	13	34	32	79	59	50	35	53	138	61	340	238	295	873	62
60/64	16	25	24	65	56	25	42	44	111	55	56	25	40	121	57	289	221	272	782	57
55/59	17	32	27	76	50	36	39	45	120	51	43	11	25	79	52	248	204	244	696	52
50/54	21	36	34	91	46	39	32	39	110	46	33	4	14	51	48	240	184	228	652	47
45/49	30	32	38	100	42	48	22	30	100	42	23	1	5	29	43	228	152	201	581	43
40/44	38	27	33	98	38	39	11	19	69	38	11		1	12	39	216	110	159	485	38
35/39	39	15	23	77	33	27	4	10	41	34	1		0	1	36	186	62	104	352	34
30/34	28	7	14	49	29	12	1	2	15	30						128	27	54	209	29
25/29	18	2	5	25	24	4	0	0	4	25						68	11	20	99	25
20/24	7	1	1	9	20	1			1	21						24	5	5	34	20
15/19	2	0		2	15											8	1	1	10	15
10/14																1	0	0	1	10
5/9																2	0		2	6
0/4																0			0	3

ADAK NAVSTA/MITCHELL FIELD ALASKA

LAT 51 53N LONG 176 39W ELEV 19 FT

MEAN FREQUENCY OF OCCURRENCE OF DRY BULB TEMPERATURE (DEGREES F) WITH MEAN COINCIDENT WET BULB TEMPERATURE (DEGREES F) FOR EACH DRY BULB TEMPERATURE RANGE

Temperature Range	MAY Obsn Hour Gp 01 to 08	MAY 09 to 16	MAY 17 to 24	MAY Total Obsn	MAY MCWB	JUNE Obsn Hour Gp 01 to 08	JUNE 09 to 16	JUNE 17 to 24	JUNE Total Obsn	JUNE MCWB	JULY Obsn Hour Gp 01 to 08	JULY 09 to 16	JULY 17 to 24	JULY Total Obsn	JULY MCWB
75/79															
70/74												0		0	62
65/69											0	2	1	3	61
60/64		0		0	55		0		0	54	2	11	3	16	57
55/59		1	0	1	52		4	1	5	51	13	35	21	69	54
50/54	0	8	1	9	47	6	35	14	55	48	36	104	63	203	49
45/49	7	59	22	88	43	39	125	82	246	44	134	89	133	356	46
40/44	99	150	139	388	40	171	75	136	382	41	62	6	26	94	42
35/39	128	29	81	238	36	24	1	7	32	37	2		0	2	39
30/34	13	1	4	18	32	0		0	0	30					
25/29	1		0	1	27										
20/24															

Temperature Range	AUGUST Obsn Hour Gp 01 to 08	AUGUST 09 to 16	AUGUST 17 to 24	AUGUST Total Obsn	AUGUST MCWB	SEPTEMBER Obsn Hour Gp 01 to 08	SEPTEMBER 09 to 16	SEPTEMBER 17 to 24	SEPTEMBER Total Obsn	SEPTEMBER MCWB	OCTOBER Obsn Hour Gp 01 to 08	OCTOBER 09 to 16	OCTOBER 17 to 24	OCTOBER Total Obsn	OCTOBER MCWB
75/79		0		0	69										
70/74		1	0	1	67										
65/69	0	4	1	5	63		0	0	0	65					
60/64	3	17	6	26	59	0	2	0	2	58		0		0	56
55/59	22	57	31	110	54	5	18	5	28	53	0	2	1	3	55
50/54	74	127	105	306	50	39	116	57	212	49	9	19	8	36	48
45/49	132	42	100	274	46	141	97	141	379	45	46	99	57	202	44
40/44	15	0	4	19	42	47	7	33	87	41	116	100	118	334	40
35/39	2		0	2	37	6	0	3	9	36	63	25	56	144	35
30/34	0		0	0	34	2		0	2	32	13	2	8	23	31
25/29											1			2	27
20/24											0			0	22

Temperature Range	NOVEMBER Obsn Hour Gp 01 to 08	09 to 16	17 to 24	Total Obsn	M C W B	DECEMBER Obsn Hour Gp 01 to 08	09 to 16	17 to 24	Total Obsn	M C W B	JANUARY Obsn Hour Gp 01 to 08	09 to 16	17 to 24	Total Obsn	M C W B	FEBRUARY Obsn Hour Gp 01 to 08	09 to 16	17 to 24	Total Obsn	M C W B
75/79																				
70/74																				
65/69																				
60/64																				
55/59																				
50/54	2	2	1	5	48	0			0	46							0		0	48
45/49	10	16	9	35	44	2	3	1	6	45	3	4	4	11	44	1	3	1	5	44
40/44	45	77	55	177	39	22	32	25	79	40	30	40	29	99	40	14	25	17	56	40
35/39	110	106	111	327	35	94	113	101	308	35	80	99	86	265	35	71	94	75	240	35
30/34	60	36	52	148	31	94	84	94	272	31	84	77	[illegible]	[illegible]	[illegible]	[illegible]	77	[illegible]	248	30
25/29	11	3	10	24	26	26	13	22	61	26	34	23	33	90	26	36	20	31	87	26
20/24	2	0	2	4	22	7	2	4	13	21	13	4	10	27	22	10	4	9	23	21
15/19	0	0		0	16	2	0	1	3	17	4	1	2	7	17	4	1	3	8	17
10/14	0			0	12	0	0		0	13	1	0	0	1	13	2	0	1	3	12
5/9											0			0	9	1			1	7

Temperature Range	MARCH Obsn Hour Gp 01 to 08	09 to 16	17 to 24	Total Obsn	M C W B	APRIL Obsn Hour Gp 01 to 08	09 to 16	17 to 24	Total Obsn	M C W B	ANNUAL TOTAL Obsn Hour Gp 01 to 08	09 to 16	17 to 24	Total Obsn	M C W B
75/79												0		0	69
70/74												1	0	1	66
65/69											0	6	2	8	62
60/64											5	30	9	44	58
55/59							0		0	42	40	117	59	216	54
50/54		0		0	45		1	0	1	46	166	412	249	827	49
45/49	1	4	0	5	43	3	18	4	25	43	519	559	554	1632	45
40/44	17	58	24	99	39	35	105	62	202	39	673	675	668	2016	40
35/39	96	124	115	335	35	123	94	121	338	36	[illegible]	[illegible]	[illegible]	[illegible]	[illegible]
30/34	100	56	93	249	31	69	21	49	139	31	520	354	469	1343	31
25/29	28	5	13	46	26	9	1	4	14	27	146	65	114	325	26
20/24	5	0	2	7	21	1		0	1	23	38	10	27	75	21
15/19	1	0	1	2	16						11	2	7	20	17
10/14	0			0	14						3	0	1	4	12
5/9											1			1	7

BARROW ALASKA

LAT 71 18N LONG 156 47W ELEV 31 FT

MEAN FREQUENCY OF OCCURRENCE OF DRY BULB TEMPERATURE (DEGREES F) WITH MEAN COINCIDENT WET BULB TEMPERATURE (DEGREES F) FOR EACH DRY BULB TEMPERATURE RANGE

Temperature Range	MAY Obsn Hour Gp 01 to 08	MAY 09 to 16	MAY 17 to 24	MAY Total Obsn	MAY MCWB	JUNE Obsn Hour Gp 01 to 08	JUNE 09 to 16	JUNE 17 to 24	JUNE Total Obsn	JUNE MCWB	JULY Obsn Hour Gp 01 to 08	JULY 09 to 16	JULY 17 to 24	JULY Total Obsn	JULY MCWB
75/79												0		0	60
70/74												0		0	63
65/69												1	1	2	58
60/64							1	0	1	54	0	4	1	5	55
55/59						0	3	1	4	51	3	8	5	16	53
50/54						1	5	2	8	48	11	14	10	35	49
45/49						3	7	5	15	44	22	29	23	74	45
40/44	0	0	0	0	38	10	21	15	46	40	32	54	44	130	40
35/39	3	8	4	15	35	35	64	49	148	35	66	87	84	237	36
30/34	14	30	24	68	31	117	110	124	351	31	105	51	79	235	32
25/29	37	59	56	152	26	57	26	39	122	27	8	1	2	11	28
20/24	63	69	70	202	21	15	3	4	22	22					
15/19	50	35	39	124	17	2	0	0	2	17					
10/14	36	26	26	88	11	0			0	14					
5/9	22	16	17	55	7										
0/4	13	5	8	26	2										
-5/-1	8	1	3	12	-3										
-10/-6	3	0	1	4	-8										
-15/-11	1			1	-12										
-20/-16															
-25/-21															

Temperature Range	AUGUST Obsn Hour Gp 01 to 08	AUGUST 09 to 16	AUGUST 17 to 24	AUGUST Total Obsn	AUGUST MCWB	SEPTEMBER Obsn Hour Gp 01 to 08	SEPTEMBER 09 to 16	SEPTEMBER 17 to 24	SEPTEMBER Total Obsn	SEPTEMBER MCWB	OCTOBER Obsn Hour Gp 01 to 08	OCTOBER 09 to 16	OCTOBER 17 to 24	OCTOBER Total Obsn	OCTOBER MCWB
75/79															
70/74		0		0	62										
65/69		1	0	1	60										
60/64	0	3	2	5	57		0	0	0	55					
55/59	1	12	4	17	53		1	0	1	53					
50/54	10	18	11	39	50		2	1	3	49					
45/49	19	25	26	70	45	2	6	3	11	44					
40/44	50	54	49	153	41	7	15	11	33	40		0	0	0	39
35/39	68	74	70	212	36	35	41	36	112	36	2	3	2	7	35
30/34	75	50	69	194	32	97	102	100	299	31	26	30	27	83	31
25/29	24	11	17	52	27	64	49	59	172	27	43	41	41	125	26
20/24	2	0	0	2	23	26	20	23	69	22	42	46	43	131	21
15/19						7	3	6	16	17	39	40	42	121	16
10/14						1	0	1	2	13	31	31	27	89	11
5/9						0		0	0	8	26	25	28	79	7
0/4						0			0	2	19	17	19	55	2
-5/-1											11	9	12	32	-3
-10/-6											6	4	5	15	-8
-15/-11											1	2	2	5	-13
-20/-16											1	0	1	2	-17
-25/-21											0			0	-22

BARROW ALASKA

Temperature Range	NOVEMBER Obsn Hour Gp 01 to 08	09 to 16	17 to 24	Total Obsn	M C W B	DECEMBER Obsn Hour Gp 01 to 08	09 to 16	17 to 24	Total Obsn	M C W B	JANUARY Obsn Hour Gp 01 to 08	09 to 16	17 to 24	Total Obsn	M C W B
75/79															
70/74															
65/69															
60/64															
55/59															
50/54															
45/49															
40/44															
35/39		0	0	0	33						0			0	35
30/34	2	1	2	5	31						2	1	1	4	31
25/29	6	6	6	18	26	1		1	2	26	3	4	3	10	26
20/24	11	11	13	35	21	2	3	3	8	21	6	5	6	17	22
15/19	19	21	18	58	16	3	3	2	8	16	6	7	7	20	16
10/14	20	18	16	54	11	5	5	6	16	11	8	8	9	25	12
5/9	25	25	24	74	6	12	9	13	34	6	9	9	11	29	6
0/4	32	35	36	103	1	20	21	21	62	1	15	15	13	43	1
-5/-1	40	38	35	113	-4	35	34	29	98	-3	18	18	18	54	-4
-10/-6	33	29	33	95	-8	37	37	35	109	-8	22	23	24	69	-9
-15/-11	23	25	27	75	-13	33	33	33	99	-13	29	30	28	87	-13
-20/-16	14	15	14	43	-18	27	26	29	82	-18	29	26	33	88	-18
-25/-21	8	9	9	26	-23	28	31	26	85	-23	33	34	32	99	-23
-30/-26	5	5	5	15	-27	22	22	25	69	-28	30	27	26	83	-28
-35/-31	1	0	1	2	-33	15	15	16	46	-33	17	22	17	56	-33
-40/-36		1		1		7	8	8	23		12	10	13	35	
-45/-41						2	2	1	5		5	6	5	16	
-50/-46											2	2	2	6	
-55/-51											0			0	

Temperature Range	FEBRUARY Obsn Hour Gp 01 to 08	09 to 16	17 to 24	Total Obsn	M C W B	MARCH Obsn Hour Gp 01 to 08	09 to 16	17 to 24	Total Obsn	M C W B	APRIL Obsn Hour Gp 01 to 08	09 to 16	17 to 24	Total Obsn	M C W B	ANNUAL TOTAL Obsn Hour Gp 01 to 08	09 to 16	17 to 24	Total Obsn	M C W B
75/79																	0		0	60
70/74																	0		0	62
65/69																	2	1	3	58
60/64																0	8	3	11	56
55/59																4	24	10	38	53
50/54																22	39	24	85	49
45/49																46	67	57	170	45
40/44																99	144	119	362	40
35/39											0	1	0	1	35	209	278	245	732	36
30/34	0	0	0	0	29						2	3	2	7	31	440	378	428	1246	31
25/29	1	2	2	5	27	1	1	0	2	26	2	8	5	15	26	247	208	231	686	26
20/24	1	0	1	2	21	2	3	2	7	21	8	16	14	38	21	178	176	179	533	21
15/19	3	2	2	7	17	2	4	3	9	17	16	14	19	49	16	147	129	138	414	17
10/14	4	3	3	10	11	3	3	5	11	12	14	22	20	56	11	122	116	113	351	11
5/9	5	6	5	16	6	5	5	4	14	6	21	33	27	81	6	125	128	129	382	6
0/4	6	8	8	22	2	8	13	8	29	1	27	33	32	92	1	140	147	145	432	1
-5/-1	10	13	12	35	-4	14	24	19	57	-4	27	40	34	101	-4	163	177	162	502	-4
-10/-6	19	19	18	56	-9	25	34	32	91	-9	32	33	35	100	-9	177	179	183	539	-8
-15/-11	25	25	25	75	-13	33	50	46	129	-13	34	24	28	86	-13	179	189	189	557	-13
-20/-16	32	35	31	98	-18	48	45	47	140	-18	29	9	17	55	-18	180	156	172	508	-18
-25/-21	32	36	34	102	-23	45	31	34	110	-23	20	2	7	29	-23	166	143	142	451	-23
-30/-26	30	29	31	90	-28	26	20	24	70	-28	7	0	1	8	-28	120	103	112	335	-28
-35/-31	25	22	23	70	-33	21	10	16	47	-33	1		1	2	-32	80	69	74	223	-33
-40/-36	17	14	17	48		10	3	5	18							46	36	43	125	
-45/-41	8	7	6	21		4	1	1	6							19	16	13	48	
-50/-46	5	3	5	13				0	0							7	5	7	19	
-55/-51	1	0	0	1												1	0	0	1	

EIELSON AFB/FAIRBANKS ALASKA

LAT 64 40N LONG 147 06W ELEV 545 FT

MEAN FREQUENCY OF OCCURRENCE OF DRY BULB TEMPERATURE (DEGREES F) WITH MEAN COINCIDENT WET BULB TEMPERATURE (DEGREES F) FOR EACH DRY BULB TEMPERATURE RANGE

Temperature Range	MAY Obsn Hour Gp 01 to 08	MAY Obsn Hour Gp 09 to 16	MAY Obsn Hour Gp 17 to 24	MAY Total Obsn	MAY MCWB	JUNE Obsn Hour Gp 01 to 08	JUNE Obsn Hour Gp 09 to 16	JUNE Obsn Hour Gp 17 to 24	JUNE Total Obsn	JUNE MCWB	JULY Obsn Hour Gp 01 to 08	JULY Obsn Hour Gp 09 to 16	JULY Obsn Hour Gp 17 to 24	JULY Total Obsn	JULY MCWB
90/94							0	0	0	64		0	0	0	66
85/89		0	0	0	68		3	1	4	63		2	1	3	63
80/84		1	1	2	62	0	7	3	10	61		9	5	14	62
75/79		2	1	3	58	0	21	13	34	59	0	23	12	35	60
70/74	0	6	3	9	54	2	37	22	61	57	1	44	27	72	58
65/69	1	17	10	28	51	7	54	40	101	55	8	59	40	107	57
60/64	1	39	20	60	48	23	54	47	124	53	27	54	58	139	55
55/59	9	53	35	97	46	51	37	53	141	50	75	38	61	174	53
50/54	23	49	49	121	43	76	22	38	136	48	93	17	35	145	49
45/49	44	33	48	125	40	54	4	18	76	44	34	3	8	45	46
40/44	59	26	42	127	37	20	0	4	24	40	9		2	11	41
35/39	56	15	25	96	33	6	0	1	7	36	2			2	37
30/34	36	3	10	49	29	1		0	1	31					
25/29	12	1	2	15	25										
20/24	2	1	1	4	20										
15/19	2	1	1	4	15										
10/14	1	0	1	.2	10										
5/9	1	0	0	1	5										
0/4	0			0	3										
-5/-1															
-10/-6															
-15/-11															
-20/-16															
-25/-21															

Temperature Range	AUGUST Obsn Hour Gp 01 to 08	AUGUST Obsn Hour Gp 09 to 16	AUGUST Obsn Hour Gp 17 to 24	AUGUST Total Obsn	AUGUST MCWB	SEPTEMBER Obsn Hour Gp 01 to 08	SEPTEMBER Obsn Hour Gp 09 to 16	SEPTEMBER Obsn Hour Gp 17 to 24	SEPTEMBER Total Obsn	SEPTEMBER MCWB	OCTOBER Obsn Hour Gp 01 to 08	OCTOBER Obsn Hour Gp 09 to 16	OCTOBER Obsn Hour Gp 17 to 24	OCTOBER Total Obsn	OCTOBER MCWB
90/94															
85/89		0		0	68										
80/84		3	1	4	64		0	0	0	59					
75/79		10	5	15	61		1	0	1	58					
70/74	0	24	11	35	59		4	1	5	56					
65/69	1	47	24	72	56	0	9	3	12	53		0		0	47
60/64	7	58	43	108	54	2	25	9	36	50	1	2	1	4	47
55/59	34	53	59	146	52	3	40	22	65	48	0	2	1	3	44
50/54	80	36	61	177	49	13	46	36	95	46	2	4	2	8	42
45/49	70	12	30	112	45	32	40	47	119	43	3	10	4	17	39
40/44	36	3	11	50	41	48	30	47	125	39	7	18	11	36	37
35/39	16	0	3	19	36	54	28	35	117	35	11	31	20	62	34
30/34	4		0	4	31	54	14	29	97	31	35	41	44	120	30
25/29	0			0	28	25	2	9	36	26	40	38	43	121	26
20/24						7	1	2	10	22	42	32	35	109	21
15/19						1		0	1	17	26	23	22	71	16
10/14						0			0	12	23	20	24	67	12
5/9											18	12	12	42	7
0/4											12	8	12	32	2
-5/-1											10	4	10	24	-3
-10/-6											9	2	4	15	-8
-15/-11											6	0	2	8	-13
-20/-16											3		0	3	-18
-25/-21											0			0	-21

EIELSON AFB/FAIRBANKS ALASKA

Temperature Range	NOVEMBER Obsn Hour Gp 01 to 08	09 to 16	17 to 24	Total Obsn	MCWB	DECEMBER Obsn Hour Gp 01 to 08	09 to 16	17 to 24	Total Obsn	MCWB	JANUARY Obsn Hour Gp 01 to 08	09 to 16	17 to 24	Total Obsn	MCWB	FEBRUARY Obsn Hour Gp 01 to 08	09 to 16	17 to 24	Total Obsn	MCWB	MARCH Obsn Hour Gp 01 to 08	09 to 16	17 to 24	Total Obsn	MCWB	APRIL Obsn Hour Gp 01 to 08	09 to 16	17 to 24	Total Obsn	MCWB	ANNUAL TOTAL Obsn Hour Gp 01 to 08	09 to 16	17 to 24	Total Obsn	MCWB
90/94																																0	0	0	64
85/89																																5	2	7	63
80/84																															0	20	10	30	62
75/79																															0	57	31	88	59
70/74																											0		0	52	3	115	64	182	58
65/69																											1	1	2	52	17	187	118	322	55
60/64																											2	1	3	49	61	234	179	474	53
55/59																											7	2	9	45	172	230	233	635	50
50/54																						1	0	1	40	0	16	6	22	41	287	191	227	705	47
45/49	1	1	0	2	38		0		0	36	1	1	1	3	39	0	0		0	37	0	3	1	4	38	2	27	15	44	38	241	134	172	547	43
40/44	2	3	2	7	36	1	1	1	3	36	0	1	0	1	35	2	2	2	6	35	2	14	6	22	35	7	40	29	76	35	193	138	157	488	38
35/39	3	5	3	11	32	3	3	4	10	31	1	1	1	3	32	1	3	2	6	31	4	22	13	39	32	21	47	45	113	32	178	155	152	485	33
30/34	5	6	6	17	29	3	3	4	10	29	4	4	5	13	30	3	4	5	12	29	15	23	18	56	29	50	32	49	131	29	210	130	170	510	30
25/29	9	12	9	30	25	4	5	3	12	25	5	4	5	14	25	6	11	6	23	25	10	24	20	54	24	48	28	35	111	24	159	125	132	416	25
20/24	16	20	19	55	21	8	8	7	23	21	8	9	7	24	21	8	15	13	36	21	14	27	26	67	20	38	18	24	80	20	143	131	134	408	21
15/19	25	27	24	76	16	10	10	10	30	16	11	12	11	34	16	13	16	15	44	16	20	28	29	77	15	25	12	15	52	16	133	129	127	389	16
10/14	28	29	28	85	12	12	12	15	39	11	11	11	12	34	11	15	24	20	59	11	21	23	25	69	11	20	4	8	32	11	131	123	133	387	11
5/9	24	25	23	72	7	13	19	16	48	6	13	15	13	41	7	18	26	22	66	6	23	19	22	64	6	11	4	5	20	6	121	120	113	354	6
0/4	25	24	25	74	2	22	24	19	65	2	17	20	18	55	2	24	29	27	80	1	27	17	19	63	1	7	2	3	12	2	134	124	123	381	2
-5/-1	24	23	26	73	-3	29	23	22	74	-3	19	25	23	67	-3	23	23	26	72	-4	24	18	20	62	-3	4	0	2	6	-3	133	116	129	378	-3
-10/-6	17	15	17	49	-8	22	22	26	70	-8	18	25	20	63	-8	25	18	22	65	-8	18	12	15	45	-8	2	0	1	3	-8	111	94	105	310	-8
-15/-11	14	12	14	40	-13	21	22	20	63	-13	24	20	24	68	-13	24	14	18	56	-13	15	9	13	37	-13	1		0	1	-13	105	77	91	273	-13
-20/-16	10	13	10	33	-18	19	19	21	59	-18	24	19	18	61	-18	14	12	14	40	-18	15	5	10	30	-18	1			1	-18	86	68	73	227	-18
-25/-21	11	10	11	32	-23	18	16	17	51	-23	15	16	19	50	-23	14	10	7	31	-23	14	2	5	21	-23						72	54	59	185	-23
-30/-26	11	9	13	33	-28	13	14	11	38	-28	15	16	16	47	-28	10	6	7	23	-28	12	1	3	16	-28						61	46	50	157	-28
-35/-31	11	4	7	22	-33	12	13	12	37	-33	21	18	19	58	-33	7	4	7	18	-33	7	0	2	9	-33						58	39	47	144	-33
-40/-36	4	1	2	7		12	12	15	39		16	12	17	45		8	4	5	17		4	0	1	5							44	29	40	113	
-45/-41	1	0	0	1		16	13	15	44		11	11	10	32		5	2	3	10		2	0	0	2							35	26	28	89	
-50/-46						8	7	6	21		12	7	8	27		4	1	2	7		2		0	2							26	15	16	57	
-55/-51						2	1	2	5		2	2	2	6		1	0	0	1												5	3	4	12	
-60/-56						1	1	2	4		0	0	0	0		0			0												1	1	2	4	
-65/-61								0	0																								0	0	

ELMENDORF AFB/ANCHORAGE ALASKA

LAT 61 15N LONG 149 48W ELEV 212 FT

MEAN FREQUENCY OF OCCURRENCE OF DRY BULB TEMPERATURE (DEGREES F) WITH MEAN COINCIDENT WET BULB TEMPERATURE (DEGREES F) FOR EACH DRY BULB TEMPERATURE RANGE

Temperature Range	MAY Obsn Hour Gp 01 to 08	MAY 09 to 16	MAY 17 to 24	MAY Total Obsn	MAY MCWB	JUNE Obsn Hour Gp 01 to 08	JUNE 09 to 16	JUNE 17 to 24	JUNE Total Obsn	JUNE MCWB	JULY Obsn Hour Gp 01 to 08	JULY 09 to 16	JULY 17 to 24	JULY Total Obsn	JULY MCWB
85/89							0	0	0	63					
80/84							1	0	1	62		1	0	1	61
75/79		0	0	0	58		1	0	1	60		1	1	2	61
70/74		1	1	2	56	0	9	4	13	57	0	16	7	23	58
65/69		7	3	10	53	1	30	16	47	55	2	42	23	67	57
60/64	1	17	9	27	49	7	59	42	108	53	20	81	62	163	54
55/59	4	49	27	80	47	46	76	74	196	50	90	81	105	276	52
50/54	21	73	56	150	44	101	51	74	226	47	117	25	48	190	49
45/49	72	70	77	219	41	71	13	27	111	44	19	1	4	24	45
40/44	82	25	54	161	38	14	0	3	17	40	1			1	42
35/39	50	3	17	70	34	0			0	35					
30/34	15	2	3	20	29										
25/29	2	1	1	4	24										
20/24	1	0	1	2	18										
15/19	0		0	0	15										
10/14															
5/9															
0/4															
-5/-1															
-10/-6															

Temperature Range	AUGUST Obsn Hour Gp 01 to 08	AUGUST 09 to 16	AUGUST 17 to 24	AUGUST Total Obsn	AUGUST MCWB	SEPTEMBER Obsn Hour Gp 01 to 08	SEPTEMBER 09 to 16	SEPTEMBER 17 to 24	SEPTEMBER Total Obsn	SEPTEMBER MCWB	OCTOBER Obsn Hour Gp 01 to 08	OCTOBER 09 to 16	OCTOBER 17 to 24	OCTOBER Total Obsn	OCTOBER MCWB
85/89															
80/84		0	0	0	64										
75/79		1	0	1	62										
70/74	0	8	3	11	60		0	0	0	59					
65/69	1	31	13	45	57	0	3	1	4	55					
60/64	8	73	49	130	54	1	18	7	26	52	0	1	0	1	48
55/59	66	94	97	257	52	7	56	28	91	50	1	2	1	4	46
50/54	119	38	72	229	49	39	78	73	190	47	2	13	6	21	44
45/49	42	2	12	56	45	84	59	81	224	44	14	38	21	73	42
40/44	11	0	1	12	40	67	19	35	121	40	32	49	43	124	38
35/39	1		0	1	35	28	6	12	46	35	47	53	55	155	34
30/34	0			0	32	11	1	2	14	30	61	41	58	160	30
25/29						2			2	25	42	30	28	100	25
20/24											23	14	21	58	21
15/19											15	6	10	31	16
10/14											8	2	4	14	12
5/9											3	0	2	5	7
0/4											1	0	1	2	2
-5/-1											1		0	1	-2
-10/-6												0		0	-6

Temperature Range	NOVEMBER Obsn Hour Gp 01 to 08	NOVEMBER Obsn Hour Gp 09 to 16	NOVEMBER Obsn Hour Gp 17 to 24	NOVEMBER Total Obsn	NOVEMBER M C W B	DECEMBER Obsn Hour Gp 01 to 08	DECEMBER Obsn Hour Gp 09 to 16	DECEMBER Obsn Hour Gp 17 to 24	DECEMBER Total Obsn	DECEMBER M C W B	JANUARY Obsn Hour Gp 01 to 08	JANUARY Obsn Hour Gp 09 to 16	JANUARY Obsn Hour Gp 17 to 24	JANUARY Total Obsn	JANUARY M C W B	FEBRUARY Obsn Hour Gp 01 to 08	FEBRUARY Obsn Hour Gp 09 to 16	FEBRUARY Obsn Hour Gp 17 to 24	FEBRUARY Total Obsn	FEBRUARY M C W B
85/89																				
80/84																				
75/79																				
70/74																				
65/69																				
60/64																				
55/59																				
50/54	1	0	1	2	41		0	0	0	44						0			0	42
45/49	2	4	1	7	40	0	1	1	2	40	0	1	0	1	40	1	0	0	1	38
40/44	7	10	6	23	38	2	2	3	7	37	2	2	2	6	37	2	4	4	10	35
35/39	15	25	19	59	34	8	8	9	25	34	5	7	5	17	34	7	17	11	35	33
30/34	41	38	38	117	31	21	24	23	68	30	16	17	16	49	31	21	33	27	81	30
25/29	34	41	38	113	25	36	37	34	107	26	16	22	23	61	25	27	40	37	104	25
20/24	35	39	39	113	21	35	40	32	107	21	37	39	34	110	21	39	46	43	128	21
15/19	31	29	30	90	16	32	30	34	96	16	34	36	35	105	16	47	33	39	119	16
10/14	25	26	24	75	11	22	25	25	72	12	28	32	28	88	11	28	22	23	73	11
5/9	23	15	17	55	7	21	22	21	64	6	32	36	33	101	6	18	12	16	46	7
0/4	14	9	13	36	2	24	21	19	64	2	31	26	32	89	2	14	9	13	36	2
-5/-1	8	4	10	22	-3	16	15	17	48	-3	22	16	22	60	-3	10	5	6	21	-3
-10/-6	5	1	3	9	-8	13	13	16	42	-8	14	10	11	35	-8	5	2	4	11	-8
-15/-11	1	0		1	-12	11	5	9	25	-13	8	3	6	17	-13	3	1	2	6	-13
-20/-16						4	2	3	9	-18	3	1	2	6	-17	1	0	0	1	-17
-25/-21						2	3	2	7	-23	0		0	0	-22					
-30/-26						1	0	1	2	-28										
-35/-31						1	0	0	1	-32										

Temperature Range	MARCH Obsn Hour Gp 01 to 08	MARCH Obsn Hour Gp 09 to 16	MARCH Obsn Hour Gp 17 to 24	MARCH Total Obsn	MARCH M C W B	APRIL Obsn Hour Gp 01 to 08	APRIL Obsn Hour Gp 09 to 16	APRIL Obsn Hour Gp 17 to 24	APRIL Total Obsn	APRIL M C W B	ANNUAL TOTAL Obsn Hour Gp 01 to 08	ANNUAL TOTAL Obsn Hour Gp 09 to 16	ANNUAL TOTAL Obsn Hour Gp 17 to 24	ANNUAL TOTAL Total Obsn	ANNUAL TOTAL M C W B
85/89												0	0	0	63
80/84												2	0	2	62
75/79												3	1	4	61
70/74											0	34	15	49	58
65/69											4	113	56	173	56
60/64							1	0	1	47	37	250	169	456	54
55/59							2	1	3	45	214	360	333	907	51
50/54		0		0	42		13	5	18	41	400	291	335	1026	48
45/49	1	5	1	7	39	1	40	18	59	39	307	234	243	784	43
40/44	3	21	10	34	36	13	69	53	135	36	236	201	214	651	38
35/39	19	45	37	101	33	64	65	85	214	33	244	229	250	723	34
30/34	34	47	45	126	29	91	29	53	173	29	311	232	265	808	30
25/29	43	41	51	135	25	46	14	18	78	25	248	226	230	704	25
20/24	41	35	38	114	20	14	5	7	26	20	225	218	215	658	21
15/19	33	25	26	84	16	7	1	2	10	16	199	160	176	535	16
10/14	29	17	17	63	11	3	0	0	3	11	143	124	121	388	11
5/9	16	6	12	34	6	1			1	6	114	91	101	306	6
0/4	12	4	7	23	1	0			0	3	96	69	85	250	2
-5/-1	8	2	4	14	-3						65	42	59	166	-3
-10/-6	7	0	1	8	-8						44	26	35	105	-8
-15/-11	2			2	-13						25	9	17	51	-13
-20/-16	1			1	-17						9	3	5	17	-18
-25/-21											2	3	2	7	-23
-30/-26											1	0	1	2	-28
-35/-31											1	0	0	1	-32

JUNEAU MAP ALASKA

LAT 58 22N LONG 134 35W ELEV 12 FT

MEAN FREQUENCY OF OCCURRENCE OF DRY BULB TEMPERATURE (DEGREES F) WITH MEAN COINCIDENT WET BULB TEMPERATURE (DEGREES F) FOR EACH DRY BULB TEMPERATURE RANGE

Temperature Range	MAY Obsn Hour Gp 01 to 08	09 to 16	17 to 24	Total Obsn	MCWB	JUNE Obsn Hour Gp 01 to 08	09 to 16	17 to 24	Total Obsn	MCWB	JULY Obsn Hour Gp 01 to 08	09 to 16	17 to 24	Total Obsn	MCWB
80/84							0	0	0	61		2	1	3	63
75/79		0	0	0	58		3	3	6	59		8	5	13	61
70/74		2	3	5	54		10	8	18	58		16	13	29	59
65/69		7	5	12	52	0	20	12	32	56	1	32	19	52	57
60/64	0	16	12	28	50	1	37	25	63	53	4	54	32	90	55
55/59	1	35	21	57	48	11	71	47	129	51	32	79	68	179	53
50/54	7	65	45	117	46	63	70	84	217	49	122	56	92	270	50
45/49	55	84	81	220	44	116	28	51	195	45	79	2	17	98	46
40/44	109	35	62	206	40	42	1	8	51	41	11		0	11	42
35/39	50	4	16	70	36	6		1	7	37	0			0	38
30/34	19		2	21	31	1			1	32					
25/29	5		0	5	27										
20/24															
15/19															

Temperature Range	AUGUST Obsn Hour Gp 01 to 08	09 to 16	17 to 24	Total Obsn	MCWB	SEPTEMBER Obsn Hour Gp 01 to 08	09 to 16	17 to 24	Total Obsn	MCWB	OCTOBER Obsn Hour Gp 01 to 08	09 to 16	17 to 24	Total Obsn	MCWB
80/84		1	0	1	62										
75/79		2	1	3	62										
70/74		8	6	14	60		0	0	0	60					
65/69	0	22	12	34	58		4	2	6	56					
60/64	1	52	25	78	56	0	17	8	25	54		0		0	49
55/59	25	88	68	181	54	7	50	27	84	52	0	4	1	5	51
50/54	118	70	107	295	50	50	97	80	227	49	11	31	17	59	48
45/49	81	6	27	114	46	91	60	86	237	46	52	85	68	205	45
40/44	19	0	2	21	42	53	10	28	91	41	87	80	88	255	40
35/39	4		0	4	38	29	1	7	37	37	46	33	40	119	36
30/34						8	0	2	10	32	29	13	25	67	31
25/29						2		0	2	28	17	2	7	26	26
20/24											6	0	1	7	22
15/19											0		0	0	18

Temperature Range	NOVEMBER Obsn Hour Gp 01 to 08	09 to 16	17 to 24	Total Obsn	MCWB	DECEMBER Obsn Hour Gp 01 to 08	09 to 16	17 to 24	Total Obsn	MCWB	JANUARY Obsn Hour Gp 01 to 08	09 to 16	17 to 24	Total Obsn	MCWB	FEBRUARY Obsn Hour Gp 01 to 08	09 to 16	17 to 24	Total Obsn	MCWB	MARCH Obsn Hour Gp 01 to 08	09 to 16	17 to 24	Total Obsn	MCWB	APRIL Obsn Hour Gp 01 to 08	09 to 16	17 to 24	Total Obsn	MCWB	ANNUAL TOTAL Obsn Hour Gp 01 to 08	09 to 16	17 to 24	Total Obsn	MCWB
80/84																																3	1	4	62
75/79																																13	9	22	61
70/74																											0		0	51		36	30	66	59
65/69																											0	0	0	52	1	85	50	136	57
60/64																											2	2	4	48	6	178	104	288	54
55/59												0	0	0	44												7	5	12	46	76	334	237	647	52
50/54	2	2	1	5	48						0	0	0	0	43							1	0	1	41	0	22	12	34	43	373	414	438	1005	18
45/49	11	17	12	40	44	3	3	3	9	43	1	1	0	0	18	1	1	0	3	43	0	8	2	10	39	2	47	28	77	40	492	343	375	1210	45
40/44	47	60	53	160	40	22	27	24	73	40	6	8	7	21	39	8	16	11	35	39	5	36	21	62	38	25	85	60	170	38	434	358	364	1156	40
35/39	67	71	68	206	36	60	66	64	190	35	43	47	45	135	35	58	78	66	202	35	48	82	67	197	34	101	63	91	255	35	512	445	465	1422	35
30/34	53	46	52	151	31	59	54	56	169	31	46	55	53	154	31	57	50	56	163	31	78	68	81	227	31	68	9	32	109	31	418	295	359	1072	31
25/29	21	16	20	57	26	28	28	28	84	26	36	37	37	110	26	27	30	35	92	25	46	27	39	112	25	35	2	7	44	26	217	142	173	532	26
20/24	15	13	13	41	20	21	18	18	57	21	31	30	30	91	21	23	19	21	63	20	32	14	20	66	20	6	2	2	10	20	134	96	105	335	21
15/19	9	8	8	25	15	14	17	13	44	15	25	24	23	72	15	18	12	14	44	16	21	7	9	37	15	2	0	0	2	16	89	68	67	224	15
10/14	8	6	7	21	10	13	15	16	44	10	21	22	21	64	11	14	8	9	31	11	9	3	4	16	11	0			0	11	65	54	57	176	11
5/9	6	2	6	14	6	15	11	14	40	6	20	13	15	48	6	10	6	6	22	6	4	1	2	7	6	0			0	8	55	33	43	131	6
0/4	2	0	0	2	2	8	5	7	20	2	11	7	10	28	1	5	2	3	10	1	2	2	2	6	0						28	16	22	66	1
-5/-1						2	2	2	6	-3	6	3	4	13	-3	4	1	2	7	-4	1	0	0	1	-4						13	6	8	27	-3
-10/-6						2	1	2	5	-8	2	1	1	4	-7	1	0		1	-7	2			2	-9						7	2	3	12	-8
-15/-11						1	0		1	-12	1	0	0	1	-12	0			0	-11											2	0	0	2	-12
-20/-16												0	0	0	-17																	0	0	0	-17

KODIAK ALASKA

LAT 57 45N LONG 152 29W ELEV 73 FT

MEAN FREQUENCY OF OCCURRENCE OF DRY BULB TEMPERATURE (DEGREES F) WITH MEAN COINCIDENT WET BULB TEMPERATURE (DEGREES F) FOR EACH DRY BULB TEMPERATURE RANGE

Temperature Range	MAY Obsn Hour Gp 01 to 08	MAY 09 to 16	MAY 17 to 24	MAY Total Obsn	MAY MCWB	JUNE Obsn Hour Gp 01 to 08	JUNE 09 to 16	JUNE 17 to 24	JUNE Total Obsn	JUNE MCWB	JULY Obsn Hour Gp 01 to 08	JULY 09 to 16	JULY 17 to 24	JULY Total Obsn	JULY MCWB
80/84												0	0	0	66
75/79		0	0	0	55		1	0	1	58	0	2	1	3	63
70/74	0	1	0	1	53	0	2	1	3	57	1	5	2	8	60
65/69	0	2	1	3	52	1	5	4	10	55	3	16	10	29	58
60/64	1	4	2	7	50	4	14	11	29	53	9	41	27	77	55
55/59	2	11	6	19	47	10	38	25	73	50	34	75	57	166	52
50/54	8	33	15	56	45	41	76	56	173	48	126	91	113	330	50
45/49	36	87	56	179	42	123	89	108	320	45	70	17	38	125	47
40/44	119	95	121	335	40	54	14	33	101	42	5		1	6	42
35/39	67	13	42	122	35	6	0	2	8	37	0			0	38
30/34	13	1	4	18	30	1		0	1	32					
25/29	3	0	1	4	25										
20/24															
15/19															

Temperature Range	AUGUST Obsn Hour Gp 01 to 08	AUGUST 09 to 16	AUGUST 17 to 24	AUGUST Total Obsn	AUGUST MCWB	SEPTEMBER Obsn Hour Gp 01 to 08	SEPTEMBER 09 to 16	SEPTEMBER 17 to 24	SEPTEMBER Total Obsn	SEPTEMBER MCWB	OCTOBER Obsn Hour Gp 01 to 08	OCTOBER 09 to 16	OCTOBER 17 to 24	OCTOBER Total Obsn	OCTOBER MCWB
80/84		0		0	65										
75/79		1	0	1	65										
70/74	1	4	2	7	61		0		0	60					
65/69	1	18	7	26	58		2	0	2	57					
60/64	9	44	23	76	55	0	14	2	16	54		0		0	48
55/59	38	93	66	197	53	9	52	21	82	52	0	5	0	5	49
50/54	147	84	129	360	50	80	119	102	301	49	2	23	8	33	46
45/49	43	3	19	65	46	99	46	88	233	45	44	76	55	175	44
40/44	8		2	10	41	35	5	19	59	40	69	75	70	214	39
35/39	1		0	1	37	15	1	7	23	35	62	46	63	171	34
30/34						2		1	3	31	42	16	33	91	30
25/29						0			0	27	20	6	13	39	25
20/24											5	1	4	10	20
15/19											2	0	2	4	17

Temperature Range	NOVEMBER Obsn Hour Gp 01 to 08	09 to 16	17 to 24	Total Obsn	MCWB	DECEMBER Obsn Hour Gp 01 to 08	09 to 16	17 to 24	Total Obsn	MCWB	JANUARY Obsn Hour Gp 01 to 08	09 to 16	17 to 24	Total Obsn	MCWB
80/84															
75/79															
70/74															
65/69															
60/64															
55/59															
50/54		0		0	44	0	0	0	0	44	0	0	0	0	42
45/49	5	13	6	24	43	1	1	1	3	39	1	1	1	1	[illegible]
40/44	47	59	50	156	40	27	35	29	91	39	14	19	17	50	39
35/39	73	77	71	221	35	68	70	70	208	35	79	91	82	252	35
30/34	56	57	62	175	30	48	53	48	149	30	62	61	57	180	30
25/29	35	21	31	87	25	37	32	34	103	25	40	33	42	115	25
20/24	18	9	14	41	21	29	28	31	88	20	28	24	25	77	20
15/19	4	2	4	10	16	21	17	20	58	16	17	12	17	46	16
10/14	2	1	2	5	11	11	8	12	31	11	5	5	6	16	12
5/9	0	0	1	1	7	5	4	3	12	6	1	0	1	2	7
0/4						0	0	1	1	2	0		0	0	1
-5/-1											0		0	0	-3

Temperature Range	FEBRUARY Obsn Hour Gp 01 to 08	09 to 16	17 to 24	Total Obsn	MCWB	MARCH Obsn Hour Gp 01 to 08	09 to 16	17 to 24	Total Obsn	MCWB	APRIL Obsn Hour Gp 01 to 08	09 to 16	17 to 24	Total Obsn	MCWB	ANNUAL TOTAL Obsn Hour Gp 01 to 08	09 to 16	17 to 24	Total Obsn	MCWB
80/84																	0	0	0	65
75/79																0	4	1	5	62
70/74																2	12	5	19	59
65/69																5	43	22	70	57
60/64												2	0	2	49	23	119	65	207	54
55/59	0	0		0	41		0		0	48	1	1	1	3	47	94	275	176	545	52
50/54	0	1	0	1	42		1	0	1	43	1	6	3	10	43	405	434	426	1265	48
45/49	[illegible]	4	[illegible]	[illegible]	40	2	9	2	13	40	3	27	10	40	40	429	374	386	1189	44
40/44	9	25	13	47	38	10	43	17	70	37	27	89	52	168	38	424	459	424	1307	39
35/39	73	82	80	235	35	72	92	94	258	35	110	79	105	294	35	626	551	616	1793	35
30/34	57	52	57	166	30	73	49	64	186	30	61	26	47	134	30	415	315	373	1103	30
25/29	30	24	26	80	25	36	24	27	87	25	26	6	16	48	25	227	146	190	563	25
20/24	25	20	21	66	20	25	15	18	58	20	9	2	4	15	20	139	99	117	355	20
15/19	16	12	16	44	16	18	11	14	43	16	3		1	4	15	81	54	74	209	16
10/14	10	2	7	19	11	9	2	8	19	11						37	18	35	90	11
5/9	1	0	2	3	7	3	1	2	6	6						10	5	9	24	6
0/4	0	0		0	2	2	0	2	4	2						2	0	3	5	2
-5/-1						0			0	-2						0		0	0	-3

NOME MAP ALASKA

LAT 64 30N LONG 165 26W ELEV 13 FT

MEAN FREQUENCY OF OCCURRENCE OF DRY BULB TEMPERATURE (DEGREES F) WITH MEAN COINCIDENT WET BULB TEMPERATURE (DEGREES F) FOR EACH DRY BULB TEMPERATURE RANGE

Temperature Range	MAY Obsn Hour Gp 01 to 08	MAY 09 to 16	MAY 17 to 24	MAY Total Obsn	MAY MCWB	JUNE Obsn Hour Gp 01 to 08	JUNE 09 to 16	JUNE 17 to 24	JUNE Total Obsn	JUNE MCWB	JULY Obsn Hour Gp 01 to 08	JULY 09 to 16	JULY 17 to 24	JULY Total Obsn	JULY MCWB
80/84							0		0	61		0		0	55
75/79							1	0	1	59		0	0	0	58
70/74						0	2	1	3	57	0	2	1	3	59
65/69		1	0	1	51	2	6	3	11	54	1	6	4	11	58
60/64	0	3	1	4	49	5	12	10	27	53	8	25	13	46	55
55/59	3	8	6	17	47	11	23	20	54	50	25	55	41	121	53
50/54	8	17	11	36	45	28	47	39	114	47	63	77	72	212	49
45/49	19	34	24	77	42	53	57	55	165	44	91	70	85	246	45
40/44	33	48	42	123	39	72	62	66	200	40	49	13	29	91	41
35/39	60	61	61	182	35	48	27	36	111	36	10		2	12	36
30/34	71	53	64	188	31	19	4	9	32	32	1			1	33
25/29	28	15	24	67	26	1	0	0	1	27					
20/24	11	4	7	22	21										
15/19	6	3	3	12	16										
10/14	5	1	3	9	11										
5/9	3		1	4	7										
0/4	1		0	1	2										
-5/-1	0			0	-4										
-10/-6	0		0	0	-8										

Temperature Range	AUGUST Obsn Hour Gp 01 to 08	AUGUST 09 to 16	AUGUST 17 to 24	AUGUST Total Obsn	AUGUST MCWB	SEPTEMBER Obsn Hour Gp 01 to 08	SEPTEMBER 09 to 16	SEPTEMBER 17 to 24	SEPTEMBER Total Obsn	SEPTEMBER MCWB	OCTOBER Obsn Hour Gp 01 to 08	OCTOBER 09 to 16	OCTOBER 17 to 24	OCTOBER Total Obsn	OCTOBER MCWB
80/84		0		0	61										
75/79		0	0	0	61										
70/74	0	1	0	1	58										
65/69	0	3	3	6	57										
60/64	4	17	8	29	55		1	0	1	53					
55/59	21	55	34	110	53	1	14	3	18	51		1		1	45
50/54	72	100	86	258	50	14	42	21	77	48	0	2	1	3	44
45/49	102	63	91	256	46	59	87	68	214	44	3	6	3	12	43
40/44	34	7	20	61	41	65	62	66	193	40	17	26	17	60	39
35/39	12	0	6	18	36	44	28	46	118	35	35	59	37	131	35
30/34	2		1	3	32	39	5	29	73	30	51	69	59	179	30
25/29						15	1	6	22	26	54	44	53	151	25
20/24						3		1	4	22	38	23	37	98	21
15/19											26	13	23	62	16
10/14											13	4	11	28	12
5/9											7	1	6	14	7
0/4											2		0	2	3
-5/-1											0			0	-1
-10/-6															

Temperature Range	NOVEMBER Obsn Hour Gp 01 to 08	09 to 16	17 to 24	Total Obsn	MCWB	DECEMBER Obsn Hour Gp 01 to 08	09 to 16	17 to 24	Total Obsn	MCWB	JANUARY Obsn Hour Gp 01 to 08	09 to 16	17 to 24	Total Obsn	MCWB
80/84															
75/79															
70/74															
65/69															
60/64															
55/59															
50/54															
45/49															
40/44	0		0	0	38		0		0	36	0	0	1	1	37
35/39	6	8	6	20	34	1	1	1	3	33	5	6	5	16	34
30/34	35	37	35	107	31	8	9	9	26	30	16	17	17	50	31
25/29	35	36	32	103	26	21	20	19	60	26	18	19	19	56	26
20/24	31	36	34	101	21	23	22	23	68	21	20	22	22	64	21
15/19	39	38	38	115	16	23	21	22	66	16	21	22	22	65	16
10/14	30	29	32	91	11	23	24	23	70	11	22	24	22	68	11
5/9	22	19	20	61	6	26	29	26	81	6	31	26	26	83	6
0/4	18	16	14	48	2	26	24	26	76	1	27	26	26	79	1
-5/-1	11	12	11	34	-3	23	24	26	73	-4	20	27	25	72	-3
-10/-6	7	5	9	21	-8	21	19	18	58	-8	20	17	20	57	-8
-15/-11	5	3	6	14	-13	16	21	20	57	-13	15	16	14	45	-13
-20/-16	1	1	1	3	-18	20	16	16	52	-18	14	14	13	41	-18
-25/-21			0	0	-21	10	9	9	28	-23	11	9	12	32	-23
-30/-26						3	4	6	13	-27	6	3	4	13	-28
-35/-31						2	2	3	7	-32	1	0	1	2	-33
-40/-36						2	2	1	5			0		0	
-45/-41								0	0						

Temperature Range	FEBRUARY Obsn Hour Gp 01 to 08	09 to 16	17 to 24	Total Obsn	MCWB	MARCH Obsn Hour Gp 01 to 08	09 to 16	17 to 24	Total Obsn	MCWB	APRIL Obsn Hour Gp 01 to 08	09 to 16	17 to 24	Total Obsn	MCWB
80/84															
75/79															
70/74															
65/69															
60/64															
55/59															
50/54												0		0	42
45/49											0	1	0	1	41
40/44							0		0	36	1	4	2	7	37
35/39	0	1	1	2	34		2	0	2	32	10	23	13	46	34
30/34	10	13	13	36	30	9	18	14	41	30	37	53	41	131	31
25/29	17	17	15	49	26	26	26	25	77	26	38	39	41	118	26
20/24	21	23	19	63	21	18	26	20	64	21	25	36	31	92	21
15/19	22	24	23	69	16	22	33	23	78	16	27	33	31	91	16
10/14	20	20	21	61	11	28	34	29	91	11	21	26	25	72	11
5/9	21	25	21	67	6	25	36	30	91	6	23	17	23	63	6
0/4	15	20	18	53	1	22	28	28	78	1	22	5	17	44	2
-5/-1	19	20	19	58	-4	26	22	22	70	-3	18	2	9	29	-3
-10/-6	16	17	19	52	-8	20	12	24	56	-8	9	1	5	15	-8
-15/-11	19	17	17	53	-13	21	7	15	43	-13	7	0	2	9	-13
-20/-16	16	14	16	46	-18	14	4	9	27	-18	2		1	3	-18
-25/-21	10	7	12	29	-23	8	1	5	14	-23	1		0	1	-23
-30/-26	10	3	9	22	-28	6	1	2	9	-28	0			0	-27
-35/-31	7	1	3	11	-32	2	0	1	3	-33					
-40/-36	0			0		1			1						
-45/-41															

Temperature Range	ANNUAL TOTAL Obsn Hour Gp 01 to 08	09 to 16	17 to 24	Total Obsn	MCWB
80/84		0		0	58
75/79		1	0	1	59
70/74	0	5	2	7	58
65/69	3	16	10	29	57
60/64	17	58	32	107	54
55/59	61	156	104	321	52
50/54	185	285	230	700	48
45/49	327	318	326	971	45
40/44	271	222	243	736	40
35/39	231	216	214	661	35
30/34	298	278	291	867	31
25/29	253	217	234	704	26
20/24	190	192	194	576	21
15/19	186	187	185	558	16
10/14	162	162	166	490	11
5/9	158	153	153	464	6
0/4	133	119	129	381	1
-5/-1	117	107	112	336	-3
-10/-6	93	71	95	259	-8
-15/-11	83	64	74	221	-13
-20/-16	67	49	56	172	-18
-25/-21	40	26	38	104	-23
-30/-26	25	11	21	57	-28
-35/-31	12	3	8	23	-32
-40/-36	3	2	1	6	
-45/-41			0	0	

DAVIS-MONTHAN AFB/TUCSON ARIZONA

LAT 32 11N LONG 110 54W ELEV 2654 FT

MEAN FREQUENCY OF OCCURRENCE OF DRY BULB TEMPERATURE (DEGREES F) WITH MEAN COINCIDENT WET BULB TEMPERATURE (DEGREES F) FOR EACH DRY BULB TEMPERATURE RANGE

Temperature Range	MAY Obsn Hour Gp 01 to 08	MAY 09 to 16	MAY 17 to 24	MAY Total Obsn	MAY MCWB	JUNE Obsn Hour Gp 01 to 08	JUNE 09 to 16	JUNE 17 to 24	JUNE Total Obsn	JUNE MCWB	JULY Obsn Hour Gp 01 to 08	JULY 09 to 16	JULY 17 to 24	JULY Total Obsn	JULY MCWB
110/114							0		0	68					
105/109							5	1	6	67		3	1	4	68
100/104		3	1	4	64		28	13	41	66		28	14	42	68
95/99		15	7	22	62	0	50	32	82	64		61	34	95	68
90/94		43	21	64	59	1	63	47	111	62	2	71	50	123	68
85/89	1	56	34	91	57	12	47	49	108	60	20	51	55	126	67
80/84	5	53	42	100	55	39	30	42	111	59	72	23	49	144	67
75/79	15	38	46	99	54	50	12	30	92	57	100	8	31	139	66
70/74	36	22	43	101	51	57	3	18	78	54	51	3	13	67	66
65/69	57	11	30	98	49	48	0	6	54	50	3	0	1	4	63
60/64	67	4	15	86	46	26		1	27	47					
55/59	41	2	6	49	44	7			7	44					
50/54	19	1	2	22	41	0			0	41					
45/49	6	0	1	7	38										
40/44	2	0		2	34										
35/39	0			0	28										
30/34															

Temperature Range	AUGUST Obsn Hour Gp 01 to 08	AUGUST 09 to 16	AUGUST 17 to 24	AUGUST Total Obsn	AUGUST MCWB	SEPTEMBER Obsn Hour Gp 01 to 08	SEPTEMBER 09 to 16	SEPTEMBER 17 to 24	SEPTEMBER Total Obsn	SEPTEMBER MCWB	OCTOBER Obsn Hour Gp 01 to 08	OCTOBER 09 to 16	OCTOBER 17 to 24	OCTOBER Total Obsn	OCTOBER MCWB
110/114															
105/109		0		0	68										
100/104		9	3	12	69		3	0	3	69					
95/99		37	20	57	69		34	10	44	66		2	0	2	61
90/94	0	75	39	114	69		54	26	80	65		18	4	22	61
85/89	5	67	51	123	69	1	64	44	109	65		41	14	55	59
80/84	39	42	62	143	68	20	47	54	121	64	0	56	23	79	58
75/79	110	14	49	173	67	57	23	52	132	63	3	52	40	95	57
70/74	84	3	20	107	66	80	11	37	128	61	21	37	50	108	55
65/69	10	0	3	13	63	55	3	13	71	57	53	21	49	123	53
60/64			0	0	61	21	0	3	24	52	70	11	37	118	50
55/59						5		1	6	48	54	6	19	79	47
50/54						1			1	43	29	2	8	39	44
45/49											12	1	3	16	40
40/44											4	1	1	6	38
35/39											0		0	0	30
30/34											0			0	26

Temperature Range	NOVEMBER					DECEMBER					JANUARY					FEBRUARY					MARCH					APRIL					ANNUAL TOTAL				
	Obsn Hour Gp 01 to 08	Obsn Hour Gp 09 to 16	Obsn Hour Gp 17 to 24	Total Obsn	MCWB	Obsn Hour Gp 01 to 08	Obsn Hour Gp 09 to 16	Obsn Hour Gp 17 to 24	Total Obsn	MCWB	Obsn Hour Gp 01 to 08	Obsn Hour Gp 09 to 16	Obsn Hour Gp 17 to 24	Total Obsn	MCWB	Obsn Hour Gp 01 to 08	Obsn Hour Gp 09 to 16	Obsn Hour Gp 17 to 24	Total Obsn	MCWB	Obsn Hour Gp 01 to 08	Obsn Hour Gp 09 to 16	Obsn Hour Gp 17 to 24	Total Obsn	MCWB	Obsn Hour Gp 01 to 08	Obsn Hour Gp 09 to 16	Obsn Hour Gp 17 to 24	Total Obsn	MCWB	Obsn Hour Gp 01 to 08	Obsn Hour Gp 09 to 16	Obsn Hour Gp 17 to 24	Total Obsn	MCWB
110/114																																0		0	68
105/109																																8	2	10	68
100/104																											0		0	62		71	31	102	67
95/99																											1	0	1	61	0	200	103	303	66
90/94							0		0	63												0	0	0	58		9	3	12	58	3	333	190	526	65
85/89		1		1	55												1	0	1	59		3	1	4	56		19	8	27	56	39	350	256	645	63
80/84		16	2	18	55		1		1	53		1	0	1	55		3	1	4	56		16	5	21	54		42	21	63	54	175	330	301	806	62
75/79		34	8	42	53		8	1	9	52		5	1	6	52		12	3	15	53	0	28	15	[illegible]	[illegible]	0	[illegible]	[illegible]	[illegible]	[illegible]	[illegible]	[illegible]	[illegible]	[illegible]	[illegible]
70/74	0	[illegible]	17	[illegible]	[illegible]		14	4	28	50		19	5	24	50	0	24	11	35	51	1	43	25	69	50	6	46	42	94	50	336	280	285	901	56
65/69	3	47	31	81	50	0	41	12	53	49	0	34	12	46	48	1	38	21	60	49	2	42	35	79	48	20	33	46	99	48	252	270	259	781	51
60/64	18	42	49	109	48	3	41	26	70	47	1	51	28	80	47	4	43	37	84	47	11	43	45	99	46	44	21	40	105	46	265	256	281	802	48
55/59	51	27	54	132	46	16	46	46	108	46	12	49	48	109	45	21	43	44	108	45	32	33	46	111	44	61	11	28	100	44	300	217	292	809	45
50/54	65	18	42	125	43	42	39	59	140	43	37	41	55	133	43	40	32	46	118	42	66	22	38	126	42	58	6	12	76	41	357	161	262	780	42
45/49	58	7	23	88	40	60	28	50	138	40	53	26	47	126	39	54	17	32	103	39	63	12	24	99	39	35	1	5	41	39	341	92	185	618	40
40/44	28	3	10	41	37	68	12	32	112	37	70	14	30	114	36	48	8	18	74	36	45	4	10	59	36	14	0	1	15	36	279	42	102	423	36
35/39	13	1	3	17	34	38	6	14	58	33	43	7	15	65	32	36	3	8	47	32	20	1	4	25	32	3	0	0	3	34	153	18	44	215	32
30/34	4	0	1	5	31	16	1	3	20	29	20	2	6	28	28	17	1	2	20	28	7	0	1	8	28	0			0	33	64	4	13	81	29
25/29	0	0		0	26	4	0	1	5	25	9	1	2	12	23	3	0	0	3	24	1			1	22						17	1	3	21	24
20/24						1			1	21	3	0	0	3	18	0			0	22	0			0	17						4	0	0	4	19
15/19											1			1	16																1			1	16

FLAGSTAFF ARIZONA

LAT 35 08N LONG 111 40W ELEV 7006 FT

MEAN FREQUENCY OF OCCURRENCE OF DRY BULB TEMPERATURE (DEGREES F) WITH MEAN COINCIDENT WET BULB TEMPERATURE (DEGREES F) FOR EACH DRY BULB TEMPERATURE RANGE

Temperature Range	MAY Obsn Hour Gp 01 to 08	MAY Obsn Hour Gp 09 to 16	MAY Obsn Hour Gp 17 to 24	MAY Total Obsn	MAY MCWB	JUNE Obsn Hour Gp 01 to 08	JUNE Obsn Hour Gp 09 to 16	JUNE Obsn Hour Gp 17 to 24	JUNE Total Obsn	JUNE MCWB	JULY Obsn Hour Gp 01 to 08	JULY Obsn Hour Gp 09 to 16	JULY Obsn Hour Gp 17 to 24	JULY Total Obsn	JULY MCWB
90/94							0		0	56					
85/89		0		0	55		4	1	5	54		9	3	12	56
80/84		2	1	3	54	0	29	10	39	52	0	49	18	67	56
75/79		9	3	12	50	2	55	22	79	51	3	74	30	107	56
70/74	1	33	12	46	48	9	56	31	96	49	14	64	35	113	56
65/69	3	55	24	82	46	20	48	37	105	47	35	33	54	122	55
60/64	12	57	33	102	44	26	30	43	99	46	48	13	57	118	54
55/59	21	33	37	91	42	34	12	39	85	44	71	5	43	119	52
50/54	30	24	40	94	40	39	4	25	68	42	54	0	10	64	47
45/49	38	17	38	93	37	40	1	18	59	38	19		0	19	43
40/44	39	10	28	77	35	34	0	11	45	35	3			3	36
35/39	47	5	19	71	32	24		4	28	31	1			1	32
30/34	37	2	11	50	29	10		0	10	27					
25/29	16	0	3	19	25	2			2	23					
20/24	5		0	5	21	0			0	21					
15/19	1			1	18										
10/14															

Temperature Range	AUGUST Obsn Hour Gp 01 to 08	AUGUST Obsn Hour Gp 09 to 16	AUGUST Obsn Hour Gp 17 to 24	AUGUST Total Obsn	AUGUST MCWB	SEPTEMBER Obsn Hour Gp 01 to 08	SEPTEMBER Obsn Hour Gp 09 to 16	SEPTEMBER Obsn Hour Gp 17 to 24	SEPTEMBER Total Obsn	SEPTEMBER MCWB	OCTOBER Obsn Hour Gp 01 to 08	OCTOBER Obsn Hour Gp 09 to 16	OCTOBER Obsn Hour Gp 17 to 24	OCTOBER Total Obsn	OCTOBER MCWB
90/94															
85/89		2	0	2	56		1		1	54					
80/84		21	6	27	56		10	1	11	54		0		0	52
75/79	0	68	22	90	56	0	43	9	52	53		6	1	7	50
70/74	5	76	28	109	56	1	61	16	78	52		28	5	33	48
65/69	21	50	45	116	56	6	59	25	90	51		53	11	64	47
60/64	36	20	55	111	54	15	38	34	87	50	1	56	17	74	45
55/59	74	9	59	142	53	27	20	51	98	49	6	43	27	76	44
50/54	63	1	26	90	49	51	8	53	112	47	17	25	40	82	42
45/49	34		7	41	44	52	1	31	84	43	31	17	56	104	40
40/44	12		0	12	39	46		16	62	38	44	9	45	98	37
35/39	2			2	35	30		2	32	34	57	5	33	95	33
30/34						10		0	10	30	52	4	10	66	29
25/29						2			2	25	30	1	3	34	26
20/24											8		0	8	21
15/19											2			2	16
10/14											0			0	14

Temperature Range	NOVEMBER Obsn Hour Gp 01 to 08	NOVEMBER Obsn Hour Gp 09 to 16	NOVEMBER Obsn Hour Gp 17 to 24	NOVEMBER Total Obsn	NOVEMBER MCWB	DECEMBER Obsn Hour Gp 01 to 08	DECEMBER Obsn Hour Gp 09 to 16	DECEMBER Obsn Hour Gp 17 to 24	DECEMBER Total Obsn	DECEMBER MCWB	JANUARY Obsn Hour Gp 01 to 08	JANUARY Obsn Hour Gp 09 to 16	JANUARY Obsn Hour Gp 17 to 24	JANUARY Total Obsn	JANUARY MCWB
90/94															
85/89															
80/84															
75/79															
70/74															
65/69		4		4	45		0		0	44					
60/64		14	1	15	43		1		1	44		0		0	41
55/59		26	4	30	41		7		7	40		4		4	41
50/54	0	39	7	46	39		22	2	24	38		15	2	17	39
45/49	3	42	18	63	37	0	41	6	47	36		28	7	35	36
40/44	17	41	38	96	36	4	42	20	66	33	3	37	17	57	33
35/39	32	27	45	104	33	20	49	34	103	31	13	51	27	91	31
30/34	49	26	52	127	29	34	38	48	120	28	28	46	52	126	28
25/29	49	13	40	102	25	49	26	56	131	24	55	34	62	151	25
20/24	46	5	23	74	20	46	12	46	104	20	45	18	34	97	20
15/19	23	1	7	31	16	43	7	19	69	16	33	8	18	59	16
10/14	9	0	4	13	11	28	2	11	41	11	28	4	13	45	11
5/9	6		1	7	6	14	0	3	17	7	20	1	8	29	6
0/4	3		0	3	2	6		1	7	2	8	1	4	13	2
-5/-1	1		0	1	-3	3	0	1	4	-3	10	0	4	14	-3
-10/-6	1			1	-7	0		0	0	-7	3		0	3	-8
-15/-11	0			0	-11	1		0	1	-13	0		0	0	-12
-20/-16											0		0	0	-18

Temperature Range	FEBRUARY Obsn Hour Gp 01 to 08	FEBRUARY Obsn Hour Gp 09 to 16	FEBRUARY Obsn Hour Gp 17 to 24	FEBRUARY Total Obsn	FEBRUARY MCWB	MARCH Obsn Hour Gp 01 to 08	MARCH Obsn Hour Gp 09 to 16	MARCH Obsn Hour Gp 17 to 24	MARCH Total Obsn	MARCH MCWB	APRIL Obsn Hour Gp 01 to 08	APRIL Obsn Hour Gp 09 to 16	APRIL Obsn Hour Gp 17 to 24	APRIL Total Obsn	APRIL MCWB
90/94															
85/89															
80/84															
75/79												1	0	1	48
70/74												5	1	6	46
65/69		1		1	44		1		1	44		17	5	22	45
60/64		3	0	3	43		6	1	7	42	0	36	11	47	43
55/59		9	2	11	41		19	5	24	40	4	49	23	76	41
50/54		21	6	27	39	0	38	12	50	38	10	45	35	90	39
45/49		31	12	43	36	2	45	26	73	35	23	33	41	97	37
40/44	4	36	19	59	34	10	42	35	87	33	37	23	45	105	35
35/39	17	42	35	94	32	27	36	41	104	31	46	17	34	97	32
30/34	30	39	53	122	29	51	30	41	122	28	53	11	26	90	29
25/29	54	25	49	128	24	57	24	42	123	24	41	3	16	60	25
20/24	45	13	31	89	20	46	7	27	80	20	19		4	23	21
15/19	31	4	10	45	16	28	1	11	40	16	6			6	16
10/14	21	1	4	26	11	16		3	19	12	2			2	12
5/9	11	0	1	12	6	5		1	6	7	0			0	7
0/4	6		1	7	2	4		0	4	2					
-5/-1	3		1	4	-3	1			1	-3					
-10/-6	1		0	1	-8	0			0	-8					
-15/-11	1		0	1	-13										
-20/-16															

Temperature Range	ANNUAL TOTAL Obsn Hour Gp 01 to 08	ANNUAL TOTAL Obsn Hour Gp 09 to 16	ANNUAL TOTAL Obsn Hour Gp 17 to 24	ANNUAL TOTAL Total Obsn	ANNUAL TOTAL MCWB
90/94		0		0	56
85/89		16	4	20	56
80/84	0	111	36	147	55
75/79	5	256	87	348	54
70/74	30	323	128	481	52
65/69	85	321	201	607	50
60/64	138	274	252	664	48
55/59	237	236	290	763	46
50/54	264	242	258	764	42
45/49	242	256	260	758	38
40/44	253	240	274	767	35
35/39	316	232	274	822	32
30/34	354	196	293	843	29
25/29	355	126	271	752	25
20/24	260	55	165	480	20
15/19	167	21	65	253	16
10/14	104	7	35	146	11
5/9	56	1	14	71	7
0/4	27	1	6	34	2
-5/-1	18	0	6	24	-3
-10/-6	5		0	5	-8
-15/-11	2		0	2	-13
-20/-16	0		0	0	-18

FORT HUACHUCA/LIBBY AAF ARIZONA

LAT 31 35N LONG 110 20W ELEV 4664 FT

MEAN FREQUENCY OF OCCURRENCE OF DRY BULB TEMPERATURE (DEGREES F) WITH MEAN COINCIDENT WET BULB TEMPERATURE (DEGREES F) FOR EACH DRY BULB TEMPERATURE RANGE

Temperature Range	MAY Obsn Hour Gp 01 to 08	MAY 09 to 16	MAY 17 to 24	MAY Total Obsn	MAY MCWB	JUNE Obsn Hour Gp 01 to 08	JUNE 09 to 16	JUNE 17 to 24	JUNE Total Obsn	JUNE MCWB	JULY Obsn Hour Gp 01 to 08	JULY 09 to 16	JULY 17 to 24	JULY Total Obsn	JULY MCWB
100/104							0		0	63		0		0	65
95/99		1	0	1	60		13	3	16	62		9	2	11	63
90/94		7	2	9	58		48	15	63	60		34	11	45	64
85/89		41	13	54	56	2	71	35	108	59	1	68	25	94	64
80/84	1	62	27	90	54	12	58	49	119	57	10	71	44	125	64
75/79	6	57	38	101	52	37	33	59	129	56	38	44	63	145	63
70/74	21	44	54	119	50	66	12	48	126	54	80	16	62	158	62
65/69	48	21	50	119	48	59	4	23	86	52	101	6	37	144	62
60/64	61	10	36	107	46	44	0	7	51	48	17	1	4	22	60
55/59	57	4	18	79	43	16		1	17	45			0	0	59
50/54	33	1	6	40	41	3			3	43					
45/49	14	1	2	17	38	0			0	42					
40/44	4	0	1	5	35										
35/39	2			2	32										
30/34															

Temperature Range	AUGUST Obsn Hour Gp 01 to 08	AUGUST 09 to 16	AUGUST 17 to 24	AUGUST Total Obsn	AUGUST MCWB	SEPTEMBER Obsn Hour Gp 01 to 08	SEPTEMBER 09 to 16	SEPTEMBER 17 to 24	SEPTEMBER Total Obsn	SEPTEMBER MCWB	OCTOBER Obsn Hour Gp 01 to 08	OCTOBER 09 to 16	OCTOBER 17 to 24	OCTOBER Total Obsn	OCTOBER MCWB
100/104															
95/99		1	0	1	65		0		0	61					
90/94		16	4	20	65		9	1	10	61		0		0	58
85/89	0	53	16	69	65		42	8	50	61		8	1	9	57
80/84	2	86	31	119	65	1	75	24	100	61		34	5	39	56
75/79	18	63	59	140	64	6	61	42	109	60		64	14	78	54
70/74	65	23	77	165	63	32	35	69	136	59	3	63	27	93	53
65/69	118	5	53	176	62	86	13	60	159	57	16	41	57	114	52
60/64	42	1	8	51	60	81	4	29	114	55	55	21	66	142	50
55/59	2		0	2	55	26	1	4	31	51	71	10	45	126	47
50/54						6	0	2	8	46	60	4	21	85	44
45/49						1		0	1	41	27	2	7	36	40
40/44						0			0	39	11	1	3	15	37
35/39											3	1	1	5	34
30/34											1	0	1	2	32

Temperature Range	NOVEMBER Obsn Hour Gp 01 to 08	NOVEMBER Obsn Hour Gp 09 to 16	NOVEMBER Obsn Hour Gp 17 to 24	NOVEMBER Total Obsn	NOVEMBER MCWB	DECEMBER Obsn Hour Gp 01 to 08	DECEMBER Obsn Hour Gp 09 to 16	DECEMBER Obsn Hour Gp 17 to 24	DECEMBER Total Obsn	DECEMBER MCWB	JANUARY Obsn Hour Gp 01 to 08	JANUARY Obsn Hour Gp 09 to 16	JANUARY Obsn Hour Gp 17 to 24	JANUARY Total Obsn	JANUARY MCWB	FEBRUARY Obsn Hour Gp 01 to 08	FEBRUARY Obsn Hour Gp 09 to 16	FEBRUARY Obsn Hour Gp 17 to 24	FEBRUARY Total Obsn	FEBRUARY MCWB
100/104																				
95/99																				
90/94																				
85/89																				
80/84		0		0	53												1	0	1	55
75/79		11	0	11	51		1		1	50		1	0	1	50		3	0	3	52
70/74		38	4	42	50		7	0	7	48		5	0	5	49		11	2	13	49
65/69	0	48	10	58	48		25	2	27	47		22	2	24	47		29	7	36	47
60/64	3	48	28	79	47	0	44	9	53	45		37	9	46	44	1	40	17	58	45
[illegible]	[illegible]	11	[illegible]	117	[illegible]	3	48	21	72	43	3	49	26	78	43	6	42	33	81	43
50/54	48	26	59	133	43	13	45	43	101	42	13	49	44	106	41	26	39	44	109	41
45/49	63	15	42	120	39	39	39	67	145	39	37	43	59	139	38	42	32	47	121	38
40/44	50	8	24	82	36	60	23	51	134	36	60	25	55	140	36	53	16	37	106	35
35/39	34	3	15	52	32	72	11	35	118	33	68	12	30	110	32	48	8	23	79	31
30/34	14	1	3	18	29	42	4	15	61	29	35	4	16	55	28	33	3	11	47	28
25/29	4	0	1	5	24	14	1	4	19	25	21	1	7	29	24	13	1	3	17	24
20/24	0			0	20	4	0	0	4	21	9	0	1	10	20	3	0	1	4	20
15/19	0			0	17	0			0	15	2	0	0	2	16	1	0	0	1	16
10/14											0	0	0	0	10	0			0	14
5/9											0			0	8					

Temperature Range	MARCH Obsn Hour Gp 01 to 08	MARCH Obsn Hour Gp 09 to 16	MARCH Obsn Hour Gp 17 to 24	MARCH Total Obsn	MARCH MCWB	APRIL Obsn Hour Gp 01 to 08	APRIL Obsn Hour Gp 09 to 16	APRIL Obsn Hour Gp 17 to 24	APRIL Total Obsn	APRIL MCWB	ANNUAL TOTAL Obsn Hour Gp 01 to 08	ANNUAL TOTAL Obsn Hour Gp 09 to 16	ANNUAL TOTAL Obsn Hour Gp 17 to 24	ANNUAL TOTAL Total Obsn	ANNUAL TOTAL MCWB
100/104												0		0	64
95/99												24	5	29	62
90/94							0	0	0	55		114	33	147	62
85/89							4	1	5	55	3	287	99	389	61
80/84		2	0	2	52		17	4	21	53	26	406	184	616	60
75/79		15	3	18	50	0	44	13	57	51	105	397	291	793	58
70/74		34	9	43	48	2	58	26	86	49	269	346	378	993	56
65/69	0	43	19	62	46	8	50	43	101	47	436	307	363	1106	54
60/64	5	46	34	85	44	[illegible]	[illegible]	[illegible]	110	[illegible]	[illegible]	[illegible]	[illegible]	[illegible]	[illegible]
[illegible]	20	39	49	108	42	56	18	47	121	43	283	252	297	832	44
50/54	45	33	51	129	40	63	9	29	101	40	310	206	299	815	41
45/49	62	21	37	120	38	45	4	15	64	38	330	157	276	763	39
40/44	52	10	26	88	35	24	1	6	31	35	314	84	203	601	36
35/39	36	4	15	55	32	12	0	1	13	32	275	39	120	434	32
30/34	21	1	4	26	29	2		0	2	31	148	13	50	211	29
25/29	5	0	1	6	24						57	3	16	76	24
20/24	1		0	1	22						17	0	2	19	20
15/19											3	0	0	3	16
10/14											0	0	0	0	10
5/9											0			0	8

LUKE AFB/GLENDALE ARIZONA

LAT 33 33N LONG 112 22W ELEV 1101 FT

MEAN FREQUENCY OF OCCURRENCE OF DRY BULB TEMPERATURE (DEGREES F) WITH MEAN COINCIDENT WET BULB TEMPERATURE (DEGREES F) FOR EACH DRY BULB TEMPERATURE RANGE

Temperature Range	MAY Obsn Hour Gp 01 to 08	MAY 09 to 16	MAY 17 to 24	MAY Total Obsn	MAY MCWB	JUNE Obsn Hour Gp 01 to 08	JUNE 09 to 16	JUNE 17 to 24	JUNE Total Obsn	JUNE MCWB	JULY Obsn Hour Gp 01 to 08	JULY 09 to 16	JULY 17 to 24	JULY Total Obsn	JULY MCWB
115/119							1	0	1	70		1	1	2	73
110/114		0	0	0	66		7	5	12	70		9	7	16	72
105/109		2	2	4	66		24	17	41	69		39	30	69	72
100/104		11	7	18	65		38	27	65	67		67	50	117	71
95/99		32	21	53	63	0	50	40	90	65	2	61	56	119	71
90/94	0	45	29	74	61	7	46	44	97	63	27	47	61	135	70
85/89	2	47	37	86	59	24	36	43	103	62	92	18	29	139	68
80/84	9	44	44	97	57	48	23	32	103	59	81	6	9	96	67
75/79	30	33	45	108	55	57	11	20	88	57	38	1	3	42	66
70/74	51	19	31	101	53	53	3	8	64	54	7	0	0	7	60
65/69	61	9	20	90	51	34	0	3	37	52	1			1	54
60/64	53	4	9	66	49	14	0	0	14	49					
55/59	31	1	3	35	46	2			2	46					
50/54	10	0	1	11	44	0			0	46					
45/49	2		0	2	38										
40/44	0			0	35										
35/39															
30/34															

Temperature Range	AUGUST Obsn Hour Gp 01 to 08	AUGUST 09 to 16	AUGUST 17 to 24	AUGUST Total Obsn	AUGUST MCWB	SEPTEMBER Obsn Hour Gp 01 to 08	SEPTEMBER 09 to 16	SEPTEMBER 17 to 24	SEPTEMBER Total Obsn	SEPTEMBER MCWB	OCTOBER Obsn Hour Gp 01 to 08	OCTOBER 09 to 16	OCTOBER 17 to 24	OCTOBER Total Obsn	OCTOBER MCWB
115/119		0		0	75										
110/114		2	1	3	74										
105/109		19	12	31	73		6	3	9	71					
100/104		52	37	89	73		26	14	40	70		0	0	0	64
95/99	1	65	49	115	72		45	25	70	69		8	2	10	66
90/94	12	58	58	128	71	1	55	42	98	67		27	9	36	64
85/89	61	36	49	146	71	11	49	45	105	66		46	20	66	62
80/84	92	13	28	133	70	39	34	48	121	65	0	50	28	78	60
75/79	64	3	11	78	69	62	17	35	114	64	4	44	41	89	59
70/74	16	0	2	18	64	63	6	20	89	60	23	35	49	107	57
65/69	3			3	54	40	1	6	47	56	51	22	49	122	55
60/64	1			1	50	19	0	1	20	53	70	10	31	111	52
55/59		0		0	41	4	0	1	5	49	62	4	14	80	48
50/54						1			1	49	27	1	4	32	44
45/49											8	1	1	10	41
40/44											2		0	2	36
35/39											1		0	1	30
30/34											0			0	27

LUKE AFB/GLENDALE ARIZONA

Temperature Range	NOVEMBER Obsn Hour Gp 01 to 08	09 to 16	17 to 24	Total Obsn	M C W B	DECEMBER Obsn Hour Gp 01 to 08	09 to 16	17 to 24	Total Obsn	M C W B	JANUARY Obsn Hour Gp 01 to 08	09 to 16	17 to 24	Total Obsn	M C W B	FEBRUARY Obsn Hour Gp 01 to 08	09 to 16	17 to 24	Total Obsn	M C W B
115/119																				
110/114																				
105/109																				
100/104																				
95/99																				
90/94		0		0	64												0		0	64
85/89		4	1	5	59		0		0	54		0		0	60		1	0	1	60
80/84		15	3	18	57		1		1	54		0	0	0	57		5	2	7	58
75/79		34	10	44	56		8	1	9	54		3	1	4	54		13	7	20	55
70/74	0	46	19	65	54		21	5	26	52		18	6	24	52		30	16	46	53
65/69	4	48	33	85	53	0	35	13	48	51		39	17	56	50	0	42	29	71	51
60/64	14	45	54	113	51	2	48	27	77	49	1	48	31	80	49	5	46	44	95	49
55/59	47	27	60	134	48	9	47	45	101	47	13	48	49	110	47	28	39	50	117	47
50/54	71	15	38	124	44	24	39	65	128	44	34	41	57	132	44	50	28	42	120	44
45/49	59	5	16	80	41	64	29	56	149	41	55	26	47	128	40	60	14	24	98	41
40/44	32	2	5	39	37	82	15	29	126	37	67	17	25	109	36	48	5	9	62	36
35/39	11	0	2	13	34	53	3	6	62	33	46	5	11	62	32	26	1	2	29	33
30/34	3			3	31	12	1	1	14	29	26	2	4	32	28	6			6	28
25/29						1			1	25	6	0	0	6	23	0			0	25
20/24											1			1	20					

Temperature Range	MARCH Obsn Hour Gp 01 to 08	09 to 16	17 to 24	Total Obsn	M C W B	APRIL Obsn Hour Gp 01 to 08	09 to 16	17 to 24	Total Obsn	M C W B	ANNUAL TOTAL Obsn Hour Gp 01 to 08	09 to 16	17 to 24	Total Obsn	M C W B
115/119												2	1	3	72
110/114												18	13	31	71
105/109												90	64	154	71
100/104							0	0	0	64		194	135	329	70
95/99							4	2	6	62	3	265	195	463	68
90/94		1	1	2	59	0	14	8	22	60	47	293	252	592	67
85/89		6	3	9	58		31	18	49	58	190	274	245	709	65
80/84		20	11	31	56	0	41	27	68	56	269	252	232	753	62
75/79	0	31	19	50	55	1	46	37	84	54	256	244	230	730	59
70/74	0	41	31	72	53	9	38	44	91	52	222	257	231	710	55
65/69	4	45	42	91	51	31	33	44	108	50	229	274	256	759	52
60/64	18	45	49	112	48	59	21	32	112	48	256	267	278	801	49
55/59	46	33	45	124	47	66	9	18	93	46	308	208	285	801	47
50/54	75	17	30	122	44	45	3	7	55	43	337	144	244	725	44
45/49	61	7	12	80	41	23	1	2	26	40	332	83	158	573	41
40/44	30	1	4	35	37	5		0	5	37	266	40	72	378	37
35/39	11	0	1	12	33	0			0	37	148	9	22	179	33
30/34	2			2	28						49	3	5	57	28
25/29	0			0	23						7	0	0	7	24
20/24		0		0	23						1	0		1	20

YUMA MCAS/IAP ARIZONA

LAT 32 39N LONG 114 37W ELEV 213 FT

MEAN FREQUENCY OF OCCURRENCE OF DRY BULB TEMPERATURE (DEGREES F) WITH MEAN COINCIDENT WET BULB TEMPERATURE (DEGREES F) FOR EACH DRY BULB TEMPERATURE RANGE

Temperature Range	MAY Obsn Hour Gp 01 to 08	MAY 09 to 16	MAY 17 to 24	MAY Total Obsn	MAY MCWB	JUNE Obsn Hour Gp 01 to 08	JUNE 09 to 16	JUNE 17 to 24	JUNE Total Obsn	JUNE MCWB	JULY Obsn Hour Gp 01 to 08	JULY 09 to 16	JULY 17 to 24	JULY Total Obsn	JULY MCWB
120/124															
115/119							1	0	1	70		1	1	2	73
110/114		1	0	1	66		9	6	15	69		14	7	21	73
105/109		3	2	5	65		27	16	43	68		50	30	80	72
100/104		14	7	21	64		42	25	67	67		70	42	112	72
95/99		37	20	57	62		55	35	90	65	1	57	51	109	72
90/94	0	50	31	81	61	3	46	44	93	64	23	39	64	126	71
85/89	2	48	36	86	59	28	34	44	106	63	112	13	39	164	70
80/84	10	42	44	96	58	55	17	37	109	61	83	3	10	96	69
75/79	33	29	45	107	56	69	6	22	97	58	22	1	3	26	64
70/74	61	16	31	108	55	53	2	7	62	57	5		0	5	58
65/69	69	7	17	93	53	24	1	2	27	54	0			0	54
60/64	41	1	12	54	50	7		1	8	51					
55/59	24	0	3	27	47	2		0	2	49					
50/54	6		0	6	45										
45/49	1			1	42										

Temperature Range	AUGUST Obsn Hour Gp 01 to 08	AUGUST 09 to 16	AUGUST 17 to 24	AUGUST Total Obsn	AUGUST MCWB	SEPTEMBER Obsn Hour Gp 01 to 08	SEPTEMBER 09 to 16	SEPTEMBER 17 to 24	SEPTEMBER Total Obsn	SEPTEMBER MCWB	OCTOBER Obsn Hour Gp 01 to 08	OCTOBER 09 to 16	OCTOBER 17 to 24	OCTOBER Total Obsn	OCTOBER MCWB
120/124							0		0	72					
115/119		0	0	0	74			0	0	72					
110/114		7	2	9	72		4	0	4	72					
105/109		45	19	64	73		28	9	37	71		0		0	68
100/104		70	38	108	73	0	49	21	70	70		13	3	16	67
95/99	0	59	49	108	73	0	55	33	88	70		33	10	43	65
90/94	16	44	72	132	72	3	48	48	99	69		45	18	63	64
85/89	104	17	47	168	72	33	33	59	125	69	0	48	31	79	63
80/84	89	5	17	111	70	71	16	42	129	67	8	39	48	95	62
75/79	28	2	3	33	66	61	5	21	87	64	31	32	53	116	60
70/74	9	0	1	10	62	46	1	6	53	59	53	22	43	118	58
65/69	1			1	55	21		1	22	56	72	10	26	108	56
60/64						3			3	53	54	3	11	68	52
55/59						0			0	46	21	1	4	26	47
50/54											8	0	1	9	44
45/49											1			1	41

YUMA MCAS/IAP ARIZONA

Temperature Range	NOVEMBER Obsn Hour Gp 01 to 08	NOVEMBER Obsn Hour Gp 09 to 16	NOVEMBER Obsn Hour Gp 17 to 24	NOVEMBER Total Obsn	NOVEMBER MCWB	DECEMBER Obsn Hour Gp 01 to 08	DECEMBER Obsn Hour Gp 09 to 16	DECEMBER Obsn Hour Gp 17 to 24	DECEMBER Total Obsn	DECEMBER MCWB	JANUARY Obsn Hour Gp 01 to 08	JANUARY Obsn Hour Gp 09 to 16	JANUARY Obsn Hour Gp 17 to 24	JANUARY Total Obsn	JANUARY MCWB
120/124															
115/119															
110/114															
105/109															
100/104															
95/99		0		0	61										
90/94		2	0	2	60										
85/89		15	3	18	59		0		0	55		0		0	58
80/84		32	6	38	58		4	0	4	56		3	0	3	56
75/79	0	44	18	62	56		20	3	23	54		13	3	16	54
70/74	2	47	34	83	54		42	11	53	51		32	11	43	52
65/69	11	42	52	105	52	0	53	26	79	50		49	24	73	50
60/64	43	30	57	130	49	6	51	51	108	48	3	50	45	98	48
55/59	66	17	41	124	46	35	39	70	144	46	28	46	63	137	46
50/54	65	8	21	94	43	71	24	55	150	42	62	29	54	145	43
45/49	36	2	7	45	40	81	12	27	120	39	73	16	32	121	40
40/44	13	1	2	16	36	43	3	4	50	36	52	7	13	72	36
35/39	3	0		3	33	11	0	1	12	31	24	2	3	29	32
30/34	0			0	31	1		0	1	29	7	0	0	7	27
25/29											0			0	22

Temperature Range	FEBRUARY Obsn Hour Gp 01 to 08	FEBRUARY Obsn Hour Gp 09 to 16	FEBRUARY Obsn Hour Gp 17 to 24	FEBRUARY Total Obsn	FEBRUARY MCWB	MARCH Obsn Hour Gp 01 to 08	MARCH Obsn Hour Gp 09 to 16	MARCH Obsn Hour Gp 17 to 24	MARCH Total Obsn	MARCH MCWB	APRIL Obsn Hour Gp 01 to 08	APRIL Obsn Hour Gp 09 to 16	APRIL Obsn Hour Gp 17 to 24	APRIL Total Obsn	APRIL MCWB	ANNUAL TOTAL Obsn Hour Gp 01 to 08	ANNUAL TOTAL Obsn Hour Gp 09 to 16	ANNUAL TOTAL Obsn Hour Gp 17 to 24	ANNUAL TOTAL Total Obsn	ANNUAL TOTAL MCWB
120/124																	0		0	72
115/119																	2	1	3	72
110/114																	35	15	50	72
105/109												0	0	0	64		153	76	229	71
100/104												3	1	4	63	0	261	137	398	71
95/99												12	5	17	61	1	308	203	512	69
90/94		0	0	0	60		4	1	5	58		27	13	40	59	45	305	291	641	67
85/89		5	1	6	58		19	8	27	57		42	24	66	58	279	274	292	845	66
80/84		14	5	19	56		35	17	52	55	0	46	31	77	57	316	256	257	829	63
75/79		26	12	38	54		42	25	67	53	3	44	42	89	55	247	264	250	761	58
70/74	0	39	22	61	52	1	45	38	84	52	23	35	46	104	53	253	281	250	784	55
65/69	3	48	40	91	50	9	43	49	101	50	57	20	38	115	52	267	273	275	815	52
60/64	18	40	49	107	48	39	35	50	124	48	70	9	23	102	50	284	219	299	802	49
55/59	45	28	48	121	46	77	16	36	129	46	53	2	12	67	47	351	149	277	777	46
50/54	63	15	30	108	42	72	6	19	97	43	25	0	4	29	44	372	82	184	638	43
45/49	57	6	12	75	39	36	2	4	42	40	7		0	7	41	292	38	82	412	40
40/44	26	1	4	31	35	12	0	0	12	36	1			1	38	147	12	23	182	36
35/39	9	0	0	9	30	2			2	31						49	2	4	55	31
30/34	2			2	27	0			0	29						10	0	0	10	27
25/29																0			0	22

BLYTHEVILLE AFB ARKANSAS

LAT 35 57N LONG 89 57W ELEV 264 FT

MEAN FREQUENCY OF OCCURRENCE OF DRY BULB TEMPERATURE (DEGREES F) WITH MEAN COINCIDENT WET BULB TEMPERATURE (DEGREES F) FOR EACH DRY BULB TEMPERATURE RANGE

Temperature Range	MAY Obsn Hour Gp 01 to 08	MAY Obsn Hour Gp 09 to 16	MAY Obsn Hour Gp 17 to 24	MAY Total Obsn	MAY MCWB	JUNE Obsn Hour Gp 01 to 08	JUNE Obsn Hour Gp 09 to 16	JUNE Obsn Hour Gp 17 to 24	JUNE Total Obsn	JUNE MCWB	JULY Obsn Hour Gp 01 to 08	JULY Obsn Hour Gp 09 to 16	JULY Obsn Hour Gp 17 to 24	JULY Total Obsn	JULY MCWB
100/104							0		0	78		2	0	2	78
95/99		0		0	71		8	1	9	76		17	3	20	79
90/94		11	2	13	71		43	10	53	75	0	58	14	72	78
85/89		33	8	41	71	2	63	25	90	74	4	75	35	114	76
80/84	2	52	22	76	69	15	58	42	115	72	22	60	62	144	74
75/79	12	52	40	104	67	45	38	64	147	70	84	26	74	184	72
70/74	44	41	60	145	65	85	22	61	168	68	87	8	44	139	69
65/69	66	31	51	148	62	58	6	27	91	64	32	2	11	45	64
60/64	52	17	36	105	58	24	1	8	33	59	14		4	18	59
55/59	37	8	17	62	53	9	0	2	11	54	4		0	4	56
50/54	21	3	9	33	48	2			2	50	0			0	52
45/49	10	0	3	13	44										
40/44	4		0	4	40										
35/39	0			0	37										
30/34															
25/29															

Temperature Range	AUGUST Obsn Hour Gp 01 to 08	AUGUST Obsn Hour Gp 09 to 16	AUGUST Obsn Hour Gp 17 to 24	AUGUST Total Obsn	AUGUST MCWB	SEPTEMBER Obsn Hour Gp 01 to 08	SEPTEMBER Obsn Hour Gp 09 to 16	SEPTEMBER Obsn Hour Gp 17 to 24	SEPTEMBER Total Obsn	SEPTEMBER MCWB	OCTOBER Obsn Hour Gp 01 to 08	OCTOBER Obsn Hour Gp 09 to 16	OCTOBER Obsn Hour Gp 17 to 24	OCTOBER Total Obsn	OCTOBER MCWB
100/104		1		1	79										
95/99		13	2	15	79		2		2	75					
90/94	0	43	10	53	77		13	2	15	77		1		1	68
85/89	2	68	25	95	75		42	8	50	74		10	0	10	70
80/84	13	65	49	127	73	2	58	20	80	71		31	3	34	67
75/79	61	39	70	170	72	20	54	43	117	69	1	38	11	50	65
70/74	79	14	57	150	69	56	36	61	153	67	6	46	26	78	62
65/69	57	3	24	84	65	54	21	47	122	63	30	41	43	114	60
60/64	26	1	9	36	60	49	8	33	90	59	40	38	48	126	56
55/59	8		2	10	56	29	4	17	50	54	45	26	40	111	52
50/54	2		0	2	52	20	2	7	29	50	40	12	38	90	48
45/49						8		2	10	46	37	4	22	63	43
40/44						2		1	3	41	28	1	14	43	39
35/39						0			0	38	16	0	3	19	35
30/34											5		0	5	31
25/29											0			0	27

BLYTHEVILLE AFB ARKANSAS

Temperature Range	NOVEMBER Obsn Hour Gp 01 to 08	NOVEMBER 09 to 16	NOVEMBER 17 to 24	NOVEMBER Total Obsn	NOVEMBER M C W B	DECEMBER Obsn Hour Gp 01 to 08	DECEMBER 09 to 16	DECEMBER 17 to 24	DECEMBER Total Obsn	DECEMBER M C W B	JANUARY Obsn Hour Gp 01 to 08	JANUARY 09 to 16	JANUARY 17 to 24	JANUARY Total Obsn	JANUARY M C W B
100/104															
95/99															
90/94															
85/89															
80/84		1	0	1	67										
75/79		6	0	6	64							0		0	66
70/74	0	17	3	20	61	1	2	1	4	64		1	0	1	64
65/69	7	26	13	46	59	3	9	3	15	61	0	6	3	9	61
60/64	14	34	24	72	56	6	18	9	33	57	8	14	9	31	58
55/59	23	37	32	92	51	13	23	17	53	52	9	14	11	34	53
50/54	35	41	40	116	47	18	30	24	72	48	9	17	13	39	47
45/49	38	35	44	117	43	23	37	32	92	43	11	28	20	59	43
40/44	38	25	37	100	38	35	42	41	118	38	18	31	29	78	38
35/39	43	11	28	82	34	45	36	48	129	34	32	40	36	108	34
30/34	26	5	13	44	29	48	27	39	114	29	54	42	56	152	29
25/29	13	1	4	18	25	32	13	19	64	25	43	25	37	105	25
20/24	3	0	2	5	20	12	6	9	27	20	29	14	15	58	20
15/19	1	0	0	1	16	9	4	5	18	16	17	7	9	33	16
10/14						3	1	1	5	11	10	5	5	20	11
5/9						1	0	0	1	6	5	2	3	10	6
0/4						1		1	2	2	2	1	1	4	1
-5/-1						0			0	-2	2		0	2	-2

Temperature Range	FEBRUARY Obsn Hour Gp 01 to 08	FEBRUARY 09 to 16	FEBRUARY 17 to 24	FEBRUARY Total Obsn	FEBRUARY M C W B	MARCH Obsn Hour Gp 01 to 08	MARCH 09 to 16	MARCH 17 to 24	MARCH Total Obsn	MARCH M C W B	APRIL Obsn Hour Gp 01 to 08	APRIL 09 to 16	APRIL 17 to 24	APRIL Total Obsn	APRIL M C W B	ANNUAL TOTAL Obsn Hour Gp 01 to 08	ANNUAL TOTAL 09 to 16	ANNUAL TOTAL 17 to 24	ANNUAL TOTAL Total Obsn	ANNUAL TOTAL M C W B
100/104																	3	0	3	78
95/99																	40	6	46	78
90/94												1		1	68	0	170	38	208	76
85/89							0		0	65		4	0	4	68	8	295	101	404	74
80/84		0		0	64		4	1	5	65		22	6	28	67	54	351	205	610	72
75/79		0	0	0	63		7	2	9	63	1	35	18	54	66	224	295	322	841	70
70/74		3	0	3	61	1	16	8	25	61	16	42	31	89	63	375	248	352	975	67
65/69	1	6	3	10	59	6	23	14	43	58	38	42	46	126	60	352	216	285	853	62
60/64	4	11	7	22	55	14	27	21	62	55	38	34	41	113	56	289	203	249	741	57
55/59	6	18	13	37	51	21	32	30	83	51	38	28	38	104	51	242	190	219	651	52
50/54	12	26	20	58	47	25	32	34	91	46	33	20	29	82	47	217	183	214	614	47
45/49	17	34	27	78	43	32	34	38	104	42	40	10	21	71	43	216	182	209	607	43
40/44	34	42	45	121	38	40	31	36	107	38	27	3	8	38	39	226	175	211	612	38
35/39	43	38	42	123	34	42	22	31	95	34	8	0	2	10	34	229	147	190	566	34
30/34	49	27	35	111	30	38	14	23	75	30	3	0	0	3	31	223	115	166	504	29
25/29	32	12	19	63	25	19	4	7	30	25						139	55	86	280	25
20/24	17	5	10	32	20	6	1	1	8	20						67	26	37	130	20
15/19	6	2	2	10	15	1	0	0	1	16						34	13	16	63	16
10/14	3	0	1	4	11	0	0	0	0	11						16	6	7	29	11
5/9	1		0	1	6	1			1	7						8	2	3	13	6
0/4																3	1	2	6	2
-5/-1																2	0	0	2	-2

FORT SMITH MAP ARKANSAS

LAT 35 20N LONG 94 22W ELEV 463 FT

MEAN FREQUENCY OF OCCURRENCE OF DRY BULB TEMPERATURE (DEGREES F) WITH MEAN COINCIDENT WET BULB TEMPERATURE (DEGREES F) FOR EACH DRY BULB TEMPERATURE RANGE

Temperature Range	MAY Obsn Hour Gp 01 to 08	MAY 09 to 16	MAY 17 to 24	MAY Total Obsn	MAY MCWB	JUNE Obsn Hour Gp 01 to 08	JUNE 09 to 16	JUNE 17 to 24	JUNE Total Obsn	JUNE MCWB	JULY Obsn Hour Gp 01 to 08	JULY 09 to 16	JULY 17 to 24	JULY Total Obsn	JULY MCWB
110/114												0		0	79
105/109												2	1	3	75
100/104							3	1	4	75		12	5	17	76
95/99		1	0	1	74		21	7	28	75		40	14	54	77
90/94		14	4	18	73	0	50	21	71	75	0	65	29	94	76
85/89		41	17	58	71	3	57	31	91	74	6	58	39	103	75
80/84	2	54	27	83	69	17	47	48	112	72	24	37	63	124	74
75/79	12	50	43	105	67	40	34	56	130	71	87	21	62	170	72
70/74	33	36	52	121	65	84	18	45	147	69	100	9	30	139	70
65/69	70	26	50	146	63	64	8	24	96	65	26	2	5	33	65
60/64	62	16	30	108	59	23	2	6	31	60	4	1	1	6	61
55/59	37	8	16	61	54	7	0	2	9	56	1		0	1	56
50/54	19	1	7	27	49	2		0	2	52	0			0	54
45/49	9	0	2	11	45	0			0	48					
40/44	3		0	3	41										
35/39	1			1	37										
30/34															
25/29															
20/24															

Temperature Range	AUGUST Obsn Hour Gp 01 to 08	AUGUST 09 to 16	AUGUST 17 to 24	AUGUST Total Obsn	AUGUST MCWB	SEPTEMBER Obsn Hour Gp 01 to 08	SEPTEMBER 09 to 16	SEPTEMBER 17 to 24	SEPTEMBER Total Obsn	SEPTEMBER MCWB	OCTOBER Obsn Hour Gp 01 to 08	OCTOBER 09 to 16	OCTOBER 17 to 24	OCTOBER Total Obsn	OCTOBER MCWB
110/114		0		0	75										
105/109		3	1	4	75										
100/104		15	5	20	75		2	0	2	70					
95/99		31	10	41	76		13	2	15	72		1	0	1	67
90/94	0	62	27	89	75		33	10	43	72		5	1	6	69
85/89	3	60	39	102	74	0	44	18	62	72		20	3	23	68
80/84	18	41	55	114	73	2	48	29	79	70	0	36	9	45	67
75/79	75	25	62	162	72	16	44	51	111	68	2	38	19	59	65
70/74	94	9	37	140	69	65	31	57	153	67	11	41	33	85	63
65/69	41	3	11	55	65	64	18	39	121	63	27	38	44	109	60
60/64	15	0	1	16	60	44	5	24	73	59	46	33	47	126	57
55/59	2			2	57	32	2	8	42	54	49	20	37	106	53
50/54						15	0	2	17	50	39	11	29	79	48
45/49						3		0	3	46	36	4	17	57	44
40/44						0			0	41	21	1	7	29	40
35/39											13	0	2	15	35
30/34											3		1	4	31
25/29											1		0	1	26
20/24											0			0	22

FORT SMITH MAP ARKANSAS

Temperature Range	NOVEMBER Obsn Hour Gp 01 to 08	09 to 16	17 to 24	Total Obsn	M C W B	DECEMBER Obsn Hour Gp 01 to 08	09 to 16	17 to 24	Total Obsn	M C W B	JANUARY Obsn Hour Gp 01 to 08	09 to 16	17 to 24	Total Obsn	M C W B
110/114															
105/109															
100/104															
95/99															
90/94															
85/89															
80/84		3		3	66		0		0	65		0		0	65
75/79	1	17	2	20	64		1		1	61		2	0	2	63
70/74	4	21	9	34	61	0	5	2	7	60	1	7	1	9	61
65/69	6	22	15	43	58	3	10	2	15	57	4	11	6	21	59
60/64	9	28	20	57	54	2	15	7	24	54	3	13	7	23	54
55/59	17	38	31	86	50	6	26	15	47	50	6	18	12	36	50
50/54	30	37	39	106	47	14	31	24	69	46	9	23	22	54	46
45/49	36	32	38	106	42	19	38	36	93	42	18	35	29	82	42
40/44	39	19	35	93	38	30	43	45	118	38	24	37	38	99	38
35/39	38	15	26	79	34	49	35	51	135	34	38	39	44	121	34
30/34	29	7	14	50	30	48	23	33	104	30	52	27	41	120	30
25/29	19	2	8	29	25	41	10	19	70	25	41	17	24	82	25
20/24	10	0	3	13	21	20	6	8	34	21	24	10	12	46	21
15/19	3	0		3	16	8	2	5	15	16	15	6	6	27	16
10/14						4	1	1	6	11	5	3	3	11	11
5/9						3	0	0	3	7	5	1	2	8	6
0/4						0	0		0	2	1	0	0	1	2
-5/-1											1		0	1	-2
-10/-6															

Temperature Range	FEBRUARY Obsn Hour Gp 01 to 08	09 to 16	17 to 24	Total Obsn	M C W B	MARCH Obsn Hour Gp 01 to 08	09 to 16	17 to 24	Total Obsn	M C W B	APRIL Obsn Hour Gp 01 to 08	09 to 16	17 to 24	Total Obsn	M C W B
110/114															
105/109															
100/104															
95/99															
90/94												1	0	1	69
85/89		0		0	65		1	0	1	66		10	2	12	67
80/84		1	0	1	63		6	2	8	63		25	10	35	66
75/79		2	1	3	60	0	12	6	18	62	2	35	22	59	64
70/74		9	3	12	58	2	21	10	33	59	13	36	29	78	62
65/69	1	15	5	21	56	7	24	17	48	56	23	37	40	100	59
60/64	3	18	14	35	52	9	31	26	66	52	39	34	41	114	56
55/59	8	23	20	51	50	16	35	31	82	49	39	31	36	106	51
50/54	17	32	32	81	46	28	34	42	104	46	44	19	31	94	47
45/49	26	33	37	96	42	41	34	42	117	42	32	9	21	62	43
40/44	38	33	38	109	38	51	24	32	107	39	30	3	7	40	39
35/39	40	28	30	98	34	41	16	22	79	34	14	0	2	16	35
30/34	44	19	28	91	30	32	8	11	51	30	3	0	1	4	31
25/29	30	7	11	48	25	15	3	4	22	25	1			1	27
20/24	10	3	2	15	20	4	1	1	6	20					
15/19	4	1	1	6	16	2	0		2	16					
10/14	1	0	0	1	10										
5/9	0	0	0	0	7										
0/4	0	0	0	0	1										
-5/-1	0			0	-4										
-10/-6	0			0	-8										

Temperature Range	ANNUAL TOTAL Obsn Hour Gp 01 to 08	09 to 16	17 to 24	Total Obsn	M C W B
110/114		0		0	77
105/109		5	2	7	75
100/104		32	11	43	75
95/99		107	33	140	76
90/94	0	230	92	322	75
85/89	12	291	149	452	73
80/84	63	298	243	604	71
75/79	235	281	324	840	69
70/74	407	243	308	958	66
65/69	336	214	258	808	61
60/64	259	196	224	679	56
55/59	220	201	208	629	51
50/54	217	188	228	633	47
45/49	220	185	222	627	43
40/44	236	160	202	598	38
35/39	234	133	177	544	34
30/34	211	84	129	424	30
25/29	148	39	66	253	25
20/24	68	20	26	114	21
15/19	32	9	12	53	16
10/14	10	4	4	18	11
5/9	8	1	2	11	6
0/4	1	0	0		2
-5/-1	1		0	1	-3
-10/-6	0			0	-8

LITTLE ROCK AFB ARKANSAS

LAT 34 55N LONG 92 09W ELEV 311 FT

MEAN FREQUENCY OF OCCURRENCE OF DRY BULB TEMPERATURE (DEGREES F) WITH MEAN COINCIDENT WET BULB TEMPERATURE (DEGREES F) FOR EACH DRY BULB TEMPERATURE RANGE

Temperature Range	MAY Obsn Hour Gp 01 to 08	MAY 09 to 16	MAY 17 to 24	MAY Total Obsn	MAY MCWB	JUNE Obsn Hour Gp 01 to 08	JUNE 09 to 16	JUNE 17 to 24	JUNE Total Obsn	JUNE MCWB	JULY Obsn Hour Gp 01 to 08	JULY 09 to 16	JULY 17 to 24	JULY Total Obsn	JULY MCWB
105/109															
100/104							0		0	77		3	0	3	78
95/99		0		0	75		7	1	8	76		25	6	31	78
90/94		9	1	10	71		42	13	55	75	0	62	24	86	77
85/89		31	12	43	70	1	68	36	105	74	3	74	46	123	75
80/84	1	59	33	93	69	12	59	58	129	72	30	48	64	142	74
75/79	12	53	50	115	67	57	39	60	156	70	99	26	69	194	72
70/74	45	39	55	139	65	89	20	50	159	68	84	9	31	124	69
65/69	71	32	47	150	62	53	5	16	74	64	22	1	6	29	64
60/64	51	16	28	95	58	19	1	4	24	59	7		1	8	59
55/59	34	7	14	55	53	7		1	8	55	2			2	56
50/54	20	2	7	29	49	1		0	1	50					
45/49	12	0	1	13	45	0			0	47					
40/44	2			2	41										
35/39															
30/34															
25/29															

Temperature Range	AUGUST Obsn Hour Gp 01 to 08	AUGUST 09 to 16	AUGUST 17 to 24	AUGUST Total Obsn	AUGUST MCWB	SEPTEMBER Obsn Hour Gp 01 to 08	SEPTEMBER 09 to 16	SEPTEMBER 17 to 24	SEPTEMBER Total Obsn	SEPTEMBER MCWB	OCTOBER Obsn Hour Gp 01 to 08	OCTOBER 09 to 16	OCTOBER 17 to 24	OCTOBER Total Obsn	OCTOBER MCWB
105/109		0		0	79										
100/104		2	0	2	77										
95/99		13	3	16	77		3	0	3	75					
90/94		55	17	72	76		22	4	26	76		2	0	2	66
85/89	1	74	38	113	74		45	15	60	73		12	2	14	70
80/84	18	55	63	136	73	2	53	34	89	71		31	8	39	67
75/79	77	36	71	184	72	28	52	56	136	70	1	39	22	62	65
70/74	91	10	41	142	69	72	36	59	167	68	11	44	35	90	63
65/69	44	3	13	60	64	60	19	39	118	63	32	44	47	123	60
60/64	15	0	2	17	60	37	6	20	63	58	42	37	44	123	56
55/59	3		0	3	56	27	2	9	38	54	44	25	40	109	52
50/54						10	0	2	12	50	48	11	31	90	48
45/49						2		1	3	45	39	3	13	55	43
40/44						1		0	1	40	21	0	5	26	39
35/39											7		1	8	36
30/34											2		0	2	31
25/29											0			0	28

LITTLE ROCK AFB ARKANSAS

Temperature Range	NOVEMBER Obsn Hour Gp 01 to 08	NOVEMBER 09 to 16	NOVEMBER 17 to 24	NOVEMBER Total Obsn	NOVEMBER MCWB	DECEMBER Obsn Hour Gp 01 to 08	DECEMBER 09 to 16	DECEMBER 17 to 24	DECEMBER Total Obsn	DECEMBER MCWB	JANUARY Obsn Hour Gp 01 to 08	JANUARY 09 to 16	JANUARY 17 to 24	JANUARY Total Obsn	JANUARY MCWB
105/109															
100/104															
95/99															
90/94															
85/89															
80/84		2	0	2	68							0		0	63
75/79		8	1	9	64		0	0	0	66		1	0	1	64
70/74	2	22	8	32	62	1	4	1	6	63		4	1	5	62
65/69	8	32	21	61	59	2	11	5	18	60	2	9	6	17	60
60/64	16	38	32	86	55	8	21	15	44	56	9	14	13	36	57
55/59	27	36	39	102	51	14	26	22	62	52	10	20	14	44	51
50/54	39	40	43	122	47	15	36	26	77	46	8	27	19	54	46
45/49	39	30	37	106	42	26	41	40	107	42	15	33	33	81	42
40/44	40	16	30	86	38	39	41	49	129	38	31	36	36	103	38
35/39	35	9	17	61	34	47	32	42	121	34	35	34	39	108	33
30/34	21	5	7	33	29	41	19	25	85	29	48	32	42	122	29
25/29	9	1	3	13	25	30	11	16	57	25	42	20	22	84	25
20/24	3	0	1	4	20	15	4	5	24	20	25	10	13	48	20
15/19	1			1	16	8	2	3	13	16	12	5	6	23	15
10/14						2	0	1	3	11	6	3	2	11	11
5/9						0	0	0	0	6	3	1	1	5	7
0/4						0			0	4	2	0	0	2	2
-5/-1											0			0	-2

Temperature Range	FEBRUARY Obsn Hour Gp 01 to 08	FEBRUARY 09 to 16	FEBRUARY 17 to 24	FEBRUARY Total Obsn	FEBRUARY MCWB	MARCH Obsn Hour Gp 01 to 08	MARCH 09 to 16	MARCH 17 to 24	MARCH Total Obsn	MARCH MCWB	APRIL Obsn Hour Gp 01 to 08	APRIL 09 to 16	APRIL 17 to 24	APRIL Total Obsn	APRIL MCWB
105/109															
100/104															
95/99															
90/94												1	0	1	68
85/89							2	1	3	67		6	2	8	67
80/84		0		0	63		5	2	7	64		25	11	36	66
75/79		1	1	2	62		9	6	15	63	2	36	25	63	65
70/74	0	5	2	7	59	2	16	12	30	59	18	44	39	101	62
65/69	0	9	6	15	56	8	24	18	50	57	35	46	45	126	59
60/64	5	16	11	32	54	15	32	30	77	54	47	38	42	127	56
55/59	8	22	19	49	50	23	35	34	92	50	42	25	38	105	51
50/54	17	31	23	71	46	27	39	37	103	45	44	14	25	83	47
45/49	22	36	38	96	42	37	35	43	115	42	29	5	9	43	43
40/44	36	38	43	117	38	54	25	33	112	38	17	1	3	21	38
35/39	38	29	35	102	33	41	15	19	75	33	5	0	0	5	34
30/34	42	20	29	91	29	25	8	11	44	29	1	0	1	2	31
25/29	35	12	13	60	25	12	2	3	17	25					
20/24	14	3	4	21	20	3	1	1	5	20					
15/19	5	1	1	7	16	1	0		1	16					
10/14	1			1	12										
5/9															
0/4															
-5/-1															

Temperature Range	ANNUAL TOTAL Obsn Hour Gp 01 to 08	ANNUAL TOTAL 09 to 16	ANNUAL TOTAL 17 to 24	ANNUAL TOTAL Total Obsn	ANNUAL TOTAL MCWB
105/109		0		0	79
100/104		5	0	5	77
95/99		48	10	58	77
90/94	0	193	59	252	76
85/89	5	312	152	469	74
80/84	63	337	273	673	71
75/79	276	300	361	937	70
70/74	415	253	334	1002	66
65/69	337	235	269	841	61
60/64	271	219	242	732	56
55/59	241	198	230	669	51
50/54	229	200	213	642	47
45/49	221	183	215	619	42
40/44	241	157	199	597	38
35/39	208	119	153	480	33
30/34	180	84	115	379	29
25/29	128	46	57	231	25
20/24	60	18	24	102	20
15/19	27	8	10	45	15
10/14	9	3	3	15	11
5/9	3	1	1	5	7
0/4	2	0	0	2	2
-5/-1	0			0	-2

ALAMEDA NAS/NIMITZ FIELD CALIFORNIA

LAT 37 47N LONG 122 19W ELEV 15 FT

MEAN FREQUENCY OF OCCURRENCE OF DRY BULB TEMPERATURE (DEGREES F) WITH MEAN COINCIDENT WET BULB TEMPERATURE (DEGREES F) FOR EACH DRY BULB TEMPERATURE RANGE

Temperature Range	MAY Obsn Hour Gp 01 to 08	MAY 09 to 16	MAY 17 to 24	MAY Total Obsn	MAY MCWB	JUNE Obsn Hour Gp 01 to 08	JUNE 09 to 16	JUNE 17 to 24	JUNE Total Obsn	JUNE MCWB	JULY Obsn Hour Gp 01 to 08	JULY 09 to 16	JULY 17 to 24	JULY Total Obsn	JULY MCWB
105/109															
100/104							0		0	70		0		0	70
95/99							0		0	69		0		0	70
90/94		0		0	63		1		1	68		1	0	1	68
85/89		0	0	0	64		3	1	4	66		2	0	2	66
80/84		3	0	3	63		8	1	9	65		7	1	8	65
75/79		5	1	6	62	0	12	3	15	63	0	13	3	16	63
70/74	0	23	4	27	60	1	52	10	63	61	1	50	8	59	61
65/69	1	62	13	76	57	6	78	31	115	59	6	98	34	138	59
60/64	14	90	41	145	55	40	60	61	161	57	34	58	71	163	57
55/59	69	52	92	213	52	119	22	99	240	54	150	17	106	273	54
50/54	141	11	90	242	49	73	4	34	111	51	56	1	25	82	51
45/49	22	0	6	28	45	1		0	1	47	2			2	49
40/44	1		0	1	43										

Temperature Range	AUGUST Obsn Hour Gp 01 to 08	AUGUST 09 to 16	AUGUST 17 to 24	AUGUST Total Obsn	AUGUST MCWB	SEPTEMBER Obsn Hour Gp 01 to 08	SEPTEMBER 09 to 16	SEPTEMBER 17 to 24	SEPTEMBER Total Obsn	SEPTEMBER MCWB	OCTOBER Obsn Hour Gp 01 to 08	OCTOBER 09 to 16	OCTOBER 17 to 24	OCTOBER Total Obsn	OCTOBER MCWB
105/109							0		0	71					
100/104		0		0	71		0		0	69					
95/99		0		0	70		1		1	66					
90/94		0	0	0	66		3	0	3	66		0		0	67
85/89		2	0	2	66		9	1	10	64		3	0	3	63
80/84		9	1	10	65	0	15	3	18	63		10	1	11	62
75/79	0	21	3	24	64	1	27	7	35	62		19	4	23	60
70/74	1	69	13	83	62	3	68	17	88	61	0	45	10	55	60
65/69	8	84	38	130	60	17	72	41	130	60	6	75	32	113	58
60/64	59	47	85	191	57	71	37	86	194	57	49	69	82	200	56
55/59	143	14	94	251	55	130	9	79	218	55	135	24	98	257	54
50/54	37	1	14	52	52	18	0	6	24	51	55	2	21	78	49
45/49	0			0	49						2		0	2	42
40/44															

ALAMEDA NAS/NIMITZ FIELD CALIFORNIA

Temperature Range	NOVEMBER Obsn Hour Gp 01 to 08	NOVEMBER 09 to 16	NOVEMBER 17 to 24	NOVEMBER Total Obsn	NOVEMBER MCWB	DECEMBER Obsn Hour Gp 01 to 08	DECEMBER 09 to 16	DECEMBER 17 to 24	DECEMBER Total Obsn	DECEMBER MCWB	JANUARY Obsn Hour Gp 01 to 08	JANUARY 09 to 16	JANUARY 17 to 24	JANUARY Total Obsn	JANUARY MCWB	FEBRUARY Obsn Hour Gp 01 to 08	FEBRUARY 09 to 16	FEBRUARY 17 to 24	FEBRUARY Total Obsn	FEBRUARY MCWB
105/109																				
100/104																				
95/99																				
90/94																				
85/89																				
80/84		1		1	61															
75/79		1	0	1	59												0		0	62
70/74		11	1	12	58		1		1	55		0		0	55		3	0	3	58
65/69	0	32	6	38	57		5	1	6	55		2	0	2	54		12	2	14	56
60/64	7	74	34	115	55	4	23	7	34	54	1	15	4	20	54	2	41	15	58	54
55/59	73	84	106	263	53	21	71	46	138	52	13	55	32	100	52	31	83	70	184	52
50/54	109	33	81	223	49	62	88	89	239	48	50	95	87	232	48	81	65	95	241	48
45/49	45	3	11	59	44	90	47	73	210	44	86	65	89	240	44	86	17	39	142	44
40/44	5		0	5	40	54	13	31	98	40	76	14	30	120	40	23	2	4	29	40
35/39						17	0	2	19	36	20	2	4	26	35	1	0		1	33
30/34						0			0	33	1	0	0	1	32					

Temperature Range	MARCH Obsn Hour Gp 01 to 08	MARCH 09 to 16	MARCH 17 to 24	MARCH Total Obsn	MARCH MCWB	APRIL Obsn Hour Gp 01 to 08	APRIL 09 to 16	APRIL 17 to 24	APRIL Total Obsn	APRIL MCWB	ANNUAL TOTAL Obsn Hour Gp 01 to 08	ANNUAL TOTAL 09 to 16	ANNUAL TOTAL 17 to 24	ANNUAL TOTAL Total Obsn	ANNUAL TOTAL MCWB
105/109												0		0	71
100/104												0		0	70
95/99												1		1	68
90/94												5	0	5	66
85/89		0		0	65		0		0	62		19	2	21	65
80/84		0		0	61		3	0	3	63	0	56	7	63	64
75/79		3	1	4	58		9	2	11	62	1	110	24	135	62
70/74		9	2	11	57	0	15	4	19	59	6	346	69	421	61
65/69	0	23	7	30	55	1	40	10	51	57	45	583	215	843	58
60/64	3	59	20	82	53	7	67	29	103	55	291	640	535	1466	56
55/59	34	91	75	200	51	48	69	76	193	52	966	591	973	2530	53
50/54	115	53	114	282	48	119	31	90	240	48	916	384	746	2046	49
45/49	83	8	27	118	44	58	5	28	91	44	475	145	273	893	44
40/44	10	1	2	13	39	6	0	1	7	40	175	30	68	273	40
35/39	2		0	2	35	0			0	37	40	2	6	48	35
30/34											1	0	0	1	32

ARCATA CALIFORNIA

LAT 40 59N LONG 124 06W ELEV 218 FT

MEAN FREQUENCY OF OCCURRENCE OF DRY BULB TEMPERATURE (DEGREES F) WITH MEAN COINCIDENT WET BULB TEMPERATURE (DEGREES F) FOR EACH DRY BULB TEMPERATURE RANGE

Temperature Range	MAY Obsn Hour Gp 01 to 08	MAY 09 to 16	MAY 17 to 24	MAY Total Obsn	MAY MCWB	JUNE Obsn Hour Gp 01 to 08	JUNE 09 to 16	JUNE 17 to 24	JUNE Total Obsn	JUNE MCWB	JULY Obsn Hour Gp 01 to 08	JULY 09 to 16	JULY 17 to 24	JULY Total Obsn	JULY MCWB
90/94															
85/89								0	0	65					
80/84							0		0	66					
75/79		0		0	60		1	0	1	65		0		0	61
70/74	0	1	0	1	61		1	0	1	63		1		1	60
65/69	0	3	1	4	58	0	6	1	7	60		13	1	14	59
60/64	1	21	4	26	56	3	56	14	73	57	2	63	19	84	57
55/59	14	110	38	162	53	41	127	84	252	54	50	135	100	285	54
50/54	104	103	128	335	50	127	48	112	287	51	160	36	116	312	51
45/49	83	8	64	155	46	51	1	26	78	46	29	0	11	40	47
40/44	36	0	12	48	41	16		2	18	42	7		0	7	42
35/39	8		1	9	37	1			1	37					
30/34	0			0	32										

Temperature Range	AUGUST Obsn Hour Gp 01 to 08	AUGUST 09 to 16	AUGUST 17 to 24	AUGUST Total Obsn	AUGUST MCWB	SEPTEMBER Obsn Hour Gp 01 to 08	SEPTEMBER 09 to 16	SEPTEMBER 17 to 24	SEPTEMBER Total Obsn	SEPTEMBER MCWB	OCTOBER Obsn Hour Gp 01 to 08	OCTOBER 09 to 16	OCTOBER 17 to 24	OCTOBER Total Obsn	OCTOBER MCWB
90/94							0		0	69					
85/89							1		1	65					
80/84		0		0	64	0	1	0	1	64		0		0	60
75/79		0		0	63	0	2	0	2	62		2	0	2	60
70/74		3	0	3	62	0	6	0	6	62	0	6	0	6	59
65/69	0	17	3	20	61	1	24	4	29	59	1	17	1	19	58
60/64	7	79	29	115	58	13	80	30	123	57	9	63	17	89	57
55/59	77	113	108	298	55	59	87	89	235	55	41	95	64	200	54
50/54	132	36	100	268	51	104	38	92	234	51	90	57	105	252	50
45/49	27	0	8	35	47	46	1	22	69	47	69	8	48	125	46
40/44	5		0	5	43	14		3	17	42	30		12	42	42
35/39						2	0		2	37	7		1	8	37
30/34											0			0	33

ARCATA CALIFORNIA

Temperature Range	NOVEMBER Obsn Hour Gp 01 to 08	NOVEMBER Obsn Hour Gp 09 to 16	NOVEMBER Obsn Hour Gp 17 to 24	NOVEMBER Total Obsn	NOVEMBER MCWB	DECEMBER Obsn Hour Gp 01 to 08	DECEMBER Obsn Hour Gp 09 to 16	DECEMBER Obsn Hour Gp 17 to 24	DECEMBER Total Obsn	DECEMBER MCWB	JANUARY Obsn Hour Gp 01 to 08	JANUARY Obsn Hour Gp 09 to 16	JANUARY Obsn Hour Gp 17 to 24	JANUARY Total Obsn	JANUARY MCWB
90/94															
85/89															
80/84		0		0	64										
75/79		1		1	60										
70/74		1	0	1	56		0	0	0	62		0		0	55
65/69	0	7	1	8	55		2	0	2	55	0	1	0	1	53
60/64	3	29	5	37	55	3	12	3	18	56	1	12	3	16	53
55/59	30	83	36	149	53	16	50	20	86	53	11	38	16	65	52
50/54	57	76	81	214	50	44	105	61	210	49	38	81	53	172	49
45/49	70	34	62	166	45	64	57	80	201	45	56	72	64	192	44
40/44	43	8	39	90	41	60	17	52	129	41	55	32	60	147	40
35/39	31	1	15	47	36	41	4	26	71	36	51	10	39	100	35
30/34	6		1	7	32	20	0	6	26	32	31	2	13	46	31

Temperature Range	FEBRUARY Obsn Hour Gp 01 to 08	FEBRUARY Obsn Hour Gp 09 to 16	FEBRUARY Obsn Hour Gp 17 to 24	FEBRUARY Total Obsn	FEBRUARY MCWB	MARCH Obsn Hour Gp 01 to 08	MARCH Obsn Hour Gp 09 to 16	MARCH Obsn Hour Gp 17 to 24	MARCH Total Obsn	MARCH MCWB	APRIL Obsn Hour Gp 01 to 08	APRIL Obsn Hour Gp 09 to 16	APRIL Obsn Hour Gp 17 to 24	APRIL Total Obsn	APRIL MCWB	ANNUAL TOTAL Obsn Hour Gp 01 to 08	ANNUAL TOTAL Obsn Hour Gp 09 to 16	ANNUAL TOTAL Obsn Hour Gp 17 to 24	ANNUAL TOTAL Total Obsn	ANNUAL TOTAL MCWB
90/94																	0		0	69
85/89																	1	0	1	65
80/84																0	1	0	1	64
75/79		0		0	57											0	6	0	6	61
70/74	0	1	0	1	59		0	0	0	56		0	0	0	53	0	20	0	20	60
65/69	0	4	1	5	55	0	2	0	2	54	0	2	0	2	55	2	98	13	113	58
60/64	3	13	5	21	55	1	8	1	10	53	0	12	2	14	54	46	448	132	626	57
55/59	13	43	18	74	52	5	35	9	49	51	6	51	15	72	52	363	967	597	1927	54
50/54	34	82	56	172	49	27	106	55	188	48	33	127	72	232	49	950	895	1031	2876	50
45/49	54	60	69	183	45	80	80	101	261	45	108	44	109	261	45	737	365	664	1766	45
40/44	54	19	47	120	40	76	16	61	153	40	60	3	33	96	41	456	95	321	872	41
35/39	46	3	25	74	36	44	1	17	62	36	28	0	8	36	36	259	19	132	410	36
30/34	19	0	3	22	31	15		2	17	32	4		0	4	33	95	2	25	122	31

BEALE AFB/MARYSVILLE CALIFORNIA

LAT 39 07N LONG 121 26W ELEV 113 FT

MEAN FREQUENCY OF OCCURRENCE OF DRY BULB TEMPERATURE (DEGREES F) WITH MEAN COINCIDENT WET BULB TEMPERATURE (DEGREES F) FOR EACH DRY BULB TEMPERATURE RANGE

Temperature Range	MAY Obsn Hour Gp 01 to 08	MAY Obsn Hour Gp 09 to 16	MAY Obsn Hour Gp 17 to 24	MAY Total Obsn	MAY MCWB	JUNE Obsn Hour Gp 01 to 08	JUNE Obsn Hour Gp 09 to 16	JUNE Obsn Hour Gp 17 to 24	JUNE Total Obsn	JUNE MCWB	JULY Obsn Hour Gp 01 to 08	JULY Obsn Hour Gp 09 to 16	JULY Obsn Hour Gp 17 to 24	JULY Total Obsn	JULY MCWB
110/114							0	0	0	73					
105/109							2	1	3	71		2	1	3	70
100/104		0		0	67		10	6	16	70		16	9	25	70
95/99		3	1	4	67		17	10	27	69		40	23	63	68
90/94		8	4	12	66	0	27	15	42	66	0	56	35	91	67
85/89		19	11	30	64	2	35	26	63	65	2	50	35	87	65
80/84	0	33	18	51	62	5	44	34	83	63	8	39	46	93	63
75/79	1	42	24	67	60	12	40	37	89	61	25	26	43	94	61
70/74	5	48	32	85	58	25	33	38	96	59	53	14	33	100	59
65/69	14	44	45	103	56	42	19	36	97	57	71	3	17	91	57
60/64	43	31	47	121	54	67	8	24	99	55	63	0	6	69	55
55/59	81	15	42	138	51	67	3	11	81	53	24	0	1	25	52
50/54	76	4	17	97	48	19	1	3	23	49	2			2	50
45/49	21	0	4	25	44	2			2	45					
40/44	6		1	7	40										
35/39	1			1	37										

Temperature Range	AUGUST Obsn Hour Gp 01 to 08	AUGUST Obsn Hour Gp 09 to 16	AUGUST Obsn Hour Gp 17 to 24	AUGUST Total Obsn	AUGUST MCWB	SEPTEMBER Obsn Hour Gp 01 to 08	SEPTEMBER Obsn Hour Gp 09 to 16	SEPTEMBER Obsn Hour Gp 17 to 24	SEPTEMBER Total Obsn	SEPTEMBER MCWB	OCTOBER Obsn Hour Gp 01 to 08	OCTOBER Obsn Hour Gp 09 to 16	OCTOBER Obsn Hour Gp 17 to 24	OCTOBER Total Obsn	OCTOBER MCWB
110/114			0	0	73										
105/109		1	0	1	73		0	0	0	70					
100/104		12	6	18	70		4	1	5	69		0		0	66
95/99		35	18	53	68		10	4	14	67		1	0	1	67
90/94		51	29	80	67		35	12	47	65		7	1	8	66
85/89	0	51	34	85	65	0	45	19	64	64		16	3	19	63
80/84	7	42	44	93	63	1	48	32	81	62		24	6	30	61
75/79	22	31	47	100	61	7	42	42	91	60	0	40	14	54	59
70/74	48	17	41	106	59	21	32	48	101	58	2	54	28	84	57
65/69	73	7	21	101	57	47	18	45	110	56	10	45	43	98	55
60/64	73	1	7	81	55	79	7	30	116	54	36	38	67	141	54
55/59	22		1	23	53	66	0	7	73	52	81	17	53	151	51
50/54	3		0	3	51	16		1	17	48	72	4	24	100	47
45/49	0			0	48	2		0	2	43	37	1	7	45	43
40/44						0			0	36	10		1	11	38
35/39											2			2	35

BEALE AFB/MARYSVILLE CALIFORNIA

Temperature Range	NOVEMBER Obsn Hour Gp 01 to 08	NOVEMBER 09 to 16	NOVEMBER 17 to 24	NOVEMBER Total Obsn	NOVEMBER MCWB	DECEMBER Obsn Hour Gp 01 to 08	DECEMBER 09 to 16	DECEMBER 17 to 24	DECEMBER Total Obsn	DECEMBER MCWB	JANUARY Obsn Hour Gp 01 to 08	JANUARY 09 to 16	JANUARY 17 to 24	JANUARY Total Obsn	JANUARY MCWB	FEBRUARY Obsn Hour Gp 01 to 08	FEBRUARY 09 to 16	FEBRUARY 17 to 24	FEBRUARY Total Obsn	FEBRUARY MCWB	MARCH Obsn Hour Gp 01 to 08	MARCH 09 to 16	MARCH 17 to 24	MARCH Total Obsn	MARCH MCWB	APRIL Obsn Hour Gp 01 to 08	APRIL 09 to 16	APRIL 17 to 24	APRIL Total Obsn	APRIL MCWB	ANNUAL TOTAL Obsn Hour Gp 01 to 08	ANNUAL TOTAL 09 to 16	ANNUAL TOTAL 17 to 24	ANNUAL TOTAL Total Obsn	ANNUAL TOTAL MCWB
110/114																																0	0	0	73
105/109																																5	2	7	71
100/104																																42	22	64	70
95/99																																106	56	162	68
90/94																															0	184	96	280	66
85/89		0		0	61																						2	1	3	63	4	218	129	351	65
80/84		1		1	59																	1	0	1	61		14	5	19	62	21	246	185	452	63
75/79		5	0	5	58		0		0	59		0		0	59		1		1	55		6	2	8	60		23	10	33	59	67	256	219	542	61
70/74		13	2	15	56		1		1	57		1		1	57		3	0	3	57		16	5	21	57	0	36	17	53	57	154	268	244	666	58
65/69		27	6	33	55	1	2	1	4	59		1	0	1	54		13	3	16	55	0	29	12	41	54	2	40	25	67	55	260	248	254	762	56
60/64	1	52	21	74	54	3	11	5	19	56	1	12	3	16	55	1	39	14	54	53	1	56	26	83	52	10	46	41	97	53	378	301	291	970	54
55/59	31	65	61	157	52	7	35	13	55	52	5	33	15	53	52	11	61	39	111	51	13	65	54	132	50	35	44	52	131	50	443	338	349	1130	51
50/54	65	50	74	189	49	24	52	33	109	48	25	56	35	116	48	33	51	60	144	48	54	50	73	177	47	70	27	50	147	47	459	295	370	1124	48
45/49	60	20	48	128	44	37	66	62	165	44	34	63	64	161	44	54	38	62	154	44	86	22	53	161	44	75	8	30	113	44	408	218	330	956	44
40/44	53	7	24	84	40	64	54	74	192	40	50	46	66	162	40	71	15	38	124	40	64	4	19	87	40	39	0	8	47	40	357	126	231	714	40
35/39	24	0	5	29	35	67	23	45	135	36	65	24	43	132	36	42	2	7	51	35	24	0	3	27	35	9		0	9	36	234	49	103	386	36
30/34	6		0	6	32	33	4	13	50	31	47	11	20	78	31	12	0	.0	12	31	6		0	6	30	0			0	33	104	15	33	152	31
25/29	0			0	24	10	0	1	11	27	20	1	2	23	26	1			1	27	1			1	27						32	1	3	36	26
20/24						1			1	23	2	0		2	22																3	0		3	23

BISHOP CALIFORNIA

LAT 37 22N LONG 118 22W ELEV 4108 FT

MEAN FREQUENCY OF OCCURRENCE OF DRY BULB TEMPERATURE (DEGREES F) WITH MEAN COINCIDENT WET BULB TEMPERATURE (DEGREES F) FOR EACH DRY BULB TEMPERATURE RANGE

Temperature Range	MAY Obsn Hour Gp 01 to 08	MAY 09 to 16	MAY 17 to 24	MAY Total Obsn	MAY MCWB	JUNE Obsn Hour Gp 01 to 08	JUNE 09 to 16	JUNE 17 to 24	JUNE Total Obsn	JUNE MCWB	JULY Obsn Hour Gp 01 to 08	JULY 09 to 16	JULY 17 to 24	JULY Total Obsn	JULY MCWB
105/109							1		1	62		1		1	62
100/104		0		0	61		8	3	11	61		20	5	25	61
95/99		2	0	2	59		23	14	37	59		65	37	102	60
90/94		7	2	9	57	0	44	34	78	57		66	62	128	59
85/89		28	12	40	55	2	49	46	97	56	3	52	69	124	58
80/84	1	43	35	79	53	10	43	51	104	54	23	29	42	94	57
75/79	3	46	47	96	51	26	36	40	102	52	59	12	24	95	56
70/74	16	39	45	100	49	45	18	24	87	51	58	3	8	69	55
65/69	34	35	35	104	47	53	10	14	77	49	50	0	1	51	52
60/64	46	22	27	95	45	48	5	8	61	47	36	0	0	36	49
55/59	51	14	20	85	43	35	2	5	42	45	17	0	0	17	46
50/54	45	7	13	65	41	15	1	2	18	43	2			2	42
45/49	33	4	6	43	39	4	1	1	6	41					
40/44	15	2	5	22	36	1			1	36					
35/39	5	0	1	6	33										
30/34	0		0	0	32										
25/29	0			0	23										
20/24															

Temperature Range	AUGUST Obsn Hour Gp 01 to 08	AUGUST 09 to 16	AUGUST 17 to 24	AUGUST Total Obsn	AUGUST MCWB	SEPTEMBER Obsn Hour Gp 01 to 08	SEPTEMBER 09 to 16	SEPTEMBER 17 to 24	SEPTEMBER Total Obsn	SEPTEMBER MCWB	OCTOBER Obsn Hour Gp 01 to 08	OCTOBER 09 to 16	OCTOBER 17 to 24	OCTOBER Total Obsn	OCTOBER MCWB
105/109		0		0	61		0		0	62					
100/104		10	1	11	61		2	0	2	60					
95/99		50	19	69	60		13	1	14	59					
90/94		66	52	118	58		37	10	47	57		2		2	57
85/89	0	53	66	119	57		56	28	84	56		17	2	19	55
80/84	8	38	55	101	56	1	48	50	99	54		37	5	42	53
75/79	30	20	34	84	54	7	34	55	96	53	0	44	20	64	51
70/74	53	8	14	75	53	14	26	44	84	51	0	45	38	83	49
65/69	56	2	6	64	51	38	15	28	81	50	5	38	47	90	47
60/64	45	0	1	46	49	47	7	13	67	48	17	28	51	96	45
55/59	34		0	34	45	48	2	6	56	46	31	17	43	91	43
50/54	14			14	42	43	0	3	46	42	46	9	22	77	41
45/49	6			6	38	28		1	29	39	50	6	12	68	38
40/44	1			1	34	12		0	12	35	51	2	6	59	35
35/39						2			2	30	33	1	2	36	32
30/34											11	0		11	28
25/29											2			2	23
20/24											0			0	21

BISHOP CALIFORNIA

Temperature Range	NOVEMBER Obsn Hour Gp 01 to 08	09 to 16	17 to 24	Total Obsn	MCWB	DECEMBER Obsn Hour Gp 01 to 08	09 to 16	17 to 24	Total Obsn	MCWB	JANUARY Obsn Hour Gp 01 to 08	09 to 16	17 to 24	Total Obsn	MCWB
105/109															
100/104															
95/99															
90/94															
85/89															
80/84		1		1	53										
75/79		8		8	51		0		0	51					
70/74		19	0	19	48		3		3	47		1		1	48
65/69		35	5	40	46		12	0	12	45		7	0	7	45
60/64	0	43	18	61	44		26	2	28	43	0	15	1	16	43
55/59	4	36	35	75	42	0	39	6	45	41		26	6	32	41
50/54	8	34	44	86	39	2	45	20	67	39	1	39	18	58	39
45/49	18	29	46	93	37	4	44	41	89	37	4	43	36	83	36
40/44	30	18	46	94	34	10	36	57	103	34	9	45	50	104	34
35/39	51	12	28	91	31	29	25	63	117	31	23	34	51	108	31
30/34	52	4	14	70	28	50	13	42	105	27	37	22	42	101	28
25/29	51	0	4	55	24	76	4	12	92	24	62	10	29	101	24
20/24	19	0		19	19	52	1	4	57	20	51	3	10	64	19
15/19	6			6	15	16	0	1	17	15	33	1	5	39	15
10/14	1			1	11	7		0	7	10	22	0	1	23	11
5/9	0			0	8	1			1	5	4	0	0	4	6
0/4											2			2	2
-5/-1											0			0	-3

Temperature Range	FEBRUARY Obsn Hour Gp 01 to 08	09 to 16	17 to 24	Total Obsn	MCWB	MARCH Obsn Hour Gp 01 to 08	09 to 16	17 to 24	Total Obsn	MCWB	APRIL Obsn Hour Gp 01 to 08	09 to 16	17 to 24	Total Obsn	MCWB	ANNUAL TOTAL Obsn Hour Gp 01 to 08	09 to 16	17 to 24	Total Obsn	MCWB
105/109																	2		2	62
100/104																	40	9	49	61
95/99																	153	71	224	60
90/94												0		0	56	0	222	160	382	58
85/89												5	1	6	54	5	260	224	489	56
80/84							0		0	50		19	8	27	51	43	258	246	547	54
75/79		0		0	51		5	1	6	49		32	19	51	50	125	237	240	602	52
70/74		5	0	5	48		22	6	28	47	1	46	37	84	48	187	235	216	638	50
65/69		20	2	22	46		42	21	63	45	8	42	44	94	46	244	258	203	705	47
60/64		28	10	38	44	1	45	35	81	42	20	35	42	97	44	260	254	208	722	45
55/59	0	39	29	68	41	6	42	49	97	40	37	23	35	95	42	263	240	234	737	42
50/54	1	41	40	82	39	20	33	49	102	38	43	17	21	81	39	240	226	232	698	39
45/49	8	39	50	97	37	31	26	34	91	35	43	11	17	71	36	229	203	244	676	37
40/44	23	29	42	94	34	41	20	28	89	33	38	5	12	55	34	231	157	246	634	34
35/39	43	16	33	92	31	48	10	16	74	30	31	2	4	37	32	265	100	198	563	31
30/34	64	7	14	85	28	51	3	9	63	28	13	0	1	14	28	278	49	122	449	28
25/29	53	1	4	58	24	32	0	1	33	23	5			5	24	281	15	50	346	24
20/24	24	0	0	24	20	15			15	20	0			0	21	161	4	14	179	20
15/19	6	0		6	15	2			2	16						63	1	6	70	15
10/14	1			1	11	0			0	13						31	0	1	32	11
5/9																5	0	0	5	6
0/4																2			2	2
-5/-1																0			0	-3

CASTLE AFB/MERCED CALIFORNIA

LAT 37 23N LONG 120 34W ELEV 188 FT

MEAN FREQUENCY OF OCCURRENCE OF DRY BULB TEMPERATURE (DEGREES F) WITH MEAN COINCIDENT WET BULB TEMPERATURE (DEGREES F) FOR EACH DRY BULB TEMPERATURE RANGE

Temperature Range	MAY Obsn Hour Gp 01 to 08	MAY 09 to 16	MAY 17 to 24	MAY Total Obsn	MAY MCWB	JUNE Obsn Hour Gp 01 to 08	JUNE 09 to 16	JUNE 17 to 24	JUNE Total Obsn	JUNE MCWB	JULY Obsn Hour Gp 01 to 08	JULY 09 to 16	JULY 17 to 24	JULY Total Obsn	JULY MCWB
110/114							1	0	1	74		0	0	0	73
105/109							3	1	4	72		3	1	4	71
100/104		0	0	0	66		9	5	14	70		17	6	23	70
95/99		3	1	4	67		16	9	25	69	0	44	22	66	69
90/94		11	5	16	65	0	30	16	46	67	0	57	33	90	67
85/89		22	10	32	63	1	38	26	65	65	3	52	37	92	65
80/84	0	34	17	51	62	5	44	33	82	63	10	38	45	93	64
75/79	1	44	27	72	60	15	42	37	94	61	30	25	47	102	61
70/74	6	51	36	93	58	28	32	38	98	59	60	10	32	102	59
65/69	17	40	45	102	56	44	17	34	95	57	73	2	18	93	57
60/64	45	27	48	120	54	65	5	27	97	54	52	0	5	57	55
55/59	80	12	38	130	51	57	2	12	71	52	19		1	20	53
50/54	72	2	18	92	48	23	0	2	25	49	2			2	49
45/49	21	0	3	24	44	1		0	1	45					
40/44	6		0	6	40	0			0	42					
35/39	0			0	36										
30/34															

Temperature Range	AUGUST Obsn Hour Gp 01 to 08	AUGUST 09 to 16	AUGUST 17 to 24	AUGUST Total Obsn	AUGUST MCWB	SEPTEMBER Obsn Hour Gp 01 to 08	SEPTEMBER 09 to 16	SEPTEMBER 17 to 24	SEPTEMBER Total Obsn	SEPTEMBER MCWB	OCTOBER Obsn Hour Gp 01 to 08	OCTOBER 09 to 16	OCTOBER 17 to 24	OCTOBER Total Obsn	OCTOBER MCWB
110/114															
105/109		0		0	70		0		0	71					
100/104		11	3	14	70		2	0	2	71					
95/99		36	14	50	69		11	3	14	69		0		0	66
90/94		57	28	85	67		30	9	39	66		7	1	8	66
85/89	0	51	35	86	66		43	20	63	65		14	3	17	64
80/84	5	42	45	92	64	0	49	29	78	63		26	9	35	62
75/79	25	28	50	103	62	6	46	43	95	62	0	41	16	57	60
70/74	55	16	42	113	59	20	34	51	105	59	1	53	31	85	58
65/69	71	5	21	97	58	47	19	49	115	57	8	50	47	105	56
60/64	63	0	9	72	55	86	6	28	120	55	35	35	61	131	54
55/59	26	1	2	29	53	58	0	8	66	52	72	17	52	141	52
50/54	2		0	2	50	20		1	21	48	79	4	23	106	48
45/49						2			2	44	42	0	4	46	44
40/44						0			0	39	9	0	1	10	39
35/39											2		0	2	33
30/34											0			0	28

CASTLE AFB/MERCED CALIFORNIA

Temperature Range	NOVEMBER Obsn Hour Gp 01 to 08	09 to 16	17 to 24	Total Obsn	M C W B	DECEMBER Obsn Hour Gp 01 to 08	09 to 16	17 to 24	Total Obsn	M C W B	JANUARY Obsn Hour Gp 01 to 08	09 to 16	17 to 24	Total Obsn	M C W B	FEBRUARY Obsn Hour Gp 01 to 08	09 to 16	17 to 24	Total Obsn	M C W B
110/114																				
105/109																				
100/104																				
95/99																				
90/94																				
85/89																				
80/84		0		0	60															
75/79		6	0	6	60															
70/74	0	18	3	21	57												2	0	2	59
65/69		32	9	41	55		4	0	4	55		2	0	2	58		14	4	18	57
60/64	2	50	27	79	54	1	17	4	22	53	0	13	5	18	55	1	38	16	55	54
55/59	21	69	58	138	52	6	33	16	55	51	8	38	21	67	52	14	63	48	125	51
50/54	54	46	69	169	48	20	47	39	106	48	20	57	44	121	48	38	54	61	153	48
45/49	64	21	46	131	44	33	60	58	151	44	40	53	56	149	44	57	35	59	151	44
40/44	59	8	21	88	40	68	54	76	198	40	52	47	64	163	40	59	14	29	102	40
35/39	31	1	6	38	36	69	26	42	137	36	65	25	42	132	36	45	3	7	55	35
30/34	9		0	9	31	40	6	12	58	31	46	11	16	73	31	12	0	1	13	31
25/29	0			0	28	11	0	1	12	27	17	1	1	19	27	0			0	26
20/24						0			0	21	1			1	22					
15/19						0			0	17										

Temperature Range	MARCH Obsn Hour Gp 01 to 08	09 to 16	17 to 24	Total Obsn	M C W B	APRIL Obsn Hour Gp 01 to 08	09 to 16	17 to 24	Total Obsn	M C W B	ANNUAL TOTAL Obsn Hour Gp 01 to 08	09 to 16	17 to 24	Total Obsn	M C W B
110/114												1	0	1	74
105/109												6	2	8	71
100/104												39	14	53	70
95/99							0	0	0	66	0	110	49	159	69
90/94							2	1	3	65	0	194	93	287	67
85/89		0	0	0	64		7	2	9	63	4	227	133	364	65
80/84		1	0	1	62		18	7	25	61	20	252	185	457	63
75/79		8	2	10	60		28	14	42	59	77	268	236	581	61
70/74		21	7	28	58	0	38	22	60	57	170	275	262	707	59
65/69		36	17	53	55	3	44	32	79	55	263	265	276	804	56
60/64	1	61	35	97	53	16	40	41	97	53	367	292	306	965	54
55/59	12	64	59	135	50	43	36	44	123	50	416	325	359	1100	51
50/54	57	42	69	168	47	67	21	45	133	47	454	273	371	1098	48
45/49	86	13	42	141	44	74	6	26	106	44	420	188	294	902	44
40/44	63	3	13	79	40	29	0	6	35	40	345	126	210	681	40
35/39	23	0	3	26	35	7		0	7	36	242	55	100	397	36
30/34	5	0	0	5	30	1			1	32	113	17	29	159	31
25/29	1			1	25						29	1	2	32	27
20/24											1			1	22
15/19											0			0	17

EDWARDS AFB CALIFORNIA

LAT 34 54N LONG 117 52W ELEV 2302 FT

MEAN FREQUENCY OF OCCURRENCE OF DRY BULB TEMPERATURE (DEGREES F) WITH MEAN COINCIDENT WET BULB TEMPERATURE (DEGREES F) FOR EACH DRY BULB TEMPERATURE RANGE

Temperature Range	MAY Obsn Hour Gp 01 to 08	MAY 09 to 16	MAY 17 to 24	MAY Total Obsn	MAY MCWB	JUNE Obsn Hour Gp 01 to 08	JUNE 09 to 16	JUNE 17 to 24	JUNE Total Obsn	JUNE MCWB	JULY Obsn Hour Gp 01 to 08	JULY 09 to 16	JULY 17 to 24	JULY Total Obsn	JULY MCWB
110/114							0		0	69		1		1	69
105/109							4	0	4	68		11	1	12	69
100/104		0		0	64		16	3	19	66		42	6	48	67
95/99		3	0	3	62	0	35	8	43	63		67	20	87	65
90/94		15	2	17	61	0	40	15	55	62	1	63	32	96	63
85/89		33	8	41	59	2	45	22	69	60	5	40	40	85	62
80/84	0	43	13	56	58	8	34	30	72	59	19	17	50	86	60
75/79	2	42	22	66	56	15	29	39	83	57	46	6	54	106	58
70/74	6	40	34	80	54	33	19	42	94	55	69	1	31	101	56
65/69	18	31	43	92	52	53	12	36	101	53	60	0	13	73	54
60/64	41	24	48	113	50	59	5	25	89	51	36		1	37	50
55/59	64	11	40	115	48	40	1	14	55	49	9		0	9	48
50/54	63	3	27	93	45	23	0	5	28	46	0			0	45
45/49	40	1	9	50	42	5		0	5	43					
40/44	12	0	2	14	38	1			1	39					
35/39	2	0		2	35										
30/34	0			0	31										
25/29															
20/24															

Temperature Range	AUGUST Obsn Hour Gp 01 to 08	AUGUST 09 to 16	AUGUST 17 to 24	AUGUST Total Obsn	AUGUST MCWB	SEPTEMBER Obsn Hour Gp 01 to 08	SEPTEMBER 09 to 16	SEPTEMBER 17 to 24	SEPTEMBER Total Obsn	SEPTEMBER MCWB	OCTOBER Obsn Hour Gp 01 to 08	OCTOBER 09 to 16	OCTOBER 17 to 24	OCTOBER Total Obsn	OCTOBER MCWB
110/114		0		0	69										
105/109		6	0	6	68		1		1	68					
100/104		37	5	42	67		5	1	6	67					
95/99		67	17	84	65		25	4	29	64		1		1	64
90/94	0	58	29	87	64		44	11	55	62		12	2	14	61
85/89	3	40	37	80	62	0	49	20	69	60		19	4	23	59
80/84	14	23	50	87	61	1	43	30	74	59		38	9	47	57
75/79	41	11	53	105	59	7	30	40	77	58	0	39	15	54	55
70/74	71	4	36	111	57	25	24	47	96	56	1	41	25	67	53
65/69	64	1	15	80	54	46	14	41	101	54	6	37	37	80	51
60/64	40	0	4	44	51	60	5	27	92	51	20	29	50	99	49
55/59	13		1	14	49	53	1	15	69	48	47	20	50	117	47
50/54	3		0	3	45	33	0	3	36	44	67	7	32	106	44
45/49	0			0	42	12		1	13	39	47	3	15	65	39
40/44						3			3	35	37	1	6	44	35
35/39						0			0	35	17	0	2	19	31
30/34											4	0	0	4	27
25/29											1		0	1	21
20/24											0			0	17

EDWARDS AFB CALIFORNIA

Temperature Range	NOVEMBER Obsn Hour Gp 01 to 08	NOVEMBER Obsn Hour Gp 09 to 16	NOVEMBER Obsn Hour Gp 17 to 24	NOVEMBER Total Obsn	NOVEMBER MCWB	DECEMBER Obsn Hour Gp 01 to 08	DECEMBER Obsn Hour Gp 09 to 16	DECEMBER Obsn Hour Gp 17 to 24	DECEMBER Total Obsn	DECEMBER MCWB	JANUARY Obsn Hour Gp 01 to 08	JANUARY Obsn Hour Gp 09 to 16	JANUARY Obsn Hour Gp 17 to 24	JANUARY Total Obsn	JANUARY MCWB
110/114															
105/109															
100/104															
95/99															
90/94															
85/89															
80/84		2		2	56		0		0	58		0		0	60
75/79		9	0	9	53		0		0	55		0		0	56
70/74		23	3	26	51		3	0	3	54		3	0	3	53
65/69		31	9	40	50	0	10	1	11	50		13	2	15	50
60/64	1	43	19	63	48	1	24	3	28	48	0	25	6	31	47
55/59	7	50	36	93	46	2	41	13	56	45	2	41	15	58	46
50/54	28	40	55	123	44	8	51	29	88	43	5	49	35	89	43
45/49	42	22	52	116	40	14	45	47	106	40	23	45	48	116	40
40/44	50	11	35	96	37	26	35	56	117	36	34	33	53	120	36
35/39	47	5	18	70	32	39	24	54	117	33	36	21	41	98	32
30/34	39	2	10	51	28	70	11	33	114	29	53	12	28	93	28
25/29	18	0	2	20	24	59	3	11	73	24	52	5	14	71	24
20/24	6	0	1	7	20	23	0	1	24	19	30	1	5	36	19
15/19	2	0	0	2	16	6	0	0	6	15	11	0	0	11	15
10/14	0			0	14	1			1	9	2		0	2	10
5/9						0			0	7	1		0	1	4
0/4											0			0	1

Temperature Range	FEBRUARY Obsn Hour Gp 01 to 08	FEBRUARY Obsn Hour Gp 09 to 16	FEBRUARY Obsn Hour Gp 17 to 24	FEBRUARY Total Obsn	FEBRUARY MCWB	MARCH Obsn Hour Gp 01 to 08	MARCH Obsn Hour Gp 09 to 16	MARCH Obsn Hour Gp 17 to 24	MARCH Total Obsn	MARCH MCWB	APRIL Obsn Hour Gp 01 to 08	APRIL Obsn Hour Gp 09 to 16	APRIL Obsn Hour Gp 17 to 24	APRIL Total Obsn	APRIL MCWB	ANNUAL TOTAL Obsn Hour Gp 01 to 08	ANNUAL TOTAL Obsn Hour Gp 09 to 16	ANNUAL TOTAL Obsn Hour Gp 17 to 24	ANNUAL TOTAL Total Obsn	ANNUAL TOTAL MCWB
110/114																	1		1	69
105/109																	22		23	68
100/104																	100	15	115	67
95/99																0	198	49	247	65
90/94												1	0	1	60	1	233	91	325	63
85/89							0	0	0	56		9	1	10	58	10	235	132	377	61
80/84		0		0	60		4	1	5	55		22	6	28	56	42	226	189	457	59
75/79		3	0	3	54		13	2	15	54		34	10	44	54	111	216	235	562	57
70/74		11	3	14	52		26	6	32	51	1	37	17	55	52	206	232	244	682	55
65/69		22	6	28	50	0	37	13	50	49	3	34	25	62	51	250	242	241	733	52
60/64	0	32	13	45	48	1	44	24	69	47	11	35	35	81	49	270	266	255	791	49
55/59	4	44	27	75	46	8	49	41	98	45	27	28	44	99	46	276	286	296	858	47
50/54	15	48	45	108	44	28	39	55	122	43	49	24	43	116	44	322	261	329	912	44
45/49	35	37	52	124	41	56	24	58	138	41	59	11	36	106	41	333	188	318	839	40
40/44	44	18	44	106	37	69	9	31	109	37	54	3	19	76	37	330	110	246	686	37
35/39	47	8	24	79	33	48	2	12	62	33	31	0	4	35	34	267	60	155	482	33
30/34	45	2	9	56	29	27	0	4	31	29	5			5	29	243	27	84	354	29
25/29	25	0	2	27	24	9	0	0	9	24	0			0	25	164	8	29	201	24
20/24	9		0	9	20	1			1	19						69	1	7	77	20
15/19	1			1	15	0			0	14						20	0	0	20	15
10/14	0			0	11											3		0	3	10
5/9																1		0	1	4
0/4																0			0	

LOS ANGELES IAP CALIFORNIA

LAT 33 56N LONG 118 24W ELEV 97 FT

MEAN FREQUENCY OF OCCURRENCE OF DRY BULB TEMPERATURE (DEGREES F) WITH MEAN COINCIDENT WET BULB TEMPERATURE (DEGREES F) FOR EACH DRY BULB TEMPERATURE RANGE

Temperature Range	MAY Obsn Hour Gp 01 to 08	MAY 09 to 16	MAY 17 to 24	MAY Total Obsn	MAY MCWB	JUNE Obsn Hour Gp 01 to 08	JUNE 09 to 16	JUNE 17 to 24	JUNE Total Obsn	JUNE MCWB	JULY Obsn Hour Gp 01 to 08	JULY 09 to 16	JULY 17 to 24	JULY Total Obsn	JULY MCWB
105/109															
100/104															
95/99		0		0	63		0		0	63		0		0	68
90/94		0		0	60		0		0	61		0		0	70
85/89	0	1		1	58	0	1	0	1	64	0	3		3	68
80/84	0	2	0	2	57	0	1	0	1	66	0	15	1	16	69
75/79	0	6	1	7	60	0	22	1	23	65	3	62	6	71	67
70/74	1	34	3	38	61	3	66	12	81	63	21	117	41	179	65
65/69	6	103	19	128	58	25	113	53	191	61	104	47	117	268	63
60/64	72	91	100	263	56	139	37	141	317	58	104	3	77	184	59
55/59	126	11	114	251	54	68	1	33	102	55	16		6	22	56
50/54	39	0	11	50	50	5		0	5	51	0			0	53
45/49	2		0	2	45	0			0	47					

Temperature Range	AUGUST Obsn Hour Gp 01 to 08	AUGUST 09 to 16	AUGUST 17 to 24	AUGUST Total Obsn	AUGUST MCWB	SEPTEMBER Obsn Hour Gp 01 to 08	SEPTEMBER 09 to 16	SEPTEMBER 17 to 24	SEPTEMBER Total Obsn	SEPTEMBER MCWB	OCTOBER Obsn Hour Gp 01 to 08	OCTOBER 09 to 16	OCTOBER 17 to 24	OCTOBER Total Obsn	OCTOBER MCWB
105/109							0		0	73					
100/104							1		1	72		1		1	67
95/99		0		0	71		2	0	2	69		1		1	65
90/94		0		0	70	0	1	0	1	69	0	3		3	63
85/89		1	0	1	70	0	5	1	6	68	0	4	0	4	62
80/84	0	16	0	16	69	2	17	2	21	68	1	10	2	13	62
75/79	2	70	6	78	67	5	49	9	63	66	1	22	3	26	63
70/74	21	121	45	187	65	16	93	35	144	64	6	65	13	84	62
65/69	119	37	132	288	63	69	63	98	230	62	34	100	64	198	61
60/64	100	2	63	165	60	122	8	91	221	60	97	40	127	264	58
55/59	6		1	7	57	26	0	4	30	56	88	2	37	127	55
50/54						0			0	53	21		1	22	50
45/49											0			0	43

LOS ANGELES IAP CALIFORNIA

Temperature Range	NOVEMBER Obsn Hour Gp 01 to 08	NOVEMBER 09 to 16	NOVEMBER 17 to 24	NOVEMBER Total Obsn	NOVEMBER MCWB	DECEMBER Obsn Hour Gp 01 to 08	DECEMBER 09 to 16	DECEMBER 17 to 24	DECEMBER Total Obsn	DECEMBER MCWB	JANUARY Obsn Hour Gp 01 to 08	JANUARY 09 to 16	JANUARY 17 to 24	JANUARY Total Obsn	JANUARY MCWB
105/109															
100/104															
95/99		0		0	60										
90/94		1		1	60		0		0	59					
85/89		4		4	59		0		0	55		0		0	60
80/84		10	0	10	56		5		5	56		3		3	57
75/79	0	19	1	20	56		10	0	10	54		7	0	7	55
70/74	0	30	5	35	57		19	2	21	53		16	1	17	54
65/69	5	61	22	88	56	0	40	8	48	53		29	5	34	53
60/64	34	78	80	192	55	10	82	36	128	53	3	60	26	89	52
55/59	86	32	97	215	52	51	69	106	226	52	33	85	86	204	51
50/54	80	4	31	115	48	92	20	78	190	48	83	38	89	210	48
45/49	31	1	5	37	43	73	2	16	91	43	81	10	33	124	43
40/44	4			4	38	19	0	2	21	38	39	1	8	48	39
35/39	0			0	33	2			2	32	9		0	9	33
30/34						0			0	29	0			0	28

Temperature Range	FEBRUARY Obsn Hour Gp 01 to 08	FEBRUARY 09 to 16	FEBRUARY 17 to 24	FEBRUARY Total Obsn	FEBRUARY MCWB	MARCH Obsn Hour Gp 01 to 08	MARCH 09 to 16	MARCH 17 to 24	MARCH Total Obsn	MARCH MCWB	APRIL Obsn Hour Gp 01 to 08	APRIL 09 to 16	APRIL 17 to 24	APRIL Total Obsn	APRIL MCWB
105/109															
100/104															
95/99															
90/94		0		0	63							0		0	59
85/89		1		1	59		1		1	56		1		1	62
80/84		2	0	2	57		3		3	56		4	0	4	62
75/79		6	0	6	56		6	0	6	55	0	6	2	8	61
70/74		15	1	16	54	0	15	2	17	56	1	20	4	25	59
65/69	2	32	6	40	53	2	41	7	50	55	3	51	12	66	58
60/64	5	72	30	107	53	5	95	31	131	54	24	114	45	183	55
55/59	48	71	95	214	52	61	71	116	248	52	113	41	141	295	53
50/54	83	23	75	181	48	108	16	82	206	49	81	3	35	119	50
45/49	66	2	16	84	43	61	0	9	70	44	17	0	1	18	45
40/44	19		1	20	38	10		1	11	40	0			0	41
35/39	1			1	34	1			1	37					
30/34															

Temperature Range	ANNUAL TOTAL Obsn Hour Gp 01 to 08	ANNUAL TOTAL 09 to 16	ANNUAL TOTAL 17 to 24	ANNUAL TOTAL Total Obsn	ANNUAL TOTAL MCWB
105/109		0		0	73
100/104		2		2	70
95/99		3	0	3	67
90/94	0	5	0	5	65
85/89	0	22	1	23	64
80/84	3	88	5	96	64
75/79	11	285	29	325	64
70/74	69	611	164	844	63
65/69	369	717	543	1629	60
60/64	715	682	847	2244	57
55/59	722	383	836	1941	53
50/54	592	104	402	1098	48
45/49	331	15	80	426	43
40/44	91	1	12	104	39
35/39	13		0	13	33
30/34	0			0	28

MCCLELLAN AFB/SACRAMENTO CALIFORNIA

LAT 38 40N LONG 121 24W ELEV 76 FT

MEAN FREQUENCY OF OCCURRENCE OF DRY BULB TEMPERATURE (DEGREES F) WITH MEAN COINCIDENT WET BULB TEMPERATURE (DEGREES F) FOR EACH DRY BULB TEMPERATURE RANGE

Temperature Range	MAY Obsn Hour Gp 01 to 08	MAY 09 to 16	MAY 17 to 24	MAY Total Obsn	MAY MCWB	JUNE Obsn Hour Gp 01 to 08	JUNE 09 to 16	JUNE 17 to 24	JUNE Total Obsn	JUNE MCWB	JULY Obsn Hour Gp 01 to 08	JULY 09 to 16	JULY 17 to 24	JULY Total Obsn	JULY MCWB
110/114							0	0	0	71					
105/109							2	1	3	70		2	1	3	70
100/104		0		0	70		8	4	12	70		16	8	24	69
95/99		2	1	3	68		16	8	24	68		36	17	53	68
90/94		8	4	12	65		25	11	36	66	0	49	25	74	67
85/89		18	7	25	64	1	34	19	54	65	0	46	27	73	66
80/84	0	34	15	49	62	3	44	26	73	63	2	38	32	72	64
75/79	1	39	20	60	60	8	42	32	82	61	12	30	38	80	62
70/74	3	46	27	76	58	18	34	35	87	60	34	21	44	99	60
65/69	10	48	39	97	56	35	21	39	95	57	65	9	36	110	58
60/64	34	34	54	122	54	65	9	39	113	55	88	1	17	106	55
55/59	82	14	53	149	52	79	3	21	103	52	42	0	3	45	53
50/54	89	3	24	116	48	30	0	4	34	49	2		0	2	50
45/49	23	0	4	27	44	2		0	2	45	0			0	46
40/44	6		0	6	40										
35/39	0			0	35										
30/34															

Temperature Range	AUGUST Obsn Hour Gp 01 to 08	AUGUST 09 to 16	AUGUST 17 to 24	AUGUST Total Obsn	AUGUST MCWB	SEPTEMBER Obsn Hour Gp 01 to 08	SEPTEMBER 09 to 16	SEPTEMBER 17 to 24	SEPTEMBER Total Obsn	SEPTEMBER MCWB	OCTOBER Obsn Hour Gp 01 to 08	OCTOBER 09 to 16	OCTOBER 17 to 24	OCTOBER Total Obsn	OCTOBER MCWB
110/114															
105/109		1	0	1	72		0	0	0	69					
100/104		13	6	19	70		3	1	4	69		0		0	67
95/99		32	15	47	68		12	4	16	67		1	0	1	65
90/94		48	23	71	67		32	11	43	65		5	1	6	65
85/89		44	24	68	66		40	17	57	64		16	3	19	63
80/84	2	42	32	76	64	1	43	25	69	63		25	8	33	61
75/79	10	31	44	85	62	3	44	33	80	61		42	15	57	59
70/74	37	23	46	106	60	15	33	45	93	59	1	50	28	79	58
65/69	69	12	36	117	58	46	22	51	119	58	9	49	46	104	56
60/64	89	2	19	110	56	81	9	36	126	55	35	36	65	136	55
55/59	40	0	3	43	54	71	1	15	87	52	89	19	56	164	52
50/54	1		0	1	51	20	0	2	22	48	68	3	19	90	48
45/49	0			0	48	4		0	4	43	32	1	6	39	43
40/44						0			0	38	11		1	12	39
35/39											3		0	3	34
30/34											0			0	27

MCCLELLAN AFB/SACRAMENTO CALIFORNIA

Temperature Range	NOVEMBER Obsn Hour Gp 01 to 08	09 to 16	17 to 24	Total Obsn	MCWB	DECEMBER Obsn Hour Gp 01 to 08	09 to 16	17 to 24	Total Obsn	MCWB	JANUARY Obsn Hour Gp 01 to 08	09 to 16	17 to 24	Total Obsn	MCWB	FEBRUARY Obsn Hour Gp 01 to 08	09 to 16	17 to 24	Total Obsn	MCWB	MARCH Obsn Hour Gp 01 to 08	09 to 16	17 to 24	Total Obsn	MCWB	APRIL Obsn Hour Gp 01 to 08	09 to 16	17 to 24	Total Obsn	MCWB	ANNUAL TOTAL Obsn Hour Gp 01 to 08	09 to 16	17 to 24	Total Obsn	MCWB
110/114																																0	0	0	71
105/109																																5	2	7	70
100/104																																40	19	59	70
95/99																																99	45	144	68
90/94																											0		0	63	0	167	75	242	66
85/89		0		0	63																						4	1	5	63	1	202	98	301	65
80/84		2	0	2	60																	1	0	1	63		16	6	22	61	8	245	144	397	63
75/79		7	0	7	59		0		0	56		0		0	57		0		0	59		7	2	9	60		25	12	37	59	34	267	196	497	61
70/74		15	3	18	57		0		0	53		0		0	55		3	0	3	59		17	7	24	57	0	37	19	56	57	108	279	254	641	59
65/69		33	9	42	55	0	5	0	5	54		1	0	1	57		13	3	16	57		29	13	42	55	1	44	28	73	55	235	286	300	821	57
60/64	3	55	31	89	54	2	13	5	20	53	1	15	5	21	55	1	42	15	58	53	1	59	30	90	52	12	44	39	95	53	412	319	355	1086	54
55/59	33	60	64	157	52	10	43	21	74	51	10	39	20	69	52	18	66	50	134	52	14	70	57	141	50	34	38	52	124	51	522	353	415	1290	52
50/54	64	43	71	178	48	28	58	46	132	48	26	61	44	131	48	43	56	66	165	48	59	45	75	179	48	76	24	49	149	48	506	293	400	1199	48
45/49	60	18	40	118	44	42	58	63	163	44	39	61	68	168	44	55	30	56	141	44	86	18	48	152	44	75	7	28	110	44	418	193	313	924	44
40/44	47	7	17	71	40	73	49	72	194	40	56	43	64	163	40	58	13	27	98	40	60	3	14	77	40	32	1	6	39	40	343	116	201	660	40
35/39	26	1	4	31	35	57	18	31	106	36	62	20	32	114	36	40	2	5	47	35	21	0	2	23	35	9		0	9	36	218	41	74	333	36
30/34	6		0	6	31	26	3	8	37	31	37	8	12	57	31	10	0	1	11	31	5		0	5	30	0			0	32	84	11	21	116	31
25/29	0			0	25	8	0	0	8	27	16	1	1	18	26	1			1	26	1			1	27						26	.	.	28	26
20/24						0			0	23	2			2	22																2			2	22

MOFFETT FIELD NAS CALIFORNIA

LAT 37 25N LONG 122 03W ELEV 34 FT

MEAN FREQUENCY OF OCCURRENCE OF DRY BULB TEMPERATURE (DEGREES F) WITH MEAN COINCIDENT WET BULB TEMPERATURE (DEGREES F) FOR EACH DRY BULB TEMPERATURE RANGE

Temperature Range	MAY Obsn Hour Gp 01 to 08	MAY 09 to 16	MAY 17 to 24	MAY Total Obsn	MAY MCWB	JUNE Obsn Hour Gp 01 to 08	JUNE 09 to 16	JUNE 17 to 24	JUNE Total Obsn	JUNE MCWB	JULY Obsn Hour Gp 01 to 08	JULY 09 to 16	JULY 17 to 24	JULY Total Obsn	JULY MCWB
105/109															
100/104							0		0	70					
95/99							0		0	71		0		0	70
90/94		0	0	0	64		2	0	2	69		1		1	68
85/89		1	0	1	64		4	1	5	67		3	1	4	67
80/84		4	1	5	64		9	3	12	66		10	2	12	66
75/79		11	3	14	63	0	22	8	30	65	0	25	7	32	65
70/74	1	22	9	32	61	3	52	23	78	62	3	66	26	95	63
65/69	3	64	26	93	58	14	86	56	156	59	15	102	72	189	61
60/64	21	98	65	184	55	64	55	82	201	57	98	39	106	243	58
55/59	78	42	91	211	52	104	10	60	174	54	116	2	33	151	55
50/54	104	5	49	158	49	52	0	8	60	50	16		1	17	51
45/49	38	0	5	43	45	3		0	3	45					
40/44	3			3	41										
35/39															

Temperature Range	AUGUST Obsn Hour Gp 01 to 08	AUGUST 09 to 16	AUGUST 17 to 24	AUGUST Total Obsn	AUGUST MCWB	SEPTEMBER Obsn Hour Gp 01 to 08	SEPTEMBER 09 to 16	SEPTEMBER 17 to 24	SEPTEMBER Total Obsn	SEPTEMBER MCWB	OCTOBER Obsn Hour Gp 01 to 08	OCTOBER 09 to 16	OCTOBER 17 to 24	OCTOBER Total Obsn	OCTOBER MCWB
105/109							0		0	71					
100/104							0	0	0	71					
95/99		0		0	69		0	0	0	67					
90/94		0	0	0	66		3	0	3	66		0		0	66
85/89		2	0	2	68		8	1	9	65		3	0	3	65
80/84	0	14	1	15	66		16	4	20	64		11	2	13	63
75/79	0	32	9	41	65	0	32	12	44	63		22	6	28	61
70/74	3	79	35	117	63	2	66	32	100	62	0	42	16	58	60
65/69	19	89	79	187	61	18	77	68	163	60	4	77	42	123	58
60/64	114	30	99	243	58	86	34	84	204	58	42	67	87	196	56
55/59	98	2	22	122	55	97	4	36	137	54	102	23	71	196	53
50/54	14		1	15	51	34	0	3	37	50	74	2	21	97	49
45/49	0			0	47	2		0	2	46	22	0	2	24	44
40/44											4			4	39
35/39											0			0	32

Temperature Range	NOVEMBER Obsn Hour Gp 01 to 08	NOVEMBER 09 to 16	NOVEMBER 17 to 24	NOVEMBER Total Obsn	NOVEMBER MCWB	DECEMBER Obsn Hour Gp 01 to 08	DECEMBER 09 to 16	DECEMBER 17 to 24	DECEMBER Total Obsn	DECEMBER MCWB	JANUARY Obsn Hour Gp 01 to 08	JANUARY 09 to 16	JANUARY 17 to 24	JANUARY Total Obsn	JANUARY MCWB	FEBRUARY Obsn Hour Gp 01 to 08	FEBRUARY 09 to 16	FEBRUARY 17 to 24	FEBRUARY Total Obsn	FEBRUARY MCWB
105/109																				
100/104																				
95/99																				
90/94																				
85/89		0		0	65															
80/84		1	0	1	63															
75/79		1	0	1	59		0		0	60							0		0	61
70/74		11	2	13	58	0	2	0	2	58		1	0	1	61		3	1	4	58
65/69	0	35	8	43	57	2	7	3	12	57		5	1	6	57		16	4	20	57
60/64	6	71	42	119	55	5	30	12	47	55	4	27	11	42	55	3	44	23	70	55
55/59	49	77	84	210	52	19	60	40	119	52	19	64	42	125	52	29	77	65	171	52
50/54	79	33	68	180	49	38	75	73	186	48	38	75	77	190	48	55	60	79	194	48
45/49	58	9	30	97	44	62	50	75	187	44	57	50	69	176	44	75	21	44	140	44
40/44	37	1	5	43	40	76	20	39	135	40	74	21	36	131	40	48	3	8	59	40
35/39	9		0	9	35	40	4	6	50	36	42	5	11	58	35	12	0	0	12	36
30/34	1		0	1	31	6	0		6	32	14	1	1	16	31	1	0	0	1	30
25/29											1			1	26					

Temperature Range	MARCH Obsn Hour Gp 01 to 08	MARCH 09 to 16	MARCH 17 to 24	MARCH Total Obsn	MARCH MCWB	APRIL Obsn Hour Gp 01 to 08	APRIL 09 to 16	APRIL 17 to 24	APRIL Total Obsn	APRIL MCWB	ANNUAL TOTAL Obsn Hour Gp 01 to 08	ANNUAL TOTAL 09 to 16	ANNUAL TOTAL 17 to 24	ANNUAL TOTAL Total Obsn	ANNUAL TOTAL MCWB
105/109												0		0	71
100/104												0	0	0	70
95/99												0	0	0	69
90/94												6	0	6	67
85/89							0	0	0	65		21	3	24	66
80/84		1	0	1	62		4	1	5	64	0	70	14	84	65
75/79		3	1	4	60		10	3	13	61	0	158	49	207	63
70/74		9	3	12	57	0	17	6	23	59	12	370	153	535	62
65/69		21	9	30	55	1	37	16	54	57	76	616	384	1076	59
60/64	3	58	25	86	53	8	71	40	119	54	454	624	676	1754	56
55/59	21	91	69	181	51	39	67	72	178	51	771	519	685	1975	53
50/54	82	54	94	230	48	82	29	70	181	48	668	333	544	1545	48
45/49	91	10	42	143	44	85	4	30	119	44	493	144	297	934	44
40/44	43	1	5	49	40	25	0	2	27	41	310	46	95	451	40
35/39	7		0	7	36	2			2	37	112	9	17	138	35
30/34	0			0	32						22	1	1	24	31
25/29											1			1	26

NORTON AFB/SAN BERNARDINO CALIFORNIA

LAT 34 06N LONG 117 14W ELEV 1156 FT

MEAN FREQUENCY OF OCCURRENCE OF DRY BULB TEMPERATURE (DEGREES F) WITH MEAN COINCIDENT WET BULB TEMPERATURE (DEGREES F) FOR EACH DRY BULB TEMPERATURE RANGE

Temperature Range	MAY Obsn Hour Gp 01 to 08	MAY Obsn Hour Gp 09 to 16	MAY Obsn Hour Gp 17 to 24	MAY Total Obsn	MAY MCWB	JUNE Obsn Hour Gp 01 to 08	JUNE Obsn Hour Gp 09 to 16	JUNE Obsn Hour Gp 17 to 24	JUNE Total Obsn	JUNE MCWB	JULY Obsn Hour Gp 01 to 08	JULY Obsn Hour Gp 09 to 16	JULY Obsn Hour Gp 17 to 24	JULY Total Obsn	JULY MCWB
110/114							0	0	0	66					
105/109							1		1	67		4	0	4	69
100/104		1		1	66		4		4	68		15	1	16	70
95/99		3	0	3	64		19	1	20	66		48	6	54	69
90/94		10	1	11	63		31	6	37	66	0	68	17	85	67
85/89	0	22	3	25	62		32	14	46	65	1	49	31	81	66
80/84	0	31	9	40	61	1	33	20	54	64	3	31	37	71	65
75/79	1	36	15	52	60	3	31	26	60	63	13	19	47	79	64
70/74	3	39	24	66	58	8	29	38	75	61	35	9	57	101	63
65/69	6	39	36	81	57	20	29	48	97	59	74	3	38	115	61
60/64	19	38	60	117	55	65	23	52	140	57	71	1	13	85	58
55/59	99	22	71	192	53	104	8	32	144	54	41		1	42	54
50/54	82	6	24	112	49	33	0	3	36	50	9			9	49
45/49	31	1	4	36	45	5		0	5	45					
40/44	6		1	7	41	1			1	42					
35/39	0			0	34										
30/34															

Temperature Range	AUGUST Obsn Hour Gp 01 to 08	AUGUST Obsn Hour Gp 09 to 16	AUGUST Obsn Hour Gp 17 to 24	AUGUST Total Obsn	AUGUST MCWB	SEPTEMBER Obsn Hour Gp 01 to 08	SEPTEMBER Obsn Hour Gp 09 to 16	SEPTEMBER Obsn Hour Gp 17 to 24	SEPTEMBER Total Obsn	SEPTEMBER MCWB	OCTOBER Obsn Hour Gp 01 to 08	OCTOBER Obsn Hour Gp 09 to 16	OCTOBER Obsn Hour Gp 17 to 24	OCTOBER Total Obsn	OCTOBER MCWB
110/114		0		0	72		0		0	71					
105/109		3		3	71		2	0	2	71					
100/104		18	1	19	71		11	0	11	69		2		2	66
95/99		54	5	59	70		30	2	32	67		12	0	12	63
90/94		60	17	77	69		43	8	51	66		26	2	28	62
85/89	1	46	29	76	68	0	43	17	60	65		28	6	34	61
80/84	5	32	42	79	66	2	35	25	62	64	0	34	10	44	59
75/79	16	18	51	85	65	8	28	34	70	63	2	39	17	58	59
70/74	45	11	58	114	64	19	23	44	86	62	4	37	27	68	58
65/69	82	4	35	121	61	41	18	53	112	60	12	35	43	90	57
60/64	73	1	9	83	58	81	7	45	133	57	43	25	69	137	55
55/59	24		0	24	54	60	1	10	71	53	75	8	46	129	52
50/54	2		0	2	50	24		2	26	49	68	2	21	91	47
45/49						4		0	4	45	34	1	5	40	43
40/44						0			0	42	8		1	9	38
35/39											1		0	1	33
30/34											1			1	30

NORTON AFB/SAN BERNARDINO CALIFORNIA

Temperature Range	NOVEMBER Obsn Hour Gp 01 to 08	NOVEMBER Obsn Hour Gp 09 to 16	NOVEMBER Obsn Hour Gp 17 to 24	NOVEMBER Total Obsn	NOVEMBER MCWB	DECEMBER Obsn Hour Gp 01 to 08	DECEMBER Obsn Hour Gp 09 to 16	DECEMBER Obsn Hour Gp 17 to 24	DECEMBER Total Obsn	DECEMBER MCWB	JANUARY Obsn Hour Gp 01 to 08	JANUARY Obsn Hour Gp 09 to 16	JANUARY Obsn Hour Gp 17 to 24	JANUARY Total Obsn	JANUARY MCWB
110/114															
105/109															
100/104															
95/99															
90/94		2		2	59							0		0	66
85/89	0	5	0	5	58		0		0	56		1		1	62
80/84	0	15	1	16	57		3	0	3	55		5	0	5	57
75/79	0	28	3	31	55		11	0	11	53	1	12	2	15	54
70/74	0	35	8	43	53		28	1	29	51	0	21	3	24	52
65/69	1	45	16	62	52	0	38	6	44	50	0	32	7	39	50
60/64	6	52	34	92	51	1	44	14	59	49	2	45	17	64	49
55/59	31	37	59	127	50	7	53	33	93	48	7	55	33	95	47
50/54	58	17	64	139	47	24	42	59	125	45	29	45	59	133	46
45/49	67	3	37	107	42	50	19	68	137	42	51	23	58	132	42
40/44	51	1	15	67	38	76	8	45	129	38	60	8	41	109	37
35/39	22	0	3	25	34	63	1	18	82	34	54	1	20	75	34
30/34	4	0	1	5	30	23	0	3	26	29	37	0	7	44	29
25/29	0			0	25	3		0	3	26	7		0	7	25
20/24						0			0	23	0			0	19

Temperature Range	FEBRUARY Obsn Hour Gp 01 to 08	FEBRUARY Obsn Hour Gp 09 to 16	FEBRUARY Obsn Hour Gp 17 to 24	FEBRUARY Total Obsn	FEBRUARY MCWB	MARCH Obsn Hour Gp 01 to 08	MARCH Obsn Hour Gp 09 to 16	MARCH Obsn Hour Gp 17 to 24	MARCH Total Obsn	MARCH MCWB	APRIL Obsn Hour Gp 01 to 08	APRIL Obsn Hour Gp 09 to 16	APRIL Obsn Hour Gp 17 to 24	APRIL Total Obsn	APRIL MCWB	ANNUAL TOTAL Obsn Hour Gp 01 to 08	ANNUAL TOTAL Obsn Hour Gp 09 to 16	ANNUAL TOTAL Obsn Hour Gp 17 to 24	ANNUAL TOTAL Total Obsn	ANNUAL TOTAL MCWB
110/114																	0	0	0	69
105/109																	10	0	10	70
100/104																	51	2	53	69
95/99							0		0	63		2		2	65		168	14	182	68
90/94		0		0	62		0		0	61		7	1	8	60	0	247	52	299	66
85/89		2		2	59		3	0	3	58		18	2	20	59	2	249	102	353	65
80/84		6	1	7	57		11	1	12	56	0	24	6	30	58	11	260	152	423	63
75/79		14	2	16	54		21	4	25	55	0	28	11	39	57	44	285	212	541	61
70/74		24	6	30	53		35	9	44	54	2	30	16	48	56	116	321	291	728	59
65/69	0	36	11	47	51	1	36	17	54	52	4	34	24	62	54	241	349	334	924	57
60/64	3	46	26	75	50	3	49	29	81	51	7	35	36	78	53	374	366	404	1144	54
55/59	15	47	49	111	50	10	49	56	115	49	41	35	59	135	51	514	315	449	1278	51
50/54	49	34	62	145	47	67	34	77	178	47	75	22	54	151	48	520	202	425	1147	47
45/49	55	12	43	110	43	80	7	37	124	44	67	6	24	97	44	444	72	276	792	43
40/44	57	2	18	77	39	60	1	14	75	39	35	1	7	43	40	354	21	142	517	38
35/39	32	0	5	37	34	22		2	24	35	9		0	9	36	203	2	48	253	34
30/34	12		1	13	30	5		0	5	30	0			0	33	82	0	12	94	29
25/29	1		0	1	25	0			0	26						11		0	11	25
20/24																0			0	22

SAN DIEGO FWF CALIFORNIA

LAT 32 43N LONG 117 09W ELEV 48 FT

MEAN FREQUENCY OF OCCURRENCE OF DRY BULB TEMPERATURE (DEGREES F) WITH MEAN COINCIDENT WET BULB TEMPERATURE (DEGREES F) FOR EACH DRY BULB TEMPERATURE RANGE

Temperature Range	MAY Obsn Hour Gp 01 to 08	MAY 09 to 16	MAY 17 to 24	MAY Total Obsn	MAY MCWB	JUNE Obsn Hour Gp 01 to 08	JUNE 09 to 16	JUNE 17 to 24	JUNE Total Obsn	JUNE MCWB	JULY Obsn Hour Gp 01 to 08	JULY 09 to 16	JULY 17 to 24	JULY Total Obsn	JULY MCWB
100/104															
95/99							0		0	64					
90/94		0		0	63		0		0	64		0		0	69
85/89		1		1	61	0	0	0	0	65		2	0	2	69
80/84	0	2	0	2	59	0	1	0	1	66	0	6	1	7	70
75/79	0	2	1	3	60	0	4	1	5	66	2	35	9	46	69
70/74	0	15	4	19	62	1	36	8	45	64	33	84	55	172	66
65/69	7	78	23	108	60	36	86	65	187	62	99	37	88	224	63
60/64	111	112	122	345	57	110	52	82	244	59	32	13	15	60	60
55/59	74	28	64	166	54	30	38	28	96	54	11	39	17	67	53
50/54	25	7	21	53	51	23	17	31	71	50	28	22	35	85	50
45/49	15	1	8	24	46	20	4	15	39	46	19	6	16	41	45
40/44	9	1	3	13	42	10	1	6	17	41	12	2	10	24	41
35/39	5	0	1	6	37	7	1	3	11	37	7	1	3	11	37
30/34	1		0	1	33	3	0	0	3	33	6	0	1	7	32
25/29						0			0	29	1			1	28

Temperature Range	AUGUST Obsn Hour Gp 01 to 08	AUGUST 09 to 16	AUGUST 17 to 24	AUGUST Total Obsn	AUGUST MCWB	SEPTEMBER Obsn Hour Gp 01 to 08	SEPTEMBER 09 to 16	SEPTEMBER 17 to 24	SEPTEMBER Total Obsn	SEPTEMBER MCWB	OCTOBER Obsn Hour Gp 01 to 08	OCTOBER 09 to 16	OCTOBER 17 to 24	OCTOBER Total Obsn	OCTOBER MCWB
100/104							0		0	64					
95/99							1	0	1	64		0		0	68
90/94		0		0	76	0	1	0	1	66		1		1	64
85/89		1	0	1	73	0	4	0	4	67		4	1	5	63
80/84	0	11	2	13	71	0	8	3	11	68		7	2	9	61
75/79	7	58	17	82	70	4	29	10	43	68	1	12	5	18	61
70/74	68	87	85	240	67	27	86	48	161	66	5	52	15	72	63
65/69	88	8	60	156	64	95	34	88	217	63	41	97	78	216	61
60/64	3	14	2	19	56	32	34	15	81	58	88	57	82	227	58
55/59	8	41	20	69	52	19	33	30	82	54	59	16	37	112	54
50/54	30	21	34	85	49	25	8	28	61	50	32	2	21	55	50
45/49	17	5	16	38	46	19	1	13	33	46	16	0	7	23	46
40/44	13	1	8	22	41	14		4	18	42	6		1	7	42
35/39	11	0	4	15	37	5		0	5	38	1			1	38
30/34	4	0		4	32	0			0	34					
25/29	0			0	29										

SAN DIEGO FWF CALIFORNIA

Temperature Range	NOVEMBER Obsn Hour Gp 01 to 08	09 to 16	17 to 24	Total Obsn	MCWB	DECEMBER Obsn Hour Gp 01 to 08	09 to 16	17 to 24	Total Obsn	MCWB	JANUARY Obsn Hour Gp 01 to 08	09 to 16	17 to 24	Total Obsn	MCWB
100/104															
95/99		0		0	65										
90/94		0		0	63										
85/89		0	0	0	61										
80/84		1	0	1	59		0	0	0	60		4	0	4	67
75/79		8	0	8	57		12	1	13	63	0	23	5	28	66
70/74	0	29	5	34	59	0	42	10	52	61	2	44	16	62	63
65/69	3	85	26	114	59	11	51	28	90	59	23	31	35	89	61
60/64	59	88	103	250	57	39	74	65	178	57	33	63	49	145	57
55/59	97	25	82	204	54	63	49	84	196	52	59	52	82	193	53
50/54	62	3	21	86	49	81	16	52	149	48	72	26	48	146	48
45/49	16	0	3	19	45	46	2	8	56	44	46	4	12	62	43
40/44	3		0	3	41	7	0	1	8	38	12	0	1	13	38
35/39						1			1	35	1			1	33
30/34															
25/29															

Temperature Range	FEBRUARY Obsn Hour Gp 01 to 08	09 to 16	17 to 24	Total Obsn	MCWB	MARCH Obsn Hour Gp 01 to 08	09 to 16	17 to 24	Total Obsn	MCWB	APRIL Obsn Hour Gp 01 to 08	09 to 16	17 to 24	Total Obsn	MCWB	ANNUAL TOTAL Obsn Hour Gp 01 to 08	09 to 16	17 to 24	Total Obsn	MCWB
100/104																	0		0	64
95/99																	1	0	1	65
90/94																0	2	0	2	65
85/89												1		1	59	0	13	1	14	65
80/84		2	0	2	66		1		1	58		2	0	2	59	0	45	8	53	67
75/79		20	4	24	66		11	1	12	64		6	1	7	60	14	220	55	289	67
70/74	3	41	17	61	64	2	43	10	55	63	0	22	5	27	62	141	581	278	1000	65
65/69	19	33	32	84	61	14	51	32	97	60	7	71	27	105	60	443	662	582	1687	62
60/64	30	60	50	140	57	33	90	77	200	57	56	100	98	254	57	626	757	760	2143	57
55/59	69	51	81	201	54	112	47	102	261	54	108	34	89	231	53	709	453	716	1878	53
50/54	66	16	35	117	49	67	6	24	97	49	49	3	14	66	50	560	147	364	1071	49
45/49	32	1	5	38	45	19	0	2	21	45	15	0	5	20	47	280	24	110	414	45
40/44	4		0	4	40	2			2	42	4		1	5	42	96	5	35	136	41
35/39	0			0	36						1			1	39	39	2	11	52	37
30/34																14	0	1	15	32
25/29																				29

TRAVIS AFB/FAIRFIELD CALIFORNIA

LAT 38 16N LONG 121 56W ELEV 62 FT

MEAN FREQUENCY OF OCCURRENCE OF DRY BULB TEMPERATURE (DEGREES F) WITH MEAN COINCIDENT WET BULB TEMPERATURE (DEGREES F) FOR EACH DRY BULB TEMPERATURE RANGE

Temperature Range	MAY Obsn Hour Gp 01 to 08	MAY Obsn Hour Gp 09 to 16	MAY Obsn Hour Gp 17 to 24	MAY Total Obsn	MAY MCWB	JUNE Obsn Hour Gp 01 to 08	JUNE Obsn Hour Gp 09 to 16	JUNE Obsn Hour Gp 17 to 24	JUNE Total Obsn	JUNE MCWB	JULY Obsn Hour Gp 01 to 08	JULY Obsn Hour Gp 09 to 16	JULY Obsn Hour Gp 17 to 24	JULY Total Obsn	JULY MCWB
110/114							0		0	71					
105/109							1	0	1	70		2	0	2	71
100/104							4	1	5	69		5	1	6	69
95/99		1	0	1	63		11	2	13	68		15	3	18	68
90/94		4	1	5	66	0	16	5	21	67	0	25	6	31	67
85/89		11	2	13	64	1	20	8	29	65	0	39	11	50	66
80/84	0	18	5	23	62	1	32	11	44	64	1	48	20	69	64
75/79	1	31	9	41	61	4	47	21	72	61	4	45	30	79	62
70/74	1	45	17	63	58	10	47	31	88	60	9	35	36	80	60
65/69	6	62	29	97	56	20	39	41	100	57	25	24	47	96	58
60/64	22	51	52	125	54	51	17	52	120	55	71	10	61	142	56
55/59	68	22	73	163	51	93	6	54	153	53	115	1	30	146	53
50/54	111	4	53	168	48	57	1	14	72	49	22		2	24	50
45/49	33	0	7	40	44	3		0	3	45			0	0	48
40/44	5		1	6	40	0			0	41					
35/39	0			0	35										
30/34	0			0	32										

Temperature Range	AUGUST Obsn Hour Gp 01 to 08	AUGUST Obsn Hour Gp 09 to 16	AUGUST Obsn Hour Gp 17 to 24	AUGUST Total Obsn	AUGUST MCWB	SEPTEMBER Obsn Hour Gp 01 to 08	SEPTEMBER Obsn Hour Gp 09 to 16	SEPTEMBER Obsn Hour Gp 17 to 24	SEPTEMBER Total Obsn	SEPTEMBER MCWB	OCTOBER Obsn Hour Gp 01 to 08	OCTOBER Obsn Hour Gp 09 to 16	OCTOBER Obsn Hour Gp 17 to 24	OCTOBER Total Obsn	OCTOBER MCWB
110/114							0		0	71					
105/109		1	0	1	70		1	0	1	70					
100/104		4	0	4	70		1	0	1	69		0		0	65
95/99		15	2	17	68		9	1	10	67		1	0	1	64
90/94		29	7	36	66		22	5	27	65		5	1	6	64
85/89		35	10	45	65	0	32	9	41	64		14	2	16	63
80/84	0	48	18	66	64	1	41	14	56	62		21	4	25	61
75/79	3	46	29	78	62	4	43	23	70	60	0	37	11	48	59
70/74	9	36	41	86	60	9	46	35	90	59	1	50	22	73	57
65/69	29	24	55	108	58	28	29	52	109	58	9	54	40	103	56
60/64	88	10	56	154	56	76	15	59	150	56	33	45	62	140	54
55/59	101	1	27	129	54	87	2	36	125	53	90	18	74	182	52
50/54	18		1	19	51	34		4	38	50	81	2	27	110	49
45/49						2			2	45	26	0	5	31	44
40/44											5		1	6	39
35/39											1			1	34
30/34															

TRAVIS AFB/FAIRFIELD CALIFORNIA

Temperature Range	NOVEMBER Obsn Hour Gp 01 to 08	09 to 16	17 to 24	Total Obsn	MCWB	DECEMBER Obsn Hour Gp 01 to 08	09 to 16	17 to 24	Total Obsn	MCWB	JANUARY Obsn Hour Gp 01 to 08	09 to 16	17 to 24	Total Obsn	MCWB
110/114															
105/109															
100/104															
95/99															
90/94															
85/89		0		0	60										
80/84		1	0	1	60										
75/79		6	1	7	58		0		0	53		0		0	55
70/74		16	1	17	56		1	0	1	53		0		0	54
65/69	0	32	8	40	54		5	1	6	51		1	0	1	53
60/64	3	57	28	88	53	1	13	4	18	52	0	13	3	16	53
55/59	35	61	70	166	51	7	39	18	64	51	7	37	19	63	52
50/54	66	40	70	176	48	25	60	45	130	47	27	64	49	140	48
45/49	67	18	43	128	44	50	60	66	176	44	39	58	65	162	44
40/44	46	6	14	66	40	75	48	73	196	40	63	45	66	174	40
35/39	17	1	5	23	36	56	18	32	106	36	64	20	33	117	35
30/34	5	0	0	5	31	27	3	8	38	31	34	9	11	54	31
25/29	1			1	28	6	0	1	7	27	13	1	1	15	27
20/24						1			1	23	1		0	1	22
15/19											0			0	19

Temperature Range	FEBRUARY Obsn Hour Gp 01 to 08	09 to 16	17 to 24	Total Obsn	MCWB	MARCH Obsn Hour Gp 01 to 08	09 to 16	17 to 24	Total Obsn	MCWB	APRIL Obsn Hour Gp 01 to 08	09 to 16	17 to 24	Total Obsn	MCWB
110/114															
105/109															
100/104															
95/99															
90/94												0		0	66
85/89							0		0	65		3	0	3	62
80/84							0	0	0	64		9	2	11	61
75/79		0		0	53		5	1	6	59	0	22	7	29	59
70/74		3	0	3	57		15	5	20	56	1	30	11	42	57
65/69		10	3	13	56	0	23	10	33	54	4	44	19	67	55
60/64	0	39	14	53	53	3	54	21	78	52	9	52	32	93	53
55/59	15	72	48	135	51	14	75	49	138	50	30	47	52	129	50
50/54	46	56	70	172	48	57	56	83	196	47	75	24	63	162	48
45/49	67	32	57	156	44	92	17	58	167	44	75	7	40	122	44
40/44	62	11	27	100	40	60	3	18	81	40	35	1	11	47	40
35/39	28	2	5	35	36	17	0	3	20	36	9	0	2	11	35
30/34	6	0	0	6	31	4		0	4	31	1			1	31
25/29	0			0	29	0			0	27					
20/24															
15/19															

Temperature Range	ANNUAL TOTAL Obsn Hour Gp 01 to 08	09 to 16	17 to 24	Total Obsn	MCWB
110/114		0		0	71
105/109		5	0	5	70
100/104		14	2	16	69
95/99		52	8	60	67
90/94	0	101	25	126	66
85/89	1	154	42	197	65
80/84	3	218	74	295	63
75/79	16	282	132	430	61
70/74	40	324	199	563	59
65/69	121	347	305	773	57
60/64	357	376	444	1177	54
55/59	662	381	550	1593	52
50/54	619	307	481	1407	48
45/49	454	192	341	987	44
40/44	351	114	211	676	40
35/39	192	41	80	313	36
30/34	77	12	19	108	31
25/29	20	1	2	23	27
20/24	2		0	2	23
15/19	0			0	19

VANDENBERG AFB/LOMPOC CALIFORNIA

LAT 34 43N LONG 120 34W ELEV 368 FT

MEAN FREQUENCY OF OCCURRENCE OF DRY BULB TEMPERATURE (DEGREES F) WITH MEAN COINCIDENT WET BULB TEMPERATURE (DEGREES F) FOR EACH DRY BULB TEMPERATURE RANGE

Temperature Range	MAY Obsn Hour Gp 01 to 08	MAY 09 to 16	MAY 17 to 24	MAY Total Obsn	MAY MCWB	JUNE Obsn Hour Gp 01 to 08	JUNE 09 to 16	JUNE 17 to 24	JUNE Total Obsn	JUNE MCWB	JULY Obsn Hour Gp 01 to 08	JULY 09 to 16	JULY 17 to 24	JULY Total Obsn	JULY MCWB
95/99															
90/94		0		0	61										
85/89	0	0		0	63							0		0	59
80/84		1	0	1	62						0	0		0	61
75/79	0	1	0	1	60	0	1		1	63	0	1	1	2	61
70/74	0	2	0	2	58	0	3	0	3	61	0	8	2	10	61
65/69	1	10	1	12	56	1	21	2	24	59	1	39	4	44	59
60/64	3	62	5	70	55	6	100	18	124	56	6	123	25	154	57
55/59	18	137	50	205	52	48	99	90	237	54	79	66	132	277	54
50/54	136	34	159	329	49	155	16	124	295	50	149	10	84	243	51
45/49	81	1	32	114	46	29		6	35	47	12	0	1	13	47
40/44	8		1	9	42	1			1	42					
35/39	0			0	37										

Temperature Range	AUGUST Obsn Hour Gp 01 to 08	AUGUST 09 to 16	AUGUST 17 to 24	AUGUST Total Obsn	AUGUST MCWB	SEPTEMBER Obsn Hour Gp 01 to 08	SEPTEMBER 09 to 16	SEPTEMBER 17 to 24	SEPTEMBER Total Obsn	SEPTEMBER MCWB	OCTOBER Obsn Hour Gp 01 to 08	OCTOBER 09 to 16	OCTOBER 17 to 24	OCTOBER Total Obsn	OCTOBER MCWB
95/99		0		0	65		0		0	62		1		1	63
90/94	0	0		0	63		1		1	61		3		3	61
85/89		0		0	63		4		4	59	0	4	0	4	60
80/84	0	0		0	62	0	5	0	5	61	0	8	0	8	58
75/79	0	3	0	3	61	1	9	1	11	61	1	12	2	15	58
70/74	1	17	1	19	61	1	21	3	25	60	3	26	3	32	57
65/69	2	67	8	77	59	5	61	10	76	59	7	57	11	75	57
60/64	11	115	46	172	57	24	99	55	178	57	24	91	43	158	56
55/59	123	41	156	320	55	114	37	130	281	55	91	42	121	254	54
50/54	108	4	37	149	52	83	4	39	126	51	87	5	56	148	50
45/49	2		0	2	47	12		2	14	46	28	0	11	39	45
40/44						1			1	42	6		1	7	39
35/39											1		0	1	34

VANDENBERG AFB/LOMPOC CALIFORNIA

Temperature Range	NOVEMBER Obsn Hour Gp 01 to 08	09 to 16	17 to 24	Total Obsn	MCWB	DECEMBER Obsn Hour Gp 01 to 08	09 to 16	17 to 24	Total Obsn	MCWB	JANUARY Obsn Hour Gp 01 to 08	09 to 16	17 to 24	Total Obsn	MCWB
95/99															
90/94															
85/89		0		0	61										
80/84		2		2	56		0		0	59		0		0	66
75/79		6		6	55		2		2	54		3	0	3	57
70/74	0	16	1	17	55		9	0	9	54	0	10	1	11	55
65/69	2	34	4	40	55	0	19	2	21	53	1	18	2	21	54
60/64	14	76	22	112	54	3	48	11	62	53	3	43	7	53	52
55/59	49	79	83	211	53	22	84	40	146	51	18	85	39	142	51
50/54	80	23	91	194	49	49	61	88	198	48	63	64	98	225	48
45/49	64	3	29	96	44	81	19	68	168	43	69	17	61	147	43
40/44	25		9	34	39	61	5	33	99	39	57	6	31	94	39
35/39	6		2	8	35	27	0	6	33	34	29	1	9	39	35
30/34	0			0	32	5		1	6	30	7		0	7	31
25/29						0		0	0	23					

Temperature Range	FEBRUARY Obsn Hour Gp 01 to 08	09 to 16	17 to 24	Total Obsn	MCWB	MARCH Obsn Hour Gp 01 to 08	09 to 16	17 to 24	Total Obsn	MCWB	APRIL Obsn Hour Gp 01 to 08	09 to 16	17 to 24	Total Obsn	MCWB
95/99															
90/94												0		0	61
85/89												1		1	60
80/84		0		0	59							1		1	59
75/79		1		1	58		2	0	2	57	0	3	0	3	59
70/74		6	0	6	56		7	0	7	55	0	7	1	8	57
65/69		15	1	16	53		17	2	19	53	3	14	3	20	56
60/64	2	43	5	50	53	4	40	7	51	52	5	47	7	59	54
55/59	15	86	35	136	51	13	107	28	148	51	16	108	33	157	51
50/54	57	60	100	217	48	66	66	126	258	48	78	54	123	255	49
45/49	79	11	62	152	44	106	9	72	187	45	102	5	67	174	45
40/44	57	1	18	76	40	48	0	12	60	40	31	0	6	37	41
35/39	13	0	2	15	35	11		1	12	35	4		0	4	36
30/34	1		0	1	31	1			1	29					
25/29															

Temperature Range	ANNUAL TOTAL Obsn Hour Gp 01 to 08	09 to 16	17 to 24	Total Obsn	MCWB
95/99		1		1	63
90/94	0	4		4	61
85/89	0	9	0	9	60
80/84	0	17	0	17	59
75/79	2	44	4	50	59
70/74	5	132	12	149	58
65/69	23	372	50	445	57
60/64	105	887	251	1243	55
55/59	606	971	937	2514	53
50/54	1111	401	1125	2637	49
45/49	665	65	411	1141	45
40/44	295	12	111	418	40
35/39	91	1	20	112	35
30/34	14		1	15	30
25/29	0		0	0	23

BUCKLEY ANGB/DENVER COLORADO

LAT 39 42N LONG 104 45W ELEV 5663 FT

MEAN FREQUENCY OF OCCURRENCE OF DRY BULB TEMPERATURE (DEGREES F) WITH MEAN COINCIDENT WET BULB TEMPERATURE (DEGREES F) FOR EACH DRY BULB TEMPERATURE RANGE

Temperature Range	MAY Obsn Hour Gp 01 to 08	MAY 09 to 16	MAY 17 to 24	MAY Total Obsn	MAY MCWB	JUNE Obsn Hour Gp 01 to 08	JUNE 09 to 16	JUNE 17 to 24	JUNE Total Obsn	JUNE MCWB	JULY Obsn Hour Gp 01 to 08	JULY 09 to 16	JULY 17 to 24	JULY Total Obsn	JULY MCWB
100/104															
95/99							2	0	2	60		2	0	2	61
90/94							12	3	15	58		31	5	36	60
85/89		4	0	4	55	0	23	6	29	58	0	62	14	76	60
80/84		20	4	24	53	1	32	12	45	57	3	60	25	88	61
75/79	0	32	9	41	52	3	44	21	68	56	10	44	37	91	60
70/74	2	41	18	61	51	9	42	30	81	55	26	29	56	111	59
65/69	5	38	25	68	50	19	38	37	94	54	62	12	60	134	57
60/64	17	39	39	95	48	45	23	48	116	52	90	5	37	132	56
55/59	34	23	43	100	46	63	11	41	115	51	45	3	13	61	53
50/54	50	22	39	111	44	58	9	29	96	48	11	0	2	13	50
45/49	56	14	34	104	42	33	5	10	48	44	1	1	1	3	45
40/44	46	11	23	80	38	9	1	2	12	41	1			1	43
35/39	24	3	9	36	35	1	0	1	2	37					
30/34	10	1	5	16	30										
25/29	3		0	3	26										
20/24															
15/19															
10/14															
5/9															

Temperature Range	AUGUST Obsn Hour Gp 01 to 08	AUGUST 09 to 16	AUGUST 17 to 24	AUGUST Total Obsn	AUGUST MCWB	SEPTEMBER Obsn Hour Gp 01 to 08	SEPTEMBER 09 to 16	SEPTEMBER 17 to 24	SEPTEMBER Total Obsn	SEPTEMBER MCWB	OCTOBER Obsn Hour Gp 01 to 08	OCTOBER 09 to 16	OCTOBER 17 to 24	OCTOBER Total Obsn	OCTOBER MCWB
100/104		0		0	64										
95/99		3	0	3	63										
90/94		18	2	20	60		0		0	60					
85/89		41	9	50	60		13	2	15	56		0		0	54
80/84	2	62	19	83	59		38	6	44	56		7		7	52
75/79	6	51	30	87	59	0	48	13	61	55		23	2	25	51
70/74	18	37	48	103	58	3	43	23	69	54	0	32	4	36	49
65/69	48	20	59	127	56	10	32	36	78	52	1	35	10	46	48
60/64	82	11	54	147	55	33	22	51	106	51	6	39	20	65	46
55/59	63	5	20	88	52	62	16	45	123	49	17	30	35	82	44
50/54	25	1	5	31	48	54	10	27	91	46	33	27	42	102	41
45/49	5	0	1	6	43	38	7	17	62	42	48	18	47	113	39
40/44	0			0	43	21	4	8	33	39	55	12	39	106	36
35/39						11	4	6	21	35	41	10	20	71	33
30/34						5	4	4	13	31	27	10	17	54	30
25/29						2		1	3	27	12	3	7	22	25
20/24						0			0	23	6	2	4	12	21
15/19											1	1	1	3	17
10/14											1	0	1	2	12
5/9											1			1	6

Temperature Range	NOVEMBER Obsn Hour Gp 01 to 08	NOVEMBER Obsn Hour Gp 09 to 16	NOVEMBER Obsn Hour Gp 17 to 24	NOVEMBER Total Obsn	NOVEMBER MCWB	DECEMBER Obsn Hour Gp 01 to 08	DECEMBER Obsn Hour Gp 09 to 16	DECEMBER Obsn Hour Gp 17 to 24	DECEMBER Total Obsn	DECEMBER MCWB	JANUARY Obsn Hour Gp 01 to 08	JANUARY Obsn Hour Gp 09 to 16	JANUARY Obsn Hour Gp 17 to 24	JANUARY Total Obsn	JANUARY MCWB	FEBRUARY Obsn Hour Gp 01 to 08	FEBRUARY Obsn Hour Gp 09 to 16	FEBRUARY Obsn Hour Gp 17 to 24	FEBRUARY Total Obsn	FEBRUARY MCWB	MARCH Obsn Hour Gp 01 to 08	MARCH Obsn Hour Gp 09 to 16	MARCH Obsn Hour Gp 17 to 24	MARCH Total Obsn	MARCH MCWB	APRIL Obsn Hour Gp 01 to 08	APRIL Obsn Hour Gp 09 to 16	APRIL Obsn Hour Gp 17 to 24	APRIL Total Obsn	APRIL MCWB	ANNUAL TOTAL Obsn Hour Gp 01 to 08	ANNUAL TOTAL Obsn Hour Gp 09 to 16	ANNUAL TOTAL Obsn Hour Gp 17 to 24	ANNUAL TOTAL Total Obsn	ANNUAL TOTAL MCWB
100/104																																0		0	64
95/99																																7	0	7	61
90/94																																61	10	71	60
85/89																															0	143	31	174	59
80/84																						0		0	53		0		0	50	6	219	66	291	58
75/79		0		0	48																	1	0	1	51		8	2	10	49	19	251	114	384	56
70/74		3		3	47		0		0	51							1		1	48		5	1	6	47		18	5	23	47	58	251	185	494	55
65/69		12	0	12	46	1	2	0	3	45		1		1	46		4	0	4	45		10	0	10	44	0	27	8	35	46	146	234	238	618	53
60/64	0	18	1	19	44	0	10	1	11	43		7	1	8	43		7	1	8	43	1	22	6	29	42	2	32	14	48	44	276	245	273	794	51
55/59	1	37	6	44	42	1	20	2	23	40	1	16	1	18	41	0	12	3	15	41	1	25	9	35	41	7	39	26	72	42	295	237	244	776	47
50/54	6	32	19	57	39	2	27	5	34	38	2	27	5	34	38	1	26	8	35	38	4	26	14	44	38	18	37	36	91	40	264	244	231	739	43
45/49	16	33	31	80	37	6	28	11	45	35	5	31	13	49	36	5	34	16	55	36	8	26	24	58	36	32	31	43	106	38	253	228	248	729	39
40/44	42	26	49	117	34	16	34	25	75	32	16	30	26	72	33	12	30	24	66	33	25	28	32	85	33	48	17	40	105	35	291	193	268	752	35
35/39	48	21	45	114	31	29	31	35	95	29	32	30	40	102	30	29	30	35	94	30	37	22	32	91	31	52	15	31	98	33	304	166	254	724	31
30/34	47	22	33	102	28	43	33	46	122	27	38	30	35	103	27	36	23	42	101	27	44	25	42	111	28	49	10	23	82	30	299	158	247	704	28
25/29	41	19	30	90	25	42	25	41	108	23	41	24	35	100	24	43	20	34	97	24	42	25	33	100	24	19	4	9	32	25	245	120	190	555	24
20/24	21	6	18	45	20	42	15	32	89	20	33	16	27	76	19	41	18	26	85	20	36	14	25	75	20	8	2	2	12	21	187	73	134	394	20
15/19	13	1	8	22	16	30	10	25	65	15	27	11	22	60	15	24	7	16	47	15	21	9	11	41	16	3	1	1	5	17	119	40	84	243	15
10/14	4	0	1	5	11	19	7	11	37	11	19	6	13	38	10	15	6	8	29	11	13	5	7	25	11	1			1	13	72	24	41	137	11
5/9	1			1	8	10	4	7	21	7	13	7	9	29	6	8	3	4	15	6	8	3	6	17	7						41	17	26	84	6
0/4						5	1	4	10	2	8	6	8	22	1	7	2	5	14	1	5	1	2	8	1						25	10	19	54	2
-5/-1						2	0	1	3	-3	6	4	4	14	-3	1	1	1	3	-4	2	0	0	2	-3						11	5	6	22	-3
-10/-6						1	0	1	2	-8	5	1	4	10	-8	1	0	0	1	-9	0		0	0	-6						7	1	5	13	-8
-15/-11						0			0	-14	2	0	2	4	-13	1		0	1	-13											3		2	5	-13
-20/-16											1	1	1	3	-18																1		1	3	-18
-25/-21											1		0	1	-24																		0	1	-24
-30/-26													0	0	-28																		0	0	-28

COLORADO SPRINGS/PETERSON COLORADO

LAT 38 49N LONG 104 43W ELEV 6145 FT

MEAN FREQUENCY OF OCCURRENCE OF DRY BULB TEMPERATURE (DEGREES F) WITH MEAN COINCIDENT WET BULB TEMPERATURE (DEGREES F) FOR EACH DRY BULB TEMPERATURE RANGE

Temperature Range	MAY Obsn Hour Gp 01 to 08	MAY 09 to 16	MAY 17 to 24	MAY Total Obsn	MAY MCWB	JUNE Obsn Hour Gp 01 to 08	JUNE 09 to 16	JUNE 17 to 24	JUNE Total Obsn	JUNE MCWB	JULY Obsn Hour Gp 01 to 08	JULY 09 to 16	JULY 17 to 24	JULY Total Obsn	JULY MCWB
100/104							0		0	58					
95/99							2	0	2	58		2	0	2	60
90/94		0		0	56		9	2	11	56		18	2	20	59
85/89		2	0	2	53	0	33	6	39	55	1	54	10	65	59
80/84		12	2	14	52	3	42	15	60	55	5	59	17	81	59
75/79	1	32	8	41	51	7	43	24	74	55	12	47	31	90	58
70/74	3	38	13	54	50	13	40	35	88	54	24	33	50	107	57
65/69	9	42	24	75	48	26	30	42	98	53	48	21	62	131	56
60/64	18	40	38	96	47	45	18	48	111	52	73	9	52	134	55
55/59	31	27	42	100	46	61	10	36	107	50	64	3	21	88	53
50/54	48	23	46	117	44	54	8	21	83	47	20	1	2	23	50
45/49	58	15	38	111	42	23	3	7	33	44	1	0	0	1	45
40/44	48	9	22	79	38	6	1	2	9	39	0			0	42
35/39	21	5	10	36	35	1	0	1	2	35					
30/34	8	2	4	14	31	1		0	1	32					
25/29	3	1	1	5	26										
20/24	1		0	1	21										
15/19															

Temperature Range	AUGUST Obsn Hour Gp 01 to 08	AUGUST 09 to 16	AUGUST 17 to 24	AUGUST Total Obsn	AUGUST MCWB	SEPTEMBER Obsn Hour Gp 01 to 08	SEPTEMBER 09 to 16	SEPTEMBER 17 to 24	SEPTEMBER Total Obsn	SEPTEMBER MCWB	OCTOBER Obsn Hour Gp 01 to 08	OCTOBER 09 to 16	OCTOBER 17 to 24	OCTOBER Total Obsn	OCTOBER MCWB
100/104															
95/99		0		0	59										
90/94		8	0	8	58		3	0	3	57					
85/89		39	5	44	58		16	2	18	55					
80/84	2	66	12	80	58	0	34	5	39	54		6	0	6	51
75/79	8	57	26	91	58	3	51	13	67	53		25	1	26	50
70/74	18	41	41	100	57	7	44	25	76	52	1	40	5	46	48
65/69	39	22	66	127	56	19	29	36	84	51	5	42	11	58	46
60/64	77	9	65	151	55	33	24	46	103	50	11	37	24	72	45
55/59	76	3	26	105	52	45	16	44	105	48	20	31	33	84	43
50/54	24	1	7	32	49	56	11	37	104	46	34	23	42	99	41
45/49	5	0	0	5	44	44	7	20	71	43	47	17	48	112	39
40/44	0			0	40	22	4	7	33	39	53	12	41	106	36
35/39						8	1	4	13	35	40	8	23	71	33
30/34						3	1	1	5	31	23	5	14	42	29
25/29						0			0	28	11	2	5	18	25
20/24											3	0	1	4	22
15/19											0			0	18

COLORADO SPRINGS/PETERSON COLORADO

Temperature Range	NOVEMBER Obsn Hour Gp 01 to 08	NOVEMBER 09 to 16	NOVEMBER 17 to 24	NOVEMBER Total Obsn	NOVEMBER M C W B	DECEMBER Obsn Hour Gp 01 to 08	DECEMBER 09 to 16	DECEMBER 17 to 24	DECEMBER Total Obsn	DECEMBER M C W B	JANUARY Obsn Hour Gp 01 to 08	JANUARY 09 to 16	JANUARY 17 to 24	JANUARY Total Obsn	JANUARY M C W B
100/104															
95/99															
90/94															
85/89															
80/84															
75/79							0		0	48					
70/74		1		1	45		0		0	48					
65/69		11		11	44	0	1	0	1	44		2		2	43
60/64	0	27	1	28	42	0	9	1	10	41		8	0	8	41
55/59	2	34	6	42	40	0	21	1	22	39		17	1	18	38
50/54	9	33	12	54	37	3	33	5	41	37	1	32	5	38	36
45/49	19	30	26	75	35	9	36	14	59	34	8	34	14	56	33
40/44	28	26	35	89	33	17	33	24	74	32	18	29	22	69	31
35/39	38	21	45	104	30	28	32	33	93	29	24	31	29	84	28
30/34	46	21	43	110	28	37	30	44	111	26	32	29	39	100	26
25/29	37	17	30	84	24	52	26	50	128	23	36	22	39	97	23
20/24	29	11	21	61	20	45	14	35	94	19	42	16	34	92	19
15/19	15	5	11	31	16	25	6	22	53	15	31	11	23	65	15
10/14	10	2	6	18	11	17	3	10	30	11	20	6	15	41	11
5/9	2	1	2	5	7	8	2	4	14	6	17	4	13	34	6
0/4	2		2	4	1	4	1	3	8	1	8	4	5	17	1
-5/-1	2		0	2	-3	2	0	2	4	-4	4	2	3	9	-3
-10/-6	0			0	-6	0		0	0	-9	4	2	3	9	-8
-15/-11						0		1	1	-12	1	0	1	2	-13
-20/-16											1		1	2	-18
-25/-21													0	0	-23
-30/-26															

Temperature Range	FEBRUARY Obsn Hour Gp 01 to 08	FEBRUARY 09 to 16	FEBRUARY 17 to 24	FEBRUARY Total Obsn	FEBRUARY M C W B	MARCH Obsn Hour Gp 01 to 08	MARCH 09 to 16	MARCH 17 to 24	MARCH Total Obsn	MARCH M C W B	APRIL Obsn Hour Gp 01 to 08	APRIL 09 to 16	APRIL 17 to 24	APRIL Total Obsn	APRIL M C W B
100/104															
95/99															
90/94															
85/89															
80/84												0		0	49
75/79		0		0	49		0		0	51		7	1	8	47
70/74		1		1	47		1	0	1	46	0	20	4	24	46
65/69		5	0	5	45		7	1	8	43	0	26	8	34	45
60/64	0	11	1	12	42	0	19	4	23	41	4	30	16	50	43
55/59	0	20	3	23	39	2	27	8	37	39	12	32	24	68	41
50/54	2	26	10	38	37	6	29	17	52	37	20	34	34	88	39
45/49	9	28	17	54	34	11	32	24	67	35	29	28	36	93	37
40/44	15	31	26	72	32	19	32	29	80	32	42	21	36	99	35
35/39	23	25	28	76	29	29	29	39	97	30	47	17	32	96	32
30/34	37	26	34	97	27	50	25	43	118	27	40	14	26	80	29
25/29	38	20	39	97	23	46	23	33	102	24	28	8	15	51	25
20/24	41	14	30	85	20	38	15	27	80	20	14	2	5	21	21
15/19	26	7	15	48	15	23	6	12	41	16	3		1	4	17
10/14	13	5	8	26	11	12	3	6	21	11	1		0	1	12
5/9	7	3	5	15	6	7	1	3	11	6	1		0	1	6
0/4	7	1	5	13	2	3	0	1	4	2	0		0	0	2
-5/-1	3	0	1	4	-3	1	0	0	1	-3	0			0	-1
-10/-6	1	0	0	1	-8	1		0	1	-7					
-15/-11	0		0	0	-13										
-20/-16	0			0	-19										
-25/-21	0		0	0	-24										
-30/-26	0			0	-26										

Temperature Range	ANNUAL TOTAL Obsn Hour Gp 01 to 08	ANNUAL TOTAL 09 to 16	ANNUAL TOTAL 17 to 24	ANNUAL TOTAL Total Obsn	ANNUAL TOTAL M C W B
100/104		0		0	58
95/99		4	0	4	59
90/94		38	4	42	58
85/89	1	144	23	168	57
80/84	10	219	51	280	57
75/79	31	262	104	397	55
70/74	66	259	173	498	54
65/69	146	238	250	634	52
60/64	261	241	296	798	50
55/59	313	241	245	799	46
50/54	277	254	238	769	42
45/49	263	230	244	737	38
40/44	268	198	244	710	34
35/39	259	169	244	672	31
30/34	277	153	248	678	27
25/29	251	119	212	582	24
20/24	213	72	153	438	20
15/19	123	35	84	242	15
10/14	73	19	45	137	11
5/9	42	11	27	80	6
0/4	24	6	16	46	2
-5/-1	12	2	6	20	-3
-10/-6	6	2	3	11	-8
-15/-11	1	0	2	3	-13
-20/-16	1		1	2	-18
-25/-21	0		0	0	-24
-30/-26	0			0	-26

GRAND JUNCTION/WALKER FIELD COLORADO

LAT 39 07N LONG 108 32W ELEV 4843 FT

MEAN FREQUENCY OF OCCURRENCE OF DRY BULB TEMPERATURE (DEGREES F) WITH MEAN COINCIDENT WET BULB TEMPERATURE (DEGREES F) FOR EACH DRY BULB TEMPERATURE RANGE

Temperature Range	MAY Obsn Hour Gp 01 to 08	MAY Obsn Hour Gp 09 to 16	MAY Obsn Hour Gp 17 to 24	MAY Total Obsn	MAY MCWB	JUNE Obsn Hour Gp 01 to 08	JUNE Obsn Hour Gp 09 to 16	JUNE Obsn Hour Gp 17 to 24	JUNE Total Obsn	JUNE MCWB	JULY Obsn Hour Gp 01 to 08	JULY Obsn Hour Gp 09 to 16	JULY Obsn Hour Gp 17 to 24	JULY Total Obsn	JULY MCWB
100/104							0	0	0	61		1	1	2	61
95/99							6	3	9	58		21	10	31	60
90/94		2	0	2	55		35	15	50	57		63	28	91	59
85/89		10	4	14	54		51	27	78	55	0	63	37	100	59
80/84		29	11	40	52	1	49	35	85	54	4	52	53	109	58
75/79	0	46	22	68	51	15	42	45	102	53	39	32	62	133	57
70/74	4	46	34	84	49	42	29	46	117	51	84	12	39	135	55
65/69	21	37	46	104	48	59	14	35	108	49	84	3	14	101	54
60/64	42	31	45	118	46	59	8	18	85	48	33	1	4	38	52
55/59	60	23	34	117	44	38	4	10	52	46	4		0	4	50
50/54	54	14	25	93	43	17	1	4	22	43	0			0	47
45/49	40	7	17	64	40	5	0	2	7	40					
40/44	18	2	6	26	37	2		0	2	37					
35/39	8	1	2	11	34	0			0	30					
30/34	1		0	1	30										
25/29															

Temperature Range	AUGUST Obsn Hour Gp 01 to 08	AUGUST Obsn Hour Gp 09 to 16	AUGUST Obsn Hour Gp 17 to 24	AUGUST Total Obsn	AUGUST MCWB	SEPTEMBER Obsn Hour Gp 01 to 08	SEPTEMBER Obsn Hour Gp 09 to 16	SEPTEMBER Obsn Hour Gp 17 to 24	SEPTEMBER Total Obsn	SEPTEMBER MCWB	OCTOBER Obsn Hour Gp 01 to 08	OCTOBER Obsn Hour Gp 09 to 16	OCTOBER Obsn Hour Gp 17 to 24	OCTOBER Total Obsn	OCTOBER MCWB
100/104															
95/99		7	3	10	60		0	0	0	59					
90/94		32	14	46	59		6	2	8	58					
85/89		57	29	86	59		27	9	36	57		0	0	0	54
80/84	2	56	39	97	58		44	19	63	55		6	1	7	54
75/79	15	49	57	121	57	1	49	30	80	54		26	5	31	52
70/74	52	31	53	136	56	11	42	43	96	53		39	12	51	50
65/69	89	12	35	136	55	38	35	50	123	51	2	47	27	76	48
60/64	70	4	15	89	54	59	20	43	122	49	15	41	40	96	46
55/59	18	0	2	20	50	63	9	29	101	47	33	37	51	121	44
50/54	2		0	2	44	45	4	8	57	44	51	25	49	125	41
45/49	0			0	40	15	2	4	21	41	63	17	34	114	39
40/44						6	1	2	9	39	52	7	21	80	36
35/39						1	0		1	33	22	2	7	31	33
30/34											9	0	2	11	29
25/29											2			2	24

Temperature Range	NOVEMBER Obsn Hour Gp 01 to 08	09 to 16	17 to 24	Total Obsn	MCWB	DECEMBER Obsn Hour Gp 01 to 08	09 to 16	17 to 24	Total Obsn	MCWB	JANUARY Obsn Hour Gp 01 to 08	09 to 16	17 to 24	Total Obsn	MCWB
100/104															
95/99															
90/94															
85/89															
80/84															
75/79															
70/74		0		0	48										
65/69		3	0	3	47										
60/64		12	2	14	45		0		0	47					
55/59	1	29	7	37	43	0	2	1	3	45		1	0	1	42
50/54	6	37	18	61	41	1	8	1	10	40	0	4	1	5	40
45/49	14	46	33	93	38	2	21	5	28	37	1	12	4	17	37
40/44	29	38	46	113	35	5	36	14	55	35	2	30	11	43	34
35/39	45	33	51	129	32	14	50	33	97	32	9	46	29	84	32
30/34	67	24	47	138	29	37	57	64	158	28	35	56	60	151	29
25/29	48	13	23	84	24	62	39	58	159	24	56	40	56	152	24
20/24	22	3	8	33	20	57	22	37	116	20	54	30	37	121	20
15/19	6	1	3	10	15	39	8	20	67	15	38	16	25	79	15
10/14	3	0	1	4	10	19	4	7	30	11	26	7	15	48	11
5/9	1			1	6	6	2	5	13	6	14	4	7	25	6
0/4						3	0	2	5	2	8	1	3	12	1
-5/-1						1	0	1	2	-3	2	1	1	4	-3
-10/-6						1	0		1	-8	0	0	0	0	-9
-15/-11						0			0	-12	0	0	0	0	-14
-20/-16											1		0	1	-18

Temperature Range	FEBRUARY Obsn Hour Gp 01 to 08	09 to 16	17 to 24	Total Obsn	MCWB	MARCH Obsn Hour Gp 01 to 08	09 to 16	17 to 24	Total Obsn	MCWB	APRIL Obsn Hour Gp 01 to 08	09 to 16	17 to 24	Total Obsn	MCWB	ANNUAL TOTAL Obsn Hour Gp 01 to 08	09 to 16	17 to 24	Total Obsn	MCWB
100/104																	1	1	2	61
95/99																	34	16	50	59
90/94																	138	59	197	58
85/89																0	208	106	314	57
80/84												3	1	4	51	7	239	159	405	56
75/79												9	3	12	49	70	253	224	547	54
70/74							3	1	4	47		[illegible]	[illegible]	[illegible]	48	133	220	237	656	53
65/69		0		0	46		9	3	12	45	1	38	19	58	46	294	198	229	721	51
60/64		3	1	4	45	0	17	7	24	43	7	39	31	77	44	285	176	206	667	48
55/59	0	8	2	10	42	2	28	16	46	41	23	37	41	101	42	242	178	193	613	44
50/54	1	17	6	24	40	7	36	25	68	39	41	35	43	119	40	225	181	180	586	41
45/49	3	28	16	47	38	19	42	39	100	37	46	30	38	114	38	208	205	192	605	38
40/44	10	43	31	84	35	37	43	47	127	34	50	18	33	101	35	211	218	211	640	35
35/39	31	48	50	129	32	53	38	47	138	31	43	6	16	65	32	226	224	235	685	32
30/34	58	36	53	147	28	58	23	38	119	28	25	1	5	31	29	290	197	269	756	29
25/29	50	21	33	104	24	45	10	20	75	24	4	0	0	4	25	267	123	190	580	24
20/24	33	9	15	57	20	21	1	5	27	19	1			1	20	188	65	102	355	20
15/19	18	6	8	32	15	6	0	1	7	15						107	31	57	195	15
10/14	10	2	6	18	11	1			1	12						59	13	29	101	11
5/9	5	1	2	8	6											26	7	14	47	6
0/4	2	1	1	4	2											13	2	6	21	1
-5/-1	1	0	0	1	-4											4	1	2	7	-3
-10/-6	1		0	1	-9											2	0	0	2	-9
-15/-11	0			0	-14											0	0	0	0	-14
-20/-16																1		0	1	-18

PUEBLO MEMORIAL APRT COLORADO

LAT 38 17N LONG 104 31W ELEV 4684 FT

MEAN FREQUENCY OF OCCURRENCE OF DRY BULB TEMPERATURE (DEGREES F) WITH MEAN COINCIDENT WET BULB TEMPERATURE (DEGREES F) FOR EACH DRY BULB TEMPERATURE RANGE

Temperature Range	MAY Obsn Hour Gp 01 to 08	MAY Obsn Hour Gp 09 to 16	MAY Obsn Hour Gp 17 to 24	MAY Total Obsn	MAY MCWB	JUNE Obsn Hour Gp 01 to 08	JUNE Obsn Hour Gp 09 to 16	JUNE Obsn Hour Gp 17 to 24	JUNE Total Obsn	JUNE MCWB	JULY Obsn Hour Gp 01 to 08	JULY Obsn Hour Gp 09 to 16	JULY Obsn Hour Gp 17 to 24	JULY Total Obsn	JULY MCWB
100/104							2	0	2	61		2	0	2	63
95/99							14	3	17	60		26	5	31	62
90/94		6	1	7	57		33	10	43	59		53	17	70	63
85/89		19	5	24	55	0	43	17	60	59	0	58	25	83	62
80/84	0	36	14	50	54	1	41	27	69	59	4	47	38	89	62
75/79	1	37	18	56	54	6	40	39	85	58	17	33	50	100	61
70/74	4	44	29	77	52	17	30	45	92	57	40	18	52	110	60
65/69	12	38	41	91	51	41	17	43	101	55	79	7	40	126	59
60/64	25	28	45	98	50	69	13	31	113	54	75	2	18	95	57
55/59	52	17	42	111	49	65	5	17	87	52	30	0	3	33	54
50/54	65	12	30	107	46	34	2	7	43	49	2			2	51
45/49	58	9	18	85	43	7	0	1	8	45					
40/44	19	2	7	28	39	1			1	42					
35/39	9	0	1	10	35										
30/34	2			2	31										
25/29	0			0	27										
20/24															

Temperature Range	AUGUST Obsn Hour Gp 01 to 08	AUGUST Obsn Hour Gp 09 to 16	AUGUST Obsn Hour Gp 17 to 24	AUGUST Total Obsn	AUGUST MCWB	SEPTEMBER Obsn Hour Gp 01 to 08	SEPTEMBER Obsn Hour Gp 09 to 16	SEPTEMBER Obsn Hour Gp 17 to 24	SEPTEMBER Total Obsn	SEPTEMBER MCWB	OCTOBER Obsn Hour Gp 01 to 08	OCTOBER Obsn Hour Gp 09 to 16	OCTOBER Obsn Hour Gp 17 to 24	OCTOBER Total Obsn	OCTOBER MCWB
100/104		1		1	63										
95/99		16	2	18	62		5	1	6	59					
90/94		46	11	57	62		19	4	23	59		1	0	1	58
85/89		58	20	78	62		33	8	41	58		8	0	8	54
80/84	2	51	33	86	62	0	42	18	60	58		25	3	28	53
75/79	8	40	50	98	61	3	39	27	69	57	0	31	6	37	52
70/74	28	23	59	110	60	9	33	41	83	55	0	36	14	50	50
65/69	79	9	51	139	59	23	25	43	91	53	3	38	23	64	49
60/64	86	3	17	106	57	41	18	39	98	52	7	32	35	74	47
55/59	36	1	5	42	53	56	13	33	102	50	16	28	36	80	45
50/54	9	0		9	47	55	6	16	77	47	32	20	46	98	43
45/49	1			1	44	35	4	7	46	43	53	14	40	107	40
40/44	0			0	39	14	1	3	18	41	62	9	24	95	37
35/39						3	1	1	5	35	45	6	14	65	34
30/34						2	0	1	3	33	21	1	5	27	29
25/29											8		1	9	25
20/24											1			1	21

Temperature Range	NOVEMBER Obsn Hour Gp 01 to 08	09 to 16	17 to 24	Total Obsn	MCWB	DECEMBER Obsn Hour Gp 01 to 08	09 to 16	17 to 24	Total Obsn	MCWB	JANUARY Obsn Hour Gp 01 to 08	09 to 16	17 to 24	Total Obsn	MCWB	FEBRUARY Obsn Hour Gp 01 to 08	09 to 16	17 to 24	Total Obsn	MCWB	MARCH Obsn Hour Gp 01 to 08	09 to 16	17 to 24	Total Obsn	MCWB	APRIL Obsn Hour Gp 01 to 08	09 to 16	17 to 24	Total Obsn	MCWB	ANNUAL TOTAL Obsn Hour Gp 01 to 08	09 to 16	17 to 24	Total Obsn	MCWB
100/104																																5	0	5	62
95/99																																61	11	72	61
90/94																																158	43	201	61
85/89																											1		1	53		220	75	295	60
80/84																						0		0	53		10	2	12	52	7	252	135	394	59
75/79		2		2	48		1		1	52							1		1	50		3	1	4	49		20	7	27	50	35	247	198	480	57
70/74		11	0	11	47		3	0	3	48		0		0	45		3	0	3	49		10	3	13	47	0	[illegible]	18	[illegible]	48	[illegible]	137	255	590	55
65/69		21	1	22	46	1	7	1	9	45		[illegible]		8	44		9	2	11	46	0	17	4	21	45	1	28	19	48	47	239	219	268	726	54
60/64	0	26	6	32	44	1	17	2	20	43		9	0	9	42	0	14	4	18	44	0	23	9	32	43	6	38	24	68	45	310	223	230	763	51
55/59	3	26	12	41	42	1	26	3	30	41		17	2	19	40	1	16	6	23	41	2	29	16	47	41	12	33	33	78	43	274	211	208	693	47
50/54	8	31	24	63	40	3	25	11	39	39	1	24	6	31	38	2	22	12	36	39	3	27	25	55	39	20	29	39	88	41	234	198	216	648	43
45/49	11	26	30	67	37	8	28	19	55	36	4	28	11	43	35	5	27	19	51	36	10	29	28	67	37	42	19	34	95	39	234	184	207	625	39
40/44	19	27	37	83	35	11	29	25	65	33	5	27	19	51	33	8	23	23	54	34	19	32	37	88	35	53	15	30	98	36	211	165	205	581	35
35/39	41	29	43	113	33	17	35	33	85	31	12	31	29	72	30	18	27	32	77	31	42	28	40	110	32	45	13	21	79	33	232	170	214	616	32
30/34	55	20	36	111	29	26	29	44	99	28	18	28	41	87	27	35	30	37	102	28	58	24	38	120	29	37	8	14	59	30	254	140	216	610	28
25/29	47	12	27	86	25	50	23	50	123	24	36	25	42	103	24	49	22	38	109	25	50	15	26	91	25	16	2	4	22	26	256	99	188	543	25
20/24	27	6	13	46	20	61	11	30	102	20	47	19	34	100	20	43	13	21	77	20	33	5	13	51	20	4	0	1	5	22	216	54	112	382	20
15/19	18	2	6	26	16	38	8	14	60	16	40	15	22	77	15	24	7	11	42	16	17	3	3	23	16	1		0	1	17	138	35	56	229	16
10/14	9	1	3	13	12	16	2	6	24	11	29	8	15	52	11	16	5	9	30	11	7	2	3	12	11	1		0	1	11	78	18	36	132	11
5/9	1	0	1	2	7	6	3	4	13	6	21	6	12	39	6	9	3	6	18	7	4	1	2	7	7	1			1	8	42	13	25	80	6
0/4	1	0	1	2	2	5	1	3	9	1	16	4	6	26	2	7	1	3	11	2	2	0	1	3	2	0			0	4	31	6	14	51	2
-5/-1	1		0	1	-2	3	0	2	5	-3	9	3	6	18	-3	4	0	2	6	-3	3		0	3	-3						20	3	10	33	-3
-10/-6	1			1	-8	2	0	0	2	-8	4	1	2	7	-8	2	0	0	2	-8	1			1	-7						10	1	2	13	-8
-15/-11	0			0	-11		0	1	1	-13	2	0	2	4	-13	1		0	1	-12											3	0	3	6	-13
-20/-16						1	0	1	2	-18	2	0	1	3	-18	0			0	-17											3	0	2	5	-18
-25/-21						1			1	-23	2	0	0	2	-23																3	0	0	3	-23
-30/-26						0			0	-26	0			0	-26																0			0	-26

TRINIDAD COLORADO

LAT 37 16N LONG 104 20W ELEV 5761 FT

MEAN FREQUENCY OF OCCURRENCE OF DRY BULB TEMPERATURE (DEGREES F) WITH MEAN COINCIDENT WET BULB TEMPERATURE (DEGREES F) FOR EACH DRY BULB TEMPERATURE RANGE

Temperature Range	MAY Obsn Hour Gp 01 to 08	MAY Obsn Hour Gp 09 to 16	MAY Obsn Hour Gp 17 to 24	MAY Total Obsn	MAY MCWB	JUNE Obsn Hour Gp 01 to 08	JUNE Obsn Hour Gp 09 to 16	JUNE Obsn Hour Gp 17 to 24	JUNE Total Obsn	JUNE MCWB	JULY Obsn Hour Gp 01 to 08	JULY Obsn Hour Gp 09 to 16	JULY Obsn Hour Gp 17 to 24	JULY Total Obsn	JULY MCWB
100/104												0		0	72
95/99							4	0	4	62		8	0	8	64
90/94		1		1	56		26	4	30	60		39	4	43	63
85/89		9	1	10	56	0	44	10	54	59	1	62	10	73	63
80/84		26	4	30	55	3	51	19	73	59	4	61	23	88	62
75/79	1	40	8	49	54	9	44	28	81	58	13	40	33	86	61
70/74	4	43	17	64	52	18	32	37	87	56	32	22	51	105	60
65/69	11	40	27	78	51	40	18	46	104	55	60	10	65	135	58
60/64	24	32	39	95	50	56	11	43	110	53	83	4	48	135	57
55/59	39	21	48	108	48	53	6	28	87	51	47	1	12	60	54
50/54	54	13	43	110	46	33	2	16	51	47	8	0	1	9	51
45/49	52	11	32	95	43	19	2	7	28	43	0		0	0	45
40/44	33	6	18	57	39	7	0	2	9	40	0			0	43
35/39	19	3	6	28	35	1			1	35					
30/34	8	[illegible]	4	13	30										
25/29	2	0	[illegible]	[illegible]	26										
20/24															

Temperature Range	AUGUST Obsn Hour Gp 01 to 08	AUGUST Obsn Hour Gp 09 to 16	AUGUST Obsn Hour Gp 17 to 24	AUGUST Total Obsn	AUGUST MCWB	SEPTEMBER Obsn Hour Gp 01 to 08	SEPTEMBER Obsn Hour Gp 09 to 16	SEPTEMBER Obsn Hour Gp 17 to 24	SEPTEMBER Total Obsn	SEPTEMBER MCWB	OCTOBER Obsn Hour Gp 01 to 08	OCTOBER Obsn Hour Gp 09 to 16	OCTOBER Obsn Hour Gp 17 to 24	OCTOBER Total Obsn	OCTOBER MCWB
100/104															
95/99		1		1	62		0		0	61					
90/94		23	1	24	62		10	0	10	59					
85/89		61	8	69	61		36	2	38	58		2		2	60
80/84	1	74	15	90	61	0	61	7	68	57		21	0	21	55
75/79	8	47	25	80	60	3	50	16	69	56	0	46	2	48	52
70/74	21	25	51	97	59	8	36	31	75	55	1	45	6	52	51
65/69	50	13	67	130	57	23	20	48	91	53	4	36	18	58	49
60/64	87	4	58	149	56	44	13	54	111	51	12	32	33	77	47
55/59	64	1	19	84	53	58	7	45	110	49	26	25	40	91	45
50/54	16	0	4	20	50	54	3	26	83	46	38	17	44	99	42
45/49	1		0	1	46	34	2	8	44	43	43	11	41	95	39
40/44						12	2	2	16	40	52	6	31	89	36
35/39						3	0	1	4	36	39	5	18	62	33
30/34						0			0	33	21	2	10	33	29
25/29											10	0	4	14	25
20/24											2		1	3	22

NOVEMBER

Temperature Range	Obsn Hour Gp 01 to 08	Obsn Hour Gp 09 to 16	Obsn Hour Gp 17 to 24	Total Obsn	MCWB
100/104					
95/99					
90/94					
85/89					
80/84					
75/79		1		1	50
70/74		11		11	48
65/69		23		23	46
60/64	0	35	2	37	44
55/59	1	35	6	42	42
50/54	5	30	18	53	39
45/49	17	28	27	72	37
40/44	29	21	39	89	34
35/39	46	17	49	112	31
30/34	52	16	36	104	28
25/29	37	10	25	72	24
20/24	23	9	17	49	20
15/19	14	3	10	27	16
10/14	8	1	5	14	11
5/9	3	0	3	6	7
0/4	3		1	4	2
-5/-1	2		1	3	-3
-10/-6	0		1	1	-8
-15/-11	0		0	0	-11
-20/-16					
-25/-21					

DECEMBER

Temperature Range	Obsn Hour Gp 01 to 08	Obsn Hour Gp 09 to 16	Obsn Hour Gp 17 to 24	Total Obsn	MCWB
100/104					
95/99					
90/94					
85/89					
80/84					
75/79					
70/74		1		1	49
65/69		6		6	45
60/64		20	0	20	43
55/59	0	29	1	30	41
50/54	2	42	6	50	38
45/49	10	36	19	65	36
40/44	14	32	27	73	33
35/39	23	26	38	87	30
30/34	42	26	51	119	27
25/29	54	15	43	112	24
20/24	39	9	28	76	20
15/19	29	3	20	52	15
10/14	19	2	7	28	11
5/9	10	0	4	14	6
0/4	4	0	3	7	2
-5/-1	1		1	2	-3
-10/-6	0		0	0	-7
-15/-11					
-20/-16					
-25/-21					

JANUARY

Temperature Range	Obsn Hour Gp 01 to 08	Obsn Hour Gp 09 to 16	Obsn Hour Gp 17 to 24	Total Obsn	MCWB
100/104					
95/99					
90/94					
85/89					
80/84					
75/79					
70/74		1		1	46
65/69		5		5	45
60/64		16	0	16	44
55/59	0	31	1	32	41
50/54	2	32	6	40	38
45/49	9	34	18	61	36
40/44	14	36	31	81	33
35/39	23	23	35	81	30
30/34	33	21	41	95	27
25/29	43	18	34	95	24
20/24	44	14	27	85	20
15/19	31	5	23	59	15
10/14	19	5	12	36	11
5/9	14	5	10	29	6
0/4	9	3	4	16	2
-5/-1	4	0	3	7	-3
-10/-6	1		1	2	-9
-15/-11	1		1	2	-12
-20/-16	0		0	0	-18
-25/-21			0	0	-22

FEBRUARY

Temperature Range	Obsn Hour Gp 01 to 08	Obsn Hour Gp 09 to 16	Obsn Hour Gp 17 to 24	Total Obsn	MCWB
100/104					
95/99					
90/94					
85/89					
80/84					
75/79		0		0	47
70/74		8		8	48
65/69		10	0	10	46
60/64	0	24	2	26	43
55/59	0	28	5	33	41
50/54	2	28	12	42	38
45/49	6	31	19	56	36
40/44	13	25	31	69	33
35/39	26	22	37	85	30
30/34	43	18	37	98	27
25/29	43	14	29	86	24
20/24	35	10	21	66	20
15/19	21	6	9	36	15
10/14	13	3	10	26	11
5/9	10	1	6	17	6
0/4	6	1	4	11	2
-5/-1	3	1	1	5	-3
-10/-6	1		1	2	-9
-15/-11	1		1	2	-14
-20/-16	1		0	1	-18
-25/-21					

MARCH

Temperature Range	Obsn Hour Gp 01 to 08	Obsn Hour Gp 09 to 16	Obsn Hour Gp 17 to 24	Total Obsn	MCWB
100/104					
95/99					
90/94					
85/89					
80/84					
75/79		1	0	1	50
70/74		8	0	8	47
65/69	0	19	2	21	45
60/64	0	33	6	39	43
55/59	3	33	13	49	40
50/54	9	35	22	66	38
45/49	13	32	30	75	36
40/44	26	24	35	85	34
35/39	35	17	37	89	31
30/34	45	14	37	96	28
25/29	40	14	26	80	24
20/24	32	10	18	60	20
15/19	22	5	9	36	16
10/14	11	3	7	21	11
5/9	6	0	3	9	6
0/4	3	1	1	5	2
-5/-1	1	0	1	2	-3
-10/-6	1		0	1	-9
-15/-11	1		0	1	-12
-20/-16					
-25/-21					

APRIL

Temperature Range	Obsn Hour Gp 01 to 08	Obsn Hour Gp 09 to 16	Obsn Hour Gp 17 to 24	Total Obsn	MCWB
100/104					
95/99					
90/94					
85/89					
80/84		6		6	51
75/79		16	2	18	50
70/74	1	30	5	36	49
65/69	2	38	11	51	47
60/64	6	36	19	61	45
55/59	12	32	30	74	43
50/54	27	22	36	85	41
45/49	36	20	41	97	39
40/44	42	15	34	91	36
35/39	45	11	26	82	33
30/34	35	11	22	68	30
25/29	22	3	11	36	25
20/24	10	0	2	12	21
15/19	1		0	1	17
10/14	1		1	2	11
5/9	0		0	0	8
0/4	0			0	4
-5/-1					
-10/-6					
-15/-11					
-20/-16					
-25/-21					

ANNUAL TOTAL

Temperature Range	Obsn Hour Gp 01 to 08	Obsn Hour Gp 09 to 16	Obsn Hour Gp 17 to 24	Total Obsn	MCWB
100/104		0		0	72
95/99		13	0	13	63
90/94		99	9	108	61
85/89	1	214	31	246	61
80/84	8	300	68	376	59
75/79	81	[illegible]	114	433	57
70/74	85	256	198	539	55
65/69	190	238	284	712	53
60/64	312	260	304	876	51
55/59	303	249	248	800	47
50/54	250	224	234	708	43
45/49	240	207	242	689	39
40/44	242	167	250	659	35
35/39	260	124	247	631	31
30/34	279	109	238	626	28
25/29	251	74	173	498	24
20/24	185	52	114	351	20
15/19	118	22	71	211	15
10/14	71	14	42	127	11
5/9	43	6	26	75	6
0/4	25	5	13	43	2
-5/-1	11	1	7	19	-3
-10/-6	3		3	6	-9
-15/-11	3		2	5	-13
-20/-16	1		0	1	-18
-25/-21			0	0	-22

DOVER AFB DELAWARE

LAT 39 08N LONG 75 28W ELEV 28 FT

MEAN FREQUENCY OF OCCURRENCE OF DRY BULB TEMPERATURE (DEGREES F) WITH MEAN COINCIDENT WET BULB TEMPERATURE (DEGREES F) FOR EACH DRY BULB TEMPERATURE RANGE

Tempera-ture Range	MAY Obsn Hour Gp 01 to 08	MAY Obsn Hour Gp 09 to 16	MAY Obsn Hour Gp 17 to 24	MAY Total Obsn	MAY MCWB	JUNE Obsn Hour Gp 01 to 08	JUNE Obsn Hour Gp 09 to 16	JUNE Obsn Hour Gp 17 to 24	JUNE Total Obsn	JUNE MCWB	JULY Obsn Hour Gp 01 to 08	JULY Obsn Hour Gp 09 to 16	JULY Obsn Hour Gp 17 to 24	JULY Total Obsn	JULY MCWB
100/104							0		0	78		1	0	1	79
95/99		0		0	76		3	0	3	76		2	0	2	76
90/94		2	0	2	73		14	3	17	75		19	3	22	75
85/89		9	2	11	70	1	32	11	44	73	0	49	17	66	74
80/84	0	18	7	25	68	4	52	26	82	71	7	76	38	121	72
75/79	2	30	16	48	65	21	51	41	113	69	49	67	69	185	70
70/74	13	40	28	81	63	54	47	60	161	66	90	29	75	194	68
65/69	29	48	36	113	60	66	28	53	147	63	66	6	37	109	64
60/64	44	47	54	145	56	54	10	35	99	59	31	0	6	37	60
55/59	60	35	53	148	52	31	2	10	43	54	4		0	4	55
50/54	54	15	37	106	48	8	0	2	10	50	0			0	50
45/49	33	3	13	49	44	1		0	1	45					
40/44	12	0	2	14	39	0			0	42					
35/39	2		0	2	34										
30/34	0			0	29										
25/29															

Tempera-ture Range	AUGUST Obsn Hour Gp 01 to 08	AUGUST Obsn Hour Gp 09 to 16	AUGUST Obsn Hour Gp 17 to 24	AUGUST Total Obsn	AUGUST MCWB	SEPTEMBER Obsn Hour Gp 01 to 08	SEPTEMBER Obsn Hour Gp 09 to 16	SEPTEMBER Obsn Hour Gp 17 to 24	SEPTEMBER Total Obsn	SEPTEMBER MCWB	OCTOBER Obsn Hour Gp 01 to 08	OCTOBER Obsn Hour Gp 09 to 16	OCTOBER Obsn Hour Gp 17 to 24	OCTOBER Total Obsn	OCTOBER MCWB
100/104															
95/99		1		1	78		0		0	76					
90/94		11	1	12	76		6	0	6	75		0		0	74
85/89	0	42	9	51	74		20	4	24	74		1	0	1	71
80/84	2	71	30	103	72	0	34	11	45	72		6	1	7	69
75/79	32	77	68	177	70	13	51	31	95	69		13	3	16	66
70/74	97	36	84	217	68	42	55	54	151	67	5	33	10	48	64
65/69	70	9	40	119	64	56	40	57	153	63	13	50	26	89	61
60/64	32	1	14	47	59	50	22	43	115	58	39	59	52	150	57
55/59	13	0	2	15	54	42	10	28	80	54	46	42	52	140	52
50/54	2			2	50	23	1	10	34	49	49	29	47	125	48
45/49						12		2	14	45	45	11	34	90	44
40/44						2		0	2	40	30	4	16	50	39
35/39						0			0	38	17	0	5	22	35
30/34											5		1	6	30
25/29											1		0	1	25

DOVER AFB DELAWARE

Temperature Range	NOVEMBER Obsn Hour Gp 01 to 08	NOVEMBER 09 to 16	NOVEMBER 17 to 24	NOVEMBER Total Obsn	NOVEMBER MCWB	DECEMBER Obsn Hour Gp 01 to 08	DECEMBER 09 to 16	DECEMBER 17 to 24	DECEMBER Total Obsn	DECEMBER MCWB	JANUARY Obsn Hour Gp 01 to 08	JANUARY 09 to 16	JANUARY 17 to 24	JANUARY Total Obsn	JANUARY MCWB
100/104															
95/99															
90/94															
85/89															
80/84		0		0	68										
75/79		2	0	2	68										
70/74	0	4	1	5	64		1		1	63		0		0	60
65/69	4	10	4	18	60	0	2	1	3	60	0	1	0	1	59
60/64	9	27	13	49	56	3	6	3	12	57	1	2	1	4	58
55/59	18	48	26	92	52	6	10	6	22	52	3	5	4	12	52
50/54	31	49	39	119	47	7	21	10	38	47	5	8	4	17	47
45/49	39	43	49	131	43	14	35	26	75	43	7	23	10	40	42
40/44	46	33	48	127	38	30	42	37	109	38	16	43	28	87	38
35/39	47	17	38	102	34	43	52	47	142	34	37	51	50	138	34
30/34	32	4	15	51	29	54	41	53	148	29	50	42	55	147	29
25/29	11	1	5	17	25	39	25	39	103	24	44	33	41	118	24
20/24	4	0	1	5	19	30	11	18	59	20	34	22	28	84	20
15/19	0			0	16	17	2	7	26	15	26	11	16	53	15
10/14						5	1	1	7	11	16	5	8	29	10
5/9						1	0		1	6	7	1	2	10	6
0/4											1		0	1	2

Temperature Range	FEBRUARY Obsn Hour Gp 01 to 08	FEBRUARY 09 to 16	FEBRUARY 17 to 24	FEBRUARY Total Obsn	FEBRUARY MCWB	MARCH Obsn Hour Gp 01 to 08	MARCH 09 to 16	MARCH 17 to 24	MARCH Total Obsn	MARCH MCWB	APRIL Obsn Hour Gp 01 to 08	APRIL 09 to 16	APRIL 17 to 24	APRIL Total Obsn	APRIL MCWB	ANNUAL TOTAL Obsn Hour Gp 01 to 08	ANNUAL TOTAL 09 to 16	ANNUAL TOTAL 17 to 24	ANNUAL TOTAL Total Obsn	ANNUAL TOTAL MCWB
100/104																	1	0	1	79
95/99																	6	0	6	76
90/94																	52	7	59	75
85/89												2	0	2	68	1	155	43	199	74
80/84							0		0	60		7	2	9	65	13	264	115	392	71
75/79							2	0	2	60	0	10	4	14	63	117	303	232	652	69
70/74		0		0	61		6	1	7	59	2	17	10	29	61	303	268	323	894	66
65/69		2	0	2	58	1	8	3	12	56	8	22	17	47	58	313	226	274	813	62
60/64	0	3	2	5	57	3	10	8	21	53	17	35	23	75	54	283	222	254	759	57
55/59	4	6	3	13	52	4	15	10	29	50	25	45	32	102	50	256	218	226	700	52
50/54	3	13	6	22	46	9	33	17	59	45	36	48	52	136	46	227	217	224	668	47
45/49	6	20	11	37	42	20	45	37	102	41	51	36	55	142	42	228	216	237	681	43
40/44	19	41	28	88	38	46	57	64	167	38	54	17	33	104	38	255	237	256	748	38
35/39	41	53	57	151	33	68	44	63	175	34	33	2	10	45	34	288	219	270	777	34
30/34	49	39	52	140	29	58	18	29	105	29	11	0	1	12	29	259	144	206	609	29
25/29	48	22	35	105	24	25	7	11	43	24	1			1	26	169	88	131	388	24
20/24	25	15	17	57	19	9	3	5	17	20						102	51	69	222	20
15/19	16	7	9	32	15	5	0	1	6	15						64	20	33	117	15
10/14	9	2	3	14	11	1			1	12						31	8	12	51	11
5/9	3	1	0	4	6	0			0	8						11	2	2	15	6
0/4	1	0		1	1											2	0	0	2	2

WILMINGTON AIRPORT DELAWARE

LAT 39 40N LONG 75 36W ELEV 78 FT

MEAN FREQUENCY OF OCCURRENCE OF DRY BULB TEMPERATURE (DEGREES F) WITH MEAN COINCIDENT WET BULB TEMPERATURE (DEGREES F) FOR EACH DRY BULB TEMPERATURE RANGE

Temperature Range	MAY Obsn Hour Gp 01 to 08	MAY 09 to 16	MAY 17 to 24	MAY Total Obsn	MAY MCWB	JUNE Obsn Hour Gp 01 to 08	JUNE 09 to 16	JUNE 17 to 24	JUNE Total Obsn	JUNE MCWB	JULY Obsn Hour Gp 01 to 08	JULY 09 to 16	JULY 17 to 24	JULY Total Obsn	JULY MCWB
100/104												1		1	74
95/99							2	0	2	77		5	1	6	74
90/94		2	0	2	71		13	2	15	74		21	5	26	74
85/89		8	2	10	70	0	35	8	43	72	1	57	16	74	73
80/84		19	5	24	67	3	49	23	75	70	6	78	42	126	70
75/79	1	32	14	47	64	14	52	42	108	67	39	56	72	167	70
70/74	8	48	28	84	62	46	44	60	150	65	93	24	70	187	68
65/69	25	50	43	118	59	65	28	55	148	62	65	6	35	106	64
60/64	48	44	57	149	56	62	12	36	110	58	35	0	8	43	59
55/59	60	28	51	139	52	35	3	12	50	54	9		0	9	55
50/54	57	13	31	101	49	13	1	3	17	50	1			1	51
45/49	32	2	13	47	44	1			1	45					
40/44	13	0	2	15	39										
35/39	3	0	0	3	35										
30/34															
25/29															

Temperature Range	AUGUST Obsn Hour Gp 01 to 08	AUGUST 09 to 16	AUGUST 17 to 24	AUGUST Total Obsn	AUGUST MCWB	SEPTEMBER Obsn Hour Gp 01 to 08	SEPTEMBER 09 to 16	SEPTEMBER 17 to 24	SEPTEMBER Total Obsn	SEPTEMBER MCWB	OCTOBER Obsn Hour Gp 01 to 08	OCTOBER 09 to 16	OCTOBER 17 to 24	OCTOBER Total Obsn	OCTOBER MCWB
100/104		1		1	73		0		0	79					
95/99		2	0	2	74		1		1	79					
90/94		9	1	10	75		4	1	5	75					
85/89	0	39	8	47	73		17	2	19	73		1	0	1	70
80/84	2	69	25	96	71	0	35	10	45	71		8	0	8	69
75/79	23	72	70	165	69	10	49	28	87	68	1	18	4	23	65
70/74	82	43	80	205	68	33	50	50	133	66	4	32	11	47	63
65/69	77	10	43	130	64	49	47	55	151	62	10	48	24	82	60
60/64	39	2	16	57	59	49	25	47	121	58	24	50	46	120	57
55/59	21		3	24	55	47	9	29	85	54	45	46	54	145	52
50/54	3		0	3	50	32	3	13	48	49	54	29	52	135	48
45/49						14	0	4	18	45	48	12	33	93	44
40/44						6		1	7	40	37	4	16	57	39
35/39						1			1	36	19	0	6	25	35
30/34											7		1	8	31
25/29											0			0	26

WILMINGTON AIRPORT DELAWARE

Tempera-ture Range	NOVEMBER Obsn Hour Gp			NOVEMBER Total Obsn	NOVEMBER MCWB	DECEMBER Obsn Hour Gp			DECEMBER Total Obsn	DECEMBER MCWB	JANUARY Obsn Hour Gp			JANUARY Total Obsn	JANUARY MCWB	FEBRUARY Obsn Hour Gp			FEBRUARY Total Obsn	FEBRUARY MCWB	MARCH Obsn Hour Gp			MARCH Total Obsn	MARCH MCWB	APRIL Obsn Hour Gp			APRIL Total Obsn	APRIL MCWB	ANNUAL TOTAL Obsn Hour Gp			ANNUAL TOTAL Total Obsn	ANNUAL TOTAL MCWB
	01 to 08	09 to 16	17 to 24			01 to 08	09 to 16	17 to 24			01 to 08	09 to 16	17 to 24			01 to 08	09 to 16	17 to 24			01 to 08	09 to 16	17 to 24			01 to 08	09 to 16	17 to 24			01 to 08	09 to 16	17 to 24		
100/104																																2		2	74
95/99																																10	1	11	75
90/94																																49	9	58	74
85/89																											2	0	2	68	1	159	36	196	72
80/84		1		1	67																						7	1	8	65	11	266	106	383	70
75/79		1		1	66																	1	0	1	58	0	14	4	18	62	88	295	234	617	68
70/74		5	0	5	62		0		0	64		0		0	63		1		1	59	0	5	1	6	58	1	17	8	26	60	267	269	308	844	66
65/69	1	11	2	14	59		2	0	2	60	0	1	1	2	60		1	0	1	57	0	5	1	6	56	5	22	12	39	57	297	231	271	799	62
60/64	5	26	9	40	56	0	3	2	5	55	2	2	2	6	57	0	3	1	4	54	1	12	5	18	52	14	32	27	73	54	279	211	256	746	57
55/59	19	38	27	84	52	4	9	4	17	53	3	5	2	10	53	1	6	2	9	50	5	22	12	39	49	29	50	39	118	51	278	216	235	729	52
50/54	23	43	33	99	47	5	18	8	31	48	4	10	5	19	48	3	17	6	26	46	7	32	20	59	45	37	42	49	128	47	239	208	220	667	48
45/49	31	48	44	123	42	14	29	20	63	43	8	24	12	44	43	8	26	17	51	42	20	49	37	106	41	54	34	53	141	43	230	224	233	687	43
40/44	45	37	47	129	38	25	48	37	110	38	18	38	25	81	38	19	46	34	99	38	43	50	60	153	38	52	15	32	99	38	258	238	254	750	38
35/39	47	21	44	112	34	40	51	48	139	34	37	65	56	158	34	43	52	52	147	34	65	42	58	165	34	32	4	12	48	34	287	235	276	798	34
30/34	45	8	24	77	30	57	42	54	153	29	57	47	64	168	29	59	36	59	154	30	57	20	34	111	29	13	0	3	16	29	295	153	239	687	29
25/29	18	1	8	27	25	35	25	36	96	25	47	27	39	113	25	41	17	28	86	25	30	8	14	52	24	3		0	3	24	174	78	125	377	25
20/24	5	0	2	7	20	33	15	25	73	20	32	16	21	69	20	23	11	12	46	20	13	3	5	21	20	0			0	21	106	45	65	216	20
15/19	2		0	2	16	23	4	11	38	15	21	9	13	43	15	14	7	9	30	15	4	0	1	5	15						64	20	34	118	15
10/14						9	1	3	13	11	12	2	6	20	11	10	2	3	15	10	2			2	11						33	5	12	50	11
5/9						2	0	0	2	6	5	1	2	8	6	3	1	1	5	6											10	2	3	15	6
0/4						0			0	2	2	0	0	2	2	1	0		1	1											3	0	0	3	2
-5/-1											0			0	-3	0			0	-3											0			0	-3

EGLIN AFB/VALPARAISO FLORIDA

LAT 30 29N LONG 86 31W ELEV 85 FT

MEAN FREQUENCY OF OCCURRENCE OF DRY BULB TEMPERATURE (DEGREES F) WITH MEAN COINCIDENT WET BULB TEMPERATURE (DEGREES F) FOR EACH DRY BULB TEMPERATURE RANGE

Temperature Range	MAY Obsn Hour Gp 01 to 08	MAY 09 to 16	MAY 17 to 24	MAY Total Obsn	MAY MCWB	JUNE Obsn Hour Gp 01 to 08	JUNE 09 to 16	JUNE 17 to 24	JUNE Total Obsn	JUNE MCWB	JULY Obsn Hour Gp 01 to 08	JULY 09 to 16	JULY 17 to 24	JULY Total Obsn	JULY MCWB
95/99							1	0	1	78		3	0	3	77
90/94		5	0	5	74	0	24	2	26	76	0	43	4	47	78
85/89	0	36	4	40	73	4	96	20	120	75	9	122	42	173	77
80/84	6	107	27	140	71	37	86	84	207	74	55	56	107	218	76
75/79	41	68	92	201	70	83	25	96	204	73	126	20	82	228	74
70/74	79	22	79	180	67	89	8	35	132	69	54	3	12	69	71
65/69	60	8	30	98	63	24	0	3	27	64	2		1	3	64
60/64	38	2	11	51	58	3		0	3	59	1		0	1	59
55/59	17	0	4	21	53	0			0	51					
50/54	5		1	6	49										
45/49	1			1	43										
40/44	0			0	40										
35/39															
30/34															

Temperature Range	AUGUST Obsn Hour Gp 01 to 08	AUGUST 09 to 16	AUGUST 17 to 24	AUGUST Total Obsn	AUGUST MCWB	SEPTEMBER Obsn Hour Gp 01 to 08	SEPTEMBER 09 to 16	SEPTEMBER 17 to 24	SEPTEMBER Total Obsn	SEPTEMBER MCWB	OCTOBER Obsn Hour Gp 01 to 08	OCTOBER 09 to 16	OCTOBER 17 to 24	OCTOBER Total Obsn	OCTOBER MCWB
95/99		2		2	78		0	0	0	73					
90/94	0	45	3	48	78		20	1	21	76		1		1	74
85/89	5	118	37	160	77	1	98	16	115	75		20	1	21	72
80/84	43	58	100	201	76	17	72	75	164	74	2	69	12	83	70
75/79	131	21	90	242	74	86	31	91	208	72	14	67	49	130	69
70/74	63	5	17	85	70	89	14	40	143	69	45	46	64	155	66
65/69	6		0	6	64	32	4	12	48	63	63	28	53	144	62
60/64	1			1	62	11	1	3	15	58	47	13	35	95	57
55/59						3	0	1	4	53	39	4	19	62	52
50/54						0		1	1	48	21	1	10	32	47
45/49						1		0	1	44	11	0	4	15	43
40/44						0			0	42	6	0	1	7	38
35/39											1			1	36
30/34											0			0	33

EGLIN AFB/VALPARAISO FLORIDA

Temperature Range	NOVEMBER Obsn Hour Gp 01 to 08	NOVEMBER Obsn Hour Gp 09 to 16	NOVEMBER Obsn Hour Gp 17 to 24	NOVEMBER Total Obsn	NOVEMBER MCWB	DECEMBER Obsn Hour Gp 01 to 08	DECEMBER Obsn Hour Gp 09 to 16	DECEMBER Obsn Hour Gp 17 to 24	DECEMBER Total Obsn	DECEMBER MCWB	JANUARY Obsn Hour Gp 01 to 08	JANUARY Obsn Hour Gp 09 to 16	JANUARY Obsn Hour Gp 17 to 24	JANUARY Total Obsn	JANUARY MCWB	FEBRUARY Obsn Hour Gp 01 to 08	FEBRUARY Obsn Hour Gp 09 to 16	FEBRUARY Obsn Hour Gp 17 to 24	FEBRUARY Total Obsn	FEBRUARY MCWB	MARCH Obsn Hour Gp 01 to 08	MARCH Obsn Hour Gp 09 to 16	MARCH Obsn Hour Gp 17 to 24	MARCH Total Obsn	MARCH MCWB	APRIL Obsn Hour Gp 01 to 08	APRIL Obsn Hour Gp 09 to 16	APRIL Obsn Hour Gp 17 to 24	APRIL Total Obsn	APRIL MCWB	ANNUAL TOTAL Obsn Hour Gp 01 to 08	ANNUAL TOTAL Obsn Hour Gp 09 to 16	ANNUAL TOTAL Obsn Hour Gp 17 to 24	ANNUAL TOTAL Total Obsn	ANNUAL TOTAL MCWB
95/99																																6	0	6	77
90/94																															0	138	10	148	77
85/89		0		0	70																						2	0	2	69	19	492	120	631	76
80/84		4		4	70																	1		1	66	0	27	2	29	71	160	480	407	1047	74
75/79	1	34	4	39	67		3		3	69		2		2	69		4	0	4	70		12	1	13	64	8	73	21	102	69	490	360	526	1376	72
70/74	17	56	28	101	66	4	24	4	32	67	1	11	2	14	66	2	16	5	23	66	3	44	10	57	64	47	82	74	203	66	493	331	370	1194	67
65/69	26	49	42	117	61	19	42	24	85	63	10	28	13	51	63	17	37	21	75	63	28	67	49	144	62	61	39	76	176	62	348	302	324	974	62
60/64	33	39	43	115	56	21	52	39	112	57	24	44	36	104	59	23	43	35	101	57	46	54	69	169	57	46	12	39	97	57	294	260	310	864	57
55/59	39	31	45	115	52	30	45	43	118	52	30	46	41	117	53	23	41	41	105	51	40	36	47	123	51	32	5	17	54	52	253	208	258	719	52
50/54	43	15	33	91	47	35	35	45	115	47	28	40	37	105	47	29	35	40	104	46	41	20	36	97	46	26	1	8	35	47	228	147	211	586	47
45/49	34	9	22	65	42	37	27	36	100	42	33	32	40	105	42	36	24	33	93	42	38	9	20	67	42	14	0	3	17	43	205	101	158	464	42
40/44	24	2	16	42	38	36	13	28	77	38	37	23	36	96	37	34	15	26	75	38	28	4	13	45	38	4		0	4	38	169	57	120	346	38
35/39	17	0	5	22	34	29	5	18	52	34	37	13	23	73	33	27	6	15	48	33	15	1	4	20	33	1			1	33	127	25	65	217	33
30/34	5	0	1	6	29	23	1	8	32	29	25	5	11	41	29	22	2	6	30	29	7	0	1	8	30						82	8	27	117	29
25/29	2	0	0	2	24	11	1	2	14	25	14	2	6	22	24	9	1	2	12	24	1			1	26						37	4	10	51	24
20/24	0			0	21	1	0	0	1	19	6	1	2	9	20	2	0	0	2	20											9	1	2	12	20
15/19						0	0	0	0	15	3	0	0	3	15	0			0	17											3	0	0	3	15
10/14						0		0	0	10	1			1	10																1		0	1	10
5/9						0			0	8	0			0	7																0			0	8

FORT MYERS/PAGE FLD FLORIDA

LAT 26 35N LONG 81 52W ELEV 15 FT

MEAN FREQUENCY OF OCCURRENCE OF DRY BULB TEMPERATURE (DEGREES F) WITH MEAN COINCIDENT WET BULB TEMPERATURE (DEGREES F) FOR EACH DRY BULB TEMPERATURE RANGE

Temperature Range	MAY Obsn Hour Gp 01 to 08	MAY 09 to 16	MAY 17 to 24	MAY Total Obsn	MAY MCWB	JUNE Obsn Hour Gp 01 to 08	JUNE 09 to 16	JUNE 17 to 24	JUNE Total Obsn	JUNE MCWB	JULY Obsn Hour Gp 01 to 08	JULY 09 to 16	JULY 17 to 24	JULY Total Obsn	JULY MCWB
95/99		2		2	74		3		3	77		1		1	78
90/94		42	1	43	74		70	3	73	76		61	3	64	78
85/89	1	121	17	139	73	5	110	24	139	76	4	110	19	133	77
80/84	13	63	47	123	72	30	39	52	121	75	35	41	58	134	76
75/79	33	15	80	128	71	85	12	109	206	74	148	27	137	312	75
70/74	92	4	84	180	69	103	5	51	159	71	61	8	31	100	72
65/69	87	1	18	106	65	16		1	17	66		0		0	68
60/64	19		2	21	60	0			0	63					
55/59	3			3	56										
50/54															

Temperature Range	AUGUST Obsn Hour Gp 01 to 08	AUGUST 09 to 16	AUGUST 17 to 24	AUGUST Total Obsn	AUGUST MCWB	SEPTEMBER Obsn Hour Gp 01 to 08	SEPTEMBER 09 to 16	SEPTEMBER 17 to 24	SEPTEMBER Total Obsn	SEPTEMBER MCWB	OCTOBER Obsn Hour Gp 01 to 08	OCTOBER 09 to 16	OCTOBER 17 to 24	OCTOBER Total Obsn	OCTOBER MCWB
95/99		0		0	80		0		0	80					
90/94		79	4	83	78		40	1	41	77		1		1	78
85/89	8	115	24	147	77	1	124	17	142	77		62	2	64	75
80/84	42	34	91	167	77	24	49	64	137	76	5	104	24	133	73
75/79	171	15	119	305	75	157	23	141	321	75	49	57	94	200	72
70/74	27	4	11	42	72	57	4	17	78	72	109	19	92	220	70
65/69	0			0	69						55	4	26	85	65
60/64											22	1	7	30	59
55/59											6	0	3	9	53
50/54											2		0	2	50

																															6		6	76
																					1		1	72		2		2	71		296	12	308	77
	13		13	75		1		1	73		1		1	70		4		4	70		30	0	30	72		59	1	60	72	19	750	104	873	75
	60	3	63	71		39	0	39	71		38		38	68		49	1	50	69	0	92	9	101	70	1	92	19	112	69	150	700	368	1218	73
5	70	26	101	69	1	74	10	85	68		81	11	92	66		69	16	85	66	7	61	35	103	67	18	50	49	117	68	674	554	827	2055	72
37	49	70	156	67	13	55	49	117	66	5	52	41	98	65	6	47	48	101	65	31	28	76	135	67	47	21	78	146	67	588	296	648	1532	68
68	23	62	153	64	54	32	68	154	64	33	36	76	145	63	39	30	60	129	63	76	20	61	157	63	81	12	57	150	64	509	158	429	1096	64
52	16	38	106	59	64	24	55	143	59	79	19	61	159	59	69	13	54	136	59	53	9	37	99	58	47	4	25	76	59	405	86	279	770	59
37	8	24	69	54	47	15	30	92	54	66	12	29	107	54	55	6	30	91	54	39	4	18	61	54	26	1	8	35	54	279	46	142	467	54
21	2	11	34	49	29	5	19	53	49	28	0	17	50	49	31	3	10	44	50	24	1	10	35	49	14		2	16	49	149	16	69	234	49
13	1	4	18	45	24	2	13	39	45	19		7	29	44	16	1	3	20	45	13	0	3	16	44	5		0	5	45	90	7	30	127	45
5		2	7	40	15	0	4	19	40	13		4	17	39	6	1	1	8	40	4			4	41	1			1	39	44	1	11	56	40
1			1	36	3			3	37	4		1	5	35	2		1	3	36											10	0	2	12	36
										1			1	29																1			1	29

HOMESTEAD AFB FLORIDA

LAT 25 29N LONG 80 24W ELEV 7 FT

MEAN FREQUENCY OF OCCURRENCE OF DRY BULB TEMPERATURE (DEGREES F) WITH MEAN COINCIDENT WET BULB TEMPERATURE (DEGREES F) FOR EACH DRY BULB TEMPERATURE RANGE

Temperature Range	MAY Obsn Hour Gp 01 to 08	MAY 09 to 16	MAY 17 to 24	MAY Total Obsn	MAY MCWB	JUNE Obsn Hour Gp 01 to 08	JUNE 09 to 16	JUNE 17 to 24	JUNE Total Obsn	JUNE MCWB	JULY Obsn Hour Gp 01 to 08	JULY 09 to 16	JULY 17 to 24	JULY Total Obsn	JULY MCWB
95/99															
90/94		1		1	74		7	0	7	78		9	0	9	78
85/89		37	3	40	75	2	91	14	107	77	5	174	35	214	77
80/84	13	138	48	199	73	49	107	93	249	75	89	50	136	275	76
75/79	104	60	134	298	71	136	27	108	271	73	143	13	71	227	74
70/74	97	10	55	162	69	52	8	25	85	71	11	2	5	18	71
65/69	27	1	7	35	64	1		0	1	66					
60/64	7		1	8	59										
55/59	1			1	55										
50/54															

Temperature Range	AUGUST Obsn Hour Gp 01 to 08	AUGUST 09 to 16	AUGUST 17 to 24	AUGUST Total Obsn	AUGUST MCWB	SEPTEMBER Obsn Hour Gp 01 to 08	SEPTEMBER 09 to 16	SEPTEMBER 17 to 24	SEPTEMBER Total Obsn	SEPTEMBER MCWB	OCTOBER Obsn Hour Gp 01 to 08	OCTOBER 09 to 16	OCTOBER 17 to 24	OCTOBER Total Obsn	OCTOBER MCWB
95/99		0		0	80										
90/94		18	1	19	78		10	1	11	78		0		0	77
85/89	4	168	35	207	78	2	132	18	152	77	0	56	3	59	76
80/84	89	46	132	267	76	67	71	123	261	76	23	124	70	217	74
75/79	141	14	74	229	74	143	24	88	255	74	102	52	115	269	72
70/74	14	2	6	22	72	28	3	10	41	71	80	13	48	141	69
65/69											30	3	11	44	63
60/64											9	0	2	11	59
55/59											2		0	2	55
50/54											0			0	47

																															0		0	80
																										1		1	76		46	2	48	78
	4		4	75		0		0	71							2		2	74		5	0	5	73		18	3	21	74	13	687	111	811	77
0	69	5	74	72		24	0	24	72		21	1	22	71.		36	3	39	72		53	7	60	72	1	84	16	101	72	331	823	634	1788	75
29	109	69	207	70	5	89	24	118	69	1	76	16	93	69	9	65	30	104	69	12	87	45	144	69	42	109	90	241	70	867	725	864	2456	72
86	35	106	227	67	60	64	85	209	66	42	67	75	184	66	48	49	65	162	67	78	60	94	232	66	108	24	101	233	67	704	337	675	1716	67
69	12	38	119	63	58	37	68	163	62	71	39	78	188	63	46	35	54	135	62	68	23	60	151	62	57	4	24	85	63	427	154	340	921	63
34	6	13	53	58	44	19	37	100	58	50	20	40	110	58	42	18	41	101	58	41	13	24	78	57	23	0	5	28	58	250	76	163	489	58
12	3	7	22	52	35	9	21	65	53	36	15	21	72	53	37	13	18	68	53	22	6	14	42	52	8		1	9	54	153	46	82	281	53
7	2	2	11	47	26	4	10	40	48	25	7	11	43	48	23	5	9	37	48	19	1	4	24	47	1		0	1	49	101	19	36	156	48
2	0	1	3	43	12	1	3	16	43	12	3	5	20	43	13	1	4	18	43	8	0	0	8	44	0			0	44	47	5	13	65	43
1		0	1	37	5	0	1	6	39	8	1	3	12	38	5	0	0	5	39	1		0	1	39						20	1	4	25	38
					2	0	0	2	35	3	0	0	3	34	1			1	34	0			0	37						6	0	0	6	35
										0			0	32																0			0	32

JACKSONVILLE/CECIL FLD NAS FLORIDA

LAT 30 13N LONG 81 53W ELEV 80 FT

MEAN FREQUENCY OF OCCURRENCE OF DRY BULB TEMPERATURE (DEGREES F) WITH MEAN COINCIDENT WET BULB TEMPERATURE (DEGREES F) FOR EACH DRY BULB TEMPERATURE RANGE

Temperature Range	MAY Obsn Hour Gp 01 to 08	MAY 09 to 16	MAY 17 to 24	MAY Total Obsn	MAY MCWB	JUNE Obsn Hour Gp 01 to 08	JUNE 09 to 16	JUNE 17 to 24	JUNE Total Obsn	JUNE MCWB	JULY Obsn Hour Gp 01 to 08	JULY 09 to 16	JULY 17 to 24	JULY Total Obsn	JULY MCWB
100/104		0	0	0	74		0		0	80		0		0	78
95/99		5	1	6	74		6	1	7	77		13	2	15	78
90/94		24	6	30	72		43	9	52	76		68	14	82	77
85/89		63	17	80	71		81	23	104	75	0	85	25	110	77
80/84	0	75	35	110	70	6	68	48	122	74	12	56	54	122	76
75/79	12	47	55	114	69	50	28	83	161	73	92	19	98	209	74
70/74	68	24	78	170	68	133	12	65	210	70	132	8	53	193	71
65/69	90	7	41	138	64	42	1	10	53	66	12	0	2	14	67
60/64	55	2	13	70	60	9		1	10	61	0			0	63
55/59	17		2	19	55	1			1	57					
50/54	5			5	50										
45/49	0			0	47										
40/44															
35/39															

Temperature Range	AUGUST Obsn Hour Gp 01 to 08	AUGUST 09 to 16	AUGUST 17 to 24	AUGUST Total Obsn	AUGUST MCWB	SEPTEMBER Obsn Hour Gp 01 to 08	SEPTEMBER 09 to 16	SEPTEMBER 17 to 24	SEPTEMBER Total Obsn	SEPTEMBER MCWB	OCTOBER Obsn Hour Gp 01 to 08	OCTOBER 09 to 16	OCTOBER 17 to 24	OCTOBER Total Obsn	OCTOBER MCWB
100/104		0		0	81										
95/99		8	1	9	78		1		1	77					
90/94		63	9	72	77		28	3	31	76		3	0	3	75
85/89	0	86	25	111	76		76	15	91	75		29	3	32	73
80/84	7	58	51	116	75	1	76	42	119	74		65	14	79	71
75/79	79	25	98	202	74	45	40	95	180	73	7	64	40	111	70
70/74	145	6	59	210	71	140	15	68	223	70	50	44	76	170	68
65/69	17	2	4	23	68	41	4	14	59	66	74	26	61	161	64
60/64	0		0	0	64	10	0	2	12	60	51	12	33	96	59
55/59						2		0	2	55	35	4	14	53	54
50/54						0			0	48	16	1	6	23	49
45/49						0			0	46	11	0	2	13	45
40/44											3		0	3	40
35/39											0			0	38

JACKSONVILLE/CECIL FLD NAS FLORIDA

Temperature Range	NOVEMBER Obsn Hour Gp 01 to 08	NOVEMBER 09 to 16	NOVEMBER 17 to 24	NOVEMBER Total Obsn	NOVEMBER MCWB	DECEMBER Obsn Hour Gp 01 to 08	DECEMBER 09 to 16	DECEMBER 17 to 24	DECEMBER Total Obsn	DECEMBER MCWB	JANUARY Obsn Hour Gp 01 to 08	JANUARY 09 to 16	JANUARY 17 to 24	JANUARY Total Obsn	JANUARY MCWB	FEBRUARY Obsn Hour Gp 01 to 08	FEBRUARY 09 to 16	FEBRUARY 17 to 24	FEBRUARY Total Obsn	FEBRUARY MCWB	MARCH Obsn Hour Gp 01 to 08	MARCH 09 to 16	MARCH 17 to 24	MARCH Total Obsn	MARCH MCWB	APRIL Obsn Hour Gp 01 to 08	APRIL 09 to 16	APRIL 17 to 24	APRIL Total Obsn	APRIL MCWB	ANNUAL TOTAL Obsn Hour Gp 01 to 08	ANNUAL TOTAL 09 to 16	ANNUAL TOTAL 17 to 24	ANNUAL TOTAL Total Obsn	ANNUAL TOTAL MCWB
100/104																																0	0	0	76
95/99																																33	5	38	77
90/94																						0		0	66		5	1	6	72		234	42	276	76
85/89		2		2	70		0		0	70							1	0	1	70		8	2	10	70		30	8	38	70	0	461	118	[illegible]	[illegible]
80/84		20	2	22	69		7	0	7	68		3	0	3	67		8	[illegible]	10	[illegible]		22	[illegible]	29	68		52	19	71	68	26	510	274	810	72
75/79		42	9	51	66		19	3	22	65		12	3	15	65		16	5	21	66		35	14	49	64	1	61	32	94	66	286	408	535	1229	71
70/74	3	50	25	78	64	1	28	12	41	64	1	22	8	31	63	2	23	14	39	63	5	43	29	77	63	17	48	56	121	64	697	323	543	1563	68
65/69	25	44	50	119	62	11	35	25	71	61	4	30	18	52	61	12	25	22	59	60	25	38	42	105	61	52	24	57	133	63	405	236	346	987	63
60/64	53	34	56	143	59	22	41	38	101	57	18	38	36	92	58	21	33	31	85	56	41	38	49	128	57	72	15	43	130	59	352	213	302	867	58
55/59	44	23	40	107	54	29	38	41	108	53	31	37	41	109	53	23	41	36	100	52	49	32	46	127	53	54	4	18	76	54	285	179	238	702	53
50/54	45	14	30	89	49	46	38	52	136	49	39	41	43	123	49	38	35	46	119	48	50	19	31	100	48	30	1	7	38	49	269	149	215	633	49
45/49	33	6	16	55	44	40	22	35	97	44	42	28	40	110	44	37	22	33	92	44	35	8	18	61	44	11		1	12	45	209	86	145	440	44
40/44	19	3	8	30	39	37	12	23	72	39	40	22	33	95	39	39	13	25	77	39	25	4	9	38	39	3		0	3	40	166	54	98	318	39
35/39	11	1	3	15	35	33	5	13	51	35	34	9	17	60	35	32	5	7	44	34	15	1	1	17	35	0			0	38	125	21	41	187	35
30/34	6	0	1	7	31	20	2	4	26	30	26	5	7	38	30	15	2	2	19	30	4	0	0	4	30						71	9	14	94	30
25/29	1	0	0	1	25	7	1	1	9	26	9	1	2	12	25	5	1	0	6	25	0			0	29						22	3	3	28	25
20/24	1		0	1	21	1	0	0	1	21	3	1		4	21	0			0	20											5	1	0	6	21
15/19						0	0		0	15																					0	0		0	15
10/14						0			0	13																					0			0	13

KEY WEST NAS FLORIDA

LAT 24 34N LONG 81 41W ELEV 6 FT

MEAN FREQUENCY OF OCCURRENCE OF DRY BULB TEMPERATURE (DEGREES F) WITH MEAN COINCIDENT WET BULB TEMPERATURE (DEGREES F) FOR EACH DRY BULB TEMPERATURE RANGE

Temperature Range	MAY Obsn Hour Gp 01 to 08	MAY 09 to 16	MAY 17 to 24	MAY Total Obsn	MAY MCWB	JUNE Obsn Hour Gp 01 to 08	JUNE 09 to 16	JUNE 17 to 24	JUNE Total Obsn	JUNE MCWB	JULY Obsn Hour Gp 01 to 08	JULY 09 to 16	JULY 17 to 24	JULY Total Obsn	JULY MCWB
95/99												0		0	81
90/94		3	0	3	78	0	15	3	18	79		22	2	24	79
85/89	1	51	11	63	75	10	128	46	184	77	17	187	81	285	77
80/84	58	153	105	316	74	156	85	153	394	76	206	33	154	393	76
75/79	148	34	113	295	72	70	10	35	115	74	25	5	9	39	74
70/74	39	6	18	63	68	3	2	2	7	71	1	0	1	2	71
65/69	3	1	1	5	65	0			0	68					
60/64															

Temperature Range	AUGUST Obsn Hour Gp 01 to 08	AUGUST 09 to 16	AUGUST 17 to 24	AUGUST Total Obsn	AUGUST MCWB	SEPTEMBER Obsn Hour Gp 01 to 08	SEPTEMBER 09 to 16	SEPTEMBER 17 to 24	SEPTEMBER Total Obsn	SEPTEMBER MCWB	OCTOBER Obsn Hour Gp 01 to 08	OCTOBER 09 to 16	OCTOBER 17 to 24	OCTOBER Total Obsn	OCTOBER MCWB
95/99			0	0	77										
90/94		23	2	25	79		7	0	7	80		0		0	79
85/89	17	187	83	287	78	5	156	39	200	78	0	63	5	68	77
80/84	203	31	148	382	76	170	63	169	402	77	74	115	112	301	75
75/79	26	7	14	47	74	60	12	30	102	75	126	56	103	285	72
70/74	2	1	1	4	72	4	2	2	8	72	43	13	26	82	67
65/69						0		0	0	68	4	1	2	7	62
60/64											0	0		0	57

NOVEMBER					DECEMB										FEBRUARY					MARCH					APRIL					ANNUAL TOTAL				
																															0	0	0	79
																										0		0	77	0	70	7	77	79
	2	0	2	76												0		0	75		2	0	2	76		16	2	18	75	50	792	267	1109	77
3	69	9	81	74		25	1	26	73		9	0	9	73		24	2	26	73		53	8	61	73	13	118	38	169	73	883	778	899	2560	75
81	105	110	296	71	25	80	46	151	71	10	83	28	121	71	31	72	48	151	72	53	97	81	231	71	115	77	127	319	71	770	638	744	2152	72
95	42	79	216	67	75	57	82	214	67	74	60	84	218	68	61	49	65	175	68	97	46	84	227	67	82	22	60	164	67	576	300	504	1380	67
45	13	31	89	62	73	51	66	190	63	76	48	71	195	63	53	36	55	144	63	53	28	45	126	62	27	6	12	45	61	334	184	283	801	63
11	7	9	27	57	49	25	39	113	57	58	29	43	130	58	51	28	35	114	58	33	19	23	75	56	2	0	1	3	56	204	108	150	462	57
4	2	1	7	52	18	7	11	36	52	22	13	16	51	52	20	11	16	47	52	11	3	6	20	52	0			0	52	75	36	50	161	52
1	0	1	2	47	7	1	2	10	48	6	5	5	16	47	8	3	5	16	48	2	0	1	3	48						24	9	14	47	48
					1	1	0	2	43	2	1	1	4	44	0	0		0	44											3	2	1	6	44

MACDILL AFB/TAMPA FLORIDA

LAT 27 51N LONG 82 30W ELEV 13 FT

MEAN FREQUENCY OF OCCURRENCE OF DRY BULB TEMPERATURE (DEGREES F) WITH MEAN COINCIDENT WET BULB TEMPERATURE (DEGREES F) FOR EACH DRY BULB TEMPERATURE RANGE

Temperature Range	MAY Obsn Hour Gp 01 to 08	MAY 09 to 16	MAY 17 to 24	MAY Total Obsn	MAY MCWB	JUNE Obsn Hour Gp 01 to 08	JUNE 09 to 16	JUNE 17 to 24	JUNE Total Obsn	JUNE MCWB
95/99		0		0	75		1	0	1	77
90/94		9	1	10	73		31	5	36	76
85/89		74	14	88	72	1	107	36	144	76
80/84	2	102	54	158	71	31	75	80	186	75
75/79	49	46	95	190	70	128	23	90	241	73
70/74	131	14	72	217	68	76	4	28	108	69
65/69	52	2	11	65	63	4			4	65
60/64	11	0	1	12	58					
55/59	1		0	1	53					
50/54										
45/49										
40/44										

Temperature Range	JULY Obsn Hour Gp 01 to 08	JULY 09 to 16	JULY 17 to 24	JULY Total Obsn	JULY MCWB	AUGUST Obsn Hour Gp 01 to 08	AUGUST 09 to 16	AUGUST 17 to 24	AUGUST Total Obsn	AUGUST MCWB
95/99		1	0	1	78		1	0	1	79
90/94		48	6	54	77		50	6	56	78
85/89	2	120	48	170	77	1	109	41	151	77
80/84	65	60	97	222	76	56	65	94	215	76
75/79	147	17	80	244	74	163	21	97	281	74
70/74	33	4	18	55	71	27	2	11	40	71
65/69	0	0	0	0	67	0			0	67
60/64										
55/59										
50/54										
45/49										
40/44										

Temperature Range	SEPTEMBER Obsn Hour Gp 01 to 08	SEPTEMBER 09 to 16	SEPTEMBER 17 to 24	SEPTEMBER Total Obsn	SEPTEMBER MCWB	OCTOBER Obsn Hour Gp 01 to 08	OCTOBER 09 to 16	OCTOBER 17 to 24	OCTOBER Total Obsn	OCTOBER MCWB
95/99		1	0	1	78					
90/94		32	4	36	77		5	0	5	76
85/89		104	27	131	76	0	59	9	68	74
80/84	20	73	78	171	75	2	84	39	125	72
75/79	154	25	110	289	73	58	58	86	202	71
70/74	62	5	20	87	70	95	31	71	197	67
65/69	3	0	1	4	62	55	8	29	92	62
60/64	0		0	0	58	22	3	10	35	57
55/59						11	1	3	15	52
50/54						4	0	1	5	47
45/49						1			1	43
40/44						0			0	40

MACDILL AFB/TAMPA FLORIDA

Temperature Range	NOVEMBER Obsn Hour Gp 01 to 08	09 to 16	17 to 24	Total Obsn	MCWB	DECEMBER Obsn Hour Gp 01 to 08	09 to 16	17 to 24	Total Obsn	MCWB	JANUARY Obsn Hour Gp 01 to 08	09 to 16	17 to 24	Total Obsn	MCWB
95/99															
90/94		0		0	72										
85/89		6	1	7	72										
80/84		35	5	40	70		10	0	10	69		3	0	3	69
75/79	3	69	25	97	68	0	38	7	45	67		26	4	30	67
70/74	27	54	60	141	66	6	49	31	86	65	1	44	19	64	65
65/69	69	39	68	176	63	35	46	61	142	62	25	47	51	123	62
60/64	68	21	44	133	58	58	44	51	153	58	57	46	59	162	58
55/59	34	9	22	65	53	50	31	42	123	53	55	36	44	135	53
50/54	23	4	8	35	48	40	17	30	87	47	39	24	36	99	48
45/49	8	2	4	14	42	28	8	16	52	42	34	14	21	69	43
40/44	6	1	2	9	38	20	4	7	31	38	22	5	10	37	38
35/39	2	0	1	3	32	7	1	2	10	33	10	3	3	16	33
30/34	0			0	27	2	0	1	3	28	3	1	1	5	28
25/29	0			0	25	1	0		1	24	1		0	1	25
20/24						0	0		0	19					

Temperature Range	FEBRUARY Obsn Hour Gp 01 to 08	09 to 16	17 to 24	Total Obsn	MCWB	MARCH Obsn Hour Gp 01 to 08	09 to 16	17 to 24	Total Obsn	MCWB	APRIL Obsn Hour Gp 01 to 08	09 to 16	17 to 24	Total Obsn	MCWB
95/99															
90/94												1	0	1	73
85/89		0		0	68		1	0	1	70		18	2	20	71
80/84		11	1	12	70		23	3	26	69		80	18	98	70
75/79		27	8	35	68	0	57	18	75	67	5	75	55	135	68
70/74	10	40	30	80	65	19	58	52	129	65	69	44	85	198	66
65/69	35	46	43	124	62	57	45	68	170	62	90	18	54	162	63
60/64	43	41	48	132	57	71	34	52	157	57	52	4	20	76	57
55/59	43	27	41	111	52	47	19	30	96	52	19	1	5	25	52
50/54	44	18	31	93	48	32	10	21	63	47	4	0	1	5	48
45/49	30	11	16	57	43	15	2	4	21	42	1		0	1	44
40/44	15	3	5	23	38	6	0	1	7	38	0			0	41
35/39	5	1	1	7	33	0			0	34					
30/34	1		0	1	28										
25/29															
20/24															

Temperature Range	ANNUAL TOTAL Obsn Hour Gp 01 to 08	09 to 16	17 to 24	Total Obsn	MCWB
95/99		4	0	4	78
90/94		176	22	198	77
85/89	4	598	178	780	75
80/84	176	621	469	1266	74
75/79	707	482	675	1864	71
70/74	556	349	497	1402	67
65/69	425	251	386	1062	62
60/64	382	193	285	860	58
55/59	260	124	187	571	53
50/54	186	73	128	387	47
45/49	117	37	61	215	43
40/44	69	13	25	107	38
35/39	24	5	7	36	33
30/34	6	1	2	9	28
25/29	2	0	0	2	24
20/24	0	0		0	19

MCCOY AFB/ORLANDO FLORIDA

LAT 28 27N LONG 81 20W ELEV 96 FT

MEAN FREQUENCY OF OCCURRENCE OF DRY BULB TEMPERATURE (DEGREES F) WITH MEAN COINCIDENT WET BULB TEMPERATURE (DEGREES F) FOR EACH DRY BULB TEMPERATURE RANGE

Temperature Range	MAY Obsn Hour Gp 01 to 08	MAY 09 to 16	MAY 17 to 24	MAY Total Obsn	MAY MCWB	JUNE Obsn Hour Gp 01 to 08	JUNE 09 to 16	JUNE 17 to 24	JUNE Total Obsn	JUNE MCWB	JULY Obsn Hour Gp 01 to 08	JULY 09 to 16	JULY 17 to 24	JULY Total Obsn	JULY MCWB
95/99		1	0	1	72		1	0	1	77		1	0	1	77
90/94		16	3	19	72		31	5	36	75		54	9	63	76
85/89		69	17	86	71		93	20	113	75		103	26	129	76
80/84	1	91	37	129	70	7	79	49	135	74	15	64	56	135	75
75/79	20	51	65	136	69	75	29	99	203	73	137	21	113	271	74
70/74	95	16	87	198	68	133	8	63	204	70	94	4	44	142	71
65/69	87	4	33	124	64	23	0	4	27	65	1	0	0	1	67
60/64	34	1	5	40	60	2			2	61	0	0		0	59
55/59	8		1	9	55	0			0	57					
50/54	1		0	1	51										
45/49	0			0	44										

Temperature Range	AUGUST Obsn Hour Gp 01 to 08	AUGUST 09 to 16	AUGUST 17 to 24	AUGUST Total Obsn	AUGUST MCWB	SEPTEMBER Obsn Hour Gp 01 to 08	SEPTEMBER 09 to 16	SEPTEMBER 17 to 24	SEPTEMBER Total Obsn	SEPTEMBER MCWB	OCTOBER Obsn Hour Gp 01 to 08	OCTOBER 09 to 16	OCTOBER 17 to 24	OCTOBER Total Obsn	OCTOBER MCWB
95/99		1	0	1	77		0		0	77		0		0	79
90/94		42	5	47	77		20	2	22	77		5	0	5	75
85/89		105	22	127	76		100	16	116	75		41	4	45	73
80/84	13	72	61	146	76	5	82	44	131	75	0	92	20	112	71
75/79	143	24	133	300	74	86	31	121	238	73	24	62	66	152	71
70/74	91	4	27	122	72	138	7	57	202	71	96	34	94	224	68
65/69	1	0	0	1	67	11	0	1	12	65	75	10	39	124	64
60/64						0			0	58	33	3	16	52	58
55/59											12	1	6	19	53
50/54											6	0	2	8	48
45/49											1		0	1	44

MCCOY AFB/ORLANDO FLORIDA

Temperature Range	NOVEMBER Obsn Hour Gp 01 to 08	09 to 16	17 to 24	Total Obsn	MCWB	DECEMBER Obsn Hour Gp 01 to 08	09 to 16	17 to 24	Total Obsn	MCWB	JANUARY Obsn Hour Gp 01 to 08	09 to 16	17 to 24	Total Obsn	MCWB
95/99															
90/94															
85/89		3	0	3	72		0		0	72		0		0	68
80/84		39	4	43	69		16	2	18	70		11	2	13	69
75/79	0	73	20	93	67	0	43	11	54	67	0	30	9	39	66
70/74	16	56	55	127	65	3	52	32	87	64	3	42	24	69	64
65/69	66	34	67	167	63	33	41	52	126	62	22	48	43	113	62
60/64	61	18	45	124	58	46	37	47	130	58	40	39	49	128	58
55/59	50	9	27	86	53	50	29	39	118	53	53	31	41	125	53
50/54	26	4	13	43	48	42	15	31	88	48	45	24	36	105	48
45/49	11	2	6	19	43	34	8	21	63	43	36	13	23	72	43
40/44	7	1	2	10	38	25	5	10	40	38	25	5	13	43	38
35/39	2	0	0	2	33	10	2	3	15	33	15	4	5	24	33
30/34	1	0	0	1	28	3	0	1	4	29	7	1	2	10	29
25/29						1	0	0	1	25	2	0	0	2	25
20/24						0			0	19	0			0	21

Temperature Range	FEBRUARY Obsn Hour Gp 01 to 08	09 to 16	17 to 24	Total Obsn	MCWB	MARCH Obsn Hour Gp 01 to 08	09 to 16	17 to 24	Total Obsn	MCWB	APRIL Obsn Hour Gp 01 to 08	09 to 16	17 to 24	Total Obsn	MCWB	ANNUAL TOTAL Obsn Hour Gp 01 to 08	09 to 16	17 to 24	Total Obsn	MCWB
95/99												0		0	73		4	0	4	76
90/94							0		0	77		3	1	4	71		171	25	196	76
85/89		2	0	2	70		6	2	8	71		25	8	33	70		547	115	662	74
80/84		14	5	19	69		28	9	37	69		65	21	86	68	41	653	310	1004	72
75/79		28	12	40	66	0	48	21	69	66	3	76	43	122	66	488	516	713	1717	71
70/74	7	39	27	73	64	12	57	43	112	64	40	47	70	157	65	728	366	623	1717	68
65/69	29	43	37	109	61	47	46	54	147	62	79	17	56	152	63	474	243	386	1103	63
60/64	36	38	44	118	57	61	31	55	147	58	68	5	30	103	58	381	172	291	844	58
55/59	41	27	35	103	53	48	18	31	97	52	34	1	10	45	53	296	116	190	602	53
50/54	32	17	34	83	48	35	9	22	66	48	12	0	2	14	48	199	69	140	408	48
45/49	39	10	19	68	43	26	3	10	39	43	3	0	0	3	44	150	36	79	265	43
40/44	24	5	7	36	38	14	1	1	16	38	1			1	39	96	17	33	146	38
35/39	10	1	4	15	34	3	0	0	3	34						40	7	12	59	33
30/34	6	0	1	7	29	0			0	31						17	1	4	22	29
25/29	0			0	25											3	0	0	3	25
20/24																0			0	20

PATRICK AFB/COCOA BEACH FLORIDA

LAT 28 14N LONG 80 36W ELEV 9 FT

MEAN FREQUENCY OF OCCURRENCE OF DRY BULB TEMPERATURE (DEGREES F) WITH MEAN COINCIDENT WET BULB TEMPERATURE (DEGREES F) FOR EACH DRY BULB TEMPERATURE RANGE

Temperature Range	MAY Obsn Hour Gp 01 to 08	MAY 09 to 16	MAY 17 to 24	MAY Total Obsn	MAY MCWB	JUNE Obsn Hour Gp 01 to 08	JUNE 09 to 16	JUNE 17 to 24	JUNE Total Obsn	JUNE MCWB	JULY Obsn Hour Gp 01 to 08	JULY 09 to 16	JULY 17 to 24	JULY Total Obsn	JULY MCWB
95/99			0	0	76		1	0	1	79		0	0	0	79
90/94		2	0	2	74		7	1	8	78		9	0	9	77
85/89		10	1	11	73	0	57	8	65	77	1	112	19	132	78
80/84	2	118	24	144	73	31	135	85	251	75	65	111	133	309	76
75/79	98	99	151	348	71	162	36	125	323	73	172	14	88	274	74
70/74	117	17	64	198	68	46	4	20	70	70	11	1	9	21	71
65/69	26	2	7	35	63	1			1	66					
60/64	5		1	6	58										
55/59	0			0	55										
50/54															

Temperature Range	AUGUST Obsn Hour Gp 01 to 08	AUGUST 09 to 16	AUGUST 17 to 24	AUGUST Total Obsn	AUGUST MCWB	SEPTEMBER Obsn Hour Gp 01 to 08	SEPTEMBER 09 to 16	SEPTEMBER 17 to 24	SEPTEMBER Total Obsn	SEPTEMBER MCWB	OCTOBER Obsn Hour Gp 01 to 08	OCTOBER 09 to 16	OCTOBER 17 to 24	OCTOBER Total Obsn	OCTOBER MCWB
95/99							0		0	77					
90/94		7	0	7	78		3	0	3	78		0		0	75
85/89	1	111	16	128	78	0	92	11	103	77		23	1	24	75
80/84	78	112	145	335	76	100	118	147	365	75	23	111	54	188	74
75/79	157	17	82	256	74	126	23	74	223	73	115	80	120	315	71
70/74	12	1	5	18	71	14	3	7	24	70	66	26	52	144	67
65/69			0	0	69	0			0	69	27	6	15	48	62
60/64											13	1	5	19	58
55/59											3	0	0	3	52
50/54											1		0		49

PATRICK AFB/COCOA BEACH FLORIDA

Temperature Range	NOVEMBER Obsn Hour Gp 01 to 08	NOVEMBER Obsn Hour Gp 09 to 16	NOVEMBER Obsn Hour Gp 17 to 24	NOVEMBER Total Obsn	NOVEMBER M C W B	DECEMBER Obsn Hour Gp 01 to 08	DECEMBER Obsn Hour Gp 09 to 16	DECEMBER Obsn Hour Gp 17 to 24	DECEMBER Total Obsn	DECEMBER M C W B	JANUARY Obsn Hour Gp 01 to 08	JANUARY Obsn Hour Gp 09 to 16	JANUARY Obsn Hour Gp 17 to 24	JANUARY Total Obsn	JANUARY M C W B
95/99															
90/94															
85/89		1		1	73		1		1	72		0		0	70
80/84		19	1	20	72		6	0	6	71		6	0	6	70
75/79	15	91	39	145	69	1	34	10	45	70		17	3	20	68
70/74	79	75	103	257	67	26	66	53	145	66	8	54	27	89	66
65/69	68	30	51	149	63	63	55	70	188	63	53	61	71	185	63
60/64	39	12	24	75	58	49	40	41	130	58	64	50	59	173	58
55/59	22	7	13	42	53	35	25	38	98	53	45	27	42	114	53
50/54	7	2	6	15	46	39	12	22	73	48	35	18	26	79	48
45/49	7	2	1	10	42	21	5	9	35	43	24	8	12	44	43
40/44	2	1	1	4	37	9	3	2	14	38	11	4	7	22	37
35/39	1	0	0	1	33	3	0	1	4	33	5	2	2	9	32
30/34						1	0	0	1	28	3	1	0	4	28
25/29						0			0	26	0			0	25

Temperature Range	FEBRUARY Obsn Hour Gp 01 to 08	FEBRUARY Obsn Hour Gp 09 to 16	FEBRUARY Obsn Hour Gp 17 to 24	FEBRUARY Total Obsn	FEBRUARY M C W B	MARCH Obsn Hour Gp 01 to 08	MARCH Obsn Hour Gp 09 to 16	MARCH Obsn Hour Gp 17 to 24	MARCH Total Obsn	MARCH M C W B	APRIL Obsn Hour Gp 01 to 08	APRIL Obsn Hour Gp 09 to 16	APRIL Obsn Hour Gp 17 to 24	APRIL Total Obsn	APRIL M C W B	ANNUAL TOTAL Obsn Hour Gp 01 to 08	ANNUAL TOTAL Obsn Hour Gp 09 to 16	ANNUAL TOTAL Obsn Hour Gp 17 to 24	ANNUAL TOTAL Total Obsn	ANNUAL TOTAL M C W B
95/99												0		0	73		1	0	1	77
90/94							0		0	70		2	0	2	74		30	1	31	77
85/89		1		1	71		3	0	3	72		8	2	10	73	2	419	58	479	77
80/84		5	1	6	71		13	3	16	71		30	6	36	71	299	784	599	1682	75
75/79	0	23	6	29	70	0	34	11	45	70	15	106	60	181	70	861	574	769	2204	72
70/74	16	44	34	94	67	32	78	55	165	66	111	71	116	298	67	538	440	545	1523	67
65/69	51	57	54	162	63	79	62	89	230	63	77	19	43	139	62	445	292	400	1137	63
60/64	48	45	54	147	58	64	34	48	146	58	26	3	9	38	57	308	185	241	734	58
55/59	39	24	39	102	52	34	15	25	74	52	9	0	3	12	52	187	98	160	445	53
50/54	32	15	24	71	48	23	7	14	44	47	2	0	0	2	48	139	54	92	285	48
45/49	25	6	9	40	43	12	2	2	16	43						89	23	33	145	43
40/44	9	3	3	15	38	3	0	0	3	38						34	11	13	58	38
35/39	3	1	0	4	33	1	0		1	34						13	3	3	19	33
30/34	1	0		1	29											5	1	0	6	28
25/29																0			0	26

PENSACOLA NAS/F SHERMAN FLD FLORIDA

LAT 30 21N LONG 87 19W ELEV 30 FT

MEAN FREQUENCY OF OCCURRENCE OF DRY BULB TEMPERATURE (DEGREES F) WITH MEAN COINCIDENT WET BULB TEMPERATURE (DEGREES F) FOR EACH DRY BULB TEMPERATURE RANGE

Temperature Range	MAY Obsn Hour Gp 01 to 08	MAY 09 to 16	MAY 17 to 24	MAY Total Obsn	MAY MCWB	JUNE Obsn Hour Gp 01 to 08	JUNE 09 to 16	JUNE 17 to 24	JUNE Total Obsn	JUNE MCWB	JULY Obsn Hour Gp 01 to 08	JULY 09 to 16	JULY 17 to 24	JULY Total Obsn	JULY MCWB
100/104															
95/99							1	0	1	77		1		1	78
90/94		2		2	71	0	20	1	21	77	0	40	2	42	79
85/89	0	35	1	36	73	8	106	18	132	76	12	130	31	173	78
80/84	13	110	30	153	73	59	82	99	240	75	74	55	125	254	76
75/79	54	61	90	205	71	92	22	91	205	73	125	18	78	221	74
70/74	90	29	82	201	68	60	8	26	94	70	34	4	12	50	71
65/69	53	8	30	91	63	17	0	5	22	65	2	0	1	3	66
60/64	21	2	9	32	58	3		0	3	58	1			1	60
55/59	10	1	4	15	53	0			0	53					
50/54	6	0	1	7	49										
45/49	0		0	0	45										
40/44	0			0	43										
35/39															

Temperature Range	AUGUST Obsn Hour Gp 01 to 08	AUGUST 09 to 16	AUGUST 17 to 24	AUGUST Total Obsn	AUGUST MCWB	SEPTEMBER Obsn Hour Gp 01 to 08	SEPTEMBER 09 to 16	SEPTEMBER 17 to 24	SEPTEMBER Total Obsn	SEPTEMBER MCWB	OCTOBER Obsn Hour Gp 01 to 08	OCTOBER 09 to 16	OCTOBER 17 to 24	OCTOBER Total Obsn	OCTOBER MCWB
100/104		0		0	79										
95/99		1		1	80		0		0	77					
90/94	0	44	2	46	79	0	22	1	23	77		0		0	77
85/89	8	123	32	163	78	3	78	15	96	76	0	19	0	19	74
80/84	68	54	120	242	76	35	85	76	196	75	5	59	15	79	72
75/79	123	21	79	223	74	83	36	88	207	73	22	67	41	130	69
70/74	43	5	14	62	71	77	13	42	132	69	42	52	68	162	66
65/69	4	0	0	4	66	27	4	13	44	64	57	31	58	146	62
60/64	1			1	62	13	1	3	17	59	54	15	34	103	58
55/59						2	0	1	3	54	32	5	20	57	53
50/54						1		0	1	49	20	1	10	31	48
45/49						0			0	45	11	0	3	14	44
40/44											4		0	4	40
35/39											1			1	37

PENSACOLA NAS/F SHERMAN FLD FLORIDA

Temperature Range	NOVEMBER Obsn Hour Gp 01 to 08	NOVEMBER 09 to 16	NOVEMBER 17 to 24	NOVEMBER Total Obsn	NOVEMBER MCWB	DECEMBER Obsn Hour Gp 01 to 08	DECEMBER 09 to 16	DECEMBER 17 to 24	DECEMBER Total Obsn	DECEMBER MCWB	JANUARY Obsn Hour Gp 01 to 08	JANUARY 09 to 16	JANUARY 17 to 24	JANUARY Total Obsn	JANUARY MCWB	FEBRUARY Obsn Hour Gp 01 to 08	FEBRUARY 09 to 16	FEBRUARY 17 to 24	FEBRUARY Total Obsn	FEBRUARY MCWB
100/104																				
95/99																				
90/94																				
85/89																				
80/84		3		3	70															
75/79	1	29	2	32	68		5		5	68		0		0	62		0		0	68
70/74	20	60	31	111	66	4	26	4	34	67		11	0	11	67	0	18	3	21	67
65/69	34	48	45	127	62	29	41	33	103	63	11	32	16	59	64	19	38	24	81	64
60/64	33	44	45	122	57	29	53	42	124	58	33	42	39	114	59	32	47	42	121	58
55/59	39	27	41	107	52	29	46	45	120	52	28	49	40	117	53	29	43	40	112	52
50/54	41	16	33	90	48	35	35	42	112	47	31	40	42	113	48	32	35	44	111	47
45/49	30	11	22	63	43	34	21	32	87	43	32	30	40	102	43	34	23	31	88	43
40/44	21	2	14	37	39	36	11	27	74	39	39	24	35	98	38	30	12	23	65	38
35/39	14	1	5	20	34	25	5	14	44	34	29	12	20	61	34	23	6	14	43	34
30/34	6	0	1	7	30	17	2	7	26	30	28	5	9	42	29	17	2	3	22	29
25/29	1	0	0	1	27	8	1	1	10	25	10	2	5	17	25	6	0	1	7	25
20/24	0			0	24	1	0	0	1	21	4	1	2	7	20	1			1	20
15/19						0	0	0	0	15	1	1	0	2	16					
10/14						0	0	0	0	11	2	0	0	2	11					
5/9						0			0	8	0			0	8					

Temperature Range	MARCH Obsn Hour Gp 01 to 08	MARCH 09 to 16	MARCH 17 to 24	MARCH Total Obsn	MARCH MCWB	APRIL Obsn Hour Gp 01 to 08	APRIL 09 to 16	APRIL 17 to 24	APRIL Total Obsn	APRIL MCWB	ANNUAL TOTAL Obsn Hour Gp 01 to 08	ANNUAL TOTAL 09 to 16	ANNUAL TOTAL 17 to 24	ANNUAL TOTAL Total Obsn	ANNUAL TOTAL MCWB
100/104												0		0	79
95/99												3	0	3	78
90/94											0	128	6	134	78
85/89							1		1	69	31	492	97	620	77
80/84		0		0	73		21	1	22	72	254	469	466	1189	75
75/79	0	8	0	8	65	10	64	17	91	70	510	331	486	1327	72
70/74	3	39	6	48	65	50	87	73	210	67	423	352	361	1136	68
65/69	31	70	47	148	63	72	47	78	197	63	356	319	350	1025	63
60/64	53	58	74	185	58	48	15	46	109	58	321	277	334	932	58
55/59	40	38	50	128	52	28	5	17	50	53	237	214	258	709	52
50/54	45	22	34	101	48	23	1	7	31	48	234	150	213	597	48
45/49	32	10	22	64	43	8		2	10	44	181	95	152	428	43
40/44	26	3	12	41	38	2		0	2	39	158	52	111	321	38
35/39	12	1	2	15	34	0			0	36	104	25	55	184	34
30/34	4	0	1	5	30						72	9	21	102	29
25/29	1			1	25						26	3	7	36	25
20/24											6	1	2	9	20
15/19											1	1	0	2	16
10/14											2	0	0	2	11
5/9											0			0	8

TYNDALL AFB/PANAMA CITY FLORIDA

LAT 30 04N LONG 85 35W ELEV 18 FT

MEAN FREQUENCY OF OCCURRENCE OF DRY BULB TEMPERATURE (DEGREES F) WITH MEAN COINCIDENT WET BULB TEMPERATURE (DEGREES F) FOR EACH DRY BULB TEMPERATURE RANGE

Temperature Range	MAY Obsn Hour Gp 01 to 08	MAY 09 to 16	MAY 17 to 24	MAY Total Obsn	MAY MCWB	JUNE Obsn Hour Gp 01 to 08	JUNE 09 to 16	JUNE 17 to 24	JUNE Total Obsn	JUNE MCWB	JULY Obsn Hour Gp 01 to 08	JULY 09 to 16	JULY 17 to 24	JULY Total Obsn	JULY MCWB
95/99							0		0	78		0		0	80
90/94		1		1	72		14	0	14	77		33	1	34	78
85/89	0	31	1	32	74	6	113	14	133	76	12	135	31	178	77
80/84	8	117	20	145	72	57	84	98	239	75	87	59	128	274	76
75/79	50	67	97	214	71	89	23	94	206	73	113	18	78	209	74
70/74	89	23	88	200	68	72	6	33	111	69	35	3	9	47	71
65/69	62	6	33	101	63	15	0	2	17	65	1		0	1	62
60/64	28	2	8	38	58	1			1	58	0			0	61
55/59	9	0	1	10	54										
50/54	1			1	49										
45/49															
40/44															

Temperature Range	AUGUST Obsn Hour Gp 01 to 08	AUGUST 09 to 16	AUGUST 17 to 24	AUGUST Total Obsn	AUGUST MCWB	SEPTEMBER Obsn Hour Gp 01 to 08	SEPTEMBER 09 to 16	SEPTEMBER 17 to 24	SEPTEMBER Total Obsn	SEPTEMBER MCWB	OCTOBER Obsn Hour Gp 01 to 08	OCTOBER 09 to 16	OCTOBER 17 to 24	OCTOBER Total Obsn	OCTOBER MCWB
95/99		1		1	79		0		0	76					
90/94		39	1	40	78		17	0	17	76		1		1	75
85/89	7	124	31	162	77	1	101	11	113	76	0	20	0	20	73
80/84	68	57	116	241	76	26	72	72	170	74	4	78	11	93	71
75/79	126	23	87	236	74	93	34	103	230	72	19	68	53	140	69
70/74	45	4	13	62	71	89	13	42	144	69	57	43	75	175	66
65/69	2	0	0	2	66	22	2	8	32	63	66	24	54	144	62
60/64						7	1	2	10	58	47	11	33	91	57
55/59						1	0	1	2	53	34	2	16	52	52
50/54						1		0	1	47	15	0	4	19	47
45/49						0			0	46	5	0	1	6	43
40/44											1	0	0	1	39

TYNDALL AFB/PANAMA CITY FLORIDA

Temperature Range	NOVEMBER Obsn Hour Gp 01 to 08	NOVEMBER 09 to 16	NOVEMBER 17 to 24	NOVEMBER Total Obsn	NOVEMBER MCWB	DECEMBER Obsn Hour Gp 01 to 08	DECEMBER 09 to 16	DECEMBER 17 to 24	DECEMBER Total Obsn	DECEMBER MCWB	JANUARY Obsn Hour Gp 01 to 08	JANUARY 09 to 16	JANUARY 17 to 24	JANUARY Total Obsn	JANUARY MCWB
95/99															
90/94															
85/89		0		0	77										
80/84		5		5	71										
75/79	0	38	2	40	68		8		8	69		2		2	66
70/74	15	66	27	108	65	4	35	5	44	66		19	0	19	65
65/69	35	48	52	135	62	21	46	27	94	62	16	38	19	73	63
60/64	42	36	53	131	57	28	52	47	127	57	29	48	42	119	59
55/59	45	25	45	115	52	35	36	50	121	52	28	44	39	111	52
50/54	46	14	32	92	47	41	35	46	122	47	33	35	45	113	48
45/49	29	6	20	55	42	47	21	39	107	42	41	29	43	113	43
40/44	19	2	8	29	37	34	9	21	64	37	42	18	34	94	38
35/39	8	1	2	11	33	24	4	9	37	33	31	10	16	57	33
30/34	1	0	0	1	27	11	2	2	15	28	17	4	7	28	28
25/29	1	0	0	1	23	3	0	0	3	24	7	1	2	10	24
20/24								0	0	18	3	0	0	3	20
15/19						0	0	0	0	14	1	0		1	15
10/14						0			0	11	0			0	11

Temperature Range	FEBRUARY Obsn Hour Gp 01 to 08	FEBRUARY 09 to 16	FEBRUARY 17 to 24	FEBRUARY Total Obsn	FEBRUARY MCWB	MARCH Obsn Hour Gp 01 to 08	MARCH 09 to 16	MARCH 17 to 24	MARCH Total Obsn	MARCH MCWB	APRIL Obsn Hour Gp 01 to 08	APRIL 09 to 16	APRIL 17 to 24	APRIL Total Obsn	APRIL MCWB	ANNUAL TOTAL Obsn Hour Gp 01 to 08	ANNUAL TOTAL 09 to 16	ANNUAL TOTAL 17 to 24	ANNUAL TOTAL Total Obsn	ANNUAL TOTAL MCWB
95/99																	1		1	78
90/94																	105	2	107	77
85/89												1		1	71	26	525	88	639	76
80/84							1		1	67	0	27	0	27	71	250	500	445	1195	75
75/79		5		5	69		12	0	12	66	9	86	18	113	69	499	384	532	1415	72
70/74	2	20	5	27	66	3	56	7	66	65	47	75	78	200	67	458	363	382	1203	67
65/69	20	41	25	86	63	33	70	55	158	62	72	35	82	189	63	365	310	357	1032	62
60/64	28	41	36	105	58	50	49	75	174	58	53	11	43	107	58	313	251	339	903	58
55/59	26	43	44	113	52	52	33	53	138	52	35	4	14	53	53	265	187	263	715	52
50/54	35	35	43	113	47	46	18	32	96	47	19	1	3	23	48	237	138	205	580	47
45/49	39	20	35	94	43	34	8	19	61	42	4	0	1	5	43	199	84	158	441	42
40/44	32	11	23	66	38	21	2	6	29	38	1			1	38	150	42	92	284	38
35/39	26	6	10	42	34	6	1	1	8	33						95	22	38	155	33
30/34	12	1	3	16	29	2		0	2	28						43	7	12	62	28
25/29	4	0	0	4	24	0			0	25						15	1	2	18	24
20/24	0			0	19											3	0	0	3	20
15/19																1	0	0	1	15
10/14																0			0	11

ATLANTA/HARTSFIELD IAP GEORGIA

LAT 33 39N LONG 84 26W ELEV 1010 FT

MEAN FREQUENCY OF OCCURRENCE OF DRY BULB TEMPERATURE (DEGREES F) WITH MEAN COINCIDENT WET BULB TEMPERATURE (DEGREES F) FOR EACH DRY BULB TEMPERATURE RANGE

Temperature Range	MAY Obsn Hour Gp 01 to 08	MAY 09 to 16	MAY 17 to 24	MAY Total Obsn	MAY MCWB	JUNE Obsn Hour Gp 01 to 08	JUNE 09 to 16	JUNE 17 to 24	JUNE Total Obsn	JUNE MCWB	JULY Obsn Hour Gp 01 to 08	JULY 09 to 16	JULY 17 to 24	JULY Total Obsn	JULY MCWB
100/104							0		0	77		1	0	1	72
95/99							4	1	5	74		5	1	6	74
90/94		4	1	5	70		29	10	39	74		30	10	40	74
85/89		33	13	46	69	0	52	25	77	72	0	61	30	91	74
80/84	0	53	28	81	67	5	65	44	114	71	5	81	57	143	73
75/79	3	57	46	106	66	31	50	62	143	69	46	51	74	171	72
70/74	32	47	62	141	64	93	28	64	185	68	147	18	69	234	70
65/69	94	30	52	176	62	82	11	28	121	64	46	2	7	55	66
60/64	59	15	26	100	58	23	1	4	28	59	5	0	1	6	60
55/59	30	7	15	52	53	5	1	1	7	55					
50/54	19	1	5	25	48	1		0	1	49					
45/49	8	0	1	9	44	0			0	44					
40/44	3	0	0	3	40										
35/39															
30/34															

Temperature Range	AUGUST Obsn Hour Gp 01 to 08	AUGUST 09 to 16	AUGUST 17 to 24	AUGUST Total Obsn	AUGUST MCWB	SEPTEMBER Obsn Hour Gp 01 to 08	SEPTEMBER 09 to 16	SEPTEMBER 17 to 24	SEPTEMBER Total Obsn	SEPTEMBER MCWB	OCTOBER Obsn Hour Gp 01 to 08	OCTOBER 09 to 16	OCTOBER 17 to 24	OCTOBER Total Obsn	OCTOBER MCWB
100/104		0		0	76										
95/99		6	1	7	74		2	0	2	72		0		0	74
90/94		30	9	39	74		9	2	11	71		1	0	1	73
85/89		72	33	105	73		31	11	42	71		3	1	4	70
80/84	3	76	58	137	72	0	60	31	91	70		16	4	20	68
75/79	47	42	76	165	71	8	57	53	118	68	1	42	14	57	64
70/74	133	19	59	211	69	72	43	71	186	67	8	52	34	94	63
65/69	54	3	11	68	65	82	21	40	143	63	28	53	54	135	60
60/64	10	0	1	11	60	49	14	23	86	59	51	39	59	149	57
55/59	0			0	56	22	2	6	30	54	60	23	40	123	52
50/54						6	1	1	8	49	51	12	24	87	48
45/49						1		0	1	45	28	4	11	43	43
40/44						0			0	42	14	2	4	20	39
35/39											7	0	1	8	33
30/34											2		0	2	29

Temperature Range	NOVEMBER Obsn Hour Gp 01 to 08	09 to 16	17 to 24	Total Obsn	MCWB	DECEMBER Obsn Hour Gp 01 to 08	09 to 16	17 to 24	Total Obsn	MCWB	JANUARY Obsn Hour Gp 01 to 08	09 to 16	17 to 24	Total Obsn	MCWB
100/104															
95/99															
90/94															
85/89															
80/84		1	0	1	67										
75/79		5	1	6	64							0		0	64
70/74	0	20	5	25	60		3	0	3	60		4	1	5	63
65/69	5	[illegible]	17	[illegible]	[illegible]	1	10	8	19	60	2	11	5	18	60
60/64	18	39	35	92	56	9	22	16	47	57	9	19	19	47	57
55/59	28	40	43	111	51	13	26	22	61	52	17	29	23	69	53
50/54	34	38	41	113	47	17	36	33	86	47	21	34	34	89	47
45/49	45	30	42	117	42	29	44	41	114	42	25	42	39	106	43
40/44	44	20	30	94	38	39	44	53	136	38	36	38	43	117	38
35/39	35	9	16	60	33	55	29	37	121	34	46	37	40	123	34
30/34	20	4	7	31	29	43	19	25	87	29	45	18	28	91	29
25/29	8	1	3	12	25	23	7	11	41	24	28	9	9	46	24
20/24	3	0	0	3	21	13	2	3	18	20	9	4	4	17	20
15/19	1	0	1	2	14	3	1	1	5	15	5	1	3	9	15
10/14	0	0	0	0	10	2	1	0	3	11	3	1	0	4	11
5/9	0	0		0	6	0	0	0	0	5	0	0	0	0	6
0/4	0			0	3	1	0		1	1	0	0		0	0
-5/-1											0	0		0	-3

Temperature Range	FEBRUARY Obsn Hour Gp 01 to 08	09 to 16	17 to 24	Total Obsn	MCWB	MARCH Obsn Hour Gp 01 to 08	09 to 16	17 to 24	Total Obsn	MCWB	APRIL Obsn Hour Gp 01 to 08	09 to 16	17 to 24	Total Obsn	MCWB	ANNUAL TOTAL Obsn Hour Gp 01 to 08	09 to 16	17 to 24	Total Obsn	MCWB
100/104																	1	0	1	73
95/99																	17	3	20	74
90/94																	103	32	135	74
85/89												2	0	2	66	0	254	113	367	72
80/84							1	0	1	64		17	7	24	64	13	370	229	612	70
75/79		2	0	2	63		9	4	13	62		38	20	58	62	136	353	350	839	69
70/74		8	3	11	60	0	10	[illegible]	[illegible]	[illegible]	[illegible]	41	30	79	61	487	301	413	1201	67
65/69	2	16	10	28	57	5	27	24	56	57	22	43	48	113	59	423	262	301	986	62
60/64	7	25	20	52	55	16	34	34	84	54	55	40	48	143	56	311	248	286	845	57
55/59	17	32	33	82	51	30	45	42	117	50	54	29	38	121	52	276	234	263	773	52
50/54	26	34	37	97	47	38	40	44	122	47	42	17	22	81	46	255	213	241	709	47
45/49	32	37	37	106	42	44	34	37	115	42	31	9	14	54	42	243	200	222	665	42
40/44	43	30	35	108	38	48	21	30	99	38	22	3	6	31	38	249	158	201	608	38
35/39	41	21	25	87	34	34	12	15	61	33	10	0	1	11	34	228	108	135	471	34
30/34	29	10	14	53	29	25	6	6	37	29	2			2	29	166	57	80	303	29
25/29	15	5	6	26	24	5	1	3	9	25						79	23	32	134	24
20/24	7	2	2	11	19	1	0	1	2	20						33	8	10	51	20
15/19	3	1	2	6	15	1	0		1	16						13	3	7	23	15
10/14	2	0	0	2	11	0	0		0	11						7	2	0	9	11
5/9	1	0		1	6											1	0	0	1	6
0/4																1	0		1	1
-5/-1																0	0		0	-3

AUGUSTA/BUSH FIELD GEORGIA

LAT 33 22N LONG 81 58W ELEV 136 FT

MEAN FREQUENCY OF OCCURRENCE OF DRY BULB TEMPERATURE (DEGREES F) WITH MEAN COINCIDENT WET BULB TEMPERATURE (DEGREES F) FOR EACH DRY BULB TEMPERATURE RANGE

Temperature Range	MAY Obsn Hour Gp 01 to 08	MAY 09 to 16	MAY 17 to 24	MAY Total Obsn	MAY MCWB	JUNE Obsn Hour Gp 01 to 08	JUNE 09 to 16	JUNE 17 to 24	JUNE Total Obsn	JUNE MCWB	JULY Obsn Hour Gp 01 to 08	JULY 09 to 16	JULY 17 to 24	JULY Total Obsn	JULY MCWB
105/109							0		0	78		0	0	0	73
100/104							2	0	2	78		2	0	2	77
95/99		3	0	3	73		17	4	21	76		17	4	21	77
90/94		24	7	31	72	0	46	15	61	75		63	20	83	76
85/89	0	51	18	69	70	2	65	28	95	74	1	81	34	116	75
80/84	1	58	28	87	69	9	61	44	114	72	13	56	58	127	74
75/79	10	50	41	101	67	40	33	62	135	71	74	25	85	184	73
70/74	41	31	59	131	66	97	13	59	169	69	127	4	42	173	71
65/69	78	18	49	145	64	60	3	20	83	65	25		4	29	66
60/64	50	8	24	82	59	21	1	6	28	60	7		1	8	61
55/59	30	3	13	46	54	9		1	10	56	1			1	57
50/54	24	1	6	31	50	2			2	52					
45/49	11	0	2	13	46										
40/44	3		0	3	42										
35/39	0			0	37										
30/34															
25/29															
20/24															

Temperature Range	AUGUST Obsn Hour Gp 01 to 08	AUGUST 09 to 16	AUGUST 17 to 24	AUGUST Total Obsn	AUGUST MCWB	SEPTEMBER Obsn Hour Gp 01 to 08	SEPTEMBER 09 to 16	SEPTEMBER 17 to 24	SEPTEMBER Total Obsn	SEPTEMBER MCWB	OCTOBER Obsn Hour Gp 01 to 08	OCTOBER 09 to 16	OCTOBER 17 to 24	OCTOBER Total Obsn	OCTOBER MCWB
105/109															
100/104		2	0	2	76		0		0	75					
95/99		19	4	23	77		5	0	5	75		1		1	76
90/94		67	18	85	76		24	5	29	74		3	0	3	75
85/89	1	76	33	110	75		56	15	71	73		13	2	15	71
80/84	9	50	51	110	74	1	60	27	88	72	0	38	7	45	68
75/79	60	26	82	168	73	17	47	57	121	71	1	46	16	63	66
70/74	124	7	48	179	70	81	27	67	175	69	13	47	36	96	64
65/69	42	1	9	52	66	70	13	41	124	65	27	46	44	117	61
60/64	11		2	13	61	43	6	19	68	60	43	29	44	116	58
55/59	1			1	57	17	1	8	26	55	46	17	41	104	54
50/54						10	0	1	11	51	43	7	29	79	50
45/49						2			2	47	31	1	17	49	45
40/44											23	1	9	33	40
35/39											14		3	17	36
30/34											6		1	7	31
25/29											1		0	1	27
20/24											0			0	23

AUGUSTA/BUSH FIELD GEORGIA

Tempera-ture Range	NOVEMBER Obsn Hour Gp 01 to 08	NOVEMBER 09 to 16	NOVEMBER 17 to 24	NOVEMBER Total Obsn	NOVEMBER M C W B	DECEMBER Obsn Hour Gp 01 to 08	DECEMBER 09 to 16	DECEMBER 17 to 24	DECEMBER Total Obsn	DECEMBER M C W B	JANUARY Obsn Hour Gp 01 to 08	JANUARY 09 to 16	JANUARY 17 to 24	JANUARY Total Obsn	JANUARY M C W B	FEBRUARY Obsn Hour Gp 01 to 08	FEBRUARY 09 to 16	FEBRUARY 17 to 24	FEBRUARY Total Obsn	FEBRUARY M C W B	MARCH Obsn Hour Gp 01 to 08	MARCH 09 to 16	MARCH 17 to 24	MARCH Total Obsn	MARCH M C W B	APRIL Obsn Hour Gp 01 to 08	APRIL 09 to 16	APRIL 17 to 24	APRIL Total Obsn	APRIL M C W B	ANNUAL TOTAL Obsn Hour Gp 01 to 08	ANNUAL TOTAL 09 to 16	ANNUAL TOTAL 17 to 24	ANNUAL TOTAL Total Obsn	ANNUAL TOTAL M C W B
105/109																																0	0	0	74
100/104																																6	0	6	77
95/99																																62	12	74	76
90/94		0		0	71																						1	0	1	73	0	228	65	293	75
85/89		2	0	2	70																	1	0	1	68		14	3	17	68	4	359	133	496	74
80/84		6	1	7	67		0		0	69		0		0	67		1	0	1	67		8	3	11	66		34	13	47	66	33	372	232	637	72
75/79		19	2	21	64		5	0	5	66		3	1	4	65		9	2	11	64		17	7	24	63	1	43	22	66	64	203	323	377	903	70
70/74	1	33	11	45	62		12	2	14	62	0	11	3	14	62	0	16	7	23	61	3	28	16	47	60	7	44	36	87	62	494	273	386	1153	67
65/69	11	41	25	77	60	4	21	9	34	60	4	21	10	35	60	5	24	14	43	58	10	37	26	73	58	27	42	51	120	60	363	267	302	932	62
60/64	22	38	33	93	56	11	31	19	61	56	9	25	20	54	56	10	30	25	65	55	20	41	40	101	55	53	32	44	129	57	300	241	277	818	57
55/59	22	36	34	92	52	17	34	28	79	52	17	35	22	74	51	23	33	31	87	51	32	41	44	117	51	50	21	32	103	53	265	221	254	740	52
50/54	27	35	39	101	47	20	41	36	97	47	22	39	31	92	47	25	36	38	99	47	37	31	40	108	47	38	8	21	67	48	248	198	241	687	48
45/49	43	20	36	99	44	31	39	38	108	43	25	35	43	103	43	34	30	37	101	43	42	22	32	96	43	27	2	12	41	44	246	149	217	612	43
40/44	35	7	28	70	39	38	32	41	111	38	35	35	44	114	38	35	24	31	90	39	42	13	23	78	39	24	0	5	29	40	235	112	181	528	39
35/39	33	3	19	55	35	36	19	38	93	34	40	26	35	101	34	34	12	21	67	34	37	4	10	51	34	11		1	12	36	205	64	127	396	34
30/34	28	1	9	38	31	39	9	22	70	30	40	11	23	74	30	27	5	12	44	30	18	3	6	27	30	2			2	32	160	29	73	262	30
25/29	14	0	2	16	26	30	3	10	43	26	31	5	12	48	25	22	2	4	28	25	7	0	1	8	26						105	10	29	144	26
20/24	3		0	3	22	16	1	4	21	21	18	1	4	23	21	7	1	1	9	20	1			1	21						45	3	9	57	21
15/19	0			0	18	6	0	1	7	17	6	0	0	6	17	2	0	0	2	16											14	0	1	15	17
10/14						1	0		1	12	0			0	12	1	0		1	11											2	0		2	12
5/9						0			0	7																					0			0	7

FORT BENNING/LAWSON AAF GEORGIA

LAT 32 21N LONG 85 OOW ELEV 232 FT

MEAN FREQUENCY OF OCCURRENCE OF DRY BULB TEMPERATURE (DEGREES F) WITH MEAN COINCIDENT WET BULB TEMPERATURE (DEGREES F) FOR EACH DRY BULB TEMPERATURE RANGE

Temperature Range	MAY Obsn Hour Gp 01 to 08	MAY 09 to 16	MAY 17 to 24	MAY Total Obsn	MAY MCWB	JUNE Obsn Hour Gp 01 to 08	JUNE 09 to 16	JUNE 17 to 24	JUNE Total Obsn	JUNE MCWB	JULY Obsn Hour Gp 01 to 08	JULY 09 to 16	JULY 17 to 24	JULY Total Obsn	JULY MCWB
100/104							0	0	0	74		0	0	0	79
95/99		0	0	0	73		7	3	10	75		6	3	9	77
90/94		14	5	19	71		36	15	51	75		45	18	63	76
85/89		46	21	67	70		66	30	96	73	0	80	31	111	75
80/84		61	30	91	69	2	64	43	109	72	2	67	50	119	74
75/79	1	53	40	94	67	30	43	58	131	71	52	40	82	174	73
70/74	34	42	62	138	66	111	19	68	198	69	165	8	60	233	70
65/69	83	19	48	150	63	68	3	17	88	65	24	1	3	28	66
60/64	59	9	25	93	59	23	1	5	29	60	4		0	4	61
55/59	38	4	13	55	54	5	0	1	6	56	1			1	56
50/54	23	1	4	28	50	1			1	50					
45/49	9		1	10	45	0			0	48					
40/44	1			1	42										
35/39	0			0	38										
30/34															

Temperature Range	AUGUST Obsn Hour Gp 01 to 08	AUGUST 09 to 16	AUGUST 17 to 24	AUGUST Total Obsn	AUGUST MCWB	SEPTEMBER Obsn Hour Gp 01 to 08	SEPTEMBER 09 to 16	SEPTEMBER 17 to 24	SEPTEMBER Total Obsn	SEPTEMBER MCWB	OCTOBER Obsn Hour Gp 01 to 08	OCTOBER 09 to 16	OCTOBER 17 to 24	OCTOBER Total Obsn	OCTOBER MCWB
100/104		0	0	0	76										
95/99		5	2	7	77		1	0	1	74					
90/94		44	17	61	75		19	6	25	74		1	0	1	73
85/89		76	33	109	75	0	60	20	80	73		13	3	16	70
80/84	1	67	47	115	74	0	59	32	91	71		40	11	51	68
75/79	44	41	80	165	73	18	49	57	124	70	2	46	21	69	66
70/74	154	13	61	228	70	89	30	68	187	69	18	51	46	115	65
65/69	40	1	7	48	65	72	15	34	121	64	33	42	48	123	61
60/64	9		1	10	60	37	6	15	58	59	49	30	44	123	58
55/59	0			0	57	16	1	5	22	55	47	16	37	100	54
50/54						6	0	1	7	50	41	6	20	67	49
45/49						1	0	1	2	45	28	2	11	41	45
40/44						1		0	1	41	16	1	5	22	41
35/39						0			0	39	11	0	1	12	36
30/34											3			3	32

Temperature Range	NOVEMBER Obsn Hour Gp 01 to 08	09 to 16	17 to 24	Total Obsn	MCWB	DECEMBER Obsn Hour Gp 01 to 08	09 to 16	17 to 24	Total Obsn	MCWB	JANUARY Obsn Hour Gp 01 to 08	09 to 16	17 to 24	Total Obsn	MCWB	FEBRUARY Obsn Hour Gp 01 to 08	09 to 16	17 to 24	Total Obsn	MCWB	MARCH Obsn Hour Gp 01 to 08	09 to 16	17 to 24	Total Obsn	MCWB	APRIL Obsn Hour Gp 01 to 08	09 to 16	17 to 24	Total Obsn	MCWB	ANNUAL TOTAL Obsn Hour Gp 01 to 08	09 to 16	17 to 24	Total Obsn	MCWB
100/104																																0	0	0	76
95/99																																19	8	27	76
90/94																											0	0	0	71		159	61	220	75
85/89		0		0	67																	0	0	0	67		9	4	13	69	0	350	142	492	73
80/84		4	1	5	68		0		0	71		0		0	70		2	0	2	66		7	3	10	64		38	20	58	66	5	409	237	651	71
75/79	0	21	5	26	64	0	5	1	6	68		2	1	3	65		5	3	8	65		18	10	28	63	0	47	26	73	64	147	370	384	901	70
70/74	2	32	15	49	62	2	14	6	22	64	0	11	4	15	62	1	15	8	24	61	[illegible]	30	[illegible]	64	60	0	[illegible]	[illegible]	[illegible]	[illegible]	[illegible]	814	[illegible]	[illegible]	[illegible]
65/69	17	40	[illegible]	79	[illegible]	[illegible]	[illegible]	13	44	60	4	15	10	29	60	5	20	17	42	58	11	31	27	69	58	36	41	55	132	61	394	251	308	953	62
60/64	22	43	36	101	56	10	33	22	65	55	11	25	19	55	56	15	25	24	64	56	20	40	43	103	55	56	29	40	125	57	315	241	274	830	57
55/59	26	34	37	97	52	17	35	33	85	51	15	31	30	76	51	18	31	30	79	50	34	39	40	113	51	45	17	25	87	53	262	208	251	721	52
50/54	32	26	39	97	48	24	37	38	99	47	22	38	33	93	47	21	32	35	88	46	32	32	37	101	46	37	7	17	61	48	239	179	224	642	47
45/49	37	21	33	91	43	30	37	41	108	42	29	36	39	104	43	27	34	32	93	42	43	25	28	96	42	30	2	8	40	44	234	157	194	585	43
40/44	40	12	25	77	39	45	31	39	115	38	37	36	40	113	38	34	28	32	94	38	42	16	21	79	38	19	1	2	22	40	235	125	164	524	39
35/39	35	5	14	54	35	33	17	27	77	34	32	23	30	85	33	34	19	25	78	34	32	7	13	52	34	8		0	8	36	185	71	110	366	34
30/34	24	2	6	32	30	36	10	19	65	30	41	18	26	85	29	36	9	13	58	29	21	2	4	27	30	1			1	32	162	41	68	271	30
25/29	9	0	1	10	26	31	4	7	42	26	37	9	11	57	25	25	3	4	32	25	10	0	0	10	26						112	16	23	151	25
20/24	2			2	21	12	1	1	14	21	13	3	3	19	20	7	1	1	9	20	1	0		1	22						35	5	5	45	21
15/19	0			0	18	2	0	0	2	16	5	1	1	7	16	2	0	0	2	15	0			0	16						9	1	1	11	16
10/14						0	0	0	0	10	2	0	0	2	11	1	0		1	12											3	0	0	3	11
5/9						0			0	7	1	0		1	6																1	0		1	6
0/4											0			0	3																0			0	3

GLYNCO NAS/BRUNSWICK GEORGIA

LAT 31 15N LONG 81 29W ELEV 25 FT

MEAN FREQUENCY OF OCCURRENCE OF DRY BULB TEMPERATURE (DEGREES F) WITH MEAN COINCIDENT WET BULB TEMPERATURE (DEGREES F) FOR EACH DRY BULB TEMPERATURE RANGE

Temperature Range	MAY Obsn Hour Gp 01 to 08	MAY 09 to 16	MAY 17 to 24	MAY Total Obsn	MAY MCWB	JUNE Obsn Hour Gp 01 to 08	JUNE 09 to 16	JUNE 17 to 24	JUNE Total Obsn	JUNE MCWB	JULY Obsn Hour Gp 01 to 08	JULY 09 to 16	JULY 17 to 24	JULY Total Obsn	JULY MCWB
95/99		1	0	1	73		2	1	3	80		4	1	5	78
90/94		12	2	14	73		21	2	23	78		45	5	50	79
85/89		38	6	44	73		73	13	86	76	0	107	27	134	78
80/84	1	81	19	101	71	9	88	50	147	75	18	65	75	158	76
75/79	15	68	58	141	70	66	41	96	203	73	113	21	96	230	74
70/74	78	31	94	203	68	117	12	66	195	70	111	6	45	162	71
65/69	84	11	47	142	65	37	2	9	48	66	6	0	1	7	66
60/64	43	5	15	63	60	8	1	2	11	61	0			0	62
55/59	19	1	5	25	55	2		1	3	57					
50/54	6		1	7	51										
45/49	1		0	1	45										
40/44	0			0	41										
35/39															

Temperature Range	AUGUST Obsn Hour Gp 01 to 08	AUGUST 09 to 16	AUGUST 17 to 24	AUGUST Total Obsn	AUGUST MCWB	SEPTEMBER Obsn Hour Gp 01 to 08	SEPTEMBER 09 to 16	SEPTEMBER 17 to 24	SEPTEMBER Total Obsn	SEPTEMBER MCWB	OCTOBER Obsn Hour Gp 01 to 08	OCTOBER 09 to 16	OCTOBER 17 to 24	OCTOBER Total Obsn	OCTOBER MCWB
95/99		2	0	2	80		0		0	77					
90/94		41	3	44	79		10	1	11	77		0		0	77
85/89		102	22	124	78		64	8	72	77		8	1	9	74
80/84	11	66	71	148	76	3	86	38	127	75	1	53	6	60	72
75/79	112	27	111	250	74	63	47	101	211	73	8	65	32	105	70
70/74	113	8	39	160	72	107	25	67	199	70	42	52	66	160	68
65/69	11	1	2	14	67	48	6	18	72	66	60	41	65	166	64
60/64	0			0	62	13	1	5	19	60	54	19	42	115	60
55/59						5	0	1	6	55	41	7	20	68	55
50/54						2		0	2	50	22	2	11	35	50
45/49											11	0	5	16	45
40/44											7		1	8	40
35/39											2		0	2	37

Temperature Range	NOVEMBER Obsn Hour Gp 01 to 08	NOVEMBER 09 to 16	NOVEMBER 17 to 24	NOVEMBER Total Obsn	NOVEMBER MCWB	DECEMBER Obsn Hour Gp 01 to 08	DECEMBER 09 to 16	DECEMBER 17 to 24	DECEMBER Total Obsn	DECEMBER MCWB	JANUARY Obsn Hour Gp 01 to 08	JANUARY 09 to 16	JANUARY 17 to 24	JANUARY Total Obsn	JANUARY MCWB	FEBRUARY Obsn Hour Gp 01 to 08	FEBRUARY 09 to 16	FEBRUARY 17 to 24	FEBRUARY Total Obsn	FEBRUARY MCWB	MARCH Obsn Hour Gp 01 to 08	MARCH 09 to 16	MARCH 17 to 24	MARCH Total Obsn	MARCH MCWB	APRIL Obsn Hour Gp 01 to 08	APRIL 09 to 16	APRIL 17 to 24	APRIL Total Obsn	APRIL MCWB	ANNUAL TOTAL Obsn Hour Gp 01 to 08	ANNUAL TOTAL 09 to 16	ANNUAL TOTAL 17 to 24	ANNUAL TOTAL Total Obsn	ANNUAL TOTAL MCWB
95/99																																9	2	11	78
90/94																											1	0	1	72		130	13	143	78
85/89		0		0	73																	2	0	2	73		11.	2	13	71	0	405	79	484	77
80/84		6	0	6	71		1		1	70		1		1	69		3	0	3	69		8	1	9	69		32	7	39	70	43	490	267	800	74
75/79		28	3	31	67		10	0	10	67		5	1	6	67		12	2	14	67		26	5	31	66	1	64	21	86	68	378	414	526	1318	72
70/74	2	47	16	65	65	0	23	4	27	64	0	16	3	19	65	1	19	7	27	64	2	41	15	58	63	18	60	55	133	65	591	340	477	1408	69
65/69	26	50	45	121	63	8	35	21	64	62	3	26	11	40	61	8	29	20	67	61	[illegible]	[illegible]	[illegible]	[illegible]	61	[illegible]	40	68	166	63	369	284	345	998	63
60/64	40	[illegible]	[illegible]	[illegible]	[illegible]	[illegible]	[illegible]	30	92	58	17	31	27	75	58	27	33	32	92	58	40	45	51	136	58	66	21	47	134	59	331	237	301	869	59
55/59	42	32	45	119	54	27	44	43	114	53	23	42	36	101	53	23	37	29	89	52	42	37	51	130	53	45	8	24	77	54	269	208	255	732	54
50/54	45	20	36	101	49	38	37	48	123	49	35	42	43	120	49	31	39	45	115	48	51	24	40	115	48	24	3	12	39	49	254	167	236	657	49
45/49	39	9	24	72	44	37	31	39	107	44	39	36	45	120	44	40	26	41	107	44	35	15	26	76	44	20	0	3	23	45	222	117	183	522	44
40/44	22	4	13	39	39	38	17	33	88	39	39	25	40	104	39	35	14	27	76	39	29	6	13	48	39	6		1	7	41	176	66	128	370	39
35/39	14	1	6	21	35	39	7	18	64	35	39	15	25	79	35	31	9	15	55	35	20	1	5	26	35	1			1	37	146	33	69	248	35
30/34	7	0	1	8	31	24	3	7	34	30	30	7	13	50	30	20	3	5	28	30	8	1	1	10	30						89	14	27	130	30
25/29	2	0	0	2	26	10	1	2	13	25	15	2	5	22	25	6	1	1	8	25	1			1	27						34	4	8	46	25
20/24	0		0	0	21	2	0	1	3	21	6	1	1	8	21	1	0		1	19											9	1	2	12	20
15/19						1	0		1	15	1	0		1	15	0			0	16											2	0		2	15
10/14						0			0	12																					0			0	12

HUNTER AAF/SAVANNAH GEORGIA

LAT 32 01N LONG 81 08W ELEV 42 FT

MEAN FREQUENCY OF OCCURRENCE OF DRY BULB TEMPERATURE (DEGREES F) WITH MEAN COINCIDENT WET BULB TEMPERATURE (DEGREES F) FOR EACH DRY BULB TEMPERATURE RANGE

Temperature Range	MAY Obsn Hour Gp 01 to 08	MAY 09 to 16	MAY 17 to 24	MAY Total Obsn	MAY MCWB	JUNE Obsn Hour Gp 01 to 08	JUNE 09 to 16	JUNE 17 to 24	JUNE Total Obsn	JUNE MCWB	JULY Obsn Hour Gp 01 to 08	JULY 09 to 16	JULY 17 to 24	JULY Total Obsn	JULY MCWB
105/109															
100/104		0		0	76		2	0	2	79		0		0	80
95/99		3	0	3	74		8	1	9	78		8	1	9	79
90/94		15	3	18	73	0	29	5	34	77		49	8	57	78
85/89	0	40	7	47	72	1	74	17	92	75	1	103	28	132	77
80/84	2	76	21	99	71	14	76	53	143	73	21	61	75	157	75
75/79	19	61	58	138	69	70	38	94	202	72	117	21	101	239	74
70/74	76	33	87	196	68	104	10	57	171	69	103	5	36	144	71
65/69	81	13	50	144	64	38	2	10	50	65	7	0	0	7	65
60/64	39	5	16	60	59	10	1	3	14	60					
55/59	23	2	4	29	54	3	0	0	3	56					
50/54	6	1	2	9	50										
45/49	2		0	2	46										
40/44	0			0	42										
35/39															
30/34															

Temperature Range	AUGUST Obsn Hour Gp 01 to 08	AUGUST 09 to 16	AUGUST 17 to 24	AUGUST Total Obsn	AUGUST MCWB	SEPTEMBER Obsn Hour Gp 01 to 08	SEPTEMBER 09 to 16	SEPTEMBER 17 to 24	SEPTEMBER Total Obsn	SEPTEMBER MCWB	OCTOBER Obsn Hour Gp 01 to 08	OCTOBER 09 to 16	OCTOBER 17 to 24	OCTOBER Total Obsn	OCTOBER MCWB
105/109		0		0	79										
100/104		1	0	1	77										
95/99		10	1	11	78		1		1	76		0		0	78
90/94		50	6	56	78		12	1	13	76		1		1	76
85/89	1	91	28	120	76		62	7	69	75		10	1	11	73
80/84	16	63	74	153	75	3	77	36	116	74		46	6	52	71
75/79	109	27	104	240	74	52	57	99	208	72	6	54	26	86	68
70/74	108	6	32	146	71	108	22	68	198	70	29	57	52	138	66
65/69	14	0	2	16	66	55	7	22	84	64	45	38	64	147	62
60/64	1			1	63	17	2	6	25	59	64	27	48	139	58
55/59						4	0	1	5	54	42	10	26	78	54
50/54						1			1	51	29	3	16	48	49
45/49											20	1	7	28	44
40/44											10	0	3	13	40
35/39											3		0	3	35
30/34											0			0	31

HUNTER AAF/SAVANNAH GEORGIA

Tempera-ture Range	NOVEMBER Obsn Hour Gp 01 to 08	09 to 16	17 to 24	Total Obsn	M C W B	DECEMBER Obsn Hour Gp 01 to 08	09 to 16	17 to 24	Total Obsn	M C W B	JANUARY Obsn Hour Gp 01 to 08	09 to 16	17 to 24	Total Obsn	M C W B
105/109															
100/104															
95/99															
90/94															
85/89		0		0	70							0		0	69
80/84		7	0	7	69		1		1	68		1		1	68
75/79		26	2	28	66		6		6	66		7	1	8	66
70/74	1	45	11	57	63		19	1	20	62	0	17	3	20	63
65/69	21	49	45	115	61	8	31	17	56	61	4	27	11	42	60
60/64	38	44	48	130	57	18	40	29	87	56	19	37	32	88	57
55/59	38	34	46	118	53	24	40	36	100	52	28	39	38	105	52
50/54	44	20	37	101	48	29	40	46	115	47	30	37	39	106	47
45/49	39	10	28	77	43	36	33	43	112	43	32	35	42	109	43
40/44	31	4	15	50	39	42	22	37	101	38	45	25	41	111	38
35/39	19	1	7	27	34	39	10	22	71	34	37	15	24	76	34
30/34	7	0	2	9	30	30	5	11	46	29	28	5	12	45	29
25/29	2		0	2	25	16	1	4	21	25	17	3	5	25	25
20/24	1			1	22	6	0	1	7	21	7	1	1	9	20
15/19						1	0	0	1	16	2	0	0	2	17
10/14						0			0	12	0	0		0	10

Tempera-ture Range	FEBRUARY Obsn Hour Gp 01 to 08	09 to 16	17 to 24	Total Obsn	M C W B	MARCH Obsn Hour Gp 01 to 08	09 to 16	17 to 24	Total Obsn	M C W B	APRIL Obsn Hour Gp 01 to 08	09 to 16	17 to 24	Total Obsn	M C W B	ANNUAL TOTAL Obsn Hour Gp 01 to 08	09 to 16	17 to 24	Total Obsn	M C W B
105/109																	0		0	79
100/104																	3	0	3	78
95/99																	30	3	33	78
90/94							0	0	0	69		1	0	1	73	0	157	23	180	77
85/89							2	1	3	68		8	1	9	69	3	390	90	483	75
80/84		3	0	3	66		10	2	12	67		33	5	38	68	56	454	272	782	73
75/79		10	2	12	64	0	25	5	30	64	1	59	18	78	66	374	391	510	1275	71
70/74	0	23	5	28	62	1	38	15	54	61	15	56	46	117	64	545	331	413	1289	68
65/69	6	36	19	61	60	21	44	38	103	60	61	42	71	164	61	351	289	349	989	62
60/64	30	35	38	103	57	40	45	50	135	56	65	27	52	144	58	341	263	322	926	57
55/59	28	36	37	101	52	39	34	45	118	52	45	11	26	82	53	274	206	259	739	52
50/54	32	32	42	106	47	48	23	42	110	47	28	4	15	47	48	244	160	239	643	48
45/49	38	25	39	102	43	35	15	27	77	43	25	1	6	32	44	227	120	192	539	43
40/44	35	13	22	70	39	35	7	15	57	38	9		1	10	40	207	71	134	412	38
35/39	25	7	12	44	34	20	4	5	29	34	2		0	2	36	145	37	70	252	34
30/34	19	3	5	27	30	9	0	2	11	30	0			0	33	93	13	32	138	29
25/29	8	1	1	10	25	2	0	0	2	26						45	5	10	60	25
20/24	2	0	0	2	21	0			0	20						16	1	2	19	21
15/19	1	0		1	15											4	0	0	4	16
10/14																0	0		0	11

MOODY AFB/VALDOSTA GEORGIA

LAT 30 58N LONG 83 12W ELEV 233 FT

MEAN FREQUENCY OF OCCURRENCE OF DRY BULB TEMPERATURE (DEGREES F) WITH MEAN COINCIDENT WET BULB TEMPERATURE (DEGREES F) FOR EACH DRY BULB TEMPERATURE RANGE

Temperature Range	MAY Obsn Hour Gp 01 to 08	MAY 09 to 16	MAY 17 to 24	MAY Total Obsn	MAY MCWB	JUNE Obsn Hour Gp 01 to 08	JUNE 09 to 16	JUNE 17 to 24	JUNE Total Obsn	JUNE MCWB
100/104							2	0	2	78
95/99		3	1	4	74		10	4	14	76
90/94		29	8	37	71		50	15	65	75
85/89	0	57	23	80	71	1	79	32	112	74
80/84	1	68	34	103	69	10	61	55	126	73
75/79	17	49	61	127	68	70	29	79	178	72
70/74	84	27	70	181	67	122	9	52	183	70
65/69	83	12	36	131	64	31	0	3	34	65
60/64	36	3	11	50	58	5		0	5	58
55/59	18	1	3	22	53	1			1	53
50/54	7	0	1	8	49					
45/49	1			1	45					
40/44										
35/39										
30/34										

Temperature Range	JULY Obsn Hour Gp 01 to 08	JULY 09 to 16	JULY 17 to 24	JULY Total Obsn	JULY MCWB	AUGUST Obsn Hour Gp 01 to 08	AUGUST 09 to 16	AUGUST 17 to 24	AUGUST Total Obsn	AUGUST MCWB
100/104		0		0	77		0		0	77
95/99		10	2	12	77		17	2	19	77
90/94		66	16	82	76		78	23	101	77
85/89		89	29	118	76	0	75	31	106	76
80/84	14	56	61	131	75	13	49	63	125	75
75/79	107	22	106	235	74	108	24	95	227	74
70/74	122	5	35	162	71	118	4	34	156	71
65/69	5			5	66	9	0	1	10	65
60/64						0	0		0	63
55/59										
50/54										
45/49										
40/44										
35/39										
30/34										

Temperature Range	SEPTEMBER Obsn Hour Gp 01 to 08	SEPTEMBER 09 to 16	SEPTEMBER 17 to 24	SEPTEMBER Total Obsn	SEPTEMBER MCWB	OCTOBER Obsn Hour Gp 01 to 08	OCTOBER 09 to 16	OCTOBER 17 to 24	OCTOBER Total Obsn	OCTOBER MCWB
100/104										
95/99		2	0	2	75					
90/94		30	5	35	75		5	1	6	75
85/89		65	18	83	74		17	3	20	72
80/84	1	66	39	106	73		49	12	61	70
75/79	33	46	91	170	72	3	55	36	94	68
70/74	145	25	72	242	70	38	54	62	154	66
65/69	51	4	12	67	65	64	35	60	159	63
60/64	8	1	4	13	60	58	20	40	118	58
55/59	3			3	55	38	8	21	67	53
50/54						27	3	10	40	48
45/49						14	1	3	18	43
40/44						4	0	1	5	39
35/39						2		0	2	35
30/34						0			0	32

MOODY AFB/VALDOSTA GEORGIA

Temperature Range	NOVEMBER Obsn Hour Gp 01 to 08	09 to 16	17 to 24	Total Obsn	MCWB	DECEMBER Obsn Hour Gp 01 to 08	09 to 16	17 to 24	Total Obsn	MCWB	JANUARY Obsn Hour Gp 01 to 08	09 to 16	17 to 24	Total Obsn	MCWB	FEBRUARY Obsn Hour Gp 01 to 08	09 to 16	17 to 24	Total Obsn	MCWB	MARCH Obsn Hour Gp 01 to 08	09 to 16	17 to 24	Total Obsn	MCWB	APRIL Obsn Hour Gp 01 to 08	09 to 16	17 to 24	Total Obsn	MCWB	ANNUAL TOTAL Obsn Hour Gp 01 to 08	09 to 16	17 to 24	Total Obsn	MCWB
100/104																																2	0	2	78
95/99																																42	9	51	77
90/94																											1	0	1	70		259	68	327	75
85/89		0		0	70																	2		2	68		16	4	20	68	1	400	140	541	74
80/84		10	1	11	68		0		0	69		1		1	68		4	1	5	67		20	3	23	67		48	18	66	67	39	432	287	758	72
75/79		28	6	34	66		11	1	12	67		11	2	13	66		15	4	19	65		28	14	42	65	0	57	32	89	65	338	375	527	1240	71
70/74	3	47	20	70	63	1	27	8	36	64		28	9	37	63	1	34	15	50	63	6	38	29	73	62	16	51	56	123	64	656	349	462	1467	68
65/69	20	48	45	113	61	11	34	30	75	62	10	32	27	69	61	17	41	36	94	61	23	42	47	112	60	60	34	64	158	62	384	282	361	1027	62
60/64	35	37	50	122	58	24	45	43	112	57	20	36	39	95	58	29	35	39	103	57	39	41	49	129	57	69	23	39	131	58	323	241	314	878	58
55/59	43	29	41	113	53	28	35	40	103	52	36	36	41	113	53	31	29	37	97	52	46	31	44	121	52	48	8	18	74	52	292	177	245	714	52
50/54	43	22	34	99	48	32	39	44	115	47	33	35	35	103	47	36	30	37	103	48	43	22	27	92	47	29	3	8	40	48	250	154	196	600	47
45/49	39	11	24	74	43	48	27	36	111	43	32	31	38	101	43	41	18	28	87	43	39	14	19	72	43	14	0	2	16	44	228	102	150	480	43
40/44	33	6	12	51	38	37	19	28	84	38	41	20	30	91	38	31	8	15	54	38	29	6	11	46	38	4		0	4	40	179	59	97	335	38
35/39	14	2	6	22	34	35	7	13	55	34	34	11	18	63	34	21	6	6	33	34	17	3	4	24	34	0			0	38	123	29	47	199	34
30/34	7	0	1	8	29	19	3	5	27	29	30	4	7	41	29	10	2	4	16	28	5	1	1	7	30						71	10	18	99	29
25/29	2	0	0	2	25	10	1	1	12	25	11	1	1	13	24	5	2	1	8	24	2			2	25						30	4	3	37	24
20/24	1			1	21	2	0		2	20	2	0		2	20	2	0		2	19											7	0		7	20
15/19																0			0	15											0			0	15

ROBINS AFB/MACON GEORGIA

LAT 32 38N LONG 83 36W ELEV . 294 FT

MEAN FREQUENCY OF OCCURRENCE OF DRY BULB TEMPERATURE (DEGREES F) WITH MEAN COINCIDENT WET BULB TEMPERATURE (DEGREES F) FOR EACH DRY BULB TEMPERATURE RANGE

	MAY					JUNE					JULY				
Temperature Range	Obsn Hour Gp			Total Obsn	M C W B	Obsn Hour Gp			Total Obsn	M C W B	Obsn Hour Gp			Total Obsn	M C W B
	01 to 08	09 to 16	17 to 24			01 to 08	09 to 16	17 to 24			01 to 08	09 to 16	17 to 24		
100/104		0		0	71		1	0	1	76		1	0	1	78
95/99		3	2	5	73		10	3	13	76		12	4	16	77
90/94		21	8	29	71		36	16	52	74		47	17	64	76
85/89		45	22	67	70		65	34	99	73	0	77	37	114	75
80/84	1	55	35	91	68	5	61	49	115	72	8	62	59	129	74
75/79	8	51	46	105	67	43	42	63	148	71	74	40	83	197	73
70/74	51	38	61	150	66	110	18	57	185	69	146	9	45	200	70
65/69	81	19	40	140	63	60	4	13	77	65	16	1	3	20	66
60/64	47	10	22	79	58	17	1	3	21	59	3	0	0	3	61
55/59	36	4	10	50	54	4	1	1	6	55	1			1	55
50/54	19	1	2	22	49	1	0		1	50					
45/49	6	0	0	6	45										
40/44	0			0	40										
35/39															
30/34															

	AUGUST					SEPTEMBER					OCTOBER				
Temperature Range	Obsn Hour Gp			Total Obsn	M C W B	Obsn Hour Gp			Total Obsn	M C W B	Obsn Hour Gp			Total Obsn	M C W B
	01 to 08	09 to 16	17 to 24			01 to 08	09 to 16	17 to 24			01 to 08	09 to 16	17 to 24		
100/104		1		1	75										
95/99		10	2	12	77		3	1	4	76					
90/94		49	20	69	76		23	6	29	74		2	0	2	71
85/89		71	39	110	75		52	22	74	73		14	3	17	70
80/84	3	62	53	118	74	0	57	35	92	71		34	11	45	67
75/79	65	39	80	184	72	17	48	61	126	71	1	50	25	76	66
70/74	136	13	47	196	70	93	31	66	190	69	17	51	47	115	65
65/69	37	2	6	45	65	68	17	32	117	64	37	41	53	131	61
60/64	7		1	8	60	36	7	13	56	59	53	31	46	130	57
55/59	1			1	57	18	2	4	24	55	49	17	32	98	53
50/54						6	0	1	7	50	40	7	19	66	49
45/49						1	0	0	1	45	27	2	8	37	44
40/44						0			0	40	15	1	4	20	40
35/39						0			0	36	8		0	8	35
30/34											2			2	32

Temperature Range	NOVEMBER Obsn Hour Gp 01 to 08	09 to 16	17 to 24	Total Obsn	MCWB	DECEMBER Obsn Hour Gp 01 to 08	09 to 16	17 to 24	Total Obsn	MCWB	JANUARY Obsn Hour Gp 01 to 08	09 to 16	17 to 24	Total Obsn	MCWB	FEBRUARY Obsn Hour Gp 01 to 08	09 to 16	17 to 24	Total Obsn	MCWB
100/104																				
95/99																				
90/94																				
85/89		1	0	1	69												0		0	69
80/84		5	1	6	68		0		0	70							1	0	1	66
75/79		20	6	26	64		6	1	7	66		2	1	3	65		5	2	7	65
70/74	2	33	17	52	61	2	15	6	23	63	0	9	4	13	61	1	11	8	20	62
65/69	18	41	31	90	59	5	21	15	41	60	4	17	11	32	59	5	17	16	38	59
60/64	25	42	40	107	56	13	32	26	71	56	9	23	20	52	56	13	27	24	64	55
55/59	28	34	42	104	51	15	35	34	84	51	17	31	28	76	51	18	32	34	84	50
50/54	32	28	38	98	47	28	38	39	105	46	21	34	36	91	47	25	37	37	99	46
45/49	37	19	31	87	43	33	38	41	112	42	28	37	43	108	42	32	33	34	99	42
40/44	43	11	20	74	39	38	32	40	110	38	36	38	38	112	38	35	28	32	95	37
35/39	35	4	10	49	34	40	18	26	84	34	42	27	32	101	33	35	19	20	74	33
30/34	19	1	3	23	30	40	10	14	64	29	42	19	23	84	29	32	9	13	54	29
25/29	4	0	1	5	25	26	3	4	33	25	31	8	10	49	25	22	3	3	28	24
20/24	1	0	0	1	20	7	0	1	8	21	12	2	2	16	20	5	1	1	7	19
15/19	0			0	16	1	0	0	1	16	4	1	1	6	15	2	0	0	2	14
10/14						1	0	0	1	11	1	0		1	10	1	0		1	10
5/9						0			0	8	1	0		1	5					

Temperature Range	MARCH Obsn Hour Gp 01 to 08	09 to 16	17 to 24	Total Obsn	MCWB	APRIL Obsn Hour Gp 01 to 08	09 to 16	17 to 24	Total Obsn	MCWB	ANNUAL TOTAL Obsn Hour Gp 01 to 08	09 to 16	17 to 24	Total Obsn	MCWB
100/104												3	0	3	76
95/99												38	12	50	76
90/94							1	0	1	71		179	67	246	75
85/89		1	0	1	67		13	6	19	68	0	339	163	502	73
80/84		5	2	7	64		35	18	53	66	17	377	263	657	71
75/79		17	9	26	62	0	46	30	76	64	208	366	407	981	70
70/74	2	27	19	48	60	9	48	46	103	62	569	303	433	1305	67
65/69	8	35	30	73	58	40	40	53	133	60	376	256	303	935	62
60/64	21	41	47	109	55	63	31	41	135	57	307	245	283	835	57
55/59	34	40	45	119	51	45	15	25	85	52	266	211	255	732	52
50/54	48	35	37	120	47	37	8	14	59	48	257	188	223	668	47
45/49	44	23	26	93	42	27	2	5	34	44	235	154	188	577	42
40/44	40	15	18	73	38	15	0	1	16	39	222	125	153	500	38
35/39	29	6	10	45	34	3		0	3	36	192	74	98	364	34
30/34	18	2	3	23	29	0			0	31	153	41	56	250	29
25/29	5	0	0	5	25						88	14	18	120	25
20/24	0	0		0	20						25	3	4	32	20
15/19											7	1	1	9	15
10/14											3	0	0	3	10
5/9											1	0		1	6

TURNER AFB/ALBANY NAS GEORGIA

LAT 31 36N LONG 84 05W ELEV 223 FT

MEAN FREQUENCY OF OCCURRENCE OF DRY BULB TEMPERATURE (DEGREES F) WITH MEAN COINCIDENT WET BULB TEMPERATURE (DEGREES F) FOR EACH DRY BULB TEMPERATURE RANGE

Temperature Range	MAY Obsn Hour Gp 01 to 08	MAY 09 to 16	MAY 17 to 24	MAY Total Obsn	MAY MCWB	JUNE Obsn Hour Gp 01 to 08	JUNE 09 to 16	JUNE 17 to 24	JUNE Total Obsn	JUNE MCWB	JULY Obsn Hour Gp 01 to 08	JULY 09 to 16	JULY 17 to 24	JULY Total Obsn	JULY MCWB
105/109							0		0	79					
100/104		0		0	70		2	1	3	78		1	0	1	77
95/99		5	1	6	72		18	5	23	76		20	4	24	77
90/94		31	13	44	71	0	50	21	71	75		68	23	91	76
85/89	0	58	28	86	70	1	67	37	105	73	1	78	38	117	76
80/84	1	60	42	103	69	13	55	54	122	72	16	55	66	137	75
75/79	19	46	57	122	68	72	30	72	174	72	115	22	90	227	73
70/74	84	29	60	173	67	113	14	43	170	69	111	4	26	141	71
65/69	81	14	33	128	63	32	2	6	40	64	5	0	0	5	66
60/64	36	4	12	52	58	8	0	1	9	59					
55/59	19	2	3	24	53	1			1	54					
50/54	7	0	0	7	48	0			0	50					
45/49	1			1	45										
40/44															
35/39															
30/34															

Temperature Range	AUGUST Obsn Hour Gp 01 to 08	AUGUST 09 to 16	AUGUST 17 to 24	AUGUST Total Obsn	AUGUST MCWB	SEPTEMBER Obsn Hour Gp 01 to 08	SEPTEMBER 09 to 16	SEPTEMBER 17 to 24	SEPTEMBER Total Obsn	SEPTEMBER MCWB	OCTOBER Obsn Hour Gp 01 to 08	OCTOBER 09 to 16	OCTOBER 17 to 24	OCTOBER Total Obsn	OCTOBER MCWB
105/109															
100/104		2	0	2	78		0		0	74					
95/99		25	6	31	77		7	1	8	74		0	0	0	76
90/94		68	25	93	76		38	10	48	74		4	0	4	74
85/89	0	73	40	113	75		63	25	88	73		19	4	23	70
80/84	12	51	68	131	74	1	59	46	106	72	0	47	15	62	68
75/79	114	25	83	222	73	48	39	81	168	71	5	52	33	90	66
70/74	109	4	25	138	71	115	22	54	191	69	28	44	55	127	65
65/69	12	1	0	13	65	49	9	16	74	64	42	39	55	136	61
60/64	1			1	60	21	3	6	30	59	61	26	42	129	58
55/59						5	0	1	6	54	45	11	25	81	53
50/54						1			1	50	33	4	13	50	48
45/49											22	1	4	27	44
40/44											8	0	1	9	39
35/39											3			3	35
30/34											0			0	32

	NOVEMBER					DECEMBER					JANUARY					FEBRUARY					MARCH					APRIL					ANNUAL TOTAL				
Temperature Range	Obsn Hour Gp 01 to 08	09 to 16	17 to 24	Total Obsn	MCWB	Obsn Hour Gp 01 to 08	09 to 16	17 to 24	Total Obsn	MCWB	Obsn Hour Gp 01 to 08	09 to 16	17 to 24	Total Obsn	MCWB	Obsn Hour Gp 01 to 08	09 to 16	17 to 24	Total Obsn	MCWB	Obsn Hour Gp 01 to 08	09 to 16	17 to 24	Total Obsn	MCWB	Obsn Hour Gp 01 to 08	09 to 16	17 to 24	Total Obsn	MCWB	Obsn Hour Gp 01 to 08	09 to 16	17 to 24	Total Obsn	MCWB
105/109																																0		0	79
100/104																																5	1	6	78
95/99																																75	17	92	76
90/94																						0		0	67		1	0	1	71	0	260	92	352	75
85/89		2	0	2	69																	3	1	4	68		19	6	25	68	2	382	179	563	73
80/84		9	1	10	68							0		0	68		3	1	4	67		13	5	18	67		45	22	67	66	43	397	320	760	71
75/79		28	[illegible]	[illegible]	64		6	0	6	65		7	1	8	66		12	5	17	66		25	14	39	63	0	49	35	84	64	373	341	478	1192	70
70/74	1	40	21	62	62	1	19	6	26	63	0	17	7	24	63	1	24	14	39	62	6	35	30	71	61	18	46	55	119	63	587	298	396	1281	67
65/69	20	43	40	103	60	7	30	21	58	60	7	26	19	52	61	12	30	26	68	60	23	43	42	108	59	57	39	52	148	61	347	276	310	933	61
60/64	37	42	48	127	57	17	34	32	83	56	17	33	31	81	57	24	34	35	93	56	37	41	50	128	56	64	24	39	127	57	323	241	296	860	57
55/59	35	32	41	108	52	23	38	40	101	52	30	36	36	102	52	26	30	36	92	52	42	35	40	117	51	43	11	19	73	52	269	195	241	705	52
50/54	41	23	39	103	48	31	41	43	115	47	24	34	38	96	47	34	31	40	105	47	45	23	30	98	46	33	4	8	45	47	249	160	211	620	47
45/49	40	12	24	76	43	38	34	44	116	43	32	34	40	106	42	36	28	31	95	43	39	16	19	74	42	19	1	3	23	43	227	126	165	518	43
40/44	38	6	12	56	39	42	24	34	100	38	41	27	37	105	38	39	16	21	76	38	31	10	10	51	38	6	0	0	6	39	205	83	115	403	38
35/39	19	2	4	25	34	39	12	19	70	34	43	18	25	86	34	25	9	11	45	34	17	3	5	25	34	0			0	35	146	44	64	254	34
30/34	6	0	1	7	30	32	6	8	46	30	33	10	9	52	29	16	4	4	24	29	7	1	1	9	30						94	21	23	138	29
25/29	2	0	0	2	25	15	2	1	18	25	14	3	4	21	25	9	1	1	11	24	2	0		2	24						42	6	6	54	25
20/24						4	1	0	5	20	6	1	1	8	20	2	0	0	2	19	0			0	22						12	2	1	15	20
15/19						0	0	0	0	15	1	0	0	1	16	1	0		1	15											2	0	0	2	15
10/14						0	0	0	0	10	0	0		0	10																0	0	0	0	10
5/9						0			0	7	0	0		0	7																0	0		0	7

BARBERS POINT NAS HAWAII

LAT 21 19N LONG 158 05W ELEV 34 FT

MEAN FREQUENCY OF OCCURRENCE OF DRY BULB TEMPERATURE (DEGREES F) WITH MEAN COINCIDENT WET BULB TEMPERATURE (DEGREES F) FOR EACH DRY BULB TEMPERATURE RANGE

Temperature Range	MAY Obsn Hour Gp 01 to 08	MAY 09 to 16	MAY 17 to 24	MAY Total Obsn	MAY MCWB	JUNE Obsn Hour Gp 01 to 08	JUNE 09 to 16	JUNE 17 to 24	JUNE Total Obsn	JUNE MCWB	JULY Obsn Hour Gp 01 to 08	JULY 09 to 16	JULY 17 to 24	JULY Total Obsn	JULY MCWB
90/94		0		0	72							0		0	74
85/89		7	0	7	73		19	1	20	72		40	4	44	74
80/84	0	132	24	156	71	2	179	52	233	71	4	174	67	245	72
75/79	25	100	99	224	69	52	42	127	221	70	91	33	141	265	71
70/74	173	8	117	298	67	174	1	59	234	68	151	1	36	188	69
65/69	48	1	7	56	65	11		1	12	66	2			2	66
60/64	2			2	63	1			1	63					

Temperature Range	AUGUST Obsn Hour Gp 01 to 08	AUGUST 09 to 16	AUGUST 17 to 24	AUGUST Total Obsn	AUGUST MCWB	SEPTEMBER Obsn Hour Gp 01 to 08	SEPTEMBER 09 to 16	SEPTEMBER 17 to 24	SEPTEMBER Total Obsn	SEPTEMBER MCWB	OCTOBER Obsn Hour Gp 01 to 08	OCTOBER 09 to 16	OCTOBER 17 to 24	OCTOBER Total Obsn	OCTOBER MCWB
90/94		0		0	73		0		0	75		1	0	1	76
85/89		53	4	57	73		57	3	60	74		35	2	37	75
80/84	3	173	72	248	72	3	164	65	232	72	6	168	52	226	73
75/79	123	21	152	296	71	107	18	148	273	71	79	42	137	258	71
70/74	119	1	19	139	69	125	1	24	150	69	145	3	56	204	68
65/69	2		0	2	68	5		0	5	67	17		1	18	66
60/64											1			1	63

Temperature Range	NOVEMBER Obsn Hour Gp 01 to 08	09 to 16	17 to 24	Total Obsn	MCWB	DECEMBER Obsn Hour Gp 01 to 08	09 to 16	17 to 24	Total Obsn	MCWB	JANUARY Obsn Hour Gp 01 to 08	09 to 16	17 to 24	Total Obsn	MCWB
90/94															
85/89		8	0	8	74		0		0	75					
80/84	1	126	17	144	72	0	53	4	57	72		30	2	32	71
75/79	33	91	112	236	70	18	141	59	218	69	11	141	61	213	69
70/74	164	13	104	281	68	110	47	139	296	67	74	63	116	253	67
65/69	39	1	7	47	65	103	6	41	150	64	122	13	60	195	64
60/64	2			2	60	13	0	5	18	60	34	1	6	41	60
55/59						3		0	3	57	5		2	7	56
50/54											2		0	2	53

Temperature Range	FEBRUARY Obsn Hour Gp 01 to 08	09 to 16	17 to 24	Total Obsn	MCWB	MARCH Obsn Hour Gp 01 to 08	09 to 16	17 to 24	Total Obsn	MCWB	APRIL Obsn Hour Gp 01 to 08	09 to 16	17 to 24	Total Obsn	MCWB	ANNUAL TOTAL Obsn Hour Gp 01 to 08	09 to 16	17 to 24	Total Obsn	MCWB
90/94																	1	0	1	75
85/89		0		0	68							0		0	75		219	14	233	74
80/84		22	1	23	71		45	3	48	70		66	5	71	71	19	1332	364	1715	72
75/79	2	120	42	164	68	2	145	56	203	68	7	142	71	220	69	550	1036	1205	2791	70
70/74	58	70	108	236	66	81	52	129	262	66	118	30	128	276	67	1492	290	1035	2817	67
65/69	121	11	65	197	63	135	6	57	198	64	105	1	34	140	64	710	39	273	1022	64
60/64	37	1	7	45	60	29	0	3	32	60	10		1	11	60	129	2	22	153	60
55/59	7		0	7	57	1		0	1	56	0			0	54	16		2	18	57
50/54																2		0	2	53

LEWISTON IDAHO

LAT 46 23N LONG 117 01W ELEV 1413 FT

MEAN FREQUENCY OF OCCURRENCE OF DRY BULB TEMPERATURE (DEGREES F) WITH MEAN COINCIDENT WET BULB TEMPERATURE (DEGREES, F) FOR EACH DRY BULB TEMPERATURE RANGE

Temperature Range	MAY Obsn Hour Gp 01 to 08	MAY 09 to 16	MAY 17 to 24	MAY Total Obsn	MAY MCWB	JUNE Obsn Hour Gp 01 to 08	JUNE 09 to 16	JUNE 17 to 24	JUNE Total Obsn	JUNE MCWB	JULY Obsn Hour Gp 01 to 08	JULY 09 to 16	JULY 17 to 24	JULY Total Obsn	JULY MCWB
100/104							0		0	69		2	1	3	68
95/99							1	0	1	70		17	4	21	65
90/94		2	0	2	66		7	2	9	67		32	11	43	64
85/89		7	2	9	65		20	5	25	64	0	45	20	65	63
80/84		13	5	18	62		47	17	64	61	2	54	33	89	60
75/79	0	24	9	33	59	3	47	28	78	60	11	42	42	95	59
70/74	1	43	21	65	57	11	42	34	87	58	32	30	46	108	57
65/69	9	42	28	79	55	34	33	45	112	57	57	15	45	117	56
60/64	25	37	36	98	53	55	19	47	121	55	74	7	32	113	54
55/59	47	39	49	135	50	67	13	38	118	52	52	3	12	67	51
50/54	68	30	52	150	47	46	10	17	73	48	20	1	3	24	49
45/49	47	9	30	86	43	21	1	9	31	45	2			2	47
40/44	37	3	18	58	40	3		0	3	40					
35/39	14	0	1	15	35	1			1	34					
30/34	1			1	32										
25/29															
20/24															

Temperature Range	AUGUST Obsn Hour Gp 01 to 08	AUGUST 09 to 16	AUGUST 17 to 24	AUGUST Total Obsn	AUGUST MCWB	SEPTEMBER Obsn Hour Gp 01 to 08	SEPTEMBER 09 to 16	SEPTEMBER 17 to 24	SEPTEMBER Total Obsn	SEPTEMBER MCWB	OCTOBER Obsn Hour Gp 01 to 08	OCTOBER 09 to 16	OCTOBER 17 to 24	OCTOBER Total Obsn	OCTOBER MCWB
100/104		1		1	67		1		1	68					
95/99		15	2	17	65		3	1	4	64					
90/94		34	9	43	63		8	1	9	63					
85/89		45	17	62	62		23	4	27	61					
80/84	1	53	29	83	61		30	9	39	59		1		1	62
75/79	6	49	42	97	59	1	43	19	63	57		5		5	59
70/74	25	28	51	104	57	5	38	29	72	56		11	1	12	59
65/69	54	12	50	116	55	15	42	41	98	54		25	3	28	55
60/64	83	8	32	123	54	37	27	46	110	52	2	45	19	66	52
55/59	57	4	15	76	51	66	19	46	131	50	20	55	40	115	50
50/54	21	1	3	25	48	62	7	27	96	47	49	54	57	160	47
45/49	2			2	44	39	1	13	53	43	56	35	58	149	43
40/44						12	0	5	17	39	51	13	43	107	39
35/39						3		1	4	36	39	5	21	65	35
30/34						1			1	33	20	1	7	28	31
25/29											11		2	13	25
20/24											2			2	22

Temperature Range	NOVEMBER					DECEMBER					JANUARY					FEBRUARY					MARCH					APRIL					ANNUAL TOTAL				
	Obsn Hour Gp 01 to 08	Obsn Hour Gp 09 to 16	Obsn Hour Gp 17 to 24	Total Obsn	M C W B	Obsn Hour Gp 01 to 08	Obsn Hour Gp 09 to 16	Obsn Hour Gp 17 to 24	Total Obsn	M C W B	Obsn Hour Gp 01 to 08	Obsn Hour Gp 09 to 16	Obsn Hour Gp 17 to 24	Total Obsn	M C W B	Obsn Hour Gp 01 to 08	Obsn Hour Gp 09 to 16	Obsn Hour Gp 17 to 24	Total Obsn	M C W B	Obsn Hour Gp 01 to 08	Obsn Hour Gp 09 to 16	Obsn Hour Gp 17 to 24	Total Obsn	M C W B	Obsn Hour Gp 01 to 08	Obsn Hour Gp 09 to 16	Obsn Hour Gp 17 to 24	Total Obsn	M C W B	Obsn Hour Gp 01 to 08	Obsn Hour Gp 09 to 16	Obsn Hour Gp 17 to 24	Total Obsn	M C W B
100/104																																4	1	5	68
95/99																																36	7	43	65
90/94																																83	23	106	64
85/89																															0	140	48	188	62
80/84																											1	0	1	57	3	199	93	295	61
75/79																											8	2	10	55	21	218	142	381	59
70/74		1		1	59																						19	4	23	54	74	212	186	472	57
65/69		1		1	55																	1	0	1	52	0	32	10	42	51	169	203	222	594	55
60/64	1	4	1	6	51												1		1	50		5		5	48	2	36	18	56	49	279	189	231	699	53
55/59	5	16	6	27	48		0		0	47						0	1	1	2	47		26	3	29	46	6	51	34	91	46	320	227	244	791	50
50/54	8	44	10	62	46	4	15	8	27	45		3	1	4	[illegible]	[illegible]	[illegible]	[illegible]	[illegible]	[illegible]	3	47	20	70	43	31	50	55	136	44	320	281	261	862	46
45/49	30	59	46	135	43	13	28	8	49	42	2	13	5	20	41	10	46	15	71	41	17	67	51	135	41	67	34	58	159	41	306	293	293	892	42
40/44	48	65	68	181	39	27	52	42	121	38	13	34	15	62	38	24	53	40	117	38	56	60	74	190	38	71	9	40	120	38	342	289	345	976	38
35/39	79	45	71	195	35	61	56	56	173	35	35	45	46	126	34	50	41	63	154	34	87	23	61	171	34	46	1	18	65	34	415	216	338	969	34
30/34	50	6	32	88	31	58	43	57	158	30	47	36	45	128	30	58	28	43	129	30	58	15	23	96	30	15		1	16	30	308	129	208	645	30
25/29	19	1	7	27	26	35	23	39	97	26	28	21	31	80	25	37	16	28	81	25	19	4	13	36	25	2			2	23	151	65	120	336	25
20/24	2			2	22	24	19	18	61	21	32	22	14	68	20	13	10	12	35	21	7	1	3	11	21	1			1	21	81	52	47	180	21
15/19						12	10	13	35	16	18	21	22	61	15	11	3	8	22	16	3		1	4	16						44	34	44	122	16
10/14						13	2	6	21	12	18	21	20	59	11	6	1	1	8	12	1			1	13						38	24	27	89	11
5/9						2		1	3	7	17	19	24	60	6	1	2		3	6											20	21	25	66	6
0/4								1	1	3	23	7	13	43	2	0	1	0	1	0											23	8	14	45	1
-5/-1											10	4	8	22	-4	0	1	2	3	-4											10	5	10	25	-4
-10/-6											5	1	5	11	-8	4		1	5	-9											9	1	6	16	-8
-15/-11											2	1	1	4	-13	2		0	2	-12											4	1	1	6	-13
-20/-16											2			2	-18																2			2	-18

MOUNTAIN HOME AFB IDAHO

LAT 43 02N LONG 115 54W ELEV 2996 FT

MEAN FREQUENCY OF OCCURRENCE OF DRY BULB TEMPERATURE (DEGREES F) WITH MEAN COINCIDENT WET BULB TEMPERATURE (DEGREES F) FOR EACH DRY BULB TEMPERATURE RANGE

Temperature Range	MAY Obsn Hour Gp 01 to 08	MAY 09 to 16	MAY 17 to 24	MAY Total Obsn	MAY MCWB	JUNE Obsn Hour Gp 01 to 08	JUNE 09 to 16	JUNE 17 to 24	JUNE Total Obsn	JUNE MCWB	JULY Obsn Hour Gp 01 to 08	JULY 09 to 16	JULY 17 to 24	JULY Total Obsn	JULY MCWB
105/109								0	0	66		1	1	2	65
100/104							2	1	3	64		7	5	12	64
95/99		0	0	0	59		6	5	11	63		25	22	47	63
90/94		3	2	5	60	0	15	11	26	62		47	37	84	61
85/89		8	6	14	58		25	18	43	60	0	51	39	90	60
80/84		19	11	30	57	1	35	25	61	58	4	49	37	90	58
75/79	0	27	18	45	55	3	36	29	68	57	15	37	41	93	57
70/74	2	32	25	59	53	11	37	34	82	55	40	20	34	94	55
65/69	8	37	32	77	51	30	33	37	100	54	67	9	22	98	53
60/64	19	41	36	96	49	50	25	32	107	52	67	2	9	78	50
55/59	32	35	40	107	47	56	17	27	100	49	38	0	3	41	47
50/54	54	26	38	118	45	51	7	16	74	47	13		0	13	43
45/49	62	13	24	99	41	29	2	4	35	43	3			3	39
40/44	41	5	10	56	38	6	0	0	6	38	0			0	35
35/39	19	1	4	24	33	1			1	34	0			0	34
30/34	8	0	1	9	29										
25/29	2			2	26										
20/24	0			0	23										
15/19															

Temperature Range	AUGUST Obsn Hour Gp 01 to 08	AUGUST 09 to 16	AUGUST 17 to 24	AUGUST Total Obsn	AUGUST MCWB	SEPTEMBER Obsn Hour Gp 01 to 08	SEPTEMBER 09 to 16	SEPTEMBER 17 to 24	SEPTEMBER Total Obsn	SEPTEMBER MCWB	OCTOBER Obsn Hour Gp 01 to 08	OCTOBER 09 to 16	OCTOBER 17 to 24	OCTOBER Total Obsn	OCTOBER MCWB
105/109		1	1	2	67										
100/104		5	3	8	64										
95/99		20	15	35	63		2	1	3	61					
90/94		39	29	68	61		10	5	15	60		0		0	59
85/89	0	45	32	77	60		20	12	32	59		2	1	3	57
80/84	3	42	32	77	58		29	17	46	57		6	2	8	55
75/79	10	37	38	85	57	1	31	23	55	55	0	13	6	19	54
70/74	32	28	40	100	55	5	41	30	76	53	0	20	10	30	52
65/69	57	15	27	99	52	13	36	36	85	51	1	30	17	48	50
60/64	65	8	16	89	50	30	31	39	100	49	4	38	24	66	48
55/59	45	5	10	60	47	52	22	32	106	46	10	42	36	88	46
50/54	23	2	4	29	45	57	12	25	94	43	28	43	45	116	43
45/49	10	0	1	11	41	40	6	13	59	40	51	28	45	124	41
40/44	2			2	37	28	2	5	35	37	53	17	34	104	37
35/39	1			1	34	9	1	2	12	33	53	7	19	79	33
30/34						4		0	4	29	34	2	7	43	29
25/29						1			1	25	10	1	1	12	25
20/24						0		0	0	20	2	0	0	2	21
15/19											1			1	16

Temperature Range	NOVEMBER					DECEMBER					JANUARY					FEBRUARY					MARCH					APRIL					ANNUAL TOTAL				
	Obsn Hour Gp 01 to 08	09 to 16	17 to 24	Total Obsn	MCWB	Obsn Hour Gp 01 to 08	09 to 16	17 to 24	Total Obsn	MCWB	Obsn Hour Gp 01 to 08	09 to 16	17 to 24	Total Obsn	MCWB	Obsn Hour Gp 01 to 08	09 to 16	17 to 24	Total Obsn	MCWB	Obsn Hour Gp 01 to 08	09 to 16	17 to 24	Total Obsn	MCWB	Obsn Hour Gp 01 to 08	09 to 16	17 to 24	Total Obsn	MCWB	Obsn Hour Gp 01 to 08	09 to 16	17 to 24	Total Obsn	MCWB
105/109																																2	2	4	66
100/104																																14	9	23	64
95/99																																53	43	96	63
90/94																															0	114	84	198	61
85/89																											0	0	0	57	0	151	108	259	60
80/84																											2	1	3	55	8	182	125	315	58
75/79																						1	0	1	53		6	3	9	53	29	188	158	375	56
70/74		1		1	50																	3	1	4	51		13	8	21	51	90	195	182	467	54
65/69		2	0	2	48												0	0	0	49		7	4	11	48		19	13	32	49	176	188	188	552	52
60/64	0	8	2	10	47		0	0	0	52			0	0	45		3	2	5	47		12	7	19	46	1	31	21	53	47	236	199	188	623	49
55/59	1	23	9	33	45		2	1	3	46	0	1	0	1	46		9	4	13	[illegible]	0	[illegible]	[illegible]	[illegible]	44	0	41	32	79	44	240	221	209	670	46
50/54	6	33	19	58	43	1	8	3	12	42	1	6	2	9	44	2	20	13	35	43	5	39	29	73	41	18	47	42	107	42	259	243	236	738	43
45/49	15	45	37	97	41	3	22	9	34	40	3	21	10	34	40	7	36	26	69	40	12	51	42	105	39	36	44	47	127	40	271	268	258	797	40
40/44	39	55	56	150	37	19	38	29	86	37	15	34	29	78	38	13	46	41	100	37	33	52	52	137	36	55	28	41	124	37	304	277	297	878	37
35/39	53	39	49	141	33	34	54	47	135	33	30	47	43	120	33	48	50	57	155	33	54	36	48	138	33	66	9	23	98	33	368	244	292	904	33
30/34	54	22	39	115	29	53	57	65	175	29	52	54	57	163	29	67	36	48	151	30	68	18	35	121	29	40	1	8	49	29	380	190	260	830	29
25/29	39	9	20	68	25	55	34	48	137	25	39	39	45	123	25	47	15	22	84	25	47	5	12	64	25	14	0	1	15	25	254	103	149	506	25
20/24	23	3	7	33	21	46	19	29	94	21	45	24	32	101	20	26	7	9	42	21	21	1	2	24	21	3		0	3	20	166	54	79	299	21
15/19	8	1	1	10	16	21	8	11	40	16	33	11	18	62	16	9	2	3	14	16	5	0	1	6	15	0			0	16	77	22	34	133	16
10/14	1	0	0	1	11	11	4	4	19	12	16	6	6	28	11	4	1	0	5	11	2		0	2	11						34	11	10	55	11
5/9	0			0	8	3	1	2	6	7	5	3	3	11	6	1	0		1	7											9	4	5	18	7
0/4						3	0	1	4	2	3	1	3	7	1	0			0	4											6		4	11	1
-5/-1						1	0		1	-3	3	1	1	5	-3																4	1	1	6	-3
-10/-6											1	0	0	1	-9																1	0	0	1	-9
-15/-11											1	0	0	1	-13																1	0	0	1	-13
-20/-16											0			0	-17																0			0	-17
-25/-21											0			0	-22																0			0	-22

POCATELLO IDAHO

LAT 42 55N LONG 112 36W ELEV 4454 FT

MEAN FREQUENCY OF OCCURRENCE OF DRY BULB TEMPERATURE (DEGREES F) WITH MEAN COINCIDENT WET BULB TEMPERATURE (DEGREES F) FOR EACH DRY BULB TEMPERATURE RANGE

Temperature Range	MAY Obsn Hour Gp 01 to 08	MAY 09 to 16	MAY 17 to 24	MAY Total Obsn	MAY MCWB	JUNE Obsn Hour Gp 01 to 08	JUNE 09 to 16	JUNE 17 to 24	JUNE Total Obsn	JUNE MCWB	JULY Obsn Hour Gp 01 to 08	JULY 09 to 16	JULY 17 to 24	JULY Total Obsn	JULY MCWB
100/104													0	0	62
95/99							1	0	1	59		8	5	13	61
90/94		0	0	0	57		7	4	11	60		32	18	50	61
85/89		3	1	4	58		18	10	28	58	0	53	31	84	60
80/84		10	4	14	56	0	30	17	47	57	2	55	35	92	59
75/79	0	18	9	27	54	2	38	25	65	55	9	45	41	95	57
70/74	1	31	19	51	52	5	41	31	77	54	25	32	46	103	55
65/69	3	37	26	66	50	17	36	37	90	52	46	16	38	100	54
60/64	11	40	31	82	48	34	26	37	97	50	63	6	22	91	51
55/59	25	38	41	104	46	51	21	33	105	48	58	1	9	68	48
50/54	46	29	43	118	44	59	13	29	101	46	32	0	2	34	45
45/49	58	22	39	119	42	43	6	13	62	43	12		0	12	42
40/44	55	14	21	90	38	22	3	4	29	39	1			1	37
35/39	35	5	12	52	34	5	0	0	5	35	0			0	34
30/34	13	1	1	15	30	1			1	31					
25/29	1			1	26										
20/24															
15/19															

Temperature Range	AUGUST Obsn Hour Gp 01 to 08	AUGUST 09 to 16	AUGUST 17 to 24	AUGUST Total Obsn	AUGUST MCWB	SEPTEMBER Obsn Hour Gp 01 to 08	SEPTEMBER 09 to 16	SEPTEMBER 17 to 24	SEPTEMBER Total Obsn	SEPTEMBER MCWB	OCTOBER Obsn Hour Gp 01 to 08	OCTOBER 09 to 16	OCTOBER 17 to 24	OCTOBER Total Obsn	OCTOBER MCWB
100/104		0		0	64										
95/99		4	2	6	62		1	0	1	59					
90/94		22	12	34	60		3	1	4	58					
85/89		47	24	71	59		14	5	19	57		0		0	56
80/84	1	53	31	85	58		30	11	41	55		5	1	6	54
75/79	6	47	34	87	56	1	35	20	56	54		14	4	18	52
70/74	16	36	50	102	55	4	38	26	68	53	0	22	7	29	51
65/69	38	21	43	102	53	9	36	36	81	51	3	28	17	48	49
60/64	59	9	29	97	51	18	34	44	96	49	5	35	23	63	47
55/59	65	5	16	86	48	36	24	41	101	46	8	36	30	74	45
50/54	40	1	5	46	45	52	14	26	92	44	22	34	44	100	43
45/49	17	0	2	19	42	54	8	17	79	40	33	29	44	106	40
40/44	6	0	1	7	38	40	4	9	53	37	51	25	39	115	37
35/39	1			1	34	18	1	3	22	34	56	12	25	93	33
30/34						6	0	0	6	30	40	7	12	59	30
25/29						1		0	1	25	22	0	2	24	25
20/24											5	0	0	5	21
15/19											1			1	17

Temperature Range	NOVEMBER Obsn Hour Gp 01 to 08	NOVEMBER 09 to 16	NOVEMBER 17 to 24	NOVEMBER Total Obsn	NOVEMBER MCWB	DECEMBER Obsn Hour Gp 01 to 08	DECEMBER 09 to 16	DECEMBER 17 to 24	DECEMBER Total Obsn	DECEMBER MCWB	JANUARY Obsn Hour Gp 01 to 08	JANUARY 09 to 16	JANUARY 17 to 24	JANUARY Total Obsn	JANUARY MCWB	FEBRUARY Obsn Hour Gp 01 to 08	FEBRUARY 09 to 16	FEBRUARY 17 to 24	FEBRUARY Total Obsn	FEBRUARY MCWB	MARCH Obsn Hour Gp 01 to 08	MARCH 09 to 16	MARCH 17 to 24	MARCH Total Obsn	MARCH MCWB	APRIL Obsn Hour Gp 01 to 08	APRIL 09 to 16	APRIL 17 to 24	APRIL Total Obsn	APRIL MCWB	ANNUAL TOTAL Obsn Hour Gp 01 to 08	ANNUAL TOTAL 09 to 16	ANNUAL TOTAL 17 to 24	ANNUAL TOTAL Total Obsn	ANNUAL TOTAL MCWB
100/104																																0	0	0	63
95/99																																14	7	21	61
90/94																																64	35	99	60
85/89																															0	135	71	206	59
80/84																											0	0	0	52	3	183	99	285	57
75/79																											[illegible]	1	4	[illegible]	[illegible]	200	134	352	56
70/74																						0		0	50		9	4	13	50	51	209	183	443	54
65/69		1		1	48																	2	1	3	48	0	19	8	27	48	116	196	206	518	51
60/64		6	1	7	47												1	0	1	47	0	5	2	7	45	1	26	14	41	46	191	188	203	582	49
55/59	1	16	4	21	44	0	0	0	0	46		0		0	45		3	1	4	45	0	14	5	19	43	5	38	28	71	44	249	196	208	653	46
50/54	5	26	15	46	42	0	3	1	4	43	0	3		3	42	1	8	4	13	42	2	18	13	33	41	17	37	39	93	41	276	186	221	683	44
45/49	15	36	27	78	40	4	10	5	19	40	2	8	4	14	39	5	15	10	30	40	8	30	21	59	39	29	38	41	108	39	280	202	223	705	40
40/44	26	40	41	107	37	12	24	17	53	37	10	13	14	37	37	14	29	21	64	37	18	44	35	97	36	43	35	45	123	36	298	231	247	776	37
35/39	36	39	44	119	33	23	46	34	103	34	24	35	29	88	33	26	45	41	112	33	35	53	54	142	33	56	23	36	115	33	315	259	278	852	33
30/34	41	36	44	121	29	43	65	55	163	30	34	51	42	127	30	49	43	48	140	30	64	44	57	165	29	57	10	21	88	30	348	257	280	885	30
25/29	48	21	31	100	25	46	43	51	140	26	35	40	45	120	25	36	32	37	105	25	59	22	33	114	25	25	2	5	32	25	273	160	204	637	25
20/24	28	11	18	57	21	42	28	40	110	21	34	34	36	104	21	29	21	27	77	21	30	12	18	60	21	6	0	0	6	20	174	106	139	419	21
15/19	21	4	8	33	16	31	16	21	68	16	29	22	24	75	16	19	13	13	45	16	18	3	7	28	16	0			0	17	119	58	73	250	16
10/14	12	1	4	17	11	21	8	12	41	12	25	18	18	61	11	17	7	10	34	11	9	1	1	11	12						84	35	45	164	11
5/9	5	1	2	8	7	14	4	6	24	7	22	12	15	49	7	11	4	6	21	7	3	0	0	3	7						55	21	29	105	7
0/4	2	1	1	4	2	7	1	3	11	2	14	6	9	29	2	6	2	3	11	2	1	0	0	1	2						30	10	16	56	2
-5/-1	1	0	0	1	-3	2	1	1	4	-3	9	3	5	17	-3	6	1	1	8	-3	1			1	-4						19	5	7	31	-3
-10/-6	0		0	0	-9	1	0	0	1	-8	4	2	3	9	-8	1	0	1	2	-8	0		0	0	-7						6	2	4	12	-8
-15/-11			0	0	-11	1	0	0	1	-13	4	1	2	7	-13	1	0	1	2	-13											6	1	3	10	-13
-20/-16											2	0	1	3	-18	2	0	0	2	-18											4	0	1	5	-18
-25/-21											1	0	0	1	-24	0			0	-23											1	0	0	1	-23
-30/-26											0			0	-27	0			0	-26											0			0	-27

CHICAGO/O HARE IAP ILLINOIS

LAT 41 59N LONG 87 54W ELEV 658 FT

MEAN FREQUENCY OF OCCURRENCE OF DRY BULB TEMPERATURE (DEGREES F) WITH MEAN COINCIDENT WET BULB TEMPERATURE (DEGREES F) FOR EACH DRY BULB TEMPERATURE RANGE

Temperature Range	MAY Obsn Hour Gp 01 to 08	MAY 09 to 16	MAY 17 to 24	MAY Total Obsn	MAY MCWB	JUNE Obsn Hour Gp 01 to 08	JUNE 09 to 16	JUNE 17 to 24	JUNE Total Obsn	JUNE MCWB	JULY Obsn Hour Gp 01 to 08	JULY 09 to 16	JULY 17 to 24	JULY Total Obsn	JULY MCWB
100/104							0		0	77		0		0	78
95/99							1	0	1	78		1	0	1	78
90/94		2	0	2	71		13	2	15	74		12	1	13	76
85/89		9	2	11	70	0	31	10	41	72	1	43	10	54	73
80/84	0	21	7	28	68	4	43	21	68	69	4	67	29	100	70
75/79	3	32	15	50	64	17	43	32	92	67	23	58	48	129	68
70/74	12	33	23	68	61	36	42	44	122	64	56	43	64	163	66
65/69	25	34	29	88	59	50	29	44	123	61	78	17	57	152	63
60/64	31	31	32	94	55	50	20	38	108	57	54	4	28	86	59
55/59	38	33	39	110	51	37	11	27	75	53	23	0	7	30	55
50/54	46	29	39	114	47	30	5	17	52	49	8		2	10	50
45/49	44	17	35	96	43	13	0	6	19	45	1		0	1	45
40/44	30	5	20	55	39	3		1	4	40					
35/39	16	2	6	24	35	0			0	36					
30/34	3		0	3	31										
25/29															
20/24															
15/19															

Temperature Range	AUGUST Obsn Hour Gp 01 to 08	AUGUST 09 to 16	AUGUST 17 to 24	AUGUST Total Obsn	AUGUST MCWB	SEPTEMBER Obsn Hour Gp 01 to 08	SEPTEMBER 09 to 16	SEPTEMBER 17 to 24	SEPTEMBER Total Obsn	SEPTEMBER MCWB	OCTOBER Obsn Hour Gp 01 to 08	OCTOBER 09 to 16	OCTOBER 17 to 24	OCTOBER Total Obsn	OCTOBER MCWB
100/104															
95/99		2		2	75		2		2	73					
90/94		17	2	19	75		8	1	9	73		0		0	66
85/89	0	31	7	38	73	0	15	3	18	72		2		2	70
80/84	3	55	21	79	71	0	24	8	32	69		11	1	12	66
75/79	18	66	42	126	68	7	35	16	58	66	0	16	3	19	63
70/74	50	48	64	162	66	19	47	30	96	63	2	26	9	37	61
65/69	68	23	60	151	63	33	50	45	128	60	9	37	20	66	59
60/64	56	6	34	96	59	48	35	53	136	57	23	38	30	91	55
55/59	33	0	13	46	55	43	19	40	102	53	32	37	41	110	51
50/54	15		4	19	50	42	5	25	72	49	38	36	43	117	47
45/49	4		1	5	46	26	1	13	40	45	49	24	42	115	44
40/44	1			1	42	14	0	6	20	41	37	13	28	78	39
35/39						5		2	7	36	29	7	18	54	35
30/34						1		0	1	32	20	1	8	29	30
25/29											6		3	9	26
20/24											2		0	2	21
15/19											0			0	18

CHICAGO/O HARE IAP ILLINOIS

Temperature Range	NOVEMBER					DECEMBER					JANUARY				
	Obsn Hour Gp 01 to 08	09 to 16	17 to 24	Total Obsn	M C W B	Obsn Hour Gp 01 to 08	09 to 16	17 to 24	Total Obsn	M C W B	Obsn Hour Gp 01 to 08	09 to 16	17 to 24	Total Obsn	M C W B
100/104															
95/99															
90/94															
85/89															
80/84															
75/79		1		1	66										
70/74		3	1	4	61										
65/69	1	8	2	11	58							0		0	63
60/64	5	11	8	24	56	0	1	0	1	54		0	0	0	58
55/59	9	20	13	42	51	0	3	2	5	53	0	1	1	2	55
50/54	10	27	19	56	47	2	7	4	13	48	1	2	1	4	50
45/49	22	38	29	89	43	4	10	6	20	43	2	5	3	10	44
40/44	33	35	38	106	38	9	21	13	43	39	4	13	5	22	39
35/39	39	36	43	118	34	28	36	34	98	34	17	34	26	77	34
30/34	46	28	35	109	30	46	52	52	150	30	45	56	54	155	30
25/29	38	17	27	82	25	42	41	44	127	25	41	40	41	122	25
20/24	18	9	14	41	20	35	27	27	89	21	34	29	30	93	20
15/19	10	3	7	20	16	22	17	18	57	16	26	22	23	71	16
10/14	5	2	4	11	11	19	14	17	50	11	20	17	19	56	11
5/9	2	1	2	5	6	12	9	12	33	6	18	15	18	51	6
0/4	2	0	1	3	1	11	5	9	25	1	16	8	15	39	1
-5/-1	1		0	1	-3	8	3	6	17	-3	11	4	7	22	-3
-10/-6						5	1	3	9	-8	7	2	3	12	-8
-15/-11						3	0	1	4	-13	4	1	1	6	-13
-20/-16						1		0	1	-17	1	0		1	-17
-25/-21											0			0	-21

Temperature Range	FEBRUARY					MARCH					APRIL					ANNUAL TOTAL				
	Obsn Hour Gp 01 to 08	09 to 16	17 to 24	Total Obsn	M C W B	Obsn Hour Gp 01 to 08	09 to 16	17 to 24	Total Obsn	M C W B	Obsn Hour Gp 01 to 08	09 to 16	17 to 24	Total Obsn	M C W B	Obsn Hour Gp 01 to 08	09 to 16	17 to 24	Total Obsn	M C W B
100/104																	0		0	77
95/99																	6	0	6	76
90/94																	52	6	58	74
85/89												1	0	1	65	1	132	32	165	72
80/84							0		0	62		4	1	5	64	11	225	88	324	70
75/79							0		0	61		9	3	12	63	68	260	159	487	67
70/74							2	0	2	57	1	18	8	27	60	176	262	243	681	64
65/69		0		0	60	0	3	1	4	55	6	19	11	36	57	270	220	269	759	61
60/64		1	0	1	55	0	5	3	8	53	13	24	18	55	54	280	176	244	700	57
55/59	1	2	1	4	52	3	9	5	17	50	14	25	22	61	50	233	160	211	604	52
50/54	1	4	2	7	47	4	15	8	27	46	25	33	32	90	46	222	163	196	581	47
45/49	2	8	4	14	43	10	22	14	46	42	35	39	36	110	42	212	164	189	565	43
40/44	4	18	10	32	38	15	39	27	81	37	44	37	49	130	38	194	181	197	572	38
35/39	18	42	30	90	34	41	57	51	149	34	50	23	35	108	34	243	237	245	725	34
30/34	53	57	61	171	30	72	50	69	191	30	33	7	20	60	30	319	251	299	869	30
25/29	45	37	46	128	25	41	24	36	101	25	14	1	5	20	25	227	160	202	589	25
20/24	30	21	28	79	21	31	14	17	62	21	4	0	1	5	20	154	100	117	371	21
15/19	23	13	16	52	16	16	5	9	30	16	1		0	1	16	98	60	73	231	16
10/14	16	9	8	33	11	9	1	4	14	11						69	43	52	164	11
5/9	9	5	8	22	6	3	0	1	4	6						44	30	41	115	6
0/4	8	5	6	19	1	3	0	0	3	2						40	18	31	89	1
-5/-1	7	2	4	13	-4	0	0		0	-3						27	9	17	53	-3
-10/-6	5	0	1	6	-8	0			0	-7						17	3	7	27	-8
-15/-11	1	0	0	1	-13											8	1	2	11	-13
-20/-16	0			0	-16											2	0	0	2	-17
-25/-21																0			0	-21

GLENVIEW NAS ILLINOIS

LAT 42 05N LONG 87 49W ELEV 659 FT

MEAN FREQUENCY OF OCCURRENCE OF DRY BULB TEMPERATURE (DEGREES F) WITH MEAN COINCIDENT WET BULB TEMPERATURE (DEGREES F) FOR EACH DRY BULB TEMPERATURE RANGE

Temperature Range	MAY Obsn Hour Gp 01 to 08	MAY Obsn Hour Gp 09 to 16	MAY Obsn Hour Gp 17 to 24	MAY Total Obsn	MAY MCWB	JUNE Obsn Hour Gp 01 to 08	JUNE Obsn Hour Gp 09 to 16	JUNE Obsn Hour Gp 17 to 24	JUNE Total Obsn	JUNE MCWB	JULY Obsn Hour Gp 01 to 08	JULY Obsn Hour Gp 09 to 16	JULY Obsn Hour Gp 17 to 24	JULY Total Obsn	JULY MCWB
100/104							0		0	80					
95/99							2	0	2	76		3	0	3	79
90/94		3	0	3	71		16	3	19	74		17	3	20	76
85/89		9	2	11	70	1	32	11	44	72	1	37	11	49	73
80/84	0	21	8	29	67	5	34	21	60	70	6	60	29	95	70
75/79	4	28	16	48	64	18	41	31	90	67	25	57	50	132	68
70/74	15	32	26	73	62	41	37	39	117	64	67	44	64	175	66
65/69	23	28	24	75	59	47	32	41	120	61	74	22	56	152	63
60/64	28	32	30	90	55	46	26	36	108	57	51	8	28	87	59
55/59	39	36	36	111	51	41	16	36	93	53	19	0	5	24	54
50/54	48	28	43	119	47	31	4	17	52	49	5		0	5	50
45/49	44	21	34	99	43	9	1	4	14	45	0			0	47
40/44	33	10	24	67	39	1			1	41					
35/39	13	1	5	19	35										
30/34	2		0	2	31										
25/29	0			0	27										
20/24															

Temperature Range	AUGUST Obsn Hour Gp 01 to 08	AUGUST Obsn Hour Gp 09 to 16	AUGUST Obsn Hour Gp 17 to 24	AUGUST Total Obsn	AUGUST MCWB	SEPTEMBER Obsn Hour Gp 01 to 08	SEPTEMBER Obsn Hour Gp 09 to 16	SEPTEMBER Obsn Hour Gp 17 to 24	SEPTEMBER Total Obsn	SEPTEMBER MCWB	OCTOBER Obsn Hour Gp 01 to 08	OCTOBER Obsn Hour Gp 09 to 16	OCTOBER Obsn Hour Gp 17 to 24	OCTOBER Total Obsn	OCTOBER MCWB
100/104															
95/99		1	0	1	81		1		1	77					
90/94		14	2	16	77		6	1	7	75					
85/89	0	40	9	49	73		11	3	14	73		2		2	69
80/84	3	49	25	77	71	1	26	9	36	71		6	2	8	67
75/79	22	57	45	124	68	8	37	20	65	68	0	15	5	20	64
70/74	54	51	65	170	66	28	41	35	104	65	3	20	12	35	62
65/69	73	24	57	154	63	41	52	46	139	61	11	29	19	59	59
60/64	54	9	35	98	59	46	37	51	134	57	29	46	32	107	56
55/59	33	2	9	44	55	45	20	42	107	53	32	42	46	120	52
50/54	7		1	8	51	42	7	21	70	49	44	41	44	129	47
45/49	1			1	46	20	2	9	31	44	44	26	42	112	43
40/44						9	1	3	13	40	38	16	29	83	39
35/39						1	0		1	37	29	5	13	47	35
30/34											14	1	4	19	31
25/29											2		0	2	26
20/24											0		0	0	20

GLENVIEW NAS ILLINOIS

Temperature Range	NOVEMBER Obsn Hour Gp 01 to 08	NOVEMBER 09 to 16	NOVEMBER 17 to 24	NOVEMBER Total Obsn	NOVEMBER MCWB	DECEMBER Obsn Hour Gp 01 to 08	DECEMBER 09 to 16	DECEMBER 17 to 24	DECEMBER Total Obsn	DECEMBER MCWB	JANUARY Obsn Hour Gp 01 to 08	JANUARY 09 to 16	JANUARY 17 to 24	JANUARY Total Obsn	JANUARY MCWB
100/104															
95/99															
90/94															
85/89															
80/84															
75/79		0		0	66										
70/74		2	1	3	62		0		0	56					
65/69	1	5	2	8	59	0	0		0	58					
60/64	5	9	8	22	56	2	1	0	3	57		1	0	1	58
55/59	8	18	11	37	51	1	3	3	7	53	0	1	2	3	53
50/54	15	32	19	66	47	3	8	4	15	48	1	2	1	4	49
45/49	27	46	35	108	43	6	13	9	28	43	2	5	2	9	43
40/44	39	43	49	131	39	12	24	18	54	39	5	12	7	24	38
35/39	46	39	44	129	34	32	40	36	108	35	19	29	27	75	34
30/34	46	26	35	107	30	48	52	52	152	30	37	40	45	122	30
25/29	29	11	20	60	25	46	43	49	138	25	36	39	35	110	25
20/24	14	5	8	27	20	31	26	26	83	20	27	33	28	88	20
15/19	5	2	5	12	15	21	15	18	54	16	28	22	26	76	16
10/14	3	1	1	5	11	17	11	16	44	11	21	23	24	68	11
5/9	1	0	1	2	7	13	6	10	29	6	21	19	20	60	6
0/4	1		0	1	2	9	4	5	18	1	20	13	15	48	1
-5/-1						5	2	3	10	-3	16	7	12	35	-4
-10/-6						2	0	1	3	-8	9	2	3	14	-8
-15/-11						0		0	0	-12	4	1	1	6	-13
-20/-16											1	0		1	-17

Temperature Range	FEBRUARY Obsn Hour Gp 01 to 08	FEBRUARY 09 to 16	FEBRUARY 17 to 24	FEBRUARY Total Obsn	FEBRUARY MCWB	MARCH Obsn Hour Gp 01 to 08	MARCH 09 to 16	MARCH 17 to 24	MARCH Total Obsn	MARCH MCWB	APRIL Obsn Hour Gp 01 to 08	APRIL 09 to 16	APRIL 17 to 24	APRIL Total Obsn	APRIL MCWB
100/104															
95/99															
90/94															
85/89												1		1	68
80/84												3	1	4	66
75/79							1	0	1	60		7	3	10	62
70/74							3	1	4	56	1	14	8	23	60
65/69						0	4	3	7	55	8	20	12	40	57
60/64		0		0	54	1	8	6	15	52	11	25	18	54	53
55/59		2	1	3	52	4	7	6	17	49	18	28	26	72	50
50/54	2	4	2	8	48	7	13	11	31	45	26	31	29	86	46
45/49	2	10	4	16	42	10	22	11	43	42	34	39	38	111	42
40/44	4	15	11	30	38	14	38	22	74	37	53	44	48	145	38
35/39	15	33	28	76	34	38	58	54	150	34	49	23	38	110	34
30/34	44	50	51	145	30	72	51	69	192	30	29	5	17	51	30
25/29	47	41	42	130	25	44	27	35	106	25	8	0	2	10	25
20/24	31	25	30	86	20	30	12	21	63	20	1		0	1	22
15/19	23	20	22	65	15	14	3	6	23	16					
10/14	20	12	14	46	11	9	1	3	13	11					
5/9	14	7	9	30	6	2	0	0	2	7					
0/4	9	4	8	21	1	1	0		1	2					
-5/-1	9	2	3	14	-4	0		0	0	-5					
-10/-6	3	0	0	3	-7	0			0	-8					
-15/-11															
-20/-16															

Temperature Range	ANNUAL TOTAL Obsn Hour Gp 01 to 08	ANNUAL TOTAL 09 to 16	ANNUAL TOTAL 17 to 24	ANNUAL TOTAL Total Obsn	ANNUAL TOTAL MCWB
100/104		0		0	80
95/99		7	0	7	78
90/94		56	9	65	75
85/89	2	132	36	170	72
80/84	15	199	95	309	70
75/79	77	243	170	490	67
70/74	209	244	251	704	65
65/69	278	216	260	754	61
60/64	273	202	244	719	57
55/59	240	175	223	638	52
50/54	231	170	192	593	48
45/49	199	185	188	572	43
40/44	208	203	211	622	38
35/39	242	228	245	715	34
30/34	292	225	273	790	30
25/29	212	161	183	556	25
20/24	134	101	113	348	20
15/19	91	62	77	230	16
10/14	70	48	58	176	11
5/9	51	32	40	123	6
0/4	40	21	28	89	1
-5/-1	30	11	18	59	-4
-10/-6	14	2	4	20	-8
-15/-11	4	1	1	6	-13
-20/-16	1	0		1	-17

MOLINE/QUAD CITY APRT ILLINOIS

LAT 41 27N LONG 90 31W ELEV 582 FT

MEAN FREQUENCY OF OCCURRENCE OF DRY BULB TEMPERATURE (DEGREES F) WITH MEAN COINCIDENT WET BULB TEMPERATURE (DEGREES F) FOR EACH DRY BULB TEMPERATURE RANGE

Tempera-ture Range	MAY Obsn Hour Gp 01 to 08	MAY 09 to 16	MAY 17 to 24	MAY Total Obsn	MAY MCWB	JUNE Obsn Hour Gp 01 to 08	JUNE 09 to 16	JUNE 17 to 24	JUNE Total Obsn	JUNE MCWB	JULY Obsn Hour Gp 01 to 08	JULY 09 to 16	JULY 17 to 24	JULY Total Obsn	JULY MCWB
100/104												0		0	74
95/99							4	0	4	76		4	1	5	78
90/94		3	1	4	71		20	6	26	74		21	6	27	76
85/89		9	3	12	69	1	36	13	50	72	1	48	20	69	73
80/84	0	24	9	33	67	7	49	30	86	70	9	71	42	122	71
75/79	4	39	21	64	64	22	47	42	111	67	32	58	58	148	69
70/74	16	41	33	90	61	43	39	54	136	65	68	31	60	159	67
65/69	29	39	42	110	59	53	24	45	122	62	66	11	42	119	64
60/64	41	38	46	125	56	54	14	30	98	58	50	3	15	68	60
55/59	46	28	41	115	52	37	6	14	57	54	17	0	3	20	56
50/54	45	17	29	91	48	18	2	4	24	50	5		0	5	51
45/49	34	6	15	55	44	5		0	5	45	0			0	48
40/44	22	2	7	31	39	1			1	42					
35/39	9	0	2	11	35										
30/34	2		0	2	32										
25/29															
20/24															
15/19															

Tempera-ture Range	AUGUST Obsn Hour Gp 01 to 08	AUGUST 09 to 16	AUGUST 17 to 24	AUGUST Total Obsn	AUGUST MCWB	SEPTEMBER Obsn Hour Gp 01 to 08	SEPTEMBER 09 to 16	SEPTEMBER 17 to 24	SEPTEMBER Total Obsn	SEPTEMBER MCWB	OCTOBER Obsn Hour Gp 01 to 08	OCTOBER 09 to 16	OCTOBER 17 to 24	OCTOBER Total Obsn	OCTOBER MCWB
100/104															
95/99		3	0	3	75		3	0	3	73					
90/94		18	4	22	75		9	1	10	73		0		0	67
85/89	0	42	14	56	73	0	16	4	20	71		4	0	4	69
80/84	5	64	34	103	71	1	27	9	37	69		14	1	15	66
75/79	23	59	51	133	69	8	39	22	69	66	0	22	6	28	63
70/74	58	42	64	164	67	23	46	34	103	63	2	32	16	50	61
65/69	66	15	44	125	63	35	46	48	129	61	13	31	24	68	58
60/64	54	5	27	86	59	42	33	43	118	57	24	36	32	92	55
55/59	28	0	9	37	55	42	15	38	95	53	32	38	38	108	51
50/54	11		2	13	51	41	5	25	71	49	36	30	40	106	47
45/49	3		0	3	46	29	1	10	40	45	40	22	40	102	43
40/44	0			0	43	12		4	16	41	42	12	25	79	39
35/39						6		1	7	37	31	5	18	54	35
30/34						1			1	33	19	1	7	27	31
25/29											6		1	7	26
20/24											2		0	2	21
15/19											0			0	17

MOLINE/QUAD CITY APRT ILLINOIS

Temperature Range	NOVEMBER Obsn Hour Gp 01 to 08	NOVEMBER Obsn Hour Gp 09 to 16	NOVEMBER Obsn Hour Gp 17 to 24	NOVEMBER Total Obsn	NOVEMBER M C W B	DECEMBER Obsn Hour Gp 01 to 08	DECEMBER Obsn Hour Gp 09 to 16	DECEMBER Obsn Hour Gp 17 to 24	DECEMBER Total Obsn	DECEMBER M C W B	JANUARY Obsn Hour Gp 01 to 08	JANUARY Obsn Hour Gp 09 to 16	JANUARY Obsn Hour Gp 17 to 24	JANUARY Total Obsn	JANUARY M C W B
100/104															
95/99															
90/94															
85/89															
80/84															
75/79		1		1	65										
70/74	0	4	1	5	60										
65/69	1	10	3	14	58		0		0	59		0		0	61
60/64	6	16	10	32	55	1	2	1	4	55		0		0	57
55/59	7	19	13	39	50	1	4	1	6	50	0	2	1	3	53
50/54	12	27	19	58	46	3	7	4	14	46	1	2	1	4	47
45/49	21	34	30	85	42	4	12	6	22	42	2	6	3	11	42
40/44	29	35	33	97	38	9	19	13	41	38	4	16	9	29	38
35/39	40	34	40	114	34	23	36	36	95	34	18	30	25	73	34
30/34	45	25	35	105	30	45	50	46	141	30	31	41	41	113	30
25/29	35	17	27	79	25	43	39	45	127	25	37	40	40	117	25
20/24	22	9	16	47	21	37	27	33	97	21	36	31	32	99	21
15/19	12	5	7	24	16	24	19	17	60	16	32	23	27	82	16
10/14	5	3	3	11	11	19	13	17	49	11	23	21	22	66	11
5/9	2	1	2	5	6	12	9	10	31	6	21	16	21	58	6
0/4	2	0	1	3	2	9	7	10	26	1	19	12	15	46	1
-5/-1	0			0	-2	7	3	5	15	-3	12	4	6	22	-3
-10/-6						7	1	2	10	-8	8	2	4	14	-8
-15/-11						2	0	1	3	-12	4	1	1	6	-13
-20/-16						1	0	0	1	-18	1	0	0	1	-17
-25/-21						0			0	-21	0			0	-23

Temperature Range	FEBRUARY Obsn Hour Gp 01 to 08	FEBRUARY Obsn Hour Gp 09 to 16	FEBRUARY Obsn Hour Gp 17 to 24	FEBRUARY Total Obsn	FEBRUARY M C W B	MARCH Obsn Hour Gp 01 to 08	MARCH Obsn Hour Gp 09 to 16	MARCH Obsn Hour Gp 17 to 24	MARCH Total Obsn	MARCH M C W B	APRIL Obsn Hour Gp 01 to 08	APRIL Obsn Hour Gp 09 to 16	APRIL Obsn Hour Gp 17 to 24	APRIL Total Obsn	APRIL M C W B	ANNUAL TOTAL Obsn Hour Gp 01 to 08	ANNUAL TOTAL Obsn Hour Gp 09 to 16	ANNUAL TOTAL Obsn Hour Gp 17 to 24	ANNUAL TOTAL Total Obsn	ANNUAL TOTAL M C W B
100/104																	0		0	74
95/99																	14	1	15	76
90/94												0		0	65		71	18	89	75
85/89												2	0	2	64	2	157	54	213	72
80/84												7	2	9	63	22	256	127	405	70
75/79							1		1	59	0	11	5	16	62	89	277	205	571	67
70/74							3	1	4	56	1	19	8	28	59	211	257	271	739	65
65/69		0		0	59	0	3	2	5	54	7	24	17	48	56	270	203	267	740	61
60/64		1	0	1	55	1	6	4	11	52	16	27	25	68	54	289	181	233	703	57
55/59	1	2	1	4	51	2	12	7	21	48	19	28	30	77	50	232	154	196	582	52
50/54	1	7	3	11	46	6	20	13	39	44	28	34	35	97	46	207	151	175	533	47
45/49	2	12	6	20	42	8	26	20	54	41	36	35	37	108	42	184	154	167	505	43
40/44	5	22	14	41	38	21	38	30	89	37	37	29	34	100	38	182	173	169	524	38
35/39	19	37	32	88	34	40	49	48	137	34	47	17	31	95	34	233	208	233	674	34
30/34	53	48	54	155	30	67	44	58	169	30	34	6	11	51	30	297	215	252	764	30
25/29	40	36	40	116	25	43	22	32	97	25	12	1	4	17	25	216	155	189	560	25
20/24	28	21	26	75	21	25	14	17	56	20	3	0	0	3	21	153	102	124	379	21
15/19	21	15	16	52	16	16	7	9	32	16						105	69	76	250	16
10/14	17	9	12	38	11	9	2	5	16	11						73	48	59	180	11
5/9	12	7	10	29	6	4	1	2	7	6						51	34	45	130	6
0/4	10	4	6	20	1	3	0	1	4	2						43	23	33	99	1
-5/-1	7	2	3	12	-3	1	0	0	1	-3						27	9	14	50	-3
-10/-6	4	1	1	6	-8	1		0	1	-8						20	4	7	31	-8
-15/-11	2		0	2	-13	1			1	-13						9	1	2	12	-13
-20/-16	0			0	-17	0			0	-17						2	0	0	2	-17
-25/-21																0			0	-22

SCOTT AFB/BELLEVILLE ILLINOIS

LAT 38 33N LONG 89 51W ELEV 453 FT

MEAN FREQUENCY OF OCCURRENCE OF DRY BULB TEMPERATURE (DEGREES F) WITH MEAN COINCIDENT WET BULB TEMPERATURE (DEGREES F) FOR EACH DRY BULB TEMPERATURE RANGE

Temperature Range	MAY Obsn Hour Gp 01 to 08	MAY 09 to 16	MAY 17 to 24	MAY Total Obsn	MAY MCWB	JUNE Obsn Hour Gp 01 to 08	JUNE 09 to 16	JUNE 17 to 24	JUNE Total Obsn	JUNE MCWB	JULY Obsn Hour Gp 01 to 08	JULY 09 to 16	JULY 17 to 24	JULY Total Obsn	JULY MCWB
100/104												2	0	2	77
95/99							3	0	3	76		7	2	9	78
90/94		2	0	2	70		25	7	32	75		32	10	42	76
85/89		18	4	22	70	1	53	19	73	73	1	66	29	96	74
80/84	0	34	13	47	68	7	59	38	104	70	9	73	54	136	72
75/79	3	46	28	77	65	29	50	56	135	68	50	47	71	168	70
70/74	19	49	45	113	63	60	31	58	149	66	94	18	53	165	68
65/69	48	37	50	135	61	69	13	35	117	63	57	3	20	80	63
60/64	55	29	44	128	57	42	6	20	68	58	25	0	8	33	59
55/59	47	21	33	101	53	25	1	6	32	54	10		1	11	54
50/54	35	8	19	62	48	7	0	1	8	50	2			2	51
45/49	26	2	9	37	43	1			1	45					
40/44	11	1	3	15	39										
35/39	3		0	3	35										
30/34	1		0	1	31										
25/29	0			0	28										

Temperature Range	AUGUST Obsn Hour Gp 01 to 08	AUGUST 09 to 16	AUGUST 17 to 24	AUGUST Total Obsn	AUGUST MCWB	SEPTEMBER Obsn Hour Gp 01 to 08	SEPTEMBER 09 to 16	SEPTEMBER 17 to 24	SEPTEMBER Total Obsn	SEPTEMBER MCWB	OCTOBER Obsn Hour Gp 01 to 08	OCTOBER 09 to 16	OCTOBER 17 to 24	OCTOBER Total Obsn	OCTOBER MCWB
100/104		1	0	1	72		0		0	71					
95/99		4	1	5	76		1	0	1	72					
90/94	0	33	6	39	75		10	2	12	73		1		1	67
85/89	0	57	22	79	73	0	28	6	34	72		5	1	6	67
80/84	6	69	44	119	71	0	44	17	61	70		16	2	18	65
75/79	36	49	62	147	70	8	49	37	94	67		28	9	37	63
70/74	75	25	60	160	67	41	50	53	144	65	4	34	20	58	61
65/69	62	8	35	105	63	53	32	44	129	62	14	40	33	87	59
60/64	43	1	14	58	59	46	18	37	101	58	33	44	41	118	55
55/59	19	1	4	24	55	38	6	26	70	53	42	35	44	121	51
50/54	5		1	6	50	32	2	15	49	49	40	25	40	105	47
45/49	1		0	1	45	19	0	4	23	45	42	15	33	90	43
40/44						5		0	5	41	38	5	18	61	39
35/39						0			0	38	23	1	8	32	35
30/34											11		1	12	30
25/29											.			.	27

SCOTT AFB/BELLEVILLE ILLINOIS

Temperature Range	NOVEMBER Obsn Hour Gp 01 to 08	NOVEMBER 09 to 16	NOVEMBER 17 to 24	NOVEMBER Total Obsn	NOVEMBER MCWB	DECEMBER Obsn Hour Gp 01 to 08	DECEMBER 09 to 16	DECEMBER 17 to 24	DECEMBER Total Obsn	DECEMBER MCWB	JANUARY Obsn Hour Gp 01 to 08	JANUARY 09 to 16	JANUARY 17 to 24	JANUARY Total Obsn	JANUARY MCWB
100/104															
95/99															
90/94															
85/89															
80/84		0		0	65										
75/79		2	0	2	64		0		0	62					
70/74	0	9	1	10	59		1		1	59		1		1	61
65/69	2	16	6	24	58	1	2	1	4	59		2	0	2	59
60/64	8	25	18	51	55	3	7	2	12	55	1	4	2	7	56
55/59	14	29	22	65	51	5	15	9	29	51	3	8	5	16	52
50/54	23	35	34	92	46	9	20	15	44	47	5	12	7	24	47
45/49	35	38	40	113	42	10	25	21	56	42	7	17	11	35	42
40/44	36	37	39	112	38	27	34	30	91	38	12	24	22	58	38
35/39	42	27	40	109	33	36	44	41	121	33	23	35	33	91	33
30/34	39	12	23	74	29	50	44	50	144	29	48	42	51	141	29
25/29	25	6	12	43	25	43	25	39	107	25	40	34	33	107	25
20/24	10	2	4	16	21	28	15	19	62	20	31	27	33	91	20
15/19	3	1	2	6	15	17	6	10	33	15	30	20	22	72	15
10/14	1	0	1	2	11	9	5	6	20	10	18	10	13	41	10
5/9	1	0	0	1	7	6	4	3	13	6	14	7	8	29	5
0/4						3	1	1	5	1	9	4	5	18	1
-5/-1						2	0	1	3	-4	6	1	2	9	-4
-10/-6						0			0	-9	3	0	0	3	-9
-15/-11											0			0	-13

Temperature Range	FEBRUARY Obsn Hour Gp 01 to 08	FEBRUARY 09 to 16	FEBRUARY 17 to 24	FEBRUARY Total Obsn	FEBRUARY MCWB	MARCH Obsn Hour Gp 01 to 08	MARCH 09 to 16	MARCH 17 to 24	MARCH Total Obsn	MARCH MCWB	APRIL Obsn Hour Gp 01 to 08	APRIL 09 to 16	APRIL 17 to 24	APRIL Total Obsn	APRIL MCWB	ANNUAL TOTAL Obsn Hour Gp 01 to 08	ANNUAL TOTAL 09 to 16	ANNUAL TOTAL 17 to 24	ANNUAL TOTAL Total Obsn	ANNUAL TOTAL MCWB
100/104																	3	0	3	75
95/99																	15	3	18	76
90/94												0		0	70	0	103	25	128	75
85/89												3	0	3	67	2	230	81	313	73
80/84		0		0	59		1	0	1	63		12	3	15	66	22	308	171	501	70
75/79		0	0	0	54		5	1	6	61	0	18	9	27	63	126	294	273	693	68
70/74		1	0	1	55		8	3	11	59	4	31	18	53	61	297	258	311	866	65
65/69		2	0	2	55	1	12	8	21	56	13	32	33	78	58	320	199	265	784	61
60/64	0	5	2	7	53	5	15	15	35	53	30	36	38	104	55	291	190	241	722	56
55/59	3	9	6	18	51	12	21	19	52	50	36	34	36	106	50	254	180	211	645	52
50/54	4	16	10	30	45	15	29	25	69	46	38	31	33	102	46	215	178	200	593	47
45/49	5	23	14	42	41	20	30	29	79	41	39	25	34	98	42	205	175	195	575	42
40/44	14	29	29	72	38	33	41	40	114	38	38	12	25	75	38	214	183	206	603	38
35/39	36	42	41	119	33	51	42	43	136	33	27	4	9	40	34	241	195	215	651	34
30/34	50	38	46	134	29	49	25	35	109	29	11	1	2	14	30	259	162	208	629	29
25/29	40	26	32	98	25	30	11	19	60	25	2		0	2	26	181	102	135	418	25
20/24	29	17	22	68	20	21	5	8	34	21						119	66	86	271	20
15/19	18	9	12	39	15	8	1	2	11	16						76	37	48	161	15
10/14	14	5	6	25	10	2	1	1	4	11						44	21	27	92	10
5/9	7	2	3	12	6	1	0	0	1	6						29	13	14	56	6
0/4	4	0	1	5	1	1		0	1	2						17	5	7	29	1
-5/-1	1		0	1	-2	0			0	-2						9	1	3	13	-4
-10/-6																3	0	0	3	-9
-15/-11																0			0	-13

SPRINGFIELD/CAPITAL ILLINOIS

LAT 39 50N LONG 89 40W ELEV 588 FT

MEAN FREQUENCY OF OCCURRENCE OF DRY BULB TEMPERATURE (DEGREES F) WITH MEAN COINCIDENT WET BULB TEMPERATURE (DEGREES F) FOR EACH DRY BULB TEMPERATURE RANGE

Temperature Range	MAY Obsn Hour Gp 01 to 08	MAY 09 to 16	MAY 17 to 24	MAY Total Obsn	MAY MCWB	JUNE Obsn Hour Gp 01 to 08	JUNE 09 to 16	JUNE 17 to 24	JUNE Total Obsn	JUNE MCWB
110/114										
105/109										
100/104							1	0	1	76
95/99							5	1	6	76
90/94		7	0	7	71	0	28	8	36	74
85/89		15	5	20	70	1	41	18	60	72
80/84	1	29	12	42	67	9	54	38	101	70
75/79	6	41	24	71	65	29	44	48	121	68
70/74	19	48	42	109	62	54	35	52	141	65
65/69	39	39	46	124	60	58	18	40	116	62
60/64	48	30	44	122	56	45	10	24	79	58
55/59	48	22	36	106	52	28	4	8	40	54
50/54	36	10	21	67	48	11		3	14	50
45/49	29	4	11	44	44	3		0	3	46
40/44	16	2	5	23	39	0			0	43
35/39	5		1	6	35					
30/34	1			1	31					
25/29										
20/24										
15/19										

Temperature Range	JULY Obsn Hour Gp 01 to 08	JULY 09 to 16	JULY 17 to 24	JULY Total Obsn	JULY MCWB	AUGUST Obsn Hour Gp 01 to 08	AUGUST 09 to 16	AUGUST 17 to 24	AUGUST Total Obsn	AUGUST MCWB
110/114		0		0	76					
105/109		0		0	78					
100/104		1	0	1	77		0		0	79
95/99		7	1	8	77		3	0	3	75
90/94	0	28	8	36	76		24	5	29	75
85/89	2	59	25	86	74	0	54	17	71	74
80/84	11	74	52	137	71	6	71	43	120	72
75/79	46	51	65	162	70	33	51	61	145	69
70/74	84	22	58	164	68	68	29	61	158	67
65/69	56	5	28	89	64	68	12	36	116	64
60/64	36	1	9	46	59	42	2	20	64	59
55/59	11	0	1	12	55	22	0	4	26	55
50/54	3			3	51	7		1	8	51
45/49						2		0	2	46
40/44						0			0	41
35/39										
30/34										
25/29										
20/24										
15/19										

Temperature Range	SEPTEMBER Obsn Hour Gp 01 to 08	SEPTEMBER 09 to 16	SEPTEMBER 17 to 24	SEPTEMBER Total Obsn	SEPTEMBER MCWB	OCTOBER Obsn Hour Gp 01 to 08	OCTOBER 09 to 16	OCTOBER 17 to 24	OCTOBER Total Obsn	OCTOBER MCWB
110/114										
105/109										
100/104		0		0	71					
95/99		5	0	5	72					
90/94		14	2	16	71		1		1	69
85/89	0	26	6	32	71		6	0	6	68
80/84	2	35	16	53	68	0	22	2	24	65
75/79	10	49	33	92	66	0	30	8	38	62
70/74	32	45	43	120	64	5	35	21	61	61
65/69	46	40	48	134	60	14	33	32	79	58
60/64	41	17	40	98	57	33	35	37	105	54
55/59	43	6	28	77	53	36	33	41	110	51
50/54	36	2	16	54	49	38	26	37	101	47
45/49	18	1	7	26	45	43	16	33	92	43
40/44	11		1	12	40	35	8	21	64	39
35/39	2			2	36	26	4	11	41	35
30/34						12	0	3	15	30
25/29						4		1	5	26
20/24						1		0	1	22
15/19						0			0	18

SPRINGFIELD/CAPITAL ILLINOIS

Temperature Range	NOVEMBER Obsn Hour Gp 01 to 08	NOVEMBER 09 to 16	NOVEMBER 17 to 24	NOVEMBER Total Obsn	NOVEMBER MCWB	DECEMBER Obsn Hour Gp 01 to 08	DECEMBER 09 to 16	DECEMBER 17 to 24	DECEMBER Total Obsn	DECEMBER MCWB	JANUARY Obsn Hour Gp 01 to 08	JANUARY 09 to 16	JANUARY 17 to 24	JANUARY Total Obsn	JANUARY MCWB	FEBRUARY Obsn Hour Gp 01 to 08	FEBRUARY 09 to 16	FEBRUARY 17 to 24	FEBRUARY Total Obsn	FEBRUARY MCWB
110/114																				
105/109																				
100/104																				
95/99																				
90/94																				
85/89																				
80/84		0		0	65															
75/79		3		3	63															
70/74	0	9	1	10	60							0		0	64		0		0	61
65/69	2	12	6	20	58		1	0	1	59		1	0	1	61		1	0	1	59
60/64	8	19	12	39	55	1	6	1	8	55	0	2	1	3	58	0	3	2	5	54
55/59	10	23	17	50	51	2	7	4	13	51	3	4	3	10	54	2	7	2	11	50
50/54	17	32	26	75	46	4	13	7	24	46	3	9	5	17	48	3	12	7	22	46
45/49	26	33	33	92	42	8	17	13	38	43	4	14	9	27	43	6	22	14	42	42
40/44	35	37	31	103	38	13	23	21	57	38	10	23	16	49	38	14	29	24	67	38
35/39	34	27	39	100	34	32	43	37	112	34	23	33	31	87	34	28	42	40	110	34
30/34	44	22	35	101	30	51	50	54	155	30	43	48	52	143	30	56	45	57	158	30
25/29	36	14	24	74	25	46	34	42	122	25	46	38	40	124	25	44	27	31	102	25
20/24	16	6	7	29	20	30	22	27	79	20	31	23	27	81	21	23	15	18	56	21
15/19	8	2	5	15	16	21	14	13	48	16	23	21	23	67	16	18	8	10	36	16
10/14	3	1	2	6	11	14	7	10	31	11	23	15	19	57	11	11	7	10	28	11
5/9	2	1	1	4	6	8	7	11	26	6	15	10	12	37	6	10	4	6	20	6
0/4	1	0	0	1	2	10	4	6	20	2	11	4	6	21	1	5	1	3	9	1
-5/-1	0		0	0	-2	4	1	2	7	-3	6	2	3	11	-4	3	1	1	5	-3
-10/-6						3	0	1	4	-8	3	1	1	5	-8	1	0	0	1	-7
-15/-11						0		0	0	-11	1	0	0	1	-12	1	0	0	1	-13
-20/-16																0			0	-18

Temperature Range	MARCH Obsn Hour Gp 01 to 08	MARCH 09 to 16	MARCH 17 to 24	MARCH Total Obsn	MARCH MCWB	APRIL Obsn Hour Gp 01 to 08	APRIL 09 to 16	APRIL 17 to 24	APRIL Total Obsn	APRIL MCWB	ANNUAL TOTAL Obsn Hour Gp 01 to 08	ANNUAL TOTAL 09 to 16	ANNUAL TOTAL 17 to 24	ANNUAL TOTAL Total Obsn	ANNUAL TOTAL MCWB
110/114												0		0	76
105/109												0		0	78
100/104												2	0	2	77
95/99												20	2	22	75
90/94											0	102	23	125	74
85/89							2	0	2	66	3	203	71	277	73
80/84		0		0	65		9	2	11	65	29	294	165	488	70
75/79		1	0	1	63	0	16	7	23	64	124	286	246	656	67
70/74		4	1	5	60	1	27	16	44	61	263	254	295	812	65
65/69	0	8	3	11	56	12	27	23	62	58	295	197	262	754	61
60/64	3	13	9	25	53	23	30	31	84	55	280	168	230	678	56
55/59	7	19	13	39	50	27	29	32	88	50	239	154	189	582	52
50/54	10	25	22	57	46	31	32	33	96	46	199	161	178	538	47
45/49	16	32	28	76	42	35	30	34	99	42	190	169	182	541	43
40/44	26	40	39	105	38	39	23	32	94	38	199	185	190	574	38
35/39	51	44	44	139	34	38	11	22	71	34	239	204	225	668	34
30/34	58	34	47	139	30	25	3	7	35	30	290	202	255	747	30
25/29	37	15	23	75	25	7	0	2	9	26	220	128	163	511	25
20/24	20	8	10	38	21	2		0	2	22	123	74	89	286	21
15/19	8	3	6	17	16						78	48	57	183	16
10/14	6	1	2	9	12						57	31	43	131	11
5/9	3	1	1	5	7						38	23	31	92	6
0/4	1	0	0	1	1						28	9	15	52	1
-5/-1	1	0	0	1	-3						14	4	6	24	-3
-10/-6	1		0	1	-7						8	1	2	11	-8
-15/-11	0			0	-12						2	0	0	2	-12
-20/-16											0			0	-18

EVANSVILLE/DRESS RGNL APRT INDIANA

LAT 38 03N   LONG 87 32W   ELEV   381 FT

MEAN FREQUENCY OF OCCURRENCE OF DRY BULB TEMPERATURE (DEGREES F) WITH MEAN COINCIDENT WET BULB TEMPERATURE (DEGREES F) FOR EACH DRY BULB TEMPERATURE RANGE

Temperature Range	MAY Obsn Hour Gp 01 to 08	MAY 09 to 16	MAY 17 to 24	MAY Total Obsn	MAY MCWB	JUNE Obsn Hour Gp 01 to 08	JUNE 09 to 16	JUNE 17 to 24	JUNE Total Obsn	JUNE MCWB	JULY Obsn Hour Gp 01 to 08	JULY 09 to 16	JULY 17 to 24	JULY Total Obsn	JULY MCWB
100/104							1	0	1	78		2	0	2	77
95/99							10	2	12	76		9	2	11	77
90/94		6	0	6	73	0	33	9	42	75	0	40	9	49	76
85/89		23	6	29	70	3	51	21	75	73	3	79	30	112	74
80/84	2	42	16	60	68	12	55	40	107	71	17	70	51	138	72
75/79	9	52	31	92	66	36	46	49	131	69	54	34	69	157	71
70/74	25	43	42	110	64	63	27	54	144	67	93	12	60	165	69
65/69	52	35	50	137	61	52	9	34	95	64	47	2	20	69	64
60/64	48	22	43	113	57	39	6	21	66	59	25	0	6	31	60
55/59	42	14	28	84	53	25	1	9	35	55	8		1	9	56
50/54	37	8	18	63	49	7	0	1	8	51	1		0	1	51
45/49	19	3	9	31	45	2		0	2	46	0			0	48
40/44	10	1	5	16	40	0			0	42					
35/39	4		1	5	36										
30/34	0		0	0	32										
25/29	0			0	28										
20/24															

Temperature Range	AUGUST Obsn Hour Gp 01 to 08	AUGUST 09 to 16	AUGUST 17 to 24	AUGUST Total Obsn	AUGUST MCWB	SEPTEMBER Obsn Hour Gp 01 to 08	SEPTEMBER 09 to 16	SEPTEMBER 17 to 24	SEPTEMBER Total Obsn	SEPTEMBER MCWB	OCTOBER Obsn Hour Gp 01 to 08	OCTOBER 09 to 16	OCTOBER 17 to 24	OCTOBER Total Obsn	OCTOBER MCWB
100/104		0	0	0	80		1		1	71					
95/99		9	1	10	76		5	0	5	72					
90/94		39	8	47	75		16	2	18	72		1		1	70
85/89	1	72	23	96	73	0	37	7	44	71		8	0	8	69
80/84	12	65	44	121	72	2	43	17	62	69	0	25	2	27	66
75/79	42	40	60	142	71	11	48	31	90	67	1	36	8	45	64
70/74	75	18	59	152	68	41	48	48	137	66	7	41	20	68	62
65/69	55	3	33	91	64	46	27	45	118	62	14	34	31	79	59
60/64	40	1	15	56	60	45	12	39	96	58	29	37	35	101	56
55/59	16		4	20	55	37	3	27	67	54	35	28	39	102	52
50/54	5		1	6	51	29	1	16	46	50	39	21	42	102	48
45/49	1			1	47	19		7	26	46	45	12	32	89	44
40/44						7		1	8	42	37	5	22	64	40
35/39						1		0	1	37	26	1	11	38	35
30/34											11		4	15	31
25/29											4		1	5	26
20/24											0			0	22

EVANSVILLE/DRESS RGNL APRT INDIANA

Temperature Range	NOVEMBER Obsn Hour Gp 01 to 08	NOVEMBER Obsn Hour Gp 09 to 16	NOVEMBER Obsn Hour Gp 17 to 24	NOVEMBER Total Obsn	NOVEMBER MCWB	DECEMBER Obsn Hour Gp 01 to 08	DECEMBER Obsn Hour Gp 09 to 16	DECEMBER Obsn Hour Gp 17 to 24	DECEMBER Total Obsn	DECEMBER MCWB	JANUARY Obsn Hour Gp 01 to 08	JANUARY Obsn Hour Gp 09 to 16	JANUARY Obsn Hour Gp 17 to 24	JANUARY Total Obsn	JANUARY MCWB
100/104															
95/99															
90/94															
85/89															
80/84		1		1	67										
75/79		5	1	6	64		0		0	65					
70/74	0	12	2	14	60		1		1	63		1	1	2	64
65/69	3	17	8	28	58	0	3	2	5	61	1	4	1	6	61
60/64	9	28	17	54	55	3	8	3	14	57	4	7	5	16	58
55/59	16	27	21	64	51	5	13	9	27	52	7	12	10	29	53
50/54	21	36	26	83	46	10	20	15	45	48	6	16	12	34	48
45/49	26	34	32	92	42	16	26	19	61	43	12	23	13	48	42
40/44	31	31	34	96	38	22	37	29	88	38	22	30	24	76	38
35/39	37	22	37	96	34	32	48	41	121	34	30	43	38	111	34
30/34	43	16	34	93	30	55	40	52	147	30	49	48	55	152	30
25/29	30	8	19	57	25	39	26	38	103	25	41	27	36	104	25
20/24	15	2	4	21	21	26	13	17	56	20	29	17	25	71	20
15/19	4	2	4	10	16	17	6	11	34	16	21	8	14	43	16
10/14	3	1	1	5	11	11	5	7	23	11	10	6	6	22	11
5/9	1	0	0	1	7	7	2	3	12	6	9	2	4	15	6
0/4	0		0	0	1	3	0	2	5	2	4	1	2	7	2
-5/-1	0		0	0	-2	1	0	0	1	-3	1	1	1	3	-3
-10/-6						0		0	0	-7	1	1	1	3	-8
-15/-11											1		0	1	-13
-20/-16											0			0	-17
-25/-21															

Temperature Range	FEBRUARY Obsn Hour Gp 01 to 08	FEBRUARY Obsn Hour Gp 09 to 16	FEBRUARY Obsn Hour Gp 17 to 24	FEBRUARY Total Obsn	FEBRUARY MCWB	MARCH Obsn Hour Gp 01 to 08	MARCH Obsn Hour Gp 09 to 16	MARCH Obsn Hour Gp 17 to 24	MARCH Total Obsn	MARCH MCWB	APRIL Obsn Hour Gp 01 to 08	APRIL Obsn Hour Gp 09 to 16	APRIL Obsn Hour Gp 17 to 24	APRIL Total Obsn	APRIL MCWB	ANNUAL TOTAL Obsn Hour Gp 01 to 08	ANNUAL TOTAL Obsn Hour Gp 09 to 16	ANNUAL TOTAL Obsn Hour Gp 17 to 24	ANNUAL TOTAL Total Obsn	ANNUAL TOTAL MCWB
100/104																	4	0	4	77
95/99																	33	5	38	76
90/94																0	135	28	163	75
85/89												3	0	3	68	7	273	87	367	73
80/84							0		0	61		19	4	23	66	45	320	174	539	70
75/79		0		0	62		4	1	5	61	1	24	11	36	64	154	289	261	704	68
70/74		1	0	1	61	1	9	3	13	60	9	29	22	60	62	314	242	311	867	66
65/69	1	4	2	7	58	2	15	9	26	58	21	35	30	86	58	294	188	265	747	61
60/64	2	10	4	16	55	7	24	15	46	54	28	34	33	95	55	279	189	236	704	57
55/59	6	17	9	32	51	13	27	22	62	50	31	29	33	93	51	241	171	212	624	52
50/54	8	23	17	48	46	22	31	30	83	46	35	28	33	96	46	220	184	211	615	47
45/49	14	29	26	69	42	26	41	39	106	42	30	22	31	83	42	210	190	208	608	43
40/44	25	36	32	93	38	41	37	40	118	38	39	14	27	80	39	234	191	214	639	39
35/39	40	44	43	127	34	44	32	41	117	34	31	4	12	47	35	245	194	224	663	34
30/34	50	29	41	120	30	48	17	31	96	30	12	1	3	16	30	268	151	220	639	30
25/29	34	12	23	69	25	25	5	11	41	25	3		0	3	26	176	78	128	382	25
20/24	18	9	11	38	20	12	3	4	19	20	0			0	23	100	44	61	205	21
15/19	10	5	7	22	15	3	1	1	5	16						55	22	37	114	16
10/14	9	3	5	17	10	2	0	0	2	11						35	15	19	69	11
5/9	4	2	1	7	6	1	0	1	2	6						22	6	9	37	6
0/4	2	0	1	3	2	1		0	1	3						10	1	5	16	2
-5/-1	1		0	1	-3	0			0	-2						3	1	1	5	-3
-10/-6	0			0	-9	0			0	-8						1	1	1	3	-8
-15/-11	0			0	-13											1		0	1	-13
-20/-16	0			0	-19											0			0	-18
-25/-21	0			0	-21											0			0	-21

GRISSOM AFB/BUNKER HILL INDIANA

LAT 40 39N LONG 86 09W ELEV 813 FT

MEAN FREQUENCY OF OCCURRENCE OF DRY BULB TEMPERATURE (DEGREES F) WITH MEAN COINCIDENT WET BULB TEMPERATURE (DEGREES F) FOR EACH DRY BULB TEMPERATURE RANGE

Tempera-ture Range	MAY Obsn Hour Gp 01 to 08	09 to 16	17 to 24	Total Obsn	MCWB	JUNE Obsn Hour Gp 01 to 08	09 to 16	17 to 24	Total Obsn	MCWB	JULY Obsn Hour Gp 01 to 08	09 to 16	17 to 24	Total Obsn	MCWB
95/99							2	0	2	74		3	0	3	76
90/94		0		0	69		11	2	13	73		10	2	12	75
85/89		7	0	7	69	1	33	9	43	72	1	42	11	54	73
80/84		22	6	28	67	4	50	23	77	69	4	73	29	106	70
75/79	2	35	14	51	64	17	53	38	108	67	22	66	55	143	68
70/74	10	42	31	83	62	37	44	54	135	64	59	38	65	162	66
65/69	30	44	42	116	60	61	28	52	141	61	79	15	53	147	63
60/64	42	35	43	120	56	50	14	33	97	57	48	2	23	73	59
55/59	39	27	39	105	51	39	4	19	62	53	25	0	8	33	54
50/54	46	19	31	96	47	23	1	9	33	49	8		2	10	49
45/49	34	11	24	69	43	7		1	8	45	2		0	2	45
40/44	29	5	13	47	39	1			1	40	0			0	43
35/39	11	0	4	15	35										
30/34	3		1	4	30										
25/29	1			1	27										
20/24															

Tempera-ture Range	AUGUST Obsn Hour Gp 01 to 08	09 to 16	17 to 24	Total Obsn	MCWB	SEPTEMBER Obsn Hour Gp 01 to 08	09 to 16	17 to 24	Total Obsn	MCWB	OCTOBER Obsn Hour Gp 01 to 08	09 to 16	17 to 24	Total Obsn	MCWB
95/99		0		0	74										
90/94		9	1	10	75		4	0	4	74					
85/89		42	9	51	74		17	3	20	73		1		1	66
80/84	2	60	23	85	70	0	32	7	39	71		7	0	7	65
75/79	18	66	46	130	68	6	46	22	74	67		21	1	22	63
70/74	43	42	61	146	66	27	44	43	114	65	2	28	8	38	61
65/69	70	19	55	144	63	43	48	43	134	61	8	35	19	62	59
60/64	57	8	33	98	59	37	27	41	105	57	23	39	36	98	56
55/59	36	1	14	51	54	45	14	37	96	53	32	39	39	110	51
50/54	15	0	5	20	50	36	5	25	66	49	37	37	43	117	47
45/49	6		1	7	46	24	2	13	39	44	44	24	39	107	43
40/44	1		0	1	42	16	0	5	21	41	41	12	35	88	39
35/39	0			0	37	5		1	6	37	35	4	18	57	35
30/34						0			0	33	19	0	7	26	30
25/29											6		2	8	27
20/24											1		0	1	22

GRISSOM AFB/BUNKER HILL INDIANA

Temperature Range	NOVEMBER Obsn Hour Gp 01 to 08	NOVEMBER 09 to 16	NOVEMBER 17 to 24	NOVEMBER Total Obsn	NOVEMBER MCWB	DECEMBER Obsn Hour Gp 01 to 08	DECEMBER 09 to 16	DECEMBER 17 to 24	DECEMBER Total Obsn	DECEMBER MCWB	JANUARY Obsn Hour Gp 01 to 08	JANUARY 09 to 16	JANUARY 17 to 24	JANUARY Total Obsn	JANUARY MCWB
95/99															
90/94															
85/89															
80/84															
75/79		0		0	66										
70/74	0	4	1	5	60										
65/69	0	6	2	8	58		1		1	60		0		0	59
60/64	4	14	8	26	56	1	2	1	4	56	0	1	0	1	57
55/59	10	22	11	43	52	3	6	3	12	53	1	2	2	5	54
50/54	15	28	21	64	47	4	11	7	22	48	2	2	2	6	50
45/49	24	42	30	96	43	10	15	12	37	43	3	8	3	14	44
40/44	36	39	43	118	39	11	24	18	53	39	9	17	11	37	39
35/39	39	38	43	120	34	28	36	32	96	34	18	31	24	73	34
30/34	45	24	43	112	30	45	49	49	143	30	37	42	46	125	30
25/29	36	13	22	71	26	47	45	48	140	25	40	35	38	113	25
20/24	20	6	11	37	21	38	24	32	94	21	29	34	28	91	21
15/19	6	2	4	12	16	21	14	18	53	16	26	29	29	84	16
10/14	2	1	2	5	11	14	9	10	33	11	24	19	28	71	11
5/9	1	0	0	1	6	9	6	5	20	7	22	14	18	54	6
0/4	1		0	1	1	8	4	8	20	2	16	8	10	34	1
-5/-1	0			0	-1	5	1	3	9	-3	10	4	5	19	-3
-10/-6						2	0	1	3	-8	6	1	3	10	-8
-15/-11						1		0	1	-13	4	1	1	6	-13
-20/-16								0	0	-16	1		0	1	-17

Temperature Range	FEBRUARY Obsn Hour Gp 01 to 08	FEBRUARY 09 to 16	FEBRUARY 17 to 24	FEBRUARY Total Obsn	FEBRUARY MCWB	MARCH Obsn Hour Gp 01 to 08	MARCH 09 to 16	MARCH 17 to 24	MARCH Total Obsn	MARCH MCWB	APRIL Obsn Hour Gp 01 to 08	APRIL 09 to 16	APRIL 17 to 24	APRIL Total Obsn	APRIL MCWB	ANNUAL TOTAL Obsn Hour Gp 01 to 08	ANNUAL TOTAL 09 to 16	ANNUAL TOTAL 17 to 24	ANNUAL TOTAL Total Obsn	ANNUAL TOTAL MCWB
95/99																	5	0	5	75
90/94																	34	5	39	74
85/89												0		0	66	2	142	32	176	73
80/84												5	1	6	65	10	249	89	348	70
75/79							1		1	59		12	3	15	63	65	300	179	544	67
70/74							5	1	6	56	1	18	7	26	61	179	265	271	715	64
65/69		0		0	58		6	2	8	54	7	22	15	44	58	298	224	283	805	61
60/64		1	0	1	55	2	8	5	15	53	16	29	26	71	54	280	180	249	709	57
55/59	0	3	1	4	51	5	13	9	27	50	26	36	35	97	50	261	167	217	645	52
50/54	2	6	3	11	48	8	18	14	40	46	29	35	33	97	46	225	162	195	582	47
45/49	4	9	5	18	43	11	25	19	55	41	31	34	37	102	42	200	170	184	554	43
40/44	5	19	11	35	38	22	40	35	97	38	41	27	35	103	38	212	183	206	601	39
35/39	18	36	31	85	34	38	54	50	142	34	43	15	28	86	34	235	214	231	680	34
30/34	41	47	48	136	30	65	38	53	156	30	30	5	17	52	30	285	205	264	754	30
25/29	43	36	39	118	25	43	24	29	96	25	13	1	3	17	26	229	154	181	564	25
20/24	34	26	30	90	21	26	12	20	58	21	2		0	2	22	150	102	121	373	21
15/19	27	18	23	68	16	16	3	8	27	16	0			0	18	96	66	82	244	16
10/14	17	12	15	44	11	7	1	3	11	11						64	42	58	164	11
5/9	13	6	8	27	6	4	0	1	5	7						49	26	32	107	6
0/4	10	4	6	20	2	1	0	0	1	2						36	16	24	76	2
-5/-1	6	1	3	10	-3	1			1	-3						22	6	11	39	-3
-10/-6	3	0	0	3	-7											11	1	4	16	-8
-15/-11																5	1	1	7	-13
-20/-16																1		0	1	-17

SOUTH BEND/ST JOSEPH APRT INDIANA

LAT 41 42N LONG 86 19W ELEV 773 FT

MEAN FREQUENCY OF OCCURRENCE OF DRY BULB TEMPERATURE (DEGREES F) WITH MEAN COINCIDENT WET BULB TEMPERATURE (DEGREES F) FOR EACH DRY BULB TEMPERATURE RANGE

Temperature Range	MAY Obsn Hour Gp 01 to 08	MAY 09 to 16	MAY 17 to 24	MAY Total Obsn	MAY MCWB	JUNE Obsn Hour Gp 01 to 08	JUNE 09 to 16	JUNE 17 to 24	JUNE Total Obsn	JUNE MCWB	JULY Obsn Hour Gp 01 to 08	JULY 09 to 16	JULY 17 to 24	JULY Total Obsn	JULY MCWB
100/104							0		0	77					
95/99							1	0	1	77		1	0	1	77
90/94		1		1	72		12	2	14	74		11	1	12	75
85/89		9	1	10	69	0	32	9	41	72	0	42	10	52	72
80/84	0	21	6	27	67	4	45	19	68	69	5	68	27	100	70
75/79	2	35	15	52	64	18	47	34	99	66	22	61	50	133	68
70/74	11	37	26	74	61	35	45	49	129	64	60	44	66	170	66
65/69	27	37	36	100	59	53	29	47	129	61	74	17	54	145	63
60/64	33	37	38	108	55	49	19	35	103	57	53	4	29	86	59
55/59	41	31	36	108	51	35	6	23	64	53	22		11	33	55
50/54	43	23	37	103	48	29	3	18	50	50	11		1	12	51
45/49	42	11	29	82	44	12	1	3	16	45	1		0	1	47
40/44	27	7	17	51	39	3		1	4	41					
35/39	18	1	7	26	36	0			0	37					
30/34	3		1	4	31										
25/29	0			0	26										
20/24															

Temperature Range	AUGUST Obsn Hour Gp 01 to 08	AUGUST 09 to 16	AUGUST 17 to 24	AUGUST Total Obsn	AUGUST MCWB	SEPTEMBER Obsn Hour Gp 01 to 08	SEPTEMBER 09 to 16	SEPTEMBER 17 to 24	SEPTEMBER Total Obsn	SEPTEMBER MCWB	OCTOBER Obsn Hour Gp 01 to 08	OCTOBER 09 to 16	OCTOBER 17 to 24	OCTOBER Total Obsn	OCTOBER MCWB
100/104															
95/99		1		1	76		2	0	2	72					
90/94		14	1	15	74		8	1	9	71		0		0	64
85/89	0	32	6	38	72	0	14	3	17	71		1		1	68
80/84	3	56	21	80	70	0	25	9	34	69		10	0	10	64
75/79	14	67	41	122	68	5	39	19	63	66	0	20	3	23	63
70/74	49	50	62	161	66	24	47	32	103	64	3	28	10	41	61
65/69	68	21	60	149	63	32	46	43	121	61	8	34	21	63	59
60/64	58	6	36	100	59	49	38	45	132	57	22	37	31	90	55
55/59	34	1	16	51	55	41	15	39	95	53	33	35	36	104	52
50/54	16		4	20	50	40	7	28	75	49	39	35	44	118	47
45/49	4		1	5	46	28	1	16	45	45	47	26	43	116	44
40/44	1			1	42	14		6	20	41	44	13	32	89	40
35/39						5		1	6	36	33	5	21	59	35
30/34						1			1	33	18	2	6	26	31
25/29											2		1	3	26
20/24											0			0	22

SOUTH BEND/ST JOSEPH, APRT INDIANA

Temperature Range	NOVEMBER Obsn Hour Gp 01 to 08	NOVEMBER Obsn Hour Gp 09 to 16	NOVEMBER Obsn Hour Gp 17 to 24	NOVEMBER Total Obsn	NOVEMBER MCWB	DECEMBER Obsn Hour Gp 01 to 08	DECEMBER Obsn Hour Gp 09 to 16	DECEMBER Obsn Hour Gp 17 to 24	DECEMBER Total Obsn	DECEMBER MCWB	JANUARY Obsn Hour Gp 01 to 08	JANUARY Obsn Hour Gp 09 to 16	JANUARY Obsn Hour Gp 17 to 24	JANUARY Total Obsn	JANUARY MCWB
100/104															
95/99															
90/94															
85/89															
80/84		0		0	65										
75/79		0	0	0	65										
70/74		3	1	4	61										
65/69	0	8	1	9	58							0	0	0	62
60/64	4	14	9	27	56		1	0	1	55	0	1	1	2	59
55/59	13	20	14	47	52	1	4	2	7	52	1	2	1	4	55
50/54	12	26	18	56	47	4	10	5	19	48	2	2	2	6	50
45/49	24	36	28	88	42	6	9	7	22	44	3	6	4	13	44
40/44	34	40	43	117	38	11	17	16	44	39	6	13	6	25	39
35/39	41	33	39	113	34	25	39	30	94	35	21	36	26	83	35
30/34	46	30	42	118	30	51	54	52	157	30	42	55	62	149	30
25/29	35	17	24	76	26	46	46	45	137	26	45	44	44	133	26
20/24	18	8	13	39	21	36	28	36	100	21	37	34	34	105	21
15/19	6	2	5	13	16	28	17	23	68	16	32	22	29	83	16
10/14	3	1	3	7	11	18	13	14	45	12	25	17	22	64	11
5/9	1	1	1	3	6	8	5	8	21	7	15	8	11	34	7
0/4	1	0	0	1	2	6	3	5	14	2	10	4	8	22	2
-5/-1	1		0	1	-3	5	1	3	9	-2	6	3	4	13	-3
-10/-6	0			0	-6	2	0	1	3	-8	4	1	1	6	-8
-15/-11						1			1	-13	2	0	0	2	-13
-20/-16						0			0	-16	0		0	0	-16

Temperature Range	FEBRUARY Obsn Hour Gp 01 to 08	FEBRUARY Obsn Hour Gp 09 to 16	FEBRUARY Obsn Hour Gp 17 to 24	FEBRUARY Total Obsn	FEBRUARY MCWB	MARCH Obsn Hour Gp 01 to 08	MARCH Obsn Hour Gp 09 to 16	MARCH Obsn Hour Gp 17 to 24	MARCH Total Obsn	MARCH MCWB	APRIL Obsn Hour Gp 01 to 08	APRIL Obsn Hour Gp 09 to 16	APRIL Obsn Hour Gp 17 to 24	APRIL Total Obsn	APRIL MCWB	ANNUAL TOTAL Obsn Hour Gp 01 to 08	ANNUAL TOTAL Obsn Hour Gp 09 to 16	ANNUAL TOTAL Obsn Hour Gp 17 to 24	ANNUAL TOTAL Total Obsn	ANNUAL TOTAL MCWB
100/104																	0		0	77
95/99																	5	0	5	75
90/94																	46	5	51	74
85/89												0		0	65	0	130	29	159	72
80/84												4	1	5	63	12	229	83	324	69
75/79							0		0	58		10	2	12	62	61	279	164	504	67
70/74							2	0	2	55	1	16	6	23	60	183	272	252	707	64
65/69		0	0	0	60		4	1	5	54	6	22	12	40	57	268	218	275	761	61
60/64	0	1	0	1	57	0	6	3	9	52	14	25	20	59	55	282	189	247	718	57
55/59	0	2	1	3	52	3	11	6	20	49	20	28	26	74	51	244	155	211	610	52
50/54	2	3	2	7	47	6	19	11	36	46	21	33	32	86	46	225	161	202	588	48
45/49	3	10	4	17	43	11	24	17	52	42	33	38	34	105	42	214	162	186	562	43
40/44	5	22	11	38	38	17	38	29	84	38	42	31	39	112	38	204	181	200	585	39
35/39	19	41	29	89	34	39	54	46	139	34	47	22	33	102	34	248	231	232	711	34
30/34	49	57	58	164	30	64	47	58	169	30	37	10	25	72	30	311	255	294	860	30
25/29	44	36	44	124	26	49	24	43	116	25	14	3	9	26	26	235	170	210	615	26
20/24	39	22	33	94	21	31	14	20	65	21	5	0	1	6	21	166	106	137	409	21
15/19	24	13	15	52	16	14	3	8	25	16	0			0	19	104	57	80	241	16
10/14	16	8	11	35	11	9	1	3	13	12						71	40	53	164	11
5/9	10	6	9	25	7	3	0	1	4	7						37	20	30	87	7
0/4	7	2	5	14	2	2		1	3	2						26	9	19	54	2
-5/-1	4	0	1	5	-3	0			0	-1						16	4	8	28	-3
-10/-6	1	0	0	1	-8											7	1	2	10	-8
-15/-11	0			0	-13											3	0	0	3	-13
-20/-16	0			0	-16											0		0	0	-16

TERRE HAUTE/HULMAN FLD INDIANA

LAT 39 27N LONG 87 18W ELEV 585 FT

MEAN FREQUENCY OF OCCURRENCE OF DRY BULB TEMPERATURE (DEGREES F) WITH MEAN COINCIDENT WET BULB TEMPERATURE (DEGREES F) FOR EACH DRY BULB TEMPERATURE RANGE

Temperature Range	MAY Obsn Hour Gp 01 to 08	MAY 09 to 16	MAY 17 to 24	MAY Total Obsn	MAY MCWB	JUNE Obsn Hour Gp 01 to 08	JUNE 09 to 16	JUNE 17 to 24	JUNE Total Obsn	JUNE MCWB	JULY Obsn Hour Gp 01 to 08	JULY 09 to 16	JULY 17 to 24	JULY Total Obsn	JULY MCWB
105/109												1		1	77
100/104							1	0	1	74		2	0	2	77
95/99							5	1	6	77		7	2	9	76
90/94		1		1	70		31	6	37	74	0	27	5	32	75
85/89		14	2	16	69	1	49	15	65	73	2	73	19	94	74
80/84	0	26	5	31	67	12	54	32	98	71	13	76	41	130	72
75/79	3	50	17	70	64	34	50	47	131	69	46	46	69	161	70
70/74	11	47	31	89	62	57	26	58	141	67	82	13	67	162	69
65/69	29	46	47	122	59	62	17	46	125	63	56	2	31	89	64
60/64	47	30	50	127	57	38	5	22	65	59	32	0	12	44	60
55/59	53	18	49	120	53	23	1	10	34	54	13		3	16	56
50/54	53	9	30	92	49	12	0	2	14	50	3			3	52
45/49	31	6	10	47	45	2		1	3	46					
40/44	15	1	5	21	41	0			0	43					
35/39	5		1	6	36										
30/34	0			0	30										
25/29															
20/24															
15/19															

Temperature Range	AUGUST Obsn Hour Gp 01 to 08	AUGUST 09 to 16	AUGUST 17 to 24	AUGUST Total Obsn	AUGUST MCWB	SEPTEMBER Obsn Hour Gp 01 to 08	SEPTEMBER 09 to 16	SEPTEMBER 17 to 24	SEPTEMBER Total Obsn	SEPTEMBER MCWB	OCTOBER Obsn Hour Gp 01 to 08	OCTOBER 09 to 16	OCTOBER 17 to 24	OCTOBER Total Obsn	OCTOBER MCWB
105/109															
100/104							0		0	71					
95/99		4		4	75		2		2	70					
90/94		21	2	23	74		7	0	7	71		1		1	72
85/89	1	54	9	64	72	0	17	1	18	69		5	0	5	67
80/84	4	74	27	105	70	1	32	5	38	68		19	1	20	67
75/79	18	58	49	125	68	4	51	17	72	66	2	25	5	32	64
70/74	62	29	68	159	68	19	58	38	115	64	6	33	12	51	62
65/69	70	9	55	134	64	47	43	51	141	61	17	42	29	88	60
60/64	49	1	27	77	60	44	22	47	113	58	19	39	31	89	55
55/59	29		10	39	55	39	8	40	87	54	33	35	38	106	51
50/54	13		1	14	51	41	1	26	68	50	41	24	42	107	48
45/49	1		0	1	46	28	0	10	38	46	40	15	40	95	44
40/44						12		3	15	41	39	5	28	72	40
35/39						6		0	6	37	30	5	14	49	35
30/34											14		5	19	31
25/29											5		2	7	26
20/24											1		0	1	21
15/19											0			0	18

TERRE HAUTE/HULMAN FLD INDIANA

Temperature Range	NOVEMBER Obsn Hour Gp 01 to 08	09 to 16	17 to 24	Total Obsn	MCWB	DECEMBER Obsn Hour Gp 01 to 08	09 to 16	17 to 24	Total Obsn	MCWB	JANUARY Obsn Hour Gp 01 to 08	09 to 16	17 to 24	Total Obsn	MCWB
105/109															
100/104															
95/99															
90/94															
85/89															
80/84		0		0	66										
75/79		1	0	1	65										
70/74		8	0	8	61		0		0	66		0		0	64
65/69	0	14	3	17	57	0	2	2	4	63		2	2	4	62
60/64	5	21	8	34	55	1	8	4	13	58	4	5	2	11	59
55/59	13	22	17	52	52	5	8	5	18	52	5	9	8	22	54
50/54	14	32	26	72	46	12	14	10	36	48	10	15	10	35	49
45/49	20	36	30	86	42	10	23	17	50	43	12	19	16	47	45
40/44	38	31	41	110	38	19	33	21	73	39	13	28	14	55	39
35/39	44	32	43	119	34	32	48	45	125	34	32	38	38	108	34
30/34	52	25	34	111	30	55	47	50	152	30	55	51	60	166	30
25/29	29	13	25	67	25	42	28	42	112	25	37	35	35	107	25
20/24	14	2	8	24	21	29	20	23	72	21	27	20	21	68	20
15/19	5	1	3	9	16	17	9	11	37	16	19	12	19	50	15
10/14	1	0	0	1	11	11	4	9	24	11	12	9	13	34	11
5/9	0	1	1	2	6	8	1	5	14	7	10	3	6	19	6
0/4	1		0	1	2	6	2	2	10	2	7	0	3	10	1
-5/-1	1		1	2	-3	0	0	0	0	-4	3		0	3	-3
-10/-6						0		1	1	-10	1			1	-8
-15/-11						1			1	-12					
-20/-16															

Temperature Range	FEBRUARY Obsn Hour Gp 01 to 08	09 to 16	17 to 24	Total Obsn	MCWB	MARCH Obsn Hour Gp 01 to 08	09 to 16	17 to 24	Total Obsn	MCWB	APRIL Obsn Hour Gp 01 to 08	09 to 16	17 to 24	Total Obsn	MCWB	ANNUAL TOTAL Obsn Hour Gp 01 to 08	09 to 16	17 to 24	Total Obsn	MCWB
105/109																	1		1	77
100/104																	3	0	3	76
95/99																	18	3	21	75
90/94																0	88	13	101	74
85/89												1		1	65	4	213	46	263	72
80/84							0		0	63		6	1	7	66	30	287	112	429	70
75/79							1		1	65		20	4	24	64	107	302	208	617	68
70/74		0		0	62		7	1	8	59	2	26	11	39	61	239	247	286	772	65
65/69	0	1	1	2	60	2	11	5	18	58	10	29	23	62	59	293	218	295	806	62
60/64	1	5	1	7	54	5	14	8	27	56	24	27	27	78	55	269	177	239	685	57
55/59	3	13	3	19	50	11	27	19	57	51	24	31	30	85	50	251	172	232	655	52
50/54	5	17	9	31	46	18	30	25	73	47	29	33	34	96	46	251	175	215	641	48
45/49	9	38	23	70	42	21	30	29	80	42	37	28	35	100	43	211	195	211	617	43
40/44	22	39	38	99	38	25	37	34	96	38	45	23	40	108	39	228	197	224	649	39
35/39	41	39	44	124	34	39	42	42	123	34	37	14	24	75	35	266	218	251	735	34
30/34	52	37	46	135	30	51	29	43	123	30	25	3	9	37	31	304	192	247	743	30
25/29	37	16	29	82	25	42	11	27	80	25	5	0	2	7	26	197	103	162	462	25
20/24	23	9	15	47	21	18	6	9	33	21	2			2	22	114	57	76	247	21
15/19	12	3	5	20	16	10	1	4	15	16	0			0	18	63	26	42	131	16
10/14	8	3	5	16	11	3	0	0	3	11						35	16	27	78	11
5/9	6	2	2	10	6	1		1	2	7						25	7	15	47	6
0/4	3	1	2	6	2	1			1	1						18	3	7	28	2
-5/-1	1	0	1	2	-4	0			0	-2						5	0	2	7	-3
-10/-6	0	0	0	0	-8											1	0	1	2	-9
-15/-11	0			0	-14											1			1	-13
-20/-16	1			1	-18											1			1	-18

DES MOINES MAP IOWA

LAT 41 32N LONG 93 39W ELEV 938 FT

MEAN FREQUENCY OF OCCURRENCE OF DRY BULB TEMPERATURE (DEGREES F) WITH MEAN COINCIDENT WET BULB TEMPERATURE (DEGREES F) FOR EACH DRY BULB TEMPERATURE RANGE

Temperature Range	MAY					JUNE					JULY				
	Obsn Hour Gp 01 to 08	09 to 16	17 to 24	Total Obsn	MCWB	Obsn Hour Gp 01 to 08	09 to 16	17 to 24	Total Obsn	MCWB	Obsn Hour Gp 01 to 08	09 to 16	17 to 24	Total Obsn	MCWB
105/109												0		0	79
100/104							0		0	76		2	0	2	76
95/99							3	0	3	77		6	3	9	76
90/94		1	0	1	69		13	5	18	74		21	8	29	75
85/89		8	2	10	69	0	31	14	45	72	1	50	24	75	73
80/84	0	20	9	29	67	4	49	33	86	70	9	63	46	118	71
75/79	2	35	20	57	64	18	48	45	111	67	29	55	60	144	69
70/74	10	44	33	87	61	39	41	51	131	65	68	36	62	166	67
65/69	25	42	43	110	59	63	28	46	137	62	81	12	33	126	64
60/64	46	39	52	137	56	57	18	27	102	58	45	3	11	59	59
55/59	58	28	43	129	52	37	7	13	57	54	13	1	1	15	55
50/54	49	19	26	94	48	17	2	3	22	50	2			2	51
45/49	30	9	14	53	44	5	0	0	5	45					
40/44	19	3	4	26	39	0			0	43					
35/39	7	0	1	8	34										
30/34	3	0	0	3	31										
25/29															
20/24															

Temperature Range	AUGUST					SEPTEMBER					OCTOBER				
	Obsn Hour Gp 01 to 08	09 to 16	17 to 24	Total Obsn	MCWB	Obsn Hour Gp 01 to 08	09 to 16	17 to 24	Total Obsn	MCWB	Obsn Hour Gp 01 to 08	09 to 16	17 to 24	Total Obsn	MCWB
105/109															
100/104		0		0	78										
95/99		6	1	7	74		1	0	1	69		0		0	66
90/94		19	7	26	74		7	1	8	71		1		1	65
85/89	0	38	17	55	73		16	4	20	71		3	0	3	66
80/84	3	56	35	94	71	0	25	12	37	68		10	2	12	65
75/79	22	57	56	135	69	6	35	23	64	65	0	20	6	26	63
70/74	61	39	60	160	67	19	39	35	93	63	2	30	16	48	60
65/69	73	21	44	138	64	27	45	47	119	60	9	34	29	72	57
60/64	56	9	22	87	59	48	37	47	132	57	24	34	36	94	55
55/59	24	2	5	31	55	52	20	38	110	53	34	36	41	111	51
50/54	8	0	2	10	51	45	10	23	78	49	40	32	38	110	46
45/49	1		0	1	46	30	3	8	41	45	45	24	34	103	43
40/44	0			0	40	10	1	2	13	40	38	14	25	77	39
35/39						2		0	2	36	30	6	14	50	34
30/34						0			0	31	17	2	5	24	30
25/29											7	0	1	8	26
20/24											2			2	21

DES MOINES MAP IOWA

Temperature Range	NOVEMBER Obsn Hour Gp 01 to 08	NOVEMBER Obsn Hour Gp 09 to 16	NOVEMBER Obsn Hour Gp 17 to 24	NOVEMBER Total Obsn	NOVEMBER MCWB	DECEMBER Obsn Hour Gp 01 to 08	DECEMBER Obsn Hour Gp 09 to 16	DECEMBER Obsn Hour Gp 17 to 24	DECEMBER Total Obsn	DECEMBER MCWB	JANUARY Obsn Hour Gp 01 to 08	JANUARY Obsn Hour Gp 09 to 16	JANUARY Obsn Hour Gp 17 to 24	JANUARY Total Obsn	JANUARY MCWB
105/109															
100/104															
95/99															
90/94															
85/89															
80/84															
75/79		0		0	63										
70/74		3	0	3	59										
65/69	0	9	2	11	56										
60/64	3	15	8	26	54	0	1		1	54					
55/59	6	20	13	39	50	0	3	2	5	51		1		1	45
50/54	12	26	23	61	46	3	8	5	16	46		4	1	5	44
45/49	20	31	25	76	42	3	13	6	22	41	1	6	2	9	41
40/44	27	30	38	95	38	7	23	16	46	38	3	16	9	28	37
35/39	41	32	38	111	34	22	31	33	86	34	13	25	25	63	34
30/34	47	30	38	115	30	40	40	43	123	30	31	31	36	98	30
25/29	32	17	21	70	25	41	39	37	117	26	35	34	34	103	26
20/24	25	13	16	54	21	35	27	30	92	21	32	30	35	97	21
15/19	11	6	9	26	16	29	22	26	77	16	28	24	22	74	16
10/14	8	4	5	17	11	23	17	20	60	11	28	23	25	76	11
5/9	4	2	2	8	6	15	9	12	36	6	20	21	24	65	6
0/4	3	0	1	4	1	12	8	8	28	2	22	15	17	54	2
-5/-1	1	0		1	-2	9	4	6	19	-3	16	10	10	36	-3
-10/-6						8	1	2	11	-8	12	5	6	23	-8
-15/-11						2	0	0	2	-13	5	1	2	8	-12
-20/-16											1	0		1	-18
-25/-21											0	0		0	-22

Temperature Range	FEBRUARY Obsn Hour Gp 01 to 08	FEBRUARY Obsn Hour Gp 09 to 16	FEBRUARY Obsn Hour Gp 17 to 24	FEBRUARY Total Obsn	FEBRUARY MCWB	MARCH Obsn Hour Gp 01 to 08	MARCH Obsn Hour Gp 09 to 16	MARCH Obsn Hour Gp 17 to 24	MARCH Total Obsn	MARCH MCWB	APRIL Obsn Hour Gp 01 to 08	APRIL Obsn Hour Gp 09 to 16	APRIL Obsn Hour Gp 17 to 24	APRIL Total Obsn	APRIL MCWB	ANNUAL TOTAL Obsn Hour Gp 01 to 08	ANNUAL TOTAL Obsn Hour Gp 09 to 16	ANNUAL TOTAL Obsn Hour Gp 17 to 24	ANNUAL TOTAL Total Obsn	ANNUAL TOTAL MCWB
105/109																	0		0	79
100/104																	2	0	2	76
95/99																	16	4	20	75
90/94																	62	21	83	74
85/89												1	0	1	65	1	147	61	209	72
80/84												5	2	7	64	16	228	139	383	70
75/79							1		1	59		10	4	14	61	77	261	214	552	67
70/74							3	1	4	55	0	17	10	27	58	199	252	268	719	64
65/69		0	0	0	57	0	4	2	6	53	5	21	17	43	56	283	216	263	762	61
60/64	0	1	0	1	53	1	6	5	12	51	11	25	24	60	53	291	188	232	711	56
55/59	0	2	1	3	46	2	11	8	21	48	21	32	27	80	50	247	163	192	602	52
50/54	0	8	2	10	44	5	16	10	31	44	29	32	37	98	46	210	157	170	537	47
45/49	2	12	7	21	41	7	21	20	48	41	36	35	39	110	42	180	154	155	489	42
40/44	4	21	15	40	38	20	33	28	81	37	37	27	32	96	38	165	168	169	502	38
35/39	19	31	30	80	34	30	41	42	113	34	41	22	29	92	34	205	188	212	605	34
30/34	46	40	49	135	30	65	47	58	170	30	41	11	16	68	30	290	201	245	736	30
25/29	36	33	35	104	26	46	27	29	102	26	15	1	3	19	25	212	151	160	523	26
20/24	33	28	29	90	21	27	17	22	66	21	4	0	0	4	21	158	115	132	405	21
15/19	22	18	20	60	16	20	11	11	42	16	1			1	17	111	81	88	280	16
10/14	20	12	13	45	11	12	6	8	26	11						91	62	71	224	11
5/9	15	9	10	34	6	8	2	3	13	7						62	43	51	156	6
0/4	11	6	7	24	2	3	1	1	5	2						51	30	34	115	2
-5/-1	9	3	3	15	-3	1	0	0	1	-3						36	17	19	72	-3
-10/-6	4	1	1	6	-8	0	0	0	0	-8						24	7	9	40	-8
-15/-11	2	0	1	3	-13	1	0	0	1	-14						10	1	3	14	-13
-20/-16	1			1	-18	0			0	-19						2	0		2	-18
-25/-21																0	0		0	-22

SIOUX CITY MAP IOWA

LAT 42 24N LONG 96 23W ELEV 1095 FT

MEAN FREQUENCY OF OCCURRENCE OF DRY BULB TEMPERATURE (DEGREES F) WITH MEAN COINCIDENT WET BULB TEMPERATURE (DEGREES F) FOR EACH DRY BULB TEMPERATURE RANGE

Temperature Range	MAY Obsn Hour Gp 01 to 08	MAY 09 to 16	MAY 17 to 24	MAY Total Obsn	MAY MCWB	JUNE Obsn Hour Gp 01 to 08	JUNE 09 to 16	JUNE 17 to 24	JUNE Total Obsn	JUNE MCWB	JULY Obsn Hour Gp 01 to 08	JULY 09 to 16	JULY 17 to 24	JULY Total Obsn	JULY MCWB
105/109							0		0	77		0	0	0	79
100/104							1	0	1	77		2	1	3	77
95/99							6	3	9	74		7	3	10	77
90/94		2	0	2	69		17	9	26	73		26	11	37	75
85/89		11	5	16	67	0	32	18	50	71	0	50	29	79	73
80/84	0	19	12	31	65	4	44	33	81	69	8	63	47	118	70
75/79	1	35	21	57	62	18	47	43	108	66	32	52	55	139	69
70/74	10	42	31	83	60	38	41	48	127	64	64	33	54	151	67
65/69	20	47	41	108	57	57	27	42	126	62	71	10	34	115	63
60/64	39	35	48	122	55	57	14	26	97	58	51	4	11	66	60
55/59	54	25	39	118	52	38	7	13	58	54	17	1	3	21	55
50/54	51	19	31	101	48	19	3	5	27	49	5		0	5	51
45/49	39	8	13	60	44	7	0	1	8	45	0			0	49
40/44	20	5	5	30	39	1			1	41					
35/39	9	1	2	12	35										
30/34	3	0	0	3	30										
25/29															
20/24															
15/19															

Temperature Range	AUGUST Obsn Hour Gp 01 to 08	AUGUST 09 to 16	AUGUST 17 to 24	AUGUST Total Obsn	AUGUST MCWB	SEPTEMBER Obsn Hour Gp 01 to 08	SEPTEMBER 09 to 16	SEPTEMBER 17 to 24	SEPTEMBER Total Obsn	SEPTEMBER MCWB	OCTOBER Obsn Hour Gp 01 to 08	OCTOBER 09 to 16	OCTOBER 17 to 24	OCTOBER Total Obsn	OCTOBER MCWB
105/109															
100/104		1	0	1	75										
95/99		7	2	9	74		2	0	2	70					
90/94		19	8	27	74		6	2	8	71		1		1	64
85/89	0	37	18	55	73		16	6	22	71		4	1	5	65
80/84	6	60	37	103	71	2	26	11	39	67		10	2	12	63
75/79	19	54	53	126	69	6	36	22	64	65	0	18	6	24	61
70/74	55	39	53	147	67	13	44	33	90	63	1	30	12	43	59
65/69	72	22	43	137	63	26	42	40	108	59	5	32	23	60	57
60/64	52	7	25	84	59	37	32	43	112	56	16	34	32	82	54
55/59	32	2	7	41	55	47	20	40	107	53	27	34	39	100	50
50/54	9	0	1	10	51	49	11	28	88	49	42	31	38	111	46
45/49	1		0	1	46	36	4	12	52	45	44	29	42	115	42
40/44	0			0	41	17	1	3	21	40	45	14	28	87	38
35/39	0			0	38	5	0	1	6	36	31	8	14	53	34
30/34						1		0	1	31	24	3	8	35	30
25/29						0			0	29	11	0	2	13	25
20/24											1	0	0	1	21
15/19											0			0	17

SIOUX CITY MAP IOWA

Tempera-ture Range	NOVEMBER Obsn Hour Gp 01 to 08	09 to 16	17 to 24	Total Obsn	MCWB	DECEMBER Obsn Hour Gp 01 to 08	09 to 16	17 to 24	Total Obsn	MCWB	JANUARY Obsn Hour Gp 01 to 08	09 to 16	17 to 24	Total Obsn	MCWB
105/109															
100/104															
95/99															
90/94															
85/89															
80/84															
75/79		0		0	55										
70/74		2	0	2	55										
65/69	0	6	1	7	54										
60/64	0	13	4	17	51		1		1	48		0		0	45
55/59	2	18	9	29	48	0	4	1	5	48		1		1	44
50/54	4	26	16	46	44	2	6	4	12	46		3	0	3	41
45/49	16	31	29	76	41	2	12	5	19	40		5	1	6	39
40/44	31	36	36	103	37	4	21	15	40	37	1	12	4	17	36
35/39	37	32	43	112	33	16	30	28	74	33	8	23	17	48	33
30/34	51	29	38	118	29	30	38	42	110	30	17	26	29	72	30
25/29	41	18	25	84	25	41	38	39	118	25	29	32	35	96	25
20/24	23	12	17	52	20	44	27	28	99	21	37	35	36	108	20
15/19	14	8	11	33	16	29	24	28	81	16	38	29	32	99	16
10/14	11	4	5	20	11	28	20	21	69	11	28	25	26	79	11
5/9	5	2	3	10	6	19	12	15	46	6	25	21	21	67	6
0/4	2	1	1	4	1	14	8	9	31	2	22	17	19	58	1
-5/-1	2	0	1	3	-3	8	5	8	21	-3	20	13	14	47	-4
-10/-6	0			0	-7	6	2	5	13	-8	16	5	10	31	-8
-15/-11						4	0	1	5	-12	7	2	2	11	-13
-20/-16						1			1	-16	3	0	0	3	-17
-25/-21											0			0	-21

Tempera-ture Range	FEBRUARY Obsn Hour Gp 01 to 08	09 to 16	17 to 24	Total Obsn	MCWB	MARCH Obsn Hour Gp 01 to 08	09 to 16	17 to 24	Total Obsn	MCWB	APRIL Obsn Hour Gp 01 to 08	09 to 16	17 to 24	Total Obsn	MCWB	ANNUAL TOTAL Obsn Hour Gp 01 to 08	09 to 16	17 to 24	Total Obsn	MCWB
105/109																	0	0	0	79
100/104																	4	1	5	76
95/99																	22	8	30	75
90/94												0	0	0	66		71	30	101	74
85/89												2	1	3	63	0	152	78	230	72
80/84												5	3	8	61	20	227	145	392	69
75/79							1	0	1	55		13	6	19	58	76	256	206	538	66
70/74							1	1	2	54	1	15	10	26	56	182	247	242	671	64
65/69							3	1	4	52	3	19	13	35	54	254	208	238	700	60
60/64		1	0	1	47	0	6	4	10	50	8	25	22	55	52	260	172	215	647	56
55/59		2	1	3	46	1	9	6	16	47	14	31	28	73	48	232	154	186	572	51
50/54	0	7	2	9	44	2	16	10	28	43	28	34	34	96	45	211	156	169	536	47
45/49	1	12	6	19	41	6	23	17	46	41	35	32	34	101	42	187	156	160	503	42
40/44	4	18	12	34	37	16	31	28	75	37	41	29	37	107	38	180	167	168	515	38
35/39	16	32	29	77	34	33	44	42	119	34	41	23	28	92	34	196	193	204	593	34
30/34	36	35	45	116	30	62	43	52	157	30	44	10	19	73	30	268	184	233	685	30
25/29	35	29	33	97	26	42	25	34	101	25	19	1	4	24	25	218	143	172	533	25
20/24	35	26	26	87	21	30	20	19	69	21	4	0	1	5	21	174	120	127	421	21
15/19	24	21	21	66	16	22	12	16	50	16	1			1	16	128	94	108	330	16
10/14	22	20	20	62	11	16	8	9	33	11						105	77	81	263	11
5/9	17	11	15	43	6	8	4	5	17	7						74	50	59	183	6
0/4	15	7	9	31	2	5	1	2	8	2						58	34	40	132	1
-5/-1	9	3	4	16	-3	2	0	1	3	-3						41	21	28	90	-4
-10/-6	7	2	2	11	-8	1	0	0	1	-7						30	9	17	56	-8
-15/-11	3	0	0	3	-12	1	0	0	1	-13						15	2	3	20	-13
-20/-16	0	0		0	-17	0		0	0	-18						4	0	0	4	-17
-25/-21	0			0	-25	0			0	-22						0			0	-22

DODGE CITY KANSAS

LAT 37 46N LONG 99 58W ELEV 2582 FT

MEAN FREQUENCY OF OCCURRENCE OF DRY BULB TEMPERATURE (DEGREES F) WITH MEAN COINCIDENT WET BULB TEMPERATURE (DEGREES F) FOR EACH DRY BULB TEMPERATURE RANGE

Temperature Range	MAY Obsn Hour Gp 01 to 08	MAY 09 to 16	MAY 17 to 24	MAY Total Obsn	MAY MCWB	JUNE Obsn Hour Gp 01 to 08	JUNE 09 to 16	JUNE 17 to 24	JUNE Total Obsn	JUNE MCWB	JULY Obsn Hour Gp 01 to 08	JULY 09 to 16	JULY 17 to 24	JULY Total Obsn	JULY MCWB
105/109												0	0	0	70
100/104		0		0	68		5	1	6	68		9	3	12	69
95/99		4	1	5	64		20	8	28	69		31	12	43	70
90/94		10	4	14	65		30	17	47	68		47	27	74	70
85/89		18	9	27	64	1	42	28	71	67	1	50	35	86	69
80/84	0	25	16	41	63	7	42	39	88	66	12	46	53	111	68
75/79	2	36	25	63	61	24	37	41	102	65	48	34	50	132	67
70/74	13	41	34	88	60	49	28	40	117	64	83	20	40	143	66
65/69	29	37	38	104	58	61	19	35	115	62	69	9	22	100	64
60/64	48	33	43	124	56	55	10	20	85	58	29	3	5	37	60
55/59	60	22	37	119	53	28	6	7	41	54	5	0	1	6	54
50/54	48	13	27	88	49	9	2	4	15	50	1	0	0	1	51
45/49	31	6	9	46	44	4	0	1	5	44	0			0	46
40/44	10	2	3	15	40	1			1	41					
35/39	4	1	2	7	35										
30/34	2	0	1	3	32										
25/29	0			0	29										
20/24															

Temperature Range	AUGUST Obsn Hour Gp 01 to 08	AUGUST 09 to 16	AUGUST 17 to 24	AUGUST Total Obsn	AUGUST MCWB	SEPTEMBER Obsn Hour Gp 01 to 08	SEPTEMBER 09 to 16	SEPTEMBER 17 to 24	SEPTEMBER Total Obsn	SEPTEMBER MCWB	OCTOBER Obsn Hour Gp 01 to 08	OCTOBER 09 to 16	OCTOBER 17 to 24	OCTOBER Total Obsn	OCTOBER MCWB
105/109		0	0	0	69										
100/104		8	3	11	69		1	0	1	65					
95/99		28	12	40	69		8	1	9	66					
90/94		44	22	66	69		19	8	27	65		3	0	3	62
85/89	0	51	34	85	68		30	13	43	65		12	2	14	61
80/84	8	47	47	102	67	0	38	25	63	64		21	6	27	60
75/79	37	34	53	124	66	6	39	36	81	62	1	26	12	39	59
70/74	82	21	41	144	65	29	34	41	104	61	1	34	20	55	56
65/69	79	11	25	115	63	52	28	41	121	59	8	37	34	79	55
60/64	31	3	9	43	59	53	19	31	103	56	26	31	40	97	53
55/59	9	1	1	11	55	47	13	26	86	52	41	31	42	114	49
50/54	1	0	1	2	50	32	8	12	52	48	51	26	41	118	46
45/49	1	0		1	47	16	3	5	24	44	49	15	24	88	42
40/44						5	1	1	7	40	38	9	16	63	38
35/39						1		0	1	37	21	2	8	31	34
30/34											8	1	1	10	30
25/29											3	1	1	5	26
20/24											1		0	1	22

DODGE CITY KANSAS

Temperature Range	NOVEMBER Obsn Hour Gp 01 to 08	NOVEMBER Obsn Hour Gp 09 to 16	NOVEMBER Obsn Hour Gp 17 to 24	NOVEMBER Total Obsn	NOVEMBER MCWB	DECEMBER Obsn Hour Gp 01 to 08	DECEMBER Obsn Hour Gp 09 to 16	DECEMBER Obsn Hour Gp 17 to 24	DECEMBER Total Obsn	DECEMBER MCWB	JANUARY Obsn Hour Gp 01 to 08	JANUARY Obsn Hour Gp 09 to 16	JANUARY Obsn Hour Gp 17 to 24	JANUARY Total Obsn	JANUARY MCWB
105/109															
100/104															
95/99															
90/94															
85/89							0		0	55					
80/84		0		0	56		0		0	56					
75/79		2	0	2	53		0		0	53		0		0	49
70/74		9	1	10	52		1		1	50		1	0	1	48
65/69	0	17	4	21	51	0	4	0	4	47		4	0	4	48
60/64	0	21	9	30	49	0	8	1	9	45		8	2	10	46
55/59	3	31	18	52	46	0	17	5	22	44	0	14	5	19	44
50/54	10	32	28	70	43	2	21	11	34	42	1	20	11	32	41
45/49	23	32	38	93	41	6	29	20	55	39	2	24	17	43	38
40/44	37	28	39	104	37	13	35	34	82	35	9	29	29	67	35
35/39	50	22	37	109	33	29	35	43	107	32	24	31	40	95	32
30/34	50	22	30	102	30	56	35	49	140	29	50	31	41	122	29
25/29	29	14	19	62	25	58	23	34	115	25	44	24	29	97	25
20/24	21	7	10	38	20	31	17	23	71	20	37	19	23	79	21
15/19	9	3	5	17	16	24	11	12	47	16	29	17	19	65	16
10/14	4	1	2	7	11	15	7	8	30	11	18	12	13	43	11
5/9	3	0	0	3	7	6	3	5	14	7	18	8	9	35	6
0/4	1	0		1	3	5	1	2	8	1	7	5	7	19	1
-5/-1						2	0	0	2	-3	7	2	3	12	-3
-10/-6						0			0	-7	2	0	1	3	-8
-15/-11											0			0	-12

Temperature Range	FEBRUARY Obsn Hour Gp 01 to 08	FEBRUARY Obsn Hour Gp 09 to 16	FEBRUARY Obsn Hour Gp 17 to 24	FEBRUARY Total Obsn	FEBRUARY MCWB	MARCH Obsn Hour Gp 01 to 08	MARCH Obsn Hour Gp 09 to 16	MARCH Obsn Hour Gp 17 to 24	MARCH Total Obsn	MARCH MCWB	APRIL Obsn Hour Gp 01 to 08	APRIL Obsn Hour Gp 09 to 16	APRIL Obsn Hour Gp 17 to 24	APRIL Total Obsn	APRIL MCWB	ANNUAL TOTAL Obsn Hour Gp 01 to 08	ANNUAL TOTAL Obsn Hour Gp 09 to 16	ANNUAL TOTAL Obsn Hour Gp 17 to 24	ANNUAL TOTAL Total Obsn	ANNUAL TOTAL MCWB
105/109																	0	0	0	69
100/104																	23	7	30	69
95/99												0		0	58		91	34	125	69
90/94							0	0	0	55		1	0	1	58		154	78	232	68
85/89		0		0	56		1	0	1	54		5	2	7	58	2	209	123	334	67
80/84		0	0	0	55		2	1	3	53		12	5	17	57	27	233	192	452	65
75/79		1	0	1	53		6	2	8	52		15	9	24	56	118	230	228	576	64
70/74		3	1	4	51		10	4	14	50	1	21	14	36	55	258	223	236	717	62
65/69		8	2	10	49	0	15	9	24	48	5	29	22	56	53	303	218	232	753	59
60/64	0	12	6	18	47	1	17	11	29	46	15	36	29	80	51	258	201	206	665	54
55/59	1	17	10	28	45	2	24	18	44	44	21	34	37	92	48	217	210	207	634	49
50/54	3	23	15	41	42	11	27	24	62	42	34	30	37	101	45	203	202	211	616	45
45/49	7	26	24	57	40	21	31	29	81	39	48	25	32	105	42	208	191	199	598	41
40/44	22	26	33	81	36	27	28	34	89	36	39	17	26	82	38	201	175	215	591	37
35/39	32	28	30	90	33	43	29	35	107	33	39	9	15	63	34	243	157	210	610	33
30/34	45	23	31	99	29	56	28	35	119	30	26	5	9	40	30	293	145	197	635	29
25/29	37	20	27	84	25	35	16	23	74	25	10	1	2	13	25	216	99	135	450	25
20/24	32	16	20	68	21	25	8	13	46	21	2	0		2	22	149	67	89	305	21
15/19	20	9	14	43	16	15	4	6	25	16	0			0	19	97	44	56	197	16
10/14	13	7	6	26	11	7	2	2	11	12						57	29	31	117	11
5/9	5	3	3	11	7	2	1	0	3	7						34	15	17	66	6
0/4	3	1	1	5	2	1	0	1	2	3						17	7	11	35	2
-5/-1	2	0		2	-2	0	0	0	0	-3						11	2	3	16	-3
-10/-6	0	0	0	0	-8	0	0		0	-8						2	0	1	3	-8
-15/-11	0			0	-13	0			0	-11						0			0	-13

FORBES ANGB/TOPEKA KANSAS

LAT 38 57N LONG 95 40W ELEV 1064 FT

MEAN FREQUENCY OF OCCURRENCE OF DRY BULB TEMPERATURE (DEGREES F) WITH MEAN COINCIDENT WET BULB TEMPERATURE (DEGREES F) FOR EACH DRY BULB TEMPERATURE RANGE

Temperature Range	MAY Obsn Hour Gp 01 to 08	MAY 09 to 16	MAY 17 to 24	MAY Total Obsn	MAY MCWB	JUNE Obsn Hour Gp 01 to 08	JUNE 09 to 16	JUNE 17 to 24	JUNE Total Obsn	JUNE MCWB	JULY Obsn Hour Gp 01 to 08	JULY 09 to 16	JULY 17 to 24	JULY Total Obsn	JULY MCWB
105/109												0		0	81
100/104												3	0	3	77
95/99		0		0	75		2	1	3	76	0	15	5	20	77
90/94		2	0	2	71		15	5	20	75		38	15	53	76
85/89		15	4	19	70		35	16	51	74	1	53	32	86	74
80/84	0	34	14	48	68	3	57	38	98	71	13	60	55	128	72
75/79	2	45	30	77	65	22	52	52	126	69	56	45	63	164	70
70/74	20	43	41	104	63	51	40	56	147	66	81	24	47	152	68
65/69	39	37	48	124	60	76	24	43	143	63	64	8	23	95	64
60/64	54	31	43	128	57	54	9	22	85	59	23	1	6	30	59
55/59	51	22	33	106	52	25	4	7	36	55	9	0	1	10	55
50/54	43	14	22	79	48	8	0	1	9	51	1			1	50
45/49	21	4	10	35	43	1			1	45					
40/44	14	1	1	16	39										
35/39	2			2	34										
30/34	1			1	31										
25/29															
20/24															

Temperature Range	AUGUST Obsn Hour Gp 01 to 08	AUGUST 09 to 16	AUGUST 17 to 24	AUGUST Total Obsn	AUGUST MCWB	SEPTEMBER Obsn Hour Gp 01 to 08	SEPTEMBER 09 to 16	SEPTEMBER 17 to 24	SEPTEMBER Total Obsn	SEPTEMBER MCWB	OCTOBER Obsn Hour Gp 01 to 08	OCTOBER 09 to 16	OCTOBER 17 to 24	OCTOBER Total Obsn	OCTOBER MCWB
105/109		1		1	77										
100/104		3	1	4	76										
95/99		10	4	14	75		1		1	76		0		0	63
90/94		40	12	52	75		9	2	11	75		1	0	1	63
85/89	0	51	27	78	73		21	7	28	73		4	0	4	67
80/84	9	57	49	115	71	0	33	15	48	69		15	3	18	66
75/79	41	41	57	139	69	8	46	34	88	67	0	24	9	33	64
70/74	70	28	51	149	67	33	45	47	125	65	4	34	20	58	61
65/69	67	12	33	112	63	45	36	47	128	62	14	36	35	85	59
60/64	44	5	11	60	59	48	25	39	112	58	29	39	37	105	55
55/59	15	0	4	19	55	49	14	29	92	53	39	37	40	116	51
50/54	2		0	2	50	36	7	16	59	49	43	29	42	114	47
45/49	0			0	46	17	2	5	24	45	43	17	33	93	43
40/44						4		1	5	40	43	9	21	73	39
35/39						0		0	0	36	20	2	5	27	34
30/34											8	1	2	11	30
25/29											3		0	3	26
20/24											0			0	23

FORBES ANGB/TOPEKA KANSAS

Temperature Range	NOVEMBER Obsn Hour Gp 01 to 08	NOVEMBER 09 to 16	NOVEMBER 17 to 24	NOVEMBER Total Obsn	NOVEMBER MCWB	DECEMBER Obsn Hour Gp 01 to 08	DECEMBER 09 to 16	DECEMBER 17 to 24	DECEMBER Total Obsn	DECEMBER MCWB	JANUARY Obsn Hour Gp 01 to 08	JANUARY 09 to 16	JANUARY 17 to 24	JANUARY Total Obsn	JANUARY MCWB
105/109															
100/104															
95/99															
90/94															
85/89															
80/84															
75/79		1	0	1	61										
70/74		8	1	9	60							0		0	57
65/69	1	17	5	23	57		2		2	53		2	0	2	53
60/64	7	21	13	41	54	2	6	3	11	53	1	2	1	4	55
55/59	9	28	20	57	50	2	12	5	19	49	1	6	3	10	49
50/54	17	34	31	82	46	5	17	10	32	45	2	11	6	19	45
45/49	28	37	37	102	42	8	24	17	49	41	3	19	11	33	41
40/44	39	32	41	112	38	19	31	32	82	38	8	24	23	55	37
35/39	48	30	40	118	34	33	38	44	115	34	20	31	33	84	33
30/34	42	18	29	89	29	48	41	46	135	29	41	34	40	115	29
25/29	25	8	13	46	25	44	28	34	106	25	41	31	31	103	25
20/24	14	4	7	25	20	39	24	25	88	20	31	27	28	86	20
15/19	5	2	3	10	16	19	10	16	45	16	28	23	28	79	16
10/14	2	1	1	4	11	12	8	8	28	11	25	18	19	62	11
5/9	1	0	0	1	7	10	4	6	20	7	22	11	14	47	6
0/4	0			0	4	5	2	3	10	1	12	7	8	27	2
-5/-1						2	0	1	3	-3	8	3	4	15	-3
-10/-6						0			0	-8	3	1	0	4	-8
-15/-11											0			0	-12

Temperature Range	FEBRUARY Obsn Hour Gp 01 to 08	FEBRUARY 09 to 16	FEBRUARY 17 to 24	FEBRUARY Total Obsn	FEBRUARY MCWB	MARCH Obsn Hour Gp 01 to 08	MARCH 09 to 16	MARCH 17 to 24	MARCH Total Obsn	MARCH MCWB	APRIL Obsn Hour Gp 01 to 08	APRIL 09 to 16	APRIL 17 to 24	APRIL Total Obsn	APRIL MCWB	ANNUAL TOTAL Obsn Hour Gp 01 to 08	ANNUAL TOTAL 09 to 16	ANNUAL TOTAL 17 to 24	ANNUAL TOTAL Total Obsn	ANNUAL TOTAL MCWB
105/109																	1		1	78
100/104																	6	1	7	77
95/99																0	28	10	38	76
90/94																	105	34	139	75
85/89							0		0	58		3	0	3	66	1	182	86	269	73
80/84							2	0	2	60		9	3	12	63	25	267	177	469	70
75/79							4	2	6	59		16	7	23	62	129	274	254	657	68
70/74		1	0	1	55	0	9	5	14	56	2	27	17	46	60	261	259	285	805	65
65/69		2	1	3	54	1	12	8	21	54	11	31	25	67	57	318	219	268	805	61
60/64		5	1	6	50	4	16	13	33	51	19	40	35	94	54	285	200	224	709	56
55/59	2	7	6	15	49	7	20	15	42	48	33	36	42	111	50	242	186	205	633	51
50/54	3	18	9	30	44	11	26	23	60	44	41	31	42	114	46	212	187	202	601	46
45/49	4	20	18	42	40	21	30	29	80	41	42	22	30	94	42	188	175	190	553	42
40/44	14	27	29	70	38	28	33	35	96	37	41	16	20	77	38	210	173	203	586	38
35/39	32	33	36	101	33	39	34	44	117	33	29	7	13	49	34	223	175	215	613	34
30/34	43	36	39	118	29	56	30	35	121	29	18	3	4	25	30	257	163	195	615	29
25/29	39	27	30	96	25	38	17	20	75	25	3	0	0	3	25	193	111	128	432	25
20/24	28	21	25	74	20	21	8	11	40	20	1			1	22	134	84	96	314	20
15/19	21	14	18	53	16	13	4	5	22	16						86	53	70	209	16
10/14	23	7	8	38	11	6	1	2	9	11						68	35	38	141	11
5/9	10	3	3	16	6	1	1	1	3	6						44	19	24	87	6
0/4	3	1	1	5	2	2	0	0	2	1						22	10	12	44	2
-5/-1	1	0	0	1	-3	0	0		0	-2						11	3	5	19	-3
-10/-6	0			0	-9											3	1	0	4	-8
-15/-11	0			0	-14											0			0	-13

FORT RILEY/MARSHALL AAF KANSAS

LAT 39 03N LONG 96 46W ELEV 1065 FT

MEAN FREQUENCY OF OCCURRENCE OF DRY BULB TEMPERATURE (DEGREES F) WITH MEAN COINCIDENT WET BULB TEMPERATURE (DEGREES F) FOR EACH DRY BULB TEMPERATURE RANGE

Temperature Range	MAY Obsn Hour Gp 01 to 08	09 to 16	17 to 24	Total Obsn	MCWB	JUNE Obsn Hour Gp 01 to 08	09 to 16	17 to 24	Total Obsn	MCWB	JULY Obsn Hour Gp 01 to 08	09 to 16	17 to 24	Total Obsn	MCWB
110/114												0	0	0	75
105/109												2	1	3	75
100/104		0		0	68		1	0	1	74		9	3	12	75
95/99		0	0	0	66		7	2	9	74		22	7	29	75
90/94		6	1	7	70	0	19	8	27	74	1	43	22	66	74
85/89		20	9	29	69	1	44	23	68	72	4	54	40	98	73
80/84	0	37	18	55	67	8	57	42	107	70	28	54	56	138	71
75/79	6	45	34	85	65	31	46	50	127	68	58	37	51	146	69
70/74	29	37	37	103	63	50	33	47	130	66	71	19	40	130	67
65/69	35	36	45	116	59	66	20	36	122	63	51	7	19	77	63
60/64	48	30	37	115	56	46	9	21	76	59	23	1	7	31	59
55/59	48	21	35	104	53	26	4	9	39	55	9	0	2	11	55
50/54	38	11	19	68	48	11	0	2	13	50	3		0	3	50
45/49	21	4	9	34	44	1		0	1	45	1			1	46
40/44	15	1	3	19	40	0			0	40	0			0	43
35/39	7	0	1	8	35										
30/34	1			1	32										
25/29	0			0	27										
20/24															

Temperature Range	AUGUST Obsn Hour Gp 01 to 08	09 to 16	17 to 24	Total Obsn	MCWB	SEPTEMBER Obsn Hour Gp 01 to 08	09 to 16	17 to 24	Total Obsn	MCWB	OCTOBER Obsn Hour Gp 01 to 08	09 to 16	17 to 24	Total Obsn	MCWB
110/114															
105/109		1		1	76										
100/104		5	2	7	75		0		0	77		0		0	64
95/99		19	6	25	74		2	0	2	74		1	0	1	63
90/94	0	43	19	62	74		15	4	19	74		1	0	1	64
85/89	1	53	35	89	72		21	9	30	71		7	1	8	67
80/84	19	52	52	123	70	1	34	21	56	69		18	5	23	65
75/79	51	36	50	137	68	16	44	32	92	66	0	27	12	39	63
70/74	65	23	42	130	66	28	45	42	115	64	8	33	24	65	61
65/69	51	12	25	88	62	38	32	44	114	61	17	34	30	81	58
60/64	39	4	12	55	59	48	23	34	105	58	28	35	32	95	54
55/59	16	0	4	20	55	43	15	31	89	53	34	36	37	107	51
50/54	4		1	5	50	33	7	16	56	49	34	27	34	95	47
45/49	1			1	46	22	2	4	28	45	41	18	33	92	43
40/44						6	0	2	8	41	35	8	23	66	39
35/39						3		1	4	37	27	2	11	40	35
30/34						0			0	34	16	1	4	21	31
25/29											6	0	[illegible]	7	26
20/24											1			1	23

FORT RILEY/MARSHALL AAF KANSAS

Temperature Range	NOVEMBER Obsn Hour Gp 01 to 08	NOVEMBER 09 to 16	NOVEMBER 17 to 24	NOVEMBER Total Obsn	NOVEMBER MCWB	DECEMBER Obsn Hour Gp 01 to 08	DECEMBER 09 to 16	DECEMBER 17 to 24	DECEMBER Total Obsn	DECEMBER MCWB	JANUARY Obsn Hour Gp 01 to 08	JANUARY 09 to 16	JANUARY 17 to 24	JANUARY Total Obsn	JANUARY MCWB
110/114															
105/109															
100/104															
95/99															
90/94															
85/89															
80/84		0		0	66										
75/79		2	0	2	62										
70/74		7	1	8	59		0		0	53		0		0	52
65/69	2	16	6	24	56	0	2		2	52		1	0	1	54
60/64	6	23	11	40	53	1	6	2	9	52	2	3	2	7	53
55/59	10	30	19	59	49	4	15	7	26	49	0	5	2	7	48
50/54	14	33	29	76	45	4	19	9	32	44	1	13	4	18	44
45/49	26	34	35	95	42	7	25	17	49	40	3	20	11	34	41
40/44	33	34	38	105	38	14	29	27	70	37	9	25	24	58	37
35/39	46	32	43	121	34	25	36	38	99	33	21	31	31	83	33
30/34	44	15	29	88	30	43	41	46	130	29	36	33	37	106	29
25/29	29	9	17	55	25	50	28	39	117	25	37	33	35	105	25
20/24	19	4	7	30	21	44	21	27	92	20	35	26	32	93	20
15/19	6	1	3	10	16	23	12	15	50	16	32	21	25	78	16
10/14	3	0	1	4	11	14	7	11	32	11	25	17	19	61	11
5/9	2		0	2	7	9	4	6	19	7	23	13	15	51	6
0/4						5	2	3	10	2	13	5	7	25	1
-5/-1						4	1	1	6	-3	8	2	3	13	-4
-10/-6						1		0	1	-7	3	0	0	3	-8
-15/-11						0			0	-11	1	0		1	-12
-20/-16											0	0		0	-18

Temperature Range	FEBRUARY Obsn Hour Gp 01 to 08	FEBRUARY 09 to 16	FEBRUARY 17 to 24	FEBRUARY Total Obsn	FEBRUARY MCWB	MARCH Obsn Hour Gp 01 to 08	MARCH 09 to 16	MARCH 17 to 24	MARCH Total Obsn	MARCH MCWB	APRIL Obsn Hour Gp 01 to 08	APRIL 09 to 16	APRIL 17 to 24	APRIL Total Obsn	APRIL MCWB	ANNUAL TOTAL Obsn Hour Gp 01 to 08	ANNUAL TOTAL 09 to 16	ANNUAL TOTAL 17 to 24	ANNUAL TOTAL Total Obsn	ANNUAL TOTAL MCWB
110/114																	0	0	0	75
105/109																	3	1	4	75
100/104																	15	5	20	75
95/99																	51	15	66	75
90/94							0		0	59		0		0	66	1	127	54	182	74
85/89							1	0	1	61		3	1	4	65	6	203	118	327	72
80/84							3	1	4	60		10	4	14	62	56	265	199	520	69
75/79		0		0	53		5	3	8	58	0	20	11	31	61	162	262	243	667	67
70/74		1	0	1	51	1	11	5	17	56	5	27	18	50	59	257	236	256	749	64
65/69		2	1	3	53	1	14	10	25	53	13	33	27	73	56	274	209	243	726	60
60/64	0	5	3	8	50	5	18	12	35	50	18	38	31	87	53	264	195	204	663	56
55/59	1	11	6	18	47	8	19	17	44	47	31	34	40	105	49	230	190	209	629	51
50/54	3	20	12	35	44	14	25	25	64	44	38	30	36	104	46	197	185	187	569	46
45/49	4	22	17	43	40	16	29	25	70	40	38	23	29	90	42	181	177	180	538	42
40/44	15	26	26	67	37	27	34	32	93	37	34	12	23	69	38	188	169	198	555	38
35/39	27	33	33	93	33	38	34	40	112	33	32	7	13	52	34	226	175	211	612	34
30/34	36	32	38	106	29	52	27	38	117	29	20	2	5	27	30	248	151	197	596	29
25/29	44	27	33	104	25	40	16	19	75	25	8	0	1	9	26	214	113	145	472	25
20/24	28	18	23	69	20	21	7	12	40	20	2		0	2	21	150	76	101	327	20
15/19	26	14	20	60	16	16	4	5	25	16	0			0	17	103	52	68	223	16
10/14	20	8	9	37	11	5	1	1	7	11						67	33	41	141	11
5/9	13	2	4	19	7	3	1	1	5	7						50	20	26	96	6
0/4	4	1	1	6	2	1	0	1	2	2						23	8	12	43	2
-5/-1	1	0	0	1	-3	1		0	1	-2						14	3	4	21	-3
-10/-6	0	0	0	0	-8											4	0	0	4	-8
-15/-11	0		0	0	-13											1	0	0	1	-12
-20/-16	0		0	0	-17											0	0	0	0	-17

GOODLAND/RENNER FLD KANSAS

LAT 39 22N LONG 101 42W ELEV 3654 FT

MEAN FREQUENCY OF OCCURRENCE OF DRY BULB TEMPERATURE (DEGREES F) WITH MEAN COINCIDENT WET BULB TEMPERATURE (DEGREES F) FOR EACH DRY BULB TEMPERATURE RANGE

Temperature Range	MAY Obsn Hour Gp 01 to 08	09 to 16	17 to 24	Total Obsn	M C W B	JUNE Obsn Hour Gp 01 to 08	09 to 16	17 to 24	Total Obsn	M C W B	JULY Obsn Hour Gp 01 to 08	09 to 16	17 to 24	Total Obsn	M C W B
105/109							1		1	67		1	0	1	68
100/104							4	1	5	66	0	9	1	10	67
95/99		1	0	1	59		19	3	22	64	0	30	5	35	67
90/94		6	0	6	59	0	30	8	38	64	0	49	14	63	67
85/89		12	3	15	59	2	38	13	53	64	3	50	21	74	66
80/84	0	24	5	29	59	4	41	23	68	63	8	45	32	85	65
75/79	1	37	11	49	58	12	33	29	74	62	22	32	47	101	64
70/74	5	35	17	57	57	26	26	37	89	61	46	18	47	111	63
65/69	11	36	29	76	55	42	20	44	106	59	77	10	46	133	62
60/64	25	36	40	101	53	58	13	37	108	57	64	3	27	94	59
55/59	42	23	43	108	51	48	8	26	82	54	23	1	8	32	55
50/54	59	17	44	120	48	32	5	13	50	50	4	0	0	4	51
45/49	50	14	33	97	44	11	1	5	17	45	1		0	1	44
40/44	34	5	14	53	40	3	0	2	5	40	0			0	42
35/39	15	1	6	22	36	1		0	1	36					
30/34	3	1	1	5	30	0			0	31					
25/29	2	0	1	3	27										
20/24															
15/19															
10/14															

Temperature Range	AUGUST Obsn Hour Gp 01 to 08	09 to 16	17 to 24	Total Obsn	M C W B	SEPTEMBER Obsn Hour Gp 01 to 08	09 to 16	17 to 24	Total Obsn	M C W B	OCTOBER Obsn Hour Gp 01 to 08	09 to 16	17 to 24	Total Obsn	M C W B
105/109															
100/104		4	0	4	66		1		1	65					
95/99		23	2	25	66		9	0	9	64					
90/94	0	47	9	56	66		18	2	20	62		1		1	59
85/89	1	52	17	70	66		31	6	37	61		10		10	57
80/84	5	48	27	80	65	1	38	10	49	60		22	1	23	56
75/79	16	32	43	91	64	3	36	20	59	59	0	27	3	30	54
70/74	36	21	56	113	62	11	32	30	73	57	1	31	6	38	53
65/69	74	12	49	135	61	26	25	38	89	56	3	36	15	54	51
60/64	74	6	30	110	59	45	18	39	102	54	9	34	24	67	50
55/59	31	2	10	43	54	46	15	37	98	51	21	28	36	85	47
50/54	8	0	3	11	49	46	10	31	87	48	36	22	43	101	45
45/49	2		0	2	43	34	5	19	56	44	50	16	42	108	41
40/44	1			1	38	19	3	6	28	40	49	11	38	98	38
35/39	0			0	35	7	0	2	9	35	41	5	20	66	34
30/34						1	0	0	1	32	26	2	12	40	30
25/29											10		5	16	26
20/24											2		1	3	21
15/19											1			1	15
10/14											0			0	11

Temperature Range	NOVEMBER Obsn Hour Gp 01 to 08	NOVEMBER Obsn Hour Gp 09 to 16	NOVEMBER Obsn Hour Gp 17 to 24	NOVEMBER Total Obsn	NOVEMBER MCWB	DECEMBER Obsn Hour Gp 01 to 08	DECEMBER Obsn Hour Gp 09 to 16	DECEMBER Obsn Hour Gp 17 to 24	DECEMBER Total Obsn	DECEMBER MCWB	JANUARY Obsn Hour Gp 01 to 08	JANUARY Obsn Hour Gp 09 to 16	JANUARY Obsn Hour Gp 17 to 24	JANUARY Total Obsn	JANUARY MCWB
105/109															
100/104															
95/99															
90/94															
85/89															
80/84							0		0	54					
75/79		1		1	51		0		0	53		0		0	55
70/74		7		7	49		1		1	48		1		1	50
65/69		17	0	17	48		3		3	46		3		3	47
60/64		20	1	21	45		10	0	10	44		8		8	44
55/59	0	28	4	32	44	0	16	1	17	42		15	0	15	42
50/54	2	37	12	51	41	1	23	2	26	40	0	21	2	23	39
45/49	10	30	23	63	39	1	32	6	39	37	1	27	7	35	37
40/44	21	25	37	83	36	6	34	15	55	34	4	33	13	50	34
35/39	42	23	46	111	33	19	34	31	84	32	13	30	29	72	32
30/34	58	17	46	121	29	44	33	52	129	29	33	28	49	110	29
25/29	50	20	32	102	25	60	24	52	136	25	50	22	37	109	25
20/24	28	7	22	57	21	43	16	36	95	21	44	17	30	91	21
15/19	15	5	10	30	16	31	10	23	64	16	30	13	26	69	16
10/14	7	1	4	12	11	21	6	12	39	12	27	9	20	56	11
5/9	3	0	3	6	7	12	4	8	24	7	17	9	13	39	6
0/4	4		1	5	2	6	2	4	12	2	14	6	9	29	2
-5/-1	0		0	0	-3	3	1	3	7	-4	8	4	7	19	-3
-10/-6	0		0	0	-7	2		1	3	-8	5	1	3	9	-8
-15/-11						0		0	0	-13	1	0	1	2	-13
-20/-16						0		0	0	-17	1		0	1	-18
-25/-21													0	0	-24

Temperature Range	FEBRUARY Obsn Hour Gp 01 to 08	FEBRUARY Obsn Hour Gp 09 to 16	FEBRUARY Obsn Hour Gp 17 to 24	FEBRUARY Total Obsn	FEBRUARY MCWB	MARCH Obsn Hour Gp 01 to 08	MARCH Obsn Hour Gp 09 to 16	MARCH Obsn Hour Gp 17 to 24	MARCH Total Obsn	MARCH MCWB	APRIL Obsn Hour Gp 01 to 08	APRIL Obsn Hour Gp 09 to 16	APRIL Obsn Hour Gp 17 to 24	APRIL Total Obsn	APRIL MCWB	ANNUAL TOTAL Obsn Hour Gp 01 to 08	ANNUAL TOTAL Obsn Hour Gp 09 to 16	ANNUAL TOTAL Obsn Hour Gp 17 to 24	ANNUAL TOTAL Total Obsn	ANNUAL TOTAL MCWB
105/109																	2	0	2	67
100/104																0	18	2	20	66
95/99																0	82	10	92	66
90/94												0		0	57	0	151	33	184	65
85/89							0		0	55		2	0	2	55	6	195	60	261	64
80/84							1	0	1	[illegible]		11	1	11	[illegible]	18	[illegible]	[illegible]	[illegible]	[illegible]
75/79		1		1	51		2	0	2	51	0	15	3	18	53	54	216	156	426	61
70/74		3	0	3	49		9	1	10	49	0	17	6	23	52	125	201	200	526	59
65/69		6	0	6	47	0	15	2	17	47	2	29	11	42	49	235	212	234	681	57
60/64		12	1	13	45	0	16	5	21	45	5	32	18	55	47	280	208	222	710	54
55/59	0	19	3	22	43	1	21	7	29	42	11	29	23	63	46	223	205	198	626	49
50/54	0	22	7	29	40	3	25	15	43	40	20	30	32	82	43	211	212	204	627	45
45/49	2	27	11	40	38	8	25	20	53	38	33	26	40	99	41	203	203	206	612	41
40/44	8	24	20	52	35	15	30	30	75	35	49	19	35	103	38	209	184	210	603	37
35/39	23	28	31	82	32	33	29	35	97	33	46	17	31	94	34	240	167	231	638	33
30/34	40	25	40	105	29	56	29	47	132	29	37	9	23	69	30	298	144	270	712	29
25/29	47	21	41	109	25	50	22	37	109	26	23	5	13	41	26	292	115	218	625	25
20/24	38	13	30	81	21	34	13	21	68	21	11	0	4	15	22	200	66	144	410	21
15/19	28	11	16	55	16	24	7	17	48	16	1		0	1	17	130	46	92	268	16
10/14	17	6	11	34	11	14	2	6	22	12	0		0	0	13	86	24	53	163	11
5/9	9	4	7	20	7	7	2	4	13	7						48	19	35	102	7
0/4	5	1	3	9	2	2	0	1	3	2						31	9	18	58	2
-5/-1	3	1	2	6	-3	0		0	0	-3						14	6	12	32	-3
-10/-6	1		1	2	-8	0		0	0	-9						8	1	5	14	-8
-15/-11	1		0	1	-13	0		0	0	-13						2	0	1	3	-13
-20/-16	1		0	1	-18	0			0	-17						2		0	2	-17
-25/-21																		0	0	-24

MCCONNELL AFB/WICHITA KANSAS

LAT 37 38N LONG 97 16W ELEV 1371 FT

MEAN FREQUENCY OF OCCURRENCE OF DRY BULB TEMPERATURE (DEGREES F) WITH MEAN COINCIDENT WET BULB TEMPERATURE (DEGREES F) FOR EACH DRY BULB TEMPERATURE RANGE

Temperature Range	MAY Obsn Hour Gp 01 to 08	MAY 09 to 16	MAY 17 to 24	MAY Total Obsn	MAY MCWB	JUNE Obsn Hour Gp 01 to 08	JUNE 09 to 16	JUNE 17 to 24	JUNE Total Obsn	JUNE MCWB	JULY Obsn Hour Gp 01 to 08	JULY 09 to 16	JULY 17 to 24	JULY Total Obsn	JULY MCWB
105/109												0	0	0	72
100/104		0		0	69		1	0	1	72		11	3	14	74
95/99		1	0	1	70		7	3	10	73		29	13	42	74
90/94		5	1	6	69		26	11	37	73		45	26	71	74
85/89		19	7	26	69		44	26	70	72	2	51	43	96	73
80/84		33	18	51	67	5	56	46	107	70	25	51	56	132	71
75/79	2	49	34	85	65	30	43	51	124	68	70	34	51	155	69
70/74	28	46	47	121	63	61	33	49	143	66	79	19	36	134	68
65/69	44	36	49	129	60	76	19	34	129	63	50	7	15	72	64
60/64	61	28	40	129	57	45	8	16	69	59	16	2	3	21	58
55/59	45	17	27	89	52	18	3	4	25	54	5	0	0	5	54
50/54	39	10	18	67	48	4	0	0	4	50	0			0	49
45/49	20	3	4	27	43										
40/44	8	0	1	9	40										
35/39	2			2	35										
30/34	0			0	33										
25/29															

Temperature Range	AUGUST Obsn Hour Gp 01 to 08	AUGUST 09 to 16	AUGUST 17 to 24	AUGUST Total Obsn	AUGUST MCWB	SEPTEMBER Obsn Hour Gp 01 to 08	SEPTEMBER 09 to 16	SEPTEMBER 17 to 24	SEPTEMBER Total Obsn	SEPTEMBER MCWB	OCTOBER Obsn Hour Gp 01 to 08	OCTOBER 09 to 16	OCTOBER 17 to 24	OCTOBER Total Obsn	OCTOBER MCWB
105/109		1	0	1	74										
100/104		9	2	11	74		0	0	0	74					
95/99		17	9	26	73		3	1	4	74					
90/94		41	20	61	73		12	4	16	73		2		2	64
85/89	2	55	39	96	71		25	12	37	71		8	2	10	67
80/84	19	53	53	125	70	1	39	23	63	69		18	6	24	65
75/79	52	39	55	146	69	14	48	42	104	67	1	29	15	45	63
70/74	75	21	43	139	66	46	43	46	135	65	9	36	25	70	61
65/69	65	8	20	93	63	52	32	46	130	62	19	36	41	96	59
60/64	28	3	6	37	58	47	20	36	103	57	36	40	37	113	55
55/59	7		1	8	55	44	12	19	75	53	38	35	42	115	51
50/54	1			1	51	22	5	8	35	49	53	23	38	114	47
45/49						10	1	3	14	45	44	14	25	83	43
40/44						2		0	2	41	32	6	13	51	39
35/39						0			0	38	13	1	2	16	35
30/34											4	1	1	6	30
25/29												0		2	26

MCCONNELL AFB/WICHITA KANSAS

Temperature Range	NOVEMBER Obsn Hour Gp 01 to 08	09 to 16	17 to 24	Total Obsn	MCWB	DECEMBER Obsn Hour Gp 01 to 08	09 to 16	17 to 24	Total Obsn	MCWB	JANUARY Obsn Hour Gp 01 to 08	09 to 16	17 to 24	Total Obsn	MCWB
105/109															
100/104															
95/99															
90/94															
85/89															
80/84															
75/79		1		1	62										
70/74		10	2	12	59		0		0	55		0	0	0	51
65/69	2	21	10	33	57		1	0	1	52		2	0	2	53
60/64	9	25	17	51	53	1	9	3	13	52	1	3	3	7	54
55/59	11	30	23	64	49	4	16	7	27	49	2	8	3	13	49
50/54	22	35	34	91	46	5	22	16	43	45	3	17	9	29	45
45/49	31	36	42	109	42	11	32	25	68	41	7	23	18	48	41
40/44	44	32	40	116	38	26	35	40	101	37	13	29	30	72	37
35/39	49	27	36	112	34	37	39	44	120	34	29	35	36	100	33
30/34	38	14	23	75	29	56	36	43	135	29	41	35	39	115	29
25/29	23	6	7	36	25	43	21	28	92	25	42	31	36	109	25
20/24	7	3	4	14	20	28	17	20	65	20	38	24	28	90	20
15/19	3	1	2	6	15	17	8	11	36	16	25	17	18	60	16
10/14	2	0	0	2	10	12	7	7	26	11	23	13	14	50	11
5/9	0			0	7	3	3	2	8	6	13	7	8	28	6
0/4						4	1	1	6	2	7	3	4	14	2
-5/-1						1	0	0	1	-3	4	1	1	6	-3
-10/-6											1	0		1	-8
-15/-11											0			0	-12

Temperature Range	FEBRUARY Obsn Hour Gp 01 to 08	09 to 16	17 to 24	Total Obsn	MCWB	MARCH Obsn Hour Gp 01 to 08	09 to 16	17 to 24	Total Obsn	MCWB	APRIL Obsn Hour Gp 01 to 08	09 to 16	17 to 24	Total Obsn	MCWB
105/109															
100/104															
95/99															
90/94												0		0	62
85/89							0		0	62		2	1	3	65
80/84							2	1	3	58		10	4	14	63
75/79		0	0	0	57		5	3	8	59	0	20	11	31	61
70/74		1	0	1	52	0	12	6	18	56	3	31	22	56	59
65/69		4	2	6	53	1	15	11	27	53	15	38	33	86	57
60/64	0	7	4	11	50	4	23	16	43	51	25	41	39	105	54
55/59	3	13	9	25	48	10	24	23	57	48	36	34	43	113	50
50/54	4	20	15	39	44	19	29	28	76	44	43	27	34	104	46
45/49	10	25	22	57	41	24	30	29	83	41	44	19	27	90	42
40/44	19	33	37	89	37	31	32	37	100	37	36	12	17	65	38
35/39	34	32	34	100	33	44	29	35	108	33	22	5	7	34	34
30/34	44	32	31	107	29	51	26	31	108	29	12	1	3	16	29
25/29	34	23	30	87	25	31	13	17	61	25	3	0	1	4	25
20/24	31	18	23	72	20	17	6	7	30	20	0	0		0	22
15/19	26	11	12	49	16	10	2	2	14	16					
10/14	10	4	5	19	11	2	1	1	4	11					
5/9	5	1	1	7	7	2	0	1	3	6					
0/4	2	0	0	2	2	1	0		1	2					
-5/-1	0			0	-4										
-10/-6															
-15/-11															

Temperature Range	ANNUAL TOTAL Obsn Hour Gp 01 to 08	09 to 16	17 to 24	Total Obsn	MCWB
105/109		1	0	1	74
100/104		21	5	26	74
95/99		57	26	83	73
90/94		131	62	193	73
85/89	4	204	130	338	71
80/84	50	262	207	519	69
75/79	169	268	262	699	67
70/74	301	252	276	829	65
65/69	324	219	261	804	61
60/64	273	209	220	702	56
55/59	223	192	201	616	51
50/54	215	188	200	603	46
45/49	201	183	195	579	42
40/44	211	179	215	605	38
35/39	230	168	194	592	33
30/34	246	145	171	562	29
25/29	177	94	120	391	25
20/24	121	68	82	271	20
15/19	81	39	45	165	16
10/14	49	25	27	101	11
5/9	23	11	12	46	6
0/4	14	4	5	23	2
-5/-1	5	1	1	7	-3
-10/-6	1	0		1	-8
-15/-11	0			0	-12

FORT CAMPBELL/CAMPBELL AAF KENTUCKY

LAT 36 40N LONG 87 29W ELEV 571 FT

MEAN FREQUENCY OF OCCURRENCE OF DRY BULB TEMPERATURE (DEGREES F) WITH MEAN COINCIDENT WET BULB TEMPERATURE (DEGREES F) FOR EACH DRY BULB TEMPERATURE RANGE

Temperature Range	MAY Obsn Hour Gp			MAY Total Obsn	MAY MCWB	JUNE Obsn Hour Gp			JUNE Total Obsn	JUNE MCWB	JULY Obsn Hour Gp			JULY Total Obsn	JULY MCWB
	01 to 08	09 to 16	17 to 24			01 to 08	09 to 16	17 to 24			01 to 08	09 to 16	17 to 24		
100/104							0		0	76		1		1	79
95/99		0		0	73		5	1	6	76		9	1	10	79
90/94		3	0	3	72		21	5	26	75	0	29	6	35	76
85/89	0	24	4	28	69	1	51	16	68	73	2	84	27	113	74
80/84	1	48	15	64	68	6	68	38	112	71	13	68	48	129	72
75/79	5	54	30	89	66	29	52	52	133	69	47	36	70	153	71
70/74	25	43	50	118	64	64	30	65	159	67	101	17	64	182	69
65/69	59	34	59	152	61	76	9	42	127	64	54	4	22	80	64
60/64	57	24	42	123	57	39	3	17	59	59	21	1	8	30	59
55/59	41	11	23	75	52	19	1	4	24	55	8		2	10	55
50/54	31	5	15	51	48	6	0	1	7	51	2			2	51
45/49	15	2	8	25	43	0		0	0	45	0			0	48
40/44	9		2	11	39	0			0	41					
35/39	4		0	4	35										
30/34															
25/29															

Temperature Range	AUGUST Obsn Hour Gp			AUGUST Total Obsn	AUGUST MCWB	SEPTEMBER Obsn Hour Gp			SEPTEMBER Total Obsn	SEPTEMBER MCWB	OCTOBER Obsn Hour Gp			OCTOBER Total Obsn	OCTOBER MCWB
	01 to 08	09 to 16	17 to 24			01 to 08	09 to 16	17 to 24			01 to 08	09 to 16	17 to 24		
100/104		1		1	77										
95/99		6	1	7	75		2	0	2	74					
90/94		32	5	37	75		9	1	10	74		0		0	73
85/89	0	69	20	89	74		39	5	44	72		5		5	68
80/84	6	69	36	111	71	1	55	15	71	70		23	1	24	66
75/79	34	44	67	145	70	8	52	38	98	68	1	37	8	46	64
70/74	89	22	73	184	68	52	43	62	157	67	4	42	20	66	62
65/69	67	4	31	102	64	56	24	50	130	63	20	45	37	102	59
60/64	33	1	11	45	59	48	10	34	92	58	35	40	47	122	56
55/59	14		3	17	55	35	4	21	60	54	45	27	41	113	52
50/54	4		0	4	50	25	1	9	35	49	40	19	39	98	47
45/49	0			0	44	9	1	3	13	45	38	7	28	73	43
40/44						4		1	5	41	33	2	18	53	39
35/39						1		0	1	37	22	0	7	29	35
30/34											10		2	12	31
25/29											2		0	2	27

Temperature Range	NOVEMBER Obsn Hour Gp 01 to 08	NOVEMBER Obsn Hour Gp 09 to 16	NOVEMBER Obsn Hour Gp 17 to 24	NOVEMBER Total Obsn	NOVEMBER MCWB	DECEMBER Obsn Hour Gp 01 to 08	DECEMBER Obsn Hour Gp 09 to 16	DECEMBER Obsn Hour Gp 17 to 24	DECEMBER Total Obsn	DECEMBER MCWB	JANUARY Obsn Hour Gp 01 to 08	JANUARY Obsn Hour Gp 09 to 16	JANUARY Obsn Hour Gp 17 to 24	JANUARY Total Obsn	JANUARY MCWB	FEBRUARY Obsn Hour Gp 01 to 08	FEBRUARY Obsn Hour Gp 09 to 16	FEBRUARY Obsn Hour Gp 17 to 24	FEBRUARY Total Obsn	FEBRUARY MCWB
100/104																				
95/99																				
90/94																				
85/89																				
80/84		1		1	68												0		0	61
75/79		5	1	6	64												0	0	0	61
70/74	0	[illegible]	8	18	[illegible]		1	0	1	62	0	1		1	62	0	2	1	3	60
65/69	6	20	9	35	58	2	7	2	11	59	1	5	2	8	59	0	7	3	10	56
60/64	10	28	17	55	55	4	17	7	28	55	4	10	7	21	56	3	12	6	21	54
55/59	20	39	29	88	51	13	20	17	50	52	8	12	10	30	52	7	16	11	34	50
50/54	29	39	36	104	47	16	27	16	59	47	10	20	13	43	46	9	20	16	45	46
45/49	34	32	37	103	43	19	28	26	73	42	13	25	19	57	42	15	27	23	65	41
40/44	35	28	41	104	38	24	40	34	98	38	20	32	25	77	38	24	35	31	90	38
35/39	37	18	30	85	34	34	40	38	112	33	23	35	33	91	33	30	37	37	104	33
30/34	35	8	21	64	30	46	33	44	123	29	44	45	50	139	29	41	32	36	109	29
25/29	19	5	11	35	25	33	18	34	85	25	42	26	36	104	25	39	17	28	84	25
20/24	10	2	4	16	21	31	10	17	58	20	30	15	26	71	20	23	10	18	51	20
15/19	4	0	2	6	16	15	3	7	25	16	25	9	12	46	16	15	5	7	27	15
10/14	1	0		1	12	7	2	3	12	11	11	6	5	22	11	9	2	3	14	11
5/9						2	0	1	3	7	10	4	5	19	6	4	1	2	7	6
0/4						1	0	1	2	2	4	2	2	8	1	2	0	1	3	2
-5/-1						1	0	0	1	-3	4	0	2	6	-3	1			1	-4
-10/-6						0		0	0	-8	1	0	0	1	-8					
-15/-11											0		0	0	-12					
-20/-16											0		0	0	-18					

Temperature Range	MARCH Obsn Hour Gp 01 to 08	MARCH Obsn Hour Gp 09 to 16	MARCH Obsn Hour Gp 17 to 24	MARCH Total Obsn	MARCH MCWB	APRIL Obsn Hour Gp 01 to 08	APRIL Obsn Hour Gp 09 to 16	APRIL Obsn Hour Gp 17 to 24	APRIL Total Obsn	APRIL MCWB	ANNUAL TOTAL Obsn Hour Gp 01 to 08	ANNUAL TOTAL Obsn Hour Gp 09 to 16	ANNUAL TOTAL Obsn Hour Gp 17 to 24	ANNUAL TOTAL Total Obsn	ANNUAL TOTAL MCWB
100/104												2		2	77
95/99												22	3	25	77
90/94											0	94	17	111	75
85/89		1		1	62		4	0	4	66	3	277	72	352	73
80/84		3	0	3	62		20	5	25	65	27	355	158	540	70
75/79		6	2	8	60	1	11	11	[illegible]	[illegible]	[illegible]	[illegible]	[illegible]	[illegible]	[illegible]
70/74	1	13	5	19	58	11	36	25	72	61	347	266	367	980	66
65/69	4	17	12	33	56	23	37	36	96	58	368	213	305	886	61
60/64	8	25	19	52	53	37	38	40	115	54	299	209	255	763	56
55/59	17	28	24	69	49	34	28	36	98	50	261	186	221	668	52
50/54	24	34	32	90	46	35	22	33	90	46	231	187	210	628	47
45/49	26	36	34	96	41	35	16	27	78	42	204	174	205	583	42
40/44	37	37	39	113	38	35	7	15	57	38	221	181	206	608	38
35/39	42	28	39	109	33	20	2	7	29	34	213	160	191	564	34
30/34	42	14	27	83	29	7		1	8	30	225	132	181	538	29
25/29	29	6	12	47	25	1	0		1	27	165	72	121	358	25
20/24	12	1	3	16	20						106	38	68	212	20
15/19	4	0	1	5	16						63	17	29	109	16
10/14	1	0	0	1	11						29	10	11	50	11
5/9	0	0	0	0	7						16	5	8	29	6
0/4	0			0	2						7	2	4	13	2
-5/-1											6	0	2	8	-3
-10/-6											1	0	0	1	-8
-15/-11											0		0	0	-12
-20/-16											0		0	0	-18

FORT KNOX/GODMAN AAF KENTUCKY

LAT 37 54N LONG 85 58W ELEV 753 FT

MEAN FREQUENCY OF OCCURRENCE OF DRY BULB TEMPERATURE (DEGREES F) WITH MEAN COINCIDENT WET BULB TEMPERATURE (DEGREES F) FOR EACH DRY BULB TEMPERATURE RANGE

Temperature Range	MAY Obsn Hour Gp 01 to 08	MAY Obsn Hour Gp 09 to 16	MAY Obsn Hour Gp 17 to 24	MAY Total Obsn	MAY MCWB	JUNE Obsn Hour Gp 01 to 08	JUNE Obsn Hour Gp 09 to 16	JUNE Obsn Hour Gp 17 to 24	JUNE Total Obsn	JUNE MCWB
100/104										
95/99							1	0	1	75
90/94		1		1	71		16	3	19	75
85/89		18	2	20	70	0	44	13	57	73
80/84	0	43	14	57	68	4	65	33	102	70
75/79	4	47	24	75	66	22	56	53	131	68
70/74	18	47	47	112	63	58	35	63	156	66
65/69	52	37	58	147	61	74	15	49	138	63
60/64	56	27	48	131	57	49	5	17	71	58
55/59	47	14	25	86	52	23	2	7	32	54
50/54	32	9	16	57	48	8	0	1	9	50
45/49	21	4	9	34	43	1		0	1	43
40/44	13	1	5	19	40	0			0	39
35/39	4	0	1	5	35	0			0	36
30/34	1		0	1	29					
25/29										

Temperature Range	JULY Obsn Hour Gp 01 to 08	JULY Obsn Hour Gp 09 to 16	JULY Obsn Hour Gp 17 to 24	JULY Total Obsn	JULY MCWB	AUGUST Obsn Hour Gp 01 to 08	AUGUST Obsn Hour Gp 09 to 16	AUGUST Obsn Hour Gp 17 to 24	AUGUST Total Obsn	AUGUST MCWB
100/104							0		0	74
95/99		1	0	1	79		3	0	3	75
90/94		21	4	25	76		23	3	26	75
85/89	1	67	18	86	74	0	62	17	79	74
80/84	7	81	44	132	72	5	70	37	112	71
75/79	37	50	71	158	70	27	50	65	142	70
70/74	98	20	75	193	68	84	30	73	187	67
65/69	68	6	28	102	64	71	9	36	116	63
60/64	27	1	7	35	59	37	2	13	52	58
55/59	8	0	2	10	54	17	0	4	21	54
50/54	2		0	2	51	5		1	6	50
45/49						1			1	45
40/44										
35/39										
30/34										
25/29										

Temperature Range	SEPTEMBER Obsn Hour Gp 01 to 08	SEPTEMBER Obsn Hour Gp 09 to 16	SEPTEMBER Obsn Hour Gp 17 to 24	SEPTEMBER Total Obsn	SEPTEMBER MCWB	OCTOBER Obsn Hour Gp 01 to 08	OCTOBER Obsn Hour Gp 09 to 16	OCTOBER Obsn Hour Gp 17 to 24	OCTOBER Total Obsn	OCTOBER MCWB
100/104										
95/99		0		0	77					
90/94		6	1	7	74		0		0	73
85/89		28	5	33	73		2	0	2	70
80/84	1	45	14	60	70		17	1	18	66
75/79	8	52	36	96	68	0	29	6	35	64
70/74	49	48	55	152	66	2	38	19	59	62
65/69	47	35	46	128	62	15	41	37	93	59
60/64	48	17	42	107	58	38	41	45	124	56
55/59	38	6	25	69	53	39	32	39	110	51
50/54	31	3	13	47	49	43	25	38	106	47
45/49	14	1	4	19	45	40	16	33	89	43
40/44	3		1	4	41	35	6	20	61	39
35/39	1			1	37	24	1	8	33	34
30/34						11	0	2	13	30
25/29						'		0	'	26

FORT KNOX/GODMAN AAF KENTUCKY

Temperature Range	NOVEMBER Obsn Hour Gp 01 to 08	NOVEMBER 09 to 16	NOVEMBER 17 to 24	NOVEMBER Total Obsn	NOVEMBER M C W B	DECEMBER Obsn Hour Gp 01 to 08	DECEMBER 09 to 16	DECEMBER 17 to 24	DECEMBER Total Obsn	DECEMBER M C W B	JANUARY Obsn Hour Gp 01 to 08	JANUARY 09 to 16	JANUARY 17 to 24	JANUARY Total Obsn	JANUARY M C W B
100/104															
95/99															
90/94															
85/89															
80/84		0		0	67										
75/79	0	2	1	3	64										
70/74	0	8	1	9	60		0	0	0	62		0		0	60
65/69	2	16	5	23	58	0	3	1	4	59	0	2	0	2	59
60/64	9	26	17	52	54	4	10	4	18	55	2	5	4	11	56
55/59	18	33	26	77	51	8	15	12	35	52	5	10	10	25	53
50/54	28	42	35	105	46	12	26	18	56	47	9	15	11	35	47
45/49	34	37	38	109	42	17	24	25	66	42	11	23	16	50	42
40/44	38	28	41	107	38	20	32	28	80	38	18	31	25	74	38
35/39	40	23	37	100	34	34	45	38	117	34	27	32	31	90	34
30/34	37	15	23	75	29	48	46	48	142	29	41	45	47	133	29
25/29	18	6	10	34	25	41	22	39	102	25	37	33	36	106	25
20/24	10	3	3	16	20	31	12	18	61	20	30	22	30	82	20
15/19	2	1	3	6	15	17	6	7	30	16	27	12	18	57	16
10/14	2	0	0	2	11	7	4	5	16	11	17	9	8	34	11
5/9	0			0	9	5	2	2	9	6	10	6	5	21	6
0/4						2	0	2	4	2	5	2	5	12	1
-5/-1						2		0	2	-3	5	1	1	7	-3
-10/-6											2	0	0	2	-8
-15/-11											1		0	1	-13
-20/-16											0			0	-17

Temperature Range	FEBRUARY Obsn Hour Gp 01 to 08	FEBRUARY 09 to 16	FEBRUARY 17 to 24	FEBRUARY Total Obsn	FEBRUARY M C W B	MARCH Obsn Hour Gp 01 to 08	MARCH 09 to 16	MARCH 17 to 24	MARCH Total Obsn	MARCH M C W B	APRIL Obsn Hour Gp 01 to 08	APRIL 09 to 16	APRIL 17 to 24	APRIL Total Obsn	APRIL M C W B	ANNUAL TOTAL Obsn Hour Gp 01 to 08	ANNUAL TOTAL 09 to 16	ANNUAL TOTAL 17 to 24	ANNUAL TOTAL Total Obsn	ANNUAL TOTAL M C W B
100/104																	0		0	74
95/99																	5	0	5	76
90/94																	67	11	78	75
85/89												2	0	2	68	1	223	55	279	73
80/84							0		0	62		15	3	18	65	17	336	146	499	70
75/79		0	0	0	66		3	1	4	61	0	24	10	34	62	98	313	267	678	68
70/74		0	0	0	61	0	10	3	13	58	6	31	23	60	60	315	267	359	941	66
65/69	1	2	1	4	60	1	13	7	21	55	17	34	29	80	57	348	213	297	858	61
60/64	1	8	4	13	54	7	21	17	45	53	35	39	44	118	54	313	202	262	777	56
55/59	4	13	8	25	51	15	21	21	57	50	36	34	36	106	50	258	180	215	653	52
50/54	8	16	13	37	46	20	30	26	76	46	33	23	32	88	45	231	189	204	624	47
45/49	11	20	18	49	41	22	36	34	92	41	34	19	30	83	42	206	180	207	593	42
40/44	21	33	30	84	38	36	40	42	118	38	38	11	20	69	38	222	182	212	616	38
35/39	28	37	35	100	34	42	32	38	112	33	25	7	10	42	34	225	177	198	600	34
30/34	46	37	42	125	29	46	25	33	104	29	13	0	2	15	30	243	168	197	608	29
25/29	37	26	30	93	25	32	11	18	61	25	2		0	2	25	168	98	133	399	25
20/24	27	14	21	62	20	18	3	6	27	21						116	54	78	248	20
15/19	16	8	11	35	15	6	1	2	9	16						68	28	41	137	16
10/14	12	4	5	21	11	2	0	0	2	11						40	17	18	75	11
5/9	7	2	2	11	6	1	0	0	1	7						23	10	9	42	6
0/4	4	1	2	7	1	0			0	1						11	3	9	23	1
-5/-1	2			2	-3	0			0	-3						9	1	1	11	-3
-10/-6																2	0	0	2	-8
-15/-11																1		0	1	-13
-20/-16																0			0	-17

BARKSDALE AFB/SHREVEPORT LOUISIANA

LAT 32 30N LONG 93 40W ELEV 167 FT

MEAN FREQUENCY OF OCCURRENCE OF DRY BULB TEMPERATURE (DEGREES F) WITH MEAN COINCIDENT WET BULB TEMPERATURE (DEGREES F) FOR EACH DRY BULB TEMPERATURE RANGE

Temperature Range	MAY Obsn Hour Gp 01 to 08	MAY 09 to 16	MAY 17 to 24	MAY Total Obsn	MAY MCWB	JUNE Obsn Hour Gp 01 to 08	JUNE 09 to 16	JUNE 17 to 24	JUNE Total Obsn	JUNE MCWB	JULY Obsn Hour Gp 01 to 08	JULY 09 to 16	JULY 17 to 24	JULY Total Obsn	JULY MCWB
105/109															
100/104												1	0	1	79
95/99							3	1	4	77		21	7	28	77
90/94		5	1	6	75		44	16	60	76		81	30	111	77
85/89		41	13	54	73	0	83	34	117	74	2	80	40	122	76
80/84	1	73	34	108	70	15	62	49	126	73	36	41	60	137	75
75/79	16	62	52	130	69	62	31	67	160	72	97	18	72	187	73
70/74	53	37	66	156	66	88	12	51	151	69	92	5	35	132	70
65/69	83	22	47	152	63	54	4	16	74	65	18	1	4	23	65
60/64	47	7	21	75	59	15	1	5	21	60	3		1	4	60
55/59	26	2	10	38	54	5		0	5	56	1			1	56
50/54	16	0	4	20	49	1			1	52					
45/49	6		1	7	46										
40/44	1			1	41										
35/39															
30/34															

Temperature Range	AUGUST Obsn Hour Gp 01 to 08	AUGUST 09 to 16	AUGUST 17 to 24	AUGUST Total Obsn	AUGUST MCWB	SEPTEMBER Obsn Hour Gp 01 to 08	SEPTEMBER 09 to 16	SEPTEMBER 17 to 24	SEPTEMBER Total Obsn	SEPTEMBER MCWB	OCTOBER Obsn Hour Gp 01 to 08	OCTOBER 09 to 16	OCTOBER 17 to 24	OCTOBER Total Obsn	OCTOBER MCWB
105/109		0		0	79										
100/104		2	1	3	77										
95/99		22	7	29	76		3	1	4	75					
90/94		73	22	95	76		32	6	38	76		3	0	3	68
85/89	2	73	35	110	75		57	17	74	74		17	3	20	71
80/84	23	48	60	131	74	2	55	33	90	72		46	9	55	68
75/79	91	21	77	189	73	40	46	60	146	71	3	49	22	74	66
70/74	90	6	39	135	70	83	31	69	183	69	18	44	40	102	64
65/69	31	1	7	39	65	55	12	32	99	64	35	40	52	127	61
60/64	9		1	10	61	30	3	17	50	59	52	26	42	120	58
55/59	1			1	55	22	1	4	27	55	44	15	38	97	53
50/54	0			0	51	7		1	8	50	38	6	26	70	49
45/49						1		0	1	45	31	1	12	44	44
40/44						1			1	40	19	0	4	23	40
35/39						0			0	37	6		0	6	36
30/34											1			1	32

Temperature Range	NOVEMBER Obsn Hour Gp 01 to 08	09 to 16	17 to 24	Total Obsn	MCWB	DECEMBER Obsn Hour Gp 01 to 08	09 to 16	17 to 24	Total Obsn	MCWB	JANUARY Obsn Hour Gp 01 to 08	09 to 16	17 to 24	Total Obsn	MCWB
105/109															
100/104															
95/99															
90/94															
85/89		0		0	72										
80/84		7	0	7	67		0		0	67		0		0	67
75/79	1	26	6	33	65		5	1	6	66		4	0	4	64
70/74	5	33	14	52	63	1	13	5	19	63	0	10	5	15	63
65/69	14	39	28	81	60	8	23	13	44	61	8	19	13	40	60
60/64	[illegible]	[illegible]	[illegible]	[illegible]	[illegible]	[illegible]	[illegible]	21	60	57	14	21	17	52	57
55/59	31	33	39	103	52	19	37	27	83	52	12	27	22	61	52
50/54	30	27	34	91	47	27	37	39	103	47	19	33	29	81	47
45/49	33	21	37	91	43	33	40	41	114	43	28	35	35	98	43
40/44	40	11	25	76	39	39	32	44	115	39	30	32	42	104	38
35/39	32	6	12	50	35	37	19	28	84	34	39	28	33	100	34
30/34	16	1	5	22	30	34	10	20	64	30	39	19	26	84	29
25/29	7	0	3	10	26	24	2	7	33	25	31	11	16	58	25
20/24	3		0	3	21	9	1	2	12	21	16	5	6	27	20
15/19	1			1	17	3	0	0	3	16	10	1	2	13	16
10/14						1	0		1	11	2	1	1	4	11
5/9						0			0	9	1	0	0	1	7
0/4											0			0	3

Temperature Range	FEBRUARY Obsn Hour Gp 01 to 08	09 to 16	17 to 24	Total Obsn	MCWB	MARCH Obsn Hour Gp 01 to 08	09 to 16	17 to 24	Total Obsn	MCWB	APRIL Obsn Hour Gp 01 to 08	09 to 16	17 to 24	Total Obsn	MCWB	ANNUAL TOTAL Obsn Hour Gp 01 to 08	09 to 16	17 to 24	Total Obsn	MCWB
105/109																	0		0	79
100/104																	3	1	4	78
95/99																	49	16	65	77
90/94																	238	75	313	76
85/89							1	0	1	66		3	1	4	70	4	355	143	502	74
80/84		2	0	2	67		6	2	8	65		34	11	45	69	77	374	258	709	72
75/79		4	1	5	64		16	7	23	64	2	53	30	85	66	312	335	395	1042	70
70/74	1	11	5	17	61	2	29	17	48	61	27	54	50	131	64	460	285	396	1141	67
65/69	4	21	11	36	59	13	37	31	81	59	46	[illegible]	50	[illegible]	[illegible]	[illegible]	[illegible]	[illegible]	[illegible]	[illegible]
60/64	11	29	23	63	55	22	37	38	97	55	46	28	43	117	57	290	215	266	771	57
55/59	16	29	29	74	51	30	38	39	107	51	43	17	30	90	53	250	199	238	687	52
50/54	22	34	33	89	46	35	34	39	108	46	36	8	16	60	48	231	179	221	631	47
45/49	30	35	41	106	42	44	23	34	101	42	23	1	7	31	44	229	156	208	593	43
40/44	39	27	35	101	38	47	16	24	87	38	13	0	3	16	39	229	118	177	524	38
35/39	41	19	26	86	34	31	7	12	50	34	5	0	0	5	35	191	79	111	381	34
30/34	32	10	15	57	30	17	3	5	25	30	1			1	32	140	43	71	254	30
25/29	21	2	3	26	25	8	1	0	9	26						91	16	29	136	25
20/24	7	1	0	8	20	1		0	1	22						36	7	8	51	21
15/19	1			1	18	0			0	18						15	1	2	18	16
10/14																3	1	1	5	11
5/9																1	0	0	1	7
0/4																0		0	0	3

ENGLAND AFB/ALEXANDRIA LOUISIANA

LAT 31 20N LONG 92 33W ELEV 89 FT

MEAN FREQUENCY OF OCCURRENCE OF DRY BULB TEMPERATURE (DEGREES F) WITH MEAN COINCIDENT WET BULB TEMPERATURE (DEGREES F) FOR EACH DRY BULB TEMPERATURE RANGE

Temperature Range	MAY Obsn Hour Gp 01 to 08	MAY 09 to 16	MAY 17 to 24	MAY Total Obsn	MAY MCWB	JUNE Obsn Hour Gp 01 to 08	JUNE 09 to 16	JUNE 17 to 24	JUNE Total Obsn	JUNE MCWB	JULY Obsn Hour Gp 01 to 08	JULY 09 to 16	JULY 17 to 24	JULY Total Obsn	JULY MCWB
100/104												0	0	0	80
95/99							6	1	7	78		17	4	21	78
90/94		11	1	12	73		60	19	79	76		81	25	106	77
85/89		57	17	74	72	0	87	35	122	75	1	82	35	118	77
80/84	2	76	35	113	71	16	55	59	130	74	25	45	66	136	75
75/79	22	55	59	136	69	75	21	75	171	72	121	19	84	224	73
70/74	68	32	71	171	67	106	8	41	155	69	91	4	31	126	70
65/69	80	11	41	132	64	30	2	9	41	65	8	0	2	10	66
60/64	42	4	15	61	59	11	0	2	13	60	1		0	1	59
55/59	21	2	7	30	54	2		0	2	56	0			0	56
50/54	12	0	1	13	50										
45/49	3		0	3	46										
40/44	0			0	43										
35/39															
30/34															

Temperature Range	AUGUST Obsn Hour Gp 01 to 08	AUGUST 09 to 16	AUGUST 17 to 24	AUGUST Total Obsn	AUGUST MCWB	SEPTEMBER Obsn Hour Gp 01 to 08	SEPTEMBER 09 to 16	SEPTEMBER 17 to 24	SEPTEMBER Total Obsn	SEPTEMBER MCWB	OCTOBER Obsn Hour Gp 01 to 08	OCTOBER 09 to 16	OCTOBER 17 to 24	OCTOBER Total Obsn	OCTOBER MCWB
100/104		0		0	77										
95/99		12	3	15	77		3	0	3	77		0		0	69
90/94		81	20	101	77	0	36	6	42	76		3		3	71
85/89	0	80	32	112	76		66	17	83	75		22	3	25	71
80/84	17	52	65	134	75	4	60	38	102	73		52	12	64	69
75/79	109	20	92	221	73	56	43	80	179	72	6	55	29	90	67
70/74	98	3	34	135	70	92	22	58	172	69	26	49	51	126	65
65/69	19	0	3	22	65	39	9	25	73	64	45	34	54	133	62
60/64	4		1	5	59	26	2	12	40	59	51	20	39	110	58
55/59	0			0	57	16	0	3	19	55	42	11	29	82	53
50/54						4		1	5	51	34	2	19	55	49
45/49						1		0	1	44	24	1	9	34	45
40/44						0		0	0	40	15	0	3	18	40
35/39						0			0	36	5		0	5	36
30/34											1			1	33

Temperature Range	NOVEMBER Obsn Hour Gp 01 to 08	09 to 16	17 to 24	Total Obsn	MCWB	DECEMBER Obsn Hour Gp 01 to 08	09 to 16	17 to 24	Total Obsn	MCWB	JANUARY Obsn Hour Gp 01 to 08	09 to 16	17 to 24	Total Obsn	MCWB	FEBRUARY Obsn Hour Gp 01 to 08	09 to 16	17 to 24	Total Obsn	MCWB
100/104																				
95/99																				
90/94																				
85/89		1		1	71												0		0	71
80/84		12	1	13	69		0		0	68		1		1	70		2	0	2	70
75/79	2	31	7	40	67	0	8	1	9	68		5	1	6	67		9	2	11	67
70/74	[illegible]	11	[illegible]	[illegible]	[illegible]	4	22	8	34	64	2	16	7	25	65	3	16	8	27	64
65/69	21	40	36	97	61	12	30	20	62	61	14	21	19	54	62	11	25	17	53	60
60/64	30	34	39	103	57	17	31	28	76	57	13	25	20	58	57	14	29	25	68	56
55/59	33	30	39	102	52	21	41	37	99	52	16	30	25	71	52	15	32	33	80	51
50/54	34	24	35	93	48	37	37	41	115	48	23	37	35	95	47	28	39	38	105	47
45/49	41	16	29	86	43	35	31	42	108	43	27	34	37	98	43	35	30	39	104	43
40/44	32	7	18	57	39	38	26	35	99	39	34	30	38	102	38	38	22	30	90	38
35/39	23	3	8	34	35	35	14	23	72	34	43	25	33	101	34	37	13	18	68	34
30/34	12	0	4	16	30	28	5	10	43	30	37	14	19	70	29	26	7	11	44	30
25/29	5	0	0	5	26	15	2	3	20	26	24	7	9	40	26	14	1	4	19	25
20/24	0			0	21	4	0	1	5	21	10	2	4	16	20	4	0	0	4	22
15/19						1	0	0	1	16	3	1	1	5	15	0			0	19
10/14						0			0	13	2	0		2	11					

Temperature Range	MARCH Obsn Hour Gp 01 to 08	09 to 16	17 to 24	Total Obsn	MCWB	APRIL Obsn Hour Gp 01 to 08	09 to 16	17 to 24	Total Obsn	MCWB	ANNUAL TOTAL Obsn Hour Gp 01 to 08	09 to 16	17 to 24	Total Obsn	MCWB
100/104												0	0	0	79
95/99												38	8	46	78
90/94											0	272	71	343	77
85/89		1	0	1	64		7	1	8	72	1	403	140	544	75
80/84		6	1	7	67		46	12	58	70	64	407	289	760	73
75/79		[illegible]	9	31	[illegible]	[illegible]	[illegible]	[illegible]	[illegible]	[illegible]	[illegible]	[illegible]	[illegible]	[illegible]	71
70/74	10	41	25	76	63	43	51	59	153	66	552	305	417	1274	67
65/69	17	41	38	96	60	48	33	54	135	62	344	246	318	908	62
60/64	26	38	44	108	56	45	22	37	104	58	280	205	262	747	57
55/59	36	36	42	114	51	40	11	21	72	53	242	193	236	671	52
50/54	40	30	38	108	47	28	4	14	46	49	240	173	222	635	48
45/49	45	17	27	89	43	19	1	5	25	44	230	130	188	548	43
40/44	38	9	15	62	39	8	0	1	9	40	203	94	140	437	39
35/39	21	5	7	33	35	3		0	3	36	167	60	89	316	34
30/34	12	1	2	15	30	1			1	31	117	27	46	190	30
25/29	4		0	4	26						62	10	16	88	26
20/24											18	2	5	25	20
15/19											4	1	1	6	16
10/14											2	0		2	11

LAKE CHARLES MAP LOUISIANA

LAT 30 07N LONG 93 13W ELEV 9 FT

MEAN FREQUENCY OF OCCURRENCE OF DRY BULB TEMPERATURE (DEGREES F) WITH MEAN COINCIDENT WET BULB TEMPERATURE (DEGREES F) FOR EACH DRY BULB TEMPERATURE RANGE

Temperature Range *	MAY Obsn Hour Gp 01 to 08	MAY 09 to 16	MAY 17 to 24	MAY Total Obsn	MAY MCWB	JUNE Obsn Hour Gp 01 to 08	JUNE 09 to 16	JUNE 17 to 24	JUNE Total Obsn	JUNE MCWB
100/104										
95/99		0		0	79		3	0	3	77
90/94		6	0	6	74		52	6	58	77
85/89	0	65	9	74	73	3	109	32	144	75
80/84	7	99	35	141	72	31	50	60	141	75
75/79	43	45	76	164	71	97	19	102	218	74
70/74	91	22	81	194	69	89	7	36	132	71
65/69	66	9	36	111	65	17	1	4	22	66
60/64	27	2	9	38	59	3	0	0	3	59
55/59	12	1	2	15	54	0			0	58
50/54	3		0	3	50					
45/49	0			0	46					
40/44										
35/39										

Temperature Range *	JULY Obsn Hour Gp 01 to 08	JULY 09 to 16	JULY 17 to 24	JULY Total Obsn	JULY MCWB	AUGUST Obsn Hour Gp 01 to 08	AUGUST 09 to 16	AUGUST 17 to 24	AUGUST Total Obsn	AUGUST MCWB
100/104		0		0	79		1		1	78
95/99		9	1	10	77		13	1	14	78
90/94		74	11	85	77		75	13	88	77
85/89	6	98	38	142	77	4	96	37	137	77
80/84	44	42	82	168	77	38	40	89	167	76
75/79	148	20	102	270	75	150	20	93	263	75
70/74	49	5	15	69	72	53	3	14	70	71
65/69	1		0	1	66	3		0	3	65
60/64						0			0	62
55/59										
50/54										
45/49										
40/44										
35/39										

Temperature Range *	SEPTEMBER Obsn Hour Gp 01 to 08	SEPTEMBER 09 to 16	SEPTEMBER 17 to 24	SEPTEMBER Total Obsn	SEPTEMBER MCWB	OCTOBER Obsn Hour Gp 01 to 08	OCTOBER 09 to 16	OCTOBER 17 to 24	OCTOBER Total Obsn	OCTOBER MCWB
100/104										
95/99		2		2	75					
90/94		37	3	40	75		3	0	3	74
85/89	0	86	18	104	75		36	2	38	72
80/84	10	66	47	123	74	0	66	12	78	70
75/79	73	32	96	201	73	12	59	40	111	69
70/74	94	14	56	164	70	38	40	62	140	67
65/69	41	3	17	61	64	54	24	56	134	63
60/64	19	0	2	21	59	57	12	38	107	58
55/59	3		0	3	54	40	7	23	70	53
50/54						29	1	11	41	49
45/49						13	1	3	17	44
40/44						3		1	4	39
35/39						1			1	36

Temperature Range	NOVEMBER Obsn Hour Gp 01 to 08	NOVEMBER 09 to 16	NOVEMBER 17 to 24	NOVEMBER Total Obsn	NOVEMBER MCWB	DECEMBER Obsn Hour Gp 01 to 08	DECEMBER 09 to 16	DECEMBER 17 to 24	DECEMBER Total Obsn	DECEMBER MCWB	JANUARY Obsn Hour Gp 01 to 08	JANUARY 09 to 16	JANUARY 17 to 24	JANUARY Total Obsn	JANUARY MCWB	FEBRUARY Obsn Hour Gp 01 to 08	FEBRUARY 09 to 16	FEBRUARY 17 to 24	FEBRUARY Total Obsn	FEBRUARY MCWB	MARCH Obsn Hour Gp 01 to 08	MARCH 09 to 16	MARCH 17 to 24	MARCH Total Obsn	MARCH MCWB	APRIL Obsn Hour Gp 01 to 08	APRIL 09 to 16	APRIL 17 to 24	APRIL Total Obsn	APRIL MCWB	ANNUAL TOTAL Obsn Hour Gp 01 to 08	ANNUAL TOTAL 09 to 16	ANNUAL TOTAL 17 to 24	ANNUAL TOTAL Total Obsn	ANNUAL TOTAL MCWB
100/104																																1		1	78
95/99																																27	2	29	77
90/94																																247	33	280	77
85/89		0		0	62																	0		0	71		6	0	6	69	13	496	136	645	75
80/84		14	0	14	71		0		0	75		0		0	70		0		0	65		6	0	6	68		42	4	46	70	130	425	329	884	74
75/79	1	38	7	46	69		11	0	11	69		11	0	11	69		16	1	17	68		36	4	40	67	6	72	26	104	68	530	379	547	1456	72
70/74	18	39	26	83	66	3	29	6	38	66	2	30	8	40	67	2	35	12	49	65	13	56	32	101	65	48	56	71	175	67	500	336	419	1255	68
65/69	22	41	38	101	62	18	37	27	82	63	21	32	28	81	64	23	37	31	91	63	40	49	55	144	62	51	33	60	144	63	357	266	352	975	63
60/64	33	36	43	112	57	20	40	33	93	58	24	31	35	90	59	24	32	36	92	58	36	37	49	122	57	48	19	42	109	58	[illegible]	[illegible]	[illegible]	[illegible]	[illegible]
55/59	38	29	41	108	52	35	42	46	[illegible]	[illegible]	[illegible]	[illegible]	[illegible]	[illegible]	[illegible]	[illegible]	31	43	103	53	38	31	44	113	52	45	9	24	78	53	269	186	259	714	53
50/54	39	20	35	94	48	38	37	44	119	48	30	37	41	108	48	40	29	39	108	48	47	17	34	98	48	25	2	10	37	49	251	143	214	608	48
45/49	39	13	29	81	43	40	25	44	109	44	37	30	41	108	43	39	20	31	90	44	35	9	18	62	43	14	0	2	16	44	217	98	168	483	43
40/44	30	7	16	53	39	41	16	27	84	39	41	18	30	89	39	36	15	18	69	39	25	5	9	39	39	4		0	4	41	180	61	101	342	39
35/39	13	1	5	19	34	28	7	14	49	34	30	9	16	55	34	18	5	9	32	35	12	2	3	17	35	0			0	36	102	24	47	173	34
30/34	7	0	1	8	30	18	4	5	27	30	22	8	7	37	30	9	1	3	13	30	3	0	0	3	30						59	13	16	88	30
25/29	1			1	25	5	1	2	8	25	7	3	5	15	25	3	0	0	3	26	0			0	28						16	4	7	27	26
20/24						2	0	0	2	21	3	1	1	5	20	0	1	1	2	20											5	2	2	9	20
15/19						0			0	18	2	1	0	3	15	1	0	0	1	16											3	1	0	4	16
10/14																0			0	13											0			0	13

NEW ORLEANS NAS LOUISIANA

LAT 29 50N LONG 90 01W ELEV 3 FT

MEAN FREQUENCY OF OCCURRENCE OF DRY BULB TEMPERATURE (DEGREES F) WITH MEAN COINCIDENT WET BULB TEMPERATURE (DEGREES F) FOR EACH DRY BULB TEMPERATURE RANGE

Temperature Range	MAY Obsn Hour Gp 01 to 08	MAY 09 to 16	MAY 17 to 24	MAY Total Obsn	MAY MCWB	JUNE Obsn Hour Gp 01 to 08	JUNE 09 to 16	JUNE 17 to 24	JUNE Total Obsn	JUNE MCWB	JULY Obsn Hour Gp 01 to 08	JULY 09 to 16	JULY 17 to 24	JULY Total Obsn	JULY MCWB
95/99							0	0	0	80		4	0	4	80
90/94		2	0	2	73		27	4	31	78		36	5	41	79
85/89	0	55	8	63	73	3	96	23	122	76	6	107	22	135	78
80/84	7	94	34	135	72	33	82	64	179	75	46	63	78	187	77
75/79	43	60	74	177	71	82	25	97	204	74	122	29	112	263	75
70/74	92	26	84	202	69	95	9	45	149	71	69	8	29	106	72
65/69	59	7	33	99	65	22	0	6	28	66	4	0	1	5	66
60/64	28	3	11	42	59	3		0	3	60	0			0	59
55/59	14	1	4	19	55	1		0	1	56					
50/54	4		0	4	50										
45/49	1			1	48										
40/44															
35/39															

Temperature Range	AUGUST Obsn Hour Gp 01 to 08	AUGUST 09 to 16	AUGUST 17 to 24	AUGUST Total Obsn	AUGUST MCWB	SEPTEMBER Obsn Hour Gp 01 to 08	SEPTEMBER 09 to 16	SEPTEMBER 17 to 24	SEPTEMBER Total Obsn	SEPTEMBER MCWB	OCTOBER Obsn Hour Gp 01 to 08	OCTOBER 09 to 16	OCTOBER 17 to 24	OCTOBER Total Obsn	OCTOBER MCWB
95/99		2	0	2	79		1		1	79					
90/94	0	44	5	49	79		17	1	18	78		1		1	77
85/89	6	106	27	139	78	1	75	11	87	77		21	1	22	74
80/84	44	63	80	187	77	22	90	57	169	75	1	61	9	71	72
75/79	130	27	107	264	75	91	40	100	231	74	21	64	41	126	70
70/74	61	6	28	95	71	77	14	48	139	70	42	53	60	155	67
65/69	7	0	2	9	65	30	2	16	48	64	60	30	59	149	63
60/64	2			2	60	14	1	4	19	59	46	13	37	96	58
55/59						3	0	1	4	54	39	5	26	70	54
50/54						1		0	1	47	23	0	12	35	49
45/49						1		0	1	44	13		4	17	45
40/44											2		0	2	40
35/39											0			0	37

Temperature Range	NOVEMBER Obsn Hour Gp 01 to 08	09 to 16	17 to 24	Total Obsn	MCWB	DECEMBER Obsn Hour Gp 01 to 08	09 to 16	17 to 24	Total Obsn	MCWB	JANUARY Obsn Hour Gp 01 to 08	09 to 16	17 to 24	Total Obsn	MCWB
95/99															
90/94															
85/89															
80/84		9		9	72		1		1	70		0		0	70
75/79	1	50	5	56	68		17	1	18	70		6	0	6	69
70/74	15	50	34	99	66	10	29	15	54	67	1	20	6	27	67
65/69	34	41	45	120	63	17	35	24	76	62	9	26	19	54	63
60/64	39	35	40	114	58	25	41	36	102	58	27	35	32	94	59
55/59	41	27	43	111	53	37	43	41	121	53	28	38	36	102	54
50/54	39	16	30	85	48	38	36	46	120	48	34	40	42	116	48
45/49	31	10	23	64	43	32	25	33	90	43	34	34	40	108	43
40/44	22	2	15	39	38	35	12	26	73	38	41	28	36	105	39
35/39	13	1	4	18	34	30	6	17	53	34	35	13	23	71	34
30/34	5	0	1	6	29	17	2	7	26	30	21	5	9	35	29
25/29	0		0	0	24	7	1	1	9	26	11	2	4	17	25
20/24						0	0	0	0	19	4	1	2	7	20
15/19						1			1	16	2	0	0	2	16
10/14											0			0	14

Temperature Range	FEBRUARY Obsn Hour Gp 01 to 08	09 to 16	17 to 24	Total Obsn	MCWB	MARCH Obsn Hour Gp 01 to 08	09 to 16	17 to 24	Total Obsn	MCWB	APRIL Obsn Hour Gp 01 to 08	09 to 16	17 to 24	Total Obsn	MCWB	ANNUAL TOTAL Obsn Hour Gp 01 to 08	09 to 16	17 to 24	Total Obsn	MCWB
95/99																	7	0	7	79
90/94																0	127	15	142	78
85/89												6	0	6	75	16	466	92	574	77
80/84		1		1	73		5	0	5	67	1	55	8	64	72	154	524	330	1008	75
75/79		10	1	11	69	0	31	5	36	68	16	74	44	134	70	506	433	587	1526	73
70/74	4	22	9	35	67	13	51	29	93	65	51	52	68	171	67	530	340	455	1325	69
65/69	14	28	21	63	63	32	47	45	124	62	59	31	58	148	63	347	247	329	923	63
60/64	16	33	27	76	57	42	39	54	135	58	46	16	34	96	58	288	216	275	779	58
55/59	25	38	39	102	53	38	37	44	119	52	30	5	17	52	54	256	194	251	701	53
50/54	39	43	48	130	48	43	22	36	101	47	23	1	8	32	49	244	158	222	624	48
45/49	30	[illegible]	[illegible]	88	43	[illegible]	12	23	73	43	12		2	14	45	201	106	159	466	43
40/44	35	16	27	78	38	28	4	11	43	39	2			2	41	165	62	115	342	39
35/39	34	6	14	54	34	12	0	2	14	34						124	26	60	210	34
30/34	15	2	4	21	30	3		0	3	30						61	9	21	91	29
25/29	2	0	0	2	26	0			0	27						20	3	5	28	25
20/24	1			1	20											5	1	2	8	20
15/19																3	0	0	3	16
10/14																0			0	14

BANGOR IAP/DOW AFB MAINE

LAT 44 48N LONG 68 50W ELEV 192 FT

MEAN FREQUENCY OF OCCURRENCE OF DRY BULB TEMPERATURE (DEGREES F) WITH MEAN COINCIDENT WET BULB TEMPERATURE (DEGREES F) FOR EACH DRY BULB TEMPERATURE RANGE

Temperature Range	MAY Obsn Hour Gp 01 to 08	MAY Obsn Hour Gp 09 to 16	MAY Obsn Hour Gp 17 to 24	MAY Total Obsn	MAY MCWB	JUNE Obsn Hour Gp 01 to 08	JUNE Obsn Hour Gp 09 to 16	JUNE Obsn Hour Gp 17 to 24	JUNE Total Obsn	JUNE MCWB	JULY Obsn Hour Gp 01 to 08	JULY Obsn Hour Gp 09 to 16	JULY Obsn Hour Gp 17 to 24	JULY Total Obsn	JULY MCWB
95/99												0		0	75
90/94		0		0	70		2	0	2	69		4	0	4	74
85/89		3	0	3	66		8	1	9	69	0	14	2	16	71
80/84		5	1	6	64	0	22	4	26	66	0	41	8	49	68
75/79		12	2	14	61	1	40	11	52	63	3	58	21	82	65
70/74	1	19	6	26	58	5	52	25	82	61	14	63	42	119	64
65/69	2	35	13	50	55	18	44	41	103	59	49	40	74	163	62
60/64	9	48	26	83	52	45	39	59	143	57	92	21	65	178	59
55/59	24	49	42	115	50	75	22	54	151	53	61	5	30	96	55
50/54	47	39	57	143	47	60	10	35	105	49	24	0	5	29	50
45/49	64	26	57	147	43	28	1	9	38	45	4		0	4	44
40/44	55	9	31	95	39	7		1	8	40	1			1	40
35/39	36	3	11	50	35	1			1	36					
30/34	10	0	1	11	31										
25/29	0		0	0	25										
20/24															
15/19															

Temperature Range	AUGUST Obsn Hour Gp 01 to 08	AUGUST Obsn Hour Gp 09 to 16	AUGUST Obsn Hour Gp 17 to 24	AUGUST Total Obsn	AUGUST MCWB	SEPTEMBER Obsn Hour Gp 01 to 08	SEPTEMBER Obsn Hour Gp 09 to 16	SEPTEMBER Obsn Hour Gp 17 to 24	SEPTEMBER Total Obsn	SEPTEMBER MCWB	OCTOBER Obsn Hour Gp 01 to 08	OCTOBER Obsn Hour Gp 09 to 16	OCTOBER Obsn Hour Gp 17 to 24	OCTOBER Total Obsn	OCTOBER MCWB
95/99															
90/94		1		1	74		1		1	74					
85/89		8	1	9	71		3	0	3	72		1		1	67
80/84	0	31	4	35	68	0	10	1	11	69		1		1	65
75/79	1	57	14	72	66	1	18	4	23	66		5	0	5	63
70/74	8	71	40	119	63	2	37	12	51	62		9	1	10	61
65/69	48	51	71	170	62	18	52	28	98	60	1	15	4	20	58
60/64	82	22	69	173	59	40	56	54	150	57	6	33	14	53	56
55/59	62	6	36	104	54	48	35	57	140	53	20	50	31	101	52
50/54	33	1	11	45	49	49	23	45	117	49	41	57	53	151	48
45/49	13	0	1	14	45	38	5	24	67	45	51	37	55	143	43
40/44	2		1	3	40	26	1	10	37	40	43	24	42	109	39
35/39	0			0	37	14		4	18	36	41	11	28	80	34
30/34						4		0	4	31	31	4	15	50	30
25/29						1			1	27	11	1	4	16	25
20/24											4		1	5	21
15/19											0			0	18

Temperature Range	NOVEMBER Obsn Hour Gp 01 to 08	NOVEMBER 09 to 16	NOVEMBER 17 to 24	NOVEMBER Total Obsn	NOVEMBER MCWB	DECEMBER Obsn Hour Gp 01 to 08	DECEMBER 09 to 16	DECEMBER 17 to 24	DECEMBER Total Obsn	DECEMBER MCWB	JANUARY Obsn Hour Gp 01 to 08	JANUARY 09 to 16	JANUARY 17 to 24	JANUARY Total Obsn	JANUARY MCWB	FEBRUARY Obsn Hour Gp 01 to 08	FEBRUARY 09 to 16	FEBRUARY 17 to 24	FEBRUARY Total Obsn	FEBRUARY MCWB	MARCH Obsn Hour Gp 01 to 08	MARCH 09 to 16	MARCH 17 to 24	MARCH Total Obsn	MARCH MCWB	APRIL Obsn Hour Gp 01 to 08	APRIL 09 to 16	APRIL 17 to 24	APRIL Total Obsn	APRIL MCWB	ANNUAL TOTAL Obsn Hour Gp 01 to 08	ANNUAL TOTAL 09 to 16	ANNUAL TOTAL 17 to 24	ANNUAL TOTAL Total Obsn	ANNUAL TOTAL MCWB
95/99																																0		0	75
90/94																																8	0	8	72
85/89																															0	37	4	41	70
80/84																															0	110	18	128	67
75/79																											1	0	1	57	6	191	52	249	65
70/74																											2	0	2	55	30	253	126	409	62
65/69		0		0	56																						5	1	6	52	136	242	232	610	60
60/64	1	3	0	4	57																	0		0	50	0	14	3	17	49	275	236	290	801	57
55/59	5	11	9	25	54	0	1		1	55												1	0	1	45	1	24	9	34	46	296	204	268	768	52
50/54	12	27	14	53	49	1	2	1	4	48	0	1		1	47		0	0	0	47		7	1	8	[illegible]	[illegible]	[illegible]	[illegible]	[illegible]	[illegible]	[illegible]	[illegible]	[illegible]	[illegible]	[illegible]
45/49	23	38	25	86	44	3	8	5	16	44	1	1	2	4	45	1	1	1	3	44	1	20	6	27	40	14	48	38	100	41	241	185	223	649	43
40/44	26	48	34	108	38	7	18	11	36	39	2	6	2	10	39	2	8	3	13	38	6	37	21	64	37	42	53	56	151	37	219	204	212	635	38
35/39	42	48	49	139	34	20	26	23	69	34	10	21	15	46	34	6	26	14	46	34	26	59	49	134	33	68	34	64	166	34	264	228	257	749	34
30/34	58	41	56	155	29	24	38	32	94	29	24	38	31	93	30	23	35	33	91	30	57	61	70	188	29	67	14	39	120	30	298	231	277	806	30
25/29	35	18	34	87	25	36	42	34	112	25	26	32	34	92	25	25	41	39	105	25	49	31	47	127	24	30	3	8	41	25	213	168	200	581	25
20/24	25	4	14	43	20	38	42	42	122	20	28	42	32	102	20	27	37	35	99	20	46	20	29	95	20	10	0	1	11	19	178	145	154	477	20
15/19	9	1	4	14	16	30	30	37	97	15	29	38	33	100	15	29	30	33	92	15	30	7	13	50	15	2		0	2	15	129	106	120	355	15
10/14	4	0	1	5	11	33	24	32	89	11	31	30	37	98	10	29	20	23	72	11	16	3	7	26	11	1			1	11	114	77	100	291	11
5/9	0		0	0	7	27	11	16	54	6	32	19	25	76	6	27	13	20	60	6	11	1	4	16	6						97	44	65	206	6
0/4						13	5	8	26	1	24	11	16	51	1	21	6	12	39	1	6		1	7	1						64	22	37	123	1
-5/-1						9	2	5	16	-3	17	6	12	35	-3	16	4	6	26	-4	2			2	-3						44	12	23	79	-3
-10/-6						4	1	1	6	-8	11	4	5	20	-8	11	2	2	15	-8	0			0	-7						26	7	8	41	-8
-15/-11						1	0	0	1	-13	8	1	2	11	-13	5	0	1	6	-13											14	1	3	18	-13
-20/-16						0			0	-17	2	0	0	2	-18	2	0	0	2	-17											4	0	0	4	-18
-25/-21											1	0		1	-23	0	0		0	-23											1	0		1	-23
-30/-26											0			0	-27	0			0	-28											0			0	-27

BRUNSWICK NAS MAINE

LAT 43 54N LONG 69 56W ELEV 75 FT

MEAN FREQUENCY OF OCCURRENCE OF DRY BULB TEMPERATURE (DEGREES F) WITH MEAN COINCIDENT WET BULB TEMPERATURE (DEGREES F) FOR EACH DRY BULB TEMPERATURE RANGE

Temperature Range	MAY Obsn Hour Gp 01 to 08	MAY 09 to 16	MAY 17 to 24	MAY Total Obsn	MAY MCWB	JUNE Obsn Hour Gp 01 to 08	JUNE 09 to 16	JUNE 17 to 24	JUNE Total Obsn	JUNE MCWB	JULY Obsn Hour Gp 01 to 08	JULY 09 to 16	JULY 17 to 24	JULY Total Obsn	JULY MCWB
90/94							2	0	2	70		2	0	2	75
85/89		1	0	1	70		4	1	5	69		10	1	11	71
80/84		3	0	3	66	0	16	2	18	67	1	29	5	35	68
75/79	0	6	1	7	62	2	35	8	45	64	3	63	15	81	65
70/74	1	17	4	22	58	7	52	21	80	62	17	73	46	136	63
65/69	2	31	9	42	56	20	48	36	104	59	56	45	79	180	62
60/64	8	49	22	79	53	52	45	66	163	57	102	22	79	203	59
55/59	28	59	41	128	50	73	27	61	161	53	52	4	20	76	55
50/54	59	48	74	181	47	60	11	37	108	50	16		3	19	49
45/49	69	23	60	152	43	23	1	8	32	45	2		0	2	44
40/44	50	8	29	87	40	4		0	4	41	0			0	42
35/39	25	2	7	34	35										
30/34	7	0	0	7	31										
25/29	0			0	26										
20/24															
15/19															

Temperature Range	AUGUST Obsn Hour Gp 01 to 08	AUGUST 09 to 16	AUGUST 17 to 24	AUGUST Total Obsn	AUGUST MCWB	SEPTEMBER Obsn Hour Gp 01 to 08	SEPTEMBER 09 to 16	SEPTEMBER 17 to 24	SEPTEMBER Total Obsn	SEPTEMBER MCWB	OCTOBER Obsn Hour Gp 01 to 08	OCTOBER 09 to 16	OCTOBER 17 to 24	OCTOBER Total Obsn	OCTOBER MCWB
90/94		0		0	69		0		0	70					
85/89		6	0	6	72		2	0	2	72					
80/84		24	3	27	69		6	1	7	68		0		0	61
75/79	1	64	11	76	66	0	19	2	21	66		3		3	63
70/74	11	72	41	124	64	3	38	11	52	63		9	0	9	60
65/69	52	54	80	186	62	16	52	29	97	60	0	16	2	18	58
60/64	90	21	75	186	59	48	59	59	166	57	6	38	17	61	56
55/59	54	7	29	90	54	47	40	62	149	53	26	55	42	123	52
50/54	31	1	9	41	49	52	18	44	114	49	46	67	59	172	48
45/49	9		1	10	45	37	4	21	62	44	52	34	55	141	43
40/44	1		0	1	40	24	1	9	34	40	46	18	39	103	39
35/39	0			0	37	12		2	14	36	41	6	22	69	34
30/34						1		0	1	31	22	2	10	34	30
25/29						0			0	27	8		1	9	26
20/24											2		0	2	22
15/19											0			0	19

NOVEMBER

Temperature Range	Obsn Hour Gp 01 to 08	Obsn Hour Gp 09 to 16	Obsn Hour Gp 17 to 24	Total Obsn	MCWB
90/94					
85/89					
80/84					
75/79					
70/74					
65/69		0		0	55
60/64	0	2	1	3	54
55/59	5	14	9	28	54
50/54	18	34	20	72	49
45/49	28	49	31	108	44
40/44	31	54	41	126	39
35/39	47	47	55	149	34
30/34	52	29	49	130	30
25/29	34	9	25	68	25
20/24	19	2	7	28	21
15/19	6	1	1	8	16
10/14	2		1	3	12
5/9					
0/4					
-5/-1					
-10/-6					
-15/-11					
-20/-16					
-25/-21					

DECEMBER

Temperature Range	Obsn Hour Gp 01 to 08	Obsn Hour Gp 09 to 16	Obsn Hour Gp 17 to 24	Total Obsn	MCWB
90/94					
85/89					
80/84					
75/79					
70/74					
65/69					
60/64		0		0	48
55/59	0	1		1	47
50/54	1	3	1	5	49
45/49	4	8	6	18	44
40/44	11	29	14	54	39
35/39	20	33	30	83	34
30/34	34	42	40	116	29
25/29	47	48	44	139	25
20/24	33	36	41	110	20
15/19	32	24	32	88	16
10/14	30	14	25	69	11
5/9	18	7	10	35	7
0/4	12	2	4	18	2
-5/-1	5	0	3	8	-3
-10/-6	2	0	0	2	-8
-15/-11	0			0	-13
-20/-16					
-25/-21					

JANUARY

Temperature Range	Obsn Hour Gp 01 to 08	Obsn Hour Gp 09 to 16	Obsn Hour Gp 17 to 24	Total Obsn	MCWB
90/94					
85/89					
80/84					
75/79					
70/74					
65/69					
60/64					
55/59					
50/54		0		0	46
45/49	1	3	2	6	44
40/44	3	16	5	24	38
35/39	17	31	25	73	34
30/34	27	43	38	108	30
25/29	35	45	42	122	24
20/24	31	41	37	109	20
15/19	33	29	36	98	15
10/14	34	20	26	80	11
5/9	25	11	20	56	6
0/4	19	5	10	34	1
-5/-1	13	3	4	20	-4
-10/-6	6	1	2	9	-8
-15/-11	3	0	0	3	-13
-20/-16	1			1	-17
-25/-21	0			0	-22

FEBRUARY

Temperature Range	Obsn Hour Gp 01 to 08	Obsn Hour Gp 09 to 16	Obsn Hour Gp 17 to 24	Total Obsn	MCWB
90/94					
85/89					
80/84					
75/79					
70/74					
65/69					
60/64					
55/59		0		0	51
50/54		0	0	0	46
45/49	1	2	1	4	41
40/44	3	15	6	24	38
35/39	11	35	22	68	33
30/34	24	46	41	111	29
25/29	32	40	43	115	24
20/24	37	38	38	113	20
15/19	31	21	26	78	15
10/14	26	14	22	62	11
5/9	21	8	12	41	6
0/4	17	4	8	29	1
-5/-1	15	2	3	20	-4
-10/-6	5	0	1	6	-8
-15/-11	2		0	2	-13
-20/-16	0			0	-17
-25/-21					

MARCH

Temperature Range	Obsn Hour Gp 01 to 08	Obsn Hour Gp 09 to 16	Obsn Hour Gp 17 to 24	Total Obsn	MCWB
90/94					
85/89					
80/84					
75/79					
70/74					
65/69					
60/64		0		0	50
55/59		1	0	1	46
50/54		7	1	8	43
45/49	1	21	6	28	40
40/44	9	54	27	90	37
35/39	41	72	66	179	33
30/34	62	46	69	177	29
25/29	56	26	43	125	24
20/24	36	13	19	68	20
15/19	21	6	10	37	15
10/14	13	1	5	19	10
5/9	6	0	1	7	6
0/4	3		0	3	2
-5/-1	1			1	-3
-10/-6					
-15/-11					
-20/-16					
-25/-21					

APRIL

Temperature Range	Obsn Hour Gp 01 to 08	Obsn Hour Gp 09 to 16	Obsn Hour Gp 17 to 24	Total Obsn	MCWB
90/94					
85/89					
80/84		0		0	64
75/79		0		0	65
70/74		1		1	56
65/69		3	0	3	53
60/64	0	13	2	15	50
55/59	1	30	7	38	46
50/54	7	45	22	74	44
45/49	24	61	47	132	41
40/44	63	52	75	190	38
35/39	73	27	61	161	34
30/34	48	7	22	77	30
25/29	17	1	3	21	25
20/24	5		1	6	20
15/19	1		0	1	15
10/14	0			0	13
5/9					
0/4					
-5/-1					
-10/-6					
-15/-11					
-20/-16					
-25/-21					

ANNUAL TOTAL

Temperature Range	Obsn Hour Gp 01 to 08	Obsn Hour Gp 09 to 16	Obsn Hour Gp 17 to 24	Total Obsn	MCWB
90/94		4	0	4	72
85/89		23	2	25	71
80/84	1	78	11	90	68
75/79	6	190	37	233	65
70/74	39	262	123	424	63
65/69	146	249	235	630	61
60/64	306	249	321	876	57
55/59	286	238	271	795	53
50/54	290	234	270	794	48
45/49	251	206	238	695	43
40/44	245	247	245	737	38
35/39	287	253	290	830	34
30/34	277	215	269	761	29
25/29	229	169	201	599	25
20/24	163	130	143	436	20
15/19	124	81	105	310	15
10/14	105	49	79	233	11
5/9	70	26	43	139	6
0/4	51	11	22	84	1
-5/-1	34	5	10	49	-3
-10/-6	13	1	3	17	-8
-15/-11	5	0	0	5	-13
-20/-16	1			1	-17
-25/-21	0			0	-22

LORING AFB MAINE

LAT 46 57N   LONG 67 53W   ELEV 746 FT

MEAN FREQUENCY OF OCCURRENCE OF DRY BULB TEMPERATURE (DEGREES F) WITH MEAN COINCIDENT WET BULB TEMPERATURE (DEGREES F) FOR EACH DRY BULB TEMPERATURE RANGE

Temperature Range	MAY Obsn Hour Gp 01 to 08	MAY 09 to 16	MAY 17 to 24	MAY Total Obsn	MAY MCWB	JUNE Obsn Hour Gp 01 to 08	JUNE 09 to 16	JUNE 17 to 24	JUNE Total Obsn	JUNE MCWB	JULY Obsn Hour Gp 01 to 08	JULY 09 to 16	JULY 17 to 24	JULY Total Obsn	JULY MCWB
90/94							0		0	71		1	0	1	71
85/89		1	0	1	66		6	1	7	66		9	1	10	70
80/84		3	1	4	63		13	5	18	65		21	6	27	68
75/79		9	3	12	60	1	21	9	31	63	1	40	17	58	65
70/74	1	14	7	22	57	3	38	22	63	60	8	65	39	112	63
65/69	2	23	13	38	54	15	51	41	107	58	37	58	58	153	61
60/64	6	34	25	65	52	38	49	53	140	56	67	36	67	170	58
55/59	17	44	33	94	49	56	36	47	139	52	74	16	42	132	54
50/54	29	46	45	120	45	58	17	36	111	48	43	2	16	61	50
45/49	54	40	49	143	42	41	7	21	69	44	15		2	17	45
40/44	62	23	42	127	38	22	1	5	28	40	2		0	2	40
35/39	46	10	22	78	34	5	0	1	6	35	0			0	37
30/34	27	2	8	37	30	0		0	0	32					
25/29	5	0	0	5	25										
20/24	1	0	0	1	20										
15/19															

Temperature Range	AUGUST Obsn Hour Gp 01 to 08	AUGUST 09 to 16	AUGUST 17 to 24	AUGUST Total Obsn	AUGUST MCWB	SEPTEMBER Obsn Hour Gp 01 to 08	SEPTEMBER 09 to 16	SEPTEMBER 17 to 24	SEPTEMBER Total Obsn	SEPTEMBER MCWB	OCTOBER Obsn Hour Gp 01 to 08	OCTOBER 09 to 16	OCTOBER 17 to 24	OCTOBER Total Obsn	OCTOBER MCWB
90/94		0		0	68										
85/89		2	0	2	70										
80/84		8	2	10	68		4	0	4	68					
75/79	0	33	9	42	65		9	2	11	65		1		1	64
70/74	3	51	24	78	63	1	22	7	30	62		4	0	4	61
65/69	22	64	52	138	61	9	37	19	65	60		9	2	11	58
60/64	57	58	65	180	58	20	46	38	104	57	2	17	10	29	56
55/59	65	24	53	142	54	34	54	50	138	52	10	28	17	55	52
50/54	53	5	32	90	49	50	40	47	137	48	26	42	32	100	48
45/49	36	2	10	48	45	52	23	42	117	44	37	54	48	139	43
40/44	10	0	1	11	41	37	4	23	64	40	46	45	48	139	39
35/39	1		0	1	37	23	0	10	33	35	48	28	43	119	34
30/34						13		2	15	31	49	18	35	102	30
25/29						1		0	1	27	22	3	11	36	26
20/24											8	0	2	10	22
15/19											1			1	17

LORING AFB MAINE

Temperature Range	NOVEMBER Obsn Hour Gp 01 to 08	09 to 16	17 to 24	Total Obsn	MCWB	DECEMBER Obsn Hour Gp 01 to 08	09 to 16	17 to 24	Total Obsn	MCWB	JANUARY Obsn Hour Gp 01 to 08	09 to 16	17 to 24	Total Obsn	MCWB
90/94															
85/89															
80/84															
75/79															
70/74															
65/69															
60/64	0	1	0	1	57										
55/59	3	5	4	12	54										
50/54	5	11	8	24	49	1	1	1	3	51					
45/49	14	15	14	43	45	2	1	2	5	46	0		0	0	45
40/44	17	31	17	65	39	4	4	3	11	40	1	1	1	3	40
35/39	27	44	33	104	34	10	15	13	38	35	3	8	4	15	34
30/34	51	60	67	178	30	21	28	23	72	30	11	18	15	44	30
25/29	52	39	44	135	25	25	31	27	83	26	19	26	24	69	25
20/24	33	24	28	85	21	29	39	37	105	21	27	34	28	89	21
15/19	21	7	18	46	16	33	42	33	108	16	25	36	32	93	16
10/14	12	3	6	21	12	32	33	36	101	11	26	39	35	100	11
5/9	5	1	1	7	7	28	24	29	81	6	32	31	37	100	6
0/4	1		0	1	2	26	16	23	65	1	34	23	29	86	1
-5/-1	0			0	-2	18	9	13	40	-3	28	16	19	63	-4
-10/-6						13	3	6	22	-8	20	10	16	46	-8
-15/-11						6	1	1	8	-13	12	4	6	22	-13
-20/-16						0	0	0	0	-17	7	2	2	11	-18
-25/-21						0			0	-25	1	0	0	1	-22
-30/-26											0			0	-27

Temperature Range	FEBRUARY Obsn Hour Gp 01 to 08	09 to 16	17 to 24	Total Obsn	MCWB	MARCH Obsn Hour Gp 01 to 08	09 to 16	17 to 24	Total Obsn	MCWB
90/94										
85/89										
80/84										
75/79										
70/74							0		0	54
65/69							0	0	0	52
60/64							0	0	0	50
55/59							0	0	0	45
50/54							1	1	2	43
45/49	0	0	1	1	44	0	6	2	8	39
40/44	1	3	1	5	39	1	23	9	33	36
35/39	4	9	7	20	34	16	44	35	95	33
30/34	8	20	12	40	29	39	58	49	146	29
25/29	19	32	29	80	25	43	44	54	141	25
20/24	27	35	34	96	20	39	31	39	109	20
15/19	26	39	33	98	16	37	20	29	86	15
10/14	28	30	36	94	11	33	14	17	64	11
5/9	30	22	26	78	6	18	6	8	32	6
0/4	25	15	20	60	1	12	2	5	19	1
-5/-1	22	9	14	45	-4	7	0	1	8	-4
-10/-6	18	5	8	31	-8	2			2	-8
-15/-11	10	3	3	16	-13	0			0	-14
-20/-16	6	1	1	8	-18	0			0	-16
-25/-21	2	0	0	2	-22					
-30/-26	0			0	-27					

Temperature Range	APRIL Obsn Hour Gp 01 to 08	09 to 16	17 to 24	Total Obsn	MCWB	ANNUAL TOTAL Obsn Hour Gp 01 to 08	09 to 16	17 to 24	Total Obsn	MCWB
90/94							1	0	1	71
85/89							18	2	20	68
80/84							49	14	63	67
75/79		0		0	55	2	113	40	155	64
70/74		0	0	0	54	16	194	99	309	62
65/69		2	0	2	53	85	244	185	514	59
60/64		4	1	5	49	190	245	259	694	56
55/59	0	12	4	16	46	259	219	250	728	52
50/54	2	24	11	37	43	267	189	229	685	48
45/49	7	40	26	73	40	258	188	217	663	43
40/44	19	51	45	115	37	222	186	195	603	38
35/39	54	56	63	173	33	237	214	231	682	34
30/34	78	36	58	172	30	297	240	269	806	30
25/29	46	9	22	77	25	232	184	211	627	25
20/24	19	3	7	29	19	183	166	175	524	20
15/19	9	2	3	14	15	152	146	148	446	16
10/14	3	0	0	3	10	134	119	130	383	11
5/9	1		0	1	6	114	84	101	299	6
0/4	0			0	2	98	56	77	231	1
-5/-1						75	34	47	156	-4
-10/-6						53	18	30	101	-8
-15/-11						28	8	10	46	-13
-20/-16						13	3	3	19	-18
-25/-21						3	0	0	3	-22
-30/-26						0			0	-27

ANDREWS AFB MARYLAND

LAT 38 49N LONG 76 52W ELEV 279 FT

MEAN FREQUENCY OF OCCURRENCE OF DRY BULB TEMPERATURE (DEGREES F) WITH MEAN COINCIDENT WET BULB TEMPERATURE (DEGREES F) FOR EACH DRY BULB TEMPERATURE RANGE

Temperature Range	MAY Obsn Hour Gp 01 to 08	MAY 09 to 16	MAY 17 to 24	MAY Total Obsn	MAY MCWB	JUNE Obsn Hour Gp 01 to 08	JUNE 09 to 16	JUNE 17 to 24	JUNE Total Obsn	JUNE MCWB	JULY Obsn Hour Gp 01 to 08	JULY 09 to 16	JULY 17 to 24	JULY Total Obsn	JULY MCWB
100/104							0		0	80		0		0	76
95/99		0	0	0	72		2	0	2	78		2	1	3	76
90/94		3	0	3	70		14	2	16	74		22	4	26	75
85/89		13	3	16	69	0	40	13	53	72	0	58	18	76	73
80/84	0	25	11	36	66	3	52	29	84	70	5	75	41	121	70
75/79	2	37	21	60	64	15	54	48	117	67	35	55	67	157	69
70/74	13	45	37	95	62	56	42	62	160	66	102	28	78	208	68
65/69	35	44	51	130	60	73	22	49	144	63	73	8	33	114	63
60/64	53	40	48	141	56	51	11	24	86	58	28	1	5	34	59
55/59	54	24	41	119	52	29	3	10	42	54	5	0	0	5	54
50/54	49	13	24	86	48	11	0	2	13	50					
45/49	29	3	10	42	44	1		0	1	45					
40/44	9	1	2	12	39										
35/39	1	0	0	1	34										
30/34	0			0	31										
25/29															

Temperature Range	AUGUST Obsn Hour Gp 01 to 08	AUGUST 09 to 16	AUGUST 17 to 24	AUGUST Total Obsn	AUGUST MCWB	SEPTEMBER Obsn Hour Gp 01 to 08	SEPTEMBER 09 to 16	SEPTEMBER 17 to 24	SEPTEMBER Total Obsn	SEPTEMBER MCWB	OCTOBER Obsn Hour Gp 01 to 08	OCTOBER 09 to 16	OCTOBER 17 to 24	OCTOBER Total Obsn	OCTOBER MCWB
100/104															
95/99		1	0	1	74		0		0	77					
90/94		16	2	18	75		8	0	8	74		0		0	75
85/89		50	14	64	73		22	5	27	73		1	0	1	72
80/84	2	71	35	108	71	0	38	15	53	71		8	1	9	67
75/79	26	63	65	154	69	9	50	34	93	68		18	3	21	65
70/74	97	34	78	209	67	43	49	49	141	66	4	37	15	56	63
65/69	71	12	37	120	63	55	39	53	147	62	14	45	32	91	60
60/64	37	1	13	51	59	52	20	42	114	57	34	50	48	132	56
55/59	11	0	3	14	54	44	10	26	80	53	46	42	48	136	52
50/54	3		0	3	50	24	2	11	37	49	50	32	47	129	47
45/49	0			0	47	12	0	3	15	45	44	11	31	86	43
40/44						2		1	3	40	32	3	16	51	38
35/39						0		0	0	36	18	1	5	24	35
30/34											7		1	8	30
25/29											0			0	26

ANDREWS AFB MARYLAND

Temperature Range	NOVEMBER Obsn Hour Gp 01 to 08	NOVEMBER 09 to 16	NOVEMBER 17 to 24	NOVEMBER Total Obsn	NOVEMBER M C W B	DECEMBER Obsn Hour Gp 01 to 08	DECEMBER 09 to 16	DECEMBER 17 to 24	DECEMBER Total Obsn	DECEMBER M C W B	JANUARY Obsn Hour Gp 01 to 08	JANUARY 09 to 16	JANUARY 17 to 24	JANUARY Total Obsn	JANUARY M C W B
100/104															
95/99															
90/94															
85/89															
80/84		1		1	69										
75/79		2	0	2	67										
70/74	1	6	2	9	61		1	0	1	59		1	0	1	59
65/69	4	14	5	23	58	0	4	1	5	58	0	1	1	2	58
60/64	8	31	17	56	55	3	7	5	15	55	1	3	1	5	55
55/59	19	42	28	89	51	6	13	7	26	50	3	5	4	12	51
50/54	31	47	41	119	46	7	20	13	40	46	4	13	6	23	45
45/49	41	41	45	127	42	16	30	27	73	42	7	24	15	46	41
40/44	47	34	46	127	37	30	44	36	110	37	22	41	32	95	37
35/39	43	16	34	93	33	45	50	50	145	33	36	46	46	128	33
30/34	33	6	15	54	29	55	41	51	147	28	55	46	55	156	29
25/29	10	1	4	15	25	37	23	32	92	24	39	32	39	110	24
20/24	4	0	2	6	20	29	11	19	59	19	34	21	23	78	19
15/19	0			0	15	13	3	6	22	15	25	10	14	49	15
10/14						6	1	1	8	10	15	5	8	28	10
5/9						1		0	1	7	6	1	2	9	6
0/4											1		0	1	2
-5/-1											0			0	-2

Temperature Range	FEBRUARY Obsn Hour Gp 01 to 08	FEBRUARY 09 to 16	FEBRUARY 17 to 24	FEBRUARY Total Obsn	FEBRUARY M C W B	MARCH Obsn Hour Gp 01 to 08	MARCH 09 to 16	MARCH 17 to 24	MARCH Total Obsn	MARCH M C W B	APRIL Obsn Hour Gp 01 to 08	APRIL 09 to 16	APRIL 17 to 24	APRIL Total Obsn	APRIL M C W B	ANNUAL TOTAL Obsn Hour Gp 01 to 08	ANNUAL TOTAL 09 to 16	ANNUAL TOTAL 17 to 24	ANNUAL TOTAL Total Obsn	ANNUAL TOTAL M C W B
100/104																	0		0	77
95/99																	5	1	6	76
90/94												1	0	1	71		64	8	72	74
85/89												5	1	6	66	0	189	54	243	72
80/84							1	0	1	61		11	4	15	63	10	282	136	428	70
75/79							4	1	5	60	1	13	8	22	61	88	296	247	631	68
70/74		0	0	0	58		8	3	11	57	2	19	13	34	58	318	270	337	925	66
65/69		2	1	3	57	1	9	5	15	55	11	29	24	64	56	337	229	292	858	61
60/64	1	3	2	6	55	4	15	10	29	52	20	36	30	86	53	292	218	245	755	56
55/59	2	10	6	18	50	7	19	17	43	48	29	39	36	104	49	255	207	226	688	51
50/54	5	14	9	28	46	12	30	24	66	44	37	42	48	127	45	233	213	225	671	46
45/49	10	21	17	48	41	24	43	38	105	41	52	28	42	122	42	236	201	228	665	42
40/44	18	40	34	92	37	46	51	55	152	37	51	15	26	92	38	257	229	248	734	37
35/39	39	46	49	134	33	60	39	50	149	33	26	2	6	34	34	268	200	240	708	33
30/34	50	43	49	142	29	56	19	30	105	29	8	0	1	9	30	264	155	202	621	29
25/29	48	23	32	103	24	25	7	9	41	24	1		0	1	25	160	86	116	362	24
20/24	24	13	15	52	19	10	3	4	17	20						101	48	63	212	19
15/19	13	6	7	26	14	4	0	0	4	16						55	19	27	101	15
10/14	10	2	3	15	10	0			0	13						31	8	12	51	10
5/9	3	0	0	3	7											10	1	2	13	6
0/4	0	0		0	2											1	0	0	1	2
-5/-1																0			0	-2

PATUXENT RIVER NAS MARYLAND

LAT 38 17N LONG 76 26W ELEV 38 FT

MEAN FREQUENCY OF OCCURRENCE OF DRY BULB TEMPERATURE (DEGREES F) WITH MEAN COINCIDENT WET BULB TEMPERATURE (DEGREES F) FOR EACH DRY BULB TEMPERATURE RANGE

Temperature Range	MAY Obsn Hour Gp 01 to 08	MAY 09 to 16	MAY 17 to 24	MAY Total Obsn	MAY MCWB	JUNE Obsn Hour Gp 01 to 08	JUNE 09 to 16	JUNE 17 to 24	JUNE Total Obsn	JUNE MCWB	JULY Obsn Hour Gp 01 to 08	JULY 09 to 16	JULY 17 to 24	JULY Total Obsn	JULY MCWB
100/104							0		0	78					
95/99		0		0	74		1	0	1	79		3	0	3	75
90/94		3	1	4	72		14	3	17	75		18	4	22	76
85/89		8	2	10	70	0	32	12	44	74	1	55	18	74	74
80/84	0	22	8	30	68	5	53	29	87	72	16	86	56	158	72
75/79	4	29	17	50	66	31	64	55	150	69	80	60	85	225	70
70/74	21	52	38	111	64	76	44	66	186	66	101	21	67	189	68
65/69	44	52	52	148	60	61	21	45	127	62	41	4	17	62	63
60/64	64	46	61	171	56	50	10	26	86	58	8	1	1	10	58
55/59	59	24	42	125	52	14	2	6	22	54	0		0	0	56
50/54	35	9	21	65	48	2		0	2	49					
45/49	18	1	6	25	44	0		0	0	45					
40/44	2	0	0	2	39										
35/39	0			0	32										
30/34															

Temperature Range	AUGUST Obsn Hour Gp 01 to 08	AUGUST 09 to 16	AUGUST 17 to 24	AUGUST Total Obsn	AUGUST MCWB	SEPTEMBER Obsn Hour Gp 01 to 08	SEPTEMBER 09 to 16	SEPTEMBER 17 to 24	SEPTEMBER Total Obsn	SEPTEMBER MCWB	OCTOBER Obsn Hour Gp 01 to 08	OCTOBER 09 to 16	OCTOBER 17 to 24	OCTOBER Total Obsn	OCTOBER MCWB
100/104															
95/99		2	0	2	77										
90/94		17	2	19	76		4	0	4	74		0		0	69
85/89	1	53	15	69	74	0	21	3	24	74		1		1	72
80/84	11	73	46	130	72	2	44	18	64	72		6	1	7	69
75/79	68	69	84	221	70	27	53	44	124	69	0	13	4	17	67
70/74	102	28	70	200	68	56	53	59	168	66	7	39	14	60	64
65/69	49	6	26	81	63	52	34	48	134	62	20	52	37	109	61
60/64	15	1	4	20	59	57	23	45	125	57	58	64	64	186	57
55/59	2	0	0	2	52	38	8	20	66	53	59	43	58	160	52
50/54	0			0	45	8	0	3	11	48	52	23	42	117	47
45/49						1		0	1	45	29	5	19	53	42
40/44											15	2	7	24	38
35/39											5	0	2	7	34
30/34											1		0	1	28

PATUXENT RIVER NAS MARYLAND

Temperature Range	NOVEMBER Obsn Hour Gp 01 to 08	NOVEMBER Obsn Hour Gp 09 to 16	NOVEMBER Obsn Hour Gp 17 to 24	NOVEMBER Total Obsn	NOVEMBER MCWB	DECEMBER Obsn Hour Gp 01 to 08	DECEMBER Obsn Hour Gp 09 to 16	DECEMBER Obsn Hour Gp 17 to 24	DECEMBER Total Obsn	DECEMBER MCWB	JANUARY Obsn Hour Gp 01 to 08	JANUARY Obsn Hour Gp 09 to 16	JANUARY Obsn Hour Gp 17 to 24	JANUARY Total Obsn	JANUARY MCWB	FEBRUARY Obsn Hour Gp 01 to 08	FEBRUARY Obsn Hour Gp 09 to 16	FEBRUARY Obsn Hour Gp 17 to 24	FEBRUARY Total Obsn	FEBRUARY MCWB	MARCH Obsn Hour Gp 01 to 08	MARCH Obsn Hour Gp 09 to 16	MARCH Obsn Hour Gp 17 to 24	MARCH Total Obsn	MARCH MCWB	APRIL Obsn Hour Gp 01 to 08	APRIL Obsn Hour Gp 09 to 16	APRIL Obsn Hour Gp 17 to 24	APRIL Total Obsn	APRIL MCWB	ANNUAL TOTAL Obsn Hour Gp 01 to 08	ANNUAL TOTAL Obsn Hour Gp 09 to 16	ANNUAL TOTAL Obsn Hour Gp 17 to 24	ANNUAL TOTAL Total Obsn	ANNUAL TOTAL MCWB
100/104																																0		0	78
95/99																																6	0	6	77
90/94																											1	0	1	64		57	10	67	75
85/89																											2	0	2	64	2	172	50	224	74
80/84		0		0	63																	0	0	0	65		9	2	11	64	34	293	160	487	72
75/79		1	0	1	64																	3	0	3	59	0	9	5	14	62	210	301	294	805	69
70/74	0	5	1	6	61		1		1	62		0		0	58		0		0	60	0	5	1	6	57	4	17	11	32	61	367	265	327	959	66
65/69	3	14	6	23	60		3	1	4	60	0	2	0	2	59	0	2	1	3	59	1	7	3	11	56	12	21	16	49	58	283	218	252	753	61
60/64	11	38	18	67	56	3	8	4	15	55	1	4	2	7	55	1	6	2	9	53	5	15	8	28	53	24	42	29	95	55	297	258	264	819	56
55/59	32	50	39	121	52	6	12	7	25	52	3	7	5	15	50	3	8	5	16	50	7	24	14	45	49	34	57	49	140	51	257	235	245	737	52
50/54	41	50	47	138	47	12	26	17	55	47	6	15	9	30	46	5	16	8	29	46	17	40	27	84	45	50	47	59	156	47	228	226	233	687	47
45/49	45	41	49	135	42	21	41	32	94	43	12	26	14	52	42	10	27	18	55	42	30	51	44	125	42	56	27	44	127	43	222	219	226	667	42
40/44	50	27	46	123	38	41	54	50	145	38	25	49	36	110	38	27	51	40	118	38	61	53	71	185	38	41	8	20	69	38	262	244	270	776	38
35/39	34	9	21	64	33	52	44	46	142	33	45	53	55	153	34	51	50	57	158	34	59	31	46	136	34	14	1	3	18	34	260	188	230	678	34
30/34	15	4	9	28	29	48	35	49	132	29	57	43	58	158	29	55	37	53	145	29	43	12	21	76	29	3	0	0	3	29	222	131	190	543	29
25/29	6	1	3	10	24	37	17	28	82	25	42	24	34	100	24	39	17	24	80	24	15	6	9	30	24	0			0	26	139	65	98	302	24
20/24	2	0	1	3	20	20	6	14	40	20	31	15	21	67	20	16	7	11	34	19	9	1	2	12	20						78	29	49	156	20
15/19						7	1	2	10	15	17	7	9	33	15	12	2	5	19	15	1			1	16						37	10	16	63	15
10/14						1	0	0	1	12	7	2	2	11	11	4	1	0	5	11											12	3	2	17	11
5/9											2	0	1	3	7	0	0		0	6											2	0	1	3	7
0/4													0	0	2																		0	0	2
-5/-1													0	0	-2																		0	0	-2

HANSCOM AFB/BEDFORD MASSACHUSETTS

LAT 42 28N LONG 71 17W ELEV 133 FT

MEAN FREQUENCY OF OCCURRENCE OF DRY BULB TEMPERATURE (DEGREES F) WITH MEAN COINCIDENT WET BULB TEMPERATURE (DEGREES F) FOR EACH DRY BULB TEMPERATURE RANGE

Temperature Range	MAY Obsn Hour Gp 01 to 08	MAY 09 to 16	MAY 17 to 24	MAY Total Obsn	MAY MCWB	JUNE Obsn Hour Gp 01 to 08	JUNE 09 to 16	JUNE 17 to 24	JUNE Total Obsn	JUNE MCWB	JULY Obsn Hour Gp 01 to 08	JULY 09 to 16	JULY 17 to 24	JULY Total Obsn	JULY MCWB
95/99							0	0	0	74		2	0	2	74
90/94		1	0	1	71		6	1	7	73		10	2	12	74
85/89		5	1	6	68		20	5	25	71		31	6	37	72
80/84		10	3	13	65	1	40	14	55	68	2	57	21	80	69
75/79	1	21	7	29	62	4	44	25	73	65	11	69	43	123	67
70/74	3	32	15	50	59	19	52	40	111	63	44	48	65	157	66
65/69	12	46	28	86	56	46	36	51	133	61	71	22	60	153	63
60/64	21	50	37	108	53	50	19	42	111	57	62	8	35	105	59
55/59	37	40	48	125	50	59	17	37	113	54	37	1	13	51	55
50/54	55	26	51	132	47	36	4	20	60	50	15		2	17	50
45/49	57	10	37	104	43	18		5	23	45	4		0	4	46
40/44	39	6	18	63	40	6		0	6	41	1			1	42
35/39	17	0	3	20	35	1			1	37					
30/34	5		0	5	31										
25/29	1			1	28										
20/24															
15/19															

Temperature Range	AUGUST Obsn Hour Gp 01 to 08	AUGUST 09 to 16	AUGUST 17 to 24	AUGUST Total Obsn	AUGUST MCWB	SEPTEMBER Obsn Hour Gp 01 to 08	SEPTEMBER 09 to 16	SEPTEMBER 17 to 24	SEPTEMBER Total Obsn	SEPTEMBER MCWB	OCTOBER Obsn Hour Gp 01 to 08	OCTOBER 09 to 16	OCTOBER 17 to 24	OCTOBER Total Obsn	OCTOBER MCWB
95/99		1		1	74		0		0	73					
90/94		7	1	8	74		2		2	75					
85/89		24	4	28	72		8	1	9	74		0		0	63
80/84	0	57	17	74	69	0	22	5	27	70		3	0	3	65
75/79	9	61	39	109	67	2	37	13	52	67		13	1	14	64
70/74	35	52	56	143	65	18	48	30	96	64	0	17	5	22	61
65/69	62	30	59	151	62	26	42	38	106	61	3	32	15	50	59
60/64	64	12	44	120	59	40	43	46	129	57	17	43	27	87	56
55/59	41	4	19	64	55	47	27	46	120	54	29	54	42	125	52
50/54	21	0	8	29	50	41	10	35	86	50	43	45	45	133	48
45/49	13		2	15	46	33	2	16	51	45	40	24	48	112	44
40/44	3		0	3	41	19	0	8	27	41	41	13	33	87	39
35/39	0		0	0	37	11		2	13	36	38	4	20	62	35
30/34	0			0	33	4		0	4	31	25	1	10	36	31
25/29						0			0	28	10	0	2	12	26
20/24											2		0	2	22
15/19											0			0	18

HANSCOM AFB/BEDFORD MASSACHUSETTS

Temperature Range	NOVEMBER Obsn Hour Gp 01 to 08	NOVEMBER 09 to 16	NOVEMBER 17 to 24	NOVEMBER Total Obsn	NOVEMBER MCWB	DECEMBER Obsn Hour Gp 01 to 08	DECEMBER 09 to 16	DECEMBER 17 to 24	DECEMBER Total Obsn	DECEMBER MCWB	JANUARY Obsn Hour Gp 01 to 08	JANUARY 09 to 16	JANUARY 17 to 24	JANUARY Total Obsn	JANUARY MCWB
95/99															
90/94															
85/89															
80/84															
75/79		0		0	65										
70/74		2	0	2	63										
65/69	0	5	3	8	61		0		0	61					
60/64	4	11	6	21	57	1	3	1	5	56	0	0		0	56
55/59	9	24	12	45	52	2	5	2	9	53	0	2	0	2	51
50/54	20	43	25	88	48	3	8	4	15	48	1	2	1	4	48
45/49	30	44	35	109	43	7	15	9	31	42	2	7	2	11	43
40/44	34	48	42	124	38	14	31	22	67	38	7	20	10	37	38
35/39	42	36	50	128	34	24	36	30	90	33	17	41	29	87	33
30/34	42	21	40	103	29	42	51	49	142	29	39	44	47	130	30
25/29	32	4	20	56	25	43	42	46	131	25	30	45	40	115	24
20/24	19	1	7	27	21	35	30	35	100	20	34	31	40	105	20
15/19	6	0	1	7	17	27	15	27	69	15	32	28	34	94	15
10/14	1		0	1	11	22	7	14	43	11	33	16	22	71	11
5/9						17	3	6	26	6	25	8	15	48	6
0/4						7	1	2	10	2	14	3	5	22	1
-5/-1						2	0	1	3	-4	6	1	2	9	-3
-10/-6						1	0	0	1	-7	4	0	1	5	-8
-15/-11						0			0	-13	2	0	0	2	-13
-20/-16											1			1	-18

Temperature Range	FEBRUARY Obsn Hour Gp 01 to 08	FEBRUARY 09 to 16	FEBRUARY 17 to 24	FEBRUARY Total Obsn	FEBRUARY MCWB	MARCH Obsn Hour Gp 01 to 08	MARCH 09 to 16	MARCH 17 to 24	MARCH Total Obsn	MARCH MCWB	APRIL Obsn Hour Gp 01 to 08	APRIL 09 to 16	APRIL 17 to 24	APRIL Total Obsn	APRIL MCWB	ANNUAL TOTAL Obsn Hour Gp 01 to 08	ANNUAL TOTAL 09 to 16	ANNUAL TOTAL 17 to 24	ANNUAL TOTAL Total Obsn	ANNUAL TOTAL MCWB
95/99																	3	0	3	74
90/94																	26	4	30	74
85/89												1	0	1	63		89	17	106	71
80/84												1	0	1	61	3	190	60	253	69
75/79							0		0	57		4	1	5	60	27	249	129	405	66
70/74							0	0	0	55	0	9	2	11	57	119	260	213	592	64
65/69		0		0	57		2	0	2	52	1	15	6	22	53	221	230	260	711	61
60/64		1		1	54		3	2	5	50	3	29	13	45	51	262	222	253	737	57
55/59	0	1	1	2	53	0	7	4	11	49	10	36	23	69	48	271	218	247	736	52
50/54	1	3	2	6	47	2	15	7	24	44	16	42	31	89	44	254	198	231	683	48
45/49	2	7	4	13	42	4	32	13	49	39	32	44	47	123	41	242	185	218	645	43
40/44	5	23	9	37	37	13	57	39	109	36	58	39	57	154	38	240	237	238	715	38
35/39	18	44	31	93	33	51	58	69	178	33	55	15	41	111	34	274	234	275	783	34
30/34	38	48	52	138	29	72	45	62	179	29	43	4	16	63	30	310	214	276	800	29
25/29	36	38	43	117	24	50	19	32	101	24	17		2	19	25	219	148	185	552	25
20/24	36	27	35	98	20	32	5	12	49	20	3		0	3	21	161	94	129	384	20
15/19	28	17	20	65	15	14	3	4	21	15	1			1	15	108	63	86	257	15
10/14	20	8	15	43	10	7	1	3	11	11	0			0	11	83	32	54	169	11
5/9	19	5	9	33	6	3	0	1	4	5	0			0	6	64	16	31	111	6
0/4	14	2	2	18	1	1		0	1	1						36	6	9	51	1
-5/-1	5	1	1	7	-3	0			0	-4						13	2	4	19	-3
-10/-6	2			2	-8	0			0	-8						7	0	1	8	-8
-15/-11	1			1	-12											3	0	0	3	-13
-20/-16																1			1	-18

OTIS AFB/FALMOUTH MASSACHUSETTS

LAT 41 39N LONG 70 31W ELEV 132 FT

MEAN FREQUENCY OF OCCURRENCE OF DRY BULB TEMPERATURE (DEGREES F) WITH MEAN COINCIDENT WET BULB TEMPERATURE (DEGREES F) FOR EACH DRY BULB TEMPERATURE RANGE

Temperature Range	MAY Obsn Hour Gp 01 to 08	MAY 09 to 16	MAY 17 to 24	MAY Total Obsn	MAY MCWB	JUNE Obsn Hour Gp 01 to 08	JUNE 09 to 16	JUNE 17 to 24	JUNE Total Obsn	JUNE MCWB	JULY Obsn Hour Gp 01 to 08	JULY 09 to 16	JULY 17 to 24	JULY Total Obsn	JULY MCWB
95/99												0		0	74
90/94							1	0	1	71		2		2	74
85/89		0		0	66		4	0	4	71	0	10	0	10	73
80/84		2	0	2	66	0	16	1	17	69	1	37	3	41	70
75/79	0	8	0	8	63	2	42	6	50	66	7	89	24	120	68
70/74	1	18	2	21	60	12	68	24	104	64	60	74	81	215	67
65/69	4	43	9	56	57	41	52	54	147	62	96	29	92	217	64
60/64	18	63	28	109	54	77	35	72	184	59	60	8	42	110	59
55/59	50	60	63	173	52	69	18	57	144	54	21		6	27	55
50/54	65	34	68	167	48	32	5	22	59	50	2		1	3	50
45/49	65	13	56	134	44	7		3	10	45	0			0	47
40/44	35	5	19	59	40	1		0	1	41					
35/39	9		3	12	35										
30/34	1		0	1	31										
25/29	0			0	28										
20/24															

Temperature Range	AUGUST Obsn Hour Gp 01 to 08	AUGUST 09 to 16	AUGUST 17 to 24	AUGUST Total Obsn	AUGUST MCWB	SEPTEMBER Obsn Hour Gp 01 to 08	SEPTEMBER 09 to 16	SEPTEMBER 17 to 24	SEPTEMBER Total Obsn	SEPTEMBER MCWB	OCTOBER Obsn Hour Gp 01 to 08	OCTOBER 09 to 16	OCTOBER 17 to 24	OCTOBER Total Obsn	OCTOBER MCWB
95/99															
90/94							0		0	73					
85/89		5		5	72		2		2	71					
80/84	0	38	2	40	71		11	1	12	72		0		0	68
75/79	8	78	21	107	68	1	33	4	38	68		4		4	65
70/74	62	73	78	213	67	20	60	26	106	65	0	19	2	21	63
65/69	78	41	81	200	63	49	56	56	161	62	8	41	11	60	61
60/64	65	12	51	128	59	50	46	57	153	58	28	55	36	119	57
55/59	25	0	13	38	54	57	27	55	139	54	58	56	59	173	53
50/54	9	0	2	11	50	37	5	29	71	49	48	42	57	147	48
45/49	1		0	1	45	18	1	10	29	44	44	21	41	106	43
40/44	0			0	41	6		2	8	40	32	8	25	65	39
35/39						1		0	1	36	20	2	13	35	34
30/34											8	0	3	11	30
25/29											2		1	3	25
20/24											0			0	21

OTIS AFB/FALMOUTH MASSACHUSETTS

Temperature Range	NOVEMBER Obsn Hour Gp 01 to 08	09 to 16	17 to 24	Total Obsn	M C W B	DECEMBER Obsn Hour Gp 01 to 08	09 to 16	17 to 24	Total Obsn	M C W B	JANUARY Obsn Hour Gp 01 to 08	09 to 16	17 to 24	Total Obsn	M C W B
95/99															
90/94															
85/89															
80/84															
75/79															
70/74		1		1	64										
65/69	0	4	1	5	62		0		0	56					
60/64	7	10	6	23	58	0	1		1	53		0		0	51
55/59	17	35	17	69	54	3	5	3	11	54	1	1	0	2	53
50/54	31	51	35	117	48	8	16	9	33	49	2	5	1	8	49
45/49	41	58	46	145	43	13	31	16	60	44	5	12	6	23	44
40/44	43	47	52	142	38	27	38	31	96	39	14	34	19	67	39
35/39	40	23	42	105	33	38	44	45	127	34	36	55	43	134	34
30/34	37	9	28	74	29	51	51	48	150	29	38	49	54	141	29
25/29	18	2	10	30	25	36	33	43	112	24	45	34	43	122	24
20/24	5	1	2	8	20	30	19	31	80	20	39	28	37	104	20
15/19	1		0	1	16	25	6	14	45	15	24	18	22	64	15
10/14	0		0	0	13	11	3	5	19	11	23	9	15	47	10
5/9						4	1	2	7	6	14	2	6	22	6
0/4						1	0	0	1	1	5	0	2	7	1
-5/-1						1		0	1	-4	2	0	0	2	-3
-10/-6											0			0	-8
-15/-11											0			0	-12

Temperature Range	FEBRUARY Obsn Hour Gp 01 to 08	09 to 16	17 to 24	Total Obsn	M C W B	MARCH Obsn Hour Gp 01 to 08	09 to 16	17 to 24	Total Obsn	M C W B	APRIL Obsn Hour Gp 01 to 08	09 to 16	17 to 24	Total Obsn	M C W B	ANNUAL TOTAL Obsn Hour Gp 01 to 08	09 to 16	17 to 24	Total Obsn	M C W B
95/99																	0		0	74
90/94																	3	0	3	74
85/89																0	21	0	21	72
80/84																1	104	7	112	70
75/79												0		0	61	18	254	55	327	68
70/74												2	0	2	58	155	315	213	683	66
65/69							0		0	53		7	0	7	55	276	273	304	853	62
60/64							2	0	2	49	1	18	2	21	52	306	250	294	850	58
55/59		0		0	52	0	8	1	9	48	7	39	13	59	49	308	249	287	844	53
50/54	1	3	2	6	48	2	15	5	22	46	22	54	30	106	46	259	230	261	750	48
45/49	4	10	5	19	43	7	39	16	62	41	42	58	55	155	42	247	243	254	744	43
40/44	10	31	12	53	38	23	65	36	124	37	68	43	77	188	38	259	271	273	803	39
35/39	32	61	47	140	34	67	62	84	213	34	61	16	47	124	35	304	263	324	891	34
30/34	48	52	56	156	29	78	42	69	189	30	32	2	14	48	30	293	205	272	770	29
25/29	43	32	44	119	24	40	11	25	76	25	7	0	1	8	25	191	112	167	470	24
20/24	33	17	28	78	20	17	3	8	28	20	1			1	19	125	68	106	299	20
15/19	20	11	17	48	15	8	2	3	13	15						78	37	56	171	15
10/14	19	5	8	32	10	3	0	1	4	10						56	17	29	102	10
5/9	11	1	4	16	6	1		1	2	6						30	4	13	47	6
0/4	3	0	1	4	1	1			1	1						10	0	3	13	1
-5/-1	1	0	0	1	-3											4	0	0	4	-3
-10/-6	0			0	-8											0			0	-8
-15/-11																0		0	0	-12

WESTOVER AFB MASSACHUSETTS

LAT 42 12N LONG 72 32W ELEV 245 FT

MEAN FREQUENCY OF OCCURRENCE OF DRY BULB TEMPERATURE (DEGREES F) WITH MEAN COINCIDENT WET BULB TEMPERATURE (DEGREES F) FOR EACH DRY BULB TEMPERATURE RANGE

Temperature Range	MAY Obsn Hour Gp 01 to 08	MAY 09 to 16	MAY 17 to 24	MAY Total Obsn	MAY MCWB	JUNE Obsn Hour Gp 01 to 08	JUNE 09 to 16	JUNE 17 to 24	JUNE Total Obsn	JUNE MCWB
100/104		0		0	71					
95/99		1	0	1	72		1	0	1	73
90/94		1	0	1	70		7	2	9	72
85/89	0	6	2	8	68		20	6	26	70
80/84	0	12	4	16	64	0	39	16	55	67
75/79	1	24	9	34	61	3	46	28	77	65
70/74	2	34	20	56	58	15	51	46	112	63
65/69	9	46	32	87	56	46	37	50	133	61
60/64	21	48	42	111	53	54	23	41	118	57
55/59	42	36	49	127	51	55	15	33	103	54
50/54	53	22	41	116	47	39	2	14	55	49
45/49	47	12	29	88	43	18	0	2	20	45
40/44	43	6	16	65	39	7		1	8	41
35/39	21	1	4	26	35	2		0	2	36
30/34	9		0	9	30	1			1	32
25/29	2			2	26					
20/24										
15/19										

Temperature Range	JULY Obsn Hour Gp 01 to 08	JULY 09 to 16	JULY 17 to 24	JULY Total Obsn	JULY MCWB	AUGUST Obsn Hour Gp 01 to 08	AUGUST 09 to 16	AUGUST 17 to 24	AUGUST Total Obsn	AUGUST MCWB
100/104		0		0	72					
95/99		1	0	1	72		0		0	76
90/94		10	2	12	73		6	1	7	74
85/89	0	31	8	39	71		24	5	29	71
80/84	1	58	25	84	68	0	54	18	72	69
75/79	8	66	47	121	66	5	64	39	108	66
70/74	42	52	65	159	65	34	53	64	151	65
65/69	78	25	62	165	63	60	31	56	147	62
60/64	59	4	27	90	59	63	13	38	114	59
55/59	34	0	8	42	54	44	2	17	63	55
50/54	20		3	23	50	22	0	6	28	50
45/49	7		0	7	46	15		3	18	45
40/44	1			1	42	5		0	5	41
35/39						1		0	1	37
30/34						0			0	31
25/29										
20/24										
15/19										

Temperature Range	SEPTEMBER Obsn Hour Gp 01 to 08	SEPTEMBER 09 to 16	SEPTEMBER 17 to 24	SEPTEMBER Total Obsn	SEPTEMBER MCWB	OCTOBER Obsn Hour Gp 01 to 08	OCTOBER 09 to 16	OCTOBER 17 to 24	OCTOBER Total Obsn	OCTOBER MCWB
100/104										
95/99										
90/94		2	0	2	74					
85/89		8	2	10	73		0		0	64
80/84		22	5	27	70		2	0	2	66
75/79	1	34	15	50	66		11	1	12	63
70/74	15	51	34	100	64	0	17	5	22	61
65/69	30	43	43	116	61	3	31	15	49	59
60/64	35	38	41	114	57	15	42	29	86	55
55/59	44	27	43	114	53	24	51	41	116	51
50/54	41	12	34	87	49	39	48	52	139	47
45/49	34	2	15	51	45	44	27	42	113	43
40/44	21	0	7	28	41	41	12	31	84	39
35/39	13		2	15	36	37	5	21	63	34
30/34	4		1	5	31	29	1	9	39	30
25/29	1			1	27	13		3	16	26
20/24						3		0	3	22
15/19						0			0	18

WESTOVER AFB MASSACHUSETTS

Temperature Range	NOVEMBER Obsn Hour Gp 01 to 08	NOVEMBER 09 to 16	NOVEMBER 17 to 24	NOVEMBER Total Obsn	NOVEMBER MCWB	DECEMBER Obsn Hour Gp 01 to 08	DECEMBER 09 to 16	DECEMBER 17 to 24	DECEMBER Total Obsn	DECEMBER MCWB	JANUARY Obsn Hour Gp 01 to 08	JANUARY 09 to 16	JANUARY 17 to 24	JANUARY Total Obsn	JANUARY MCWB
100/104															
95/99															
90/94															
85/89															
80/84															
75/79															
70/74		1		1	62										
65/69	1	4	2	7	61										
60/64	3	9	5	17	56	0	1	1	2	56		0		0	51
55/59	9	23	14	46	52	1	3	2	6	52	0	1	0	1	50
50/54	17	40	25	82	47	2	7	2	11	47	1	1	2	4	49
45/49	25	41	34	100	42	6	12	7	25	42	1	3	1	5	42
40/44	36	52	40	128	38	11	25	16	52	37	5	17	7	29	37
35/39	41	40	51	132	33	22	40	33	95	33	17	38	29	84	33
30/34	45	24	45	114	29	44	53	54	151	29	37	49	43	129	29
25/29	33	6	16	55	25	47	46	46	139	24	29	41	41	111	24
20/24	19	1	7	27	21	36	30	36	102	20	33	33	38	104	20
15/19	8	0	1	9	17	26	18	26	70	15	33	31	35	99	15
10/14	1			1	13	22	8	14	44	11	33	19	27	79	10
5/9						13	4	6	23	6	24	8	14	46	6
0/4						10	2	2	14	2	14	4	6	24	1
-5/-1						6	0	1	7	-3	8	2	3	13	-3
-10/-6						1		0	1	-8	6	0	1	7	-8
-15/-11						0			0	-13	5	0	0	5	-13
-20/-16						0			0	-16	1			1	-18
-25/-21											0			0	-22

Temperature Range	FEBRUARY Obsn Hour Gp 01 to 08	FEBRUARY 09 to 16	FEBRUARY 17 to 24	FEBRUARY Total Obsn	FEBRUARY MCWB	MARCH Obsn Hour Gp 01 to 08	MARCH 09 to 16	MARCH 17 to 24	MARCH Total Obsn	MARCH MCWB	APRIL Obsn Hour Gp 01 to 08	APRIL 09 to 16	APRIL 17 to 24	APRIL Total Obsn	APRIL MCWB	ANNUAL TOTAL Obsn Hour Gp 01 to 08	ANNUAL TOTAL 09 to 16	ANNUAL TOTAL 17 to 24	ANNUAL TOTAL Total Obsn	ANNUAL TOTAL MCWB
100/104																	0		0	71
95/99																	3	0	3	72
90/94												0		0	62		26	5	31	73
85/89												0		0	64	0	89	23	112	71
80/84												2	0	2	62	1	189	68	258	68
75/79							0		0	59		6	1	7	58	18	251	140	409	65
70/74							1		1	56	0	11	4	15	56	108	271	238	617	64
65/69		0		0	57		3	1	4	53	0	16	8	24	53	227	236	269	732	61
60/64		0		0	56		3	2	5	51	3	29	17	49	50	253	210	243	706	56
55/59	0	1	0	1	52	0	8	5	13	48	11	38	29	78	48	264	205	241	710	52
50/54	1	2	2	5	47	1	19	10	30	43	19	42	37	98	44	255	195	228	678	47
45/49	1	8	4	13	41	6	32	19	57	40	35	41	43	119	41	239	178	199	616	42
40/44	4	19	12	35	37	16	49	37	102	36	52	37	50	139	37	242	217	217	676	38
35/39	19	40	27	86	33	43	57	63	163	33	53	15	36	104	34	269	236	266	771	33
30/34	38	51	55	144	29	74	46	59	179	29	38	3	13	54	29	319	227	279	825	29
25/29	35	39	43	117	24	51	19	32	102	24	20	0	2	22	25	231	151	183	565	24
20/24	37	27	34	98	20	31	7	11	49	20	5		0	5	21	164	98	126	388	20
15/19	28	18	21	67	15	15	2	5	22	15	2		0	2	16	112	69	88	269	15
10/14	20	9	13	42	10	6	2	3	11	10	1			1	11	83	38	57	178	10
5/9	17	7	10	34	6	3	0	0	3	6	0			0	8	57	19	30	106	6
0/4	11	2	3	16	1	0		0	0	1						35	8	11	54	1
-5/-1	7	0	1	8	-3	0			0	-4						21	2	5	28	-3
-10/-6	4	0		4	-8	0			0	-8						11	0	1	12	-8
-15/-11	1			1	-13	0			0	-13						6	0	0	6	-13
-20/-16	0			0	-17											1			1	-18
-25/-21																0			0	-22

KINCHELOE AFB MICHIGAN

LAT 46 15N   LONG 84 28W   ELEV 799 FT

MEAN FREQUENCY OF OCCURRENCE OF DRY BULB TEMPERATURE (DEGREES F) WITH MEAN COINCIDENT WET BULB TEMPERATURE (DEGREES F) FOR EACH DRY BULB TEMPERATURE RANGE

Temperature Range	MAY Obsn Hour Gp 01 to 08	MAY 09 to 16	MAY 17 to 24	MAY Total Obsn	MAY MCWB	JUNE Obsn Hour Gp 01 to 08	JUNE 09 to 16	JUNE 17 to 24	JUNE Total Obsn	JUNE MCWB	JULY Obsn Hour Gp 01 to 08	JULY 09 to 16	JULY 17 to 24	JULY Total Obsn	JULY MCWB
90/94							0		0	76		1		1	72
85/89		1		1	70		5	1	6	71		8	1	9	71
80/84		2	1	3	66		14	5	19	68		27	8	35	68
75/79		6	2	8	63	0	27	10	37	65	1	49	20	70	65
70/74	0	16	6	22	59	2	40	19	61	61	6	64	35	105	63
65/69	1	27	12	40	55	10	45	32	87	59	29	48	52	129	61
60/64	7	36	22	65	53	27	44	44	115	56	60	34	58	152	58
55/59	16	38	31	85	50	50	38	49	137	53	64	13	40	117	54
50/54	31	47	39	117	46	60	23	41	124	49	46	3	24	73	50
45/49	50	38	48	136	42	50	5	26	81	44	29	0	8	37	45
40/44	53	23	42	118	38	25	0	10	35	40	11		2	13	41
35/39	45	10	26	81	34	12		3	15	36	1		0	1	37
30/34	30	4	14	48	30	4		0	4	32					
25/29	12	0	4	16	26	0			0	27					
20/24	4		1	5	21										
15/19	0			0	18										
10/14															

Temperature Range	AUGUST Obsn Hour Gp 01 to 08	AUGUST 09 to 16	AUGUST 17 to 24	AUGUST Total Obsn	AUGUST MCWB	SEPTEMBER Obsn Hour Gp 01 to 08	SEPTEMBER 09 to 16	SEPTEMBER 17 to 24	SEPTEMBER Total Obsn	SEPTEMBER MCWB	OCTOBER Obsn Hour Gp 01 to 08	OCTOBER 09 to 16	OCTOBER 17 to 24	OCTOBER Total Obsn	OCTOBER MCWB
90/94															
85/89		2	0	2	71		0		0	72					
80/84		22	4	26	69	0	4	1	5	73		1		1	71
75/79	0	41	14	55	66	0	14	4	18	67		2	0	2	66
70/74	5	57	29	91	63	4	26	11	41	64	0	7	1	8	62
65/69	29	54	50	133	61	11	40	22	73	61	1	15	5	21	59
60/64	59	46	60	165	58	25	48	37	110	58	6	22	11	39	56
55/59	64	21	49	134	54	44	45	45	134	54	17	33	26	76	53
50/54	43	5	27	75	50	51	36	53	140	49	37	50	41	128	48
45/49	29	1	10	40	46	44	17	33	94	45	45	41	45	131	44
40/44	15		3	18	41	30	7	22	59	40	40	38	48	126	39
35/39	3		0	3	37	19	1	8	28	36	42	25	37	104	35
30/34	0			0	33	9	0	3	12	31	42	12	24	78	30
25/29						1		0	1	27	14	3	8	25	26
20/24						0			0	23	3	0	1	4	21
15/19											1		0	1	18
10/14													0	0	13

KINCHELOE AFB MICHIGAN

Temperature Range	NOVEMBER Obsn Hour Gp 01 to 08	NOVEMBER 09 to 16	NOVEMBER 17 to 24	NOVEMBER Total Obsn	NOVEMBER MCWB	DECEMBER Obsn Hour Gp 01 to 08	DECEMBER 09 to 16	DECEMBER 17 to 24	DECEMBER Total Obsn	DECEMBER MCWB
90/94										
85/89										
80/84										
75/79										
70/74										
65/69										
60/64	0	1		1	57					
55/59	1	4	2	7	52		0		0	52
50/54	2	9	5	16	48		1	0	1	47
45/49	11	24	13	48	44	1	2	2	5	44
40/44	27	38	31	96	40	3	4	3	10	39
35/39	40	47	47	134	35	15	20	17	52	34
30/34	65	55	62	182	30	36	41	40	117	30
25/29	43	35	39	117	25	34	41	36	111	25
20/24	24	17	22	63	21	33	41	42	116	21
15/19	15	6	10	31	17	33	34	36	103	16
10/14	7	2	5	14	11	27	29	29	85	11
5/9	3	1	2	6	7	23	17	21	61	7
0/4	1	1	1	3	2	17	10	14	41	2
-5/-1	0		0	0	-3	15	4	5	24	-3
-10/-6			0	0	-7	6	2	2	10	-8
-15/-11						1	0	0	1	-12
-20/-16						0	0		0	-18
-25/-21						0			0	-22
-30/-26										
-35/-31										

Temperature Range	JANUARY Obsn Hour Gp 01 to 08	JANUARY 09 to 16	JANUARY 17 to 24	JANUARY Total Obsn	JANUARY MCWB	FEBRUARY Obsn Hour Gp 01 to 08	FEBRUARY 09 to 16	FEBRUARY 17 to 24	FEBRUARY Total Obsn	FEBRUARY MCWB
90/94										
85/89										
80/84										
75/79										
70/74										
65/69										
60/64										
55/59										
50/54										
45/49										
40/44		0	0	0	39	1	2	1	4	38
35/39	3	8	4	15	34	2	7	4	13	34
30/34	17	24	20	61	30	11	23	16	50	30
25/29	26	35	33	94	26	23	33	29	85	25
20/24	29	32	32	93	21	27	34	36	97	20
15/19	27	35	38	100	16	28	35	37	100	16
10/14	37	37	35	109	11	28	30	30	88	11
5/9	30	29	32	91	6	32	24	27	83	6
0/4	27	22	26	75	1	24	17	18	59	1
-5/-1	23	15	15	53	-4	19	10	13	42	-4
-10/-6	16	8	9	33	-8	14	7	9	30	-8
-15/-11	8	3	4	15	-13	9	3	3	15	-13
-20/-16	3	1	1	5	-18	5	1	1	7	-17
-25/-21	1	0		1	-22	2	0	0	2	-22
-30/-26	0	0		0	-27	0			0	-27
-35/-31	0	0		0	-33					

Temperature Range	MARCH Obsn Hour Gp 01 to 08	MARCH 09 to 16	MARCH 17 to 24	MARCH Total Obsn	MARCH MCWB	APRIL Obsn Hour Gp 01 to 08	APRIL 09 to 16	APRIL 17 to 24	APRIL Total Obsn	APRIL MCWB
90/94										
85/89										
80/84										
75/79							1	0	1	60
70/74							1	0	1	58
65/69							5	2	7	55
60/64						0	9	3	12	52
55/59		0	0	0	50	1	16	7	24	47
50/54	0	2	0	2	43	5	29	15	49	44
45/49	1	7	3	11	39	11	36	28	75	41
40/44	3	19	8	30	37	31	46	38	115	38
35/39	9	37	24	70	33	48	50	54	152	34
30/34	35	54	54	143	29	63	31	53	147	30
25/29	47	47	55	149	25	44	12	29	85	25
20/24	41	31	39	111	20	23	3	8	34	21
15/19	30	26	28	84	16	9	1	2	12	16
10/14	28	16	23	67	11	4	0	1	5	11
5/9	26	5	8	39	6	1	0	0	1	7
0/4	18	2	3	23	2	0		0	0	2
-5/-1	6	0	1	7	-3	0			0	-5
-10/-6	2	1	1	4	-8					
-15/-11	1	0	0	1	-14					
-20/-16	1		0	1	-18					
-25/-21	0		0	0	-23					
-30/-26										
-35/-31										

Temperature Range	ANNUAL TOTAL Obsn Hour Gp 01 to 08	ANNUAL TOTAL 09 to 16	ANNUAL TOTAL 17 to 24	ANNUAL TOTAL Total Obsn	ANNUAL TOTAL MCWB
90/94		1		1	73
85/89		16	2	18	71
80/84	0	70	19	89	69
75/79	1	140	50	191	65
70/74	17	211	101	329	63
65/69	81	234	175	490	60
60/64	184	240	235	659	57
55/59	257	208	249	714	53
50/54	275	205	245	725	48
45/49	271	171	216	658	44
40/44	239	177	208	624	39
35/39	239	205	224	668	34
30/34	312	244	286	842	30
25/29	244	206	233	683	25
20/24	184	158	181	523	21
15/19	143	137	151	431	16
10/14	131	114	123	368	11
5/9	115	76	90	281	6
0/4	87	52	62	201	1
-5/-1	63	29	34	126	-3
-10/-6	38	18	21	77	-8
-15/-11	19	6	7	32	-13
-20/-16	9	2	2	13	-18
-25/-21	3	0	0	3	-22
-30/-26	0	0		0	-27
-35/-31	0	0		0	-33

K I SAWYER AFB MICHIGAN

LAT 46 21N LONG 87 24W ELEV 1220 FT

MEAN FREQUENCY OF OCCURRENCE OF DRY BULB TEMPERATURE (DEGREES F) WITH MEAN COINCIDENT WET BULB TEMPERATURE (DEGREES F) FOR EACH DRY BULB TEMPERATURE RANGE

Temperature Range	MAY					JUNE					JULY				
	Obsn Hour Gp 01 to 08	09 to 16	17 to 24	Total Obsn	M C W B	Obsn Hour Gp 01 to 08	09 to 16	17 to 24	Total Obsn	M C W B	Obsn Hour Gp 01 to 08	09 to 16	17 to 24	Total Obsn	M C W B
100/104							0	0	0	82					
95/99							0		0	79		1	0	1	76
90/94		1	0	1	69		2	1	3	72		3	1	4	72
85/89		2	1	3	68		9	4	13	69		9	3	12	70
80/84		4	1	5	64	0	16	6	22	66	0	27	12	39	68
75/79	0	6	4	10	62	1	24	13	38	63	2	47	24	73	65
70/74	1	15	8	24	58	4	38	22	64	61	8	59	43	110	63
65/69	3	25	14	42	56	13	37	33	83	58	37	49	52	138	61
60/64	7	33	24	64	53	33	37	43	113	56	60	32	49	141	57
55/59	20	38	30	88	50	42	34	36	112	52	56	13	34	103	54
50/54	29	37	37	103	46	54	27	42	123	48	42	6	19	67	49
45/49	45	35	37	117	42	47	11	26	84	44	29	2	8	39	45
40/44	47	26	40	113	38	26	4	11	41	40	11	0	2	13	41
35/39	42	17	27	86	34	13	0	3	16	35	3		0	3	37
30/34	34	8	18	60	30	7		1	8	31	0			0	33
25/29	16	1	6	23	25	1			1	26					
20/24	5			5	21										
15/19	0			0	18										
10/14															

Temperature Range	AUGUST					SEPTEMBER					OCTOBER				
	Obsn Hour Gp 01 to 08	09 to 16	17 to 24	Total Obsn	M C W B	Obsn Hour Gp 01 to 08	09 to 16	17 to 24	Total Obsn	M C W B	Obsn Hour Gp 01 to 08	09 to 16	17 to 24	Total Obsn	M C W B
100/104															
95/99															
90/94		2	1	3	73										
85/89		6	2	8	70		1	0	1	73					
80/84		24	8	32	68		4	1	5	70		1		1	65
75/79	0	37	18	55	66	1	16	5	22	66		5	1	6	62
70/74	7	50	35	92	63	2	27	13	42	63		10	3	13	60
65/69	23	49	47	119	61	9	33	26	68	61	2	14	8	24	58
60/64	53	39	54	146	58	19	36	34	89	57	4	19	13	36	55
55/59	58	29	41	128	54	41	43	43	127	53	13	28	24	65	52
50/54	52	11	25	88	50	50	39	42	131	49	29	40	36	105	48
45/49	31	2	12	45	45	47	28	39	114	45	39	37	41	117	44
40/44	16	0	4	20	41	34	10	23	67	40	39	41	41	121	39
35/39	8		1	9	36	26	2	9	37	35	45	33	39	117	35
30/34	1			1	33	9	0	4	13	31	50	16	31	97	30
25/29						2	0	1	3	27	21	4	9	34	26
20/24						1		0	1	22	6	1	2	9	22
15/19											1	0	0	1	17
10/14											0			0	13

K I SAWYER AFB MICHIGAN

Temperature Range	NOVEMBER Obsn Hour Gp 01 to 08	NOVEMBER 09 to 16	NOVEMBER 17 to 24	NOVEMBER Total Obsn	NOVEMBER MCWB	DECEMBER Obsn Hour Gp 01 to 08	DECEMBER 09 to 16	DECEMBER 17 to 24	DECEMBER Total Obsn	DECEMBER MCWB	JANUARY Obsn Hour Gp 01 to 08	JANUARY 09 to 16	JANUARY 17 to 24	JANUARY Total Obsn	JANUARY MCWB	FEBRUARY Obsn Hour Gp 01 to 08	FEBRUARY 09 to 16	FEBRUARY 17 to 24	FEBRUARY Total Obsn	FEBRUARY MCWB	MARCH Obsn Hour Gp 01 to 08	MARCH 09 to 16	MARCH 17 to 24	MARCH Total Obsn	MARCH MCWB	APRIL Obsn Hour Gp 01 to 08	APRIL 09 to 16	APRIL 17 to 24	APRIL Total Obsn	APRIL MCWB	ANNUAL TOTAL Obsn Hour Gp 01 to 08	ANNUAL TOTAL 09 to 16	ANNUAL TOTAL 17 to 24	ANNUAL TOTAL Total Obsn	ANNUAL TOTAL MCWB
100/104																																0	0	0	82
95/99																																1	0	1	76
90/94																																8	3	11	72
85/89																																27	10	37	70
80/84																											0	0	0	61	0	76	28	104	67
75/79																											1	0	1	56	4	136	65	205	65
70/74																											2	1	3	57	22	201	125	348	62
65/69		0		0	55																						4	1	5	52	87	211	181	479	60
60/64	0	1	0	1	55																	1	0	1	48	0	10	4	14	50	176	208	221	605	56
55/59	0	3	1	4	49		1		1	51											0	1	1	2	48	1	18	8	27	47	231	208	218	657	52
50/54	1	9	4	14	47	0	1	1	2	49							0	0	0	40	0	6	3	9	44	5	24	18	47	44	262	200	227	689	48
45/49	6	16	12	34	44	1	2	1	4	45							1	1	2	37	2	7	6	15	41	18	33	28	79	42	265	174	211	650	44
40/44	16	26	24	66	39	2	3	2	7	40	0	1	0	1	36		2	1	3	34	5	17	9	31	37	26	42	37	105	38	222	172	194	588	39
35/39	34	47	41	122	35	7	13	9	29	35	3	9	5	17	34	2	7	5	14	32	8	29	25	62	33	39	45	49	133	33	230	202	213	645	34
30/34	64	62	67	193	30	25	27	29	81	31	15	21	20	56	30	9	17	13	39	29	37	48	44	129	29	58	41	52	151	30	309	240	279	828	30
25/29	59	40	44	143	25	29	36	36	101	25	23	26	26	75	25	16	33	30	79	25	40	47	47	134	25	49	15	31	95	26	256	202	230	688	25
20/24	31	22	25	78	21	52	59	52	163	21	31	39	41	111	21	30	42	35	107	21	33	37	38	108	20	27	4	9	40	21	216	204	202	622	21
15/19	16	10	12	38	16	44	48	46	138	16	32	37	32	101	16	38	33	35	106	16	34	28	29	91	16	10	1	2	13	16	175	157	156	488	16
10/14	6	3	5	14	11	28	28	31	87	11	34	40	37	111	11	33	32	35	100	11	25	18	22	65	11	2	0	1	3	12	128	121	131	380	11
5/9	6	1	3	10	7	20	15	17	52	6	31	25	30	86	6	25	24	25	74	6	24	6	15	45	6	2		0	2	7	108	71	90	269	6
0/4	1	0	0	1	4	17	9	13	39	2	24	22	21	67	1	26	14	19	59	1	21	2	7	30	2	1			1	3	90	47	60	197	1
-5/-1						13	4	8	25	-3	18	14	18	50	-3	16	12	12	40	-4	13	1	1	15	-3	0			0	-2	60	31	39	130	-3
-10/-6						8	2	3	13	-8	16	8	10	34	-8	13	4	8	25	-8	3	0	1	4	-8						40	14	22	76	-8
-15/-11						2	1	1	4	-13	10	3	5	18	-13	9	3	3	15	-13	3	0	0	3	-13						24	7	9	40	-13
-20/-16								0	0	-16	7	2	3	12	-17	6	1	1	8	-17	0			0	-18						13	3	4	20	-17
-25/-21											3	1	0	4	-23	1	0		1	-22	0			0	-21						4	1	0	5	-23
-30/-26												0		0	-27																	0		0	-27

LANSING/CAPITAL CITY APRT MICHIGAN

LAT 42 47N LONG 84 36W ELEV 841 FT

MEAN FREQUENCY OF OCCURRENCE OF DRY BULB TEMPERATURE (DEGREES F) WITH MEAN COINCIDENT WET BULB TEMPERATURE (DEGREES F) FOR EACH DRY BULB TEMPERATURE RANGE

Tempera-ture Range	MAY Obsn Hour Gp 01 to 08	MAY 09 to 16	MAY 17 to 24	MAY Total Obsn	MAY MCWB	JUNE Obsn Hour Gp 01 to 08	JUNE 09 to 16	JUNE 17 to 24	JUNE Total Obsn	JUNE MCWB	JULY Obsn Hour Gp 01 to 08	JULY 09 to 16	JULY 17 to 24	JULY Total Obsn	JULY MCWB
100/104															
95/99							1	0	1	75					
90/94							6	2	8	74		7	2	9	74
85/89		4	1	5	71		24	9	33	72		33	12	45	71
80/84		13	4	17	67	1	36	19	56	69	1	62	31	94	69
75/79	1	25	13	39	64	7	47	32	86	66	10	59	48	117	66
70/74	6	33	22	61	61	24	48	50	122	63	43	50	61	154	65
65/69	15	43	32	90	57	53	38	50	141	61	60	27	46	133	62
60/64	24	43	43	110	54	50	23	35	108	57	64	10	31	105	59
55/59	38	35	45	118	51	44	10	25	79	53	42	1	14	57	55
50/54	48	24	39	111	47	34	6	15	55	49	21		2	23	50
45/49	50	15	24	89	43	20	1	2	23	45	7			7	46
40/44	35	10	17	62	39	6		0	6	41					
35/39	20	2	6	28	35	0			0	37					
30/34	9	0	1	10	31										
25/29	2			2	27										
20/24															

Tempera-ture Range	AUGUST Obsn Hour Gp 01 to 08	AUGUST 09 to 16	AUGUST 17 to 24	AUGUST Total Obsn	AUGUST MCWB	SEPTEMBER Obsn Hour Gp 01 to 08	SEPTEMBER 09 to 16	SEPTEMBER 17 to 24	SEPTEMBER Total Obsn	SEPTEMBER MCWB	OCTOBER Obsn Hour Gp 01 to 08	OCTOBER 09 to 16	OCTOBER 17 to 24	OCTOBER Total Obsn	OCTOBER MCWB
100/104		0		0	79										
95/99		1	0	1	76		0		0	75					
90/94		5	1	6	71		3	1	4	73					
85/89		16	5	21	71		7	3	10	72		1		1	67
80/84	1	44	17	62	69	0	16	6	22	70		6	0	6	64
75/79	3	57	36	96	66	3	27	16	46	66		14	3	17	62
70/74	22	62	58	142	64	18	46	28	92	64	2	23	9	34	60
65/69	55	42	60	157	62	25	48	40	113	60	7	30	20	57	58
60/64	73	18	43	134	59	39	42	46	127	57	18	33	29	80	55
55/59	52	3	20	75	55	43	32	44	119	53	25	35	32	92	51
50/54	26		7	33	50	41	13	29	83	49	34	35	38	107	47
45/49	13		1	14	46	40	4	18	62	45	45	36	47	128	44
40/44	3			3	42	19	0	7	26	41	40	23	34	97	39
35/39	0			0	38	8	0	2	10	37	40	9	22	71	35
30/34						4		0	4	33	25	2	9	36	31
25/29											10		4	14	26
20/24											2			2	22

LANSING/CAPITAL CITY APRT MICHIGAN

Temperature Range	NOVEMBER					DECEMBER					JANUARY				
	Obsn Hour Gp 01 to 08	09 to 16	17 to 24	Total Obsn	M C W B	Obsn Hour Gp 01 to 08	09 to 16	17 to 24	Total Obsn	M C W B	Obsn Hour Gp 01 to 08	09 to 16	17 to 24	Total Obsn	M C W B
100/104															
95/99															
90/94															
85/89															
80/84															
75/79		1		1	64										
70/74	1	2	1	4	62										
65/69	0	7	1	8	57								0	0	60
60/64	2	10	5	17	55	0	0	0	0	56	0	0	0	0	60
55/59	11	19	15	45	52	1	4	1	6	50	1	2	1	4	54
50/54	12	23	16	51	47	3	5	6	14	47	1	2	3	6	49
45/49	19	34	25	78	43	4	8	6	18	43	3	4	3	10	44
40/44	32	49	46	127	39	10	14	11	35	39	6	10	8	24	40
35/39	47	40	50	137	35	21	27	26	74	35	20	29	21	70	34
30/34	52	28	38	118	30	46	54	45	145	30	38	48	47	133	30
25/29	35	19	24	78	26	47	48	53	148	26	49	47	49	145	26
20/24	18	7	12	37	21	40	41	34	115	21	33	39	36	108	20
15/19	6	2	5	13	17	29	24	28	81	16	35	28	31	94	16
10/14	2	0	1	3	13	22	14	20	56	11	22	19	22	63	11
5/9	1	1	0	2	7	13	6	9	28	7	19	11	15	45	6
0/4	1	0	1	2	2	7	2	6	15	1	10	5	7	22	1
-5/-1			0	0	-1	6	1	2	9	-3	6	2	3	11	-3
-10/-6						1	0	0	1	-7	4	1	1	6	-8
-15/-11						0			0	-13	1	0	0	1	-12

Temperature Range	FEBRUARY					MARCH					APRIL					ANNUAL TOTAL				
	Obsn Hour Gp 01 to 08	09 to 16	17 to 24	Total Obsn	M C W B	Obsn Hour Gp 01 to 08	09 to 16	17 to 24	Total Obsn	M C W B	Obsn Hour Gp 01 to 08	09 to 16	17 to 24	Total Obsn	M C W B	Obsn Hour Gp 01 to 08	09 to 16	17 to 24	Total Obsn	M C W B
100/104																	0		0	79
95/99																	2	0	2	75
90/94																	21	6	27	73
85/89												0		0	69		85	30	115	71
80/84												3	1	4	64	3	180	78	261	69
75/79							0	0	0	58		6	3	9	62	24	236	151	411	66
70/74							1	1	2	55		9	6	15	59	116	274	236	626	63
65/69							2	1	3	53	2	16	11	29	56	217	253	261	731	60
60/64		0		0	57		5	2	7	52	9	19	18	46	54	279	203	252	734	57
55/59	0	1	1	2	55	2	8	5	15	50	13	29	21	63	50	272	179	224	675	52
50/54	1	2	2	5	48	6	12	10	28	46	22	29	34	85	46	249	151	201	601	48
45/49	1	8	3	12	43	6	17	13	36	41	31	37	33	101	42	239	164	175	578	43
40/44	6	12	9	27	38	14	29	21	64	38	30	33	40	103	38	201	180	193	574	39
35/39	12	30	23	65	34	30	52	44	126	34	48	33	39	120	34	246	222	233	701	34
30/34	40	58	51	149	30	59	53	61	173	30	48	18	25	91	30	321	261	277	859	30
25/29	45	46	48	139	25	47	35	42	124	25	25	4	8	37	25	260	199	228	687	25
20/24	39	29	31	99	21	33	22	24	79	20	8	1	3	12	21	173	139	140	452	21
15/19	31	17	28	76	16	24	9	14	47	16	3	0	0	3	16	128	80	106	314	16
10/14	19	12	14	45	11	14	2	7	23	11	0			0	11	79	47	64	190	11
5/9	14	6	8	28	6	7	2	3	12	7						54	26	35	115	6
0/4	9	3	5	17	1	4	0	1	5	2						31	10	20	61	1
-5/-1	7	1	1	9	-3	2	0	0	2	-3						21	4	6	31	-3
-10/-6	2	0		2	-8											7	1	1	9	-8
-15/-11																1	0	0	1	-12

MUSKEGON/MUSKEGON CO APRT MICHIGAN

LAT 43 10N   LONG 86 14W   ELEV 625 FT

MEAN FREQUENCY OF OCCURRENCE OF DRY BULB TEMPERATURE (DEGREES F) WITH MEAN COINCIDENT WET BULB TEMPERATURE (DEGREES F) FOR EACH DRY BULB TEMPERATURE RANGE

Temperature Range	MAY Obsn Hour Gp 01 to 08	MAY 09 to 16	MAY 17 to 24	MAY Total Obsn	MAY MCWB	JUNE Obsn Hour Gp 01 to 08	JUNE 09 to 16	JUNE 17 to 24	JUNE Total Obsn	JUNE MCWB	JULY Obsn Hour Gp 01 to 08	JULY 09 to 16	JULY 17 to 24	JULY Total Obsn	JULY MCWB
95/99															
90/94		0		0	74		0	0	0	73		3	1	4	74
85/89		1	0	1	70		7	5	12	71		16	7	23	72
80/84		4	3	7	68	0	29	15	44	69	1	47	22	70	70
75/79	0	16	8	24	64	6	47	29	82	67	12	75	48	135	67
70/74	4	28	19	51	61	18	55	43	116	63	47	64	64	175	65
65/69	10	40	26	76	58	44	45	52	141	61	62	30	53	145	62
60/64	25	51	42	118	54	57	39	43	139	57	67	11	37	115	59
55/59	36	52	46	134	51	48	15	31	94	53	37	2	14	53	55
50/54	51	31	48	130	47	34	2	17	53	49	18		2	20	50
45/49	60	16	35	111	44	25	1	5	31	45	4		0	4	47
40/44	40	7	15	62	39	7		0	7	41	0			0	43
35/39	18	1	5	24	35	1			1	36					
30/34	4		0	4	30	0			0	32					
25/29	1			1	27										
20/24															

Temperature Range	AUGUST Obsn Hour Gp 01 to 08	AUGUST 09 to 16	AUGUST 17 to 24	AUGUST Total Obsn	AUGUST MCWB	SEPTEMBER Obsn Hour Gp 01 to 08	SEPTEMBER 09 to 16	SEPTEMBER 17 to 24	SEPTEMBER Total Obsn	SEPTEMBER MCWB	OCTOBER Obsn Hour Gp 01 to 08	OCTOBER 09 to 16	OCTOBER 17 to 24	OCTOBER Total Obsn	OCTOBER MCWB
95/99		0		0	76										
90/94		2	1	3	75		1		1	69					
85/89		13	4	17	71		5	1	6	72					
80/84	1	35	16	52	70	0	13	7	20	70		2	0	2	69
75/79	8	70	36	114	67	6	24	15	45	68		5	1	6	65
70/74	34	70	59	163	65	13	43	26	82	64	1	17	9	27	62
65/69	58	37	63	158	62	27	56	40	123	61	11	31	18	60	60
60/64	61	18	44	123	59	47	55	53	155	57	20	40	28	88	56
55/59	47	3	20	70	55	44	27	46	117	53	32	44	42	118	52
50/54	29	0	5	34	51	48	11	34	93	49	39	48	46	133	48
45/49	9		1	10	46	30	4	14	48	45	44	30	47	121	43
40/44	1			1	42	15	0	4	19	41	43	19	32	94	39
35/39						8		1	9	37	38	10	16	64	35
30/34						2		0	2	32	15	2	7	24	31
25/29						0			0	29	5		2	7	27
20/24											1		0	1	22

MUSKEGON/MUSKEGON CO APRT MICHIGAN

Temperature Range	NOVEMBER Obsn Hour Gp 01 to 08	NOVEMBER 09 to 16	NOVEMBER 17 to 24	NOVEMBER Total Obsn	NOVEMBER MCWB	DECEMBER Obsn Hour Gp 01 to 08	DECEMBER 09 to 16	DECEMBER 17 to 24	DECEMBER Total Obsn	DECEMBER MCWB	JANUARY Obsn Hour Gp 01 to 08	JANUARY 09 to 16	JANUARY 17 to 24	JANUARY Total Obsn	JANUARY MCWB	FEBRUARY Obsn Hour Gp 01 to 08	FEBRUARY 09 to 16	FEBRUARY 17 to 24	FEBRUARY Total Obsn	FEBRUARY MCWB
95/99																				
90/94																				
85/89																				
80/84																				
75/79		0	0	0	66															
70/74		1	1	2	64															
65/69		2	1	3	59															
60/64	2	7	5	14	57		0	0	0	57		0	0	0	58					
55/59	9	15	11	35	53	1	2	2	5	52			1	1	54	0			0	50
50/54	19	32	22	73	48	2	7	6	15	48	0	1	1	2	49	0	0	0	0	45
45/49	29	42	33	104	43	5	6	4	15	44	3	3	3	9	45	1	2	2	5	42
40/44	45	50	57	152	38	13	18	16	47	40	4	9	8	21	40	3	11	5	19	38
35/39	52	41	50	143	34	26	33	29	88	35	25	34	29	88	35	19	31	26	76	35
30/34	45	27	32	104	30	54	55	52	161	30	49	51	51	151	30	48	53	53	154	30
25/29	22	15	18	55	25	50	54	57	161	25	40	46	46	132	26	36	51	49	136	25
20/24	12	7	8	27	21	40	37	39	116	21	43	35	37	115	21	39	32	37	108	21
15/19	3	1	2	6	17	31	22	25	78	16	29	27	28	84	16	31	21	25	77	16
10/14	1	0	0	1	11	21	12	13	46	12	27	24	26	77	11	20	14	16	50	11
5/9	1	1	0	2	7	5	3	3	11	7	16	13	12	41	7	14	5	8	27	6
0/4	0		0	0	3	1	0	1	2	1	7	3	6	16	2	7	2	3	12	2
-5/-1			0	0	-4	1		1	2	-3	4	1	1	6	-2	4	0	0	4	-3
-10/-6	0		0	0	-9			0	0	-7	1	0		1	-8	1	0		1	-7
-15/-11	1			1	-12						0			0	-11					

Temperature Range	MARCH Obsn Hour Gp 01 to 08	MARCH 09 to 16	MARCH 17 to 24	MARCH Total Obsn	MARCH MCWB	APRIL Obsn Hour Gp 01 to 08	APRIL 09 to 16	APRIL 17 to 24	APRIL Total Obsn	APRIL MCWB	ANNUAL TOTAL Obsn Hour Gp 01 to 08	ANNUAL TOTAL 09 to 16	ANNUAL TOTAL 17 to 24	ANNUAL TOTAL Total Obsn	ANNUAL TOTAL MCWB
95/99												0		0	76
90/94												6	2	8	74
85/89												42	17	59	72
80/84							1	0	1	65	2	131	63	196	70
75/79							3	1	4	61	32	240	138	410	67
70/74		0		0	59	0	8	5	13	59	117	286	226	629	64
65/69		1	0	1	55	1	13	10	24	56	213	255	263	731	61
60/64	0	4	2	6	51	7	19	15	41	53	286	244	269	799	57
55/59	2	6	5	13	50	13	27	21	61	50	269	193	239	701	52
50/54	6	13	9	28	47	20	32	29	81	46	266	177	219	662	48
45/49	8	17	14	39	42	26	44	35	105	42	244	165	193	602	43
40/44	15	27	21	63	38	40	37	42	119	38	226	178	200	604	39
35/39	37	50	48	135	34	57	39	51	147	34	281	239	255	775	35
30/34	53	52	59	164	30	50	14	24	88	30	320	254	278	852	30
25/29	45	42	45	132	25	20	3	6	29	26	219	211	223	653	25
20/24	37	22	26	85	20	3	0	1	4	21	175	133	148	456	21
15/19	21	9	11	41	16	1			1	18	116	80	91	287	16
10/14	13	2	6	21	11						82	52	61	195	11
5/9	7	2	2	11	7						43	24	25	92	7
0/4	2	1	1	4	1						17	6	11	34	2
-5/-1	2		0	2	-3						11	1	2	14	-3
-10/-6											2	0	0	2	-8
-15/-11											1			1	-12

SELFRIDGE ANGB/MT CLEMENS MICHIGAN

LAT 42 36N LONG 82 50W ELEV 583 FT

MEAN FREQUENCY OF OCCURRENCE OF DRY BULB TEMPERATURE (DEGREES F) WITH MEAN COINCIDENT WET BULB TEMPERATURE (DEGREES F) FOR EACH DRY BULB TEMPERATURE RANGE

Temperature Range	MAY Obsn Hour Gp 01 to 08	MAY 09 to 16	MAY 17 to 24	MAY Total Obsn	MAY MCWB	JUNE Obsn Hour Gp 01 to 08	JUNE 09 to 16	JUNE 17 to 24	JUNE Total Obsn	JUNE MCWB	JULY Obsn Hour Gp 01 to 08	JULY 09 to 16	JULY 17 to 24	JULY Total Obsn	JULY MCWB
95/99							0	0	0	77		1	0	1	74
90/94		1	0	1	72		7	2	9	74		5	2	7	74
85/89		4	1	5	69	0	18	7	25	72	0	30	10	40	72
80/84		10	3	13	67	2	34	18	54	69	1	57	28	86	70
75/79	1	19	10	30	64	7	43	29	79	67	14	69	55	138	67
70/74	5	26	17	48	62	24	49	43	116	64	52	54	70	176	65
65/69	15	41	29	85	58	48	42	52	142	61	73	23	47	143	62
60/64	22	44	37	103	55	53	31	42	126	57	56	7	25	88	58
55/59	38	38	47	123	51	45	13	28	86	53	32	2	9	43	54
50/54	48	34	41	123	47	34	4	15	53	48	18		2	20	50
45/49	44	21	32	97	43	20		4	24	44	3		0	3	45
40/44	43	9	23	75	39	6		1	7	40	1			1	40
35/39	24	1	6	31	34	1			1	35					
30/34	5		1	6	30										
25/29	1		0	1	26										
20/24	0			0	22										
15/19															

Temperature Range	AUGUST Obsn Hour Gp 01 to 08	AUGUST 09 to 16	AUGUST 17 to 24	AUGUST Total Obsn	AUGUST MCWB	SEPTEMBER Obsn Hour Gp 01 to 08	SEPTEMBER 09 to 16	SEPTEMBER 17 to 24	SEPTEMBER Total Obsn	SEPTEMBER MCWB	OCTOBER Obsn Hour Gp 01 to 08	OCTOBER 09 to 16	OCTOBER 17 to 24	OCTOBER Total Obsn	OCTOBER MCWB
95/99		0		0	75										
90/94		5	1	6	76		0		0	75					
85/89		22	7	29	73		8	1	9	74		1	0	1	64
80/84	1	48	23	72	70		20	7	27	71		3	0	3	68
75/79	9	61	40	110	68	5	36	18	59	68		8	2	10	65
70/74	37	59	65	161	65	23	52	40	115	65	1	20	8	29	62
65/69	69	37	60	166	62	40	47	51	138	62	6	27	18	51	60
60/64	62	14	31	107	59	42	38	48	128	57	20	44	33	97	57
55/59	40	2	16	58	54	37	22	37	96	53	29	46	43	118	52
50/54	22	1	4	27	50	44	13	23	80	49	45	44	52	141	48
45/49	7		1	8	46	31	3	9	43	45	44	32	41	117	43
40/44	1		0	1	41	12	1	6	19	41	45	17	30	92	39
35/39						6		0	6	36	33	6	14	53	35
30/34						0			0	31	15	1	5	21	30
25/29						0			0	28	8		2	10	26
20/24											1		0	1	22
15/19											0			0	17

SELFRIDGE ANGB/MT CLEMENS MICHIGAN

Temperature Range	NOVEMBER Obsn Hour Gp 01 to 08	NOVEMBER Obsn Hour Gp 09 to 16	NOVEMBER Obsn Hour Gp 17 to 24	NOVEMBER Total Obsn	NOVEMBER MCWB	DECEMBER Obsn Hour Gp 01 to 08	DECEMBER Obsn Hour Gp 09 to 16	DECEMBER Obsn Hour Gp 17 to 24	DECEMBER Total Obsn	DECEMBER MCWB	JANUARY Obsn Hour Gp 01 to 08	JANUARY Obsn Hour Gp 09 to 16	JANUARY Obsn Hour Gp 17 to 24	JANUARY Total Obsn	JANUARY MCWB
95/99															
90/94															
85/89															
80/84															
75/79		0		0	66										
70/74		0	0	0	62										
65/69	0	2	1	3	57										
60/64	2	7	3	12	56		0	1	1	57		1	0	1	56
55/59	6	19	11	36	52	1	2	2	5	54	1	0	0	1	54
50/54	16	32	25	73	48	2	5	3	10	48	1	1	0	2	48
45/49	29	45	38	112	43	6	9	6	21	43	1	2	2	5	44
40/44	43	52	51	146	39	13	25	21	59	39	3	10	6	19	39
35/39	50	38	45	133	34	27	39	39	105	34	14	27	22	63	34
30/34	43	29	37	109	30	45	53	47	145	30	41	45	48	134	30
25/29	29	11	19	59	25	50	53	50	153	25	42	42	38	122	25
20/24	15	4	7	26	21	40	31	37	108	21	34	40	36	110	20
15/19	5	1	3	9	16	28	17	21	66	16	32	32	35	99	16
10/14	1	0	1	2	12	17	10	15	42	11	30	26	32	88	11
5/9	0	0	0	0	7	13	4	5	22	7	26	15	19	60	6
0/4	0			0	4	5	1	2	8	2	14	5	8	27	2
-5/-1						1	0	0	1	-3	10	1	2	13	-3
-10/-6											1	0	0	1	-8
-15/-11											1	0	0	1	-12

Temperature Range	FEBRUARY Obsn Hour Gp 01 to 08	FEBRUARY Obsn Hour Gp 09 to 16	FEBRUARY Obsn Hour Gp 17 to 24	FEBRUARY Total Obsn	FEBRUARY MCWB	MARCH Obsn Hour Gp 01 to 08	MARCH Obsn Hour Gp 09 to 16	MARCH Obsn Hour Gp 17 to 24	MARCH Total Obsn	MARCH MCWB	APRIL Obsn Hour Gp 01 to 08	APRIL Obsn Hour Gp 09 to 16	APRIL Obsn Hour Gp 17 to 24	APRIL Total Obsn	APRIL MCWB	ANNUAL TOTAL Obsn Hour Gp 01 to 08	ANNUAL TOTAL Obsn Hour Gp 09 to 16	ANNUAL TOTAL Obsn Hour Gp 17 to 24	ANNUAL TOTAL Total Obsn	ANNUAL TOTAL MCWB
95/99																	1	0	1	75
90/94																	18	5	23	74
85/89												0	0	0	66	0	83	26	109	72
80/84												2	1	3	64	4	174	80	258	70
75/79												5	2	7	64	36	241	156	433	67
70/74							1	0	1	57	0	8	4	12	60	142	269	247	658	65
65/69							3	1	4	54	2	15	8	25	57	253	237	267	757	61
60/64		0		0	54	0	4	2	6	51	6	22	14	42	54	263	212	236	711	57
55/59		0		0	51	2	6	4	12	49	13	31	22	66	50	244	181	219	644	52
50/54	0	1	1	2	47	3	10	5	18	46	21	39	34	94	46	254	184	205	643	48
45/49	1	5	2	8	42	5	20	14	39	41	35	40	46	121	42	226	177	195	598	43
40/44	4	15	9	28	38	10	35	24	69	37	41	40	44	125	38	222	204	215	641	39
35/39	17	31	27	75	34	39	60	56	155	34	54	28	40	122	34	265	230	249	744	34
30/34	34	46	43	123	30	73	53	69	195	30	43	10	19	72	30	299	237	269	805	30
25/29	36	45	43	124	25	45	32	36	113	25	20	2	6	28	25	231	185	194	610	25
20/24	39	31	37	107	20	32	15	22	69	20	4	0	1	5	21	165	121	140	426	21
15/19	39	20	29	88	16	20	6	11	37	16	1		0	1	17	125	76	99	300	16
10/14	22	16	17	55	11	13	2	4	19	11						83	54	69	206	11
5/9	15	9	11	35	6	5	1	1	7	6						59	29	36	124	6
0/4	10	3	5	18	1	1	0	0	1	2						30	9	15	54	2
-5/-1	6	1	1	8	-3											17	2	3	22	-3
-10/-6	1	0		1	-7											2	0	0	2	-7
-15/-11																1	0	0	1	-12

TRAVERSE CITY APRT MICHIGAN

LAT 44 45N LONG 85 35W ELEV 624 FT

MEAN FREQUENCY OF OCCURRENCE OF DRY BULB TEMPERATURE (DEGREES F) WITH MEAN COINCIDENT WET BULB TEMPERATURE (DEGREES F) FOR EACH DRY BULB TEMPERATURE RANGE

Temperature Range	MAY Obsn Hour Gp 01 to 08	09 to 16	17 to 24	Total Obsn	MCWB	JUNE Obsn Hour Gp 01 to 08	09 to 16	17 to 24	Total Obsn	MCWB	JULY Obsn Hour Gp 01 to 08	09 to 16	17 to 24	Total Obsn	MCWB
100/104															
95/99							1	0	1	73		1	0	1	77
90/94		1	0	1	70		5	1	6	73		7	1	8	72
85/89		3	1	4	68		14	4	18	71		25	7	32	71
80/84		8	3	11	65	1	31	10	42	67	1	47	21	69	68
75/79	0	19	9	28	62	6	38	25	69	65	8	60	38	106	66
70/74	4	24	15	43	60	17	42	35	94	63	30	50	53	133	64
65/69	12	33	21	66	57	32	41	42	115	60	49	37	58	144	62
60/64	20	38	27	85	54	45	33	44	122	57	71	18	40	129	58
55/59	29	35	36	100	51	48	21	39	108	53	49	5	21	75	55
50/54	38	38	42	118	47	40	11	22	73	49	28	0	6	34	50
45/49	43	27	40	110	43	29	3	13	45	45	9		1	10	46
40/44	43	15	32	90	39	14	0	3	17	41	3		0	3	42
35/39	31	6	17	54	35	7		1	8	37	0			0	38
30/34	20	1	5	26	31	2		0	2	32					
25/29	7		0	7	27										
20/24	1			1	23										

Temperature Range	AUGUST Obsn Hour Gp 01 to 08	09 to 16	17 to 24	Total Obsn	MCWB	SEPTEMBER Obsn Hour Gp 01 to 08	09 to 16	17 to 24	Total Obsn	MCWB	OCTOBER Obsn Hour Gp 01 to 08	09 to 16	17 to 24	Total Obsn	MCWB
100/104		0		0	73										
95/99		1	0	1	74		0		0	75					
90/94		5	1	6	72		2	0	2	73					
85/89		14	5	19	72		7	2	9	72					
80/84	0	38	15	53	69	0	8	5	13	70		2	0	2	64
75/79	6	54	31	91	67	5	19	10	34	68		8	1	9	62
70/74	24	57	51	132	64	11	34	18	63	63	0	15	5	20	60
65/69	55	45	55	155	62	15	46	30	91	60	4	22	13	39	58
60/64	62	25	47	134	58	34	52	46	132	57	14	34	21	69	56
55/59	49	8	29	86	54	50	42	51	143	53	23	46	34	103	52
50/54	31	1	10	42	50	49	22	39	110	49	39	38	46	123	48
45/49	15		3	18	46	36	7	23	66	45	48	40	48	136	44
40/44	5			5	42	24	1	11	36	41	53	28	46	127	40
35/39	0			0	37	10		3	13	36	39	11	23	73	35
30/34						3		0	3	31	22	2	9	33	31
25/29						0			0	28	6		2	8	27
20/24											1			1	23

TRAVERSE CITY APRT MICHIGAN

Temperature Range	NOVEMBER Obsn Hour Gp 01 to 08	NOVEMBER 09 to 16	NOVEMBER 17 to 24	NOVEMBER Total Obsn	NOVEMBER MCWB	DECEMBER Obsn Hour Gp 01 to 08	DECEMBER 09 to 16	DECEMBER 17 to 24	DECEMBER Total Obsn	DECEMBER MCWB	JANUARY Obsn Hour Gp 01 to 08	JANUARY 09 to 16	JANUARY 17 to 24	JANUARY Total Obsn	JANUARY MCWB	FEBRUARY Obsn Hour Gp 01 to 08	FEBRUARY 09 to 16	FEBRUARY 17 to 24	FEBRUARY Total Obsn	FEBRUARY MCWB
100/104																				
95/99																				
90/94																				
85/89																				
80/84																				
75/79																				
70/74		1	0	1	61															
65/69	0	3	1	4	58															
60/64	2	6	3	11	55		1	0	1	53										
55/59	8	10	10	28	52	0	2	1	3	51										
50/54	7	20	11	38	47	3	2	2	7	47			0	0	49		1	0	1	43
45/49	19	33	25	77	43	2	3	4	9	43	1	1	1	3	45	1	2	1	4	43
40/44	33	47	38	118	39	5	13	8	26	39	2	4	3	9	39	1	7	4	12	38
35/39	54	49	55	158	35	29	32	29	90	35	9	20	14	43	34	10	24	16	50	34
30/34	56	36	49	141	30	47	53	51	151	30	38	44	40	122	30	32	45	40	117	30
25/29	32	21	28	81	26	45	50	50	145	25	44	54	48	146	25	36	47	44	127	25
20/24	14	10	11	35	21	42	42	38	122	21	46	39	47	132	21	45	41	46	132	21
15/19	9	3	5	17	16	33	31	34	98	16	35	36	34	105	16	31	24	29	84	16
10/14	3	2	2	7	11	25	14	23	62	11	31	27	31	89	11	24	18	21	63	11
5/9	2	1	1	4	7	11	4	7	22	7	22	14	18	54	7	19	8	13	40	7
0/4	1	0	0	1	3	4	1	2	7	2	12	7	7	26	2	10	5	7	22	2
-5/-1	1		0	1	-3	1	0	0	1	-3	4	2	3	9	-3	7	2	3	12	-3
-10/-6						0	0		0	-6	3	1	1	5	-8	4	1	1	6	-8
-15/-11											1	0		1	-13	2		0	2	-13
-20/-16											0			0	-17	1	0	0	1	-19
-25/-21																1			1	-23

Temperature Range	MARCH Obsn Hour Gp 01 to 08	MARCH 09 to 16	MARCH 17 to 24	MARCH Total Obsn	MARCH MCWB	APRIL Obsn Hour Gp 01 to 08	APRIL 09 to 16	APRIL 17 to 24	APRIL Total Obsn	APRIL MCWB	ANNUAL TOTAL Obsn Hour Gp 01 to 08	ANNUAL TOTAL 09 to 16	ANNUAL TOTAL 17 to 24	ANNUAL TOTAL Total Obsn	ANNUAL TOTAL MCWB
100/104												0		0	73
95/99												3	0	3	74
90/94												20	3	23	73
85/89							0		0	65		63	19	82	71
80/84							2	1	3	61	2	136	55	193	68
75/79							4	2	6	59	25	202	116	343	66
70/74		0		0	51	0	7	3	10	57	86	230	180	496	63
65/69		1	0	1	53	2	11	6	19	55	169	239	226	634	60
60/64		1	1	2	51	3	17	10	30	52	251	225	239	715	57
55/59	0	2	2	4	49	8	24	17	49	49	264	195	240	699	53
50/54	1	5	3	9	46	15	31	21	67	45	251	169	202	622	48
45/49	2	12	5	19	41	28	36	32	96	42	233	164	196	593	43
40/44	8	25	13	46	37	36	39	45	120	38	227	179	203	609	39
35/39	24	52	37	113	34	46	39	44	129	34	259	233	239	731	34
30/34	48	57	63	168	30	56	22	41	119	30	324	260	298	882	30
25/29	50	43	53	146	25	31	4	13	48	26	251	219	238	708	25
20/24	44	29	37	110	21	11	2	3	16	21	204	163	182	549	21
15/19	29	13	18	60	16	2	1	1	4	17	139	108	121	368	16
10/14	20	4	10	34	12	2		0	2	11	105	65	87	257	11
5/9	10	1	5	16	7	1		0	1	6	65	28	44	137	7
0/4	6	1	1	8	2						33	14	17	64	2
-5/-1	5	0	0	5	-2						18	4	6	28	-3
-10/-6	1	0	0	1	-8						8	2	2	12	-8
-15/-11	0		0	0	-13						3	0	0	3	-13
-20/-16	0		0	0	-19						1	0	0	1	-18
-25/-21	1		0	1	-23						2		0	2	-23

WURTSMITH AFB/OSCODA MICHIGAN

LAT 44 27N LONG 83 24W ELEV 634 FT

MEAN FREQUENCY OF OCCURRENCE OF DRY BULB TEMPERATURE (DEGREES F) WITH MEAN COINCIDENT WET BULB TEMPERATURE (DEGREES F) FOR EACH DRY BULB TEMPERATURE RANGE

Temperature Range	MAY Obsn Hour Gp 01 to 08	MAY 09 to 16	MAY 17 to 24	MAY Total Obsn	MAY MCWB	JUNE Obsn Hour Gp 01 to 08	JUNE 09 to 16	JUNE 17 to 24	JUNE Total Obsn	JUNE MCWB	JULY Obsn Hour Gp 01 to 08	JULY 09 to 16	JULY 17 to 24	JULY Total Obsn	JULY MCWB
95/99		0		0	74		1	0	1	71		1	0	1	69
90/94		1	0	1	71		5	2	7	71		5	1	6	72
85/89		3	1	4	69		13	4	17	70		15	5	20	71
80/84		8	3	11	65	0	21	10	31	68	0	38	12	50	68
75/79	0	13	5	18	63	3	28	16	47	65	5	50	30	85	66
70/74	2	18	11	31	61	9	37	26	72	62	24	62	54	140	64
65/69	10	22	19	51	58	28	42	37	107	60	49	50	64	163	62
60/64	16	32	21	69	54	39	47	50	136	56	69	22	48	139	58
55/59	21	39	30	90	50	58	29	49	136	53	52	5	25	82	54
50/54	36	39	43	118	46	49	15	31	95	49	33	0	7	40	49
45/49	50	40	50	140	43	29	2	12	43	44	13		2	15	45
40/44	45	24	37	106	39	18	0	4	22	40	2			2	41
35/39	37	8	21	66	35	5		1	6	36	0			0	37
30/34	21	0	6	27	30	1		0	1	31					
25/29	8		1	9	26										
20/24	1			1	21										
15/19															

Temperature Range	AUGUST Obsn Hour Gp 01 to 08	AUGUST 09 to 16	AUGUST 17 to 24	AUGUST Total Obsn	AUGUST MCWB	SEPTEMBER Obsn Hour Gp 01 to 08	SEPTEMBER 09 to 16	SEPTEMBER 17 to 24	SEPTEMBER Total Obsn	SEPTEMBER MCWB	OCTOBER Obsn Hour Gp 01 to 08	OCTOBER 09 to 16	OCTOBER 17 to 24	OCTOBER Total Obsn	OCTOBER MCWB
95/99		0	0	0	73										
90/94		2	1	3	74		1		1	76					
85/89		12	3	15	71		3	1	4	74		0		0	65
80/84		29	11	40	70		10	3	13	70		0	0	0	66
75/79	2	48	22	72	67	1	23	10	34	67		6	1	7	63
70/74	18	61	47	126	65	11	36	23	70	65		11	3	14	60
65/69	50	57	68	175	62	22	46	34	102	61	2	18	11	31	59
60/64	68	28	51	147	59	33	48	46	127	58	8	31	19	58	56
55/59	47	8	26	81	54	41	41	46	128	53	26	49	36	111	52
50/54	35	2	16	53	50	46	22	37	105	49	41	47	48	136	48
45/49	24	0	2	26	45	39	9	24	72	44	37	42	49	128	43
40/44	4		0	4	41	27	2	11	40	40	47	27	39	113	39
35/39	0			0	38	15	0	5	20	36	46	12	26	84	35
30/34						6		1	7	32	28	4	13	45	30
25/29						0			0	28	10	0	3	13	26
20/24											3		0	3	21
15/19											0		0	0	17

WURTSMITH AFB/OSCODA MICHIGAN

Temperature Range	NOVEMBER Obsn Hour Gp 01 to 08	NOVEMBER 09 to 16	NOVEMBER 17 to 24	NOVEMBER Total Obsn	NOVEMBER MCWB	DECEMBER Obsn Hour Gp 01 to 08	DECEMBER 09 to 16	DECEMBER 17 to 24	DECEMBER Total Obsn	DECEMBER MCWB	JANUARY Obsn Hour Gp 01 to 08	JANUARY 09 to 16	JANUARY 17 to 24	JANUARY Total Obsn	JANUARY MCWB	FEBRUARY Obsn Hour Gp 01 to 08	FEBRUARY 09 to 16	FEBRUARY 17 to 24	FEBRUARY Total Obsn	FEBRUARY MCWB
95/99																				
90/94																				
85/89																				
80/84																				
75/79																				
70/74		0		0	59															
65/69	0	1	0	1	58															
60/64	1	3	1	5	55		0		0	52										
55/59	1	9	5	15	53		1	0	1	51										
50/54	12	20	16	48	48	0	3	1	4	49							0		0	39
45/49	19	40	27	86	43	3	3	4	10	43	1	1	0	2	43	0	2	1	3	43
40/44	36	47	45	128	39	7	12	8	27	39	1	2	1	4	39	2	5	3	10	37
35/39	49	48	46	143	34	23	32	28	83	35	6	16	12	34	34	6	19	12	37	34
30/34	49	40	48	137	30	45	51	48	144	30	30	42	36	108	30	23	40	35	98	30
25/29	37	20	30	87	25	46	55	50	151	25	36	42	42	120	25	31	45	42	118	25
20/24	21	8	13	42	21	41	41	40	122	21	36	42	37	115	21	38	39	39	116	20
15/19	9	2	6	17	16	29	25	29	83	16	35	39	35	109	16	31	30	33	94	16
10/14	6	1	2	9	12	20	14	19	53	11	30	32	34	96	11	28	19	26	73	11
5/9	1	0	1	2	7	18	7	12	37	7	28	17	27	72	6	28	14	17	59	6
0/4						11	2	5	18	2	19	9	13	41	2	16	7	10	33	1
-5/-1						4	1	2	7	-3	14	4	6	24	-3	12	3	4	19	-3
-10/-6						1	0	0	1	-7	9	1	4	14	-8	6	1	2	9	-8
-15/-11						0		0	0	-13	3	0	0	3	-12	2	0	1	3	-13
-20/-16											0	0		0	-18	1			1	-17

Temperature Range	MARCH Obsn Hour Gp 01 to 08	MARCH 09 to 16	MARCH 17 to 24	MARCH Total Obsn	MARCH MCWB	APRIL Obsn Hour Gp 01 to 08	APRIL 09 to 16	APRIL 17 to 24	APRIL Total Obsn	APRIL MCWB	ANNUAL TOTAL Obsn Hour Gp 01 to 08	ANNUAL TOTAL 09 to 16	ANNUAL TOTAL 17 to 24	ANNUAL TOTAL Total Obsn	ANNUAL TOTAL MCWB
95/99												2	0	2	71
90/94												14	4	18	72
85/89							0	0	0	64		46	14	60	71
80/84							2	1	3	64	0	108	40	148	68
75/79							2	2	4	62	11	170	86	267	66
70/74		0		0	56		5	1	6	59	64	230	165	459	64
65/69		1	0	1	52	1	7	3	11	56	162	244	236	642	61
60/64		2	1	3	53	3	13	6	22	53	237	226	243	706	57
55/59	0	4	1	5	48	6	20	13	39	50	252	205	231	688	52
50/54	1	5	3	9	45	11	27	19	57	45	264	180	221	665	48
45/49	3	11	7	21	41	22	43	33	98	42	240	193	211	644	43
40/44	5	23	13	41	37	36	54	48	138	38	230	196	209	635	39
35/39	19	51	34	104	33	55	41	52	148	34	261	227	237	725	34
30/34	56	60	70	186	30	53	23	43	119	30	312	260	300	872	30
25/29	51	46	54	151	25	34	3	16	53	25	253	211	238	702	25
20/24	38	27	31	96	20	16	1	3	20	21	194	158	163	515	21
15/19	27	12	18	57	16	4		1	5	16	135	108	122	365	16
10/14	25	4	11	40	11	2			2	12	111	70	92	273	11
5/9	13	1	3	17	7	0			0	8	88	39	60	187	6
0/4	6	0	2	8	2						52	18	30	100	2
-5/-1	2	0	0	2	-3						32	8	12	52	-3
-10/-6	1		0	1	-9						17	2	6	25	-8
-15/-11											5	0	1	6	-12
-20/-16											1	0		1	-17

DULUTH IAP MINNESOTA

LAT 46 50N LONG 92 11W ELEV 1428 FT

MEAN FREQUENCY OF OCCURRENCE OF DRY BULB TEMPERATURE (DEGREES F) WITH MEAN COINCIDENT WET BULB TEMPERATURE (DEGREES F) FOR EACH DRY BULB TEMPERATURE RANGE

Temperature Range	MAY Obsn Hour Gp 01 to 08	MAY 09 to 16	MAY 17 to 24	MAY Total Obsn	MAY MCWB	JUNE Obsn Hour Gp 01 to 08	JUNE 09 to 16	JUNE 17 to 24	JUNE Total Obsn	JUNE MCWB	JULY Obsn Hour Gp 01 to 08	JULY 09 to 16	JULY 17 to 24	JULY Total Obsn	JULY MCWB
90/94							1	0	1	70		1		1	73
85/89		1	0	1	65		5	2	7	68		10	3	13	71
80/84		4	2	6	62	0	14	4	18	66	0	32	10	42	68
75/79		8	3	11	59	1	27	11	39	64	2	51	21	74	65
70/74	1	19	7	27	56	6	37	19	62	61	14	56	36	106	63
65/69	2	25	13	40	54	16	41	27	84	58	38	45	51	134	61
60/64	9	36	20	65	51	33	47	46	126	56	62	34	57	153	58
55/59	22	40	32	94	49	53	37	54	144	53	69	12	44	125	55
50/54	36	40	45	121	46	60	22	46	128	49	46	5	23	74	50
45/49	49	29	45	123	43	41	8	22	71	45	15	1	3	19	46
40/44	52	24	40	116	39	23	1	8	32	40	2		0	2	42
35/39	40	14	26	80	34	6		1	7	36	0			0	38
30/34	29	5	13	47	31	2			2	31					
25/29	7	1	2	10	26										
20/24	1	0	0	1	22										
15/19															
10/14															

Temperature Range	AUGUST Obsn Hour Gp 01 to 08	AUGUST 09 to 16	AUGUST 17 to 24	AUGUST Total Obsn	AUGUST MCWB	SEPTEMBER Obsn Hour Gp 01 to 08	SEPTEMBER 09 to 16	SEPTEMBER 17 to 24	SEPTEMBER Total Obsn	SEPTEMBER MCWB	OCTOBER Obsn Hour Gp 01 to 08	OCTOBER 09 to 16	OCTOBER 17 to 24	OCTOBER Total Obsn	OCTOBER MCWB
90/94		1	0	1	71										
85/89		7	1	8	71		1	0	1	74		0		0	64
80/84	0	21	6	27	68		3	1	4	70		1		1	62
75/79	1	37	14	52	65	0	10	2	12	65		3	0	3	61
70/74	10	52	29	91	63	3	19	7	29	62	0	9	1	10	58
65/69	29	55	47	131	61	7	34	14	55	59	1	14	5	20	56
60/64	54	43	55	152	58	16	45	30	91	56	3	23	11	37	52
55/59	75	22	54	151	55	36	49	43	128	53	12	33	19	64	50
50/54	51	9	30	90	50	53	40	56	149	49	22	36	33	91	47
45/49	22	1	10	33	46	56	27	50	133	45	45	43	49	137	44
40/44	5		1	6	42	41	9	24	74	40	49	40	50	139	39
35/39	1			1	37	18	2	9	29	35	47	28	40	115	34
30/34						9		3	12	31	44	13	27	84	30
25/29						1		0	1	27	16	3	8	27	26
20/24											6	1	3	10	21
15/19											2	0	1	3	17
10/14											0			0	13

DULUTH IAP MINNESOTA

Temperature Range	NOVEMBER Obsn Hour Gp 01 to 08	09 to 16	17 to 24	Total Obsn	M C W B	DECEMBER Obsn Hour Gp 01 to 08	09 to 16	17 to 24	Total Obsn	M C W B	JANUARY Obsn Hour Gp 01 to 08	09 to 16	17 to 24	Total Obsn	M C W B
90/94															
85/89															
80/84															
75/79															
70/74															
65/69		0		0	53										
60/64		1	0	1	49										
55/59	0	4	1	5	48										
50/54	2	9	3	14	47	0	1	1	2	48					
45/49	6	16	9	31	43	1	1	1	3	45					
40/44	15	24	21	60	38	1	3	1	5	39		1		1	35
35/39	28	42	36	106	34	4	10	6	20	34	1	4	3	8	33
30/34	52	45	51	148	30	17	22	22	61	30	6	11	8	25	30
25/29	48	33	42	123	26	26	36	32	94	26	16	25	18	59	25
20/24	27	26	28	81	21	35	42	38	115	21	27	39	36	102	21
15/19	21	18	16	55	16	29	34	34	97	16	32	35	30	97	16
10/14	16	12	16	44	11	31	30	29	90	11	27	25	31	83	11
5/9	10	4	10	24	6	24	21	23	68	6	20	27	25	72	6
0/4	7	2	4	13	2	24	23	23	70	1	24	24	26	74	1
-5/-1	4	2	2	8	-4	18	15	19	52	-4	24	23	23	70	-4
-10/-6	2	0	1	3	-8	16	7	14	37	-8	24	16	22	62	-8
-15/-11	1	0	0	1	-13	17	3	5	25	-13	22	10	14	46	-13
-20/-16	0	0		0	-17	4	0	1	5	-17	13	5	7	25	-18
-25/-21						0	0	0	0	-23	7	2	3	12	-23
-30/-26						0			0	-28	4	1	1	6	-28
-35/-31											1			1	-32

Temperature Range	FEBRUARY Obsn Hour Gp 01 to 08	09 to 16	17 to 24	Total Obsn	M C W B	MARCH Obsn Hour Gp 01 to 08	09 to 16	17 to 24	Total Obsn	M C W B	APRIL Obsn Hour Gp 01 to 08	09 to 16	17 to 24	Total Obsn	M C W B
90/94															
85/89												1		1	62
80/84												1	0	1	59
75/79												2	1	3	55
70/74											0	3	1	4	54
65/69												7	3	10	51
60/64							0	0	0	46	1	11	4	16	48
55/59							1	0	1	45	2	15	9	26	46
50/54		0	0	0	42	0	1	0	1	42	6	19	13	38	43
45/49		1	0	1	40	1	5	2	8	40	16	29	25	70	40
40/44		3	2	5	36	2	15	6	23	36	24	42	32	98	37
35/39	3	7	5	15	33	8	33	21	62	33	36	47	50	133	33
30/34	10	20	13	43	30	27	50	40	117	29	71	42	60	173	30
25/29	21	37	32	90	25	37	50	54	141	25	44	12	28	84	25
20/24	29	40	35	104	21	52	41	49	142	21	22	6	9	37	21
15/19	26	34	35	95	16	37	24	29	90	16	10	2	4	16	16
10/14	27	27	29	83	11	24	13	20	57	11	5	0	1	6	11
5/9	28	20	26	74	6	21	9	13	43	6	0	0	0	0	6
0/4	25	14	22	61	1	16	4	8	28	1	1	0	0	1	1
-5/-1	20	11	12	43	-4	13	1	3	17	-4	0			0	-3
-10/-6	16	5	7	28	-8	7	0	1	8	-8					
-15/-11	9	3	4	16	-13	2	0	0	2	-13					
-20/-16	7	1	1	9	-18	1	0	0	1	-18					
-25/-21	3	0		3	-23	0			0	-23					
-30/-26	0			0	-26										
-35/-31															

Temperature Range	ANNUAL TOTAL Obsn Hour Gp 01 to 08	09 to 16	17 to 24	Total Obsn	M C W B
90/94		3	0	3	71
85/89		25	6	31	70
80/84	0	76	23	99	67
75/79	4	138	52	194	64
70/74	34	195	100	329	62
65/69	93	221	160	474	59
60/64	178	240	223	641	56
55/59	269	213	256	738	52
50/54	276	182	250	708	48
45/49	252	161	216	629	44
40/44	214	162	185	561	39
35/39	192	187	197	576	34
30/34	267	208	237	712	30
25/29	216	197	216	629	25
20/24	199	195	198	592	21
15/19	157	147	149	453	16
10/14	130	107	126	363	11
5/9	103	81	97	281	6
0/4	97	67	83	247	1
-5/-1	79	52	59	190	-4
-10/-6	65	28	45	138	-8
-15/-11	51	16	23	90	-13
-20/-16	25	6	9	40	-18
-25/-21	10	2	3	15	-23
-30/-26	4	1	1	6	-28
-35/-31	1			1	-32

INTERNATIONAL FALLS IAP MINNESOTA

LAT 48 34N LONG 93 23W ELEV 1179 FT

MEAN FREQUENCY OF OCCURRENCE OF DRY BULB TEMPERATURE (DEGREES F) WITH MEAN COINCIDENT WET BULB TEMPERATURE (DEGREES F) FOR EACH DRY BULB TEMPERATURE RANGE

Temperature Range	MAY Obsn Hour Gp 01 to 08	MAY 09 to 16	MAY 17 to 24	MAY Total Obsn	MAY MCWB	JUNE Obsn Hour Gp 01 to 08	JUNE 09 to 16	JUNE 17 to 24	JUNE Total Obsn	JUNE MCWB	JULY Obsn Hour Gp 01 to 08	JULY 09 to 16	JULY 17 to 24	JULY Total Obsn	JULY MCWB
95/99							1		1	68					
90/94							2	1	3	68		1	0	1	72
85/89		0		0	60		8	2	10	68		12	4	16	70
80/84		5	1	6	60	0	19	8	27	66		37	13	50	67
75/79		11	3	14	57	2	37	17	56	63	1	54	25	80	65
70/74	0	25	11	36	55	7	44	29	80	61	11	56	38	105	63
65/69	1	30	16	47	53	16	45	38	99	58	29	52	56	137	61
60/64	9	37	25	71	52	42	43	45	130	56	72	25	60	157	59
55/59	22	42	42	106	49	56	28	47	131	53	69	8	35	112	55
50/54	34	40	46	120	46	46	10	30	86	49	41	2	14	57	51
45/49	54	26	41	121	42	35	3	16	54	45	19		3	22	46
40/44	43	20	30	93	38	25	1	5	31	40	6		0	6	41
35/39	37	9	18	64	34	9		1	10	36					
30/34	34	3	12	49	30	3		0	3	32					
25/29	12	0	2	14	26										
20/24	3	0	0	3	21										
15/19															

Temperature Range	AUGUST Obsn Hour Gp 01 to 08	AUGUST 09 to 16	AUGUST 17 to 24	AUGUST Total Obsn	AUGUST MCWB	SEPTEMBER Obsn Hour Gp 01 to 08	SEPTEMBER 09 to 16	SEPTEMBER 17 to 24	SEPTEMBER Total Obsn	SEPTEMBER MCWB	OCTOBER Obsn Hour Gp 01 to 08	OCTOBER 09 to 16	OCTOBER 17 to 24	OCTOBER Total Obsn	OCTOBER MCWB
95/99															
90/94		2	0	2	71										
85/89		7	2	9	69							0		0	64
80/84	0	26	8	34	67		4	1	5	70		2	0	2	61
75/79	1	46	19	66	65	0	10	4	14	64		6	1	7	60
70/74	6	62	38	106	63	1	25	9	35	62		12	3	15	58
65/69	27	53	48	128	61	7	33	15	55	59	1	17	8	26	56
60/64	50	35	55	140	58	15	40	26	81	56	3	21	12	36	53
55/59	70	14	46	130	55	26	49	41	116	53	7	34	21	62	50
50/54	51	3	20	74	50	44	42	49	135	49	23	36	33	92	47
45/49	30	1	12	43	46	50	24	39	113	44	42	35	41	118	43
40/44	11		1	12	41	41	10	30	81	40	46	40	48	134	39
35/39	1			1	37	29	3	19	51	36	47	31	41	119	35
30/34	0			0	34	20	0	7	27	31	42	12	30	84	30
25/29						7		0	7	27	26	3	10	39	26
20/24						0			0	23	8	0	2	10	22
15/19											3		1	4	17

INTERNATIONAL FALLS IAP MINNESOTA

Temperature Range	NOVEMBER Obsn Hour Gp 01 to 08	NOVEMBER Obsn Hour Gp 09 to 16	NOVEMBER Obsn Hour Gp 17 to 24	NOVEMBER Total Obsn	NOVEMBER MCWB	DECEMBER Obsn Hour Gp 01 to 08	DECEMBER Obsn Hour Gp 09 to 16	DECEMBER Obsn Hour Gp 17 to 24	DECEMBER Total Obsn	DECEMBER MCWB
95/99										
90/94										
85/89										
80/84										
75/79										
70/74										
65/69										
60/64		1		1	50					
55/59		4	1	5	48		1		1	50
50/54	4	7	3	14	48		0	1	1	48
45/49	1	12	5	18	42	0	1		1	44
40/44	7	19	15	41	38	1	2	0	3	40
35/39	19	36	29	84	34	3	9	6	18	34
30/34	56	51	54	161	30	13	21	13	47	30
25/29	50	43	45	138	26	17	20	24	61	26
20/24	35	28	32	95	21	24	35	35	94	21
15/19	22	17	22	61	16	30	29	22	81	16
10/14	18	10	14	42	11	31	28	28	87	11
5/9	11	6	8	25	7	21	24	26	71	6
0/4	6	3	5	14	2	22	22	23	67	1
-5/-1	2	3	3	8	-3	24	21	22	67	-4
-10/-6	4	1	3	8	-8	18	19	17	54	-9
-15/-11	3	1	1	5	-13	11	9	16	36	-13
-20/-16	2	1	0	3	-18	14	5	10	29	-18
-25/-21	0		0	0	-23	12	2	4	18	-23
-30/-26	0		0	0	-26	5	1	1	7	-27
-35/-31						2			2	-33
-40/-36										

Temperature Range	JANUARY Obsn Hour Gp 01 to 08	JANUARY Obsn Hour Gp 09 to 16	JANUARY Obsn Hour Gp 17 to 24	JANUARY Total Obsn	JANUARY MCWB	FEBRUARY Obsn Hour Gp 01 to 08	FEBRUARY Obsn Hour Gp 09 to 16	FEBRUARY Obsn Hour Gp 17 to 24	FEBRUARY Total Obsn	FEBRUARY MCWB
95/99										
90/94										
85/89										
80/84										
75/79										
70/74										
65/69										
60/64										
55/59										
50/54							1	0	1	44
45/49		0		0	39		1	1	2	41
40/44		1		1	35	1	2	2	5	38
35/39		1	1	2	34	1	4	3	8	33
30/34	4	9	7	20	30	6	15	9	30	29
25/29	10	21	14	45	25	10	24	23	57	25
20/24	18	22	22	62	21	21	30	26	77	21
15/19	19	26	20	65	16	18	29	21	68	16
10/14	20	24	20	64	11	19	27	25	71	11
5/9	23	29	27	79	6	19	28	27	74	6
0/4	25	30	24	79	1	21	21	24	66	1
-5/-1	21	27	25	73	-4	22	16	23	61	-4
-10/-6	21	23	29	73	-9	24	13	19	56	-9
-15/-11	23	18	24	65	-14	24	8	11	43	-13
-20/-16	27	12	20	59	-18	17	3	7	27	-18
-25/-21	17	5	10	32	-23	10	1	3	14	-23
-30/-26	12	2	3	17	-28	8	1	1	10	-28
-35/-31	7	1	1	9	-33	3			3	-33
-40/-36	2	0		2		0			0	

Temperature Range	MARCH Obsn Hour Gp 01 to 08	MARCH Obsn Hour Gp 09 to 16	MARCH Obsn Hour Gp 17 to 24	MARCH Total Obsn	MARCH MCWB	APRIL Obsn Hour Gp 01 to 08	APRIL Obsn Hour Gp 09 to 16	APRIL Obsn Hour Gp 17 to 24	APRIL Total Obsn	APRIL MCWB
95/99										
90/94										
85/89							0		0	60
80/84							1		1	58
75/79							2	0	2	57
70/74		0	0	0	55		4	1	5	53
65/69		0	0	0	53	0	6	3	9	51
60/64		1	0	1	50	0	8	5	13	48
55/59	0	1	1	2	48	2	18	9	29	45
50/54	1	8	3	12	43	4	25	17	46	43
45/49	1	13	5	19	39	11	35	25	71	40
40/44	1	22	11	34	35	21	42	37	100	36
35/39	10	33	27	70	33	36	42	50	128	33
30/34	24	50	41	115	29	61	34	46	141	30
25/29	36	39	51	126	25	48	15	28	91	25
20/24	46	33	39	118	20	30	7	14	51	21
15/19	40	19	22	81	16	18	3	6	27	16
10/14	29	15	18	62	11	9	0	2	11	11
5/9	17	7	11	35	6	2			2	7
0/4	15	5	10	30	1	0			0	4
-5/-1	9	2	4	15	-4					
-10/-6	10	1	3	14	-9					
-15/-11	6	0	0	6	-13					
-20/-16	2			2	-17					
-25/-21	1	0		1	-22					
-30/-26	0		0	0	-29					
-35/-31	1			1	-33					
-40/-36	0			0						

Temperature Range	ANNUAL TOTAL Obsn Hour Gp 01 to 08	ANNUAL TOTAL Obsn Hour Gp 09 to 16	ANNUAL TOTAL Obsn Hour Gp 17 to 24	ANNUAL TOTAL Total Obsn	ANNUAL TOTAL MCWB
95/99		1		1	68
90/94		5	1	6	70
85/89		[illegible]	[illegible]	[illegible]	[illegible]
80/84	0	94	31	125	67
75/79	4	166	69	239	64
70/74	25	228	129	382	61
65/69	81	236	184	501	59
60/64	191	211	228	630	56
55/59	252	199	243	694	52
50/54	248	174	216	638	48
45/49	243	151	188	582	43
40/44	203	159	179	541	38
35/39	192	168	195	555	34
30/34	263	195	219	677	30
25/29	216	165	197	578	25
20/24	185	155	170	510	21
15/19	150	123	114	387	16
10/14	126	104	107	337	11
5/9	93	94	99	286	6
0/4	89	81	86	256	1
-5/-1	78	69	77	224	-4
-10/-6	77	57	71	205	-9
-15/-11	67	36	52	155	-13
-20/-16	62	21	37	120	-18
-25/-21	40	8	17	65	-23
-30/-26	25	4	5	34	-28
-35/-31	13	1	1	15	-33
-40/-36	2	0		2	

MINNEAPOLIS-ST PAUL IAP MINNESOTA

LAT 44 53N   LONG 93 13W   ELEV 834 FT

MEAN FREQUENCY OF OCCURRENCE OF DRY BULB TEMPERATURE (DEGREES F) WITH MEAN COINCIDENT WET BULB TEMPERATURE (DEGREES F) FOR EACH DRY BULB TEMPERATURE RANGE

Temperature Range	MAY Obsn Hour Gp 01 to 08	MAY 09 to 16	MAY 17 to 24	MAY Total Obsn	MAY MCWB	JUNE Obsn Hour Gp 01 to 08	JUNE 09 to 16	JUNE 17 to 24	JUNE Total Obsn	JUNE MCWB	JULY Obsn Hour Gp 01 to 08	JULY 09 to 16	JULY 17 to 24	JULY Total Obsn	JULY MCWB
100/104												0		0	80
95/99							2	1	3	74		3	1	4	77
90/94		1	0	1	67		9	4	13	72		11	5	16	75
85/89		5	2	7	66	0	17	10	27	71	0	37	15	52	71
80/84		14	6	20	64	2	37	20	59	68	4	58	36	98	69
75/79	1	25	14	40	62	10	48	34	92	65	16	60	52	128	67
70/74	5	35	24	64	59	28	49	47	124	63	53	48	63	164	65
65/69	16	39	34	89	57	50	36	50	136	60	78	23	48	149	63
60/64	35	42	46	123	54	62	25	41	128	57	61	8	23	92	59
55/59	48	34	47	129	51	43	10	22	75	53	29	1	5	35	55
50/54	51	24	36	111	47	29	5	10	44	49	7		1	8	51
45/49	45	18	22	85	43	13	0	2	15	45	0			0	47
40/44	29	8	12	49	39	2			2	42					
35/39	13	2	3	18	34										
30/34	5	0	2	7	30										
25/29	1	0	0	1	27										
20/24															
15/19															

Temperature Range	AUGUST Obsn Hour Gp 01 to 08	AUGUST 09 to 16	AUGUST 17 to 24	AUGUST Total Obsn	AUGUST MCWB	SEPTEMBER Obsn Hour Gp 01 to 08	SEPTEMBER 09 to 16	SEPTEMBER 17 to 24	SEPTEMBER Total Obsn	SEPTEMBER MCWB	OCTOBER Obsn Hour Gp 01 to 08	OCTOBER 09 to 16	OCTOBER 17 to 24	OCTOBER Total Obsn	OCTOBER MCWB
100/104															
95/99		1	0	1	75		0		0	76					
90/94		12	3	15	74		4	1	5	75					
85/89	0	27	11	38	72		7	2	9	73		1	0	1	65
80/84	3	46	27	76	69	1	13	7	21	69		7	0	7	63
75/79	12	59	43	114	67	6	26	13	45	65	0	11	3	14	62
70/74	41	48	61	150	65	8	40	24	72	62	1	17	7	25	59
65/69	69	33	57	159	62	16	41	35	92	59	3	28	16	47	56
60/64	67	16	29	112	59	34	41	47	122	56	12	34	28	74	54
55/59	37	5	13	55	54	51	36	47	134	53	27	37	36	100	51
50/54	16	0	3	19	50	56	23	35	114	49	37	37	45	119	47
45/49	4		0	4	46	35	8	22	65	44	50	33	40	123	43
40/44	0			0	41	25	2	7	34	40	43	26	36	105	39
35/39						6	0	1	7	36	38	11	22	71	34
30/34						1			1	32	23	6	11	40	30
25/29						0			0	28	9	1	3	13	25
20/24											4	0	1	5	21
15/19											0		0	0	18

MINNEAPOLIS-ST PAUL IAP MINNESOTA

Temperature Range	NOVEMBER Obsn Hour Gp 01 to 08	NOVEMBER Obsn Hour Gp 09 to 16	NOVEMBER Obsn Hour Gp 17 to 24	NOVEMBER Total Obsn	NOVEMBER MCWB	DECEMBER Obsn Hour Gp 01 to 08	DECEMBER Obsn Hour Gp 09 to 16	DECEMBER Obsn Hour Gp 17 to 24	DECEMBER Total Obsn	DECEMBER MCWB
100/104										
95/99										
90/94										
85/89										
80/84										
75/79										
70/74		0		0	55					
65/69	0	2		2	54					
60/64	0	6	2	8	53		0		0	53
55/59	2	12	7	21	50	0	0	1	1	50
50/54	7	18	11	36	47	2	1	0	3	49
45/49	11	28	19	58	42	1	2	2	5	44
40/44	23	32	32	87	38	3	11	4	18	38
35/39	39	37	42	118	34	11	20	18	49	34
30/34	48	36	42	126	30	24	33	34	91	30
25/29	39	25	30	94	25	38	43	39	120	26
20/24	29	18	22	69	21	36	36	34	106	21
15/19	15	14	17	46	16	31	27	30	88	16
10/14	13	6	11	30	11	28	21	25	74	11
5/9	7	3	2	12	7	22	21	21	64	6
0/4	4	2	2	8	1	19	17	18	54	1
-5/-1	2	1	1	4	-3	14	8	11	33	-3
-10/-6	0	0		0	-8	11	4	6	21	-8
-15/-11	0			0	-13	5	1	2	8	-12
-20/-16						2	0	0	2	-18
-25/-21										
-30/-26										

Temperature Range	JANUARY Obsn Hour Gp 01 to 08	JANUARY Obsn Hour Gp 09 to 16	JANUARY Obsn Hour Gp 17 to 24	JANUARY Total Obsn	JANUARY MCWB	FEBRUARY Obsn Hour Gp 01 to 08	FEBRUARY Obsn Hour Gp 09 to 16	FEBRUARY Obsn Hour Gp 17 to 24	FEBRUARY Total Obsn	FEBRUARY MCWB
100/104										
95/99										
90/94										
85/89										
80/84										
75/79										
70/74										
65/69										
60/64										
55/59							1	0	1	47
50/54							1	0	1	43
45/49		0		0	38		3	1	4	40
40/44	0	3	1	4	36	1	10	4	15	37
35/39	4	12	9	25	33	8	20	16	44	34
30/34	14	20	18	52	30	23	36	37	96	30
25/29	22	38	33	93	25	30	32	32	94	25
20/24	31	33	35	99	21	25	32	30	87	21
15/19	31	27	28	86	16	30	31	33	94	16
10/14	29	29	30	88	11	33	22	25	80	11
5/9	29	25	27	81	6	21	16	19	56	6
0/4	24	24	23	71	1	19	10	12	41	1
-5/-1	21	16	20	57	-3	16	7	7	30	-4
-10/-6	17	11	13	41	-8	10	3	4	17	-8
-15/-11	15	7	7	29	-13	4	1	2	7	-13
-20/-16	6	2	3	11	-18	2	0	1	3	-17
-25/-21	4	0	2	6	-23	0	0	0	0	-23
-30/-26	1			1	-27	0		0	0	-26

Temperature Range	MARCH Obsn Hour Gp 01 to 08	MARCH Obsn Hour Gp 09 to 16	MARCH Obsn Hour Gp 17 to 24	MARCH Total Obsn	MARCH MCWB	APRIL Obsn Hour Gp 01 to 08	APRIL Obsn Hour Gp 09 to 16	APRIL Obsn Hour Gp 17 to 24	APRIL Total Obsn	APRIL MCWB
100/104										
95/99										
90/94							0		0	63
85/89							2	0	2	61
80/84							3	1	4	61
75/79		0		0	54		6	3	9	59
70/74		0	0	0	58	0	9	5	14	57
65/69		1	0	1	54	1	15	11	27	54
60/64	0	1	1	2	52	5	21	17	43	51
55/59	0	4	2	6	48	12	22	23	57	48
50/54	1	10	5	16	44	20	33	28	81	45
45/49	1	13	9	23	40	28	35	33	96	41
40/44	10	24	20	54	37	39	39	41	119	38
35/39	24	41	37	102	34	50	29	39	118	34
30/34	40	54	58	152	29	45	18	25	88	30
25/29	52	38	43	133	25	26	6	11	43	25
20/24	41	25	29	95	20	10	1	3	14	20
15/19	27	16	20	63	16	2	0	0	2	16
10/14	18	10	12	40	11	1	0	0	1	10
5/9	15	7	7	29	6	0			0	8
0/4	10	3	3	16	1					
-5/-1	5	0	2	7	-3					
-10/-6	2	0	0	2	-8					
-15/-11	1			1	-13					
-20/-16		0	0	0	-18					
-25/-21	0	0		0	-24					
-30/-26	0			0	-27					

Temperature Range	ANNUAL TOTAL Obsn Hour Gp 01 to 08	ANNUAL TOTAL Obsn Hour Gp 09 to 16	ANNUAL TOTAL Obsn Hour Gp 17 to 24	ANNUAL TOTAL Total Obsn	ANNUAL TOTAL MCWB
100/104		0		0	80
95/99		6	2	8	76
90/94		37	13	50	74
85/89	0	96	40	136	71
80/84	10	178	97	285	68
75/79	45	235	162	442	66
70/74	136	246	231	613	63
65/69	233	218	251	702	60
60/64	276	194	234	704	56
55/59	249	162	203	614	52
50/54	226	152	174	552	47
45/49	188	140	150	478	43
40/44	175	155	157	487	38
35/39	193	172	187	552	34
30/34	223	203	227	653	30
25/29	217	183	191	591	25
20/24	176	145	154	475	21
15/19	136	115	128	379	16
10/14	122	88	103	313	11
5/9	94	72	76	242	6
0/4	76	56	58	190	1
-5/-1	58	32	41	131	-3
-10/-6	40	18	23	81	-8
-15/-11	25	9	11	45	-13
-20/-16	10	2	4	16	-18
-25/-21	4	0	2	6	-23
-30/-26	1		0	1	-27

COLUMBUS AFB MISSISSIPPI

LAT 33 39N LONG 88 27W ELEV 219 FT

MEAN FREQUENCY OF OCCURRENCE OF DRY BULB TEMPERATURE (DEGREES F) WITH MEAN COINCIDENT WET BULB TEMPERATURE (DEGREES F) FOR EACH DRY BULB TEMPERATURE RANGE

Tempera-ture Range	MAY Obsn Hour Gp 01 to 08	MAY Obsn Hour Gp 09 to 16	MAY Obsn Hour Gp 17 to 24	MAY Total Obsn	MAY MCWB	JUNE Obsn Hour Gp 01 to 08	JUNE Obsn Hour Gp 09 to 16	JUNE Obsn Hour Gp 17 to 24	JUNE Total Obsn	JUNE MCWB	JULY Obsn Hour Gp 01 to 08	JULY Obsn Hour Gp 09 to 16	JULY Obsn Hour Gp 17 to 24	JULY Total Obsn	JULY MCWB
100/104							0		0	79		1	0	1	77
95/99		1	0	1	73		10	1	11	77		16	3	19	78
90/94		14	2	16	73		49	11	60	76		62	15	77	77
85/89		43	12	55	71	1	73	27	101	74	2	77	32	111	76
80/84	1	65	26	92	69	11	56	44	111	73	14	54	53	121	74
75/79	11	52	42	105	68	42	31	66	139	71	73	26	83	182	73
70/74	42	39	63	144	66	94	15	62	171	69	119	11	54	184	70
65/69	76	20	52	148	63	59	5	21	85	65	32	1	7	40	66
60/64	49	9	26	84	59	24	0	7	31	60	7		1	8	61
55/59	32	3	16	51	54	6		1	7	56	1		0	1	57
50/54	22	1	7	30	50	1		0	1	51					
45/49	11	0	2	13	46	1		0	1	47					
40/44	3		0	3	41	0			0	43					
35/39	0			0	38										
30/34															

Tempera-ture Range	AUGUST Obsn Hour Gp 01 to 08	AUGUST Obsn Hour Gp 09 to 16	AUGUST Obsn Hour Gp 17 to 24	AUGUST Total Obsn	AUGUST MCWB	SEPTEMBER Obsn Hour Gp 01 to 08	SEPTEMBER Obsn Hour Gp 09 to 16	SEPTEMBER Obsn Hour Gp 17 to 24	SEPTEMBER Total Obsn	SEPTEMBER MCWB	OCTOBER Obsn Hour Gp 01 to 08	OCTOBER Obsn Hour Gp 09 to 16	OCTOBER Obsn Hour Gp 17 to 24	OCTOBER Total Obsn	OCTOBER MCWB
100/104		0		0	77										
95/99		8	1	9	78		2	0	2	75					
90/94		53	9	62	77		23	2	25	75		1		1	69
85/89	1	84	26	111	76		60	10	70	74		18	1	19	70
80/84	9	65	48	122	74	2	64	27	93	71		36	5	41	68
75/79	60	31	88	179	73	19	46	54	119	70	1	46	14	61	66
70/74	121	7	60	188	70	77	27	72	176	68	15	49	33	97	65
65/69	41	0	13	54	65	64	14	42	120	64	35	44	54	133	62
60/64	12		3	15	60	40	3	19	62	60	44	29	47	120	58
55/59	4		0	4	56	21	1	10	32	55	41	16	38	95	53
50/54	0			0	52	13	0	3	16	51	35	6	27	68	49
45/49						4		1	5	46	36	1	19	56	45
40/44						1		0	1	41	25		8	33	40
35/39						0			0	37	12		2	14	36
30/34											4		0	4	31

COLUMBUS AFB MISSISSIPPI

Temperature Range	NOVEMBER Obsn Hour Gp 01 to 08	NOVEMBER 09 to 16	NOVEMBER 17 to 24	NOVEMBER Total Obsn	NOVEMBER MCWB	DECEMBER Obsn Hour Gp 01 to 08	DECEMBER 09 to 16	DECEMBER 17 to 24	DECEMBER Total Obsn	DECEMBER MCWB	JANUARY Obsn Hour Gp 01 to 08	JANUARY 09 to 16	JANUARY 17 to 24	JANUARY Total Obsn	JANUARY MCWB	FEBRUARY Obsn Hour Gp 01 to 08	FEBRUARY 09 to 16	FEBRUARY 17 to 24	FEBRUARY Total Obsn	FEBRUARY MCWB	MARCH Obsn Hour Gp 01 to 08	MARCH 09 to 16	MARCH 17 to 24	MARCH Total Obsn	MARCH MCWB	APRIL Obsn Hour Gp 01 to 08	APRIL 09 to 16	APRIL 17 to 24	APRIL Total Obsn	APRIL MCWB	ANNUAL TOTAL Obsn Hour Gp 01 to 08	ANNUAL TOTAL 09 to 16	ANNUAL TOTAL 17 to 24	ANNUAL TOTAL Total Obsn	ANNUAL TOTAL MCWB
100/104																																1	0	1	78
95/99																																37	5	42	77
90/94																																[illegible]	[illegible]	[illegible]	[illegible]
85/89																						1	0	1	67		8	1	9	70	4	364	109	477	74
80/84		3	0	3	66												1	0	1	66		6	1	7	65		40	12	52	67	37	390	216	643	72
75/79		14	1	15	64		3	0	3	66		1		1	63		3	0	3	65		15	7	22	63	1	47	27	75	65	207	315	382	904	70
70/74	2	30	7	39	62	0	8	2	10	63	0	7	1	8	62	1	9	3	13	61	3	25	14	42	61	15	48	42	105	63	489	275	413	1177	67
65/69	8	34	21	63	60	5	17	9	31	61	2	14	10	26	60	4	15	8	27	59	11	33	26	70	58	47	40	54	141	61	384	237	317	938	62
60/64	18	42	29	89	55	13	26	20	59	57	10	19	14	43	56	6	24	17	47	55	20	39	32	91	54	53	28	40	121	57	296	219	255	770	57
55/59	26	36	34	96	52	17	32	24	73	52	15	25	20	60	51	13	28	23	64	50	30	36	38	104	51	38	19	30	87	52	244	196	234	674	52
50/54	35	34	45	114	48	25	41	30	96	47	17	34	25	76	47	21	35	31	87	46	30	34	36	100	46	35	9	21	65	48	234	194	225	653	47
45/49	40	22	37	99	43	25	40	39	104	42	24	33	33	90	42	25	36	35	96	42	32	25	33	90	42	28	2	10	40	44	226	159	209	594	43
40/44	35	14	31	80	39	37	37	43	117	38	28	36	37	101	38	31	33	39	103	38	40	20	31	91	38	18	0	4	22	40	218	140	193	551	38
35/39	33	7	19	59	34	39	25	38	102	34	32	31	41	104	34	41	22	34	97	34	41	9	19	69	34	6		0	6	36	204	94	153	451	34
30/34	24	3	10	37	30	40	13	27	80	29	43	21	33	97	29	39	11	20	70	29	29	5	9	43	30	1			1	32	180	53	99	332	29
25/29	14	0	4	18	26	28	4	12	44	25	38	14	18	70	25	25	5	10	40	25	8	1	2	11	25						113	24	46	183	25
20/24	4	0	1	5	20	13	1	3	17	21	19	7	9	35	20	11	2	3	16	20	3	0	0	3	22						50	10	16	76	20
15/19	1			1	16	4	1	1	6	16	9	4	4	17	16	5	0	1	6	16	0			0	16						19	5	6	30	16
10/14						1	0	0	1	11	5	1	2	8	11	1			1	12											7	1	2	10	11
5/9						0	0	0	0	7	2	1	1	4	6																2	1	1	4	6
0/4						1			1	3	2	0	0	2	2																3	0	0	3	2
-5/-1											0			0	-2																0			0	-2

JACKSON/ALLEN THOMPSON FLD MISSISSIPPI

LAT 32 19N LONG 90 05W ELEV 310 FT

MEAN FREQUENCY OF OCCURRENCE OF DRY BULB TEMPERATURE (DEGREES F) WITH MEAN COINCIDENT WET BULB TEMPERATURE (DEGREES F) FOR EACH DRY BULB TEMPERATURE RANGE

Temperature Range	MAY Obsn Hour Gp 01 to 08	MAY Obsn Hour Gp 09 to 16	MAY Obsn Hour Gp 17 to 24	MAY Total Obsn	MAY MCWB	JUNE Obsn Hour Gp 01 to 08	JUNE Obsn Hour Gp 09 to 16	JUNE Obsn Hour Gp 17 to 24	JUNE Total Obsn	JUNE MCWB	JULY Obsn Hour Gp 01 to 08	JULY Obsn Hour Gp 09 to 16	JULY Obsn Hour Gp 17 to 24	JULY Total Obsn	JULY MCWB
100/104							2	0	2	78		2		2	77
95/99		1	0	1	73		17	3	20	77		22	4	26	77
90/94		17	2	19	72		53	14	67	75	0	80	20	100	76
85/89	0	68	18	86	71	2	79	29	110	74	2	83	31	116	76
80/84	3	65	27	95	70	20	53	48	121	73	28	42	58	128	75
75/79	21	44	52	117	68	66	24	75	165	72	103	15	89	207	73
70/74	59	27	65	151	67	97	9	53	159	69	103	5	45	153	71
65/69	88	16	51	155	64	39	3	14	56	65	10	0	1	11	66
60/64	40	7	19	66	59	11	1	4	16	60	1			1	61
55/59	20	3	8	31	54	4		0	4	55					
50/54	11	1	5	17	49	0			0	51					
45/49	6		1	7	45	0			0	48					
40/44	1			1	43										
35/39															
30/34															
25/29															

Temperature Range	AUGUST Obsn Hour Gp 01 to 08	AUGUST Obsn Hour Gp 09 to 16	AUGUST Obsn Hour Gp 17 to 24	AUGUST Total Obsn	AUGUST MCWB	SEPTEMBER Obsn Hour Gp 01 to 08	SEPTEMBER Obsn Hour Gp 09 to 16	SEPTEMBER Obsn Hour Gp 17 to 24	SEPTEMBER Total Obsn	SEPTEMBER MCWB	OCTOBER Obsn Hour Gp 01 to 08	OCTOBER Obsn Hour Gp 09 to 16	OCTOBER Obsn Hour Gp 17 to 24	OCTOBER Total Obsn	OCTOBER MCWB
100/104		5	0	5	76		1		1	75					
95/99		25	4	29	76		7	0	7	73		0		0	75
90/94		76	17	93	76		38	4	42	73		6	0	6	73
85/89	3	83	33	119	75	0	69	15	84	72		28	3	31	70
80/84	22	39	57	118	74	4	60	31	95	71	0	45	8	53	67
75/79	84	16	87	187	73	31	35	69	135	70	5	50	24	79	66
70/74	109	4	45	158	70	92	19	73	184	69	28	45	42	115	65
65/69	24	0	4	28	65	56	7	30	93	64	45	37	54	136	62
60/64	4		1	5	60	35	3	15	53	59	45	19	42	106	57
55/59	2			2	57	16		3	19	54	38	11	34	83	52
50/54						6		0	6	50	36	5	22	63	48
45/49						1			1	45	30	2	11	43	44
40/44											14	0	6	20	40
35/39											6		1	7	35
30/34											2		0	2	31
25/29											0			0	29

JACKSON/ALLEN THOMPSON FLD MISSISSIPPI

Tempera-ture Range	NOVEMBER Obsn Hour Gp 01 to 08	NOVEMBER 09 to 16	NOVEMBER 17 to 24	NOVEMBER Total Obsn	NOVEMBER MCWB	DECEMBER Obsn Hour Gp 01 to 08	DECEMBER 09 to 16	DECEMBER 17 to 24	DECEMBER Total Obsn	DECEMBER MCWB	JANUARY Obsn Hour Gp 01 to 08	JANUARY 09 to 16	JANUARY 17 to 24	JANUARY Total Obsn	JANUARY MCWB	FEBRUARY Obsn Hour Gp 01 to 08	FEBRUARY 09 to 16	FEBRUARY 17 to 24	FEBRUARY Total Obsn	FEBRUARY MCWB	MARCH Obsn Hour Gp 01 to 08	MARCH 09 to 16	MARCH 17 to 24	MARCH Total Obsn	MARCH MCWB	APRIL Obsn Hour Gp 01 to 08	APRIL 09 to 16	APRIL 17 to 24	APRIL Total Obsn	APRIL MCWB	ANNUAL TOTAL Obsn Hour Gp 01 to 08	ANNUAL TOTAL 09 to 16	ANNUAL TOTAL 17 to 24	ANNUAL TOTAL Total Obsn	ANNUAL TOTAL MCWB
100/104																																10	0	10	76
95/99																																72	11	83	76
90/94																															0	270	57	327	75
85/89		0		0	72							0		0	64							0		0	69		11	1	12	69	7	421	130	558	73
80/84		7	0	7	68		1		1	67		1		1	67		2	0	2	67		10	1	11	67		37	10	47	67	77	362	240	679	72
75/79	0	22	3	25	65		6	0	6	67		7	1	8	67		13	2	15	65		23	9	32	65	2	51	22	75	65	312	306	433	1051	70
70/74	7	36	15	58	63	2	15	4	21	63	2	23	7	32	64	2	24	12	38	63	5	33	21	59	62	18	41	42	101	63	524	281	424	1229	67
65/69	12	34	25	71	59	6	26	15	47	60	17	25	24	66	62	12	29	19	60	60	23	37	30	90	59	40	34	49	123	61	372	248	316	936	62
60/64	20	33	28	81	55	18	35	26	79	57	18	24	23	65	57	20	36	31	87	56	24	41	39	104	55	49	31	43	123	57	285	230	271	786	57
55/59	27	37	35	99	51	21	35	27	83	52	19	27	24	70	52	24	29	35	88	52	34	35	39	108	51	45	22	32	99	52	250	199	237	686	52
50/54	34	28	37	99	47	27	41	36	104	47	21	33	29	83	47	35	28	32	95	47	33	29	39	101	47	37	9	21	67	48	240	174	221	635	47
45/49	33	21	36	90	43	36	37	41	114	43	30	35	38	103	43	37	26	35	98	43	42	19	31	92	42	25	3	16	44	43	240	143	209	592	43
40/44	39	14	31	84	38	38	25	40	103	38	33	31	35	99	39	32	15	26	73	39	36	12	21	69	38	19	0	5	24	40	212	97	164	473	39
35/39	34	7	17	58	34	37	16	31	84	34	38	21	31	90	34	28	12	14	54	35	31	6	14	51	34	6	0	0	6	36	180	62	108	350	34
30/34	21	2	9	32	30	34	7	18	59	30	33	12	20	65	30	17	5	10	32	30	16	2	3	21	30	0			0	33	123	28	60	211	30
25/29	9	0	4	13	25	19	2	7	28	25	22	5	10	37	25	10	3	3	16	25	3	0	1	4	24						63	10	25	98	25
20/24	4	0	0	4	21	8	1	2	11	21	11	3	5	19	21	5	0	2	7	20	1			1	22						29	4	9	42	21
15/19	0			0	18	2	0	0	2	16	1	0	1	2	15	1	1	0	2	16											4	1	1	6	16
10/14						1		0	1	10	1	1	1	3	10	0	0	1	1	12											2	1	2	5	11
5/9						0			0	8	1	0	1	2	5	1	0	0	1	7											2	0	1	3	6
0/4											1		0	1	2	0			0	3											1		0	1	2

KEESLER AFB/BILOXI MISSISSIPPI

LAT 30 25N LONG 88 55W ELEV 26 FT

MEAN FREQUENCY OF OCCURRENCE OF DRY BULB TEMPERATURE (DEGREES F) WITH MEAN COINCIDENT WET BULB TEMPERATURE (DEGREES F) FOR EACH DRY BULB TEMPERATURE RANGE

Temperature Range	MAY Obsn Hour Gp 01 to 08	MAY 09 to 16	MAY 17 to 24	MAY Total Obsn	MAY MCWB	JUNE Obsn Hour Gp 01 to 08	JUNE 09 to 16	JUNE 17 to 24	JUNE Total Obsn	JUNE MCWB	JULY Obsn Hour Gp 01 to 08	JULY 09 to 16	JULY 17 to 24	JULY Total Obsn	JULY MCWB
100/104							0		0	83		0		0	80
95/99		1	0	1	80		3	0	3	80		7	1	8	79
90/94		6	0	6	76	0	35	4	39	78		60	8	68	79
85/89	0	60	8	68	74	6	118	46	170	77	10	120	62	192	78
80/84	16	104	60	180	73	71	59	104	234	75	93	44	99	236	76
75/79	80	48	98	226	71	95	19	63	177	73	115	15	67	197	74
70/74	80	20	55	155	67	53	5	21	79	69	30	2	11	43	71
65/69	41	7	18	66	63	13	0	2	15	64	0	0	0	0	67
60/64	18	2	5	25	57	1			1	58					
55/59	9	0	2	11	52	0			0	54					
50/54	4		0	4	48										
45/49	0			0	45										
40/44															
35/39															

Temperature Range	AUGUST Obsn Hour Gp 01 to 08	AUGUST 09 to 16	AUGUST 17 to 24	AUGUST Total Obsn	AUGUST MCWB	SEPTEMBER Obsn Hour Gp 01 to 08	SEPTEMBER 09 to 16	SEPTEMBER 17 to 24	SEPTEMBER Total Obsn	SEPTEMBER MCWB	OCTOBER Obsn Hour Gp 01 to 08	OCTOBER 09 to 16	OCTOBER 17 to 24	OCTOBER Total Obsn	OCTOBER MCWB
100/104		0		0	80										
95/99		6	1	7	79		1		1	76					
90/94	0	75	9	84	79		27	1	28	78		1		1	76
85/89	8	107	62	177	78	1	91	18	110	76	0	22	1	23	75
80/84	73	38	98	209	76	25	70	78	173	75	4	57	15	76	72
75/79	126	19	68	213	74	90	35	88	213	73	18	72	43	133	69
70/74	37	3	10	50	70	83	14	44	141	69	38	45	67	150	67
65/69	4		0	4	64	30	3	9	42	62	57	29	56	142	62
60/64	0			0	60	10	1	2	13	58	55	14	34	103	57
55/59						1			1	54	35	7	21	63	52
50/54											25	2	9	36	47
45/49											10	0	2	12	43
40/44											4		0	4	38
35/39											0			0	36

KEESLER AFB/BILOXI MISSISSIPPI

Temperature Range	NOVEMBER Obsn Hour Gp 01 to 08	NOVEMBER Obsn Hour Gp 09 to 16	NOVEMBER Obsn Hour Gp 17 to 24	NOVEMBER Total Obsn	NOVEMBER MCWB	DECEMBER Obsn Hour Gp 01 to 08	DECEMBER Obsn Hour Gp 09 to 16	DECEMBER Obsn Hour Gp 17 to 24	DECEMBER Total Obsn	DECEMBER MCWB	JANUARY Obsn Hour Gp 01 to 08	JANUARY Obsn Hour Gp 09 to 16	JANUARY Obsn Hour Gp 17 to 24	JANUARY Total Obsn	JANUARY MCWB
100/104															
95/99															
90/94															
85/89															
80/84		3		3	72										
75/79	1	24	2	27	70		3		3	69		3		3	70
70/74	11	52	23	86	67	1	16	2	19	66	1	16	3	20	67
65/69	34	51	48	133	62	17	42	23	82	63	17	41	23	81	64
60/64	36	41	49	126	57	33	48	47	128	59	39	46	47	132	59
55/59	35	29	39	103	52	34	49	43	126	53	30	47	43	120	53
50/54	40	21	38	99	47	34	39	49	122	47	29	37	40	106	48
45/49	40	14	23	77	43	38	28	39	105	43	32	23	37	92	43
40/44	21	4	14	39	38	38	13	25	76	38	41	18	30	89	38
35/39	13	1	5	19	33	28	6	13	47	34	29	10	15	54	34
30/34	7	0	1	8	29	17	3	6	26	29	20	5	6	31	29
25/29	1			1	24	6	1	1	8	25	7	2	2	11	24
20/24						1	0	0	1	20	2	1	1	4	20
15/19						0	0	0	0	15	1	0	0	1	15
10/14						0			0	11	1	0		1	10

Temperature Range	FEBRUARY Obsn Hour Gp 01 to 08	FEBRUARY Obsn Hour Gp 09 to 16	FEBRUARY Obsn Hour Gp 17 to 24	FEBRUARY Total Obsn	FEBRUARY MCWB	MARCH Obsn Hour Gp 01 to 08	MARCH Obsn Hour Gp 09 to 16	MARCH Obsn Hour Gp 17 to 24	MARCH Total Obsn	MARCH MCWB	APRIL Obsn Hour Gp 01 to 08	APRIL Obsn Hour Gp 09 to 16	APRIL Obsn Hour Gp 17 to 24	APRIL Total Obsn	APRIL MCWB
100/104															
95/99															
90/94												0		0	67
85/89												2	0	2	68
80/84		0		0	70		2		2	70	0	31	4	35	72
75/79		5	0	5	69	0	20	3	23	68	15	72	35	122	70
70/74	4	26	10	40	66	11	53	24	88	66	52	67	75	194	67
65/69	21	48	32	101	63	45	63	60	168	62	62	40	67	169	62
60/64	37	45	47	129	58	44	52	65	161	57	41	19	34	94	57
55/59	34	36	46	116	53	37	30	44	111	51	32	6	16	54	52
50/54	38	27	38	103	48	43	15	25	83	47	23	2	7	32	47
45/49	33	19	25	77	43	31	9	18	58	42	12		1	13	43
40/44	27	9	13	49	38	27	4	8	39	38	2			2	39
35/39	14	5	8	27	33	7	1	1	9	33					
30/34	13	2	2	17	29	2		0	2	28					
25/29	2	1	1	4	25	0			0	26					
20/24	1	0	0	1	20										
15/19	1	0	0	1	16										
10/14															

Temperature Range	ANNUAL TOTAL Obsn Hour Gp 01 to 08	ANNUAL TOTAL Obsn Hour Gp 09 to 16	ANNUAL TOTAL Obsn Hour Gp 17 to 24	ANNUAL TOTAL Total Obsn	ANNUAL TOTAL MCWB
100/104		0		0	81
95/99		18	2	20	79
90/94	0	204	22	226	79
85/89	25	520	197	742	77
80/84	282	408	458	1148	75
75/79	540	335	467	1342	72
70/74	401	319	345	1065	67
65/69	341	324	338	1003	63
60/64	314	268	330	912	58
55/59	247	204	254	705	52
50/54	236	143	206	585	47
45/49	196	93	145	434	43
40/44	160	48	90	298	38
35/39	91	23	42	156	34
30/34	59	10	15	84	29
25/29	16	4	4	24	25
20/24	4	1	1	6	20
15/19	2	0	0	2	15
10/14	1	0		1	11

MERIDIAN NAS/MCCAIN FIELD MISSISSIPPI

LAT 32 33N LONG 88 34W ELEV 317 FT

MEAN FREQUENCY OF OCCURRENCE OF DRY BULB TEMPERATURE (DEGREES F) WITH MEAN COINCIDENT WET BULB TEMPERATURE (DEGREES F) FOR EACH DRY BULB TEMPERATURE RANGE

Tempera-ture Range	MAY Obsn Hour Gp 01 to 08	MAY 09 to 16	MAY 17 to 24	MAY Total Obsn	MAY MCWB	JUNE Obsn Hour Gp 01 to 08	JUNE 09 to 16	JUNE 17 to 24	JUNE Total Obsn	JUNE MCWB	JULY Obsn Hour Gp 01 to 08	JULY 09 to 16	JULY 17 to 24	JULY Total Obsn	JULY MCWB
100/104							1		1	78		1	0	1	79
95/99		0		0	71		8	1	9	75		18	3	21	77
90/94		12	1	13	72		48	11	59	74		71	14	85	76
85/89		54	13	67	71	1	71	22	94	73	3	82	25	110	75
80/84	1	75	25	101	68	11	65	37	113	72	15	44	45	104	74
75/79	8	48	33	89	67	26	28	49	103	71	53	20	69	142	72
70/74	35	31	55	121	66	72	15	69	156	69	110	9	74	193	70
65/69	63	18	63	144	63	81	4	38	123	65	57	2	14	73	66
60/64	68	6	33	107	59	34	0	10	44	60	8	0	3	11	61
55/59	35	4	16	55	55	12		2	14	56	2		1	3	57
50/54	24	0	7	31	51	4		0	4	51	1			1	52
45/49	10		2	12	46	1			1	47					
40/44	4			4	42										
35/39															
30/34															
25/29															

Tempera-ture Range	AUGUST Obsn Hour Gp 01 to 08	AUGUST 09 to 16	AUGUST 17 to 24	AUGUST Total Obsn	AUGUST MCWB	SEPTEMBER Obsn Hour Gp 01 to 08	SEPTEMBER 09 to 16	SEPTEMBER 17 to 24	SEPTEMBER Total Obsn	SEPTEMBER MCWB	OCTOBER Obsn Hour Gp 01 to 08	OCTOBER 09 to 16	OCTOBER 17 to 24	OCTOBER Total Obsn	OCTOBER MCWB
100/104															
95/99		7	1	8	77		2		2	76					
90/94		55	9	64	77		25	3	28	74		4		4	68
85/89	0	86	22	108	75		67	12	79	73		23	2	25	68
80/84	8	56	38	102	74	2	60	24	86	71		40	7	47	68
75/79	39	30	72	141	73	13	40	45	98	70	0	43	14	57	66
70/74	113	12	78	203	70	66	26	70	162	69	15	50	29	94	64
65/69	60	1	24	85	66	68	15	45	128	65	25	41	46	112	61
60/64	21		4	25	60	44	4	28	76	60	38	27	50	115	57
55/59	6		1	7	57	25	1	10	36	55	48	14	39	101	54
50/54	1			1	53	16	0	2	18	51	47	5	30	82	49
45/49						3		1	4	47	33	0	18	51	45
40/44						1		0	1	41	22		9	31	41
35/39						0			0	36	12		3	15	37
30/34											6		1	7	32
25/29											.			.	28

Temperature Range	NOVEMBER Obsn Hour Gp 01 to 08	09 to 16	17 to 24	Total Obsn	MCWB	DECEMBER Obsn Hour Gp 01 to 08	09 to 16	17 to 24	Total Obsn	MCWB	JANUARY Obsn Hour Gp 01 to 08	09 to 16	17 to 24	Total Obsn	MCWB
100/104															
95/99															
90/94															
85/89															
80/84		6		6	67		0		0	68		0		0	67
75/79		23	1	24	64		6	0	6	67		4	0	4	68
70/74	1	33	9	43	62	1	15	5	21	65	0	9	3	12	62
65/69	9	42	22	73	59	11	23	14	48	62	5	16	10	31	61
60/64	19	39	32	90	56	12	25	16	53	57	12	24	16	52	57
55/59	25	37	35	97	52	15	36	21	72	52	13	29	22	64	53
50/54	40	31	44	115	48	21	42	34	97	48	19	33	28	80	48
45/49	38	16	33	87	44	28	39	36	103	43	24	36	31	91	43
40/44	35	8	28	71	39	36	29	41	106	39	28	34	39	101	39
35/39	31	4	20	55	35	34	18	33	85	35	35	28	32	95	35
30/34	27	1	10	38	31	38	9	27	74	30	39	17	30	86	30
25/29	10	0	4	14	26	35	3	16	54	26	34	9	20	63	26
20/24	3	0	1	4	21	12	1	3	16	22	20	5	9	34	21
15/19	1		0	1	17	3	1	0	4	16	10	2	4	16	16
10/14						1	0	0	1	11	4	1	2	7	11
5/9						1		0	1	5	3	0	1	4	6
0/4						0			0	3	2			2	3

Temperature Range	FEBRUARY Obsn Hour Gp 01 to 08	09 to 16	17 to 24	Total Obsn	MCWB	MARCH Obsn Hour Gp 01 to 08	09 to 16	17 to 24	Total Obsn	MCWB	APRIL Obsn Hour Gp 01 to 08	09 to 16	17 to 24	Total Obsn	MCWB	ANNUAL TOTAL Obsn Hour Gp 01 to 08	09 to 16	17 to 24	Total Obsn	MCWB
100/104																	2	0	2	78
95/99																	35	5	40	77
90/94																	215	38	253	75
85/89		0		0	71		3	0	3	65		15	3	18	70	4	401	99	504	73
80/84		1	0	1	67		10	2	12	65		46	14	60	67	37	403	192	632	71
75/79		5	1	6	67		22	6	28	63	4	54	25	83	65	143	323	315	781	69
70/74	1	10	4	15	64	4	32	18	54	61	19	46	43	108	64	437	288	457	1182	67
65/69	6	20	10	36	59	13	35	28	76	59	44	38	54	136	62	442	255	368	1065	63
60/64	6	24	18	48	54	24	33	33	90	55	56	25	44	125	58	342	207	287	836	58
55/59	13	34	16	63	50	26	34	32	92	51	35	11	25	71	53	255	200	220	675	53
50/54	17	37	33	87	46	27	31	36	94	46	34	5	18	57	49	251	184	232	667	48
45/49	26	32	36	94	42	38	28	36	102	43	21	1	10	32	44	222	152	203	577	43
40/44	27	30	35	92	38	36	13	25	74	39	17		4	21	40	206	114	181	501	39
35/39	35	19	31	85	34	30	6	17	53	35	8		1	9	36	185	75	137	397	35
30/34	41	8	24	73	30	32	1	11	44	30	2			2	31	185	36	103	324	30
25/29	32	3	12	47	26	14	0	3	17	26						126	15	55	196	26
20/24	16	1	3	20	21	3		0	3	22						54	7	16	77	21
15/19	3		0	3	17											17	3	4	24	16
10/14	1			1	12											6	1	2	9	11
5/9																4	0	1	5	6
0/4																2			2	3

COLUMBIA REGIONAL APRT MISSOURI

LAT 38 58N LONG 92 22W ELEV 778 FT

MEAN FREQUENCY OF OCCURRENCE OF DRY BULB TEMPERATURE (DEGREES F) WITH MEAN COINCIDENT WET BULB TEMPERATURE (DEGREES F) FOR EACH DRY BULB TEMPERATURE RANGE

Temperature Range	MAY Obsn Hour Gp 01 to 08	MAY 09 to 16	MAY 17 to 24	MAY Total Obsn	MAY MCWB	JUNE Obsn Hour Gp 01 to 08	JUNE 09 to 16	JUNE 17 to 24	JUNE Total Obsn	JUNE MCWB	JULY Obsn Hour Gp 01 to 08	JULY 09 to 16	JULY 17 to 24	JULY Total Obsn	JULY MCWB
110/114												1	0	1	74
105/109												1	0	1	73
100/104							1	0	1	75		4	1	5	74
95/99							7	2	9	75	0	16	3	19	75
90/94		3	0	3	70		24	6	30	74	0	38	13	51	75
85/89		20	5	25	70	1	47	20	68	73	2	62	29	93	73
80/84	0	35	13	48	67	9	53	38	100	71	15	58	52	125	71
75/79	5	42	29	76	65	30	48	49	127	68	51	43	62	156	70
70/74	21	47	42	110	63	51	32	52	135	66	84	19	55	158	68
65/69	41	38	51	130	60	68	18	42	128	63	61	6	27	94	64
60/64	58	34	45	137	57	47	7	22	76	59	26	1	6	33	60
55/59	51	18	31	100	53	23	3	8	34	54	7	0	0	7	56
50/54	34	9	22	65	48	9	0	2	11	51	1			1	51
45/49	21	1	8	30	44	2			2	47	0			0	49
40/44	12	1	2	15	40										
35/39	4		0	4	36										
30/34	0			0	32										
25/29															
20/24															

Temperature Range	AUGUST Obsn Hour Gp 01 to 08	AUGUST 09 to 16	AUGUST 17 to 24	AUGUST Total Obsn	AUGUST MCWB	SEPTEMBER Obsn Hour Gp 01 to 08	SEPTEMBER 09 to 16	SEPTEMBER 17 to 24	SEPTEMBER Total Obsn	SEPTEMBER MCWB	OCTOBER Obsn Hour Gp 01 to 08	OCTOBER 09 to 16	OCTOBER 17 to 24	OCTOBER Total Obsn	OCTOBER MCWB
110/114															
105/109															
100/104		1	0	1	73		0		0	67					
95/99		14	3	17	74		7	1	8	70					
90/94		40	12	52	73		16	3	19	70		1		1	67
85/89	1	57	25	83	72		28	8	36	69		7	1	8	66
80/84	8	58	46	112	70	1	41	20	62	67		25	2	27	64
75/79	40	43	65	148	69	10	43	35	88	65	1	28	10	39	62
70/74	80	23	52	155	67	35	44	44	123	64	4	36	25	65	60
65/69	66	8	30	104	64	47	33	48	128	61	18	34	36	88	58
60/64	35	2	12	49	59	50	18	40	108	57	34	39	40	113	55
55/59	14	0	3	17	56	41	9	26	76	53	43	36	44	123	51
50/54	4		0	4	51	33	1	12	46	49	46	22	36	104	47
45/49	1			1	47	17	0	3	20	45	41	11	30	82	42
40/44						5		0	5	41	32	6	16	54	39
35/39						0			0	36	19	2	6	27	34
30/34											8	0	1	9	30
25/29											2		0	2	26
20/24											0			0	21

Temperature Range	NOVEMBER Obsn Hour Gp 01 to 08	09 to 16	17 to 24	Total Obsn	MCWB	DECEMBER Obsn Hour Gp 01 to 08	09 to 16	17 to 24	Total Obsn	MCWB	JANUARY Obsn Hour Gp 01 to 08	09 to 16	17 to 24	Total Obsn	MCWB
110/114															
105/109															
100/104															
95/99															
90/94															
85/89															
80/84		0		0	64										
75/79		4	0	4	62							0		0	62
70/74	0	12	2	14	59		0		0	57		1	0	1	57
65/69	4	17	8	29	57	0	3	0	3	55		2	0	2	55
60/64	9	21	15	45	54	1	9	3	13	52	2	5	3	10	54
55/59	11	26	21	58	49	3	11	6	20	49	2	10	6	18	50
50/54	17	30	28	75	45	7	19	12	38	45	5	13	6	24	46
45/49	30	33	36	99	42	10	22	17	49	42	7	21	15	43	41
40/44	41	34	36	111	37	18	31	29	78	37	14	25	25	64	37
35/39	36	27	34	97	33	36	37	41	114	34	23	35	32	90	34
30/34	35	17	28	80	29	49	43	45	137	30	45	37	40	122	30
25/29	29	10	16	55	25	41	28	37	106	25	44	34	35	113	25
20/24	15	5	10	30	20	28	20	23	71	21	29	24	27	80	20
15/19	8	2	5	15	16	22	9	14	45	16	22	17	28	67	16
10/14	4	1	1	6	11	12	7	10	29	11	24	13	15	52	11
5/9	2	0	1	3	6	9	5	5	19	6	16	7	8	31	6
0/4	0		0	0	2	7	2	4	13	2	7	4	4	15	2
-5/-1						3	0	1	4	-3	6	1	3	10	-3
-10/-6						1	0		1	-7	3	1	1	5	-8

Temperature Range	FEBRUARY Obsn Hour Gp 01 to 08	09 to 16	17 to 24	Total Obsn	MCWB	MARCH Obsn Hour Gp 01 to 08	09 to 16	17 to 24	Total Obsn	MCWB	APRIL Obsn Hour Gp 01 to 08	09 to 16	17 to 24	Total Obsn	MCWB
110/114															
105/109															
100/104															
95/99															
90/94															
85/89												4	1	5	64
80/84							1		1	61		13	4	17	64
75/79		0		0	58		4	1	5	60		21	9	30	62
70/74		1	0	1	58	0	8	4	12	57	3	29	18	50	59
65/69		3	1	4	55	1	13	7	21	54	17	28	24	69	57
60/64	1	7	2	10	51	5	17	12	34	51	25	28	33	86	54
55/59	1	14	7	22	48	9	20	18	47	48	28	32	35	95	50
50/54	6	18	15	39	45	13	25	23	61	44	36	27	35	98	46
45/49	12	27	21	60	42	20	31	30	81	41	35	24	30	89	42
40/44	21	31	30	82	38	30	37	37	104	37	38	21	26	85	38
35/39	29	34	40	103	34	50	41	44	135	34	34	11	19	64	34
30/34	57	36	43	136	30	53	27	36	116	30	19	2	5	26	30
25/29	35	24	29	88	25	33	14	21	68	25	5	0	1	6	25
20/24	22	11	16	49	21	17	6	10	33	21	1			1	21
15/19	15	9	8	32	16	11	2	3	16	16					
10/14	11	6	8	25	11	3	1	1	5	11					
5/9	8	2	3	13	6	2	0	1	3	6					
0/4	2	1	1	4	2	1	0	0	1	1					
-5/-1	2	0	1	3	-4	1	0	0	1	-3					
-10/-6	1		0	1	-7	0			0	-8					

Temperature Range	ANNUAL TOTAL Obsn Hour Gp 01 to 08	09 to 16	17 to 24	Total Obsn	MCWB
110/114		1	0	1	74
105/109		1	0	1	73
100/104		6	1	7	73
95/99	0	44	9	53	74
90/94	0	100	81	188	74
85/89	4	225	89	318	72
80/84	33	284	175	492	69
75/79	137	276	260	673	67
70/74	278	252	294	824	65
65/69	323	203	274	800	61
60/64	293	188	233	714	56
55/59	233	179	205	617	51
50/54	211	164	191	566	46
45/49	196	170	190	556	42
40/44	211	186	201	598	38
35/39	231	187	216	634	34
30/34	266	162	198	626	30
25/29	189	110	139	438	25
20/24	112	66	86	264	21
15/19	78	39	58	175	16
10/14	54	28	35	117	11
5/9	37	14	18	69	6
0/4	17	7	9	33	2
-5/-1	12	1	5	18	-3
-10/-6	5		1	7	-7

FT LEONARD WOOD/FORNEY AAF MISSOURI

LAT 37 45N LONG 92 09W ELEV 1158 FT

MEAN FREQUENCY OF OCCURRENCE OF DRY BULB TEMPERATURE (DEGREES F) WITH MEAN COINCIDENT WET BULB TEMPERATURE (DEGREES F) FOR EACH DRY BULB TEMPERATURE RANGE

Temperature Range	MAY Obsn Hour Gp 01 to 08	MAY 09 to 16	MAY 17 to 24	MAY Total Obsn	MAY MCWB	JUNE Obsn Hour Gp 01 to 08	JUNE 09 to 16	JUNE 17 to 24	JUNE Total Obsn	JUNE MCWB	JULY Obsn Hour Gp 01 to 08	JULY 09 to 16	JULY 17 to 24	JULY Total Obsn	JULY MCWB
100/104												1		1	77
95/99							1		1	76		11	3	14	76
90/94		0		0	67		11	2	13	76		38	11	49	76
85/89		11	3	14	67	0	46	13	59	74	0	59	27	86	74
80/84		46	14	60	66	2	67	31	100	71	10	59	52	121	72
75/79	1	46	27	74	65	21	48	58	127	69	47	46	69	162	70
70/74	16	45	49	110	63	60	31	62	153	67	95	27	57	179	68
65/69	47	37	50	134	60	72	23	44	139	63	53	6	20	79	64
60/64	55	24	40	119	56	50	9	20	79	59	28	1	7	36	59
55/59	49	24	35	108	53	23	4	8	35	55	11	1	2	14	55
50/54	39	11	20	70	48	10	0	3	13	51	3			3	51
45/49	28	2	10	40	44	2			2	46	0			0	47
40/44	9	1	1	11	39										
35/39	3		0	3	35										
30/34	1			1	31										
25/29															

Temperature Range	AUGUST Obsn Hour Gp 01 to 08	AUGUST 09 to 16	AUGUST 17 to 24	AUGUST Total Obsn	AUGUST MCWB	SEPTEMBER Obsn Hour Gp 01 to 08	SEPTEMBER 09 to 16	SEPTEMBER 17 to 24	SEPTEMBER Total Obsn	SEPTEMBER MCWB	OCTOBER Obsn Hour Gp 01 to 08	OCTOBER 09 to 16	OCTOBER 17 to 24	OCTOBER Total Obsn	OCTOBER MCWB
100/104		1	0	1	78										
95/99		5	1	6	75		1	0	1	70					
90/94		21	5	26	74		5	1	6	73		0		0	66
85/89	0	49	17	66	73		25	4	29	72		3	0	3	66
80/84	4	68	34	106	70	1	36	14	51	70		14	2	16	66
75/79	27	52	62	141	69	5	50	32	87	67		25	5	30	63
70/74	69	32	71	172	67	33	49	52	134	65	2	35	19	56	60
65/69	73	15	38	126	63	59	40	55	154	62	18	37	36	91	59
60/64	48	4	16	68	59	44	19	42	105	58	33	43	38	114	55
55/59	17	1	4	22	54	46	9	26	81	53	35	36	44	115	50
50/54	8		0	8	50	35	5	10	50	49	38	29	42	109	46
45/49	1			1	46	13	2	4	19	45	41	18	34	93	43
40/44						4		1	5	41	43	6	21	70	39
35/39						1		0	1	36	26	1	6	33	35
30/34						0			0	33	10		1	11	31
25/29											3			3	27

Temperature Range	NOVEMBER					DECEMBER					JANUARY				
	Obsn Hour Gp 01 to 08	09 to 16	17 to 24	Total Obsn	MCWB	Obsn Hour Gp 01 to 08	09 to 16	17 to 24	Total Obsn	MCWB	Obsn Hour Gp 01 to 08	09 to 16	17 to 24	Total Obsn	MCWB
100/104															
95/99															
90/94															
85/89															
80/84															
75/79		6	0	6	63							0		0	61
70/74		12	3	15	59		2	0	2	61		2	0	2	59
65/69	4	26	11	41	56	1	6	3	10	58		4	2	6	55
60/64	12	26	25	63	55	5	11	7	23	55	2	8	4	14	54
55/59	22	29	29	80	51	8	16	12	36	51	7	12	10	29	51
50/54	27	27	31	85	46	11	24	19	54	46	11	21	16	48	46
45/49	27	27	30	84	42	14	27	22	63	41	10	22	17	49	41
40/44	37	35	37	109	38	27	38	40	105	37	16	29	29	74	36
35/39	38	29	36	103	33	39	34	40	113	33	24	22	32	78	33
30/34	37	15	22	74	30	48	40	47	135	30	37	35	35	107	29
25/29	21	4	8	33	24	41	26	28	95	25	38	31	31	100	25
20/24	8	2	5	15	20	28	17	22	67	21	32	27	31	90	20
15/19	2	2	1	5	15	15	4	4	23	16	26	16	19	61	16
10/14	3	0	1	4	12	7	3	2	12	11	19	9	12	40	11
5/9	2	0		2	7	2	0	1	3	6	16	6	5	27	6
0/4						1	0	1	2	1	5	2	4	11	1
-5/-1						0			0	-1	5	1	1	7	-3
-10/-6											2	0		2	-7

Temperature Range	FEBRUARY					MARCH				
	Obsn Hour Gp 01 to 08	09 to 16	17 to 24	Total Obsn	MCWB	Obsn Hour Gp 01 to 08	09 to 16	17 to 24	Total Obsn	MCWB
100/104										
95/99										
90/94										
85/89										
80/84							2	0	2	60
75/79							9	2	11	60
70/74		0		0	51	0	12	7	19	57
65/69		2	1	3	51	3	13	11	27	54
60/64	0	6	3	9	52	8	24	18	50	52
55/59	2	11	7	20	47	12	20	21	53	48
50/54	6	21	12	39	44	18	26	28	72	45
45/49	8	25	19	52	41	20	25	28	73	41
40/44	13	27	32	72	37	31	26	29	86	37
35/39	35	35	39	109	33	36	30	32	98	33
30/34	47	36	42	125	29	44	33	37	114	29
25/29	33	28	28	89	24	40	16	19	75	25
20/24	32	17	24	73	20	20	9	12	41	20
15/19	27	9	13	49	15	14	2	2	18	16
10/14	12	4	4	20	11	2	0		2	12
5/9	5	1	2	8	7					
0/4	4	1	0	5	2					
-5/-1	0			0	-2					
-10/-6										

Temperature Range	APRIL					ANNUAL TOTAL				
	Obsn Hour Gp 01 to 08	09 to 16	17 to 24	Total Obsn	MCWB	Obsn Hour Gp 01 to 08	09 to 16	17 to 24	Total Obsn	MCWB
100/104							2	0	2	77
95/99							18	4	22	76
90/94		0		0	63		75	19	94	75
85/89		4	1	5	64	0	197	65	262	73
80/84		14	4	18	64	17	306	151	474	70
75/79	0	25	13	38	61	101	307	268	676	67
70/74	5	33	22	60	59	280	280	342	902	65
65/69	17	38	35	90	56	347	247	306	900	61
60/64	31	37	46	114	53	316	212	266	794	56
55/59	42	32	39	113	50	274	195	237	706	51
50/54	39	22	30	91	46	245	186	211	642	46
45/49	42	17	22	81	42	206	165	186	557	42
40/44	35	10	16	61	39	215	172	206	593	37
35/39	15	5	7	27	34	217	156	192	565	33
30/34	11	2	3	16	30	235	161	187	583	29
25/29	1			1	27	177	105	114	396	25
20/24						120	72	94	286	20
15/19						84	33	39	156	16
10/14						43	16	19	78	11
5/9						25	7	8	40	6
0/4						10	3	5	18	1
-5/-1						5	1	1	7	-3
-10/-6						2	0		2	-7

RICHARDS-GEBAUR AFB/GRANDVIEW MISSOURI

LAT 38 51N LONG 94 33W ELEV 1090 FT

MEAN FREQUENCY OF OCCURRENCE OF DRY BULB TEMPERATURE (DEGREES F) WITH MEAN COINCIDENT WET BULB TEMPERATURE (DEGREES F) FOR EACH DRY BULB TEMPERATURE RANGE

Temperature Range	MAY Obsn Hour Gp 01 to 08	MAY 09 to 16	MAY 17 to 24	MAY Total Obsn	MAY MCWB	JUNE Obsn Hour Gp 01 to 08	JUNE 09 to 16	JUNE 17 to 24	JUNE Total Obsn	JUNE MCWB	JULY Obsn Hour Gp 01 to 08	JULY 09 to 16	JULY 17 to 24	JULY Total Obsn	JULY MCWB
100/104												0	0	0	77
95/99							0	0	0	78		4	2	6	77
90/94		1		1	70		7	2	9	75		31	10	41	77
85/89		12	3	15	70		34	13	47	73	0	54	26	80	75
80/84		33	13	46	68	1	60	34	95	71	10	66	52	128	72
75/79	1	46	29	76	65	18	56	55	129	69	49	54	66	169	70
70/74	19	47	43	109	63	55	43	59	157	66	85	27	58	170	67
65/69	43	36	50	129	60	76	24	45	145	63	68	8	25	101	63
60/64	58	31	47	136	56	55	11	23	89	59	27	2	7	36	59
55/59	49	24	31	104	52	25	4	8	37	54	6	0	2	8	54
50/54	40	12	21	73	48	8	1	2	11	50	3		0	3	50
45/49	22	6	10	38	43	2		0	2	46	0			0	47
40/44	13	0	3	16	39										
35/39	3		0	3	34										
30/34															
25/29															
20/24															

Temperature Range	AUGUST Obsn Hour Gp 01 to 08	AUGUST 09 to 16	AUGUST 17 to 24	AUGUST Total Obsn	AUGUST MCWB	SEPTEMBER Obsn Hour Gp 01 to 08	SEPTEMBER 09 to 16	SEPTEMBER 17 to 24	SEPTEMBER Total Obsn	SEPTEMBER MCWB	OCTOBER Obsn Hour Gp 01 to 08	OCTOBER 09 to 16	OCTOBER 17 to 24	OCTOBER Total Obsn	OCTOBER MCWB
100/104		1	0	1	77										
95/99		7	2	9	75		0		0	72					
90/94		26	9	35	75		6	2	8	74		1		1	64
85/89	0	55	24	79	73		22	5	27	72		4	1	5	66
80/84	5	61	44	110	71	0	30	14	44	70		12	2	14	66
75/79	37	50	62	149	69	6	49	32	87	67		24	7	31	63
70/74	78	32	54	164	67	31	48	47	126	65	3	35	21	59	61
65/69	62	11	34	107	63	53	39	50	142	62	14	35	34	83	59
60/64	46	5	15	66	59	48	24	40	112	57	34	43	39	116	55
55/59	14	0	4	18	55	49	13	28	90	53	43	37	42	122	51
50/54	5		1	6	50	32	6	16	54	49	41	29	40	110	46
45/49	0			0	47	16	3	5	24	45	44	19	32	95	42
40/44						4		1	5	40	35	8	20	63	38
35/39						1		0	1	36	23	2	7	32	34
30/34						0			0	33	9	0	3	12	30
25/29											2		0	2	26
20/24											0			0	22

Temperature Range	NOVEMBER Obsn Hour Gp 01 to 08	NOVEMBER 09 to 16	NOVEMBER 17 to 24	NOVEMBER Total Obsn	NOVEMBER MCWB	DECEMBER Obsn Hour Gp 01 to 08	DECEMBER 09 to 16	DECEMBER 17 to 24	DECEMBER Total Obsn	DECEMBER MCWB	JANUARY Obsn Hour Gp 01 to 08	JANUARY 09 to 16	JANUARY 17 to 24	JANUARY Total Obsn	JANUARY MCWB
100/104															
95/99															
90/94															
85/89															
80/84		0		0	65										
75/79		1	0	1	62										
70/74	0	9	1	10	61		0		0	60		0		0	59
65/69	2	16	7	25	58	0	2	0	2	57		2	0	2	56
60/64	7	24	13	44	54	3	6	3	12	55	1	2	2	5	55
55/59	10	28	21	59	50	3	11	6	20	50	2	6	3	11	51
50/54	19	32	31	82	45	6	16	9	31	46	2	10	5	17	46
45/49	28	35	35	98	42	9	26	17	52	41	5	17	11	33	41
40/44	41	32	41	114	38	23	33	33	89	38	9	25	25	59	37
35/39	49	33	37	119	34	35	37	42	114	33	24	30	32	86	33
30/34	39	18	28	85	29	47	40	48	135	29	39	33	38	110	29
25/29	22	8	14	44	25	41	31	33	105	25	37	33	33	103	25
20/24	12	4	7	23	20	34	22	24	80	20	32	27	30	89	20
15/19	7	2	3	12	15	21	10	15	46	16	27	23	26	76	15
10/14	2	0	1	3	11	12	7	9	28	11	23	17	18	58	11
5/9	1	0	0	1	6	7	5	4	16	6	21	11	13	45	6
0/4	0			0	3	4	2	4	10	2	13	7	7	27	1
-5/-1						3	1	1	5	-3	6	3	5	14	-4
-10/-6						1	0		1	-7	5	1	1	7	-8
-15/-11											0	0		0	-13

Temperature Range	FEBRUARY Obsn Hour Gp 01 to 08	FEBRUARY 09 to 16	FEBRUARY 17 to 24	FEBRUARY Total Obsn	FEBRUARY MCWB	MARCH Obsn Hour Gp 01 to 08	MARCH 09 to 16	MARCH 17 to 24	MARCH Total Obsn	MARCH MCWB	APRIL Obsn Hour Gp 01 to 08	APRIL 09 to 16	APRIL 17 to 24	APRIL Total Obsn	APRIL MCWB	ANNUAL TOTAL Obsn Hour Gp 01 to 08	ANNUAL TOTAL 09 to 16	ANNUAL TOTAL 17 to 24	ANNUAL TOTAL Total Obsn	ANNUAL TOTAL MCWB
100/104																	1	0	1	77
95/99																	11	4	15	76
90/94																	72	23	95	75
85/89												2	0	2	65	0	183	72	255	73
80/84							1	0	1	60		7	2	9	64	16	270	161	447	70
75/79							5	1	6	59		18	7	25	62	111	303	259	673	68
70/74		0	0	0	56	0	8	5	13	57	3	26	16	45	60	274	275	304	853	65
65/69		2	1	3	53	2	12	7	21	54	10	35	30	75	57	330	222	283	835	61
60/64		4	1	5	50	4	16	13	33	52	21	38	34	93	54	304	206	237	747	56
55/59	1	6	5	12	49	10	18	16	44	48	35	34	44	113	50	247	181	210	638	51
50/54	4	17	9	30	45	12	23	21	56	44	38	31	34	103	46	210	177	189	576	46
45/49	6	23	16	45	41	19	33	29	81	41	43	22	34	99	42	194	184	189	567	42
40/44	17	27	30	74	38	28	31	34	93	37	42	17	21	80	38	212	173	208	593	38
35/39	32	33	38	103	33	39	37	44	120	33	25	7	13	45	34	231	179	213	623	33
30/34	43	36	39	118	29	55	32	37	124	29	17	3	4	24	30	249	162	197	608	29
25/29	37	28	28	93	25	34	17	21	72	25	4	0	1	5	25	177	117	130	424	25
20/24	25	23	24	72	20	22	9	12	43	20	1			1	22	126	85	97	308	20
15/19	24	14	20	58	15	12	4	5	21	16						91	53	69	213	16
10/14	20	8	8	36	11	7	1	1	9	11						64	33	37	134	11
5/9	10	3	3	16	6	2	1	1	4	7						41	20	21	82	6
0/4	4	1	2	7	2	1	0	0	1	1						22	10	13	45	2
-5/-1	1	0	0	1	-3	1		0	1	-3						11	4	6	21	-3
-10/-6	0			0	-6											6	1	1	8	-8
-15/-11																0	0		0	-13

ST LOUIS/LAMBERT IAP MISSOURI

LAT 38 45N LONG 90 23W ELEV 535 FT

MEAN FREQUENCY OF OCCURRENCE OF DRY BULB TEMPERATURE (DEGREES F) WITH MEAN COINCIDENT WET BULB TEMPERATURE (DEGREES F) FOR EACH DRY BULB TEMPERATURE RANGE

Temperature Range	MAY Obsn Hour Gp 01 to 08	MAY 09 to 16	MAY 17 to 24	MAY Total Obsn	MAY MCWB	JUNE Obsn Hour Gp 01 to 08	JUNE 09 to 16	JUNE 17 to 24	JUNE Total Obsn	JUNE MCWB	JULY Obsn Hour Gp 01 to 08	JULY 09 to 16	JULY 17 to 24	JULY Total Obsn	JULY MCWB
110/114												0	0	0	76
105/109												1	0	1	76
100/104							2	1	3	75		3	1	4	76
95/99		0		0	72		8	3	11	75		12	4	16	75
90/94		4	1	5	71	0	29	10	39	74	0	37	14	51	75
85/89		21	6	27	70	2	46	25	73	73	3	64	37	104	73
80/84	0	37	18	55	67	15	57	45	117	70	23	67	63	153	71
75/79	7	46	33	86	65	38	43	49	130	68	61	40	67	168	70
70/74	28	45	41	114	63	59	28	53	140	66	93	18	44	155	68
65/69	46	39	52	137	60	64	16	35	115	62	45	4	15	64	63
60/64	59	27	43	129	57	36	7	14	57	58	19	1	3	23	59
55/59	43	16	27	86	52	18	2	5	25	54	4		0	4	54
50/54	31	9	16	56	48	6	0	1	7	50	0			0	51
45/49	19	3	7	29	43	1			1	46					
40/44	12	1	2	15	39										
35/39	2		0	2	34										
30/34	0			0	31										
25/29															

Temperature Range	AUGUST Obsn Hour Gp 01 to 08	AUGUST 09 to 16	AUGUST 17 to 24	AUGUST Total Obsn	AUGUST MCWB	SEPTEMBER Obsn Hour Gp 01 to 08	SEPTEMBER 09 to 16	SEPTEMBER 17 to 24	SEPTEMBER Total Obsn	SEPTEMBER MCWB	OCTOBER Obsn Hour Gp 01 to 08	OCTOBER 09 to 16	OCTOBER 17 to 24	OCTOBER Total Obsn	OCTOBER MCWB
110/114															
105/109															
100/104		2	0	2	76		1	0	1	68					
95/99		12	2	14	75		5	1	6	71					
90/94		36	12	48	74		16	4	20	71		2		2	68
85/89	1	59	30	90	73	0	28	11	39	70		7	0	7	67
80/84	15	66	55	136	71	4	40	24	68	68		24	4	28	65
75/79	55	42	64	161	69	18	45	37	100	66	1	31	12	44	63
70/74	78	22	50	150	67	41	48	47	136	64	8	36	25	69	61
65/69	56	8	24	88	63	46	34	51	131	60	19	35	40	94	58
60/64	31	1	9	41	59	49	15	34	98	56	40	36	44	120	55
55/59	10	1	1	12	55	41	6	21	68	53	42	34	39	115	50
50/54	2			2	51	28	1	8	37	49	42	24	37	103	47
45/49						12	0	2	14	44	43	12	28	83	43
40/44						3		0	3	41	32	7	13	52	39
35/39											15	2	6	23	34
30/34											6	0	1	7	30
25/29															26

Temperature Range	NOVEMBER Obsn Hour Gp 01 to 08	09 to 16	17 to 24	Total Obsn	MCWB	DECEMBER Obsn Hour Gp 01 to 08	09 to 16	17 to 24	Total Obsn	MCWB	JANUARY Obsn Hour Gp 01 to 08	09 to 16	17 to 24	Total Obsn	MCWB
110/114															
105/109															
100/104															
95/99															
90/94															
85/89															
80/84		1		1	65										
75/79		4	0	4	63							0		0	64
70/74	0	12	2	14	59		1		1	61		1	1	2	62
65/69	3	15	10	28	58		3	1	4	57	1	3	0	4	56
60/64	9	24	16	49	54	2	8	2	12	54	3	7	4	14	56
55/59	14	26	24	64	50	3	12	7	22	50	4	10	7	21	51
50/54	23	31	32	86	45	9	19	16	44	46	5	14	9	28	46
45/49	32	33	31	96	42	10	21	17	48	42	10	17	15	42	42
40/44	37	35	36	108	38	24	31	30	85	38	14	26	23	63	37
35/39	36	26	37	99	33	40	45	42	127	33	26	36	36	98	34
30/34	42	17	27	86	29	50	44	49	143	29	49	46	47	142	30
25/29	24	12	15	51	25	41	26	38	105	25	44	32	37	113	25
20/24	12	3	6	21	20	28	16	17	61	20	27	21	29	77	20
15/19	4	1	3	8	15	15	8	11	34	15	25	17	18	60	15
10/14	3	1	1	5	11	11	7	9	27	11	19	11	12	42	11
5/9	2	0	0	2	6	8	4	5	17	6	10	5	6	21	6
0/4	0		0	0	3	5	1	2	8	2	6	3	3	12	1
-5/-1						2	0	0	2	-3	4	1	2	7	-3
-10/-6						0			0	-6	1	0	0	1	-7

Temperature Range	FEBRUARY Obsn Hour Gp 01 to 08	09 to 16	17 to 24	Total Obsn	MCWB	MARCH Obsn Hour Gp 01 to 08	09 to 16	17 to 24	Total Obsn	MCWB	APRIL Obsn Hour Gp 01 to 08	09 to 16	17 to 24	Total Obsn	MCWB	ANNUAL TOTAL Obsn Hour Gp 01 to 08	09 to 16	17 to 24	Total Obsn	MCWB
110/114																	0	0	0	76
105/109																	1	0	1	76
100/104																	8	2	10	74
95/99																	37	10	47	76
90/94												0		0	68	0	124	41	165	74
85/89							0		0	64		5	1	6	66	6	230	110	346	72
80/84		0		0	61		1	0	1	62		15	4	19	65	57	308	213	578	70
75/79		0		0	59		4	1	5	61	0	21	12	33	62	180	276	275	731	67
70/74		1	1	2	59		8	4	12	58	8	26	21	55	60	315	246	289	850	65
65/69	0	3	1	4	55	1	12	7	20	54	17	29	29	75	58	298	201	265	764	60
60/64	1	7	3	11	51	5	17	13	35	52	28	27	32	87	54	282	177	217	676	56
55/59	3	12	7	22	49	11	22	20	53	49	31	32	31	94	50	224	173	189	586	51
50/54	8	21	15	44	46	16	28	27	71	45	34	33	31	98	45	204	180	192	576	46
45/49	12	27	23	62	42	21	31	30	82	41	34	22	32	88	42	194	166	185	545	42
40/44	21	34	31	86	38	38	41	40	119	37	39	20	27	86	38	220	195	202	617	38
35/39	37	39	44	120	33	53	42	49	144	34	34	8	15	57	34	243	198	229	670	34
30/34	56	37	45	138	30	51	23	31	105	30	12	1	3	16	30	266	168	203	637	30
25/29	35	18	24	77	25	27	10	17	54	25	3	0	0	3	25	175	98	131	404	25
20/24	20	11	12	43	20	15	5	6	26	20	0			0	22	102	56	70	228	20
15/19	11	7	8	26	15	7	1	2	10	16						62	34	42	138	15
10/14	9	4	6	19	11	2	1	1	4	11						44	24	29	97	11
5/9	6	1	2	9	6	1	0	0	1	6						27	10	13	50	6
0/4	2	1	1	4	1	0	0	0	0	1						13	5	6	24	2
-5/-1	2	0	0	2	-3	0			0	-3						8	1	2	11	-3
-10/-6	0		0	0	-7											1	0	0	1	-7

SPRINGFIELD MAP MISSOURI

LAT 37 14N LONG 93 23W ELEV 1268 FT

MEAN FREQUENCY OF OCCURRENCE OF DRY BULB TEMPERATURE (DEGREES F) WITH MEAN COINCIDENT WET BULB TEMPERATURE (DEGREES F) FOR EACH DRY BULB TEMPERATURE RANGE

Temperature Range	MAY Obsn Hour Gp 01 to 08	09 to 16	17 to 24	Total Obsn	MCWB	JUNE Obsn Hour Gp 01 to 08	09 to 16	17 to 24	Total Obsn	MCWB	JULY Obsn Hour Gp 01 to 08	09 to 16	17 to 24	Total Obsn	MCWB
110/114												0		0	77
105/109												1	0	1	74
100/104							0	0	0	73		2	0	2	74
95/99							9	2	11	74	0	10	3	13	74
90/94		1	0	1	76		23	6	29	74	0	42	13	55	75
85/89		17	3	20	70	1	45	15	61	73	2	63	26	91	74
80/84	0	41	14	55	69	8	57	31	96	71	12	59	42	113	72
75/79	3	46	24	73	66	24	42	50	116	69	41	39	65	145	71
70/74	18	46	46	110	64	58	32	59	149	67	96	23	63	182	69
65/69	47	41	54	142	61	74	20	44	138	64	69	7	29	105	65
60/64	71	30	49	150	58	42	8	22	72	60	21	1	6	28	60
55/59	47	16	29	92	53	21	3	7	31	55	7		1	8	56
50/54	30	7	18	55	49	10	1	3	14	51	1			1	51
45/49	21	3	8	32	44	2		0	2	46					
40/44	8	1	1	10	40	0			0	43					
35/39	3	0	1	4	36										
30/34	1		0	1	32										
25/29															
20/24															

Temperature Range	AUGUST Obsn Hour Gp 01 to 08	09 to 16	17 to 24	Total Obsn	MCWB	SEPTEMBER Obsn Hour Gp 01 to 08	09 to 16	17 to 24	Total Obsn	MCWB	OCTOBER Obsn Hour Gp 01 to 08	09 to 16	17 to 24	Total Obsn	MCWB
110/114															
105/109															
100/104		2	0	2	74		0		0	70					
95/99		15	4	19	74		5	0	5	70					
90/94	0	40	10	50	74		14	3	17	70		1		1	66
85/89	1	64	25	90	72	0	33	9	42	70		7	0	7	67
80/84	7	56	42	105	71	2	42	16	60	68		24	3	27	66
75/79	31	39	63	133	70	6	46	32	84	66	0	32	8	40	63
70/74	92	21	59	172	68	32	45	53	130	65	4	41	19	64	61
65/69	67	8	30	105	64	64	30	55	149	62	18	36	39	93	60
60/64	35	2	11	48	60	54	16	35	105	58	39	35	48	122	56
55/59	10	0	3	13	55	38	6	22	66	53	45	31	39	115	52
50/54	4		0	4	51	27	2	12	41	49	43	22	37	102	48
45/49	1			1	47	13	0	3	16	45	36	11	28	75	43
40/44						3		0	3	41	32	5	18	55	39
35/39						0			0	38	17	2	6	25	35
30/34											10	1	3	14	30
25/29											2		0	2	25
20/24											0			0	22

SPRINGFIELD MAP MISSOURI

Temperature Range	NOVEMBER Obsn Hour Gp 01 to 08	NOVEMBER 09 to 16	NOVEMBER 17 to 24	NOVEMBER Total Obsn	NOVEMBER MCWB	DECEMBER Obsn Hour Gp 01 to 08	DECEMBER 09 to 16	DECEMBER 17 to 24	DECEMBER Total Obsn	DECEMBER MCWB	JANUARY Obsn Hour Gp 01 to 08	JANUARY 09 to 16	JANUARY 17 to 24	JANUARY Total Obsn	JANUARY MCWB	FEBRUARY Obsn Hour Gp 01 to 08	FEBRUARY 09 to 16	FEBRUARY 17 to 24	FEBRUARY Total Obsn	FEBRUARY MCWB
110/114																				
105/109																				
100/104																				
95/99																				
90/94																				
85/89																				
80/84		0		0	63												0		0	63
75/79		4		4	64		0		0	63		0		0	64		1	0	1	59
70/74	0	14	1	15	61		1	0	1	56		2	0	2	59		3	1	4	58
65/69	4	22	7	33	58	0	4	0	4	55	1	6	1	8	56	0	5	2	7	55
60/64	7	24	15	46	55	2	11	3	16	53	3	10	4	17	55	2	12	5	19	52
55/59	13	25	21	59	50	3	16	7	26	50	4	14	8	26	51	3	18	9	30	49
50/54	20	33	31	84	46	9	23	15	47	46	7	16	11	34	46	8	26	19	53	46
45/49	30	32	39	101	42	14	33	23	70	42	9	25	17	51	42	18	30	28	76	42
40/44	41	32	33	106	38	24	34	34	92	38	17	26	29	72	37	25	29	34	88	38
35/39	34	21	34	89	34	33	33	43	109	34	26	32	36	94	34	38	31	37	106	34
30/34	32	14	27	73	30	50	41	47	138	30	45	39	42	126	30	45	29	38	112	30
25/29	30	10	17	57	25	42	23	32	97	25	46	30	36	112	25	35	18	23	76	25
20/24	16	5	8	29	21	31	13	22	66	21	28	21	28	77	21	20	11	15	46	20
15/19	8	2	5	15	16	19	6	9	34	16	22	11	14	47	16	15	7	8	30	16
10/14	4	1	1	6	11	10	6	6	22	11	20	8	10	38	11	10	2	3	15	11
5/9	1	0	0	1	6	6	2	5	13	6	8	5	5	18	6	3	1	1	5	6
0/4						4	1	1	6	2	6	2	3	11	1	2	1	0	3	1
-5/-1						1			1	-3	3	1	1	5	-4	0	0	0	0	-4
-10/-6											1	0	0	1	-7	0		0	0	-8

Temperature Range	MARCH Obsn Hour Gp 01 to 08	MARCH 09 to 16	MARCH 17 to 24	MARCH Total Obsn	MARCH MCWB	APRIL Obsn Hour Gp 01 to 08	APRIL 09 to 16	APRIL 17 to 24	APRIL Total Obsn	APRIL MCWB	ANNUAL TOTAL Obsn Hour Gp 01 to 08	ANNUAL TOTAL 09 to 16	ANNUAL TOTAL 17 to 24	ANNUAL TOTAL Total Obsn	ANNUAL TOTAL MCWB
110/114												0		0	77
105/109												1	0	1	74
100/104												4	0	4	74
95/99											0	39	9	48	74
90/94							0		0	72	0	121	32	153	74
85/89		0		0	58		3	0	3	66	4	232	78	314	72
80/84		2	0	2	63		14	3	17	65	29	295	151	475	70
75/79		5	1	6	61	0	25	9	34	63	105	279	252	636	68
70/74	0	11	3	14	58	4	33	21	58	61	304	272	325	901	66
65/69	3	17	9	29	56	15	32	30	77	58	362	228	300	890	62
60/64	6	22	17	45	52	33	33	34	100	55	315	204	249	768	57
55/59	10	25	19	54	49	34	27	38	99	51	235	181	203	619	52
50/54	17	27	29	73	45	32	25	33	90	46	208	182	208	598	47
45/49	24	33	36	93	41	38	24	29	91	42	206	191	211	608	42
40/44	37	31	39	107	38	32	15	23	70	38	219	173	211	603	38
35/39	56	33	39	128	34	28	8	15	51	35	235	160	211	606	34
30/34	37	23	29	89	30	17	2	5	24	30	237	149	191	577	30
25/29	34	11	17	62	26	6	0	0	6	26	195	92	125	412	25
20/24	12	4	6	22	21	0		0	0	21	107	54	79	240	21
15/19	10	2	3	15	16	0			0	19	74	28	39	141	16
10/14	2	1	1	4	11						46	18	21	85	11
5/9	1	0	1	2	6						19	8	12	39	6
0/4	1			1	2						13	4	4	21	2
-5/-1											4	1	1	6	-4
-10/-6											1	0	0	1	-7

BILLINGS/LOGAN IAP MONTANA

LAT 45 48N   LONG 108 32W   ELEV 3567 FT

MEAN FREQUENCY OF OCCURRENCE OF DRY BULB TEMPERATURE (DEGREES F) WITH MEAN COINCIDENT WET BULB TEMPERATURE (DEGREES F) FOR EACH DRY BULB TEMPERATURE RANGE

Temperature Range	MAY Obsn Hour Gp 01 to 08	MAY 09 to 16	MAY 17 to 24	MAY Total Obsn	MAY MCWB	JUNE Obsn Hour Gp 01 to 08	JUNE 09 to 16	JUNE 17 to 24	JUNE Total Obsn	JUNE MCWB	JULY Obsn Hour Gp 01 to 08	JULY 09 to 16	JULY 17 to 24	JULY Total Obsn	JULY MCWB
105/109															
100/104												2	0	2	68
95/99							1	1	2	64		9	3	12	66
90/94		1		1	61		5	2	7	63		29	13	42	64
85/89		3	1	4	60		15	7	22	63		42	26	68	63
80/84		10	3	13	59	0	25	15	40	61	1	45	41	87	62
75/79		19	10	29	57	1	37	22	60	59	8	45	44	97	60
70/74	1	27	15	43	55	6	44	34	84	57	33	37	44	114	58
65/69	4	39	27	70	52	19	41	42	102	56	61	23	35	119	56
60/64	12	42	39	93	50	51	34	44	129	53	71	9	25	105	54
55/59	32	37	44	113	48	64	20	36	120	51	50	5	11	66	51
50/54	55	31	42	128	46	58	13	26	97	48	18	1	4	23	48
45/49	64	21	36	121	43	30	4	8	42	44	3	0	1	4	45
40/44	51	11	21	83	39	8	1	2	11	40	1			1	41
35/39	19	5	5	29	35	1	1	1	3	36					
30/34	5	2	3	10	31	1	1	1	3	33					
25/29	3	1	1	5	27										
20/24	1	0	1	2	21										
15/19	1			1	17										
10/14	0			0	14										

Temperature Range	AUGUST Obsn Hour Gp 01 to 08	AUGUST 09 to 16	AUGUST 17 to 24	AUGUST Total Obsn	AUGUST MCWB	SEPTEMBER Obsn Hour Gp 01 to 08	SEPTEMBER 09 to 16	SEPTEMBER 17 to 24	SEPTEMBER Total Obsn	SEPTEMBER MCWB	OCTOBER Obsn Hour Gp 01 to 08	OCTOBER 09 to 16	OCTOBER 17 to 24	OCTOBER Total Obsn	OCTOBER MCWB
105/109		0		0	68										
100/104		1	0	1	67		0		0	63					
95/99		5	2	7	65		1	0	1	63					
90/94		23	10	33	63		4	1	5	62					
85/89		35	20	55	62		11	4	15	60		1		1	58
80/84	1	44	33	78	61		21	9	30	59		7	1	8	56
75/79	7	46	44	97	59	0	26	17	43	57		13	3	16	54
70/74	20	39	45	104	57	3	35	29	67	55	0	23	9	32	52
65/69	50	26	40	116	56	12	35	33	80	53	1	25	19	45	50
60/64	75	17	28	120	54	28	34	39	101	50	7	34	29	70	48
55/59	61	8	17	86	51	45	27	38	110	48	20	33	37	90	45
50/54	27	3	7	37	48	58	19	28	105	45	34	32	40	106	43
45/49	7	0	1	8	44	46	13	19	78	42	54	30	35	119	40
40/44	1			1	39	28	11	14	53	39	51	19	30	100	37
35/39						13	3	5	21	35	35	16	22	73	33
30/34						6	2	3	11	31	29	12	16	57	30
25/29						0		0	0	26	13	4	5	22	26
20/24											3	1	1	5	22
15/19													0	0	16
10/14															

BILLINGS/LOGAN IAP MONTANA

Temperature Range	NOVEMBER Obsn Hour Gp 01 to 08	09 to 16	17 to 24	Total Obsn	M C W B	DECEMBER Obsn Hour Gp 01 to 08	09 to 16	17 to 24	Total Obsn	M C W B	JANUARY Obsn Hour Gp 01 to 08	09 to 16	17 to 24	Total Obsn	M C W B
105/109															
100/104															
95/99															
90/94															
85/89															
80/84															
75/79															
70/74															
65/69		3		3	49		0		0	47		0		0	48
60/64	0	9	2	11	46		1	0	1	45		1	0	1	45
55/59	2	19	8	29	44		4	1	5	42	0	3	1	4	42
50/54	8	26	18	52	41	1	13	4	18	40	1	7	3	11	40
45/49	17	35	28	80	38	5	22	11	38	37	5	19	12	36	37
40/44	34	37	42	113	35	24	38	33	95	34	16	28	24	68	34
35/39	44	31	43	118	32	37	42	48	127	31	26	30	32	88	31
30/34	48	29	34	111	29	46	37	43	126	28	33	30	34	97	28
25/29	29	17	21	67	25	38	23	34	95	24	32	26	28	86	24
20/24	21	10	15	46	20	33	18	23	74	20	26	20	22	68	20
15/19	14	8	10	32	16	18	13	11	42	16	22	16	20	58	16
10/14	9	6	7	22	11	14	12	15	41	11	17	17	14	48	11
5/9	6	3	4	13	7	11	8	8	27	7	17	11	14	42	6
0/4	4	3	4	11	2	7	7	7	21	1	13	11	13	37	2
-5/-1	2	2	2	6	-3	7	4	5	16	-3	9	10	9	28	-4
-10/-6	1	1	1	3	-8	3	2	3	8	-8	13	10	11	34	-8
-15/-11	1	0	0	1	-13	2	1	1	4	-12	9	7	7	23	-13
-20/-16	0	0		0	-18	1	0	1	2	-18	7	2	5	14	-18
-25/-21						1	0	1	2	-23	1	1	0	2	-22
-30/-26							0		0	-26	0	0		0	-27

Temperature Range	FEBRUARY Obsn Hour Gp 01 to 08	09 to 16	17 to 24	Total Obsn	M C W B	MARCH Obsn Hour Gp 01 to 08	09 to 16	17 to 24	Total Obsn	M C W B	APRIL Obsn Hour Gp 01 to 08	09 to 16	17 to 24	Total Obsn	M C W B	ANNUAL TOTAL Obsn Hour Gp 01 to 08	09 to 16	17 to 24	Total Obsn	M C W B
105/109																	0		0	68
100/104																	3	0	3	67
95/99																	16	6	22	65
90/94																	62	26	88	64
85/89												0	0	0	55		107	58	165	62
80/84												2	1	3	55	2	154	103	259	60
75/79							0		0	51		4	2	6	53	16	190	142	348	58
70/74		0		0	50		2	0	2	50		11	5	16	51	63	218	181	462	56
65/69		1	0	1	49		5	2	7	48	0	14	8	22	49	147	212	206	565	54
60/64		2	0	2	47		10	4	14	46	2	23	17	42	47	246	216	227	689	51
55/59	0	8	3	11	44	0	15	9	24	43	5	29	22	56	45	279	208	227	714	48
50/54	2	14	8	24	41	3	20	17	40	41	15	33	29	77	42	280	212	226	718	44
45/49	6	23	16	45	38	9	27	22	58	38	29	37	40	106	39	275	231	229	735	40
40/44	20	33	27	80	34	22	38	32	92	35	43	31	39	113	37	299	247	264	810	36
35/39	32	33	37	102	32	39	35	41	115	32	50	24	32	106	33	296	220	266	782	32
30/34	38	29	40	107	28	50	31	41	122	29	48	19	27	94	30	304	192	242	738	29
25/29	37	22	27	86	25	44	21	27	92	25	33	10	14	57	26	229	124	157	510	25
20/24	23	15	18	56	20	28	13	15	56	20	12	2	4	18	21	147	79	99	325	20
15/19	16	13	12	41	16	17	11	13	41	16	3	0	1	4	17	91	61	67	219	16
10/14	14	11	13	38	11	11	7	8	26	11	1	0		1	12	66	53	57	176	11
5/9	12	9	10	31	6	8	5	5	18	7						54	36	41	131	6
0/4	10	6	8	24	2	5	4	4	13	2						39	31	36	106	2
-5/-1	6	3	4	13	-3	5	3	3	11	-3						29	22	23	74	-3
-10/-6	4	1	2	7	-8	3	2	3	8	-8						24	16	20	60	-8
-15/-11	2	0	0	2	-13	3	0	1	4	-12						17	8	9	34	-13
-20/-16	1		0	1	-18	1		0	1	-17						10	2	6	18	-18
-25/-21	0			0	-21											2	1		4	-23
-30/-26																0	0		0	-26

GLASGOW AFB MONTANA

LAT 48 25N LONG 106 32W ELEV 2760 FT

MEAN FREQUENCY OF OCCURRENCE OF DRY BULB TEMPERATURE (DEGREES F) WITH MEAN COINCIDENT WET BULB TEMPERATURE (DEGREES F) FOR EACH DRY BULB TEMPERATURE RANGE

Temperature Range	MAY Obsn Hour Gp 01 to 08	MAY 09 to 16	MAY 17 to 24	MAY Total Obsn	MAY MCWB	JUNE Obsn Hour Gp 01 to 08	JUNE 09 to 16	JUNE 17 to 24	JUNE Total Obsn	JUNE MCWB	JULY Obsn Hour Gp 01 to 08	JULY 09 to 16	JULY 17 to 24	JULY Total Obsn	JULY MCWB
100/104												0	0	0	68
95/99							0	0	0	64		3	2	5	66
90/94		0		0	61		1	0	1	64		14	6	20	65
85/89		1	0	1	62		8	4	12	62		32	18	50	63
80/84		6	3	9	59		19	9	28	60	2	49	29	80	62
75/79		13	7	20	56	2	37	21	60	59	8	60	45	113	60
70/74	0	20	11	31	54	5	42	30	77	57	27	47	46	120	59
65/69	4	29	22	55	52	20	50	40	110	55	59	24	49	132	57
60/64	10	38	29	77	49	42	40	46	128	54	71	13	34	118	55
55/59	24	41	41	106	47	64	25	44	133	51	55	4	15	74	52
50/54	41	39	41	121	45	61	15	31	107	48	20	1	4	25	48
45/49	56	32	43	131	42	37	3	12	52	44	4		1	5	45
40/44	59	17	32	108	39	9		2	11	40	1		0	1	39
35/39	35	8	12	55	34	1			1	35					
30/34	14	3	4	21	30										
25/29	2	0	2	4	26										
20/24	2		0	2	22										
15/19															
10/14															

Temperature Range	AUGUST Obsn Hour Gp 01 to 08	AUGUST 09 to 16	AUGUST 17 to 24	AUGUST Total Obsn	AUGUST MCWB	SEPTEMBER Obsn Hour Gp 01 to 08	SEPTEMBER 09 to 16	SEPTEMBER 17 to 24	SEPTEMBER Total Obsn	SEPTEMBER MCWB	OCTOBER Obsn Hour Gp 01 to 08	OCTOBER 09 to 16	OCTOBER 17 to 24	OCTOBER Total Obsn	OCTOBER MCWB
100/104		0		0	65										
95/99		3	1	4	63										
90/94		15	6	21	62		1	0	1	63					
85/89	0	29	13	42	62		7	2	9	61					
80/84	1	40	22	63	60		12	4	16	59		1		1	56
75/79	7	47	38	92	58	0	20	10	30	57		4	1	5	53
70/74	19	43	43	105	57	1	30	16	47	55		14	3	17	53
65/69	40	29	43	112	55	6	32	28	66	53	0	15	7	22	51
60/64	61	25	38	124	53	21	34	33	88	50	2	30	16	48	48
55/59	64	12	28	104	51	34	32	36	102	48	10	38	26	74	46
50/54	39	4	12	55	47	48	27	41	116	45	25	40	41	106	43
45/49	14	1	4	19	43	51	23	29	103	42	38	40	40	118	40
40/44	3			3	40	39	11	21	71	38	55	29	43	127	37
35/39	0			0	38	23	7	12	42	34	50	18	39	107	33
30/34						12	3	5	20	30	41	12	19	72	30
25/29						3	1	2	6	24	18	5	7	30	25
20/24						1	0	0	1	22	6	3	5	14	22
15/19											2		2	4	17
10/14											1			1	12

GLASGOW AFB MONTANA

Temperature Range	NOVEMBER Obsn Hour Gp 01 to 08	NOVEMBER Obsn Hour Gp 09 to 16	NOVEMBER Obsn Hour Gp 17 to 24	NOVEMBER Total Obsn	NOVEMBER MCWB	DECEMBER Obsn Hour Gp 01 to 08	DECEMBER Obsn Hour Gp 09 to 16	DECEMBER Obsn Hour Gp 17 to 24	DECEMBER Total Obsn	DECEMBER MCWB	JANUARY Obsn Hour Gp 01 to 08	JANUARY Obsn Hour Gp 09 to 16	JANUARY Obsn Hour Gp 17 to 24	JANUARY Total Obsn	JANUARY MCWB
100/104															
95/99															
90/94															
85/89															
80/84															
75/79															
70/74															
65/69		1		1	48										
60/64	0	2	0	2	48										
55/59	0	4	1	5	45										
50/54		13	4	17	42		1	0	1	42					
45/49	2	20	8	30	39	1	5	1	7	39		1	0	1	38
40/44	15	26	23	64	36	3	15	7	25	36	2	8	4	14	36
35/39	23	36	32	91	32	14	18	18	50	32	11	18	11	40	33
30/34	38	44	47	129	29	23	31	25	79	29	14	23	23	60	29
25/29	50	29	41	120	25	32	32	34	98	25	20	21	25	66	25
20/24	42	19	30	91	21	31	29	34	94	21	25	16	20	61	21
15/19	18	12	13	43	16	29	26	30	85	16	25	26	21	72	16
10/14	14	12	12	38	11	25	17	19	61	12	21	21	24	66	12
5/9	13	9	12	34	7	23	17	21	61	7	24	19	19	62	7
0/4	12	7	10	29	2	19	23	17	59	1	22	26	29	77	2
-5/-1	5	4	3	12	-3	15	15	15	45	-3	21	22	20	63	-3
-10/-6	3	2	4	9	-8	11	8	13	32	-8	20	23	17	60	-9
-15/-11	2	1	0	3	-13	10	7	9	26	-13	18	14	20	52	-13
-20/-16	1		0	1	-18	7	3	3	13	-18	16	8	12	36	-18
-25/-21						2	1	3	6	-23	7	2	2	11	-22
-30/-26						2	0	1	3	-28	1	1	0	2	-27
-35/-31											0			0	-34
-40/-36															

Temperature Range	FEBRUARY Obsn Hour Gp 01 to 08	FEBRUARY Obsn Hour Gp 09 to 16	FEBRUARY Obsn Hour Gp 17 to 24	FEBRUARY Total Obsn	FEBRUARY MCWB	MARCH Obsn Hour Gp 01 to 08	MARCH Obsn Hour Gp 09 to 16	MARCH Obsn Hour Gp 17 to 24	MARCH Total Obsn	MARCH MCWB	APRIL Obsn Hour Gp 01 to 08	APRIL Obsn Hour Gp 09 to 16	APRIL Obsn Hour Gp 17 to 24	APRIL Total Obsn	APRIL MCWB	ANNUAL TOTAL Obsn Hour Gp 01 to 08	ANNUAL TOTAL Obsn Hour Gp 09 to 16	ANNUAL TOTAL Obsn Hour Gp 17 to 24	ANNUAL TOTAL Total Obsn	ANNUAL TOTAL MCWB
100/104																	0	0	0	67
95/99																	6	3	9	65
90/94																	31	12	43	64
85/89																0	77	37	114	62
80/84												1	0	1	55	3	128	67	198	61
75/79												1	0	1	53	17	182	122	321	59
70/74							1		1	51		2	1	3	52	52	199	150	401	57
65/69							1	1	2	51	0	5	2	7	49	129	186	192	507	55
60/64							3	2	5	47	0	14	8	22	47	207	199	206	612	52
55/59							6	4	10	44	2	29	16	47	45	253	191	211	655	49
50/54		0	0	0	42	0	11	6	17	42	4	34	26	64	42	238	185	206	629	45
45/49	0	3	2	5	41	2	20	14	36	39	18	35	35	88	39	223	183	189	595	41
40/44	2	8	8	18	37	9	26	22	57	36	34	30	35	99	36	231	170	197	598	37
35/39	9	16	16	41	33	25	33	27	85	33	49	35	40	124	33	240	189	207	636	33
30/34	18	28	28	74	30	38	32	38	108	29	61	31	43	135	30	259	207	232	698	29
25/29	26	28	27	81	26	43	24	31	98	25	40	15	20	75	25	234	155	189	578	25
20/24	34	26	30	90	21	25	27	23	75	21	20	6	9	35	21	186	126	151	463	21
15/19	26	19	22	67	16	25	18	22	65	16	7	1	2	10	17	132	102	112	346	16
10/14	21	25	16	62	12	22	14	19	55	12	2	0	1	3	12	106	89	91	286	12
5/9	19	21	18	58	7	15	9	10	34	7	0	0		0	8	94	75	80	249	7
0/4	21	20	19	60	2	10	10	11	31	1	1		0	1	0	85	86	86	257	2
-5/-1	17	12	16	45	-3	10	7	8	25	-4						68	60	62	190	-3
-10/-6	13	10	15	38	-8	10	6	7	23	-8						57	49	56	162	-8
-15/-11	13	3	5	21	-13	9	1	4	14	-13						52	26	38	116	-13
-20/-16	3	1	2	6	-18	4	0	1	5	-18						31	12	18	61	-18
-25/-21	1	1	0	2	-23	1		0	1	-21						11	4	5	20	-22
-30/-26	0	0	1	1	-28											3	1	2	6	-28
-35/-31	1	0	0	1	-32											1	0	0	1	-33
-40/-36	0			0												0			0	

HELENA MONTANA

LAT 46 36N LONG 112 00W ELEV 3828 FT

MEAN FREQUENCY OF OCCURRENCE OF DRY BULB TEMPERATURE (DEGREES F) WITH MEAN COINCIDENT WET BULB TEMPERATURE (DEGREES F) FOR EACH DRY BULB TEMPERATURE RANGE

Temperature Range	MAY Obsn Hour Gp 01 to 08	MAY 09 to 16	MAY 17 to 24	MAY Total Obsn	MAY MCWB	JUNE Obsn Hour Gp 01 to 08	JUNE 09 to 16	JUNE 17 to 24	JUNE Total Obsn	JUNE MCWB	JULY Obsn Hour Gp 01 to 08	JULY 09 to 16	JULY 17 to 24	JULY Total Obsn	JULY MCWB
100/104												0	0	0	60
95/99							0	0	0	58		3	1	4	61
90/94							2	1	3	59		13	7	20	61
85/89		1	0	1	58		7	3	10	59		33	19	52	60
80/84		5	2	7	56		14	8	22	58	0	43	27	70	59
75/79		11	6	17	55	0	29	18	47	57	1	46	32	79	58
70/74		23	12	35	53	1	39	23	63	55	8	45	43	96	56
65/69	0	33	21	54	51	5	45	36	86	53	29	33	44	106	55
60/64	5	40	27	72	49	25	42	42	109	51	61	18	38	117	53
55/59	18	44	41	103	47	53	32	45	130	49	73	9	23	105	50
50/54	39	37	44	120	44	72	22	39	133	47	52	3	10	65	47
45/49	60	30	44	134	41	53	6	16	75	43	19	1	2	22	44
40/44	67	13	33	113	38	22	2	6	30	39	5	0	0	5	41
35/39	37	6	11	54	34	7	1	2	10	35	0			0	36
30/34	16	4	5	25	31	2	0	0	2	32					
25/29	3	0	1	4	27										
20/24	1		0	1	20										
15/19	0			0	17										
10/14															

Temperature Range	AUGUST Obsn Hour Gp 01 to 08	AUGUST 09 to 16	AUGUST 17 to 24	AUGUST Total Obsn	AUGUST MCWB	SEPTEMBER Obsn Hour Gp 01 to 08	SEPTEMBER 09 to 16	SEPTEMBER 17 to 24	SEPTEMBER Total Obsn	SEPTEMBER MCWB	OCTOBER Obsn Hour Gp 01 to 08	OCTOBER 09 to 16	OCTOBER 17 to 24	OCTOBER Total Obsn	OCTOBER MCWB
100/104		0	0	0	61										
95/99		1	1	2	60		0	0	0	61					
90/94		9	4	13	60		2	0	2	60					
85/89		23	13	36	59		5	2	7	58					
80/84		36	20	56	58		13	5	18	57		1	0	1	53
75/79	0	46	30	76	57		22	10	32	55		6	1	7	53
70/74	5	47	39	91	55	0	31	17	48	54		12	4	16	51
65/69	21	38	45	104	54	3	34	27	64	52	0	21	8	29	50
60/64	46	26	40	112	52	8	36	35	79	50	2	28	14	44	48
55/59	69	15	34	118	50	26	36	41	103	47	7	35	26	68	46
50/54	65	5	15	85	47	45	26	37	108	45	15	40	36	91	43
45/49	32	1	5	38	44	59	19	31	109	42	34	40	45	119	40
40/44	7	0	1	8	40	52	9	21	82	38	46	28	47	121	37
35/39	1		0	1	36	30	6	8	44	34	57	17	31	105	34
30/34						13	2	4	19	30	43	13	21	77	30
25/29						3	0	1	4	27	27	4	11	42	26
20/24						0		0	0	23	13	2	3	18	21
15/19											3	1	1	5	16
10/14											1	0	0	1	12

HELENA MONTANA

Temperature Range	NOVEMBER Obsn Hour Gp 01 to 08	09 to 16	17 to 24	Total Obsn	MCWB	DECEMBER Obsn Hour Gp 01 to 08	09 to 16	17 to 24	Total Obsn	MCWB	JANUARY Obsn Hour Gp 01 to 08	09 to 16	17 to 24	Total Obsn	MCWB
100/104															
95/99															
90/94															
85/89															
80/84															
75/79															
70/74		0		0	50										
65/69		1		1	48										
60/64		3	1	4	46							0		0	46
55/59	1	9	5	15	44	0	0		0	43		1		1	43
50/54	4	18	8	30	41	0	3	1	4	40	1	5	2	8	41
45/49	9	30	15	54	39	6	12	9	27	38	3	9	6	18	38
40/44	21	43	37	101	35	13	24	14	51	35	10	19	17	46	35
35/39	34	37	43	114	32	23	43	31	97	32	20	29	27	76	32
30/34	39	31	37	107	29	38	43	42	123	28	26	30	30	86	28
25/29	40	23	32	95	25	36	34	39	109	25	25	27	28	80	24
20/24	31	15	20	66	21	33	25	36	94	20	27	22	24	73	20
15/19	23	11	14	48	16	34	22	25	81	16	25	20	21	66	16
10/14	15	7	10	32	11	22	13	16	51	11	23	19	17	59	11
5/9	8	5	6	19	7	14	9	10	33	6	16	13	17	46	6
0/4	6	3	4	13	2	10	6	8	24	2	16	13	11	40	1
-5/-1	3	2	3	8	-3	6	5	6	17	-3	15	11	10	36	-3
-10/-6	3	2	2	7	-8	2	4	4	10	-8	10	13	11	34	-8
-15/-11	1	1	1	3	-13	7	3	3	13	-13	9	7	10	26	-13
-20/-16	1	0	1	2	-18	2	1	2	5	-18	10	7	10	27	-18
-25/-21	1	0	0	1	-22	1	0	0	1	-22	7	2	4	13	-23
-30/-26	0	0	0	0	-28		0	0	0	-28	3	0	1	4	-28
-35/-31	0			0	-34	0		0	0	-33	1	0	1	2	-33
-40/-36	0			0		0			0		1	0	0	1	

Temperature Range	FEBRUARY Obsn Hour Gp 01 to 08	09 to 16	17 to 24	Total Obsn	MCWB	MARCH Obsn Hour Gp 01 to 08	09 to 16	17 to 24	Total Obsn	MCWB	APRIL Obsn Hour Gp 01 to 08	09 to 16	17 to 24	Total Obsn	MCWB	ANNUAL TOTAL Obsn Hour Gp 01 to 08	09 to 16	17 to 24	Total Obsn	MCWB
100/104																	0	0	0	61
95/99																	4	2	6	61
90/94																	26	12	38	60
85/89												0		0	54		69	37	106	59
80/84												0	0	0	53	0	112	62	174	58
75/79												3	1	4	52	1	163	98	262	57
70/74							0	0	0	49		5	3	8	50	14	202	141	357	55
65/69		0		0	48		2	1	3	47	0	11	6	17	48	58	218	188	464	53
60/64		1	0	1	46		5	2	7	45	0	20	10	30	46	147	219	209	575	50
55/59	1	2	1	4	44	0	8	4	12	43	2	25	16	43	44	250	216	236	702	48
50/54	0	7	3	10	41	1	17	8	26	41	9	34	29	72	41	303	217	232	752	45
45/49	3	14	8	25	38	4	27	20	51	38	17	44	38	99	39	299	233	239	771	41
40/44	10	23	19	52	35	12	39	30	81	35	35	40	43	118	35	300	240	268	808	36
35/39	23	44	36	103	32	29	45	46	120	32	59	30	44	133	33	320	258	279	857	33
30/34	38	39	46	123	28	58	36	52	146	29	58	19	28	105	29	331	217	265	813	29
25/29	43	25	34	102	25	52	22	28	102	25	33	8	15	56	25	262	143	189	594	25
20/24	24	18	19	61	21	29	14	17	60	20	20	1	6	27	21	178	97	125	400	21
15/19	22	15	14	51	16	19	11	12	42	16	6	0	1	7	16	132	80	88	300	16
10/14	15	11	13	39	11	14	7	8	29	11	1	0	0	1	11	91	57	64	212	11
5/9	14	10	10	34	6	8	6	8	22	6	1	0	0	1	7	61	43	51	155	6
0/4	11	7	9	27	1	7	3	3	13	1	0			0	3	50	32	35	117	1
-5/-1	7	4	6	17	-3	5	3	3	11	-3						36	25	28	89	-3
-10/-6	7	1	3	11	-8	4	2	2	8	-8						26	22	22	70	-8
-15/-11	2	1	1	4	-13	2	2	2	6	-13						21	14	17	52	-13
-20/-16	2	1	0	3	-17	2	0	1	3	-18						17	9	14	40	-18
-25/-21	1	0	0	1	-23	1		0	1	-23						11	2	4	17	-23
-30/-26	1		0	1	-27	0			0	-27						4	0	1	5	-28
-35/-31																1	0	1	2	-33
-40/-36																	0	0	1	

MALMSTROM AFB MONTANA

LAT 47 30N LONG 111 11W ELEV 3525 FT

MEAN FREQUENCY OF OCCURRENCE OF DRY BULB TEMPERATURE (DEGREES F) WITH MEAN COINCIDENT WET BULB TEMPERATURE (DEGREES F) FOR EACH DRY BULB TEMPERATURE RANGE

Temperature Range	MAY Obsn Hour Gp 01 to 08	MAY 09 to 16	MAY 17 to 24	MAY Total Obsn	MAY MCWB	JUNE Obsn Hour Gp 01 to 08	JUNE 09 to 16	JUNE 17 to 24	JUNE Total Obsn	JUNE MCWB	JULY Obsn Hour Gp 01 to 08	JULY 09 to 16	JULY 17 to 24	JULY Total Obsn	JULY MCWB
105/109															
100/104												0	0	0	62
95/99							0	0	0	58		2	1	3	62
90/94		0		0	60		3	1	4	60		13	7	20	61
85/89		2	0	2	58		8	4	12	61		33	18	51	61
80/84		8	3	11	57		19	8	27	59	0	49	29	78	60
75/79		15	7	22	55	1	32	17	50	57	4	50	35	89	58
70/74	0	26	14	40	53	3	39	27	69	55	14	47	41	102	56
65/69	3	34	23	60	51	13	40	34	87	54	35	29	45	109	55
60/64	12	35	28	75	49	29	41	41	111	52	60	15	36	111	53
55/59	22	39	38	99	46	55	30	45	130	50	70	6	24	100	50
50/54	37	36	46	119	44	69	20	40	129	47	47	3	10	60	47
45/49	61	29	39	129	42	48	7	16	71	44	14	0	2	16	43
40/44	60	15	31	106	38	15	1	4	20	39	5		0	5	38
35/39	36	6	12	54	34	5	0	1	6	35	0			0	33
30/34	13	2	3	18	30	1	0	0	1	31					
25/29	3	0	1	4	26	0			0	28					
20/24	1		0	1	22										
15/19	0			0	19										
10/14															
5/9															
0/4															

Temperature Range	AUGUST Obsn Hour Gp 01 to 08	AUGUST 09 to 16	AUGUST 17 to 24	AUGUST Total Obsn	AUGUST MCWB	SEPTEMBER Obsn Hour Gp 01 to 08	SEPTEMBER 09 to 16	SEPTEMBER 17 to 24	SEPTEMBER Total Obsn	SEPTEMBER MCWB	OCTOBER Obsn Hour Gp 01 to 08	OCTOBER 09 to 16	OCTOBER 17 to 24	OCTOBER Total Obsn	OCTOBER MCWB
105/109		0	0	0	65										
100/104		1	0	1	64										
95/99		4	2	6	62		1	0	1	61					
90/94		20	9	29	61		3	1	4	59					
85/89		35	18	53	60		10	3	13	59		1	0	1	56
80/84	0	36	22	58	58		17	6	23	57		4	0	4	55
75/79	3	40	30	73	57	0	21	11	32	56		11	2	13	53
70/74	12	41	42	95	55	4	31	19	54	54	0	19	4	23	52
65/69	33	33	43	109	53	6	35	26	67	52	1	23	9	33	49
60/64	56	19	37	112	51	24	37	36	97	49	7	30	19	56	47
55/59	63	11	26	100	49	36	26	38	100	47	20	35	30	85	45
50/54	51	5	14	70	46	50	22	34	106	44	34	38	43	115	42
45/49	23	1	5	29	43	47	16	30	93	42	42	31	39	112	39
40/44	5		1	6	38	35	11	18	64	38	46	21	37	104	36
35/39	1			1	36	21	6	9	36	34	38	13	27	78	33
30/34		0		0	25	11	5	7	23	30	29	10	18	57	29
25/29						4	1	1	6	26	18	9	11	38	26
20/24						0			0	22	10	2	5	17	22
15/19											2	2	1	5	17
10/14											1	0	1	2	12
5/9											0	0	0	0	7
0/4											0		0	0	2

MALMSTROM AFB MONTANA

Temperature Range	NOVEMBER Obsn Hour Gp 01 to 08	NOVEMBER 09 to 16	NOVEMBER 17 to 24	NOVEMBER Total Obsn	NOVEMBER MCWB	DECEMBER Obsn Hour Gp 01 to 08	DECEMBER 09 to 16	DECEMBER 17 to 24	DECEMBER Total Obsn	DECEMBER MCWB	JANUARY Obsn Hour Gp 01 to 08	JANUARY 09 to 16	JANUARY 17 to 24	JANUARY Total Obsn	JANUARY MCWB
105/109															
100/104															
95/99															
90/94															
85/89															
80/84															
75/79		0		0	53										
70/74		1		1	51										
65/69		2		2	47										
60/64	0	7	1	8	46		1		1	44		1		1	46
55/59	2	16	5	23	44	1	5	1	7	42		3	0	3	43
50/54	12	30	17	59	41	3	17	5	25	40	2	10	4	16	41
45/49	20	33	27	80	38	13	23	19	55	37	10	19	12	41	38
40/44	34	40	37	111	35	26	31	27	84	35	20	30	27	77	35
35/39	40	34	40	114	32	31	35	32	98	31	30	28	33	91	32
30/34	37	24	38	99	29	29	32	31	92	28	29	23	26	78	28
25/29	33	15	27	75	25	28	22	31	81	24	20	18	19	57	24
20/24	22	11	13	46	21	31	16	27	74	20	21	16	20	57	20
15/19	13	7	11	31	16	17	12	17	46	16	15	14	14	43	16
10/14	8	8	11	27	11	13	9	9	31	11	16	14	14	44	11
5/9	8	4	5	17	6	11	12	11	34	6	15	13	11	39	6
0/4	6	4	5	15	2	13	13	13	39	1	13	13	15	41	1
-5/-1	3	3	3	9	-3	12	11	13	36	-3	14	14	14	42	-3
-10/-6	2	1	1	4	-9	10	6	6	22	-8	17	13	13	43	-8
-15/-11	1	0	1	2	-13	3	1	3	7	-13	12	10	12	34	-13
-20/-16	1		0	1	-17	1	1	1	3	-18	7	5	6	18	-18
-25/-21						1	1	1	3	-23	4	3	4	11	-23
-30/-26						1	0	0	1	-27	2	0	1	3	-28
-35/-31						0	0	0	0	-33	1	0	0	1	-32
-40/-36						0	0	0	0						
-45/-41						0	0		0						

Temperature Range	FEBRUARY Obsn Hour Gp 01 to 08	FEBRUARY 09 to 16	FEBRUARY 17 to 24	FEBRUARY Total Obsn	FEBRUARY MCWB	MARCH Obsn Hour Gp 01 to 08	MARCH 09 to 16	MARCH 17 to 24	MARCH Total Obsn	MARCH MCWB	APRIL Obsn Hour Gp 01 to 08	APRIL 09 to 16	APRIL 17 to 24	APRIL Total Obsn	APRIL MCWB	ANNUAL TOTAL Obsn Hour Gp 01 to 08	ANNUAL TOTAL 09 to 16	ANNUAL TOTAL 17 to 24	ANNUAL TOTAL Total Obsn	ANNUAL TOTAL MCWB
105/109																	0	0	0	65
100/104																	1	0	1	63
95/99																	7	3	10	62
90/94																	39	18	57	61
85/89												0		0	57		89	43	132	60
80/84												1	0	1	55	0	134	68	202	59
75/79							0		0	52		2	1	3	53	8	171	103	282	57
70/74							1	0	1	49	0	6	2	8	51	33	211	149	393	55
65/69		0		0	48		3	1	4	47		9	4	13	49	91	208	185	484	53
60/64		3	0	3	47		9	3	12	46	1	19	10	30	46	189	217	211	617	50
55/59	0	7	2	9	44	2	13	5	20	43	3	33	18	54	44	274	224	232	730	47
50/54	3	16	6	25	41	2	22	12	36	40	13	37	29	79	41	323	256	260	839	44
45/49	7	21	14	42	38	9	33	23	65	38	24	39	37	100	38	318	252	263	833	40
40/44	17	31	24	72	35	24	37	33	94	35	38	32	44	114	36	325	249	283	857	36
35/39	28	30	34	92	32	34	31	41	106	32	49	24	38	111	33	313	207	267	787	32
30/34	35	22	34	91	28	47	27	36	110	29	58	21	31	110	30	289	166	224	679	29
25/29	31	19	25	75	24	39	17	29	85	25	29	10	16	55	25	205	111	160	476	25
20/24	26	17	19	62	21	30	14	19	63	21	16	5	8	29	21	157	81	111	349	21
15/19	19	14	16	49	16	14	9	11	34	16	6	1	1	8	17	86	59	71	216	16
10/14	14	14	15	43	11	11	12	9	32	11	2	0	0	2	12	65	57	59	181	11
5/9	12	12	13	37	6	11	9	11	31	7	1		0	1	7	58	50	51	159	6
0/4	16	11	11	38	2	8	5	5	18	2	0			0		56	46	49	151	2
-5/-1	6	4	6	16	-3	7	4	5	16	-3						42	36	41	119	-3
-10/-6	5	2	5	12	-8	5	2	3	10	-8						39	24	28	91	-8
-15/-11	5	1	2	8	-13	4	1	1	6	-13						25	13	19	57	-13
-20/-16	0		0	0	-17	1	0	0	1	-17						10	6	7	23	-18
-25/-21						0			0	-22						5	4	5	14	-23
-30/-26																3	0	1	4	-28
-35/-31																1	0	0	1	-32
-40/-36																0	0	0	0	
-45/-41																0	0		0	

MISSOULA MONTANA

LAT 46 55N LONG 114 05W ELEV 3190 FT

MEAN FREQUENCY OF OCCURRENCE OF DRY BULB TEMPERATURE (DEGREES F) WITH MEAN COINCIDENT WET BULB TEMPERATURE (DEGREES F) FOR EACH DRY BULB TEMPERATURE RANGE

Temperature Range	MAY Obsn Hour Gp 01 to 08	MAY 09 to 16	MAY 17 to 24	MAY Total Obsn	MAY MCWB	JUNE Obsn Hour Gp 01 to 08	JUNE 09 to 16	JUNE 17 to 24	JUNE Total Obsn	JUNE MCWB	JULY Obsn Hour Gp 01 to 08	JULY 09 to 16	JULY 17 to 24	JULY Total Obsn	JULY MCWB
100/104												0	1	1	66
95/99							0	0	0	65		3	2	5	64
90/94		0	0	0	63		2	1	3	63		16	10	26	62
85/89		1	0	1	59		6	4	10	62		33	20	53	61
80/84		6	3	9	58		15	9	24	60	0	40	28	68	60
75/79		11	7	18	56		25	16	41	58	0	40	32	72	58
70/74		21	11	32	54	0	34	22	56	56	3	44	36	83	57
65/69	0	29	19	48	52	4	43	32	79	54	19	34	42	95	55
60/64	3	38	28	69	50	15	44	40	99	52	47	23	37	107	53
55/59	13	45	39	97	48	40	35	47	122	50	67	10	25	102	51
50/54	37	41	47	125	45	74	26	42	142	48	64	4	11	79	48
45/49	56	31	46	133	42	61	9	20	90	44	35	1	3	39	44
40/44	66	18	30	114	39	34	1	6	41	40	12		0	12	40
35/39	50	5	15	70	35	9	0	1	10	36	2			2	36
30/34	20	1	3	24	31	2			2	32					
25/29	2		0	2	25										
20/24	0			0	21										
15/19															

Temperature Range	AUGUST Obsn Hour Gp 01 to 08	AUGUST 09 to 16	AUGUST 17 to 24	AUGUST Total Obsn	AUGUST MCWB	SEPTEMBER Obsn Hour Gp 01 to 08	SEPTEMBER 09 to 16	SEPTEMBER 17 to 24	SEPTEMBER Total Obsn	SEPTEMBER MCWB	OCTOBER Obsn Hour Gp 01 to 08	OCTOBER 09 to 16	OCTOBER 17 to 24	OCTOBER Total Obsn	OCTOBER MCWB
100/104		1	0	1	64										
95/99		1	1	2	62		0	0	0	64					
90/94		9	5	14	62		1	1	2	61					
85/89		24	15	39	60		5	3	8	60					
80/84	0	36	22	58	59		13	7	20	58		0	0	0	58
75/79	0	40	29	69	57	0	20	11	31	56		2	0	2	54
70/74	3	41	36	80	56	0	27	17	44	54		7	3	10	52
65/69	10	35	39	84	54	2	32	24	58	53		14	5	19	52
60/64	31	32	43	106	53	7	40	37	84	51	0	20	10	30	49
55/59	69	18	34	121	50	22	37	42	101	49	2	30	19	51	47
50/54	77	9	17	103	47	41	33	41	115	46	8	46	34	88	45
45/49	44	2	7	53	44	63	20	30	113	43	31	45	54	130	42
40/44	13	0	0	13	41	56	10	19	85	39	52	42	54	148	39
35/39	1			1	36	35	2	7	44	35	62	26	41	129	35
30/34	0			0	33	10	0	1	11	31	55	12	22	89	31
25/29						2			2	27	29	4	5	38	27
20/24						0			0	24	9	0	0	9	22
15/19											0			0	18

MISSOULA MONTANA

Temperature Range	NOVEMBER Obsn Hour Gp 01 to 08	NOVEMBER 09 to 16	NOVEMBER 17 to 24	NOVEMBER Total Obsn	NOVEMBER MCWB	DECEMBER Obsn Hour Gp 01 to 08	DECEMBER 09 to 16	DECEMBER 17 to 24	DECEMBER Total Obsn	DECEMBER MCWB	JANUARY Obsn Hour Gp 01 to 08	JANUARY 09 to 16	JANUARY 17 to 24	JANUARY Total Obsn	JANUARY MCWB	FEBRUARY Obsn Hour Gp 01 to 08	FEBRUARY 09 to 16	FEBRUARY 17 to 24	FEBRUARY Total Obsn	FEBRUARY MCWB
100/104																				
95/99																				
90/94																				
85/89																				
80/84																				
75/79																				
70/74																				
65/69																				
60/64		0		0	48															
55/59	0	3	1	4	46		0		0	43	0	0		0	46		1		1	45
50/54	1	9	3	13	43	0	1	0	1	41	0	1	0	1	44	0	1	0	1	43
45/49	4	23	11	38	41	1	4	1	6	40	1	4	2	7	40	1	6	3	10	40
40/44	13	41	31	85	38	6	14	9	29	37	4	12	9	25	37	5	20	10	35	37
35/39	41	50	51	142	34	19	45	28	92	34	16	35	27	78	34	13	48	37	98	33
30/34	56	47	57	160	30	52	59	63	174	30	34	39	40	113	30	54	61	68	183	30
25/29	49	34	41	124	26	53	44	54	151	26	35	39	38	112	26	52	37	47	136	26
20/24	36	17	21	74	21	43	30	36	109	21	38	34	36	108	21	35	19	25	79	21
15/19	18	7	13	38	17	24	22	23	69	16	35	23	27	85	16	24	14	13	51	16
10/14	12	3	5	20	12	24	14	15	53	12	26	18	18	62	11	18	9	11	38	11
5/9	5	3	3	11	7	10	8	10	28	7	15	14	15	44	6	11	4	4	19	6
0/4	2	2	1	5	1	8	4	4	16	1	12	11	14	37	1	4	3	3	10	1
-5/-1	2	1	2	5	-3	4	1	3	8	-3	9	9	11	29	-3	2	1	1	4	-3
-10/-6	1	0	1	2	-8	1	1	1	3	-8	10	6	6	22	-8	2	1	1	4	-8
-15/-11	0	0	0	0	-13	1	1	0	2	-13	6	3	3	12	-13	1	0	0	1	-13
-20/-16	0			0	-18	1	1	0	2	-17	4	2	1	7	-18	2	0		2	-18
-25/-21						0	0	0	0	-23	2	0	0	2	-22	0			0	-22
-30/-26						0	0		0	-28	0	0		0	-27					
-35/-31											0			0	-31					

Temperature Range	MARCH Obsn Hour Gp 01 to 08	MARCH 09 to 16	MARCH 17 to 24	MARCH Total Obsn	MARCH MCWB	APRIL Obsn Hour Gp 01 to 08	APRIL 09 to 16	APRIL 17 to 24	APRIL Total Obsn	APRIL MCWB	ANNUAL TOTAL Obsn Hour Gp 01 to 08	ANNUAL TOTAL 09 to 16	ANNUAL TOTAL 17 to 24	ANNUAL TOTAL Total Obsn	ANNUAL TOTAL MCWB
100/104												1	1	2	65
95/99												4	3	7	63
90/94												28	17	45	62
85/89												69	42	111	61
80/84							0	0	0	54	0	110	69	179	59
75/79							2	1	3	54	0	140	96	236	57
70/74							5	2	7	52	6	179	127	312	55
65/69		0	0	0	49		10	6	16	49	35	197	167	399	54
60/64		3	1	4	47		18	11	29	47	103	218	207	528	52
55/59		7	4	11	44	1	26	18	45	45	214	212	229	655	49
50/54	0	12	6	18	42	4	44	30	78	42	306	227	231	764	46
45/49	1	27	17	45	39	19	54	49	122	40	317	226	243	786	42
40/44	8	46	37	91	36	45	48	55	148	37	314	252	260	826	38
35/39	36	58	56	150	33	67	25	43	135	33	351	294	306	951	34
30/34	72	43	62	177	29	67	8	22	97	30	422	270	338	1030	30
25/29	60	25	33	118	25	30	0	3	33	25	312	183	221	716	26
20/24	33	12	14	59	21	6	0	0	6	21	200	112	132	444	21
15/19	17	6	9	32	16	1	0		1	15	119	72	85	276	16
10/14	11	4	4	19	11						91	48	53	192	11
5/9	4	2	3	9	6						45	31	35	111	6
0/4	3	1	1	5	1						29	21	23	73	1
-5/-1	2	0	0	2	-3						19	12	17	48	-3
-10/-6	1			1	-8						15	8	9	32	-8
-15/-11	0			0	-11						8	4	3	15	-13
-20/-16											7	3	1	11	-17
-25/-21											2	0	0	2	-22
-30/-26											0	0		0	-27
-35/-31											0			0	-31

GRAND ISLAND NEBRASKA

LAT 40 58N LONG 98 19W ELEV 1841 FT

MEAN FREQUENCY OF OCCURRENCE OF DRY BULB TEMPERATURE (DEGREES F) WITH MEAN COINCIDENT WET BULB TEMPERATURE (DEGREES F) FOR EACH DRY BULB TEMPERATURE RANGE

Temperature Range	MAY Obsn Hour Gp 01 to 08	MAY 09 to 16	MAY 17 to 24	MAY Total Obsn	MAY MCWB	JUNE Obsn Hour Gp 01 to 08	JUNE 09 to 16	JUNE 17 to 24	JUNE Total Obsn	JUNE MCWB	JULY Obsn Hour Gp 01 to 08	JULY 09 to 16	JULY 17 to 24	JULY Total Obsn	JULY MCWB
105/109							0		0	74		1	0	1	73
100/104							3	1	4	73		6	2	8	72
95/99		0	0	0	73		7	3	10	72		15	7	22	72
90/94		4	1	5	67		19	9	28	72		28	13	41	72
85/89		8	3	11	67	0	30	18	48	70	1	51	30	82	71
80/84		19	10	29	65	5	45	33	83	68	9	56	43	108	69
75/79	1	30	17	48	62	17	44	38	99	66	31	45	48	124	67
70/74	6	40	28	74	60	34	40	44	118	64	61	29	50	140	66
65/69	17	47	39	103	57	54	25	39	118	61	73	13	38	124	63
60/64	41	39	49	129	55	60	16	32	108	58	53	4	13	70	60
55/59	56	29	43	128	52	43	6	15	64	54	18	1	3	22	56
50/54	57	18	33	108	48	18	4	6	28	49	2		0	2	51
45/49	39	7	14	60	44	6	0	2	8	45	0			0	47
40/44	16	4	6	26	39	3		1	4	40					
35/39	11	1	3	15	35	0			0	37					
30/34	4	1	1	6	31										
25/29	1			1	27										
20/24															
15/19															

Temperature Range	AUGUST Obsn Hour Gp 01 to 08	AUGUST 09 to 16	AUGUST 17 to 24	AUGUST Total Obsn	AUGUST MCWB	SEPTEMBER Obsn Hour Gp 01 to 08	SEPTEMBER 09 to 16	SEPTEMBER 17 to 24	SEPTEMBER Total Obsn	SEPTEMBER MCWB	OCTOBER Obsn Hour Gp 01 to 08	OCTOBER 09 to 16	OCTOBER 17 to 24	OCTOBER Total Obsn	OCTOBER MCWB
105/109			0	0	75										
100/104		2	1	3	72										
95/99		10	4	14	72		3	1	4	68					
90/94		33	13	46	71		11	4	15	68		1		1	64
85/89	0	40	23	63	71		19	7	26	66		5	1	6	61
80/84	6	56	41	103	69	0	27	15	42	65		12	2	14	61
75/79	22	47	47	116	67	6	36	23	65	63		22	6	28	59
70/74	58	32	51	141	66	18	38	31	87	61	0	29	13	42	57
65/69	72	19	38	129	63	24	35	36	95	59	4	35	22	61	55
60/64	53	7	20	80	59	40	30	42	112	56	16	36	34	86	53
55/59	26	2	9	37	55	51	19	36	106	53	26	35	37	98	49
50/54	10	0	1	11	51	45	13	27	85	48	39	28	40	107	46
45/49	2		0	2	47	32	5	12	49	44	46	23	38	107	42
40/44	1		0	1	41	15	2	5	22	40	45	14	29	88	38
35/39						7		1	8	36	39	6	15	60	34
30/34						1		0	1	31	19	2	8	29	30
25/29						0			0	26	9	1	2	12	25
20/24											3		0	3	21
15/19											0			0	18

GRAND ISLAND NEBRASKA

Temperature Range	NOVEMBER Obsn Hour Gp 01 to 08	09 to 16	17 to 24	Total Obsn	M C W B	DECEMBER Obsn Hour Gp 01 to 08	09 to 16	17 to 24	Total Obsn	M C W B	JANUARY Obsn Hour Gp 01 to 08	09 to 16	17 to 24	Total Obsn	M C W B	FEBRUARY Obsn Hour Gp 01 to 08	09 to 16	17 to 24	Total Obsn	M C W B
105/109																				
100/104																				
95/99																				
90/94																				
85/89																				
80/84																				
75/79		1		1	53		0		0	55							0		0	56
70/74		4	0	4	53		0		0	52		0		0	50		1	0	1	54
65/69		10	1	11	52		1	0	1	48		1		1	48		2	0	2	50
60/64	0	14	4	18	49		3	0	3	46		1	0	1	45		4	1	5	48
55/59	1	23	9	33	46		8	1	9	45		3	0	3	44		7	2	9	45
50/54	5	29	18	52	44	1	14	4	19	42		8	2	10	41	0	13	6	19	42
45/49	14	32	27	73	40	3	20	8	31	40	0	13	4	17	38	3	17	9	29	40
40/44	27	34	38	99	37	6	28	17	51	36	1	21	10	32	36	5	25	19	49	37
35/39	40	30	42	112	33	17	31	32	80	33	10	29	26	65	33	20	30	32	82	33
30/34	53	23	42	118	29	38	37	45	120	29	24	29	40	93	29	43	31	44	118	30
25/29	39	18	22	79	25	47	29	40	116	25	38	31	35	104	25	38	26	32	96	25
20/24	24	12	19	55	20	47	27	35	109	21	40	27	32	99	21	37	20	22	79	21
15/19	20	6	10	36	16	28	16	21	65	16	32	24	25	81	16	24	19	19	62	16
10/14	7	3	3	13	11	24	16	18	58	11	26	20	21	67	11	17	15	17	49	11
5/9	6	1	3	10	6	15	10	15	40	6	25	13	18	56	6	16	8	13	37	6
0/4	3	0	1	4	1	12	5	7	24	2	22	16	17	55	1	11	3	5	19	2
-5/-1	1		0	1	-3	5	2	3	10	-3	16	7	11	34	-3	6	1	2	9	-3
-10/-6						5	1	2	8	-8	7	3	6	16	-8	3	0	0	3	-8
-15/-11						1	0	0	1	-12	4	1	1	6	-12	1			1	-13
-20/-16											2	0		2	-18	0			0	-16
-25/-21											1	0		1	-22					

Temperature Range	MARCH Obsn Hour Gp 01 to 08	09 to 16	17 to 24	Total Obsn	M C W B	APRIL Obsn Hour Gp 01 to 08	09 to 16	17 to 24	Total Obsn	M C W B	ANNUAL TOTAL Obsn Hour Gp 01 to 08	09 to 16	17 to 24	Total Obsn	M C W B
105/109												1	0	1	73
100/104												11	4	15	72
95/99												35	15	50	72
90/94							1	0	1	60		97	40	137	71
85/89							2	1	3	62	1	155	83	239	69
80/84		0	0	0	59		6	2	8	60	20	221	146	387	67
75/79		1	0	1	55		11	6	17	59	77	237	185	499	65
70/74	0	4	1	5	54	0	17	9	26	56	177	234	227	638	63
65/69	0	7	3	10	52	3	20	15	38	54	247	215	231	693	60
60/64	0	10	6	16	49	8	28	22	58	51	271	192	223	686	56
55/59	2	12	8	22	47	15	33	28	76	48	238	178	191	607	51
50/54	3	21	16	40	43	27	36	38	101	45	207	184	191	582	46
45/49	12	28	21	61	40	40	28	35	103	42	197	173	170	540	42
40/44	17	29	33	79	37	43	24	32	99	38	179	181	190	550	37
35/39	31	33	35	99	34	39	21	26	86	34	214	181	212	607	33
30/34	55	36	43	134	30	40	11	21	72	30	277	170	244	691	30
25/29	49	27	33	109	25	18	1	4	23	25	239	133	168	540	25
20/24	32	20	23	75	21	6		1	7	21	189	106	132	427	21
15/19	19	10	13	42	16	2			2	17	125	75	88	288	16
10/14	14	6	7	27	11	0			0	13	88	60	66	214	11
5/9	9	3	4	16	6						71	35	53	159	6
0/4	4	0	2	6	2						52	24	32	108	2
-5/-1	1	0	0	1	-3						29	10	16	55	-3
-10/-6	1	0		1	-7						16	4	8	28	-8
-15/-11	0	0		0	-13						6	1	1	8	-12
-20/-16	0			0	-18						2	0		2	-17
-25/-21												0			-22

NORTH PLATTE/LEE BIRD FLD NEBRASKA

LAT 41 08N LONG 100 41W ELEV 2775 FT

MEAN FREQUENCY OF OCCURRENCE OF DRY BULB TEMPERATURE (DEGREES F) WITH MEAN COINCIDENT WET BULB TEMPERATURE (DEGREES F) FOR EACH DRY BULB TEMPERATURE RANGE

Temperature Range	MAY Obsn Hour Gp 01 to 08	MAY 09 to 16	MAY 17 to 24	MAY Total Obsn	MAY MCWB	JUNE Obsn Hour Gp 01 to 08	JUNE 09 to 16	JUNE 17 to 24	JUNE Total Obsn	JUNE MCWB	JULY Obsn Hour Gp 01 to 08	JULY 09 to 16	JULY 17 to 24	JULY Total Obsn	JULY MCWB
110/114												0	0	0	70
105/109							0	0	0	71		1	0	1	69
100/104							2	1	3	70		3	1	4	70
95/99		0	0	0	61		7	3	10	69		12	6	18	70
90/94		1	1	2	63		14	7	21	69		29	15	44	70
85/89		7	3	10	63		26	15	41	68	0	44	27	71	69
80/84		15	8	23	62	2	41	29	72	66	4	57	42	103	67
75/79	0	26	14	40	61	7	43	33	83	64	18	47	46	111	66
70/74	2	38	25	65	58	22	41	41	104	63	49	33	46	128	65
65/69	9	46	31	86	56	47	33	40	120	60	74	14	38	126	63
60/64	23	44	46	113	54	61	19	34	114	58	63	6	22	91	59
55/59	52	33	45	130	52	53	9	23	85	54	30	1	5	36	55
50/54	62	18	37	117	48	31	5	9	45	50	8	0	1	9	51
45/49	44	12	20	76	44	12	1	3	16	45	1			1	46
40/44	30	6	13	49	40	4		1	5	40	1			1	42
35/39	17	2	3	22	36	2		0	2	37					
30/34	7	1	1	9	31										
25/29	1		0	1	26										
20/24	0			0	22										
15/19															
10/14															

Temperature Range	AUGUST Obsn Hour Gp 01 to 08	AUGUST 09 to 16	AUGUST 17 to 24	AUGUST Total Obsn	AUGUST MCWB	SEPTEMBER Obsn Hour Gp 01 to 08	SEPTEMBER 09 to 16	SEPTEMBER 17 to 24	SEPTEMBER Total Obsn	SEPTEMBER MCWB	OCTOBER Obsn Hour Gp 01 to 08	OCTOBER 09 to 16	OCTOBER 17 to 24	OCTOBER Total Obsn	OCTOBER MCWB
110/114															
105/109															
100/104		2	1	3	69		0	0	0	65					
95/99		10	4	14	69		3	1	4	66					
90/94		28	11	39	69		10	2	12	66		0		0	60
85/89	0	43	22	65	68		18	7	25	65		6	1	7	59
80/84	2	49	34	85	67		28	14	42	63		12	2	14	58
75/79	11	49	48	108	66	3	35	22	60	61		21	6	27	57
70/74	41	36	52	129	65	9	38	28	75	60	0	25	10	35	55
65/69	71	21	40	132	62	21	33	36	90	58	1	32	18	51	53
60/64	70	8	26	104	59	36	30	39	105	55	8	36	28	72	51
55/59	33	2	8	43	55	44	21	37	102	52	17	34	35	86	48
50/54	13	0	2	15	50	46	14	25	85	48	28	29	38	95	46
45/49	3	0	1	4	46	39	8	17	64	44	37	20	36	93	42
40/44	2			2	42	25	3	9	37	40	47	18	34	99	39
35/39	0			0	37	13	0	2	15	36	47	10	22	79	35
30/34						3		0	3	31	31	4	11	46	31
25/29						1		0	1	27	21	1	6	28	26
20/24						0			0	23	8	0	1	9	22
15/19											2			2	16
10/14											0			0	12

NORTH PLATTE/LEE BIRD FLD NEBRASKA

Temperature Range	NOVEMBER Obsn Hour Gp 01 to 08	NOVEMBER 09 to 16	NOVEMBER 17 to 24	NOVEMBER Total Obsn	NOVEMBER MCWB	DECEMBER Obsn Hour Gp 01 to 08	DECEMBER 09 to 16	DECEMBER 17 to 24	DECEMBER Total Obsn	DECEMBER MCWB	JANUARY Obsn Hour Gp 01 to 08	JANUARY 09 to 16	JANUARY 17 to 24	JANUARY Total Obsn	JANUARY MCWB
110/114															
105/109															
100/104															
95/99															
90/94															
85/89															
80/84															
75/79		0		0	53										
70/74		5	0	5	51		0		0	51		0		0	50
65/69		8	1	9	49		1	0	1	49		1	0	1	47
60/64		13	3	16	47	0	4	0	4	45		3	0	3	45
55/59	0	22	6	28	44	0	9	1	10	43		6	1	7	43
50/54	1	29	13	43	42	0	14	3	17	41		12	3	15	40
45/49	6	30	23	59	39	1	21	8	30	38	0	17	6	23	38
40/44	15	28	33	76	36	2	31	14	47	35	1	26	12	39	35
35/39	30	30	44	104	33	12	33	30	75	32	5	27	24	56	32
30/34	44	29	44	117	29	28	34	42	104	29	17	31	38	86	29
25/29	55	19	33	107	25	42	32	50	124	25	35	26	42	103	25
20/24	42	12	18	72	21	57	23	38	118	21	50	26	29	105	21
15/19	22	7	10	39	16	41	16	20	77	16	39	23	28	90	16
10/14	10	4	5	19	11	23	15	18	56	11	26	17	19	62	11
5/9	8	2	3	13	6	20	8	13	41	6	26	10	17	53	6
0/4	4	0	2	6	1	11	4	6	21	2	18	13	13	44	1
-5/-1	2	0	1	3	-3	8	2	3	13	-3	16	7	9	32	-4
-10/-6	1			1	-8	4	0	2	6	-8	9	3	4	16	-8
-15/-11						1	0	0	1	-13	3	1	2	6	-13
-20/-16						0			0	-17	2	0	0	2	-17
-25/-21											1			1	-22

Temperature Range	FEBRUARY Obsn Hour Gp 01 to 08	FEBRUARY 09 to 16	FEBRUARY 17 to 24	FEBRUARY Total Obsn	FEBRUARY MCWB	MARCH Obsn Hour Gp 01 to 08	MARCH 09 to 16	MARCH 17 to 24	MARCH Total Obsn	MARCH MCWB	APRIL Obsn Hour Gp 01 to 08	APRIL 09 to 16	APRIL 17 to 24	APRIL Total Obsn	APRIL MCWB	ANNUAL TOTAL Obsn Hour Gp 01 to 08	ANNUAL TOTAL 09 to 16	ANNUAL TOTAL 17 to 24	ANNUAL TOTAL Total Obsn	ANNUAL TOTAL MCWB
110/114																	0	0	0	70
105/109																	1	0	1	69
100/104																	7	3	10	70
95/99																	32	14	46	69
90/94																	82	36	118	69
85/89												2	1	3	57	0	146	76	222	67
80/84							0	0	0	54		6	2	8	57	8	208	131	347	65
75/79		0	0	0	53		2	1	3	52		8	4	12	55	39	231	174	444	64
70/74		1	0	1	51		5	2	7	50	0	14	8	22	54	123	236	212	571	61
65/69		3	1	4	49		7	3	10	49	0	22	15	37	51	223	221	223	667	59
60/64		5	2	7	46	0	9	6	15	47	3	27	20	50	49	264	204	226	694	55
55/59		11	3	14	44	0	15	9	24	44	10	34	27	71	47	239	197	200	636	50
50/54	0	15	7	22	41	2	22	15	39	42	20	33	32	85	44	211	191	185	587	46
45/49	1	21	12	34	39	7	27	22	56	39	29	28	34	91	41	180	185	182	547	41
40/44	4	20	18	42	36	11	29	26	66	36	43	26	34	103	38	185	187	194	566	37
35/39	12	30	30	72	33	28	34	34	96	33	47	21	26	94	34	213	187	215	615	33
30/34	30	31	40	101	30	57	34	42	133	30	43	15	25	83	30	260	179	243	682	30
25/29	49	26	35	110	25	48	28	37	113	25	29	4	11	44	26	281	136	214	631	25
20/24	40	19	24	83	21	36	18	23	77	21	12	0	2	14	21	245	98	135	478	21
15/19	29	18	19	66	16	23	8	13	44	16	3		0	3	17	159	72	90	321	16
10/14	23	13	16	52	11	17	5	9	31	11	0		0	0	14	99	54	67	220	11
5/9	15	6	9	30	7	11	3	4	18	6						80	29	46	155	6
0/4	8	3	5	16	2	5	1	2	8	2						46	21	28	95	1
-5/-1	5	1	2	8	-3	1	0	0	1	-3						32	10	15	57	-3
-10/-6	3	0	0	3	-8	0	0	0	0	-8						17	3	6	26	-8
-15/-11	2	0	0	2	-13	0	0	0	0	-13						6	1	2	9	-13
-20/-16	1		0	1	-18	1		0	1	-18						4	0	0	4	-17
-25/-21	0			0	-22	0			0	-21										-22

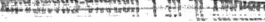

OFFUTT AFB NEBRASKA

LAT 41 07N LONG 95 55W ELEV 1048 FT

MEAN FREQUENCY OF OCCURRENCE OF DRY BULB TEMPERATURE (DEGREES F) WITH MEAN COINCIDENT WET BULB TEMPERATURE (DEGREES F) FOR EACH DRY BULB TEMPERATURE RANGE

Temperature Range	MAY Obsn Hour Gp 01 to 08	MAY 09 to 16	MAY 17 to 24	MAY Total Obsn	MAY MCWB	JUNE Obsn Hour Gp 01 to 08	JUNE 09 to 16	JUNE 17 to 24	JUNE Total Obsn	JUNE MCWB	JULY Obsn Hour Gp 01 to 08	JULY 09 to 16	JULY 17 to 24	JULY Total Obsn	JULY MCWB
105/109													0	0	78
100/104							0		0	75		1	1	2	78
95/99		0	0	0	67		3	1	4	74		7	3	10	77
90/94		2	1	3	66		12	5	17	73		24	11	35	76
85/89		12	4	16	68		31	17	48	71	0	49	30	79	73
80/84		25	14	39	67	2	45	32	79	70	8	63	52	123	71
75/79	1	35	26	62	64	14	53	51	118	67	37	55	61	153	69
70/74	14	41	35	90	61	42	46	54	142	64	78	37	57	172	67
65/69	28	40	43	111	58	69	31	42	142	61	74	11	27	112	63
60/64	51	36	45	132	55	62	13	26	101	58	36	2	7	45	59
55/59	48	28	39	115	51	31	6	9	46	54	11		1	12	54
50/54	46	18	25	89	47	15	0	2	17	49	3		0	3	50
45/49	31	8	12	51	43	4		0	4	45	0			0	42
40/44	19	2	4	25	39	0			0	41					
35/39	7		1	8	34										
30/34	2	1		3	30										
25/29	0			0	25										
20/24															

Temperature Range	AUGUST Obsn Hour Gp 01 to 08	AUGUST 09 to 16	AUGUST 17 to 24	AUGUST Total Obsn	AUGUST MCWB	SEPTEMBER Obsn Hour Gp 01 to 08	SEPTEMBER 09 to 16	SEPTEMBER 17 to 24	SEPTEMBER Total Obsn	SEPTEMBER MCWB	OCTOBER Obsn Hour Gp 01 to 08	OCTOBER 09 to 16	OCTOBER 17 to 24	OCTOBER Total Obsn	OCTOBER MCWB
105/109															
100/104		0	0	0	77										
95/99		3	1	4	76		0		0	72					
90/94		19	6	25	75		5	1	6	74		1		1	64
85/89	0	45	23	68	73		12	5	17	73		2	0	2	66
80/84	5	59	44	108	71	0	23	13	36	70		8	2	10	66
75/79	25	53	57	135	69	7	35	25	67	67	0	19	7	26	63
70/74	63	40	57	160	66	17	44	33	94	64	3	26	15	44	60
65/69	73	19	39	131	63	30	43	47	120	61	8	33	27	68	58
60/64	52	8	16	76	59	45	35	47	127	57	17	37	36	90	54
55/59	23	1	5	29	55	53	26	36	115	53	34	39	38	111	51
50/54	6		0	6	50	45	11	22	78	49	38	31	39	108	46
45/49	1			1	45	30	5	10	45	44	44	24	37	105	43
40/44	0			0	42	9	1	2	12	40	42	18	25	85	38
35/39						3	0	0	3	36	35	7	15	57	34
30/34						1		0	1	31	19	2	4	25	30
25/29						0			0	28	5	0	1	6	26
20/24											2			2	22

OFFUTT AFB NEBRASKA

Temperature Range	NOVEMBER Obsn Hour Gp 01 to 08	NOVEMBER Obsn Hour Gp 09 to 16	NOVEMBER Obsn Hour Gp 17 to 24	NOVEMBER Total Obsn	NOVEMBER MCWB	DECEMBER Obsn Hour Gp 01 to 08	DECEMBER Obsn Hour Gp 09 to 16	DECEMBER Obsn Hour Gp 17 to 24	DECEMBER Total Obsn	DECEMBER MCWB	JANUARY Obsn Hour Gp 01 to 08	JANUARY Obsn Hour Gp 09 to 16	JANUARY Obsn Hour Gp 17 to 24	JANUARY Total Obsn	JANUARY MCWB	FEBRUARY Obsn Hour Gp 01 to 08	FEBRUARY Obsn Hour Gp 09 to 16	FEBRUARY Obsn Hour Gp 17 to 24	FEBRUARY Total Obsn	FEBRUARY MCWB	MARCH Obsn Hour Gp 01 to 08	MARCH Obsn Hour Gp 09 to 16	MARCH Obsn Hour Gp 17 to 24	MARCH Total Obsn	MARCH MCWB	APRIL Obsn Hour Gp 01 to 08	APRIL Obsn Hour Gp 09 to 16	APRIL Obsn Hour Gp 17 to 24	APRIL Total Obsn	APRIL MCWB	ANNUAL TOTAL Obsn Hour Gp 01 to 08	ANNUAL TOTAL Obsn Hour Gp 09 to 16	ANNUAL TOTAL Obsn Hour Gp 17 to 24	ANNUAL TOTAL Total Obsn	ANNUAL TOTAL MCWB
105/109																																	0	0	78
100/104																																1	1	2	77
95/99																																13	5	18	76
90/94																											0		0	70		63	24	87	75
85/89																						0	0	0	64		2	1	3	63	0	153	80	233	72
80/84		0		0	63																	1	0	1	60		7	3	10	62	15	231	160	406	70
75/79		1		1	61																	2	1	3	57		10	6	16	60	84	263	234	581	67
70/74		1	0	1	59												0		0	52	1	7	3	11	55	1	19	12	32	58	219	261	266	746	64
65/69	0	8	3	11	55		0		0	51							0		0	51	1	7	5	13	53	5	24	20	49	55	288	216	253	757	60
60/64	1	14	7	22	52		2	0	2	51		0		0	47		1	0	1	49	1	10	7	18	50	11	30	26	67	52	276	188	217	681	56
55/59	2	20	11	33	49	1	6	3	10	49		2	0	2	45		3	1	4	48	3	13	11	27	47	19	38	36	93	48	225	182	190	597	51
50/54	8	30	24	62	46	3	13	5	21	44		3	1	4	42	1	10	4	15	44	8	17	16	41	44	39	35	40	114	45	212	168	178	558	46
45/49	21	35	31	87	42	3	15	10	28	41	0	9	5	14	39	2	17	9	28	41	10	25	22	57	40	40	32	38	110	42	186	170	174	530	42
40/44	34	34	42	110	38	5	20	19	44	37	3	16	10	29	37	3	21	19	43	37	20	31	31	82	37	44	25	31	100	38	179	168	183	530	38
35/39	44	38	43	125	34	23	35	35	93	33	12	26	28	66	34	19	27	32	78	33	37	44	42	123	34	40	13	17	70	34	220	190	213	623	34
30/34	55	30	39	124	29	42	41	48	131	29	29	28	37	94	30	41	33	40	114	30	57	36	47	140	30	28	5	8	41	30	274	176	223	673	30
25/29	35	15	21	71	25	46	34	38	118	25	36	30	32	98	25	36	31	32	99	25	45	24	25	94	25	10	0	1	11	25	213	134	150	497	25
20/24	19	9	9	37	20	39	29	28	96	20	33	31	29	93	21	31	26	24	81	20	27	14	19	60	20	3		0	3	21	154	109	109	372	20
15/19	12	3	7	22	16	33	24	27	84	16	25	26	24	75	16	21	22	24	67	15	18	8	10	36	16	0			0	16	109	83	92	284	16
10/14	5	1	2	8	11	22	12	14	48	11	29	25	28	82	11	23	18	20	61	11	10	6	5	21	11						89	62	69	220	11
5/9	3	1	1	5	6	12	9	9	30	6	27	23	22	72	6	21	10	11	42	6	7	2	2	11	6						70	45	45	160	6
0/4	0	0	1	1	2	9	4	5	18	1	22	15	18	55	1	15	5	5	25	1	1	1	1	3	2						47	25	30	102	1
-5/-1		0	0	0	-3	4	2	4	10	-3	16	9	11	36	-3	6	1	2	9	-3	1	0	0	1	-3						27	12	17	56	-3
-10/-6	0	0		0	-8	4	1	1	6	-8	9	4	4	17	-8	2	0	1	3	-8	1	0	0	1	-8						16	5	6	27	-8
-15/-11	0			0	-11	1	0	0	1	-12	6	1	1	8	-13	1	0	0	1	-13	1			1	-13						9	1	1	11	-13
-20/-16											1	0		1	-17	0			0	-17											1	0		1	-17

SCOTTSBLUFF NEBRASKA

LAT 41 52N LONG 103 36W ELEV 3958 FT

MEAN FREQUENCY OF OCCURRENCE OF DRY BULB TEMPERATURE (DEGREES F) WITH MEAN COINCIDENT WET BULB TEMPERATURE (DEGREES F) FOR EACH DRY BULB TEMPERATURE RANGE

Temperature Range	MAY Obsn Hour Gp 01 to 08	MAY 09 to 16	MAY 17 to 24	MAY Total Obsn	MAY MCWB	JUNE Obsn Hour Gp 01 to 08	JUNE 09 to 16	JUNE 17 to 24	JUNE Total Obsn	JUNE MCWB	JULY Obsn Hour Gp 01 to 08	JULY 09 to 16	JULY 17 to 24	JULY Total Obsn	JULY MCWB
105/109												0	0	0	65
100/104							1	0	1	62		2	0	2	66
95/99							6	1	7	63		15	2	17	65
90/94		2	0	2	60		18	4	22	64		39	9	48	66
85/89		7	1	8	59		30	9	39	63	0	52	19	71	65
80/84		18	4	22	58	1	39	18	58	62	2	54	31	87	64
75/79	0	29	9	38	57	4	42	28	74	60	10	43	44	97	63
70/74	1	36	15	52	55	14	39	35	88	59	33	26	50	109	61
65/69	5	38	26	69	53	32	31	42	105	57	70	12	49	131	60
60/64	16	39	35	90	51	54	16	42	112	55	75	4	31	110	57
55/59	35	34	48	117	50	62	9	33	104	53	44	1	11	56	54
50/54	58	21	46	125	47	44	6	19	69	49	13	0	2	15	50
45/49	59	12	34	105	43	21	2	7	30	45	2		0	2	45
40/44	42	8	20	70	39	5	0	1	6	40	1			1	41
35/39	21	3	7	31	35	2	0	1	3	35					
30/34	7	1	3	11	31	1	0	0	1	32					
25/29	2	0	1	3	25										
20/24	0			0	21										
15/19															
10/14															

Temperature Range	AUGUST Obsn Hour Gp 01 to 08	AUGUST 09 to 16	AUGUST 17 to 24	AUGUST Total Obsn	AUGUST MCWB	SEPTEMBER Obsn Hour Gp 01 to 08	SEPTEMBER 09 to 16	SEPTEMBER 17 to 24	SEPTEMBER Total Obsn	SEPTEMBER MCWB	OCTOBER Obsn Hour Gp 01 to 08	OCTOBER 09 to 16	OCTOBER 17 to 24	OCTOBER Total Obsn	OCTOBER MCWB
105/109															
100/104		0		0	64										
95/99		7	1	8	65		1		1	64					
90/94		29	5	34	65		8	1	9	62					
85/89		54	13	67	64		26	3	29	61		3		3	57
80/84	1	54	23	78	64		34	8	42	59		14	1	15	55
75/79	4	49	38	91	62	0	36	14	50	58		23	2	25	53
70/74	23	30	50	103	61	2	37	23	62	56	0	29	5	34	52
65/69	52	14	56	122	59	8	30	34	72	54	0	32	11	43	50
60/64	81	6	40	127	57	26	25	41	92	53	2	35	19	56	48
55/59	57	2	14	73	53	48	16	42	106	51	7	31	31	69	46
50/54	21	1	6	28	49	49	13	33	95	46	23	30	42	95	44
45/49	8	0	1	9	45	54	9	23	86	43	42	20	51	113	41
40/44	2		0	2	41	32	4	14	50	39	59	14	38	111	37
35/39	0			0	39	14	1	4	19	35	56	10	26	92	34
30/34						4		1	5	31	37	5	14	56	30
25/29						1			1	26	17	1	7	25	25
20/24						0			0	24	4	0	1	5	21
15/19											1		0	1	16
10/14											0			0	14

SCOTTSBLUFF NEBRASKA

Tempera- ture Range	NOVEMBER Obsn Hour Gp					DECEMBER Obsn Hour Gp					JANUARY Obsn Hour Gp					FEBRUARY Obsn Hour Gp					MARCH Obsn Hour Gp					APRIL Obsn Hour Gp					ANNUAL TOTAL Obsn Hour Gp				
	01 to 08	09 to 16	17 to 24	Total Obsn	M C W B	01 to 08	09 to 16	17 to 24	Total Obsn	M C W B	01 to 08	09 to 16	17 to 24	Total Obsn	M C W B	01 to 08	09 to 16	17 to 24	Total Obsn	M C W B	01 to 08	09 to 16	17 to 24	Total Obsn	M C W B	01 to 08	09 to 16	17 to 24	Total Obsn	M C W B	01 to 08	09 to 16	17 to 24	Total Obsn	M C W B
105/109																																0	0	0	65
100/104																																3	0	3	64
95/99																																29	4	33	64
90/94																																96	19	115	65
85/89																											1	0	1	55	0	173	45	218	64
80/84																											5	1	6	53	4	218	86	308	62
75/79		0		0	53												0		0	51		1	0	1	51		11	2	13	52	18	234	137	389	60
70/74		3		3	49												1	0	1	49		4	1	5	48		17	5	22	50	73	222	184	479	58
65/69		9	0	9	47		0		0	45		0		0	48	0	3	0	3	46		8	2	10	47	0	21	10	31	49	167	198	230	595	56
60/64	0	19	1	20	45	1	4	0	5	45		3		3	44	0	9	1	10	45		14	4	18	45	1	29	14	44	47	256	203	228	687	53
55/59	1	25	4	30	43	0	11	1	12	42		10	0	10	42	0	14	2	16	42	0	19	7	26	42	5	28	23	56	44	259	200	216	675	49
50/54	2	30	10	42	40	2	18	2	22	40	0	16	2	18	39	1	17	6	24	40	2	25	12	39	40	14	32	29	75	42	229	209	209	647	45
45/49	5	33	21	59	38	3	26	5	34	37	3	25	5	33	37	3	27	11	41	37	6	28	19	53	37	25	31	35	91	40	231	213	212	656	40
40/44	17	30	32	79	35	5	33	14	52	34	9	34	17	60	34	6	30	18	54	34	12	34	29	75	35	44	22	37	103	37	234	209	220	663	36
35/39	30	27	47	104	32	17	38	31	86	31	9	32	27	68	31	13	28	31	72	31	30	32	34	96	32	48	20	33	101	33	240	191	241	672	32
30/34	52	23	46	121	29	34	37	50	121	28	23	31	40	94	28	34	30	39	103	28	50	32	47	129	29	50	16	28	94	30	292	175	268	735	29
25/29	53	17	32	102	25	49	29	48	126	24	40	24	38	102	24	48	22	40	110	25	52	22	39	113	25	32	6	18	56	25	294	121	223	638	25
20/24	35	10	19	64	21	42	21	35	98	20	44	21	34	99	20	38	15	27	80	20	39	14	23	76	21	15	0	5	20	21	217	81	144	442	20
15/19	19	8	13	40	16	36	13	26	75	16	33	16	24	73	16	27	14	19	60	16	22	6	15	43	16	5		1	6	16	143	57	98	298	16
10/14	10	3	7	20	11	28	8	17	53	11	24	11	19	54	11	24	7	15	46	11	18	4	9	31	11	1		0	1	13	105	33	67	205	11
5/9	8	1	4	13	6	16	5	10	31	7	20	9	15	44	6	14	4	7	25	7	10	2	4	16	7						68	21	40	129	6
0/4	5	1	2	8	1	8	2	4	14	2	18	8	11	37	2	6	1	4	11	2	4	1	2	7	2						41	13	23	77	2
-5/-1	1	0	2	3	-3	4	1	2	7	-3	13	4	8	25	-3	4	1	2	7	-3	2	0	1	3	-3						24	6	15	45	-3
-10/-6	1			1	-9	3	1	1	5	-8	7	2	5	14	-8	2	0	0	2	-8	1	0	0	1	-8						14	3	6	23	-8
-15/-11						1	0	1	2	-13	3	1	2	6	-13	0	0	0	0	-13	1		0	1	-13						5	1	3	9	-13
-20/-16						0	0	0	0	-18	3	0	1	4	-18	1		0	1	-18											4	0	1	5	-18
-25/-21						0	0		0	-23	0			0	-23	0			0	-23											0	0		0	-23
-30/-26											0	0		0	-28	0			0	-27											0	0		0	-28

ELY NEVADA

LAT 39 17N LONG 114 51W ELEV 6253 FT

MEAN FREQUENCY OF OCCURRENCE OF DRY BULB TEMPERATURE (DEGREES F) WITH MEAN COINCIDENT WET BULB TEMPERATURE (DEGREES F) FOR EACH DRY BULB TEMPERATURE RANGE

Temperature Range	MAY Obsn Hour Gp 01 to 08	MAY 09 to 16	MAY 17 to 24	MAY Total Obsn	MAY MCWB	JUNE Obsn Hour Gp 01 to 08	JUNE 09 to 16	JUNE 17 to 24	JUNE Total Obsn	JUNE MCWB	JULY Obsn Hour Gp 01 to 08	JULY 09 to 16	JULY 17 to 24	JULY Total Obsn	JULY MCWB
95/99							0		0	59					
90/94							2		2	57		7		7	59
85/89		0		0	53		13	2	15	54		70	13	83	56
80/84		2		2	51	0	33	6	39	52		86	24	110	54
75/79		18	2	20	49	1	43	10	54	51	7	50	28	85	53
70/74		41	7	48	48	5	38	19	62	50	19	24	44	87	52
65/69	2	42	17	61	47	8	28	25	61	48	29	9	51	89	50
60/64	8	42	28	78	45	18	29	36	83	47	37	1	44	82	48
55/59	18	32	38	88	43	24	23	41	88	45	48	1	32	81	45
50/54	25	23	40	88	41	40	15	45	100	43	48	0	10	58	42
45/49	36	14	35	85	39	48	10	30	88	40	36	0	3	39	37
40/44	50	16	34	100	36	48	3	16	67	38	20			20	33
35/39	48	12	24	84	33	34	1	8	43	35	3			3	30
30/34	38	5	17	60	30	13	2	3	18	31	0			0	26
25/29	17	1	6	24	26	1			1	24					
20/24	5		2	7	22										
15/19	1			1	18										
10/14	0			0	13										

Temperature Range	AUGUST Obsn Hour Gp 01 to 08	AUGUST 09 to 16	AUGUST 17 to 24	AUGUST Total Obsn	AUGUST MCWB	SEPTEMBER Obsn Hour Gp 01 to 08	SEPTEMBER 09 to 16	SEPTEMBER 17 to 24	SEPTEMBER Total Obsn	SEPTEMBER MCWB	OCTOBER Obsn Hour Gp 01 to 08	OCTOBER 09 to 16	OCTOBER 17 to 24	OCTOBER Total Obsn	OCTOBER MCWB
95/99															
90/94		4	0	4	58		1		1	54					
85/89		44	4	48	56		7		7	53					
80/84		81	18	99	55		45	3	48	53		0		0	52
75/79	3	61	19	83	53		61	8	69	51		14		14	50
70/74	11	36	37	84	52	1	50	15	66	50		35	2	37	48
65/69	23	11	54	88	50	5	35	27	67	48		53	4	57	47
60/64	39	7	51	97	48	15	20	41	76	46	1	52	10	63	45
55/59	51	2	40	93	46	23	12	47	82	44	8	37	32	77	43
50/54	53	0	18	71	42	40	6	43	89	41	15	16	42	73	41
45/49	38	0	5	43	37	45	3	34	82	39	33	15	45	93	38
40/44	16		3	19	33	53	1	15	69	34	32	13	46	91	36
35/39	11		1	12	30	33		7	40	31	46	6	33	85	32
30/34	3			3	27	17		2	19	27	54	3	25	82	28
25/29	1			1	25	8			8	24	37	2	8	47	24
20/24						0			0	19	16		2	18	20
15/19											5		1	6	16
10/14											0			0	13

ELY NEVADA

Temperature Range	NOVEMBER Obsn Hour Gp 01 to 08	NOVEMBER 09 to 16	NOVEMBER 17 to 24	NOVEMBER Total Obsn	NOVEMBER MCWB	DECEMBER Obsn Hour Gp 01 to 08	DECEMBER 09 to 16	DECEMBER 17 to 24	DECEMBER Total Obsn	DECEMBER MCWB	JANUARY Obsn Hour Gp 01 to 08	JANUARY 09 to 16	JANUARY 17 to 24	JANUARY Total Obsn	JANUARY MCWB
95/99															
90/94															
85/89															
80/84															
75/79															
70/74															
65/69		2		2	44										
60/64		17	0	17	43		1		1	43		0		0	41
55/59		30	1	31	42		4		4	40		2		2	40
50/54	0	44	6	50	40		12	0	12	38		8		8	37
45/49	3	34	18	55	38	3	34	2	39	37		20	2	22	36
40/44	16	31	26	73	35	5	53	12	70	34	5	30	11	46	34
35/39	20	26	36	82	32	17	44	27	88	32	16	45	17	78	31
30/34	36	24	55	115	29	24	37	36	97	28	23	41	25	89	28
25/29	52	14	38	104	25	25	33	40	98	24	25	31	31	87	24
20/24	41	9	20	70	20	31	17	44	92	20	22	32	37	91	19
15/19	24	6	21	51	16	47	8	40	95	15	23	18	39	80	15
10/14	20	1	9	30	11	44	4	21	69	11	35	9	31	75	11
5/9	10	1	5	16	7	27	1	15	43	6	35	8	20	63	6
0/4	7	1	3	11	2	13	1	6	20	1	27	3	15	45	2
-5/-1	5		3	8	-4	7		4	11	-4	15	2	8	25	-3
-10/-6	4		0	4	-8	4		1	5	-8	9	1	8	18	-8
-15/-11	1			1	-13	0			0	-12	7	0	2	9	-14
-20/-16											5		1	6	-18
-25/-21											1			1	-22

Temperature Range	FEBRUARY Obsn Hour Gp 01 to 08	FEBRUARY 09 to 16	FEBRUARY 17 to 24	FEBRUARY Total Obsn	FEBRUARY MCWB	MARCH Obsn Hour Gp 01 to 08	MARCH 09 to 16	MARCH 17 to 24	MARCH Total Obsn	MARCH MCWB	APRIL Obsn Hour Gp 01 to 08	APRIL 09 to 16	APRIL 17 to 24	APRIL Total Obsn	APRIL MCWB
95/99															
90/94															
85/89															
80/84															
75/79												2		2	48
70/74												12	2	14	47
65/69							1		1	44		18	3	21	45
60/64		4		4	44		10	0	10	43	1	25	6	32	43
55/59		7	0	7	41		17	3	20	41	3	44	15	62	42
50/54		16	2	18	39	1	27	7	35	38	7	31	26	64	39
45/49	1	22	4	27	37	3	27	11	41	36	15	27	35	77	37
40/44	5	35	16	56	35	9	41	23	73	33	26	21	42	89	35
35/39	16	44	31	91	32	20	40	36	96	31	44	26	35	105	32
30/34	24	36	40	100	29	36	39	47	122	28	63	21	40	124	29
25/29	30	29	42	101	24	42	30	44	116	24	39	10	21	70	25
20/24	35	17	40	92	20	51	13	43	107	20	28	2	12	42	21
15/19	39	8	21	68	16	39	2	19	60	16	8	0	2	10	16
10/14	32	5	15	52	11	23	1	11	35	11	4		0	4	11
5/9	18	2	6	26	6	13		3	16	7	2		1	3	7
0/4	13	1	5	19	1	6		1	7	3	0		1	1	1
-5/-1	5		1	6	-3	3		0	3	-3	1			1	-3
-10/-6	4		0	4	-8	0			0	-7					
-15/-11	1		0	1	-14										
-20/-16	1			1	-17										
-25/-21															

Temperature Range	ANNUAL TOTAL Obsn Hour Gp 01 to 08	ANNUAL TOTAL 09 to 16	ANNUAL TOTAL 17 to 24	ANNUAL TOTAL Total Obsn	ANNUAL TOTAL MCWB
95/99		0		0	59
90/94		14	0	14	58
85/89		134	19	153	55
80/84	0	247	51	298	54
75/79	11	249	67	327	52
70/74	36	236	126	398	50
65/69	67	199	181	447	48
60/64	119	208	216	543	46
55/59	175	211	249	635	44
50/54	229	198	239	666	41
45/49	261	206	224	691	38
40/44	285	244	244	773	35
35/39	308	244	255	807	32
30/34	331	208	290	829	29
25/29	277	150	230	657	24
20/24	229	90	200	519	20
15/19	186	42	143	371	15
10/14	158	20	87	265	11
5/9	105	12	50	167	6
0/4	66	6	31	103	2
-5/-1	36	2	16	54	-3
-10/-6	21	1	9	31	-8
-15/-11	9	0	2	11	-14
-20/-16	6		1	7	-18
-25/-21	1			1	-22

FALLON NAS/VAN VOORHIS FLD NEVADA

LAT 39 25N LONG 118 42W ELEV 3934 FT

MEAN FREQUENCY OF OCCURRENCE OF DRY BULB TEMPERATURE (DEGREES F) WITH MEAN COINCIDENT WET BULB TEMPERATURE (DEGREES F) FOR EACH DRY BULB TEMPERATURE RANGE

Temperature Range	MAY Obsn Hour Gp 01 to 08	MAY 09 to 16	MAY 17 to 24	MAY Total Obsn	MAY MCWB	JUNE Obsn Hour Gp 01 to 08	JUNE 09 to 16	JUNE 17 to 24	JUNE Total Obsn	JUNE MCWB
105/109										
100/104							2	0	2	63
95/99		0		0	62		11	4	15	62
90/94		3	1	4	60		25	9	34	61
85/89		13	3	16	59	0	37	18	55	59
80/84		29	10	39	57	2	39	24	65	57
75/79	1	40	19	60	55	6	40	32	78	56
70/74	3	42	25	70	53	15	32	38	85	54
65/69	10	38	37	85	51	34	25	41	100	52
60/64	24	30	42	96	49	49	15	32	96	51
55/59	43	24	40	107	46	57	7	22	86	49
50/54	54	16	31	101	44	46	4	15	65	46
45/49	54	9	24	87	41	23	1	4	28	43
40/44	37	2	11	50	37	7	0	1	8	39
35/39	16	1	2	19	33	1			1	34
30/34	5	0	1	6	30					
25/29	1		0	1	26					
20/24	0			0	23					
15/19										

Temperature Range	JULY Obsn Hour Gp 01 to 08	JULY 09 to 16	JULY 17 to 24	JULY Total Obsn	JULY MCWB	AUGUST Obsn Hour Gp 01 to 08	AUGUST 09 to 16	AUGUST 17 to 24	AUGUST Total Obsn	AUGUST MCWB
105/109			0	0	62					
100/104		5	1	6	64		3	1	4	64
95/99		35	12	47	63		24	8	32	63
90/94		65	26	91	62		55	19	74	61
85/89	1	61	33	95	60	0	59	25	84	60
80/84	7	47	39	93	59	3	50	31	84	58
75/79	21	22	47	90	58	13	31	44	88	57
70/74	38	9	45	92	56	30	14	50	94	56
65/69	59	2	33	94	54	48	8	39	95	54
60/64	65	1	10	76	52	67	2	20	89	51
55/59	40	0	2	42	49	51	1	8	60	48
50/54	14		0	14	46	25		2	27	45
45/49	1			1	41	9	0	0	9	42
40/44	0			0	39	1			1	38
35/39						0			0	35
30/34										
25/29										
20/24										
15/19										

Temperature Range	SEPTEMBER Obsn Hour Gp 01 to 08	SEPTEMBER 09 to 16	SEPTEMBER 17 to 24	SEPTEMBER Total Obsn	SEPTEMBER MCWB	OCTOBER Obsn Hour Gp 01 to 08	OCTOBER 09 to 16	OCTOBER 17 to 24	OCTOBER Total Obsn	OCTOBER MCWB
105/109										
100/104										
95/99		1	0	1	61					
90/94		13	2	15	60		0		0	61
85/89		40	10	50	59		3	0	3	59
80/84	0	49	16	65	57		15	1	16	56
75/79	1	44	24	69	55		28	5	33	54
70/74	7	36	33	76	54		39	9	48	52
65/69	15	26	42	83	52	1	45	19	65	50
60/64	32	16	43	91	50	6	41	29	76	48
55/59	57	10	36	103	47	16	36	39	91	45
50/54	57	5	21	83	44	28	23	44	95	43
45/49	42	1	9	52	41	53	12	45	110	40
40/44	17	0	3	20	37	52	6	34	92	37
35/39	8		1	9	33	49	1	17	67	33
30/34	3			3	29	29	0	5	34	29
25/29	1			1	25	11		1	12	25
20/24	0			0	21	3		0	3	21
15/19						0			0	18

FALLON NAS/VAN VOORHIS FLD NEVADA

Temperature Range	NOVEMBER Obsn Hour Gp 01 to 08	NOVEMBER Obsn Hour Gp 09 to 16	NOVEMBER Obsn Hour Gp 17 to 24	NOVEMBER Total Obsn	NOVEMBER MCWB	DECEMBER Obsn Hour Gp 01 to 08	DECEMBER Obsn Hour Gp 09 to 16	DECEMBER Obsn Hour Gp 17 to 24	DECEMBER Total Obsn	DECEMBER MCWB	JANUARY Obsn Hour Gp 01 to 08	JANUARY Obsn Hour Gp 09 to 16	JANUARY Obsn Hour Gp 17 to 24	JANUARY Total Obsn	JANUARY MCWB
105/109															
100/104															
95/99															
90/94															
85/89															
80/84		0		0	55										
75/79		0		0	52										
70/74		4		4	51										
65/69		12	0	12	49		0		0	51		1		1	47
60/64	0	27	3	30	47	0	5	0	5	48		4	0	4	47
55/59	1	34	11	46	44	1	13	2	16	45		12	2	14	44
50/54	7	47	21	75	42	2	27	5	34	42	1	28	9	38	42
45/49	15	46	38	99	40	5	45	14	64	39	6	37	19	62	39
40/44	33	34	49	116	37	15	46	26	87	36	15	48	30	93	36
35/39	40	21	44	105	33	19	42	41	102	33	25	47	43	115	33
30/34	50	10	36	96	29	36	37	53	126	29	37	37	49	123	29
25/29	35	5	24	64	25	43	21	52	116	25	44	18	41	103	25
20/24	34	1	12	47	21	54	8	36	98	21	47	10	33	90	21
15/19	19	0	2	21	17	46	1	15	62	17	34	4	14	52	16
10/14	4		0	4	12	21	1	4	26	12	23	2	5	30	12
5/9	0			0	9	5	0	1	6	7	10	1	2	13	7
0/4						1			1	2	4	0	1	5	2
-5/-1						0			0	-3	2		1	3	-3
-10/-6											1			1	-7
-15/-11											0			0	-11

Temperature Range	FEBRUARY Obsn Hour Gp 01 to 08	FEBRUARY Obsn Hour Gp 09 to 16	FEBRUARY Obsn Hour Gp 17 to 24	FEBRUARY Total Obsn	FEBRUARY MCWB	MARCH Obsn Hour Gp 01 to 08	MARCH Obsn Hour Gp 09 to 16	MARCH Obsn Hour Gp 17 to 24	MARCH Total Obsn	MARCH MCWB	APRIL Obsn Hour Gp 01 to 08	APRIL Obsn Hour Gp 09 to 16	APRIL Obsn Hour Gp 17 to 24	APRIL Total Obsn	APRIL MCWB
105/109															
100/104															
95/99															
90/94															
85/89												0		0	59
80/84							0		0	56		4	1	5	54
75/79							3	1	4	52		15	4	19	53
70/74		0		0	50		7	2	9	50		25	8	33	51
65/69		3	0	3	50		19	4	23	48	0	34	17	51	49
60/64		13	2	15	47	0	29	11	40	45	3	37	26	66	46
55/59	0	28	8	36	45	2	44	21	67	43	9	41	36	86	44
50/54	4	37	18	59	42	7	44	35	86	41	26	34	39	99	41
45/49	9	43	30	82	39	20	41	44	105	38	39	26	40	105	39
40/44	20	43	43	106	36	38	33	46	117	35	54	17	36	107	36
35/39	37	30	48	115	33	49	18	41	108	32	53	5	23	81	33
30/34	50	18	38	106	29	63	7	30	100	29	39	1	8	48	29
25/29	49	5	25	79	25	46	1	9	56	25	14	0	2	16	25
20/24	32	2	8	42	21	17		3	20	21	2			2	22
15/19	17	1	3	21	16	5			5	17	0			0	19
10/14	6	0	1	7	12	1			1	13					
5/9	1		0	1	7										
0/4															
-5/-1															
-10/-6															
-15/-11															

Temperature Range	ANNUAL TOTAL Obsn Hour Gp 01 to 08	ANNUAL TOTAL Obsn Hour Gp 09 to 16	ANNUAL TOTAL Obsn Hour Gp 17 to 24	ANNUAL TOTAL Total Obsn	ANNUAL TOTAL MCWB
105/109			0	0	62
100/104		10	2	12	64
95/99		71	24	95	63
90/94		161	57	218	61
85/89	1	213	89	303	59
80/84	12	233	122	367	58
75/79	42	223	176	441	56
70/74	93	208	210	511	54
65/69	167	213	232	612	52
60/64	246	220	218	684	49
55/59	277	250	227	754	46
50/54	271	265	240	776	43
45/49	276	261	267	804	40
40/44	289	229	279	797	36
35/39	297	165	260	722	33
30/34	312	110	220	642	29
25/29	244	50	154	448	25
20/24	189	21	92	302	21
15/19	121	6	34	161	16
10/14	55	3	10	68	12
5/9	16	1	3	20	7
0/4	5	0	1	6	2
-5/-1	2		1	3	-3
-10/-6	1			1	-7
-15/-11	0			0	-11

NELLIS AFB/LAS VEGAS NEVADA

LAT 36 15N LONG 115 02W ELEV 1868 FT

MEAN FREQUENCY OF OCCURRENCE OF DRY BULB TEMPERATURE (DEGREES F) WITH MEAN COINCIDENT WET BULB TEMPERATURE (DEGREES F) FOR EACH DRY BULB TEMPERATURE RANGE

Temperature Range	MAY Obsn Hour Gp 01 to 08	MAY 09 to 16	MAY 17 to 24	MAY Total Obsn	MAY MCWB	JUNE Obsn Hour Gp 01 to 08	JUNE 09 to 16	JUNE 17 to 24	JUNE Total Obsn	JUNE MCWB	JULY Obsn Hour Gp 01 to 08	JULY 09 to 16	JULY 17 to 24	JULY Total Obsn	JULY MCWB
115/119							0	0	0	71		0	0	0	66
110/114							6	2	8	67		13	4	17	68
105/109		0		0	65		20	8	28	66		44	19	63	68
100/104		6	2	8	63	0	43	21	64	64	0	77	41	118	66
95/99		22	8	30	61	2	48	29	79	62	5	64	51	120	65
90/94	0	44	19	63	59	8	45	39	92	60	27	35	56	118	64
85/89	2	51	31	84	57	22	34	45	101	58	58	11	44	113	62
80/84	10	41	40	91	55	43	22	41	106	56	68	3	24	95	60
75/79	27	28	45	100	53	47	15	28	90	54	51	1	8	60	57
70/74	41	24	38	103	51	53	6	16	75	52	27	1	2	30	53
65/69	54	16	30	100	49	36	2	8	46	50	10		0	10	48
60/64	53	10	19	82	47	20	0	2	22	48	2			2	44
55/59	38	3	12	53	45	6		1	7	46	0			0	42
50/54	18	1	3	22	42	1			1	44					
45/49	4	0	0	4	39										
40/44	1		0	1	38										
35/39															
30/34															
25/29															

Temperature Range	AUGUST Obsn Hour Gp 01 to 08	AUGUST 09 to 16	AUGUST 17 to 24	AUGUST Total Obsn	AUGUST MCWB	SEPTEMBER Obsn Hour Gp 01 to 08	SEPTEMBER 09 to 16	SEPTEMBER 17 to 24	SEPTEMBER Total Obsn	SEPTEMBER MCWB	OCTOBER Obsn Hour Gp 01 to 08	OCTOBER 09 to 16	OCTOBER 17 to 24	OCTOBER Total Obsn	OCTOBER MCWB
115/119		0		0	71										
110/114		5	1	6	70										
105/109		29	11	40	69		4	0	4	67					
100/104	0	65	31	96	68		23	6	29	65		0		0	64
95/99	2	67	46	115	67		43	14	57	64		4	0	4	62
90/94	16	49	56	121	66	1	52	27	80	62		19	3	22	60
85/89	51	24	52	127	64	7	48	41	96	61		35	9	44	58
80/84	79	6	32	117	63	18	35	44	97	59	1	46	18	65	56
75/79	56	2	14	72	60	40	21	45	106	57	4	45	30	79	54
70/74	29	1	4	34	56	58	10	34	102	54	12	38	40	90	52
65/69	12	0	1	13	52	59	2	19	80	51	30	31	48	109	50
60/64	2		0	2	46	35	1	7	43	47	52	18	44	114	48
55/59	1			1	44	16	0	2	18	43	62	8	33	103	45
50/54	0			0	39	4		0	4	39	48	3	16	67	42
45/49						1			1	36	27	1	4	32	38
40/44											8	1	2	11	34
35/39											3		1	4	28
30/34											1			1	24
25/29											0			0	21

NELLIS AFB/LAS VEGAS NEVADA

Temperature Range	NOVEMBER Obsn Hour Gp 01 to 08	09 to 16	17 to 24	Total Obsn	MCWB	DECEMBER Obsn Hour Gp 01 to 08	09 to 16	17 to 24	Total Obsn	MCWB	JANUARY Obsn Hour Gp 01 to 08	09 to 16	17 to 24	Total Obsn	MCWB
115/119															
110/114															
105/109															
100/104															
95/99															
90/94															
85/89															
80/84		3		3	55										
75/79		16	1	17	53		0		0	51		1		1	56
70/74	0	31	5	36	51		3		3	49		3	1	4	52
65/69	1	48	17	66	49		14	1	15	48	0	15	2	17	49
60/64	6	47	32	85	47	2	34	6	42	47	1	38	10	49	46
55/59	21	45	50	116	45	3	54	18	75	44	4	48	23	75	44
50/54	44	29	58	131	42	11	52	41	104	42	15	50	42	107	41
45/49	59	14	42	115	39	25	43	57	125	38	28	41	53	122	38
40/44	52	5	24	81	35	41	29	61	131	35	36	29	49	114	34
35/39	36	1	8	45	32	60	14	42	116	31	53	15	36	104	31
30/34	16		2	18	27	71	5	19	95	28	55	6	22	83	27
25/29	3		0	3	24	27	0	4	31	24	39	1	8	48	23
20/24	0			0	19	7	0	0	7	19	13	1	2	16	18
15/19						1		0	1	14	3		0	3	14
10/14						0			0	10	0			0	9

Temperature Range	FEBRUARY Obsn Hour Gp 01 to 08	09 to 16	17 to 24	Total Obsn	MCWB	MARCH Obsn Hour Gp 01 to 08	09 to 16	17 to 24	Total Obsn	MCWB	APRIL Obsn Hour Gp 01 to 08	09 to 16	17 to 24	Total Obsn	MCWB	ANNUAL TOTAL Obsn Hour Gp 01 to 08	09 to 16	17 to 24	Total Obsn	MCWB
115/119																	0	0	0	69
110/114																	24	7	31	68
105/109																	97	38	135	68
100/104																0	214	101	315	66
95/99												1	0	1	60	9	249	148	406	65
90/94							0		0	58		10	2	12	58	52	254	202	508	63
85/89							2	0	2	56		19	7	26	56	140	224	229	593	60
80/84		1		1	56		9	3	12	54	0	34	15	49	54	219	200	217	636	58
75/79		7	1	8	54		23	8	31	52	2	44	28	74	52	227	203	208	638	55
70/74		16	5	21	51	0	39	18	57	50	9	42	39	90	50	229	214	202	645	52
65/69	1	28	11	40	49	3	46	31	80	48	25	36	41	102	47	231	238	209	678	49
60/64	3	46	24	73	46	12	48	43	103	45	41	27	39	107	45	229	269	226	724	47
55/59	14	51	42	107	44	31	40	51	122	43	54	18	32	104	43	250	267	264	781	44
50/54	30	39	53	122	41	54	25	44	123	40	52	8	24	84	41	277	207	281	765	41
45/49	47	24	45	116	38	61	11	30	102	37	39	2	11	52	38	291	136	242	669	38
40/44	51	10	29	90	35	50	4	14	68	34	16	0	2	18	35	255	78	181	514	35
35/39	45	3	12	60	31	25	0	4	29	30	3	0		3	31	225	33	103	361	31
30/34	24	0	3	27	27	9		1	10	26	0			0	27	176	11	47	234	27
25/29	9		1	10	23	2		0	2	21						80	1	13	94	23
20/24	1			1	18	1			1	17						22	1	2	25	18
15/19																4		0	4	14
10/14																0			0	9

STEAD AFB/RENO NEVADA

LAT 39 40N LONG 119 52W ELEV 5023 FT

MEAN FREQUENCY OF OCCURRENCE OF DRY BULB TEMPERATURE (DEGREES F) WITH MEAN COINCIDENT WET BULB TEMPERATURE (DEGREES F) FOR EACH DRY BULB TEMPERATURE RANGE

Temperature Range	MAY Obsn Hour Gp			MAY Total Obsn	MAY MCWB	JUNE Obsn Hour Gp			JUNE Total Obsn	JUNE MCWB	JULY Obsn Hour Gp			JULY Total Obsn	JULY MCWB
	01 to 08	09 to 16	17 to 24			01 to 08	09 to 16	17 to 24			01 to 08	09 to 16	17 to 24		
95/99							1	0	1	61		2	0	2	61
90/94							8	1	9	59		21	4	25	60
85/89		1		1	56		18	6	24	58		60	15	75	58
80/84		6	1	7	55	0	33	12	45	56	1	69	32	102	56
75/79	0	18	4	22	53	2	42	20	64	54	6	53	41	100	55
70/74	0	34	11	45	51	5	43	29	77	52	18	28	51	97	53
65/69	2	43	19	64	49	14	34	37	85	50	36	11	49	96	51
60/64	7	39	30	76	47	29	26	40	95	48	54	4	35	93	49
55/59	19	35	40	94	45	44	19	40	103	46	61	0	15	76	46
50/54	35	30	44	109	43	51	9	25	85	44	44	0	5	49	43
45/49	50	23	40	113	40	50	5	19	74	41	21		1	22	40
40/44	56	12	34	102	37	31	2	8	41	38	7			7	36
35/39	46	5	17	68	33	11	0	2	13	34	1			1	33
30/34	22	2	7	31	29	3		0	3	30					
25/29	8	1	1	10	26	1			1	26					
20/24	1		0	1	22										
15/19	0		0	0	17										
10/14	0			0	13										

Temperature Range	AUGUST Obsn Hour Gp			AUGUST Total Obsn	AUGUST MCWB	SEPTEMBER Obsn Hour Gp			SEPTEMBER Total Obsn	SEPTEMBER MCWB	OCTOBER Obsn Hour Gp			OCTOBER Total Obsn	OCTOBER MCWB
	01 to 08	09 to 16	17 to 24			01 to 08	09 to 16	17 to 24			01 to 08	09 to 16	17 to 24		
95/99		0	0	0	60		0		0	57					
90/94		15	2	17	59		3	0	3	58					
85/89		45	12	57	57		16	2	18	56		0		0	57
80/84	0	62	23	85	55		41	8	49	54		6	0	6	55
75/79	2	52	34	88	54	0	47	17	64	53		20	2	22	52
70/74	13	42	47	102	52	2	47	29	78	51		39	6	45	50
65/69	26	19	52	97	51	8	34	40	82	49	0	37	12	49	48
60/64	46	8	42	96	49	21	23	42	86	47	2	43	25	70	47
55/59	60	3	23	86	46	38	16	39	93	45	11	35	39	85	44
50/54	51	1	10	62	42	50	9	31	90	42	22	31	41	94	42
45/49	33		3	36	39	53	4	18	75	39	35	18	41	94	39
40/44	13		0	13	36	39	0	9	48	36	50	12	40	102	36
35/39	2		0	2	32	20	0	3	23	32	53	6	26	85	32
30/34	1			1	29	7		0	7	28	44	1	9	54	29
25/29						1		0	1	23	20	0	5	25	25
20/24						1			1	20	9		1	10	20
15/19						0			0	15	2			2	16
10/14											0			0	13

STEAD AFB/RENO NEVADA

Temperature Range	NOVEMBER					DECEMBER					JANUARY					FEBRUARY				
	Obsn Hour Gp 01 to 08	09 to 16	17 to 24	Total Obsn	M C W B	Obsn Hour Gp 01 to 08	09 to 16	17 to 24	Total Obsn	M C W B	Obsn Hour Gp 01 to 08	09 to 16	17 to 24	Total Obsn	M C W B	Obsn Hour Gp 01 to 08	09 to 16	17 to 24	Total Obsn	M C W B
95/99																				
90/94																				
85/89																				
80/84																				
75/79																				
70/74		1		1	51															
65/69		8	0	8	48		1		1	47							0		0	49
60/64		21	1	22	46		3	0	3	44		1		1	44		5	0	5	45
55/59	0	33	6	39	43	0	10	0	10	43		7	0	7	43	0	14	2	16	43
50/54	5	43	19	67	41	2	32	3	37	41	1	18	4	23	41	2	27	8	37	41
45/49	17	38	32	87	39	8	41	16	65	39	6	31	12	49	38	6	40	21	67	38
40/44	25	35	40	100	36	16	46	33	95	36	16	47	27	90	35	17	45	35	97	36
35/39	28	30	42	100	32	25	42	38	105	32	28	50	43	121	32	28	38	41	107	32
30/34	43	19	43	105	29	25	33	46	104	29	34	38	48	120	29	40	32	50	122	29
25/29	52	9	31	92	25	33	25	46	104	25	36	27	42	105	25	51	14	36	101	25
20/24	36	3	16	55	20	50	11	34	95	20	37	15	30	82	20	38	4	18	60	20
15/19	23	1	6	30	16	47	3	20	70	16	30	7	21	58	16	22	2	7	31	16
10/14	9	0	2	11	12	29	1	7	37	11	24	4	12	40	11	12	1	3	16	12
5/9	2		1	3	7	9	0	3	12	7	20	2	5	27	7	5	1	1	7	7
0/4	1		0	1	2	3	0	0	3	2	10	1	2	13	2	2	0	1	3	1
-5/-1	0			0	-1	1		0	1	-4	4	0	1	5	-3	1	0	1	2	-4
-10/-6						0			0	-6	2	0	1	3	-8	1		0	1	-8
-15/-11											1		0	1	-13	0			0	-14
-20/-16											1			1	-18					

Temperature Range	MARCH					APRIL					ANNUAL TOTAL				
	Obsn Hour Gp 01 to 08	09 to 16	17 to 24	Total Obsn	M C W B	Obsn Hour Gp 01 to 08	09 to 16	17 to 24	Total Obsn	M C W B	Obsn Hour Gp 01 to 08	09 to 16	17 to 24	Total Obsn	M C W B
95/99												3	0	3	61
90/94												47	7	54	59
85/89												140	35	175	57
80/84							0		0	55	1	217	76	294	55
75/79							2	0	2	52	10	234	118	362	54
70/74		2	0	2	49		15	2	17	49	38	251	175	464	52
65/69		4	1	5	47		29	7	36	47	86	220	217	523	50
60/64		15	3	18	44	1	35	15	51	45	160	223	233	616	47
55/59	0	27	7	34	42	4	39	27	70	43	237	238	238	713	45
50/54	3	41	17	61	40	10	38	34	82	41	276	279	241	796	42
45/49	10	50	33	93	37	28	30	39	97	38	317	280	275	872	39
40/44	25	41	51	117	35	44	25	43	112	35	339	265	320	924	36
35/39	46	34	51	131	32	52	17	37	106	32	340	222	300	862	32
30/34	52	23	43	118	28	51	8	23	82	29	322	156	269	747	29
25/29	56	7	28	91	25	31	2	12	45	25	289	85	201	575	25
20/24	37	2	11	50	20	15	0	2	17	21	224	35	112	371	20
15/19	16	0	2	18	16	3			3	17	143	13	56	212	16
10/14	4		0	4	12	0			0	13	78	6	24	108	11
5/9	1			1	8						37	3	10	50	7
0/4											16	1	3	20	2
-5/-1											6	0	2	8	-3
-10/-6											3	0	1	4	-8
-15/-11											1		0	1	-13
-20/-16											1			1	-18

TONOPAH MAP NEVADA

LAT 38 04N LONG 117 05W ELEV 5426 FT

MEAN FREQUENCY OF OCCURRENCE OF DRY BULB TEMPERATURE (DEGREES F) WITH MEAN COINCIDENT WET BULB TEMPERATURE (DEGREES F) FOR EACH DRY BULB TEMPERATURE RANGE

Tempera-ture Range	MAY Obsn Hour Gp 01 to 08	MAY 09 to 16	MAY 17 to 24	MAY Total Obsn	MAY MCWB	JUNE Obsn Hour Gp 01 to 08	JUNE 09 to 16	JUNE 17 to 24	JUNE Total Obsn	JUNE MCWB	JULY Obsn Hour Gp 01 to 08	JULY 09 to 16	JULY 17 to 24	JULY Total Obsn	JULY MCWB
100/104							0		0	61		1		1	63
95/99							6	1	7	60		11	2	13	61
90/94		0		0	58		16	5	21	58		56	15	71	59
85/89		3	0	3	56	0	41	16	57	55	0	80	31	111	57
80/84		19	3	22	53	2	51	25	78	53	6	60	40	106	56
75/79	0	43	13	56	51	7	45	30	82	52	20	29	47	96	54
70/74	3	47	21	71	49	17	35	38	90	50	33	9	50	92	53
65/69	8	41	32	81	47	31	19	39	89	48	53	2	39	94	51
60/64	19	32	40	91	45	43	12	33	88	46	68	0	18	86	49
55/59	33	24	41	98	43	47	7	25	79	44	44	0	6	50	43
50/54	47	18	39	104	41	49	5	17	71	41	17		1	18	39
45/49	56	11	26	93	38	31	2	8	41	39	5			5	35
40/44	43	7	20	70	35	10	1	3	14	38	0			0	33
35/39	26	2	9	37	32	3	0	0	3	34					
30/34	11	0	3	14	29	0			0	32					
25/29	2		0	2	24										
20/24	0			0	20										
15/19															

Tempera-ture Range	AUGUST Obsn Hour Gp 01 to 08	AUGUST 09 to 16	AUGUST 17 to 24	AUGUST Total Obsn	AUGUST MCWB	SEPTEMBER Obsn Hour Gp 01 to 08	SEPTEMBER 09 to 16	SEPTEMBER 17 to 24	SEPTEMBER Total Obsn	SEPTEMBER MCWB	OCTOBER Obsn Hour Gp 01 to 08	OCTOBER 09 to 16	OCTOBER 17 to 24	OCTOBER Total Obsn	OCTOBER MCWB
100/104															
95/99		4	0	4	60										
90/94		37	6	43	59		7	0	7	58					
85/89		75	23	98	57		32	4	36	56		1		1	53
80/84	1	68	34	103	56	0	60	12	72	54		9	1	10	53
75/79	11	41	40	92	54	1	54	22	77	52		36	2	38	51
70/74	26	16	50	92	53	6	37	30	73	50		42	7	49	49
65/69	40	5	47	92	51	14	23	40	77	48	1	52	16	69	47
60/64	63	2	29	94	49	28	14	48	90	46	4	37	28	69	45
55/59	60	0	14	74	43	50	8	40	98	44	13	31	41	85	43
50/54	34		4	38	39	69	4	28	101	41	35	19	49	103	40
45/49	11		1	12	36	46	1	11	58	37	55	8	47	110	37
40/44	2		0	2	32	19	0	3	22	34	65	7	33	105	34
35/39	0			0	31	5			5	31	48	4	15	67	31
30/34						0			0	25	17	1	8	26	28
25/29											8		1	9	23
20/24											2		0	2	20
15/19											0			0	16

TONOPAH MAP NEVADA

Temperature Range	NOVEMBER Obsn Hour Gp 01 to 08	NOVEMBER 09 to 16	NOVEMBER 17 to 24	NOVEMBER Total Obsn	NOVEMBER MCWB	DECEMBER Obsn Hour Gp 01 to 08	DECEMBER 09 to 16	DECEMBER 17 to 24	DECEMBER Total Obsn	DECEMBER MCWB	JANUARY Obsn Hour Gp 01 to 08	JANUARY 09 to 16	JANUARY 17 to 24	JANUARY Total Obsn	JANUARY MCWB
100/104															
95/99															
90/94															
85/89															
80/84															
75/79															
70/74		1		1	47		0		0	43					
65/69		8		8	46		0		0	46					
60/64		28	1	29	44		3		3	44		1		1	43
55/59		40	6	46	42		14	0	14	41		7	0	7	41
50/54	2	43	15	60	40	0	31	2	33	39		23	1	24	39
45/49	8	37	26	71	37	2	48	9	59	37	1	32	7	40	37
40/44	20	30	45	95	34	6	50	23	79	35	4	48	20	72	34
35/39	42	24	49	115	31	15	47	43	105	31	13	49	36	98	32
30/34	64	19	50	133	28	35	33	64	132	28	36	37	57	130	28
25/29	55	7	29	91	24	79	16	59	154	24	53	25	51	129	24
20/24	31	1	12	44	19	64	4	32	100	20	56	13	35	104	20
15/19	12	0	5	17	15	30	1	11	42	15	39	8	19	66	15
10/14	6		2	8	11	10	0	4	14	10	20	3	11	34	11
5/9	1			1	7	5		1	6	6	13	1	7	21	6
0/4						1			1	2	8	0	2	10	1
-5/-1											3	0	1	4	-3
-10/-6											1	0	0	1	-7
-15/-11											0			0	-13

Temperature Range	FEBRUARY Obsn Hour Gp 01 to 08	FEBRUARY 09 to 16	FEBRUARY 17 to 24	FEBRUARY Total Obsn	FEBRUARY MCWB	MARCH Obsn Hour Gp 01 to 08	MARCH 09 to 16	MARCH 17 to 24	MARCH Total Obsn	MARCH MCWB
100/104										
95/99										
90/94										
85/89										
80/84										
75/79							0		0	46
70/74							2	0	2	46
65/69		1		1	44		11	1	12	45
60/64		9	0	9	43		25	5	30	43
55/59		20	2	22	42	0	38	13	51	41
50/54		29	8	37	39	2	45	22	69	38
45/49	2	40	20	62	37	8	38	33	79	36
40/44	12	47	35	94	35	25	34	45	104	33
35/39	25	36	49	110	31	46	27	49	122	31
30/34	52	24	46	122	28	69	16	43	128	27
25/29	56	10	34	100	24	47	9	23	79	24
20/24	39	4	16	59	19	33	1	11	45	19
15/19	23	2	8	33	15	14	0	3	17	15
10/14	11	1	3	15	11	4		1	5	11
5/9	3	0	1	4	6	1			1	7
0/4	1			1	2					
-5/-1										
-10/-6										
-15/-11										

Temperature Range	APRIL Obsn Hour Gp 01 to 08	APRIL 09 to 16	APRIL 17 to 24	APRIL Total Obsn	APRIL MCWB	ANNUAL TOTAL Obsn Hour Gp 01 to 08	ANNUAL TOTAL 09 to 16	ANNUAL TOTAL 17 to 24	ANNUAL TOTAL Total Obsn	ANNUAL TOTAL MCWB
100/104							1		1	63
95/99							21	3	24	60
90/94							116	26	142	59
85/89						0	232	74	306	57
80/84		1	0	1	52	9	268	115	392	55
75/79		11	2	13	49	39	259	156	454	53
70/74		23	5	28	48	85	212	201	498	51
65/69	0	39	12	51	46	147	201	226	574	48
60/64	2	47	23	72	43	227	210	225	662	46
55/59	9	42	33	84	41	256	231	221	708	43
50/54	21	29	43	93	39	276	246	229	751	40
45/49	35	19	42	96	36	260	236	230	726	37
40/44	54	16	36	106	34	260	240	263	763	34
35/39	55	11	23	89	31	278	200	273	751	31
30/34	39	3	14	56	27	323	133	285	741	28
25/29	18	0	6	24	24	318	67	203	588	24
20/24	6		1	7	20	231	23	107	361	20
15/19	1			1	15	119	11	46	176	15
10/14	0			0	11	51	4	21	76	11
5/9						23	1	9	33	6
0/4						10	0	2	12	1
-5/-1						3	0	1	4	-3
-10/-6						1	0	0	1	-7
-15/-11						0			0	-13

WINNEMUCCA MAP NEVADA

LAT 40 54N LONG 117 48W ELEV 4301 FT

MEAN FREQUENCY OF OCCURRENCE OF DRY BULB TEMPERATURE (DEGREES F) WITH MEAN COINCIDENT WET BULB TEMPERATURE (DEGREES F) FOR EACH DRY BULB TEMPERATURE RANGE

Temperature Range	MAY Obsn Hour Gp 01 to 08	MAY Obsn Hour Gp 09 to 16	MAY Obsn Hour Gp 17 to 24	MAY Total Obsn	MAY MCWB	JUNE Obsn Hour Gp 01 to 08	JUNE Obsn Hour Gp 09 to 16	JUNE Obsn Hour Gp 17 to 24	JUNE Total Obsn	JUNE MCWB
100/104							1	0	1	63
95/99							6	1	7	61
90/94		2	0	2	59		10	5	15	59
85/89		7	2	9	57	0	25	11	36	57
80/84		20	6	26	56	1	38	19	58	55
75/79	1	33	13	47	53	5	39	21	65	53
70/74	3	40	18	61	51	11	33	27	71	52
65/69	10	31	25	66	49	24	34	36	94	50
60/64	16	35	37	88	48	29	27	38	94	48
55/59	27	30	38	95	45	36	17	31	84	46
50/54	39	21	38	98	43	47	9	29	85	44
45/49	48	17	33	98	41	40	2	12	54	41
40/44	41	11	23	75	38	26	1	7	34	37
35/39	38	2	11	51	34	12		2	14	33
30/34	16		3	19	30	6		0	6	29
25/29	6		0	6	25	2			2	24
20/24	1			1	20					
15/19	1			1	16					
10/14										
5/9										

Temperature Range	JULY Obsn Hour Gp 01 to 08	JULY Obsn Hour Gp 09 to 16	JULY Obsn Hour Gp 17 to 24	JULY Total Obsn	JULY MCWB	AUGUST Obsn Hour Gp 01 to 08	AUGUST Obsn Hour Gp 09 to 16	AUGUST Obsn Hour Gp 17 to 24	AUGUST Total Obsn	AUGUST MCWB
100/104		0		0	63		0		0	60
95/99		28	7	35	61		12	2	14	60
90/94		71	30	101	59		48	15	63	58
85/89	2	64	29	95	58	0	67	28	95	57
80/84	10	42	35	87	57	2	56	24	82	55
75/79	25	24	37	86	55	16	34	32	82	54
70/74	33	12	45	90	53	24	17	37	78	51
65/69	40	7	31	78	51	30	9	38	77	50
60/64	46	2	23	71	49	29	4	32	65	47
55/59	36		8	44	46	35	1	26	62	45
50/54	30		3	33	42	43		9	52	41
45/49	18		0	18	38	38		3	41	38
40/44	8			8	35	21			21	34
35/39	1			1	32	10			10	31
30/34	0			0	29	1			1	27
25/29										
20/24										
15/19										
10/14										
5/9										

Temperature Range	SEPTEMBER Obsn Hour Gp 01 to 08	SEPTEMBER Obsn Hour Gp 09 to 16	SEPTEMBER Obsn Hour Gp 17 to 24	SEPTEMBER Total Obsn	SEPTEMBER MCWB	OCTOBER Obsn Hour Gp 01 to 08	OCTOBER Obsn Hour Gp 09 to 16	OCTOBER Obsn Hour Gp 17 to 24	OCTOBER Total Obsn	OCTOBER MCWB
100/104										
95/99		5	1	6	60					
90/94		18	1	19	60					
85/89		42	7	49	57		0		0	56
80/84	0	49	14	63	55		14		14	54
75/79	2	44	20	66	53		33	2	35	52
70/74	7	32	29	68	51		33	5	38	50
65/69	16	24	34	74	49	0	43	10	53	48
60/64	21	13	37	71	46	6	34	21	61	46
55/59	23	9	35	67	44	13	32	27	72	44
50/54	30	3	27	60	41	20	27	38	85	42
45/49	36	1	18	55	39	28	17	47	92	39
40/44	42	1	11	54	35	33	9	47	89	36
35/39	38	1	4	43	32	38	6	26	70	32
30/34	17		0	17	27	41	2	17	60	29
25/29	6			6	23	42		5	47	24
20/24	1			1	19	17		2	19	20
15/19						6		1	7	15
10/14						3			3	12
5/9						0			0	9

WINNEMUCCA MAP NEVADA

Temperature Range	NOVEMBER					DECEMBER					JANUARY					FEBRUARY					MARCH					APRIL					ANNUAL TOTAL				
	Obsn Hour Gp			Total Obsn	M C W B	Obsn Hour Gp			Total Obsn	M C W B	Obsn Hour Gp			Total Obsn	M C W B	Obsn Hour Gp			Total Obsn	M C W B	Obsn Hour Gp			Total Obsn	M C W B	Obsn Hour Gp			Total Obsn	M C W B	Obsn Hour Gp			Total Obsn	M C W B
	01 to 08	09 to 16	17 to 24			01 to 08	09 to 16	17 to 24			01 to 08	09 to 16	17 to 24			01 to 08	09 to 16	17 to 24			01 to 08	09 to 16	17 to 24			01 to 08	09 to 16	17 to 24			01 to 08	09 to 16	17 to 24		
100/104																																1	0	1	63
95/99																																51	11	62	60
90/94																																149	51	200	59
85/89																															2	205	77	284	57
80/84																											1		1	54	13	220	98	331	56
75/79																											11	2	13	51	49	218	127	394	54
70/74		1		1	49																	3	0	3	48		26	6	32	50	78	197	167	442	51
65/69		9		9	47												2		2	47		8	1	9	46	1	37	14	52	47	121	204	189	514	49
60/64	0	32		32	45							3		3	48		8	1	9	45		17	4	21	44	5	42	21	68	45	152	217	214	583	47
55/59	1	35	3	39	44	1	4	1	6	46		8	1	9	45		17	1	18	43	1	34	12	47	42	10	39	30	79	44	183	226	213	622	44
50/54	1	38	13	52	41	2	16	3	21	43	1	18	3	22	42	1	24	10	35	41	1	42	22	65	40	23	34	47	104	41	238	232	242	712	42
45/49	8	31	31	70	39	7	34	8	49	39	11	28	17	56	40	4	31	16	51	38	11	36	31	78	38	35	21	40	96	39	284	218	256	758	39
40/44	20	32	38	90	36	10	45	19	74	36	17	46	31	94	36	15	41	25	81	35	28	37	41	106	35	46	15	39	100	36	307	238	281	826	36
35/39	28	33	40	101	32	20	57	34	111	33	32	54	46	132	33	22	40	43	105	32	34	30	46	110	32	39	12	20	71	32	312	235	272	819	32
30/34	32	18	47	97	29	41	51	58	150	30	49	40	56	145	30	43	35	51	129	29	55	28	38	121	29	35	4	13	52	28	336	178	283	797	29
25/29	43	6	30	79	25	34	24	48	106	25	42	27	31	100	25	45	19	45	109	25	40	13	30	83	24	24	1	5	30	25	284	90	194	568	25
20/24	40	2	17	59	20	34	11	34	79	21	26	14	26	66	21	34	5	19	58	20	35	2	17	54	21	12		1	13	21	200	34	116	350	21
15/19	29	2	12	43	16	26	5	22	53	16	21	8	19	48	16	30	2	9	41	16	25		4	29	16	5			5	16	143	17	67	227	16
10/14	20	0	7	27	11	24	1	12	37	11	18	2	10	30	11	17	1	2	20	11	11		1	12	11	3			3	12	96	4	32	132	11
5/9	11		4	15	7	30	0	5	35	7	13	1	6	20	7	6	0	2	8	7	5		0	5	7						65	1	17	83	7
0/4	5		0	5	2	12	0	2	14	2	9		1	10	2	4			4	2	1			1	2						31	0	3	34	2
-5/-1	1			1	-2	3		1	4	-4	6		1	7	-3	2			2	-2	1			1	-2						13		2	15	-3
-10/-6						3		0	3	-8	2		0	2	-7	1			1	-7											6		0	6	-7
-15/-11						1			1	-13	0			0	-12																1			1	-13

PEASE AFB/PORTSMOUTH NEW HAMPSHIRE

LAT 43 04N LONG 70 49W ELEV 101 FT

MEAN FREQUENCY OF OCCURRENCE OF DRY BULB TEMPERATURE (DEGREES F) WITH MEAN COINCIDENT WET BULB TEMPERATURE (DEGREES F) FOR EACH DRY BULB TEMPERATURE RANGE

Temperature Range	MAY Obsn Hour Gp 01 to 08	MAY 09 to 16	MAY 17 to 24	MAY Total Obsn	MAY MCWB	JUNE Obsn Hour Gp 01 to 08	JUNE 09 to 16	JUNE 17 to 24	JUNE Total Obsn	JUNE MCWB	JULY Obsn Hour Gp 01 to 08	JULY 09 to 16	JULY 17 to 24	JULY Total Obsn	JULY MCWB
100/104												0		0	72
95/99		0	0	0	71		0		0	76		1		1	75
90/94		1	0	1	71		4	0	4	73		7	1	8	74
85/89		3	1	4	69		15	4	19	71	0	24	5	29	72
80/84	0	9	3	12	65	0	31	11	42	68	1	43	16	60	69
75/79	1	13	5	19	62	3	43	20	66	65	9	66	33	108	67
70/74	2	23	11	36	59	17	44	37	98	63	34	59	58	151	65
65/69	9	35	21	65	57	40	44	45	129	60	73	32	72	177	63
60/64	18	50	28	96	53	54	31	47	132	57	83	15	52	150	59
55/59	29	49	43	121	50	65	20	46	131	54	38	1	10	49	55
50/54	62	40	60	162	48	46	8	28	82	50	10		0	10	50
45/49	65	18	52	135	44	14	0	3	17	46	1			1	47
40/44	42	6	21	69	40	2			2	42					
35/39	18	2	4	24	36										
30/34	2			2	31										
25/29	0			0	27										
20/24															

Temperature Range	AUGUST Obsn Hour Gp 01 to 08	AUGUST 09 to 16	AUGUST 17 to 24	AUGUST Total Obsn	AUGUST MCWB	SEPTEMBER Obsn Hour Gp 01 to 08	SEPTEMBER 09 to 16	SEPTEMBER 17 to 24	SEPTEMBER Total Obsn	SEPTEMBER MCWB	OCTOBER Obsn Hour Gp 01 to 08	OCTOBER 09 to 16	OCTOBER 17 to 24	OCTOBER Total Obsn	OCTOBER MCWB
100/104															
95/99		0		0	76										
90/94		5	0	5	74		1	0	1	75					
85/89		17	4	21	72		7	1	8	74		0		0	64
80/84	0	44	13	57	70		15	4	19	71		2	0	2	64
75/79	6	57	28	91	67	1	25	12	38	67		8	1	9	63
70/74	29	66	52	147	64	14	45	22	81	64	0	14	4	18	61
65/69	60	41	68	169	62	25	50	34	109	61	2	26	8	36	58
60/64	81	15	59	155	59	43	48	56	147	57	12	40	26	78	56
55/59	45	4	21	70	55	50	33	56	139	53	31	59	46	136	52
50/54	22	0	2	24	50	52	14	38	104	49	50	50	55	155	48
45/49	4		1	5	46	33	1	14	48	45	48	31	54	133	43
40/44	1		0	1	38	15	0	3	18	40	48	13	32	93	38
35/39						5		0	5	36	38	5	16	59	34
30/34						0			0	33	15	1	6	22	30
25/29											4		1	5	26
20/24											0			0	22

Temperature Range	NOVEMBER Obsn Hour Gp 01 to 08	NOVEMBER Obsn Hour Gp 09 to 16	NOVEMBER Obsn Hour Gp 17 to 24	NOVEMBER Total Obsn	NOVEMBER MCWB	DECEMBER Obsn Hour Gp 01 to 08	DECEMBER Obsn Hour Gp 09 to 16	DECEMBER Obsn Hour Gp 17 to 24	DECEMBER Total Obsn	DECEMBER MCWB	JANUARY Obsn Hour Gp 01 to 08	JANUARY Obsn Hour Gp 09 to 16	JANUARY Obsn Hour Gp 17 to 24	JANUARY Total Obsn	JANUARY MCWB
100/104															
95/99															
90/94															
85/89															
80/84															
75/79		0		0	65										
70/74		1	0	1	62										
65/69		2	1	3	60										
60/64	1	6	3	10	56	0	0	0	0	53					
55/59	7	19	9	35	52	1	3	1	5	51	0	1		1	48
50/54	21	36	23	80	48	2	6	3	11	47	1	1	0	2	48
45/49	30	51	36	117	43	5	13	6	24	43	0	5	2	7	42
40/44	32	49	47	128	38	13	28	19	60	38	4	16	8	28	38
35/39	51	45	55	151	34	22	36	34	92	33	16	34	24	74	33
30/34	51	23	45	119	29	41	47	45	133	29	36	46	49	131	29
25/29	34	6	16	56	25	46	46	46	138	24	35	41	42	118	25
20/24	10	1	3	14	21	38	35	44	117	20	34	37	39	110	20
15/19	3	0	1	4	16	31	20	28	79	15	36	29	36	101	15
10/14	1		0	1	11	28	9	14	51	11	33	21	23	77	10
5/9						13	3	5	21	6	24	10	16	50	6
0/4						4	2	1	7	1	15	4	6	25	1
-5/-1						2	0	1	3	-4	7	2	2	11	-3
-10/-6						1	0	0	1	-8	4	1	1	6	-9
-15/-11											1	0		1	-13
-20/-16											0			0	-16

Temperature Range	FEBRUARY Obsn Hour Gp 01 to 08	FEBRUARY Obsn Hour Gp 09 to 16	FEBRUARY Obsn Hour Gp 17 to 24	FEBRUARY Total Obsn	FEBRUARY MCWB	MARCH Obsn Hour Gp 01 to 08	MARCH Obsn Hour Gp 09 to 16	MARCH Obsn Hour Gp 17 to 24	MARCH Total Obsn	MARCH MCWB	APRIL Obsn Hour Gp 01 to 08	APRIL Obsn Hour Gp 09 to 16	APRIL Obsn Hour Gp 17 to 24	APRIL Total Obsn	APRIL MCWB	ANNUAL TOTAL Obsn Hour Gp 01 to 08	ANNUAL TOTAL Obsn Hour Gp 09 to 16	ANNUAL TOTAL Obsn Hour Gp 17 to 24	ANNUAL TOTAL Total Obsn	ANNUAL TOTAL MCWB
100/104																	0		0	72
95/99																	1	0	1	74
90/94												0		0	64		18	1	19	74
85/89												0	0	0	63	0	66	15	81	72
80/84												1		1	61	1	145	47	193	69
75/79							0		0	57		2	0	2	59	20	214	99	333	66
70/74							0	0	0	57	0	4	1	5	57	96	256	185	537	64
65/69		0		0	56		1	0	1	53	1	7	2	10	54	210	238	251	699	61
60/64		0		0	54		1	1	2	49	1	18	6	25	51	293	224	278	795	57
55/59		0		0	48	0	4	1	5	48	6	33	14	53	48	272	226	247	745	52
50/54		2	1	3	46	1	12	4	17	44	10	48	25	83	44	277	217	239	733	48
45/49	2	5	3	10	42	3	23	11	37	40	29	54	50	133	41	234	201	232	667	43
40/44	4	19	9	32	37	9	56	33	98	36	67	47	74	188	38	237	234	246	717	38
35/39	15	36	27	78	33	47	69	70	186	33	63	22	50	135	34	275	249	280	804	34
30/34	32	49	48	129	29	78	47	73	198	29	48	5	16	69	30	303	218	282	803	29
25/29	35	38	47	120	24	54	23	35	112	24	13	0	1	14	25	221	154	188	563	24
20/24	40	32	34	106	20	31	8	13	52	20	2		0	2	19	155	113	133	401	20
15/19	30	21	27	78	15	15	3	4	22	15	0			0	16	115	73	96	284	15
10/14	27	13	15	55	10	5	1	3	9	10						94	44	55	193	10
5/9	20	5	9	34	6	3	0	1	4	6						60	18	31	109	6
0/4	13	3	4	20	1	1		0	1	1						33	9	11	53	1
-5/-1	6	1	1	8	-4											15	3	4	22	-4
-10/-6	1			1	-8											6	1	1	8	-8
-15/-11																1	0		1	-13
-20/-16																0			0	-16

MCGUIRE AFB NEW JERSEY

LAT 40 01N LONG 74 36W ELEV 133 FT

MEAN FREQUENCY OF OCCURRENCE OF DRY BULB TEMPERATURE (DEGREES F) WITH MEAN COINCIDENT WET BULB TEMPERATURE (DEGREES F) FOR EACH DRY BULB TEMPERATURE RANGE

Temperature Range	MAY Obsn Hour Gp 01 to 08	MAY Obsn Hour Gp 09 to 16	MAY Obsn Hour Gp 17 to 24	MAY Total Obsn	MAY MCWB	JUNE Obsn Hour Gp 01 to 08	JUNE Obsn Hour Gp 09 to 16	JUNE Obsn Hour Gp 17 to 24	JUNE Total Obsn	JUNE MCWB	JULY Obsn Hour Gp 01 to 08	JULY Obsn Hour Gp 09 to 16	JULY Obsn Hour Gp 17 to 24	JULY Total Obsn	JULY MCWB
100/104												0		0	74
95/99			0	0	70		2	0	2	77		2	0	2	74
90/94		2	0	2	72		11	2	13	75		16	2	18	74
85/89		8	2	10	69	0	32	10	42	72	0	47	14	61	73
80/84		17	6	23	66	2	51	22	75	69	4	76	34	114	70
75/79	1	32	13	46	64	10	51	39	100	67	28	64	60	152	69
70/74	7	41	24	72	61	44	48	52	144	65	82	32	74	188	67
65/69	19	50	37	106	58	60	27	54	141	62	76	10	47	133	63
60/64	37	44	47	128	55	60	14	37	111	58	44	1	15	60	59
55/59	55	29	52	136	52	42	3	19	64	54	13		1	14	54
50/54	56	17	42	115	48	18	0	4	22	49	1			1	50
45/49	50	6	20	76	44	4		0	4	45					
40/44	19	1	5	25	39	0			0	42					
35/39	4		1	5	34										
30/34	1			1	30										
25/29															

Temperature Range	AUGUST Obsn Hour Gp 01 to 08	AUGUST Obsn Hour Gp 09 to 16	AUGUST Obsn Hour Gp 17 to 24	AUGUST Total Obsn	AUGUST MCWB	SEPTEMBER Obsn Hour Gp 01 to 08	SEPTEMBER Obsn Hour Gp 09 to 16	SEPTEMBER Obsn Hour Gp 17 to 24	SEPTEMBER Total Obsn	SEPTEMBER MCWB	OCTOBER Obsn Hour Gp 01 to 08	OCTOBER Obsn Hour Gp 09 to 16	OCTOBER Obsn Hour Gp 17 to 24	OCTOBER Total Obsn	OCTOBER MCWB
100/104															
95/99															
90/94		8	1	9	75		5	0	5	74					
85/89		43	8	51	74		20	3	23	73		1		1	72
80/84	1	68	26	95	71	0	35	10	45	70		6	1	7	69
75/79	22	68	57	147	69	6	49	26	81	68	1	18	3	22	65
70/74	71	41	74	186	67	36	49	49	134	66	3	35	10	48	63
65/69	75	16	52	143	63	47	40	50	137	62	11	45	25	81	60
60/64	49	3	22	74	59	52	28	48	128	58	29	50	45	124	56
55/59	22	0	7	29	54	45	11	33	89	53	39	42	46	127	52
50/54	7		0	7	49	33	3	16	52	49	50	30	51	131	47
45/49	0			0	45	13	0	4	17	44	48	14	37	99	43
40/44						6		1	7	40	35	5	19	59	39
35/39						2		0	2	36	22	2	8	32	34
30/34											9		2	11	30
25/29											2		0	2	25

MCGUIRE AFB NEW JERSEY

Temperature Range	NOVEMBER Obsn Hour Gp 01 to 08	NOVEMBER Obsn Hour Gp 09 to 16	NOVEMBER Obsn Hour Gp 17 to 24	NOVEMBER Total Obsn	NOVEMBER MCWB	DECEMBER Obsn Hour Gp 01 to 08	DECEMBER Obsn Hour Gp 09 to 16	DECEMBER Obsn Hour Gp 17 to 24	DECEMBER Total Obsn	DECEMBER MCWB	JANUARY Obsn Hour Gp 01 to 08	JANUARY Obsn Hour Gp 09 to 16	JANUARY Obsn Hour Gp 17 to 24	JANUARY Total Obsn	JANUARY MCWB
100/104															
95/99															
90/94															
85/89															
80/84		0		0	69										
75/79		1	0	1	69		0		0	62					
70/74	1	4	1	6	64		1	0	1	62		0		0	59
65/69	2	10	3	15	59	0	2	1	3	58		1	0	1	56
60/64	6	24	12	42	56	1	3	1	5	56	1	1	1	3	58
55/59	18	38	22	78	52	5	10	5	20	52	2	3	2	7	53
50/54	26	52	36	114	47	8	19	9	36	47	4	7	4	15	48
45/49	37	47	46	130	42	13	27	24	64	43	6	20	8	34	42
40/44	45	34	50	129	38	23	39	30	92	38	16	34	22	72	38
35/39	45	20	39	104	33	38	50	45	133	33	30	51	44	125	34
30/34	41	7	23	71	29	55	48	56	159	29	43	44	57	144	29
25/29	14	1	6	21	25	39	27	40	106	24	46	34	38	118	24
20/24	5	0	1	6	20	31	16	21	68	20	35	28	34	97	19
15/19	1			1	16	24	6	13	43	15	30	16	22	68	15
10/14						8	1	2	11	11	22	7	11	40	11
5/9						2	0	1	3	7	10	3	4	17	6
0/4						1		0	1	1	3	0	0	3	2
-5/-1															

Temperature Range	FEBRUARY Obsn Hour Gp 01 to 08	FEBRUARY Obsn Hour Gp 09 to 16	FEBRUARY Obsn Hour Gp 17 to 24	FEBRUARY Total Obsn	FEBRUARY MCWB	MARCH Obsn Hour Gp 01 to 08	MARCH Obsn Hour Gp 09 to 16	MARCH Obsn Hour Gp 17 to 24	MARCH Total Obsn	MARCH MCWB
100/104										
95/99										
90/94										
85/89										
80/84							0		0	60
75/79							2	0	2	58
70/74							4	1	5	57
65/69		1	0	1	57		7	2	9	54
60/64		3	1	4	56	1	10	5	16	53
55/59	2	5	5	12	52	3	15	9	27	49
50/54	4	11	5	20	46	5	28	16	49	44
45/49	4	18	10	32	42	13	41	29	83	41
40/44	14	35	21	70	38	37	49	52	138	37
35/39	36	50	47	133	33	62	51	65	178	34
30/34	45	44	59	148	29	66	27	44	137	29
25/29	48	27	39	114	24	36	9	16	61	24
20/24	29	16	19	64	19	15	3	6	24	20
15/19	23	9	12	44	15	6	2	1	9	15
10/14	12	3	5	20	10	2		0	2	11
5/9	7	1	2	10	6	0			0	6
0/4	1	0	0	1	1					
-5/-1	0	0		0	-4					

Temperature Range	APRIL Obsn Hour Gp 01 to 08	APRIL Obsn Hour Gp 09 to 16	APRIL Obsn Hour Gp 17 to 24	APRIL Total Obsn	APRIL MCWB	ANNUAL TOTAL Obsn Hour Gp 01 to 08	ANNUAL TOTAL Obsn Hour Gp 09 to 16	ANNUAL TOTAL Obsn Hour Gp 17 to 24	ANNUAL TOTAL Total Obsn	ANNUAL TOTAL MCWB
100/104							0		0	74
95/99							4	0	4	76
90/94		0		0	67		42	5	47	74
85/89		2	0	2	66	0	153	37	190	73
80/84		6	1	7	64	7	259	100	366	70
75/79		10	3	13	61	68	295	201	564	68
70/74	0	15	7	22	59	244	270	292	806	65
65/69	2	23	13	38	55	292	232	284	808	61
60/64	12	33	21	66	53	292	214	255	761	57
55/59	23	44	31	98	50	269	200	232	701	52
50/54	30	42	42	114	46	242	209	225	676	47
45/49	46	35	54	135	42	234	208	232	674	42
40/44	54	22	45	121	38	249	219	245	713	38
35/39	46	6	20	72	34	285	230	269	784	34
30/34	21	1	4	26	30	281	171	245	697	29
25/29	4		0	4	25	189	98	139	426	24
20/24	1			1	20	116	63	81	260	20
15/19	0			0	17	84	33	48	165	15
10/14						44	11	18	73	11
5/9						19	4	7	30	6
0/4						5	0	0	5	2
-5/-1						0	0		0	-4

NEWARK IAP NEW JERSEY

LAT 40 42N LONG 74 10W ELEV 7 FT

MEAN FREQUENCY OF OCCURRENCE OF DRY BULB TEMPERATURE (DEGREES F) WITH MEAN COINCIDENT WET BULB TEMPERATURE (DEGREES F) FOR EACH DRY BULB TEMPERATURE RANGE

Temperature Range	MAY Obsn Hour Gp 01 to 08	MAY 09 to 16	MAY 17 to 24	MAY Total Obsn	MAY MCWB	JUNE Obsn Hour Gp 01 to 08	JUNE 09 to 16	JUNE 17 to 24	JUNE Total Obsn	JUNE MCWB	JULY Obsn Hour Gp 01 to 08	JULY 09 to 16	JULY 17 to 24	JULY Total Obsn	JULY MCWB
105/109															
100/104							0	0	0	81		0		0	75
95/99		0		0	71		4	1	5	75		7	2	9	74
90/94		2	1	3	71	0	14	4	18	73		23	8	31	73
85/89		8	2	10	69	1	30	12	43	70	1	52	21	74	71
80/84	0	16	7	23	65	4	43	25	72	68	8	69	43	120	69
75/79	1	26	14	41	63	17	50	39	106	66	42	56	71	169	68
70/74	11	38	23	72	60	43	46	55	144	64	91	28	70	189	67
65/69	20	54	40	114	58	64	31	52	147	61	77	9	29	115	62
60/64	42	48	55	145	55	67	17	37	121	57	26	2	4	32	58
55/59	67	31	53	151	51	35	4	14	53	53	2	0	1	3	54
50/54	61	16	38	115	47	8	0	1	9	49					
45/49	37	8	14	59	43	0			0	47					
40/44	9	0	2	11	38										
35/39	0		0	0	36										
30/34															

Temperature Range	AUGUST Obsn Hour Gp 01 to 08	AUGUST 09 to 16	AUGUST 17 to 24	AUGUST Total Obsn	AUGUST MCWB	SEPTEMBER Obsn Hour Gp 01 to 08	SEPTEMBER 09 to 16	SEPTEMBER 17 to 24	SEPTEMBER Total Obsn	SEPTEMBER MCWB	OCTOBER Obsn Hour Gp 01 to 08	OCTOBER 09 to 16	OCTOBER 17 to 24	OCTOBER Total Obsn	OCTOBER MCWB
105/109							0		0	75					
100/104		0		0	73		0	0	0	75					
95/99		4	1	5	74		0	0	0	75					
90/94		14	3	17	74		7	1	8	74		0		0	75
85/89	0	35	12	47	72	0	14	4	18	73		2	0	2	71
80/84	4	63	33	100	70	1	31	13	45	70		8	1	9	67
75/79	30	70	67	167	68	12	49	28	89	68	0	19	5	24	64
70/74	78	47	80	205	66	33	45	46	124	65	4	29	13	46	62
65/69	83	13	43	139	63	44	49	58	151	61	11	42	31	84	59
60/64	41	2	9	52	58	58	29	50	137	57	33	58	53	144	56
55/59	12	0	1	13	54	48	12	27	87	52	47	43	57	147	51
50/54	0			0	49	29	3	9	41	48	55	28	47	130	47
45/49						11	0	2	13	43	50	13	27	90	43
40/44						3		0	3	39	33	4	11	48	38
35/39						0			0	38	13	1	4	18	34
30/34											1	0	0	1	30

Temperature Range	NOVEMBER Obsn Hour Gp 01 to 08	NOVEMBER 09 to 16	NOVEMBER 17 to 24	NOVEMBER Total Obsn	NOVEMBER MCWB	DECEMBER Obsn Hour Gp 01 to 08	DECEMBER 09 to 16	DECEMBER 17 to 24	DECEMBER Total Obsn	DECEMBER MCWB	JANUARY Obsn Hour Gp 01 to 08	JANUARY 09 to 16	JANUARY 17 to 24	JANUARY Total Obsn	JANUARY MCWB
105/109															
100/104															
95/99															
90/94															
85/89		0		0	67										
80/84		1		1	66										
75/79		1	0	1	66										
70/74		4	0	4	60							0		0	64
65/69	1	12	5	18	59		1	0	1	54		0	0	0	60
60/64	6	22	11	39	55	0	3	1	4	55	1	1	1	3	57
55/59	18	40	31	89	52	5	10	6	21	53	2	3	1	6	53
50/54	32	47	45	124	47	6	15	8	29	48	3	10	5	18	48
45/49	38	44	44	126	42	12	25	21	58	43	8	19	14	41	43
40/44	46	38	46	130	37	25	47	39	111	38	18	42	33	93	38
35/39	51	21	39	111	33	49	56	55	160	34	43	57	55	155	33
30/34	36	8	14	58	29	53	40	50	143	29	53	50	58	161	29
25/29	8	1	4	13	24	39	28	32	99	24	48	31	39	118	24
20/24	3	1	1	5	19	27	15	22	64	19	32	20	23	75	19
15/19	1	0		1	15	21	7	10	38	15	21	9	14	44	15
10/14						8	2	3	13	10	12	2	5	19	11
5/9						2	0	1	3	6	5	1	1	7	6
0/4						0		0	0	1	1	0		1	2
-5/-1															

Temperature Range	FEBRUARY Obsn Hour Gp 01 to 08	FEBRUARY 09 to 16	FEBRUARY 17 to 24	FEBRUARY Total Obsn	FEBRUARY MCWB	MARCH Obsn Hour Gp 01 to 08	MARCH 09 to 16	MARCH 17 to 24	MARCH Total Obsn	MARCH MCWB	APRIL Obsn Hour Gp 01 to 08	APRIL 09 to 16	APRIL 17 to 24	APRIL Total Obsn	APRIL MCWB
105/109															
100/104															
95/99															
90/94												0		0	68
85/89												2	0	2	66
80/84												6	2	8	63
75/79							1	0	1	58		7	3	10	60
70/74		0		0	58		2	1	3	55	1	17	7	25	58
65/69		1	0	1	57	0	3	1	4	53	4	18	13	35	56
60/64		2	0	2	53	0	10	4	14	51	12	32	22	66	52
55/59	1	5	2	8	50	3	16	10	29	48	21	44	33	98	49
50/54	2	11	7	20	46	8	30	21	59	44	43	45	56	144	46
45/49	6	25	14	45	41	17	47	34	98	40	60	44	53	157	42
40/44	20	42	37	99	37	43	54	60	157	37	56	20	38	114	38
35/39	49	55	58	162	33	77	47	63	187	33	31	4	10	45	33
30/34	50	38	52	140	29	53	25	33	111	28	10	2	2	14	29
25/29	42	20	24	86	24	27	9	12	48	24	1	0	0	1	23
20/24	24	13	16	53	19	16	3	6	25	19	0		0	0	19
15/19	14	7	8	29	14	3	1	1	5	14					
10/14	10	3	4	17	10	2		0	2	9					
5/9	4	1	2	7	6										
0/4	1	0	0	1	1										
-5/-1	0	0		0	-2										

Temperature Range	ANNUAL TOTAL Obsn Hour Gp 01 to 08	ANNUAL TOTAL 09 to 16	ANNUAL TOTAL 17 to 24	ANNUAL TOTAL Total Obsn	ANNUAL TOTAL MCWB
105/109		0		0	75
100/104		0	0	0	76
95/99		15	4	19	74
90/94	0	60	17	77	74
85/89	2	143	51	196	71
80/84	17	237	124	378	69
75/79	102	279	227	608	67
70/74	261	256	295	812	65
65/69	304	233	272	809	60
60/64	286	226	247	759	56
55/59	261	208	236	705	51
50/54	247	205	237	689	47
45/49	239	225	223	687	42
40/44	253	247	266	766	38
35/39	313	241	284	838	33
30/34	256	163	209	628	29
25/29	165	89	111	365	24
20/24	102	52	68	222	19
15/19	60	24	33	117	15
10/14	32	7	12	51	10
5/9	11	2	4	17	6
0/4	2	0	0	2	1
-5/-1	0	0		0	-2

ALBUQUERQUE IAP/KIRTLAND AFB NEW MEXICO

LAT 35 03N LONG 106 37W ELEV 5311 FT

MEAN FREQUENCY OF OCCURRENCE OF DRY BULB TEMPERATURE (DEGREES F) WITH MEAN COINCIDENT WET BULB TEMPERATURE (DEGREES F) FOR EACH DRY BULB TEMPERATURE RANGE

Temperature Range	MAY Obsn Hour Gp 01 to 08	MAY 09 to 16	MAY 17 to 24	MAY Total Obsn	MAY MCWB	JUNE Obsn Hour Gp 01 to 08	JUNE 09 to 16	JUNE 17 to 24	JUNE Total Obsn	JUNE MCWB	JULY Obsn Hour Gp 01 to 08	JULY 09 to 16	JULY 17 to 24	JULY Total Obsn	JULY MCWB
100/104							0	0	0	59		2	0	2	63
95/99		1	0	1	57		16	5	21	60		20	6	26	62
90/94		5	1	6	57		47	20	67	59		52	19	71	62
85/89		22	5	27	55	0	57	34	91	57	0	65	34	99	62
80/84		46	20	66	53	3	55	46	104	56	6	57	49	112	61
75/79	0	52	31	83	52	18	36	54	108	55	35	35	59	129	60
70/74	7	48	44	99	50	54	18	43	115	53	80	13	49	142	60
65/69	24	35	52	111	48	76	8	23	107	52	93	3	24	120	59
60/64	56	20	44	120	47	52	2	11	65	49	31	1	7	39	58
55/59	66	12	26	104	45	26	0	3	29	46	2		0	2	53
50/54	48	6	14	68	42	9		1	10	43	0			0	53
45/49	29	1	8	38	40	1			1	41					
40/44	13	0	3	16	35	0			0	42					
35/39	5		0	5	32										
30/34	0			0	28										

Temperature Range	AUGUST Obsn Hour Gp 01 to 08	AUGUST 09 to 16	AUGUST 17 to 24	AUGUST Total Obsn	AUGUST MCWB	SEPTEMBER Obsn Hour Gp 01 to 08	SEPTEMBER 09 to 16	SEPTEMBER 17 to 24	SEPTEMBER Total Obsn	SEPTEMBER MCWB	OCTOBER Obsn Hour Gp 01 to 08	OCTOBER 09 to 16	OCTOBER 17 to 24	OCTOBER Total Obsn	OCTOBER MCWB
100/104															
95/99		6	1	7	62		0		0	61					
90/94		40	12	52	62		13	1	14	59					
85/89		65	24	89	62		40	11	51	58		2	0	2	57
80/84	1	66	45	112	62		57	26	83	57		15	1	16	55
75/79	13	45	64	122	60	1	52	44	97	56		40	10	50	53
70/74	68	20	62	150	60	18	38	61	117	55	0	48	21	69	52
65/69	109	4	35	148	59	59	22	51	132	54	2	45	42	89	50
60/64	53	0	6	59	57	79	13	31	123	52	20	39	58	117	48
55/59	4			4	53	54	5	11	70	49	50	29	52	131	46
50/54						25	1	3	29	46	68	18	35	121	43
45/49						3	0	1	4	44	59	8	21	88	40
40/44						0			0	40	36	4	7	47	37
35/39											11	0	1	12	33
30/34											2			2	29

Temperature Range	NOVEMBER Obsn Hour Gp 01 to 08	NOV 09 to 16	NOV 17 to 24	NOV Total Obsn	NOV MCWB	DECEMBER Obsn Hour Gp 01 to 08	DEC 09 to 16	DEC 17 to 24	DEC Total Obsn	DEC MCWB	JANUARY Obsn Hour Gp 01 to 08	JAN 09 to 16	JAN 17 to 24	JAN Total Obsn	JAN MCWB	FEBRUARY Obsn Hour Gp 01 to 08	FEB 09 to 16	FEB 17 to 24	FEB Total Obsn	FEB MCWB
100/104																				
95/99																				
90/94																				
85/89																				
80/84																				
75/79																				
70/74		2		2	48		0		0	47							0		0	49
65/69		14	2	16	47		0	0	0	44		1		1	47		6	1	7	46
60/64		29	8	37	45		6	1	7	44		5	0	5	44		18	5	23	44
55/59	0	43	21	64	43		16	3	19	42		15	4	19	42		26	12	38	42
50/54	7	45	42	94	40	1	33	12	46	39	0	30	14	44	39	1	34	26	61	39
45/49	29	40	55	124	38	5	39	30	74	37	4	44	27	75	37	9	39	41	89	37
40/44	55	30	49	134	35	16	51	49	116	34	15	46	47	108	34	30	34	45	109	34
35/39	59	20	31	110	32	38	44	57	139	31	39	42	58	139	31	47	30	38	115	31
30/34	45	11	21	77	28	64	34	54	152	28	60	32	49	141	28	54	18	28	100	27
25/29	31	4	8	43	24	67	17	29	113	24	58	18	26	102	24	43	11	14	68	24
20/24	10	1	3	14	19	35	5	9	49	20	38	8	12	58	19	20	4	8	32	20
15/19	4	0	0	4	15	17	2	3	22	15	16	4	6	26	15	10	2	4	16	15
10/14	1			1	11	3	0	1	4	10	12	2	3	17	10	6	0	1	7	11
5/9						1	0	0	1	6	4	1	1	6	5	1	0	1	2	6
0/4											1	0	1	2	1	0	0	0	0	1
-5/-1											1	0	0	1	-4	0			0	-4
-10/-6											0			0	-6					

Temperature Range	MARCH Obsn Hour Gp 01 to 08	MAR 09 to 16	MAR 17 to 24	MAR Total Obsn	MAR MCWB	APRIL Obsn Hour Gp 01 to 08	APR 09 to 16	APR 17 to 24	APR Total Obsn	APR MCWB	ANNUAL TOTAL Obsn Hour Gp 01 to 08	ANN 09 to 16	ANN 17 to 24	ANN Total Obsn	ANN MCWB
100/104												2	0	2	63
95/99												43	12	55	61
90/94												157	53	210	61
85/89							0		0	[illegible]	[illegible]	[illegible]	[illegible]	[illegible]	[illegible]
80/84							9	2	11	52	10	305	189	504	58
75/79		2		2	49		23	8	31	50	67	285	270	622	56
70/74		8	2	10	47		43	20	63	48	227	238	302	767	55
65/69		23	8	31	45	1	44	32	77	46	364	205	270	839	53
60/64	0	36	19	55	43	9	41	45	95	44	300	210	235	745	49
55/59	3	42	31	76	41	30	31	44	105	42	235	219	207	661	44
50/54	14	39	44	97	39	51	24	38	113	40	224	230	229	683	41
45/49	33	40	47	120	36	56	15	28	99	37	228	226	258	712	38
40/44	50	28	38	116	34	51	6	15	72	35	266	199	253	718	35
35/39	59	19	33	111	31	30	1	7	38	32	288	156	225	669	31
30/34	45	9	19	73	27	10	0	1	11	28	280	104	172	556	28
25/29	30	2	8	40	23	1			1	23	230	52	85	367	24
20/24	13	0	1	14	19						116	18	33	167	19
15/19	2		0	2	15						49	8	13	70	15
10/14	0			0	11						22	2	5	29	10
5/9											6	1	2	9	5
0/4											1	0	1	2	1
-5/-1											1	0	0	1	-4
-10/-6											0			0	-6

CANNON AFB/CLOVIS NEW MEXICO

LAT 34 23N LONG 103 19W ELEV 4283 FT

MEAN FREQUENCY OF OCCURRENCE OF DRY BULB TEMPERATURE (DEGREES F) WITH MEAN COINCIDENT WET BULB TEMPERATURE (DEGREES F) FOR EACH DRY BULB TEMPERATURE RANGE

Temperature Range	MAY Obsn Hour Gp 01 to 08	MAY 09 to 16	MAY 17 to 24	MAY Total Obsn	MAY MCWB	JUNE Obsn Hour Gp 01 to 08	JUNE 09 to 16	JUNE 17 to 24	JUNE Total Obsn	JUNE MCWB	JULY Obsn Hour Gp 01 to 08	JULY 09 to 16	JULY 17 to 24	JULY Total Obsn	JULY MCWB
105/109							0		0	65		0		0	65
100/104							1	0	1	64		1	0	1	66
95/99		1		1	60		10	3	13	63		14	3	17	66
90/94		9	1	10	59		32	10	42	62		53	15	68	66
85/89		29	9	38	58	0	57	22	79	62		68	29	97	65
80/84		45	17	62	56	2	53	29	84	62	4	54	38	96	65
75/79	1	49	24	74	55	10	40	40	90	61	23	31	55	109	64
70/74	7	43	34	84	54	35	25	49	109	60	61	17	60	138	62
65/69	20	31	45	96	53	66	12	43	121	59	107	7	37	151	61
60/64	49	20	49	118	52	73	7	28	108	56	49	2	10	61	59
55/59	69	12	38	119	50	41	3	12	56	53	4	0	1	5	56
50/54	55	6	19	80	46	11	0	3	14	48					
45/49	31	3	10	44	42	2		0	2	43					
40/44	11	0	2	13	37	0			0	41					
35/39	4		0	4	33										
30/34	1			1	27										
25/29															
20/24															

Temperature Range	AUGUST Obsn Hour Gp 01 to 08	AUGUST 09 to 16	AUGUST 17 to 24	AUGUST Total Obsn	AUGUST MCWB	SEPTEMBER Obsn Hour Gp 01 to 08	SEPTEMBER 09 to 16	SEPTEMBER 17 to 24	SEPTEMBER Total Obsn	SEPTEMBER MCWB	OCTOBER Obsn Hour Gp 01 to 08	OCTOBER 09 to 16	OCTOBER 17 to 24	OCTOBER Total Obsn	OCTOBER MCWB
105/109															
100/104		0		0	65										
95/99		7	1	8	66		1	0	1	63					
90/94		38	8	46	65		7	1	8	63		0		0	55
85/89	0	61	20	81	65		34	5	39	62		6	0	6	57
80/84	2	59	31	92	64		50	13	63	62		26	3	29	56
75/79	13	45	44	102	64	2	52	24	78	61		37	7	44	54
70/74	45	23	65	133	62	10	40	40	90	60	0	41	12	53	53
65/69	101	10	59	170	61	38	25	58	121	59	4	37	23	64	52
60/64	73	3	17	93	58	80	16	51	147	56	14	36	43	93	50
55/59	14	1	2	17	55	60	7	28	95	52	38	24	51	113	48
50/54	1	1	1	3	52	34	5	12	51	48	60	15	49	124	45
45/49						11	3	6	20	43	67	11	31	109	41
40/44						6	1	2	9	40	39	9	17	65	38
35/39						0			0	36	17	5	10	32	34
30/34											7	0	2	9	29
25/29											1		0	1	25
20/24											0			0	21

Temperature Range	NOVEMBER Obsn Hour Gp 01 to 08	09 to 16	17 to 24	Total Obsn	MCWB	DECEMBER Obsn Hour Gp 01 to 08	09 to 16	17 to 24	Total Obsn	MCWB
105/109										
100/104										
95/99										
90/94										
[illegible]										
80/84		0		0	52					
75/79		4		4	52		0		0	52
70/74		21	0	21	50		2		2	51
65/69		27	4	31	48		10	0	10	47
60/64	0	39	10	49	46		25	1	26	45
55/59	3	37	22	62	45	0	33	7	40	42
50/54	15	34	40	89	42	3	35	17	55	40
45/49	35	26	44	105	39	9	38	27	74	37
40/44	54	23	49	126	36	22	33	42	97	35
35/39	58	16	36	110	33	41	26	49	116	31
30/34	43	9	21	73	29	66	19	46	131	28
25/29	21	5	9	35	24	56	14	34	104	25
20/24	7	0	4	11	20	30	9	15	54	20
15/19	3		1	4	15	14	3	8	25	16
10/14	1		0	1	11	4	1	2	7	11
5/9	0			0	7	2	0	0	2	7
0/4						0		0	0	1
-5/-1						0			0	-4
-10/-6						0			0	-6
-15/-11						0			0	-11

Temperature Range	JANUARY Obsn Hour Gp 01 to 08	09 to 16	17 to 24	Total Obsn	MCWB	FEBRUARY Obsn Hour Gp 01 to 08	09 to 16	17 to 24	Total Obsn	MCWB
105/109										
100/104										
95/99										
90/94										
[illegible]										
80/84							0		0	53
75/79		0		0	49		1	0	1	51
70/74		2	0	2	48		5	1	6	49
65/69		12	1	13	46		13	2	15	47
60/64		20	4	24	44	0	20	5	25	45
55/59		28	7	35	42	1	29	12	42	42
50/54	2	35	15	52	40	5	34	21	60	40
45/49	7	34	25	66	37	10	31	30	71	38
40/44	19	32	38	89	34	26	24	37	87	35
35/39	38	27	45	110	31	37	25	39	101	32
30/34	53	21	42	116	28	52	17	34	103	28
25/29	47	15	28	90	24	44	12	22	78	24
20/24	36	9	18	63	20	26	6	13	45	20
15/19	19	6	11	36	15	14	4	5	23	16
10/14	13	4	8	25	11	5	1	2	8	12
5/9	8	2	5	15	6	2		1	3	7
0/4	3	1	2	6	1	0			0	4
-5/-1	2	0	1	3	-3					
-10/-6	1	0	0	1	-8					
-15/-11	0			0	-12					

Temperature Range	MARCH Obsn Hour Gp 01 to 08	09 to 16	17 to 24	Total Obsn	MCWB	APRIL Obsn Hour Gp 01 to 08	09 to 16	17 to 24	Total Obsn	MCWB	ANNUAL TOTAL Obsn Hour Gp 01 to 08	09 to 16	17 to 24	Total Obsn	MCWB
105/109												0		0	65
100/104												2	0	2	65
95/99												33	7	40	65
90/94							1	0	1	57		140	35	175	64
[illegible]		0		0	57		5	1	6	55	0	260	86	346	63
80/84		2	0	2	53		16	4	20	53	8	305	135	448	61
75/79		9	2	11	50		32	11	43	52	49	300	207	556	60
70/74		19	5	24	48	1	39	18	58	50	159	277	284	720	58
65/69	0	27	10	37	47	4	40	26	70	48	340	251	308	899	56
60/64	0	33	17	50	44	10	36	37	83	47	348	257	272	877	52
55/59	4	35	27	66	42	25	26	41	92	45	259	235	248	742	47
50/54	15	31	34	80	40	47	20	41	108	43	248	216	252	716	43
45/49	25	26	38	89	38	58	13	30	101	40	255	185	241	681	39
40/44	46	21	38	105	35	49	8	17	74	36	272	151	242	665	36
35/39	51	18	31	100	32	27	3	9	39	33	273	120	219	612	32
30/34	47	13	23	83	28	15	1	5	21	29	284	80	173	537	28
25/29	33	10	16	59	25	5	0	1	6	26	207	56	110	373	24
20/24	17	3	6	26	20	0		0	0	22	116	27	56	199	20
15/19	7	1	2	10	16						57	14	27	98	16
10/14	3		1	4	12						26	6	13	45	11
5/9	0			0	9						12	2	6	20	6
0/4											3	1	2	6	1
-5/-1											2	0	1	3	-3
-10/-6											1	0	0	1	-8
-15/-11											0			0	-12

FARMINGTON MAP NEW MEXICO

LAT 36 44N LONG 108 14W ELEV 5503 FT

MEAN FREQUENCY OF OCCURRENCE OF DRY BULB TEMPERATURE (DEGREES F) WITH MEAN COINCIDENT WET BULB TEMPERATURE (DEGREES F) FOR EACH DRY BULB TEMPERATURE RANGE

Temperature Range	MAY Obsn Hour Gp 01 to 08	MAY 09 to 16	MAY 17 to 24	MAY Total Obsn	MAY MCWB	JUNE Obsn Hour Gp 01 to 08	JUNE 09 to 16	JUNE 17 to 24	JUNE Total Obsn	JUNE MCWB	JULY Obsn Hour Gp 01 to 08	JULY 09 to 16	JULY 17 to 24	JULY Total Obsn	JULY MCWB
100/104							0		0	62		0		0	66
95/99							6	2	8	61		15	3	18	63
90/94		1	0	1	57		35	14	49	60		56	22	78	62
85/89		13	3	16	56		51	28	79	58		68	36	104	61
80/84		36	14	50	54	0	55	37	92	56	1	52	45	98	60
75/79		54	25	79	52	4	43	43	90	54	10	35	52	97	59
70/74	1	47	33	81	51	20	30	42	92	53	50	15	47.	112	58
65/69	7	37	43	87	49	44	14	38	96	51	96	5	30	131	56
60/64	24	28	43	95	47	62	4	23	89	48	72	1	12	85	54
55/59	46	18	38	102	45	63	1	9	73	45	18		1	19	48
50/54	68	10	25	103	42	34	0	3	37	42	2	0		2	43
45/49	56	4	16	76	39	11		1	12	39					
40/44	32	1	6	39	36	2		0	2	35					
35/39	13	0	1	14	34	1			1	31					
30/34	1			1	28										
25/29															
20/24															

Temperature Range	AUGUST Obsn Hour Gp 01 to 08	AUGUST 09 to 16	AUGUST 17 to 24	AUGUST Total Obsn	AUGUST MCWB	SEPTEMBER Obsn Hour Gp 01 to 08	SEPTEMBER 09 to 16	SEPTEMBER 17 to 24	SEPTEMBER Total Obsn	SEPTEMBER MCWB	OCTOBER Obsn Hour Gp 01 to 08	OCTOBER 09 to 16	OCTOBER 17 to 24	OCTOBER Total Obsn	OCTOBER MCWB
100/104		0		0	65										
95/99		5	1	6	64										
90/94		30	9	39	63		5	0	5	60					
85/89		62	25	87	62		32	7	39	59		0		0	57
80/84		60	37	97	61		50	19	69	58		7	0	7	56
75/79	4	49	53	106	60	0	48	32	80	56		28	4	32	53
70/74	30	29	57	116	59	3	45	45	93	55		41	14	55	51
65/69	82	9	45	136	58	19	30	49	98	53	0	44	27	71	49
60/64	88	2	20	110	56	51	18	43	112	51	4	38	40	82	48
55/59	35		2	37	50	73	8	28	109	48	17	32	43	92	46
50/54	8	0		8	43	56	3	12	71	44	37	30	46	113	43
45/49	1			1	40	29	1	4	34	41	65	18	43	126	40
40/44						10	0	1	11	38	71	8	22	101	37
35/39						1			1	35	34	2	8	44	32
30/34											14	0	2	16	28
25/29											5			5	24
20/24											0			0	20

Temperature Range	NOVEMBER Obsn Hour Gp 01 to 08	NOVEMBER 09 to 16	NOVEMBER 17 to 24	NOVEMBER Total Obsn	NOVEMBER MCWB	DECEMBER Obsn Hour Gp 01 to 08	DECEMBER 09 to 16	DECEMBER 17 to 24	DECEMBER Total Obsn	DECEMBER MCWB	JANUARY Obsn Hour Gp 01 to 08	JANUARY 09 to 16	JANUARY 17 to 24	JANUARY Total Obsn	JANUARY MCWB
100/104															
95/99															
90/94															
85/89															
80/84															
75/79															
70/74		0		0	48										
65/69		5		5	47										
60/64		16	3	19	46		0		0	42		1		1	43
55/59	0	32	9	41	43		6	0	6	42		4	0	4	42
50/54	2	42	22	66	41		15	2	17	40		8	1	9	41
45/49	11	42	38	91	39	0	34	8	42	37		19	5	24	37
40/44	22	42	43	107	36	4	40	24	68	35	2	37	16	55	35
35/39	37	33	45	115	32	18	41	40	99	32	13	49	35	97	32
30/34	63	20	47	130	29	35	42	49	126	29	36	52	59	147	29
25/29	64	7	22	93	25	48	33	52	133	25	46	35	53	134	25
20/24	23	1	8	32	20	60	20	35	115	21	45	21	35	101	21
15/19	13	0	2	15	16	43	9	21	73	16	42	13	20	75	16
10/14	4		0	4	11	22	4	8	34	12	26	6	10	42	11
5/9	1			1	8	9	1	5	15	7	18	4	8	30	6
0/4						6	1	2	9	2	10	2	3	15	2
-5/-1						2	0	0	2	-2	6	0	2	8	-3
-10/-6						0	0	0	0	-9	2	0	0	2	-8
-15/-11						0	0	1	1	-12	1		0	1	-14
-20/-16						1		0	1	-18					

Temperature Range	FEBRUARY Obsn Hour Gp 01 to 08	FEBRUARY 09 to 16	FEBRUARY 17 to 24	FEBRUARY Total Obsn	FEBRUARY MCWB	MARCH Obsn Hour Gp 01 to 08	MARCH 09 to 16	MARCH 17 to 24	MARCH Total Obsn	MARCH MCWB	APRIL Obsn Hour Gp 01 to 08	APRIL 09 to 16	APRIL 17 to 24	APRIL Total Obsn	APRIL MCWB	ANNUAL TOTAL Obsn Hour Gp 01 to 08	ANNUAL TOTAL 09 to 16	ANNUAL TOTAL 17 to 24	ANNUAL TOTAL Total Obsn	ANNUAL TOTAL MCWB
100/104																	0		0	63
95/99																	26	6	32	63
90/94																	127	45	172	61
85/89												0		0	54		226	99	325	60
80/84												[illegible]	[illegible]	[illegible]	[illegible]	1	[illegible]	[illegible]	410	[illegible]
75/79							0		0	49		16	4	20	50	18	273	213	504	56
70/74							5	1	6	47		29	12	41	49	104	241	251	596	54
65/69		1		1	49		11	4	15	46	0	42	21	63	46	248	198	257	703	53
60/64		6	1	7	47		22	8	30	44	2	39	29	70	44	303	175	222	700	50
55/59		13	4	17	44	0	37	19	56	42	8	36	37	81	42	260	187	190	637	45
50/54	0	26	10	36	41	3	41	28	72	39	25	34	42	101	40	235	209	191	635	42
45/49	2	34	22	58	38	11	40	39	90	37	44	23	38	105	38	230	215	214	659	39
40/44	9	47	37	93	35	26	42	45	113	35	58	13	30	101	35	236	230	224	690	36
35/39	30	41	45	116	33	48	30	49	127	32	52	5	19	76	32	247	201	242	690	32
30/34	44	27	51	122	29	67	15	35	117	29	36	0	6	42	29	296	156	249	701	29
25/29	60	15	33	108	25	51	4	17	72	24	11		1	12	24	285	94	178	557	25
20/24	42	9	11	62	21	32	0	4	36	20	3			3	20	205	51	93	349	20
15/19	21	4	6	31	16	10	0		10	15	0			0	16	129	26	49	204	16
10/14	9	1	3	13	12	1			1	11						62	11	21	94	11
5/9	5	0	1	6	7											33	5	14	52	7
0/4	3			3	2											19	3	5	27	2
-5/-1	1			1	-2											9	0	2	11	-3
-10/-6																2	0	0	2	-8
-15/-11																1	0	1	2	-13
-20/-16																2	0	0	2	-18

HOLLOMAN AFB/ALAMOGORDO NEW MEXICO

LAT 32 51N LONG 106 06W ELEV 4093 FT

MEAN FREQUENCY OF OCCURRENCE OF DRY BULB TEMPERATURE (DEGREES F) WITH MEAN COINCIDENT WET BULB TEMPERATURE (DEGREES F) FOR EACH DRY BULB TEMPERATURE RANGE

Tempera-ture Range	MAY Obsn Hour Gp			MAY Total Obsn	MAY MCWB	JUNE Obsn Hour Gp			JUNE Total Obsn	JUNE MCWB	JULY Obsn Hour Gp			JULY Total Obsn	JULY MCWB
	01 to 08	09 to 16	17 to 24			01 to 08	09 to 16	17 to 24			01 to 08	09 to 16	17 to 24		
105/109							0		0	67		1	0	1	66
100/104							7	3	10	65		6	2	8	65
95/99		2	0	2	60		28	12	40	62		30	15	45	64
90/94		20	6	26	58	0	57	30	87	61	0	64	33	97	65
85/89		43	20	63	56	2	61	39	102	60	2	69	47	118	64
80/84	1	62	33	96	55	12	48	46	106	58	18	45	63	126	63
75/79	5	52	41	98	53	34	24	48	106	57	60	20	48	128	62
70/74	19	38	47	104	51	59	11	32	102	56	93	10	30	133	61
65/69	42	19	47	108	49	62	4	20	86	53	64	2	9	75	60
60/64	62	8	31	101	47	44	1	8	53	50	11	0	1	12	58
55/59	56	2	15	73	44	21	0	2	23	45		0		0	54
50/54	38	1	5	44	41	5		0	5	41					
45/49	17	0	2	19	37	1			1	39					
40/44	5		0	5	32	0			0	30					
35/39	2		0	2	29										
30/34	0			0	23										
25/29	0			0	19										

Tempera-ture Range	AUGUST Obsn Hour Gp			AUGUST Total Obsn	AUGUST MCWB	SEPTEMBER Obsn Hour Gp			SEPTEMBER Total Obsn	SEPTEMBER MCWB	OCTOBER Obsn Hour Gp			OCTOBER Total Obsn	OCTOBER MCWB
	01 to 08	09 to 16	17 to 24			01 to 08	09 to 16	17 to 24			01 to 08	09 to 16	17 to 24		
105/109															
100/104		0	0	0	64		0		0	68					
95/99		16	5	21	65		3	1	4	65					
90/94		52	22	74	65		15	4	19	64		0		0	62
85/89	0	65	37	102	64		48	17	65	62		5	1	6	58
80/84	6	60	57	123	63	0	64	35	99	61		25	6	31	56
75/79	35	34	63	132	62	6	50	50	106	60	0	44	14	58	55
70/74	91	16	43	150	61	31	35	60	126	59	1	58	29	88	53
65/69	84	4	19	107	60	70	17	44	131	57	9	45	44	98	52
60/64	27	0	2	29	56	78	5	20	103	54	25	35	56	116	50
55/59	5		0	5	52	35	2	7	44	50	57	22	48	127	47
50/54						13	1	3	17	45	66	9	29	104	44
45/49						5	0	0	5	41	47	4	14	65	40
40/44						0		0	0	36	28	1	5	34	36
35/39						0			0	33	12		1	13	32
30/34											3		0	3	27
25/29											0			0	24

Temperature Range	NOVEMBER Obsn Hour Gp 01 to 08	09 to 16	17 to 24	Total Obsn	MCWB	DECEMBER Obsn Hour Gp 01 to 08	09 to 16	17 to 24	Total Obsn	MCWB	JANUARY Obsn Hour Gp 01 to 08	09 to 16	17 to 24	Total Obsn	MCWB	FEBRUARY Obsn Hour Gp 01 to 08	09 to 16	17 to 24	Total Obsn	MCWB	MARCH Obsn Hour Gp 01 to 08	09 to 16	17 to 24	Total Obsn	MCWB	APRIL Obsn Hour Gp 01 to 08	09 to 16	17 to 24	Total Obsn	MCWB	ANNUAL TOTAL Obsn Hour Gp 01 to 08	09 to 16	17 to 24	Total Obsn	MCWB
105/109																																1	0	1	67
100/104																																13	5	18	65
95/99																																79	33	112	64
90/94																						0		0	[illegible]		1	[illegible]	1	[illegible]	0	209	95	304	63
85/89																						0	0	0	54		8	2	10	55	4	299	163	466	61
80/84																						2	1	3	53		23	9	32	53	37	329	250	616	60
75/79		1		1	54												2	0	2	53		12	4	16	50	0	44	20	64	51	140	283	288	711	58
70/74		20	2	22	51		1		1	49		2	0	2	49		8	2	10	49		27	12	39	48	2	53	35	90	49	296	279	292	867	56
65/69	0	37	10	47	48		6	0	6	48		10	2	12	47		16	6	22	47	1	40	22	63	46	9	45	44	98	47	341	245	267	853	53
60/64	2	43	22	67	46	0	23	5	28	45	1	20	8	29	45	0	32	16	48	45	4	41	33	78	44	26	34	49	109	44	280	242	251	773	48
55/59	9	46	35	90	44	2	37	14	53	43	2	36	17	55	43	4	40	27	71	42	14	41	43	98	42	42	20	37	99	42	247	246	245	738	44
50/54	22	39	47	108	42	7	45	25	77	41	5	43	24	72	41	12	38	36	86	40	29	36	42	107	40	59	9	26	94	40	256	221	237	714	41
45/49	34	29	47	110	39	16	43	41	100	38	14	41	40	95	38	26	34	39	99	38	45	23	38	106	37	49	3	12	64	37	254	177	233	664	38
40/44	54	17	39	110	35	24	37	48	109	35	27	36	47	110	35	34	26	38	98	34	52	14	27	93	34	32	1	4	37	33	256	132	208	596	35
35/39	54	6	23	83	32	41	31	55	127	32	35	27	44	106	31	41	16	31	88	31	43	7	16	66	31	16		1	17	30	244	87	171	502	31
30/34	37	3	10	50	28	69	17	39	125	28	56	17	34	107	28	47	7	16	70	27	35	3	8	46	27	4			4	26	251	47	107	405	28
25/29	19	0	3	22	23	49	7	17	73	24	47	7	17	71	24	32	4	8	44	24	18	1	2	21	23	0			0	23	165	19	47	231	24
20/24	7		0	7	19	27	2	4	33	19	32	5	9	46	19	16	1	3	20	19	6	0	1	7	18						88	8	17	113	19
15/19	1			1	16	11	0	1	12	15	16	2	4	22	15	8	0	1	9	15	1			1	15						37	2	6	45	15
10/14						2			2	11	5	1	2	8	10	2		0	2	11	0			0	11						9	1	2	12	10
5/9						0			0	5	5	1	1	7	5	0			0	8	0			0	6						5	1	1	7	5
0/4						0			0	3	2	0	1	3	1																2	0	1	3	1
-5/-1											1	0	0	1	-4																1	0	0	1	-4
-10/-6											0			0	-9																0			0	-9
-15/-11											0			0	-11																0			0	-11

ALBANY NEW YORK

LAT 42 45N   LONG 73 48W   ELEV 275 FT

MEAN FREQUENCY OF OCCURRENCE OF DRY BULB TEMPERATURE (DEGREES F) WITH MEAN COINCIDENT WET BULB TEMPERATURE (DEGREES F) FOR EACH DRY BULB TEMPERATURE RANGE

Temperature Range	MAY Obsn Hour Gp 01 to 08	MAY 09 to 16	MAY 17 to 24	MAY Total Obsn	MAY MCWB	JUNE Obsn Hour Gp 01 to 08	JUNE 09 to 16	JUNE 17 to 24	JUNE Total Obsn	JUNE MCWB	JULY Obsn Hour Gp 01 to 08	JULY 09 to 16	JULY 17 to 24	JULY Total Obsn	JULY MCWB
95/99							1	0	1	76		4	0	4	74
90/94		1	0	1	70		6	1	7	73		14	4	18	73
85/89		4	1	5	67	0	23	8	31	70		37	12	49	71
80/84		13	5	18	65	1	39	17	57	68	2	55	27	84	68
75/79	1	25	10	36	63	6	49	31	86	65	12	64	44	120	67
70/74	3	35	21	59	60	23	45	42	110	63	44	47	62	153	65
65/69	12	45	37	94	57	49	39	52	140	61	80	21	59	160	63
60/64	29	42	42	113	54	56	24	45	125	57	58	4	28	90	59
55/59	44	38	46	128	51	53	12	30	95	53	32	1	10	43	55
50/54	52	26	37	115	47	36	3	12	51	49	16		2	18	51
45/49	52	14	32	98	43	12		2	14	45	3			3	46
40/44	34	5	14	53	39	4		0	4	41	0			0	41
35/39	14	0	3	17	35	1			1	37					
30/34	7		0	7	31										
25/29	1			1	28										
20/24															

Temperature Range	AUGUST Obsn Hour Gp 01 to 08	AUGUST 09 to 16	AUGUST 17 to 24	AUGUST Total Obsn	AUGUST MCWB	SEPTEMBER Obsn Hour Gp 01 to 08	SEPTEMBER 09 to 16	SEPTEMBER 17 to 24	SEPTEMBER Total Obsn	SEPTEMBER MCWB	OCTOBER Obsn Hour Gp 01 to 08	OCTOBER 09 to 16	OCTOBER 17 to 24	OCTOBER Total Obsn	OCTOBER MCWB
95/99		1	0	1	75		1	0	1	76					
90/94		6	1	7	73		1	0	1	76					
85/89		21	5	26	71		9	2	11	73		0	0	0	62
80/84	1	48	18	67	69	0	18	5	23	71		2	0	2	67
75/79	6	64	38	108	66	2	30	14	46	67		11	1	12	64
70/74	29	60	57	146	65	15	40	28	83	64	1	18	7	26	62
65/69	62	32	63	157	63	24	48	34	106	60	4	28	13	45	58
60/64	65	12	42	119	59	37	47	47	131	57	11	44	27	82	55
55/59	47	3	18	68	55	46	28	46	120	53	30	47	43	120	52
50/54	27		6	33	51	45	13	34	92	49	38	43	48	129	47
45/49	11		0	11	47	38	4	20	62	45	50	33	47	130	44
40/44	1			1	43	19	0	7	26	41	43	14	34	91	39
35/39						10		2	12	36	36	7	17	60	35
30/34						4		0	4	32	24	1	10	35	31
25/29						0			0	28	9		1	10	27
20/24											2			2	22

Temperature Range	NOVEMBER Obsn Hour Gp 01 to 08	09 to 16	17 to 24	Total Obsn	MCWB	DECEMBER Obsn Hour Gp 01 to 08	09 to 16	17 to 24	Total Obsn	MCWB	JANUARY Obsn Hour Gp 01 to 08	09 to 16	17 to 24	Total Obsn	MCWB
95/99															
90/94															
85/89															
80/84		0		0	64										
75/79		0		0	65										
70/74		0		0	64										
65/69	1	3	1	5	59										
60/64	2	11	4	17	56	0	0	0	0	57	0	0	0	0	56
55/59	7	18	13	38	52	2	3	2	7	54	1	1	0	2	54
50/54	17	34	23	74	48	3	5	5	13	48	1	2	1	4	49
45/49	26	42	32	100	43	5	11	7	23	43	2	3	3	8	45
40/44	38	46	43	127	38	10	20	12	42	38	8	15	8	31	39
35/39	40	43	45	128	34	27	43	33	103	34	21	33	29	83	34
30/34	45	28	43	116	30	45	51	50	146	30	34	43	38	115	30
25/29	35	11	25	71	25	41	39	46	126	25	33	43	39	115	25
20/24	20	2	8	30	21	35	32	32	99	20	31	37	38	106	20
15/19	6	1	3	10	17	28	22	23	73	16	32	30	35	97	16
10/14	2	0	1	3	12	21	10	19	50	11	29	19	25	73	11
5/9	1			1	8	15	6	9	30	7	22	13	16	51	6
0/4						8	4	5	17	2	18	7	10	35	2
-5/-1						5	1	2	8	-3	10	1	3	14	-3
-10/-6						2	0	1	3	-8	3	0	2	5	-8
-15/-11						1		0	1	-12	2	0	0	2	-13
-20/-16						1			1	-17	1			1	-17
-25/-21											0			0	-23

Temperature Range	FEBRUARY Obsn Hour Gp 01 to 08	09 to 16	17 to 24	Total Obsn	MCWB	MARCH Obsn Hour Gp 01 to 08	09 to 16	17 to 24	Total Obsn	MCWB	APRIL Obsn Hour Gp 01 to 08	09 to 16	17 to 24	Total Obsn	MCWB	ANNUAL TOTAL Obsn Hour Gp 01 to 08	09 to 16	17 to 24	Total Obsn	MCWB
95/99																	7	0	7	75
90/94												0		0	63		28	6	34	73
85/89												1	0	1	65	0	95	28	123	71
80/84												2	1	3	63	4	177	73	254	68
75/79							0	0	0	57		5	2	7	60	27	248	140	415	66
70/74							1	0	1	55	0	11	5	16	57	115	257	222	594	64
65/69							1	1	2	54	2	18	11	31	55	234	235	271	740	61
60/64		0		0	56		3	1	4	51	5	25	16	46	51	263	212	252	727	57
55/59		1		1	50	1	6	3	10	49	11	32	25	68	49	274	190	236	700	52
50/54	1	3	2	6	47	3	12	8	23	45	24	42	36	102	45	263	183	214	660	48
45/49	1	7	4	12	42	5	27	15	47	41	37	42	43	122	42	242	183	205	630	43
40/44	6	18	11	35	38	14	45	31	90	37	52	39	45	136	38	229	202	205	636	38
35/39	21	42	32	95	34	36	55	54	145	33	55	18	36	109	34	261	241	251	753	34
30/34	36	46	46	128	30	67	46	59	172	30	33	5	16	54	30	295	220	262	777	30
25/29	35	36	39	110	25	47	27	38	112	25	15	0	3	18	25	216	156	191	563	25
20/24	34	26	30	90	20	37	14	22	73	20	4	1	0	5	20	163	112	130	405	20
15/19	24	19	24	67	15	18	7	10	35	15	2	0	1	3	16	110	79	96	285	16
10/14	21	12	16	49	11	11	2	4	17	11						84	43	65	192	11
5/9	17	7	11	35	6	5	1	2	8	6						60	27	38	125	6
0/4	8	5	6	19	1	3	0	1	4	2						37	16	22	75	2
-5/-1	11	1	4	16	-3	1	0	0	1	-4						27	3	9	39	-3
-10/-6	5	0	1	6	-8	0		0	0	-8						10	0	4	14	-8
-15/-11	2	0		2	-13	0			0	-14						5	0	0	5	-13
-20/-16	1			1	-17	0			0	-17						3			3	-17
-25/-21																0			0	-23

GRIFFISS AFB/ROME NEW YORK

LAT 43 14N LONG 75 25W ELEV 514 FT

MEAN FREQUENCY OF OCCURRENCE OF DRY BULB TEMPERATURE (DEGREES F) WITH MEAN COINCIDENT WET BULB TEMPERATURE (DEGREES F) FOR EACH DRY BULB TEMPERATURE RANGE

Temperature Range	MAY Obsn Hour Gp 01 to 08	MAY 09 to 16	MAY 17 to 24	MAY Total Obsn	MAY MCWB	JUNE Obsn Hour Gp 01 to 08	JUNE 09 to 16	JUNE 17 to 24	JUNE Total Obsn	JUNE MCWB	JULY Obsn Hour Gp 01 to 08	JULY 09 to 16	JULY 17 to 24	JULY Total Obsn	JULY MCWB
100/104												0		0	72
95/99							0		0	80		0	0	0	73
90/94		0		0	70		3	1	4	74		6	1	7	72
85/89		3	1	4	70		17	5	22	71		22	8	30	70
80/84		9	4	13	66	0	30	14	44	67	0	47	19	66	68
75/79		19	8	27	63	2	44	23	69	65	6	65	39	110	66
70/74	2	28	15	45	60	15	48	40	103	63	28	57	56	141	64
65/69	8	36	26	70	57	38	42	47	127	60	64	37	60	161	62
60/64	25	43	36	104	54	49	30	42	121	57	65	13	37	115	59
55/59	33	40	39	112	51	50	21	37	108	53	43	1	20	64	54
50/54	41	34	42	117	47	42	6	23	71	49	28		7	35	50
45/49	47	23	40	110	43	27	0	6	33	44	12		1	13	46
40/44	41	10	23	74	39	12		2	14	40	2			2	42
35/39	31	3	12	46	34	4		0	4	35					
30/34	16	1	3	20	30	0			0	31					
25/29	3		0	3	26										
20/24	0			0	22										
15/19															

Temperature Range	AUGUST Obsn Hour Gp 01 to 08	AUGUST 09 to 16	AUGUST 17 to 24	AUGUST Total Obsn	AUGUST MCWB	SEPTEMBER Obsn Hour Gp 01 to 08	SEPTEMBER 09 to 16	SEPTEMBER 17 to 24	SEPTEMBER Total Obsn	SEPTEMBER MCWB	OCTOBER Obsn Hour Gp 01 to 08	OCTOBER 09 to 16	OCTOBER 17 to 24	OCTOBER Total Obsn	OCTOBER MCWB
100/104															
95/99		0	0	0	70										
90/94		3	0	3	73		1	0	1	74					
85/89		17	4	21	71		8	2	10	73		0		0	63
80/84	0	42	15	57	69		17	5	22	71		1	0	1	62
75/79	4	56	32	92	67	3	29	14	46	68		8	1	9	64
70/74	24	62	49	135	65	13	44	28	85	64		16	3	19	61
65/69	52	42	62	156	62	28	45	37	110	61	3	27	10	40	59
60/64	63	21	45	129	58	34	38	40	112	57	11	36	22	69	56
55/59	48	5	25	78	54	43	33	44	120	53	23	40	35	98	52
50/54	34	1	10	45	50	45	19	36	100	49	37	46	49	132	47
45/49	16		4	20	46	36	6	20	62	45	43	36	46	125	43
40/44	6		1	7	42	23	1	9	33	40	50	25	41	116	39
35/39	1			1	36	11		4	15	35	41	11	26	78	35
30/34						4		0	4	31	27	2	10	39	30
25/29						0			0	27	9	0	3	12	26
20/24											3		1	4	21
15/19											1			1	18

GRIFFISS AFB/ROME NEW YORK

Temperature Range	NOVEMBER Obsn Hour Gp 01 to 08	NOVEMBER Obsn Hour Gp 09 to 16	NOVEMBER Obsn Hour Gp 17 to 24	NOVEMBER Total Obsn	NOVEMBER MCWB	DECEMBER Obsn Hour Gp 01 to 08	DECEMBER Obsn Hour Gp 09 to 16	DECEMBER Obsn Hour Gp 17 to 24	DECEMBER Total Obsn	DECEMBER MCWB	JANUARY Obsn Hour Gp 01 to 08	JANUARY Obsn Hour Gp 09 to 16	JANUARY Obsn Hour Gp 17 to 24	JANUARY Total Obsn	JANUARY MCWB
100/104															
95/99															
90/94															
85/89															
80/84															
75/79		0		0	67										
70/74		0		0	60		0		0	60					
65/69	1	2	1	4	59		0	0	0	58		0		0	54
60/64	2	6	3	11	55		1	0	1	55					
55/59	5	15	7	27	51	1	3	2	6	52	0	0	0	0	53
50/54	14	30	19	63	47	3	4	2	9	47	1	1	1	3	49
45/49	30	42	36	108	43	4	5	5	14	43	0	2	0	2	42
40/44	37	46	39	122	38	9	18	15	42	38	4	8	5	17	38
35/39	45	45	44	134	34	25	37	28	90	34	18	24	20	62	33
30/34	48	33	47	128	30	44	44	50	138	30	30	40	36	106	30
25/29	33	14	28	75	25	41	39	37	117	25	29	37	36	102	25
20/24	15	5	9	29	21	34	39	39	112	20	31	36	34	101	20
15/19	7	1	3	11	16	28	24	28	80	16	32	34	34	100	15
10/14	2	0	2	4	12	20	17	18	55	11	30	27	28	85	11
5/9	1		0	1	8	14	8	12	34	6	22	18	24	64	6
0/4	0			0	3	10	4	7	21	2	17	10	15	42	1
-5/-1						9	2	4	15	-3	13	6	8	27	-4
-10/-6						4	1	1	6	-8	10	3	4	17	-8
-15/-11						2	0	0	2	-12	5	1	2	8	-13
-20/-16						0			0	-17	4	0	1	5	-18
-25/-21											2		0	2	-23
-30/-26											0			0	-27

Temperature Range	FEBRUARY Obsn Hour Gp 01 to 08	FEBRUARY Obsn Hour Gp 09 to 16	FEBRUARY Obsn Hour Gp 17 to 24	FEBRUARY Total Obsn	FEBRUARY MCWB	MARCH Obsn Hour Gp 01 to 08	MARCH Obsn Hour Gp 09 to 16	MARCH Obsn Hour Gp 17 to 24	MARCH Total Obsn	MARCH MCWB	APRIL Obsn Hour Gp 01 to 08	APRIL Obsn Hour Gp 09 to 16	APRIL Obsn Hour Gp 17 to 24	APRIL Total Obsn	APRIL MCWB	ANNUAL TOTAL Obsn Hour Gp 01 to 08	ANNUAL TOTAL Obsn Hour Gp 09 to 16	ANNUAL TOTAL Obsn Hour Gp 17 to 24	ANNUAL TOTAL Total Obsn	ANNUAL TOTAL MCWB
100/104																	0		0	72
95/99																	0	0	0	72
90/94																	13	2	15	73
85/89												1	0	1	64		68	20	88	71
80/84												2	1	3	63	0	148	58	206	68
75/79							0	0	0	58		5	2	7	61	15	226	119	360	66
70/74							1	0	1	55	0	8	3	11	58	82	264	194	540	64
65/69							1	0	1	53	1	12	8	21	55	195	244	251	690	61
60/64							2	1	3	50	5	21	13	39	52	254	211	239	704	57
55/59						0	4	2	6	47	9	29	23	61	48	255	191	234	680	52
50/54	0	1	0	1	46	1	9	3	13	44	19	33	30	82	45	265	184	222	671	48
45/49	2	3	3	8	43	4	15	10	29	41	26	36	32	94	41	247	168	203	618	43
40/44	4	10	6	20	38	10	30	23	63	37	37	42	42	121	38	235	190	206	631	38
35/39	15	27	23	65	34	30	54	50	134	33	48	34	43	125	34	269	235	250	754	34
30/34	31	40	35	106	30	61	60	65	186	30	50	13	31	94	30	311	233	277	821	30
25/29	29	39	36	104	25	48	34	42	124	25	30	3	10	43	25	222	166	192	580	25
20/24	30	33	35	98	20	36	21	27	84	20	11	0	2	13	21	160	134	147	441	20
15/19	26	27	31	84	15	24	9	15	48	16	2	0	0	2	16	120	95	111	326	16
10/14	25	21	22	68	11	18	5	6	29	11	1		0	1	11	96	70	76	242	11
5/9	23	12	17	52	6	10	1	3	14	6	0			0	7	70	39	56	165	6
0/4	16	7	9	32	1	4	1	1	6	1	0			0	2	47	22	32	101	1
-5/-1	12	3	3	18	-4	2		0	2	-3						36	11	15	62	-4
-10/-6	6	1	2	9	-8	1			1	-8						21	5	7	33	-8
-15/-11	3	0	1	4	-13											10	1	3	14	-13
-20/-16	1	0		1	-18											5	0	1	6	-18
-25/-21	0			0	-22											2		0	2	-23
-30/-26																0			0	-27

NEWBURGH/STEWART APRT NEW YORK

LAT 41 30N LONG 74 06W ELEV 471 FT

MEAN FREQUENCY OF OCCURRENCE OF DRY BULB TEMPERATURE (DEGREES F) WITH MEAN COINCIDENT WET BULB TEMPERATURE (DEGREES F) FOR EACH DRY BULB TEMPERATURE RANGE

Temperature Range	MAY Obsn Hour Gp 01 to 08	MAY 09 to 16	MAY 17 to 24	MAY Total Obsn	MAY MCWB	JUNE Obsn Hour Gp 01 to 08	JUNE 09 to 16	JUNE 17 to 24	JUNE Total Obsn	JUNE MCWB	JULY Obsn Hour Gp 01 to 08	JULY 09 to 16	JULY 17 to 24	JULY Total Obsn	JULY MCWB
100/104												0		0	75
95/99							1	0	1	76		3	1	4	74
90/94		0		0	71		8	2	10	73		11	3	14	74
85/89		7	1	8	70		26	7	33	70		39	11	50	72
80/84		13	4	17	67	1	39	18	58	68	2	64	32	98	69
75/79	1	22	10	33	63	6	46	35	87	65	14	64	50	128	67
70/74	4	38	21	63	60	28	46	49	123	64	59	42	69	170	66
65/69	16	41	34	91	57	51	37	50	138	61	78	19	51	148	63
60/64	27	49	42	118	54	57	23	40	120	57	53	5	23	81	58
55/59	40	38	47	125	51	55	13	27	95	53	29	0	6	35	54
50/54	55	22	44	121	47	28	1	10	39	49	11		1	12	50
45/49	53	13	29	95	43	10		2	12	45	1			1	46
40/44	36	4	13	53	39	3		0	3	41	0			0	44
35/39	14	0	3	17	35	0			0	36					
30/34	2		0	2	31										
25/29	0			0	27										
20/24															

Temperature Range	AUGUST Obsn Hour Gp 01 to 08	AUGUST 09 to 16	AUGUST 17 to 24	AUGUST Total Obsn	AUGUST MCWB	SEPTEMBER Obsn Hour Gp 01 to 08	SEPTEMBER 09 to 16	SEPTEMBER 17 to 24	SEPTEMBER Total Obsn	SEPTEMBER MCWB	OCTOBER Obsn Hour Gp 01 to 08	OCTOBER 09 to 16	OCTOBER 17 to 24	OCTOBER Total Obsn	OCTOBER MCWB
100/104															
95/99		1		1	77										
90/94		6	1	7	75		2	0	2	72					
85/89		26	7	33	72		10	1	11	72		1		1	70
80/84	0	54	21	75	69		25	8	33	70		5	0	5	67
75/79	9	67	46	122	67	2	36	21	59	67		12	3	15	64
70/74	43	52	67	162	65	19	46	35	100	64	2	18	9	29	62
65/69	76	31	59	166	62	29	47	40	116	61	6	34	16	56	59
60/64	64	9	30	103	58	48	40	50	138	57	18	44	34	96	56
55/59	35	1	13	49	54	53	24	42	119	53	31	53	44	128	51
50/54	17	0	4	21	50	43	9	26	78	49	42	38	48	128	47
45/49	5		0	5	45	26	1	12	39	44	49	26	42	117	43
40/44	1		0	1	39	15	0	3	18	40	47	12	32	91	39
35/39	0			0	36	4		1	5	36	31	3	14	48	34
30/34						2		0	2	32	18	1	5	24	30
25/29						0			0	28	4		1	5	25
20/24											0		0	0	21

NEWBURGH/STEWART APRT NEW YORK

Temperature Range	NOVEMBER Obsn Hour Gp 01 to 08	NOVEMBER Obsn Hour Gp 09 to 16	NOVEMBER Obsn Hour Gp 17 to 24	NOVEMBER Total Obsn	NOVEMBER MCWB	DECEMBER Obsn Hour Gp 01 to 08	DECEMBER Obsn Hour Gp 09 to 16	DECEMBER Obsn Hour Gp 17 to 24	DECEMBER Total Obsn	DECEMBER MCWB	JANUARY Obsn Hour Gp 01 to 08	JANUARY Obsn Hour Gp 09 to 16	JANUARY Obsn Hour Gp 17 to 24	JANUARY Total Obsn	JANUARY MCWB
100/104															
95/99															
90/94															
85/89															
80/84															
75/79															
70/74		2	0	2	58										
65/69	1	6	3	10	60		0	0	0	61					
60/64	4	12	5	21	55	0	1	1	2	57	0	0	0	0	58
55/59	10	28	14	52	51	1	3	3	7	53	1	1	1	3	53
50/54	18	33	27	78	47	3	8	3	14	48	1	2	1	4	48
45/49	30	44	36	110	42	4	14	7	25	42	2	6	2	10	43
40/44	35	49	41	125	38	16	27	18	61	38	7	18	9	34	38
35/39	45	37	51	133	33	27	46	39	112	33	21	41	32	94	33
30/34	51	22	40	113	29	46	56	58	160	29	39	58	51	148	29
25/29	31	5	15	51	25	49	39	42	130	25	38	40	41	119	24
20/24	11	2	5	18	20	35	25	32	92	20	38	32	42	112	20
15/19	4	0	1	5	16	27	16	23	66	15	34	24	30	88	15
10/14	0			0	12	19	9	15	43	11	29	16	21	66	11
5/9						14	3	5	22	6	20	8	11	39	6
0/4						5	1	1	7	2	9	3	5	17	1
-5/-1						1		0	1	-3	5	1	2	8	-3
-10/-6						0			0	-6	3	0	1	4	-9
-15/-11											1			1	-13
-20/-16											0			0	-17

Temperature Range	FEBRUARY Obsn Hour Gp 01 to 08	FEBRUARY Obsn Hour Gp 09 to 16	FEBRUARY Obsn Hour Gp 17 to 24	FEBRUARY Total Obsn	FEBRUARY MCWB	MARCH Obsn Hour Gp 01 to 08	MARCH Obsn Hour Gp 09 to 16	MARCH Obsn Hour Gp 17 to 24	MARCH Total Obsn	MARCH MCWB	APRIL Obsn Hour Gp 01 to 08	APRIL Obsn Hour Gp 09 to 16	APRIL Obsn Hour Gp 17 to 24	APRIL Total Obsn	APRIL MCWB	ANNUAL TOTAL Obsn Hour Gp 01 to 08	ANNUAL TOTAL Obsn Hour Gp 09 to 16	ANNUAL TOTAL Obsn Hour Gp 17 to 24	ANNUAL TOTAL Total Obsn	ANNUAL TOTAL MCWB
100/104																	0		0	75
95/99																	5	1	6	75
90/94																	27	6	33	74
85/89												1	0	1	64		110	27	137	71
80/84												4	1	5	63	3	204	84	291	69
75/79		0		0	60		0	0	0	56		9	3	12	60	32	256	168	456	66
70/74		0		0	60		2	0	2	56	0	11	6	17	58	155	257	256	668	64
65/69		0		0	54		3	1	4	53	2	18	10	30	55	259	236	264	759	61
60/64		0	0	0	52	0	5	2	7	51	7	28	19	54	52	278	216	246	740	56
55/59	0	3	1	4	50	1	9	6	16	49	13	38	31	82	48	269	211	235	715	52
50/54	1	5	3	9	47	4	21	10	35	44	27	38	40	105	45	250	177	217	644	47
45/49	2	10	5	17	42	7	35	21	63	41	42	44	44	130	41	231	193	200	624	42
40/44	7	23	14	44	37	18	50	42	110	37	50	31	43	124	38	235	214	215	664	38
35/39	25	46	38	109	33	52	50	64	166	33	52	15	29	96	34	271	238	271	780	33
30/34	38	44	49	131	29	69	42	53	164	30	33	2	13	48	29	298	225	269	792	29
25/29	38	35	40	113	25	45	19	28	92	25	10	1	1	12	25	215	139	168	522	25
20/24	34	23	30	87	20	28	8	12	48	20	2		0	2	20	148	90	121	359	20
15/19	30	16	20	66	15	13	2	6	21	15	0		0	0	15	108	58	80	246	15
10/14	20	10	13	43	11	8	2	2	12	11						76	37	51	164	11
5/9	14	5	9	28	6	2	0	0	2	6						50	16	25	91	6
0/4	9	2	3	14	1	1		0	1	2						24	6	9	39	1
-5/-1	3	0	1	4	-3	0			0	-4						9	1	3	13	-3
-10/-6	2	0	0	2	-8	0			0	-8						5	0	1	6	-8
-15/-11	1	0	0	1	-13											2	0	0	2	-13
-20/-16	1			1	-18											1			1	-18

NIAGARA FALLS IAP NEW YORK

LAT 43 06N LONG 78 57W ELEV 590 FT

MEAN FREQUENCY OF OCCURRENCE OF DRY BULB TEMPERATURE (DEGREES F) WITH MEAN COINCIDENT WET BULB TEMPERATURE (DEGREES F) FOR EACH DRY BULB TEMPERATURE RANGE

Temperature Range	MAY Obsn Hour Gp 01 to 08	MAY 09 to 16	MAY 17 to 24	MAY Total Obsn	MAY MCWB	JUNE Obsn Hour Gp 01 to 08	JUNE 09 to 16	JUNE 17 to 24	JUNE Total Obsn	JUNE MCWB	JULY Obsn Hour Gp 01 to 08	JULY 09 to 16	JULY 17 to 24	JULY Total Obsn	JULY MCWB
95/99															
90/94							3	0	3	77		7	1	8	74
85/89		1		1	70		17	3	20	72		35	9	44	72
80/84		6	2	8	68	1	36	13	50	69	2	62	26	90	70
75/79	0	22	5	27	66	8	47	23	78	67	14	67	46	127	67
70/74	3	34	11	48	62	22	55	46	123	64	52	47	66	165	65
65/69	13	38	27	78	59	46	42	56	144	61	74	23	59	156	62
60/64	23	42	34	99	56	59	24	48	131	57	61	7	31	99	58
55/59	35	35	42	112	52	46	12	31	89	54	33	0	9	42	55
50/54	43	36	45	124	48	41	5	15	61	49	12		1	13	51
45/49	55	23	47	125	44	15	1	5	21	45	1			1	47
40/44	46	10	27	83	40	2		0	2	41					
35/39	25	2	8	35	35	0			0	37					
30/34	7		1	8	31										
25/29															
20/24															

Temperature Range	AUGUST Obsn Hour Gp 01 to 08	AUGUST 09 to 16	AUGUST 17 to 24	AUGUST Total Obsn	AUGUST MCWB	SEPTEMBER Obsn Hour Gp 01 to 08	SEPTEMBER 09 to 16	SEPTEMBER 17 to 24	SEPTEMBER Total Obsn	SEPTEMBER MCWB	OCTOBER Obsn Hour Gp 01 to 08	OCTOBER 09 to 16	OCTOBER 17 to 24	OCTOBER Total Obsn	OCTOBER MCWB
95/99							1		1	76					
90/94		5	0	5	73		3	0	3	76					
85/89		19	3	22	73	0	9	2	11	73					
80/84	1	49	15	65	70	0	17	5	22	70		1		1	66
75/79	14	68	41	123	68	3	29	15	47	67		7	1	8	66
70/74	39	62	66	167	65	22	40	27	89	65	1	17	3	21	63
65/69	72	31	65	168	63	31	52	37	120	61	11	31	15	57	60
60/64	55	12	38	105	58	35	44	44	123	57	16	44	26	86	56
55/59	47	3	18	68	54	47	32	50	129	53	24	42	34	100	52
50/54	16		3	19	50	45	12	36	93	49	43	47	50	140	48
45/49	5		0	5	46	32	2	19	53	44	51	38	56	145	44
40/44						18	0	5	23	40	48	15	38	101	40
35/39						5		1	6	36	35	7	21	63	35
30/34						1			1	31	17	1	4	22	31
25/29											2		1	3	26
20/24											0			0	22

NIAGARA FALLS IAP NEW YORK

Temperature Range	NOVEMBER Obsn Hour Gp 01 to 08	NOVEMBER 09 to 16	NOVEMBER 17 to 24	NOVEMBER Total Obsn	NOVEMBER MCWB	DECEMBER Obsn Hour Gp 01 to 08	DECEMBER 09 to 16	DECEMBER 17 to 24	DECEMBER Total Obsn	DECEMBER MCWB	JANUARY Obsn Hour Gp 01 to 08	JANUARY 09 to 16	JANUARY 17 to 24	JANUARY Total Obsn	JANUARY MCWB
95/99															
90/94															
85/89															
80/84															
75/79															
70/74		2		2	64										
65/69	0	5	2	7	58										
60/64	4	13	5	22	56		1		1	56					
55/59	10	21	12	43	53		5	1	6	52		0	0	0	50
50/54	18	26	26	70	48	4	5	4	13	48	2	2	2	6	49
45/49	28	34	34	96	43	6	8	10	24	44	4	6	3	13	44
40/44	41	45	42	128	39	20	29	19	68	39	6	7	7	20	39
35/39	52	43	48	143	34	37	49	46	132	35	16	24	24	64	34
30/34	48	35	40	123	30	62	65	63	190	30	45	51	46	142	31
25/29	26	8	21	55	26	47	34	42	123	25	40	58	50	148	25
20/24	8	6	6	20	20	28	25	25	78	20	42	46	38	126	21
15/19	3	1	3	7	16	21	19	21	61	16	39	24	33	96	16
10/14	2	0	1	3	12	15	7	14	36	11	28	20	28	76	11
5/9	0			0	6	7	2	2	11	7	19	7	12	38	7
0/4						1		1	2	3	6	2	2	10	2
-5/-1						0		0	0	-2	1	0	1	2	-3
-10/-6												0	1	1	-8
-15/-11											1	0		1	-13
-20/-16											0			0	-16

Temperature Range	FEBRUARY Obsn Hour Gp 01 to 08	FEBRUARY 09 to 16	FEBRUARY 17 to 24	FEBRUARY Total Obsn	FEBRUARY MCWB	MARCH Obsn Hour Gp 01 to 08	MARCH 09 to 16	MARCH 17 to 24	MARCH Total Obsn	MARCH MCWB	APRIL Obsn Hour Gp 01 to 08	APRIL 09 to 16	APRIL 17 to 24	APRIL Total Obsn	APRIL MCWB
95/99															
90/94															
85/89															
80/84												1	0	1	68
75/79												4	0	4	65
70/74							0		0	54		9	3	12	61
65/69							1	0	1	56	1	17	6	24	58
60/64		1	0	1	53	0	3	1	4	54	5	26	16	47	54
55/59	0	1	0	1	50	2	4	4	10	50	13	38	24	75	51
50/54	1	4	4	9	47	2	12	3	17	46	22	35	34	91	48
45/49	3	7	2	12	42	5	23	11	39	42	38	39	44	121	43
40/44	7	14	10	31	38	13	36	22	71	38	44	35	45	124	39
35/39	18	33	27	78	34	32	56	49	137	34	59	26	37	122	35
30/34	52	64	58	174	30	78	53	72	203	30	42	8	24	74	30
25/29	44	43	47	134	25	54	41	47	142	25	14	1	5	20	26
20/24	37	26	33	96	21	35	13	29	77	21	2	1	2	5	20
15/19	23	11	15	49	16	18	5	9	32	16	2	0	0	2	14
10/14	20	12	17	49	11	6	1	1	8	11	0			0	11
5/9	12	4	6	22	7	1	0	0	1	8					
0/4	5	3	3	11	2										
-5/-1	2	0	0	2	-2										
-10/-6															
-15/-11															
-20/-16															

Temperature Range	ANNUAL TOTAL Obsn Hour Gp 01 to 08	ANNUAL TOTAL 09 to 16	ANNUAL TOTAL 17 to 24	ANNUAL TOTAL Total Obsn	ANNUAL TOTAL MCWB
95/99		1		1	76
90/94		18	1	19	75
85/89	0	81	17	98	72
80/84	4	172	61	237	70
75/79	39	244	131	414	67
70/74	139	266	222	627	65
65/69	248	240	267	755	61
60/64	258	217	243	718	57
55/59	257	193	225	675	53
50/54	249	184	223	656	48
45/49	243	181	231	655	44
40/44	245	191	215	651	39
35/39	279	240	261	780	35
30/34	352	277	308	937	30
25/29	227	185	213	625	25
20/24	152	117	133	402	21
15/19	106	60	81	247	16
10/14	71	40	61	172	11
5/9	39	13	20	72	7
0/4	12	5	6	23	2
-5/-1	3	0	1	4	-2
-10/-6		0	1	1	-8
-15/-11	1	0		1	-13
-20/-16	0			0	-16

PLATTSBURG AFB NEW YORK

LAT 44 39N LONG 73 28W ELEV 235 FT

MEAN FREQUENCY OF OCCURRENCE OF DRY BULB TEMPERATURE (DEGREES F) WITH MEAN COINCIDENT WET BULB TEMPERATURE (DEGREES F) FOR EACH DRY BULB TEMPERATURE RANGE

Temperature Range	MAY Obsn Hour Gp 01 to 08	MAY 09 to 16	MAY 17 to 24	MAY Total Obsn	MAY MCWB	JUNE Obsn Hour Gp 01 to 08	JUNE 09 to 16	JUNE 17 to 24	JUNE Total Obsn	JUNE MCWB	JULY Obsn Hour Gp 01 to 08	JULY 09 to 16	JULY 17 to 24	JULY Total Obsn	JULY MCWB
95/99		0		0	67		0		0	73		0		0	72
90/94		1	0	1	69		2	1	3	73		3	1	4	73
85/89		1	0	1	68		6	3	9	69		9	4	13	71
80/84		4	2	6	65	0	17	9	26	68	1	34	16	51	69
75/79	0	10	6	16	63	4	36	22	62	65	8	67	38	113	66
70/74	2	18	12	32	59	12	54	38	104	62	25	68	56	149	64
65/69	5	34	22	61	56	33	54	51	138	60	68	49	66	183	61
60/64	16	42	35	93	53	56	42	51	149	56	75	15	44	134	58
55/59	35	52	43	130	50	61	22	41	124	53	48	2	19	69	53
50/54	49	48	52	149	46	44	5	19	68	49	18		4	22	49
45/49	55	26	39	120	42	20	1	5	26	44	5		0	5	45
40/44	42	9	23	74	38	8		1	9	40	0			0	41
35/39	30	3	10	43	34	2			2	37					
30/34	11	1	3	15	30										
25/29	2		0	2	25										
20/24	0			0	23										
15/19															

Temperature Range	AUGUST Obsn Hour Gp 01 to 08	AUGUST 09 to 16	AUGUST 17 to 24	AUGUST Total Obsn	AUGUST MCWB	SEPTEMBER Obsn Hour Gp 01 to 08	SEPTEMBER 09 to 16	SEPTEMBER 17 to 24	SEPTEMBER Total Obsn	SEPTEMBER MCWB	OCTOBER Obsn Hour Gp 01 to 08	OCTOBER 09 to 16	OCTOBER 17 to 24	OCTOBER Total Obsn	OCTOBER MCWB
95/99		0		0	74										
90/94		1	0	1	74		0		0	74					
85/89		5	1	6	71		3	0	3	73		0		0	64
80/84	0	24	7	31	69		9	3	12	71		0	0	0	65
75/79	2	56	28	86	67	1	21	11	33	68		2	1	3	63
70/74	22	74	53	149	64	10	37	24	71	64	0	7	2	9	61
65/69	55	53	61	169	61	24	52	35	111	61	1	17	7	25	58
60/64	63	27	52	142	58	32	51	46	129	56	11	36	21	68	56
55/59	53	7	32	92	53	45	38	45	128	53	25	50	36	111	52
50/54	38	1	11	50	49	44	23	37	104	48	39	53	52	144	47
45/49	12	0	2	14	45	40	6	23	69	44	49	39	45	133	43
40/44	2		0	2	41	25	0	12	37	40	43	27	38	108	38
35/39	0			0	36	13		4	17	36	39	13	26	78	34
30/34						3		1	4	31	25	2	14	41	30
25/29						0			0	28	13	1	5	19	25
20/24											3		1	4	22
15/19											0			0	18

PLATTSBURG AFB NEW YORK

Temperature Range	NOVEMBER Obsn Hour Gp 01 to 08	09 to 16	17 to 24	Total Obsn	MCWB	DECEMBER Obsn Hour Gp 01 to 08	09 to 16	17 to 24	Total Obsn	MCWB	JANUARY Obsn Hour Gp 01 to 08	09 to 16	17 to 24	Total Obsn	MCWB	FEBRUARY Obsn Hour Gp 01 to 08	09 to 16	17 to 24	Total Obsn	MCWB	MARCH Obsn Hour Gp 01 to 08	09 to 16	17 to 24	Total Obsn	MCWB	APRIL Obsn Hour Gp 01 to 08	09 to 16	17 to 24	Total Obsn	MCWB	ANNUAL TOTAL Obsn Hour Gp 01 to 08	09 to 16	17 to 24	Total Obsn	MCWB
95/99																																0		0	72
90/94																																7	2	9	73
85/89																											0	0	0	63		24	8	32	70
80/84																											1	0	1	61	1	89	37	127	69
75/79																											1	1	2	59	15	193	107	315	66
70/74		0		0	62																	0		0	54	0	3	1	4	58	71	261	186	518	63
65/69	0	0	0	0	57																	0	0	0	53	1	8	5	14	54	187	267	247	701	60
60/64	2	3	2	7	55			0	0	55												0	1	1	49	1	12	8	21	51	256	228	260	744	56
55/59	4	11	5	20	51	0	1	1	2	52	0			0	51							1	1	2	47	4	24	17	45	47	275	208	240	723	52
50/54	13	26	19	58	48	2	2	2	6	48	0	0	0	0	45		0		0	45	0	6	2	8	43	12	36	26	74	44	259	200	224	683	47
45/49	25	38	26	89	43	4	7	4	15	42	1	2	1	4	42	0	1	0	1	42	2	13	7	22	40	23	49	41	113	41	236	182	193	611	43
40/44	36	47	42	125	38	10	16	12	38	38	3	6	2	11	38	3	7	6	16	38	8	34	22	64	37	46	51	48	145	37	226	197	206	629	38
35/39	35	47	40	122	34	22	30	24	76	34	16	23	19	58	34	10	18	13	41	34	30	50	47	127	33	61	37	53	151	33	258	221	236	715	34
30/34	51	42	54	147	29	30	35	37	102	30	20	28	27	75	29	23	30	28	81	29	47	53	57	157	29	54	15	28	97	29	264	206	249	719	29
25/29	37	19	32	88	25	33	43	38	114	25	22	34	30	86	25	24	35	32	91	25	54	42	46	142	24	24	3	9	36	25	209	177	192	578	25
20/24	23	5	12	40	20	37	37	35	109	20	28	33	34	95	20	24	38	34	96	20	40	27	33	100	20	9	1	2	12	20	164	141	151	456	20
15/19	10	1	6	17	16	31	28	31	90	16	27	34	27	88	15	30	33	35	98	15	29	12	19	60	15	4		0	4	15	131	108	118	357	15
10/14	4	1	1	6	11	27	22	26	75	11	31	32	30	93	11	28	23	24	75	11	19	6	9	34	11	0		0	0	10	109	84	90	283	11
5/9	1	0	1	2	6	23	16	21	60	6	29	23	25	77	6	26	18	21	65	6	9	2	4	15	6						88	59	72	219	6
0/4	0			0	2	14	5	11	30	1	23	17	23	63	1	18	12	14	44	1	7	1	1	9	1						62	35	49	146	1
-5/-1						9	3	4	16	-3	20	10	15	45	-4	15	6	8	29	-4	1		0	1	-3						45	19	27	91	-3
-10/-6						4	1	3	8	-8	15	4	8	27	-8	14	2	6	22	-8	1			1	-8						34	7	17	58	-8
-15/-11						2	0	1	3	-13	7	2	4	13	-13	5	0	2	7	-13											14	2	7	23	-13
-20/-16						1		0	1	-18	3	0	2	5	-18	2	0	1	3	-18											6	0	3	9	-18
-25/-21						0			0	-21	2	0	0	2	-23	1			1	-22											3	0	0	3	-22
-30/-26											1			1	-27																1			1	-27

SUFFOLK CO/WESTHAMPTON BCH NEW YORK

LAT 40 51N LONG 72 38W ELEV 67 FT

MEAN FREQUENCY OF OCCURRENCE OF DRY BULB TEMPERATURE (DEGREES F) WITH MEAN COINCIDENT WET BULB TEMPERATURE (DEGREES F) FOR EACH DRY BULB TEMPERATURE RANGE

Temperature Range	MAY Obsn Hour Gp 01 to 08	MAY 09 to 16	MAY 17 to 24	MAY Total Obsn	MAY MCWB	JUNE Obsn Hour Gp 01 to 08	JUNE 09 to 16	JUNE 17 to 24	JUNE Total Obsn	JUNE MCWB	JULY Obsn Hour Gp 01 to 08	JULY 09 to 16	JULY 17 to 24	JULY Total Obsn	JULY MCWB
95/99												1		1	71
90/94							3	0	3	71		4	0	4	73
85/89		1	0	1	67	0	9	1	10	70	1	13	1	15	74
80/84	0	4	0	4	66	2	16	3	21	68	3	39	7	49	71
75/79	0	7	2	9	63	5	41	11	57	67	14	96	36	146	69
70/74	2	19	4	25	60	18	64	33	115	64	77	71	99	247	67
65/69	9	45	14	68	58	54	60	62	176	62	86	21	73	180	64
60/64	24	64	39	127	55	77	37	75	189	59	46	4	25	75	59
55/59	54	60	69	183	52	53	11	43	107	55	16	0	6	22	55
50/54	66	34	68	168	48	23	0	9	32	50	5		1	6	50
45/49	54	12	39	105	44	7		1	8	45	1			1	45
40/44	28	3	12	43	40	1		0	1	42					
35/39	9	0	2	11	35	1		0	1	36					
30/34	2			2	31	0			0	32					
25/29	0			0	25										
20/24															
15/19															

Temperature Range	AUGUST Obsn Hour Gp 01 to 08	AUGUST 09 to 16	AUGUST 17 to 24	AUGUST Total Obsn	AUGUST MCWB	SEPTEMBER Obsn Hour Gp 01 to 08	SEPTEMBER 09 to 16	SEPTEMBER 17 to 24	SEPTEMBER Total Obsn	SEPTEMBER MCWB	OCTOBER Obsn Hour Gp 01 to 08	OCTOBER 09 to 16	OCTOBER 17 to 24	OCTOBER Total Obsn	OCTOBER MCWB
95/99															
90/94		1	0	1	77		0		0	71					
85/89	0	7	0	7	74		2	0	2	72					
80/84	1	41	3	45	71		11	1	12	71		1		1	68
75/79	13	86	35	134	70	3	37	9	49	69		5	0	5	67
70/74	73	80	95	248	67	25	68	36	129	66	2	18	3	23	64
65/69	81	27	72	180	64	53	63	61	177	62	10	44	16	70	62
60/64	44	5	31	80	59	55	40	60	155	58	32	70	46	148	57
55/59	23	0	9	32	54	47	18	40	105	53	48	55	58	161	52
50/54	10		2	12	50	34	2	22	58	49	46	35	49	130	48
45/49	3		1	4	45	16	0	8	24	44	43	15	36	94	43
40/44	0			0	41	5		2	7	40	35	4	24	63	39
35/39	0			0	38	2		1	3	36	23	1	11	35	35
30/34											6	0	4	10	30
25/29											1		1	2	26
20/24											0		0	0	21
15/19											0		0	0	17

SUFFOLK CO/WESTHAMPTON BCH NEW YORK

Temperature Range	NOVEMBER Obsn Hour Gp 01 to 08	NOVEMBER 09 to 16	NOVEMBER 17 to 24	NOVEMBER Total Obsn	NOVEMBER MCWB	DECEMBER Obsn Hour Gp 01 to 08	DECEMBER 09 to 16	DECEMBER 17 to 24	DECEMBER Total Obsn	DECEMBER MCWB	JANUARY Obsn Hour Gp 01 to 08	JANUARY 09 to 16	JANUARY 17 to 24	JANUARY Total Obsn	JANUARY MCWB	FEBRUARY Obsn Hour Gp 01 to 08	FEBRUARY 09 to 16	FEBRUARY 17 to 24	FEBRUARY Total Obsn	FEBRUARY MCWB	MARCH Obsn Hour Gp 01 to 08	MARCH 09 to 16	MARCH 17 to 24	MARCH Total Obsn	MARCH MCWB	APRIL Obsn Hour Gp 01 to 08	APRIL 09 to 16	APRIL 17 to 24	APRIL Total Obsn	APRIL MCWB	ANNUAL TOTAL Obsn Hour Gp 01 to 08	ANNUAL TOTAL 09 to 16	ANNUAL TOTAL 17 to 24	ANNUAL TOTAL Total Obsn	ANNUAL TOTAL MCWB
95/99																																1		1	71
90/94																																8	0	8	73
85/89																															1	32	2	35	72
80/84																											1	0	1	64	6	113	14	133	70
75/79																											2	0	2	61	35	274	93	402	69
70/74		1		1	61																					0	3	0	3	58	197	324	270	791	66
65/69	0	2	0	2	62							0		0	55							1	0	1	53	0	10	1	11	55	293	273	299	865	62
60/64	5	15	8	28	58		0		0	49		0		0	52							1	0	1	49	2	18	4	24	52	285	254	288	827	58
55/59	22	45	23	90	54	1	4	1	6	53	0	1	1	2	52		1		1	51	0	6	1	7	47	8	40	16	64	50	272	241	267	780	53
50/54	31	54	41	126	48	11	21	9	41	49	3	3	2	8	48	0	6	1	7	47	2	23	7	32	45	31	59	41	131	47	262	237	252	751	48
45/49	39	56	44	139	43	15	29	22	66	44	6	17	7	30	44	4	18	8	30	43	11	47	24	82	42	55	65	68	188	43	254	259	258	771	43
40/44	42	39	49	130	38	24	46	33	103	39	18	36	23	77	39	18	42	23	83	39	35	65	53	153	38	66	34	69	169	39	272	269	288	829	39
35/39	43	21	38	102	33	41	51	43	135	34	35	57	44	136	34	37	53	48	138	34	67	58	81	206	34	40	8	27	75	34	298	249	295	842	34
30/34	34	6	24	64	29	43	44	51	138	29	45	50	54	149	29	49	44	58	151	29	63	29	51	143	29	28	2	10	40	30	270	175	252	697	29
25/29	17	1	10	28	25	42	28	38	108	25	42	37	47	126	24	39	29	38	106	24	41	12	21	74	25	7	0	2	9	25	189	107	157	453	25
20/24	6	1	3	10	21	30	16	26	72	20	39	27	33	99	20	30	18	20	68	20	18	3	7	28	20	2		0	2	21	125	65	89	279	20
15/19	1		0	1	16	24	6	16	46	15	28	13	23	64	15	21	9	15	45	15	8	2	2	12	15	1		0	1	16	83	30	56	169	15
10/14	0			0	14	11	2	6	19	11	18	4	10	32	11	16	4	9	29	11	2	0	1	3	11						47	10	26	83	11
5/9						5	1	2	8	6	10	2	4	16	6	7	1	2	10	6	1		0	1	7						23	4	8	35	6
0/4						1	0	0	1	2	3	0	1	4	2	3	0	0	3	2	0			0	2						7	0	1	8	2
-5/-1											0		0	0	-2	1		0	1	-3	0			0	-1						1		0	1	-2
-10/-6																0			0	-9											0			0	-9
-15/-11											0			0	-12																0			0	-12

SYRACUSE/HANCOCK IAP NEW YORK

LAT 43 07N LONG 76·07W ELEV 410 FT

MEAN FREQUENCY OF OCCURRENCE OF DRY BULB TEMPERATURE (DEGREES F) WITH MEAN COINCIDENT WET BULB TEMPERATURE (DEGREES F) FOR EACH DRY BULB TEMPERATURE RANGE

Temperature Range	MAY Obsn Hour Gp 01 to 08	MAY 09 to 16	MAY 17 to 24	MAY Total Obsn	MAY MCWB	JUNE Obsn Hour Gp 01 to 08	JUNE 09 to 16	JUNE 17 to 24	JUNE Total Obsn	JUNE MCWB	JULY Obsn Hour Gp 01 to 08	JULY 09 to 16	JULY 17 to 24	JULY Total Obsn	JULY MCWB
95/99							1	0	1	76		1	0	1	72
90/94		0		0	72		4	1	5	74		10	2	12	73
85/89		5	1	6	69	0	22	7	29	71	0	34	9	43	71
80/84	0	15	4	19	66	2	35	17	54	68	3	59	27	89	69
75/79	1	26	11	38	64	8	48	31	87	65	17	61	49	127	66
70/74	7	32	22	61	60	30	48	46	124	63	47	48	64	159	65
65/69	18	41	32	91	57	44	39	48	131	60	71	24	54	149	62
60/64	30	37	36	103	55	49	25	42	116	57	62	9	32	103	58
55/59	40	36	39	115	51	52	14	32	98	53	37	1	10	48	54
50/54	45	32	43	120	47	37	5	12	54	49	11		1	12	50
45/49	50	19	37	106	43	15	0	4	19	45	1			1	46
40/44	35	5	15	55	39	2		0	2	41					
35/39	18	1	6	25	35	0			0	36					
30/34	5	0	0	5	31										
25/29	0			0	26										

Temperature Range	AUGUST Obsn Hour Gp 01 to 08	AUGUST 09 to 16	AUGUST 17 to 24	AUGUST Total Obsn	AUGUST MCWB	SEPTEMBER Obsn Hour Gp 01 to 08	SEPTEMBER 09 to 16	SEPTEMBER 17 to 24	SEPTEMBER Total Obsn	SEPTEMBER MCWB	OCTOBER Obsn Hour Gp 01 to 08	OCTOBER 09 to 16	OCTOBER 17 to 24	OCTOBER Total Obsn	OCTOBER MCWB
95/99		0		0	73		1		1	74					
90/94		6	1	7	72		4	0	4	74					
85/89	0	19	5	24	71	0	13	3	16	72		1		1	66
80/84	2	46	18	66	68	2	19	8	29	70		4	0	4	65
75/79	11	65	40	116	67	7	27	17	51	67		12	2	14	64
70/74	35	60	60	155	65	15	40	24	79	63	2	21	7	30	61
65/69	63	34	58	155	62	27	47	36	110	60	7	31	16	54	58
60/64	57	14	43	114	58	37	43	42	122	57	14	36	28	78	55
55/59	52	1	20	73	54	46	30	51	127	53	28	44	41	113	52
50/54	24	0	4	28	50	50	14	36	100	49	43	41	48	132	47
45/49	5			5	46	32	4	15	51	45	49	32	45	126	43
40/44	0			0	43	17	0	6	23	40	49	19	37	105	39
35/39						7		1	8	36	34	5	18	57	35
30/34						1			1	30	18	2	6	26	31
25/29						0			0	28	3	0		3	27

SYRACUSE/HANCOCK IAP NEW YORK

Temperature Range	NOVEMBER Obsn Hour Gp 01 to 08	NOVEMBER Obsn Hour Gp 09 to 16	NOVEMBER Obsn Hour Gp 17 to 24	NOVEMBER Total Obsn	NOVEMBER M C W B	DECEMBER Obsn Hour Gp 01 to 08	DECEMBER Obsn Hour Gp 09 to 16	DECEMBER Obsn Hour Gp 17 to 24	DECEMBER Total Obsn	DECEMBER M C W B	JANUARY Obsn Hour Gp 01 to 08	JANUARY Obsn Hour Gp 09 to 16	JANUARY Obsn Hour Gp 17 to 24	JANUARY Total Obsn	JANUARY M C W B
95/99															
90/94															
85/89															
80/84		0		0	67										
75/79		1		1	64										
70/74	0	2	1	3	60							0		0	59
65/69	1	5	3	9	58		0		0	59	0	0	0	0	58
60/64	5	12	6	23	54	0	2	1	3	55	1	0	1	2	56
55/59	8	21	9	38	51	2	3	3	8	52	1	3	2	6	52
50/54	22	32	25	79	47	3	7	4	14	47	2	2	2	6	48
45/49	29	38	39	106	43	8	11	10	29	42	4	5	3	12	43
40/44	40	43	40	123	38	14	22	19	55	38	10	13	9	32	38
35/39	41	37	42	120	34	30	36	30	96	34	21	31	28	80	34
30/34	52	32	47	131	30	53	50	51	154	30	37	42	39	118	30
25/29	27	12	20	59	26	36	40	40	116	25	33	41	38	112	25
20/24	10	4	5	19	21	33	32	32	97	21	36	40	40	116	21
15/19	3	1	3	7	16	32	20	29	81	16	31	29	34	94	16
10/14	2	0	0	2	12	17	13	15	45	11	32	22	27	81	11
5/9	0			0	7	9	6	8	23	7	20	12	15	47	6
0/4						7	3	3	13	2	14	5	6	25	2
-5/-1						4	2	2	8	-3	5	1	2	8	-3
-10/-6						1	0	0	1	-7	1	0	0	1	-8
-15/-11						0	0	0	0	-13	0	0	0	0	-13
-20/-16						0			0	-18	0	0		0	-18
-25/-21											0	0		0	-22

Temperature Range	FEBRUARY Obsn Hour Gp 01 to 08	FEBRUARY Obsn Hour Gp 09 to 16	FEBRUARY Obsn Hour Gp 17 to 24	FEBRUARY Total Obsn	FEBRUARY M C W B	MARCH Obsn Hour Gp 01 to 08	MARCH Obsn Hour Gp 09 to 16	MARCH Obsn Hour Gp 17 to 24	MARCH Total Obsn	MARCH M C W B	APRIL Obsn Hour Gp 01 to 08	APRIL Obsn Hour Gp 09 to 16	APRIL Obsn Hour Gp 17 to 24	APRIL Total Obsn	APRIL M C W B
95/99															
90/94															
85/89												1	0	1	64
80/84												3	1	4	64
75/79							0	0	0	54	0	5	2	7	62
70/74							1	0	1	54	1	11	4	16	58
65/69						0	2	1	3	52	3	17	9	29	55
60/64	0	1	1	2	55	1	3	1	5	52	8	22	17	47	53
55/59	0	2	1	3	50	2	6	3	11	49	15	31	23	69	49
50/54	2	3	2	7	46	4	13	8	25	45	20	36	33	89	46
45/49	3	5	5	13	42	6	21	13	40	41	38	40	42	120	42
40/44	8	15	10	33	38	14	36	26	76	38	46	37	46	129	38
35/39	22	39	28	89	34	37	49	51	137	34	51	25	35	111	34
30/34	38	46	47	131	30	62	53	60	175	30	40	10	21	71	30
25/29	39	39	43	121	25	51	32	42	125	25	12	2	4	18	25
20/24	32	26	31	89	21	31	19	23	73	20	4	1	1	6	20
15/19	23	20	23	66	16	20	8	14	42	16	1	0	1	2	16
10/14	21	14	16	51	11	12	4	5	21	11	0			0	11
5/9	16	8	12	36	6	5	1	1	7	6					
0/4	11	4	3	18	2	2	0	0	2	2					
-5/-1	5	2	2	9	-3	0	0	0	0	-3					
-10/-6	3	0	1	4	-9	0	0	0	0	-7					
-15/-11	1	0	0	1	-12	0			0	-14					
-20/-16	0			0	-16										
-25/-21															

Temperature Range	ANNUAL TOTAL Obsn Hour Gp 01 to 08	ANNUAL TOTAL Obsn Hour Gp 09 to 16	ANNUAL TOTAL Obsn Hour Gp 17 to 24	ANNUAL TOTAL Total Obsn	ANNUAL TOTAL M C W B
95/99		3	0	3	74
90/94		24	4	28	73
85/89	0	95	25	120	71
80/84	9	181	75	265	68
75/79	44	245	152	441	66
70/74	137	263	228	628	63
65/69	234	240	257	731	60
60/64	264	204	250	718	56
55/59	283	192	234	709	52
50/54	263	185	218	666	47
45/49	240	175	213	628	43
40/44	235	190	208	633	38
35/39	261	223	239	723	34
30/34	306	235	271	812	30
25/29	201	166	187	554	25
20/24	146	122	132	400	21
15/19	110	78	104	292	16
10/14	84	53	63	200	11
5/9	50	27	36	113	6
0/4	34	12	12	58	2
-5/-1	14	5	6	25	-3
-10/-6	5	0	1	6	-8
-15/-11	1	0	0	1	-13
-20/-16	0	0		0	-18
-25/-21	0	0		0	-22

CHERRY POINT MCAS NORTH CAROLINA

LAT 34 54N LONG 76 53W ELEV 29 FT

MEAN FREQUENCY OF OCCURRENCE OF DRY BULB TEMPERATURE (DEGREES F) WITH MEAN COINCIDENT WET BULB TEMPERATURE (DEGREES F) FOR EACH DRY BULB TEMPERATURE RANGE

Temperature Range	MAY Obsn Hour Gp 01 to 08	MAY 09 to 16	MAY 17 to 24	MAY Total Obsn	MAY MCWB	JUNE Obsn Hour Gp 01 to 08	JUNE 09 to 16	JUNE 17 to 24	JUNE Total Obsn	JUNE MCWB	JULY Obsn Hour Gp 01 to 08	JULY 09 to 16	JULY 17 to 24	JULY Total Obsn	JULY MCWB
100/104							0		0	78					
95/99		0		0	72		2	0	2	78		2	0	2	79
90/94		5		5	73		11	1	12	78		26	2	28	78
85/89		20	1	21	71	1	50	6	57	75	1	95	18	114	76
80/84	1	50	9	60	69	10	82	33	125	73	23	79	67	169	75
75/79	9	70	29	108	67	47	56	76	179	71	103	36	98	237	73
70/74	44	52	70	166	66	87	23	73	183	69	97	9	53	159	70
65/69	69	28	65	162	63	61	11	35	107	64	18	1	8	27	66
60/64	58	15	44	117	58	23	2	12	37	60	6		2	8	61
55/59	40	6	21	67	54	10	1	3	14	55	1		0	1	58
50/54	20	1	8	29	49	1		0	1	52					
45/49	6	1	1	8	45	0		0	0	47					
40/44	1		0	1	40	0			0	44					
35/39	1		0	1	34										
30/34	0			0	29										
25/29															

Temperature Range	AUGUST Obsn Hour Gp 01 to 08	AUGUST 09 to 16	AUGUST 17 to 24	AUGUST Total Obsn	AUGUST MCWB	SEPTEMBER Obsn Hour Gp 01 to 08	SEPTEMBER 09 to 16	SEPTEMBER 17 to 24	SEPTEMBER Total Obsn	SEPTEMBER MCWB	OCTOBER Obsn Hour Gp 01 to 08	OCTOBER 09 to 16	OCTOBER 17 to 24	OCTOBER Total Obsn	OCTOBER MCWB
100/104															
95/99		3	0	3	78		0		0	79					
90/94		24	2	26	78		5	0	5	76		0		0	73
85/89	0	82	15	97	76		39	3	42	75		3	0	3	73
80/84	19	81	58	158	75	3	79	22	104	73	0	20	1	21	71
75/79	91	43	97	231	73	34	60	68	162	71	5	50	13	68	69
70/74	100	15	64	179	70	84	35	76	195	68	21	62	45	128	66
65/69	34	1	12	47	65	65	15	45	125	64	49	56	60	165	62
60/64	5	0	1	6	60	33	5	18	56	59	58	32	53	143	58
55/59	0		0	0	57	14	1	6	21	55	40	16	40	96	53
50/54						6		3	9	50	35	6	20	61	49
45/49						1			1	46	22	2	11	35	44
40/44											11	0	4	15	39
35/39											5		1	6	35
30/34											1		0	1	31
25/29													0		27

CHERRY POINT MCAS NORTH CAROLINA

Temperature Range	NOVEMBER Obsn Hour Gp 01 to 08	09 to 16	17 to 24	Total Obsn	MCWB	DECEMBER Obsn Hour Gp 01 to 08	09 to 16	17 to 24	Total Obsn	MCWB	JANUARY Obsn Hour Gp 01 to 08	09 to 16	17 to 24	Total Obsn	MCWB
100/104															
95/99															
90/94															
85/89															
80/84		2		2	70		0		0	69					
75/79		13	1	14	67		3	0	3	67		1		1	65
70/74	3	30	7	40	64	0	13	1	14	64		7	0	7	62
65/69	14	44	24	82	61	10	20	10	40	61	3	15	5	23	60
60/64	23	49	38	110	57	15	26	22	63	58	8	20	15	43	57
55/59	39	41	45	125	52	17	38	26	81	52	14	27	21	62	52
50/54	40	31	47	118	48	21	42	30	93	47	14	34	22	70	47
45/49	41	18	37	96	43	27	37	43	107	43	27	36	40	103	43
40/44	41	8	26	75	39	39	35	42	116	38	43	42	48	133	39
35/39	25	3	10	38	34	41	19	33	93	34	40	32	39	111	34
30/34	11	1	4	16	30	42	10	25	77	30	43	22	36	101	29
25/29	3	0	1	4	25	22	4	11	37	25	36	9	16	61	25
20/24	0			0	19	10	2	5	17	21	13	2	6	21	20
15/19						4	0	0	4	17	6	1	1	8	16
10/14						0			0	12	1			1	11

Temperature Range	FEBRUARY Obsn Hour Gp 01 to 08	09 to 16	17 to 24	Total Obsn	MCWB	MARCH Obsn Hour Gp 01 to 08	09 to 16	17 to 24	Total Obsn	MCWB	APRIL Obsn Hour Gp 01 to 08	09 to 16	17 to 24	Total Obsn	MCWB	ANNUAL TOTAL Obsn Hour Gp 01 to 08	09 to 16	17 to 24	Total Obsn	MCWB
100/104																	0		0	78
95/99																	7	0	7	78
90/94												0	0	0	68		71	5	76	77
85/89							0		0	69		6	0	6	68	2	295	43	340	75
80/84		0		0	68		2		2	65		17	1	18	66	56	412	191	659	73
75/79		2	0	2	65		9	1	10	63	0	40	6	46	65	289	383	389	1061	71
70/74		9	0	9	62	1	18	3	22	61	6	43	23	72	62	443	316	415	1174	67
65/69	3	15	5	23	60	5	30	14	49	59	32	47	53	132	60	363	283	336	982	62
60/64	12	23	18	53	57	18	40	29	87	56	51	40	54	145	56	310	252	306	868	57
55/59	14	26	20	60	52	27	44	42	113	51	39	28	45	112	51	255	228	269	752	52
50/54	19	35	27	81	46	37	41	49	127	47	48	14	33	95	48	241	204	239	684	47
45/49	27	36	41	104	43	45	34	46	125	43	36	4	17	57	43	232	168	236	636	43
40/44	33	38	42	113	38	43	18	35	96	38	21	1	7	29	39	232	142	204	578	39
35/39	42	24	34	100	34	41	7	21	69	34	6	0	1	7	35	201	85	139	425	34
30/34	38	12	23	73	29	22	3	8	33	30	1		0	1	31	158	48	96	302	29
25/29	25	4	10	39	25	8	1	1	10	26						95	18	39	152	25
20/24	9	1	2	12	20	1			1	21						33	5	13	51	20
15/19	2	0	0	2	15											12	1	1	14	16
10/14	1			1	12											2			2	11

ELIZABETH CITY CGAS/MAP NORTH CAROLINA

LAT 36 16N LONG 76 11W ELEV 12 FT

MEAN FREQUENCY OF OCCURRENCE OF DRY BULB TEMPERATURE (DEGREES F) WITH MEAN COINCIDENT WET BULB TEMPERATURE (DEGREES F) FOR EACH DRY BULB TEMPERATURE RANGE

Temperature Range	MAY Obsn Hour Gp 01 to 08	MAY 09 to 16	MAY 17 to 24	MAY Total Obsn	MAY MCWB	JUNE Obsn Hour Gp 01 to 08	JUNE 09 to 16	JUNE 17 to 24	JUNE Total Obsn	JUNE MCWB	JULY Obsn Hour Gp 01 to 08	JULY 09 to 16	JULY 17 to 24	JULY Total Obsn	JULY MCWB
100/104												1	0	1	80
95/99		0		0	74		4	0	4	78		5	0	5	78
90/94		5	0	5	73	0	22	3	25	77	0	34	4	38	77
85/89		19	3	22	71	1	49	11	61	74	1	82	19	102	75
80/84	0	40	9	49	69	8	61	31	100	72	20	76	55	151	74
75/79	8	55	26	89	67	43	56	61	160	70	98	39	96	233	72
70/74	37	52	53	142	65	81	30	67	178	68	86	10	59	155	70
65/69	63	40	59	162	62	56	14	46	116	64	32	2	12	46	66
60/64	54	21	47	122	58	34	2	16	52	60	10	0	2	12	61
55/59	44	12	33	89	54	13		5	18	56	1			1	58
50/54	30	3	14	47	50	4		0	4	52					
45/49	9	0	3	12	45	0			0	49					
40/44	2		1	3	41										
35/39															
30/34															
25/29															

Temperature Range	AUGUST Obsn Hour Gp 01 to 08	AUGUST 09 to 16	AUGUST 17 to 24	AUGUST Total Obsn	AUGUST MCWB	SEPTEMBER Obsn Hour Gp 01 to 08	SEPTEMBER 09 to 16	SEPTEMBER 17 to 24	SEPTEMBER Total Obsn	SEPTEMBER MCWB	OCTOBER Obsn Hour Gp 01 to 08	OCTOBER 09 to 16	OCTOBER 17 to 24	OCTOBER Total Obsn	OCTOBER MCWB
100/104															
95/99		1		1	78		0		0	78		0		0	78
90/94		25	2	27	78		7	0	7	77		1		1	77
85/89	0	76	14	90	76	0	31	3	34	75		3	0	3	73
80/84	15	75	45	135	74	3	60	14	77	72	0	16	1	17	70
75/79	81	55	95	231	73	33	66	53	152	71	3	34	8	45	68
70/74	97	16	68	181	70	70	46	72	188	68	13	55	23	91	65
65/69	36	1	19	56	65	60	21	54	135	64	40	63	51	154	62
60/64	15		4	19	61	43	8	29	80	59	55	41	59	155	58
55/59	3		0	3	57	21	0	11	32	55	45	21	45	111	54
50/54	0		0	0	52	9	0	3	12	51	38	10	35	83	49
45/49						2		1	3	46	29	3	18	50	45
40/44						0			0	43	17	0	7	24	40
35/39											7	0	1	8	35
30/34											1		0	1	30
25/29											1			1	26

ELIZABETH CITY CGAS/MAP NORTH CAROLINA

Temperature Range	NOVEMBER Obsn Hour Gp 01 to 08	NOVEMBER 09 to 16	NOVEMBER 17 to 24	NOVEMBER Total Obsn	NOVEMBER MCWB	DECEMBER Obsn Hour Gp 01 to 08	DECEMBER 09 to 16	DECEMBER 17 to 24	DECEMBER Total Obsn	DECEMBER MCWB	JANUARY Obsn Hour Gp 01 to 08	JANUARY 09 to 16	JANUARY 17 to 24	JANUARY Total Obsn	JANUARY MCWB
100/104															
95/99															
90/94															
85/89															
80/84		1		1	67							0		0	68
75/79		9	0	9	66		1		1	66		2		2	65
70/74	1	23	4	28	63		6	0	6	63		6	0	6	62
65/69	9	36	16	60	61	4	16	5	25	61	1	15	5	21	60
60/64	22	42	31	95	57	9	21	13	43	57	13	20	14	47	57
55/59	31	41	36	108	52	16	25	18	59	53	16	23	19	58	52
50/54	32	42	41	115	48	18	35	25	78	48	14	29	21	64	47
45/49	41	27	42	110	44	24	47	33	104	43	21	42	31	94	43
40/44	46	12	38	96	39	31	40	43	114	38	35	41	46	122	38
35/39	31	4	19	54	35	40	31	44	115	34	46	35	43	124	34
30/34	20	2	9	31	30	51	18	34	103	29	45	22	37	104	29
25/29	7	0	2	9	25	30	7	22	59	25	33	9	22	64	25
20/24	1	0	1	2	21	16	2	8	26	20	18	3	8	29	20
15/19						7	0	1	8	16	6	0	1	7	16
10/14						1			1	11	1			1	12
5/9						0			0	9					

Temperature Range	FEBRUARY Obsn Hour Gp 01 to 08	FEBRUARY 09 to 16	FEBRUARY 17 to 24	FEBRUARY Total Obsn	FEBRUARY MCWB	MARCH Obsn Hour Gp 01 to 08	MARCH 09 to 16	MARCH 17 to 24	MARCH Total Obsn	MARCH MCWB	APRIL Obsn Hour Gp 01 to 08	APRIL 09 to 16	APRIL 17 to 24	APRIL Total Obsn	APRIL MCWB
100/104															
95/99															
90/94												1		1	68
85/89												8	1	9	67
80/84		0		0	68		3	0	3	65		20	3	23	66
75/79		1		1	62		9	1	10	63	1	29	9	39	64
70/74		7	1	8	61	1	16	4	21	61	7	33	22	62	62
65/69	2	12	4	18	59	7	26	15	48	59	31	38	40	109	60
60/64	8	22	12	42	56	17	29	22	68	55	46	40	40	126	56
55/59	12	26	20	58	52	22	34	30	86	51	39	33	40	112	51
50/54	22	35	24	81	47	27	45	36	108	46	37	27	39	103	47
45/49	31	41	40	112	43	45	43	50	138	43	36	8	29	73	43
40/44	35	37	46	118	38	52	26	49	127	38	29	2	13	44	39
35/39	39	22	34	95	34	39	11	25	75	34	12	1	3	16	35
30/34	38	13	24	75	29	27	5	11	43	29	3		0	3	31
25/29	23	4	12	39	25	9	1	4	14	25	0			0	25
20/24	9	3	5	17	20	3		0	3	21					
15/19	4	0	1	5	15										
10/14	1			1	11										
5/9															

Temperature Range	ANNUAL TOTAL Obsn Hour Gp 01 to 08	ANNUAL TOTAL 09 to 16	ANNUAL TOTAL 17 to 24	ANNUAL TOTAL Total Obsn	ANNUAL TOTAL MCWB
100/104		1	0	1	80
95/99		10	0	10	78
90/94	0	95	9	104	77
85/89	2	268	51	321	75
80/84	46	352	158	556	72
75/79	267	356	349	972	71
70/74	393	300	373	1066	67
65/69	341	283	326	950	62
60/64	326	246	289	861	58
55/59	263	215	257	735	53
50/54	231	226	238	695	48
45/49	238	211	247	696	43
40/44	247	158	243	648	39
35/39	214	104	169	487	34
30/34	185	60	115	360	29
25/29	103	21	62	186	25
20/24	47	8	22	77	20
15/19	17	0	3	20	16
10/14	3			3	11
5/9	0			0	9

FORT BRAGG/SIMMONS AAF NORTH CAROLINA

LAT 35 08N LONG 78 56W ELEV 242 FT

MEAN FREQUENCY OF OCCURRENCE OF DRY BULB TEMPERATURE (DEGREES F) WITH MEAN COINCIDENT WET BULB TEMPERATURE (DEGREES F) FOR EACH DRY BULB TEMPERATURE RANGE

Temperature Range	MAY Obsn Hour Gp 01 to 08	09 to 16	17 to 24	Total Obsn	MCWB	JUNE Obsn Hour Gp 01 to 08	09 to 16	17 to 24	Total Obsn	MCWB	JULY Obsn Hour Gp 01 to 08	09 to 16	17 to 24	Total Obsn	MCWB
100/104							2	1	3	76					
95/99		3	0	3	73		7	1	8	74		8	2	10	77
90/94		13	4	17	70		26	7	33	74		34	11	45	76
85/89		25	9	34	68	1	62	24	87	72	0	84	30	114	74
80/84	1	44	18	63	66	6	71	43	120	70	8	68	53	129	73
75/79	3	50	40	93	64	31	41	58	130	69	59	37	77	173	72
70/74	25	50	57	132	62	83	22	76	181	68	138	16	67	221	70
65/69	64	32	48	144	60	81	5	24	110	63	37	1	9	47	66
60/64	55	17	33	105	57	28	1	3	32	58	5		0	5	61
55/59	47	11	26	84	53	10	2	2	14	54	0			0	58
50/54	40	4	12	56	49	1	0	2	3	51					
45/49	11		1	12	44										
40/44	2			2	40										
35/39															
30/34															

Temperature Range	AUGUST Obsn Hour Gp 01 to 08	09 to 16	17 to 24	Total Obsn	MCWB	SEPTEMBER Obsn Hour Gp 01 to 08	09 to 16	17 to 24	Total Obsn	MCWB	OCTOBER Obsn Hour Gp 01 to 08	09 to 16	17 to 24	Total Obsn	MCWB
100/104		0	0	0	75										
95/99		13	3	16	76		4	0	4	76					
90/94		30	9	39	76		16	2	18	75					
85/89	1	61	23	85	75		42	11	53	72		9	1	10	67
80/84	9	67	48	124	72	1	63	30	94	70		29	5	34	68
75/79	53	47	73	173	71	14	50	51	115	69	1	46	18	65	65
70/74	111	24	69	204	69	60	35	64	159	67	11	58	46	115	64
65/69	50	5	19	74	65	65	21	46	132	63	52	48	66	166	62
60/64	19		4	23	59	54	7	27	88	59	63	33	48	144	57
55/59	5		0	5	55	33	1	6	40	54	45	16	29	90	52
50/54						9	0	1	10	50	27	6	18	51	47
45/49						3			3	46	22	2	11	35	43
40/44											19	0	5	24	38
35/39											7		2	9	34
30/34											2			2	31

FORT BRAGG/SIMMONS AAF NORTH CAROLINA

Temperature Range	NOVEMBER Obsn Hour Gp 01 to 08	09 to 16	17 to 24	Total Obsn	M C W B	DECEMBER Obsn Hour Gp 01 to 08	09 to 16	17 to 24	Total Obsn	M C W B	JANUARY Obsn Hour Gp 01 to 08	09 to 16	17 to 24	Total Obsn	M C W B
100/104															
95/99															
90/94															
85/89															
80/84		2		2	71		1		1	70					
75/79		11	1	12	64		5	1	6	67		2	0	2	63
70/74	2	22	7	31	61	1	18	8	27	63		8	1	9	59
65/69	5	40	15	60	57	9	19	12	40	59	2	11	4	17	57
60/64	15	43	32	90	55	13	26	24	63	56	3	15	12	30	54
55/59	27	35	35	97	50	20	25	25	70	51	13	21	19	53	51
50/54	34	35	43	112	46	22	38	32	92	46	13	22	21	56	46
45/49	38	24	40	102	41	25	44	37	106	41	18	36	31	85	42
40/44	44	18	37	99	37	31	32	36	99	37	29	44	43	116	37
35/39	30	7	18	55	33	31	23	30	84	32	40	32	38	110	33
30/34	24	3	8	35	28	49	14	26	89	28	52	31	34	117	29
25/29	15	1	4	20	25	28	3	15	46	25	38	20	32	90	24
20/24	4	0	0	4	21	16	0	1	17	21	24	5	10	39	19
15/19	1			1	16	2			2	17	14	2	2	18	15
10/14											3			3	11

Temperature Range	FEBRUARY Obsn Hour Gp 01 to 08	09 to 16	17 to 24	Total Obsn	M C W B	MARCH Obsn Hour Gp 01 to 08	09 to 16	17 to 24	Total Obsn	M C W B
100/104										
95/99										
90/94										
85/89							1	0	1	64
80/84							5	2	7	62
75/79							12	5	17	61
70/74		5	1	6	60	1	21	12	34	59
65/69	0	12	6	18	56	3	24	22	49	56
60/64	3	18	15	36	52	11	35	33	79	53
55/59	11	23	17	51	48	25	39	38	102	49
50/54	12	38	25	75	43	43	43	45	131	45
45/49	16	35	34	85	40	40	34	31	105	40
40/44	28	33	43	104	36	41	19	31	91	36
35/39	44	28	38	110	32	30	9	17	56	32
30/34	53	21	30	104	28	41	4	11	56	28
25/29	33	8	12	53	24	11	0	1	12	24
20/24	13	2	3	18	20	2			2	21
15/19	7	0	1	8	15					
10/14	2	0		2	11					

Temperature Range	APRIL Obsn Hour Gp 01 to 08	09 to 16	17 to 24	Total Obsn	M C W B	ANNUAL TOTAL Obsn Hour Gp 01 to 08	09 to 16	17 to 24	Total Obsn	M C W B
100/104							2	1	3	76
95/99							35	6	41	76
90/94		1		1	64		120	33	153	75
85/89		13	5	18	65	2	297	103	402	72
80/84		26	11	37	63	25	376	210	611	70
75/79	0	38	19	57	61	161	339	343	843	68
70/74	7	45	36	88	58	439	324	444	1207	66
65/69	26	44	50	120	57	394	262	321	977	61
60/64	44	34	39	117	54	313	229	270	812	56
55/59	40	21	37	98	50	276	194	234	704	51
50/54	48	13	26	87	47	249	199	225	673	46
45/49	46	3	12	61	42	219	178	197	594	41
40/44	23	2	6	31	39	217	148	201	566	37
35/39	6			6	35	188	99	143	430	33
30/34						221	73	109	403	28
25/29						125	32	64	221	24
20/24						59	7	14	80	20
15/19						24	2	3	29	15
10/14						5	0		5	11

GREENSBORO NORTH CAROLINA

LAT 36 05N LONG 79 57W ELEV 897 FT

MEAN FREQUENCY OF OCCURRENCE OF DRY BULB TEMPERATURE (DEGREES F) WITH MEAN COINCIDENT WET BULB TEMPERATURE (DEGREES F) FOR EACH DRY BULB TEMPERATURE RANGE

Temperature Range	MAY Obsn Hour Gp 01 to 08	09 to 16	17 to 24	Total Obsn	MCWB	JUNE Obsn Hour Gp 01 to 08	09 to 16	17 to 24	Total Obsn	MCWB	JULY Obsn Hour Gp 01 to 08	09 to 16	17 to 24	Total Obsn	MCWB
100/104							0		0	75		0		0	76
95/99							4	2	6	75		4	1	5	74
90/94		4	1	5	71	0	20	5	25	73		25	4	29	74
85/89		22	6	28	68	1	49	17	67	71	0	69	22	91	73
80/84	0	44	17	61	66	4	61	33	98	70	4	73	40	117	71
75/79	3	52	29	84	65	17	50	49	116	68	24	50	66	140	70
70/74	13	50	47	110	63	60	33	64	157	67	109	21	82	212	69
65/69	56	35	60	151	61	81	15	46	142	64	82	4	28	114	65
60/64	69	23	43	135	58	51	6	19	76	60	24	0	4	28	60
55/59	51	10	26	87	53	21	1	5	27	55	5		1	6	55
50/54	29	6	13	48	49	6	0	1	7	50	1		0	1	52
45/49	19	2	5	26	45	1		0	1	46					
40/44	7		1	8	40	0			0	43					
35/39	2		0	2	37										
30/34	0			0	32										
25/29															
20/24															

Temperature Range	AUGUST Obsn Hour Gp 01 to 08	09 to 16	17 to 24	Total Obsn	MCWB	SEPTEMBER Obsn Hour Gp 01 to 08	09 to 16	17 to 24	Total Obsn	MCWB	OCTOBER Obsn Hour Gp 01 to 08	09 to 16	17 to 24	Total Obsn	MCWB
100/104															
95/99		2		2	74		1	0	1	71					
90/94		23	4	27	74		8	2	10	71		2	0	2	72
85/89		62	19	81	73		24	6	30	71		4	1	5	69
80/84	2	68	35	105	71		48	15	63	70	0	16	2	18	66
75/79	15	54	65	134	70	3	56	36	95	68	0	31	6	37	63
70/74	105	28	84	217	69	42	47	60	149	67	3	40	18	61	61
65/69	84	7	32	123	65	63	29	49	141	63	15	46	37	98	60
60/64	32	3	9	44	60	51	17	38	106	59	32	44	47	123	56
55/59	9	0	1	10	56	40	6	23	69	54	45	35	46	126	53
50/54	1		0	1	51	27	3	9	39	50	48	19	41	108	48
45/49						12	1	3	16	46	41	8	30	79	44
40/44						3		0	3	41	34	1	14	49	40
35/39						0			0	38	20	0	5	25	35
30/34											7		1	8	30
25/29											2		0	2	26
20/24											0			0	21

GREENSBORO NORTH CAROLINA

Temperature Range	NOVEMBER Obsn Hour Gp 01 to 08	09 to 16	17 to 24	Total Obsn	M C W B	DECEMBER Obsn Hour Gp 01 to 08	09 to 16	17 to 24	Total Obsn	M C W B	JANUARY Obsn Hour Gp 01 to 08	09 to 16	17 to 24	Total Obsn	M C W B
100/104															
95/99															
90/94															
85/89															
80/84		1		1	65										
75/79		7	0	7	62		0		0	59		0		0	63
70/74	0	16	3	19	59		2		2	59		3	0	3	61
65/69	5	26	10	41	58	0	6	2	8	58		7	2	9	58
60/64	12	34	22	68	56	5	18	6	29	56	4	15	9	28	56
55/59	18	39	27	84	51	7	21	14	42	52	12	22	15	49	51
50/54	22	38	36	96	46	9	28	19	56	46	12	27	19	58	46
45/49	33	33	41	107	42	18	43	29	90	42	12	37	26	75	42
40/44	39	24	37	100	38	29	41	38	108	38	24	41	38	103	37
35/39	42	15	31	88	34	34	39	44	117	33	46	41	47	134	33
30/34	39	5	22	66	30	51	30	45	126	29	46	31	44	121	29
25/29	19	1	8	28	25	46	13	32	91	24	40	15	30	85	25
20/24	8	0	2	10	21	27	6	13	46	20	28	6	11	45	20
15/19	2	1	1	4	16	15	2	5	22	16	13	3	6	22	16
10/14	1	0	0	1	12	5	0	1	6	11	8	0	1	9	11
5/9						1	0	0	1	7	2	0		2	7
0/4						1			1	2	0			0	3

Temperature Range	FEBRUARY Obsn Hour Gp 01 to 08	09 to 16	17 to 24	Total Obsn	M C W B	MARCH Obsn Hour Gp 01 to 08	09 to 16	17 to 24	Total Obsn	M C W B	APRIL Obsn Hour Gp 01 to 08	09 to 16	17 to 24	Total Obsn	M C W B	ANNUAL TOTAL Obsn Hour Gp 01 to 08	09 to 16	17 to 24	Total Obsn	M C W B
100/104																	0		0	76
95/99																	11	3	14	74
90/94												0		0	65	0	82	16	98	73
85/89												6	1	7	65	1	236	72	309	72
80/84							0		0	60		20	6	26	64	10	331	148	489	69
75/79		0		0	58		5	2	7	61		26	11	37	62	62	331	264	657	68
70/74		2	0	2	57		12	4	16	58	2	30	23	55	59	334	284	385	1003	66
65/69	1	9	2	12	56	3	22	12	37	55	15	36	35	86	57	405	242	315	962	62
60/64	2	17	8	27	53	10	29	22	61	53	37	40	45	122	55	329	246	272	847	57
55/59	8	25	18	51	50	14	36	33	83	49	42	33	38	113	50	272	228	247	747	52
50/54	13	32	25	70	45	23	41	33	97	45	41	25	32	98	46	232	219	228	679	47
45/49	19	36	35	90	42	31	35	39	105	41	37	15	23	75	42	223	210	231	664	42
40/44	28	34	39	101	37	41	32	42	115	38	29	7	16	52	38	234	180	225	639	38
35/39	42	31	41	114	34	51	21	33	105	34	24	1	7	32	34	261	148	208	617	34
30/34	48	22	31	101	29	43	10	20	73	29	12		2	14	30	246	98	165	509	29
25/29	33	9	16	58	25	21	3	6	30	25	2			2	25	163	41	92	296	25
20/24	18	4	5	27	20	8	2	3	13	20						89	18	34	141	20
15/19	8	1	2	11	15	2	0	0	2	16						40	7	14	61	16
10/14	3	1	1	5	11	1			1	11						18	1	3	22	11
5/9	1	0	0	1	6	0			0	7						4	0	0	4	7
0/4	1		0	1	1											2		0	2	2

SEYMOUR JOHNSON AFB NORTH CAROLINA

LAT 35 20N LONG 77 58W ELEV 109 FT

MEAN FREQUENCY OF OCCURRENCE OF DRY BULB TEMPERATURE (DEGREES F) WITH MEAN COINCIDENT WET BULB TEMPERATURE (DEGREES F) FOR EACH DRY BULB TEMPERATURE RANGE

Temperature Range	MAY Obsn Hour Gp 01 to 08	MAY 09 to 16	MAY 17 to 24	MAY Total Obsn	MAY MCWB	JUNE Obsn Hour Gp 01 to 08	JUNE 09 to 16	JUNE 17 to 24	JUNE Total Obsn	JUNE MCWB	JULY Obsn Hour Gp 01 to 08	JULY 09 to 16	JULY 17 to 24	JULY Total Obsn	JULY MCWB
100/104							0		0	77		0	0	0	76
95/99		0		0	71		7	2	9	76		5	1	6	77
90/94		10	3	13	70		25	6	31	75		33	8	41	77
85/89		30	11	41	69	0	54	21	75	73	0	77	27	104	75
80/84	0	45	19	64	68	5	63	38	106	71	8	75	51	134	74
75/79	4	60	38	102	66	36	50	62	148	70	74	42	88	204	73
70/74	35	45	61	141	65	86	27	67	180	68	123	14	64	201	70
65/69	71	28	53	152	62	64	11	33	108	64	34	1	8	43	65
60/64	57	17	33	107	57	34	3	7	44	59	8	0	2	10	60
55/59	42	10	19	71	53	11	1	3	15	54	1			1	57
50/54	26	2	9	37	49	3	0	0	3	50					
45/49	9	1	2	12	45	1			1	45					
40/44	2		0	2	40										
35/39	1		0	1	36										
30/34															
25/29															

Temperature Range	AUGUST Obsn Hour Gp 01 to 08	AUGUST 09 to 16	AUGUST 17 to 24	AUGUST Total Obsn	AUGUST MCWB	SEPTEMBER Obsn Hour Gp 01 to 08	SEPTEMBER 09 to 16	SEPTEMBER 17 to 24	SEPTEMBER Total Obsn	SEPTEMBER MCWB	OCTOBER Obsn Hour Gp 01 to 08	OCTOBER 09 to 16	OCTOBER 17 to 24	OCTOBER Total Obsn	OCTOBER MCWB
100/104		0		0	76										
95/99		4	1	5	77		0		0	77					
90/94		30	7	37	77		8	1	9	76		0		0	72
85/89		70	24	94	75		46	8	54	74		6	0	6	70
80/84	6	75	49	130	73	0	63	23	86	71		21	3	24	69
75/79	69	45	86	200	72	17	56	55	128	70	2	45	13	60	67
70/74	109	19	61	189	70	70	37	70	177	68	15	52	35	102	65
65/69	46	4	17	67	65	62	19	46	127	63	30	51	51	132	61
60/64	15	1	3	19	60	47	10	26	83	59	52	37	50	139	57
55/59	2		0	2	55	29	1	9	39	55	43	23	41	107	53
50/54	0			0	48	11	0	3	14	50	38	10	28	76	48
45/49	0			0	47	3		0	3	46	31	4	15	50	44
40/44						0			0	43	21	1	7	29	39
35/39											13	0	3	16	35
30/34											3		0	3	31
25/29											1			1	26

SEYMOUR JOHNSON AFB NORTH CAROLINA

Temperature Range	NOVEMBER Obsn Hour Gp 01 to 08	09 to 16	17 to 24	Total Obsn	M C W B	DECEMBER Obsn Hour Gp 01 to 08	09 to 16	17 to 24	Total Obsn	M C W B	JANUARY Obsn Hour Gp 01 to 08	09 to 16	17 to 24	Total Obsn	M C W B
100/104															
95/99															
90/94															
85/89															
80/84		4	0	4	69		0		0	72		0		0	65
75/79	0	13	1	14	65		2	0	2	67		1	0	1	66
70/74	2	25	8	35	62	0	11	2	13	63	0	7	2	9	62
65/69	9	37	22	68	59	6	15	9	30	60	3	11	5	19	59
60/64	19	44	33	96	56	11	23	18	52	56	6	16	11	33	55
55/59	26	41	39	106	51	14	27	21	62	51	12	23	20	55	51
50/54	40	32	43	115	47	21	36	28	85	46	12	27	23	62	46
45/49	39	24	38	101	43	20	39	38	97	42	19	37	33	89	42
40/44	39	14	30	83	38	28	38	40	106	37	37	41	42	120	38
35/39	37	5	16	58	34	42	31	39	112	33	40	33	38	111	33
30/34	19	1	7	27	29	51	17	31	99	29	41	28	36	105	29
25/29	8	0	2	10	25	32	7	16	55	25	39	16	24	79	25
20/24	2			2	20	18	2	5	25	20	26	5	10	41	20
15/19						4	1	1	6	16	9	2	2	13	16
10/14						1	0	0	1	11	3	0	0	3	11
5/9							0		0	5	0			0	6
0/4													0	0	1

Temperature Range	FEBRUARY Obsn Hour Gp 01 to 08	09 to 16	17 to 24	Total Obsn	M C W B	MARCH Obsn Hour Gp 01 to 08	09 to 16	17 to 24	Total Obsn	M C W B	APRIL Obsn Hour Gp 01 to 08	09 to 16	17 to 24	Total Obsn	M C W B	ANNUAL TOTAL Obsn Hour Gp 01 to 08	09 to 16	17 to 24	Total Obsn	M C W B
100/104																	0	0	0	76
95/99												0		0	73		16	4	20	77
90/94												3	1	4	68		109	26	135	76
85/89							0	0	0	64		13	4	17	66	0	296	95	391	73
80/84		0	0	0	65		3	0	3	63		22	10	32	65	19	371	193	583	71
75/79		2	0	2	65		11	3	14	61	1	33	15	49	63	203	360	361	924	70
70/74	1	8	2	11	61	1	18	8	27	60	6	39	31	76	61	448	302	411	1161	67
65/69	2	13	7	22	59	7	26	20	53	57	31	39	48	118	59	365	255	319	939	61
60/64	9	16	17	42	55	14	34	31	79	54	44	37	44	125	55	316	238	275	829	57
55/59	11	23	18	52	50	20	38	37	95	49	38	29	35	102	51	249	216	242	707	51
50/54	13	33	27	73	45	32	41	42	115	45	38	17	29	84	47	234	198	232	664	47
45/49	23	34	37	94	42	43	35	42	120	42	43	5	17	65	43	231	179	222	632	42
40/44	34	36	35	105	37	48	22	35	105	38	30	3	7	40	39	239	155	196	590	38
35/39	40	32	41	113	33	42	12	18	72	33	10		1	11	35	225	113	156	494	33
30/34	46	18	27	91	29	28	5	7	40	29	0			0	32	188	69	108	365	29
25/29	29	7	9	45	24	10	1	3	14	25						119	31	54	204	25
20/24	11	2	3	16	20	2	0		2	21						59	9	18	86	20
15/19	4	1	1	6	15											17	4	4	25	16
10/14	1			1	12											5	0	0	5	11
5/9																0	0		0	5
0/4																	0	0	0	

BISMARCK MAP NORTH DAKOTA

LAT 46 46N LONG 100 45W ELEV 1647 FT

MEAN FREQUENCY OF OCCURRENCE OF DRY BULB TEMPERATURE (DEGREES F) WITH MEAN COINCIDENT WET BULB TEMPERATURE (DEGREES F) FOR EACH DRY BULB TEMPERATURE RANGE

Temperature Range	MAY Obsn Hour Gp 01 to 08	MAY 09 to 16	MAY 17 to 24	MAY Total Obsn	MAY MCWB	JUNE Obsn Hour Gp 01 to 08	JUNE 09 to 16	JUNE 17 to 24	JUNE Total Obsn	JUNE MCWB	JULY Obsn Hour Gp 01 to 08	JULY 09 to 16	JULY 17 to 24	JULY Total Obsn	JULY MCWB
105/109												0	0	0	71
100/104							0		0	67		1	0	1	72
95/99							2	1	3	68		5	2	7	70
90/94		1	0	1	63		6	3	9	69		20	11	31	69
85/89		4	2	6	63		15	8	23	67	0	33	19	52	69
80/84		11	6	17	61	0	30	18	48	66	1	51	33	85	66
75/79	0	22	11	33	59	2	43	28	73	63	7	53	42	102	65
70/74	1	31	19	51	56	10	44	37	91	61	26	43	44	113	63
65/69	5	38	27	70	54	30	37	42	109	59	53	26	42	121	61
60/64	15	43	37	95	52	47	29	44	120	57	66	12	35	113	58
55/59	29	35	42	106	49	59	22	35	116	53	61	2	16	79	54
50/54	47	25	41	113	47	52	8	18	78	49	27	1	3	31	50
45/49	60	20	32	112	43	25	2	5	32	45	7		0	7	46
40/44	43	8	16	67	39	11	1	2	14	40	0			0	42
35/39	26	6	8	40	34	2	0	0	2	37					
30/34	15	3	6	24	31	0			0	33					
25/29	5		1	6	26										
20/24	1			1	22										
15/19															
10/14															
5/9															

Temperature Range	AUGUST Obsn Hour Gp 01 to 08	AUGUST 09 to 16	AUGUST 17 to 24	AUGUST Total Obsn	AUGUST MCWB	SEPTEMBER Obsn Hour Gp 01 to 08	SEPTEMBER 09 to 16	SEPTEMBER 17 to 24	SEPTEMBER Total Obsn	SEPTEMBER MCWB	OCTOBER Obsn Hour Gp 01 to 08	OCTOBER 09 to 16	OCTOBER 17 to 24	OCTOBER Total Obsn	OCTOBER MCWB
105/109		0	0	0	69		0		0	65					
100/104		2	1	3	69		0	0	0	67					
95/99		8	4	12	68		2	0	2	66		0		0	60
90/94		17	9	26	67		4	1	5	67		0	0	0	62
85/89		31	18	49	66		8	4	12	64		2	0	2	58
80/84	0	46	26	72	64	0	17	7	24	62		6	1	7	58
75/79	5	47	36	88	63	0	24	13	37	59		11	3	14	57
70/74	19	43	42	104	62	3	32	18	53	58		16	5	21	55
65/69	48	26	45	119	60	8	36	25	69	55	1	24	10	35	53
60/64	62	15	34	111	57	14	35	34	83	53	3	28	17	48	50
55/59	53	9	22	84	53	34	32	40	106	51	8	34	28	70	47
50/54	38	3	9	50	49	49	25	42	116	47	18	32	38	88	45
45/49	16	0	2	18	45	56	15	30	101	43	33	34	41	108	41
40/44	5		0	5	40	38	8	16	62	39	53	26	38	117	38
35/39	1			1	36	27	2	7	36	35	49	20	33	102	34
30/34	0			0	32	9	0	1	10	30	47	11	22	80	30
25/29						3		0	3	27	23	3	9	35	26
20/24						1			1	22	9	1	2	12	21
15/19											2	0	1	3	16
10/14											1		0	1	11
5/9											0			0	6

BISMARCK MAP NORTH DAKOTA

Temperature Range	NOVEMBER Obsn Hour Gp 01 to 08	NOVEMBER 09 to 16	NOVEMBER 17 to 24	NOVEMBER Total Obsn	NOVEMBER MCWB	DECEMBER Obsn Hour Gp 01 to 08	DECEMBER 09 to 16	DECEMBER 17 to 24	DECEMBER Total Obsn	DECEMBER MCWB	JANUARY Obsn Hour Gp 01 to 08	JANUARY 09 to 16	JANUARY 17 to 24	JANUARY Total Obsn	JANUARY MCWB	FEBRUARY Obsn Hour Gp 01 to 08	FEBRUARY 09 to 16	FEBRUARY 17 to 24	FEBRUARY Total Obsn	FEBRUARY MCWB
105/109																				
100/104																				
95/99																				
90/94																				
85/89																				
80/84																				
75/79																				
70/74		0		0	53															
65/69		2		2	49												0	0	0	50
60/64		4	1	5	48												0	0	0	48
55/59	0	9	1	10	45		1		1	45							2	0	2	46
50/54	1	16	6	23	42		2	0	2	41		1	0	1	41		2	1	3	43
45/49	3	23	11	37	40	0	7	1	8	39		3	0	3	38		4	2	6	40
40/44	11	27	24	62	36	2	14	4	20	36	2	8	3	13	36	2	10	7	19	37
35/39	25	37	42	104	33	8	24	17	49	33	4	10	10	24	33	6	16	14	36	33
30/34	48	34	46	128	30	21	26	28	75	29	7	13	11	31	29	15	24	22	61	30
25/29	43	25	34	102	25	27	28	33	88	25	14	20	19	53	25	25	28	26	79	26
20/24	36	22	26	84	21	30	30	34	94	21	17	26	22	65	21	22	24	27	73	21
15/19	26	14	15	55	16	32	26	29	87	16	25	24	23	72	16	20	23	23	66	16
10/14	17	10	14	41	11	30	19	22	71	11	28	29	26	83	11	23	25	27	75	11
5/9	9	7	5	21	6	24	21	20	65	6	26	25	28	79	6	28	24	23	75	6
0/4	8	5	6	19	2	23	22	23	68	1	33	24	28	85	1	26	18	21	65	2
-5/-1	7	3	7	17	-3	21	14	19	54	-3	24	23	25	72	-3	22	14	15	51	-3
-10/-6	6	1	2	9	-8	12	8	10	30	-8	20	18	21	59	-8	14	7	9	30	-8
-15/-11	2	0	1	3	-13	10	4	6	20	-13	19	12	16	47	-13	10	2	4	16	-13
-20/-16	1	0	0	1	-17	4	2	3	9	-18	14	7	10	31	-18	5	1	3	9	-18
-25/-21	0	0	0	0	-23	3	1	1	5	-23	8	2	4	14	-23	3	0	1	4	-23
-30/-26	0		0	0	-27	1	0	0	1	-27	4	1	2	7	-28	2	0		2	-27
-35/-31						0	0		0	-33	2	0	0	2	-33	0			0	-32
-40/-36											1	0	0	1						
-45/-41											0			0						

Temperature Range	MARCH Obsn Hour Gp 01 to 08	MARCH 09 to 16	MARCH 17 to 24	MARCH Total Obsn	MARCH MCWB	APRIL Obsn Hour Gp 01 to 08	APRIL 09 to 16	APRIL 17 to 24	APRIL Total Obsn	APRIL MCWB	ANNUAL TOTAL Obsn Hour Gp 01 to 08	ANNUAL TOTAL 09 to 16	ANNUAL TOTAL 17 to 24	ANNUAL TOTAL Total Obsn	ANNUAL TOTAL MCWB
105/109												0	0	0	70
100/104												3	1	4	70
95/99												17	7	24	68
90/94							1	0	1	60		49	24	73	68
85/89							1	1	2	60	0	94	52	146	67
80/84		0		0	55		3	1	4	58	1	164	92	257	64
75/79		0	0	0	53		5	2	7	56	14	205	135	354	62
70/74		1	1	2	51		8	5	13	54	59	218	171	448	60
65/69		2	1	3	50	1	15	8	24	51	146	206	200	552	58
60/64		2	1	3	48	1	19	13	33	48	208	187	216	611	54
55/59		5	3	8	45	4	24	17	45	46	248	175	204	627	51
50/54	0	8	4	12	42	11	31	25	67	43	243	154	187	584	46
45/49	1	14	8	23	39	21	30	33	84	40	222	152	165	539	42
40/44	4	22	17	43	36	32	34	36	102	37	203	158	163	524	38
35/39	18	36	31	85	33	43	32	38	113	33	209	183	200	592	34
30/34	41	40	48	129	30	55	26	33	114	30	258	177	217	652	30
25/29	40	32	36	108	25	40	7	19	66	25	220	143	177	540	25
20/24	36	26	27	89	21	24	2	5	31	21	176	131	143	450	21
15/19	27	19	22	68	16	5	2	1	8	16	137	108	114	359	16
10/14	21	15	15	51	11	3	1	1	5	11	123	99	105	327	11
5/9	19	12	11	42	6	1	0	0	1	7	107	89	87	283	6
0/4	15	6	9	30	2	0		0	0	3	105	75	87	267	1
-5/-1	9	4	5	18	-3	0			0	-2	83	58	71	212	-3
-10/-6	6	2	4	12	-8						58	36	46	140	-8
-15/-11	5	1	1	7	-13						46	19	28	93	-13
-20/-16	3	0	1	4	-18						27	10	17	54	-18
-25/-21	1		0	1	-23						15	3	6	24	-23
-30/-26	0			0	-26						7	1	2	10	-28
-35/-31											2	0	0	2	-33
-40/-36											1	0	0	1	
-45/-41											0			0	

GRAND FORKS AFB NORTH DAKOTA

LAT 47 57N LONG 97 24W ELEV 911 FT

MEAN FREQUENCY OF OCCURRENCE OF DRY BULB TEMPERATURE (DEGREES F) WITH MEAN COINCIDENT WET BULB TEMPERATURE (DEGREES F) FOR EACH DRY BULB TEMPERATURE RANGE

Temperature Range	MAY Obsn Hour Gp 01 to 08	MAY 09 to 16	MAY 17 to 24	MAY Total Obsn	MAY MCWB	JUNE Obsn Hour Gp 01 to 08	JUNE 09 to 16	JUNE 17 to 24	JUNE Total Obsn	JUNE MCWB	JULY Obsn Hour Gp 01 to 08	JULY 09 to 16	JULY 17 to 24	JULY Total Obsn	JULY MCWB
100/104		0		0	65										
95/99		0	0	0	66		1	0	1	72		1	1	2	74
90/94		1	0	1	71		5	2	7	70		7	3	10	72
85/89		3	1	4	66		11	5	16	70		21	10	31	71
80/84		8	4	12	62	0	22	13	35	67		50	23	73	68
75/79	1	15	8	24	59	3	38	24	65	64	4	65	40	109	66
70/74	1	26	16	43	56	10	49	36	95	61	20	57	53	130	64
65/69	3	34	22	59	54	27	47	46	120	59	54	30	51	135	62
60/64	12	36	30	78	52	51	37	50	138	57	72	12	40	124	58
55/59	24	34	36	94	50	62	22	36	120	53	57	4	19	80	54
50/54	41	39	44	124	46	44	7	18	69	49	29	1	8	38	50
45/49	49	24	39	112	42	26	2	8	36	44	9	0	2	11	45
40/44	49	17	26	92	39	11	1	3	15	40	2			2	41
35/39	36	7	15	58	34	5	0	0	5	36	0			0	38
30/34	23	3	5	31	30	1			1	28					
25/29	7	1	1	9	26	0			0	24					
20/24	2	1	1	4	21										
15/19	0	0	0	0	17										
10/14	0			0	14										
5/9	0			0	7										
0/4	0			0	3										

Temperature Range	AUGUST Obsn Hour Gp 01 to 08	AUGUST 09 to 16	AUGUST 17 to 24	AUGUST Total Obsn	AUGUST MCWB	SEPTEMBER Obsn Hour Gp 01 to 08	SEPTEMBER 09 to 16	SEPTEMBER 17 to 24	SEPTEMBER Total Obsn	SEPTEMBER MCWB	OCTOBER Obsn Hour Gp 01 to 08	OCTOBER 09 to 16	OCTOBER 17 to 24	OCTOBER Total Obsn	OCTOBER MCWB
100/104		0		0	69										
95/99		2	1	3	70		0	0	0	76					
90/94		14	5	19	70		1	1	2	71					
85/89		26	12	38	69		6	2	8	68		1		1	63
80/84	0	36	21	57	67		13	5	18	66		2	0	2	61
75/79	4	49	33	86	64	1	20	10	31	63		6	1	7	60
70/74	16	49	39	104	62	3	26	17	46	60	0	10	3	13	57
65/69	37	37	47	121	60	10	37	25	72	58	0	15	6	21	55
60/64	65	21	43	129	57	21	41	34	96	55	3	25	14	42	52
55/59	54	11	27	92	53	36	38	40	114	51	10	38	26	74	49
50/54	43	2	14	59	49	41	31	38	110	47	22	40	32	94	46
45/49	20	0	4	24	45	49	16	37	102	44	39	37	47	123	42
40/44	6		1	7	41	43	8	22	73	40	43	34	43	120	38
35/39	2		0	2	35	26	3	7	36	35	55	26	37	118	34
30/34	1			1	32	7	1	1	9	30	46	12	23	81	30
25/29						2		0	2	26	21	3	11	35	26
20/24						1			1	23	8	0	3	11	21
15/19											2		0	2	17
10/14															
5/9															
0/4															

GRAND FORKS AFB NORTH DAKOTA

Temperature Range	NOVEMBER Obsn Hour Gp 01 to 08	09 to 16	17 to 24	Total Obsn	MCWB	DECEMBER Obsn Hour Gp 01 to 08	09 to 16	17 to 24	Total Obsn	MCWB	JANUARY Obsn Hour Gp 01 to 08	09 to 16	17 to 24	Total Obsn	MCWB
100/104															
95/99															
90/94															
85/89															
80/84															
75/79															
70/74															
65/69		0		0	52										
60/64		1		1	47										
55/59	0	4	1	5	46		0		0	42					
50/54	0	8	2	10	44		0	0	0	43					
45/49	4	15	7	26	41		2	1	3	41					
40/44	9	22	17	48	38		3	2	5	36	0	2	1	3	36
35/39	20	36	37	93	34	3	8	4	15	33	4	8	6	18	33
30/34	52	47	52	151	30	12	20	14	46	30	6	7	7	20	29
25/29	48	40	39	127	25	22	23	23	68	26	11	12	10	33	25
20/24	38	27	33	98	21	26	23	27	76	21	13	11	12	36	21
15/19	27	17	19	63	16	25	29	26	80	16	15	18	19	52	16
10/14	18	11	15	44	11	27	30	31	88	11	18	23	20	61	11
5/9	11	6	10	27	6	29	33	31	93	6	22	27	28	77	6
0/4	8	3	6	17	2	29	26	27	82	1	25	32	25	82	1
-5/-1	3	1	2	6	-3	25	22	22	69	-3	28	36	34	98	-4
-10/-6	1	0	1	2	-8	22	16	16	54	-8	37	30	32	99	-8
-15/-11	1	0		1	-13	14	8	15	37	-13	27	20	24	71	-13
-20/-16	0		0	0	-19	8	3	7	18	-18	23	13	18	54	-18
-25/-21			0	0	-22	4	1	2	7	-23	11	5	7	23	-23
-30/-26						1	0	1	2	-28	7	2	3	12	-28
-35/-31						1	0		1	-33	3	0	0	3	-32
-40/-36															

Temperature Range	FEBRUARY Obsn Hour Gp 01 to 08	09 to 16	17 to 24	Total Obsn	MCWB	MARCH Obsn Hour Gp 01 to 08	09 to 16	17 to 24	Total Obsn	MCWB	APRIL Obsn Hour Gp 01 to 08	09 to 16	17 to 24	Total Obsn	MCWB	ANNUAL TOTAL Obsn Hour Gp 01 to 08	09 to 16	17 to 24	Total Obsn	MCWB
100/104																	0		0	67
95/99																	4	2	6	71
90/94																	28	11	39	71
85/89																	68	30	98	70
80/84												0	0	0	57	0	131	66	197	67
75/79							0	0	0	54		2	0	2	56	13	195	116	324	64
70/74							0	0	0	55		3	1	4	55	50	220	165	435	61
65/69							1	0	1	52		7	4	11	54	131	208	201	540	59
60/64						0	2	1	3	50	1	14	7	22	50	225	189	219	633	56
55/59		0		0	48	0	3	2	5	49	3	21	14	38	48	246	175	201	622	52
50/54		0	0	0	45	0	5	4	9	45	7	27	23	57	45	227	160	183	570	47
45/49			0	0	42	1	7	4	12	41	16	35	34	85	42	213	138	183	534	43
40/44	0	1	1	2	37	4	11	9	24	38	32	37	38	107	38	199	136	163	498	38
35/39	2	7	6	15	34	14	26	25	65	34	52	39	45	136	34	219	160	182	561	34
30/34	9	16	16	41	30	35	39	40	114	30	63	33	42	138	30	255	178	200	633	30
25/29	18	23	22	63	26	32	36	35	103	25	37	15	19	71	25	198	153	160	511	25
20/24	22	26	19	67	21	28	35	31	94	21	18	7	10	35	21	156	130	136	422	21
15/19	19	23	22	64	16	32	26	28	86	16	7	1	2	10	16	127	114	116	357	16
10/14	20	24	25	69	11	25	22	25	72	11	4	0	1	5	12	112	110	117	339	11
5/9	22	25	27	74	6	25	19	19	63	6	1			1	8	110	110	115	335	6
0/4	24	23	23	70	1	19	9	14	42	1	1		0	1	1	106	93	95	294	1
-5/-1	23	22	22	67	-4	18	4	6	28	-3						97	85	86	268	-4
-10/-6	23	17	20	60	-8	9	1	3	13	-8						92	64	72	228	-8
-15/-11	18	10	11	39	-13	3	0	1	4	-13						63	38	51	152	-13
-20/-16	14	6	6	26	-18	1		0	1	-18						46	22	31	99	-18
-25/-21	6	2	3	11	-23	0	0		0	-23						21	8	12	41	-23
-30/-26	3	1	1	5	-28	0		0	0	-28						11	3	5	19	-28
-35/-31	2	0	0	2	-32	0			0	-31						6	0	0	6	-32
-40/-36	0			0												0			0	

MINOT AFB NORTH DAKOTA

LAT 48 25N LONG 101 21W ELEV 1668 FT

MEAN FREQUENCY OF OCCURRENCE OF DRY BULB TEMPERATURE (DEGREES F) WITH MEAN COINCIDENT WET BULB TEMPERATURE (DEGREES F) FOR EACH DRY BULB TEMPERATURE RANGE

Temperature Range	MAY Obsn Hour Gp 01 to 08	MAY 09 to 16	MAY 17 to 24	MAY Total Obsn	MAY MCWB	JUNE Obsn Hour Gp 01 to 08	JUNE 09 to 16	JUNE 17 to 24	JUNE Total Obsn	JUNE MCWB	JULY Obsn Hour Gp 01 to 08	JULY 09 to 16	JULY 17 to 24	JULY Total Obsn	JULY MCWB
105/109												0	0	0	72
100/104												0	0	0	72
95/99							0		0	65		3	1	4	70
90/94		1	1	2	67		5	2	7	65		11	7	18	69
85/89		2	1	3	64		12	6	18	65		25	15	40	68
80/84		8	4	12	60	0	21	12	33	65	0	40	24	64	66
75/79	0	12	8	20	58	2	32	22	56	62	3	56	41	100	64
70/74	1	24	14	39	55	5	51	36	92	60	16	55	47	118	62
65/69	3	33	22	58	53	20	45	42	107	58	51	38	46	135	60
60/64	10	35	30	75	51	46	38	51	135	56	70	15	41	126	57
55/59	22	37	36	95	48	64	24	41	129	52	67	4	20	91	53
50/54	39	42	47	128	45	58	8	19	85	49	29	1	5	35	49
45/49	52	24	38	114	42	28	4	7	39	44	10	0	1	11	45
40/44	55	16	28	99	38	12	0	1	13	39	1			1	41
35/39	38	10	13	61	34	3		0	3	35	0			0	37
30/34	20	3	4	27	30	2			2	30					
25/29	6	1	1	8	25										
20/24	3	0	0	3	21										
15/19															
10/14															
5/9															

Temperature Range	AUGUST Obsn Hour Gp 01 to 08	AUGUST 09 to 16	AUGUST 17 to 24	AUGUST Total Obsn	AUGUST MCWB	SEPTEMBER Obsn Hour Gp 01 to 08	SEPTEMBER 09 to 16	SEPTEMBER 17 to 24	SEPTEMBER Total Obsn	SEPTEMBER MCWB	OCTOBER Obsn Hour Gp 01 to 08	OCTOBER 09 to 16	OCTOBER 17 to 24	OCTOBER Total Obsn	OCTOBER MCWB
105/109		0		0	69										
100/104		1	0	1	70										
95/99		5	2	7	67		1	0	1	73					
90/94		18	9	27	67		3	1	4	66		0		0	61
85/89		26	16	42	65		8	3	11	65		0	0	0	61
80/84	1	39	24	64	64		12	7	19	62		2	0	2	58
75/79	4	43	31	78	62	0	22	10	32	60		5	1	6	57
70/74	15	37	39	91	60	2	27	17	46	58		12	3	15	55
65/69	29	36	42	107	58	9	29	21	59	56	0	16	6	22	52
60/64	59	26	39	124	56	17	36	32	85	53	1	27	13	41	49
55/59	66	12	28	106	53	32	37	42	111	51	10	35	25	70	47
50/54	45	5	14	64	49	46	28	38	112	47	22	38	33	93	44
45/49	22	0	4	26	45	46	21	32	99	43	30	34	39	103	41
40/44	5		1	6	40	46	11	22	79	39	48	32	47	127	38
35/39	2			2	36	28	4	9	41	35	52	29	40	121	34
30/34	0			0	32	12	1	4	17	30	50	12	26	88	30
25/29						2	0	1	3	26	23	4	9	36	26
20/24						0			0	21	8	2	4	14	21
15/19						0			0	18	2		1	3	17
10/14											1	0	0	1	12
5/9											0			0	8

MINOT AFB NORTH DAKOTA

Temperature Range	NOVEMBER Obsn Hour Gp 01 to 08	09 to 16	17 to 24	Total Obsn	MCWB	DECEMBER Obsn Hour Gp 01 to 08	09 to 16	17 to 24	Total Obsn	MCWB	JANUARY Obsn Hour Gp 01 to 08	09 to 16	17 to 24	Total Obsn	MCWB
105/109															
100/104															
95/99															
90/94															
85/89															
80/84															
75/79															
70/74		0		0	50										
65/69		1	0	1	48										
60/64		2	0	2	48										
55/59	0	5	1	6	44		0		0	41					
50/54	0	12	3	15	42		2		2	41		0		0	41
45/49	2	17	9	28	40	0	3	0	3	38		1		1	39
40/44	10	26	17	53	36	1	8	3	12	36	2	5	3	10	37
35/39	25	35	37	97	33	6	15	10	31	33	7	15	11	33	33
30/34	41	42	45	128	29	17	21	20	58	29	10	12	14	36	29
25/29	48	33	43	124	25	23	21	25	69	25	15	12	15	42	25
20/24	43	22	32	97	21	29	30	28	87	21	15	16	14	45	21
15/19	26	16	17	59	16	26	24	27	77	16	16	19	21	56	16
10/14	16	14	14	44	11	25	25	23	73	11	17	18	14	49	11
5/9	8	8	11	27	6	21	26	29	76	6	21	26	20	67	6
0/4	9	3	8	20	2	31	25	26	82	1	30	33	29	92	1
-5/-1	7	3	2	12	-3	24	20	25	69	-3	30	29	31	90	-4
-10/-6	1	1	1	3	-8	20	14	19	53	-8	23	22	29	74	-8
-15/-11	1	0	1	2	-13	16	9	10	35	-13	25	22	22	69	-13
-20/-16	1	0		1	-19	5	3	3	11	-18	20	11	14	45	-18
-25/-21						3	2	1	6	-23	11	5	7	23	-23
-30/-26						0	0	0	0	-27	5	2	1	8	-28
-35/-31						1	0		1	-32	2	0	0	2	-32

Temperature Range	FEBRUARY Obsn Hour Gp 01 to 08	09 to 16	17 to 24	Total Obsn	MCWB	MARCH Obsn Hour Gp 01 to 08	09 to 16	17 to 24	Total Obsn	MCWB	APRIL Obsn Hour Gp 01 to 08	09 to 16	17 to 24	Total Obsn	MCWB	ANNUAL TOTAL Obsn Hour Gp 01 to 08	09 to 16	17 to 24	Total Obsn	MCWB
105/109																	0	0	0	71
100/104																	1	0	1	70
95/99																	9	3	12	69
90/94																	38	20	58	67
85/89												0	0	0	57		73	41	114	66
80/84												1	1	2	56	1	123	72	196	64
75/79							0	0	0	54		2	1	3	54	9	172	114	295	62
70/74							1	0	1	52		4	2	6	54	39	211	158	408	60
65/69							1	0	1	49		8	4	12	51	112	207	183	502	57
60/64							3	2	5	48	0	16	10	26	48	203	198	218	619	54
55/59		0		0	45		5	2	7	45	2	23	16	41	46	263	182	211	656	51
50/54		0	0	0	43	0	8	5	13	43	7	28	25	60	43	246	172	189	607	46
45/49		1	1	2	40	1	11	7	19	40	16	33	31	80	41	207	149	169	525	42
40/44	1	7	3	11	36	4	15	12	31	37	31	33	35	99	37	216	153	172	541	38
35/39	6	13	11	30	33	16	29	27	72	34	49	36	48	133	33	232	186	206	624	34
30/34	14	20	19	53	29	36	37	44	117	30	68	36	40	144	30	270	184	216	670	30
25/29	21	24	29	74	25	41	32	39	112	25	31	14	18	63	25	210	141	180	531	25
20/24	28	27	26	81	21	33	27	26	86	20	22	6	7	35	21	181	130	137	448	21
15/19	24	27	23	74	16	26	26	26	78	16	9	1	2	12	16	129	113	117	359	16
10/14	22	23	23	68	11	24	21	23	68	11	3	0	1	4	11	108	101	98	307	11
5/9	15	23	22	60	6	23	15	16	54	6	1			1	7	89	98	98	285	6
0/4	19	20	24	63	1	16	10	11	37	1						105	91	98	294	1
-5/-1	23	15	18	56	-3	14	5	5	24	-3						98	72	81	251	-3
-10/-6	21	12	11	44	-8	8	1	2	11	-8						73	50	62	185	-8
-15/-11	14	7	10	31	-13	3	0	0	3	-13						59	38	43	140	-13
-20/-16	10	4	4	18	-18	2	0		2	-17						38	18	21	77	-18
-25/-21	4	1	1	6	-23	0	0		0	-22						18	8	9	35	-23
-30/-26	1	0	1	2	-28	1		0	1	-28						7	2	2	11	-28
-35/-31	0			0	-32											3	0	0	3	-32

AKRON/AKRON-GANTON APRT OHIO

LAT 40 55N LONG 81 26W ELEV 1208 FT

MEAN FREQUENCY OF OCCURRENCE OF DRY BULB TEMPERATURE (DEGREES F) WITH MEAN COINCIDENT WET BULB TEMPERATURE (DEGREES F) FOR EACH DRY BULB TEMPERATURE RANGE

Temperature Range	MAY Obsn Hour Gp 01 to 08	MAY 09 to 16	MAY 17 to 24	MAY Total Obsn	MAY MCWB	JUNE Obsn Hour Gp 01 to 08	JUNE 09 to 16	JUNE 17 to 24	JUNE Total Obsn	JUNE MCWB
100/104							0		0	74
95/99							1	0	1	74
90/94							3	1	4	74
85/89		1	0	1	69		19	4	23	72
80/84	0	12	2	14	67	1	41	16	58	69
75/79	0	30	11	41	64	5	47	28	80	66
70/74	4	41	24	69	61	21	51	49	121	64
65/69	15	38	35	88	59	59	43	55	157	62
60/64	42	43	45	130	56	54	21	39	114	58
55/59	44	37	39	120	51	45	9	27	81	54
50/54	41	23	38	102	48	36	4	16	56	50
45/49	42	13	28	83	44	17	2	5	24	46
40/44	37	9	17	63	40	2		0	2	42
35/39	17	1	7	25	36	0			0	39
30/34	6		1	7	31					
25/29	0			0	27					
20/24										

Temperature Range	JULY Obsn Hour Gp 01 to 08	JULY 09 to 16	JULY 17 to 24	JULY Total Obsn	JULY MCWB	AUGUST Obsn Hour Gp 01 to 08	AUGUST 09 to 16	AUGUST 17 to 24	AUGUST Total Obsn	AUGUST MCWB
100/104										
95/99		0		0	74		0		0	68
90/94		5	1	6	72		7	1	8	71
85/89		33	8	41	71		21	4	25	71
80/84	1	59	23	83	69	1	56	19	76	69
75/79	8	68	44	120	67	4	73	38	115	67
70/74	44	56	72	172	66	35	53	66	154	66
65/69	85	21	59	165	63	80	29	63	172	63
60/64	64	5	27	96	59	69	8	37	114	59
55/59	32	1	12	45	54	38	0	15	53	55
50/54	13		2	15	51	17		5	22	50
45/49	1			1	48	4		0	4	47
40/44										
35/39										
30/34										
25/29										
20/24										

Temperature Range	SEPTEMBER Obsn Hour Gp 01 to 08	SEPTEMBER 09 to 16	SEPTEMBER 17 to 24	SEPTEMBER Total Obsn	SEPTEMBER MCWB	OCTOBER Obsn Hour Gp 01 to 08	OCTOBER 09 to 16	OCTOBER 17 to 24	OCTOBER Total Obsn	OCTOBER MCWB
100/104										
95/99		1		1	71					
90/94		4	0	4	70					
85/89		12	3	15	71		1		1	68
80/84	0	25	7	32	68		4	0	4	66
75/79	1	34	18	53	66		16	1	17	62
70/74	16	45	34	95	64	0	25	6	31	60
65/69	39	50	43	132	61	8	29	20	57	59
60/64	44	40	47	131	57	13	38	31	82	55
55/59	47	21	41	109	53	33	39	40	112	52
50/54	44	6	29	79	49	39	40	42	121	48
45/49	29	2	12	43	45	46	34	46	126	44
40/44	15	1	5	21	40	58	15	40	113	40
35/39	4		1	5	36	33	6	17	56	35
30/34	1		0	1	32	15	3	4	22	31
25/29						2	0	1	3	27
20/24						1		0	1	23

AKRON/AKRON-CANTON APRT OHIO

Tempera-ture Range	NOVEMBER					DECEMBER					JANUARY					FEBRUARY					MARCH					APRIL					ANNUAL TOTAL				
	Obsn Hour Gp 01 to 08	Obsn Hour Gp 09 to 16	Obsn Hour Gp 17 to 24	Total Obsn	M C W B	Obsn Hour Gp 01 to 08	Obsn Hour Gp 09 to 16	Obsn Hour Gp 17 to 24	Total Obsn	M C W B	Obsn Hour Gp 01 to 08	Obsn Hour Gp 09 to 16	Obsn Hour Gp 17 to 24	Total Obsn	M C W B	Obsn Hour Gp 01 to 08	Obsn Hour Gp 09 to 16	Obsn Hour Gp 17 to 24	Total Obsn	M C W B	Obsn Hour Gp 01 to 08	Obsn Hour Gp 09 to 16	Obsn Hour Gp 17 to 24	Total Obsn	M C W B	Obsn Hour Gp 01 to 08	Obsn Hour Gp 09 to 16	Obsn Hour Gp 17 to 24	Total Obsn	M C W B	Obsn Hour Gp 01 to 08	Obsn Hour Gp 09 to 16	Obsn Hour Gp 17 to 24	Total Obsn	M C W B
100/104																																0		0	74
95/99																																2	0	2	72
90/94																																19	3	22	72
85/89																																87	19	106	71
80/84																											3	0	3	65	3	200	67	270	69
75/79		1		1	64																	0		0	58		10	2	12	63	18	279	142	439	66
70/74		1	0	1	62							0		0	61							1	0	1	56	0	18	7	25	59	120	291	258	669	64
65/69	1	10	3	14	57		0		0	57	0	0	1	1	58		0	0	0	54		4	1	5	54	3	24	14	41	56	290	248	294	832	61
60/64	3	14	8	25	55	0	2	1	3	54	1	1	0	2	57		1	1	2	54	1	8	4	13	54	13	24	24	61	54	304	205	264	773	57
55/59	12	21	14	47	51	2	7	3	12	52	3	4	4	11	55	2	4	3	9	51	4	12	9	25	51	22	25	26	73	51	284	180	233	697	52
50/54	15	24	23	62	47	6	12	8	26	48	4	8	5	17	50	3	9	6	18	48	9	19	12	40	46	28	27	30	85	47	255	172	216	643	48
45/49	25	30	29	84	43	9	15	10	34	44	9	9	8	26	45	5	14	11	30	42	11	25	23	59	42	34	33	36	103	43	232	177	208	617	43
40/44	30	38	31	99	39	15	21	21	57	39	9	16	15	40	39	15	24	22	61	39	21	31	25	77	38	33	30	29	92	39	235	185	205	625	39
35/39	36	35	42	113	34	27	37	31	95	35	15	31	26	72	35	20	34	30	84	34	28	42	42	112	34	41	27	35	103	34	221	213	231	665	35
30/34	50	36	45	131	30	46	52	48	146	30	44	49	42	135	30	41	52	52	145	30	54	50	51	155	30	41	15	27	83	31	298	257	270	825	30
25/29	38	18	23	79	26	43	42	47	132	26	47	49	49	145	25	48	41	38	127	26	51	35	41	127	26	18	3	7	28	26	247	188	206	641	26
20/24	18	8	13	39	21	39	27	34	100	21	44	40	40	124	21	35	20	27	82	21	36	15	26	77	21	5	1	2	8	21	178	111	142	431	21
15/19	7	3	4	14	16	23	20	22	65	16	27	21	28	76	16	24	11	14	49	16	15	5	10	30	16	1		1	2	17	97	60	79	236	16
10/14	4	1	4	9	11	22	9	14	45	11	25	14	18	57	11	13	8	11	32	11	11	2	4	17	12						75	34	51	160	11
5/9	1	1	2	4	7	9	3	6	18	7	13	5	8	26	7	5	3	6	14	7	4	0	1	5	8						32	12	23	67	7
0/4	0	0		0	3	3	2	2	7	1	5	1	3	9	2	8	2	2	12	2	1			1	2						17	5	7	29	2
-5/-1	0			0	-1	2	1	1	4	-3	2	0	0	2	-3	1	1	0	2	-3											5	2	1	8	-3
-10/-6						2	0	0	2	-7	0			0	-7	1	0	1	2	-8											3	0		4	-8
-15/-11						0			0	-12																					0			0	-12

CINCINNATI APRT/COVINGTON OHIO

LAT 39 03N   LONG 84 40W   ELEV 869 FT

MEAN FREQUENCY OF OCCURRENCE OF DRY BULB TEMPERATURE (DEGREES F) WITH MEAN COINCIDENT WET BULB TEMPERATURE (DEGREES F) FOR EACH DRY BULB TEMPERATURE RANGE

Temperature Range	MAY Obsn Hour Gp 01 to 08	MAY Obsn Hour Gp 09 to 16	MAY Obsn Hour Gp 17 to 24	MAY Total Obsn	MAY MCWB	JUNE Obsn Hour Gp 01 to 08	JUNE Obsn Hour Gp 09 to 16	JUNE Obsn Hour Gp 17 to 24	JUNE Total Obsn	JUNE MCWB	JULY Obsn Hour Gp 01 to 08	JULY Obsn Hour Gp 09 to 16	JULY Obsn Hour Gp 17 to 24	JULY Total Obsn	JULY MCWB
100/104												0	0	0	78
95/99							1	0	1	76		2	1	3	74
90/94		1	0	1	70		12	3	15	73		21	7	28	73
85/89		11	4	15	69	0	34	14	48	71	0	53	24	77	72
80/84		26	11	37	67	2	57	34	93	69	3	71	45	119	70
75/79	1	41	25	67	64	13	55	46	114	67	25	61	67	153	69
70/74	10	45	40	95	62	51	42	62	155	66	91	30	69	190	68
65/69	40	46	50	136	60	72	24	45	141	63	77	9	28	114	64
60/64	53	34	49	136	57	50	11	24	85	58	38	1	6	45	59
55/59	50	21	31	102	52	34	3	8	45	54	12		1	13	55
50/54	45	13	21	79	48	14	1	2	17	50	2		0	2	50
45/49	27	7	9	43	43	3		1	4	45	0			0	48
40/44	15	3	6	24	39										
35/39	7	0	2	9	35										
30/34	1		0	1	31										
25/29	0			0	28										
20/24															
15/19															

Temperature Range	AUGUST Obsn Hour Gp 01 to 08	AUGUST Obsn Hour Gp 09 to 16	AUGUST Obsn Hour Gp 17 to 24	AUGUST Total Obsn	AUGUST MCWB	SEPTEMBER Obsn Hour Gp 01 to 08	SEPTEMBER Obsn Hour Gp 09 to 16	SEPTEMBER Obsn Hour Gp 17 to 24	SEPTEMBER Total Obsn	SEPTEMBER MCWB	OCTOBER Obsn Hour Gp 01 to 08	OCTOBER Obsn Hour Gp 09 to 16	OCTOBER Obsn Hour Gp 17 to 24	OCTOBER Total Obsn	OCTOBER MCWB
100/104		0	0	0	74		0		0	69					
95/99		3	0	3	72		1	0	1	67					
90/94		19	5	24	72		8	2	10	70					
85/89		48	20	68	71	0	21	8	29	70		3	0	3	69
80/84	1	70	40	111	69	0	30	16	46	67		13	3	16	64
75/79	17	56	65	138	68	5	46	33	84	66		27	8	35	62
70/74	72	37	64	173	67	32	50	48	130	64	5	35	23	63	61
65/69	79	15	37	131	63	46	45	49	140	60	14	36	35	85	59
60/64	49	2	13	64	59	46	25	40	111	57	30	39	46	115	55
55/59	23		3	26	55	41	10	26	77	53	38	35	42	115	51
50/54	6		0	6	51	36	4	12	52	49	49	29	37	115	47
45/49	0			0	48	23	1	4	28	44	46	18	30	94	43
40/44						8	0	1	9	40	34	8	15	57	39
35/39						2		0	2	36	20	4	5	29	35
30/34											8	1	3	12	30
25/29											3	0	1	4	26
20/24											1	0	0	1	20
15/19											0			0	17

CINCINNATI APRT/COVINGTON OHIO

Temperature Range	NOVEMBER Obsn Hour Gp 01 to 08	NOVEMBER Obsn Hour Gp 09 to 16	NOVEMBER Obsn Hour Gp 17 to 24	NOVEMBER Total Obsn	NOVEMBER MCWB	DECEMBER Obsn Hour Gp 01 to 08	DECEMBER Obsn Hour Gp 09 to 16	DECEMBER Obsn Hour Gp 17 to 24	DECEMBER Total Obsn	DECEMBER MCWB
100/104										
95/99										
90/94										
85/89										
80/84		0		0	67					
75/79		1	0	1	64					
70/74	1	5	2	8	60		0		0	61
65/69	2	11	6	19	57	0	2	1	3	59
60/64	5	20	14	39	54	1	6	4	11	55
55/59	16	28	23	67	51	5	12	8	25	51
50/54	23	29	28	80	46	13	14	15	42	47
45/49	26	38	34	98	42	13	24	19	56	43
40/44	31	32	39	102	38	20	27	29	76	38
35/39	41	31	36	108	34	35	43	35	113	34
30/34	45	25	32	102	30	41	45	54	140	29
25/29	30	12	15	57	25	44	32	33	109	25
20/24	13	4	6	23	21	30	19	25	74	20
15/19	3	1	2	6	16	21	10	11	42	16
10/14	1	1	2	4	11	10	7	7	24	11
5/9	1	0	0	1	6	6	4	5	15	6
0/4	1	0		1	2	5	1	2	8	2
-5/-1						3	0	0	3	-3
-10/-6						0	0		0	-7
-15/-11										
-20/-16										

Temperature Range	JANUARY Obsn Hour Gp 01 to 08	JANUARY Obsn Hour Gp 09 to 16	JANUARY Obsn Hour Gp 17 to 24	JANUARY Total Obsn	JANUARY MCWB	FEBRUARY Obsn Hour Gp 01 to 08	FEBRUARY Obsn Hour Gp 09 to 16	FEBRUARY Obsn Hour Gp 17 to 24	FEBRUARY Total Obsn	FEBRUARY MCWB
100/104										
95/99										
90/94										
85/89										
80/84										
75/79										
70/74		0	0	0	62		0		0	56
65/69	0	1	1	2	60	1	1	1	3	58
60/64	3	6	4	13	58	1	7	5	13	55
55/59	7	8	7	22	54	4	11	8	23	51
50/54	9	14	14	37	48	8	16	14	38	46
45/49	9	19	17	45	43	11	26	23	60	42
40/44	16	25	24	65	38	21	31	31	83	38
35/39	32	38	35	105	34	36	40	43	119	34
30/34	49	50	52	151	30	50	39	43	132	30
25/29	39	35	37	111	25	39	24	25	88	25
20/24	32	22	27	81	20	21	11	14	46	20
15/19	21	13	15	49	16	14	7	8	29	15
10/14	14	9	7	30	11	6	5	5	16	11
5/9	9	5	4	18	6	5	4	2	11	6
0/4	4	2	2	8	1	5	2	2	9	2
-5/-1	3	1	2	6	-3	1	0	1	2	-3
-10/-6	1	0	0	1	-7	1	0		1	-8
-15/-11	0	0	0	0	-13	0	0		0	-13
-20/-16	1	0		1	-16					

Temperature Range	MARCH Obsn Hour Gp 01 to 08	MARCH Obsn Hour Gp 09 to 16	MARCH Obsn Hour Gp 17 to 24	MARCH Total Obsn	MARCH MCWB	APRIL Obsn Hour Gp 01 to 08	APRIL Obsn Hour Gp 09 to 16	APRIL Obsn Hour Gp 17 to 24	APRIL Total Obsn	APRIL MCWB
100/104										
95/99										
90/94										
85/89							1	0	1	65
80/84							9	3	12	64
75/79		1	0	1	58		18	9	27	62
70/74		5	3	8	57	2	24	18	44	60
65/69	1	10	6	17	55	15	23	26	64	57
60/64	7	19	15	41	54	25	30	31	86	54
55/59	11	20	20	51	50	26	33	32	91	50
50/54	15	23	25	63	45	31	31	32	94	46
45/49	20	31	30	81	41	32	28	33	93	41
40/44	35	40	40	115	38	42	22	29	93	38
35/39	42	40	43	125	33	38	16	19	73	34
30/34	52	34	37	123	29	21	5	6	32	30
25/29	35	15	18	68	25	7	1	1	9	25
20/24	18	5	7	30	21	0			0	21
15/19	8	3	3	14	16					
10/14	3	1	1	5	11					
5/9	2	0	0	2	6					
0/4	0			0	3					
-5/-1										
-10/-6										
-15/-11										
-20/-16										

Temperature Range	ANNUAL TOTAL Obsn Hour Gp 01 to 08	ANNUAL TOTAL Obsn Hour Gp 09 to 16	ANNUAL TOTAL Obsn Hour Gp 17 to 24	ANNUAL TOTAL Total Obsn	ANNUAL TOTAL MCWB
100/104		0	0	0	74
95/99		7	1	8	73
90/94		61	17	78	73
85/89	0	171	70	241	71
80/84	6	276	152	434	69
75/79	61	306	253	620	67
70/74	264	273	329	866	65
65/69	347	223	285	855	61
60/64	308	200	251	759	56
55/59	267	181	209	657	51
50/54	251	174	200	625	47
45/49	210	192	200	602	42
40/44	222	188	214	624	38
35/39	253	212	218	683	34
30/34	267	199	227	693	30
25/29	197	119	130	446	25
20/24	115	61	79	255	20
15/19	67	34	39	140	16
10/14	34	23	22	79	11
5/9	23	13	11	47	6
0/4	15	5	6	26	2
-5/-1	7	1	3	11	-3
-10/-6	2	0	0	2	-7
-15/-11	0	0	0	0	-13
-20/-16	1	0		1	-16

TOLEDO/TOLEDO EXPRESS APRT OHIO

LAT 41 36N LONG 83 48W ELEV 669 FT

MEAN FREQUENCY OF OCCURRENCE OF DRY BULB TEMPERATURE (DEGREES F) WITH MEAN COINCIDENT WET BULB TEMPERATURE (DEGREES F) FOR EACH DRY BULB TEMPERATURE RANGE

Temperature Range	MAY Obsn Hour Gp 01 to 08	MAY 09 to 16	MAY 17 to 24	MAY Total Obsn	MAY MCWB	JUNE Obsn Hour Gp 01 to 08	JUNE 09 to 16	JUNE 17 to 24	JUNE Total Obsn	JUNE MCWB	JULY Obsn Hour Gp 01 to 08	JULY 09 to 16	JULY 17 to 24	JULY Total Obsn	JULY MCWB
95/99		0		0	71		0		0	74		0		0	76
90/94		3	1	4	71		10	4	14	71		9	3	12	74
85/89		7	3	10	70		24	11	35	71		36	14	50	71
80/84		21	9	30	67	1	41	22	64	69		60	31	91	69
75/79	1	26	17	44	64	7	46	34	87	66	7	67	49	123	67
70/74	12	36	24	72	62	28	49	47	124	64	42	50	68	160	66
65/69	24	41	36	101	59	50	36	50	136	61	76	20	50	146	63
60/64	32	37	43	112	55	51	22	37	110	58	68	5	24	97	59
55/59	35	31	37	103	51	39	10	21	70	54	35	0	8	43	55
50/54	43	25	38	106	47	37	2	10	49	50	16		2	18	51
45/49	39	13	24	76	43	23	1	3	27	45	4		0	4	46
40/44	37	7	13	57	39	5		0	5	42	0			0	44
35/39	20	1	4	25	35	0			0	39					
30/34	5		0	5	31										
25/29	1			1	28										
20/24															
15/19															

Temperature Range	AUGUST Obsn Hour Gp 01 to 08	AUGUST 09 to 16	AUGUST 17 to 24	AUGUST Total Obsn	AUGUST MCWB	SEPTEMBER Obsn Hour Gp 01 to 08	SEPTEMBER 09 to 16	SEPTEMBER 17 to 24	SEPTEMBER Total Obsn	SEPTEMBER MCWB	OCTOBER Obsn Hour Gp 01 to 08	OCTOBER 09 to 16	OCTOBER 17 to 24	OCTOBER Total Obsn	OCTOBER MCWB
95/99		0		0	79										
90/94		8	2	10	75		5	1	6	73		0		0	65
85/89		26	11	37	73		13	3	16	72		1	0	1	65
80/84	0	54	25	79	70		24	10	34	70		8	1	9	63
75/79	8	64	44	116	68	2	36	21	59	67		18	5	23	62
70/74	30	55	65	150	66	22	47	39	108	65	2	25	11	38	60
65/69	70	29	50	149	63	35	43	44	122	61	4	31	20	55	58
60/64	64	9	32	105	59	39	38	40	117	57	14	43	37	94	55
55/59	42	2	14	58	55	41	23	35	99	53	29	36	38	103	51
50/54	26		5	31	51	37	10	25	72	49	39	36	42	117	47
45/49	8		0	8	46	31	2	14	47	45	44	25	42	111	44
40/44	1			1	42	19	0	7	26	41	52	17	30	99	39
35/39	0			0	38	10		1	11	36	32	7	15	54	35
30/34						3		0	3	32	21	1	5	27	31
25/29						0			0	28	9	0	2	11	26
20/24											2		0	2	22
15/19											0			0	19

TOLEDO/TOLEDO EXPRESS APRT OHIO

Temperature Range	NOVEMBER Obsn Hour Gp 01 to 08	09 to 16	17 to 24	Total Obsn	MCWB	DECEMBER Obsn Hour Gp 01 to 08	09 to 16	17 to 24	Total Obsn	MCWB	JANUARY Obsn Hour Gp 01 to 08	09 to 16	17 to 24	Total Obsn	MCWB
95/99															
90/94															
85/89															
80/84															
75/79		0		0	68										
70/74		3	1	4	59										
65/69	2	6	3	11	59										
60/64	4	13	7	24	55		1		1	54					
55/59	14	25	18	57	53	1	7	3	11	52	1	0	1	2	55
50/54	15	26	23	64	47	4	7	8	19	48	1	2	2	5	49
45/49	20	39	31	90	43	5	12	10	27	43	1	4	2	7	43
40/44	34	40	43	117	39	10	19	16	45	39	4	14	6	24	38
35/39	38	36	38	112	34	28	35	29	92	35	14	28	26	68	34
30/34	43	27	40	110	30	38	47	47	132	30	45	52	50	147	30
25/29	35	16	22	73	26	47	46	47	140	26	39	44	41	124	25
20/24	24	6	10	40	21	37	29	29	95	21	33	38	37	108	20
15/19	8	3	3	14	16	28	20	25	73	16	32	28	31	91	16
10/14	2	1	2	5	11	14	13	18	45	11	34	19	24	77	11
5/9	1	0	1	2	7	12	7	9	28	6	18	10	15	43	6
0/4	1		0	1	3	12	4	6	22	2	15	6	8	29	2
-5/-1						8	2	2	12	-3	7	2	3	12	-3
-10/-6						2	0	0	2	-8	5	1	1	7	-7
-15/-11						0			0	-11	1	0	0	1	-13
-20/-16											0		0	0	-16

Temperature Range	FEBRUARY Obsn Hour Gp 01 to 08	09 to 16	17 to 24	Total Obsn	MCWB	MARCH Obsn Hour Gp 01 to 08	09 to 16	17 to 24	Total Obsn	MCWB	APRIL Obsn Hour Gp 01 to 08	09 to 16	17 to 24	Total Obsn	MCWB	ANNUAL TOTAL Obsn Hour Gp 01 to 08	09 to 16	17 to 24	Total Obsn	MCWB
95/99																	0		0	75
90/94																	35	11	46	73
85/89												1		1	69		108	42	150	72
80/84												6	2	8	64	1	214	100	315	69
75/79							1	0	1	66		10	4	14	63	25	268	174	467	67
70/74							2	1	3	57	0	13	9	22	60	136	280	265	681	64
65/69		0	0	0	56		4	2	6	56	4	19	14	37	57	265	229	269	763	61
60/64		0	0	0	54	0	5	5	10	53	17	24	19	60	55	289	197	244	730	57
55/59		1	1	2	53	2	8	7	17	50	13	26	24	63	50	252	169	207	628	52
50/54	1	3	3	7	49	6	12	9	27	46	22	35	31	88	46	247	158	198	603	48
45/49	3	9	6	18	43	8	19	16	43	41	29	33	37	99	42	215	157	185	557	43
40/44	3	16	10	29	38	19	42	32	93	38	38	35	41	114	38	222	190	198	610	39
35/39	21	35	33	89	34	39	56	53	148	34	50	25	34	109	34	252	223	233	708	34
30/34	44	51	46	141	30	61	55	61	177	30	40	11	21	72	30	300	244	270	814	30
25/29	37	47	43	127	25	52	26	34	112	25	21	1	4	26	25	241	180	193	614	25
20/24	41	30	39	110	20	28	10	16	54	21	5			5	21	170	113	131	414	21
15/19	35	11	19	65	16	14	4	8	26	16	1		0	1	17	118	66	86	270	16
10/14	16	11	10	37	11	12	2	2	16	11	1			1	13	79	46	56	181	11
5/9	10	7	9	26	6	4	0	1	5	7						45	24	35	104	6
0/4	8	2	2	12	2	2			2	2						38	12	16	66	2
-5/-1	3	0	2	5	-3	0			0	-2						18	4	7	29	-3
-10/-6	2	0	0	2	-7											9	1	1	11	-7
-15/-11																1	0	0	1	-13
-20/-16																0		0	0	-16

WRIGHT-PATTERSON AFB/DAYTON OHIO

LAT 39 49N LONG 84 03W ELEV 824 FT

MEAN FREQUENCY OF OCCURRENCE OF DRY BULB TEMPERATURE (DEGREES F) WITH MEAN COINCIDENT WET BULB TEMPERATURE (DEGREES F) FOR EACH DRY BULB TEMPERATURE RANGE

Temperature Range	MAY Obsn Hour Gp 01 to 08	MAY Obsn Hour Gp 09 to 16	MAY Obsn Hour Gp 17 to 24	MAY Total Obsn	MAY MCWB	JUNE Obsn Hour Gp 01 to 08	JUNE Obsn Hour Gp 09 to 16	JUNE Obsn Hour Gp 17 to 24	JUNE Total Obsn	JUNE MCWB	JULY Obsn Hour Gp 01 to 08	JULY Obsn Hour Gp 09 to 16	JULY Obsn Hour Gp 17 to 24	JULY Total Obsn	JULY MCWB
100/104							0		0	81					
95/99							0	0	0	80		1	0	1	75
90/94		1	0	1	70		12	4	16	73		11	3	14	75
85/89		9	3	12	69	0	32	15	47	71		50	23	73	72
80/84		25	9	34	67	1	53	34	88	69	2	70	46	118	70
75/79	1	34	23	58	65	13	55	49	117	67	22	62	68	152	68
70/74	9	42	40	91	62	44	43	56	143	64	75	37	62	174	66
65/69	37	45	52	134	60	69	27	44	140	62	77	14	35	126	63
60/64	46	35	44	125	56	44	12	25	81	58	46	3	9	58	58
55/59	41	25	32	98	51	42	3	11	56	54	20	0	1	21	54
50/54	45	17	21	83	48	23	1	2	26	49	5		0	5	50
45/49	34	10	15	59	43	3		0	3	45	0			0	48
40/44	24	4	8	36	39	1			1	41					
35/39	9	0	1	10	35										
30/34	2		0	2	30										
25/29	0			0	27										
20/24															

Temperature Range	AUGUST Obsn Hour Gp 01 to 08	AUGUST Obsn Hour Gp 09 to 16	AUGUST Obsn Hour Gp 17 to 24	AUGUST Total Obsn	AUGUST MCWB	SEPTEMBER Obsn Hour Gp 01 to 08	SEPTEMBER Obsn Hour Gp 09 to 16	SEPTEMBER Obsn Hour Gp 17 to 24	SEPTEMBER Total Obsn	SEPTEMBER MCWB	OCTOBER Obsn Hour Gp 01 to 08	OCTOBER Obsn Hour Gp 09 to 16	OCTOBER Obsn Hour Gp 17 to 24	OCTOBER Total Obsn	OCTOBER MCWB
100/104		0		0	80										
95/99		1	0	1	76		1	0	1	71					
90/94		12	3	15	75		5	1	6	73					
85/89		43	17	60	73		20	7	27	72		1		1	67
80/84	1	66	39	106	70		35	16	51	69		8	1	9	65
75/79	16	61	62	139	68	6	43	33	82	67		20	6	26	63
70/74	58	39	62	159	66	34	45	52	131	65	1	25	16	42	61
65/69	66	20	39	125	63	46	39	40	125	61	10	36	27	73	59
60/64	61	6	20	87	59	38	30	39	107	57	24	43	42	109	55
55/59	34	1	5	40	54	37	13	26	76	53	35	38	43	116	51
50/54	10		1	11	50	40	7	16	63	49	39	33	41	113	47
45/49	2		0	2	46	25	2	7	34	45	43	25	33	101	43
40/44	0			0	41	11	0	1	12	41	44	13	24	81	39
35/39						3		0	3	37	32	5	10	47	35
30/34						0			0	33	14	1	4	19	31
25/29											5	0	1	6	26
20/24											1		0	1	22

WRIGHT-PATTERSON AFB/DAYTON OHIO

Temperature Range	NOVEMBER					DECEMBER					JANUARY				
	Obsn Hour Gp 01 to 08	09 to 16	17 to 24	Total Obsn	MCWB	Obsn Hour Gp 01 to 08	09 to 16	17 to 24	Total Obsn	MCWB	Obsn Hour Gp 01 to 08	09 to 16	17 to 24	Total Obsn	MCWB
100/104															
95/99															
90/94															
85/89															
80/84															
75/79		1	0	1	64										
70/74	1	4	1	6	60							0		0	59
65/69	1	8	5	14	59		1	1	2	59		0	0	0	58
60/64	5	18	12	35	55	2	6	3	11	55	1	2	2	5	56
55/59	13	26	19	58	51	4	9	7	20	52	2	4	3	9	53
50/54	21	33	33	87	47	9	12	12	33	48	5	7	5	17	49
45/49	32	43	37	112	43	13	20	18	51	43	7	13	10	30	43
40/44	39	39	39	117	38	19	27	25	71	38	13	23	21	57	38
35/39	40	29	43	112	34	28	39	32	99	34	23	33	31	87	34
30/34	43	24	29	96	30	44	48	51	143	30	38	41	43	122	29
25/29	27	11	14	52	25	46	38	42	126	25	41	35	39	115	25
20/24	12	3	5	20	21	35	21	25	81	21	27	32	29	88	20
15/19	4	2	2	8	16	20	11	14	45	16	29	23	30	82	16
10/14	1	0	1	2	12	12	7	9	28	11	28	16	17	61	11
5/9	0	0	0	0	6	6	4	4	14	7	15	9	9	33	6
0/4	0	0		0	2	6	2	3	11	2	9	5	5	19	2
-5/-1						3	0	0	3	-3	7	2	3	12	-3
-10/-6						1			1	-7	3	1	0	4	-7
-15/-11											1	0	0	1	-13
-20/-16											0		0	0	-16

Temperature Range	FEBRUARY					MARCH					APRIL					ANNUAL TOTAL				
	Obsn Hour Gp 01 to 08	09 to 16	17 to 24	Total Obsn	MCWB	Obsn Hour Gp 01 to 08	09 to 16	17 to 24	Total Obsn	MCWB	Obsn Hour Gp 01 to 08	09 to 16	17 to 24	Total Obsn	MCWB	Obsn Hour Gp 01 to 08	09 to 16	17 to 24	Total Obsn	MCWB
100/104																	0		0	80
95/99																	3	0	3	75
90/94																	41	11	52	74
85/89												1	0	1	69	0	156	65	221	72
80/84												7	2	9	66	4	264	147	415	69
75/79							2	0	2	58	0	15	8	23	63	58	293	249	600	67
70/74		0		0	63		6	3	9	57	2	19	16	37	60	224	260	308	792	65
65/69		1	0	1	57	1	8	5	14	54	11	26	20	57	57	318	225	268	811	61
60/64	1	3	2	6	54	5	13	10	28	53	22	37	34	93	54	295	208	242	745	56
55/59	2	5	4	11	52	9	15	16	40	50	26	34	37	97	50	265	173	204	642	52
50/54	4	8	6	18	47	8	21	19	48	45	31	35	36	102	46	240	174	192	606	47
45/49	6	14	12	32	42	19	30	28	77	42	35	29	33	97	42	219	186	193	598	43
40/44	11	22	22	55	38	29	40	35	104	38	38	21	30	89	38	229	189	205	623	38
35/39	24	41	35	100	34	42	46	51	139	33	41	14	17	72	34	242	207	220	669	34
30/34	40	44	47	131	30	54	38	41	133	29	27	3	6	36	30	262	199	221	682	30
25/29	42	35	35	112	25	40	19	24	83	25	6	0	0	6	26	207	138	155	500	25
20/24	34	20	26	80	20	24	8	11	43	21	1		0	1	22	134	84	96	314	20
15/19	24	15	17	56	16	12	3	3	18	16	0			0	18	89	54	66	209	16
10/14	15	7	8	30	11	4	1	1	6	12						60	31	36	127	11
5/9	10	6	5	21	6	2	0	0	2	7						33	19	18	70	6
0/4	7	2	2	11	2	0			0	2						22	9	10	41	2
-5/-1	3	0	1	4	-3											13	2	4	19	-3
-10/-6	0			0	-6											4	1	0	5	-7
-15/-11																1	0	0	1	-13
-20/-16																0		0	0	-16

ALTUS AFB OKLAHOMA

LAT 34 39N LONG 99 16W ELEV 1378 FT

MEAN FREQUENCY OF OCCURRENCE OF DRY BULB TEMPERATURE (DEGREES F) WITH MEAN COINCIDENT WET BULB TEMPERATURE (DEGREES F) FOR EACH DRY BULB TEMPERATURE RANGE

Temperature Range	MAY Obsn Hour Gp 01 to 08	MAY 09 to 16	MAY 17 to 24	MAY Total Obsn	MAY MCWB	JUNE Obsn Hour Gp 01 to 08	JUNE 09 to 16	JUNE 17 to 24	JUNE Total Obsn	JUNE MCWB	JULY Obsn Hour Gp 01 to 08	JULY 09 to 16	JULY 17 to 24	JULY Total Obsn	JULY MCWB
110/114															
105/109							1	0	1	71		4	1	5	73
100/104		1	1	2	67		5	3	8	73		24	13	37	73
95/99		4	3	7	68		26	14	40	73		53	33	86	73
90/94		16	7	23	69		44	29	73	72	0	57	43	100	73
85/89		35	20	55	67	1	53	44	98	71	6	49	53	108	72
80/84	1	47	34	82	66	18	51	53	122	70	46	34	54	134	70
75/79	7	47	44	98	65	55	27	43	125	69	95	16	31	142	69
70/74	39	40	48	127	63	77	17	31	125	66	80	9	16	105	68
65/69	64	27	42	133	61	59	12	16	87	63	18	2	3	23	64
60/64	65	18	32	115	57	24	4	5	33	59	3	0	1	4	58
55/59	39	7	14	60	53	6	0	1	7	55	0			0	57
50/54	20	3	4	27	48	1			1	51					
45/49	9	0	1	10	44										
40/44	3		0	3	39										
35/39															
30/34															
25/29															

Temperature Range	AUGUST Obsn Hour Gp 01 to 08	AUGUST 09 to 16	AUGUST 17 to 24	AUGUST Total Obsn	AUGUST MCWB	SEPTEMBER Obsn Hour Gp 01 to 08	SEPTEMBER 09 to 16	SEPTEMBER 17 to 24	SEPTEMBER Total Obsn	SEPTEMBER MCWB	OCTOBER Obsn Hour Gp 01 to 08	OCTOBER 09 to 16	OCTOBER 17 to 24	OCTOBER Total Obsn	OCTOBER MCWB
110/114		0	0	0	73										
105/109		4	1	5	73										
100/104		19	9	28	73		3	1	4	72					
95/99		39	21	60	73		12	5	17	72					
90/94	0	55	37	92	72		27	13	40	72		7	1	8	65
85/89	3	54	51	108	71	0	37	23	60	71		16	6	22	66
80/84	28	40	57	125	70	4	44	39	87	69		26	11	37	65
75/79	80	24	46	150	69	26	42	45	113	67	0	32	23	55	63
70/74	96	10	21	127	67	66	33	42	141	66	8	39	32	79	61
65/69	33	2	5	40	62	55	23	37	115	62	25	42	40	107	58
60/64	7	1	1	9	58	45	11	23	79	58	42	36	44	122	55
55/59	2	0	0	2	55	30	5	9	44	53	57	25	43	125	52
50/54	0			0	47	11	2	3	16	49	51	16	27	94	48
45/49						2	0	0	2	46	37	7	14	58	43
40/44						0			0	41	20	3	5	28	39
35/39											7	0	1	8	35
30/34											1	0		1	31
25/29											0			0	28

ALTUS AFB OKLAHOMA

Temperature Range	NOVEMBER Obsn Hour Gp 01 to 08	NOVEMBER 09 to 16	NOVEMBER 17 to 24	NOVEMBER Total Obsn	NOVEMBER MCWB	DECEMBER Obsn Hour Gp 01 to 08	DECEMBER 09 to 16	DECEMBER 17 to 24	DECEMBER Total Obsn	DECEMBER MCWB	JANUARY Obsn Hour Gp 01 to 08	JANUARY 09 to 16	JANUARY 17 to 24	JANUARY Total Obsn	JANUARY MCWB
110/114															
105/109															
100/104															
95/99															
90/94															
85/89		0		0	60										
80/84		3	0	3	61		0		0	58		0	0	0	56
75/79		12	3	15	60		0	0	0	55		1	0	1	57
70/74	1	17	8	26	59		4	1	5	54		4	1	5	54
65/69	3	27	16	46	56		10	3	13	52		8	4	12	53
60/64	8	31	24	63	53	0	19	8	27	50	1	12	8	21	51
55/59	15	37	32	84	50	5	28	16	49	48	4	20	13	37	48
50/54	31	33	41	105	46	9	34	27	70	45	3	26	19	48	44
45/49	46	32	43	121	42	19	39	43	101	41	13	34	29	76	41
40/44	44	25	35	104	38	36	34	44	114	38	24	34	41	99	37
35/39	45	16	25	86	34	49	30	44	123	33	37	30	38	105	33
30/34	30	5	9	44	30	61	27	33	121	30	54	29	35	118	29
25/29	11	2	3	16	25	39	14	19	72	25	40	19	26	85	25
20/24	4	1	1	6	20	20	6	8	34	21	32	14	16	62	20
15/19	1			1	14	6	2	3	11	16	19	9	12	40	16
10/14						4	0	0	4	12	12	5	4	21	11
5/9						0	0		0	7	7	2	2	11	6
0/4											2	0	0	2	2
-5/-1											1	0	0	1	-3

Temperature Range	FEBRUARY Obsn Hour Gp 01 to 08	FEBRUARY 09 to 16	FEBRUARY 17 to 24	FEBRUARY Total Obsn	FEBRUARY MCWB	MARCH Obsn Hour Gp 01 to 08	MARCH 09 to 16	MARCH 17 to 24	MARCH Total Obsn	MARCH MCWB	APRIL Obsn Hour Gp 01 to 08	APRIL 09 to 16	APRIL 17 to 24	APRIL Total Obsn	APRIL MCWB	ANNUAL TOTAL Obsn Hour Gp 01 to 08	ANNUAL TOTAL 09 to 16	ANNUAL TOTAL 17 to 24	ANNUAL TOTAL Total Obsn	ANNUAL TOTAL MCWB
110/114																	0	0	0	73
105/109																	9	2	11	73
100/104							0	0	0	66		0		0	64		52	27	79	73
95/99							0	0	0	66		1	0	1	65		135	76	211	73
90/94		0	0	0	61		1	1	2	62		5	2	7	63	0	212	133	345	72
85/89		0	0	0	63		3	1	4	59		12	6	18	64	10	259	204	473	70
80/84		1	0	1	58		6	4	10	58	0	22	12	34	62	97	274	264	635	68
75/79		2	1	3	57		10	6	16	58	1	32	23	56	61	264	245	265	774	67
70/74		5	3	8	54	0	16	11	27	55	6	39	30	75	59	373	233	244	850	64
65/69	0	9	6	15	53	3	27	19	49	53	21	38	43	102	57	281	227	234	742	59
60/64	1	19	11	31	50	8	26	26	60	51	39	37	42	118	55	243	214	225	682	55
55/59	5	23	19	47	47	16	31	32	79	48	52	25	37	114	51	231	201	216	648	50
50/54	7	29	27	63	44	24	30	34	88	45	49	18	23	90	46	206	191	205	602	46
45/49	20	30	35	85	41	35	33	37	105	41	36	8	14	58	43	217	183	216	616	42
40/44	32	33	39	104	38	53	28	33	114	38	20	3	7	30	38	232	160	204	596	38
35/39	43	28	32	103	34	45	19	23	87	34	11	1	1	13	34	237	124	164	525	34
30/34	44	20	26	90	29	37	12	14	63	29	3	1	1	5	29	230	94	118	442	29
25/29	39	15	16	70	25	19	4	4	27	25	2		0	2	26	150	54	68	272	25
20/24	23	8	8	39	21	5	2	2	9	21						84	31	35	150	20
15/19	6	2	2	10	16	2	1	1	4	16						34	14	18	66	16
10/14	2	0	0	2	11	2	0		2	12						20	5	4	29	11
5/9	1		0	1	7	0			0	9						8	2	2	12	6
0/4	0			0	3											2	0	0	2	2
-5/-1																1	0	0	1	-3

FORT SILL/POST AAF OKLAHOMA

LAT 34 39N LONG 98 24W ELEV 1187 FT

MEAN FREQUENCY OF OCCURRENCE OF DRY BULB TEMPERATURE (DEGREES F) WITH MEAN COINCIDENT WET BULB TEMPERATURE (DEGREES F) FOR EACH DRY BULB TEMPERATURE RANGE

Temperature Range	MAY Obsn Hour Gp 01 to 08	MAY 09 to 16	MAY 17 to 24	MAY Total Obsn	MAY MCWB	JUNE Obsn Hour Gp 01 to 08	JUNE 09 to 16	JUNE 17 to 24	JUNE Total Obsn	JUNE MCWB	JULY Obsn Hour Gp 01 to 08	JULY 09 to 16	JULY 17 to 24	JULY Total Obsn	JULY MCWB
105/109								0	0	76		2	0	2	74
100/104		0	0	0	70		3	1	4	74		18	8	26	74
95/99		2	1	3	69		18	9	27	74		50	28	78	74
90/94		9	5	14	71		42	25	67	74	0	61	42	103	74
85/89		29	16	45	69	1	57	42	100	72	7	50	53	110	73
80/84	0	49	30	79	68	15	51	56	122	71	44	37	58	139	71
75/79	5	52	48	105	66	55	33	52	140	69	99	19	36	154	70
70/74	42	45	52	139	64	80	21	31	132	67	75	7	18	100	68
65/69	64	32	44	140	61	57	11	16	84	64	20	3	3	26	64
60/64	66	18	33	117	58	24	4	7	35	60	3	0	1	4	59
55/59	39	9	14	62	53	7	1	1	9	55	1			1	57
50/54	20	3	6	29	48	1		0	1	49					
45/49	9	1	1	11	44										
40/44	2			2	40										
35/39	0			0	36										
30/34															
25/29															

Temperature Range	AUGUST Obsn Hour Gp 01 to 08	AUGUST 09 to 16	AUGUST 17 to 24	AUGUST Total Obsn	AUGUST MCWB	SEPTEMBER Obsn Hour Gp 01 to 08	SEPTEMBER 09 to 16	SEPTEMBER 17 to 24	SEPTEMBER Total Obsn	SEPTEMBER MCWB	OCTOBER Obsn Hour Gp 01 to 08	OCTOBER 09 to 16	OCTOBER 17 to 24	OCTOBER Total Obsn	OCTOBER MCWB
105/109		2	1	3	76										
100/104		16	6	22	74		2	0	2	75					
95/99		38	20	58	74		9	3	12	73					
90/94		55	35	90	73		26	11	37	73		5	1	6	65
85/89	2	53	49	104	72	0	39	23	62	71		13	4	17	67
80/84	27	43	58	128	71	3	46	38	87	69		29	11	40	66
75/79	81	25	50	156	69	29	43	49	121	67	0	30	20	50	64
70/74	97	12	24	133	67	63	33	44	140	66	12	41	38	91	62
65/69	32	3	5	40	63	60	23	37	120	62	26	44	41	111	59
60/64	7	1	1	9	58	43	12	22	77	58	44	39	44	127	55
55/59	2	0	0	2	55	27	5	8	40	53	52	26	40	118	51
50/54						11	2	4	17	49	46	13	27	86	47
45/49						3		0	3	45	41	6	15	62	43
40/44						0			0	42	20	3	5	28	39
35/39											5	1	1	7	35
30/34											1	0	0	1	31
25/29											1				27

FORT SILL/POST AAF OKLAHOMA

Temperature Range	NOVEMBER					DECEMBER					JANUARY					FEBRUARY				
	Obsn Hour Gp 01 to 08	09 to 16	17 to 24	Total Obsn	MCWB	Obsn Hour Gp 01 to 08	09 to 16	17 to 24	Total Obsn	MCWB	Obsn Hour Gp 01 to 08	09 to 16	17 to 24	Total Obsn	MCWB	Obsn Hour Gp 01 to 08	09 to 16	17 to 24	Total Obsn	MCWB
105/109																				
100/104																				
95/99																				
90/94																				
85/89																				
80/84		2	0	2	61		0		0	58		0		0	55		1	0	1	61
75/79		12	2	14	61		1	0	1	58		0	0	0	57		2	1	3	56
70/74	1	20	11	32	60		3	1	4	56		4	1	5	54		5	2	7	56
65/69	5	25	16	48	57		10	3	13	55		7	4	11	54	0	11	6	17	54
60/64	12	35	26	73	53	2	20	10	32	52	2	14	9	25	52	1	18	13	32	51
55/59	17	35	33	85	50	8	29	19	56	49	5	19	13	37	49	6	24	19	49	48
50/54	35	34	43	112	46	11	36	30	77	45	6	26	21	53	45	9	28	29	66	44
45/49	41	32	38	111	42	23	38	46	107	41	15	33	31	79	41	23	30	35	88	41
40/44	48	24	36	108	38	37	34	42	113	37	30	34	40	104	38	37	33	39	109	37
35/39	45	13	20	78	34	54	31	40	125	33	40	33	39	112	33	44	29	31	104	33
30/34	23	5	8	36	29	54	25	28	107	30	48	30	34	112	29	41	20	25	86	29
25/29	8	2	3	13	25	33	13	16	62	25	41	20	24	85	25	35	14	13	62	25
20/24	4	0	1	5	20	16	7	9	32	21	27	11	15	53	20	18	7	8	33	20
15/19	0	0	0	0	14	4	2	3	9	15	17	10	10	37	16	6	2	2	10	16
10/14	0			0	11	4	1	1	6	11	8	4	4	16	11	2	0	0	2	11
5/9						1	0		1	7	6	2	3	11	6					
0/4											2	0		2	2					
-5/-1											0			0	-1					

Temperature Range	MARCH					APRIL					ANNUAL TOTAL				
	Obsn Hour Gp 01 to 08	09 to 16	17 to 24	Total Obsn	MCWB	Obsn Hour Gp 01 to 08	09 to 16	17 to 24	Total Obsn	MCWB	Obsn Hour Gp 01 to 08	09 to 16	17 to 24	Total Obsn	MCWB
105/109												4	1	5	75
100/104		0	0	0	69							39	15	54	74
95/99		0	0	0	67		0		0	69		117	61	178	74
90/94		1	0	1	64		2	1	3	65	0	201	120	321	73
85/89		3	1	4	62		9	4	13	65	10	253	192	455	71
80/84		5	4	9	61		20	10	30	64	89	283	265	637	69
75/79		11	6	17	59	0	33	22	55	62	269	261	286	816	67
70/74	1	18	12	31	56	7	40	37	84	61	378	249	271	898	65
65/69	4	25	19	48	54	33	42	43	118	59	301	236	239	776	60
60/64	10	29	27	66	52	42	39	45	126	55	256	229	238	723	55
55/59	20	29	32	81	48	50	26	34	110	51	234	203	213	650	50
50/54	27	33	37	97	45	45	17	24	86	46	211	192	221	624	46
45/49	39	29	35	103	41	30	8	13	51	42	224	177	214	615	42
40/44	46	27	33	106	38	20	2	5	27	38	240	157	200	597	38
35/39	46	20	21	87	33	10	1	2	13	34	244	128	154	526	33
30/34	31	11	14	56	29	3	1	1	5	30	201	92	110	403	29
25/29	15	4	4	23	25	1		0	1	26	134	53	60	247	25
20/24	5	2	1	8	20	0			0	23	70	27	34	131	20
15/19	2	1	1	4	15						29	15	16	60	16
10/14	1	0		1	12						15	5	5	25	11
5/9											7	2	3	12	6
0/4											2	0		2	2
-5/-1											0			0	-1

TINKER AFB/OKLAHOMA CITY OKLAHOMA

LAT 35 25N LONG 97 23W ELEV 1291 FT

MEAN FREQUENCY OF OCCURRENCE OF DRY BULB TEMPERATURE (DEGREES F) WITH MEAN COINCIDENT WET BULB TEMPERATURE (DEGREES F) FOR EACH DRY BULB TEMPERATURE RANGE

Temperature Range	MAY Obsn Hour Gp 01 to 08	MAY Obsn Hour Gp 09 to 16	MAY Obsn Hour Gp 17 to 24	MAY Total Obsn	MAY MCWB	JUNE Obsn Hour Gp 01 to 08	JUNE Obsn Hour Gp 09 to 16	JUNE Obsn Hour Gp 17 to 24	JUNE Total Obsn	JUNE MCWB	JULY Obsn Hour Gp 01 to 08	JULY Obsn Hour Gp 09 to 16	JULY Obsn Hour Gp 17 to 24	JULY Total Obsn	JULY MCWB
105/109												0		0	72
100/104							0		0	72		7	2	9	73
95/99		0		0	72		3	1	4	74		36	15	51	74
90/94		3	1	4	72		30	12	42	74		59	32	91	74
85/89		21	7	28	70		57	31	88	73	3	53	47	103	73
80/84	0	46	25	71	68	7	63	57	127	71	30	44	68	142	71
75/79	5	54	45	104	66	43	42	66	151	69	95	30	46	171	70
70/74	38	49	57	144	64	91	23	42	156	67	81	14	28	123	68
65/69	66	32	50	148	61	64	14	20	98	63	31	3	8	42	64
60/64	60	22	33	115	57	25	6	8	39	59	6	1	1	8	59
55/59	40	14	20	74	53	9	1	2	12	54	1		0	1	55
50/54	24	5	8	37	48	1	0	0	1	50	0			0	51
45/49	11	1	2	14	44										
40/44	3	0	0	3	40										
35/39	0			0	35										
30/34															
25/29															

Temperature Range	AUGUST Obsn Hour Gp 01 to 08	AUGUST Obsn Hour Gp 09 to 16	AUGUST Obsn Hour Gp 17 to 24	AUGUST Total Obsn	AUGUST MCWB	SEPTEMBER Obsn Hour Gp 01 to 08	SEPTEMBER Obsn Hour Gp 09 to 16	SEPTEMBER Obsn Hour Gp 17 to 24	SEPTEMBER Total Obsn	SEPTEMBER MCWB	OCTOBER Obsn Hour Gp 01 to 08	OCTOBER Obsn Hour Gp 09 to 16	OCTOBER Obsn Hour Gp 17 to 24	OCTOBER Total Obsn	OCTOBER MCWB
105/109		1	0	1	73										
100/104		6	2	8	74		1	0	1	75					
95/99		23	9	32	73		6	1	7	73		0		0	61
90/94		50	24	74	73		19	6	25	72		3	0	3	64
85/89	1	63	42	106	72		33	16	49	71		9	2	11	67
80/84	17	49	64	130	70	3	43	31	77	69		23	7	30	66
75/79	72	33	59	164	69	23	49	51	123	67	0	32	17	49	64
70/74	99	16	37	152	67	57	39	49	145	65	10	38	36	84	62
65/69	46	4	10	60	63	56	24	42	122	62	32	42	41	115	59
60/64	11	1	1	13	58	52	16	28	96	58	43	39	46	128	55
55/59	3	0	0	3	56	32	7	10	49	53	43	32	45	120	51
50/54						11	3	5	19	49	53	17	29	99	47
45/49						4	0	0	4	45	37	8	17	62	43
40/44						1			1	41	21	4	6	31	39
35/39											7	1	1	9	35
30/34											1	0	1	2	30
25/29											1			1	26

Temperature Range	NOVEMBER Obsn Hour Gp 01 to 08	09 to 16	17 to 24	Total Obsn	MCWB	DECEMBER Obsn Hour Gp 01 to 08	09 to 16	17 to 24	Total Obsn	MCWB	JANUARY Obsn Hour Gp 01 to 08	09 to 16	17 to 24	Total Obsn	MCWB
105/109															
100/104															
95/99															
90/94															
85/89															
80/84		0	0	0	63										
75/79		6	1	7	61		0		0	58		0		0	54
70/74	1	21	7	29	60		1	0	1	55		1	0	1	55
65/69	5	27	20	52	57	0	8	1	9	53		5	2	7	53
60/64	15	30	26	71	54	3	16	8	27	53	3	12	7	22	53
55/59	20	35	32	87	50	9	23	17	49	50	5	15	12	32	49
50/54	28	34	39	101	45	10	35	26	71	45	8	26	21	55	45
45/49	42	30	39	111	42	23	37	41	101	41	15	29	25	69	41
40/44	39	28	33	100	37	37	35	42	114	37	25	33	36	94	37
35/39	46	18	27	91	34	49	35	42	126	33	34	32	37	103	33
30/34	27	7	11	45	29	51	26	30	107	29	48	34	37	119	29
25/29	10	3	6	19	24	29	15	18	62	25	40	24	27	91	25
20/24	6	1	1	8	20	22	10	12	44	20	25	15	21	61	20
15/19	1	0	0	1	15	7	5	7	19	16	19	11	12	42	16
10/14	0			0	10	6	2	2	10	11	15	8	7	30	11
5/9						2	0	0	2	7	5	3	4	12	6
0/4						1	0	0	1	2	6	1	1	8	2
-5/-1											1	0		1	-2

Temperature Range	FEBRUARY Obsn Hour Gp 01 to 08	09 to 16	17 to 24	Total Obsn	MCWB	MARCH Obsn Hour Gp 01 to 08	09 to 16	17 to 24	Total Obsn	MCWB	APRIL Obsn Hour Gp 01 to 08	09 to 16	17 to 24	Total Obsn	MCWB	ANNUAL TOTAL Obsn Hour Gp 01 to 08	09 to 16	17 to 24	Total Obsn	MCWB
105/109																	1	0	1	73
100/104																	14	4	18	74
95/99																	68	26	94	74
90/94							0		0	62		1	0	1	66		165	75	240	73
85/89		0		0	62		1	0	1	60		5	2	7	66	4	242	147	393	72
80/84		1	0	1	60		3	1	4	62		15	6	21	64	57	287	259	603	70
75/79		1	0	1	56	0	8	4	12	60	0	30	17	47	62	238	285	306	829	67
70/74		4	1	5	55	0	15	9	24	57	8	40	36	84	61	385	261	302	948	65
65/69	0	8	5	13	53	3	22	16	41	55	27	43	42	112	58	330	232	257	819	60
60/64	2	12	8	22	51	11	28	26	65	52	41	37	45	123	54	272	220	237	729	55
55/59	6	20	16	42	49	19	28	27	74	48	47	27	37	111	50	234	202	218	654	50
50/54	11	27	24	62	45	26	31	36	93	45	43	20	26	89	46	215	198	214	627	46
45/49	21	30	32	83	41	34	31	34	99	41	34	14	17	65	42	221	180	207	608	41
40/44	31	34	40	105	37	42	28	37	107	37	23	5	9	37	38	222	167	203	592	37
35/39	37	31	34	102	33	41	24	25	90	33	11	2	3	16	34	225	143	169	537	33
30/34	40	23	29	92	29	39	18	20	77	29	4	0		4	30	210	108	128	446	29
25/29	35	15	20	70	25	21	8	7	36	25	1	1	1	3	26	137	66	79	282	25
20/24	26	13	10	49	20	8	2	2	12	20						87	41	46	174	20
15/19	11	4	4	19	16	2	1	1	4	16						40	21	24	85	16
10/14	3	1	1	5	12	2	1	1	4	11						26	12	11	49	11
5/9	1	0		1	7	1	0		1	8						9	3	4	16	6
0/4	0			0	3	0			0	4						7	1	1	9	2
-5/-1																1	0		1	-2

TULSA IAP OKLAHOMA

LAT 36 12N LONG 95 54W ELEV 650 FT

MEAN FREQUENCY OF OCCURRENCE OF DRY BULB TEMPERATURE (DEGREES F) WITH MEAN COINCIDENT WET BULB TEMPERATURE (DEGREES F) FOR EACH DRY BULB TEMPERATURE RANGE

Temperature Range	MAY Obsn Hour Gp 01 to 08	MAY 09 to 16	MAY 17 to 24	MAY Total Obsn	MAY MCWB	JUNE Obsn Hour Gp 01 to 08	JUNE 09 to 16	JUNE 17 to 24	JUNE Total Obsn	JUNE MCWB	JULY Obsn Hour Gp 01 to 08	JULY 09 to 16	JULY 17 to 24	JULY Total Obsn	JULY MCWB
110/114												1	0	1	76
105/109												3	2	5	75
100/104							2	1	3	75		11	4	15	75
95/99		0		0	75		15	5	20	75	0	41	17	58	75
90/94		6	1	7	73		46	18	64	75	1	62	33	96	75
85/89		27	10	37	72	2	60	39	101	74	11	56	49	116	74
80/84	1	49	25	75	69	24	49	56	129	72	52	33	61	146	73
75/79	15	51	45	111	67	64	31	53	148	70	84	24	44	152	72
70/74	36	43	48	127	64	66	23	38	127	67	70	12	29	111	69
65/69	60	34	51	145	62	51	11	20	82	64	24	4	8	36	65
60/64	58	21	37	116	58	22	4	8	34	59	6	1	2	9	61
55/59	41	11	21	73	54	9	1	2	12	54	1			1	58
50/54	24	4	8	36	49	2			2	51					
45/49	8	1	2	11	44										
40/44	3		1	4	40										
35/39	1			1	35										
30/34															
25/29															

Temperature Range	AUGUST Obsn Hour Gp 01 to 08	AUGUST 09 to 16	AUGUST 17 to 24	AUGUST Total Obsn	AUGUST MCWB	SEPTEMBER Obsn Hour Gp 01 to 08	SEPTEMBER 09 to 16	SEPTEMBER 17 to 24	SEPTEMBER Total Obsn	SEPTEMBER MCWB	OCTOBER Obsn Hour Gp 01 to 08	OCTOBER 09 to 16	OCTOBER 17 to 24	OCTOBER Total Obsn	OCTOBER MCWB
110/114															
105/109		5	1	6	73										
100/104		19	6	25	74		3	0	3	71					
95/99		33	14	47	74		14	3	17	70		0		0	67
90/94	0	57	34	91	74		36	11	47	70		5	1	6	69
85/89	12	60	46	118	72	1	40	24	65	69		16	3	19	67
80/84	36	43	58	137	72	6	47	34	87	68	0	30	9	39	65
75/79	82	21	54	157	71	28	41	52	121	66	4	32	20	56	64
70/74	76	8	25	109	68	57	32	50	139	65	14	40	33	87	61
65/69	30	3	8	41	64	59	19	35	113	62	24	42	44	110	58
60/64	10	1	2	13	59	44	5	22	71	57	44	35	46	125	55
55/59	3	0	0	3	54	31	1	7	39	53	49	25	38	112	51
50/54						14	1	1	16	50	44	13	30	87	47
45/49						2		0	2	46	34	6	15	55	43
40/44											23	2	5	30	39
35/39											8	1	2	11	34
30/34											3		1	4	29
25/29											1			1	27

Temperature Range	NOVEMBER Obsn Hour Gp 01 to 08	NOVEMBER Obsn Hour Gp 09 to 16	NOVEMBER Obsn Hour Gp 17 to 24	NOVEMBER Total Obsn	NOVEMBER MCWB	DECEMBER Obsn Hour Gp 01 to 08	DECEMBER Obsn Hour Gp 09 to 16	DECEMBER Obsn Hour Gp 17 to 24	DECEMBER Total Obsn	DECEMBER MCWB	JANUARY Obsn Hour Gp 01 to 08	JANUARY Obsn Hour Gp 09 to 16	JANUARY Obsn Hour Gp 17 to 24	JANUARY Total Obsn	JANUARY MCWB
110/114															
105/109															
100/104															
95/99															
90/94															
85/89															
80/84		1		1	64										
75/79		9	1	10	61		2		2	59		0	0	0	64
70/74	3	23	7	33	60		3	2	5	57		5	1	6	59
65/69	8	26	13	47	56	1	7	3	11	54	3	10	6	19	58
60/64	7	25	20	52	52	4	16	6	26	51	6	12	8	26	55
55/59	11	35	31	77	48	7	29	17	53	49	9	18	12	39	49
50/54	25	35	39	99	45	11	35	27	73	45	9	24	20	53	46
45/49	47	27	37	111	42	20	40	40	100	41	10	31	28	69	41
40/44	37	22	33	92	37	37	42	50	129	37	24	32	34	90	38
35/39	36	20	26	82	33	49	30	39	118	33	41	35	41	117	34
30/34	32	12	18	62	29	51	20	30	101	29	47	31	38	116	30
25/29	19	5	12	36	25	34	13	21	68	25	37	19	26	82	25
20/24	11	1	4	16	20	21	6	7	34	20	30	15	20	65	21
15/19	4	0	0	4	16	7	4	4	15	15	19	9	8	36	16
10/14	1			1	10	4	1	3	8	11	8	4	4	16	11
5/9						3	0	0	3	6	3	1	2	6	6
0/4						0			0	3	0	0	1	1	1
-5/-1											1			1	-3

Temperature Range	FEBRUARY Obsn Hour Gp 01 to 08	FEBRUARY Obsn Hour Gp 09 to 16	FEBRUARY Obsn Hour Gp 17 to 24	FEBRUARY Total Obsn	FEBRUARY MCWB	MARCH Obsn Hour Gp 01 to 08	MARCH Obsn Hour Gp 09 to 16	MARCH Obsn Hour Gp 17 to 24	MARCH Total Obsn	MARCH MCWB	APRIL Obsn Hour Gp 01 to 08	APRIL Obsn Hour Gp 09 to 16	APRIL Obsn Hour Gp 17 to 24	APRIL Total Obsn	APRIL MCWB	ANNUAL TOTAL Obsn Hour Gp 01 to 08	ANNUAL TOTAL Obsn Hour Gp 09 to 16	ANNUAL TOTAL Obsn Hour Gp 17 to 24	ANNUAL TOTAL Total Obsn	ANNUAL TOTAL MCWB
110/114																	1	0	1	76
105/109																	8	3	11	74
100/104																	35	11	46	74
95/99																0	103	39	142	74
90/94							0		0	59		1	0	1	68	1	213	98	312	74
85/89							1	0	1	61		5	2	7	65	26	265	173	464	72
80/84		1	0	1	61		4	1	5	61		19	7	26	66	119	276	251	646	70
75/79		2	0	2	57		8	4	12	60	0	32	17	49	63	277	253	290	820	68
70/74		5	2	7	58	2	15	12	29	58	9	33	32	74	62	333	242	279	854	65
65/69	1	13	6	20	55	6	23	11	40	54	28	36	36	100	58	295	228	241	764	60
60/64	4	22	11	37	52	9	26	19	54	51	37	36	36	109	54	251	204	217	672	55
55/59	9	25	21	55	49	14	31	31	76	48	34	34	38	106	50	218	210	218	646	50
50/54	14	30	33	77	46	24	33	37	94	45	38	24	31	93	46	205	199	226	630	46
45/49	24	30	33	87	42	39	37	42	118	42	41	15	25	81	42	225	187	222	634	42
40/44	36	26	37	99	38	46	26	35	107	38	31	5	13	49	38	237	155	208	600	38
35/39	42	25	29	96	34	40	20	23	83	34	16	1	3	20	34	233	132	163	528	34
30/34	35	18	23	76	30	37	14	20	71	30	5	0	0	5	30	210	95	130	435	30
25/29	25	13	17	55	25	16	4	6	26	25	1	1	1	3	26	133	55	83	271	25
20/24	20	8	7	35	21	9	3	3	15	21	0			0	22	91	33	41	165	21
15/19	9	4	4	17	16	3	1	1	5	16						42	18	17	77	16
10/14	3	1	1	5	12	1	1	1	3	11						17	7	9	33	11
5/9	2	0	0	2	6	2		0	2	7						10	1	2	13	6
0/4	0	0		0	1											0	0		1	1
-5/-1																1			1	-3

VANCE AFB/ENID OKLAHOMA

LAT 36 21N LONG 97 55W ELEV 1307 FT

MEAN FREQUENCY OF OCCURRENCE OF DRY BULB TEMPERATURE (DEGREES F) WITH MEAN COINCIDENT WET BULB TEMPERATURE (DEGREES F) FOR EACH DRY BULB TEMPERATURE RANGE

Temperature Range	MAY Obsn Hour Gp 01 to 08	MAY Obsn Hour Gp 09 to 16	MAY Obsn Hour Gp 17 to 24	MAY Total Obsn	MAY MCWB	JUNE Obsn Hour Gp 01 to 08	JUNE Obsn Hour Gp 09 to 16	JUNE Obsn Hour Gp 17 to 24	JUNE Total Obsn	JUNE MCWB	JULY Obsn Hour Gp 01 to 08	JULY Obsn Hour Gp 09 to 16	JULY Obsn Hour Gp 17 to 24	JULY Total Obsn	JULY MCWB
110/114							0		0	73		1	0	1	73
105/109							1	0	1	74		5	1	6	72
100/104		0	0	0	73		9	2	11	74		21	6	27	74
95/99		3	1	4	70		28	10	38	75		42	20	62	75
90/94		12	4	16	70	0	44	21	65	74	1	56	33	90	74
85/89		26	10	36	70	4	49	35	88	73	10	50	44	104	73
80/84	1	37	20	58	68	21	44	49	114	71	36	37	55	128	72
75/79	10	42	35	87	66	54	31	50	135	69	83	21	49	153	70
70/74	29	46	41	116	64	65	18	38	121	67	81	12	32	125	68
65/69	47	39	55	141	61	53	11	22	86	64	30	3	7	40	65
60/64	68	24	47	139	59	30	4	9	43	60	6	1	1	8	60
55/59	48	11	24	83	54	8	1	3	12	53	1	0	0	1	56
50/54	31	6	8	45	49	5		0	5	49					
45/49	9	2	2	13	44	0			0	46					
40/44	3	1	2	6	40										
35/39	1		0	1	36										
30/34	0			0	31										
25/29															
20/24															

Temperature Range	AUGUST Obsn Hour Gp 01 to 08	AUGUST Obsn Hour Gp 09 to 16	AUGUST Obsn Hour Gp 17 to 24	AUGUST Total Obsn	AUGUST MCWB	SEPTEMBER Obsn Hour Gp 01 to 08	SEPTEMBER Obsn Hour Gp 09 to 16	SEPTEMBER Obsn Hour Gp 17 to 24	SEPTEMBER Total Obsn	SEPTEMBER MCWB	OCTOBER Obsn Hour Gp 01 to 08	OCTOBER Obsn Hour Gp 09 to 16	OCTOBER Obsn Hour Gp 17 to 24	OCTOBER Total Obsn	OCTOBER MCWB
110/114		0		0	73										
105/109		5	1	6	75		0		0	74					
100/104		22	6	28	75		2	1	3	71					
95/99		40	17	57	74		19	4	23	70		1	0	1	68
90/94	1	56	32	89	73		30	10	40	69		6	1	7	68
85/89	6	53	44	103	72	0	38	20	58	68		16	4	20	66
80/84	33	37	54	124	71	5	41	34	80	67	0	25	8	33	65
75/79	77	22	50	149	70	22	42	46	110	65	3	32	18	53	63
70/74	79	9	32	120	68	56	32	46	134	64	10	36	31	77	61
65/69	41	2	8	51	64	54	19	38	111	61	25	36	41	102	59
60/64	9	1	1	11	59	48	10	28	86	57	38	37	41	116	55
55/59	2	0	1	3	55	39	4	9	52	53	50	27	43	120	51
50/54	1	0		1	51	13	2	4	19	49	47	18	33	98	47
45/49						2	1	0	3	45	42	8	18	68	43
40/44						0			0	41	18	4	6	28	39
35/39											10	2	2	14	34
30/34											3	0	2	5	31
25/29											1		0	1	25
20/24											0			0	24

Temperature Range	NOVEMBER					DECEMBER					JANUARY				
	Obsn Hour Gp			Total Obsn	M C W B	Obsn Hour Gp			Total Obsn	M C W B	Obsn Hour Gp			Total Obsn	M C W B
	01 to 08	09 to 16	17 to 24			01 to 08	09 to 16	17 to 24			01 to 08	09 to 16	17 to 24		
110/114															
105/109															
100/104															
95/99															
90/94															
85/89															
80/84		1		1	61		0		0	59					
75/79		7	0	7	60		1		1	56		0	0	0	61
70/74	0	18	2	20	58		2	0	2	54		2	0	2	53
65/69	3	23	11	37	56		6	2	8	52		7	1	8	54
60/64	6	27	18	51	53	2	14	4	20	51	2	12	6	20	52
55/59	11	37	32	80	48	5	22	11	38	49	3	18	10	31	48
50/54	20	35	36	91	45	6	36	18	60	45	6	25	17	48	45
45/49	43	28	44	115	42	18	41	36	95	41	11	26	24	61	41
40/44	48	23	34	105	38	27	39	49	115	37	22	38	34	94	38
35/39	41	16	27	84	33	50	35	50	135	33	33	28	44	105	34
30/34	33	12	16	61	29	64	24	35	123	29	55	26	35	116	30
25/29	18	10	13	41	25	34	13	24	71	25	40	22	27	89	25
20/24	13	2	6	21	20	25	7	10	42	21	30	19	23	72	20
15/19	4	0	0	4	15	12	5	4	21	16	21	14	13	48	16
10/14	1	0		1	11	4	2	3	9	11	14	8	9	31	11
5/9						2	0	1	3	7	6	2	3	11	7
0/4						1			1	3	2	1	1	4	1
-5/-1											1	0	0	1	-3
-10/-6											0			0	-7

Temperature Range	FEBRUARY					MARCH					APRIL					ANNUAL TOTAL				
	Obsn Hour Gp			Total Obsn	M C W B	Obsn Hour Gp			Total Obsn	M C W B	Obsn Hour Gp			Total Obsn	M C W B	Obsn Hour Gp			Total Obsn	M C W B
	01 to 08	09 to 16	17 to 24			01 to 08	09 to 16	17 to 24			01 to 08	09 to 16	17 to 24			01 to 08	09 to 16	17 to 24		
110/114																	1	0	1	73
105/109																	11	2	13	74
100/104																	54	15	69	74
95/99												0		0	65		133	52	185	74
90/94												2	0	2	64	2	206	101	309	73
85/89							1	0	1	58		8	2	10	66	20	241	159	420	71
80/84		0	0	0	59		4	1	5	60		16	6	22	65	96	242	227	565	70
75/79		2	0	2	59		6	3	9	59		19	12	31	62	249	225	263	737	68
70/74		5	1	6	56	0	14	7	21	57	5	29	22	56	60	325	223	252	800	65
65/69		10	4	14	54	3	18	12	33	54	18	34	29	81	58	274	208	230	712	60
60/64	2	19	10	31	52	6	30	18	54	51	27	35	37	99	54	244	214	220	678	55
55/59	5	25	17	47	48	11	32	27	70	48	40	34	43	117	51	223	211	220	654	50
50/54	10	29	27	66	45	25	33	35	93	45	39	27	33	99	46	203	211	211	625	46
45/49	24	26	34	84	42	35	30	40	105	42	39	20	28	87	42	223	182	226	631	42
40/44	34	31	33	98	38	41	29	40	110	38	38	11	17	66	39	231	176	215	622	38
35/39	39	27	32	98	34	48	21	27	96	34	24	3	8	35	35	246	132	190	568	34
30/34	45	23	31	99	30	38	20	22	80	30	9	0	2	11	30	247	105	143	495	30
25/29	30	12	19	61	25	27	6	11	44	25	2	1	1	4	26	152	64	95	311	25
20/24	19	8	8	35	21	9	2	3	14	21						96	38	50	184	20
15/19	12	5	5	22	16	4	1	1	6	16						53	25	23	101	16
10/14	4	1	2	7	11	1	0		1	12						24	11	14	49	11
5/9	1	0	0	1	6											9	2	4	15	7
0/4	0	0		0	2											3	1	1	5	2
-5/-1	0			0	-3											1	0	0	1	-3
-10/-6																0			0	-7

ASTORIA OREGON

LAT 46 09N LONG 123 53W ELEV 8 FT

MEAN FREQUENCY OF OCCURRENCE OF DRY BULB TEMPERATURE (DEGREES F) WITH MEAN COINCIDENT WET BULB TEMPERATURE (DEGREES F) FOR EACH DRY BULB TEMPERATURE RANGE

Temperature Range	MAY Obsn Hour Gp 01 to 08	MAY 09 to 16	MAY 17 to 24	MAY Total Obsn	MAY MCWB	JUNE Obsn Hour Gp 01 to 08	JUNE 09 to 16	JUNE 17 to 24	JUNE Total Obsn	JUNE MCWB	JULY Obsn Hour Gp 01 to 08	JULY 09 to 16	JULY 17 to 24	JULY Total Obsn	JULY MCWB
100/104												0		0	68
95/99												0	0	0	71
90/94							0	0	0	68		1	0	1	70
85/89		0	0	0	62		0	0	0	66		1	0	1	69
80/84		1	0	1	62		1	0	1	68	0	2	1	3	67
75/79		2	0	2	61		2	0	2	66	0	5	1	6	65
70/74	0	5	1	6	60	0	6	1	7	63	1	14	3	18	63
65/69	1	11	3	15	58	1	25	6	32	60	2	76	17	95	60
60/64	2	40	9	51	55	11	99	37	147	56	26	121	78	225	57
55/59	23	100	50	173	52	74	91	102	267	54	149	28	125	302	55
50/54	89	78	106	273	49	111	16	82	209	51	51	1	22	74	51
45/49	82	10	63	155	45	34	0	10	44	46	18		2	20	47
40/44	38	0	14	52	41	8		1	9	43	1			1	43
35/39	13		1	14	37	0			0	39					
30/34	1		0	1	31										

Temperature Range	AUGUST Obsn Hour Gp 01 to 08	AUGUST 09 to 16	AUGUST 17 to 24	AUGUST Total Obsn	AUGUST MCWB	SEPTEMBER Obsn Hour Gp 01 to 08	SEPTEMBER 09 to 16	SEPTEMBER 17 to 24	SEPTEMBER Total Obsn	SEPTEMBER MCWB	OCTOBER Obsn Hour Gp 01 to 08	OCTOBER 09 to 16	OCTOBER 17 to 24	OCTOBER Total Obsn	OCTOBER MCWB
100/104															
95/99															
90/94							0		0	69					
85/89		0		0	66		2	0	2	67					
80/84		1		1	69		4	1	5	65		0		0	61
75/79		3	0	3	66		6	2	8	64		2	0	2	61
70/74	0	21	3	24	63	0	20	2	22	62		7	0	7	60
65/69	1	95	20	116	60	3	59	12	74	60	0	19	2	21	58
60/64	37	110	90	237	58	21	98	58	177	58	7	56	17	80	56
55/59	139	18	115	272	56	100	46	104	250	55	52	102	78	232	54
50/54	55	0	20	75	52	65	4	44	113	51	77	46	79	202	50
45/49	15		1	16	47	37	0	15	52	47	57	13	47	117	46
40/44	0			0	43	15		1	16	42	35	3	21	59	42
35/39						0			0	39	17	0	4	21	37
30/34											3		0	3	33

Temperature Range	NOVEMBER Obsn Hour Gp 01 to 08	NOVEMBER 09 to 16	NOVEMBER 17 to 24	NOVEMBER Total Obsn	NOVEMBER MCWB	DECEMBER Obsn Hour Gp 01 to 08	DECEMBER 09 to 16	DECEMBER 17 to 24	DECEMBER Total Obsn	DECEMBER MCWB	JANUARY Obsn Hour Gp 01 to 08	JANUARY 09 to 16	JANUARY 17 to 24	JANUARY Total Obsn	JANUARY MCWB
100/104															
95/99															
90/94															
85/89															
80/84															
75/79															
70/74															
65/69		1	0	1	56							0		0	49
60/64	1	6	0	7	53	0	1	0	1	52	0	1		1	49
55/59	11	50	19	80	53	5	10	5	20	52	2	7	1	10	51
50/54	50	86	62	198	49	32	62	34	128	49	22	48	29	99	49
45/49	61	58	72	191	45	56	90	70	216	45	48	77	64	189	45
40/44	51	27	42	120	40	65	54	76	195	40	64	58	66	188	40
35/39	37	7	33	77	36	56	22	39	117	36	57	34	44	135	36
30/34	22	3	9	34	31	25	8	20	53	31	32	17	30	79	31
25/29	5	2	3	10	25	7	1	3	11	26	13	5	9	27	25
20/24	1	0	1	2	19	1	1	0	2	19	7	1	4	12	20
15/19	1		0	1	16	1		0	1	14	3	0	0	3	16

Temperature Range	FEBRUARY Obsn Hour Gp 01 to 08	FEBRUARY 09 to 16	FEBRUARY 17 to 24	FEBRUARY Total Obsn	FEBRUARY MCWB	MARCH Obsn Hour Gp 01 to 08	MARCH 09 to 16	MARCH 17 to 24	MARCH Total Obsn	MARCH MCWB	APRIL Obsn Hour Gp 01 to 08	APRIL 09 to 16	APRIL 17 to 24	APRIL Total Obsn	APRIL MCWB	ANNUAL TOTAL Obsn Hour Gp 01 to 08	ANNUAL TOTAL 09 to 16	ANNUAL TOTAL 17 to 24	ANNUAL TOTAL Total Obsn	ANNUAL TOTAL MCWB
100/104																	0		0	68
95/99																	0	0	0	71
90/94																	1	0	1	69
85/89																	3	0	3	67
80/84												0		0	62	0	9	2	11	65
75/79												1	0	1	58	0	21	3	24	64
70/74							0		0	57		1	0	1	55	1	74	10	85	62
65/69		1		1	53		2	0	2	53	0	6	1	7	55	8	295	61	364	60
60/64	0	3	0	3	51		4	1	5	52	0	10	3	13	53	105	549	293	947	57
55/59	4	14	6	24	52	0	15	2	17	49	2	40	10	52	50	561	521	617	1699	54
50/54	19	55	31	105	48	7	67	24	98	47	32	106	60	198	48	610	569	593	1772	49
45/49	52	85	67	204	45	59	108	94	261	44	88	67	101	256	45	607	508	606	1721	45
40/44	65	46	64	175	40	84	41	83	208	40	74	8	53	135	41	500	237	421	1158	40
35/39	47	16	39	102	36	57	10	34	101	36	33	0	11	44	37	317	89	205	611	36
30/34	26	3	13	42	31	34	1	11	46	31	11		1	12	33	154	32	84	270	31
25/29	8	1	2	11	26	6		0	6	27	0			0	29	39	9	17	65	26
20/24	3	0	1	4	21	0			0	23						12	2	6	20	20
15/19																5	0	0	5	16

EUGENE OREGON

LAT 44 07N LONG 123 13W ELEV 359 FT

MEAN FREQUENCY OF OCCURRENCE OF DRY BULB TEMPERATURE (DEGREES F) WITH MEAN COINCIDENT WET BULB TEMPERATURE (DEGREES F) FOR EACH DRY BULB TEMPERATURE RANGE

Temperature Range	MAY Obsn Hour Gp 01 to 08	MAY 09 to 16	MAY 17 to 24	MAY Total Obsn	MAY MCWB	JUNE Obsn Hour Gp 01 to 08	JUNE 09 to 16	JUNE 17 to 24	JUNE Total Obsn	JUNE MCWB	JULY Obsn Hour Gp 01 to 08	JULY 09 to 16	JULY 17 to 24	JULY Total Obsn	JULY MCWB
105/109												0		0	70
100/104							0		0	76		1	0	1	69
95/99							1	0	1	67		4	2	6	68
90/94		0		0	69		2	1	3	70		13	7	20	67
85/89		1	0	1	66		7	4	11	67		26	18	44	65
80/84		7	3	10	64		15	9	24	64		37	23	60	63
75/79		12	7	19	61	0	29	17	46	62	1	48	32	81	62
70/74	0	25	13	38	59	2	39	26	67	60	5	50	38	93	60
65/69	1	40	25	66	56	7	55	37	99	57	17	43	44	104	58
60/64	8	55	34	97	54	24	59	52	135	55	54	24	45	123	56
55/59	32	61	59	152	51	77	26	55	158	53	91	3	30	124	53
50/54	82	37	64	183	49	83	6	29	118	50	60		7	67	50
45/49	72	10	31	113	45	36	0	8	44	46	18		1	19	46
40/44	40	1	11	52	41	10		1	11	42	2			2	42
35/39	12		1	13	37	1			1	38					
30/34	2			2	33										
25/29															

Temperature Range	AUGUST Obsn Hour Gp 01 to 08	AUGUST 09 to 16	AUGUST 17 to 24	AUGUST Total Obsn	AUGUST MCWB	SEPTEMBER Obsn Hour Gp 01 to 08	SEPTEMBER 09 to 16	SEPTEMBER 17 to 24	SEPTEMBER Total Obsn	SEPTEMBER MCWB	OCTOBER Obsn Hour Gp 01 to 08	OCTOBER 09 to 16	OCTOBER 17 to 24	OCTOBER Total Obsn	OCTOBER MCWB
105/109															
100/104		0		0	69										
95/99		3	1	4	67		1	0	1	67					
90/94		8	5	13	66		6	1	7	65					
85/89		22	11	33	65		10	4	14	64		1		1	61
80/84		36	21	57	63		21	7	28	62		3	1	4	61
75/79	0	46	28	74	62		33	16	49	61		7	2	9	60
70/74	2	53	36	91	60	0	45	23	68	59		16	4	20	59
65/69	12	50	52	114	58	3	54	39	96	57		29	11	40	57
60/64	61	26	55	142	57	29	47	61	137	56	4	50	25	79	55
55/59	91	4	29	124	54	63	18	53	134	54	29	65	59	153	53
50/54	56	0	9	65	50	70	4	26	100	50	55	45	67	167	50
45/49	22		1	23	46	48	0	7	55	46	68	23	51	142	46
40/44	3			3	43	20		2	22	42	46	9	22	77	41
35/39						6			6	37	35	1	6	42	37
30/34						1			1	34	12		1	13	32
25/29											1			1	27

EUGENE OREGON

Temperature Range	NOVEMBER Obsn Hour Gp 01 to 08	09 to 16	17 to 24	Total Obsn	M C W B	DECEMBER Obsn Hour Gp 01 to 08	09 to 16	17 to 24	Total Obsn	M C W B	JANUARY Obsn Hour Gp 01 to 08	09 to 16	17 to 24	Total Obsn	M C W B
105/109															
100/104															
95/99															
90/94															
85/89															
80/84															
75/79															
70/74		0		0	59										
65/69		2		2	57		0		0	61					
60/64	0	12	2	14	55	0	2	1	3	57	0	1		1	54
55/59	8	40	17	65	52	2	17	4	23	53	1	12	4	17	51
50/54	30	65	47	142	49	18	43	30	91	49	11	34	25	70	48
45/49	52	53	63	168	45	43	61	54	158	45	33	50	44	127	45
40/44	50	37	52	139	41	67	62	73	202	41	39	52	49	140	40
35/39	48	19	39	106	36	56	39	49	144	36	55	44	50	149	36
30/34	29	9	15	53	32	46	19	33	98	32	52	31	38	121	31
25/29	16	1	2	19	27	11	4	4	19	27	22	15	19	56	26
20/24	5	0	3	8	21	4	1	0	5	21	15	6	12	33	21
15/19	2		0	2	17	0	0	1	1	16	11	3	6	20	16
10/14						1	0	0	1	10	5	0	1	6	12
5/9											2	0	0	2	7
0/4											1		0	1	2
-5/-1											0			0	-2

Temperature Range	FEBRUARY Obsn Hour Gp 01 to 08	09 to 16	17 to 24	Total Obsn	M C W B	MARCH Obsn Hour Gp 01 to 08	09 to 16	17 to 24	Total Obsn	M C W B
105/109										
100/104										
95/99										
90/94										
85/89										
80/84										
75/79										
70/74							1	0	1	57
65/69		1		1	55		2	1	3	56
60/64		7	1	8	54		12	4	16	52
55/59	1	20	9	30	51	0	32	15	47	49
50/54	15	52	35	102	48	8	69	42	119	47
45/49	35	60	61	156	44	46	78	78	202	44
40/44	52	46	52	150	40	81	41	67	189	40
35/39	57	25	42	124	36	68	12	32	112	36
30/34	44	9	19	72	31	39	2	8	49	32
25/29	13	1	2	16	27	6		1	7	28
20/24	3	1	1	5	20	0			0	24
15/19	1	1	0	2	17					
10/14	0	0	0	0	12					
5/9	0	0	1	1	7					
0/4	1		0	1	2					
-5/-1	1			1	-2					

Temperature Range	APRIL Obsn Hour Gp 01 to 08	09 to 16	17 to 24	Total Obsn	M C W B	ANNUAL TOTAL Obsn Hour Gp 01 to 08	09 to 16	17 to 24	Total Obsn	M C W B
105/109							0		0	70
100/104							1	0	1	70
95/99							9	3	12	68
90/94							29	14	43	67
85/89							67	37	104	65
80/84		1	0	1	63		120	64	184	63
75/79		4	1	5	59	1	179	103	283	61
70/74		11	5	16	57	9	240	145	394	59
65/69	0	21	10	31	55	40	297	219	556	57
60/64	0	38	19	57	52	180	333	299	812	55
55/59	4	61	42	107	50	399	359	376	1134	52
50/54	36	67	66	169	47	524	422	447	1393	49
45/49	77	31	59	167	44	550	366	458	1374	45
40/44	68	7	31	106	40	478	255	360	1093	40
35/39	41	1	7	49	36	379	141	226	746	36
30/34	13		0	13	32	238	70	114	422	32
25/29	0			0	29	69	21	28	118	27
20/24						27	8	16	51	21
15/19						14	4	7	25	16
10/14						6	0	1	7	12
5/9						2	0	1	3	7
0/4						2		0	2	2
-5/-1						1			1	-2

KINGSLEY FIELD OREGON

LAT 42 09N LONG 121 44W ELEV 4092 FT

MEAN FREQUENCY OF OCCURRENCE OF DRY BULB TEMPERATURE (DEGREES F) WITH MEAN COINCIDENT WET BULB TEMPERATURE (DEGREES F) FOR EACH DRY BULB TEMPERATURE RANGE

Temperature Range	MAY Obsn Hour Gp 01 to 08	MAY 09 to 16	MAY 17 to 24	MAY Total Obsn	MAY MCWB	JUNE Obsn Hour Gp 01 to 08	JUNE 09 to 16	JUNE 17 to 24	JUNE Total Obsn	JUNE MCWB	JULY Obsn Hour Gp 01 to 08	JULY 09 to 16	JULY 17 to 24	JULY Total Obsn	JULY MCWB
95/99												1	0	1	63
90/94							2	1	3	60		14	6	20	62
85/89		0		0	55		9	3	12	60		36	14	50	60
80/84		9	2	11	56		20	8	28	58		53	26	79	59
75/79		24	9	33	54		35	17	52	56	0	59	39	98	57
70/74		33	15	48	52	1	35	21	57	55	8	43	42	93	56
65/69		44	23	67	50	9	40	34	83	53	25	25	45	95	54
60/64	7	41	35	83	48	22	41	43	106	51	39	12	35	86	52
55/59	24	33	43	100	46	41	30	41	112	49	54	4	24	82	50
50/54	40	30	41	111	43	54	17	34	105	46	67	1	12	80	47
45/49	53	19	35	107	41	48	8	24	80	43	36	1	3	40	43
40/44	44	11	26	81	37	36	2	10	48	38	17		1	18	40
35/39	42	5	15	62	33	20	2	3	25	34	2		1	3	35
30/34	31	1	6	38	29	7	0	3	10	31	1			1	31
25/29	8		1	9	25	2			2	27					
20/24	1			1	21										

Temperature Range	AUGUST Obsn Hour Gp 01 to 08	AUGUST 09 to 16	AUGUST 17 to 24	AUGUST Total Obsn	AUGUST MCWB	SEPTEMBER Obsn Hour Gp 01 to 08	SEPTEMBER 09 to 16	SEPTEMBER 17 to 24	SEPTEMBER Total Obsn	SEPTEMBER MCWB	OCTOBER Obsn Hour Gp 01 to 08	OCTOBER 09 to 16	OCTOBER 17 to 24	OCTOBER Total Obsn	OCTOBER MCWB
95/99															
90/94		12	3	15	60		1		1	66					
85/89		39	14	53	59		8	1	9	59					
80/84		51	25	76	58		32	9	41	57					
75/79		42	27	69	57		43	15	58	56		2		2	53
70/74	2	39	39	80	56		42	24	66	54		13	2	15	51
65/69	17	29	42	88	54	1	37	33	71	53		24	4	28	49
60/64	35	16	40	91	52	10	31	43	84	51		35	10	45	47
55/59	61	12	30	103	50	28	24	46	98	49	1	39	26	66	45
50/54	66	7	16	89	47	62	14	39	115	46	9	45	41	95	43
45/49	48	2	10	60	44	70	7	18	95	43	28	47	43	118	41
40/44	16		3	19	40	43	1	9	53	39	41	35	60	136	38
35/39	5			5	37	17		4	21	36	72	8	43	123	34
30/34						7			7	32	67	1	17	85	30
25/29						3			3	26	25		2	27	26
20/24						1			1	23	6			6	22

KINGSLEY FIELD OREGON

Temperature Range	NOVEMBER Obsn Hour Gp 01 to 08	NOVEMBER 09 to 16	NOVEMBER 17 to 24	NOVEMBER Total Obsn	NOVEMBER MCWB	DECEMBER Obsn Hour Gp 01 to 08	DECEMBER 09 to 16	DECEMBER 17 to 24	DECEMBER Total Obsn	DECEMBER MCWB	JANUARY Obsn Hour Gp 01 to 08	JANUARY 09 to 16	JANUARY 17 to 24	JANUARY Total Obsn	JANUARY MCWB
95/99															
90/94															
85/89															
80/84															
75/79															
70/74															
65/69		2		2	50										
60/64		7		7	48										
55/59		16	3	19	46										
50/54	7	38	13	58	44	1	2	2	5	47		1		1	41
45/49	14	43	30	87	41	3	15	3	21	40		8	1	9	39
40/44	20	51	42	113	38	19	37	19	75	38	5	31	16	52	36
35/39	47	39	56	142	34	21	43	42	106	33	31	58	43	132	33
30/34	54	27	51	132	30	57	61	63	181	30	61	71	83	215	30
25/29	44	12	28	84	26	41	45	51	137	26	52	39	51	142	25
20/24	39	5	15	59	21	36	25	33	94	21	40	21	28	89	21
15/19	12	1	2	15	17	31	12	21	64	16	23	10	11	44	16
10/14	5		1	6	13	22	6	10	38	12	16	5	11	32	12
5/9	0			0	8	10	3	3	16	7	14	3	4	21	7
0/4						6		2	8	2	4	2	2	8	3
-5/-1						2	0	1	3	-2	3	0		3	-2
-10/-6						1			1	-7	1	0		1	-8
-15/-11											0			0	-11

Temperature Range	FEBRUARY Obsn Hour Gp 01 to 08	FEBRUARY 09 to 16	FEBRUARY 17 to 24	FEBRUARY Total Obsn	FEBRUARY MCWB	MARCH Obsn Hour Gp 01 to 08	MARCH 09 to 16	MARCH 17 to 24	MARCH Total Obsn	MARCH MCWB	APRIL Obsn Hour Gp 01 to 08	APRIL 09 to 16	APRIL 17 to 24	APRIL Total Obsn	APRIL MCWB	ANNUAL TOTAL Obsn Hour Gp 01 to 08	ANNUAL TOTAL 09 to 16	ANNUAL TOTAL 17 to 24	ANNUAL TOTAL Total Obsn	ANNUAL TOTAL MCWB
95/99																	1	0	1	63
90/94																	29	10	39	61
85/89																	92	32	124	59
80/84																	165	70	235	58
75/79												1		1	51	0	206	107	313	56
70/74							4	1	5	50		7	2	9	50	11	216	146	373	54
65/69		0		0	45		8	4	12	47		16	6	22	48	52	225	191	468	52
60/64		2	0	2	46		13	3	16	46		21	10	31	46	113	219	219	551	50
55/59		8	1	9	43		18	8	26	43	0	28	15	43	44	209	212	237	658	48
50/54		10	4	14	42		29	18	47	41	6	33	24	63	41	312	227	244	783	45
45/49	3	31	15	49	39	5	41	25	71	38	11	45	33	89	38	319	267	240	826	41
40/44	12	49	32	93	36	27	43	49	119	35	24	51	49	124	36	304	311	316	931	37
35/39	37	52	55	144	33	46	47	50	143	32	58	28	52	138	33	398	282	364	1044	33
30/34	68	48	75	191	29	65	32	58	155	29	70	10	37	117	29	488	251	393	1132	30
25/29	61	17	30	108	26	67	13	23	103	25	48	1	11	60	25	351	127	197	675	25
20/24	27	4	8	39	21	29	2	10	41	21	21		1	22	21	200	57	95	352	21
15/19	12	1	2	15	17	8		1	9	16	3			3	18	89	24	37	150	16
10/14	2	1	1	4	12	1	1		2	12						46	13	23	82	12
5/9	1			1	8	1			1	8						26	6	7	39	7
0/4	1	0		1	4											11	2	4	17	3
-5/-1																5	0	1	6	-2
-10/-6																2	0		2	-7
-15/-11																0			0	-11

MEDFORD OREGON

LAT 42 22N LONG 122 52W ELEV 1298 FT

MEAN FREQUENCY OF OCCURRENCE OF DRY BULB TEMPERATURE (DEGREES F) WITH MEAN COINCIDENT WET BULB TEMPERATURE (DEGREES F) FOR EACH DRY BULB TEMPERATURE RANGE

Temperature Range	MAY Obsn Hour Gp 01 to 08	MAY 09 to 16	MAY 17 to 24	MAY Total Obsn	MAY MCWB	JUNE Obsn Hour Gp 01 to 08	JUNE 09 to 16	JUNE 17 to 24	JUNE Total Obsn	JUNE MCWB	JULY Obsn Hour Gp 01 to 08	JULY 09 to 16	JULY 17 to 24	JULY Total Obsn	JULY MCWB
105/109							0	0	0	71		0	0	0	71
100/104							1	0	1	70		5	2	7	70
95/99			0	0	71		4	2	6	68		16	8	24	68
90/94		2	1	3	65		10	6	16	66		32	18	50	66
85/89		9	3	12	64		20	11	31	64		43	24	67	64
80/84		15	7	22	61		28	15	43	62	0	44	30	74	62
75/79		23	11	34	59	0	36	22	58	60	2	43	36	81	61
70/74		30	17	47	57	3	40	30	73	58	13	35	41	89	59
65/69	1	36	24	61	55	12	41	38	91	56	38	21	41	100	57
60/64	9	43	35	87	52	33	34	43	110	54	68	8	30	106	55
55/59	28	43	46	117	50	67	20	41	128	52	75	1	13	89	52
50/54	57	32	49	138	47	67	5	26	98	48	39	0	3	42	48
45/49	73	12	37	122	44	40	1	7	48	45	13		0	13	45
40/44	57	2	14	73	40	14		1	15	41	1			1	41
35/39	20	0	2	22	36	2		0	2	36	0			0	37
30/34	3		0	3	32	0			0	33					
25/29	0			0	28										

Temperature Range	AUGUST Obsn Hour Gp 01 to 08	AUGUST 09 to 16	AUGUST 17 to 24	AUGUST Total Obsn	AUGUST MCWB	SEPTEMBER Obsn Hour Gp 01 to 08	SEPTEMBER 09 to 16	SEPTEMBER 17 to 24	SEPTEMBER Total Obsn	SEPTEMBER MCWB	OCTOBER Obsn Hour Gp 01 to 08	OCTOBER 09 to 16	OCTOBER 17 to 24	OCTOBER Total Obsn	OCTOBER MCWB
105/109							0		0	69					
100/104		3	1	4	68		1	0	1	68					
95/99		12	5	17	67		6	2	8	66		0		0	64
90/94		27	12	39	66		14	5	19	65		2	0	2	63
85/89		39	22	61	64		22	9	31	63		4	1	5	62
80/84	0	44	28	72	62		31	15	46	61		9	2	11	61
75/79	1	41	33	75	61		34	19	53	60		13	4	17	59
70/74	7	40	42	89	59	1	37	30	68	58	0	20	7	27	57
65/69	27	25	47	99	57	6	38	39	83	56	0	33	14	47	55
60/64	62	13	37	112	55	27	30	45	102	54	2	40	27	69	53
55/59	83	3	16	102	52	56	19	42	117	52	12	48	47	107	51
50/54	53	0	5	58	49	68	5	23	96	48	45	40	58	143	49
45/49	14		0	14	45	49	1	9	59	44	67	24	49	140	45
40/44	1			1	41	24	0	2	26	41	59	11	28	98	41
35/39						8		0	8	36	39	4	9	52	37
30/34						1			1	32	20	1	1	22	32
25/29											4			4	28

MEDFORD OREGON

Temperature Range	NOVEMBER Obsn Hour Gp 01 to 08	NOVEMBER Obsn Hour Gp 09 to 16	NOVEMBER Obsn Hour Gp 17 to 24	NOVEMBER Total Obsn	NOVEMBER MCWB	DECEMBER Obsn Hour Gp 01 to 08	DECEMBER Obsn Hour Gp 09 to 16	DECEMBER Obsn Hour Gp 17 to 24	DECEMBER Total Obsn	DECEMBER MCWB	JANUARY Obsn Hour Gp 01 to 08	JANUARY Obsn Hour Gp 09 to 16	JANUARY Obsn Hour Gp 17 to 24	JANUARY Total Obsn	JANUARY MCWB
105/109															
100/104															
95/99															
90/94															
85/89															
80/84															
75/79		0		0	57										
70/74		1		1	56		0		0	58					
65/69	0	6	1	7	53		0		0	59		0	0	0	51
60/64	1	13	3	17	51	0	2	1	3	55		1	1	2	49
55/59	4	28	9	41	49	2	8	2	12	51	1	7	2	10	48
50/54	10	45	29	84	47	5	19	11	35	47	4	16	10	30	46
45/49	33	53	52	138	44	18	42	28	88	44	12	37	24	73	43
40/44	56	47	67	170	41	43	63	58	164	40	34	60	53	147	40
35/39	52	27	42	121	36	62	55	64	181	36	50	59	60	169	36
30/34	44	14	27	85	31	58	41	57	156	32	80	45	64	189	31
25/29	26	4	9	39	27	44	16	26	86	27	36	16	23	75	27
20/24	12	1	2	15	22	14	1	2	17	22	17	4	8	29	22
15/19	2			2	18	2		0	2	17	9	1	3	13	17
10/14											3	0	1	4	12
5/9											1	0	0	1	7
0/4													0		2

Temperature Range	FEBRUARY Obsn Hour Gp 01 to 08	FEBRUARY Obsn Hour Gp 09 to 16	FEBRUARY Obsn Hour Gp 17 to 24	FEBRUARY Total Obsn	FEBRUARY MCWB	MARCH Obsn Hour Gp 01 to 08	MARCH Obsn Hour Gp 09 to 16	MARCH Obsn Hour Gp 17 to 24	MARCH Total Obsn	MARCH MCWB	APRIL Obsn Hour Gp 01 to 08	APRIL Obsn Hour Gp 09 to 16	APRIL Obsn Hour Gp 17 to 24	APRIL Total Obsn	APRIL MCWB
105/109															
100/104															
95/99															
90/94												0		0	64
85/89												1	0	1	61
80/84							0	0	0	58		4	1	5	60
75/79							1	1	2	58		11	4	15	57
70/74		0		0	53		3	1	4	54		17	9	26	55
65/69		2	0	2	52		9	4	13	52		27	14	41	53
60/64	1	7	3	11	50		18	8	26	50	0	37	23	60	51
55/59	2	19	7	28	48	1	32	15	48	47	4	47	37	88	48
50/54	4	42	27	73	46	5	50	36	91	45	26	48	50	124	46
45/49	20	54	48	122	43	22	63	59	144	42	56	32	49	137	43
40/44	38	48	55	141	40	56	47	61	164	39	65	13	34	112	39
35/39	49	31	50	130	36	79	19	46	144	35	59	2	15	76	36
30/34	59	16	27	102	31	59	6	13	78	31	27	0	3	30	31
25/29	36	3	6	45	27	20	0	3	23	27	3			3	28
20/24	10	1	1	12	22	4	0		4	22					
15/19	1	0	0	1	16	0			0	18					
10/14	1		0	1	12										
5/9	0	0		0	8										
0/4															

Temperature Range	ANNUAL TOTAL Obsn Hour Gp 01 to 08	ANNUAL TOTAL Obsn Hour Gp 09 to 16	ANNUAL TOTAL Obsn Hour Gp 17 to 24	ANNUAL TOTAL Total Obsn	ANNUAL TOTAL MCWB
105/109		0	0	0	70
100/104		10	3	13	69
95/99		38	17	55	68
90/94		87	42	129	66
85/89		138	70	208	64
80/84	0	175	98	273	62
75/79	3	202	130	335	60
70/74	24	223	177	424	58
65/69	84	238	222	544	56
60/64	203	246	256	705	53
55/59	335	275	277	887	51
50/54	383	302	327	1012	47
45/49	417	319	362	1098	44
40/44	448	291	373	1112	40
35/39	420	197	288	905	36
30/34	351	123	192	666	31
25/29	169	39	67	275	27
20/24	57	7	13	77	22
15/19	14	1	3	18	17
10/14	4	0	1	5	12
5/9	1	0	0	1	7
0/4			0		2

PENDLETON OREGON

LAT 45 41N LONG 118 51W ELEV 1482 FT

MEAN FREQUENCY OF OCCURRENCE OF DRY BULB TEMPERATURE (DEGREES F) WITH MEAN COINCIDENT WET BULB TEMPERATURE (DEGREES F) FOR EACH DRY BULB TEMPERATURE RANGE

Temperature Range	MAY Obsn Hour Gp 01 to 08	MAY 09 to 16	MAY 17 to 24	MAY Total Obsn	MAY MCWB	JUNE Obsn Hour Gp 01 to 08	JUNE 09 to 16	JUNE 17 to 24	JUNE Total Obsn	JUNE MCWB	JULY Obsn Hour Gp 01 to 08	JULY 09 to 16	JULY 17 to 24	JULY Total Obsn	JULY MCWB
110/114															
105/109							0		0	69		0	0	0	69
100/104							1	0	1	67		4	2	6	66
95/99							2	1	3	65		16	9	25	65
90/94		1	0	1	64	0	10	5	15	63		35	19	54	63
85/89		5	1	6	63	0	19	8	27	62	1	45	26	72	61
80/84		12	5	17	61	1	29	15	45	60	6	47	35	88	60
75/79	0	22	10	32	58	3	36	24	63	58	14	41	40	95	58
70/74	2	33	18	53	56	11	45	32	88	56	35	31	44	110	56
65/69	8	43	27	78	54	27	46	43	116	54	57	19	34	110	54
60/64	20	50	40	110	51	46	33	46	125	52	66	6	25	97	52
55/59	38	44	49	131	49	68	14	39	121	50	46	1	11	58	49
50/54	65	27	53	145	46	57	4	22	83	47	20	1	2	23	46
45/49	66	10	33	109	42	24	2	6	32	43	3		0	3	42
40/44	40	2	11	53	38	4			4	39	0			0	40
35/39	8		1	9	34										
30/34	1			1	29										
25/29	0		0	0	24										
20/24															

Temperature Range	AUGUST Obsn Hour Gp 01 to 08	AUGUST 09 to 16	AUGUST 17 to 24	AUGUST Total Obsn	AUGUST MCWB	SEPTEMBER Obsn Hour Gp 01 to 08	SEPTEMBER 09 to 16	SEPTEMBER 17 to 24	SEPTEMBER Total Obsn	SEPTEMBER MCWB	OCTOBER Obsn Hour Gp 01 to 08	OCTOBER 09 to 16	OCTOBER 17 to 24	OCTOBER Total Obsn	OCTOBER MCWB
110/114		0	0	0	70										
105/109		0	0	0	68										
100/104		1	0	1	66		0	0	0	65					
95/99		8	3	11	64		2	0	2	64					
90/94		24	11	35	63		4	1	5	63					
85/89	0	39	19	58	61		17	4	21	61		0		0	60
80/84	1	47	29	77	60	0	30	11	41	59		3	0	3	59
75/79	7	49	37	93	58	1	40	19	60	57	0	8	1	9	57
70/74	24	40	48	112	56	5	45	30	80	55	1	18	4	23	56
65/69	50	25	47	122	54	17	43	44	104	53	2	33	9	44	54
60/64	77	12	35	124	52	44	34	52	130	51	6	50	24	80	52
55/59	58	2	16	76	50	71	17	42	130	49	20	52	44	116	49
50/54	27	0	3	30	47	58	6	26	90	46	54	47	63	164	46
45/49	3			3	43	31	1	8	40	42	66	27	57	150	43
40/44	0			0	37	10		2	12	38	54	8	31	93	39
35/39						2		0	2	35	34	2	11	47	35
30/34											10	0	2	12	31
25/29											1		0	1	27
20/24											0			0	23

PENDLETON OREGON

Temperature Range	NOVEMBER Obsn Hour Gp 01 to 08	NOVEMBER Obsn Hour Gp 09 to 16	NOVEMBER Obsn Hour Gp 17 to 24	NOVEMBER Total Obsn	NOVEMBER MCWB	DECEMBER Obsn Hour Gp 01 to 08	DECEMBER Obsn Hour Gp 09 to 16	DECEMBER Obsn Hour Gp 17 to 24	DECEMBER Total Obsn	DECEMBER MCWB	JANUARY Obsn Hour Gp 01 to 08	JANUARY Obsn Hour Gp 09 to 16	JANUARY Obsn Hour Gp 17 to 24	JANUARY Total Obsn	JANUARY MCWB
110/114															
105/109															
100/104															
95/99															
90/94															
85/89															
80/84															
75/79															
70/74		0		0	53										
65/69	0	2	0	2	53		0	0	0	50					
60/64	2	9	3	14	51		1	0	1	51	0	2	0	2	50
55/59	5	19	7	31	48	2	7	4	13	49	1	7	2	10	47
50/54	15	46	25	86	45	8	20	10	38	45	11	18	12	41	45
45/49	38	54	43	135	42	20	37	24	81	42	19	31	21	71	42
40/44	44	41	50	135	39	34	45	38	117	38	29	45	35	109	38
35/39	45	29	46	120	35	52	41	54	147	35	46	36	49	131	34
30/34	42	21	35	98	31	55	43	52	150	31	45	32	41	118	31
25/29	28	10	17	55	26	45	35	43	123	26	31	24	31	86	26
20/24	12	5	8	25	21	20	11	13	44	22	20	15	16	51	22
15/19	5	2	3	10	17	6	4	5	15	17	11	10	9	30	16
10/14	2	2	2	6	11	3	3	3	9	12	10	13	10	33	11
5/9	2	1	1	4	7	1	0	1	2	6	9	8	8	25	6
0/4	0	0	0	0	2	0	1	0	1	2	6	6	8	20	2
-5/-1	1		0	1	-3	1	1	1	3	-3	4	2	3	9	-3
-10/-6						0	0	0	0	-9	3	1	2	6	-8
-15/-11						0		0	0	-11	1	0	1	2	-12
-20/-16											0		0	0	-18

Temperature Range	FEBRUARY Obsn Hour Gp 01 to 08	FEBRUARY Obsn Hour Gp 09 to 16	FEBRUARY Obsn Hour Gp 17 to 24	FEBRUARY Total Obsn	FEBRUARY MCWB	MARCH Obsn Hour Gp 01 to 08	MARCH Obsn Hour Gp 09 to 16	MARCH Obsn Hour Gp 17 to 24	MARCH Total Obsn	MARCH MCWB	APRIL Obsn Hour Gp 01 to 08	APRIL Obsn Hour Gp 09 to 16	APRIL Obsn Hour Gp 17 to 24	APRIL Total Obsn	APRIL MCWB
110/114															
105/109															
100/104															
95/99															
90/94															
85/89												0		0	62
80/84												2	0	2	59
75/79							1	0	1	56		5	2	7	57
70/74							2	1	3	55	0	11	3	14	54
65/69		0		0	51		5	1	6	52	1	24	10	35	52
60/64	0	5	1	6	50	0	12	3	15	49	3	44	19	66	49
55/59	2	16	4	22	47	2	27	11	40	47	12	56	35	103	47
50/54	9	30	17	56	45	12	53	27	92	44	29	53	52	134	44
45/49	23	45	32	100	41	24	70	54	148	41	56	32	60	148	41
40/44	34	48	49	131	38	61	45	62	168	38	76	12	42	130	38
35/39	58	36	53	147	34	72	22	54	148	34	47	2	15	64	34
30/34	55	24	42	121	30	54	8	26	88	30	13		1	14	30
25/29	21	8	13	42	26	16	2	6	24	25	1			1	25
20/24	8	5	5	18	21	4	1	1	6	21					
15/19	6	2	3	11	16	2	1	1	4	17					
10/14	3	1	2	6	11	1		0	1	12					
5/9	1	1	1	3	7										
0/4	1	1	0	2	2										
-5/-1	0	1	1	2	-3										
-10/-6	1	0	1	2	-8										
-15/-11	1	0	0	1	-14										
-20/-16	1		0	1	-17										

Temperature Range	ANNUAL TOTAL Obsn Hour Gp 01 to 08	ANNUAL TOTAL Obsn Hour Gp 09 to 16	ANNUAL TOTAL Obsn Hour Gp 17 to 24	ANNUAL TOTAL Total Obsn	ANNUAL TOTAL MCWB
110/114		0	0	0	70
105/109		0	0	0	69
100/104		6	2	8	66
95/99		28	13	41	65
90/94	0	74	36	110	63
85/89	1	125	58	184	61
80/84	8	170	95	273	60
75/79	25	202	133	360	58
70/74	78	225	180	483	56
65/69	162	240	215	617	54
60/64	264	258	248	770	51
55/59	325	262	264	851	49
50/54	365	305	312	982	45
45/49	373	309	338	1020	42
40/44	386	246	320	952	38
35/39	364	168	283	815	34
30/34	275	128	199	602	31
25/29	143	79	110	332	26
20/24	64	37	43	144	21
15/19	30	19	21	70	16
10/14	19	19	17	55	11
5/9	13	10	11	34	6
0/4	7	8	8	23	2
-5/-1	6	4	5	15	-3
-10/-6	4	1	3	8	-8
-15/-11	2	0	1	3	-13
-20/-16	1		0	1	-17

PORTLAND IAP OREGON

LAT 45 36N LONG 122 36W ELEV 21 FT

MEAN FREQUENCY OF OCCURRENCE OF DRY BULB TEMPERATURE (DEGREES F) WITH MEAN COINCIDENT WET BULB TEMPERATURE (DEGREES F) FOR EACH DRY BULB TEMPERATURE RANGE

Temperature Range	MAY Obsn Hour Gp 01 to 08	MAY 09 to 16	MAY 17 to 24	MAY Total Obsn	MAY MCWB	JUNE Obsn Hour Gp 01 to 08	JUNE 09 to 16	JUNE 17 to 24	JUNE Total Obsn	JUNE MCWB	JULY Obsn Hour Gp 01 to 08	JULY 09 to 16	JULY 17 to 24	JULY Total Obsn	JULY MCWB
100/104												1	0	1	72
95/99							0	0	0	64		2	1	3	70
90/94		0		0	62		3	1	4	67		6	3	9	68
85/89		2	1	3	63		4	2	6	67		13	6	19	67
80/84		8	3	11	63	0	11	5	16	64	0	29	15	44	66
75/79		10	6	16	61	0	18	11	29	62	0	37	26	63	64
70/74	0	18	10	28	59	1	34	21	56	60	4	50	41	95	61
65/69	1	33	20	54	56	5	49	35	89	58	13	58	55	126	59
60/64	8	50	35	93	54	31	69	60	160	56	75	45	63	183	57
55/59	38	70	64	172	51	95	44	75	214	53	120	9	36	165	54
50/54	90	45	69	204	49	88	8	29	125	50	33	0	2	35	50
45/49	77	12	34	123	45	20	1	2	23	46	2			2	47
40/44	29	1	6	36	41	1			1	43	0			0	44
35/39	4		0	4	36										
30/34	1		0	1	33										

Temperature Range	AUGUST Obsn Hour Gp 01 to 08	AUGUST 09 to 16	AUGUST 17 to 24	AUGUST Total Obsn	AUGUST MCWB	SEPTEMBER Obsn Hour Gp 01 to 08	SEPTEMBER 09 to 16	SEPTEMBER 17 to 24	SEPTEMBER Total Obsn	SEPTEMBER MCWB	OCTOBER Obsn Hour Gp 01 to 08	OCTOBER 09 to 16	OCTOBER 17 to 24	OCTOBER Total Obsn	OCTOBER MCWB
100/104															
95/99		1	1	2	68		0	0	0	65					
90/94		5	1	6	69		3	0	3	65					
85/89		11	5	16	67		8	2	10	64		0		0	64
80/84		24	12	36	65		16	6	22	63		2	0	2	63
75/79		35	22	57	63		25	10	35	62		6	1	7	60
70/74	2	56	39	97	61	0	37	20	57	60		13	3	16	59
65/69	13	63	60	136	60	4	52	41	97	58	0	29	10	39	57
60/64	84	44	74	202	57	37	63	72	172	57	7	51	30	88	56
55/59	113	9	31	153	54	91	29	65	185	54	40	65	69	174	53
50/54	32	0	2	34	51	69	5	20	94	51	79	55	72	206	50
45/49	3			3	47	29	1	4	34	46	62	19	44	125	46
40/44						8	0	0	8	42	43	7	17	67	41
35/39						1			1	38	15	1	2	18	37
30/34											2			2	33

PORTLAND IAP OREGON

Temperature Range	NOVEMBER Obsn Hour Gp 01 to 08	NOVEMBER Obsn Hour Gp 09 to 16	NOVEMBER Obsn Hour Gp 17 to 24	NOVEMBER Total Obsn	NOVEMBER MCWB	DECEMBER Obsn Hour Gp 01 to 08	DECEMBER Obsn Hour Gp 09 to 16	DECEMBER Obsn Hour Gp 17 to 24	DECEMBER Total Obsn	DECEMBER MCWB	JANUARY Obsn Hour Gp 01 to 08	JANUARY Obsn Hour Gp 09 to 16	JANUARY Obsn Hour Gp 17 to 24	JANUARY Total Obsn	JANUARY MCWB
100/104															
95/99															
90/94															
85/89															
80/84															
75/79															
70/74															
65/69		1		1	54										
60/64	0	5	1	6	54		1	0	1	57		0		0	55
55/59	6	33	11	50	51	2	8	4	14	53	2	9	3	14	51
50/54	30	69	48	147	49	11	27	14	52	49	10	21	15	46	48
45/49	59	63	70	192	45	36	61	44	141	44	29	47	36	112	44
40/44	67	43	58	168	40	77	85	91	253	40	53	67	68	188	40
35/39	39	18	33	90	36	67	45	61	173	36	70	48	60	178	36
30/34	25	6	13	44	31	38	16	27	81	31	41	28	31	100	31
25/29	11	2	3	16	26	14	3	4	21	26	21	15	16	52	25
20/24	2	1	2	5	20	1	0	0	1	21	11	9	11	31	20
15/19	1		0	1	16	0	1	1	2	14	7	3	5	15	15
10/14	0			0	13	1	1	1	3	10	3	1	2	6	11
5/9						0		0	0	6	1	0	0	1	7
0/4											0			0	2
-5/-1											0			0	-1

Temperature Range	FEBRUARY Obsn Hour Gp 01 to 08	FEBRUARY Obsn Hour Gp 09 to 16	FEBRUARY Obsn Hour Gp 17 to 24	FEBRUARY Total Obsn	FEBRUARY MCWB	MARCH Obsn Hour Gp 01 to 08	MARCH Obsn Hour Gp 09 to 16	MARCH Obsn Hour Gp 17 to 24	MARCH Total Obsn	MARCH MCWB	APRIL Obsn Hour Gp 01 to 08	APRIL Obsn Hour Gp 09 to 16	APRIL Obsn Hour Gp 17 to 24	APRIL Total Obsn	APRIL MCWB	ANNUAL TOTAL Obsn Hour Gp 01 to 08	ANNUAL TOTAL Obsn Hour Gp 09 to 16	ANNUAL TOTAL Obsn Hour Gp 17 to 24	ANNUAL TOTAL Total Obsn	ANNUAL TOTAL MCWB
100/104																	1	0	1	72
95/99																	3	2	5	68
90/94																	17	5	22	68
85/89												0		0	68		38	16	54	67
80/84												1	0	1	64	0	91	41	132	65
75/79												3	0	3	58	0	134	76	210	63
70/74							1	0	1	56		9	4	13	56	7	218	138	363	61
65/69		0		0	51		3	1	4	54	0	17	8	25	53	36	305	230	571	58
60/64		4	1	5	52		9	4	13	51	1	31	17	49	51	243	372	357	972	56
55/59	3	13	5	21	50	1	26	12	39	48	8	53	37	98	50	519	368	412	1299	53
50/54	14	41	25	80	47	9	58	39	106	46	38	69	64	171	47	503	398	399	1300	49
45/49	30	68	56	154	43	52	80	73	205	43	77	43	68	188	44	476	395	431	1302	44
40/44	67	59	74	200	40	88	50	78	216	40	84	12	37	133	40	517	324	429	1270	40
35/39	59	25	43	127	36	62	16	33	111	36	28	1	4	33	36	345	154	236	735	36
30/34	35	8	15	58	31	30	4	7	41	32	5	0	0	5	33	177	62	93	332	31
25/29	10	3	3	16	26	7	1	1	9	26	0			0	28	63	24	27	114	26
20/24	3	1	1	5	20	0			0	21						17	11	14	42	20
15/19	1	1	1	3	16											9	5	7	21	15
10/14	0	0	1	1	10											4	2	4	10	10
5/9	1	0	0	1	7											2	0	0	2	7
0/4	0	0		0	2											0	0		0	2
-5/-1	0			0	-1											0			0	-1

HARRISBURG IAP/OLMSTED PENNSYLVANIA

LAT 40 12N LONG 76 46W ELEV 308 FT

MEAN FREQUENCY OF OCCURRENCE OF DRY BULB TEMPERATURE (DEGREES F) WITH MEAN COINCIDENT WET BULB TEMPERATURE (DEGREES F) FOR EACH DRY BULB TEMPERATURE RANGE

Temperature Range	MAY Obsn Hour Gp 01 to 08	MAY 09 to 16	MAY 17 to 24	MAY Total Obsn	MAY MCWB	JUNE Obsn Hour Gp 01 to 08	JUNE 09 to 16	JUNE 17 to 24	JUNE Total Obsn	JUNE MCWB	JULY Obsn Hour Gp 01 to 08	JULY 09 to 16	JULY 17 to 24	JULY Total Obsn	JULY MCWB
100/104							0		0	78		1	0	1	74
95/99		0		0	74		4	1	5	77		7	1	8	75
90/94		2	0	2	72	0	15	5	20	74		28	9	37	74
85/89		12	3	15	69	0	35	14	49	71	0	53	22	75	72
80/84	0	20	9	29	67	3	49	30	82	69	5	68	49	122	70
75/79	1	35	21	57	63	15	46	45	106	67	35	53	66	154	68
70/74	9	42	34	85	61	47	39	55	141	65	83	27	61	171	67
65/69	25	47	49	121	59	59	28	46	133	61	73	9	29	111	63
60/64	48	40	51	139	56	59	15	28	102	58	37	2	10	49	59
55/59	58	30	40	128	52	42	6	14	62	53	13		0	13	55
50/54	53	15	25	93	48	13	2	3	18	50	1			1	51
45/49	36	5	12	53	44	1		0	1	45					
40/44	14	0	2	16	39										
35/39	3	1	0	4	34										
30/34	0			0	32										
25/29															

Temperature Range	AUGUST Obsn Hour Gp 01 to 08	AUGUST 09 to 16	AUGUST 17 to 24	AUGUST Total Obsn	AUGUST MCWB	SEPTEMBER Obsn Hour Gp 01 to 08	SEPTEMBER 09 to 16	SEPTEMBER 17 to 24	SEPTEMBER Total Obsn	SEPTEMBER MCWB	OCTOBER Obsn Hour Gp 01 to 08	OCTOBER 09 to 16	OCTOBER 17 to 24	OCTOBER Total Obsn	OCTOBER MCWB
100/104		1	0	1	76		0		0	76					
95/99		4	0	4	75		1	0	1	75					
90/94		14	3	17	75		7	0	7	75		0		0	74
85/89	0	38	12	50	73		17	5	22	73		2	0	2	71
80/84	2	61	35	98	70	0	30	14	44	70		6	1	7	68
75/79	21	64	63	148	69	7	42	30	79	68	0	17	5	22	65
70/74	65	42	71	178	67	31	47	44	122	65	5	25	12	42	63
65/69	84	20	44	148	63	42	43	51	136	61	7	39	23	69	59
60/64	46	4	16	66	59	51	34	42	127	57	16	45	38	99	56
55/59	22		4	26	54	45	14	31	90	53	36	50	49	135	52
50/54	8		0	8	50	32	5	16	53	49	49	38	52	139	47
45/49	0			0	48	20	0	5	25	45	56	19	39	114	43
40/44						7		1	8	40	43	6	21	70	39
35/39						3			3	36	26	2	7	35	35
30/34						0			0	32	9	0	1	10	31
25/29											1			1	26

HARRISBURG IAP/OLMSTED PENNSYLVANIA

Temperature Range	NOVEMBER Obsn Hour Gp 01 to 08	NOVEMBER Obsn Hour Gp 09 to 16	NOVEMBER Obsn Hour Gp 17 to 24	NOVEMBER Total Obsn	NOVEMBER MCWB	DECEMBER Obsn Hour Gp 01 to 08	DECEMBER Obsn Hour Gp 09 to 16	DECEMBER Obsn Hour Gp 17 to 24	DECEMBER Total Obsn	DECEMBER MCWB	JANUARY Obsn Hour Gp 01 to 08	JANUARY Obsn Hour Gp 09 to 16	JANUARY Obsn Hour Gp 17 to 24	JANUARY Total Obsn	JANUARY MCWB
100/104															
95/99															
90/94															
85/89															
80/84															
75/79															
70/74	0	3	0	3	62										
65/69	2	7	4	13	59		0	0	0	61		0		0	55
60/64	4	15	6	25	55	0	2	2	4	55	1	1	1	3	56
55/59	10	31	20	61	51	4	5	4	13	53	0	1	1	2	53
50/54	22	42	28	92	47	4	13	6	23	47	2	4	2	8	47
45/49	30	50	43	123	42	7	22	14	43	43	2	14	6	22	42
40/44	41	47	51	139	38	22	42	35	99	38	14	33	20	67	37
35/39	54	28	49	131	34	43	54	55	152	34	35	59	55	149	34
30/34	43	14	28	85	30	59	48	52	159	29	58	60	67	185	29
25/29	26	2	8	36	26	37	29	37	103	24	51	35	46	132	25
20/24	5	1	2	8	20	33	20	25	78	20	35	23	23	81	20
15/19	2	0	0	2	15	21	9	14	44	15	24	11	16	51	15
10/14						12	3	4	19	11	15	5	8	28	11
5/9						3	0	1	4	7	6	2	3	11	6
0/4						2	0	0	2	2	3	1	1	5	1
-5/-1						0	0	0	0	-3	1	0	0	1	-3
-10/-6						0			0	-7	0			0	-6

Temperature Range	FEBRUARY Obsn Hour Gp 01 to 08	FEBRUARY Obsn Hour Gp 09 to 16	FEBRUARY Obsn Hour Gp 17 to 24	FEBRUARY Total Obsn	FEBRUARY MCWB	MARCH Obsn Hour Gp 01 to 08	MARCH Obsn Hour Gp 09 to 16	MARCH Obsn Hour Gp 17 to 24	MARCH Total Obsn	MARCH MCWB	APRIL Obsn Hour Gp 01 to 08	APRIL Obsn Hour Gp 09 to 16	APRIL Obsn Hour Gp 17 to 24	APRIL Total Obsn	APRIL MCWB
100/104															
95/99															
90/94												1	0	1	69
85/89												3	0	3	67
80/84												8	3	11	65
75/79							1	0	1	58	0	12	6	18	62
70/74		0		0	58		3	1	4	56	2	15	12	29	59
65/69		0	1	1	58		4	2	6	54	6	21	19	46	57
60/64	0	2	1	3	54	1	11	6	18	52	15	31	25	71	54
55/59	2	4	3	9	51	4	16	11	31	50	23	40	37	100	50
50/54	2	10	6	18	46	6	29	18	53	45	39	42	45	126	46
45/49	5	20	13	38	41	14	38	36	88	41	50	38	45	133	42
40/44	14	41	29	84	38	36	55	55	146	37	54	20	33	107	38
35/39	37	53	51	141	34	68	50	61	179	34	34	7	12	53	34
30/34	61	42	59	162	29	64	27	38	129	29	13	1	3	17	30
25/29	45	21	29	95	25	33	10	14	57	24	3	0	0	3	24
20/24	24	15	15	54	20	16	3	5	24	20	0			0	20
15/19	13	9	12	34	15	4	0	1	5	16					
10/14	14	4	5	23	11	2			2	11					
5/9	6	1	2	9	7										
0/4	2	0	0	2	2										
-5/-1	0			0	-3										
-10/-6	0			0	-6										

Temperature Range	ANNUAL TOTAL Obsn Hour Gp 01 to 08	ANNUAL TOTAL Obsn Hour Gp 09 to 16	ANNUAL TOTAL Obsn Hour Gp 17 to 24	ANNUAL TOTAL Total Obsn	ANNUAL TOTAL MCWB
100/104		2	0	2	76
95/99		16	2	18	75
90/94	0	67	17	84	74
85/89	0	160	56	216	72
80/84	10	242	141	393	69
75/79	79	270	236	585	67
70/74	242	243	290	775	65
65/69	298	218	268	784	61
60/64	278	202	226	706	56
55/59	259	197	214	670	52
50/54	231	200	201	632	47
45/49	221	206	213	640	43
40/44	245	244	247	736	38
35/39	303	254	290	847	34
30/34	307	192	248	747	29
25/29	196	97	134	427	25
20/24	113	62	70	245	20
15/19	64	29	43	136	15
10/14	43	12	17	72	11
5/9	15	3	6	24	6
0/4	7	1	1	9	1
-5/-1	1	0	0	1	-3
-10/-6	0			0	-7

PITTSBURGH/GTR PITTSBURGH IAP PA

LAT 40 30N LONG 80 13W ELEV 1137 FT

MEAN FREQUENCY OF OCCURRENCE OF DRY BULB TEMPERATURE (DEGREES F) WITH MEAN COINCIDENT WET BULB TEMPERATURE (DEGREES F) FOR EACH DRY BULB TEMPERATURE RANGE

Temperature Range	MAY Obsn Hour Gp 01 to 08	MAY 09 to 16	MAY 17 to 24	MAY Total Obsn	MAY MCWB	JUNE Obsn Hour Gp 01 to 08	JUNE 09 to 16	JUNE 17 to 24	JUNE Total Obsn	JUNE MCWB	JULY Obsn Hour Gp 01 to 08	JULY 09 to 16	JULY 17 to 24	JULY Total Obsn	JULY MCWB
95/99							0		0	72		0		0	72
90/94		0	0	0	71		4	0	4	72		4	1	5	72
85/89		4	1	5	69		23	6	29	71		35	10	45	71
80/84		19	6	25	66		47	22	69	68	0	66	30	96	69
75/79	0	35	17	52	63	4	50	33	87	66	7	65	52	124	67
70/74	6	42	30	78	60	26	52	54	132	64	49	48	72	169	66
65/69	21	43	44	108	59	56	33	52	141	61	82	23	54	159	63
60/64	47	39	48	134	55	59	19	41	119	58	66	6	24	96	59
55/59	40	27	37	104	51	46	9	21	76	53	29	0	6	35	54
50/54	46	19	29	94	47	33	3	9	45	49	13		1	14	50
45/49	39	12	20	71	43	14	1	2	17	45	2			2	45
40/44	30	7	13	50	39	2		0	2	41	0			0	41
35/39	15	0	3	18	35	0			0	38					
30/34	4	0	0	4	30										
25/29	1			1	27										
20/24															
15/19															

Temperature Range	AUGUST Obsn Hour Gp 01 to 08	AUGUST 09 to 16	AUGUST 17 to 24	AUGUST Total Obsn	AUGUST MCWB	SEPTEMBER Obsn Hour Gp 01 to 08	SEPTEMBER 09 to 16	SEPTEMBER 17 to 24	SEPTEMBER Total Obsn	SEPTEMBER MCWB	OCTOBER Obsn Hour Gp 01 to 08	OCTOBER 09 to 16	OCTOBER 17 to 24	OCTOBER Total Obsn	OCTOBER MCWB
95/99		1		1	69		1		1	73					
90/94		6	1	7	71		3	1	4	70					
85/89		20	5	25	71		14	2	16	71		0		0	72
80/84	0	62	22	84	69	0	27	10	37	69		6	0	6	65
75/79	4	67	48	119	67	1	42	20	63	66		19	3	22	62
70/74	32	53	71	156	66	14	45	39	98	64	1	27	12	40	60
65/69	82	29	61	172	63	40	41	50	131	61	8	34	23	65	58
60/64	67	9	28	104	59	49	37	47	133	57	15	40	39	94	54
55/59	41	1	9	51	54	44	19	33	96	53	31	37	43	111	51
50/54	19	0	2	21	50	44	8	25	77	48	44	37	44	125	47
45/49	3		0	3	45	29	3	10	42	45	52	28	37	117	43
40/44	0			0	41	13	0	2	15	40	46	15	30	91	39
35/39						6		0	6	36	33	5	12	50	35
30/34						0			0	33	16	2	4	22	31
25/29											4	0	0	4	26
20/24											0			0	22
15/19											0			0	17

PITTSBURGH/GTR PITTSBURGH IAP PA

Temperature Range	NOVEMBER Obsn Hour Gp 01 to 08	NOVEMBER Obsn Hour Gp 09 to 16	NOVEMBER Obsn Hour Gp 17 to 24	NOVEMBER Total Obsn	NOVEMBER MCWB	DECEMBER Obsn Hour Gp 01 to 08	DECEMBER Obsn Hour Gp 09 to 16	DECEMBER Obsn Hour Gp 17 to 24	DECEMBER Total Obsn	DECEMBER MCWB	JANUARY Obsn Hour Gp 01 to 08	JANUARY Obsn Hour Gp 09 to 16	JANUARY Obsn Hour Gp 17 to 24	JANUARY Total Obsn	JANUARY MCWB
95/99															
90/94															
85/89															
80/84		0		0	66										
75/79		0	0	0	64										
70/74		3	1	4	60										
65/69	0	11	2	13	55	0	1	0	1	57		0		0	58
60/64	4	18	12	34	54	1	4	3	8	54	0	1	1	2	56
55/59	14	22	19	55	50	2	8	5	15	51	2	3	3	8	52
50/54	20	31	27	78	46	8	13	8	29	47	4	7	5	16	47
45/49	31	34	36	101	42	13	14	16	43	42	5	11	9	25	42
40/44	33	39	38	110	38	17	28	24	69	38	15	21	22	58	38
35/39	40	38	40	118	34	31	33	33	97	34	24	36	29	89	34
30/34	52	26	42	120	30	45	48	51	144	30	38	42	47	127	30
25/29	28	10	15	53	25	44	43	41	128	25	44	45	41	130	25
20/24	12	4	5	21	21	33	25	26	84	20	36	32	34	102	20
15/19	3	2	2	7	16	21	16	22	59	15	29	24	25	78	15
10/14	2	1	2	5	11	18	9	12	39	11	25	16	18	59	11
5/9	0	0	0	0	7	10	4	6	20	6	13	6	10	29	6
0/4	1	0	0	1	1	3	1	2	6	1	8	3	4	15	1
-5/-1						2	1	0	3	-3	4	1	1	6	-3
-10/-6											2	0	0	2	-7
-15/-11											0	0		0	-13
-20/-16											0	0		0	-17

Temperature Range	FEBRUARY Obsn Hour Gp 01 to 08	FEBRUARY Obsn Hour Gp 09 to 16	FEBRUARY Obsn Hour Gp 17 to 24	FEBRUARY Total Obsn	FEBRUARY MCWB	MARCH Obsn Hour Gp 01 to 08	MARCH Obsn Hour Gp 09 to 16	MARCH Obsn Hour Gp 17 to 24	MARCH Total Obsn	MARCH MCWB	APRIL Obsn Hour Gp 01 to 08	APRIL Obsn Hour Gp 09 to 16	APRIL Obsn Hour Gp 17 to 24	APRIL Total Obsn	APRIL MCWB	ANNUAL TOTAL Obsn Hour Gp 01 to 08	ANNUAL TOTAL Obsn Hour Gp 09 to 16	ANNUAL TOTAL Obsn Hour Gp 17 to 24	ANNUAL TOTAL Total Obsn	ANNUAL TOTAL MCWB
95/99																	2		2	71
90/94																	17	3	20	72
85/89												1		1	67		97	24	121	71
80/84												6	2	8	63	0	233	92	325	68
75/79							1	0	1	57		13	5	18	62	16	292	178	486	66
70/74							3	1	4	56	1	22	11	34	59	129	295	291	715	64
65/69		1	0	1	55	0	6	2	8	54	5	22	19	46	56	294	244	307	845	61
60/64	1	2	1	4	53	2	11	6	19	52	18	27	29	74	54	329	213	279	821	56
55/59	2	5	4	11	51	6	17	15	38	49	29	32	34	95	50	286	180	229	695	52
50/54	4	10	8	22	45	11	20	20	51	45	31	32	35	98	46	277	180	213	670	47
45/49	7	14	15	36	41	13	28	25	66	41	31	28	32	91	42	239	173	202	614	42
40/44	13	23	21	57	38	28	35	35	98	38	37	25	29	91	37	234	193	214	641	38
35/39	26	37	32	95	33	40	44	45	129	33	38	22	24	84	34	253	215	218	686	34
30/34	44	46	51	141	29	54	43	48	145	29	32	7	18	57	30	285	214	261	760	30
25/29	36	32	33	101	25	44	24	29	97	25	15	2	4	21	25	216	156	163	535	25
20/24	32	22	24	78	20	25	10	15	50	20	4	0	0	4	21	142	93	104	339	20
15/19	21	13	16	50	15	15	4	6	25	16	0			0	18	89	59	71	219	15
10/14	18	9	10	37	11	7	1	2	10	11						70	36	44	150	11
5/9	8	5	7	20	6	3	0	0	3	7						34	15	23	72	6
0/4	7	2	2	11	2	0			0	4						19	6	8	33	1
-5/-1	3	1	0	4	-3											9	3	1	13	-3
-10/-6	2	0		2	-7											4	0	0	4	-7
-15/-11																0	0		0	-13
-20/-16																0	0		0	-17

WILKES-BARRE-SCRANTON APRT PENNSYLVANIA

LAT 41 20N LONG 75 44W ELEV 930 FT

MEAN FREQUENCY OF OCCURRENCE OF DRY BULB TEMPERATURE (DEGREES F) WITH MEAN COINCIDENT WET BULB TEMPERATURE (DEGREES F) FOR EACH DRY BULB TEMPERATURE RANGE

Temperature Range	MAY Obsn Hour Gp 01 to 08	MAY 09 to 16	MAY 17 to 24	MAY Total Obsn	MAY MCWB	JUNE Obsn Hour Gp 01 to 08	JUNE 09 to 16	JUNE 17 to 24	JUNE Total Obsn	JUNE MCWB	JULY Obsn Hour Gp 01 to 08	JULY 09 to 16	JULY 17 to 24	JULY Total Obsn	JULY MCWB
100/104															
95/99							1	0	1	77		1	0	1	72
90/94		1	0	1	69		4	1	5	74		11	2	13	72
85/89		5	1	6	68		21	6	27	71		33	9	42	71
80/84		16	4	20	65	1	43	18	62	68	1	61	27	89	68
75/79	1	25	11	37	62	6	47	32	85	65	8	62	48	118	67
70/74	4	41	24	69	59	25	47	48	120	63	50	48	69	167	65
65/69	15	41	36	92	58	49	35	53	137	61	81	24	56	161	63
60/64	33	40	46	119	55	53	26	42	121	57	60	6	28	94	58
55/59	43	36	45	124	51	53	10	27	90	53	34	1	9	44	54
50/54	56	26	38	120	47	40	4	12	56	49	13		0	13	50
45/49	49	13	28	90	43	12		1	13	45	1			1	46
40/44	33	4	11	48	39	2			2	40					
35/39	12	1	2	15	34	0			0	37					
30/34	2		0	2	30										
25/29															
20/24															

Temperature Range	AUGUST Obsn Hour Gp 01 to 08	AUGUST 09 to 16	AUGUST 17 to 24	AUGUST Total Obsn	AUGUST MCWB	SEPTEMBER Obsn Hour Gp 01 to 08	SEPTEMBER 09 to 16	SEPTEMBER 17 to 24	SEPTEMBER Total Obsn	SEPTEMBER MCWB	OCTOBER Obsn Hour Gp 01 to 08	OCTOBER 09 to 16	OCTOBER 17 to 24	OCTOBER Total Obsn	OCTOBER MCWB
100/104							0		0	75					
95/99		1		1	72		0		0	75					
90/94		6	1	7	71		2	0	2	73					
85/89		19	3	22	71		8	1	9	72		1		1	68
80/84	0	49	17	66	69	0	21	5	26	69		4	0	4	68
75/79	5	64	40	109	67	2	32	17	51	67		13	2	15	63
70/74	34	59	67	160	65	15	42	31	88	64	1	19	8	28	62
65/69	72	37	66	175	63	32	46	41	119	61	6	31	16	53	58
60/64	68	12	35	115	59	43	43	51	137	57	16	39	32	87	55
55/59	40	2	15	57	54	51	29	45	125	53	26	48	46	120	51
50/54	23		3	26	50	42	13	29	84	49	44	40	43	127	47
45/49	6			6	46	30	3	14	47	44	47	27	45	119	43
40/44						18	0	5	23	40	48	17	32	97	39
35/39						6		1	7	36	37	7	18	62	34
30/34						2			2	32	19	2	6	27	30
25/29											5		0	5	27
20/24											0			0	23

WILKES-BARRE-SCRANTON APRT PENNSYLVANIA

Temperature Range	NOVEMBER Obsn Hour Gp			Total Obsn	MCWB	DECEMBER Obsn Hour Gp			Total Obsn	MCWB	JANUARY Obsn Hour Gp			Total Obsn	MCWB
	01 to 08	09 to 16	17 to 24			01 to 08	09 to 16	17 to 24			01 to 08	09 to 16	17 to 24		
100/104															
95/99															
90/94															
85/89															
80/84															
75/79		1		1	65										
70/74		1	0	1	61										
65/69	1	5	1	7	58		0		0	59		0		0	58
60/64	2	14	5	21	55		1	1	2	57	0	1	0	1	56
55/59	9	19	15	43	52	3	3	4	10	54	1	1	1	3	54
50/54	19	31	26	76	47	4	7	5	16	47	3	3	2	8	50
45/49	28	38	33	99	43	7	14	7	28	43	3	9	5	17	44
40/44	32	48	39	119	38	12	24	20	56	38	12	20	15	47	39
35/39	47	40	48	135	34	32	44	40	116	34	26	36	32	94	34
30/34	51	29	45	125	29	50	53	52	155	29	42	52	51	145	29
25/29	32	11	18	61	25	46	39	41	126	25	42	50	45	137	24
20/24	14	3	7	24	21	31	29	32	92	20	38	35	39	112	20
15/19	3	1	2	6	16	27	17	22	66	15	29	22	26	77	15
10/14	2	0	0	2	11	19	10	14	43	11	27	13	19	59	10
5/9						10	4	7	21	6	15	5	8	28	6
0/4						6	1	2	9	1	5	1	2	8	1
-5/-1						2	0	0	2	-3	4	1	1	6	-3
-10/-6											1			1	-7
-15/-11															

Temperature Range	FEBRUARY Obsn Hour Gp			Total Obsn	MCWB	MARCH Obsn Hour Gp			Total Obsn	MCWB	APRIL Obsn Hour Gp			Total Obsn	MCWB
	01 to 08	09 to 16	17 to 24			01 to 08	09 to 16	17 to 24			01 to 08	09 to 16	17 to 24		
100/104															
95/99															
90/94															
85/89												1	0	1	63
80/84												4	1	5	63
75/79							0		0	55		9	3	12	60
70/74		0		0	59		1	0	1	53	1	12	8	21	59
65/69		0		0	57		3	1	4	52	4	20	13	37	55
60/64		0	0	0	56	0	5	2	7	51	11	24	19	54	53
55/59	1	3	1	5	50	3	10	7	20	50	18	33	29	80	49
50/54	2	5	4	11	47	5	17	10	32	45	26	36	36	98	46
45/49	3	10	6	19	42	9	28	20	57	41	39	36	39	114	42
40/44	9	22	15	46	38	18	43	34	95	37	41	33	40	114	38
35/39	25	43	38	106	34	46	55	59	160	33	47	21	33	101	34
30/34	50	49	49	148	29	65	42	54	161	29	36	9	16	61	30
25/29	37	39	45	121	25	42	23	32	97	25	13	1	3	17	25
20/24	32	20	25	77	20	30	13	16	59	20	4	0	1	5	20
15/19	23	14	18	55	15	17	6	9	32	15	1		0	1	16
10/14	17	10	12	39	10	8	2	3	13	11					
5/9	13	5	8	26	6	4	0	1	5	6					
0/4	8	2	3	13	2	0			0	3					
-5/-1	3	0	1	4	-3										
-10/-6	1	0		1	-9										
-15/-11	0			0	-11										

Temperature Range	ANNUAL TOTAL Obsn Hour Gp			Total Obsn	MCWB
	01 to 08	09 to 16	17 to 24		
100/104		0		0	75
95/99		3	0	3	74
90/94		24	4	28	72
85/89		88	20	108	71
80/84	2	198	72	272	68
75/79	22	253	153	428	66
70/74	130	270	255	655	64
65/69	260	242	283	785	61
60/64	286	211	261	758	56
55/59	282	195	244	721	52
50/54	277	182	208	667	47
45/49	234	178	198	610	43
40/44	225	211	211	647	38
35/39	278	247	271	796	34
30/34	317	236	273	826	29
25/29	217	163	184	564	25
20/24	149	100	120	369	20
15/19	100	60	77	237	15
10/14	73	35	48	156	11
5/9	42	14	24	80	6
0/4	19	4	7	30	1
-5/-1	9	1	2	12	-3
-10/-6	2	0		2	-8
-15/-11	0			0	-11

WILLIAMSPORT PENNSYLVANIA

LAT 41 15N LONG 76 55W ELEV 524 FT

MEAN FREQUENCY OF OCCURRENCE OF DRY BULB TEMPERATURE (DEGREES F) WITH MEAN COINCIDENT WET BULB TEMPERATURE (DEGREES F) FOR EACH DRY BULB TEMPERATURE RANGE

Temperature Range	MAY Obsn Hour Gp 01 to 08	09 to 16	17 to 24	Total Obsn	MCWB	JUNE Obsn Hour Gp 01 to 08	09 to 16	17 to 24	Total Obsn	MCWB	JULY Obsn Hour Gp 01 to 08	09 to 16	17 to 24	Total Obsn	MCWB
100/104							0		0	76		0		0	72
95/99		0		0	69		2	1	3	75		4	1	5	73
90/94		2	0	2	68		10	3	13	72		19	6	25	72
85/89		7	2	9	67	0	27	11	38	70		38	17	55	71
80/84		16	7	23	64	1	43	26	70	68	1	60	36	97	68
75/79	0	28	15	43	62	6	48	38	92	65	9	62	51	122	67
70/74	3	39	30	72	60	22	44	48	114	63	44	40	63	147	66
65/69	12	47	42	101	57	48	36	50	134	61	79	20	47	146	64
60/64	34	45	45	124	55	63	19	36	118	58	62	5	23	90	59
55/59	54	33	47	134	51	54	9	20	83	54	37		6	43	55
50/54	53	19	34	106	47	34	2	6	42	50	16		0	16	51
45/49	52	9	18	79	44	11		1	12	45	1			1	46
40/44	27	1	6	34	39	2			2	41	0			0	42
35/39	12	1	1	14	35	0			0	38					
30/34	2			2	31										
25/29															
20/24															

Temperature Range	AUGUST Obsn Hour Gp 01 to 08	09 to 16	17 to 24	Total Obsn	MCWB	SEPTEMBER Obsn Hour Gp 01 to 08	09 to 16	17 to 24	Total Obsn	MCWB	OCTOBER Obsn Hour Gp 01 to 08	09 to 16	17 to 24	Total Obsn	MCWB
100/104		0		0	77		0		0	76					
95/99		3	0	3	73		1		1	74					
90/94		7	2	9	73		3	0	3	73		0		0	68
85/89		24	7	31	71		11	3	14	71		1		1	69
80/84	0	54	25	79	69		23	9	32	69		5	1	6	66
75/79	4	64	50	118	67	2	32	18	52	66		12	3	15	63
70/74	30	56	63	149	66	13	43	36	92	64	1	21	8	30	61
65/69	70	29	57	156	63	33	47	44	124	61	4	30	18	52	58
60/64	71	10	30	111	60	42	40	47	129	57	11	42	33	86	55
55/59	40	1	12	53	55	47	24	38	109	54	27	46	41	114	51
50/54	25		2	27	51	42	10	27	79	50	37	46	48	131	47
45/49	7		0	7	47	35	4	12	51	45	53	27	50	130	44
40/44						20	1	4	25	41	53	12	28	93	39
35/39						6		0	6	36	36	5	14	55	35
30/34						1			1	32	22	0	4	26	31
25/29											4		0	4	27
20/24											0			0	23

WILLIAMSPORT PENNSYLVANIA

Temperature Range	NOVEMBER Obsn Hour Gp 01 to 08	NOVEMBER 09 to 16	NOVEMBER 17 to 24	NOVEMBER Total Obsn	NOVEMBER MCWB	DECEMBER Obsn Hour Gp 01 to 08	DECEMBER 09 to 16	DECEMBER 17 to 24	DECEMBER Total Obsn	DECEMBER MCWB	JANUARY Obsn Hour Gp 01 to 08	JANUARY 09 to 16	JANUARY 17 to 24	JANUARY Total Obsn	JANUARY MCWB
100/104															
95/99															
90/94															
85/89															
80/84		0		0	66										
75/79		0	0	0	65										
70/74		1	0	1	63										
65/69	1	5	2	8	58										
60/64	2	10	4	16	55		1	0	1	56		0	0	0	55
55/59	7	24	17	48	51	1	3	2	6	53	1	1	2	4	53
50/54	19	36	24	79	47	3	7	3	13	47	3	2	2	7	49
45/49	27	44	34	105	42	6	16	10	32	43	4	8	4	16	43
40/44	31	52	46	129	38	13	28	19	60	38	10	22	12	44	38
35/39	50	37	51	138	34	29	54	43	126	34	32	50	44	126	34
30/34	50	21	37	108	30	53	54	63	170	29	52	65	64	181	29
25/29	33	7	17	57	26	49	36	42	127	25	42	42	48	132	24
20/24	15	2	5	22	21	35	25	29	89	20	40	27	33	100	20
15/19	3	1	2	6	15	25	14	19	58	15	24	16	19	59	15
10/14	1			1	12	15	6	10	31	11	20	8	12	40	11
5/9						11	3	4	18	6	11	3	4	18	6
0/4						4	1	1	6	1	3	2	2	7	2
-5/-1						2	0	0	2	-3	4	1	1	6	-3
-10/-6						2	0	0	2	-8	2	0	0	2	-8
-15/-11						1			1	-13	0			0	-12

Temperature Range	FEBRUARY Obsn Hour Gp 01 to 08	FEBRUARY 09 to 16	FEBRUARY 17 to 24	FEBRUARY Total Obsn	FEBRUARY MCWB	MARCH Obsn Hour Gp 01 to 08	MARCH 09 to 16	MARCH 17 to 24	MARCH Total Obsn	MARCH MCWB	APRIL Obsn Hour Gp 01 to 08	APRIL 09 to 16	APRIL 17 to 24	APRIL Total Obsn	APRIL MCWB	ANNUAL TOTAL Obsn Hour Gp 01 to 08	ANNUAL TOTAL 09 to 16	ANNUAL TOTAL 17 to 24	ANNUAL TOTAL Total Obsn	ANNUAL TOTAL MCWB
100/104																				
95/99																	0		0	75
90/94																	10	2	12	73
85/89												0	0	0	64		41	11	52	72
80/84												2	1	3	64	0	110	41	151	70
75/79												6	3	9	62	2	207	107	316	68
70/74							0		0	55	0	9	5	14	60	21	255	180	456	66
65/69		0	0	0	57		1	0	1	53	1	13	10	24	57	114	258	258	630	64
60/64		0	0	0	54		3	1	4	52	3	19	15	37	55	250	236	276	762	61
55/59	1	2	1	4	49	2	7	4	13	51	10	27	22	59	52	297	206	244	747	57
50/54	1	5	2	8	46	2	11	7	20	48	16	39	34	89	49	287	193	227	707	52
45/49	3	12	7	22	41	4	21	13	38	44	28	38	35	101	45	265	186	196	647	47
40/44	9	31	19	59	37	10	35	26	71	40	43	42	41	126	42	252	197	203	652	43
35/39	29	56	49	134	33	23	54	45	122	37	49	32	40	121	38	237	233	219	689	38
30/34	52	52	62	166	29	48	55	59	162	33	44	12	27	83	34	286	270	288	844	34
25/29	43	27	35	105	24	60	38	53	151	29	31	3	7	41	29	323	233	290	846	29
20/24	28	17	21	66	20	50	15	25	90	24	11	0	2	13	25	232	127	169	528	25
15/19	24	11	12	47	15	25	6	11	42	20	3		0	3	20	146	77	99	322	20
10/14	14	7	8	29	10	16	2	3	21	15	0			0	18	92	44	55	191	15
5/9	10	3	6	19	6	5	0	1	6	11						55	21	31	107	11
0/4	8	1	1	10	2	4		0	4	6						36	9	14	59	6
-5/-1	2	0		2	-3	0			0	4						15	4	4	23	2
-10/-6	0	0		0	-9											8	1	1	10	-3
-15/-11																4	0	0	4	-8
																1			1	-12

QUONSET POINT NAS RHODE ISLAND

LAT 41 36N LONG 71 25W ELEV 30 FT

MEAN FREQUENCY OF OCCURRENCE OF DRY BULB TEMPERATURE (DEGREES F) WITH MEAN COINCIDENT WET BULB TEMPERATURE (DEGREES F) FOR EACH DRY BULB TEMPERATURE RANGE

Temperature Range	MAY Obsn Hour Gp 01 to 08	MAY 09 to 16	MAY 17 to 24	MAY Total Obsn	MAY MCWB	JUNE Obsn Hour Gp 01 to 08	JUNE 09 to 16	JUNE 17 to 24	JUNE Total Obsn	JUNE MCWB	JULY Obsn Hour Gp 01 to 08	JULY 09 to 16	JULY 17 to 24	JULY Total Obsn	JULY MCWB
100/104												0		0	77
95/99												1	0	1	75
90/94		0	0	0	70		4	1	5	72		6	1	7	75
85/89		1	0	1	69		13	2	15	71	1	24	3	28	73
80/84	0	4	0	4	66	1	24	6	31	69	3	56	14	73	70
75/79	1	13	3	17	63	5	45	16	66	66	15	74	39	128	68
70/74	2	27	7	36	60	19	57	37	113	64	67	57	85	209	67
65/69	8	46	15	69	57	47	47	58	152	62	88	24	80	192	64
60/64	25	62	44	131	55	76	33	68	177	58	60	4	24	88	59
55/59	53	54	67	174	52	63	14	41	118	55	13	0	1	14	54
50/54	74	26	67	167	48	25	2	11	38	50	1		0	1	50
45/49	58	11	36	105	44	4		0	4	45					
40/44	24	3	9	36	40										
35/39	3		0	3	33										
30/34	0			0	31										
25/29															
20/24															

Temperature Range	AUGUST Obsn Hour Gp 01 to 08	AUGUST 09 to 16	AUGUST 17 to 24	AUGUST Total Obsn	AUGUST MCWB	SEPTEMBER Obsn Hour Gp 01 to 08	SEPTEMBER 09 to 16	SEPTEMBER 17 to 24	SEPTEMBER Total Obsn	SEPTEMBER MCWB	OCTOBER Obsn Hour Gp 01 to 08	OCTOBER 09 to 16	OCTOBER 17 to 24	OCTOBER Total Obsn	OCTOBER MCWB
100/104															
95/99															
90/94		4		4	76		0		0	78					
85/89	0	21	1	22	73		6	0	6	73		1		1	71
80/84	2	53	11	66	71		18	2	20	71		2		2	64
75/79	13	71	39	123	69	3	33	10	46	69		6	0	6	64
70/74	60	63	82	205	67	23	58	32	113	65	1	19	3	23	63
65/69	88	26	76	190	63	42	54	56	152	62	5	39	14	58	60
60/64	56	9	31	96	59	53	43	63	159	57	33	62	50	145	57
55/59	20	1	6	27	54	56	23	44	123	53	50	53	56	159	52
50/54	7		1	8	49	36	4	24	64	49	47	38	55	140	48
45/49	1			1	43	20	1	6	27	44	47	19	40	106	43
40/44						7	0	1	8	39	36	7	20	63	38
35/39						1		0	1	35	19	2	9	30	34
30/34											9	0	2	11	30
25/29											1		0	1	25
20/24											0		0	0	20

QUONSET POINT NAS RHODE ISLAND

Temperature Range	NOVEMBER Obsn Hour Gp 01 to 08	09 to 16	17 to 24	Total Obsn	M C W B	DECEMBER Obsn Hour Gp 01 to 08	09 to 16	17 to 24	Total Obsn	M C W B	JANUARY Obsn Hour Gp 01 to 08	09 to 16	17 to 24	Total Obsn	M C W B
100/104															
95/99															
90/94															
85/89															
80/84															
75/79															
70/74		0		0	59										
65/69		3	0	3	61		0		0	56					
60/64	5	13	7	25	58		1		1	54		1	0	1	50
55/59	19	37	23	79	53	3	7	2	12	52	1	1	0	2	51
50/54	31	52	40	123	48	6	15	9	30	48	2	6	2	10	47
45/49	43	50	49	142	43	12	23	15	50	43	5	12	6	23	43
40/44	39	42	48	129	38	19	37	32	88	38	13	29	20	62	39
35/39	42	29	39	110	33	42	48	49	139	34	32	52	45	129	34
30/34	34	11	24	69	29	47	45	49	141	29	41	48	53	142	29
25/29	20	2	8	30	25	38	35	36	109	24	45	40	47	132	24
20/24	6	1	2	9	20	35	22	31	88	20	41	29	36	106	20
15/19	1	0	0	1	16	27	9	14	50	16	29	18	21	68	15
10/14						13	4	6	23	11	21	7	12	40	10
5/9						4	1	2	7	6	12	4	5	21	6
0/4						1	1	1	3	1	5	1	1	7	1
-5/-1						0	0	0	0	-3	1	0	0	1	-4
-10/-6						1		0	1	-9	1		0	1	-8

Temperature Range	FEBRUARY Obsn Hour Gp 01 to 08	09 to 16	17 to 24	Total Obsn	M C W B	MARCH Obsn Hour Gp 01 to 08	09 to 16	17 to 24	Total Obsn	M C W B	APRIL Obsn Hour Gp 01 to 08	09 to 16	17 to 24	Total Obsn	M C W B
100/104															
95/99															
90/94															
85/89												0		0	67
80/84												0	0	0	66
75/79												4	0	4	60
70/74							0		0	54	0	7	1	8	58
65/69							1		1	50	1	10	3	14	55
60/64		0		0	51	0	3	0	3	49	3	28	8	39	52
55/59		2	0	2	48	0	10	3	13	47	10	39	20	69	49
50/54	1	5	1	7	47	2	23	10	35	44	30	58	42	130	46
45/49	5	16	8	29	43	11	44	23	78	41	56	51	69	176	42
40/44	11	36	20	67	38	31	64	57	152	37	71	34	66	171	39
35/39	38	53	49	140	34	77	51	76	204	34	49	7	27	83	34
30/34	49	46	60	155	29	62	34	49	145	29	19	1	2	22	29
25/29	37	31	36	104	24	39	12	18	69	24	1		0	1	24
20/24	33	18	23	74	20	13	4	7	24	19	1			1	19
15/19	20	9	13	42	15	8	2	3	13	15					
10/14	15	5	8	28	10	3	0	1	4	10					
5/9	11	2	4	17	6	1		0	1	6					
0/4	3	1	1	5	2	0			0	3					
-5/-1	2	0	0	2	-3										
-10/-6	0			0	-6										

Temperature Range	ANNUAL TOTAL Obsn Hour Gp 01 to 08	09 to 16	17 to 24	Total Obsn	M C W B
100/104		0		0	77
95/99		1	0	1	75
90/94		14	2	16	74
85/89	1	66	6	73	73
80/84	6	157	33	196	70
75/79	37	246	107	390	68
70/74	172	288	247	707	65
65/69	279	250	302	831	62
60/64	311	259	295	865	57
55/59	288	241	263	792	52
50/54	262	229	262	753	48
45/49	262	227	252	741	43
40/44	251	252	273	776	38
35/39	303	242	294	839	34
30/34	261	185	239	685	29
25/29	181	120	145	446	24
20/24	129	74	99	302	20
15/19	85	38	51	174	15
10/14	52	16	27	95	10
5/9	28	7	11	46	6
0/4	9	3	3	15	1
-5/-1	3	0	0	3	-3
-10/-6	2		0	2	-8

CHARLESTON AFB/MAP SOUTH CAROLINA

LAT 32 54N LONG 80 02W ELEV 45 FT

MEAN FREQUENCY OF OCCURRENCE OF DRY BULB TEMPERATURE (DEGREES F) WITH MEAN COINCIDENT WET BULB TEMPERATURE (DEGREES F) FOR EACH DRY BULB TEMPERATURE RANGE

Temperature Range	MAY Obsn Hour Gp 01 to 08	MAY 09 to 16	MAY 17 to 24	MAY Total Obsn	MAY MCWB	JUNE Obsn Hour Gp 01 to 08	JUNE 09 to 16	JUNE 17 to 24	JUNE Total Obsn	JUNE MCWB	JULY Obsn Hour Gp 01 to 08	JULY 09 to 16	JULY 17 to 24	JULY Total Obsn	JULY MCWB
100/104							0		0	78		0		0	79
95/99		2	0	2	74		7	1	8	78		4	0	4	80
90/94		14	2	16	72		26	3	29	77		36	3	39	78
85/89	0	34	5	39	71	1	70	12	83	76	1	92	18	111	77
80/84	2	74	14	90	70	14	79	42	135	74	20	77	61	158	76
75/79	17	65	46	128	68	57	42	83	182	73	92	30	110	232	74
70/74	59	34	79	172	67	96	12	73	181	70	111	8	52	171	71
65/69	76	17	62	155	64	50	2	20	72	66	21	0	3	24	66
60/64	49	6	27	82	60	17	1	5	23	61	3		0	3	61
55/59	29	1	9	39	55	4	0	1	5	56	0			0	59
50/54	12	1	3	16	50	0			0	53					
45/49	4	0	1	5	46										
40/44	0		0	0	42										
35/39	0			0	36										
30/34															
25/29															

Temperature Range	AUGUST Obsn Hour Gp 01 to 08	AUGUST 09 to 16	AUGUST 17 to 24	AUGUST Total Obsn	AUGUST MCWB	SEPTEMBER Obsn Hour Gp 01 to 08	SEPTEMBER 09 to 16	SEPTEMBER 17 to 24	SEPTEMBER Total Obsn	SEPTEMBER MCWB	OCTOBER Obsn Hour Gp 01 to 08	OCTOBER 09 to 16	OCTOBER 17 to 24	OCTOBER Total Obsn	OCTOBER MCWB
100/104		0		0	79										
95/99		4	0	4	78										
90/94		36	3	39	78		7	0	7	76		1		1	74
85/89	0	93	17	110	77		56	4	60	75		9	0	9	73
80/84	16	77	60	153	75	3	79	26	108	74	0	40	3	43	70
75/79	81	28	102	211	74	30	54	70	154	72	5	53	18	76	68
70/74	109	9	55	173	71	92	30	83	205	70	18	56	43	117	66
65/69	36	1	10	47	66	71	11	39	121	65	43	44	57	144	63
60/64	5		1	6	62	28	3	15	46	60	54	26	52	132	59
55/59						12	0	3	15	55	54	14	37	105	54
50/54						4		0	4	51	32	4	21	57	49
45/49											21	1	11	33	45
40/44											14	0	4	18	40
35/39											4	0	1	5	36
30/34											1		0	1	32
25/29											0			0	27

CHARLESTON AFB/MAP SOUTH CAROLINA

Temperature Range	NOVEMBER Obsn Hour Gp 01 to 08	NOVEMBER 09 to 16	NOVEMBER 17 to 24	NOVEMBER Total Obsn	NOVEMBER MCWB	DECEMBER Obsn Hour Gp 01 to 08	DECEMBER 09 to 16	DECEMBER 17 to 24	DECEMBER Total Obsn	DECEMBER MCWB	JANUARY Obsn Hour Gp 01 to 08	JANUARY 09 to 16	JANUARY 17 to 24	JANUARY Total Obsn	JANUARY MCWB
100/104															
95/99															
90/94															
85/89		0		0	70										
80/84		6	0	6	70		0		0	69		0		0	66
75/79		24	1	25	66		5		5	67		9	0	9	66
70/74	3	41	11	55	64	0	19	2	21	63		18	2	20	63
65/69	19	47	34	100	61	9	26	16	51	61	4	28	12	44	60
60/64	30	39	38	107	57	14	36	23	73	57	20	35	31	86	57
55/59	31	35	39	105	52	20	40	32	92	52	21	34	30	85	52
50/54	35	27	40	102	48	24	38	33	95	47	30	37	38	105	48
45/49	42	14	32	88	44	33	35	43	111	43	33	34	40	107	43
40/44	31	5	25	61	39	38	24	39	101	38	34	26	40	100	38
35/39	29	2	14	45	35	42	15	32	89	34	40	17	29	86	34
30/34	15	0	5	20	30	38	6	17	61	30	35	6	19	60	30
25/29	5	0	1	6	25	20	2	8	30	25	20	2	7	29	25
20/24	1	0	0	1	19	8	0	1	9	21	10	0	1	11	21
15/19	0	0	0	0	15	2	0	0	2	16	1		0	1	17
10/14						0		0	0	10					
5/9						0			0	8					

Temperature Range	FEBRUARY Obsn Hour Gp 01 to 08	FEBRUARY 09 to 16	FEBRUARY 17 to 24	FEBRUARY Total Obsn	FEBRUARY MCWB	MARCH Obsn Hour Gp 01 to 08	MARCH 09 to 16	MARCH 17 to 24	MARCH Total Obsn	MARCH MCWB	APRIL Obsn Hour Gp 01 to 08	APRIL 09 to 16	APRIL 17 to 24	APRIL Total Obsn	APRIL MCWB	ANNUAL TOTAL Obsn Hour Gp 01 to 08	ANNUAL TOTAL 09 to 16	ANNUAL TOTAL 17 to 24	ANNUAL TOTAL Total Obsn	ANNUAL TOTAL MCWB
100/104																	0		0	78
95/99																	17	1	18	78
90/94							0		0	61		1		1	72		121	11	132	77
85/89		0		0	68		1	0	1	67		5	1	6	70	2	360	57	419	76
80/84		2	0	2	66		9	1	10	66		30	3	33	67	55	473	210	738	73
75/79		7	1	8	64		23	2	25	64	1	57	11	69	66	283	397	444	1124	71
70/74	0	22	2	24	61	2	35	12	49	61	11	52	34	97	63	501	336	448	1285	68
65/69	5	35	17	57	60	18	42	35	95	60	42	47	69	158	61	394	300	374	1068	63
60/64	22	37	31	90	57	33	42	43	118	56	57	28	54	139	57	332	253	320	905	58
55/59	27	35	38	100	52	35	36	43	114	52	47	14	34	95	53	280	209	266	755	53
50/54	28	33	39	100	47	37	28	45	110	47	34	5	21	60	48	236	173	240	649	48
45/49	37	24	38	99	43	45	16	32	93	43	25	1	10	36	44	240	125	207	572	43
40/44	34	15	30	79	38	34	10	22	66	39	16	0	3	19	40	201	80	163	444	39
35/39	33	8	17	58	34	27	3	8	38	34	7		1	8	35	182	45	102	329	34
30/34	24	4	8	36	30	12	2	4	18	30	0			0	32	125	18	53	196	30
25/29	11	1	2	14	25	4	0	0	4	25						60	5	18	83	25
20/24	3	0	0	3	20	0			0	21						22	0	2	24	21
15/19	1	0		1	15											4	0	0	4	16
10/14																0		0	0	10
5/9																0			0	8

GREENVILLE-SPARTANBURG APRT SO CAROLINA

LAT 34 54N LONG 82 13W ELEV 957 FT

MEAN FREQUENCY OF OCCURRENCE OF DRY BULB TEMPERATURE (DEGREES F) WITH MEAN COINCIDENT WET BULB TEMPERATURE (DEGREES F) FOR EACH DRY BULB TEMPERATURE RANGE

Tempera-ture Range	MAY Obsn Hour Gp 01 to 08	MAY 09 to 16	MAY 17 to 24	MAY Total Obsn	MAY M C W B	JUNE Obsn Hour Gp 01 to 08	JUNE 09 to 16	JUNE 17 to 24	JUNE Total Obsn	JUNE M C W B	JULY Obsn Hour Gp 01 to 08	JULY 09 to 16	JULY 17 to 24	JULY Total Obsn	JULY M C W B
100/104															
95/99		0		0	69		3	1	4	74		2	1	3	74
90/94		7	2	9	69		21	6	27	74		27	7	34	74
85/89		33	12	45	68	0	49	21	70	72		75	28	103	73
80/84	0	49	25	74	67	4	64	41	109	70	3	79	53	135	72
75/79	4	50	41	95	65	19	53	55	127	68	34	47	82	163	71
70/74	25	43	62	130	64	74	31	67	172	67	152	17	66	235	69
65/69	83	31	52	166	62	97	16	38	151	64	52	2	11	65	65
60/64	70	23	33	126	58	37	4	8	49	59	6		0	6	59
55/59	37	9	15	61	53	9	0	1	10	54	1			1	55
50/54	17	3	6	26	48	1	0	0	1	50					
45/49	10		1	11	43										
40/44	2			2	39										
35/39	0			0	35										
30/34															

Tempera-ture Range	AUGUST Obsn Hour Gp 01 to 08	AUGUST 09 to 16	AUGUST 17 to 24	AUGUST Total Obsn	AUGUST M C W B	SEPTEMBER Obsn Hour Gp 01 to 08	SEPTEMBER 09 to 16	SEPTEMBER 17 to 24	SEPTEMBER Total Obsn	SEPTEMBER M C W B	OCTOBER Obsn Hour Gp 01 to 08	OCTOBER 09 to 16	OCTOBER 17 to 24	OCTOBER Total Obsn	OCTOBER M C W B
100/104		0		0	75										
95/99		3	1	4	74		1		1	73					
90/94		32	8	40	74		9	2	11	71					
85/89	0	73	30	103	74		34	10	44	72		1		1	70
80/84	3	70	57	130	72		51	27	78	70		17	2	19	66
75/79	35	45	77	157	71	4	53	51	108	68		36	10	46	64
70/74	134	19	57	210	69	70	44	66	180	67	4	44	27	75	62
65/69	63	5	16	84	65	72	29	46	147	63	20	52	44	116	60
60/64	12	1	2	15	60	48	12	23	83	58	44	50	61	155	56
55/59	1			1	55	30	5	10	45	54	59	27	46	132	52
50/54						13	1	3	17	50	45	15	36	96	48
45/49						3	1	1	5	46	44	6	16	66	44
40/44											23	1	5	29	39
35/39											8	0	1	9	34
30/34											2		0	2	30

GREENVILLE-SPARTANBURG APRT SO CAROLINA

Tempera-ture Range	NOVEMBER Obsn Hour Gp			Total Obsn	M C W B	DECEMBER Obsn Hour Gp			Total Obsn	M C W B	JANUARY Obsn Hour Gp			Total Obsn	M C W B
	01 to 08	09 to 16	17 to 24			01 to 08	09 to 16	17 to 24			01 to 08	09 to 16	17 to 24		
100/104															
95/99															
90/94															
85/89															
80/84		2	0	2	68										
75/79		9	1	10	64		1		1	62					
70/74		21	6	27	60		4	0	4	58		2	0	2	62
65/69	4	36	19	59	58	1	12	2	15	57	1	6	2	9	57
60/64	23	46	32	101	56	5	22	12	39	56	4	14	7	25	55
55/59	27	39	46	112	50	12	26	22	60	51	7	24	14	45	50
50/54	41	34	46	121	46	16	33	32	81	46	9	32	25	66	45
45/49	43	27	40	110	42	25	41	37	103	42	24	42	39	105	41
40/44	43	16	27	86	37	37	45	45	127	37	32	46	50	128	37
35/39	34	6	16	56	33	44	33	45	122	33	51	39	50	140	33
30/34	18	2	6	26	28	49	21	34	104	29	52	27	36	115	29
25/29	6	1	2	9	24	36	7	14	57	24	38	11	18	67	24
20/24	3	0	0	3	20	16	2	4	22	19	20	4	6	30	19
15/19	0			0	18	5	1	1	7	15	8	2	2	12	14
10/14						2	0	1	3	10	2	0		2	10
5/9						1			1	6	0			0	6
0/4															

Tempera-ture Range	FEBRUARY Obsn Hour Gp			Total Obsn	M C W B	MARCH Obsn Hour Gp			Total Obsn	M C W B	APRIL Obsn Hour Gp			Total Obsn	M C W B	ANNUAL TOTAL Obsn Hour Gp			Total Obsn	M C W B
	01 to 08	09 to 16	17 to 24			01 to 08	09 to 16	17 to 24			01 to 08	09 to 16	17 to 24			01 to 08	09 to 16	17 to 24		
100/104																	0		0	75
95/99												0		0	72		9	3	12	74
90/94												0		0	65		96	25	121	73
85/89												8	2	10	67	0	273	103	376	72
80/84							2	1	3	60		22	9	31	65	10	356	215	581	70
75/79		0		0	66		7	2	9	62		28	17	45	62	96	329	336	761	68
70/74		4	1	5	59	0	16	8	24	59	3	36	29	68	60	462	281	389	1132	66
65/69	0	10	5	15	56	2	23	16	41	56	20	39	44	103	58	415	261	295	971	61
60/64	3	18	II	32	54	12	36	27	75	53	48	40	49	137	55	312	266	265	843	56
55/59	13	31	28	72	51	18	44	41	103	49	52	34	39	125	51	266	239	262	767	51
50/54	18	33	30	81	46	33	39	46	118	46	44	20	25	89	46	237	210	249	696	46
45/49	25	37	41	103	42	46	35	43	124	42	38	10	18	66	42	258	199	236	693	42
40/44	36	37	41	114	37	54	26	32	112	38	23	3	7	33	38	250	174	207	631	37
35/39	50	29	34	113	33	46	10	20	76	33	12	0	1	13	33	245	117	167	529	33
30/34	39	15	20	74	28	24	6	7	37	28	1			1	29	185	71	103	359	29
25/29	22	5	8	35	24	8	3	3	14	24						110	27	45	182	24
20/24	10	2	3	15	19	4	1	2	7	21						53	9	15	77	19
15/19	5	1	1	7	14	1	0	0	1	16						19	4	4	27	15
10/14	1	0	1	2	10	1			1	12						6	0	2	8	10
5/9	1	0		1	5											2	0		2	6
0/4	0			0	3											0			0	3

MYRTLE BEACH AFB SOUTH CAROLINA

LAT 33 41N LONG 78 56W ELEV 25 FT

MEAN FREQUENCY OF OCCURRENCE OF DRY BULB TEMPERATURE (DEGREES F) WITH MEAN COINCIDENT WET BULB TEMPERATURE (DEGREES F) FOR EACH DRY BULB TEMPERATURE RANGE

Tempera-ture Range	MAY Obsn Hour Gp 01 to 08	MAY 09 to 16	MAY 17 to 24	MAY Total Obsn	MAY MCWB	JUNE Obsn Hour Gp 01 to 08	JUNE 09 to 16	JUNE 17 to 24	JUNE Total Obsn	JUNE MCWB	JULY Obsn Hour Gp 01 to 08	JULY 09 to 16	JULY 17 to 24	JULY Total Obsn	JULY MCWB
100/104							0		0	78					
95/99							2	0	2	79		2		2	79
90/94		3	0	3	72		9	2	11	78		19	2	21	79
85/89		13	1	14	73	1	40	7	48	77	1	88	20	109	78
80/84	1	43	9	53	71	12	97	43	152	74	27	97	84	208	76
75/79	11	86	43	140	69	58	67	106	231	72	105	33	99	237	73
70/74	61	63	92	216	67	90	19	58	167	69	91	8	38	137	70
65/69	71	24	59	154	63	50	4	19	73	65	19	0	4	23	65
60/64	49	10	26	85	59	21	2	4	27	60	4		0	4	61
55/59	33	5	12	50	54	7	0	1	8	55	0			0	58
50/54	17	1	4	22	50	1		0	1	51					
45/49	5	1	1	7	46										
40/44	1		0	1	40										
35/39	0			0	35										
30/34															

Tempera-ture Range	AUGUST Obsn Hour Gp 01 to 08	AUGUST 09 to 16	AUGUST 17 to 24	AUGUST Total Obsn	AUGUST MCWB	SEPTEMBER Obsn Hour Gp 01 to 08	SEPTEMBER 09 to 16	SEPTEMBER 17 to 24	SEPTEMBER Total Obsn	SEPTEMBER MCWB	OCTOBER Obsn Hour Gp 01 to 08	OCTOBER 09 to 16	OCTOBER 17 to 24	OCTOBER Total Obsn	OCTOBER MCWB
100/104															
95/99		2	0	2	80		0		0	80					
90/94		15	2	17	79		3	0	3	76		0		0	77
85/89	0	82	14	96	78		32	2	34	76		2	0	2	74
80/84	21	102	89	212	75	6	96	39	141	74	0	25	2	27	71
75/79	96	34	92	222	73	38	58	85	181	71	8	57	22	87	69
70/74	92	10	40	142	70	76	34	59	169	68	22	59	48	129	66
65/69	31	3	10	44	65	59	13	34	106	64	40	49	54	143	62
60/64	8	0	1	9	60	40	3	15	58	59	51	31	45	127	58
55/59						16	1	5	22	54	45	16	36	97	53
50/54						4	0	1	5	50	36	7	23	66	49
45/49						1			1	46	23	1	11	35	44
40/44											14	0	6	20	40
35/39											7		1	8	35
30/34											2		0	2	31

MYRTLE BEACH AFB SOUTH CAROLINA

Temperature Range	NOVEMBER Obsn Hour Gp 01 to 08	NOVEMBER 09 to 16	NOVEMBER 17 to 24	NOVEMBER Total Obsn	NOVEMBER MCWB	DECEMBER Obsn Hour Gp 01 to 08	DECEMBER 09 to 16	DECEMBER 17 to 24	DECEMBER Total Obsn	DECEMBER MCWB	JANUARY Obsn Hour Gp 01 to 08	JANUARY 09 to 16	JANUARY 17 to 24	JANUARY Total Obsn	JANUARY MCWB	FEBRUARY Obsn Hour Gp 01 to 08	FEBRUARY 09 to 16	FEBRUARY 17 to 24	FEBRUARY Total Obsn	FEBRUARY MCWB
100/104																				
95/99																				
90/94																				
85/89																				
80/84		1		1	69		0		0	71							0		0	67
75/79	0	10	1	11	68	0	3		3	66		1		1	64		1	0	1	66
70/74	5	33	6	44	64	1	8	1	10	64		4	0	4	63	0	5	0	5	61
65/69	20	56	30	106	61	9	26	8	43	61	3	13	2	18	60	3	15	4	22	60
60/64	23	49	46	118	57	17	31	27	75	58	11	24	16	51	58	12	30	22	64	57
55/59	34	35	41	110	52	20	39	28	87	52	15	33	28	76	53	21	34	27	82	52
50/54	37	29	37	103	48	24	45	37	106	47	25	39	33	97	48	24	39	40	103	47
45/49	38	17	33	88	43	24	37	41	102	42	25	43	38	106	43	28	40	40	108	42
40/44	34	7	26	67	39	35	29	39	103	38	31	36	42	109	38	32	30	36	98	38
35/39	29	2	13	44	34	39	18	33	90	34	45	27	33	105	34	39	20	32	91	33
30/34	15	0	5	20	30	41	8	23	72	30	38	17	34	89	29	39	8	16	63	29
25/29	5	0	1	6	26	27	3	10	40	25	32	7	18	57	25	17	2	5	24	25
20/24	1		0	1	19	9	1	1	11	21	18	3	4	25	20	7	1	1	9	20
15/19	0			0	17	1	0	0	1	16	4	1	0	5	16	1	0	0	1	15
10/14						0			0	12	1			1	12	0			0	9
5/9																0			0	7

Temperature Range	MARCH Obsn Hour Gp 01 to 08	MARCH 09 to 16	MARCH 17 to 24	MARCH Total Obsn	MARCH MCWB	APRIL Obsn Hour Gp 01 to 08	APRIL 09 to 16	APRIL 17 to 24	APRIL Total Obsn	APRIL MCWB	ANNUAL TOTAL Obsn Hour Gp 01 to 08	ANNUAL TOTAL 09 to 16	ANNUAL TOTAL 17 to 24	ANNUAL TOTAL Total Obsn	ANNUAL TOTAL MCWB
100/104												0		0	78
95/99												6	0	6	79
90/94							1	0	1	70		50	6	56	78
85/89		0	0	0	66		3	1	4	68	2	260	45	307	77
80/84		1	0	1	64		9	2	11	67	67	471	268	806	74
75/79		4	1	5	64	1	36	5	42	66	317	390	454	1161	72
70/74	0	18	3	21	61	9	53	30	92	64	447	314	375	1136	68
65/69	6	36	14	56	60	41	54	62	157	61	352	293	300	945	62
60/64	26	45	43	114	57	58	46	61	165	57	320	271	306	897	58
55/59	37	50	52	139	52	42	27	39	108	52	270	240	269	779	53
50/54	36	44	53	133	47	34	8	22	64	48	238	212	250	700	48
45/49	47	26	39	112	43	29	4	14	47	44	220	169	217	606	43
40/44	38	14	25	77	38	19	0	4	23	40	204	116	178	498	38
35/39	32	5	13	50	34	6		1	7	36	197	72	126	395	34
30/34	19	3	4	26	29	1			1	32	155	36	82	273	29
25/29	6	0	1	7	26						87	12	35	134	25
20/24	1			1	21						36	5	6	47	21
15/19											6	1	0	7	16
10/14											1			1	11
5/9											0			0	7

SHAW AFB/SUMTER SOUTH CAROLINA

LAT 33 58N LONG 80 28W ELEV 252 FT

MEAN FREQUENCY OF OCCURRENCE OF DRY BULB TEMPERATURE (DEGREES F) WITH MEAN COINCIDENT WET BULB TEMPERATURE (DEGREES F) FOR EACH DRY BULB TEMPERATURE RANGE

Tempera-ture Range	MAY Obsn Hour Gp 01 to 08	MAY 09 to 16	MAY 17 to 24	MAY Total Obsn	MAY MCWB	JUNE Obsn Hour Gp 01 to 08	JUNE 09 to 16	JUNE 17 to 24	JUNE Total Obsn	JUNE MCWB	JULY Obsn Hour Gp 01 to 08	JULY 09 to 16	JULY 17 to 24	JULY Total Obsn	JULY MCWB
105/109							0	0	0	78					
100/104							2	0	2	77		0	0	0	80
95/99		2	0	2	72		6	2	8	76		7	1	8	78
90/94		13	4	17	71		34	12	46	75		46	12	58	76
85/89		41	14	55	69	1	60	26	87	73	0	79	33	112	75
80/84	0	57	29	86	68	6	64	45	115	71	10	70	57	137	74
75/79	7	54	46	107	66	39	44	64	147	70	82	36	91	209	72
70/74	60	43	67	160	65	111	22	67	200	68	136	9	52	197	70
65/69	87	21	48	156	63	62	5	20	87	64	18		2	20	64
60/64	49	9	24	82	57	18	1	3	22	59	2			2	60
55/59	34	5	12	51	53	4	0	1	5	54					
50/54	17	2	3	22	49	0			0	50					
45/49	3	1	1	5	44										
40/44	1			1	40										
35/39															
30/34															

Tempera-ture Range	AUGUST Obsn Hour Gp 01 to 08	AUGUST 09 to 16	AUGUST 17 to 24	AUGUST Total Obsn	AUGUST MCWB	SEPTEMBER Obsn Hour Gp 01 to 08	SEPTEMBER 09 to 16	SEPTEMBER 17 to 24	SEPTEMBER Total Obsn	SEPTEMBER MCWB	OCTOBER Obsn Hour Gp 01 to 08	OCTOBER 09 to 16	OCTOBER 17 to 24	OCTOBER Total Obsn	OCTOBER MCWB
105/109															
100/104		0	0	0	79										
95/99		7	1	8	78		1		1	78					
90/94		41	11	52	77		15	2	17	75		0		0	70
85/89	0	80	31	111	75		56	14	70	73		8	1	9	70
80/84	8	64	54	126	74	1	62	32	95	71		31	5	36	68
75/79	77	38	91	206	72	20	50	66	136	70	2	48	19	69	66
70/74	124	14	49	187	70	91	32	70	193	68	19	55	44	118	64
65/69	31	2	10	43	64	63	16	32	111	63	37	47	58	142	61
60/64	7	0	1	8	59	40	6	18	64	58	58	31	50	139	57
55/59	0			0	55	17	1	6	24	54	47	19	37	103	52
50/54						7	0	1	8	49	40	8	20	68	48
45/49						1		0	1	45	25	1	9	35	43
40/44											14	0	4	18	38
35/39											5		1	6	34
30/34											1		0	1	30

SHAW AFB/SUMTER SOUTH CAROLINA

Temperature Range	NOVEMBER Obsn Hour Gp 01 to 08	NOVEMBER 09 to 16	NOVEMBER 17 to 24	NOVEMBER Total Obsn	NOVEMBER MCWB	DECEMBER Obsn Hour Gp 01 to 08	DECEMBER 09 to 16	DECEMBER 17 to 24	DECEMBER Total Obsn	DECEMBER MCWB	JANUARY Obsn Hour Gp 01 to 08	JANUARY 09 to 16	JANUARY 17 to 24	JANUARY Total Obsn	JANUARY MCWB
105/109															
100/104															
95/99															
90/94															
85/89		1		1	69										
80/84		3	0	3	69		0		0	69					
75/79		18	2	20	64		4	1	5	65		3	0	3	63
70/74	3	32	11	46	61	1	13	3	17	62		9	2	11	61
65/69	10	45	27	82	59	5	21	11	37	59	3	14	8	25	59
60/64	22	41	40	103	55	12	27	22	61	56	7	20	15	42	55
55/59	35	36	47	118	51	15	33	26	74	50	12	29	22	63	50
50/54	44	32	44	120	46	25	41	42	108	46	20	32	33	85	46
45/49	46	20	34	100	42	34	40	40	114	41	29	38	41	108	42
40/44	35	9	21	65	38	36	30	41	107	37	38	37	40	115	37
35/39	26	3	10	39	33	44	22	35	101	33	44	33	39	116	33
30/34	15	1	3	19	29	43	12	18	73	29	46	20	29	95	29
25/29	2	0	1	3	24	24	4	8	36	24	31	8	14	53	24
20/24	1	0	0	1	19	8	1	2	11	20	12	3	3	18	20
15/19	0		0	0	16	2	0	0	2	15	5	1	1	7	15
10/14						1	0		1	10	1	0		1	10
5/9						0			0	7	0			0	7

Temperature Range	FEBRUARY Obsn Hour Gp 01 to 08	FEBRUARY 09 to 16	FEBRUARY 17 to 24	FEBRUARY Total Obsn	FEBRUARY MCWB	MARCH Obsn Hour Gp 01 to 08	MARCH 09 to 16	MARCH 17 to 24	MARCH Total Obsn	MARCH MCWB	APRIL Obsn Hour Gp 01 to 08	APRIL 09 to 16	APRIL 17 to 24	APRIL Total Obsn	APRIL MCWB	ANNUAL TOTAL Obsn Hour Gp 01 to 08	ANNUAL TOTAL 09 to 16	ANNUAL TOTAL 17 to 24	ANNUAL TOTAL Total Obsn	ANNUAL TOTAL MCWB
105/109																	0	0	0	78
100/104																	2	0	2	77
95/99												0		0	75		23	4	27	77
90/94												2	0	2	70		151	41	192	75
85/89							1	0	1	65		14	4	18	67	1	340	123	464	73
80/84		0	0	0	65		5	2	7	63		30	13	43	66	25	386	237	648	71
75/79		4	1	5	64	0	16	5	21	61	1	39	24	64	63	228	354	410	992	69
70/74	0	10	4	14	60	1	23	14	38	59	9	44	40	93	61	545	306	423	1274	67
65/69	3	16	11	30	58	7	31	25	63	57	35	41	53	129	59	361	259	305	925	61
60/64	12	25	19	56	55	22	41	41	104	54	59	34	44	137	56	308	235	277	820	56
55/59	15	27	26	68	50	32	42	44	118	50	46	21	31	98	51	257	213	252	722	51
50/54	18	38	37	93	45	39	36	43	118	46	43	10	22	75	47	253	199	245	697	46
45/49	33	37	39	109	41	51	26	35	112	42	30	3	7	40	43	252	166	206	624	42
40/44	34	29	39	102	37	42	16	24	82	37	16	1	2	19	39	216	122	171	509	37
35/39	47	21	27	95	33	32	6	10	48	33	2			2	34	200	85	122	407	33
30/34	35	11	15	61	28	16	4	3	23	28	0			0	29	156	48	68	272	29
25/29	20	3	4	27	24	6	1	1	8	25						83	16	28	127	24
20/24	5	1	1	7	19	1			1	19						27	5	6	38	20
15/19	2	0	0	2	14											9	1	1	11	15
10/14	1			1	10											3	0		3	10
5/9	0			0	7											0			0	7

ELLSWORTH AFB/RAPID CITY SOUTH DAKOTA

LAT 44 08N LONG 103 06W ELEV 3276 FT

MEAN FREQUENCY OF OCCURRENCE OF DRY BULB TEMPERATURE (DEGREES F) WITH MEAN COINCIDENT WET BULB TEMPERATURE (DEGREES F) FOR EACH DRY BULB TEMPERATURE RANGE

Temperature Range	MAY Obsn Hour Gp 01 to 08	MAY 09 to 16	MAY 17 to 24	MAY Total Obsn	MAY MCWB	JUNE Obsn Hour Gp 01 to 08	JUNE 09 to 16	JUNE 17 to 24	JUNE Total Obsn	JUNE MCWB	JULY Obsn Hour Gp 01 to 08	JULY 09 to 16	JULY 17 to 24	JULY Total Obsn	JULY MCWB
105/109							0		0	67		0		0	71
100/104							1		1	67		1	0	1	67
95/99		0		0	66		2	1	3	66		8	2	10	67
90/94		0	0	0	66		6	2	8	65	0	23	7	30	67
85/89		4	1	5	61	0	15	5	20	65	1	43	17	61	67
80/84	0	12	3	15	60	2	25	12	39	64	4	58	33	95	65
75/79	0	19	7	26	59	5	39	21	65	63	18	53	46	117	63
70/74	1	28	15	44	56	14	52	35	101	60	45	35	55	135	61
65/69	9	36	26	71	54	31	42	48	121	58	73	18	48	139	59
60/64	18	45	36	99	52	58	31	53	142	55	67	7	29	103	56
55/59	38	38	41	117	49	68	17	39	124	52	29	1	8	38	53
50/54	55	30	49	134	47	42	8	18	68	48	9		2	11	48
45/49	57	19	36	112	43	14	2	5	21	43	1		0	1	44
40/44	42	9	20	71	39	4	0	2	6	39	0		0	0	40
35/39	18	5	9	32	35	1	0	0	1	34					
30/34	6	2	4	12	30	0	0		0	32					
25/29	3	0	0	3	27										
20/24	0		0	0	24										
15/19															

Temperature Range	AUGUST Obsn Hour Gp 01 to 08	AUGUST 09 to 16	AUGUST 17 to 24	AUGUST Total Obsn	AUGUST MCWB	SEPTEMBER Obsn Hour Gp 01 to 08	SEPTEMBER 09 to 16	SEPTEMBER 17 to 24	SEPTEMBER Total Obsn	SEPTEMBER MCWB	OCTOBER Obsn Hour Gp 01 to 08	OCTOBER 09 to 16	OCTOBER 17 to 24	OCTOBER Total Obsn	OCTOBER MCWB
105/109							0		0	67					
100/104		2	0	2	65		1	0	1	66					
95/99		12	3	15	66		1	0	1	66					
90/94		34	10	44	65		8	1	9	62		1		1	59
85/89	0	43	18	61	64	0	16	4	20	61		2		2	58
80/84	4	47	30	81	63	1	25	9	35	60	0	10	1	11	56
75/79	17	40	43	100	61	2	29	14	45	58	0	13	2	15	54
70/74	46	32	52	130	59	7	37	25	69	56	1	19	5	25	53
65/69	59	19	40	118	57	20	32	35	87	54	4	30	13	47	50
60/64	58	12	30	100	54	37	27	36	100	52	11	35	22	68	48
55/59	39	6	15	60	51	45	23	36	104	49	23	36	32	91	46
50/54	16	2	7	25	47	48	17	32	97	46	36	32	40	108	43
45/49	7	0	1	8	44	39	12	20	71	42	42	26	44	112	40
40/44	1			1	39	23	8	17	48	38	46	19	37	102	37
35/39						13	3	7	23	34	40	11	25	76	33
30/34						5	0	2	7	30	26	7	17	50	29
25/29						1			1	26	13	3	8	24	26
20/24											5	1	2	8	21
15/19											2	1	0	3	17

ELLSWORTH AFB/RAPID CITY SOUTH DAKOTA

Temperature Range	NOVEMBER Obsn Hour Gp 01 to 08	09 to 16	17 to 24	Total Obsn	MCWB	DECEMBER Obsn Hour Gp 01 to 08	09 to 16	17 to 24	Total Obsn	MCWB	JANUARY Obsn Hour Gp 01 to 08	09 to 16	17 to 24	Total Obsn	MCWB
105/109															
100/104															
95/99															
90/94															
85/89															
80/84															
75/79															
70/74		2		2	50		0		0	47					
65/69		5	0	5	48		1		1	45		0		0	50
60/64	1	14	1	16	46	0	4	0	4	45		2		2	45
55/59	2	22	3	27	44	1	10	1	12	43	0	7	0	7	43
50/54	5	29	12	46	41	3	15	3	21	40	2	11	3	16	40
45/49	15	32	26	73	38	5	22	9	36	37	5	17	7	29	38
40/44	32	32	40	104	35	16	28	21	65	35	13	26	16	55	35
35/39	41	29	42	112	33	29	30	32	91	31	22	26	26	74	32
30/34	46	27	44	117	29	37	32	42	111	28	26	27	28	81	28
25/29	46	21	31	98	25	38	28	36	102	24	27	23	32	82	24
20/24	24	11	20	55	20	33	21	30	84	20	30	17	28	75	20
15/19	13	7	9	29	16	22	15	20	57	16	27	19	20	66	16
10/14	10	4	7	21	11	22	17	19	58	11	23	21	20	64	11
5/9	3	2	3	8	6	21	13	16	50	6	18	16	20	54	6
0/4	2	1	1	4	2	10	7	10	27	2	17	16	17	50	1
-5/-1	1	1	1	3	-3	5	2	5	12	-3	15	12	15	42	-3
-10/-6	1	0	0	1	-9	4	1	2	7	-8	14	6	10	30	-8
-15/-11	0		0	0	-12	1	1	1	3	-13	7	2	5	14	-13
-20/-16						1	0	1	2	-18	1	0	1	2	-18
-25/-21						0			0	-21	0	0	0	0	-22

Temperature Range	FEBRUARY Obsn Hour Gp 01 to 08	09 to 16	17 to 24	Total Obsn	MCWB	MARCH Obsn Hour Gp 01 to 08	09 to 16	17 to 24	Total Obsn	MCWB	APRIL Obsn Hour Gp 01 to 08	09 to 16	17 to 24	Total Obsn	MCWB
105/109															
100/104															
95/99															
90/94															
85/89												0		0	55
80/84							0		0	55		3	0	3	55
75/79							1	0	1	52	0	6	1	7	53
70/74		0		0	52		3	1	4	50	0	12	4	16	52
65/69		2	0	2	49		6	2	8	48	1	16	7	24	50
60/64	0	5	0	5	46	1	12	3	16	46	2	22	13	37	48
55/59	1	8	2	11	44	1	15	7	23	44	7	31	22	60	45
50/54	2	12	6	20	41	6	18	11	35	41	19	32	31	82	43
45/49	6	18	9	33	38	9	22	20	51	38	35	35	37	107	40
40/44	12	25	15	52	35	18	30	25	73	35	47	28	37	112	37
35/39	20	24	28	72	32	30	31	36	97	32	45	23	37	105	33
30/34	28	24	30	82	28	45	37	42	124	29	48	21	33	102	30
25/29	35	24	31	90	25	44	25	38	107	25	24	8	12	44	25
20/24	29	21	27	77	20	35	20	27	82	21	8	2	3	13	20
15/19	22	16	23	61	16	24	11	15	50	16	3	1	1	5	15
10/14	23	20	17	60	11	15	9	9	33	11	1		0	1	10
5/9	19	12	17	48	7	7	4	6	17	6	0		0	0	7
0/4	14	9	11	34	2	5	2	3	10	1					
-5/-1	9	3	6	18	-3	5	2	2	9	-3					
-10/-6	2	1	1	4	-7	1	0	1	2	-8					
-15/-11	1	0	0	1	-13	0		0	0	-13					
-20/-16	1		0	1	-17	0		0	0	-17					
-25/-21															

Temperature Range	ANNUAL TOTAL Obsn Hour Gp 01 to 08	09 to 16	17 to 24	Total Obsn	MCWB
105/109		0		0	69
100/104		5	0	5	66
95/99		23	6	29	66
90/94	0	72	20	92	65
85/89	1	123	45	169	65
80/84	11	180	88	279	63
75/79	42	200	134	376	61
70/74	114	220	192	526	59
65/69	197	207	219	623	56
60/64	253	216	223	692	52
55/59	254	214	206	674	49
50/54	243	206	214	663	44
45/49	235	205	214	654	40
40/44	254	205	230	689	36
35/39	259	182	242	683	33
30/34	267	177	242	686	29
25/29	231	132	188	551	25
20/24	164	93	137	394	20
15/19	113	70	88	271	16
10/14	94	71	72	237	11
5/9	68	47	62	177	6
0/4	48	35	42	125	2
-5/-1	35	20	29	84	-3
-10/-6	22	8	14	44	-8
-15/-11	9	3	6	18	-13
-20/-16	3	0	2	5	-18
-25/-21	0	0	0	0	-21

HURON SOUTH DAKOTA

LAT 44 23N LONG 98 13W ELEV 1281 FT

MEAN FREQUENCY OF OCCURRENCE OF DRY BULB TEMPERATURE (DEGREES F) WITH MEAN COINCIDENT WET BULB TEMPERATURE (DEGREES F) FOR EACH DRY BULB TEMPERATURE RANGE

Temperature Range	MAY Obsn Hour Gp 01 to 08	MAY 09 to 16	MAY 17 to 24	MAY Total Obsn	MAY MCWB	JUNE Obsn Hour Gp 01 to 08	JUNE 09 to 16	JUNE 17 to 24	JUNE Total Obsn	JUNE MCWB	JULY Obsn Hour Gp 01 to 08	JULY 09 to 16	JULY 17 to 24	JULY Total Obsn	JULY MCWB
105/109							0		0	70		0	0	0	77
100/104							1	1	2	72		3	1	4	75
95/99		0	0	0	62		5	2	7	73		11	5	16	74
90/94		1	0	1	68		12	7	19	72		24	12	36	73
85/89		7	3	10	66		22	12	34	71		46	25	71	71
80/84		13	6	19	64	2	36	22	60	68	4	59	39	102	69
75/79	0	25	14	39	61	9	45	35	89	66	19	48	45	112	67
70/74	2	35	22	59	59	23	46	39	108	64	49	33	49	131	66
65/69	9	46	31	86	57	43	34	45	122	61	65	17	41	123	63
60/64	25	42	45	112	55	55	21	38	114	58	59	6	22	87	59
55/59	47	33	41	121	52	51	10	24	85	54	34	0	7	41	55
50/54	48	22	37	107	48	33	6	12	51	50	15		1	16	51
45/49	49	14	28	91	44	17	1	3	21	46	3		0	3	47
40/44	34	7	13	54	40	6		1	7	41					
35/39	18	2	4	24	35	1		0	1	37					
30/34	10	1	3	14	31	0			0	31					
25/29	4		0	4	26										
20/24	1		0	1	23										
15/19	0			0	17										
10/14															

Temperature Range	AUGUST Obsn Hour Gp 01 to 08	AUGUST 09 to 16	AUGUST 17 to 24	AUGUST Total Obsn	AUGUST MCWB	SEPTEMBER Obsn Hour Gp 01 to 08	SEPTEMBER 09 to 16	SEPTEMBER 17 to 24	SEPTEMBER Total Obsn	SEPTEMBER MCWB	OCTOBER Obsn Hour Gp 01 to 08	OCTOBER 09 to 16	OCTOBER 17 to 24	OCTOBER Total Obsn	OCTOBER MCWB
105/109															
100/104		2	1	3	74		0	0	0	68		0		0	68
95/99		10	4	14	72		3	1	4	71		0	0	0	64
90/94		22	10	32	71		6	3	9	70		1		1	63
85/89	0	38	20	58	70		13	5	18	67		3	1	4	62
80/84	2	52	33	87	68	1	22	11	34	64		8	1	9	61
75/79	13	52	44	109	67	4	29	17	50	62		14	5	19	60
70/74	38	36	51	125	65	10	36	25	71	61	1	23	8	32	57
65/69	61	22	40	123	62	16	41	33	90	58	2	28	16	46	55
60/64	59	9	27	95	59	28	35	38	101	55	6	30	24	60	52
55/59	44	4	14	62	55	43	23	37	103	52	18	34	30	82	49
50/54	21	0	4	25	50	49	16	33	98	48	30	33	39	102	46
45/49	7		0	7	46	41	11	21	73	44	39	30	38	107	42
40/44	2		0	2	41	29	2	11	42	40	48	24	36	108	39
35/39	1			1	37	16	0	2	18	36	43	13	25	81	34
30/34						4		1	5	32	33	6	14	53	30
25/29						1		0	1	28	17	1	7	25	26
20/24						0			0	22	7	0	2	9	21
15/19											3		0	3	17
10/14											0			0	12

HURON SOUTH DAKOTA

Temperature Range	NOVEMBER Obsn Hour Gp 01 to 08	NOVEMBER Obsn Hour Gp 09 to 16	NOVEMBER Obsn Hour Gp 17 to 24	NOVEMBER Total Obsn	NOVEMBER MCWB	DECEMBER Obsn Hour Gp 01 to 08	DECEMBER Obsn Hour Gp 09 to 16	DECEMBER Obsn Hour Gp 17 to 24	DECEMBER Total Obsn	DECEMBER MCWB	JANUARY Obsn Hour Gp 01 to 08	JANUARY Obsn Hour Gp 09 to 16	JANUARY Obsn Hour Gp 17 to 24	JANUARY Total Obsn	JANUARY MCWB
105/109															
100/104															
95/99															
90/94															
85/89															
80/84															
75/79		0		0	56										
70/74		2	0	2	54										
65/69		5	1	6	51										
60/64		7	1	8	48		0		0	49		0		0	45
55/59	0	11	4	15	46		1	0	1	47		1		1	44
50/54	1	24	9	34	44		4	1	5	43		2	0	2	40
45/49	5	26	16	47	41	1	9	2	12	40		3	0	3	39
40/44	13	32	29	74	37	2	12	7	21	37	0	6	2	8	35
35/39	32	33	42	107	33	9	23	20	52	34	2	11	8	21	33
30/34	51	33	40	124	30	20	28	28	76	30	8	19	16	43	29
25/29	45	25	36	106	26	29	35	36	100	26	19	28	25	72	25
20/24	35	15	25	75	21	40	33	37	110	21	27	32	32	91	21
15/19	26	11	16	53	16	39	26	27	92	16	33	30	36	99	16
10/14	11	7	8	26	11	24	24	25	73	11	31	27	28	86	11
5/9	8	4	5	17	6	26	19	23	68	6	30	25	23	78	6
0/4	6	3	4	13	2	19	14	16	49	2	25	22	22	69	2
-5/-1	3	1	2	6	-3	17	10	14	41	-3	23	20	21	64	-3
-10/-6	2	0	1	3	-8	8	5	6	19	-8	21	14	18	53	-8
-15/-11	1	0	0	1	-12	7	3	5	15	-13	17	6	11	34	-13
-20/-16	0		0	0	-17	4	0	2	6	-18	9	2	5	16	-18
-25/-21			0	0	-21	2	0	0	2	-22	4	0	1	5	-23
-30/-26											1	0	0	1	-27
-35/-31											0			0	-31
-40/-36															

Temperature Range	FEBRUARY Obsn Hour Gp 01 to 08	FEBRUARY Obsn Hour Gp 09 to 16	FEBRUARY Obsn Hour Gp 17 to 24	FEBRUARY Total Obsn	FEBRUARY MCWB	MARCH Obsn Hour Gp 01 to 08	MARCH Obsn Hour Gp 09 to 16	MARCH Obsn Hour Gp 17 to 24	MARCH Total Obsn	MARCH MCWB	APRIL Obsn Hour Gp 01 to 08	APRIL Obsn Hour Gp 09 to 16	APRIL Obsn Hour Gp 17 to 24	APRIL Total Obsn	APRIL MCWB	ANNUAL TOTAL Obsn Hour Gp 01 to 08	ANNUAL TOTAL Obsn Hour Gp 09 to 16	ANNUAL TOTAL Obsn Hour Gp 17 to 24	ANNUAL TOTAL Total Obsn	ANNUAL TOTAL MCWB
105/109																	0	0	0	76
100/104																	6	3	9	74
95/99																	29	12	41	73
90/94												0	0	0	61		66	32	98	72
85/89							0		0	64		1	1	2	62	0	130	67	197	70
80/84							0	0	0	59		4	2	6	60	9	194	114	317	67
75/79							1	0	1	57		8	3	11	58	45	222	163	430	65
70/74							1	1	2	53		12	6	18	56	123	224	201	548	63
65/69		0	0	0	52		1	1	2	52	0	19	11	30	53	196	213	219	628	60
60/64		0	0	0	50	0	3	2	5	49	3	24	17	44	50	235	177	214	626	56
55/59		2	1	3	46	0	6	3	9	46	10	25	19	54	48	247	150	180	577	52
50/54		3	1	4	43	1	10	6	17	42	18	28	28	74	45	216	148	171	535	47
45/49	0	6	3	9	41	2	17	11	30	40	26	31	35	92	42	190	148	157	495	43
40/44	2	13	6	21	37	7	26	19	52	37	39	31	36	106	38	182	153	160	495	38
35/39	8	22	18	48	34	24	36	36	96	34	43	29	36	108	34	197	169	191	557	34
30/34	23	29	35	87	30	50	46	49	145	30	49	20	30	99	30	248	182	216	646	30
25/29	29	27	30	86	26	41	29	39	109	26	30	6	11	47	26	215	151	184	550	26
20/24	28	27	27	82	21	34	23	28	85	21	15	1	4	20	21	187	131	155	473	21
15/19	27	24	22	73	16	29	19	20	68	16	4	1	1	6	16	161	111	122	394	16
10/14	22	21	21	64	12	21	11	12	44	12	2	0	0	2	12	111	90	94	295	11
5/9	19	21	22	62	6	11	10	11	32	7	0			0	8	94	79	84	257	6
0/4	22	15	18	55	2	13	4	5	22	2						85	58	65	208	2
-5/-1	17	7	10	34	-3	7	2	3	12	-3						67	40	50	157	-3
-10/-6	13	3	6	22	-8	4	1	1	6	-8						48	23	32	103	-8
-15/-11	7	1	2	10	-13	3	0	1	4	-13						35	10	19	64	-13
-20/-16	3	1	1	5	-18	1	0		1	-17						17	3	8	28	-18
-25/-21	2	0	0	2	-23	0			0	-23						8	0	1	9	-23
-30/-26	1		0	1	-27											2	0	0	2	-27
-35/-31	0			0	-35											0			0	-33
-40/-36	0		0	0												0		0	0	

SIOUX FALLS/FOSS FLD SOUTH DAKOTA

LAT 43 34N LONG 96 44W ELEV 1418 FT

MEAN FREQUENCY OF OCCURRENCE OF DRY BULB TEMPERATURE (DEGREES F) WITH MEAN COINCIDENT WET BULB TEMPERATURE (DEGREES F) FOR EACH DRY BULB TEMPERATURE RANGE

Temperature Range	MAY Obsn Hour Gp 01 to 08	09 to 16	17 to 24	Total Obsn	MCWB	JUNE Obsn Hour Gp 01 to 08	09 to 16	17 to 24	Total Obsn	MCWB	JULY Obsn Hour Gp 01 to 08	09 to 16	17 to 24	Total Obsn	MCWB
100/104							0		0	72		1	0	1	76
95/99							3	1	4	73		5	2	7	75
90/94		1	1	2	69		13	6	19	72		23	10	33	73
85/89		7	3	10	66	0	25	13	38	70	0	42	23	65	70
80/84		15	8	23	63	1	36	24	61	67	3	57	40	100	68
75/79	0	28	16	44	60	12	45	37	94	65	23	55	50	128	67
70/74	6	36	23	65	59	30	48	43	121	63	51	40	51	142	65
65/69	12	45	35	92	56	44	33	44	121	60	68	19	39	126	62
60/64	29	42	44	115	54	60	20	36	116	57	57	4	26	87	59
55/59	52	31	42	125	51	43	8	22	73	53	33	1	6	40	55
50/54	47	21	34	102	47	30	6	11	47	49	11		1	12	51
45/49	45	14	26	85	43	15	1	3	19	45	1		0	1	47
40/44	31	5	10	46	39	3		0	3	41					
35/39	15	3	5	23	34	1			1	36					
30/34	7	0	2	9	30										
25/29	3		0	3	26										
20/24	0			0	23										
15/19															

Temperature Range	AUGUST Obsn Hour Gp 01 to 08	09 to 16	17 to 24	Total Obsn	MCWB	SEPTEMBER Obsn Hour Gp 01 to 08	09 to 16	17 to 24	Total Obsn	MCWB	OCTOBER Obsn Hour Gp 01 to 08	09 to 16	17 to 24	Total Obsn	MCWB
100/104		1	0	1	74										
95/99		6	2	8	72		1	0	1	66					
90/94		20	7	27	72		7	2	9	70		1		1	63
85/89	1	34	17	52	71		10	4	14	68		2	0	2	63
80/84	3	50	30	83	69	1	20	9	30	65		7	1	8	61
75/79	14	53	46	113	67	6	31	15	52	63		15	4	19	59
70/74	41	44	52	137	65	12	38	25	75	61	1	23	10	34	57
65/69	64	26	47	137	62	16	41	36	93	58	3	31	19	53	55
60/64	58	12	31	101	59	32	40	42	114	55	13	33	28	74	53
55/59	43	3	12	58	55	42	25	42	109	52	21	36	34	91	49
50/54	17	0	3	20	50	50	17	35	102	48	35	30	39	104	46
45/49	6		0	6	46	44	8	20	72	44	42	29	34	105	42
40/44	1		0	1	41	23	1	8	32	40	46	24	38	108	38
35/39	1			1	37	11	0	2	13	36	36	11	22	69	34
30/34						3	0	1	4	31	27	5	13	45	29
25/29						1			1	27	16	1	6	23	25
20/24											6	0	1	7	21
15/19											1			1	17

SIOUX FALLS/FOSS FLD SOUTH DAKOTA

Temperature Range	NOVEMBER					DECEMBER					JANUARY				
	Obsn Hour Gp 01 to 08	Obsn Hour Gp 09 to 16	Obsn Hour Gp 17 to 24	Total Obsn	MCWB	Obsn Hour Gp 01 to 08	Obsn Hour Gp 09 to 16	Obsn Hour Gp 17 to 24	Total Obsn	MCWB	Obsn Hour Gp 01 to 08	Obsn Hour Gp 09 to 16	Obsn Hour Gp 17 to 24	Total Obsn	MCWB
100/104															
95/99															
90/94															
85/89															
80/84															
75/79															
70/74		1		1	52										
65/69		5	0	5	52										
60/64		9	2	11	49		0		0	48					
55/59	0	15	7	22	47		2	0	2	48		0		0	41
50/54	3	21	11	35	44	1	4	2	7	46		1	0	1	40
45/49	11	31	22	64	41	1	7	3	11	41		4	1	5	38
40/44	23	32	30	85	37	3	16	9	28	36		7	3	10	36
35/39	36	34	41	111	33	11	24	23	58	33	3	15	11	29	32
30/34	48	32	43	123	29	25	33	30	88	29	13	27	19	59	29
25/29	44	24	32	100	25	34	37	37	108	25	19	29	27	75	25
20/24	29	14	21	64	20	45	37	34	116	21	32	32	36	100	20
15/19	21	9	13	43	16	33	27	32	92	16	35	33	35	103	16
10/14	8	6	8	22	11	24	21	24	69	11	32	24	29	85	11
5/9	8	4	4	16	6	24	18	19	61	6	27	24	23	74	6
0/4	5	1	3	9	1	17	10	13	40	1	22	21	21	64	1
-5/-1	3	1	2	6	-3	13	7	10	30	-3	20	16	19	55	-4
-10/-6	1	0	0	1	-8	7	3	7	17	-8	21	10	14	45	-9
-15/-11	0	0	0	0	-13	7	1	4	12	-13	14	4	9	27	-13
-20/-16	0			0	-17	2	0	1	3	-18	7	1	1	9	-18
-25/-21						0			0	-24	1	0	0	1	-23
-30/-26											0			0	-26

Temperature Range	FEBRUARY					MARCH					APRIL					ANNUAL TOTAL				
	Obsn Hour Gp 01 to 08	Obsn Hour Gp 09 to 16	Obsn Hour Gp 17 to 24	Total Obsn	MCWB	Obsn Hour Gp 01 to 08	Obsn Hour Gp 09 to 16	Obsn Hour Gp 17 to 24	Total Obsn	MCWB	Obsn Hour Gp 01 to 08	Obsn Hour Gp 09 to 16	Obsn Hour Gp 17 to 24	Total Obsn	MCWB	Obsn Hour Gp 01 to 08	Obsn Hour Gp 09 to 16	Obsn Hour Gp 17 to 24	Total Obsn	MCWB
100/104																	2	0	2	75
95/99																	15	5	20	73
90/94												1	0	1	61		66	26	92	72
85/89												1	0	1	60	1	121	60	182	70
80/84												3	2	5	59	8	188	114	310	67
75/79							1	0	1	55		8	4	12	58	55	236	172	463	65
70/74							1	0	1	53	0	15	7	22	55	141	246	211	598	62
65/69		0	0	0	50		1	1	2	51	2	18	12	32	53	209	219	233	661	59
60/64		0	0	0	47	0	3	2	5	49	4	21	16	41	50	253	184	227	664	56
55/59		2	0	2	46	0	6	3	9	46	12	29	21	62	47	246	158	189	593	51
50/54		5	1	6	42	2	11	6	19	43	18	29	30	77	44	214	145	173	532	47
45/49	1	7	4	12	41	3	18	12	33	40	30	30	35	95	41	199	149	160	508	42
40/44	3	13	7	23	37	9	26	21	56	37	42	35	35	112	37	184	159	161	504	38
35/39	9	30	21	60	33	27	42	38	107	33	42	26	32	100	33	192	185	195	572	33
30/34	29	30	35	94	30	50	46	54	150	30	48	18	30	96	30	250	191	227	668	29
25/29	28	31	33	92	25	48	31	38	117	25	27	5	12	44	25	220	158	185	563	25
20/24	29	27	29	85	20	32	23	23	78	21	12	1	2	15	20	185	134	146	465	20
15/19	34	25	27	86	16	28	16	21	65	16	3	0	1	4	16	155	110	129	394	16
10/14	22	21	21	64	11	15	10	11	36	11	1			1	11	102	82	93	277	11
5/9	20	17	20	57	6	13	8	9	30	6						92	71	75	238	6
0/4	18	9	13	40	1	10	2	4	16	2						72	43	54	169	1
-5/-1	14	5	8	27	-4	6	1	1	8	-3						56	30	40	126	-4
-10/-6	11	2	3	16	-8	4	0	1	5	-8						44	15	25	84	-8
-15/-11	4	1	1	6	-13	1	0	0	1	-14						26	6	14	46	-13
-20/-16	2	0	0	2	-19	1			1	-18						12	1	2	15	-18
-25/-21	1	0		1	-23											2	0	0	2	-23
-30/-26	0			0	-29											0			0	-28

BRISTOL/TRI CITY APRT TENNESSEE

LAT 36 29N LONG 82 24W ELEV 1507 FT

MEAN FREQUENCY OF OCCURRENCE OF DRY BULB TEMPERATURE (DEGREES F) WITH MEAN COINCIDENT WET BULB TEMPERATURE (DEGREES F), FOR EACH DRY BULB TEMPERATURE RANGE

Temperature Range	MAY Obsn Hour Gp 01 to 08	MAY 09 to 16	MAY 17 to 24	MAY Total Obsn	MAY MCWB	JUNE Obsn Hour Gp 01 to 08	JUNE 09 to 16	JUNE 17 to 24	JUNE Total Obsn	JUNE MCWB	JULY Obsn Hour Gp 01 to 08	JULY 09 to 16	JULY 17 to 24	JULY Total Obsn	JULY MCWB
100/104												0		0	74
95/99							0		0	76		2	1	3	73
90/94		1		1	71		11	4	15	73		11	3	14	73
85/89		14	4	18	69		35	15	50	71		54	21	75	72
80/84		41	17	58	66	1	59	34	94	69	0	75	44	119	70
75/79	1	54	32	87	64	7	61	50	118	67	9	65	65	139	69
70/74	6	51	47	104	62	39	44	67	150	66	69	34	75	178	68
65/69	33	38	59	130	60	84	21	48	153	64	116	6	34	156	65
60/64	74	26	43	143	58	71	7	18	96	60	37	0	6	43	60
55/59	59	13	25	97	53	29	1	4	34	55	12		1	13	55
50/54	40	6	13	59	49	8	1	1	10	50	4			4	50
45/49	21	2	6	29	44	1			1	46	0			0	47
40/44	11	1	2	14	40	0			0	44					
35/39	3		0	3	36										
30/34	0			0	31										
25/29															
20/24															

Temperature Range	AUGUST Obsn Hour Gp 01 to 08	AUGUST 09 to 16	AUGUST 17 to 24	AUGUST Total Obsn	AUGUST MCWB	SEPTEMBER Obsn Hour Gp 01 to 08	SEPTEMBER 09 to 16	SEPTEMBER 17 to 24	SEPTEMBER Total Obsn	SEPTEMBER MCWB	OCTOBER Obsn Hour Gp 01 to 08	OCTOBER 09 to 16	OCTOBER 17 to 24	OCTOBER Total Obsn	OCTOBER MCWB
100/104															
95/99		1	0	1	71		1	0	1	68					
90/94		12	3	15	72		5	1	6	68		0		0	70
85/89		50	16	66	72		24	6	30	69		2	0	2	69
80/84	0	75	40	115	70		47	23	70	68		12	2	14	65
75/79	5	64	58	127	69	1	51	35	87	66		30	9	39	63
70/74	55	35	75	165	68	16	52	56	124	64	0	43	22	65	60
65/69	106	9	44	159	65	62	34	58	154	62	10	44	37	91	58
60/64	60	3	10	73	60	57	16	36	109	58	28	38	54	120	56
55/59	17		1	18	55	54	7	16	77	54	38	33	46	117	51
50/54	5		0	5	52	30	2	6	38	50	50	24	34	108	48
45/49	0			0	48	16	0	2	18	46	49	13	24	86	44
40/44						5		0	5	41	36	7	11	54	39
35/39						0			0	39	21	2	6	29	35
30/34											14	0	2	16	30
25/29											2	0	0	2	25
20/24											2			2	21

BRISTOL/TRI CITY APRT TENNESSEE

Tempera-ture Range	NOVEMBER					DECEMBER					JANUARY				
	Obsn Hour Gp 01 to 08	09 to 16	17 to 24	Total Obsn	M C W B	Obsn Hour Gp 01 to 08	09 to 16	17 to 24	Total Obsn	M C W B	Obsn Hour Gp 01 to 08	09 to 16	17 to 24	Total Obsn	M C W B
100/104															
95/99															
90/94															
85/89															
80/84															
75/79		3	0	3	64		0		0	62		0		0	61
70/74	1	11	2	14	59		1	0	1	59		2	0	2	60
65/69	3	20	9	32	57	0	5	1	6	57		3	1	4	58
60/64	8	27	18	53	54	2	10	5	17	55	2	9	6	17	55
55/59	12	32	27	71	50	8	17	13	38	52	9	18	15	42	52
50/54	23	34	39	96	46	11	26	19	56	47	17	25	22	64	47
45/49	25	37	38	100	42	13	29	27	69	43	20	32	31	83	42
40/44	39	29	37	105	38	21	38	37	96	38	25	39	37	101	38
35/39	40	23	30	93	34	40	43	46	129	34	32	35	38	105	34
30/34	44	16	21	81	30	52	35	42	129	29	46	40	45	131	29
25/29	29	6	12	47	25	35	22	31	88	25	36	21	25	82	25
20/24	11	2	3	16	21	35	11	14	60	20	26	14	14	54	20
15/19	4	0	1	5	17	15	4	8	27	16	19	6	8	33	16
10/14	1		0	1	12	10	2	3	15	11	9	2	3	14	11
5/9	1	1	1	3	6	4	1	1	6	6	3	1	2	6	6
0/4						1	0	0	1	1	2	1	1	4	1
-5/-1						0	0	0	0	-4	2	0	0	2	-3
-10/-6						0			0	-8	0	0		0	-7

Tempera-ture Range	FEBRUARY					MARCH					APRIL					ANNUAL TOTAL				
	Obsn Hour Gp 01 to 08	09 to 16	17 to 24	Total Obsn	M C W B	Obsn Hour Gp 01 to 08	09 to 16	17 to 24	Total Obsn	M C W B	Obsn Hour Gp 01 to 08	09 to 16	17 to 24	Total Obsn	M C W B	Obsn Hour Gp 01 to 08	09 to 16	17 to 24	Total Obsn	M C W B
100/104																	0		0	74
95/99																	4	1	5	71
90/94																	40	11	51	72
85/89							0		0	61		2	0	2	65		181	62	243	71
80/84							0		0	61		14	5	19	63	1	323	165	489	69
75/79		0		0	57		3	1	4	60		23	12	35	61	23	354	262	639	67
70/74		2	0	2	57	0	9	4	13	58	1	30	21	52	59	187	314	369	870	65
65/69		7	3	10	56	1	16	9	26	55	9	38	33	80	56	424	241	336	1001	62
60/64	2	14	7	23	52	4	27	21	52	52	24	33	42	99	54	369	210	266	845	57
55/59	6	24	18	48	50	15	34	34	83	50	37	30	39	106	50	296	209	239	744	52
50/54	13	30	29	72	46	21	37	36	94	46	44	27	33	104	46	266	212	232	710	47
45/49	22	36	37	95	42	39	38	43	120	42	34	22	22	78	42	240	209	230	679	43
40/44	26	33	36	95	38	39	32	35	106	38	35	13	20	68	38	237	192	215	644	38
35/39	39	29	37	105	33	33	26	29	88	33	32	5	11	48	34	240	163	197	600	34
30/34	43	25	27	95	29	51	17	22	90	29	19	1	3	23	30	269	134	162	565	29
25/29	37	12	16	65	25	27	6	8	41	25	4			4	25	170	67	92	329	25
20/24	18	6	8	32	20	9	2	3	14	21	0			0	20	101	35	42	178	20
15/19	9	3	3	15	15	4	0	1	5	16						51	13	21	85	16
10/14	5	2	2	9	11	1	0	1	2	12						26	6	9	41	11
5/9	3	1	1	5	6	1			1	7						12	4	5	21	6
0/4	1	0		1	2	0			0	4						4	1	1	6	1
-5/-1	1			1	-2											3	0	0	3	-3
-10/-6																0	0		0	-8

KNOXVILLE/ALCOA ANG STA TENNESSEE

LAT 35 49N LONG 83 59W ELEV 980 FT

MEAN FREQUENCY OF OCCURRENCE OF DRY BULB TEMPERATURE (DEGREES F) WITH MEAN COINCIDENT WET BULB TEMPERATURE (DEGREES F) FOR EACH DRY BULB TEMPERATURE RANGE

Tempera-ture Range	MAY Obsn Hour Gp 01 to 08	MAY 09 to 16	MAY 17 to 24	MAY Total Obsn	MAY MCWB	JUNE Obsn Hour Gp 01 to 08	JUNE 09 to 16	JUNE 17 to 24	JUNE Total Obsn	JUNE MCWB	JULY Obsn Hour Gp 01 to 08	JULY 09 to 16	JULY 17 to 24	JULY Total Obsn	JULY MCWB
100/104							0	0	0	77		0	0	0	71
95/99							3	2	5	75		6	2	8	74
90/94		3	1	4	70		18	8	26	74		33	14	47	74
85/89		22	10	32	69	0	49	24	73	72	0	68	35	103	73
80/84		51	25	76	67	3	66	43	112	70	5	73	53	131	72
75/79	3	58	42	103	65	26	54	61	141	69	45	47	76	168	71
70/74	24	46	55	125	64	70	31	59	160	67	132	19	57	208	69
65/69	66	31	54	151	61	83	13	31	127	64	52	2	10	64	65
60/64	67	21	30	118	58	41	3	8	52	59	11	0	1	12	60
55/59	41	11	18	70	53	14	1	2	17	55	2			2	56
50/54	26	3	8	37	49	3		0	3	50	0			0	51
45/49	13	2	4	19	44	0			0	45					
40/44	7	0	0	7	40										
35/39	0			0	39										
30/34															
25/29															

Tempera-ture Range	AUGUST Obsn Hour Gp 01 to 08	AUGUST 09 to 16	AUGUST 17 to 24	AUGUST Total Obsn	AUGUST MCWB	SEPTEMBER Obsn Hour Gp 01 to 08	SEPTEMBER 09 to 16	SEPTEMBER 17 to 24	SEPTEMBER Total Obsn	SEPTEMBER MCWB	OCTOBER Obsn Hour Gp 01 to 08	OCTOBER 09 to 16	OCTOBER 17 to 24	OCTOBER Total Obsn	OCTOBER MCWB
100/104							1	0	1	71					
95/99		4	1	5	74		2	1	3	71					
90/94		29	10	39	73		10	3	13	70		0	0	0	71
85/89		63	30	93	72		34	14	48	70		4	1	5	71
80/84	2	72	50	124	71	1	53	29	83	69		17	4	21	67
75/79	34	50	79	163	70	7	49	46	102	67	0	35	15	50	64
70/74	113	23	58	194	69	49	48	61	158	66	5	48	32	85	62
65/69	72	6	17	95	65	70	28	49	147	63	24	42	46	112	60
60/64	24	1	2	27	60	54	12	24	90	59	39	39	52	130	57
55/59	3		0	3	57	36	4	9	49	54	46	30	39	115	53
50/54	0			0	51	18	1	3	22	50	47	19	30	96	48
45/49						5		0	5	45	44	9	18	71	44
40/44						0			0	42	25	4	6	35	39
35/39											11	2	4	17	35
30/34											5	0	1	6	30
25/29											2			2	26

Temperature Range	NOVEMBER Obsn Hour Gp 01 to 08	09 to 16	17 to 24	Total Obsn	M C W B	DECEMBER Obsn Hour Gp 01 to 08	09 to 16	17 to 24	Total Obsn	M C W B	JANUARY Obsn Hour Gp 01 to 08	09 to 16	17 to 24	Total Obsn	M C W B
100/104															
95/99															
90/94															
85/89															
80/84		1		1	66										
75/79	0	3	1	4	63		0		0	65		0		0	64
70/74	2	12	4	18	61	0	2	1	3	62		3	1	4	62
65/69	4	21	12	37	57	3	7	4	14	59	3	9	7	19	60
60/64	10	29	23	62	55	5	12	11	28	56	9	13	15	37	57
55/59	17	32	31	80	51	9	22	14	45	52	11	17	15	43	52
50/54	22	38	36	96	47	14	28	26	68	48	15	27	23	65	47
45/49	34	39	43	116	43	23	39	33	95	43	20	35	31	86	43
40/44	42	30	39	111	38	28	47	50	125	38	31	39	41	111	39
35/39	45	19	29	93	34	47	42	47	136	34	41	39	44	124	34
30/34	42	11	15	68	30	52	28	32	112	29	50	36	39	125	30
25/29	16	3	5	24	25	39	14	19	72	25	30	15	18	63	25
20/24	4	1	1	6	21	16	5	6	27	21	21	8	9	38	20
15/19	2	0	0	2	16	7	2	2	11	16	8	4	4	16	16
10/14	0	0	1	1	10	3	1	1	5	11	5	2	2	9	11
5/9	0	0	0	0	6	1	0	0	1	6	2	0	1	3	6
0/4						1	0		1	2	0	0	0	0	1
-5/-1						0			0	-1					

Temperature Range	FEBRUARY Obsn Hour Gp 01 to 08	09 to 16	17 to 24	Total Obsn	M C W B	MARCH Obsn Hour Gp 01 to 08	09 to 16	17 to 24	Total Obsn	M C W B	APRIL Obsn Hour Gp 01 to 08	09 to 16	17 to 24	Total Obsn	M C W B	ANNUAL TOTAL Obsn Hour Gp 01 to 08	09 to 16	17 to 24	Total Obsn	M C W B
100/104																	1	0	1	72
95/99																	15	6	21	74
90/94												0		0	70		93	36	129	73
85/89												3	1	4	66	0	243	115	358	72
80/84							1	0	1	66		17	7	24	65	11	351	211	573	70
75/79		0		0	62	0	5	3	8	63	0	28	18	46	62	115	329	341	785	68
70/74	0	5	2	7	60	2	13	8	23	60	6	36	31	73	60	403	286	369	1058	66
65/69	3	11	7	21	57	7	22	16	45	57	22	36	38	96	58	409	228	291	928	61
60/64	6	20	17	43	54	10	30	26	66	53	36	38	43	117	55	312	218	252	782	56
55/59	11	28	27	66	51	17	35	35	87	50	40	32	35	107	51	247	212	225	684	52
50/54	23	34	37	94	47	31	39	45	115	46	41	23	29	93	47	240	212	237	689	47
45/49	31	38	37	106	43	42	38	40	120	42	35	17	20	72	42	247	217	226	690	43
40/44	34	32	34	100	38	41	28	32	101	38	29	9	14	52	38	237	189	216	642	38
35/39	41	26	31	98	34	43	22	25	90	33	21	2	4	27	34	249	152	184	585	34
30/34	34	14	15	63	29	33	11	13	57	29	8	0	1	9	30	224	100	116	440	30
25/29	19	7	8	34	25	17	4	4	25	25	0			0	26	123	43	54	220	25
20/24	11	5	4	20	20	4	1	1	6	20						56	20	21	97	20
15/19	4	2	2	8	16	2	0	1	3	15						23	8	9	40	16
10/14	2	1	2	5	10	1	0		1	11						11	4	6	21	11
5/9	2	0	0	2	6	0	0		0	8						5	0	1	6	6
0/4	1	0		1	2											2	0	0	2	2
-5/-1	0			0	-2											0			0	-1

MEMPHIS NAS/MILLINGTON TENNESSEE

LAT 35 20N LONG 89 53W ELEV 322 FT

MEAN FREQUENCY OF OCCURRENCE OF DRY BULB TEMPERATURE (DEGREES F) WITH MEAN COINCIDENT WET BULB TEMPERATURE (DEGREES F) FOR EACH DRY BULB TEMPERATURE RANGE

	MAY					JUNE					JULY				
Temperature Range	Obsn Hour Gp 01 to 08	09 to 16	17 to 24	Total Obsn	MCWB	Obsn Hour Gp 01 to 08	09 to 16	17 to 24	Total Obsn	MCWB	Obsn Hour Gp 01 to 08	09 to 16	17 to 24	Total Obsn	MCWB
100/104							0		0	74		1		1	78
95/99							4	1	5	76		10	2	12	78
90/94		8	2	10	73		42	13	55	75		54	18	72	77
85/89		34	11	45	71	1	70	30	101	73	3	83	43	129	75
80/84	2	61	30	93	69	18	64	55	137	72	29	62	66	157	74
75/79	15	54	52	121	67	55	37	71	163	70	90	27	77	194	72
70/74	51	38	60	149	65	94	18	49	161	68	94	10	36	140	69
65/69	73	26	45	144	62	48	3	16	67	63	23	2	6	31	63
60/64	52	18	26	96	57	19	1	4	24	59	8	0	1	9	59
55/59	29	7	13	49	52	4	0	0	4	55	1			1	56
50/54	16	2	8	26	47	0			0	50					
45/49	9		1	10	43										
40/44	1			1	39										
35/39															
30/34															

	AUGUST					SEPTEMBER					OCTOBER				
Temperature Range	Obsn Hour Gp 01 to 08	09 to 16	17 to 24	Total Obsn	MCWB	Obsn Hour Gp 01 to 08	09 to 16	17 to 24	Total Obsn	MCWB	Obsn Hour Gp 01 to 08	09 to 16	17 to 24	Total Obsn	MCWB
100/104		0		0	78		0		0	78					
95/99		6	1	7	78		2	0	2	76					
90/94		49	13	62	77		12	2	14	76					
85/89	0	81	32	113	75		47	12	59	74		8	1	9	70
80/84	15	67	62	144	73	2	60	26	88	71		34	5	39	68
75/79	75	32	78	185	72	26	56	60	142	70	1	44	17	62	66
70/74	102	11	49	162	69	74	34	63	171	68	12	44	32	88	63
65/69	41	2	10	53	64	57	18	40	115	63	29	40	47	116	60
60/64	12	0	3	15	59	42	7	23	72	58	47	38	48	133	56
55/59	2			2	54	26	3	9	38	54	46	24	42	112	52
50/54						9	1	4	14	49	45	13	34	92	48
45/49						2		1	3	44	38	3	17	58	44
40/44						1		0	1	40	24	0	5	29	39
35/39											5		1	6	35
30/34											1			1	31

MEMPHIS NAS/MILLINGTON TENNESSEE

Temperature Range	NOVEMBER Obsn Hour Gp 01 to 08	09 to 16	17 to 24	Total Obsn	MCWB	DECEMBER Obsn Hour Gp 01 to 08	09 to 16	17 to 24	Total Obsn	MCWB	JANUARY Obsn Hour Gp 01 to 08	09 to 16	17 to 24	Total Obsn	MCWB
100/104															
95/99															
90/94															
85/89															
80/84		1	0	1	69										
75/79		6	1	7	65										
70/74	2	23	6	31	62	0	3	0	3	63	0	2	1	3	64
65/69	8	27	16	51	60	2	10	5	17	61	2	7	5	14	61
60/64	16	37	31	84	56	7	19	10	36	57	8	14	9	31	58
55/59	27	40	35	102	51	17	26	20	63	53	10	18	14	42	53
50/54	36	36	41	113	47	19	31	30	80	48	9	22	18	49	47
45/49	40	30	40	110	43	24	38	29	91	43	13	30	26	69	43
40/44	40	21	37	98	38	36	45	45	126	39	28	34	34	96	38
35/39	36	10	18	64	34	45	35	44	124	34	36	40	42	118	34
30/34	20	6	9	35	29	44	22	35	101	29	50	36	47	133	30
25/29	10	2	4	16	25	29	11	17	57	25	39	19	27	85	25
20/24	3	0	2	5	20	12	5	7	24	20	25	12	12	49	20
15/19	2	0	0	2	17	8	3	3	14	16	13	7	8	28	16
10/14						2	1	1	4	11	8	3	4	15	11
5/9						1	0	1	2	6	4	1	2	7	6
0/4						0		0	0	3	2	1	1	4	2
-5/-1								0	0	-4	1		0	1	-2
-10/-6						0			0	-9					
-15/-11						0			0	-12					

Temperature Range	FEBRUARY Obsn Hour Gp 01 to 08	09 to 16	17 to 24	Total Obsn	MCWB	MARCH Obsn Hour Gp 01 to 08	09 to 16	17 to 24	Total Obsn	MCWB	APRIL Obsn Hour Gp 01 to 08	09 to 16	17 to 24	Total Obsn	MCWB
100/104															
95/99															
90/94												0		0	68
85/89												4	1	5	69
80/84		0		0	63		3	1	4	63		23	9	32	67
75/79		1	0	1	63		8	4	12	63	3	40	23	66	65
70/74	1	4	1	6	62	2	16	9	27	61	17	47	36	100	62
65/69	1	7	4	12	59	7	22	16	45	58	37	40	47	124	60
60/64	5	16	10	31	56	16	32	26	74	54	46	33	44	123	56
55/59	9	20	19	48	52	22	32	30	84	51	38	26	35	99	51
50/54	15	29	22	66	47	26	37	40	103	46	40	16	25	81	47
45/49	25	33	36	94	43	41	38	40	119	42	33	9	14	56	43
40/44	32	38	39	109	38	43	28	39	110	38	19	2	5	26	39
35/39	38	32	34	104	34	43	19	26	88	34	7	1	1	9	35
30/34	42	24	32	98	29	33	10	14	57	30	1		0	1	32
25/29	30	12	17	59	25	13	3	3	19	25					
20/24	17	5	7	29	20	2	0	1	3	21					
15/19	6	2	2	10	15	0	0	0	0	14					
10/14	3	1	1	5	11	0			0	10					
5/9	2		0	2	6										
0/4															
-5/-1															
-10/-6															
-15/-11															

Temperature Range	ANNUAL TOTAL Obsn Hour Gp 01 to 08	09 to 16	17 to 24	Total Obsn	MCWB
100/104		1		1	78
95/99		22	4	26	77
90/94		165	48	213	76
85/89	4	327	130	461	74
80/84	66	375	254	695	72
75/79	265	305	383	953	70
70/74	449	250	342	1041	66
65/69	328	204	257	789	61
60/64	278	215	235	728	56
55/59	231	196	217	644	52
50/54	215	187	222	624	47
45/49	225	181	204	610	43
40/44	224	168	204	596	38
35/39	210	137	166	513	34
30/34	191	98	137	426	29
25/29	121	47	68	236	25
20/24	59	22	29	110	20
15/19	29	12	13	54	16
10/14	13	5	6	24	11
5/9	7	1	3	11	6
0/4	2	1	1	4	2
-5/-1	1		0	1	-2
-10/-6	0			0	-9
-15/-11	0			0	-12

SEWART AFB/SMYRNA APRT TENNESSEE

LAT 36 00N LONG 86 32W ELEV 543 FT

MEAN FREQUENCY OF OCCURRENCE OF DRY BULB TEMPERATURE (DEGREES F) WITH MEAN COINCIDENT WET BULB TEMPERATURE (DEGREES F) FOR EACH DRY BULB TEMPERATURE RANGE

Temperature Range	MAY Obsn Hour Gp 01 to 08	MAY 09 to 16	MAY 17 to 24	MAY Total Obsn	MAY MCWB	JUNE Obsn Hour Gp 01 to 08	JUNE 09 to 16	JUNE 17 to 24	JUNE Total Obsn	JUNE MCWB	JULY Obsn Hour Gp 01 to 08	JULY 09 to 16	JULY 17 to 24	JULY Total Obsn	JULY MCWB
100/104							0		0	77		1	0	1	77
95/99							2	0	2	74		10	1	11	75
90/94		6	1	7	71	0	28	6	34	74	0	44	10	54	75
85/89		29	6	35	70	0	62	19	81	72	2	81	28	111	74
80/84	1	52	17	70	68	7	63	35	105	70	11	66	49	126	72
75/79	6	53	28	87	66	23	49	49	121	69	46	33	74	153	71
70/74	23	43	51	117	65	60	24	62	146	67	113	12	63	188	69
65/69	62	32	61	155	62	79	9	43	131	64	51	2	17	70	65
60/64	58	19	37	114	58	43	4	17	64	59	16		5	21	60
55/59	40	9	23	72	53	20	0	6	26	55	7		1	8	55
50/54	28	3	14	45	49	7		1	8	51	2		0	2	52
45/49	16	2	7	25	45	2		0	2	46					
40/44	11		3	14	40	1		0	1	42					
35/39	2		0	2	36	0			0	38					
30/34	0			0	32										
25/29															
20/24															

Temperature Range	AUGUST Obsn Hour Gp 01 to 08	AUGUST 09 to 16	AUGUST 17 to 24	AUGUST Total Obsn	AUGUST MCWB	SEPTEMBER Obsn Hour Gp 01 to 08	SEPTEMBER 09 to 16	SEPTEMBER 17 to 24	SEPTEMBER Total Obsn	SEPTEMBER MCWB	OCTOBER Obsn Hour Gp 01 to 08	OCTOBER 09 to 16	OCTOBER 17 to 24	OCTOBER Total Obsn	OCTOBER MCWB
100/104		1	0	1	73		1	0	1	71					
95/99		11	1	12	76		3	0	3	72					
90/94	0	44	10	54	75		16	2	18	71		1		1	73
85/89	1	69	24	94	73	0	39	9	48	71		4	0	4	71
80/84	9	67	44	120	72	2	56	19	77	69		27	2	29	66
75/79	39	35	67	141	71	11	50	37	98	68	1	40	9	50	64
70/74	95	16	63	174	69	43	42	59	144	66	8	42	21	71	62
65/69	56	4	27	87	65	60	22	52	134	63	16	43	35	94	59
60/64	32	1	9	42	60	51	9	31	91	59	36	36	42	114	56
55/59	11		3	14	56	35	2	16	53	55	33	29	42	104	52
50/54	3		0	3	51	21	0	10	31	50	44	17	39	100	48
45/49	0			0	48	13	1	4	18	46	39	8	29	76	44
40/44						4		1	5	42	34	2	17	53	40
35/39						1		0	1	37	22	1	8	31	35
30/34											11		3	14	31
25/29											4		0	4	27
20/24											0			0	22

Temperature Range	NOVEMBER Obsn Hour Gp 01 to 08	NOVEMBER Obsn Hour Gp 09 to 16	NOVEMBER Obsn Hour Gp 17 to 24	NOVEMBER Total Obsn	NOVEMBER MCWB	DECEMBER Obsn Hour Gp 01 to 08	DECEMBER Obsn Hour Gp 09 to 16	DECEMBER Obsn Hour Gp 17 to 24	DECEMBER Total Obsn	DECEMBER MCWB	JANUARY Obsn Hour Gp 01 to 08	JANUARY Obsn Hour Gp 09 to 16	JANUARY Obsn Hour Gp 17 to 24	JANUARY Total Obsn	JANUARY MCWB
100/104															
95/99															
90/94															
85/89															
80/84		1		1	65										
75/79		5	I	6	64		0		0	63					
70/74	2	18	3	23	60		2	0	2	61		1	0	1	61
65/69	5	27	9	41	58	1	8	1	10	59	1	7	2	10	59
60/64	11	32	20	63	54	6	18	9	33	56	6	12	8	26	56
55/59	19	37	29	85	51	12	27	18	57	52	7	18	13	38	52
50/54	28	36	35	99	47	16	31	23	70	47	11	23	14	48	46
45/49	33	32	39	104	43	23	34	28	85	42	19	33	25	77	43
40/44	34	23	36	93	39	30	38	35	103	38	21	34	32	87	38
35/39	40	16	31	87	34	34	39	42	115	34	31	41	41	113	34
30/34	31	9	22	62	30	39	27	41	107	29	46	37	46	129	29
25/29	20	4	10	34	25	35	15	29	79	25	34	20	32	86	25
20/24	11	1	5	17	21	29	6	15	50	21	32	10	19	61	20
15/19	5	0	1	6	17	14	3	6	23	16	19	8	8	35	16
10/14	0			0	13	5	1	2	8	11	11	4	4	19	11
5/9						2	0	1	3	7	4	2	2	8	6
0/4						0	0	0	0	2	3	1	1	5	2
-5/-1						1		0	1	-4	2	0	1	3	-3
-10/-6						1		0	1	-8	1	0	0	1	-8
-15/-11											0			0	-12

Temperature Range	FEBRUARY Obsn Hour Gp 01 to 08	FEBRUARY Obsn Hour Gp 09 to 16	FEBRUARY Obsn Hour Gp 17 to 24	FEBRUARY Total Obsn	FEBRUARY MCWB	MARCH Obsn Hour Gp 01 to 08	MARCH Obsn Hour Gp 09 to 16	MARCH Obsn Hour Gp 17 to 24	MARCH Total Obsn	MARCH MCWB	APRIL Obsn Hour Gp 01 to 08	APRIL Obsn Hour Gp 09 to 16	APRIL Obsn Hour Gp 17 to 24	APRIL Total Obsn	APRIL MCWB	ANNUAL TOTAL Obsn Hour Gp 01 to 08	ANNUAL TOTAL Obsn Hour Gp 09 to 16	ANNUAL TOTAL Obsn Hour Gp 17 to 24	ANNUAL TOTAL Total Obsn	ANNUAL TOTAL MCWB
100/104																	3	0	3	74
95/99																	26	2	28	75
90/94																0	139	29	168	74
85/89												5	1	6	67	3	289	87	379	73
80/84		0		0	62		2	0	2	63		22	5	27	66	30	356	171	557	70
75/79		0	0	0	62		8	1	9	62	1	40	15	56	63	127	313	281	721	68
70/74	0	3	1	4	60	1	17	6	24	60	8	40	27	75	61	353	260	356	969	66
65/69	1	10	6	17	58	7	23	14	44	57	29	39	42	110	59	368	226	309	903	62
60/64	4	17	9	30	54	12	29	22	63	54	40	33	41	114	55	315	210	250	775	57
55/59	10	23	14	47	51	18	36	28	82	49	39	26	39	104	51	251	207	232	690	52
50/54	17	25	23	65	47	28	33	36	97	46	34	21	30	85	47	239	189	225	653	47
45/49	18	30	25	73	42	28	32	37	97	42	35	11	22	68	43	226	183	216	625	43
40/44	28	33	37	98	38	34	30	36	100	38	28	3	12	43	39	225	163	209	597	38
35/39	33	32	35	100	34	37	21	32	90	34	17	1	5	23	35	217	151	194	562	34
30/34	34	22	30	86	29	41	11	23	75	30	7		2	9	30	209	106	167	482	30
25/29	33	16	22	71	25	26	4	10	40	25	2		0	2	27	154	59	103	316	25
20/24	19	6	11	36	20	11	1	3	15	21						102	24	53	179	20
15/19	14	3	6	23	16	4	0	1	5	16						56	14	22	92	16
10/14	7	2	3	12	11	1	0	0	1	12						24	7	9	40	11
5/9	4	0	1	5	7	0			0	7						10	2	4	16	7
0/4	2	0	0	2	2											5	1	1	7	2
-5/-1	0			0	-2											3	0	1	4	-3
-10/-6																2	0	0	2	-8
-15/-11																0			0	-12

AMARILLO TEXAS

LAT 35 14N LONG 101 42W ELEV 3604 FT

MEAN FREQUENCY OF OCCURRENCE OF DRY BULB TEMPERATURE (DEGREES F) WITH MEAN COINCIDENT WET BULB TEMPERATURE (DEGREES F) FOR EACH DRY BULB TEMPERATURE RANGE

Temperature Range	MAY Obsn Hour Gp 01 to 08	MAY 09 to 16	MAY 17 to 24	MAY Total Obsn	MAY MCWB	JUNE Obsn Hour Gp 01 to 08	JUNE 09 to 16	JUNE 17 to 24	JUNE Total Obsn	JUNE MCWB
105/109							0	0	0	68
100/104		0		0	64		4	1	5	68
95/99		4	1	5	63		16	8	24	66
90/94		13	6	19	61		36	19	55	66
85/89		26	13	39	60	0	46	28	74	66
80/84	0	35	22	57	60	4	48	39	91	65
75/79	1	39	29	69	58	22	38	44	104	64
70/74	11	39	38	88	57	52	25	41	118	63
65/69	31	32	39	102	56	66	12	31	109	61
60/64	54	24	39	117	54	58	8	19	85	58
55/59	59	19	32	110	52	27	4	7	38	54
50/54	50	11	18	79	48	9	1	2	12	49
45/49	27	5	10	42	44	2	0	1	3	44
40/44	10	1	1	12	39	0			0	42
35/39	3	1	1	5	35					
30/34	1	0	0	1	30					
25/29	0			0	28					

Temperature Range	JULY Obsn Hour Gp 01 to 08	JULY 09 to 16	JULY 17 to 24	JULY Total Obsn	JULY MCWB	AUGUST Obsn Hour Gp 01 to 08	AUGUST 09 to 16	AUGUST 17 to 24	AUGUST Total Obsn	AUGUST MCWB
105/109										
100/104		2	1	3	68		1	0	1	68
95/99		24	9	33	68		18	5	23	68
90/94		52	28	80	68		53	23	76	67
85/89	0	59	36	95	68	0	60	33	93	67
80/84	6	51	47	104	66	3	51	44	98	66
75/79	37	34	56	127	65	23	36	58	117	65
70/74	86	18	43	147	64	82	18	52	152	63
65/69	87	7	22	116	63	100	7	25	132	62
60/64	29	2	5	36	60	33	3	5	41	59
55/59	3		1	4	55	6	1	1	8	55
50/54						1	0		1	52
45/49						0			0	48
40/44										
35/39										
30/34										
25/29										

Temperature Range	SEPTEMBER Obsn Hour Gp 01 to 08	SEPTEMBER 09 to 16	SEPTEMBER 17 to 24	SEPTEMBER Total Obsn	SEPTEMBER MCWB	OCTOBER Obsn Hour Gp 01 to 08	OCTOBER 09 to 16	OCTOBER 17 to 24	OCTOBER Total Obsn	OCTOBER MCWB
105/109										
100/104										
95/99		2	1	3	65					
90/94		19	6	25	65		2	0	2	63
85/89		39	15	54	64		13	2	15	59
80/84	0	45	25	70	63		26	9	35	58
75/79	2	42	36	80	62		33	13	46	57
70/74	24	35	49	108	60	1	37	22	60	56
65/69	60	24	48	132	59	8	36	37	81	54
60/64	69	18	33	120	56	26	35	46	107	52
55/59	45	9	16	70	52	44	25	45	114	49
50/54	27	5	7	39	48	63	19	35	117	46
45/49	9	1	3	13	44	53	14	25	92	42
40/44	3	1	1	5	41	33	5	10	48	38
35/39						16	2	4	22	34
30/34						4	1	1	6	30
25/29						*			*	27

Temperature Range	NOVEMBER Obsn Hour Gp 01 to 08	NOVEMBER 09 to 16	NOVEMBER 17 to 24	NOVEMBER Total Obsn	NOVEMBER MCWB	DECEMBER Obsn Hour Gp 01 to 08	DECEMBER 09 to 16	DECEMBER 17 to 24	DECEMBER Total Obsn	DECEMBER MCWB	JANUARY Obsn Hour Gp 01 to 08	JANUARY 09 to 16	JANUARY 17 to 24	JANUARY Total Obsn	JANUARY MCWB
105/109															
100/104															
95/99															
90/94															
85/89															
80/84		0		0	56		0		0	54		0		0	54
75/79		5	0	5	52		1		1	52		1	0	1	51
70/74		16	3	19	51		4	0	4	49		4	1	5	49
65/69	0	24	6	30	49		11	2	13	47		11	2	13	47
60/64	1	30	15	46	48	1	19	6	26	45	0	15	6	21	45
55/59	5	30	24	59	45	1	22	12	35	43	1	22	12	35	43
50/54	12	32	36	80	43	5	29	20	54	41	5	28	19	52	40
45/49	30	28	39	97	40	10	33	29	72	38	10	29	26	65	37
40/44	46	24	41	111	36	20	35	40	95	35	20	31	34	85	34
35/39	53	21	30	104	33	39	32	45	116	32	36	28	41	105	32
30/34	44	16	24	84	29	65	28	42	135	29	46	26	37	109	28
25/29	29	9	12	50	25	54	16	28	98	25	48	17	25	90	25
20/24	11	3	7	21	20	27	9	11	47	20	30	15	16	61	20
15/19	7	1	3	11	15	12	5	9	26	16	22	9	12	43	15
10/14	3	0	0	3	11	9	3	3	15	12	14	5	7	26	11
5/9	1			1	8	3	1	1	5	7	9	4	5	18	6
0/4						1	0	0	1	2	4	2	2	8	1
-5/-1						0			0	-2	2	1	1	4	-3
-10/-6											2	0	0	2	-8
-15/-11															

Temperature Range	FEBRUARY Obsn Hour Gp 01 to 08	FEBRUARY 09 to 16	FEBRUARY 17 to 24	FEBRUARY Total Obsn	FEBRUARY MCWB	MARCH Obsn Hour Gp 01 to 08	MARCH 09 to 16	MARCH 17 to 24	MARCH Total Obsn	MARCH MCWB	APRIL Obsn Hour Gp 01 to 08	APRIL 09 to 16	APRIL 17 to 24	APRIL Total Obsn	APRIL MCWB
105/109															
100/104															
95/99															
90/94												1	0	1	56
85/89		0		0	58		0	0	0	53		11	4	15	56
80/84		1	0	1	55		2	1	3	52		17	9	26	55
75/79		2	1	3	51		10	4	14	51		23	12	35	53
70/74		8	3	11	50	0	19	9	28	49	0	29	21	50	52
65/69	0	15	7	22	47	0	23	15	38	47	4	32	28	64	50
60/64	1	20	10	31	46	1	29	21	51	45	17	34	34	85	49
55/59	2	22	16	40	44	6	29	27	62	43	29	29	37	95	47
50/54	7	25	24	56	41	15	29	31	75	41	46	22	34	102	44
45/49	16	28	30	74	39	27	27	35	89	38	44	18	25	87	41
40/44	28	23	30	81	36	42	26	34	102	35	44	13	19	76	37
35/39	34	25	31	90	32	50	21	30	101	32	31	8	10	49	34
30/34	43	20	30	93	29	45	16	21	82	29	17	2	4	23	30
25/29	37	16	18	71	25	31	9	11	51	25	6	1	1	8	25
20/24	25	10	13	48	21	17	4	6	27	20	1	0		1	22
15/19	20	6	9	35	16	9	1	2	12	16					
10/14	6	3	2	11	12	3	0	0	3	11					
5/9	3	0	1	4	7	0	0	0	0	7					
0/4	0	0	0	0	3	0			0	3					
-5/-1	0	0		0	-3										
-10/-6	0	0	0	0	-8										
-15/-11	0			0	-12										

Temperature Range	ANNUAL TOTAL Obsn Hour Gp 01 to 08	ANNUAL TOTAL 09 to 16	ANNUAL TOTAL 17 to 24	ANNUAL TOTAL Total Obsn	ANNUAL TOTAL MCWB
105/109		0	0	0	68
100/104		7	2	9	68
95/99		64	24	88	67
90/94		176	82	258	66
85/89	0	254	131	385	65
80/84	13	276	196	485	63
75/79	85	264	253	602	62
70/74	256	252	282	790	60
65/69	356	234	262	852	57
60/64	290	237	239	766	53
55/59	228	212	230	670	48
50/54	240	201	226	667	44
45/49	228	183	223	634	40
40/44	246	159	210	615	36
35/39	262	138	192	592	32
30/34	265	109	159	533	29
25/29	206	68	95	369	25
20/24	111	41	53	205	20
15/19	70	22	35	127	16
10/14	35	11	12	58	11
5/9	16	5	7	28	6
0/4	5	2	2	9	1
-5/-1	2	1	1	4	-3
-10/-6	2	0	0	2	-8
-15/-11	0			0	-12

BERGSTROM AFB/AUSTIN TEXAS

LAT 30 12N LONG 97 40W ELEV 541 FT

MEAN FREQUENCY OF OCCURRENCE OF DRY BULB TEMPERATURE (DEGREES F) WITH MEAN COINCIDENT WET BULB TEMPERATURE (DEGREES F) FOR EACH DRY BULB TEMPERATURE RANGE

Temperature Range	MAY Obsn Hour Gp 01 to 08	MAY 09 to 16	MAY 17 to 24	MAY Total Obsn	MAY MCWB	JUNE Obsn Hour Gp 01 to 08	JUNE 09 to 16	JUNE 17 to 24	JUNE Total Obsn	JUNE MCWB	JULY Obsn Hour Gp 01 to 08	JULY 09 to 16	JULY 17 to 24	JULY Total Obsn	JULY MCWB
105/109												0	0	0	74
100/104							0	0	0	71		5	3	8	74
95/99		2	1	3	73		16	9	25	75		52	30	82	75
90/94		16	7	23	73		64	33	97	75		80	50	130	75
85/89		52	26	78	72	0	72	48	120	74	1	68	59	128	74
80/84	1	70	47	118	71	20	55	65	140	73	43	34	67	144	74
75/79	40	55	71	166	70	106	23	55	184	72	145	8	33	186	73
70/74	89	30	56	175	67	82	7	22	111	69	55	1	7	63	70
65/69	62	14	26	102	63	25	2	7	34	65	4	0	0	4	63
60/64	32	7	11	50	58	5	1	1	7	59	1		0	1	59
55/59	16	1	3	20	53	1			1	55					
50/54	7		0	7	49										
45/49	1			1	45										
40/44															
35/39															
30/34															

Temperature Range	AUGUST Obsn Hour Gp 01 to 08	AUGUST 09 to 16	AUGUST 17 to 24	AUGUST Total Obsn	AUGUST MCWB	SEPTEMBER Obsn Hour Gp 01 to 08	SEPTEMBER 09 to 16	SEPTEMBER 17 to 24	SEPTEMBER Total Obsn	SEPTEMBER MCWB	OCTOBER Obsn Hour Gp 01 to 08	OCTOBER 09 to 16	OCTOBER 17 to 24	OCTOBER Total Obsn	OCTOBER MCWB
105/109		0	0	0	73										
100/104		8	4	12	74		0	0	0	76					
95/99		48	28	76	74		11	5	16	74		0		0	70
90/94		76	41	117	74		43	17	60	74		6	1	7	73
85/89	1	61	56	118	74		61	34	95	73		28	9	37	71
80/84	42	38	68	148	73	7	55	56	118	72	0	52	22	74	69
75/79	129	13	40	182	72	78	39	64	181	71	15	53	45	113	68
70/74	66	3	9	78	69	86	19	38	143	68	37	44	55	136	65
65/69	7	0	1	8	63	38	9	17	64	63	50	29	46	125	61
60/64	3	0		3	58	20	4	7	31	58	51	21	35	107	57
55/59						8	0	2	10	54	43	9	20	72	52
50/54						2		0	2	50	29	5	12	46	48
45/49						0		0	0	45	16	0	3	19	44
40/44											4	0	1	5	40
35/39											2			2	36
30/34											0			0	33

Temperature Range	NOVEMBER Obsn Hour Gp 01 to 08	NOVEMBER 09 to 16	NOVEMBER 17 to 24	NOVEMBER Total Obsn	NOVEMBER MCWB	DECEMBER Obsn Hour Gp 01 to 08	DECEMBER 09 to 16	DECEMBER 17 to 24	DECEMBER Total Obsn	DECEMBER MCWB	JANUARY Obsn Hour Gp 01 to 08	JANUARY 09 to 16	JANUARY 17 to 24	JANUARY Total Obsn	JANUARY MCWB
105/109															
100/104															
95/99															
90/94															
85/89		2	0	2	65							1	0	1	59
80/84		14	2	16	67		2	0	2	63		1	0	1	63
75/79	1	30	11	42	66		9	2	11	64		7	2	9	63
70/74	10	41	29	80	63	3	25	11	39	63	1	17	9	27	62
65/69	24	38	40	102	61	17	32	23	72	60	13	23	20	56	61
60/64	34	36	40	110	56	17	34	29	80	55	12	27	22	61	55
55/59	39	30	40	109	52	20	38	39	97	51	16	32	32	80	51
50/54	37	22	31	90	47	32	37	42	111	47	27	35	39	101	47
45/49	36	16	25	77	43	40	29	41	110	43	30	32	38	100	43
40/44	31	7	14	52	39	47	23	34	104	39	39	29	31	99	38
35/39	15	3	5	23	34	37	11	16	64	34	44	23	29	96	34
30/34	11	1	2	14	30	22	6	8	36	29	34	13	15	62	29
25/29	1		0	1	24	9	1	3	13	25	19	6	7	32	25
20/24						3		0	3	21	7	3	3	13	20
15/19											3	1	1	5	15
10/14											1			1	11

Temperature Range	FEBRUARY Obsn Hour Gp 01 to 08	FEBRUARY 09 to 16	FEBRUARY 17 to 24	FEBRUARY Total Obsn	FEBRUARY MCWB	MARCH Obsn Hour Gp 01 to 08	MARCH 09 to 16	MARCH 17 to 24	MARCH Total Obsn	MARCH MCWB	APRIL Obsn Hour Gp 01 to 08	APRIL 09 to 16	APRIL 17 to 24	APRIL Total Obsn	APRIL MCWB	ANNUAL TOTAL Obsn Hour Gp 01 to 08	ANNUAL TOTAL 09 to 16	ANNUAL TOTAL 17 to 24	ANNUAL TOTAL Total Obsn	ANNUAL TOTAL MCWB
105/109																	0	0	0	73
100/104																	13	7	20	74
95/99							0	0	0	67		0		0	58		129	73	202	75
90/94		0	0	0	67		1	0	1	67		2	1	3	69		288	150	438	74
85/89		1	0	1	65		3	1	4	67		11	5	16	71	2	360	238	600	73
80/84		3	1	4	66		11	5	16	64		45	22	67	69	113	380	355	848	72
75/79		9	4	13	63		25	14	39	63	5	59	46	110	67	519	330	387	1236	70
70/74	1	16	11	28	60	4	41	31	76	62	56	51	65	172	66	490	295	343	1128	66
65/69	9	26	21	56	59	26	46	46	118	60	59	35	45	139	62	334	254	292	880	61
60/64	16	32	28	76	55	34	35	47	116	56	40	21	29	90	57	265	218	249	732	56
55/59	19	33	36	88	51	38	29	34	101	51	34	10	17	61	52	234	182	223	639	51
50/54	34	35	42	111	47	45	25	31	101	47	25	5	8	38	48	238	164	205	607	47
45/49	43	31	34	108	43	40	15	19	74	42	13	1	2	16	43	219	124	162	505	43
40/44	40	19	24	83	39	30	11	13	54	38	6	0	1	7	39	197	89	118	404	38
35/39	31	13	14	58	34	18	4	6	28	34	2	0		2	34	149	54	70	273	34
30/34	21	5	7	33	30	10	1	1	12	29						98	26	33	157	29
25/29	9	1	1	11	25	3	0		3	25						41	8	11	60	25
20/24	1			1	22	0			0	23						11	3	3	17	20
15/19	0			0	18											3	1	1	5	15
10/14																1			1	11

BROWNSVILLE IAP TEXAS

LAT 25 54N LONG 97 26W ELEV 19 FT

MEAN FREQUENCY OF OCCURRENCE OF DRY BULB TEMPERATURE (DEGREES F) WITH MEAN COINCIDENT WET BULB TEMPERATURE (DEGREES F) FOR EACH DRY BULB TEMPERATURE RANGE

Temperature Range	MAY Obsn Hour Gp 01 to 08	MAY 09 to 16	MAY 17 to 24	MAY Total Obsn	MAY MCWB	JUNE Obsn Hour Gp 01 to 08	JUNE 09 to 16	JUNE 17 to 24	JUNE Total Obsn	JUNE MCWB	JULY Obsn Hour Gp 01 to 08	JULY 09 to 16	JULY 17 to 24	JULY Total Obsn	JULY MCWB
100/104												0		0	72
95/99		0		0	79		2		2	78		5	0	5	76
90/94		16	0	16	77		68	3	71	77		126	7	133	77
85/89	0	106	11	117	75	3	126	41	170	76	5	99	57	161	77
80/84	22	96	69	187	74	61	33	115	209	77	71	13	134	218	77
75/79	116	20	118	254	73	133	9	76	218	75	157	4	49	210	75
70/74	70	6	38	114	69	39	2	6	47	71	15	0	1	16	72
65/69	28	2	9	39	65	3		1	4	66					
60/64	10	1	3	14	59	0			0	62					
55/59	2		0	2	53										
50/54	0			0	50										
45/49															

Temperature Range	AUGUST Obsn Hour Gp 01 to 08	AUGUST 09 to 16	AUGUST 17 to 24	AUGUST Total Obsn	AUGUST MCWB	SEPTEMBER Obsn Hour Gp 01 to 08	SEPTEMBER 09 to 16	SEPTEMBER 17 to 24	SEPTEMBER Total Obsn	SEPTEMBER MCWB	OCTOBER Obsn Hour Gp 01 to 08	OCTOBER 09 to 16	OCTOBER 17 to 24	OCTOBER Total Obsn	OCTOBER MCWB
100/104		0		0	76										
95/99		7	0	7	77		3		3	76					
90/94		141	12	153	77		61	3	64	77		10	0	10	77
85/89	5	77	56	138	77	2	107	31	140	76		68	6	74	75
80/84	74	17	144	235	77	44	45	108	197	76	9	98	39	146	73
75/79	152	5	34	191	75	117	19	78	214	74	57	42	88	187	72
70/74	17	1	1	19	71	59	4	17	80	70	72	18	65	155	68
65/69	0			0	68	18	1	3	22	65	55	5	32	92	64
60/64						1			1	61	34	4	12	50	59
55/59											16	2	5	23	54
50/54											5	1	2	8	50
45/49											0			0	44

Temperature Range	NOVEMBER					DECEMBER					JANUARY					FEBRUARY					MARCH					APRIL					ANNUAL TOTAL				
	Obsn Hour Gp 01 to 08	Obsn Hour Gp 09 to 16	Obsn Hour Gp 17 to 24	Total Obsn	M C W B	Obsn Hour Gp 01 to 08	Obsn Hour Gp 09 to 16	Obsn Hour Gp 17 to 24	Total Obsn	M C W B	Obsn Hour Gp 01 to 08	Obsn Hour Gp 09 to 16	Obsn Hour Gp 17 to 24	Total Obsn	M C W B	Obsn Hour Gp 01 to 08	Obsn Hour Gp 09 to 16	Obsn Hour Gp 17 to 24	Total Obsn	M C W B	Obsn Hour Gp 01 to 08	Obsn Hour Gp 09 to 16	Obsn Hour Gp 17 to 24	Total Obsn	M C W B	Obsn Hour Gp 01 to 08	Obsn Hour Gp 09 to 16	Obsn Hour Gp 17 to 24	Total Obsn	M C W B	Obsn Hour Gp 01 to 08	Obsn Hour Gp 09 to 16	Obsn Hour Gp 17 to 24	Total Obsn	M C W B
100/104																																0		[illegible]	[illegible]
95/99																						0		0	67		1		1	73		18	0	18	76
90/94		1		1	72												0	0	0	66		1	0	1	66		6	0	6	74		430	25	455	77
85/89		7	0	7	74		1	0	1	68		1		1	63		2		2	67		9	0	9	70		29	2	31	73	15	632	204	851	76
80/84	0	60	4	64	72		16	1	17	70		13	0	13	70		22	1	23	69		47	3	50	70	1	91	17	109	72	282	551	635	1468	75
75/79	18	57	39	114	70	1	53	8	62	68		56	7	63	68	0	55	11	66	68	4	70	28	102	69	50	67	86	203	71	805	457	622	1884	73
70/74	48	39	60	147	68	19	45	42	106	66	22	48	48	118	66	21	48	47	116	66	63	53	79	195	67	96	27	81	204	69	541	291	485	1317	68
65/69	43	29	52	124	63	46	40	53	139	63	43	37	50	130	63	59	33	57	149	63	72	28	64	164	63	47	11	33	91	64	414	186	354	954	63
60/64	45	18	34	97	58	36	30	38	104	58	42	29	46	117	58	40	25	41	106	58	39	17	32	88	58	25	5	16	46	58	272	129	222	623	58
55/59	33	12	23	68	53	37	23	41	101	53	36	23	34	93	53	36	16	30	82	54	29	12	22	63	53	17	3	6	26	54	206	91	161	458	53
50/54	25	10	15	50	48	45	20	33	98	49	35	18	26	79	49	25	9	16	50	49	20	7	11	38	49	3	0	0	3	49	158	65	103	326	49
45/49	19	6	11	36	44	33	11	19	63	44	29	9	18	56	44	20	5	10	35	45	14	3	6	23	44	1			1	44	116	34	64	214	44
40/44	8	1	3	12	39	22	7	10	39	40	25	7	11	43	40	13	6	7	26	40	6	1	2	9	39						74	22	33	129	40
35/39	2	0	0	2	36	6	1	3	10	34	10	3	4	17	35	7	2	3	12	35	1	0		1	34						26	6	10	42	35
30/34	0			0	32	2	1	0	3	30	2	3	3	8	29	1	0	0	1	29											5	4	3	12	29
25/29						0			0	28	3	2	2	7	25	1	0	0	1	26											4	2	2	8	25
20/24											0			0	18	0	0		0	21											0	0		0	20

CARSWELL AFB/FORT WORTH TEXAS

LAT 32 47N LONG 97 26W ELEV 650 FT

MEAN FREQUENCY OF OCCURRENCE OF DRY BULB TEMPERATURE (DEGREES F) WITH MEAN COINCIDENT WET BULB TEMPERATURE (DEGREES F) FOR EACH DRY BULB TEMPERATURE RANGE

Temperature Range	MAY Obsn Hour Gp 01 to 08	MAY Obsn Hour Gp 09 to 16	MAY Obsn Hour Gp 17 to 24	MAY Total Obsn	MAY MCWB	JUNE Obsn Hour Gp 01 to 08	JUNE Obsn Hour Gp 09 to 16	JUNE Obsn Hour Gp 17 to 24	JUNE Total Obsn	JUNE MCWB	JULY Obsn Hour Gp 01 to 08	JULY Obsn Hour Gp 09 to 16	JULY Obsn Hour Gp 17 to 24	JULY Total Obsn	JULY MCWB
105/109												0	0	0	74
100/104		0		0	75		1	0	1	76		19	8	27	75
95/99		2	1	3	75		21	10	31	75		60	33	93	75
90/94		11	5	16	73		58	33	91	74	0	73	49	122	74
85/89		43	22	65	71	1	69	53	123	73	13	50	66	129	73
80/84	1	61	43	105	69	28	49	64	141	72	81	27	52	160	72
75/79	22	56	59	137	68	93	23	46	162	70	100	12	29	141	71
70/74	70	39	56	165	65	78	13	25	116	68	47	5	10	62	68
65/69	77	22	38	137	62	30	4	6	40	64	6	0	0	6	62
60/64	43	9	17	69	58	8	2	3	13	59	1			1	58
55/59	22	3	7	32	53	2		0	2	54					
50/54	13	0	1	14	49										
45/49	1			1	44										
40/44															
35/39															
30/34															

Temperature Range	AUGUST Obsn Hour Gp 01 to 08	AUGUST Obsn Hour Gp 09 to 16	AUGUST Obsn Hour Gp 17 to 24	AUGUST Total Obsn	AUGUST MCWB	SEPTEMBER Obsn Hour Gp 01 to 08	SEPTEMBER Obsn Hour Gp 09 to 16	SEPTEMBER Obsn Hour Gp 17 to 24	SEPTEMBER Total Obsn	SEPTEMBER MCWB	OCTOBER Obsn Hour Gp 01 to 08	OCTOBER Obsn Hour Gp 09 to 16	OCTOBER Obsn Hour Gp 17 to 24	OCTOBER Total Obsn	OCTOBER MCWB
105/109		1	0	1	76										
100/104		17	7	24	74		1	0	1	74					
95/99		54	26	80	74		16	5	21	74					
90/94	0	68	44	112	73		37	16	53	73		7	1	8	69
85/89	11	53	60	124	72	0	50	33	83	72		18	5	23	69
80/84	65	33	59	157	71	12	50	50	112	70		40	17	57	68
75/79	101	17	39	157	70	65	38	56	159	69	7	45	33	85	66
70/74	59	5	11	75	68	72	28	43	143	66	32	46	50	128	63
65/69	10	0	1	11	63	49	13	26	88	62	44	38	47	129	60
60/64	2	1	1	4	59	27	5	8	40	57	50	28	43	121	56
55/59						11	2	3	16	53	46	16	30	92	51
50/54						2	0	1	3	49	42	6	15	63	47
45/49						1			1	46	20	3	5	28	43
40/44											5	1	1	7	39
35/39											1	0	0	1	34
30/34											0			0	32

CARSWELL AFB/FORT WORTH TEXAS

Temperature Range	NOVEMBER Obsn Hour Gp 01 to 08	09 to 16	17 to 24	Total Obsn	MCWB	DECEMBER Obsn Hour Gp 01 to 08	09 to 16	17 to 24	Total Obsn	MCWB	JANUARY Obsn Hour Gp 01 to 08	09 to 16	17 to 24	Total Obsn	MCWB
105/109															
100/104															
95/99															
90/94															
85/89		1	0	1	66							0		0	58
80/84		8	1	9	65		1		1	62		0	0	0	61
75/79	1	21	8	30	63		4	1	5	62		4	1	5	59
70/74	5	32	18	55	61	0	13	3	16	59		11	3	14	58
65/69	15	34	29	78	58	4	22	13	39	57	3	15	10	28	58
60/64	24	35	37	96	55	13	31	20	64	54	9	20	16	45	54
55/59	33	36	40	109	51	12	33	32	77	49	7	28	22	57	49
50/54	41	29	41	111	46	27	36	41	104	46	23	35	37	95	46
45/49	42	22	31	95	42	41	34	46	121	42	27	32	39	98	42
40/44	40	15	22	77	38	52	33	39	124	38	39	30	37	106	38
35/39	25	5	10	40	33	45	22	29	96	34	42	26	31	99	33
30/34	10	2	4	16	29	29	12	15	56	29	40	21	25	86	29
25/29	3	0	0	3	25	17	4	7	28	25	27	11	13	51	24
20/24	1	0		1	20	6	2	2	10	20	16	8	9	33	20
15/19						1	0		1	15	7	4	4	15	15
10/14						0			0	12	6	2	1	9	11
5/9											0	0		0	8

Temperature Range	FEBRUARY Obsn Hour Gp 01 to 08	09 to 16	17 to 24	Total Obsn	MCWB	MARCH Obsn Hour Gp 01 to 08	09 to 16	17 to 24	Total Obsn	MCWB	APRIL Obsn Hour Gp 01 to 08	09 to 16	17 to 24	Total Obsn	MCWB
105/109															
100/104															
95/99							0	0	0	69		1	0	1	65
90/94							1	0	1	67		1	0	1	69
85/89		1	0	1	60		3	1	4	65		9	4	13	68
80/84		2	1	3	61		8	4	12	64		34	17	51	67
75/79		5	2	7	59		17	9	26	61	2	43	36	81	65
70/74		12	5	17	57	2	26	19	47	59	26	51	51	128	63
65/69	1	18	14	33	55	11	34	32	77	57	49	41	49	139	60
60/64	9	24	20	53	53	24	35	39	98	54	56	30	37	123	56
55/59	15	27	30	72	49	32	33	36	101	50	44	18	25	87	51
50/54	25	33	39	97	45	41	28	39	108	45	31	10	15	56	47
45/49	36	32	38	106	41	48	28	29	105	42	21	2	4	27	42
40/44	46	31	35	112	37	41	19	20	80	38	9	0	1	10	38
35/39	39	19	21	79	33	25	10	13	48	33	2	1	0	3	34
30/34	33	14	15	62	29	15	4	5	24	29	1	0	0	1	32
25/29	15	4	5	24	25	6	1	1	8	25					
20/24	3	1	1	5	21	2	0	0	2	21					
15/19	1	0		1	17	0			0	16					
10/14															
5/9															

Temperature Range	ANNUAL TOTAL Obsn Hour Gp 01 to 08	09 to 16	17 to 24	Total Obsn	MCWB
105/109		1	0	1	75
100/104		38	15	53	75
95/99		154	75	229	74
90/94	0	256	148	404	73
85/89	25	297	244	566	72
80/84	187	313	308	808	70
75/79	391	285	319	995	68
70/74	391	281	294	966	65
65/69	299	241	265	805	60
60/64	266	220	241	727	55
55/59	224	196	225	645	50
50/54	245	177	229	651	46
45/49	237	153	192	582	42
40/44	232	129	155	516	38
35/39	179	83	104	366	33
30/34	128	53	64	245	29
25/29	68	20	26	114	25
20/24	28	11	12	51	20
15/19	9	4	4	17	15
10/14	6	2	1	9	11
5/9	0	0		0	8

CORPUS CHRISTI NAS TEXAS

LAT 27 42N LONG 97 17W ELEV 19 FT

MEAN FREQUENCY OF OCCURRENCE OF DRY BULB TEMPERATURE (DEGREES F) WITH MEAN COINCIDENT WET BULB TEMPERATURE (DEGREES F) FOR EACH DRY BULB TEMPERATURE RANGE

Temperature Range	MAY Obsn Hour Gp 01 to 08	MAY Obsn Hour Gp 09 to 16	MAY Obsn Hour Gp 17 to 24	MAY Total Obsn	MAY MCWB	JUNE Obsn Hour Gp 01 to 08	JUNE Obsn Hour Gp 09 to 16	JUNE Obsn Hour Gp 17 to 24	JUNE Total Obsn	JUNE MCWB	JULY Obsn Hour Gp 01 to 08	JULY Obsn Hour Gp 09 to 16	JULY Obsn Hour Gp 17 to 24	JULY Total Obsn	JULY MCWB
95/99												0		0	79
90/94		1		1	76		21	1	22	80		65	5	70	79
85/89	0	40	4	44	76	5	147	40	192	78	10	154	71	235	78
80/84	16	124	57	197	75	134	60	160	354	76	180	25	164	369	77
75/79	134	63	137	334	73	88	10	36	134	74	57	3	8	68	75
70/74	72	13	38	123	69	10	2	3	15	68	1	0	0	1	69
65/69	16	5	9	30	63	2	0	0	2	64	0			0	61
60/64	10	3	2	15	60										
55/59	0			0	54										
50/54															
45/49															

Temperature Range	AUGUST Obsn Hour Gp 01 to 08	AUGUST Obsn Hour Gp 09 to 16	AUGUST Obsn Hour Gp 17 to 24	AUGUST Total Obsn	AUGUST MCWB	SEPTEMBER Obsn Hour Gp 01 to 08	SEPTEMBER Obsn Hour Gp 09 to 16	SEPTEMBER Obsn Hour Gp 17 to 24	SEPTEMBER Total Obsn	SEPTEMBER MCWB	OCTOBER Obsn Hour Gp 01 to 08	OCTOBER Obsn Hour Gp 09 to 16	OCTOBER Obsn Hour Gp 17 to 24	OCTOBER Total Obsn	OCTOBER MCWB
95/99		2		2	79		0		0	76					
90/94		63	6	69	79		26	1	27	79		1		1	78
85/89	6	142	67	215	78	3	115	31	149	78	0	39	3	42	77
80/84	175	30	161	366	77	110	65	152	327	76	22	85	53	160	74
75/79	62	9	14	85	75	92	23	41	156	73	79	61	91	231	71
70/74	4	1	1	6	70	25	8	11	44	68	63	34	58	155	67
65/69	0			0	62	8	3	3	14	63	44	16	27	87	61
60/64						2	0	0	2	58	27	8	11	46	58
55/59											10	4	4	18	52
50/54											2	1	1	4	49
45/49											1	0	0	1	43

CORPUS CHRISTI NAS TEXAS

Temperature Range	NOVEMBER Obsn Hour Gp 01 to 08	NOVEMBER 09 to 16	NOVEMBER 17 to 24	NOVEMBER Total Obsn	NOVEMBER MCWB	DECEMBER Obsn Hour Gp 01 to 08	DECEMBER 09 to 16	DECEMBER 17 to 24	DECEMBER Total Obsn	DECEMBER MCWB	JANUARY Obsn Hour Gp 01 to 08	JANUARY 09 to 16	JANUARY 17 to 24	JANUARY Total Obsn	JANUARY MCWB
95/99															
90/94															
85/89		2	0	2	71		0		0	74					
80/84		31	2	33	73		2		2	70		0		0	73
75/79	18	57	38	113	71		27	1	28	69		6	1	7	69
70/74	54	44	62	160	68	19	48	37	104	67	1	32	7	40	67
65/69	50	34	50	134	63	41	37	49	127	63	26	35	38	99	64
60/64	38	28	38	104	57	44	43	49	136	58	40	39	52	131	59
55/59	32	22	26	80	52	43	33	44	120	53	35	39	46	120	54
50/54	25	13	16	54	47	45	27	35	107	48	52	42	45	139	48
45/49	15	4	6	25	43	31	19	20	70	43	44	26	32	102	44
40/44	6	3	2	11	38	18	10	11	39	38	27	14	15	56	39
35/39	2	1	1	4	35	6	2	2	10	34	14	8	8	30	34
30/34		0		0	32	2	0	0	2	29	5	4	2	11	29
25/29											2	2	2	6	23
20/24											2	1	0	3	19

Temperature Range	FEBRUARY Obsn Hour Gp 01 to 08	FEBRUARY 09 to 16	FEBRUARY 17 to 24	FEBRUARY Total Obsn	FEBRUARY MCWB	MARCH Obsn Hour Gp 01 to 08	MARCH 09 to 16	MARCH 17 to 24	MARCH Total Obsn	MARCH MCWB	APRIL Obsn Hour Gp 01 to 08	APRIL 09 to 16	APRIL 17 to 24	APRIL Total Obsn	APRIL MCWB	ANNUAL TOTAL Obsn Hour Gp 01 to 08	ANNUAL TOTAL 09 to 16	ANNUAL TOTAL 17 to 24	ANNUAL TOTAL Total Obsn	ANNUAL TOTAL MCWB
95/99																	2		2	79
90/94												0		0	74		177	13	190	79
85/89		0	0	0	66		0	0	0	62		3	0	3	71	24	642	216	882	78
80/84		1	0	1	66		3	0	3	65	0	42	6	48	73	637	468	755	1860	76
75/79		13	1	14	68		30	4	34	68	24	97	49	170	71	554	399	421	1374	72
70/74	2	34	13	49	66	9	73	35	117	67	102	63	113	278	69	362	352	378	1092	68
65/69	33	46	44	123	63	75	60	89	224	63	73	23	50	146	64	368	259	359	986	63
60/64	51	43	58	152	58	67	37	60	164	58	24	9	17	50	57	303	210	287	800	58
55/59	46	34	47	127	53	46	20	33	99	52	12	4	5	21	53	224	156	205	585	53
50/54	40	25	31	96	48	27	14	17	58	47	4	1		5	49	195	123	145	463	48
45/49	26	14	17	57	44	14	8	8	30	43						131	71	83	285	43
40/44	16	9	9	34	39	8	2	2	12	39						75	38	39	152	39
35/39	6	4	3	13	34	1	0	0	1	33						29	15	14	58	34
30/34	3	0	0	3	30											10	4	2	16	29
25/29																2	2	2	6	23
20/24																2	1	0	3	19

DYESS AFB/ABILENE TEXAS

LAT 32 25N LONG 99 51W ELEV 1789 FT

MEAN FREQUENCY OF OCCURRENCE OF DRY BULB TEMPERATURE (DEGREES F) WITH MEAN COINCIDENT WET BULB TEMPERATURE (DEGREES F) FOR EACH DRY BULB TEMPERATURE RANGE

Temperature Range	MAY Obsn Hour Gp 01 to 08	MAY 09 to 16	MAY 17 to 24	MAY Total Obsn	MAY MCWB	JUNE Obsn Hour Gp 01 to 08	JUNE 09 to 16	JUNE 17 to 24	JUNE Total Obsn	JUNE MCWB	JULY Obsn Hour Gp 01 to 08	JULY 09 to 16	JULY 17 to 24	JULY Total Obsn	JULY MCWB
105/109		0	0	0	64		0	0	0	70		0		0	71
100/104		0	0	0	64		4	2	6	72		9	5	14	71
95/99		4	2	6	67		15	9	24	72		49	31	80	71
90/94		18	8	26	67		42	27	69	71		66	43	109	71
85/89	0	36	21	57	67	1	60	43	104	70	4	59	56	119	70
80/84	1	50	38	89	66	14	56	57	127	69	54	38	55	147	68
75/79	17	50	51	118	65	68	35	52	155	68	105	15	35	155	68
70/74	57	41	47	145	63	84	17	30	131	65	63	8	20	91	67
65/69	66	26	38	130	60	49	8	13	70	63	19	2	3	24	64
60/64	55	13	26	94	57	20	3	5	28	59	2	0	0	2	58
55/59	30	7	10	47	52	3	1	1	5	54	0			0	51
50/54	11	2	4	17	48	1		0	1	49					
45/49	7	1	1	9	44										
40/44	3		0	3	39										
35/39	0			0	30										
30/34															

Temperature Range	AUGUST Obsn Hour Gp 01 to 08	AUGUST 09 to 16	AUGUST 17 to 24	AUGUST Total Obsn	AUGUST MCWB	SEPTEMBER Obsn Hour Gp 01 to 08	SEPTEMBER 09 to 16	SEPTEMBER 17 to 24	SEPTEMBER Total Obsn	SEPTEMBER MCWB	OCTOBER Obsn Hour Gp 01 to 08	OCTOBER 09 to 16	OCTOBER 17 to 24	OCTOBER Total Obsn	OCTOBER MCWB
105/109		0	0	0	72										
100/104		8	3	11	71		1	0	1	71					
95/99		43	23	66	71		9	4	13	70		1	0	1	66
90/94	0	64	36	100	70		28	13	41	70		5	1	6	67
85/89	3	57	47	107	69	0	46	24	70	69		16	6	22	65
80/84	42	41	57	140	68	6	48	40	94	67		33	13	46	65
75/79	89	22	48	159	67	42	43	48	133	66	2	43	28	73	63
70/74	76	9	27	112	66	71	30	49	150	65	27	47	44	118	61
65/69	30	2	5	37	62	53	19	34	106	62	42	37	44	123	58
60/64	6	1	1	8	58	34	9	18	61	57	44	29	38	111	55
55/59	2	0	0	2	55	23	4	8	35	53	41	19	35	95	51
50/54	0			0	51	9	2	2	13	48	45	11	21	77	47
45/49						1	0	0	1	44	26	5	12	43	43
40/44						1			1	39	16	3	5	24	38
35/39											4	0	1	5	35
30/34											1			1	30

DYESS AFB/ABILENE TEXAS

Temperature Range	NOVEMBER Obsn Hour Gp 01 to 08	NOVEMBER 09 to 16	NOVEMBER 17 to 24	NOVEMBER Total Obsn	NOVEMBER MCWB	DECEMBER Obsn Hour Gp 01 to 08	DECEMBER 09 to 16	DECEMBER 17 to 24	DECEMBER Total Obsn	DECEMBER MCWB	JANUARY Obsn Hour Gp 01 to 08	JANUARY 09 to 16	JANUARY 17 to 24	JANUARY Total Obsn	JANUARY MCWB
105/109															
100/104															
95/99															
90/94															
85/89		1		1	61		0		0	55		0		0	57
80/84		6	1	7	61		1	0	1	57		1	0	1	56
75/79		20	5	25	60		3	0	3	56		5	1	6	55
70/74	2	28	14	44	58		13	3	16	54		12	4	16	53
65/69	8	30	28	66	56	1	22	9	32	53	0	16	10	26	52
60/64	29	35	35	99	53	9	31	21	61	51	6	23	18	47	50
55/59	29	31	35	95	49	16	35	29	80	48	13	27	24	64	47
50/54	36	32	36	104	45	29	33	36	98	44	21	30	32	83	44
45/49	44	27	36	107	42	33	31	40	104	40	26	34	35	95	40
40/44	39	16	27	82	37	36	26	35	97	37	38	29	33	100	36
35/39	29	10	16	55	34	54	24	32	110	33	37	23	31	91	33
30/34	15	4	6	25.	29	37	16	25	78	29	39	17	25	81	29
25/29	7	1	2	10	24	19	8	12	39	25	30	15	15	60	24
20/24	1	0	0	1	20	10	3	3	16	20	17	8	8	33	20
15/19	0			0	15	6	1	1	8	16	11	5	7	23	15
10/14						1	0	0	1	12	7	3	3	13	11
5/9						0			0	8	4	1	1	6	6
0/4											0			0	4

Temperature Range	FEBRUARY Obsn Hour Gp 01 to 08	FEBRUARY 09 to 16	FEBRUARY 17 to 24	FEBRUARY Total Obsn	FEBRUARY MCWB	MARCH Obsn Hour Gp 01 to 08	MARCH 09 to 16	MARCH 17 to 24	MARCH Total Obsn	MARCH MCWB	APRIL Obsn Hour Gp 01 to 08	APRIL 09 to 16	APRIL 17 to 24	APRIL Total Obsn	APRIL MCWB	ANNUAL TOTAL Obsn Hour Gp 01 to 08	ANNUAL TOTAL 09 to 16	ANNUAL TOTAL 17 to 24	ANNUAL TOTAL Total Obsn	ANNUAL TOTAL MCWB
105/109																	0	0	0	69
100/104																	22	10	32	71
95/99							0		0	65		1	1	2	63		122	70	192	71
90/94							2	1	3	62		6	3	9	63	0	231	132	363	70
85/89		0	0	0	62		5	3	8	59		17	9	26	63	8	297	209	514	69
80/84		3	1	4	57		9	4	13	58		28	17	45	62	117	314	283	714	67
75/79		6	3	9	55		14	9	23	57	1	39	29	69	61	324	295	309	928	65
70/74	0	10	5	15	54	2	26	20	48	55	20	42	41	103	59	402	283	304	989	63
65/69	1	19	12	32	52	8	34	28	70	53	45	35	41	121	57	322	250	265	837	58
60/64	7	23	20	50	50	24	33	33	90	51	46	28	36	110	54	282	228	251	761	54
55/59	15	29	27	71	47	32	31	35	98	48	43	19	27	89	50	247	203	231	681	49
50/54	23	30	31	84	44	32	28	33	93	44	36	14	21	71	46	243	182	216	641	45
45/49	28	29	38	95	41	38	24	29	91	41	26	8	10	44	42	229	159	201	589	41
40/44	42	26	32	100	37	38	16	22	76	37	13	2	3	18	37	226	118	157	501	37
35/39	43	20	25	88	33	33	12	17	62	33	7	0	1	8	33	207	89	123	419	33
30/34	29	13	15	57	29	26	10	10	46	29	2	1	1	4	30	149	61	82	292	29
25/29	21	11	10	42	25	9	3	3	15	25	1			1	27	87	38	42	167	25
20/24	12	5	6	23	21	4	1	1	6	20						44	17	18	79	20
15/19	3	1	1	5	16	1	0	0	1	16						21	7	9	37	16
10/14	1		0	1	11	0			0	10						9	3	3	15	11
5/9	0			0	7	0			0	8						4	1	1	6	6
0/4																0			0	4

ELLINGTON AFB/HOUSTON TEXAS

LAT 29 37N LONG 95 10W ELEV 40 FT

MEAN FREQUENCY OF OCCURRENCE OF DRY BULB TEMPERATURE (DEGREES F) WITH MEAN COINCIDENT WET BULB TEMPERATURE (DEGREES F) FOR EACH DRY BULB TEMPERATURE RANGE

Temperature Range	MAY Obsn Hour Gp 01 to 08	MAY 09 to 16	MAY 17 to 24	MAY Total Obsn	MAY MCWB	JUNE Obsn Hour Gp 01 to 08	JUNE 09 to 16	JUNE 17 to 24	JUNE Total Obsn	JUNE MCWB	JULY Obsn Hour Gp 01 to 08	JULY 09 to 16	JULY 17 to 24	JULY Total Obsn	JULY MCWB
100/104												0		0	80
95/99		0		0	78		4	0	4	78		16	2	18	79
90/94		4	1	5	76		56	7	63	77		87	19	106	78
85/89		52	6	58	74	4	103	36	143	76	5	93	44	142	77
80/84	4	103	32	139	72	28	48	64	140	75	39	34	80	153	76
75/79	50	57	82	189	71	100	19	92	211	73	148	13	89	250	74
70/74	95	21	79	195	69	83	9	34	126	70	51	4	13	68	70
65/69	55	9	33	97	64	21	1	5	27	65	4	0	1	5	65
60/64	27	2	13	42	59	3	0	1	4	59	1			1	59
55/59	15	1	2	18	54	1			1	54					
50/54	3		0	3	50										
45/49	0			0	48										
40/44															
35/39															

Temperature Range	AUGUST Obsn Hour Gp 01 to 08	AUGUST 09 to 16	AUGUST 17 to 24	AUGUST Total Obsn	AUGUST MCWB	SEPTEMBER Obsn Hour Gp 01 to 08	SEPTEMBER 09 to 16	SEPTEMBER 17 to 24	SEPTEMBER Total Obsn	SEPTEMBER MCWB	OCTOBER Obsn Hour Gp 01 to 08	OCTOBER 09 to 16	OCTOBER 17 to 24	OCTOBER Total Obsn	OCTOBER MCWB
100/104		1	0	1	77		0		0	77					
95/99		15	2	17	78		2	0	2	77		0		0	78
90/94		81	16	97	78		29	2	31	77		2		2	77
85/89	3	90	38	131	77	0	89	20	109	76		34	2	36	74
80/84	33	41	81	155	76	14	67	54	135	75	1	65	13	79	72
75/79	152	17	95	264	74	92	35	94	221	73	17	65	43	125	69
70/74	55	3	14	72	71	79	14	50	143	70	47	39	68	154	67
65/69	5	1	1	7	65	35	4	16	55	64	58	25	51	134	63
60/64	1		0	1	59	14	1	3	18	59	48	12	36	96	58
55/59	0			0	55	5	0	1	6	56	36	5	22	63	53
50/54						0		0	0	49	26	2	10	38	49
45/49						0			0	45	11	0	2	13	45
40/44											2		0	2	40
35/39											1			1	37

ELLINGTON AFB/HOUSTON TEXAS

Temperature Range	NOVEMBER Obsn Hour Gp 01 to 08	09 to 16	17 to 24	Total Obsn	MCWB	DECEMBER Obsn Hour Gp 01 to 08	09 to 16	17 to 24	Total Obsn	MCWB	JANUARY Obsn Hour Gp 01 to 08	09 to 16	17 to 24	Total Obsn	MCWB
100/104															
95/99															
90/94															
85/89		2		2	71										
80/84		20	1	21	71		1		1	69		2	0	2	70
75/79	4	48	10	62	69		19	1	20	68		12	1	13	68
70/74	19	45	32	96	66	6	33	14	53	66	2	28	10	40	65
65/69	38	40	47	125	63	21	38	28	87	63	21	28	26	75	63
60/64	37	30	42	109	58	31	41	40	112	58	24	32	28	84	58
55/59	32	24	35	91	53	33	38	43	114	53	26	34	36	96	53
50/54	36	18	35	89	48	35	32	42	109	48	29	36	43	108	48
45/49	35	8	22	65	44	42	25	41	108	44	33	28	37	98	43
40/44	22	4	10	36	39	36	13	23	72	39	42	24	32	98	39
35/39	10	1	4	15	34	26	6	12	44	35	33	14	23	70	34
30/34	5	0	0	5	30	13	2	4	19	30	24	6	9	39	29
25/29	0			0	26	4	0	1	5	25	10	3	3	16	25
20/24						1	0		1	21	3	1	2	6	20
15/19											2	0	0	2	15

Temperature Range	FEBRUARY Obsn Hour Gp 01 to 08	09 to 16	17 to 24	Total Obsn	MCWB	MARCH Obsn Hour Gp 01 to 08	09 to 16	17 to 24	Total Obsn	MCWB	APRIL Obsn Hour Gp 01 to 08	09 to 16	17 to 24	Total Obsn	MCWB	ANNUAL TOTAL Obsn Hour Gp 01 to 08	09 to 16	17 to 24	Total Obsn	MCWB
100/104																	1	0	1	77
95/99																	37	4	41	78
90/94												0		0	74		259	45	304	78
85/89		0		0	66		0		0	70		4	0	4	73	12	467	146	625	76
80/84		3	0	3	69		7	1	8	67		50	6	56	71	119	441	332	892	74
75/79		10	1	11	67		30	6	36	66	10	82	36	128	70	573	407	550	1530	72
70/74	2	26	10	38	65	8	54	25	87	65	72	53	82	207	68	519	329	431	1279	68
65/69	19	34	24	77	62	34	52	50	136	62	53	31	55	139	63	364	263	337	964	63
60/64	19	35	30	84	57	44	42	55	141	57	41	14	35	90	58	290	209	283	782	58
55/59	27	38	40	105	53	45	27	44	116	52	35	5	18	58	53	255	172	241	668	53
50/54	41	34	44	119	48	41	17	32	90	47	17	1	6	24	48	228	140	212	580	48
45/49	39	21	37	97	43	34	11	23	68	43	10		1	11	44	204	93	163	460	43
40/44	37	14	22	73	39	24	5	9	38	39	2			2	38	165	60	96	321	39
35/39	22	6	11	39	35	13	1	3	17	34	0			0	37	105	28	53	186	34
30/34	14	2	4	20	30	4	0	0	4	30						60	10	17	87	30
25/29	4	0	0	4	26	0			0	26						18	3	4	25	25
20/24																4	1	2	7	20
15/19																2	0	0	2	15

FORT BLISS/BIGGS AAF TEXAS

LAT 31 51N LONG 106 23W ELEV 3947 FT

MEAN FREQUENCY OF OCCURRENCE OF DRY BULB TEMPERATURE (DEGREES F) WITH MEAN COINCIDENT WET BULB TEMPERATURE (DEGREES F) FOR EACH DRY BULB TEMPERATURE RANGE

Temperature Range	MAY Obsn Hour Gp 01 to 08	MAY 09 to 16	MAY 17 to 24	MAY Total Obsn	MAY MCWB	JUNE Obsn Hour Gp 01 to 08	JUNE 09 to 16	JUNE 17 to 24	JUNE Total Obsn	JUNE MCWB	JULY Obsn Hour Gp 01 to 08	JULY 09 to 16	JULY 17 to 24	JULY Total Obsn	JULY MCWB
105/109		0		0	63		1	0	1	64		0	0	0	68
100/104		1	0	1	62		12	4	16	64		9	3	12	66
95/99		4	1	5	61		40	19	59	63		39	16	55	66
90/94		26	11	37	59	1	67	44	112	61	0	66	40	106	65
85/89	1	52	29	82	57	9	60	54	123	60	5	65	54	124	65
80/84	3	62	47	112	55	29	38	51	118	59	32	40	59	131	64
75/79	18	49	55	122	53	66	16	40	122	58	84	18	46	148	63
70/74	45	30	46	121	52	68	5	18	91	57	91	7	24	122	63
65/69	60	15	29	104	50	43	1	7	51	54	33	3	6	42	63
60/64	59	8	18	85	48	20	0	2	22	50	3	0	1	4	60
55/59	37	2	8	47	45	4		0	4	46					
50/54	17	0	2	19	41	1			1	40					
45/49	6		1	7	37										
40/44	2		0	2	35										
35/39	0			0	29										
30/34															

Temperature Range	AUGUST Obsn Hour Gp 01 to 08	AUGUST 09 to 16	AUGUST 17 to 24	AUGUST Total Obsn	AUGUST MCWB	SEPTEMBER Obsn Hour Gp 01 to 08	SEPTEMBER 09 to 16	SEPTEMBER 17 to 24	SEPTEMBER Total Obsn	SEPTEMBER MCWB	OCTOBER Obsn Hour Gp 01 to 08	OCTOBER 09 to 16	OCTOBER 17 to 24	OCTOBER Total Obsn	OCTOBER MCWB
105/109															
100/104		1	0	1	69										
95/99		25	8	33	66		6	1	7	64					
90/94		68	32	100	65		38	9	47	63		1	0	1	62
85/89	1	73	53	127	65	0	57	26	83	62		16	2	18	60
80/84	16	51	68	135	64	3	59	48	110	61		47	13	60	58
75/79	73	24	59	156	63	19	45	64	128	60	2	54	30	86	56
70/74	108	5	22	135	62	68	24	54	146	59	9	53	45	107	55
65/69	48	1	5	54	61	83	9	28	120	57	27	38	54	119	53
60/64	3	0	0	3	60	50	2	7	59	54	47	24	51	122	51
55/59						13	1	2	16	51	66	10	34	110	48
50/54						3	0	0	3	46	56	3	12	71	44
45/49						0			0	43	29	1	5	35	40
40/44											11	1	1	13	37
35/39											1			1	33
30/34											0			0	28

FORT BLISS/BIGGS AAF TEXAS

Temperature Range	NOVEMBER Obsn Hour Gp 01 to 08	NOVEMBER Obsn Hour Gp 09 to 16	NOVEMBER Obsn Hour Gp 17 to 24	NOVEMBER Total Obsn	NOVEMBER MCWB	DECEMBER Obsn Hour Gp 01 to 08	DECEMBER Obsn Hour Gp 09 to 16	DECEMBER Obsn Hour Gp 17 to 24	DECEMBER Total Obsn	DECEMBER MCWB	JANUARY Obsn Hour Gp 01 to 08	JANUARY Obsn Hour Gp 09 to 16	JANUARY Obsn Hour Gp 17 to 24	JANUARY Total Obsn	JANUARY MCWB	FEBRUARY Obsn Hour Gp 01 to 08	FEBRUARY Obsn Hour Gp 09 to 16	FEBRUARY Obsn Hour Gp 17 to 24	FEBRUARY Total Obsn	FEBRUARY MCWB
105/109																				
100/104																				
95/99																				
90/94																				
85/89																				
80/84		1		1	56												0		0	55
75/79		6	1	7	54		0		0	52		0		0	59		3	1	4	53
70/74	0	33	7	40	51		6	1	7	51		3	1	4	51		13	5	18	49
65/69	2	44	22	68	49	0	14	5	19	48		15	6	21	48	0	25	14	39	47
60/64	8	45	35	88	47	3	35	16	54	46	2	34	20	56	46	4	35	28	67	45
55/59	20	38	41	99	45	7	44	28	79	44	7	41	29	77	43	14	38	33	85	43
50/54	31	31	45	107	42	14	46	38	98	41	16	48	40	104	41	21	40	40	101	40
45/49	45	23	41	109	39	23	42	49	114	38	28	41	44	113	38	35	28	38	101	37
40/44	53	13	29	95	36	38	29	47	114	35	38	31	44	113	35	39	19	29	87	34
35/39	45	5	14	64	32	54	18	37	109	32	48	20	35	103	31	42	12	19	73	31
30/34	24	2	4	30	28	58	10	22	90	28	49	8	18	75	28	35	5	10	50	27
25/29	11	0	2	13	24	34	2	7	43	24	34	3	6	43	24	19	3	5	27	23
20/24	2	0	0	2	20	12	1	1	14	20	17	1	3	21	19	9	1	2	12	20
15/19	0			0	16	3	0	0	3	16	5	1	2	8	14	4	1	1	6	16
10/14						1			1	11	3	1	0	4	10	1	0	0	1	12
5/9						0			0	6	0	0	1	1	6	0			0	9
0/4											1	0	0	1	0					
-5/-1											0	0		0	-4					
-10/-6											0			0	-8					

Temperature Range	MARCH Obsn Hour Gp 01 to 08	MARCH Obsn Hour Gp 09 to 16	MARCH Obsn Hour Gp 17 to 24	MARCH Total Obsn	MARCH MCWB	APRIL Obsn Hour Gp 01 to 08	APRIL Obsn Hour Gp 09 to 16	APRIL Obsn Hour Gp 17 to 24	APRIL Total Obsn	APRIL MCWB	ANNUAL TOTAL Obsn Hour Gp 01 to 08	ANNUAL TOTAL Obsn Hour Gp 09 to 16	ANNUAL TOTAL Obsn Hour Gp 17 to 24	ANNUAL TOTAL Total Obsn	ANNUAL TOTAL MCWB
105/109												1	0	1	65
100/104												23	7	30	65
95/99							0	0	0	59		114	45	159	65
90/94							1	0	1	57	1	267	136	404	63
85/89						0	9	4	13	55	16	332	222	570	62
80/84		4	1	5	53		33	15	48	53	83	335	302	720	60
75/79		20	8	28	51	1	55	39	95	51	263	290	343	896	58
70/74	1	39	23	63	49	10	53	50	113	49	400	271	296	967	56
65/69	6	42	40	88	47	32	39	48	119	48	334	246	264	844	52
60/64	21	43	45	109	45	44	27	38	109	46	264	253	261	778	48
55/59	36	40	41	117	43	57	14	26	97	43	261	228	242	731	44
50/54	41	27	36	104	40	46	6	12	64	41	246	201	225	672	41
45/49	49	19	26	94	38	33	2	6	41	38	248	156	210	614	38
40/44	38	9	16	63	34	13	1	1	15	34	232	103	167	502	35
35/39	30	4	9	43	31	3	0		3	31	223	59	114	396	31
30/34	17	1	2	20	27	0			0	27	183	26	56	265	28
25/29	7	1	1	9	23						105	9	21	135	24
20/24	1		0	1	21						41	3	6	50	20
15/19	0		0	0	15						12	2	3	17	15
10/14	0			0	13						5	1	0	6	11
5/9											0	0	1	1	7
0/4											1	0	0	1	0
-5/-1											0	0		0	-4
-10/-6											0			0	-8

FORT HOOD/ROBERT GRAY AAF TEXAS

LAT 31 04N LONG 97 50W ELEV 1015 FT

MEAN FREQUENCY OF OCCURRENCE OF DRY BULB TEMPERATURE (DEGREES F) WITH MEAN COINCIDENT WET BULB TEMPERATURE (DEGREES F) FOR EACH DRY BULB TEMPERATURE RANGE

Temperature Range	MAY Obsn Hour Gp 01 to 08	MAY Obsn Hour Gp 09 to 16	MAY Obsn Hour Gp 17 to 24	MAY Total Obsn	MAY MCWB	JUNE Obsn Hour Gp 01 to 08	JUNE Obsn Hour Gp 09 to 16	JUNE Obsn Hour Gp 17 to 24	JUNE Total Obsn	JUNE MCWB	JULY Obsn Hour Gp 01 to 08	JULY Obsn Hour Gp 09 to 16	JULY Obsn Hour Gp 17 to 24	JULY Total Obsn	JULY MCWB
105/109												0		0	74
100/104							0	0	0	73		4	2	6	73
95/99		1	0	1	76		9	4	13	73		40	23	63	73
90/94		8	4	12	74		51	25	76	73		76	46	122	73
85/89		37	19	56	71	0	74	45	119	72	2	72	60	134	73
80/84	1	58	39	98	69	12	61	63	136	71	34	43	64	141	72
75/79	14	64	59	137	68	80	27	56	163	70	130	11	40	181	71
70/74	74	44	64	182	67	104	12	32	148	69	72	2	12	86	69
65/69	81	24	37	142	63	35	4	11	50	64	9	1	1	11	65
60/64	47	9	20	76	59	7	2	2	11	60	1			1	58
55/59	23	3	6	32	54	2	0	1	3	55					
50/54	7	1		8	50	1			1	50					
45/49	1			1	45										
40/44															
35/39															

Temperature Range	AUGUST Obsn Hour Gp 01 to 08	AUGUST Obsn Hour Gp 09 to 16	AUGUST Obsn Hour Gp 17 to 24	AUGUST Total Obsn	AUGUST MCWB	SEPTEMBER Obsn Hour Gp 01 to 08	SEPTEMBER Obsn Hour Gp 09 to 16	SEPTEMBER Obsn Hour Gp 17 to 24	SEPTEMBER Total Obsn	SEPTEMBER MCWB	OCTOBER Obsn Hour Gp 01 to 08	OCTOBER Obsn Hour Gp 09 to 16	OCTOBER Obsn Hour Gp 17 to 24	OCTOBER Total Obsn	OCTOBER MCWB
105/109		1	1	2	73										
100/104		12	6	18	73		1	0	1	73					
95/99		38	20	58	73		9	3	12	74					
90/94	0	77	43	120	73		34	14	48	74		5	1	6	67
85/89	3	59	56	118	72		54	28	82	72		21	7	28	69
80/84	41	40	62	143	72	8	56	53	117	71	0	44	18	62	67
75/79	109	14	42	165	71	56	45	57	158	70	10	56	38	104	66
70/74	84	7	18	109	69	86	26	54	166	67	32	48	59	139	64
65/69	10	0	2	12	63	54	11	23	88	62	48	37	47	132	60
60/64	1			1	59	24	3	6	33	58	50	22	42	114	56
55/59						9	0	2	11	53	54	8	23	85	51
50/54						2		0	2	46	35	4	10	49	47
45/49						1			1	44	15	3	5	23	43
40/44											4	0	0	4	40
35/39											0			0	35

FORT HOOD/ROBERT GRAY AAF TEXAS

Temperature Range	NOVEMBER Obsn Hour Gp 01 to 08	NOVEMBER 09 to 16	NOVEMBER 17 to 24	NOVEMBER Total Obsn	NOVEMBER MCWB	DECEMBER Obsn Hour Gp 01 to 08	DECEMBER 09 to 16	DECEMBER 17 to 24	DECEMBER Total Obsn	DECEMBER MCWB	JANUARY Obsn Hour Gp 01 to 08	JANUARY 09 to 16	JANUARY 17 to 24	JANUARY Total Obsn	JANUARY MCWB
105/109															
100/104															
95/99															
90/94															
85/89		2	0	2	63							0		0	61
80/84		10	2	12	63		1		1	62		1	0	1	59
75/79		26	7	33	64		4	0	4	60		5	1	6	60
70/74	4	37	23	64	62	1	19	6	26	61	0	12	6	18	60
65/69	25	36	38	99	60	9	27	14	50	59	8	22	15	45	58
60/64	35	42	45	122	56	15	30	25	70	55	12	25	24	61	55
55/59	38	33	42	113	51	14	33	33	80	50	16	30	30	76	50
50/54	42	22	33	97	47	28	39	44	111	46	27	38	37	102	46
45/49	37	18	29	84	42	43	34	42	119	42	31	33	40	104	42
40/44	37	12	16	65	38	50	26	36	112	38	35	25	31	91	38
35/39	15	2	5	22	34	43	19	24	86	34	42	24	27	93	33
30/34	7	0	1	8	29	25	12	15	52	29	35	14	18	67	29
25/29	0			0	25	15	4	7	26	25	18	10	10	38	24
20/24						6	1	1	8	21	12	5	5	22	20
15/19						1			1	17	8	4	4	16	15
10/14											3	1	1	5	12

Temperature Range	FEBRUARY Obsn Hour Gp 01 to 08	FEBRUARY 09 to 16	FEBRUARY 17 to 24	FEBRUARY Total Obsn	FEBRUARY MCWB	MARCH Obsn Hour Gp 01 to 08	MARCH 09 to 16	MARCH 17 to 24	MARCH Total Obsn	MARCH MCWB	APRIL Obsn Hour Gp 01 to 08	APRIL 09 to 16	APRIL 17 to 24	APRIL Total Obsn	APRIL MCWB
105/109															
100/104															
95/99												1	0	1	66
90/94							1	1	2	67		3	1	4	69
85/89		1	0	1	61		3	1	4	65		9	3	12	70
80/84		2	1	3	61		9	4	13	64		38	17	55	67
75/79		6	2	8	61		20	13	33	62	1	55	39	95	66
70/74	0	14	8	22	57	2	40	27	69	60	32	53	62	147	64
65/69	5	22	16	43	56	27	44	42	113	58	68	38	53	159	62
60/64	10	29	25	64	53	35	37	46	118	55	54	23	34	111	56
55/59	14	30	29	73	49	35	28	35	98	50	37	14	19	70	52
50/54	29	31	41	101	45	41	28	30	99	46	26	5	9	40	47
45/49	39	33	38	110	42	41	18	24	83	42	16	1	2	19	43
40/44	47	31	33	111	38	26	11	14	51	37	4		0	4	37
35/39	40	13	17	70	33	24	6	9	39	33	1			1	36
30/34	25	9	9	43	29	12	2	3	17	29					
25/29	11	3	4	18	25	3	1	1	5	24					
20/24	3	0	1	4	21	2			2	20					
15/19	1			1	17										
10/14															

Temperature Range	ANNUAL TOTAL Obsn Hour Gp 01 to 08	ANNUAL TOTAL 09 to 16	ANNUAL TOTAL 17 to 24	ANNUAL TOTAL Total Obsn	ANNUAL TOTAL MCWB
105/109		1	1	2	73
100/104		17	8	25	73
95/99		98	50	148	73
90/94	0	255	135	390	73
85/89	5	332	219	556	72
80/84	96	363	323	782	70
75/79	400	333	354	1087	69
70/74	491	314	371	1176	66
65/69	379	266	299	944	61
60/64	291	222	269	782	56
55/59	242	179	220	641	51
50/54	238	168	204	610	46
45/49	224	140	180	544	42
40/44	203	105	130	438	38
35/39	165	64	82	311	33
30/34	104	37	46	187	29
25/29	47	18	22	87	24
20/24	23	6	7	36	20
15/19	10	4	4	18	15
10/14	3	1	1	5	12

KELLY AFB/SAN ANTONIO TEXAS

LAT 29 23N LONG 98 35W ELEV 690 FT

MEAN FREQUENCY OF OCCURRENCE OF DRY BULB TEMPERATURE (DEGREES F) WITH MEAN COINCIDENT WET BULB TEMPERATURE (DEGREES F) FOR EACH DRY BULB TEMPERATURE RANGE

Temperature Range	MAY Obsn Hour Gp 01 to 08	MAY 09 to 16	MAY 17 to 24	MAY Total Obsn	MAY MCWB	JUNE Obsn Hour Gp 01 to 08	JUNE 09 to 16	JUNE 17 to 24	JUNE Total Obsn	JUNE MCWB	JULY Obsn Hour Gp 01 to 08	JULY 09 to 16	JULY 17 to 24	JULY Total Obsn	JULY MCWB
105/109												0		0	74
100/104		0	0	0	74		1	1	2	73		5	2	7	74
95/99		2	1	3	73		18	9	27	75		47	31	78	74
90/94		20	9	29	73		58	32	90	74		74	45	119	74
85/89		50	27	77	72		72	47	119	74	0	63	55	118	74
80/84	0	68	48	116	71	13	57	65	135	73	24	47	70	141	73
75/79	40	60	73	173	70	120	26	61	207	72	168	10	37	215	73
70/74	100	30	56	186	68	84	6	20	110	69	54	2	6	62	70
65/69	60	13	24	97	63	17	1	4	22	64	2		0	2	64
60/64	29	4	7	40	58	5	0	1	6	60	0			0	56
55/59	12	0	3	15	53	1			1	55					
50/54	5		0	5	48										
45/49	2			2	46										
40/44															
35/39															

Temperature Range	AUGUST Obsn Hour Gp 01 to 08	AUGUST 09 to 16	AUGUST 17 to 24	AUGUST Total Obsn	AUGUST MCWB	SEPTEMBER Obsn Hour Gp 01 to 08	SEPTEMBER 09 to 16	SEPTEMBER 17 to 24	SEPTEMBER Total Obsn	SEPTEMBER MCWB	OCTOBER Obsn Hour Gp 01 to 08	OCTOBER 09 to 16	OCTOBER 17 to 24	OCTOBER Total Obsn	OCTOBER MCWB
105/109		0		0	74										
100/104		7	4	11	74		0	0	0	76					
95/99		44	29	73	74		9	4	13	74		0	0	0	75
90/94		71	41	112	74		40	16	56	74		6	2	8	73
85/89	0	62	54	116	73		61	36	97	73		21	8	29	71
80/84	30	47	69	146	73	5	63	57	125	72	0	52	23	75	69
75/79	157	12	40	209	72	96	41	73	210	72	17	60	50	127	68
70/74	50	4	10	64	69	77	15	32	124	68	43	49	59	151	65
65/69	9	1	0	10	63	31	7	14	52	63	53	31	46	130	62
60/64	2			2	57	22	3	7	32	58	48	16	31	95	57
55/59						8		1	9	54	37	9	17	63	52
50/54						1		0	1	48	29	3	9	41	49
45/49											14	0	2	16	44
40/44											5		0	5	39
35/39											1			1	36

KELLY AFB/SAN ANTONIO TEXAS

Temperature Range	NOVEMBER Obsn Hour Gp 01 to 08	NOVEMBER Obsn Hour Gp 09 to 16	NOVEMBER Obsn Hour Gp 17 to 24	NOVEMBER Total Obsn	NOVEMBER MCWB	DECEMBER Obsn Hour Gp 01 to 08	DECEMBER Obsn Hour Gp 09 to 16	DECEMBER Obsn Hour Gp 17 to 24	DECEMBER Total Obsn	DECEMBER MCWB	JANUARY Obsn Hour Gp 01 to 08	JANUARY Obsn Hour Gp 09 to 16	JANUARY Obsn Hour Gp 17 to 24	JANUARY Total Obsn	JANUARY MCWB
105/109															
100/104															
95/99															
90/94		0		0	62										
85/89		1	0	1	67							1	0	1	60
80/84		13	3	16	67		1	0	1	65		1	0	1	63
75/79	1	34	13	48	66		9	2	11	64		6	2	8	62
70/74	11	46	32	89	64	1	27	11	39	62	0	16	8	24	61
65/69	31	41	43	115	61	18	38	29	85	61	13	28	21	62	60
60/64	38	37	43	118	56	21	39	34	94	56	14	35	28	77	56
55/59	34	28	39	101	51	24	39	39	102	51	20	35	33	88	51
50/54	37	20	29	86	47	34	36	44	114	47	28	37	45	110	47
45/49	34	12	22	68	43	41	27	40	108	43	33	31	37	101	42
40/44	27	6	11	44	39	38	20	30	88	38	45	28	32	105	38
35/39	15	1	3	19	34	41	10	14	65	34	38	16	24	78	34
30/34	8	1	2	11	30	20	3	4	27	29	32	9	11	52	29
25/29	2		0	2	26	9	0	0	9	25	16	3	4	23	24
20/24	0			0	21	1			1	21	7	2	2	11	19
15/19											2	0	0	2	15
10/14											1			1	10

Temperature Range	FEBRUARY Obsn Hour Gp 01 to 08	FEBRUARY Obsn Hour Gp 09 to 16	FEBRUARY Obsn Hour Gp 17 to 24	FEBRUARY Total Obsn	FEBRUARY MCWB	MARCH Obsn Hour Gp 01 to 08	MARCH Obsn Hour Gp 09 to 16	MARCH Obsn Hour Gp 17 to 24	MARCH Total Obsn	MARCH MCWB	APRIL Obsn Hour Gp 01 to 08	APRIL Obsn Hour Gp 09 to 16	APRIL Obsn Hour Gp 17 to 24	APRIL Total Obsn	APRIL MCWB	ANNUAL TOTAL Obsn Hour Gp 01 to 08	ANNUAL TOTAL Obsn Hour Gp 09 to 16	ANNUAL TOTAL Obsn Hour Gp 17 to 24	ANNUAL TOTAL Total Obsn	ANNUAL TOTAL MCWB
105/109																	0		0	74
100/104							0	0	0	68							13	7	20	74
95/99							0	0	0	64		1	0	1	74		121	74	195	74
90/94		0		0	64		2	1	3	66		4	2	6	70		275	148	423	74
85/89		1	1	2	65		4	2	6	65		18	9	27	70	0	354	239	593	73
80/84		4	2	6	64		12	6	18	64		43	24	67	69	72	408	367	847	72
75/79		10	5	15	62		28	16	44	62	5	57	46	108	67	604	353	418	1375	70
70/74	1	19	12	32	60	3	37	32	72	62	53	53	62	168	66	477	304	340	1121	66
65/69	12	29	24	65	58	30	52	51	133	60	63	35	47	145	62	339	276	303	918	61
60/64	17	35	30	82	55	40	41	46	127	56	43	18	26	87	57	279	228	253	760	56
55/59	24	37	38	99	51	41	28	35	104	51	31	9	14	54	52	232	185	219	636	51
50/54	36	35	42	113	47	40	22	27	89	46	24	3	8	35	48	234	156	204	594	47
45/49	43	25	33	101	43	39	13	19	71	42	12	0	2	14	43	218	108	155	481	43
40/44	38	18	21	77	39	29	7	10	46	38	6	0	0	6	39	188	79	104	371	38
35/39	29	9	11	49	34	18	2	3	23	33	2			2	33	144	38	55	237	34
30/34	16	4	4	24	30	6	0	1	7	29	0			0	30	82	17	22	121	29
25/29	9	0	1	10	26	2	0		2	25						38	3	5	46	25
20/24	0			0	21											8	2	2	12	20
15/19																2	0	0	2	15
10/14																1			1	10

LAUGHLIN AFB TEXAS

LAT 29 22N LONG 100 47W ELEV 1081 FT

MEAN FREQUENCY OF OCCURRENCE OF DRY BULB TEMPERATURE (DEGREES F) WITH MEAN COINCIDENT WET BULB TEMPERATURE (DEGREES F) FOR EACH DRY BULB TEMPERATURE RANGE

Temperature Range	MAY Obsn Hour Gp 01 to 08	MAY 09 to 16	MAY 17 to 24	MAY Total Obsn	MAY MCWB	JUNE Obsn Hour Gp 01 to 08	JUNE 09 to 16	JUNE 17 to 24	JUNE Total Obsn	JUNE MCWB	JULY Obsn Hour Gp 01 to 08	JULY 09 to 16	JULY 17 to 24	JULY Total Obsn	JULY MCWB
105/109							1	0	1	71		1	0	1	72
100/104		1	0	1	69		3	3	6	72		7	6	13	73
95/99		5	6	11	70		27	25	52	72		45	47	92	73
90/94		30	25	55	70		59	57	116	72		64	59	123	73
85/89		52	46	98	70	1	59	61	121	72	6	60	68	134	73
80/84	3	59	62	124	69	35	55	59	149	72	68	54	43	165	72
75/79	45	56	58	159	68	132	28	24	184	71	137	15	19	171	71
70/74	104	31	27	162	66	61	7	9	77	68	36	2	5	43	70
65/69	62	10	17	89	62	10	0	2	12	64	1			1	67
60/64	21	4	5	30	57	1	0	0	1	60					
55/59	10	1	2	13	53	1			1	57					
50/54	2			2	45										
45/49	0			0	42										
40/44															

Temperature Range	AUGUST Obsn Hour Gp 01 to 08	AUGUST 09 to 16	AUGUST 17 to 24	AUGUST Total Obsn	AUGUST MCWB	SEPTEMBER Obsn Hour Gp 01 to 08	SEPTEMBER 09 to 16	SEPTEMBER 17 to 24	SEPTEMBER Total Obsn	SEPTEMBER MCWB	OCTOBER Obsn Hour Gp 01 to 08	OCTOBER 09 to 16	OCTOBER 17 to 24	OCTOBER Total Obsn	OCTOBER MCWB
105/109															
100/104		6	6	12	73		1	1	2	71		0		0	69
95/99		53	46	99	73		18	11	29	72		2	1	3	68
90/94		71	59	130	73		53	36	89	72		10	5	15	71
85/89	9	61	71	141	72	0	65	51	116	71		33	17	50	69
80/84	79	44	43	166	72	22	56	65	143	70	2	55	39	96	68
75/79	121	12	21	154	71	106	33	45	184	70	23	55	52	130	67
70/74	37	1	3	41	68	71	12	25	108	66	60	45	55	160	65
65/69	3			3	64	27	3	6	36	61	59	26	36	121	61
60/64						12	0	1	13	56	45	13	25	83	56
55/59						2			2	53	28	7	10	45	52
50/54											20	3	6	29	48
45/49											9	1	2	12	43
40/44											3			3	39

LAUGHLIN AFB TEXAS

Temperature Range	NOVEMBER Obsn Hour Gp 01 to 08	09 to 16	17 to 24	Total Obsn	MCWB	DECEMBER Obsn Hour Gp 01 to 08	09 to 16	17 to 24	Total Obsn	MCWB	JANUARY Obsn Hour Gp 01 to 08	09 to 16	17 to 24	Total Obsn	MCWB
105/109															
100/104															
95/99															
90/94		0		0	67										
85/89		2	0	2	60		1	0	1	58					
80/84		6	2	8	63		1	0	1	60		1	0	1	60
75/79		19	9	28	62		9	2	11	58		5	3	8	59
70/74	5	40	22	67	61		18	8	26	58		12	5	17	57
65/69	19	48	40	107	59	3	28	19	50	56	4	25	18	47	56
60/64	31	47	51	129	55	11	44	39	94	53	8	36	28	72	53
55/59	38	33	46	117	51	28	43	43	114	50	16	40	39	95	50
50/54	49	24	38	111	46	29	38	47	114	46	31	42	51	124	46
45/49	50	12	20	82	42	52	31	47	130	42	48	41	51	140	43
40/44	30	5	7	42	38	59	20	30	109	38	58	23	28	109	38
35/39	12	4	4	20	34	42	12	11	65	34	47	11	13	71	34
30/34	5	1	2	8	30	18	2	2	22	30	19	7	7	33	29
25/29	1			1	26	4	0		4	26	9	3	3	15	23
20/24						1			1	22	6	1	2	9	18
15/19											2	1	0	3	16
10/14											0			0	11
5/9											1			1	8

Temperature Range	FEBRUARY Obsn Hour Gp 01 to 08	09 to 16	17 to 24	Total Obsn	MCWB	MARCH Obsn Hour Gp 01 to 08	09 to 16	17 to 24	Total Obsn	MCWB	APRIL Obsn Hour Gp 01 to 08	09 to 16	17 to 24	Total Obsn	MCWB
105/109															
100/104							0	0	0	65		0		0	65
95/99							1	1	2	64		3	2	5	65
90/94		1	0	1	61		2	1	3	63		13	10	23	66
85/89		2	2	4	60		10	7	17	63	0	27	23	50	67
80/84		7	4	11	60		23	18	41	61	0	39	36	75	66
75/79		18	12	30	59	0	34	29	63	59	9	49	49	107	64
70/74	0	28	23	51	57	7	38	35	80	58	54	46	46	146	64
65/69	11	34	30	75	57	25	40	40	105	56	57	31	32	120	60
60/64	24	33	38	95	53	46	36	43	125	53	49	17	22	88	55
55/59	37	34	38	109	50	52	26	32	110	49	36	12	11	59	51
50/54	40	26	31	97	46	42	22	22	86	45	24	4	6	34	47
45/49	43	19	22	84	42	36	11	13	60	41	7	1	2	10	43
40/44	31	12	12	55	38	25	4	5	34	37	4	0	0	4	38
35/39	19	6	9	34	33	9	1	2	12	33	0			0	37
30/34	12	5	3	20	29	5	1		6	28					
25/29	6	0	1	7	25	1			1	24					
20/24	1			1	21										
15/19															
10/14															
5/9															

Temperature Range	ANNUAL TOTAL Obsn Hour Gp 01 to 08	09 to 16	17 to 24	Total Obsn	MCWB
105/109		2	0	2	72
100/104		18	16	34	72
95/99		154	139	293	72
90/94		303	252	555	72
85/89	16	372	346	734	71
80/84	209	400	371	980	70
75/79	573	333	323	1229	68
70/74	435	280	263	978	64
65/69	281	245	240	766	59
60/64	248	230	252	730	54
55/59	248	196	221	665	50
50/54	237	159	201	597	46
45/49	245	116	157	518	42
40/44	210	64	82	356	38
35/39	129	34	39	202	34
30/34	59	16	14	89	29
25/29	21	3	4	28	24
20/24	8	1	2	11	19
15/19	2	1	0	3	16
10/14	0			0	11
5/9	1			1	8

PERRIN AFB/SHERMAN TEXAS

LAT 33 43N LONG 96 40W ELEV 763 FT

MEAN FREQUENCY OF OCCURRENCE OF DRY BULB TEMPERATURE (DEGREES F) WITH MEAN COINCIDENT WET BULB TEMPERATURE (DEGREES F) FOR EACH DRY BULB TEMPERATURE RANGE

Temperature Range	MAY Obsn Hour Gp 01 to 08	MAY 09 to 16	MAY 17 to 24	MAY Total Obsn	MAY MCWB	JUNE Obsn Hour Gp 01 to 08	JUNE 09 to 16	JUNE 17 to 24	JUNE Total Obsn	JUNE MCWB	JULY Obsn Hour Gp 01 to 08	JULY 09 to 16	JULY 17 to 24	JULY Total Obsn	JULY MCWB
105/109												0		0	76
100/104							0	0	0	73		9	3	12	75
95/99		1	0	1	72		9	3	12	75		47	21	68	75
90/94		7	2	9	73		43	19	62	74		70	40	110	74
85/89		32	12	44	71	1	64	41	106	73	9	56	61	126	73
80/84	1	62	34	97	69	17	61	62	140	72	64	37	65	166	72
75/79	14	58	61	133	68	73	34	59	166	70	108	20	42	170	71
70/74	64	42	60	166	65	87	18	37	142	67	55	8	16	79	69
65/69	76	26	43	145	62	44	8	14	66	64	11	0	2	13	64
60/64	54	12	23	89	58	15	2	4	21	59	1		0	1	60
55/59	21	7	10	38	52	3	0	1	4	55					
50/54	14	1	3	18	49	1		0	1	51					
45/49	3		0	3	44										
40/44	1			1	39										
35/39															
30/34															

Temperature Range	AUGUST Obsn Hour Gp 01 to 08	AUGUST 09 to 16	AUGUST 17 to 24	AUGUST Total Obsn	AUGUST MCWB	SEPTEMBER Obsn Hour Gp 01 to 08	SEPTEMBER 09 to 16	SEPTEMBER 17 to 24	SEPTEMBER Total Obsn	SEPTEMBER MCWB	OCTOBER Obsn Hour Gp 01 to 08	OCTOBER 09 to 16	OCTOBER 17 to 24	OCTOBER Total Obsn	OCTOBER MCWB
105/109		1	0	1	74										
100/104		13	4	17	74		0		0	74					
95/99		42	19	61	74		10	2	12	73		0	0	0	69
90/94	1	64	36	101	73		30	10	40	73		6	1	7	66
85/89	10	61	57	128	72	0	46	25	71	71		13	3	16	68
80/84	53	39	66	158	71	9	49	45	103	70		34	11	45	67
75/79	95	21	45	161	70	46	45	57	148	68	5	42	30	77	65
70/74	72	6	18	96	67	75	33	52	160	66	27	48	45	120	62
65/69	14	1	2	17	63	59	18	32	109	62	47	43	49	139	59
60/64	3	0	0	3	58	30	6	13	49	57	49	30	46	125	55
55/59						16	3	4	23	53	47	19	35	101	51
50/54						3	0	1	4	48	41	9	20	70	46
45/49						1			1	43	21	4	6	31	43
40/44											8	1	2	11	39
35/39											1	0	0	1	34
30/34											1			1	30

PERRIN AFB/SHERMAN TEXAS

Temperature Range	NOVEMBER					DECEMBER					JANUARY				
	Obsn Hour Gp 01 to 08	09 to 16	17 to 24	Total Obsn	MCWB	Obsn Hour Gp 01 to 08	09 to 16	17 to 24	Total Obsn	MCWB	Obsn Hour Gp 01 to 08	09 to 16	17 to 24	Total Obsn	MCWB
105/109															
100/104															
95/99															
90/94															
85/89															
80/84		2	0	2	65							0		0	58
75/79		15	3	18	63		2	0	2	63		1	0	1	61
70/74	3	29	13	45	62		6	1	7	61		5	1	6	60
65/69	14	32	25	71	59	4	16	9	29	58	2	13	7	22	58
60/64	24	38	39	101	55	11	28	17	56	55	9	15	14	38	56
55/59	28	34	36	98	50	14	33	28	75	50	7	23	18	48	50
50/54	40	38	42	120	46	17	36	37	90	45	16	35	26	77	46
45/49	44	25	37	106	42	36	37	46	119	42	24	33	38	95	42
40/44	36	18	25	79	38	47	34	39	120	37	34	32	41	107	38
35/39	28	7	14	49	33	50	26	34	110	34	44	35	38	117	34
30/34	16	3	5	24	29	34	17	21	72	29	47	24	27	98	29
25/29	6	1	1	8	24	21	7	10	38	24	28	14	20	62	25
20/24	1	0		1	19	8	3	4	15	20	18	8	8	34	20
15/19	0			0	15	3	1	1	5	16	10	5	6	21	15
10/14						1	0	0	1	11	6	3	3	12	11
5/9						0			0	7	4	1	0	5	6
0/4											0			0	4

Temperature Range	FEBRUARY					MARCH					APRIL					ANNUAL TOTAL				
	Obsn Hour Gp 01 to 08	09 to 16	17 to 24	Total Obsn	MCWB	Obsn Hour Gp 01 to 08	09 to 16	17 to 24	Total Obsn	MCWB	Obsn Hour Gp 01 to 08	09 to 16	17 to 24	Total Obsn	MCWB	Obsn Hour Gp 01 to 08	09 to 16	17 to 24	Total Obsn	MCWB
105/109																	1	0	1	74
100/104																	22	7	29	74
95/99																	109	45	154	74
90/94							0	0	0	63		0	0	0	66	1	220	108	329	74
85/89		0	0	0	71		1	0	1	66		4	1	5	68	20	277	200	497	72
80/84		1	0	1	64		5	2	7	66		19	8	27	67	144	309	293	746	70
75/79		2	1	3	59		12	6	18	62	0	39	24	63	65	341	291	328	960	68
70/74		7	3	10	58	0	21	15	36	60	17	53	48	118	63	400	276	309	985	65
65/69	0	14	8	22	56	10	31	25	66	58	43	48	52	143	60	324	250	268	842	60
60/64	8	21	16	45	54	23	36	35	94	54	54	35	43	132	55	281	223	250	754	56
55/59	12	27	28	67	50	23	31	37	91	49	52	21	32	105	51	223	198	229	650	50
50/54	20	31	31	82	45	39	32	39	110	46	32	13	19	64	46	223	195	218	636	46
45/49	33	36	39	108	42	43	30	35	108	42	24	5	8	37	42	229	170	209	608	42
40/44	42	32	38	112	38	44	26	25	95	38	13	1	3	17	38	225	144	173	542	38
35/39	39	23	30	92	33	32	13	17	62	34	4	1	0	5	34	198	105	133	436	33
30/34	39	18	18	75	29	21	7	9	37	30	1	0	1	2	31	159	69	81	309	29
25/29	21	8	9	38	25	9	2	2	13	25						85	32	42	159	25
20/24	8	2	3	13	21	3	0	1	4	20						38	13	16	67	20
15/19	3	0	0	3	16	1	0		1	16						17	6	7	30	16
10/14																7	3	3	13	11
5/9																4	1	0	5	6
0/4																0			0	4

WACO/JAMES CONNALLY ARPT TEXAS

LAT 31 38N LONG 97 04W ELEV 475 FT

MEAN FREQUENCY OF OCCURRENCE OF DRY BULB TEMPERATURE (DEGREES F) WITH MEAN COINCIDENT WET BULB TEMPERATURE (DEGREES F) FOR EACH DRY BULB TEMPERATURE RANGE

Temperature Range	MAY Obsn Hour Gp 01 to 08	MAY 09 to 16	MAY 17 to 24	MAY Total Obsn	MAY MCWB	JUNE Obsn Hour Gp 01 to 08	JUNE 09 to 16	JUNE 17 to 24	JUNE Total Obsn	JUNE MCWB	JULY Obsn Hour Gp 01 to 08	JULY 09 to 16	JULY 17 to 24	JULY Total Obsn	JULY MCWB
105/109												1	0	1	76
100/104							2	1	3	74		13	6	19	75
95/99		2	1	3	74		24	11	35	76		67	35	102	75
90/94		21	7	28	73	0	69	34	103	75	0	77	46	123	75
85/89		52	25	77	71	1	72	51	124	74	6	57	61	124	74
80/84	2	64	44	110	70	24	44	65	133	73	67	24	62	153	73
75/79	29	51	63	143	69	100	18	47	165	72	130	7	30	167	72
70/74	77	32	53	162	67	82	8	23	113	69	41	2	8	51	70
65/69	76	16	34	126	63	26	4	8	38	65	3	0		3	65
60/64	38	7	15	60	59	5	1	1	7	60					
55/59	16	2	5	23	53	1		0	1	55					
50/54	9	1	1	11	49	0			0	53					
45/49	2	0	0	2	43										
40/44	0			0	41										
35/39															

Temperature Range	AUGUST Obsn Hour Gp 01 to 08	AUGUST 09 to 16	AUGUST 17 to 24	AUGUST Total Obsn	AUGUST MCWB	SEPTEMBER Obsn Hour Gp 01 to 08	SEPTEMBER 09 to 16	SEPTEMBER 17 to 24	SEPTEMBER Total Obsn	SEPTEMBER MCWB	OCTOBER Obsn Hour Gp 01 to 08	OCTOBER 09 to 16	OCTOBER 17 to 24	OCTOBER Total Obsn	OCTOBER MCWB
105/109		2	0	2	75		0		0	77					
100/104		24	10	34	75		3	1	4	74					
95/99		60	31	91	75		21	5	26	73		1		1	69
90/94	0	68	45	113	74		52	22	74	73		12	2	14	69
85/89	8	56	61	125	73	1	59	36	96	72		30	8	38	69
80/84	70	27	56	153	73	12	47	58	117	71	0	46	21	67	68
75/79	110	10	36	156	72	74	32	59	165	70	13	45	42	100	67
70/74	50	2	8	60	69	78	16	35	129	67	34	44	53	131	64
65/69	9	0	1	10	63	45	7	16	68	62	51	33	45	129	60
60/64	1			1	60	21	2	6	29	57	47	20	34	101	56
55/59	0			0	57	8	0	1	9	54	43	11	28	82	52
50/54						1			1	48	36	4	12	52	47
45/49						0			0	43	18	1	3	22	43
40/44											5	0	1	6	38
35/39											2	0	0	2	34

WACO/JAMES CONNALLY APRT TEXAS

Temperature Range	NOVEMBER Obsn Hour Gp 01 to 08	NOVEMBER 09 to 16	NOVEMBER 17 to 24	NOVEMBER Total Obsn	NOVEMBER MCWB	DECEMBER Obsn Hour Gp 01 to 08	DECEMBER 09 to 16	DECEMBER 17 to 24	DECEMBER Total Obsn	DECEMBER MCWB	JANUARY Obsn Hour Gp 01 to 08	JANUARY 09 to 16	JANUARY 17 to 24	JANUARY Total Obsn	JANUARY MCWB
105/109															
100/104															
95/99															
90/94															
85/89		2		2	66		0		0	68					
80/84		11	2	13	68		1		1	65		1		1	63
75/79	1	23	10	34	66		7	1	8	63		7	1	8	64
70/74	11	31	20	62	63	1	17	5	23	61	1	17	7	25	61
65/69	18	37	28	83	59	8	25	17	50	59	11	23	16	50	60
60/64	24	38	39	101	56	14	32	25	71	55	13	25	23	61	55
55/59	34	35	45	114	51	15	35	31	81	50	14	30	31	75	50
50/54	41	27	34	102	47	23	38	44	105	47	19	35	39	93	47
45/49	38	17	32	87	42	43	37	47	127	43	36	33	39	108	43
40/44	36	11	17	64	38	52	27	39	118	39	40	27	35	102	38
35/39	24	6	9	39	34	47	15	22	84	34	42	19	24	85	34
30/34	10	1	3	14	29	26	8	10	44	29	36	14	16	66	30
25/29	3	0	0	3	25	11	4	6	21	25	16	8	8	32	25
20/24	0			0	22	7	1	1	9	21	10	4	5	19	20
15/19						0	0	0	0	16	7	4	5	16	16
10/14						0			0	13	3	1	0	4	11
5/9											0			0	8

Temperature Range	FEBRUARY Obsn Hour Gp 01 to 08	FEBRUARY 09 to 16	FEBRUARY 17 to 24	FEBRUARY Total Obsn	FEBRUARY MCWB	MARCH Obsn Hour Gp 01 to 08	MARCH 09 to 16	MARCH 17 to 24	MARCH Total Obsn	MARCH MCWB	APRIL Obsn Hour Gp 01 to 08	APRIL 09 to 16	APRIL 17 to 24	APRIL Total Obsn	APRIL MCWB
105/109															
100/104															
95/99												0		0	67
90/94		0		0	60		0	0	0	69		2	1	3	69
85/89		1	0	1	61		3	1	4	67		13	4	17	68
80/84		3	1	4	63		12	5	17	65		40	18	58	67
75/79		9	3	12	61		24	13	37	63	1	49	37	87	66
70/74	0	20	10	30	60	4	36	28	68	61	30	49	54	133	64
65/69	7	26	22	55	59	24	40	37	101	59	57	36	45	138	61
60/64	18	28	30	76	55	27	34	39	100	55	47	26	35	108	56
55/59	22	29	31	82	51	35	31	38	104	50	38	16	25	79	52
50/54	27	31	37	95	47	44	29	35	108	46	32	7	15	54	48
45/49	39	29	33	101	43	42	17	24	83	42	21	2	4	27	43
40/44	42	22	27	91	39	33	11	14	58	38	10	0	1	11	39
35/39	32	14	18	64	34	21	7	8	36	33	3	0	0	3	34
30/34	23	7	8	38	30	14	3	5	22	30	0			0	31
25/29	10	4	4	18	26	4	0	0	4	25					
20/24	3	1	1	5	21	1			1	21					
15/19	1	0	0	1	16										
10/14	1	0	0	1	11										
5/9	0			0	8										

Temperature Range	ANNUAL TOTAL Obsn Hour Gp 01 to 08	ANNUAL TOTAL 09 to 16	ANNUAL TOTAL 17 to 24	ANNUAL TOTAL Total Obsn	ANNUAL TOTAL MCWB
105/109		3	0	3	75
100/104		42	18	60	75
95/99		175	83	258	75
90/94	0	301	157	458	74
85/89	16	345	247	608	73
80/84	175	320	332	827	71
75/79	458	282	342	1082	69
70/74	409	274	304	987	65
65/69	335	247	269	851	61
60/64	255	213	247	715	56
55/59	226	189	235	650	51
50/54	232	172	217	621	47
45/49	239	136	182	557	43
40/44	218	98	134	450	38
35/39	171	61	81	313	34
30/34	109	33	42	184	30
25/29	44	16	18	78	25
20/24	21	6	7	34	20
15/19	8	4	5	17	16
10/14	4	1	0	5	11
5/9	0			0	8

WEBB AFB/BIG SPRING TEXAS

LAT 32 13N LONG 101 31W ELEV 2561 FT

MEAN FREQUENCY OF OCCURRENCE OF DRY BULB TEMPERATURE (DEGREES F) WITH MEAN COINCIDENT WET BULB TEMPERATURE (DEGREES F) FOR EACH DRY BULB TEMPERATURE RANGE

Temperature Range	MAY Obsn Hour Gp 01 to 08	MAY 09 to 16	MAY 17 to 24	MAY Total Obsn	MAY MCWB	JUNE Obsn Hour Gp 01 to 08	JUNE 09 to 16	JUNE 17 to 24	JUNE Total Obsn	JUNE MCWB	JULY Obsn Hour Gp 01 to 08	JULY 09 to 16	JULY 17 to 24	JULY Total Obsn	JULY MCWB
105/109							1	0	1	71		0	0	0	72
100/104		2	1	3	65		7	5	12	69		4	3	7	70
95/99		10	5	15	64		22	14	36	69		37	27	64	69
90/94		25	13	38	64		45	32	77	69		66	44	110	69
85/89		40	25	65	64	1	53	47	101	68	1	57	52	110	68
80/84	1	47	39	87	63	13	52	55	120	67	24	48	60	132	67
75/79	10	45	50	105	63	61	33	46	140	66	100	23	39	162	66
70/74	51	35	47	133	62	91	16	24	131	64	90	9	19	118	65
65/69	73	24	34	131	59	50	7	11	68	61	29	3	4	36	63
60/64	62	12	22	96	56	20	4	6	30	58	3			3	60
55/59	33	6	9	48	52	4	0	1	5	54					
50/54	12	3	3	18	47	1			1	48					
45/49	5	1	0	6	43	0			0	44					
40/44	1	0	0	1	40										
35/39															

Temperature Range	AUGUST Obsn Hour Gp 01 to 08	AUGUST 09 to 16	AUGUST 17 to 24	AUGUST Total Obsn	AUGUST MCWB	SEPTEMBER Obsn Hour Gp 01 to 08	SEPTEMBER 09 to 16	SEPTEMBER 17 to 24	SEPTEMBER Total Obsn	SEPTEMBER MCWB	OCTOBER Obsn Hour Gp 01 to 08	OCTOBER 09 to 16	OCTOBER 17 to 24	OCTOBER Total Obsn	OCTOBER MCWB
105/109		0	0	0	72										
100/104		6	3	9	69		0	0	0	68					
95/99		32	20	52	70		5	2	7	67		0		0	63
90/94		59	40	99	69		28	13	41	68		4	1	5	62
85/89	0	57	51	108	68		41	24	65	67		21	8	29	63
80/84	20	49	59	128	67	1	49	43	93	66		33	14	47	62
75/79	89	28	45	162	66	19	50	55	124	65	0	36	25	61	61
70/74	93	12	25	130	64	77	33	51	161	63	10	44	45	99	59
65/69	39	4	5	48	62	74	20	34	128	61	41	39	50	130	58
60/64	6	1	1	8	57	45	10	12	67	57	51	29	43	123	54
55/59	2	0	0	2	54	18	3	3	24	52	48	21	31	100	50
50/54						6	1	1	8	48	50	11	18	79	46
45/49						1		0	1	44	30	7	8	45	43
40/44											13	2	3	18	39
35/39											4	1	1	6	35

WEBB AFB/BIG SPRING TEXAS

Temperature Range	NOVEMBER Obsn Hour Gp 01 to 08	NOVEMBER 09 to 16	NOVEMBER 17 to 24	NOVEMBER Total Obsn	NOVEMBER MCWB	DECEMBER Obsn Hour Gp 01 to 08	DECEMBER 09 to 16	DECEMBER 17 to 24	DECEMBER Total Obsn	DECEMBER MCWB	JANUARY Obsn Hour Gp 01 to 08	JANUARY 09 to 16	JANUARY 17 to 24	JANUARY Total Obsn	JANUARY MCWB
105/109															
100/104															
95/99															
90/94															
85/89		0		0	61										
80/84		4	0	4	58		1	0	1	57		1	0	1	54
75/79		18	5	23	57		2	1	3	55		3	1	4	53
70/74		24	10	34	56		9	2	11	52		10	4	14	52
65/69	3	27	19	49	54		19	7	26	51		16	8	24	50
60/64	10	34	36	80	52	1	28	16	45	49	1	21	16	38	48
55/59	27	33	44	104	49	7	29	29	65	47	7	26	25	58	46
50/54	42	33	42	117	45	18	36	39	93	44	12	30	34	76	43
45/49	49	28	35	112	41	27	33	44	104	40	22	31	40	93	40
40/44	45	20	28	93	37	42	30	41	113	36	38	31	36	105	36
35/39	35	12	15	62	33	60	24	32	116	33	48	27	33	108	33
30/34	18	4	5	27	29	47	20	21	88	29	48	22	23	93	29
25/29	8	1	1	10	24	31	11	11	53	25	33	14	14	61	24
20/24	2	0	0	2	21	13	4	4	21	21	19	9	6	34	20
15/19	0			0	14	3	1	1	5	16	10	5	5	20	15
10/14						0			0	10	7	2	3	12	10
5/9						0			0	8	3	1	0	4	7
0/4											0	0		0	2
-5/-1											0	0		0	-3
-10/-6											0			0	-7

Temperature Range	FEBRUARY Obsn Hour Gp 01 to 08	FEBRUARY 09 to 16	FEBRUARY 17 to 24	FEBRUARY Total Obsn	FEBRUARY MCWB	MARCH Obsn Hour Gp 01 to 08	MARCH 09 to 16	MARCH 17 to 24	MARCH Total Obsn	MARCH MCWB	APRIL Obsn Hour Gp 01 to 08	APRIL 09 to 16	APRIL 17 to 24	APRIL Total Obsn	APRIL MCWB	ANNUAL TOTAL Obsn Hour Gp 01 to 08	ANNUAL TOTAL 09 to 16	ANNUAL TOTAL 17 to 24	ANNUAL TOTAL Total Obsn	ANNUAL TOTAL MCWB
105/109																	1	0	1	71
100/104																	19	12	31	69
95/99												1	0	1	63		107	68	175	69
90/94							1	0	1	60		8	4	12	61		236	147	383	68
85/89		1	0	1	60		4	1	5	57		19	11	30	59	2	293	219	514	66
80/84		2	1	3	58		9	5	14	55	0	35	21	56	59	59	330	297	686	65
75/79		5	2	7	54	0	15	10	25	55	1	33	29	63	57	280	291	308	879	64
70/74		11	6	17	52	0	28	18	46	53	8	38	39	85	56	420	269	290	979	61
65/69	0	18	12	30	50	3	32	30	65	51	35	31	41	107	55	347	240	255	842	57
60/64	2	24	22	48	49	13	34	36	83	50	48	29	36	113	52	262	226	246	734	53
55/59	11	27	27	65	47	28	31	41	100	47	51	19	26	96	49	236	195	236	667	48
50/54	18	29	36	83	44	42	26	36	104	43	45	13	17	75	45	246	182	226	654	44
45/49	35	31	37	103	40	49	23	26	98	40	30	10	11	51	42	248	164	201	613	41
40/44	42	26	33	101	37	41	17	18	76	37	14	3	3	20	38	236	129	162	527	37
35/39	44	20	20	84	33	29	14	13	56	32	6	0	0	6	33	226	98	114	438	33
30/34	32	15	13	60	29	28	9	10	47	29	2	1	1	4	31	175	71	73	319	29
25/29	23	8	7	38	25	10	4	2	16	25	1			1	28	106	38	35	179	25
20/24	12	6	6	24	21	4	1	1	6	20						50	20	17	87	20
15/19	4	2	1	7	16	1	0	0	1	16						18	8	7	33	16
10/14	1	0		1	12											8	2	3	13	11
5/9	0	0		0	9											3	1	0	4	7
0/4																0	0		0	2
-5/-1																0	0		0	-3
-10/-6																0			0	-7

DUGWAY PG/MICHAELS AAF UTAH

LAT 40 12N LONG 112 56W ELEV 4340 FT

MEAN FREQUENCY OF OCCURRENCE OF DRY BULB TEMPERATURE (DEGREES F) WITH MEAN COINCIDENT WET BULB TEMPERATURE (DEGREES F) FOR EACH DRY BULB TEMPERATURE RANGE

Temperature Range	MAY Obsn Hour Gp 01 to 08	MAY 09 to 16	MAY 17 to 24	MAY Total Obsn	MAY MCWB	JUNE Obsn Hour Gp 01 to 08	JUNE 09 to 16	JUNE 17 to 24	JUNE Total Obsn	JUNE MCWB	JULY Obsn Hour Gp 01 to 08	JULY 09 to 16	JULY 17 to 24	JULY Total Obsn	JULY MCWB
105/109							0		0	64		0		0	63
100/104							1	0	1	63		9	3	12	63
95/99							11	5	16	61		43	22	65	62
90/94		4	1	5	58		29	17	46	59		67	37	104	61
85/89		12	6	18	56	0	36	24	60	58	2	63	44	109	60
80/84	0	30	14	44	55	3	42	30	75	57	13	39	48	100	59
75/79	0	37	22	59	53	11	37	36	84	55	40	17	45	102	57
70/74	4	39	30	73	51	24	32	39	95	53	62	8	33	103	56
65/69	13	35	35	83	49	37	25	33	95	52	68	2	12	82	53
60/64	30	31	40	101	47	54	15	26	95	50	44	0	3	47	49
55/59	38	27	35	100	45	51	7	18	76	48	15	0	1	16	46
50/54	51	18	30	99	43	35	4	8	47	46	4		0	4	43
45/49	53	9	21	83	41	18	1	2	21	43	1			1	39
40/44	35	5	10	50	37	6	0	1	7	39	0			0	34
35/39	18	1	4	23	33	1		0	1	34					
30/34	5	0	1	6	30	0			0	26					
25/29	2			2	25										
20/24															
15/19															

Temperature Range	AUGUST Obsn Hour Gp 01 to 08	AUGUST 09 to 16	AUGUST 17 to 24	AUGUST Total Obsn	AUGUST MCWB	SEPTEMBER Obsn Hour Gp 01 to 08	SEPTEMBER 09 to 16	SEPTEMBER 17 to 24	SEPTEMBER Total Obsn	SEPTEMBER MCWB	OCTOBER Obsn Hour Gp 01 to 08	OCTOBER 09 to 16	OCTOBER 17 to 24	OCTOBER Total Obsn	OCTOBER MCWB
105/109															
100/104		2	0	2	62		0		0	62					
95/99		25	10	35	62		3	0	3	60					
90/94		57	27	84	61		16	5	21	59					
85/89	0	62	36	98	60		38	15	53	58		2	0	2	55
80/84	4	47	45	96	59	0	43	23	66	56		13	3	16	54
75/79	28	29	51	108	57	2	39	30	71	55		24	8	32	53
70/74	58	15	43	116	56	13	34	37	84	53	0	34	14	48	51
65/69	68	7	24	99	54	24	26	40	90	51	3	38	21	62	49
60/64	50	3	8	61	51	37	19	34	90	48	9	39	30	78	47
55/59	24	1	3	28	46	48	12	27	87	46	16	36	37	89	45
50/54	10	0	1	11	42	51	7	16	74	43	25	26	44	95	42
45/49	3			3	38	34	3	7	44	39	41	18	41	100	39
40/44	1			1	35	19	1	4	24	35	54	12	30	96	36
35/39	0			0	30	9	0	1	10	32	55	4	15	74	32
30/34						3		0	3	29	34	1	5	40	29
25/29						0			0	25	10		1	11	24
20/24											1			1	20
15/19											0			0	16

DUGWAY PG/MICHALES AAF UTAH

Temperature Range	NOVEMBER Obsn Hour Gp 01 to 08	09 to 16	17 to 24	Total Obsn	MCWB	DECEMBER Obsn Hour Gp 01 to 08	09 to 16	17 to 24	Total Obsn	MCWB
105/109										
100/104										
95/99										
90/94										
85/89										
80/84										
75/79										
70/74		1	0	1	50					
65/69		7	1	8	48					
60/64		19	4	23	46		0	0	0	50
55/59	2	31	13	46	44	0	2	1	3	46
50/54	10	31	21	62	42	3	10	4	17	43
45/49	12	33	28	73	39	5	22	8	35	40
40/44	20	38	38	96	36	11	38	18	67	36
35/39	33	36	46	115	32	15	49	35	99	33
30/34	56	24	42	122	29	29	48	49	126	29
25/29	44	12	23	79	25	46	38	57	141	25
20/24	29	6	14	49	20	53	25	42	120	21
15/19	19	2	6	27	16	42	11	20	73	16
10/14	9	0	2	11	12	29	4	8	41	12
5/9	2	1	1	4	6	11	1	3	15	7
0/4	2		1	3	1	4	0	2	6	2
-5/-1	1		0	1	-3	2	0	0	2	-2
-10/-6	0		0	0	-7					
-15/-11										
-20/-16										

Temperature Range	JANUARY Obsn Hour Gp 01 to 08	09 to 16	17 to 24	Total Obsn	MCWB	FEBRUARY Obsn Hour Gp 01 to 08	09 to 16	17 to 24	Total Obsn	MCWB
105/109										
100/104										
95/99										
90/94										
85/89										
80/84										
75/79										
70/74										
65/69		0		0	52		1	0	1	47
60/64		1		1	47		5	1	6	46
55/59		4	1	5	45	0	10	5	15	44
50/54	1	11	4	16	42	3	20	11	34	42
45/49	3	17	9	29	39	6	29	20	55	39
40/44	12	39	20	71	36	11	35	30	76	36
35/39	21	38	34	93	33	26	42	42	110	33
30/34	33	46	51	130	29	46	39	46	131	29
25/29	38	39	44	121	25	51	25	35	111	25
20/24	37	24	30	91	21	33	11	18	62	20
15/19	31	14	23	68	16	24	5	8	37	16
10/14	30	9	15	54	11	12	2	4	18	11
5/9	20	4	10	34	7	6	1	2	9	7
0/4	13	2	4	19	2	3	0	2	5	2
-5/-1	4	0	2	6	-3	2		0	2	-3
-10/-6	3	0	1	4	-9	1		0	1	-7
-15/-11	2	0	0	2	-13	0			0	-11
-20/-16	0			0	-16					

Temperature Range	MARCH Obsn Hour Gp 01 to 08	09 to 16	17 to 24	Total Obsn	MCWB	APRIL Obsn Hour Gp 01 to 08	09 to 16	17 to 24	Total Obsn	MCWB
105/109										
100/104										
95/99										
90/94										
85/89							0	0	0	56
80/84		0		0	50		3	1	4	53
75/79		1	0	1	50		12	5	17	52
70/74		3	2	5	49		23	12	35	50
65/69		10	4	14	47	1	29	19	49	47
60/64	0	19	8	27	45	6	33	24	63	46
55/59	2	25	15	42	43	13	38	33	84	43
50/54	5	34	25	64	41	26	39	39	104	41
45/49	10	40	34	84	38	34	32	43	109	39
40/44	32	44	46	122	35	54	18	34	106	36
35/39	46	36	43	125	32	57	9	19	85	33
30/34	56	25	38	119	29	34	4	10	48	29
25/29	43	10	25	78	24	12	0	2	14	25
20/24	33	2	7	42	20	3			3	20
15/19	14	1	1	16	16	0			0	17
10/14	4	0	1	5	11					
5/9	2	0	0	2	6					
0/4	1			1	2					
-5/-1	0			0	-3					
-10/-6	0			0	-6					
-15/-11										
-20/-16										

Temperature Range	ANNUAL TOTAL Obsn Hour Gp 01 to 08	09 to 16	17 to 24	Total Obsn	MCWB
105/109		0		0	64
100/104		12	3	15	63
95/99		82	37	119	62
90/94		173	87	260	60
85/89	2	213	125	340	59
80/84	20	217	164	401	57
75/79	81	196	197	474	56
70/74	161	189	210	560	53
65/69	214	180	189	583	51
60/64	230	184	178	592	48
55/59	209	193	189	591	45
50/54	224	200	203	627	42
45/49	220	204	213	637	39
40/44	255	230	231	716	36
35/39	281	215	239	735	33
30/34	296	187	242	725	29
25/29	246	124	187	557	25
20/24	189	68	111	368	21
15/19	130	33	58	221	16
10/14	84	15	30	129	11
5/9	41	7	16	64	7
0/4	23	2	9	34	2
-5/-1	9	0	2	11	-3
-10/-6	4	0	1	5	-8
-15/-11	2	0	0	2	-13
-20/-16	0			0	-16

HILL AFB/OGDEN UTAH

LAT 41 07N LONG 111 58W ELEV 4785 FT

MEAN FREQUENCY OF OCCURRENCE OF DRY BULB TEMPERATURE (DEGREES F) WITH MEAN COINCIDENT WET BULB TEMPERATURE (DEGREES F) FOR EACH DRY BULB TEMPERATURE RANGE

Temperature Range	MAY Obsn Hour Gp 01 to 08	MAY 09 to 16	MAY 17 to 24	MAY Total Obsn	MAY MCWB	JUNE Obsn Hour Gp 01 to 08	JUNE 09 to 16	JUNE 17 to 24	JUNE Total Obsn	JUNE MCWB	JULY Obsn Hour Gp 01 to 08	JULY 09 to 16	JULY 17 to 24	JULY Total Obsn	JULY MCWB
100/104							0		0	64		0	0	0	64
95/99							2	1	3	62		7	3	10	62
90/94		0	0	0	59		11	6	17	60		41	23	64	62
85/89		3	1	4	58		23	13	36	59	0	69	41	110	60
80/84		14	6	20	55	1	33	22	56	58	4	61	55	120	59
75/79	0	25	13	38	54	5	38	33	76	56	25	41	58	124	57
70/74	2	36	25	63	52	21	37	38	96	54	73	21	42	136	55
65/69	13	40	39	92	50	40	36	38	114	52	83	6	20	109	53
60/64	29	40	42	111	48	50	29	35	114	50	48	2	6	56	51
55/59	44	33	41	118	46	50	18	27	95	48	13	0	1	14	48
50/54	58	28	37	123	43	48	9	21	78	46	3		0	3	44
45/49	52	16	24	92	41	21	3	5	29	43					
40/44	32	8	12	52	37	4	0	1	5	38					
35/39	13	4	6	23	34	1			1	36					
30/34	5	2	2	9	30										
25/29	1		0	1	25										
20/24	0			0	21										

Temperature Range	AUGUST Obsn Hour Gp 01 to 08	AUGUST 09 to 16	AUGUST 17 to 24	AUGUST Total Obsn	AUGUST MCWB	SEPTEMBER Obsn Hour Gp 01 to 08	SEPTEMBER 09 to 16	SEPTEMBER 17 to 24	SEPTEMBER Total Obsn	SEPTEMBER MCWB	OCTOBER Obsn Hour Gp 01 to 08	OCTOBER 09 to 16	OCTOBER 17 to 24	OCTOBER Total Obsn	OCTOBER MCWB
100/104		0		0	67										
95/99		4	1	5	63		0	0	0	62					
90/94		31	15	46	62		2	0	2	61					
85/89		56	30	86	61		12	4	16	59		0		0	58
80/84	1	58	45	104	59		32	14	46	57		1	0	1	56
75/79	17	45	61	123	58	2	40	25	67	55		10	2	12	53
70/74	64	27	48	139	56	11	42	39	92	53	0	19	8	27	51
65/69	87	14	26	127	54	29	31	44	104	51	3	31	17	51	50
60/64	44	8	13	65	51	46	32	41	119	49	11	40	29	80	47
55/59	19	3	7	29	47	53	22	31	106	46	25	41	39	105	45
50/54	10	2	3	15	44	44	14	22	80	43	40	35	49	124	42
45/49	5	0	1	6	40	31	9	12	52	40	57	32	44	133	39
40/44	0			0	35	15	2	6	23	36	55	22	32	109	36
35/39	0			0	33	9	0	2	11	33	34	10	17	61	33
30/34						1	1	1	3	31	17	5	7	29	28
25/29						0			0	27	4	1	2	7	24
20/24											2	0	1	3	20

HILL AFB/OGDEN UTAH

Temperature Range	NOVEMBER Obsn Hour Gp 01 to 08	NOVEMBER Obsn Hour Gp 09 to 16	NOVEMBER Obsn Hour Gp 17 to 24	NOVEMBER Total Obsn	NOVEMBER MCWB	DECEMBER Obsn Hour Gp 01 to 08	DECEMBER Obsn Hour Gp 09 to 16	DECEMBER Obsn Hour Gp 17 to 24	DECEMBER Total Obsn	DECEMBER MCWB	JANUARY Obsn Hour Gp 01 to 08	JANUARY Obsn Hour Gp 09 to 16	JANUARY Obsn Hour Gp 17 to 24	JANUARY Total Obsn	JANUARY MCWB	FEBRUARY Obsn Hour Gp 01 to 08	FEBRUARY Obsn Hour Gp 09 to 16	FEBRUARY Obsn Hour Gp 17 to 24	FEBRUARY Total Obsn	FEBRUARY MCWB	MARCH Obsn Hour Gp 01 to 08	MARCH Obsn Hour Gp 09 to 16	MARCH Obsn Hour Gp 17 to 24	MARCH Total Obsn	MARCH MCWB	APRIL Obsn Hour Gp 01 to 08	APRIL Obsn Hour Gp 09 to 16	APRIL Obsn Hour Gp 17 to 24	APRIL Total Obsn	APRIL MCWB	ANNUAL TOTAL Obsn Hour Gp 01 to 08	ANNUAL TOTAL Obsn Hour Gp 09 to 16	ANNUAL TOTAL Obsn Hour Gp 17 to 24	ANNUAL TOTAL Total Obsn	ANNUAL TOTAL MCWB
100/104																																0	0	0	65
95/99																																13	5	18	62
90/94																																85	44	129	61
85/89																															0	163	89	252	60
80/84																											0	0	0	54	6	199	142	347	58
75/79																											3	1	4	52	49	202	193	444	56
70/74		0		0	52																	0	0	0	50		8	5	13	50	171	190	205	566	54
65/69		1	0	1	47												0		0	49		5	2	7	47	1	18	10	29	48	256	182	196	634	52
60/64		9	1	10	45												1	0	1	49	0	10	5	15	45	5	23	20	48	46	233	194	192	619	49
55/59	1	18	7	26	44	0	0	0	0	45		0	0	0	44		5	2	7	45	2	18	12	32	43	11	32	26	69	43	218	190	193	601	46
50/54	10	29	21	60	41	1	3	1	5	42	0	2	1	3	42	2	13	9	24	42	5	26	23	54	41	26	39	38	103	41	247	200	225	672	43
45/49	20	36	34	90	39	7	12	8	27	39	5	12	7	24	39	10	25	21	56	39	21	34	33	88	38	33	42	40	115	38	262	221	229	712	39
40/44	42	46	45	133	36	14	29	17	60	36	13	24	19	56	36	19	32	32	83	36	35	42	43	120	35	52	39	45	136	36	281	244	252	777	36
35/39	52	40	47	139	32	28	42	36	106	33	35	44	38	117	33	40	43	45	128	32	53	42	50	145	32	61	24	33	118	33	326	249	274	849	32
30/34	50	38	49	137	29	42	54	57	153	29	31	48	48	127	29	51	46	49	146	29	57	39	42	138	28	44	10	20	74	29	298	243	275	816	29
25/29	41	16	27	84	25	58	51	59	168	25	49	49	51	149	24	42	28	34	104	24	37	20	24	81	24	6	0	1	7	25	238	165	198	601	24
20/24	16	4	6	26	20	49	36	37	122	20	47	34	41	122	20	31	21	21	73	20	21	8	9	38	20	1			1	20	167	103	115	385	20
15/19	6	1	3	10	16	33	13	24	70	16	32	19	22	73	15	16	6	9	31	16	12	2	3	17	15						99	41	61	201	16
10/14	1	0		1	12	13	6	7	26	11	16	8	11	35	11	9	3	3	15	11	3	1	1	5	10						42	18	22	82	11
5/9						4	2	1	7	6	11	4	7	22	6	4	1	1	6	6	1	0		1	6						20	7	9	36	6
0/4						1	0	0	1	2	5	2	2	9	2	1	0		1	1	0			0	3						7	2	2	11	2
-5/-1						0	0		0	-2	1	1	1	3	-4	0			0	-1											1	1	1	3	-3
-10/-6											1	0	0	1	-8																1	0	0	1	-8
-15/-11											1	0	0	1	-13																1	0	0	1	-13

WENDOVER AF RANGE UTAH

LAT 40 44N LONG 114 02W ELEV 4237 FT

MEAN FREQUENCY OF OCCURRENCE OF DRY BULB TEMPERATURE (DEGREES F) WITH MEAN COINCIDENT WET BULB TEMPERATURE (DEGREES F) FOR EACH DRY BULB TEMPERATURE RANGE

Temperature Range	MAY Obsn Hour Gp 01 to 08	MAY 09 to 16	MAY 17 to 24	MAY Total Obsn	MAY MCWB	JUNE Obsn Hour Gp 01 to 08	JUNE 09 to 16	JUNE 17 to 24	JUNE Total Obsn	JUNE MCWB	JULY Obsn Hour Gp 01 to 08	JULY 09 to 16	JULY 17 to 24	JULY Total Obsn	JULY MCWB
100/104							1	0	1	61		2	1	3	63
95/99							4	3	7	61		22	10	32	62
90/94		1	0	1	60	0	13	9	22	59		52	31	83	61
85/89		7	4	11	58	1	34	21	56	58	5	70	55	130	60
80/84		22	11	33	56	2	42	32	76	56	28	57	61	146	58
75/79	1	36	24	61	54	16	46	47	109	55	58	31	53	142	57
70/74	10	41	36	87	52	40	41	42	123	53	84	11	27	122	55
65/69	28	45	40	113	50	57	31	36	124	51	51	3	9	63	53
60/64	39	38	40	117	48	52	16	25	93	49	19	0	2	21	50
55/59	51	27	35	113	46	40	8	16	64	47	3			3	45
50/54	54	18	29	101	43	20	2	6	28	44	0			0	41
45/49	38	9	17	64	40	9	1	2	12	40					
40/44	20	3	10	33	36	3		0	3	39					
35/39	7	1	1	9	33										
30/34	0			0	33										
25/29															

Temperature Range	AUGUST Obsn Hour Gp 01 to 08	AUGUST 09 to 16	AUGUST 17 to 24	AUGUST Total Obsn	AUGUST MCWB	SEPTEMBER Obsn Hour Gp 01 to 08	SEPTEMBER 09 to 16	SEPTEMBER 17 to 24	SEPTEMBER Total Obsn	SEPTEMBER MCWB	OCTOBER Obsn Hour Gp 01 to 08	OCTOBER 09 to 16	OCTOBER 17 to 24	OCTOBER Total Obsn	OCTOBER MCWB
100/104		0		0	61										
95/99		8	3	11	61		1	0	1	60					
90/94		47	23	70	60		10	3	13	58					
85/89	1	70	47	118	59	0	23	11	34	57					
80/84	13	64	59	136	58	2	39	23	64	56		2	1	3	54
75/79	46	40	58	144	56	7	48	33	88	54		9	3	12	52
70/74	79	15	38	132	55	19	46	46	111	52		22	9	31	51
65/69	73	4	15	92	53	39	38	46	123	50	3	37	19	59	49
60/64	27	0	4	31	50	59	21	40	120	48	9	54	33	96	47
55/59	7		0	7	47	55	10	23	88	45	24	57	54	135	45
50/54	1			1	45	37	3	9	49	43	50	37	56	143	42
45/49						14	1	4	19	39	69	20	39	128	39
40/44						6		1	7	37	52	8	24	84	36
35/39						1			1	34	31	2	8	41	33
30/34											10	0	2	12	30
25/29											1			1	24

WENDOVER AF RANGE UTAH

Temperature Range	NOVEMBER Obsn Hour Gp 01 to 08	NOVEMBER 09 to 16	NOVEMBER 17 to 24	NOVEMBER Total Obsn	NOVEMBER M C W B	DECEMBER Obsn Hour Gp 01 to 08	DECEMBER 09 to 16	DECEMBER 17 to 24	DECEMBER Total Obsn	DECEMBER M C W B	JANUARY Obsn Hour Gp 01 to 08	JANUARY 09 to 16	JANUARY 17 to 24	JANUARY Total Obsn	JANUARY M C W B	FEBRUARY Obsn Hour Gp 01 to 08	FEBRUARY 09 to 16	FEBRUARY 17 to 24	FEBRUARY Total Obsn	FEBRUARY M C W B	MARCH Obsn Hour Gp 01 to 08	MARCH 09 to 16	MARCH 17 to 24	MARCH Total Obsn	MARCH M C W B	APRIL Obsn Hour Gp 01 to 08	APRIL 09 to 16	APRIL 17 to 24	APRIL Total Obsn	APRIL M C W B	ANNUAL TOTAL Obsn Hour Gp 01 to 08	ANNUAL TOTAL 09 to 16	ANNUAL TOTAL 17 to 24	ANNUAL TOTAL Total Obsn	ANNUAL TOTAL M C W B
100/104																																3	1	4	62
95/99																																35	16	51	61
90/94																															0	123	66	189	60
85/89																															7	204	138	349	59
80/84																											0		0	52	45	226	187	458	57
75/79																											8	2	10	52	128	218	220	566	55
70/74		0		0	50																	1	0	1	51		15	9	24	50	232	192	207	631	53
65/69		3	0	3	48																	3	1	4	48	2	31	17	50	48	253	195	183	631	51
60/64	1	6	2	9	46		0		0	49		0		0	44		2	0	2	47	0	9	4	13	45	8	40	34	82	46	214	186	184	584	48
55/59	2	17	7	26	45	1	2	1	4	48		2	1	3	42	0	9	4	13	45	1	28	15	44	43	22	51	47	120	44	206	211	203	620	45
50/54	8	30	17	55	42	1	4	3	8	43	1	5	3	9	41	2	18	12	32	42	8	44	30	82	41	42	46	47	135	41	224	207	212	643	42
45/49	10	42	30	82	39	3	16	6	25	39	2	14	6	22	39	7	29	20	56	39	23	48	48	119	38	56	28	39	123	39	231	208	211	650	39
40/44	25	49	41	115	36	9	31	16	56	36	8	33	22	63	36	14	41	33	88	36	38	50	49	137	35	53	16	29	98	35	228	231	225	684	36
35/39	46	44	54	144	32	27	55	43	125	33	22	50	46	118	33	35	44	44	123	32	58	38	45	141	32	38	5	13	56	32	265	239	254	758	32
30/34	64	29	44	137	28	43	66	64	173	29	44	54	53	151	29	44	38	43	125	28	63	22	35	120	28	18	1	3	22	28	286	210	244	740	29
25/29	38	13	24	75	24	63	52	69	184	25	56	47	53	156	25	54	27	39	120	25	40	5	18	63	24	2			2	24	254	144	203	601	24
20/24	27	6	12	45	20	58	17	32	107	21	51	27	37	115	21	38	11	19	68	20	14	0	2	16	19						188	61	102	351	20
15/19	13	1	5	19	15	32	4	11	47	16	34	13	18	65	16	19	4	6	29	16	3			3	15						101	22	40	163	16
10/14	4	0	1	5	11	9	1	2	12	12	22	3	8	33	11	8	1	3	12	12	0			0	13						43	5	14	62	12
5/9	1		0	1	7	3		1	4	8	8	0	2	10	7	3	0	0	3	7											15	0	3	18	7
0/4											1		0	1	3	0			0	3													0		3

FORT BELVOIR/DAVISON AAF VIRGINIA

LAT 38 43N LONG 77 11W ELEV 69 FT

MEAN FREQUENCY OF OCCURRENCE OF DRY BULB TEMPERATURE (DEGREES F) WITH MEAN COINCIDENT WET BULB TEMPERATURE (DEGREES F) FOR EACH DRY BULB TEMPERATURE RANGE

Temperature Range	MAY Obsn Hour Gp 01 to 08	MAY Obsn Hour Gp 09 to 16	MAY Obsn Hour Gp 17 to 24	MAY Total Obsn	MAY MCWB	JUNE Obsn Hour Gp 01 to 08	JUNE Obsn Hour Gp 09 to 16	JUNE Obsn Hour Gp 17 to 24	JUNE Total Obsn	JUNE MCWB	JULY Obsn Hour Gp 01 to 08	JULY Obsn Hour Gp 09 to 16	JULY Obsn Hour Gp 17 to 24	JULY Total Obsn	JULY MCWB
100/104							0		0	80		0		0	79
95/99		0	0	0	72		2	1	3	77		2	0	2	77
90/94		4	1	5	69		14	2	16	75		23	4	27	75
85/89		13	4	17	69	0	40	14	54	73	0	63	21	84	74
80/84	0	25	11	36	67	2	56	30	88	71	5	75	44	124	71
75/79	2	37	20	59	64	12	60	46	I18	67	35	54	64	153	70
70/74	10	51	35	96	62	49	38	57	144	66	87	24	70	181	69
65/69	30	44	47	121	60	68	20	46	134	63	72	5	32	109	64
60/64	49	37	46	132	56	48	8	25	81	59	32	1	10	43	60
55/59	55	22	39	116	53	36	2	15	53	55	14		2	16	55
50/54	45	12	26	83	49	18		4	22	51	3		0	3	51
45/49	32	3	12	47	45	5		1	6	46					
40/44	17	1	6	24	40	2			2	42					
35/39	7		1	8	36										
30/34	2		0	2	31										
25/29	0			0	29										
20/24															

Temperature Range	AUGUST Obsn Hour Gp 01 to 08	AUGUST Obsn Hour Gp 09 to 16	AUGUST Obsn Hour Gp 17 to 24	AUGUST Total Obsn	AUGUST MCWB	SEPTEMBER Obsn Hour Gp 01 to 08	SEPTEMBER Obsn Hour Gp 09 to 16	SEPTEMBER Obsn Hour Gp 17 to 24	SEPTEMBER Total Obsn	SEPTEMBER MCWB	OCTOBER Obsn Hour Gp 01 to 08	OCTOBER Obsn Hour Gp 09 to 16	OCTOBER Obsn Hour Gp 17 to 24	OCTOBER Total Obsn	OCTOBER MCWB
100/104															
95/99		2	0	2	78		0		0	83					
90/94		20	4	24	76		7	1	8	75		1		1	69
85/89	0	55	18	73	74		31	6	37	73		2	0	2	71
80/84	2	74	38	114	72	0	41	15	56	70		8	1	9	68
75/79	29	61	61	151	70	8	51	34	93	68	0	23	4	27	66
70/74	82	30	71	183	68	38	46	48	132	66	6	39	16	61	63
65/69	73	6	34	113	64	49	34	43	126	62	16	49	30	95	60
60/64	35	1	15	51	60	42	20	40	102	58	25	48	39	112	56
55/59	21	0	6	27	55	46	8	31	85	54	36	42	45	123	52
50/54	6		1	7	51	32	2	15	49	50	46	25	43	114	48
45/49	1			1	46	16		6	22	45	41	8	33	82	44
40/44						7		1	8	42	32	2	22	56	40
35/39						1		0	1	36	28	0	11	39	35
30/34											15		3	18	31
25/29											4		1	5	27
20/24											0			0	23

FORT BELVOIR/DAVISON AAF VIRGINIA

Temperature Range	NOVEMBER Obsn Hour Gp 01 to 08	NOVEMBER 09 to 16	NOVEMBER 17 to 24	NOVEMBER Total Obsn	NOVEMBER MCWB	DECEMBER Obsn Hour Gp 01 to 08	DECEMBER 09 to 16	DECEMBER 17 to 24	DECEMBER Total Obsn	DECEMBER MCWB	JANUARY Obsn Hour Gp 01 to 08	JANUARY 09 to 16	JANUARY 17 to 24	JANUARY Total Obsn	JANUARY MCWB
100/104															
95/99															
90/94															
85/89		0		0	71										
80/84		0	0	0	69										
75/79		3	1	4	64		0		0	57					
70/74	1	6	2	9	61	0	1	1	2	60		1	0	1	60
65/69	3	17	6	26	58	0	4	1	5	58		1	1	2	59
60/64	8	31	16	55	55	2	6	3	11	55	1	3	1	5	53
55/59	17	41	23	81	51	5	13	7	25	51	2	7	4	13	50
50/54	27	46	35	108	46	6	20	11	37	46	3	11	7	21	45
45/49	27	41	39	107	42	12	26	23	61	42	7	27	15	49	41
40/44	36	31	47	114	38	25	45	32	102	38	19	39	29	87	38
35/39	43	16	38	97	34	34	51	44	129	33	30	45	42	117	33
30/34	44	5	23	72	30	51	42	54	147	29	45	49	50	144	29
25/29	26	1	9	36	26	43	23	39	105	25	45	31	46	122	24
20/24	8	0	1	9	21	32	12	21	65	20	36	18	26	80	20
15/19	1		0	1	17	23	3	8	34	16	28	11	14	53	15
10/14						12	1	3	16	11	17	4	7	28	11
5/9						3	0	0	3	7	9	1	4	14	7
0/4						1		0	1	1	4	0	1	5	2
-5/-1						0			0	-1	2	0	0	2	-3
-10/-6											1			1	-7

Temperature Range	FEBRUARY Obsn Hour Gp 01 to 08	FEBRUARY 09 to 16	FEBRUARY 17 to 24	FEBRUARY Total Obsn	FEBRUARY MCWB	MARCH Obsn Hour Gp 01 to 08	MARCH 09 to 16	MARCH 17 to 24	MARCH Total Obsn	MARCH MCWB	APRIL Obsn Hour Gp 01 to 08	APRIL 09 to 16	APRIL 17 to 24	APRIL Total Obsn	APRIL MCWB	ANNUAL TOTAL Obsn Hour Gp 01 to 08	ANNUAL TOTAL 09 to 16	ANNUAL TOTAL 17 to 24	ANNUAL TOTAL Total Obsn	ANNUAL TOTAL MCWB
100/104																	0		0	79
95/99												0		0	69		6	1	7	77
90/94												1	0	1	68	0	70	12	82	75
85/89												5	1	6	65	0	209	64	273	73
80/84							2	0	2	62		11	5	16	62	9	292	144	445	70
75/79							4	2	6	59	0	14	7	21	60	86	307	239	632	68
70/74		1	0	1	58		8	4	12	57	2	20	13	35	58	275	265	317	857	66
65/69		2	1	3	57	1	11	6	18	55	8	30	22	60	56	320	223	269	812	62
60/64	0	3	3	6	53	3	13	10	26	52	17	37	31	85	53	262	208	239	709	57
55/59	2	10	6	18	49	7	21	18	46	48	27	40	36	103	49	268	206	232	706	52
50/54	5	15	9	29	45	8	32	24	64	44	34	39	43	116	46	233	202	218	653	47
45/49	8	26	14	48	41	21	45	38	104	41	44	28	40	112	42	214	204	221	639	42
40/44	16	42	38	96	37	39	50	48	137	37	49	13	29	91	39	242	223	252	717	38
35/39	35	44	44	123	33	53	36	44	133	33	33	2	9	44	34	264	194	233	691	33
30/34	44	39	47	130	29	56	18	34	108	29	19	0	4	23	30	276	153	215	644	29
25/29	47	25	35	107	24	32	7	15	54	25	6		1	7	26	203	87	146	436	25
20/24	29	10	16	55	20	19	2	5	26	20	1			1	21	125	42	69	236	20
15/19	17	4	7	28	15	5	0	1	6	16						74	18	30	122	16
10/14	12	2	3	17	11	2		0	2	11						43	7	13	63	11
5/9	6	0	0	6	6	1		0	1	7						19	1	4	24	7
0/4	2			2	2	0			0	4						7	0	1	8	2
-5/-1						0			0	-2						2	0	0	2	-3
-10/-6																1			1	-7

LANGLEY AFB/HAMPTON VIRGINIA

LAT 37 05N LONG 76 21W ELEV 10 FT

MEAN FREQUENCY OF OCCURRENCE OF DRY BULB TEMPERATURE (DEGREES F) WITH MEAN COINCIDENT WET BULB TEMPERATURE (DEGREES F) FOR EACH DRY BULB TEMPERATURE RANGE

Temperature Range	MAY Obsn Hour Gp 01 to 08	09 to 16	17 to 24	Total Obsn	MCWB	JUNE Obsn Hour Gp 01 to 08	09 to 16	17 to 24	Total Obsn	MCWB	JULY Obsn Hour Gp 01 to 08	09 to 16	17 to 24	Total Obsn	MCWB
95/99		0		0	76		2	0	2	78		3	0	3	78
90/94		2	0	2	74		15	3	18	77		23	4	27	77
85/89		13	3	16	71	1	39	15	55	75	0	56	19	75	76
80/84	0	32	10	42	69	5	55	33	93	73	12	81	52	145	74
75/79	3	40	25	68	67	33	58	52	143	70	92	62	93	247	72
70/74	30	49	44	123	65	87	45	70	202	68	101	21	66	188	69
65/69	57	46	50	153	61	64	19	45	128	63	33	2	13	48	65
60/64	57	41	53	151	57	32	7	18	57	59	8	0	2	10	60
55/59	51	18	39	108	53	13	1	3	17	55	2		0	2	56
50/54	33	6	19	58	49	3		1	4	50					
45/49	11	1	4	16	45	1		0	1	46					
40/44	5		1	6	40	0			0	43					
35/39	1		0	1	36										
30/34															
25/29															

Temperature Range	AUGUST Obsn Hour Gp 01 to 08	09 to 16	17 to 24	Total Obsn	MCWB	SEPTEMBER Obsn Hour Gp 01 to 08	09 to 16	17 to 24	Total Obsn	MCWB	OCTOBER Obsn Hour Gp 01 to 08	09 to 16	17 to 24	Total Obsn	MCWB
95/99		2	0	2	79										
90/94		17	3	20	78		3	0	3	77					
85/89	0	49	14	63	76		24	3	27	75		2		2	73
80/84	11	83	44	138	74	1	49	17	67	73		7	1	8	71
75/79	82	65	94	241	72	28	65	51	144	71	2	20	6	28	69
70/74	97	28	69	194	69	71	52	66	189	68	12	52	21	85	66
65/69	41	4	19	64	64	58	30	54	142	63	35	62	53	150	62
60/64	12	0	4	16	60	45	15	33	93	58	59	50	58	167	58
55/59	4		1	5	55	26	2	12	40	54	44	34	46	124	52
50/54	1		0	1	51	9		4	13	50	40	14	35	89	48
45/49						2		1	3	46	31	5	17	53	44
40/44						0			0	43	16	1	8	25	39
35/39											9	0	2	11	35
30/34											1		0	1	30
25/29											0			0	26

LANGLEY AFB/HAMPTON VIRGINIA

Temperature Range	NOVEMBER Obsn Hour Gp 01 to 08	NOVEMBER 09 to 16	NOVEMBER 17 to 24	NOVEMBER Total Obsn	NOVEMBER MCWB	DECEMBER Obsn Hour Gp 01 to 08	DECEMBER 09 to 16	DECEMBER 17 to 24	DECEMBER Total Obsn	DECEMBER MCWB	JANUARY Obsn Hour Gp 01 to 08	JANUARY 09 to 16	JANUARY 17 to 24	JANUARY Total Obsn	JANUARY MCWB
95/99															
90/94															
85/89															
80/84		1		1	70										
75/79		5	1	6	66		1		1	67		0		0	62
70/74	2	14	3	19	63	0	4	1	5	63		3		3	60
65/69	5	25	12	42	61	1	9	3	13	60	0	6	2	8	60
60/64	20	40	29	89	57	7	13	10	30	57	4	11	7	22	55
55/59	32	49	39	120	52	13	18	14	45	52	8	13	10	31	52
50/54	37	48	47	132	47	16	32	25	73	47	11	18	12	41	46
45/49	42	34	44	120	43	26	46	35	107	43	17	33	25	75	42
40/44	46	17	37	100	38	39	46	44	129	38	33	47	45	125	38
35/39	28	5	18	51	34	40	38	44	122	33	43	45	46	134	33
30/34	19	1	9	29	29	47	28	41	116	29	45	36	46	127	29
25/29	6	0	2	8	25	35	9	21	65	25	44	23	35	102	24
20/24	1	0		1	20	17	3	8	28	20	28	9	13	50	20
15/19						6	1	2	9	16	11	3	5	19	15
10/14						1		0	1	12	3	1	1	5	11
5/9											1			1	7

Temperature Range	FEBRUARY Obsn Hour Gp 01 to 08	FEBRUARY 09 to 16	FEBRUARY 17 to 24	FEBRUARY Total Obsn	FEBRUARY MCWB	MARCH Obsn Hour Gp 01 to 08	MARCH 09 to 16	MARCH 17 to 24	MARCH Total Obsn	MARCH MCWB	APRIL Obsn Hour Gp 01 to 08	APRIL 09 to 16	APRIL 17 to 24	APRIL Total Obsn	APRIL MCWB
95/99												0		0	68
90/94												2	0	2	68
85/89												4	1	5	67
80/84							3	0	3	63		11	3	14	66
75/79							6	1	7	61	0	18	10	28	64
70/74	0	3	0	3	60	0	9	3	12	59	5	26	15	46	62
65/69	1	6	3	10	58	3	15	9	27	58	22	29	26	77	60
60/64	4	10	7	21	56	10	19	16	45	54	30	41	34	105	55
55/59	6	12	10	28	51	13	28	22	63	50	39	44	44	127	51
50/54	10	22	15	47	46	21	38	27	86	46	40	40	48	128	47
45/49	18	34	29	81	42	38	54	56	148	42	54	20	40	114	43
40/44	34	47	47	128	38	63	48	64	175	38	35	4	15	54	39
35/39	46	45	50	141	33	55	20	31	106	33	11	1	2	14	35
30/34	49	28	38	115	29	27	8	14	49	28	3	0	1	4	31
25/29	33	11	18	62	24	14	2	5	21	24					
20/24	16	4	7	27	20	3	0	0	3	20					
15/19	6	1	1	8	15										
10/14	1	0	0	1	11										
5/9	0			0	8										

Temperature Range	ANNUAL TOTAL Obsn Hour Gp 01 to 08	ANNUAL TOTAL 09 to 16	ANNUAL TOTAL 17 to 24	ANNUAL TOTAL Total Obsn	ANNUAL TOTAL MCWB
95/99		7	0	7	78
90/94		62	10	72	77
85/89	1	187	55	243	75
80/84	29	322	160	511	73
75/79	240	340	333	913	71
70/74	405	306	358	1069	67
65/69	320	253	289	862	62
60/64	288	247	271	806	57
55/59	251	219	240	710	52
50/54	221	218	233	672	47
45/49	240	227	251	718	43
40/44	271	210	261	742	38
35/39	233	154	193	580	33
30/34	191	101	149	441	29
25/29	132	45	81	258	24
20/24	65	16	28	109	20
15/19	23	5	8	36	15
10/14	5	1	1	7	11
5/9	1	0	0	1	7

RICHMOND/BYRD IAP VIRGINIA

LAT 37 30N LONG 77 20W ELEV 164 FT

MEAN FREQUENCY OF OCCURRENCE OF DRY BULB TEMPERATURE (DEGREES F) WITH MEAN COINCIDENT WET BULB TEMPERATURE (DEGREES F) FOR EACH DRY BULB TEMPERATURE RANGE

Temperature Range	MAY Obsn Hour Gp 01 to 08	MAY 09 to 16	MAY 17 to 24	MAY Total Obsn	MAY MCWB	JUNE Obsn Hour Gp 01 to 08	JUNE 09 to 16	JUNE 17 to 24	JUNE Total Obsn	JUNE MCWB	JULY Obsn Hour Gp 01 to 08	JULY 09 to 16	JULY 17 to 24	JULY Total Obsn	JULY MCWB
100/104							0	0	0	76		2	0	2	77
95/99		1	0	1	73		6	1	7	76		12	2	14	76
90/94		8	1	9	73	0	31	7	38	75	0	44	11	55	76
85/89		24	6	30	70	1	49	18	68	73	1	69	26	96	74
80/84	1	37	14	52	68	5	54	29	88	70	11	64	44	119	72
75/79	4	45	26	75	65	23	48	49	120	68	46	39	66	151	71
70/74	18	48	40	106	63	62	30	57	149	67	104	14	64	182	69
65/69	47	37	52	136	61	65	15	44	124	64	57	4	27	88	65
60/64	55	29	46	130	57	46	6	24	76	59	22	0	6	28	60
55/59	51	12	37	100	53	29	2	10	41	55	7		1	8	56
50/54	40	7	17	64	49	9		1	10	51	0			0	52
45/49	23	1	6	30	45	1		0	1	47					
40/44	8	0	2	10	40										
35/39	2			2	36										
30/34	0			0	32										
25/29															
20/24															

Temperature Range	AUGUST Obsn Hour Gp 01 to 08	AUGUST 09 to 16	AUGUST 17 to 24	AUGUST Total Obsn	AUGUST MCWB	SEPTEMBER Obsn Hour Gp 01 to 08	SEPTEMBER 09 to 16	SEPTEMBER 17 to 24	SEPTEMBER Total Obsn	SEPTEMBER MCWB	OCTOBER Obsn Hour Gp 01 to 08	OCTOBER 09 to 16	OCTOBER 17 to 24	OCTOBER Total Obsn	OCTOBER MCWB
100/104		1		1	73		1		1	74					
95/99		5	0	5	76		2	0	2	74					
90/94		29	5	34	76		11	1	12	75		2	0	2	72
85/89	0	62	18	80	74		30	6	36	73		6	0	6	71
80/84	4	65	35	104	72	1	41	15	57	71	0	14	2	16	68
75/79	33	56	68	157	71	10	54	33	97	69	0	29	6	35	65
70/74	98	23	74	195	69	43	46	55	144	67	7	40	17	64	63
65/69	67	7	34	108	65	55	33	50	138	63	16	44	29	89	60
60/64	32	1	13	46	60	47	14	39	100	59	28	47	46	121	57
55/59	13		1	14	56	42	7	26	75	55	47	38	51	136	53
50/54	1			1	51	25	1	10	36	50	47	20	46	113	49
45/49						12	0	4	16	45	43	7	29	79	44
40/44						4		1	5	41	31	1	15	47	40
35/39						1			1	38	19	0	6	25	35
30/34											8		1	9	30
25/29											1			1	27
20/24											0			0	21

RICHMOND/BYRD IAP VIRGINIA

Temperature Range	NOVEMBER					DECEMBER					JANUARY				
	Obsn Hour Gp 01 to 08	Obsn Hour Gp 09 to 16	Obsn Hour Gp 17 to 24	Total Obsn	MCWB	Obsn Hour Gp 01 to 08	Obsn Hour Gp 09 to 16	Obsn Hour Gp 17 to 24	Total Obsn	MCWB	Obsn Hour Gp 01 to 08	Obsn Hour Gp 09 to 16	Obsn Hour Gp 17 to 24	Total Obsn	MCWB
100/104															
95/99															
90/94															
85/89		0		0	67										
80/84		2		2	67										
75/79		7	1	8	63		1		1	64		1		1	65
70/74	1	17	2	20	61		3	0	3	61		3	1	4	62
65/69	5	25	10	40	58	1	8	3	12	59	1	8	4	13	58
60/64	12	33	23	68	56	6	16	8	30	56	5	14	8	27	55
55/59	20	38	27	85	51	7	19	12	38	51	10	16	12	38	51
50/54	23	37	33	93	46	12	23	17	52	46	12	22	17	51	46
45/49	33	36	40	109	42	17	38	25	80	42	14	34	21	69	41
40/44	37	27	42	106	38	23	47	40	110	38	24	47	42	113	38
35/39	45	12	36	93	34	39	40	47	126	33	40	44	50	134	33
30/34	42	5	19	66	30	46	31	42	119	29	50	31	45	126	29
25/29	16	1	5	22	25	43	15	31	89	25	41	17	26	84	24
20/24	5	0	1	6	20	30	6	15	51	20	26	7	16	49	20
15/19	1		0	1	16	18	1	6	25	16	17	3	5	25	16
10/14						5	0	0	5	11	7	1	2	10	11
5/9						0		0	0	6	1		0	1	6
0/4						0		0	0	3	1			1	2

Temperature Range	FEBRUARY					MARCH					APRIL					ANNUAL TOTAL				
	Obsn Hour Gp 01 to 08	Obsn Hour Gp 09 to 16	Obsn Hour Gp 17 to 24	Total Obsn	MCWB	Obsn Hour Gp 01 to 08	Obsn Hour Gp 09 to 16	Obsn Hour Gp 17 to 24	Total Obsn	MCWB	Obsn Hour Gp 01 to 08	Obsn Hour Gp 09 to 16	Obsn Hour Gp 17 to 24	Total Obsn	MCWB	Obsn Hour Gp 01 to 08	Obsn Hour Gp 09 to 16	Obsn Hour Gp 17 to 24	Total Obsn	MCWB
100/104																	4	0	4	76
95/99												0		0	68		26	3	29	75
90/94												3	1	4	67	0	128	26	154	75
85/89							0		0	59		11	2	13	66	2	251	76	329	73
80/84							3	0	3	62		19	6	25	64	22	299	145	466	70
75/79		1		1	60		7	2	9	60	1	25	12	38	63	117	313	263	693	69
70/74		4	1	5	58	1	11	4	16	58	6	28	19	53	60	340	267	334	941	66
65/69	0	7	3	10	57	3	20	10	33	56	16	33	31	80	58	333	241	297	871	62
60/64	2	14	7	23	54	9	26	19	54	53	32	35	39	106	55	296	235	278	809	57
55/59	8	20	15	43	50	12	31	24	67	49	35	35	36	106	50	281	218	252	751	52
50/54	10	28	22	60	45	17	34	31	82	45	41	28	40	109	47	237	200	234	671	47
45/49	20	38	31	89	42	28	43	43	114	41	35	15	29	79	42	226	212	228	666	42
40/44	29	37	38	104	38	48	38	52	138	38	35	6	18	59	38	239	203	250	692	38
35/39	38	33	43	114	34	58	19	33	110	34	27	1	7	35	34	269	149	222	640	34
30/34	47	23	34	104	29	38	10	18	66	29	10	1	1	12	30	241	101	160	502	29
25/29	36	10	19	65	25	22	5	8	35	25	2		0	2	27	161	48	89	298	25
20/24	18	4	8	30	20	9	1	3	13	20						88	18	43	149	20
15/19	12	3	3	18	15	3		1	4	16						51	7	15	73	16
10/14	4	1	1	6	11	0			0	13						16	2	3	21	11
5/9	0	0		0	5											1	0	0	1	6
0/4																1		0	1	2

ROANOKE/WOODRUM ARPT VIRGINIA

LAT 37 19N LONG 79 58W ELEV 1193 FT

MEAN FREQUENCY OF OCCURRENCE OF DRY BULB TEMPERATURE (DEGREES F) WITH MEAN COINCIDENT WET BULB TEMPERATURE (DEGREES F) FOR EACH DRY BULB TEMPERATURE RANGE

Temperature Range	MAY Obsn Hour Gp 01 to 08	MAY 09 to 16	MAY 17 to 24	MAY Total Obsn	MAY MCWB	JUNE Obsn Hour Gp 01 to 08	JUNE 09 to 16	JUNE 17 to 24	JUNE Total Obsn	JUNE MCWB	JULY Obsn Hour Gp 01 to 08	JULY 09 to 16	JULY 17 to 24	JULY Total Obsn	JULY MCWB
100/104												1	0	1	75
95/99		0		0	73		3	1	4	74		6	1	7	73
90/94		3	0	3	69		19	5	24	72		25	6	31	72
85/89		20	5	25	67	0	45	15	60	70	1	59	22	82	71
80/84	1	38	14	53	65	2	55	28	85	68	3	74	41	118	69
75/79	3	46	29	78	63	14	52	50	116	67	23	48	66	137	69
70/74	14	47	42	103	61	42	35	62	139	65	91	27	76	194	67
65/69	42	35	54	131	60	79	19	49	147	63	86	7	31	124	64
60/64	61	27	47	135	57	56	8	23	87	59	31	1	5	37	59
55/59	56	19	32	107	52	33	3	6	42	55	11		0	11	54
50/54	40	10	17	67	48	10	1	2	13	50	1			1	50
45/49	23	3	7	33	43	3		0	3	46					
40/44	8	0	1	9	39	0			0	43					
35/39	2		0	2	34										
30/34															
25/29															

Temperature Range	AUGUST Obsn Hour Gp 01 to 08	AUGUST 09 to 16	AUGUST 17 to 24	AUGUST Total Obsn	AUGUST MCWB	SEPTEMBER Obsn Hour Gp 01 to 08	SEPTEMBER 09 to 16	SEPTEMBER 17 to 24	SEPTEMBER Total Obsn	SEPTEMBER MCWB	OCTOBER Obsn Hour Gp 01 to 08	OCTOBER 09 to 16	OCTOBER 17 to 24	OCTOBER Total Obsn	OCTOBER MCWB
100/104		0		0	72										
95/99		3	1	4	71		2	0	2	70					
90/94		22	3	25	72		6	1	7	70		1		1	69
85/89		54	17	71	71		25	6	31	70		5	0	5	68
80/84	1	67	35	103	69		37	15	52	68		13	2	15	64
75/79	16	55	61	132	68	2	47	31	80	66	0	28	7	35	62
70/74	80	32	80	192	67	28	47	52	127	65	2	35	19	56	60
65/69	90	11	39	140	64	58	41	57	156	62	13	40	35	88	58
60/64	43	3	10	56	60	52	22	43	117	58	29	43	47	119	55
55/59	13		1	14	55	47	8	23	78	54	46	39	48	133	52
50/54	3		0	3	51	30	3	10	43	49	50	28	44	122	47
45/49	0			0	47	15	1	3	19	45	48	11	29	88	43
40/44						6		1	7	41	35	4	10	49	39
35/39						1			1	37	16	1	4	21	34
30/34											8	0	2	10	30
25/29											1		0	1	25

ROANOKE/WOODRUM APRT VIRGINIA

Temperature Range	NOVEMBER Obsn Hour Gp 01 to 08	NOVEMBER Obsn Hour Gp 09 to 16	NOVEMBER Obsn Hour Gp 17 to 24	NOVEMBER Total Obsn	NOVEMBER MCWB	DECEMBER Obsn Hour Gp 01 to 08	DECEMBER Obsn Hour Gp 09 to 16	DECEMBER Obsn Hour Gp 17 to 24	DECEMBER Total Obsn	DECEMBER MCWB	JANUARY Obsn Hour Gp 01 to 08	JANUARY Obsn Hour Gp 09 to 16	JANUARY Obsn Hour Gp 17 to 24	JANUARY Total Obsn	JANUARY MCWB
100/104															
95/99															
90/94															
85/89															
80/84		0		0	65										
75/79		3	0	3	62							1		1	63
70/74		11	2	13	58		1		1	60		2	0	2	60
65/69	3	19	8	30	56	1	4	1	6	57		5	2	7	57
60/64	9	27	19	55	53	2	9	4	15	53	2	8	5	15	54
55/59	19	35	31	85	50	7	19	12	38	50	7	17	11	35	50
50/54	27	39	38	104	46	8	24	21	53	45	11	20	17	48	45
45/49	33	35	39	107	41	20	30	29	79	41	15	29	27	71	41
40/44	40	33	38	111	37	27	43	37	107	37	31	43	39	113	37
35/39	41	21	33	95	33	44	44	45	133	33	44	47	47	138	33
30/34	40	12	20	72	29	53	36	44	133	29	50	39	48	137	29
25/29	17	3	9	29	25	35	22	28	85	24	36	20	28	84	24
20/24	8	1	2	11	20	25	10	17	52	20	27	11	15	53	19
15/19	2	0	0	2	16	18	4	7	29	15	16	5	7	28	15
10/14	1	0	0	1	10	4	1	1	6	10	6	1	3	10	10
5/9			0	0	8	3	0	0	3	6	3	0	0	3	5
0/4						0			0	2	0	0		0	0
-5/-1											0			0	-4

Temperature Range	FEBRUARY Obsn Hour Gp 01 to 08	FEBRUARY Obsn Hour Gp 09 to 16	FEBRUARY Obsn Hour Gp 17 to 24	FEBRUARY Total Obsn	FEBRUARY MCWB	MARCH Obsn Hour Gp 01 to 08	MARCH Obsn Hour Gp 09 to 16	MARCH Obsn Hour Gp 17 to 24	MARCH Total Obsn	MARCH MCWB	APRIL Obsn Hour Gp 01 to 08	APRIL Obsn Hour Gp 09 to 16	APRIL Obsn Hour Gp 17 to 24	APRIL Total Obsn	APRIL MCWB	ANNUAL TOTAL Obsn Hour Gp 01 to 08	ANNUAL TOTAL Obsn Hour Gp 09 to 16	ANNUAL TOTAL Obsn Hour Gp 17 to 24	ANNUAL TOTAL Total Obsn	ANNUAL TOTAL MCWB
100/104																	1	0	1	75
95/99																	14	3	17	73
90/94												1		1	66		77	15	92	72
85/89												6	1	7	64	1	214	66	281	70
80/84							1	0	1	57		16	5	21	62	7	301	140	448	68
75/79		0		0	57		4	1	5	57		24	11	35	60	58	308	256	622	66
70/74		1	0	1	56	0	8	4	12	56	3	28	21	52	58	260	274	358	892	65
65/69	0	5	2	7	54	2	17	9	28	54	13	31	31	75	56	387	234	318	939	61
60/64	1	13	5	19	50	5	22	17	44	51	27	29	38	94	53	318	212	263	793	56
55/59	5	18	13	36	48	11	29	27	67	48	35	32	38	105	50	290	219	242	751	51
50/54	11	25	22	58	44	24	31	32	87	44	42	32	34	108	46	257	213	237	707	46
45/49	19	32	30	81	41	31	39	37	107	40	43	24	27	94	41	250	204	228	682	42
40/44	31	37	41	109	37	38	41	41	120	37	39	14	24	77	37	255	215	232	702	37
35/39	44	39	45	128	33	57	33	45	135	33	24	3	7	34	33	273	188	226	687	33
30/34	48	29	34	111	29	47	15	24	86	29	11	0	3	14	29	257	131	175	563	29
25/29	31	13	16	60	24	20	4	7	31	24	2	0	0	2	25	142	62	88	292	24
20/24	19	6	9	34	19	6	3	3	12	19						85	31	46	162	19
15/19	8	4	4	16	15	6	0	1	7	15						50	13	19	82	15
10/14	5	1	2	8	10	0			0	12						16	3	6	25	10
5/9	2	1	0	3	5											8	1	0	9	6
0/4	0	0		0	2											0	0		0	1
-5/-1																0			0	-4

FAIRCHILD AFB/SPOKANE WASHINGTON

LAT 47 37N LONG 117 38W ELEV 2462 FT

MEAN FREQUENCY OF OCCURRENCE OF DRY BULB TEMPERATURE (DEGREES F) WITH MEAN COINCIDENT WET BULB TEMPERATURE (DEGREES F) FOR EACH DRY BULB TEMPERATURE RANGE

Temperature Range	MAY Obsn Hour Gp 01 to 08	MAY 09 to 16	MAY 17 to 24	MAY Total Obsn	MAY MCWB	JUNE Obsn Hour Gp 01 to 08	JUNE 09 to 16	JUNE 17 to 24	JUNE Total Obsn	JUNE MCWB	JULY Obsn Hour Gp 01 to 08	JULY 09 to 16	JULY 17 to 24	JULY Total Obsn	JULY MCWB
100/104												1	0	1	66
95/99							0	0	0	65		5	2	7	64
90/94		0		0	60		4	2	6	64		21	9	30	63
85/89		2	1	3	62		12	6	18	62		38	23	61	61
80/84		6	2	8	59	0	19	11	30	61	1	43	30	74	59
75/79	0	14	7	21	57	1	33	20	54	58	7	48	42	97	58
70/74	1	27	15	43	54	7	42	33	82	56	26	41	49	116	56
65/69	4	38	25	67	52	19	46	39	104	54	51	29	40	120	54
60/64	12	41	35	88	50	36	41	49	126	52	63	15	27	105	52
55/59	30	43	43	116	48	58	27	44	129	50	52	6	18	76	49
50/54	53	41	50	144	45	61	12	28	101	47	35	1	7	43	46
45/49	60	24	40	124	42	45	3	8	56	43	12		2	14	42
40/44	52	9	22	83	39	11	0	1	12	39	1			1	38
35/39	27	1	8	36	34	2		0	2	36	0			0	34
30/34	8	0	1	9	31										
25/29	1			1	27										
20/24															
15/19															

Temperature Range	AUGUST Obsn Hour Gp 01 to 08	AUGUST 09 to 16	AUGUST 17 to 24	AUGUST Total Obsn	AUGUST MCWB	SEPTEMBER Obsn Hour Gp 01 to 08	SEPTEMBER 09 to 16	SEPTEMBER 17 to 24	SEPTEMBER Total Obsn	SEPTEMBER MCWB	OCTOBER Obsn Hour Gp 01 to 08	OCTOBER 09 to 16	OCTOBER 17 to 24	OCTOBER Total Obsn	OCTOBER MCWB
100/104		1	0	1	65										
95/99		6	2	8	63										
90/94		15	7	22	62		1	0	1	61					
85/89		30	15	45	60		6	2	8	61					
80/84	0	41	27	68	59		18	5	23	59		0		0	58
75/79	3	41	34	78	57	0	27	13	40	57		5	0	5	55
70/74	20	42	46	108	55	1	34	23	58	54		8	2	10	54
65/69	44	33	41	118	53	7	41	32	80	52		14	5	19	52
60/64	58	24	36	118	51	25	46	46	117	50	0	25	12	37	50
55/59	61	12	28	101	50	48	34	46	128	48	6	42	27	75	48
50/54	43	3	10	56	47	61	25	42	128	46	23	58	44	125	45
45/49	15	0	1	16	43	56	7	22	85	42	51	54	66	171	42
40/44	3			3	40	31	1	7	39	38	69	27	55	151	39
35/39	0			0	36	8	0	1	9	33	60	9	27	96	35
30/34						2		0	2	28	29	4	9	42	30
25/29						0			0	25	7	1	1	9	26
20/24											1	0	0	1	20
15/19											0			0	16

FAIRCHILD AFB/SPOKANE WASHINGTON

Temperature Range	NOVEMBER Obsn Hour Gp 01 to 08	09 to 16	17 to 24	Total Obsn	MCWB	DECEMBER Obsn Hour Gp 01 to 08	09 to 16	17 to 24	Total Obsn	MCWB	JANUARY Obsn Hour Gp 01 to 08	09 to 16	17 to 24	Total Obsn	MCWB	FEBRUARY Obsn Hour Gp 01 to 08	09 to 16	17 to 24	Total Obsn	MCWB	MARCH Obsn Hour Gp 01 to 08	09 to 16	17 to 24	Total Obsn	MCWB	APRIL Obsn Hour Gp 01 to 08	09 to 16	17 to 24	Total Obsn	MCWB	ANNUAL TOTAL Obsn Hour Gp 01 to 08	09 to 16	17 to 24	Total Obsn	MCWB
100/104																																2	0	2	66
95/99																																11	4	15	63
90/94																																41	18	59	62
85/89																																88	47	135	61
80/84																											0	0	0	59	1	127	75	203	59
75/79																											1	0	1	56	11	169	116	296	57
70/74																						0		0	52		3	1	4	54	55	197	169	421	55
65/69		0		0	50																	2	0	2	51		8	3	11	51	125	211	185	521	53
60/64		0		0	46												0		0	50		4	1	5	49	0	18	9	27	49	194	214	215	623	51
55/59		2	0	2	46							0		0	53		1	0	1	48		9	4	13	46	3	37	19	59	46	258	213	229	700	48
50/54	1	13	3	17	45		1	0	1	45	0	0		0	48		7	2	9	45	0	23	11	34	43	8	58	37	103	43	285	242	234	761	45
45/49	9	37	20	66	42	1	6	2	9	42	1	5	1	7	42	2	18	10	30	42	5	46	28	79	40	26	65	60	151	40	283	265	260	808	42
40/44	40	63	51	154	39	11	27	16	54	39	9	22	15	46	39	14	41	29	84	38	30	62	56	148	37	68	39	66	173	37	339	291	318	948	38
35/39	53	54	63	170	34	36	49	51	136	35	34	43	43	120	35	38	65	63	166	34	55	52	66	173	33	84	10	36	130	34	397	283	358	1038	34
30/34	72	41	61	174	30	75	69	70	214	31	53	55	57	165	30	80	53	69	202	30	88	31	53	172	30	44	1	8	53	30	451	254	328	1033	30
25/29	39	21	28	88	26	58	53	55	166	26	50	46	47	143	26	48	23	30	101	26	44	13	19	76	25	7	0	0	7	26	254	157	180	591	26
20/24	18	5	9	32	21	36	26	30	92	21	38	31	34	103	21	24	10	11	45	21	17	4	6	27	20	0	0		0	21	134	76	90	300	21
15/19	6	2	3	11	16	18	10	13	41	17	22	20	20	62	16	10	4	7	21	16	6	1	2	9	15						62	37	45	144	16
10/14	1	0	1	2	11	5	2	5	12	12	15	12	15	42	11	5	1	2	8	11	2	0	1	3	10						28	15	24	67	11
5/9	1	0	0	1	6	3	2	2	7	7	12	8	9	29	6	2	0	0	2	7	1	0	0	1	5						19	10	11	40	6
0/4	0			0	3	2	1	2	5	2	7	4	4	15	1	1	0	0	1	3	0			0	2						10	5	6	21	1
-5/-1						0	1	1	2	-4	4	2	2	8	-3																4	3	3	10	-3
-10/-6						0	1	1	2	-9	1	0	1	2	-8																1	1	2	4	-9
-15/-11						1	1	1	3	-14	1		0	1	-13																2	1	1	4	-13
-20/-16						1	0	0	1	-17	0			0	-16																1	0	0	1	-17

MCCHORD AFB/TACOMA WASHINGTON

LAT 47 09N LONG 122 29W ELEV 322 FT

MEAN FREQUENCY OF OCCURRENCE OF DRY BULB TEMPERATURE (DEGREES F) WITH MEAN COINCIDENT WET BULB TEMPERATURE (DEGREES F) FOR EACH DRY BULB TEMPERATURE RANGE

Temperature Range	MAY Obsn Hour Gp			MAY Total Obsn	MAY MCWB	JUNE Obsn Hour Gp			JUNE Total Obsn	JUNE MCWB	JULY Obsn Hour Gp			JULY Total Obsn	JULY MCWB
	01 to 08	09 to 16	17 to 24			01 to 08	09 to 16	17 to 24			01 to 08	09 to 16	17 to 24		
95/99							0		0	66		0	0	0	70
90/94		0		0	64		1	0	1	67		3	2	5	69
85/89		2	0	2	63		3	2	5	66		10	8	18	67
80/84		3	2	5	62		10	6	16	64		21	13	34	65
75/79		8	5	13	60		16	11	27	62	0	34	23	57	63
70/74		15	9	24	58	1	31	19	51	60	2	51	37	90	60
65/69	1	32	18	51	56	4	48	34	86	57	8	59	51	118	58
60/64	3	53	33	89	53	18	70	58	146	55	39	51	60	150	56
55/59	21	63	60	144	51	68	49	65	182	53	100	17	45	162	54
50/54	66	55	65	186	48	97	11	38	146	49	77	1	10	88	50
45/49	86	15	40	141	44	43	1	8	52	46	21		1	22	46
40/44	49	2	14	65	40	9		0	9	42	1			1	41
35/39	17		3	20	36	0			0	39	0			0	38
30/34	5		0	5	32										
25/29															
20/24															

Temperature Range	AUGUST Obsn Hour Gp			AUGUST Total Obsn	AUGUST MCWB	SEPTEMBER Obsn Hour Gp			SEPTEMBER Total Obsn	SEPTEMBER MCWB	OCTOBER Obsn Hour Gp			OCTOBER Total Obsn	OCTOBER MCWB
	01 to 08	09 to 16	17 to 24			01 to 08	09 to 16	17 to 24			01 to 08	09 to 16	17 to 24		
95/99		0	0	0	68										
90/94		2	1	3	68		0	0	0	69					
85/89		6	3	9	66		1	0	1	66					
80/84		17	9	26	64		4	2	6	63		0		0	63
75/79		34	19	53	63	0	16	5	21	62		1	0	1	63
70/74	1	53	36	90	60		29	13	42	60		6	1	7	60
65/69	5	66	49	120	58	1	53	27	81	58	0	20	4	24	58
60/64	42	55	69	166	57	12	72	56	140	56	4	41	15	60	55
55/59	104	16	49	169	54	62	48	75	185	53	21	69	45	135	52
50/54	69	1	12	82	50	79	14	41	134	50	55	69	73	197	49
45/49	24		1	25	46	50	1	18	69	46	67	30	65	162	45
40/44	3			3	41	29		3	32	41	50	11	31	92	41
35/39						6		0	6	36	34	2	11	47	36
30/34						1			1	32	15	0	2	17	32
25/29											2		0	2	26
20/24											1			1	22

Temperature Range	NOVEMBER Obsn Hour Gp 01 to 08	09 to 16	17 to 24	Total Obsn	MCWB	DECEMBER Obsn Hour Gp 01 to 08	09 to 16	17 to 24	Total Obsn	MCWB	JANUARY Obsn Hour Gp 01 to 08	09 to 16	17 to 24	Total Obsn	MCWB
95/99															
90/94															
85/89															
80/84															
75/79															
70/74															
65/69		0		0	54										
60/64		4	0	4	54	0	1		1	52	0	0	0	0	54
55/59	4	21	6	31	52	2	5	2	9	51	1	6	3	10	52
50/54	22	67	35	124	49	15	33	18	66	49	14	26	17	57	48
45/49	58	73	68	199	45	37	58	43	138	45	30	50	42	122	44
40/44	60	43	63	166	41	57	68	71	196	40	46	66	55	167	40
35/39	41	22	38	101	36	64	50	61	175	36	58	57	60	175	35
30/34	33	9	23	65	31	46	24	37	107	31	52	25	42	119	31
25/29	19	1	5	25	27	17	4	11	32	27	24	13	18	55	26
20/24	3	0	0	3	23	8	1	2	11	22	13	4	6	23	21
15/19						2	1	1	4	16	5	1	3	9	16
10/14						1	1	1	3	11	2	0	1	3	11
5/9						1	0	0	1	7	2	0	0	2	8
0/4						1		0	1	3	0			0	2

Temperature Range	FEBRUARY Obsn Hour Gp 01 to 08	09 to 16	17 to 24	Total Obsn	MCWB	MARCH Obsn Hour Gp 01 to 08	09 to 16	17 to 24	Total Obsn	MCWB	APRIL Obsn Hour Gp 01 to 08	09 to 16	17 to 24	Total Obsn	MCWB
95/99															
90/94															
85/89															
80/84												0		0	54
75/79												1	0	1	58
70/74		0		0	56		1	0	1	55		4	2	6	55
65/69		1	0	1	54		3	1	4	53	0	9	4	13	54
60/64		4	1	5	51		9	3	12	50	0	19	9	28	51
55/59	2	15	5	22	50	0	25	11	36	48	1	47	26	74	49
50/54	10	45	26	81	47	8	60	32	100	46	17	88	58	163	46
45/49	32	65	53	150	43	30	78	67	175	43	63	55	74	192	44
40/44	57	56	63	176	40	71	52	74	197	39	89	15	51	155	40
35/39	53	25	49	127	35	62	16	43	121	35	46	1	16	63	36
30/34	43	11	20	74	31	51	3	17	71	31	22		1	23	31
25/29	22	1	5	28	27	23	1	1	25	27	2			2	28
20/24	4	0	1	5	21	2		0	2	21					
15/19	2		0	2	17	0			0	17					
10/14			0	0	10										
5/9															
0/4															

Temperature Range	ANNUAL TOTAL Obsn Hour Gp 01 to 08	09 to 16	17 to 24	Total Obsn	MCWB
95/99		0	0	0	69
90/94		6	3	9	68
85/89		22	13	35	66
80/84		55	32	87	64
75/79	0	110	63	173	62
70/74	4	190	117	311	60
65/69	19	291	188	498	58
60/64	118	379	304	801	55
55/59	386	381	392	1159	52
50/54	529	470	425	1424	48
45/49	541	426	480	1447	44
40/44	521	313	425	1259	40
35/39	381	173	281	835	36
30/34	268	72	142	482	31
25/29	109	20	40	169	27
20/24	31	5	9	45	21
15/19	9	2	4	15	16
10/14	3	1	2	6	11
5/9	3	0	0	3	8
0/4			0		3

MOSES LAKE/GRANT CO WASHINGTON

LAT 47 12N LONG 119 19W ELEV 1185 FT

MEAN FREQUENCY OF OCCURRENCE OF DRY BULB TEMPERATURE (DEGREES F) WITH MEAN COINCIDENT WET BULB TEMPERATURE (DEGREES F) FOR EACH DRY BULB TEMPERATURE RANGE

Temperature Range	MAY Obsn Hour Gp 01 to 08	MAY 09 to 16	MAY 17 to 24	MAY Total Obsn	MAY MCWB	JUNE Obsn Hour Gp 01 to 08	JUNE 09 to 16	JUNE 17 to 24	JUNE Total Obsn	JUNE MCWB	JULY Obsn Hour Gp 01 to 08	JULY 09 to 16	JULY 17 to 24	JULY Total Obsn	JULY MCWB
110/114															
105/109												0	0	0	66
100/104							1	0	1	67		4	2	6	67
95/99		0	0	0	67		3	2	5	66		20	10	30	66
90/94		3	1	4	65		9	4	13	63		38	22	60	64
85/89		6	3	9	62	0	19	10	29	62	1	44	30	75	62
80/84		16	7	23	60	1	35	19	55	60	6	51	40	97	61
75/79	1	29	15	45	58	4	48	29	81	58	18	42	43	103	59
70/74	3	40	22	65	56	13	56	41	110	56	38	31	42	111	57
65/69	9	48	33	90	53	30	43	46	119	54	58	12	31	101	55
60/64	26	50	46	122	50	58	20	46	124	52	65	5	19	89	52
55/59	42	35	49	126	48	67	6	29	102	50	45	1	7	53	50
50/54	64	16	44	124	46	48	1	12	61	46	15		1	16	47
45/49	61	3	21	85	42	16		1	17	43	2		0	2	43
40/44	30	0	5	35	38	2		0	2	39	0			0	40
35/39	11		1	12	34	1			1	35					
30/34	2			2	30										
25/29	0			0	23										
20/24															

Temperature Range	AUGUST Obsn Hour Gp 01 to 08	AUGUST 09 to 16	AUGUST 17 to 24	AUGUST Total Obsn	AUGUST MCWB	SEPTEMBER Obsn Hour Gp 01 to 08	SEPTEMBER 09 to 16	SEPTEMBER 17 to 24	SEPTEMBER Total Obsn	SEPTEMBER MCWB	OCTOBER Obsn Hour Gp 01 to 08	OCTOBER 09 to 16	OCTOBER 17 to 24	OCTOBER Total Obsn	OCTOBER MCWB
110/114		0	0	0	70										
105/109		0	0	0	68										
100/104		2	1	3	66										
95/99		11	4	15	65		1		1	67					
90/94	0	25	13	38	63		5	1	6	64					
85/89	1	40	20	61	62		18	5	23	62		0		0	59
80/84	2	48	31	81	60		27	11	38	60		2	0	2	58
75/79	8	50	45	103	59	0	39	20	59	58		9	1	10	57
70/74	27	39	47	113	57	3	50	33	86	55		16	5	21	56
65/69	52	22	43	117	55	15	44	42	101	53	1	32	11	44	54
60/64	70	9	29	108	53	35	32	51	118	51	2	48	22	72	51
55/59	57	1	12	70	50	59	18	45	122	49	13	54	42	109	49
50/54	25	0	2	27	47	65	5	22	92	46	38	44	59	141	46
45/49	6		0	6	43	42	0	8	50	42	59	29	56	144	42
40/44	0			0	41	15		1	16	38	68	10	36	114	39
35/39						3		0	3	33	41	3	11	55	35
30/34						1			1	29	20	0	4	24	30
25/29											7		1	8	26
20/24											1		0	1	23

MOSES LAKE/GRANT CO WASHINGTON

Temperature Range	NOVEMBER Obsn Hour Gp 01 to 08	NOVEMBER Obsn Hour Gp 09 to 16	NOVEMBER Obsn Hour Gp 17 to 24	NOVEMBER Total Obsn	NOVEMBER MCWB	DECEMBER Obsn Hour Gp 01 to 08	DECEMBER Obsn Hour Gp 09 to 16	DECEMBER Obsn Hour Gp 17 to 24	DECEMBER Total Obsn	DECEMBER MCWB	JANUARY Obsn Hour Gp 01 to 08	JANUARY Obsn Hour Gp 09 to 16	JANUARY Obsn Hour Gp 17 to 24	JANUARY Total Obsn	JANUARY MCWB
110/114															
105/109															
100/104															
95/99															
90/94															
85/89															
80/84															
75/79															
70/74															
65/69		0		0	54										
60/64	0	3	0	3	50		0		0	51					
55/59	1	12	2	15	48		1		1	46	0	1	0	1	48
50/54	4	33	9	46	45	1	4	2	7	44	1	5	2	8	46
45/49	16	51	36	103	43	3	16	4	23	41	3	14	7	24	42
40/44	44	50	54	148	39	14	35	19	68	38	II	27	I8	56	38
35/39	51	39	50	140	35	36	53	49	138	34	32	45	34	1II	35
30/34	49	28	45	122	30	80	65	82	227	31	59	59	68	186	31
25/29	41	13	27	81	26	52	39	46	137	26	48	35	41	124	26
20/24	21	6	10	37	21	32	19	21	72	21	33	26	29	88	21
15/19	7	3	4	14	16	15	8	10	33	16	23	15	19	57	16
10/14	3	1	1	5	11	7	4	6	17	11	15	12	11	38	11
5/9	2	0	1	3	6	5	2	4	11	6	11	6	10	27	6
0/4	0			0	2	2	0	2	4	2	7	2	5	14	1
-5/-1						1	1	1	3	-4	4	1	2	7	-3
-10/-6						0	0	0	0	-9	2	0	1	3	-9
-15/-11						1		0	1	-12	0	0	0	0	-14
-20/-16											1		0	1	-19

Temperature Range	FEBRUARY Obsn Hour Gp 01 to 08	FEBRUARY Obsn Hour Gp 09 to 16	FEBRUARY Obsn Hour Gp 17 to 24	FEBRUARY Total Obsn	FEBRUARY MCWB	MARCH Obsn Hour Gp 01 to 08	MARCH Obsn Hour Gp 09 to 16	MARCH Obsn Hour Gp 17 to 24	MARCH Total Obsn	MARCH MCWB	APRIL Obsn Hour Gp 01 to 08	APRIL Obsn Hour Gp 09 to 16	APRIL Obsn Hour Gp 17 to 24	APRIL Total Obsn	APRIL MCWB	ANNUAL TOTAL Obsn Hour Gp 01 to 08	ANNUAL TOTAL Obsn Hour Gp 09 to 16	ANNUAL TOTAL Obsn Hour Gp 17 to 24	ANNUAL TOTAL Total Obsn	ANNUAL TOTAL MCWB
110/114																	0	0	0	70
105/109																	0	0	0	67
100/104																	7	3	10	67
95/99																	35	16	51	66
90/94																0	80	41	121	64
85/89												0		0	63	2	127	68	197	62
80/84												2	1	3	61	9	181	109	299	60
75/79							0		0	58		4	1	5	57	31	221	154	406	58
70/74							1	0	1	54		14	5	19	54	84	247	195	526	56
65/69							4	1	5	52	0	30	12	42	52	165	235	219	619	54
60/64		1		1	51		12	3	15	48	1	51	24	76	49	257	231	240	728	51
55/59		7	1	8	49	1	27	9	37	46	9	61	42	112	46	294	224	238	756	48
50/54	1	16	5	22	44	1	56	24	81	43	28	51	56	135	44	291	231	238	760	45
45/49	7	34	17	58	41	14	63	52	129	40	58	21	56	135	41	287	231	258	776	42
40/44	18	46	38	102	38	50	43	59	162	37	74	5	32	111	38	326	216	262	804	38
35/39	42	52	58	152	34	64	25	50	139	33	48	0	10	58	34	329	217	263	809	34
30/34	67	38	54	159	30	67	11	33	111	30	17		1	18	29	362	201	287	850	30
25/29	48	17	27	92	26	36	3	10	49	25	4		0	4	26	236	107	152	495	26
20/24	20	7	13	40	21	10	1	3	14	20	0			0	23	117	59	76	252	21
15/19	11	3	6	20	17	4	0	1	5	16						60	29	40	129	16
10/14	6	2	3	11	11	1	0	0	1	11						32	19	21	72	11
5/9	1	0	1	2	6	0			0	6						19	8	16	43	6
0/4	1	0	1	2	1											10	2	8	20	1
-5/-1	1	0	0	1	-4											6	2	3	11	-3
-10/-6	1			1	-8											3	0	1	4	-8
-15/-11																1	0	0	1	-13
-20/-16																1		0	1	-19

SEATTLE NSA WASHINGTON

LAT 47 41N LONG 122 15W ELEV 47 FT

MEAN FREQUENCY OF OCCURRENCE OF DRY BULB TEMPERATURE (DEGREES F) WITH MEAN COINCIDENT WET BULB TEMPERATURE (DEGREES F) FOR EACH DRY BULB TEMPERATURE RANGE

Temperature Range	MAY Obsn Hour Gp 01 to 08	MAY 09 to 16	MAY 17 to 24	MAY Total Obsn	MAY MCWB	JUNE Obsn Hour Gp 01 to 08	JUNE 09 to 16	JUNE 17 to 24	JUNE Total Obsn	JUNE MCWB	JULY Obsn Hour Gp 01 to 08	JULY 09 to 16	JULY 17 to 24	JULY Total Obsn	JULY MCWB
95/99		0		0	65		0		0	67		0	0	0	79
90/94		0		0	67		1	0	1	69		2	1	3	72
85/89		1	0	1	65		2	2	4	68		9	5	14	69
80/84		5	2	7	64		7	4	11	66		20	13	33	67
75/79		8	4	12	62	0	16	10	26	64	0	31	25	56	65
70/74		16	9	25	60	1	33	21	55	61	2	53	41	96	62
65/69	1	32	21	54	57	6	55	41	102	58	15	63	55	133	60
60/64	6	53	39	98	54	30	66	65	161	56	70	52	72	194	57
55/59	33	66	65	164	52	103	47	69	219	54	131	17	33	181	54
50/54	98	50	69	217	49	92	12	26	130	50	29	1	2	32	51
45/49	81	15	34	130	45	9	0	1	10	47	1		0	1	48
40/44	28	1	4	33	41										
35/39	2		0	2	37										

Temperature Range	AUGUST Obsn Hour Gp 01 to 08	AUGUST 09 to 16	AUGUST 17 to 24	AUGUST Total Obsn	AUGUST MCWB	SEPTEMBER Obsn Hour Gp 01 to 08	SEPTEMBER 09 to 16	SEPTEMBER 17 to 24	SEPTEMBER Total Obsn	SEPTEMBER MCWB	OCTOBER Obsn Hour Gp 01 to 08	OCTOBER 09 to 16	OCTOBER 17 to 24	OCTOBER Total Obsn	OCTOBER MCWB
95/99		1	0	1	69										
90/94	0	1	0	1	67		0	0	0	70					
85/89		5	2	7	68		1	0	1	67					
80/84		17	9	26	66		5	2	7	65		0		0	67
75/79		30	19	49	64		16	5	21	64		1	0	1	64
70/74	1	54	38	93	62	0	31	15	46	62		5	1	6	60
65/69	10	66	62	138	60	2	56	37	95	59		19	4	23	58
60/64	88	58	81	227	58	39	70	78	187	57	7	49	24	80	56
55/59	120	16	35	171	55	101	48	76	225	54	40	77	73	190	53
50/54	28	0	3	31	51	78	12	25	115	51	90	67	92	249	50
45/49	1			1	48	18	1	2	21	47	80	24	46	150	46
40/44						1			1	43	29	5	8	42	42
35/39											3	0	0	3	38

SEATTLE NSA WASHINGTON

Temperature Range	NOVEMBER Obsn Hour Gp 01 to 08	NOVEMBER 09 to 16	NOVEMBER 17 to 24	NOVEMBER Total Obsn	NOVEMBER MCWB	DECEMBER Obsn Hour Gp 01 to 08	DECEMBER 09 to 16	DECEMBER 17 to 24	DECEMBER Total Obsn	DECEMBER MCWB	JANUARY Obsn Hour Gp 01 to 08	JANUARY 09 to 16	JANUARY 17 to 24	JANUARY Total Obsn	JANUARY MCWB
95/99															
90/94															
85/89															
80/84															
75/79															
70/74															
65/69		0		0	56										
60/64	0	3	1	4	54		0		0	52		0		0	51
55/59	4	24	8	36	52	0	4	2	6	52		4	1	5	50
50/54	37	74	54	165	49	18	39	24	81	49	9	21	14	44	48
45/49	77	73	86	236	45	64	79	74	217	45	42	64	57	163	45
40/44	66	43	60	169	40	68	68	73	209	40	72	80	76	228	40
35/39	38	15	24	77	36	58	39	53	150	36	72	50	64	186	36
30/34	13	5	4	22	32	27	13	17	57	31	29	16	22	67	31
25/29	2	1	1	4	25	7	3	2	12	27	12	9	9	30	25
20/24		1	1	2	19	2	1	2	5	20	6	3	5	14	20
15/19	2	0	1	3	16	1	2	1	4	15	5	1	1	7	16
10/14	0			0	14	1	1	1	3	11	0			0	13
5/9						0			0	8					

Temperature Range	FEBRUARY Obsn Hour Gp 01 to 08	FEBRUARY 09 to 16	FEBRUARY 17 to 24	FEBRUARY Total Obsn	FEBRUARY MCWB	MARCH Obsn Hour Gp 01 to 08	MARCH 09 to 16	MARCH 17 to 24	MARCH Total Obsn	MARCH MCWB	APRIL Obsn Hour Gp 01 to 08	APRIL 09 to 16	APRIL 17 to 24	APRIL Total Obsn	APRIL MCWB
95/99															
90/94															
85/89															
80/84															
75/79												1	0	1	59
70/74		0		0	56		0		0	55		4	1	5	58
65/69		1	0	1	55		3	1	4	54		12	4	16	55
60/64		3	1	4	52		9	3	12	52	0	21	12	33	52
55/59	1	13	5	19	50	0	23	9	32	49	2	50	32	84	50
50/54	11	40	25	76	48	6	57	36	99	47	24	81	71	176	47
45/49	43	73	68	184	44	49	86	87	222	44	99	56	83	238	44
40/44	77	60	74	211	40	102	53	78	233	40	87	13	32	132	41
35/39	61	27	40	128	36	67	15	28	110	36	26	0	5	31	37
30/34	24	6	9	39	31	22	2	4	28	31	1		0	1	33
25/29	5	1	2	8	25	1	1	1	3	26					
20/24	2	1	0	3	19	1		0	1	20					
15/19	1	0	0	1	16										
10/14															
5/9															

Temperature Range	ANNUAL TOTAL Obsn Hour Gp 01 to 08	ANNUAL TOTAL 09 to 16	ANNUAL TOTAL 17 to 24	ANNUAL TOTAL Total Obsn	ANNUAL TOTAL MCWB
95/99		1	0	1	71
90/94	0	4	1	5	70
85/89		18	9	27	68
80/84		54	30	84	66
75/79	0	103	63	166	64
70/74	4	196	126	326	62
65/69	34	307	225	566	59
60/64	240	384	376	1000	57
55/59	535	389	408	1332	53
50/54	520	454	441	1415	49
45/49	564	471	538	1573	45
40/44	530	323	405	1258	40
35/39	327	146	214	687	36
30/34	116	42	56	214	31
25/29	27	15	15	57	25
20/24	11	6	8	25	20
15/19	9	3	3	15	16
10/14	1	1	1	3	12
5/9	0			0	8

CHARLESTON/KANAWHA APRT WEST VIRGINIA

LAT 38 22N LONG 81 36W ELEV 939 FT

MEAN FREQUENCY OF OCCURRENCE OF DRY BULB TEMPERATURE (DEGREES F) WITH MEAN COINCIDENT WET BULB TEMPERATURE (DEGREES F) FOR EACH DRY BULB TEMPERATURE RANGE

Temperature Range	MAY Obsn Hour Gp 01 to 08	MAY 09 to 16	MAY 17 to 24	MAY Total Obsn	MAY MCWB	JUNE Obsn Hour Gp 01 to 08	JUNE 09 to 16	JUNE 17 to 24	JUNE Total Obsn	JUNE MCWB	JULY Obsn Hour Gp 01 to 08	JULY 09 to 16	JULY 17 to 24	JULY Total Obsn	JULY MCWB
100/104												0		0	78
95/99							1		1	76		2	0	2	76
90/94		1	0	1	70		13	4	17	74		20	5	25	73
85/89		17	6	23	67		37	14	51	71		52	18	70	72
80/84	0	38	15	53	65	2	55	27	84	69	2	73	41	116	70
75/79	4	41	28	73	63	12	51	46	109	67	14	55	63	132	69
70/74	13	43	38	94	61	39	41	56	136	66	77	32	74	183	68
65/69	34	40	52	126	60	64	25	49	138	63	89	13	35	137	65
60/64	53	29	44	126	57	51	12	27	90	59	39	3	10	52	61
55/59	44	18	30	92	53	40	4	12	56	55	20		2	22	56
50/54	44	13	20	77	49	26	2	4	32	51	6		0	6	52
45/49	28	7	11	46	44	7		0	7	47	1			1	47
40/44	20	2	4	26	40	0			0	42					
35/39	6		0	6	36										
30/34	1			1	32										
25/29	0			0	29										
20/24															

Temperature Range	AUGUST Obsn Hour Gp 01 to 08	AUGUST 09 to 16	AUGUST 17 to 24	AUGUST Total Obsn	AUGUST MCWB	SEPTEMBER Obsn Hour Gp 01 to 08	SEPTEMBER 09 to 16	SEPTEMBER 17 to 24	SEPTEMBER Total Obsn	SEPTEMBER MCWB	OCTOBER Obsn Hour Gp 01 to 08	OCTOBER 09 to 16	OCTOBER 17 to 24	OCTOBER Total Obsn	OCTOBER MCWB
100/104		0		0	70		1		1	72					
95/99		3	0	3	72		1	0	1	71					
90/94		15	4	19	74		8	2	10	70		0		0	70
85/89		44	14	58	72		30	8	38	70		4	0	4	68
80/84	1	70	35	106	71	0	41	17	58	68		12	2	14	65
75/79	11	56	58	125	69	3	43	30	76	66	0	31	8	39	62
70/74	65	40	73	178	68	29	45	50	124	65	3	37	21	61	61
65/69	83	15	43	141	65	51	33	50	134	62	10	38	34	82	58
60/64	50	4	15	69	61	46	20	40	106	58	24	34	44	102	56
55/59	25	1	5	31	56	44	12	26	82	54	40	31	40	111	52
50/54	11	0	1	12	52	36	4	12	52	50	48	29	41	118	48
45/49	2			2	48	21	1	3	25	46	45	19	30	94	44
40/44						8	0	1	9	42	34	8	17	59	40
35/39						3		0	3	37	26	4	8	38	36
30/34						0			0	34	15	1	3	19	31
25/29											2		0	2	27
20/24											1			1	22

Temperature Range	NOVEMBER Obsn Hour Gp 01 to 08	09 to 16	17 to 24	Total Obsn	MCWB	DECEMBER Obsn Hour Gp 01 to 08	09 to 16	17 to 24	Total Obsn	MCWB	JANUARY Obsn Hour Gp 01 to 08	09 to 16	17 to 24	Total Obsn	MCWB
100/104															
95/99															
90/94															
85/89															
80/84		1		1	64										
75/79		4	1	5	61		1	0	1	61		0	0	0	63
70/74	2	13	4	19	59		2	1	3	57		3	1	4	60
65/69	5	21	13	39	56	1	6	3	10	56	2	4	3	9	57
60/64	10	24	20	54	52	5	10	8	23	54	6	10	9	25	54
55/59	22	26	28	76	49	10	15	13	38	51	10	15	13	38	50
50/54	24	30	29	83	46	14	23	19	56	46	12	19	19	50	46
45/49	23	29	30	82	42	15	26	25	66	42	15	25	23	63	42
40/44	31	29	32	92	38	27	34	32	93	38	19	28	27	74	38
35/39	39	28	34	101	34	31	36	40	107	34	32	34	35	101	34
30/34	43	19	27	89	30	49	39	42	130	29	46	43	47	136	30
25/29	28	10	13	51	25	35	29	30	94	25	34	28	28	90	25
20/24	9	3	5	17	21	28	15	18	61	20	29	19	22	70	20
15/19	4	1	2	7	15	14	7	10	31	15	18	12	12	42	15
10/14	1	0	1	2	11	12	5	5	22	11	13	6	6	25	11
5/9	1	1	0	2	7	4	1	1	6	6	6	1	3	10	6
0/4						2	0		2	2	3	1	1	5	1
-5/-1						0			0	-2	1	0	0	1	-3
-10/-6											1	0	0	1	-8
-15/-11											0	0		0	-12

Temperature Range	FEBRUARY Obsn Hour Gp 01 to 08	09 to 16	17 to 24	Total Obsn	MCWB	MARCH Obsn Hour Gp 01 to 08	09 to 16	17 to 24	Total Obsn	MCWB	APRIL Obsn Hour Gp 01 to 08	09 to 16	17 to 24	Total Obsn	MCWB	ANNUAL TOTAL Obsn Hour Gp 01 to 08	09 to 16	17 to 24	Total Obsn	MCWB
100/104																	1		1	73
95/99																	7	0	7	74
90/94												0		0	66		57	15	72	73
85/89							0		0	59		6	2	8	63		190	62	252	71
80/84							1	0	1	58		17	8	25	62	5	308	145	458	69
75/79		0		0	63		3	2	5	59	1	25	15	41	60	45	310	251	606	67
70/74	0	2	0	2	56	0	11	5	16	56	9	26	23	58	58	237	295	346	878	65
65/69	1	5	2	8	55	4	14	9	27	54	17	27	30	74	56	361	241	323	925	61
60/64	4	10	10	24	52	10	21	20	51	52	29	29	34	92	54	327	206	281	814	56
55/59	7	16	15	38	49	15	25	25	65	49	32	28	34	94	50	309	191	243	743	52
50/54	12	22	19	53	45	20	29	27	76	45	29	27	27	83	46	282	198	218	698	47
45/49	17	30	28	75	41	24	34	36	94	41	31	24	26	81	42	229	195	212	636	42
40/44	25	29	32	86	38	35	35	38	108	37	35	18	23	76	38	234	183	206	623	38
35/39	36	33	33	102	34	41	33	35	109	33	33	10	14	57	34	247	178	199	624	34
30/34	43	34	38	115	30	47	28	32	107	29	19	3	5	27	30	263	167	194	624	30
25/29	29	17	21	67	25	28	10	12	50	25	5	0	1	6	26	161	94	105	360	25
20/24	23	11	12	46	20	12	4	4	20	20	1	0		1	22	103	52	61	216	20
15/19	12	7	5	24	15	7	1	2	10	15						55	28	31	114	15
10/14	9	4	5	18	11	2	0	0	2	11						37	15	17	69	11
5/9	3	2	2	7	6	0			0	8						14	5	6	25	6
0/4	3	1	0	4	1											8	2	1	11	1
-5/-1	1			1	-2											2	0	0	2	-2
-10/-6																1	0	0	1	-8
-15/-11																0	0		0	-12

ELKINS/RANDOLPH CO APRT WEST VIRGINIA

LAT 38 53N LONG 79 51W ELEV 1948 FT

MEAN FREQUENCY OF OCCURRENCE OF DRY BULB TEMPERATURE (DEGREES F) WITH MEAN COINCIDENT WET BULB TEMPERATURE (DEGREES F) FOR EACH DRY BULB TEMPERATURE RANGE

Temperature Range	MAY Obsn Hour Gp 01 to 08	MAY 09 to 16	MAY 17 to 24	MAY Total Obsn	MAY MCWB	JUNE Obsn Hour Gp 01 to 08	JUNE 09 to 16	JUNE 17 to 24	JUNE Total Obsn	JUNE MCWB	JULY Obsn Hour Gp 01 to 08	JULY 09 to 16	JULY 17 to 24	JULY Total Obsn	JULY MCWB
95/99												0		0	76
90/94							1		1	72		1	0	1	74
85/89		1		1	68		13	3	16	72		19	3	22	72
80/84		13	3	16	65	0	42	11	53	69	0	64	16	80	70
75/79	0	39	12	51	63	2	58	23	83	66	3	70	32	105	68
70/74	5	50	23	78	60	12	53	39	104	64	15	56	53	124	66
65/69	14	45	34	93	58	34	37	53	124	63	60	26	73	159	64
60/64	33	38	50	121	57	58	23	52	133	59	84	10	45	139	61
55/59	42	29	45	116	53	49	8	31	88	55	47	1	18	66	56
50/54	49	17	36	102	49	43	3	20	66	51	25		7	32	52
45/49	41	10	22	73	45	29	1	7	37	47	12		1	13	47
40/44	32	6	16	54	40	12	1	2	15	42	2			2	42
35/39	20	1	6	27	35	1			1	38					
30/34	10	0	1	11	31										
25/29	1			1	27										
20/24															
15/19															
10/14															

Temperature Range	AUGUST Obsn Hour Gp 01 to 08	AUGUST 09 to 16	AUGUST 17 to 24	AUGUST Total Obsn	AUGUST MCWB	SEPTEMBER Obsn Hour Gp 01 to 08	SEPTEMBER 09 to 16	SEPTEMBER 17 to 24	SEPTEMBER Total Obsn	SEPTEMBER MCWB	OCTOBER Obsn Hour Gp 01 to 08	OCTOBER 09 to 16	OCTOBER 17 to 24	OCTOBER Total Obsn	OCTOBER MCWB
95/99							0		0	68					
90/94		1	0	1	69		2	0	2	68					
85/89		11	1	12	71		6	1	7	67		0		0	66
80/84		49	10	59	70		26	3	29	68		4		4	65
75/79	1	76	24	101	67	0	42	10	52	66		14	1	15	61
70/74	12	60	48	120	66	2	53	25	80	63	0	33	5	38	58
65/69	53	33	74	160	64	24	44	44	112	62	3	36	14	53	56
60/64	76	12	52	140	61	46	34	55	135	58	11	37	25	73	54
55/59	53	4	25	82	56	43	18	38	99	55	16	34	37	87	52
50/54	32	1	10	43	52	38	11	32	81	50	31	29	43	103	48
45/49	17	0	3	20	47	40	3	18	61	46	41	30	43	114	44
40/44	4		0	4	43	29	1	9	39	42	47	18	38	103	40
35/39						12	0	3	15	37	37	8	22	67	36
30/34						6		1	7	32	36	4	15	55	31
25/29						1			1	28	20	0	5	25	27
20/24											5		1	6	22
15/19											1		0	1	17
10/14											0			0	13

Temperature Range	NOVEMBER Obsn Hour Gp 01 to 08	09 to 16	17 to 24	Total Obsn	M C W B	DECEMBER Obsn Hour Gp 01 to 08	09 to 16	17 to 24	Total Obsn	M C W B	JANUARY Obsn Hour Gp 01 to 08	09 to 16	17 to 24	Total Obsn	M C W B
95/99															
90/94															
85/89															
80/84															
75/79		1		1	61		0		0	60		0		0	58
70/74		4	1	5	59		0		0	60		1	0	1	58
65/69	1	15	2	18	56	0	1	0	1	56	0	3	1	4	57
60/64	5	25	10	40	53	1	7	2	10	54	1	4	2	7	55
55/59	12	25	17	54	50	5	12	7	24	51	7	10	7	24	51
50/54	19	29	24	72	46	10	17	12	39	48	11	17	12	40	47
45/49	23	26	26	75	43	14	24	17	55	43	11	20	18	49	42
40/44	23	29	30	82	38	20	30	24	74	38	18	27	24	69	37
35/39	27	30	34	91	34	21	34	33	88	33	22	32	28	82	34
30/34	43	30	43	116	29	37	38	47	122	29	39	42	44	125	29
25/29	39	15	31	85	25	43	36	35	114	25	40	33	35	108	25
20/24	31	9	15	55	21	32	26	28	86	20	30	25	32	87	21
15/19	11	3	5	19	16	25	13	17	55	15	28	17	20	65	15
10/14	5	0	3	8	11	20	8	16	44	11	18	11	14	43	11
5/9	2	1	1	4	6	11	3	7	21	6	11	3	7	21	6
0/4	1			1	2	6	0	2	8	2	7	1	3	11	1
-5/-1						2	0	0	2	-2	3	1	1	5	-3
-10/-6						1			1	-6	2	0	0	2	-7
-15/-11											1		0	1	-14
-20/-16											0			0	-17

Temperature Range	FEBRUARY Obsn Hour Gp 01 to 08	09 to 16	17 to 24	Total Obsn	M C W B	MARCH Obsn Hour Gp 01 to 08	09 to 16	17 to 24	Total Obsn	M C W B	APRIL Obsn Hour Gp 01 to 08	09 to 16	17 to 24	Total Obsn	M C W B	ANNUAL TOTAL Obsn Hour Gp 01 to 08	09 to 16	17 to 24	Total Obsn	M C W B
95/99																	0		0	70
90/94																	5	0	5	70
85/89												0		0	61		50	8	58	71
80/84							0		0	58		4	1	5	62	0	202	44	246	69
75/79							1	0	1	56		19	4	23	61	6	320	106	432	66
70/74		0		0	55		3	1	4	54	1	26	10	37	59	47	339	205	591	63
65/69		3	0	3	53	0	11	2	13	53	6	27	16	49	56	195	281	313	789	61
60/64	1	4	2	7	53	5	16	9	30	52	13	29	28	70	53	334	239	332	905	58
55/59	4	13	8	25	50	9	21	12	42	49	26	29	35	90	51	313	204	280	797	53
50/54	8	17	12	37	46	14	24	24	62	46	32	27	34	93	47	312	192	266	770	48
45/49	12	27	20	59	41	16	29	22	67	41	29	25	27	81	42	285	195	224	704	43
40/44	22	29	29	80	38	21	35	37	93	38	30	22	28	80	38	260	198	237	695	39
35/39	24	30	29	83	34	33	34	36	103	34	36	19	28	83	34	233	188	219	640	34
30/34	36	37	41	114	29	50	36	47	133	29	35	10	23	68	30	292	197	262	751	30
25/29	32	27	32	91	25	44	23	34	101	25	23	2	5	30	26	243	136	177	556	25
20/24	33	16	22	71	21	30	9	15	54	21	9	1	1	11	22	170	86	114	370	21
15/19	19	8	13	40	16	14	3	5	22	16	1	0	0	1	16	99	44	60	203	16
10/14	14	7	7	28	11	7	1	2	10	12	0			0	14	64	27	42	133	11
5/9	8	3	6	17	7	3	0	1	4	7						35	10	22	67	6
0/4	6	1	3	10	1	2		0	2	3						22	2	8	32	2
-5/-1	4	0	1	5	-3											9	1	2	12	-3
-10/-6	1	0	0	1	-7											4	0	0	4	-7
-15/-11	1			1	-13											2		0	2	-13
-20/-16	0			0	-16											0			0	-16

HUNTINGTON WEST VIRGINIA

LAT 38 25N LONG 82 30W ELEV 565 FT

MEAN FREQUENCY OF OCCURRENCE OF DRY BULB TEMPERATURE (DEGREES F) WITH MEAN COINCIDENT WET BULB TEMPERATURE (DEGREES F) FOR EACH DRY BULB TEMPERATURE RANGE

Temperature Range	MAY Obsn Hour Gp 01 to 08	09 to 16	17 to 24	Total Obsn	MCWB	JUNE Obsn Hour Gp 01 to 08	09 to 16	17 to 24	Total Obsn	MCWB	JULY Obsn Hour Gp 01 to 08	09 to 16	17 to 24	Total Obsn	MCWB
105/109												0		0	82
100/104												1	0	1	79
95/99							3	0	3	78		7	1	8	76
90/94		4	0	4	71		18	4	22	75		27	5	32	75
85/89		23	6	29	69	0	40	13	53	72	0	58	18	76	73
80/84	0	41	14	55	67	1	56	24	81	70	2	65	35	102	71
75/79	2	42	23	67	65	10	52	43	105	68	17	53	61	131	71
70/74	11	46	38	95	63	36	35	56	127	67	80	27	75	182	69
65/69	30	38	49	117	61	62	21	49	132	64	81	9	36	126	65
60/64	59	27	47	133	58	57	9	31	97	60	41	1	13	55	61
55/59	46	15	32	93	53	42	4	15	61	55	21		3	24	56
50/54	42	9	22	73	49	25	1	5	31	51	5		0	5	52
45/49	31	4	13	48	45	6	0	0	6	47	0			0	48
40/44	20	1	4	25	41	0		0	0	41					
35/39	6		0	6	36		0	0	0	32					
30/34	1			1	32	0	0	0	0	28					
25/29						0			0	23					
20/24															
15/19						0		0	0	17					

Temperature Range	AUGUST Obsn Hour Gp 01 to 08	09 to 16	17 to 24	Total Obsn	MCWB	SEPTEMBER Obsn Hour Gp 01 to 08	09 to 16	17 to 24	Total Obsn	MCWB	OCTOBER Obsn Hour Gp 01 to 08	09 to 16	17 to 24	Total Obsn	MCWB
105/109															
100/104		0		0	73		1		1	74					
95/99		6	0	6	75		3	0	3	73					
90/94		22	4	26	75		12	2	14	72		1		1	70
85/89	0	54	14	68	73		30	6	36	71		5	0	5	70
80/84	1	64	29	94	71	0	41	14	55	69		17	2	19	66
75/79	12	54	51	117	70	4	43	25	72	67	0	30	8	38	64
70/74	63	32	73	168	69	28	47	45	120	66	2	38	16	56	61
65/69	81	13	46	140	65	46	33	50	129	63	10	37	30	77	59
60/64	51	2	20	73	61	45	18	41	104	59	27	39	41	107	56
55/59	25	0	8	33	56	43	8	31	82	55	30	30	38	98	52
50/54	13	0	2	15	52	39	3	19	61	51	44	27	44	115	49
45/49	2			2	48	24	1	6	31	46	53	15	34	102	45
40/44						11		2	13	42	34	6	20	60	40
35/39						1		0	1	37	29	3	12	44	36
30/34											14	1	3	18	31
25/29											3	0	1	4	26
20/24											2		0	2	22
15/19											0			0	18

HUNTINGTON WEST VIRGINIA

Temperature Range	NOVEMBER Obsn Hour Gp 01 to 08	NOVEMBER Obsn Hour Gp 09 to 16	NOVEMBER Obsn Hour Gp 17 to 24	NOVEMBER Total Obsn	NOVEMBER MCWB	DECEMBER Obsn Hour Gp 01 to 08	DECEMBER Obsn Hour Gp 09 to 16	DECEMBER Obsn Hour Gp 17 to 24	DECEMBER Total Obsn	DECEMBER MCWB	JANUARY Obsn Hour Gp 01 to 08	JANUARY Obsn Hour Gp 09 to 16	JANUARY Obsn Hour Gp 17 to 24	JANUARY Total Obsn	JANUARY MCWB
105/109															
100/104															
95/99															
90/94															
85/89															
80/84		2		2	66										
75/79		4	1	5	62		0		0	62		0		0	63
70/74	1	12	3	16	59		2	0	2	59		1	0	1	60
65/69	1	17	7	25	56	1	5	1	7	58	1	5	2	8	58
60/64	8	24	14	46	53	2	11	4	17	54	4	8	5	17	55
55/59	13	29	21	63	51	7	15	11	33	52	7	14	10	31	51
50/54	20	31	30	81	47	11	20	16	47	47	12	21	18	51	47
45/49	28	32	34	94	43	15	26	19	60	43	15	24	22	61	43
40/44	30	33	35	98	39	19	35	29	83	38	19	29	25	73	38
35/39	39	28	39	106	34	36	44	44	124	34	33	43	38	114	34
30/34	46	17	32	95	30	49	39	48	136	30	47	41	48	136	30
25/29	36	7	16	59	26	40	25	33	98	25	36	27	33	96	25
20/24	11	2	5	18	21	31	11	19	61	21	30	15	20	65	21
15/19	5	1	2	8	16	16	8	13	37	16	21	9	12	42	16
10/14	1	0	1	2	11	13	4	7	24	11	11	6	8	25	11
5/9	1	0	0	1	8	6	2	2	10	7	6	2	3	11	7
0/4						2	1	0	3	2	4	1	2	7	1
-5/-1						1	0		1	-3	3	0	0	3	-3
-10/-6											0	0	0	0	-8
-15/-11											1	0		1	-11

Temperature Range	FEBRUARY Obsn Hour Gp 01 to 08	FEBRUARY Obsn Hour Gp 09 to 16	FEBRUARY Obsn Hour Gp 17 to 24	FEBRUARY Total Obsn	FEBRUARY MCWB	MARCH Obsn Hour Gp 01 to 08	MARCH Obsn Hour Gp 09 to 16	MARCH Obsn Hour Gp 17 to 24	MARCH Total Obsn	MARCH MCWB	APRIL Obsn Hour Gp 01 to 08	APRIL Obsn Hour Gp 09 to 16	APRIL Obsn Hour Gp 17 to 24	APRIL Total Obsn	APRIL MCWB	ANNUAL TOTAL Obsn Hour Gp 01 to 08	ANNUAL TOTAL Obsn Hour Gp 09 to 16	ANNUAL TOTAL Obsn Hour Gp 17 to 24	ANNUAL TOTAL Total Obsn	ANNUAL TOTAL MCWB
105/109																	0		0	82
100/104																	2	0	2	76
95/99																	19	1	20	76
90/94												1		1	67		85	15	100	74
85/89							0		0	60		9	2	11	65	0	219	59	278	72
80/84							1	0	1	59		17	7	24	64	4	304	125	433	70
75/79		0		0	61		5	1	6	58	1	24	11	36	62	46	307	224	577	68
70/74	0	3	0	3	58	0	9	4	13	57	4	24	16	44	59	225	276	326	827	66
65/69	1	5	2	8	56	2	16	11	29	55	14	27	26	67	57	330	226	309	865	62
60/64	2	10	7	19	53	9	21	16	46	53	24	33	38	95	54	329	203	277	809	57
55/59	6	15	12	33	50	12	26	22	60	50	31	30	34	95	51	283	186	237	706	53
50/54	8	23	17	48	46	16	27	27	70	46	32	28	32	92	47	267	190	232	689	48
45/49	17	27	23	67	42	26	37	35	98	42	35	22	30	87	43	252	188	216	656	43
40/44	24	34	32	90	38	36	36	38	110	38	37	16	23	76	38	230	190	208	628	39
35/39	34	38	38	110	34	45	38	42	125	34	31	7	16	54	34	254	201	229	684	34
30/34	45	33	41	119	30	47	20	31	98	30	23	1	5	29	31	272	152	208	632	30
25/29	34	16	25	75	25	30	7	13	50	25	7	0	1	8	26	186	82	122	390	25
20/24	24	9	12	45	21	17	3	5	25	21	1			1	23	116	40	61	217	21
15/19	13	6	7	26	16	6	1	2	9	16						61	25	36	122	16
10/14	8	3	4	15	11	2	0	0	2	11						35	13	20	68	11
5/9	4	1	2	7	7	1			1	7						18	5	7	30	7
0/4	3	0	1	4	1	0			0	4						9	2	3	14	2
-5/-1	1			1	-3											5	0	0	5	-3
-10/-6																0	0	0	0	-8
-15/-11																1	0		1	-11

GREEN BAY/AUSTIN-STRAUBEL WISCONSIN

LAT 44 29N LONG 88 08W ELEV 682 FT

MEAN FREQUENCY OF OCCURRENCE OF DRY BULB TEMPERATURE (DEGREES F) WITH MEAN COINCIDENT WET BULB TEMPERATURE (DEGREES F) FOR EACH DRY BULB TEMPERATURE RANGE

Temperature Range	MAY Obsn Hour Gp 01 to 08	MAY 09 to 16	MAY 17 to 24	MAY Total Obsn	MAY MCWB	JUNE Obsn Hour Gp 01 to 08	JUNE 09 to 16	JUNE 17 to 24	JUNE Total Obsn	JUNE MCWB	JULY Obsn Hour Gp 01 to 08	JULY 09 to 16	JULY 17 to 24	JULY Total Obsn	JULY MCWB
95/99							0		0	71		0	0	0	79
90/94		0		0	67		4	1	5	73		3	0	3	75
85/89		2	0	2	69		12	2	14	73		24	4	28	72
80/84		8	2	10	68	1	33	10	44	70	1	54	18	73	69
75/79	0	21	6	27	64	6	44	21	71	67	10	68	33	111	67
70/74	2	31	14	47	60	16	53	36	105	63	32	52	54	138	65
65/69	11	39	23	73	58	39	45	48	132	61	58	31	59	148	63
60/64	23	43	33	99	55	50	31	49	130	57	66	11	51	128	59
55/59	37	38	44	119	52	51	14	37	102	54	51	4	22	77	55
50/54	44	31	44	119	47	43	4	23	70	50	22	0	6	28	51
45/49	46	20	38	104	43	22	0	10	32	45	7		1	8	47
40/44	41	12	27	80	39	10		2	12	41	0			0	43
35/39	28	4	12	44	35	2		0	2	37					
30/34	13	0	4	17	31	0			0	33					
25/29	3		0	3	27										
20/24															
15/19															

Temperature Range	AUGUST Obsn Hour Gp 01 to 08	AUGUST 09 to 16	AUGUST 17 to 24	AUGUST Total Obsn	AUGUST MCWB	SEPTEMBER Obsn Hour Gp 01 to 08	SEPTEMBER 09 to 16	SEPTEMBER 17 to 24	SEPTEMBER Total Obsn	SEPTEMBER MCWB	OCTOBER Obsn Hour Gp 01 to 08	OCTOBER 09 to 16	OCTOBER 17 to 24	OCTOBER Total Obsn	OCTOBER MCWB
95/99		1		1	74										
90/94		5	1	6	73		2	0	2	73					
85/89	0	16	3	19	73		7	1	8	72		0		0	66
80/84	1	41	12	54	70	0	9	3	12	70		1		1	64
75/79	5	58	26	89	67	3	22	8	33	67		8	0	8	63
70/74	27	61	46	134	65	11	39	15	65	64	0	16	2	18	61
65/69	54	41	59	154	63	16	48	29	93	60	2	23	9	34	58
60/64	61	21	54	136	59	32	46	42	120	57	10	38	18	66	56
55/59	53	4	31	88	55	44	40	52	136	53	24	47	37	108	52
50/54	28		14	42	51	51	20	44	115	49	37	43	44	124	48
45/49	15		3	18	46	39	5	27	71	45	39	34	47	120	44
40/44	4		0	4	42	25	0	12	37	41	49	24	42	115	40
35/39	0			0	38	14		5	19	36	43	12	31	86	35
30/34						5		1	6	31	28	3	13	44	31
25/29						0		0	0	28	10	0	5	15	26
20/24											4		1	5	22
15/19											1		0	1	17

GREEN BAY/AUSTIN-STRAUBEL WISCONSIN

Temperature Range	NOVEMBER Obsn Hour Gp 01 to 08	09 to 16	17 to 24	Total Obsn	M C W B	DECEMBER Obsn Hour Gp 01 to 08	09 to 16	17 to 24	Total Obsn	M C W B	JANUARY Obsn Hour Gp 01 to 08	09 to 16	17 to 24	Total Obsn	M C W B
95/99															
90/94															
85/89															
80/84															
75/79															
70/74		0		0	57										
65/69		2	0	2	58										
60/64	1	6	2	9	56		0		0	54					
55/59	4	11	7	22	52	0	1		1	53					
50/54	8	18	9	35	48	1	I	I	3	50					
45/49	13	29	22	64	43	2	4	3	9	44		1		1	41
40/44	22	41	30	93	39	3	7	4	I4	39	1	3	1	5	39
35/39	42	43	44	129	34	13	25	I8	56	35	4	14	6	24	34
30/34	55	42	52	149	30	38	46	42	126	30	22	35	31	88	30
25/29	41	24	33	98	25	33	46	39	II8	25	37	44	41	122	26
20/24	24	11	18	53	21	37	37	37	III	21	32	37	32	101	21
15/19	11	7	11	29	16	31	28	30	89	16	29	30	28	87	16
10/14	8	3	7	18	11	22	21	24	67	11	26	28	30	84	11
5/9	4	2	2	8	6	21	17	22	60	6	25	21	27	73	6
0/4	3	1	1	5	2	23	9	17	49	1	20	15	22	57	1
-5/-1	2	0	1	3	-3	13	3	8	24	-3	22	10	14	46	-3
-10/-6	1		0	1	-7	7	1	3	11	-8	14	5	9	28	-8
-15/-11						3	0		3	-13	9	3	4	16	-13
-20/-16						1	0		1	-17	4	1	1	6	-18
-25/-21											1	0	0	1	-23
-30/-26											1	0		:	-28

Temperature Range	FEBRUARY Obsn Hour Gp 01 to 08	09 to 16	17 to 24	Total Obsn	M C W B	MARCH Obsn Hour Gp 01 to 08	09 to 16	17 to 24	Total Obsn	M C W B
95/99										
90/94										
85/89										
80/84										
75/79										
70/74							0		0	56
65/69							0	0	0	54
60/64							1	0	1	56
55/59							3	1	4	50
50/54		0		0	39	1	5	3	9	46
45/49		2	0	2	41	2	10	4	16	42
40/44	1	6	3	10	38	5	24	10	39	37
35/39	7	18	11	36	34	21	53	37	111	34
30/34	25	43	36	104	30	49	58	67	174	30
25/29	32	42	35	109	25	56	44	51	151	25
20/24	28	39	35	102	21	38	27	32	97	20
15/19	29	28	36	93	16	24	14	19	57	16
10/14	30	21	27	78	11	23	6	15	44	11
5/9	25	11	18	54	6	17	2	7	26	7
0/4	19	8	12	39	1	7	1	1	9	2
-5/-1	13	4	6	23	-3	3	0	1	4	-3
-10/-6	8	1	3	12	-8	1	0		1	-8
-15/-11	5	0	1	6	-13	0	0	0	0	-14
-20/-16	2	0	0	2	-18	1	0	0	1	-18
-25/-21	1		0	1	-23	0		0	0	-23
-30/-26						0			0	-27

Temperature Range	APRIL Obsn Hour Gp 01 to 08	09 to 16	17 to 24	Total Obsn	M C W B	ANNUAL TOTAL Obsn Hour Gp 01 to 08	09 to 16	17 to 24	Total Obsn	M C W B
95/99							1	0	1	75
90/94							14	2	16	74
85/89		0		0	64	0	61	10	71	72
80/84		1	0	1	62	3	147	45	195	70
75/79		5	1	6	60	24	226	95	345	67
70/74		9	2	11	57	88	261	169	518	64
65/69	1	12	5	18	55	181	241	232	654	61
60/64	3	19	9	31	52	246	216	258	720	57
55/59	7	23	16	46	49	271	185	247	703	53
50/54	14	32	25	71	46	249	154	213	616	48
45/49	26	41	34	101	42	211	146	189	546	44
40/44	41	43	47	131	38	202	160	178	540	39
35/39	52	34	45	131	34	226	203	209	638	34
30/34	55	16	39	110	30	290	243	285	818	30
25/29	29	3	10	42	25	241	203	214	658	25
20/24	8	1	4	13	21	171	152	159	482	21
15/19	3	0	0	3	16	128	107	124	359	16
10/14	1		0	1	11	110	79	103	292	11
5/9	0			0	7	92	53	76	221	6
0/4						72	34	53	159	1
-5/-1						53	17	30	100	-3
-10/-6						31	7	15	53	-8
-15/-11						17	3	5	25	-13
-20/-16						8	1	1	10	-18
-25/-21						2	0	0	2	-23
-30/-26						1	0		1	-28

LA CROSSE MAP WISCONSIN

LAT 43 52N LONG 91 15W ELEV 651 FT

MEAN FREQUENCY OF OCCURRENCE OF DRY BULB TEMPERATURE (DEGREES F) WITH MEAN COINCIDENT WET BULB TEMPERATURE (DEGREES F) FOR EACH DRY BULB TEMPERATURE RANGE

Temperature Range	MAY Obsn Hour Gp 01 to 08	MAY 09 to 16	MAY 17 to 24	MAY Total Obsn	MAY MCWB	JUNE Obsn Hour Gp 01 to 08	JUNE 09 to 16	JUNE 17 to 24	JUNE Total Obsn	JUNE MCWB	JULY Obsn Hour Gp 01 to 08	JULY 09 to 16	JULY 17 to 24	JULY Total Obsn	JULY MCWB
100/104												0		0	78
95/99							1	0	1	75		2	0	2	78
90/94		0		0	71	0	8	2	10	74		10	3	13	77
85/89		6	2	8	69	0	20	9	29	72	0	35	15	50	72
80/84	0	15	6	21	65	1	40	22	63	69	4	56	34	94	70
75/79	1	30	15	46	63	11	52	40	103	66	19	63	53	135	68
70/74	9	34	26	69	60	34	49	47	130	64	51	51	63	165	66
65/69	19	44	39	102	58	54	36	47	137	61	76	25	49	150	63
60/64	34	43	46	123	55	56	21	39	116	58	62	6	26	94	60
55/59	53	31	43	127	52	44	10	23	77	54	28	1	5	34	56
50/54	49	21	35	105	47	27	3	9	39	50	8		1	9	52
45/49	42	16	22	80	43	11	0	1	12	46	0			0	49
40/44	27	5	9	41	39	2		0	2	42					
35/39	11	1	4	16	34										
30/34	3	0	1	4	30										
25/29	0			0	28										
20/24															
15/19															

Temperature Range	AUGUST Obsn Hour Gp 01 to 08	AUGUST 09 to 16	AUGUST 17 to 24	AUGUST Total Obsn	AUGUST MCWB	SEPTEMBER Obsn Hour Gp 01 to 08	SEPTEMBER 09 to 16	SEPTEMBER 17 to 24	SEPTEMBER Total Obsn	SEPTEMBER MCWB	OCTOBER Obsn Hour Gp 01 to 08	OCTOBER 09 to 16	OCTOBER 17 to 24	OCTOBER Total Obsn	OCTOBER MCWB
100/104		0		0	72										
95/99		2	0	2	75		0		0	71					
90/94		10	3	13	74		4	0	4	74		0		0	63
85/89	0	24	10	34	72		7	2	9	74		0	0	0	64
80/84	3	48	26	77	70	0	11	7	18	70		4	0	4	64
75/79	13	59	45	117	68	7	28	14	49	67		12	2	14	62
70/74	44	52	58	154	66	12	41	23	76	63	1	20	10	31	60
65/69	67	35	53	155	63	19	45	37	101	60	7	31	18	56	58
60/64	63	15	35	113	59	36	45	48	129	57	16	35	28	79	55
55/59	41	3	14	58	55	53	34	49	136	53	31	38	39	108	51
50/54	15		3	18	51	51	18	35	104	49	35	37	44	116	47
45/49	3		0	3	47	38	6	16	60	45	47	34	39	120	43
40/44	1		0	1	42	16	0	6	22	41	46	22	37	105	39
35/39	0			0	37	6		1	7	36	34	11	21	66	34
30/34						1			1	32	23	4	7	34	30
25/29											5	0	2	7	25
20/24											2		0	2	22
15/19											0			0	19

LA CROSSE MAP WISCONSIN

Temperature Range	NOVEMBER Obsn Hour Gp			Total Obsn	MCWB	DECEMBER Obsn Hour Gp			Total Obsn	MCWB	JANUARY Obsn Hour Gp			Total Obsn	MCWB	FEBRUARY Obsn Hour Gp			Total Obsn	MCWB	MARCH Obsn Hour Gp			Total Obsn	MCWB	APRIL Obsn Hour Gp			Total Obsn	MCWB	ANNUAL TOTAL Obsn Hour Gp			Total Obsn	MCWB
	01 to 08	09 to 16	17 to 24			01 to 08	09 to 16	17 to 24			01 to 08	09 to 16	17 to 24			01 to 08	09 to 16	17 to 24			01 to 08	09 to 16	17 to 24			01 to 08	09 to 16	17 to 24			01 to 08	09 to 16	17 to 24		
100/104																																0		0	76
95/99																																5	0	5	76
90/94																											0		0	62	0	32	8	40	75
85/89																											1	0	1	63	0	93	38	131	72
80/84																											3	1	4	61	8	177	96	281	69
75/79																						0	0	0	51		7	2	9	59	51	251	171	473	66
70/74		1		1	58																	0	0	0	56	1	10	5	16	57	152	258	232	642	64
65/69	0	3	0	3	56																	1	0	1	54	4	19	11	34	54	246	239	254	739	61
60/64	2	7	4	13	55	0	0	0	0	54							0		0	51	1	2	1	4	51	7	22	20	49	52	277	196	247	720	57
55/59	6	15	8	29	51	1	1	1	3	52							1		1	45		5	3	8	48	14	26	25	65	49	271	165	210	646	52
50/54	8	24	15	47	47	2	1	2	5	49		0		0	45	0	2	1	3	44	2	11	5	18	44	23	33	31	87	45	220	150	181	551	47
45/49	15	26	23	64	42	1	4	2	7	43		1	0	1	40	1	5	2	8	41	3	15	9	27	40	31	38	37	106	41	192	145	151	488	43
40/44	25	34	33	92	38	5	13	7	25	38	0	6	2	8	37	2	12	5	19	37	9	31	22	62	37	39	38	40	117	38	172	161	161	494	38
35/39	41	38	39	118	34	14	24	23	61	34	10	20	16	46	34	10	28	22	60	33	27	48	44	119	33	51	26	35	112	34	204	196	205	605	34
30/34	50	35	46	131	30	33	42	42	117	30	20	34	30	84	30	32	41	43	116	30	50	55	61	166	30	41	12	22	75	30	253	223	252	728	30
25/29	38	24	28	90	25	38	47	40	125	25	30	34	34	98	25	32	34	36	102	25	51	34	41	126	25	21	3	8	32	25	215	176	189	580	25
20/24	21	16	17	54	20	37	34	32	103	21	32	36	32	100	21	28	35	31	94	20	37	22	26	85	20	6	1	1	8	21	163	144	139	446	21
15/19	14	8	14	36	16	32	23	29	84	16	28	27	31	86	16	27	27	26	80	16	25	13	16	54	16	0	0	0	0	16	126	98	116	340	16
10/14	8	5	8	21	11	25	21	18	64	11	30	30	27	87	11	27	15	21	63	11	17	7	10	34	11	1		0	1	10	108	78	84	270	11
5/9	7	2	2	11	7	19	18	22	59	6	26	21	23	70	6	22	11	16	49	6	14	3	5	22	6						88	55	68	211	6
0/4	4	1	2	7	1	13	11	13	37	2	20	17	20	57	1	18	8	9	35	1	7	1	2	10	2						62	38	46	146	1
-5/-1	1	0	1	2	-3	11	5	11	27	-3	20	13	17	50	-4	10	4	7	21	-3	3	0	1	4	-4						45	22	37	104	-3
-10/-6	0			0	-7	10	3	5	18	-8	15	7	9	31	-8	7	2	3	12	-8	1	0	0	1	-8						33	12	17	62	-8
-15/-11						5	0	1	6	-13	8	3	5	16	-13	5	1	1	7	-13	0	0		0	-14						18	4	7	29	-13
-20/-16						1	0		1	-17	5	1	1	7	-18	2	0	1	3	-18	0		0	0	-18						8	1	2	11	-18
-25/-21						0			0	-22	2	0	1	3	-23	1			1	-22	0	0		0	-23						3	0	1	4	-23
-30/-26											1	0	0	1	-28						0			0	-27						1	0	0	1	-28
-35/-31											0	0		0	-33																0	0		0	-33

MADISON/TRAUX FIELD WISCONSIN

LAT 43 08N LONG 89 20W ELEV 858 FT

MEAN FREQUENCY OF OCCURRENCE OF DRY BULB TEMPERATURE (DEGREES F) WITH MEAN COINCIDENT WET BULB TEMPERATURE (DEGREES F) FOR EACH DRY BULB TEMPERATURE RANGE

Temperature Range	MAY Obsn Hour Gp 01 to 08	MAY 09 to 16	MAY 17 to 24	MAY Total Obsn	MAY MCWB	JUNE Obsn Hour Gp 01 to 08	JUNE 09 to 16	JUNE 17 to 24	JUNE Total Obsn	JUNE MCWB	JULY Obsn Hour Gp 01 to 08	JULY 09 to 16	JULY 17 to 24	JULY Total Obsn	JULY MCWB
100/104												0		0	80
95/99							1		1	76		2	0	2	77
90/94		0		0	71		10	2	12	73		12	2	14	74
85/89		5	1	6	68	0	24	7	31	72	0	40	10	50	71
80/84		17	4	21	67	2	45	17	64	69	4	66	29	99	69
75/79	1	31	11	43	63	12	51	32	95	66	18	62	45	125	67
70/74	6	39	21	66	60	27	43	46	116	64	46	40	59	145	66
65/69	18	41	32	91	58	48	34	48	130	61	63	19	56	138	63
60/64	36	38	44	118	55	49	20	43	112	57	64	7	33	104	59
55/59	40	32	43	115	51	49	8	28	85	54	35	1	12	48	55
50/54	45	21	37	103	47	29	4	13	46	49	15		2	17	51
45/49	41	16	28	85	43	17	0	4	21	45	3		0	3	47
40/44	34	6	18	58	40	6		1	7	41					
35/39	18	2	8	28	35	1			1	37					
30/34	9		2	11	30										
25/29	1			1	26										
20/24															
15/19															

Temperature Range	AUGUST Obsn Hour Gp 01 to 08	AUGUST 09 to 16	AUGUST 17 to 24	AUGUST Total Obsn	AUGUST MCWB	SEPTEMBER Obsn Hour Gp 01 to 08	SEPTEMBER 09 to 16	SEPTEMBER 17 to 24	SEPTEMBER Total Obsn	SEPTEMBER MCWB	OCTOBER Obsn Hour Gp 01 to 08	OCTOBER 09 to 16	OCTOBER 17 to 24	OCTOBER Total Obsn	OCTOBER MCWB
100/104		0		0	72										
95/99		2		2	73		1		1	71					
90/94		11	2	13	74		3	0	3	74					
85/89	0	26	8	34	72	0	12	2	14	72		1		1	65
80/84	2	54	19	75	70	0	15	6	21	70		3	0	3	65
75/79	11	67	38	116	68	4	30	13	47	66	0	15	1	16	64
70/74	39	48	56	143	66	14	49	21	84	63	0	24	7	31	60
65/69	61	27	55	143	63	18	45	33	96	60	5	33	17	55	58
60/64	60	11	43	114	59	40	43	47	130	57	18	37	26	81	55
55/59	43	1	20	64	55	45	27	49	121	53	26	38	35	99	51
50/54	21		7	28	51	47	13	36	96	49	34	36	40	110	47
45/49	10		1	11	46	36	3	19	58	45	42	31	45	118	43
40/44	2			2	42	19	0	10	29	41	44	17	37	98	39
35/39	0			0	39	11		3	14	36	39	11	25	75	35
30/34						4		0	4	32	28	2	10	40	30
25/29						0			0	28	8	0	4	12	26
20/24											2		1	3	20
15/19											1			1	17

MADISON/TRAUX FIELD WISCONSIN

Temperature Range	NOVEMBER Obsn Hour Gp 01 to 08	09 to 16	17 to 24	Total Obsn	MCWB	DECEMBER Obsn Hour Gp 01 to 08	09 to 16	17 to 24	Total Obsn	MCWB	JANUARY Obsn Hour Gp 01 to 08	09 to 16	17 to 24	Total Obsn	MCWB
100/104															
95/99															
90/94															
85/89															
80/84															
75/79		0		0	62										
70/74		1	0	1	61										
65/69	0	4	0	4	56										
60/64	2	9	4	15	55		0		0	54					
55/59	6	16	10	32	51	1	2	0	3	52					
50/54	7	21	14	42	47	0	3	2	5	48		1		1	46
45/49	16	28	21	65	43	2	7	4	13	43	0	2	1	3	44
40/44	23	38	28	89	38	4	15	5	24	38	2	7	2	11	38
35/39	34	38	45	117	34	14	25	20	59	34	6	23	13	42	34
30/34	58	36	46	140	30	42	47	48	137	30	26	37	36	99	30
25/29	40	26	32	98	25	39	48	46	133	25	39	45	41	125	26
20/24	23	11	18	52	21	40	35	31	I06	21	34	35	34	103	21
15/19	12	5	12	29	16	27	24	26	77	16	29	28	30	87	16
10/14	8	3	6	17	11	21	I8	21	60	11	32	27	28	87	11
5/9	4	2	3	9	6	20	I4	20	54	6	20	18	22	60	6
0/4	2	1	1	4	1	16	7	14	37	1	20	13	21	54	1
-5/-1	1		1	2	-3	11	4	8	23	-3	17	7	12	36	-3
-10/-6	0			0	-7	9	I	3	13	-8	14	4	6	24	-8
-15/-11						2	0	0	2	-13	5	1	2	8	-13
-20/-16						1			I	-17	3	0	1	4	-18
-25/-21						0			0	-21	0	0	0	0	-22
-30/-26											1		0	1	-28
-35/-31											0			0	-33
-40/-36											0			0	

Temperature Range	FEBRUARY Obsn Hour Gp 01 to 08	09 to 16	17 to 24	Total Obsn	MCWB	MARCH Obsn Hour Gp 01 to 08	09 to 16	17 to 24	Total Obsn	MCWB	APRIL Obsn Hour Gp 01 to 08	09 to 16	17 to 24	Total Obsn	MCWB
100/104															
95/99															
90/94															
85/89												1		1	62
80/84												3	1	4	62
75/79												7	2	9	60
70/74							1	0	1	55	0	14	4	18	57
65/69							1	0	1	55	2	19	10	31	55
60/64						0	3	1	4	52	7	24	17	48	53
55/59		0		0	50	0	5	2	7	49	14	28	23	65	49
50/54	1	3	0	4	46	1	10	5	16	45	20	30	30	80	45
45/49	1	5	2	8	42	4	21	9	34	41	30	39	35	104	42
40/44	2	14	5	21	37	9	29	18	56	37	39	34	42	115	38
35/39	10	30	21	61	34	24	54	45	123	34	47	26	38	111	34
30/34	35	47	43	125	30	60	56	67	183	30	47	12	29	88	30
25/29	36	45	43	124	25	56	33	45	134	25	25	2	9	36	25
20/24	36	31	39	106	20	32	20	27	79	20	7	0	2	9	20
15/19	27	18	25	70	16	26	9	14	49	16	1	0	0	1	16
10/14	24	13	18	55	11	14	3	10	27	11	1			1	9
5/9	22	8	11	41	6	10	1	4	15	7					
0/4	11	5	9	25	1	4	1	1	6	2					
-5/-1	9	3	5	17	-4	3	0	0	3	-3					
-10/-6	7	1	2	10	-8	2	0	0	2	-8					
-15/-11	2	0	1	3	-13	0			0	-13					
-20/-16	1		0	1	-18	0	0	0	0	-19					
-25/-21	0		0	0	-23	0			0	-23					
-30/-26	0			0	-26	0			0	-27					
-35/-31															
-40/-36															

Temperature Range	ANNUAL TOTAL Obsn Hour Gp 01 to 08	09 to 16	17 to 24	Total Obsn	MCWB
100/104		0		0	76
95/99		6	0	6	75
90/94		36	6	42	74
85/89	0	109	28	137	72
80/84	8	203	76	287	69
75/79	46	263	142	451	66
70/74	132	259	214	605	64
65/69	215	223	251	689	61
60/64	276	192	258	726	57
55/59	259	158	222	639	52
50/54	220	142	186	548	48
45/49	202	152	169	523	43
40/44	184	160	166	510	39
35/39	204	209	218	631	34
30/34	309	237	281	827	30
25/29	244	199	220	663	25
20/24	174	132	152	458	20
15/19	123	84	107	314	16
10/14	100	64	83	247	11
5/9	76	43	60	179	6
0/4	53	27	46	126	1
-5/-1	41	14	26	81	-3
-10/-6	32	6	11	49	-8
-15/-11	9	1	3	13	-13
-20/-16	5	0	1	6	-18
-25/-21	0	0	0	0	-23
-30/-26	1		0	1	-28
-35/-31	0			0	-33
-40/-36	0			0	

CASPER IAP WYOMING

LAT 42 55N LONG 106 28W ELEV 5338 FT

MEAN FREQUENCY OF OCCURRENCE OF DRY BULB TEMPERATURE (DEGREES F) WITH MEAN COINCIDENT WET BULB TEMPERATURE (DEGREES F) FOR EACH DRY BULB TEMPERATURE RANGE

Temperature Range	MAY Obsn Hour Gp 01 to 08	MAY 09 to 16	MAY 17 to 24	MAY Total Obsn	MAY MCWB	JUNE Obsn Hour Gp 01 to 08	JUNE 09 to 16	JUNE 17 to 24	JUNE Total Obsn	JUNE MCWB	JULY Obsn Hour Gp 01 to 08	JULY 09 to 16	JULY 17 to 24	JULY Total Obsn	JULY MCWB
100/104												1	0	1	62
95/99							1	0	1	58		4	1	5	60
90/94							8	2	10	56		29	9	38	58
85/89		2	0	2	55		23	8	31	56	0	59	24	83	58
80/84		8	2	10	54	0	34	14	48	55	2	58	31	91	58
75/79		20	6	26	52	3	41	21	65	55	10	42	40	92	57
70/74	1	34	13	48	51	6	38	27	71	54	28	29	47	104	56
65/69	3	38	21	62	50	18	36	41	95	52	48	16	45	109	55
60/64	9	36	30	75	48	34	27	40	101	51	67	8	30	105	53
55/59	24	39	41	104	47	56	18	37	111	49	55	3	15	73	51
50/54	39	31	44	114	45	66	9	29	104	47	29	1	5	35	48
45/49	59	24	43	126	42	39	3	14	56	44	7		1	8	45
40/44	61	11	32	104	39	14	1	4	19	40	1		0	1	41
35/39	35	5	12	52	35	3	1	1	5	35					
30/34	14	1	3	18	31	1	1	1	3	31					
25/29	1	1	1	3	25	0		0	0	28					
20/24	1	0	1	2	21										
15/19	1		0	1	18										
10/14															

Temperature Range	AUGUST Obsn Hour Gp 01 to 08	AUGUST 09 to 16	AUGUST 17 to 24	AUGUST Total Obsn	AUGUST MCWB	SEPTEMBER Obsn Hour Gp 01 to 08	SEPTEMBER 09 to 16	SEPTEMBER 17 to 24	SEPTEMBER Total Obsn	SEPTEMBER MCWB	OCTOBER Obsn Hour Gp 01 to 08	OCTOBER 09 to 16	OCTOBER 17 to 24	OCTOBER Total Obsn	OCTOBER MCWB
100/104															
95/99		0	0	0	57										
90/94		16	4	20	58		1	0	1	58					
85/89		52	17	69	57		15	2	17	56		0		0	54
80/84	1	64	26	91	57		31	8	39	54		2	0	2	52
75/79	6	49	37	92	56	0	39	14	53	53		13	1	14	50
70/74	22	33	49	104	55	4	37	25	66	52		26	4	30	48
65/69	48	16	50	114	54	13	32	33	78	50	0	34	8	42	47
60/64	66	10	36	112	52	23	29	38	90	48	6	34	17	57	45
55/59	59	5	16	80	49	37	19	39	95	46	14	34	31	79	43
50/54	31	2	9	42	47	43	13	29	85	44	25	29	38	92	41
45/49	10	1	3	14	43	53	11	23	87	41	36	26	42	104	39
40/44	5		1	6	39	36	8	17	61	38	56	22	42	120	36
35/39	1			1	36	21	4	9	34	34	47	15	29	91	33
30/34						8	2	3	13	31	37	8	22	67	29
25/29						2		1	3	26	18	4	10	32	26
20/24						0		0	0	23	7	1	2	10	21
15/19											2		1	3	16
10/14													0	0	14

CASPER IAP WYOMING

Temperature Range	NOVEMBER					DECEMBER					JANUARY				
	Obsn Hour Gp 01 to 08	Obsn Hour Gp 09 to 16	Obsn Hour Gp 17 to 24	Total Obsn	MCWB	Obsn Hour Gp 01 to 08	Obsn Hour Gp 09 to 16	Obsn Hour Gp 17 to 24	Total Obsn	MCWB	Obsn Hour Gp 01 to 08	Obsn Hour Gp 09 to 16	Obsn Hour Gp 17 to 24	Total Obsn	MCWB
100/104															
95/99															
90/94															
85/89															
80/84															
75/79															
70/74															
65/69		1		1	47										
60/64		8	0	8	44										
55/59		17	2	19	42		1		1	41		0		0	42
50/54	3	26	10	39	39	1	7	1	9	39		4	0	4	39
45/49	13	37	22	72	37	2	22	5	29	37	1	17	3	21	36
40/44	31	38	36	105	34	12	35	18	65	34	7	33	13	53	33
35/39	39	29	41	109	32	32	45	38	115	31	25	42	37	104	31
30/34	42	27	39	108	28	43	47	48	138	28	38	38	43	119	27
25/29	40	20	34	94	25	41	35	44	120	24	39	30	39	108	24
20/24	31	16	18	65	21	41	23	33	97	20	38	28	34	100	20
15/19	15	11	15	41	16	34	16	25	75	16	29	17	24	70	15
10/14	11	5	9	25	11	16	7	16	39	11	22	12	18	52	11
5/9	7	2	6	15	7	10	5	11	26	7	17	8	11	36	6
0/4	5	1	4	10	2	8	2	5	15	2	10	7	7	24	1
-5/-1	2	1	2	5	-4	4	2	3	9	-3	8	5	8	21	-3
-10/-6	2	0	1	3	-8	3	1	2	6	-8	5	5	4	14	-9
-15/-11	0			0	-12	1	0	1	2	-13	4	2	4	10	-13
-20/-16						1	0	0	1	-17	3	1	2	6	-18
-25/-21						0		0	0	-24	2	0	1	3	-23
-30/-26						0		0	0	-27	0		0	0	-27

Temperature Range	FEBRUARY					MARCH					APRIL				
	Obsn Hour Gp 01 to 08	Obsn Hour Gp 09 to 16	Obsn Hour Gp 17 to 24	Total Obsn	MCWB	Obsn Hour Gp 01 to 08	Obsn Hour Gp 09 to 16	Obsn Hour Gp 17 to 24	Total Obsn	MCWB	Obsn Hour Gp 01 to 08	Obsn Hour Gp 09 to 16	Obsn Hour Gp 17 to 24	Total Obsn	MCWB
100/104															
95/99															
90/94															
85/89															
80/84												0		0	52
75/79												3	0	3	50
70/74							0		0	48		11	2	13	48
65/69							3	1	4	45	0	20	6	26	46
60/64		2		2	44		8	2	10	43	1	24	10	35	44
55/59		5	1	6	42	0	13	4	17	42	4	25	18	47	42
50/54	1	11	3	15	39	1	20	8	29	39	11	31	25	67	40
45/49	3	22	8	33	37	5	30	16	51	37	20	31	33	84	38
40/44	14	30	20	64	34	16	35	30	81	34	34	32	37	103	36
35/39	21	31	29	81	31	29	34	40	103	32	47	24	38	109	33
30/34	26	31	33	90	28	46	35	40	121	28	54	19	32	105	30
25/29	37	33	37	107	24	41	27	38	106	25	40	16	24	80	25
20/24	43	23	33	99	20	40	22	28	90	21	21	4	12	37	21
15/19	30	15	27	72	16	29	11	18	58	16	8	0	2	10	17
10/14	20	9	13	42	11	18	4	11	33	11	1		0	1	12
5/9	11	4	8	23	6	9	4	5	18	7					
0/4	7	4	5	16	2	6	2	4	12	2					
-5/-1	4	2	4	10	-3	4	1	2	7	-3					
-10/-6	4	0	1	5	-8	3	0	1	4	-8					
-15/-11	2	0	1	3	-13	1	0	0	1	-13					
-20/-16	0			0	-18	0			0	-17					
-25/-21															
-30/-26															

Temperature Range	ANNUAL TOTAL				
	Obsn Hour Gp 01 to 08	Obsn Hour Gp 09 to 16	Obsn Hour Gp 17 to 24	Total Obsn	MCWB
100/104		1	0	1	62
95/99		5	1	6	60
90/94		54	15	69	58
85/89	0	151	51	202	57
80/84	3	197	81	281	56
75/79	19	207	119	345	55
70/74	61	208	167	436	53
65/69	130	196	205	531	52
60/64	206	186	203	595	50
55/59	249	179	204	632	47
50/54	250	184	201	635	43
45/49	248	224	213	685	39
40/44	287	245	250	782	36
35/39	300	230	274	804	32
30/34	309	209	264	782	28
25/29	259	166	228	653	25
20/24	222	117	161	500	20
15/19	148	70	112	330	16
10/14	88	37	67	192	11
5/9	54	23	41	118	6
0/4	36	16	25	77	2
-5/-1	22	11	19	52	-3
-10/-6	17	6	9	32	-8
-15/-11	8	2	6	16	-13
-20/-16	4	1	2	7	-18
-25/-21	2	0	1	3	-23
-30/-26	0		0	0	-27

CHEYENNE MAP WYOMING

LAT 41 09N LONG 104 49W ELEV 6126 FT

MEAN-FREQUENCY OF OCCURRENCE OF DRY BULB TEMPERATURE (DEGREES F) WITH MEAN COINCIDENT WET BULB TEMPERATURE (DEGREES F) FOR EACH DRY BULB TEMPERATURE RANGE

Temperature Range	MAY Obsn Hour Gp 01 to 08	MAY 09 to 16	MAY 17 to 24	MAY Total Obsn	MAY MCWB	JUNE Obsn Hour Gp 01 to 08	JUNE 09 to 16	JUNE 17 to 24	JUNE Total Obsn	JUNE MCWB	JULY Obsn Hour Gp 01 to 08	JULY 09 to 16	JULY 17 to 24	JULY Total Obsn	JULY MCWB
100/104							0		0	60					
95/99							0	0	0	58		1	0	1	60
90/94							2	0	2	56	0	9	1	10	59
85/89		1		1	55		17	3	20	57	0	42	6	48	58
80/84		6	1	7	53	1	33	8	42	56	2	61	17	80	58
75/79	0	16	3	19	52	4	43	17	64	56	8	50	28	86	58
70/74	1	30	9	40	51	8	41	26	75	55	17	39	40	96	57
65/69	4	38	13	55	50	14	36	38	88	53	31	27	60	118	56
60/64	9	41	27	77	48	30	28	46	104	52	67	12	53	132	54
55/59	21	38	37	96	46	58	20	44	122	50	73	6	30	109	52
50/54	42	30	47	119	45	62	11	33	106	48	39	2	11	52	49
45/49	54	20	47	121	42	41	5	18	64	44	10	1	2	13	45
40/44	58	15	34	107	39	15	2	4	21	39	1	0	0	1	41
35/39	37	7	20	64	35	4	1	2	7	35	0			0	39
30/34	18	5	8	31	31	2	1	1	4	31					
25/29	2	1	1	4	26	1		0	1	27					
20/24	2	1	2	5	22										
15/19	1			1	18										
10/14															

Temperature Range	AUGUST Obsn Hour Gp 01 to 08	AUGUST 09 to 16	AUGUST 17 to 24	AUGUST Total Obsn	AUGUST MCWB	SEPTEMBER Obsn Hour Gp 01 to 08	SEPTEMBER 09 to 16	SEPTEMBER 17 to 24	SEPTEMBER Total Obsn	SEPTEMBER MCWB	OCTOBER Obsn Hour Gp 01 to 08	OCTOBER 09 to 16	OCTOBER 17 to 24	OCTOBER Total Obsn	OCTOBER MCWB
100/104															
95/99															
90/94		4	0	4	58		1		1	59					
85/89		26	3	29	58		6	1	7	56					
80/84	0	61	11	72	57		28	3	31	55		1		1	53
75/79	5	62	22	89	57	1	48	9	58	54		15	0	15	51
70/74	13	43	38	94	56	3	41	15	59	52	0	32	3	35	49
65/69	27	26	56	109	55	10	32	27	69	51	1	40	6	47	47
60/64	60	14	62	136	54	20	26	38	84	49	5	38	12	55	45
55/59	82	6	40	128	51	37	20	49	106	47	12	31	27	70	43
50/54	45	4	12	61	48	55	14	39	108	45	27	26	38	91	41
45/49	11	1	4	16	44	49	10	27	86	42	43	22	50	115	38
40/44	5		1	6	39	35	8	18	61	38	58	18	48	124	36
35/39	0			0	39	19	3	9	31	35	46	11	29	86	32
30/34						8	1	4	13	31	32	10	20	62	29
25/29						2	0	1	3	26	16	3	11	30	26
20/24						0			0	22	7	1	3	11	21
15/19											1	0	1	2	17
10/14											0		0	0	13

CHEYENNE MAP WYOMING

Temperature Range	NOVEMBER Obsn Hour Gp 01 to 08	09 to 16	17 to 24	Total Obsn	MCWB	DECEMBER Obsn Hour Gp 01 to 08	09 to 16	17 to 24	Total Obsn	MCWB	JANUARY Obsn Hour Gp 01 to 08	09 to 16	17 to 24	Total Obsn	MCWB
100/104															
95/99															
90/94															
85/89															
80/84															
75/79															
70/74		0		0	45										
65/69		4		4	44		0		0	46					
60/64		16		16	43		1		1	42		1		1	42
55/59	0	26	2	28	40	1	10	1	12	41		6	0	6	39
50/54	4	35	10	49	38	1	21	1	23	38	1	17	1	19	37
45/49	18	35	23	76	36	5	31	8	44	35	4	28	6	38	35
40/44	34	29	40	103	33	22	40	22	84	32	15	36	18	69	32
35/39	38	21	40	99	30	36	38	42	116	30	27	37	32	96	29
30/34	38	23	39	100	28	39	34	50	123	27	34	30	42	106	26
25/29	36	19	33	88	24	43	29	42	114	23	40	27	41	108	23
20/24	30	16	21	67	20	42	20	35	97	20	38	22	29	89	19
15/19	18	10	15	43	16	26	9	20	55	15	26	15	28	69	15
10/14	12	3	11	26	11	15	6	12	33	11	24	9	18	51	10
5/9	6	2	3	11	6	8	2	7	17	6	12	5	11	28	6
0/4	2	1	3	6	1	5	3	5	13	1	12	5	7	24	1
-5/-1	2	1	2	5	-3	2	1	2	5	-3	4	3	5	12	-4
-10/-6	1			1	-7	1	0	1	2	-9	4	3	3	10	-8
-15/-11						0		0	0	-14	2	2	3	7	-13
-20/-16						0			0	-17	3	1	2	6	-18
-25/-21						0			0	-21	1	0	1	2	-23
-30/-26											0	0	0	0	-26

Temperature Range	FEBRUARY Obsn Hour Gp 01 to 08	09 to 16	17 to 24	Total Obsn	MCWB	MARCH Obsn Hour Gp 01 to 08	09 to 16	17 to 24	Total Obsn	MCWB	APRIL Obsn Hour Gp 01 to 08	09 to 16	17 to 24	Total Obsn	MCWB
100/104															
95/99															
90/94															
85/89															
80/84												0	0	0	51
75/79												2	0	2	49
70/74							0		0	48		10	1	11	48
65/69		1	0	1	45		4	0	4	44	1	18	5	24	46
60/64		4	0	4	42	0	7	1	8	42	1	27	9	37	44
55/59		10	1	11	41	0	16	4	20	40	5	27	17	49	42
50/54	2	19	4	25	38	1	25	7	33	38	9	31	22	62	40
45/49	5	26	11	42	36	5	25	14	44	35	21	32	34	87	38
40/44	15	30	22	67	33	15	34	24	73	33	34	28	38	100	35
35/39	24	32	29	85	30	28	31	37	96	31	49	23	39	111	32
30/34	32	29	35	96	27	41	33	47	121	28	53	18	32	103	29
25/29	35	25	36	96	23	47	28	37	112	24	33	14	19	66	25
20/24	38	19	31	88	20	40	26	33	99	20	22	8	17	47	21
15/19	31	10	23	64	15	31	11	18	60	16	9	1	4	14	17
10/14	16	8	14	38	11	19	5	13	37	11	2		1	3	12
5/9	10	3	8	21	6	9	2	7	18	6	1		0	1	7
0/4	7	4	5	16	1	5	2	4	11	2	0		0	0	2
-5/-1	4	1	3	8	-3	3	0	1	4	-3	0			0	-2
-10/-6	3	0	2	5	-8	2	0	1	3	-8					
-15/-11	1	0	0	1	-14	0			0	-11					
-20/-16	0		0	0	-18										
-25/-21			0	0	-23										
-30/-26															

Temperature Range	ANNUAL TOTAL Obsn Hour Gp 01 to 08	09 to 16	17 to 24	Total Obsn	MCWB
100/104		0		0	60
95/99		1	0	1	59
90/94	0	16	1	17	59
85/89	0	92	13	105	58
80/84	3	190	40	233	57
75/79	18	236	79	333	56
70/74	42	236	132	410	54
65/69	88	226	205	519	53
60/64	192	215	248	655	51
55/59	289	216	252	757	48
50/54	288	235	225	748	44
45/49	266	236	244	746	39
40/44	307	240	269	816	35
35/39	308	204	279	791	31
30/34	297	184	278	759	28
25/29	255	146	221	622	24
20/24	219	113	171	503	20
15/19	143	56	109	308	15
10/14	88	31	69	188	11
5/9	46	14	36	96	6
0/4	31	15	24	70	1
-5/-1	15	6	13	34	-3
-10/-6	11	3	7	21	-8
-15/-11	3	2	3	8	-13
-20/-16	3	1	2	6	-18
-25/-21	1	0	1	2	-23
-30/-26	0	0	0	0	-26

ROCK SPRINGS WYOMING

LAT 41 36N   LONG 109 04W   ELEV 6745 FT

MEAN FREQUENCY OF OCCURRENCE OF DRY BULB TEMPERATURE (DEGREES F) WITH MEAN COINCIDENT WET BULB TEMPERATURE (DEGREES F) FOR EACH DRY BULB TEMPERATURE RANGE

Temperature Range	MAY Obsn Hour Gp 01 to 08	MAY 09 to 16	MAY 17 to 24	MAY Total Obsn	MAY MCWB	JUNE Obsn Hour Gp 01 to 08	JUNE 09 to 16	JUNE 17 to 24	JUNE Total Obsn	JUNE MCWB	JULY Obsn Hour Gp 01 to 08	JULY 09 to 16	JULY 17 to 24	JULY Total Obsn	JULY MCWB
95/99												0		0	59
90/94							1	0	1	54		2	0	2	57
85/89		0	0	0	51		5	1	6	53		23	7	30	55
80/84		1	0	1	52	0	24	9	33	53	0	64	29	93	55
75/79		6	2	8	51	0	39	20	59	52	1	67	37	105	54
70/74		24	7	31	48	1	46	28	75	50	7	48	51	106	52
65/69	0	41	18	59	47	10	39	38	87	49	36	27	55	118	51
60/64	3	41	28	72	45	31	36	44	111	47	81	11	44	136	49
55/59	16	37	38	91	43	52	23	35	110	45	73	4	17	94	47
50/54	35	32	43	110	42	53	13	30	96	44	37	1	6	44	45
45/49	49	29	39	117	40	47	9	20	76	41	11	0	2	13	42
40/44	58	20	33	111	37	30	3	10	43	38	2		0	2	39
35/39	45	11	24	80	34	11	2	4	17	34	0			0	38
30/34	29	4	12	45	30	4	0	1	5	30					
25/29	9	1	3	13	26	1		0	1	26					
20/24	3	0	1	4	21										
15/19	0		0	0	19										
10/14		0		0	13										

Temperature Range	AUGUST Obsn Hour Gp 01 to 08	AUGUST 09 to 16	AUGUST 17 to 24	AUGUST Total Obsn	AUGUST MCWB	SEPTEMBER Obsn Hour Gp 01 to 08	SEPTEMBER 09 to 16	SEPTEMBER 17 to 24	SEPTEMBER Total Obsn	SEPTEMBER MCWB	OCTOBER Obsn Hour Gp 01 to 08	OCTOBER 09 to 16	OCTOBER 17 to 24	OCTOBER Total Obsn	OCTOBER MCWB
95/99															
90/94		0	0	0	57										
85/89		10	3	13	55		2	0	2	53					
80/84		48	17	65	54		10	2	12	53					
75/79		61	27	88	53		31	9	40	51		1		1	51
70/74	1	56	42	99	53		45	22	67	49		13	1	14	47
65/69	20	39	59	118	51	2	39	33	74	48		27	6	33	46
60/64	64	20	53	137	50	16	37	45	98	46	0	36	16	52	44
55/59	88	8	30	126	48	35	29	44	108	44	4	37	29	70	42
50/54	47	4	12	63	45	53	19	34	106	42	15	37	44	96	40
45/49	19	1	4	24	41	57	12	23	92	39	35	30	48	113	37
40/44	7	0	2	9	37	41	10	15	66	37	57	28	38	123	35
35/39	2		0	2	34	23	5	8	36	34	58	20	27	105	32
30/34	0		0	0	32	10	1	4	15	29	44	14	25	83	28
25/29						3		1	4	26	24	5	8	37	25
20/24						0			0	22	8	2	4	14	21
15/19											3	1	1	5	17
10/14											0			0	12

ROCK SPRINGS WYOMING

Temperature Range	NOVEMBER Obsn Hour Gp 01 to 08	NOVEMBER Obsn Hour Gp 09 to 16	NOVEMBER Obsn Hour Gp 17 to 24	NOVEMBER Total Obsn	NOVEMBER MCWB	DECEMBER Obsn Hour Gp 01 to 08	DECEMBER Obsn Hour Gp 09 to 16	DECEMBER Obsn Hour Gp 17 to 24	DECEMBER Total Obsn	DECEMBER MCWB	JANUARY Obsn Hour Gp 01 to 08	JANUARY Obsn Hour Gp 09 to 16	JANUARY Obsn Hour Gp 17 to 24	JANUARY Total Obsn	JANUARY MCWB
95/99															
90/94															
85/89															
80/84															
75/79															
70/74															
65/69															
60/64		1		1	44										
55/59		7	0	7	41										
50/54		17	3	20	38		0	0	0	39		0		0	38
45/49	1	26	12	39	36	1	4	0	5	37		3		3	37
40/44	10	36	29	75	34	1	21	4	26	34	0	12	2	14	34
35/39	34	42	47	123	31	9	37	23	69	31	7	25	15	47	32
30/34	48	33	45	126	28	30	49	46	125	28	19	42	33	94	28
25/29	44	28	35	107	24	46	46	51	143	24	32	44	42	118	24
20/24	39	25	27	91	20	49	40	46	135	20	41	36	45	122	20
15/19	26	14	19	59	16	43	25	36	104	16	42	33	36	111	15
10/14	19	7	13	39	11	29	13	20	62	11	36	23	27	86	11
5/9	8	3	6	17	6	18	8	12	38	6	25	14	21	60	6
0/4	5	2	2	9	2	12	4	6	22	2	21	7	12	40	2
-5/-1	3	0	1	4	-3	5	2	3	10	-3	11	4	5	20	-3
-10/-6	1		0	1	-8	3	1	1	5	-8	7	4	3	14	-8
-15/-11			0	0	-12	2	0	0	2	-13	4	2	2	8	-13
-20/-16						0			0	-16	2	1	2	5	-18
-25/-21											1	0	0	1	-23
-30/-26											0	0	0	0	-27

Temperature Range	FEBRUARY Obsn Hour Gp 01 to 08	FEBRUARY Obsn Hour Gp 09 to 16	FEBRUARY Obsn Hour Gp 17 to 24	FEBRUARY Total Obsn	FEBRUARY MCWB	MARCH Obsn Hour Gp 01 to 08	MARCH Obsn Hour Gp 09 to 16	MARCH Obsn Hour Gp 17 to 24	MARCH Total Obsn	MARCH MCWB	APRIL Obsn Hour Gp 01 to 08	APRIL Obsn Hour Gp 09 to 16	APRIL Obsn Hour Gp 17 to 24	APRIL Total Obsn	APRIL MCWB	ANNUAL TOTAL Obsn Hour Gp 01 to 08	ANNUAL TOTAL Obsn Hour Gp 09 to 16	ANNUAL TOTAL Obsn Hour Gp 17 to 24	ANNUAL TOTAL Total Obsn	ANNUAL TOTAL MCWB
95/99																	0		0	59
90/94																	3	0	3	57
85/89																	40	11	51	55
80/84																0	147	57	204	54
75/79																1	205	95	301	53
70/74												1	0	1	47	9	233	151	393	51
65/69							0	0	0	43		9	2	11	45	68	221	211	500	49
60/64							2	0	2	41		21	7	28	43	195	205	237	637	47
55/59		0		0	44		5	1	6	40	1	29	14	44	40	269	179	208	656	45
50/54		3	1	4	40		12	4	16	38	6	34	24	64	38	246	172	201	619	42
45/49	0	9	2	11	37	1	19	8	28	36	15	33	33	81	36	236	175	191	602	38
40/44	2	19	9	30	34	4	31	19	54	33	33	36	40	109	34	245	216	201	662	35
35/39	12	35	24	71	32	18	41	36	95	31	45	34	41	120	31	264	252	249	765	32
30/34	26	39	41	106	28	43	44	49	136	28	53	26	39	118	28	306	252	295	853	28
25/29	37	38	39	114	24	49	38	46	133	24	45	14	24	83	25	290	214	249	753	24
20/24	43	32	39	114	20	46	28	38	112	20	31	4	13	48	20	260	167	213	640	20
15/19	36	23	29	88	16	38	17	24	79	16	10	0	2	12	17	198	113	147	458	16
10/14	25	12	18	55	11	25	6	14	45	11	1		0	1	12	135	61	92	288	11
5/9	17	7	12	36	6	13	2	5	20	7						81	34	56	171	6
0/4	13	4	6	23	1	6	1	2	9	1						57	18	28	103	2
-5/-1	6	2	3	11	-3	4	0	0	4	-3						29	8	12	49	-3
-10/-6	4	1	1	6	-8	0			0	-6						15	6	5	26	-8
-15/-11	2	0	0	2	-13											8	2	2	12	-13
-20/-16	0		0	0	-16											2	1	2	5	-17
-25/-21																1	0	0	1	-23
-30/-26																0	0	0	0	-27

SHERIDAN WYOMING

LAT 44 46N LONG 106 58W ELEV 3964 FT

MEAN FREQUENCY OF OCCURRENCE OF DRY BULB TEMPERATURE (DEGREES F) WITH MEAN COINCIDENT WET BULB TEMPERATURE (DEGREES F) FOR EACH DRY BULB TEMPERATURE RANGE

Temperature Range	MAY Obsn Hour Gp 01 to 08	MAY 09 to 16	MAY 17 to 24	MAY Total Obsn	MAY MCWB	JUNE Obsn Hour Gp 01 to 08	JUNE 09 to 16	JUNE 17 to 24	JUNE Total Obsn	JUNE MCWB	JULY Obsn Hour Gp 01 to 08	JULY 09 to 16	JULY 17 to 24	JULY Total Obsn	JULY MCWB
105/109												0		0	66
100/104												2	0	2	65
95/99							1	0	1	62		11	2	13	63
90/94		0		0	59		5	2	7	62		35	10	45	63
85/89		3	0	3	58	0	15	5	20	62	0	49	20	69	62
80/84		10	3	13	57	0	29	12	41	61	3	49	28	80	61
75/79	0	22	5	27	56	2	41	19	62	59	11	43	38	92	60
70/74	1	31	14	46	54	7	44	27	78	57	29	31	49	109	58
65/69	5	35	21	61	52	18	39	38	95	56	50	16	44	110	57
60/64	13	39	35	87	50	40	30	48	118	54	68	8	34	110	55
55/59	23	38	40	101	48	61	20	42	123	52	49	4	13	66	52
50/54	49	29	44	122	46	59	11	32	102	48	28	1	7	36	49
45/49	60	23	43	126	43	34	3	11	48	44	10	1	2	13	45
40/44	53	10	27	90	39	12	1	4	17	40	1		0	1	41
35/39	28	4	11	43	35	4	1	1	6	36					
30/34	10	2	3	15	30	2	0	1	3	32					
25/29	3	2	2	7	26	0			0	29					
20/24	2	0	1	3	21										
15/19	0		0	0	17										
10/14	0			0	13										
5/9															

Temperature Range	AUGUST Obsn Hour Gp 01 to 08	AUGUST 09 to 16	AUGUST 17 to 24	AUGUST Total Obsn	AUGUST MCWB	SEPTEMBER Obsn Hour Gp 01 to 08	SEPTEMBER 09 to 16	SEPTEMBER 17 to 24	SEPTEMBER Total Obsn	SEPTEMBER MCWB	OCTOBER Obsn Hour Gp 01 to 08	OCTOBER 09 to 16	OCTOBER 17 to 24	OCTOBER Total Obsn	OCTOBER MCWB
105/109															
100/104		1		1	62										
95/99		6	2	8	62		1	0	1	62					
90/94		25	6	31	61		6	1	7	59		0		0	56
85/89	0	46	16	62	61	0	19	3	22	58		2		2	56
80/84	2	57	25	84	60	0	24	7	31	57	0	10	1	11	54
75/79	7	46	33	86	59	1	31	12	44	56	0	18	2	20	52
70/74	21	32	46	99	57	4	37	18	59	54	1	23	4	28	51
65/69	41	18	45	104	55	10	29	30	69	52	3	30	8	41	49
60/64	64	10	42	116	54	23	28	39	90	50	3	30	16	49	47
55/59	61	6	19	86	51	38	21	37	96	48	9	27	26	62	45
50/54	36	1	11	48	48	47	15	36	98	45	21	29	40	90	43
45/49	14	0	3	17	44	49	13	25	87	42	40	26	45	111	40
40/44	3		0	3	39	35	10	20	65	39	51	21	40	112	37
35/39	0			0	37	22	5	10	37	35	52	17	29	98	34
30/34						8	1	4	13	31	38	11	26	75	30
25/29						3		0	3	26	20	2	8	30	26
20/24						1			1	22	8	1	2	11	22
15/19											2		1	3	17
10/14											1		0	1	12
5/9											1		0	1	8

SHERIDAN WYOMING

Temperature Range	NOVEMBER Obsn Hour Gp 01 to 08	NOVEMBER 09 to 16	NOVEMBER 17 to 24	NOVEMBER Total Obsn	NOVEMBER MCWB	DECEMBER Obsn Hour Gp 01 to 08	DECEMBER 09 to 16	DECEMBER 17 to 24	DECEMBER Total Obsn	DECEMBER MCWB	JANUARY Obsn Hour Gp 01 to 08	JANUARY 09 to 16	JANUARY 17 to 24	JANUARY Total Obsn	JANUARY MCWB	FEBRUARY Obsn Hour Gp 01 to 08	FEBRUARY 09 to 16	FEBRUARY 17 to 24	FEBRUARY Total Obsn	FEBRUARY MCWB
105/109																				
100/104																				
95/99																				
90/94																				
85/89																				
80/84																				
75/79		0		0	51															
70/74		1		1	49							0		0	51		0		0	50
65/69		4	0	4	47		0	0	0	44		0	0	0	48		1	0	1	48
60/64	1	10	1	12	45	0	2	0	2	44	0	1	1	2	45	0	2	0	2	46
55/59	2	18	4	24	43	2	7	1	10	42	0	2	1	3	43	1	7	2	10	43
50/54	5	23	7	35	41	3	11	2	16	40	2	7	2	11	40	3	12	5	20	41
45/49	7	32	14	53	38	6	20	6	32	37	3	17	5	25	37	4	19	6	29	38
40/44	16	32	27	75	36	8	28	11	47	34	6	24	10	40	34	6	31	13	50	35
35/39	31	31	47	109	33	17	40	29	86	32	14	34	23	71	32	16	33	30	79	32
30/34	44	27	45	116	29	35	43	49	127	29	26	36	31	93	28	41	33	46	120	29
25/29	51	22	33	106	25	43	28	42	113	25	34	32	38	104	24	38	23	34	95	25
20/24	29	14	18	61	21	44	22	36	102	20	35	21	35	91	20	31	19	24	74	21
15/19	18	11	15	44	16	31	17	23	71	16	30	16	26	72	16	24	16	22	62	16
10/14	14	8	14	36	11	21	9	18	48	11	30	16	18	64	11	16	12	16	44	11
5/9	12	3	8	23	7	18	8	12	38	6	18	12	15	45	6	15	7	11	33	6
0/4	7	2	4	13	2	7	6	7	20	2	12	10	11	33	1	13	4	8	25	2
-5/-1	2	1	2	5	-3	6	5	7	18	-3	11	9	10	30	-3	8	2	4	14	-3
-10/-6	2	0	2	4	-8	6	2	2	10	-8	8	8	10	26	-8	4	0	2	6	-8
-15/-11	1	0	0	1	-13	1	0	2	3	-13	9	4	6	19	-13	3	0	1	4	-13
-20/-16	1	0	0	1	-18	1	0	0	1	-17	7	1	5	13	-18	1		0	1	-18
-25/-21	0		0	0	-22	1	1	1	3	-23	4	0	1	5	-23	0			0	-22
-30/-26											1		1	2	-27					
-35/-31											0			0	-32					

Temperature Range	MARCH Obsn Hour Gp 01 to 08	MARCH 09 to 16	MARCH 17 to 24	MARCH Total Obsn	MARCH MCWB	APRIL Obsn Hour Gp 01 to 08	APRIL 09 to 16	APRIL 17 to 24	APRIL Total Obsn	APRIL MCWB	ANNUAL TOTAL Obsn Hour Gp 01 to 08	ANNUAL TOTAL 09 to 16	ANNUAL TOTAL 17 to 24	ANNUAL TOTAL Total Obsn	ANNUAL TOTAL MCWB
105/109												0		0	66
100/104												3	0	3	64
95/99												19	4	23	62
90/94												71	19	90	62
85/89							0		0	55	0	134	44	178	61
80/84							1	0	1	54	5	180	76	261	60
75/79							4	1	5	52	21	205	110	336	58
70/74		2	0	2	49	0	11	2	13	50	63	212	160	435	56
65/69		6	1	7	47	1	17	6	24	48	128	195	193	516	54
60/64	0	7	3	10	45	2	23	11	36	46	214	190	230	634	52
55/59	1	14	5	20	43	5	31	18	54	44	252	195	208	655	48
50/54	3	21	10	34	41	9	30	24	63	42	265	190	220	675	45
45/49	6	28	16	50	38	19	33	34	86	40	252	215	210	677	41
40/44	12	36	28	76	35	40	29	46	115	37	243	222	226	691	37
35/39	30	36	38	104	32	51	25	38	114	33	265	226	256	747	33
30/34	49	31	46	126	29	54	25	33	112	30	307	209	284	800	29
25/29	49	29	37	115	25	34	10	20	64	26	275	148	214	637	25
20/24	31	14	23	68	21	19	2	6	27	21	200	93	145	438	21
15/19	24	9	12	45	16	6	0	2	8	17	135	69	101	305	16
10/14	13	6	11	30	11	1			1	12	96	51	77	224	11
5/9	14	4	7	25	7	0			0	8	78	34	53	165	7
0/4	6	4	4	14	2						45	26	34	105	2
-5/-1	4	1	4	9	-3						31	18	27	76	-3
-10/-6	3	0	2	5	-8						23	10	18	51	-8
-15/-11	2		0	2	-13						16	4	9	29	-13
-20/-16	1			1	-17						11	1	5	17	-18
-25/-21											5		2	8	-23
-30/-26											1		1	2	-27
-35/-31											0			0	-32

CHAPTER 4

DATA FOR USE IN CALCULATING ENERGY CONSUMPTION ESTIMATES FOR SITES OUTSIDE THE UNITED STATES

AFRICA

CAIRO IAP UNITED ARAB REPUBLIC/EGYPT

LAT 30 08N LONG 31 24E ELEV 367 FT

MEAN FREQUENCY OF OCCURRENCE OF DRY BULB TEMPERATURE (DEGREES F) WITH MEAN COINCIDENT WET BULB TEMPERATURE (DEGREES F) FOR EACH DRY BULB TEMPERATURE RANGE

Tempera-ture Range	MAY Obsn Hour Gp 01 to 08	MAY 09 to 16	MAY 17 to 24	MAY Total Obsn	MAY MCWB	JUNE Obsn Hour Gp 01 to 08	JUNE 09 to 16	JUNE 17 to 24	JUNE Total Obsn	JUNE MCWB	JULY Obsn Hour Gp 01 to 08	JULY 09 to 16	JULY 17 to 24	JULY Total Obsn	JULY MCWB
110/114							1		1	69					
105/109		1	0	1	65		3	0	3	68		0		0	79
100/104		5	1	6	67	0	15	5	20	68		4	1	5	73
95/99		19	6	25	65	0	29	13	42	68		20	9	29	71
90/94	1	33	16	50	64	2	59	34	95	68	0	64	37	101	71
85/89	3	50	27	80	63	4	62	48	114	67	1	84	52	137	70
80/84	6	56	45	107	62	13	40	48	101	67	7	53	59	119	70
75/79	13	55	57	125	62	38	27	62	127	67	79	23	70	172	70
70/74	43	22	52	117	61	110	3	26	139	66	134	0	19	153	68
65/69	92	7	37	136	61	68	0	3	71	63	25		I	26	65
60/64	81		7	88	58	4			4	59					
55/59	9			9	55	0			0	59					

Tempera-ture Range	AUGUST Obsn Hour Gp 01 to 08	AUGUST 09 to 16	AUGUST 17 to 24	AUGUST Total Obsn	AUGUST MCWB	SEPTEMBER Obsn Hour Gp 01 to 08	SEPTEMBER 09 to 16	SEPTEMBER 17 to 24	SEPTEMBER Total Obsn	SEPTEMBER MCWB	OCTOBER Obsn Hour Gp 01 to 08	OCTOBER 09 to 16	OCTOBER 17 to 24	OCTOBER Total Obsn	OCTOBER MCWB
110/114															
105/109		0	0	0	75										
100/104		2	0	2	73		2	1	3	68					
95/99		18	5	23	72		13	1	14	69		4	0	4	66
90/94	0	78	35	113	71		59	21	80	70	0	20	3	23	66
85/89	1	78	55	134	71	1	74	41	116	69		39	11	50	67
80/84	5	52	65	122	71	4	57	52	113	69	1	64	29	94	66
75/79	92	19	70	181	71	44	31	88	163	69	9	85	66	160	64
70/74	139	1	17	157	69	138	3	32	173	68	63	25	80	168	64
65/69	10		0	10	66	49	0	3	52	65	93	11	49	153	62
60/64		0		0	61	4		0	4	60	73	1	10	84	58
55/59	0		0	0	58	0			0	59	9		1	10	55

OΛIRO IAP UNITED ARAB REPUBLIC/EGYPT

Temperature Range	NOVEMBER Obsn Hour Gp 01 to 08	09 to 16	17 to 24	Total Obsn	M C W B	DECEMBER Obsn Hour Gp 01 to 08	09 to 16	17 to 24	Total Obsn	M C W B	JANUARY Obsn Hour Gp 01 to 08	09 to 16	17 to 24	Total Obsn	M C W B
110/114															
105/109															
100/104															
95/99															
90/94		1	0	1	68										
85/89		1	1	2	65							1		1	61
80/84		9	1	10	63		3	0	3	60		2		2	59
75/79	1	61	13	75	62	1	9	1	11	57		6	1	7	58
70/74	5	92	41	138	61	1	29	6	36	57	1	22	5	28	55
65/69	18	49	81	148	59	3	82	22	107	55	3	57	18	78	53
60/64	96	22	73	191	57	11	72	69	152	53	11	82	56	149	52
55/59	91	4	30	125	53	72	43	102	217	51	36	57	99	192	50
50/54	27	0	1	28	49	117	9	42	168	48	131	19	62	212	47
45/49	2	0		2	46	35	2	6	43	44	55	2	7	64	43
40/44	0			0	43	8			8	40	9	0	1	10	40
35/39						0			0	36	1			1	34

Temperature Range	FEBRUARY Obsn Hour Gp 01 to 08	09 to 16	17 to 24	Total Obsn	M C W B	MARCH Obsn Hour Gp 01 to 08	09 to 16	17 to 24	Total Obsn	M C W B	APRIL Obsn Hour Gp 01 to 08	09 to 16	17 to 24	Total Obsn	M C W B
110/114															
105/109												1	0	1	66
100/104												4	2	6	65
95/99							2	0	2	62	0	7	2	9	64
90/94		0		0	61		10	2	12	59	1	14	6	21	62
85/89		2	1	3	57		12	5	17	58	2	20	10	32	61
80/84		6	2	8	57	2	17	9	28	57	4	31	18	53	60
75/79	2	16	6	24	55	7	36	19	62	56	11	53	36	100	58
70/74	3	35	14	52	55	12	43	31	86	55	15	52	46	113	57
65/69	4	60	32	96	53	18	62	44	124	54	27	40	49	116	56
60/64	15	66	58	139	52	30	47	54	131	53	63	15	51	129	55
55/59	47	33	76	156	50	80	16	62	158	51	95	2	19	116	53
50/54	115	5	35	155	47	83	2	20	105	48	19	0	1	20	49
45/49	36		1	37	44	16		0	16	43	1			1	45
40/44	2	0		2	41	1			1	41					
35/39	0			0	38										

Temperature Range	ANNUAL TOTAL Obsn Hour Gp 01 to 08	09 to 16	17 to 24	Total Obsn	M C W B
110/114		1		1	69
105/109		5	0	5	68
100/104	0	32	10	42	68
95/99	0	112	36	148	68
90/94	4	338	154	496	69
85/89	12	423	251	686	68
80/84	42	390	328	760	66
75/79	297	421	489	1207	65
70/74	664	327	369	1360	63
65/69	410	368	339	1117	58
60/64	388	305	378	1071	55
55/59	439	155	389	983	51
50/54	492	35	161	688	47
45/49	145	4	14	163	44
40/44	20	0	1	21	40
35/39	1			1	35

ASIA

TEHRAN/MEHRABAD IAP IRAN

LAT 35 41N LONG 51 19E ELEV 3949 FT

MEAN FREQUENCY OF OCCURRENCE OF DRY BULB TEMPERATURE (DEGREES F) WITH MEAN COINCIDENT WET BULB TEMPERATURE (DEGREES F) FOR EACH DRY BULB TEMPERATURE RANGE

Temperature Range	MAY Obsn Hour Gp 01 to 08	MAY 09 to 16	MAY 17 to 24	MAY Total Obsn	MAY MCWB	JUNE Obsn Hour Gp 01 to 08	JUNE 09 to 16	JUNE 17 to 24	JUNE Total Obsn	JUNE MCWB	JULY Obsn Hour Gp 01 to 08	JULY 09 to 16	JULY 17 to 24	JULY Total Obsn	JULY MCWB
105/109												1	0	1	65
100/104						0	8	2	10	62		25	11	36	63
95/99		2		2	58	0	35	17	52	60	0	64	38	102	62
90/94		12	4	16	58	1	62	35	98	59	5	71	52	128	61
85/89	0	39	13	52	57	9	68	46	123	58	28	51	68	147	60
80/84	4	49	27	80	56	27	39	50	116	57	59	28	43	130	59
75/79	20	62	53	135	54	62	19	50	131	55	84	8	24	116	58
70/74	35	41	49	125	53	65	7	23	95	54	50	1	10	61	57
65/69	64	28	46	138	52	47	1	11	59	52	19	0	2	21	56
60/64	54	11	29	94	51	20	0	6	26	50	2		1	3	52
55/59	45	3	21	69	49	7		0	7	48	0			0	47
50/54	22	1	5	28	46	1	0		1	44					
45/49	4			4	43										
40/44															

Temperature Range	AUGUST Obsn Hour Gp 01 to 08	AUGUST 09 to 16	AUGUST 17 to 24	AUGUST Total Obsn	AUGUST MCWB	SEPTEMBER Obsn Hour Gp 01 to 08	SEPTEMBER 09 to 16	SEPTEMBER 17 to 24	SEPTEMBER Total Obsn	SEPTEMBER MCWB	OCTOBER Obsn Hour Gp 01 to 08	OCTOBER 09 to 16	OCTOBER 17 to 24	OCTOBER Total Obsn	OCTOBER MCWB
105/109															
100/104		11	1	12	62										
95/99	0	69	31	100	61		15	2	17	59					
90/94	2	73	47	122	60	0	38	14	52	58		1		1	58
85/89	14	54	62	130	59	2	60	24	86	57		15	2	17	56
80/84	45	27	57	129	57	9	59	49	117	56		36	6	42	55
75/79	104	11	33	148	56	35	43	63	141	54	2	68	21	91	52
70/74	60	2	13	75	55	59	16	48	123	52	9	60	45	114	51
65/69	18	1	3	22	53	71	6	27	104	50	36	36	58	130	49
60/64	5	0	1	6	51	47	2	10	59	49	68	22	61	151	48
55/59			0	0	47	14	1	3	18	46	76	8	38	122	45
50/54						4	1	1	6	46	44	2	14	60	43
45/49											11	0	2	13	40
40/44											1			1	36

TEHRAN/MEHRABAD IAP IRAN

Temperature Range	NOVEMBER Obsn Hour Gp 01 to 08	NOVEMBER 09 to 16	NOVEMBER 17 to 24	NOVEMBER Total Obsn	NOVEMBER MCWB	DECEMBER Obsn Hour Gp 01 to 08	DECEMBER 09 to 16	DECEMBER 17 to 24	DECEMBER Total Obsn	DECEMBER MCWB	JANUARY Obsn Hour Gp 01 to 08	JANUARY 09 to 16	JANUARY 17 to 24	JANUARY Total Obsn	JANUARY MCWB
105/109															
100/104															
95/99															
90/94															
85/89															
80/84															
75/79		3	0	3	51										
70/74		12	1	13	50										
65/69	1	29	6	36	48	0	1		1	49			0	0	48
60/64	5	53	16	74	46		5		5	46		5	1	6	46
55/59	17	74	46	137	45		29	2	31	43		12	2	14	43
50/54	58	43	73	174	43	5	51	20	76	41	1	16	7	24	41
45/49	62	21	49	132	40	24	60	46	130	39	5	36	15	56	38
40/44	55	4	32	91	36	51	54	64	169	36	15	54	32	101	35
35/39	25	2	12	39	31	67	29	60	156	33	48	47	56	151	33
30/34	15	1	5	21	27	59	15	39	113	29	72	50	67	189	29
25/29	3			3	25	30	5	11	46	25	54	21	41	116	25
20/24						7	0	5	12	20	34	7	21	62	21
15/19						4		1	5	17	13	1	5	19	16
10/14											5	0	2	7	11
5/9											1			1	7

Temperature Range	FEBRUARY Obsn Hour Gp 01 to 08	FEBRUARY 09 to 16	FEBRUARY 17 to 24	FEBRUARY Total Obsn	FEBRUARY MCWB	MARCH Obsn Hour Gp 01 to 08	MARCH 09 to 16	MARCH 17 to 24	MARCH Total Obsn	MARCH MCWB	APRIL Obsn Hour Gp 01 to 08	APRIL 09 to 16	APRIL 17 to 24	APRIL Total Obsn	APRIL MCWB	ANNUAL TOTAL Obsn Hour Gp 01 to 08	ANNUAL TOTAL 09 to 16	ANNUAL TOTAL 17 to 24	ANNUAL TOTAL Total Obsn	ANNUAL TOTAL MCWB
105/109																	1	0	1	65
100/104																0	44	14	58	62
95/99																0	185	88	273	61
90/94																8	257	152	417	60
85/89												0		0	51	53	287	215	555	58
80/84							0		0	53		9	1	10	53	144	247	233	624	57
75/79							1	0	1	51	1	36	14	51	52	308	251	258	817	55
70/74		0		0	48		6	2	8	48	4	39	26	69	51	282	184	217	683	53
65/69		3	0	3	45		18	7	25	47	19	52	43	114	49	275	175	203	653	50
60/64		15	2	17	44	3	40	23	66	46	36	50	49	135	48	240	203	199	642	48
55/59	1	24	10	35	43	20	72	43	135	44	62	28	50	140	46	242	251	215	708	45
50/54	6	43	29	78	41	41	56	63	160	42	61	17	36	114	44	243	230	248	721	42
45/49	21	42	39	102	38	58	26	48	132	39	34	5	13	52	41	219	190	212	621	39
40/44	40	36	43	119	36	60	15	35	110	37	15	2	5	22	38	237	165	211	613	36
35/39	54	26	40	120	33	43	11	16	70	33	6	1	2	9	34	243	116	186	545	33
30/34	51	23	31	105	29	18	3	8	29	30	3	0	0	3	31	218	92	150	460	29
25/29	25	9	19	53	25	4	0	1	5	27		0		0	28	116	35	72	223	25
20/24	15	2	9	26	21	0			0	19						56	9	35	100	21
15/19	10	1	2	13	16											27	2	8	37	16
10/14	2			2	13											7	0	2	9	11
5/9																1			1	7

ASIA (CONT)

TEL AVIV ISRAEL

LAT 32 00N LONG 34 34E ELEV 131 FT

MEAN FREQUENCY OF OCCURRENCE OF DRY BULB TEMPERATURE (DEGREES F) WITH MEAN COINCIDENT WET BULB TEMPERATURE (DEGREES F) FOR EACH DRY BULB TEMPERATURE RANGE

Temperature Range	MAY Obsn Hour Gp 01 to 08	MAY 09 to 16	MAY 17 to 24	MAY Total Obsn	MAY MCWB	JUNE Obsn Hour Gp 01 to 08	JUNE 09 to 16	JUNE 17 to 24	JUNE Total Obsn	JUNE MCWB	JULY Obsn Hour Gp 01 to 08	JULY 09 to 16	JULY 17 to 24	JULY Total Obsn	JULY MCWB
110/114		1		1	69										
105/109		2		2	67										
100/104		2	1	3	66		1		1	69		0		0	79
95/99	1	4	2	7	65	0	6	2	8	68		1	0	1	71
90/94	1	14	5	20	66		16	3	19	70	0	22	4	26	73
85/89	2	20	6	28	65	1	52	11	64	70		102	16	118	72
80/84	1	40	14	55	65	5	121	40	166	69	10	113	66	189	71
75/79	9	104	37	150	64	46	41	75	162	68	65	9	91	165	70
70/74	39	50	61	150	63	46	2	67	115	66	77	1	60	138	67
65/69	51	9	60	120	61	76	0	34	110	63	85	0	10	95	64
60/64	59	1	47	107	59	56		8	64	60	10			10	60
55/59	68	0	15	83	55	10		0	10	56					
50/54	14		1	15	51	0			0	46					
45/49	2			2	44										
40/44	0			0	39										

Temperature Range	AUGUST Obsn Hour Gp 01 to 08	AUGUST 09 to 16	AUGUST 17 to 24	AUGUST Total Obsn	AUGUST MCWB	SEPTEMBER Obsn Hour Gp 01 to 08	SEPTEMBER 09 to 16	SEPTEMBER 17 to 24	SEPTEMBER Total Obsn	SEPTEMBER MCWB	OCTOBER Obsn Hour Gp 01 to 08	OCTOBER 09 to 16	OCTOBER 17 to 24	OCTOBER Total Obsn	OCTOBER MCWB
110/114															
105/109															
100/104							0		0	78					
95/99		2	0	2	72		3	0	3	69		2		2	70
90/94		30	3	33	72		11	1	12	73		8	0	8	66
85/89		152	24	176	73		98	5	103	72	1	23	2	26	68
80/84	19	59	76	154	72	9	118	58	185	71	4	100	13	117	68
75/79	64	4	87	155	71	64	8	95	167	70	14	90	66	170	66
70/74	101	0	56	157	67	67	0	62	129	67	46	18	75	139	65
65/69	58	1	3	62	64	85	0	17	102	63	59	6	47	112	63
60/64	6			6	58	16		1	17	60	84	2	41	127	59
55/59						0			0	59	37	0	4	41	55
50/54											3			3	50
45/49															
40/44															

TEL AVIV ISRAEL

Temperature Range	NOVEMBER Obsn Hour Gp 01 to 08	NOVEMBER 09 to 16	NOVEMBER 17 to 24	NOVEMBER Total Obsn	NOVEMBER MCWB	DECEMBER Obsn Hour Gp 01 to 08	DECEMBER 09 to 16	DECEMBER 17 to 24	DECEMBER Total Obsn	DECEMBER MCWB	JANUARY Obsn Hour Gp 01 to 08	JANUARY 09 to 16	JANUARY 17 to 24	JANUARY Total Obsn	JANUARY MCWB
110/114															
105/109															
100/104															
95/99															
90/94		3	0	3	66							0		0	60
85/89		5	1	6	63							2		2	57
80/84	2	19	2	23	62	0	2		2	63		2	0	2	56
75/79	2	76	8	86	62	0	12	1	13	60	0	5	3	8	56
70/74	3	86	42	131	61	1	35	5	41	58	2	23	3	28	55
65/69	11	30	43	84	59	4	75	14	93	57	4	43	9	56	55
60/64	64	14	77	155	57	11	68	51	130	55	8	81	36	125	54
55/59	96	6	57	159	54	59	44	94	197	52	23	64	62	149	51
50/54	56	1	9	66	50	105	9	64	178	49	88	23	101	212	49
45/49	6		1	7	44	50	3	15	68	44	91	4	31	126	44
40/44	0			0	40	14		4	18	39	26	1	2	29	40
35/39						3			3	36	6			6	36
30/34						0	0		0	33	1			1	32

Temperature Range	FEBRUARY Obsn Hour Gp 01 to 08	FEBRUARY 09 to 16	FEBRUARY 17 to 24	FEBRUARY Total Obsn	FEBRUARY MCWB	MARCH Obsn Hour Gp 01 to 08	MARCH 09 to 16	MARCH 17 to 24	MARCH Total Obsn	MARCH MCWB	APRIL Obsn Hour Gp 01 to 08	APRIL 09 to 16	APRIL 17 to 24	APRIL Total Obsn	APRIL MCWB	ANNUAL TOTAL Obsn Hour Gp 01 to 08	ANNUAL TOTAL 09 to 16	ANNUAL TOTAL 17 to 24	ANNUAL TOTAL Total Obsn	ANNUAL TOTAL MCWB
110/114																	1		1	69
105/109																	2		2	67
100/104												3	0	3	66		6	1	7	68
95/99												6	1	7	65	1	24	5	30	67
90/94		0		0	57		3		3	62		9	4	13	64	1	116	20	137	70
85/89		1		1	61		9	1	10	61	1	7	3	11	63	5	471	69	545	71
80/84		2	1	3	59	1	15	4	20	59	4	14	7	25	61	55	605	281	941	69
75/79	1	10	2	13	57	5	23	9	37	59	5	37	13	55	61	275	419	487	1181	67
70/74		29	6	35	55	6	31	16	53	57	8	69	28	105	60	396	344	481	1221	64
65/69	1	52	10	63	55	8	56	25	89	56	11	62	42	115	58	453	334	314	1101	61
60/64	8	75	38	121	53	22	73	58	153	55	47	26	69	142	56	391	340	426	1157	57
55/59	26	39	67	132	51	53	29	70	152	53	72	7	49	128	53	444	189	418	1051	53
50/54	81	14	73	168	49	91	7	53	151	49	70	0	24	94	50	508	54	325	887	49
45/49	80	2	24	106	45	61	0	12	63	45	22		1	23	45	302	9	84	395	45
40/44	24	0	2	26	41	10	0	0	10	41	1			1	41	75	1	8	84	40
35/39	4		0	4	37	1			1	37						14		0	14	36
30/34																1	0		1	32

ASIA (CONT)

ITAZUKE AUX AIRFIELD JAPAN

LAT 33 35N LONG 130 27E ELEV 00 FT

MEAN FREQUENCY OF OCCURRENCE OF DRY BULB TEMPERATURE (DEGREES F) WITH MEAN COINCIDENT WET BULB TEMPERATURE (DEGREES F) FOR EACH DRY BULB TEMPERATURE RANGE

Temperature Range	MAY Obsn Hour Gp 01 to 08	MAY 09 to 16	MAY 17 to 24	MAY Total Obsn	MAY MCWB	JUNE Obsn Hour Gp 01 to 08	JUNE 09 to 16	JUNE 17 to 24	JUNE Total Obsn	JUNE MCWB	JULY Obsn Hour Gp 01 to 08	JULY 09 to 16	JULY 17 to 24	JULY Total Obsn	JULY MCWB
100/104															
95/99												1	0	1	80
90/94							1	0	1	77		36	4	40	79
85/89		1	0	1	64		15	2	17	73	2	94	36	132	77
80/84		14	2	16	67	4	48	13	65	71	56	62	94	212	76
75/79	2	45	11	58	66	18	77	44	139	70	128	38	78	244	74
70/74	10	71	35	116	64	51	66	81	198	67	50	16	30	96	70
65/69	37	72	71	180	61	89	28	69	186	64	9	2	6	17	65
60/64	89	39	79	207	59	54	5	27	86	60	2	0	0	2	60
55/59	59	6	36	101	55	20		4	24	55	0			0	56
50/54	35	0	11	46	50	3		0	3	51	0	0		0	43
45/49	13		2	15	46										
40/44	3		0	3	42										
35/39	0			0	37										

Temperature Range	AUGUST Obsn Hour Gp 01 to 08	AUGUST 09 to 16	AUGUST 17 to 24	AUGUST Total Obsn	AUGUST MCWB	SEPTEMBER Obsn Hour Gp 01 to 08	SEPTEMBER 09 to 16	SEPTEMBER 17 to 24	SEPTEMBER Total Obsn	SEPTEMBER MCWB	OCTOBER Obsn Hour Gp 01 to 08	OCTOBER 09 to 16	OCTOBER 17 to 24	OCTOBER Total Obsn	OCTOBER MCWB
100/104		0		0	77										
95/99		4	0	4	79		0		0	78					
90/94		44	7	51	78		8	0	8	78					
85/89	3	105	38	146	77	0	38	7	45	76		1		1	74
80/84	47	73	97	217	76	6	62	29	97	73		10	1	11	70
75/79	144	20	91	255	74	53	71	66	190	71	1	34	6	41	67
70/74	48	1	15	64	70	67	45	67	179	68	13	84	25	122	64
65/69	6	0	1	7	65	58	15	46	119	64	29	74	56	159	61
60/64						35	1	19	55	60	50	32	70	152	57
55/59						16		4	20	56	62	12	51	125	54
50/54						4		1	5	51	52	1	31	84	50
45/49						0		0	0	46	33	0	8	41	45
40/44											7		1	8	41
35/39											0			0	37

ITAZUKE AUX AIRFIELD JAPAN

Temperature Range	NOVEMBER Obsn Hour Gp 01 to 08	09 to 16	17 to 24	Total Obsn	MCWB	DECEMBER Obsn Hour Gp 01 to 08	09 to 16	17 to 24	Total Obsn	MCWB	JANUARY Obsn Hour Gp 01 to 08	09 to 16	17 to 24	Total Obsn	MCWB
100/104															
95/99															
90/94															
85/89															
80/84															
75/79	0	1		1	63										
70/74	1	16	1	18	62										
65/69	5	53	11	69	59		4	0	4	57		1	0	1	57
60/64	22	69	39	130	56	1	18	3	22	54	1	5	2	8	54
55/59	32	56	54	142	52	7	47	16	70	51	2	15	4	21	51
50/54	54	28	65	147	48	24	66	44	134	47	10	40	20	70	46
45/49	61	14	42	117	44	51	59	69	179	42	25	59	43	127	42
40/44	46	4	21	71	40	76	35	66	177	38	53	64	67	184	37
35/39	18	0	6	24	35	59	15	38	112	34	85	44	72	201	33
30/34	3		1	4	31	27	4	11	42	30	61	20	36	117	30
25/29						2	0	0	2	27	11	1	3	15	26
20/24						0			0	23	0		0	0	23
15/19															

Temperature Range	FEBRUARY Obsn Hour Gp 01 to 08	09 to 16	17 to 24	Total Obsn	MCWB	MARCH Obsn Hour Gp 01 to 08	09 to 16	17 to 24	Total Obsn	MCWB
100/104										
95/99										
90/94										
85/89										
80/84										
75/79							1		1	61
70/74		0		0	56	0	3	0	3	59
65/69	0	3	1	4	57	1	10	5	16	58
60/64	1	7	3	11	54	6	28	11	45	54
55/59	4	18	8	30	51	10	53	25	88	50
50/54	13	45	22	80	46	29	66	52	147	46
45/49	28	57	46	131	42	44	56	63	163	42
40/44	42	49	55	I46	38	64	25	57	146	38
35/39	63	35	57	155	33	58	5	28	91	34
30/34	60	9	27	96	30	31	1	8	40	31
25/29	13	0	4	17	26	4		1	5	27
20/24	1		0	1	21	0			0	24
15/19	0			0	17					

Temperature Range	APRIL Obsn Hour Gp 01 to 08	09 to 16	17 to 24	Total Obsn	MCWB	ANNUAL TOTAL Obsn Hour Gp 01 to 08	09 to 16	17 to 24	Total Obsn	MCWB
100/104							0		0	77
95/99							5	0	5	79
90/94							89	11	100	78
85/89		0		0	71	5	254	83	342	77
80/84		1	0	1	70	113	270	236	619	75
75/79	0	8	1	9	66	346	295	297	938	72
70/74	2	27	8	37	62	242	329	262	833	66
65/69	12	47	21	80	60	246	309	287	842	62
60/64	28	70	50	148	56	289	274	303	866	57
55/59	49	56	67	172	53	261	263	269	793	53
50/54	58	23	51	132	48	282	269	297	848	48
45/49	48	6	30	84	44	303	251	303	857	43
40/44	27	1	9	37	40	318	178	276	772	38
35/39	14		3	17	35	297	99	204	600	34
30/34	2		0	2	32	184	34	83	301	30
25/29	0			0	26	30	1	8	39	26
20/24						1		0	1	22
15/19						0			0	17

ASIA (CONT)

KADENA AB/OKINAWA

LAT 26 21N LONG 127 46E ELEV 140 FT

MEAN FREQUENCY OF OCCURRENCE OF DRY BULB TEMPERATURE (DEGREES F) WITH MEAN COINCIDENT WET BULB TEMPERATURE (DEGREES F) FOR EACH DRY BULB TEMPERATURE RANGE

Temperature Range	MAY Obsn Hour Gp 01 to 08	MAY 09 to 16	MAY 17 to 24	MAY Total Obsn	MAY MCWB	JUNE Obsn Hour Gp 01 to 08	JUNE 09 to 16	JUNE 17 to 24	JUNE Total Obsn	JUNE MCWB	JULY Obsn Hour Gp 01 to 08	JULY 09 to 16	JULY 17 to 24	JULY Total Obsn	JULY MCWB
95/99															
90/94		0		0	81		2		2	79		26	2	28	80
85/89		9	0	9	77	1	67	10	78	79	10	165	52	227	79
80/84	3	72	17	92	75	54	87	83	224	77	162	49	167	378	78
75/79	76	110	95	281	72	115	63	97	275	74	75	7	27	109	75
70/74	109	48	99	256	68	56	18	43	117	69	1	1	0	2	71
65/69	46	9	30	85	64	14	3	7	24	65					
60/64	13	1	6	20	59	1	0	0	1	62					
55/59	1	0	0	1	56										
50/54	0			0	51										

Temperature Range	AUGUST Obsn Hour Gp 01 to 08	AUGUST 09 to 16	AUGUST 17 to 24	AUGUST Total Obsn	AUGUST MCWB	SEPTEMBER Obsn Hour Gp 01 to 08	SEPTEMBER 09 to 16	SEPTEMBER 17 to 24	SEPTEMBER Total Obsn	SEPTEMBER MCWB	OCTOBER Obsn Hour Gp 01 to 08	OCTOBER 09 to 16	OCTOBER 17 to 24	OCTOBER Total Obsn	OCTOBER MCWB
95/99		0		0	80										
90/94		14	1	15	80		2		2	79		0		0	80
85/89	5	151	38	194	79	1	113	13	127	78		14	1	15	77
80/84	138	71	163	372	77	84	108	128	320	76	6	87	21	114	74
75/79	98	11	45	154	75	124	16	83	223	74	73	107	95	275	71
70/74	8	1	1	10	71	28	2	14	44	68	108	37	93	238	67
65/69						4		2	6	62	49	3	32	84	62
60/64											12		7	19	58
55/59											0		0	0	55
50/54															

KADENA AB/OKINAWA

Temperature Range	NOVEMBER Obsn Hour Gp 01 to 08	NOVEMBER 09 to 16	NOVEMBER 17 to 24	NOVEMBER Total Obsn	NOVEMBER MCWB	DECEMBER Obsn Hour Gp 01 to 08	DECEMBER 09 to 16	DECEMBER 17 to 24	DECEMBER Total Obsn	DECEMBER MCWB	JANUARY Obsn Hour Gp 01 to 08	JANUARY 09 to 16	JANUARY 17 to 24	JANUARY Total Obsn	JANUARY MCWB
95/99															
90/94															
85/89		0		0	78	0			0	75					
80/84		12	0	12	73		0		0	73		0		0	75
75/79	10	90	23	123	69	0	12	0	12	69	0	6	1	7	71
70/74	70	90	88	248	66	10	65	21	96	64	6	29	10	45	66
65/69	95	40	81	216	61	59	91	76	226	61	26	55	37	118	61
60/64	53	7	41	101	57	87	56	82	225	57	49	72	53	174	56
55/59	11		6	17	54	67	20	56	143	52	82	63	86	231	51
50/54	1		0	1	50	21	3	12	36	48	68	20	53	141	47
45/49						4	1	1	6	44	15	1	7	23	43
40/44						0			0	41	1		0	1	40
35/39											0			0	36

Temperature Range	FEBRUARY Obsn Hour Gp 01 to 08	FEBRUARY 09 to 16	FEBRUARY 17 to 24	FEBRUARY Total Obsn	FEBRUARY MCWB	MARCH Obsn Hour Gp 01 to 08	MARCH 09 to 16	MARCH 17 to 24	MARCH Total Obsn	MARCH MCWB	APRIL Obsn Hour Gp 01 to 08	APRIL 09 to 16	APRIL 17 to 24	APRIL Total Obsn	APRIL MCWB	ANNUAL TOTAL Obsn Hour Gp 01 to 08	ANNUAL TOTAL 09 to 16	ANNUAL TOTAL 17 to 24	ANNUAL TOTAL Total Obsn	ANNUAL TOTAL MCWB
95/99																	0		0	80
90/94																	44	3	47	80
85/89											0	0		0	76	17	519	114	650	79
80/84		0		0	72		1		1	72		25	2	27	74	447	512	581	1540	77
75/79		8	1	9	68	0	21	4	25	70	16	66	33	115	71	587	517	504	1608	73
70/74	5	36	13	54	65	20	59	33	112	66	71	92	81	244	67	492	478	496	1466	67
65/69	36	53	44	133	62	56	75	70	201	62	77	43	76	196	63	462	372	455	1289	62
60/64	47	66	59	172	57	70	63	67	200	57	51	10	36	97	58	383	275	351	1009	57
55/59	66	47	63	176	52	60	26	54	140	52	20	3	10	33	53	307	159	275	741	52
50/54	50	13	36	99	47	34	3	19	56	48	4	0	1	5	48	178	39	121	338	47
45/49	18	1	7	26	43	7		1	8	45	0			0	44	44	3	16	63	43
40/44	2		0	2	40	0		0	0	41						3		0	3	40
35/39	0			0	36											0			0	36

MISAWA AB JAPAN

LAT 40 40N LONG 141 00E ELEV 110 FT

MEAN FREQUENCY OF OCCURRENCE OF DRY BULB TEMPERATURE (DEGREES F) WITH MEAN COINCIDENT WET BULB TEMPERATURE (DEGREES F) FOR EACH DRY BULB TEMPERATURE RANGE

Temperature Range	MAY Obsn Hour Gp 01 to 08	MAY 09 to 16	MAY 17 to 24	MAY Total Obsn	MAY MCWB	JUNE Obsn Hour Gp 01 to 08	JUNE 09 to 16	JUNE 17 to 24	JUNE Total Obsn	JUNE MCWB	JULY Obsn Hour Gp 01 to 08	JULY 09 to 16	JULY 17 to 24	JULY Total Obsn	JULY MCWB
95/99															
90/94												2		2	75
85/89		0		0	61		1		1	72	0	14	1	15	75
80/84		3	0	3	62	0	7	0	7	68	4	37	11	52	73
75/79	0	12	1	13	60	1	20	3	24	65	18	47	30	95	70
70/74	2	25	5	32	58	7	42	12	61	63	45	55	47	147	68
65/69	8	42	13	63	56	22	57	33	112	61	66	47	71	184	64
60/64	19	57	26	102	54	55	58	66	179	58	72	30	56	158	60
55/59	41	55	57	153	51	89	35	78	202	55	35	13	27	75	56
50/54	78	36	84	198	48	52	16	39	107	50	6	2	4	12	51
45/49	70	14	49	133	45	14	4	8	26	46	1		0	1	47
40/44	25	3	11	39	40	1		0	1	41					
35/39	4	0	1	5	35	0			0	37					
30/34	0			0	32										

Temperature Range	AUGUST Obsn Hour Gp 01 to 08	AUGUST 09 to 16	AUGUST 17 to 24	AUGUST Total Obsn	AUGUST MCWB	SEPTEMBER Obsn Hour Gp 01 to 08	SEPTEMBER 09 to 16	SEPTEMBER 17 to 24	SEPTEMBER Total Obsn	SEPTEMBER MCWB	OCTOBER Obsn Hour Gp 01 to 08	OCTOBER 09 to 16	OCTOBER 17 to 24	OCTOBER Total Obsn	OCTOBER MCWB
95/99		1		1	78										
90/94		6	1	7	77		0		0	78					
85/89	1	21	3	25	75		2	0	2	75					
80/84	7	40	13	60	73	1	12	1	14	71					
75/79	26	65	37	128	71	3	33	7	43	68		1		1	64
70/74	77	73	87	237	68	18	74	33	125	65	0	10	1	11	61
65/69	99	37	88	224	65	55	76	77	208	62	1	42	4	47	58
60/64	35	6	17	58	61	80	37	77	194	58	19	84	38	141	56
55/59	2		1	3	57	55	6	33	94	54	47	71	62	180	52
50/54	0			0	53	21	0	10	31	49	67	32	77	176	48
45/49						5		1	6	45	63	6	48	117	44
40/44						0			0	42	38	2	15	55	39
35/39											11		3	14	36
30/34											1		0	1	32

MISAWA AB JAPAN

Temperature Range	NOVEMBER Obsn Hour Gp 01 to 08	NOVEMBER 09 to 16	NOVEMBER 17 to 24	NOVEMBER Total Obsn	NOVEMBER MCWB	DECEMBER Obsn Hour Gp 01 to 08	DECEMBER 09 to 16	DECEMBER 17 to 24	DECEMBER Total Obsn	DECEMBER MCWB	JANUARY Obsn Hour Gp 01 to 08	JANUARY 09 to 16	JANUARY 17 to 24	JANUARY Total Obsn	JANUARY MCWB
95/99															
90/94															
85/89															
80/84															
75/79															
70/74		0		0	61										
65/69	0	4	0	4	54										
60/64	2	19	2	23	54		1		1	51					
55/59	10	43	15	68	51	1	2	1	4	50		0		0	49
50/54	25	52	39	116	46	3	13	5	21	46	0	1	0	1	46
45/49	46	50	55	151	42	8	26	12	46	42	1	3	1	5	42
40/44	59	36	57	152	38	24	46	32	102	37	5	14	7	26	37
35/39	59	22	44	125	34	56	65	61	182	33	19	53	25	97	33
30/34	30	10	23	63	30	75	56	73	204	29	52	85	69	206	29
25/29	8	2	4	14	26	54	32	43	129	25	91	69	86	246	25
20/24	1	0	0	1	22	23	6	20	49	21	63	19	50	132	21
15/19						3	0	2	5	16	15	3	9	27	17
10/14						0			0	13	2	1	1	4	12
5/9													0	0	6

Temperature Range	FEBRUARY Obsn Hour Gp 01 to 08	FEBRUARY 09 to 16	FEBRUARY 17 to 24	FEBRUARY Total Obsn	FEBRUARY MCWB	MARCH Obsn Hour Gp 01 to 08	MARCH 09 to 16	MARCH 17 to 24	MARCH Total Obsn	MARCH MCWB	APRIL Obsn Hour Gp 01 to 08	APRIL 09 to 16	APRIL 17 to 24	APRIL Total Obsn	APRIL MCWB	ANNUAL TOTAL Obsn Hour Gp 01 to 08	ANNUAL TOTAL 09 to 16	ANNUAL TOTAL 17 to 24	ANNUAL TOTAL Total Obsn	ANNUAL TOTAL MCWB
95/99																	1		1	78
90/94																	8	1	9	77
85/89																1	38	4	43	75
80/84																12	99	25	136	72
75/79												1		1	56	48	179	78	305	69
70/74											0	5	0	5	55	149	284	185	618	66
65/69							1		1	50	1	13	3	17	54	252	319	289	860	62
60/64							2	0	2	50	4	25	8	37	51	286	319	290	895	57
55/59		0		0	48	1	7	2	10	47	11	46	15	72	48	292	278	291	861	53
50/54	0	3		3	44	2	15	6	23	44	24	56	32	112	45	278	226	296	800	48
45/49	1	6	3	10	41	8	30	13	51	41	51	48	65	164	42	268	187	255	710	43
40/44	6	23	10	39	37	24	57	34	115	37	69	34	71	174	38	251	215	237	703	38
35/39	22	45	31	98	33	49	70	63	182	33	53	10	35	98	34	273	265	263	801	33
30/34	48	78	59	185	29	79	44	79	202	29	26	2	11	39	30	311	275	314	900	29
25/29	67	51	72	190	25	56	17	36	109	25	3	0	1	4	26	279	171	242	692	25
20/24	61	15	39	115	21	23	4	13	40	21						171	44	122	337	21
15/19	18	3	10	31	17	5	0	2	7	17						41	6	23	70	17
10/14	2		0	2	12											4	1	1	6	12
5/9																		0	0	6

YOKOTA AB JAPAN

LAT 35 44N LONG 139 20E ELEV 455 FT

MEAN FREQUENCY OF OCCURRENCE OF DRY BULB TEMPERATURE (DEGREES F) WITH MEAN COINCIDENT WET BULB TEMPERATURE (DEGREES F) FOR EACH DRY BULB TEMPERATURE RANGE

Temperature Range	MAY Obsn Hour Gp 01 to 08	MAY 09 to 16	MAY 17 to 24	MAY Total Obsn	MAY MCWB	JUNE Obsn Hour Gp 01 to 08	JUNE 09 to 16	JUNE 17 to 24	JUNE Total Obsn	JUNE MCWB	JULY Obsn Hour Gp 01 to 08	JULY 09 to 16	JULY 17 to 24	JULY Total Obsn	JULY MCWB
95/99							0		0	79		1		1	81
90/94		0		0	70		2	0	2	78		19	1	20	79
85/89		2		2	71		9	1	10	74	0	55	10	65	77
80/84		10	1	11	66	0	28	5	33	70	6	59	31	96	75
75/79	0	37	6	43	64	4	61	21	86	68	62	56	91	209	73
70/74	4	62	20	86	62	25	69	59	153	66	109	39	81	229	70
65/69	19	67	52	138	60	89	43	95	227	64	61	16	29	106	66
60/64	63	41	82	186	58	83	21	42	146	60	8	3	4	15	61
55/59	93	22	63	178	54	30	5	16	51	55	2	0	1	3	57
50/54	51	6	20	77	50	8	0	1	9	51					
45/49	15	0	5	20	45	0			0	45					
40/44	3			3	41										
35/39	0			0	38										

Temperature Range	AUGUST Obsn Hour Gp 01 to 08	AUGUST 09 to 16	AUGUST 17 to 24	AUGUST Total Obsn	AUGUST MCWB	SEPTEMBER Obsn Hour Gp 01 to 08	SEPTEMBER 09 to 16	SEPTEMBER 17 to 24	SEPTEMBER Total Obsn	SEPTEMBER MCWB	OCTOBER Obsn Hour Gp 01 to 08	OCTOBER 09 to 16	OCTOBER 17 to 24	OCTOBER Total Obsn	OCTOBER MCWB
95/99		2		2	80		0		0	79					
90/94		30	1	31	79		3	0	3	78					
85/89	1	86	17	104	77		15	1	16	76		0		0	71
80/84	13	64	50	127	75	1	45	8	54	73		3		3	69
75/79	107	43	120	270	73	15	64	43	122	71	0	12	1	13	65
70/74	102	20	51	173	70	66	59	79	204	68	1	40	5	46	62
65/69	25	3	9	37	66	94	39	70	203	64	15	75	36	126	60
60/64	1		0	1	63	47	13	33	93	60	51	66	76	193	57
55/59						15	2	7	24	55	84	41	83	208	54
50/54						3		0	3	51	63	10	37	110	50
45/49						0			0	47	26	1	8	35	45
40/44											8	0	1	9	41
35/39											0			0	37

YOKOTA AB JAPAN

Tempera-ture Range	NOVEMBER					DECEMBER					JANUARY					FEBRUARY					MARCH					APRIL					ANNUAL TOTAL				
	Obsn Hour Gp			Total Obsn	M C W B	Obsn Hour Gp			Total Obsn	M C W B	Obsn Hour Gp			Total Obsn	M C W B	Obsn Hour Gp			Total Obsn	M C W B	Obsn Hour Gp			Total Obsn	M C W B	Obsn Hour Gp			Total Obsn	M C W B	Obsn Hour Gp			Total Obsn	M C W B
	01 to 08	09 to 16	17 to 24			01 to 08	09 to 16	17 to 24			01 to 08	09 to 16	17 to 24			01 to 08	09 to 16	17 to 24			01 to 08	09 to 16	17 to 24			01 to 08	09 to 16	17 to 24			01 to 08	09 to 16	17 to 24		
95/99																																3		3	80
90/94																																54	2	56	79
85/89																															1	167	29	197	77
80/84																											1	0	1	68	20	210	95	325	74
75/79		1		1	63												0	0	0	59		0	0	0	62		8	1	9	63	188	282	283	753	71
70/74		6	0	6	60		0		0	59	0	0		0	51		0	0	0	54		2	0	2	60	0	23	3	26	60	307	320	298	925	67
65/69	0	27	2	29	57		4	0	4	55		0		0	57		2	0	2	53	0	9	2	11	55	2	40	14	56	57	305	325	309	939	62
60/64	2	55	15	72	54	0	7	1	8	52		2	0	2	51		5	0	5	50	1	21	6	28	52	13	56	38	107	55	269	290	297	856	57
55/59	28	68	49	145	52	2	36	4	42	48	0	9	1	10	46	0	14	2	16	47	4	42	16	62	48	41	53	61	155	52	299	292	303	894	52
50/54	51	51	66	168	48	5	69	15	89	44	2	30	5	37	42	2	35	8	45	43	9	57	30	96	44	59	37	61	157	47	253	295	243	791	47
45/49	65	23	61	149	44	18	72	46	136	41	3	78	14	95	38	8	63	23	94	39	23	56	52	131	41	64	16	39	119	43	222	309	248	779	42
40/44	52	8	33	93	39	49	43	81	173	38	17	80	53	150	36	21	64	56	141	36	61	42	69	172	38	42	4	18	64	39	253	241	311	805	37
35/39	30	1	12	43	35	70	15	67	152	34	41	35	79	155	32	51	27	70	148	33	67	16	48	131	33	14	0	4	18	34	273	94	280	647	33
30/34	11		2	13	31	75	2	29	106	30	84	12	70	166	29	75	12	48	135	29	57	3	24	84	29	4		0	4	30	306	29	173	508	29
25/29	1		0	1	27	26	0	5	31	25	75	1	23	99	24	50	2	15	67	25	22	0	3	25	25	0			0	26	174	3	46	223	25
20/24						4		0	4	21	23		2	25	21	17		1	18	21	4		0	4	20						48		3	51	21
15/19						0			0	18	3		0	3	16	1			1	17	0			0	16						4		0	4	16
10/14											0			0	12																0			0	12

OSAN AB KOREA

LAT 37 08N LONG 127 02E ELEV 35 FT

MEAN FREQUENCY OF OCCURRENCE OF DRY BULB TEMPERATURE (DEGREES F) WITH MEAN COINCIDENT WET BULB TEMPERATURE (DEGREES F) FOR EACH DRY BULB TEMPERATURE RANGE

Temperature Range	MAY Obsn Hour Gp 01 to 08	MAY 09 to 16	MAY 17 to 24	MAY Total Obsn	MAY MCWB	JUNE Obsn Hour Gp 01 to 08	JUNE 09 to 16	JUNE 17 to 24	JUNE Total Obsn	JUNE MCWB	JULY Obsn Hour Gp 01 to 08	JULY 09 to 16	JULY 17 to 24	JULY Total Obsn	JULY MCWB
95/99							0		0	72		1	0	1	80
90/94							2	0	2	70		16	2	18	79
85/89		2		2	66		14	1	15	71	0	56	11	67	77
80/84		16	1	17	64	0	48	8	56	69	15	81	44	140	75
75/79	0	50	8	58	62	4	81	31	116	67	95	60	104	259	73
70/74	3	69	23	95	60	34	60	66	160	66	88	27	65	180	70
65/69	20	59	49	128	59	83	27	83	193	63	37	4	15	56	65
60/64	48	36	75	159	57	79	7	42	128	59	9	1	3	13	60
55/59	79	12	58	149	53	33	1	8	42	55	1			1	56
50/54	61	4	29	94	49	7	0	1	8	51					
45/49	29	0	5	34	45	0			0	48					
40/44	8		0	8	41										
35/39	0			0	34										
30/34															
25/29															

Temperature Range	AUGUST Obsn Hour Gp 01 to 08	AUGUST 09 to 16	AUGUST 17 to 24	AUGUST Total Obsn	AUGUST MCWB	SEPTEMBER Obsn Hour Gp 01 to 08	SEPTEMBER 09 to 16	SEPTEMBER 17 to 24	SEPTEMBER Total Obsn	SEPTEMBER MCWB	OCTOBER Obsn Hour Gp 01 to 08	OCTOBER 09 to 16	OCTOBER 17 to 24	OCTOBER Total Obsn	OCTOBER MCWB
95/99		2	0	2	79										
90/94		23	2	25	78										
85/89	1	84	14	99	77		8	0	8	74					
80/84	19	81	56	156	75	0	40	5	45	70		1		1	64
75/79	100	43	103	246	73	7	75	22	104	69		9	0	9	63
70/74	91	13	59	163	70	34	73	59	166	66		41	3	44	60
65/69	33	2	12	47	66	59	35	71	165	63	4	68	14	86	58
60/64	4	0	1	5	61	59	8	49	116	59	13	61	40	114	55
55/59	0			0	58	46	1	25	72	55	37	40	60	137	52
50/54						23		7	30	50	52	21	60	133	49
45/49						9		1	10	46	59	6	42	107	45
40/44						2		0	2	42	47	2	24	73	40
35/39						0			0	38	29		6	35	36
30/34											6		0	6	31
25/29											0			0	28

OSAN AB KOREA

Temperature Range	NOVEMBER Obsn Hour Gp 01 to 08	09 to 16	17 to 24	Total Obsn	MCWB	DECEMBER Obsn Hour Gp 01 to 08	09 to 16	17 to 24	Total Obsn	MCWB
95/99										
90/94										
85/89										
80/84										
75/79										
70/74		0		0	59					
65/69		6	0	6	56		0		0	56
60/64	1	26	3	30	54		1		1	54
55/59	7	47	14	68	51		5	0	5	51
50/54	16	50	34	100	47	0	15	5	20	47
45/49	32	41	50	123	43	5	26	12	43	42
40/44	48	33	51	132	39	16	39	21	76	38
35/39	49	21	37	107	34	25	51	37	113	34
30/34	46	12	31	89	30	50	46	61	157	29
25/29	29	4	16	49	25	53	33	48	134	25
20/24	10	1	2	13	21	43	20	33	96	20
15/19	2		1	3	15	30	8	21	59	16
10/14	0			0	12	17	3	8	28	11
5/9	0			0	9	5	0	3	8	7
0/4						2		0	2	2
-5/-1						0			0	-3
-10/-6										
-15/-11										
-20/-16										

Temperature Range	JANUARY Obsn Hour Gp 01 to 08	09 to 16	17 to 24	Total Obsn	MCWB	FEBRUARY Obsn Hour Gp 01 to 08	09 to 16	17 to 24	Total Obsn	MCWB
95/99										
90/94										
85/89										
80/84										
75/79										
70/74										
65/69										
60/64										
55/59						0	2		2	49
50/54		1		1	44	0	6	1	7	45
45/49	1	6	1	8	40	1	17	4	22	41
40/44	0	23	4	27	37	5	36	15	56	37
35/39	10	41	21	72	33	16	57	33	106	33
30/34	30	56	47	133	29	41	44	60	145	29
25/29	38	47	56	141	25	48	32	51	131	24
20/24	45	34	46	125	20	45	21	33	99	20
15/19	43	23	34	100	15	31	6	18	55	16
10/14	34	11	22	67	11	21	2	6	29	11
5/9	24	3	13	40	6	10	0	2	12	7
0/4	15	1	3	19	2	3	0	0	3	2
-5/-1	5	0	1	6	-3	1	0	0	1	-3
-10/-6	2	0	0	2	-7	1	0	0	1	-8
-15/-11	1			1	-13	0		0	0	-13
-20/-16	0			0	-16	0			0	-17

Temperature Range	MARCH Obsn Hour Gp 01 to 08	09 to 16	17 to 24	Total Obsn	MCWB	APRIL Obsn Hour Gp 01 to 08	09 to 16	17 to 24	Total Obsn	MCWB
95/99										
90/94										
85/89										
80/84							0		0	62
75/79							6	0	6	62
70/74		0		0	56	0	19	3	22	59
65/69		2		2	53	3	37	11	51	56
60/64	0	10	1	11	51	7	45	24	76	53
55/59	1	22	7	30	49	24	54	43	121	50
50/54	4	39	16	59	45	37	46	56	139	47
45/49	11	48	32	91	42	58	25	52	135	43
40/44	25	51	46	122	37	49	6	32	87	39
35/39	48	45	58	151	33	37	2	14	53	35
30/34	80	24	60	164	29	21	0	3	24	30
25/29	55	5	23	83	25	4	0	0	4	26
20/24	19	1	3	23	21	0			0	23
15/19	4		1	5	16					
10/14	1			1	12					
5/9										
0/4										
-5/-1										
-10/-6										
-15/-11										
-20/-16										

Temperature Range	ANNUAL TOTAL Obsn Hour Gp 01 to 08	09 to 16	17 to 24	Total Obsn	MCWB
95/99		3	0	3	79
90/94		41	4	45	78
85/89	1	164	26	191	76
80/84	34	267	114	415	73
75/79	206	324	268	798	71
70/74	250	302	278	830	66
65/69	239	240	255	734	61
60/64	220	195	238	653	57
55/59	228	184	215	627	52
50/54	200	182	209	591	48
45/49	205	169	199	573	43
40/44	200	190	193	583	38
35/39	214	217	206	637	34
30/34	274	183	262	719	29
25/29	228	123	196	547	25
20/24	164	77	118	359	20
15/19	110	37	75	222	16
10/14	73	16	36	125	11
5/9	39	3	18	60	6
0/4	20	1	3	24	2
-5/-1	6	0	1	7	-3
-10/-6	3	0	0	3	-7
-15/-11	1		0	1	-13
-20/-16	0			0	-17

DHAHRAN AB SAUDI ARABIA

LAT 26 16N LONG 50 10E ELEV 78 FT

MEAN FREQUENCY OF OCCURRENCE OF DRY BULB TEMPERATURE (DEGREES F) WITH MEAN COINCIDENT WET BULB TEMPERATURE (DEGREES F) FOR EACH DRY BULB TEMPERATURE RANGE

Temperature Range	MAY Obsn Hour Gp 01 to 08	MAY 09 to 16	MAY 17 to 24	MAY Total Obsn	MAY MCWB	JUNE Obsn Hour Gp 01 to 08	JUNE 09 to 16	JUNE 17 to 24	JUNE Total Obsn	JUNE MCWB	JULY Obsn Hour Gp 01 to 08	JULY 09 to 16	JULY 17 to 24	JULY Total Obsn	JULY MCWB
120/124															
115/119		0		0	71		1		1	73		2		2	75
110/114		3		3	72		17	0	17	72		29	0	29	74
105/109		16	0	16	71		69	3	72	71	0	95	5	100	74
100/104	0	43	3	46	70	2	93	19	114	71	4	94	28	126	75
95/99	3	77	14	94	70	17	50	48	115	70	33	26	67	126	74
90/94	15	67	35	117	69	58	10	79	147	70	84	2	91	177	74
85/89	45	32	75	152	69	85	1	62	148	69	100	0	51	151	74
80/84	90	8	82	180	68	62		25	87	70	25		6	31	74
75/79	70	2	31	103	67	15		3	18	70	1		0	1	73
70/74	21	0	7	28	64	2		0	2	68					
65/69	3		0	3	60	0			0	60					
60/64	0			0	55										

Temperature Range	AUGUST Obsn Hour Gp 01 to 08	AUGUST 09 to 16	AUGUST 17 to 24	AUGUST Total Obsn	AUGUST MCWB	SEPTEMBER Obsn Hour Gp 01 to 08	SEPTEMBER 09 to 16	SEPTEMBER 17 to 24	SEPTEMBER Total Obsn	SEPTEMBER MCWB	OCTOBER Obsn Hour Gp 01 to 08	OCTOBER 09 to 16	OCTOBER 17 to 24	OCTOBER Total Obsn	OCTOBER MCWB
120/124		0		0	77										
115/119		2		2	75		0		0	73					
110/114		28	0	28	74		3		3	72		0		0	71
105/109	0	88	3	91	75		33	0	33	73		2		2	71
100/104	4	98	21	123	77	0	78	3	81	74		13		13	70
95/99	23	30	56	109	77	3	89	20	112	75		53	1	54	71
90/94	67	2	96	165	77	20	32	58	110	75	1	87	9	97	72
85/89	110	0	64	174	76	68	4	93	165	75	7	67	42	116	72
80/84	42		9	51	76	106	0	54	160	73	41	22	97	160	72
75/79	2			2	72	41	0	10	51	70	102	4	73	179	70
70/74						3		1	4	65	75	0	22	97	66
65/69											19		4	23	61
60/64											3		0	3	56

DHAHRAN AB SAUDI ARABIA

Temperature Range	NOVEMBER Obsn Hour Gp 01 to 08	09 to 16	17 to 24	Total Obsn	MCWB	DECEMBER Obsn Hour Gp 01 to 08	09 to 16	17 to 24	Total Obsn	MCWB	JANUARY Obsn Hour Gp 01 to 08	09 to 16	17 to 24	Total Obsn	MCWB
120/124															
115/119															
110/114															
105/109															
100/104															
95/99		1		1	68							0		0	62
90/94		11	0	11	68							0		0	64
85/89	0	50	2	52	69		1		1	68		0	0	0	61
80/84	3	77	19	99	68		6		6	65		1	0	1	61
75/79	27	60	62	149	68	0	45	3	48	64		11	1	12	62
70/74	65	27	85	177	65	10	87	25	122	63	0	53	6	59	60
65/69	76	10	52	138	61	34	61	74	169	61	9	91	38	138	59
60/64	53	2	17	72	56	66	33	94	193	57	50	58	89	197	56
55/59	12	1	3	16	50	89	11	40	140	53	83	24	78	185	53
50/54	3	0	0	3	43	39	3	9	51	47	70	7	28	105	48
45/49	0			0	38	8	0	2	10	41	28	1	7	36	43
40/44						2		0	2	37	6	0	1	7	37
35/39											1			1	33

Temperature Range	FEBRUARY Obsn Hour Gp 01 to 08	09 to 16	17 to 24	Total Obsn	MCWB	MARCH Obsn Hour Gp 01 to 08	09 to 16	17 to 24	Total Obsn	MCWB	APRIL Obsn Hour Gp 01 to 08	09 to 16	17 to 24	Total Obsn	MCWB	ANNUAL TOTAL Obsn Hour Gp 01 to 08	09 to 16	17 to 24	Total Obsn	MCWB
120/124																	0		0	77
115/119																	5		5	74
110/114												0		0	70		80	0	80	73
105/109												1		1	70	0	304	11	315	73
100/104												5	0	5	68	10	424	74	508	74
95/99							1		1	65		19	1	20	67	79	346	207	632	73
90/94		0		0	64		5	0	5	65	0	40	4	44	67	245	256	372	873	73
85/89		1	0	1	64		18	1	19	64	3	72	13	88	66	418	246	403	1067	72
80/84		5	0	5	63	0	38	6	44	63	18	60	48	126	66	387	217	346	950	70
75/79		25	3	28	61	3	70	23	96	62	54	32	78	164	65	315	249	287	851	67
70/74	1	59	14	74	60	28	70	62	160	61	88	9	66	163	63	293	305	288	886	63
65/69	18	77	52	147	59	77	35	82	194	60	56	2	23	81	60	292	276	325	893	60
60/64	62	41	81	184	56	85	9	55	149	56	18	0	6	24	57	337	143	342	822	57
55/59	77	12	53	142	53	40	2	17	59	52	4		1	5	52	305	50	192	547	53
50/54	45	4	17	66	48	13	0	2	15	48	1		0	1	47	171	14	56	241	48
45/49	18	1	4	23	42	2		0	2	43						56	2	13	71	42
40/44	3	0	0	3	37											11	0	1	12	37
35/39	1			1	31											2			2	32

TAIPEI IAP TAIWAN

LAT 25 04N LONG 121 33E ELEV 30 FT

MEAN FREQUENCY OF OCCURRENCE OF DRY BULB TEMPERATURE (DEGREES F) WITH MEAN COINCIDENT WET BULB TEMPERATURE (DEGREES F) FOR EACH DRY BULB TEMPERATURE RANGE

Temperature Range	MAY Obsn Hour Gp 01 to 08	MAY 09 to 16	MAY 17 to 24	MAY Total Obsn	MAY MCWB	JUNE Obsn Hour Gp 01 to 08	JUNE 09 to 16	JUNE 17 to 24	JUNE Total Obsn	JUNE MCWB	JULY Obsn Hour Gp 01 to 08	JULY 09 to 16	JULY 17 to 24	JULY Total Obsn	JULY MCWB
95/99							1		1	78		12	0	12	81
90/94		11	1	12	79	0	49	3	52	80	1	109	11	121	81
85/89		60	8	68	78	3	82	26	111	79	8	86	50	144	79
80/84	11	68	40	119	76	34	50	70	154	77	89	33	132	254	77
75/79	84	63	97	244	73	138	42	101	281	75	146	7	54	207	76
70/74	108	35	72	215	70	55	14	34	103	71	4	1	0	5	71
65/69	35	11	26	72	65	10	2	6	18	67					
60/64	8	1	3	12	61										
55/59	1		1	2	56	0			0	55					
50/54	1			1	53										
45/49															

Temperature Range	AUGUST Obsn Hour Gp 01 to 08	AUGUST 09 to 16	AUGUST 17 to 24	AUGUST Total Obsn	AUGUST MCWB	SEPTEMBER Obsn Hour Gp 01 to 08	SEPTEMBER 09 to 16	SEPTEMBER 17 to 24	SEPTEMBER Total Obsn	SEPTEMBER MCWB	OCTOBER Obsn Hour Gp 01 to 08	OCTOBER 09 to 16	OCTOBER 17 to 24	OCTOBER Total Obsn	OCTOBER MCWB
95/99		7		7	80		0		0	81					
90/94	0	97	9	106	80		41	1	42	80		2		2	78
85/89	8	98	46	152	79	2	84	14	100	78	0	37	0	37	77
80/84	83	37	125	245	77	35	70	71	176	76	6	49	16	71	75
75/79	146	9	67	222	75	143	37	125	305	74	57	85	70	212	72
70/74	12		1	13	71	46	8	22	76	70	93	55	88	236	68
65/69						10	0	6	16	66	58	18	59	135	65
60/64						4		1	5	61	24	1	12	37	61
55/59						0			0	58	6		3	9	56
50/54											2		1	3	52
45/49											1			1	46

																															20	0	20	80
	0		0	74																	0		0	76		1	0	1	77	1	310	25	336	80
0	5		5	74							0		0	74		1		1	73		2		2	75		16	6	16	76	21	471	144	636	78
0	21	1	22	73		7	0	7	73		3	0	3	71		5	0	5	71		12	2	14	72	1	57		64	74	259	412	463	1134	76
9	59	18	86	70	0	24	3	27	69		13	1	14	68	0	22	5	27	68	0	42	11	53	69	15	56	49	120	72	738	459	601	1798	74
46	69	66	181	67	7	53	20	80	66	0	35	9	44	65	2	30	11	43	66	11	40	30	81	66	72	47	70	189	69	456	387	423	1266	68
93	52	89	234	64	41	66	66	173	63	13	41	36	90	63	14	47	32	93	63	38	40	41	119	64	73	35	57	165	64	385	312	418	1115	64
68	28	51	147	59	96	51	83	230	59	78	56	69	203	60	73	49	68	190	60	92	62	81	235	59	49	18	37	104	60	492	266	405	1163	60
21	5	15	41	55	62	31	44	137	55	89	65	74	228	54	75	36	60	171	55	73	43	62	178	55	22	7	13	42	55	349	187	272	808	55
2		1	3	51	30	14	22	66	48	50	31	46	127	50	39	28	37	104	50	24	7	15	46	50	9	3	6	18	50	157	83	128	368	50
					8	2	7	17	44	13	3	13	29	45	19	7	11	37	45	4	0	3	7	45	1		0	1	47	46	12	34	92	45
					3		2	5	41	3		1	4	42	1	0	0	1	41	4		2	6	41						11	0	5	16	41
					0		0	0	38	1			1	39	1			1	38	2		0	2	38						4		0	4	38

ASIA (CONT)

BANGKOK DON MUANG IAP THAILAND

LAT 13 55N LONG 100 37E ELEV 12 FT

MEAN FREQUENCY OF OCCURRENCE OF DRY BULB TEMPERATURE (DEGREES F) WITH MEAN COINCIDENT WET BULB TEMPERATURE (DEGREES F) FOR EACH DRY BULB TEMPERATURE RANGE

Temperature Range	MAY Obsn Hour Gp 01 to 08	MAY 09 to 16	MAY 17 to 24	MAY Total Obsn	MAY MCWB	JUNE Obsn Hour Gp 01 to 08	JUNE 09 to 16	JUNE 17 to 24	JUNE Total Obsn	JUNE MCWB	JULY Obsn Hour Gp 01 to 08	JULY 09 to 16	JULY 17 to 24	JULY Total Obsn	JULY MCWB
100/104		4	0	4	83										
95/99		36	6	42	81		15	2	17	81		7	1	8	82
90/94		84	19	103	81		104	15	119	81		86	14	100	81
85/89	11	76	62	149	80	4	89	57	150	79	1	104	47	152	79
80/84	80	37	105	222	78	85	24	108	217	78	66	44	119	229	78
75/79	154	8	53	215	76	148	4	54	206	76	180	7	65	252	76
70/74	1	0	1	2	73	1	0	0	1	73	1		1	2	73
65/69															

Temperature Range	AUGUST Obsn Hour Gp 01 to 08	AUGUST 09 to 16	AUGUST 17 to 24	AUGUST Total Obsn	AUGUST MCWB	SEPTEMBER Obsn Hour Gp 01 to 08	SEPTEMBER 09 to 16	SEPTEMBER 17 to 24	SEPTEMBER Total Obsn	SEPTEMBER MCWB	OCTOBER Obsn Hour Gp 01 to 08	OCTOBER 09 to 16	OCTOBER 17 to 24	OCTOBER Total Obsn	OCTOBER MCWB
100/104															
95/99		3		3	82		0		0	81					
90/94		71	9	80	81		54	6	60	81		24	2	26	80
85/89	1	121	42	164	79	1	119	48	168	79	1	140	46	187	79
80/84	59	45	113	217	78	60	54	112	226	78	57	66	129	252	77
75/79	187	7	84	278	76	177	13	72	262	76	180	17	67	264	76
70/74	2	0	1	3	72	3		2	5	73	10	2	3	15	71
65/69											1		0	1	67

																					1		1	81		2	0	2	82		7	0	7	82
						0		0	77		2	0	2	76		5	0	5	78		43	3	46	79		75	7	82	81		186	19	205	81
	22	1	23	79		38	4	42	77		61	11	72	77		84	15	99	78		113	32	145	79		89	32	121	80		830	160	990	80
	104	27	231	77		81	27	108	75		79	39	118	75		68	39	107	76	0	48	48	96	78	5	49	67	121	79	24	1078	549	1651	78
16	80	97	193	75	1	73	67	141	73	1	51	56	108	73	2	39	71	112	76	36	30	120	186	77	91	18	104	213	78	554	561	1201	2316	77
139	30	96	265	74	87	41	104	232	73	61	37	95	193	73	102	22	85	209	74	170	8	39	217	75	132	7	30	169	75	1717	201	844	2762	75
65	4	15	84	69	88	13	36	137	69	103	12	32	147	69	95	5	13	113	70	36	1	3	40	71	12	0	1	13	72	417	37	108	562	70
17	0	4	21	64	53	3	10	66	65	50	5	11	66	64	21	0	0	21	65	2			2	65	0			0	67	144	8	25	177	64
3			3	60	18		1	19	61	29	1	3	33	60	4			4	61											54	1	4	59	60
					1			1	57	4		0	4	55																5		0	5	56
										0			0	51																0			0	51

NAKHON PHANOM THAILAND

LAT 17 23N LONG 104 30E ELEV 577 FT

MEAN FREQUENCY OF OCCURRENCE OF DRY BULB TEMPERATURE (DEGREES F) WITH MEAN COINCIDENT WET BULB TEMPERATURE (DEGREES F) FOR EACH DRY BULB TEMPERATURE RANGE

Temperature Range	MAY Obsn Hour Gp 01 to 08	MAY 09 to 16	MAY 17 to 24	MAY Total Obsn	MAY MCWB	JUNE Obsn Hour Gp 01 to 08	JUNE 09 to 16	JUNE 17 to 24	JUNE Total Obsn	JUNE MCWB	JULY Obsn Hour Gp 01 to 08	JULY 09 to 16	JULY 17 to 24	JULY Total Obsn	JULY MCWB
100/104		3	0	3	81		0		0	85		0		0	84
95/99		19	5	24	80		4	0	4	84		4	0	4	83
90/94	1	72	24	97	79		34	9	43	81		30	8	38	81
85/89	7	74	58	139	78	1	85	41	127	79	1	85	38	124	79
80/84	70	54	91	215	77	59	78	116	253	78	56	90	109	255	78
75/79	143	22	63	228	75	155	36	71	262	76	172	38	89	299	76
70/74	27	4	6	37	72	25	3	2	30	73	18	2	3	23	73
65/69	1	0		1	66										
60/64															

Temperature Range	AUGUST Obsn Hour Gp 01 to 08	AUGUST 09 to 16	AUGUST 17 to 24	AUGUST Total Obsn	AUGUST MCWB	SEPTEMBER Obsn Hour Gp 01 to 08	SEPTEMBER 09 to 16	SEPTEMBER 17 to 24	SEPTEMBER Total Obsn	SEPTEMBER MCWB	OCTOBER Obsn Hour Gp 01 to 08	OCTOBER 09 to 16	OCTOBER 17 to 24	OCTOBER Total Obsn	OCTOBER MCWB
100/104															
95/99		0		0	80		1		1	82		3		3	78
90/94		19	3	22	80		25	2	27	78		33	2	35	77
85/89		79	27	106	79	0	83	21	104	77		105	18	123	74
80/84	33	91	106	230	78	11	84	82	177	77	7	78	68	153	73
75/79	190	56	108	354	76	164	42	123	329	75	81	22	113	216	72
70/74	25	2	5	32	73	60	5	11	76	71	112	7	41	160	69
65/69						4		0	4	65	44	0	6	50	64
60/64											4		0	4	61

																1	0	1	72		9	1	10	76		10	2	12	77		23	3	26	77
						0		0	79		2	0	2	75		14	3	17	73		38	14	52	76		42	11	53	78		127	33	160	77
	13	0	13	74		11	0	11	74		16	3	19	74		30	13	43	74		56	31	87	75	0	73	37	110	76	1	412	132	545	77
	82	10	92	72		57	10	67	71		42	13	55	72		47	27	74	72	2	60	51	113	73	9	54	60	123	75	20	853	374	1247	76
1	86	39	126	70		82	29	111	69		62	31	93	68	2	44	38	84	69	28	44	65	137	72	63	35	67	165	74	330	828	841	1999	75
15	47	83	145	68	5	57	53	115	66	2	58	48	108	66	36	38	48	122	68	82	26	48	156	70	93	18	45	156	72	1138	460	892	2490	73
80	11	71	162	67	31	30	68	129	65	30	40	60	130	64	49	28	38	115	65	71	11	27	109	67	58	6	16	80	69	586	149	348	1083	67
89	2	29	120	63	74	10	54	138	62	65	20	48	133	62	48	16	30	94	62	43	3	10	56	63	13	1	2	16	63	381	52	179	612	62
40		7	47	60	82	1	23	106	59	69	6	31	106	58	50	6	19	75	58	15	0	3	18	58	4		1	5	58	264	13	84	361	58
11	0	1	12	55	36		7	43	54	56	0	11	67	54	25	1	6	32	54	7		0	7	54						135	1	25	161	54
4			4	52	15		2	17	49	19		2	21	49	11		1	12	50	0			0	51						49		5	54	49
0			0	48	5		0	5	45	8			8	44	2			2	46											15		0	15	45
					0			0	41	0			0	40																0			0	40

INCIRLIK AB/ADANA TURKEY

LAT 37 00N LONG 35 20E ELEV 239 FT

MEAN FREQUENCY OF OCCURRENCE OF DRY BULB TEMPERATURE (DEGREES F) WITH MEAN COINCIDENT WET BULB TEMPERATURE (DEGREES F) FOR EACH DRY BULB TEMPERATURE RANGE

Temperature Range	MAY Obsn Hour Gp 01 to 08	MAY 09 to 16	MAY 17 to 24	MAY Total Obsn	MAY MCWB	JUNE Obsn Hour Gp 01 to 08	JUNE 09 to 16	JUNE 17 to 24	JUNE Total Obsn	JUNE MCWB	JULY Obsn Hour Gp 01 to 08	JULY 09 to 16	JULY 17 to 24	JULY Total Obsn	JULY MCWB
110/114															
105/109							0		0	73		1		1	74
100/104		0		0	70		3	0	3	70		6	0	6	71
95/99		8	0	8	67	0	12	1	13	70	0	29	2	31	73
90/94		15	3	18	67	0	42	4	46	71	1	100	14	115	74
85/89	1	28	6	35	66	2	77	19	98	70	5	86	43	134	73
80/84	2	48	12	62	66	11	71	40	122	69	41	25	79	145	73
75/79	9	61	24	94	65	40	26	65	131	68	88	1	88	177	72
70/74	25	53	50	128	63	72	6	68	146	67	89	0	19	108	68
65/69	57	26	68	151	61	76	2	33	111	63	22		2	24	64
60/64	74	7	55	136	59	35	1	9	45	60	2		0	2	58
55/59	62	2	26	90	55	4		0	4	56	0			0	52
50/54	17	0	4	21	51										
45/49	1	0	0	1	46										
40/44	0			0	43										

Temperature Range	AUGUST Obsn Hour Gp 01 to 08	AUGUST 09 to 16	AUGUST 17 to 24	AUGUST Total Obsn	AUGUST MCWB	SEPTEMBER Obsn Hour Gp 01 to 08	SEPTEMBER 09 to 16	SEPTEMBER 17 to 24	SEPTEMBER Total Obsn	SEPTEMBER MCWB	OCTOBER Obsn Hour Gp 01 to 08	OCTOBER 09 to 16	OCTOBER 17 to 24	OCTOBER Total Obsn	OCTOBER MCWB
110/114		1		1	73										
105/109		3	0	3	74										
100/104	0	11	1	12	72		3	0	3	68		0		0	69
95/99	0	45	3	48	74		13	0	13	67		2	0	2	66
90/94	1	110	18	129	74	0	57	3	60	69		14	0	14	64
85/89	6	67	48	121	74	1	92	17	110	69	0	44	2	46	64
80/84	56	11	100	167	74	13	57	45	115	68	1	76	11	88	63
75/79	90	0	61	151	71	36	15	68	119	67	12	61	31	104	62
70/74	81		16	97	67	74	3	62	139	64	26	31	51	108	60
65/69	13		1	14	62	81	1	35	117	61	58	14	62	134	59
60/64	0		0	0	53	31		10	41	56	86	6	56	148	56
55/59						4		1	5	50	49	0	28	77	52
50/54											13		5	18	46
45/49											3		2	5	40
40/44											1		1	2	37

INCIRLIK AB/ADANA TURKEY

Temperature Range	NOVEMBER Obsn Hour Gp 01 to 08	09 to 16	17 to 24	Total Obsn	M C W B	DECEMBER Obsn Hour Gp 01 to 08	09 to 16	17 to 24	Total Obsn	M C W B	JANUARY Obsn Hour Gp 01 to 08	09 to 16	17 to 24	Total Obsn	M C W B	FEBRUARY Obsn Hour Gp 01 to 08	09 to 16	17 to 24	Total Obsn	M C W B
110/114																				
105/109																				
100/104																				
95/99																				
90/94		1		1	62															
85/89		5		5	62															
80/84	0	21	1	22	60		0		0	60										
75/79	1	47	3	51	59		2		2	56							1		1	57
70/74	3	57	14	74	58		10	0	10	55		0		0	57	0	6	1	7	56
65/69	19	50	36	105	56	0	31	1	32	53		9	0	9	54	1	20	3	24	55
60/64	47	32	52	131	54	5	63	12	80	52	1	45	4	50	52	2	45	12	59	53
55/59	70	17	60	147	51	31	77	50	158	50	16	80	32	128	49	12	62	33	107	50
50/54	51	10	40	101	47	87	48	93	228	48	55	70	72	197	47	48	52	60	160	47
45/49	28	1	21	50	42	67	15	57	139	43	67	29	62	158	43	68	29	59	156	43
40/44	15		12	27	37	37	2	26	65	38	60	12	44	116	38	45	8	34	87	38
35/39	5		2	7	33	16	1	7	24	33	30	2	22	54	32	34	1	17	52	33
30/34	0			0	30	4		2	6	29	16	0	10	26	28	14		5	19	28
25/29						0		0	0	24	3		1	4	24	1		0	1	25
20/24											1		0	1	19					
15/19											0		0	0	14					

Temperature Range	MARCH Obsn Hour Gp 01 to 08	09 to 16	17 to 24	Total Obsn	M C W B	APRIL Obsn Hour Gp 01 to 08	09 to 16	17 to 24	Total Obsn	M C W B	ANNUAL TOTAL Obsn Hour Gp 01 to 08	09 to 16	17 to 24	Total Obsn	M C W B
110/114												1		1	73
105/109												4	0	4	73
100/104											0	23	1	24	71
95/99							0		0	65	0	109	6	115	72
90/94							1		1	67	2	340	42	384	72
85/89							6	1	7	64	15	405	136	556	71
80/84		3		3	60	0	20	3	23	62	124	332	291	747	69
75/79		12	2	14	59	1	37	7	45	61	277	263	349	889	67
70/74	2	23	5	30	57	6	59	18	83	59	378	248	304	930	64
65/69	5	50	14	69	55	17	71	39	127	58	349	274	294	917	59
60/64	15	73	36	124	53	47	32	71	150	56	345	304	317	966	55
55/59	43	58	69	170	51	77	10	63	150	54	368	306	362	1036	51
50/54	73	25	64	162	48	65	3	32	100	50	409	208	370	987	48
45/49	60	5	36	101	43	22	0	7	29	45	316	79	244	639	43
40/44	34	0	16	50	38	4		1	5	40	196	22	134	352	38
35/39	13		6	19	33	1		0	1	35	99	4	54	157	33
30/34	3		0	3	29						37	0	17	54	28
25/29	0			0	26						4		1	5	24
20/24											1		0	1	19
15/19											0		0	0	14

SAIGON/TAN SON NHUT VIETNAM

LAT 10 49N LONG 106 39E ELEV 33 FT

MEAN FREQUENCY OF OCCURRENCE OF DRY BULB TEMPERATURE (DEGREES F) WITH MEAN COINCIDENT WET BULB TEMPERATURE (DEGREES F) FOR EACH DRY BULB TEMPERATURE RANGE

Temperature Range	MAY Obsn Hour Gp 01 to 08	MAY 09 to 16	MAY 17 to 24	MAY Total Obsn	MAY MCWB	JUNE Obsn Hour Gp 01 to 08	JUNE 09 to 16	JUNE 17 to 24	JUNE Total Obsn	JUNE MCWB	JULY Obsn Hour Gp 01 to 08	JULY 09 to 16	JULY 17 to 24	JULY Total Obsn	JULY MCWB
100/104		0		0	79										
95/99		20	0	20	79		0		0	80		4		4	81
90/94	0	98	8	106	79		77	6	83	79		47	5	52	79
85/89	14	79	60	153	79	5	97	27	129	79	4	103	26	133	78
80/84	115	39	115	269	78	91	55	123	269	78	66	74	100	240	77
75/79	118	12	65	195	76	142	10	82	234	76	175	19	114	308	76
70/74	0	0	0	0	72	2	0	1	3	73	4	0	3	7	72
65/69															

Temperature Range	AUGUST Obsn Hour Gp 01 to 08	AUGUST 09 to 16	AUGUST 17 to 24	AUGUST Total Obsn	AUGUST MCWB	SEPTEMBER Obsn Hour Gp 01 to 08	SEPTEMBER 09 to 16	SEPTEMBER 17 to 24	SEPTEMBER Total Obsn	SEPTEMBER MCWB	OCTOBER Obsn Hour Gp 01 to 08	OCTOBER 09 to 16	OCTOBER 17 to 24	OCTOBER Total Obsn	OCTOBER MCWB
100/104															
95/99		0		0	80							0		0	80
90/94		45	3	48	79		35	1	36	79		34	0	34	79
85/89	1	111	19	131	78	1	101	15	117	78	1	116	13	130	78
80/84	40	80	111	231	77	36	81	103	220	77	27	77	102	206	77
75/79	200	12	112	324	76	186	22	114	322	76	187	19	121	327	75
70/74	7		3	10	73	17	1	7	25	72	32	1	11	44	72
65/69											0			0	66

Temperature Range	NOVEMBER Obsn Hour Gp 01 to 08	NOVEMBER Obsn Hour Gp 09 to 16	NOVEMBER Obsn Hour Gp 17 to 24	NOVEMBER Total Obsn	NOVEMBER MCWB	DECEMBER Obsn Hour Gp 01 to 08	DECEMBER Obsn Hour Gp 09 to 16	DECEMBER Obsn Hour Gp 17 to 24	DECEMBER Total Obsn	DECEMBER MCWB	JANUARY Obsn Hour Gp 01 to 08	JANUARY Obsn Hour Gp 09 to 16	JANUARY Obsn Hour Gp 17 to 24	JANUARY Total Obsn	JANUARY MCWB
100/104															
95/99							0		0	79		0		0	72
90/94		37	1	38	77		37	1	38	76		48	3	51	74
85/89		116	17	133	76		109	22	131	75		92	22	114	74
80/84	10	74	106	190	75	5	79	87	171	74	1	74	77	152	73
75/79	176	13	107	296	74	124	22	120	266	73	105	29	126	260	72
70/74	52	0	10	62	70	93	1	17	111	69	114	5	19	138	69
65/69	2			2	64	24		0	24	65	25	0	1	26	65
60/64						1			1	61	2			2	60

Temperature Range	FEBRUARY Obsn Hour Gp 01 to 08	FEBRUARY Obsn Hour Gp 09 to 16	FEBRUARY Obsn Hour Gp 17 to 24	FEBRUARY Total Obsn	FEBRUARY MCWB	MARCH Obsn Hour Gp 01 to 08	MARCH Obsn Hour Gp 09 to 16	MARCH Obsn Hour Gp 17 to 24	MARCH Total Obsn	MARCH MCWB	APRIL Obsn Hour Gp 01 to 08	APRIL Obsn Hour Gp 09 to 16	APRIL Obsn Hour Gp 17 to 24	APRIL Total Obsn	APRIL MCWB	ANNUAL TOTAL Obsn Hour Gp 01 to 08	ANNUAL TOTAL Obsn Hour Gp 09 to 16	ANNUAL TOTAL Obsn Hour Gp 17 to 24	ANNUAL TOTAL Total Obsn	ANNUAL TOTAL MCWB
100/104							0		0	76							0		0	78
95/99		3		3	75		17		17	77		24	0	24	78		68	0	68	78
90/94		65	4	69	75		107	6	113	76	0	126	6	132	77	0	756	44	800	77
85/89		91	24	115	73	1	83	45	129	75	8	70	65	143	77	35	1168	355	1558	77
80/84	4	48	82	134	73	39	36	123	198	75	129	19	148	296	76	563	736	1277	2576	76
75/79	127	16	107	250	72	186	4	73	263	73	100	1	20	121	75	1826	179	1161	3166	74
70/74	80	1	7	88	69	22		1	23	70	3			3	72	426	9	79	514	70
65/69	13			13	65	0			0	67						64	0	1	65	65
60/64																3			3	60

ATLANTIC OCEAN

LAJES FIELD AZORES

LAT 38 46N LONG 27 06W ELEV 109 FT

MEAN FREQUENCY OF OCCURRENCE OF DRY BULB TEMPERATURE (DEGREES F) WITH MEAN COINCIDENT WET BULB TEMPERATURE (DEGREES F) FOR EACH DRY BULB TEMPERATURE RANGE

Temperature Range	MAY					JUNE					JULY				
	Obsn Hour Gp 01 to 08	09 to 16	17 to 24	Total Obsn	MCWB	Obsn Hour Gp 01 to 08	09 to 16	17 to 24	Total Obsn	MCWB	Obsn Hour Gp 01 to 08	09 to 16	17 to 24	Total Obsn	MCWB
85/89															
80/84							0		0	69	0	4	0	4	71
75/79		0		0	65	0	12	1	13	67	5	44	9	58	69
70/74	1	13	1	15	63	14	73	24	111	65	47	141	83	271	66
65/69	20	97	32	149	61	80	114	99	293	62	136	57	130	323	63
60/64	112	117	127	356	57	107	39	97	243	59	53	1	26	80	59
55/59	91	20	79	190	53	33	1	17	51	54	7		1	8	55
50/54	23	0	9	32	50	6		2	8	50	0			0	52
45/49	2		0	2	46	0			0	48					

Temperature Range	AUGUST					SEPTEMBER					OCTOBER				
	Obsn Hour Gp 01 to 08	09 to 16	17 to 24	Total Obsn	MCWB	Obsn Hour Gp 01 to 08	09 to 16	17 to 24	Total Obsn	MCWB	Obsn Hour Gp 01 to 08	09 to 16	17 to 24	Total Obsn	MCWB
85/89							0		0	73					
80/84		12	1	13	72		6	0	6	72		1		1	70
75/79	10	96	24	130	69	6	60	11	77	69	1	10	1	12	69
70/74	100	128	134	362	66	71	129	97	297	66	23	75	27	125	66
65/69	103	12	76	191	63	109	41	104	254	62	103	124	113	340	62
60/64	30	0	13	43	59	44	3	24	71	59	92	37	88	217	58
55/59	5		1	6	56	7		3	10	55	25	1	16	42	54
50/54						1		0	1	50	4	0	2	6	50
45/49											1			1	45

Temperature Range	NOVEMBER Obsn Hour Gp 01 to 08	09 to 16	17 to 24	Total Obsn	M C W B	DECEMBER Obsn Hour Gp 01 to 08	09 to 16	17 to 24	Total Obsn	M C W B	JANUARY Obsn Hour Gp 01 to 08	09 to 16	17 to 24	Total Obsn	M C W B
85/89															
80/84															
75/79															
70/74	1	10	1	12	66		2	0	2	64		0		0	64
65/69	36	77	38	151	62	17	45	18	80	61	4	19	5	28	61
60/64	112	120	125	357	57	89	119	97	305	58	67	99	74	240	58
55/59	68	30	62	160	53	96	73	96	265	53	107	106	109	322	53
50/54	18	3	14	35	49	38	9	32	79	49	53	23	52	128	48
45/49	4	0	1	5	46	8	0	5	13	45	14	1	8	23	45
40/44						1		0	1	42	2		1	3	42

Temperature Range	FEBRUARY Obsn Hour Gp 01 to 08	09 to 16	17 to 24	Total Obsn	M C W B	MARCH Obsn Hour Gp 01 to 08	09 to 16	17 to 24	Total Obsn	M C W B	APRIL Obsn Hour Gp 01 to 08	09 to 16	17 to 24	Total Obsn	M C W B
85/89															
80/84															
75/79															
70/74							0		0	60		2		2	63
65/69	0	7	1	8	60	1	18	3	22	60	4	40	6	50	60
60/64	32	78	44	154	57	47	113	59	219	57	64	141	83	288	57
55/59	98	104	109	311	53	112	100	128	340	53	118	50	118	286	53
50/54	69	31	58	158	48	71	16	52	139	49	47	6	29	82	49
45/49	20	3	11	34	44	15	1	6	22	45	7	0	3	10	46
40/44	4	0	2	6	41	1	0	0	1	42	0		0	0	42

Temperature Range	ANNUAL TOTAL Obsn Hour Gp 01 to 08	09 to 16	17 to 24	Total Obsn	M C W B
85/89	0	0		0	73
80/84	0	23		24	72
75/79	22	222	46	290	69
70/74	257	573	367	1197	66
65/69	613	651	625	1889	62
60/64	849	867	857	2573	58
55/59	767	485	739	1991	53
50/54	330	88	250	668	49
45/49	71	5	34	110	45
40/44	8	0	3	11	41

BERMUDA NAS/KINDLEY AFB

LAT 32 22N LONG 64 41W ELEV 10 FT

MEAN FREQUENCY OF OCCURRENCE OF DRY BULB TEMPERATURE (DEGREES F) WITH MEAN COINCIDENT WET BULB TEMPERATURE (DEGREES F) FOR EACH DRY BULB TEMPERATURE RANGE

Temperature Range	MAY Obsn Hour Gp 01 to 08	MAY Obsn Hour Gp 09 to 16	MAY Obsn Hour Gp 17 to 24	MAY Total Obsn	MAY MCWB	JUNE Obsn Hour Gp 01 to 08	JUNE Obsn Hour Gp 09 to 16	JUNE Obsn Hour Gp 17 to 24	JUNE Total Obsn	JUNE MCWB	JULY Obsn Hour Gp 01 to 08	JULY Obsn Hour Gp 09 to 16	JULY Obsn Hour Gp 17 to 24	JULY Total Obsn	JULY MCWB
90/94												0	0	0	78
85/89							1	0	1	77	0	27	4	31	76
80/84		0	0	0	72	1	59	11	71	74	52	169	109	330	75
75/79	2	55	10	67	70	108	136	135	379	72	180	47	129	356	73
70/74	92	136	120	348	67	116	40	85	241	69	16	5	6	27	70
65/69	129	53	104	286	62	15	4	8	27	64	0	0	0	0	69
60/64	25	4	14	43	56			0	0	64					
55/59	0			0	54										

Temperature Range	AUGUST Obsn Hour Gp 01 to 08	AUGUST Obsn Hour Gp 09 to 16	AUGUST Obsn Hour Gp 17 to 24	AUGUST Total Obsn	AUGUST MCWB	SEPTEMBER Obsn Hour Gp 01 to 08	SEPTEMBER Obsn Hour Gp 09 to 16	SEPTEMBER Obsn Hour Gp 17 to 24	SEPTEMBER Total Obsn	SEPTEMBER MCWB	OCTOBER Obsn Hour Gp 01 to 08	OCTOBER Obsn Hour Gp 09 to 16	OCTOBER Obsn Hour Gp 17 to 24	OCTOBER Total Obsn	OCTOBER MCWB
90/94		0	0	0	80		0		0	75					
85/89	0	52	6	58	76		14	1	15	76		1	0	1	77
80/84	116	166	161	443	75	35	154	75	264	74	4	44	8	56	74
75/79	128	27	78	233	73	184	66	152	402	72	100	128	114	342	71
70/74	4	2	3	9	71	21	6	12	39	67	124	64	110	298	66
65/69	0	0		0	69	0	0	0	0	66	19	10	16	45	60
60/64											1		1	2	56
55/59															

																															0	0	0	78
																														0	95	11	106	76
	0		0	75																										208	592	364	1164	75
5	37	8	50	70		1		1	69												0		0	67		2	0	2	68	707	499	626	1832	72
98	133	112	343	66	22	64	28	114	66	4	24	6	34	66	1	18	2	21	66	2	22	4	28	66	6	65	16	87	66	506	579	504	1589	67
119	66	106	291	60	108	114	114	336	61	69	102	81	252	62	56	89	74	219	62	62	99	74	235	62	104	117	123	344	62	681	654	700	2035	62
18	4	14	36	56	100	59	91	250	55	113	89	109	311	56	101	80	90	271	56	104	91	109	304	56	104	52	84	240	55	566	379	512	1457	56
0	0	0	0	55	16	10	14	40	52	52	30	45	127	51	54	32	50	136	50	73	32	56	161	51	26	4	17	47	51	221	108	182	511	51
					1	1	1	3	48	9	3	7	19	47	12	4	7	23	48	7	2	4	13	48	1		0	1	49	30	10	19	59	48
										0			0	45	1	0	0	1	45	0	0		0	44						1	0	0	1	45

KEFLAVIK NAS ICELAND

LAT 63 59N LONG 22 36W ELEV 103 FT

MEAN FREQUENCY OF OCCURRENCE OF DRY BULB TEMPERATURE (DEGREES F) WITH MEAN COINCIDENT WET BULB TEMPERATURE (DEGREES F) FOR EACH DRY BULB TEMPERATURE RANGE

Temperature Range	MAY Obsn Hour Gp 01 to 08	MAY 09 to 16	MAY 17 to 24	MAY Total Obsn	MAY MCWB	JUNE Obsn Hour Gp 01 to 08	JUNE 09 to 16	JUNE 17 to 24	JUNE Total Obsn	JUNE MCWB	JULY Obsn Hour Gp 01 to 08	JULY 09 to 16	JULY 17 to 24	JULY Total Obsn	JULY MCWB
65/69		0		0	52							0	0	0	56
60/64		2	0	2	51		2	0	2	54	0	12	4	16	53
55/59	0	5	2	7	50	1	26	9	36	51	12	84	38	134	51
50/54	8	52	23	83	47	43	117	85	245	48	112	121	142	375	49
45/49	68	104	98	270	44	146	88	122	356	45	105	30	59	194	45
40/44	93	59	83	235	39	45	7	22	74	40	18	1	5	24	40
35/39	52	21	29	102	34	5		2	7	35	0			0	35
30/34	23	5	13	41	29										
25/29	4	0	1	5	25										
20/24	0		0	0	21										
15/19															

Temperature Range	AUGUST Obsn Hour Gp 01 to 08	AUGUST 09 to 16	AUGUST 17 to 24	AUGUST Total Obsn	AUGUST MCWB	SEPTEMBER Obsn Hour Gp 01 to 08	SEPTEMBER 09 to 16	SEPTEMBER 17 to 24	SEPTEMBER Total Obsn	SEPTEMBER MCWB	OCTOBER Obsn Hour Gp 01 to 08	OCTOBER 09 to 16	OCTOBER 17 to 24	OCTOBER Total Obsn	OCTOBER MCWB
65/69		0	0	0	55										
60/64		4	1	5	53		1		1	56					
55/59	6	69	27	102	51	6	16	5	27	52	0	0	0	0	52
50/54	106	142	140	388	49	43	92	61	196	49	13	27	17	57	50
45/49	111	30	70	211	45	95	97	106	298	44	59	84	66	209	45
40/44	24	2	10	36	40	71	29	52	152	40	80	71	83	234	40
35/39	1			1	36	23	6	14	43	35	65	47	54	166	35
30/34						2	0	1	3	30	25	14	22	61	30
25/29											3	3	5	11	24
20/24											2	1	1	4	19
15/19											0			0	16

KEFLAVIK NAS ICELAND

Temperature Range	NOVEMBER Obsn Hour Gp 01 to 08	NOVEMBER Obsn Hour Gp 09 to 16	NOVEMBER Obsn Hour Gp 17 to 24	NOVEMBER Total Obsn	NOVEMBER MCWB	DECEMBER Obsn Hour Gp 01 to 08	DECEMBER Obsn Hour Gp 09 to 16	DECEMBER Obsn Hour Gp 17 to 24	DECEMBER Total Obsn	DECEMBER MCWB	JANUARY Obsn Hour Gp 01 to 08	JANUARY Obsn Hour Gp 09 to 16	JANUARY Obsn Hour Gp 17 to 24	JANUARY Total Obsn	JANUARY MCWB
65/69															
60/64															
55/59															
50/54	2	2	2	6	49										
45/49	29	32	29	90	45	11	10	7	28	45	12	9	10	31	45
40/44	46	52	49	147	40	32	34	37	103	40	33	37	36	106	40
35/39	57	56	54	167	35	64	67	62	193	35	65	72	65	202	35
30/34	62	56	60	178	30	68	67	69	204	30	60	56	62	178	30
25/29	30	30	32	92	25	42	40	42	124	25	37	36	36	109	25
20/24	14	12	13	39	20	21	21	21	63	20	26	26	23	75	20
15/19	2	1	2	5	16	8	8	9	25	16	9	8	12	29	16
10/14						2	1	1	4	12	4	4	4	12	10
5/9											1	1	1	3	7
0/4															

Temperature Range	FEBRUARY Obsn Hour Gp 01 to 08	FEBRUARY Obsn Hour Gp 09 to 16	FEBRUARY Obsn Hour Gp 17 to 24	FEBRUARY Total Obsn	FEBRUARY MCWB	MARCH Obsn Hour Gp 01 to 08	MARCH Obsn Hour Gp 09 to 16	MARCH Obsn Hour Gp 17 to 24	MARCH Total Obsn	MARCH MCWB	APRIL Obsn Hour Gp 01 to 08	APRIL Obsn Hour Gp 09 to 16	APRIL Obsn Hour Gp 17 to 24	APRIL Total Obsn	APRIL MCWB	ANNUAL TOTAL Obsn Hour Gp 01 to 08	ANNUAL TOTAL Obsn Hour Gp 09 to 16	ANNUAL TOTAL Obsn Hour Gp 17 to 24	ANNUAL TOTAL Total Obsn	ANNUAL TOTAL MCWB
65/69																	0	0	0	55
60/64																0	21	5	26	53
55/59												0		0	46	25	200	81	306	51
50/54							0		0	48	0	6	1	7	47	327	559	471	1357	49
45/49	12	14	12	38	45	9	30	13	52	44	21	59	35	115	44	678	587	627	1892	44
40/44	24	36	29	89	40	50	58	58	166	40	60	81	75	216	39	576	467	539	1582	40
35/39	64	60	56	180	35	54	45	51	150	35	79	49	71	199	35	529	423	458	1410	35
30/34	52	50	57	159	30	51	52	52	155	30	48	29	34	111	30	391	329	370	1090	30
25/29	35	36	36	107	25	39	38	40	117	25	17	11	14	42	25	207	194	206	607	25
20/24	24	20	24	68	20	32	18	26	76	20	10	3	7	20	20	129	101	115	345	20
15/19	12	6	7	25	16	9	5	5	19	16	3	2	2	7	15	43	30	37	110	16
10/14	1	1	2	4	11	3	1	1	5	11	1	1	1	3	10	11	8	9	28	11
5/9	1	1	1	3	7	1	0	1	2	6	1		0	1	5	4	2	3	9	6
0/4	1	0		1	2	0	0		0	4						1	0		.	2

CARIBBEAN SEA

GUANTANAMO BAY NAS CUBA

LAT 19 54N LONG 75 09W ELEV [illegible] FT

MEAN FREQUENCY OF OCCURRENCE OF DRY BULB TEMPERATURE (DEGREES F) WITH MEAN COINCIDENT WET BULB TEMPERATURE (DEGREES F) FOR EACH DRY BULB TEMPERATURE RANGE

Temperature Range	MAY Obsn Hour Gp 01 to 08	MAY Obsn Hour Gp 09 to 16	MAY Obsn Hour Gp 17 to 24	MAY Total Obsn	MAY MCWB	JUNE Obsn Hour Gp 01 to 08	JUNE Obsn Hour Gp 09 to 16	JUNE Obsn Hour Gp 17 to 24	JUNE Total Obsn	JUNE MCWB	JULY Obsn Hour Gp 01 to 08	JULY Obsn Hour Gp 09 to 16	JULY Obsn Hour Gp 17 to 24	JULY Total Obsn	JULY MCWB
100/104												0		0	77
95/99		0		0	79		1	0	1	79		10	1	11	79
90/94		39	2	41	78		76	7	83	79		99	16	115	79
85/89	0	115	28	143	77	0	106	46	152	78	0	108	76	184	77
80/84	21	77	124	222	75	41	49	138	228	76	56	29	133	218	76
75/79	165	15	87	267	73	185	8	46	239	74	187	1	21	209	74
70/74	60	1	7	68	70	14	1	3	18	72	4		1	5	72
65/69	2			2	65	0			0	69					

Temperature Range	AUGUST Obsn Hour Gp 01 to 08	AUGUST Obsn Hour Gp 09 to 16	AUGUST Obsn Hour Gp 17 to 24	AUGUST Total Obsn	AUGUST MCWB	SEPTEMBER Obsn Hour Gp 01 to 08	SEPTEMBER Obsn Hour Gp 09 to 16	SEPTEMBER Obsn Hour Gp 17 to 24	SEPTEMBER Total Obsn	SEPTEMBER MCWB	OCTOBER Obsn Hour Gp 01 to 08	OCTOBER Obsn Hour Gp 09 to 16	OCTOBER Obsn Hour Gp 17 to 24	OCTOBER Total Obsn	OCTOBER MCWB
100/104															
95/99		9	1	10	80		3	0	3	80		1		1	81
90/94		96	16	112	80		86	9	95	80		50	2	52	79
85/89	0	101	75	176	78	0	101	57	158	78	0	110	28	138	77
80/84	55	37	130	222	76	37	44	135	216	76	16	63	128	207	76
75/79	188	5	26	219	74	200	6	39	245	74	206	23	87	316	74
70/74	5	0	0	5	72	3	0	1	4	71	26	1	2	29	71
65/69											0		0	0	68

100/104																																0		0	77
95/99																																24	2	26	80
90/94		12	0	12	78		1		1	76		0	0	0	75		1	0	1	75		3	0	3	75		15	1	16	77		478	53	531	79
85/89		96	12	108	76		59	5	64	75		58	5	63	74		63	8	71	74		95	14	109	75		114	23	137	76	0	1126	377	1503	77
80/84	3	89	81	173	74		109	45	154	73	0	89	38	127	73	0	77	43	120	73	1	87	68	156	73	7	81	102	190	74	237	831	1165	2233	75
75/79	98	39	124	261	72	24	57	134	215	71	7	59	118	184	71	15	54	114	183	71	45	52	127	224	71	109	28	100	237	71	1429	347	1023	2799	73
70/74	128	4	23	155	70	176	21	60	257	69	144	35	72	251	68	135	24	50	209	68	159	11	36	206	68	106	2	13	121	69	960	100	268	1328	69
65/69	10		1	11	65	47	1	·5	53	65	84	7	13	104	65	63	4	7	74	64	41	0	2	43	64	18		0	18	64	265	12	28	305	64
60/64	0			0	62	1			1	61	12	1	1	14	59	10	0	1	11	59	1			1	61	0			0	61	24	1	2	27	59
55/59											1			1	56	1			1	55											2			2	55

RAMEY AFB/AGUADILLA PUERTO RICO

LAT 18 30N LONG 67 08W ELEV 200 FT

MEAN FREQUENCY OF OCCURRENCE OF DRY BULB TEMPERATURE (DEGREES F) WITH MEAN COINCIDENT WET BULB TEMPERATURE (DEGREES F) FOR EACH DRY BULB TEMPERATURE RANGE

Temperature Range	MAY Obsn Hour Gp 01 to 08	MAY 09 to 16	MAY 17 to 24	MAY Total Obsn	MAY MCWB	JUNE Obsn Hour Gp 01 to 08	JUNE 09 to 16	JUNE 17 to 24	JUNE Total Obsn	JUNE MCWB	JULY Obsn Hour Gp 01 to 08	JULY 09 to 16	JULY 17 to 24	JULY Total Obsn	JULY MCWB
95/99												0		0	76
90/94		0	0	0	76		0	0	0	77		0	0	0	75
85/89		47	4	51	76		82	10	92	77		98	10	108	77
80/84	10	167	71	248	74	14	140	101	255	75	18	136	126	280	76
75/79	115	32	148	295	72	162	16	120	298	73	188	13	109	310	73
70/74	121	2	24	147	70	64	1	9	74	70	42	1	3	46	70
65/69	2	0	0	2	66	0			0	66					

Temperature Range	AUGUST Obsn Hour Gp 01 to 08	AUGUST 09 to 16	AUGUST 17 to 24	AUGUST Total Obsn	AUGUST MCWB	SEPTEMBER Obsn Hour Gp 01 to 08	SEPTEMBER 09 to 16	SEPTEMBER 17 to 24	SEPTEMBER Total Obsn	SEPTEMBER MCWB	OCTOBER Obsn Hour Gp 01 to 08	OCTOBER 09 to 16	OCTOBER 17 to 24	OCTOBER Total Obsn	OCTOBER MCWB
95/99															
90/94		1	0	1	76		1		1	78		1		1	78
85/89		116	11	127	77		130	8	138	77		112	6	118	77
80/84	17	115	116	248	76	15	95	100	210	76	8	119	84	211	75
75/79	180	13	115	308	74	169	12	127	308	73	144	13	141	298	73
70/74	52	3	6	61	71	57	1	6	64	71	95	2	17	114	70
65/69	0			0	67	0			0	60	0			0	67

																															0		0	76
	0		0	77																	0		0	77		0		0	76		3	0	3	77
	45	1	46	76		4		4	74		2	0	2	73		3	0	3	73		7	0	7	74		14	1	15	76		660	51	711	77
4	156	58	218	74	0	143	24	167	73		116	16	132	72		103	16	119	72		154	30	184	72	1	165	38	204	73	87	1609	780	2476	74
88	36	140	264	72	43	90	140	273	71	16	112	123	251	70	8	102	108	218	70	28	81	146	255	70	66	58	155	279	71	1207	578	1572	3357	72
139	2	41	182	70	166	11	78	255	69	161	18	101	280	68	146	16	94	256	68	170	5	69	244	68	154	3	45	202	69	1367	65	493	1925	69
10		0	10	66	37	0	5	42	65	68	0	7	75	65	65	1	6	72	65	49	0	3	52	64	19		1	20	64	250	1	22	273	65
0			0	61	1			1	61	3	0	0	3	60	5		0	5	60	0			0	60						9	0	0	9	60

CENTRAL AMERICA

HOWARD AFB/BALBOA PANAMA CANAL ZONE

LAT 8 55N LONG 79 36W ELEV [illegible] FT

MEAN FREQUENCY OF OCCURRENCE OF DRY BULB TEMPERATURE (DEGREES F) WITH MEAN COINCIDENT WET BULB TEMPERATURE (DEGREES F) FOR EACH DRY BULB TEMPERATURE RANGE

Temperature Range	MAY Obsn Hour Gp 01 to 08	MAY 09 to 16	MAY 17 to 24	MAY Total Obsn	MAY MCWB	JUNE Obsn Hour Gp 01 to 08	JUNE 09 to 16	JUNE 17 to 24	JUNE Total Obsn	JUNE MCWB	JULY Obsn Hour Gp 01 to 08	JULY 09 to 16	JULY 17 to 24	JULY Total Obsn	JULY MCWB
95/99												0		0	81
90/94		13	0	13	78		8	0	8	81		13	0	13	81
85/89	0	100	11	111	77	1	84	8	93	79	0	104	11	115	78
80/84	35	101	96	232	76	34	117	95	246	76	36	101	105	242	76
75/79	188	33	133	354	74	177	30	126	333	74	197	28	129	354	74
70/74	25	1	7	33	71	29	1	10	40	71	15	2	3	20	71
65/69	0		0	0	68										

Temperature Range	AUGUST Obsn Hour Gp 01 to 08	AUGUST 09 to 16	AUGUST 17 to 24	AUGUST Total Obsn	AUGUST MCWB	SEPTEMBER Obsn Hour Gp 01 to 08	SEPTEMBER 09 to 16	SEPTEMBER 17 to 24	SEPTEMBER Total Obsn	SEPTEMBER MCWB	OCTOBER Obsn Hour Gp 01 to 08	OCTOBER 09 to 16	OCTOBER 17 to 24	OCTOBER Total Obsn	OCTOBER MCWB
95/99												0		0	82
90/94		3		3	79		2		2	80		2		2	81
85/89		82	4	86	78		71	2	73	78		57	1	58	78
80/84	22	122	80	224	76	21	127	75	223	77	13	148	61	222	77
75/79	188	39	155	382	74	175	31	146	352	74	182	40	170	392	74
70/74	37	2	9	48	71	36	1	8	45	72	52	1	15	68	72
65/69	0			0	64										

100/104																						0		0	80							0		0	80
95/99																	0		0	77		1		1	77		2		2	77		3		3	78
90/94		0		0	80		10		10	78		18		18	76		37	1	38	76		62	1	63	75		46	2	48	76		214	4	218	77
85/89		60	1	61	78	0	103	9	112	77		132	13	145	75		116	22	138	75		130	33	163	75		116	28	144	75	1	1155	143	1299	77
80/84	10	130	45	185	77	16	103	62	181	76	7	80	66	153	74	6	62	55	123	74	23	51	75	149	74	31	61	80	172	74	254	1203	895	2352	76
75/79	191	48	180	419	74	174	30	161	365	74	175	18	156	349	72	150	9	137	296	72	187	4	136	327	72	170	14	125	309	73	154	324	1754	4232	74
70/74	39	1	13	53	72	55	1	15	71	70	62	0	12	74	70	66	0	10	76	70	37	0	3	40	70	37	0	5	42	70	490	10	110	610	71
65/69	0			0	69	3			3	67	3	0	0	3	67	2			2	66	1			1	69	2			2	65	11	0	0	11	67
60/64											0			0	64																0			0	64

EUROPE

RAMSTEIN AB/LANDSTUHL GERMANY

LAT 49 26N LONG 7 36E ELEV 780 FT

MEAN FREQUENCY OF OCCURRENCE OF DRY BULB TEMPERATURE (DEGREES F) WITH MEAN COINCIDENT WET BULB TEMPERATURE (DEGREES F) FOR EACH DRY BULB TEMPERATURE RANGE

Temperature Range	MAY Obsn Hour Gp 01 to 08	MAY 09 to 16	MAY 17 to 24	MAY Total Obsn	MAY MCWB	JUNE Obsn Hour Gp 01 to 08	JUNE 09 to 16	JUNE 17 to 24	JUNE Total Obsn	JUNE MCWB	JULY Obsn Hour Gp 01 to 08	JULY 09 to 16	JULY 17 to 24	JULY Total Obsn	JULY MCWB
95/99												1	0	1	71
90/94							1	0	1	68		3	2	5	70
85/89		0		0	66		3	1	4	67		11	6	17	68
80/84		3	1	4	63		12	6	18	65		19	9	28	66
75/79		12	6	18	61	0	28	14	42	63	1	33	21	55	64
70/74	0	23	12	35	59	1	42	26	69	61	3	45	32	80	61
65/69	1	35	23	59	57	8	52	41	101	59	15	53	44	112	59
60/64	8	52	38	98	54	34	51	53	138	57	44	52	61	157	57
55/59	31	57	55	143	51	64	38	56	158	54	81	29	49	159	54
50/54	63	46	58	167	48	69	13	31	113	50	65	4	19	88	50
45/49	60	16	37	113	45	43	2	11	56	46	31		4	35	46
40/44	46	4	13	63	40	18	0	1	19	41	9		0	9	41
35/39	26	0	4	30	36	3		0	3	36	0			0	38
30/34	10		1	11	32	1			1	32					
25/29	2		0	2	27										
20/24	0			0	24										

Temperature Range	AUGUST Obsn Hour Gp 01 to 08	AUGUST 09 to 16	AUGUST 17 to 24	AUGUST Total Obsn	AUGUST MCWB	SEPTEMBER Obsn Hour Gp 01 to 08	SEPTEMBER 09 to 16	SEPTEMBER 17 to 24	SEPTEMBER Total Obsn	SEPTEMBER MCWB	OCTOBER Obsn Hour Gp 01 to 08	OCTOBER 09 to 16	OCTOBER 17 to 24	OCTOBER Total Obsn	OCTOBER MCWB
95/99															
90/94		1	0	1	69										
85/89		4	2	6	68		1	0	1	67					
80/84		14	6	20	67		5	1	6	66					
75/79	0	25	12	37	64		13	5	18	64		1	0	1	63
70/74	1	43	26	70	62	1	33	13	47	61		6	1	7	61
65/69	9	62	49	120	60	3	48	28	79	59	0	17	4	21	58
60/64	50	62	67	179	58	17	57	46	120	57	6	37	18	61	56
55/59	72	31	53	156	55	45	51	57	153	54	20	49	38	107	53
50/54	66	5	27	98	51	63	25	52	140	50	43	62	57	162	49
45/49	36	0	6	42	46	49	6	27	82	46	55	42	57	154	45
40/44	13		1	14	42	38	1	8	47	41	45	23	41	109	41
35/39	2			2	38	19	0	2	21	36	39	8	21	68	36
30/34						5			5	32	27	3	9	39	31
25/29											13	0	2	15	27
20/24											1		0	1	23

RAMSTEIN AB/LANDSTUHL GERMANY

Temperature Range	NOVEMBER Obsn Hour Gp 01 to 08	NOVEMBER 09 to 16	NOVEMBER 17 to 24	NOVEMBER Total Obsn	NOVEMBER MCWB	DECEMBER Obsn Hour Gp 01 to 08	DECEMBER 09 to 16	DECEMBER 17 to 24	DECEMBER Total Obsn	DECEMBER MCWB	JANUARY Obsn Hour Gp 01 to 08	JANUARY 09 to 16	JANUARY 17 to 24	JANUARY Total Obsn	JANUARY MCWB	FEBRUARY Obsn Hour Gp 01 to 08	FEBRUARY 09 to 16	FEBRUARY 17 to 24	FEBRUARY Total Obsn	FEBRUARY MCWB
95/99																				
90/94																				
85/89																				
80/84																				
75/79																				
70/74																				
65/69		0		0	58												0	0	0	54
60/64	0	2	1	3	54												2	0	2	53
55/59	4	10	8	22	52	1	2	1	4	53		1		1	49	0	5	3	8	50
50/54	14	30	15	59	48	5	7	6	18	48	1	4	3	8	47	5	14	10	29	47
45/49	36	54	45	135	44	15	23	18	56	44	16	23	18	57	44	20	32	25	77	44
40/44	53	54	62	169	40	31	44	36	111	40	30	40	33	103	40	33	44	39	116	39
35/39	55	51	53	159	36	46	56	55	157	35	41	53	52	146	35	37	50	47	134	35
30/34	53	31	45	129	31	65	57	61	183	31	61	57	59	177	31	47	38	50	135	30
25/29	19	6	10	35	27	40	32	35	107	26	33	33	38	104	26	39	23	31	93	26
20/24	5	1	1	7	22	19	16	19	54	21	26	21	24	71	21	20	9	11	40	21
15/19	2	0		2	18	13	7	11	31	17	18	10	10	38	16	11	4	4	19	17
10/14						9	3	5	17	12	12	4	6	22	12	5	1	2	8	12
5/9						4	1	2	7	8	6	1	3	10	7	4	0	1	5	7
0/4						1	0	0	1	3	3	1	2	6	2	1	0	0	1	2
-5/-1											1	0	0	1	-3	1	0		1	-3
-10/-6											0	0		0	-6	0	0		0	-8

Temperature Range	MARCH Obsn Hour Gp 01 to 08	MARCH 09 to 16	MARCH 17 to 24	MARCH Total Obsn	MARCH MCWB	APRIL Obsn Hour Gp 01 to 08	APRIL 09 to 16	APRIL 17 to 24	APRIL Total Obsn	APRIL MCWB	ANNUAL TOTAL Obsn Hour Gp 01 to 08	ANNUAL TOTAL 09 to 16	ANNUAL TOTAL 17 to 24	ANNUAL TOTAL Total Obsn	ANNUAL TOTAL MCWB
95/99												1	0	1	71
90/94												5	2	7	70
85/89							0		0	61		19	9	28	68
80/84							1	0	1	61		54	23	77	66
75/79		0	0	0	55		2	1	3	60	1	114	59	174	63
70/74		1	0	1	55		8	4	12	56	6	201	114	321	61
65/69		3	1	4	53		17	8	25	54	36	287	198	521	59
60/64		7	3	10	51	1	29	15	45	52	160	351	302	813	56
55/59	0	16	8	24	49	3	37	29	69	49	321	326	357	1004	53
50/54	6	36	23	65	47	24	52	49	125	47	424	298	350	1072	49
45/49	27	52	49	128	43	50	47	53	150	44	438	297	350	1085	44
40/44	45	48	54	147	39	54	35	44	133	39	415	293	332	1040	40
35/39	47	42	47	136	35	49	11	25	85	35	364	271	306	941	35
30/34	52	29	36	117	30	39	2	9	50	31	360	217	270	847	31
25/29	37	10	20	67	26	17		3	20	27	200	104	139	443	26
20/24	19	2	5	26	21	3			3	22	93	49	60	202	21
15/19	10	1	1	12	17	0			0	19	54	22	26	102	17
10/14	3	0	0	3	12						29	8	13	50	12
5/9	2			2	7						16	2	6	24	7
0/4	0			0	4						5	1	2	8	2
-5/-1											2	0	0	2	-3
-10/-6											0	0		0	-7

STUTTGART/ECHTERDINGEN AB GERMANY

LAT 48 41N LONG 0 10E ELEV 1300 FT

MEAN FREQUENCY OF OCCURRENCE OF DRY BULB TEMPERATURE (DEGREES F) WITH MEAN COINCIDENT WET BULB TEMPERATURE (DEGREES F) FOR EACH DRY BULB TEMPERATURE RANGE

Temperature Range	MAY Obsn Hour Gp 01 to 08	MAY 09 to 16	MAY 17 to 24	MAY Total Obsn	MAY MCWB	JUNE Obsn Hour Gp 01 to 08	JUNE 09 to 16	JUNE 17 to 24	JUNE Total Obsn	JUNE MCWB	JULY Obsn Hour Gp 01 to 08	JULY 09 to 16	JULY 17 to 24	JULY Total Obsn	JULY MCWB
95/99												0		0	74
90/94							0		0	67		2	0	2	70
85/89		0		0	66		1		1	66		7	1	8	69
80/84		1	0	1	63		9	2	11	66	1	22	5	28	66
75/79		9	1	10	61	0	29	7	36	63	1	34	15	50	64
70/74	0	27	7	34	59	3	45	18	66	61	9	47	26	82	62
65/69	3	35	15	53	56	11	47	31	89	59	24	49	43	116	59
60/64	12	43	31	86	54	48	50	60	158	57	58	56	64	178	57
55/59	39	57	54	150	51	69	38	65	172	53	84	25	64	173	54
50/54	60	46	67	173	48	68	17	40	125	49	58	5	25	88	50
45/49	76	23	48	147	44	33	4	14	51	45	11	0	3	14	45
40/44	42	6	19	67	40	7	0	2	9	40	2		0	2	41
35/39	12	1	3	16	36	1	0	0	1	37					
30/34	4	0	2	6	32										
25/29	1			1	28										
20/24															

Temperature Range	AUGUST Obsn Hour Gp 01 to 08	AUGUST 09 to 16	AUGUST 17 to 24	AUGUST Total Obsn	AUGUST MCWB	SEPTEMBER Obsn Hour Gp 01 to 08	SEPTEMBER 09 to 16	SEPTEMBER 17 to 24	SEPTEMBER Total Obsn	SEPTEMBER MCWB	OCTOBER Obsn Hour Gp 01 to 08	OCTOBER 09 to 16	OCTOBER 17 to 24	OCTOBER Total Obsn	OCTOBER MCWB
95/99															
90/94		1		1	69										
85/89		4	0	4	69		1		1	67					
80/84		19	3	22	67		8	0	8	66		0		0	64
75/79	1	29	10	40	64		17	2	19	63		1		1	63
70/74	3	40	20	63	62	1	36	9	46	61		6	0	6	60
65/69	16	51	36	103	59	4	45	23	72	59	0	19	1	20	57
60/64	58	69	72	199	57	27	57	58	142	57	2	39	11	52	55
55/59	83	32	71	186	54	60	49	65	174	53	17	53	38	108	52
50/54	68	5	33	106	50	76	23	54	153	49	43	56	60	159	48
45/49	16		3	19	46	51	4	24	79	45	59	37	65	161	44
40/44	2			2	41	18		5	23	41	56	25	44	125	40
35/39	0			0	39	4		0	4	37	47	10	24	81	36
30/34						0			0	33	20	1	3	24	32
25/29											4		0	4	28
20/24											0			0	24

STUTTGART/ECHTERDINGEN AB GERMANY

Temperature Range	NOVEMBER Obsn Hour Gp 01 to 08	09 to 16	17 to 24	Total Obsn	MCWB	DECEMBER Obsn Hour Gp 01 to 08	09 to 16	17 to 24	Total Obsn	MCWB	JANUARY Obsn Hour Gp 01 to 08	09 to 16	17 to 24	Total Obsn	MCWB
95/99															
90/94															
85/89															
80/84															
75/79															
70/74															
65/69		0		0	55										
60/64	0	3	0	3	52		0		0	51					
55/59	3	13	5	21	50	0	1	1	2	52		0		0	46
50/54	6	25	11	42	47	5	6	4	15	47	0	5	0	5	46
45/49	22	47	35	104	43	11	24	13	48	43	6	18	13	37	42
40/44	56	58	59	173	40	25	33	31	89	39	22	35	24	81	39
35/39	69	52	68	189	36	38	49	44	131	35	43	54	53	150	35
30/34	52	29	42	123	31	65	62	66	193	31	62	54	65	181	31
25/29	22	11	16	49	27	47	41	45	133	26	45	37	41	123	26
20/24	7	1	2	10	22	26	16	20	62	21	25	22	22	69	21
15/19	1	0	0	1	18	16	8	13	37	17	17	11	15	43	17
10/14	1	0		1	12	11	5	7	23	12	14	8	11	33	12
5/9						4	2	3	9	7	8	3	5	16	7
0/4						1	0	1	2	2	5	1	1	7	3
-5/-1						1	0		1	-2	0	0		0	-2
-10/-6															
-15/-11															

Temperature Range	FEBRUARY Obsn Hour Gp 01 to 08	09 to 16	17 to 24	Total Obsn	MCWB	MARCH Obsn Hour Gp 01 to 08	09 to 16	17 to 24	Total Obsn	MCWB	APRIL Obsn Hour Gp 01 to 08	09 to 16	17 to 24	Total Obsn	MCWB
95/99															
90/94															
85/89															
80/84												0	0	0	59
75/79												2	0	2	58
70/74							1		1	52		9	2	11	56
65/69		0		0	53		1	0	1	51		14	4	18	53
60/64		3	0	3	52		14	1	15	50	2	33	13	48	51
55/59	0	6	2	8	48	0	24	7	31	48	8	44	27	79	49
50/54	5	14	8	27	46	3	39	23	65	45	32	46	54	132	47
45/49	9	25	17	51	43	28	46	53	127	43	64	38	53	155	43
40/44	25	36	31	92	39	51	40	49	140	39	48	30	36	114	39
35/39	39	41	45	125	35	59	36	47	142	35	49	21	34	104	35
30/34	44	42	46	132	30	46	34	37	117	30	30	4	14	48	31
25/29	37	25	32	94	26	34	13	25	72	25	6	0	2	8	27
20/24	22	14	18	54	21	19	1	6	26	21	0			0	23
15/19	13	8	11	32	16	6	0	1	7	16					
10/14	14	4	7	25	12	1			1	13					
5/9	6	2	4	12	7										
0/4	5	3	2	10	2										
-5/-1	2	1	1	4	-2										
-10/-6	1	0	0	1	-8										
-15/-11	1			1	-12										

Temperature Range	ANNUAL TOTAL Obsn Hour Gp 01 to 08	09 to 16	17 to 24	Total Obsn	MCWB
95/99		0		0	74
90/94		3	0	3	69
85/89		13	1	14	68
80/84	1	59	10	70	66
75/79	2	121	35	158	64
70/74	16	211	82	309	61
65/69	58	261	153	472	58
60/64	207	367	310	884	56
55/59	363	342	399	1104	52
50/54	424	287	379	1090	48
45/49	386	266	341	993	44
40/44	354	263	300	917	39
35/39	361	264	318	943	35
30/34	323	226	275	824	31
25/29	196	127	161	484	26
20/24	99	54	68	221	21
15/19	53	27	40	120	17
10/14	41	17	25	83	12
5/9	18	7	12	37	7
0/4	11	4	4	19	2
-5/-1	3	1	1	5	-2
-10/-6	1	0	0	1	-8
-15/-11	1			*	-12

TEMPELHOF AB/BERLIN GERMANY

LAT 52 29N LONG 13 24E ELEV 161 FT

MEAN FREQUENCY OF OCCURRENCE OF DRY BULB TEMPERATURE (DEGREES F) WITH MEAN COINCIDENT WET BULB TEMPERATURE (DEGREES F) FOR EACH DRY BULB TEMPERATURE RANGE

Temperature Range	MAY Obsn Hour Gp 01 to 08	MAY 09 to 16	MAY 17 to 24	MAY Total Obsn	MAY MCWB	JUNE Obsn Hour Gp 01 to 08	JUNE 09 to 16	JUNE 17 to 24	JUNE Total Obsn	JUNE MCWB	JULY Obsn Hour Gp 01 to 08	JULY 09 to 16	JULY 17 to 24	JULY Total Obsn	JULY MCWB
100/104												0		0	68
95/99												1	0	1	69
90/94							1		1	69		4	1	5	69
85/89		1		1	64		5	1	6	66		7	2	9	68
80/84		3	1	4	63	0	15	4	19	63	1	19	8	28	66
75/79	0	9	2	11	60	1	36	15	52	62	2	34	16	52	64
70/74	2	27	9	38	58	7	47	30	84	60	12	54	37	103	61
65/69	3	35	21	59	55	18	48	45	111	58	38	55	54	147	59
60/64	15	51	41	107	53	62	45	63	170	56	76	51	70	197	57
55/59	49	58	59	166	51	79	33	54	166	52	79	21	44	144	54
50/54	73	40	63	176	48	54	8	23	85	49	35	4	14	53	50
45/49	65	18	37	120	44	14	1	4	19	44	5	0	1	6	46
40/44	31	5	13	49	40	4	0	1	5	39					
35/39	9	0	3	12	36	0			0	37					
30/34	1		0	1	32										
25/29															
20/24															

Temperature Range	AUGUST Obsn Hour Gp 01 to 08	AUGUST 09 to 16	AUGUST 17 to 24	AUGUST Total Obsn	AUGUST MCWB	SEPTEMBER Obsn Hour Gp 01 to 08	SEPTEMBER 09 to 16	SEPTEMBER 17 to 24	SEPTEMBER Total Obsn	SEPTEMBER MCWB	OCTOBER Obsn Hour Gp 01 to 08	OCTOBER 09 to 16	OCTOBER 17 to 24	OCTOBER Total Obsn	OCTOBER MCWB
100/104															
95/99		0		0	68										
90/94		2	0	2	70										
85/89		4	1	5	68		1		1	67					
80/84	0	11	3	14	66		3	0	3	67		0		0	66
75/79	1	25	10	36	64		13	2	15	64		1		1	63
70/74	5	48	26	79	62	0	33	10	43	61		4	0	4	61
65/69	24	66	47	137	59	4	47	25	76	58		15	2	17	58
60/64	67	68	78	213	57	28	63	54	145	56	1	28	11	40	55
55/59	102	22	66	190	54	69	53	71	193	53	21	64	43	128	52
50/54	43	2	16	61	50	77	23	52	152	49	57	68	70	195	49
45/49	6		1	7	46	45	4	21	70	45	85	52	76	213	45
40/44						15	0	4	19	41	57	13	38	108	40
35/39						2			2	37	22	2	6	30	36
30/34											5	1	1	7	32
25/29											1	0	*	2	25
20/24											0			0	22

TEMPELHOF AB/BERLIN GERMANY

Tempera-ture Range	NOVEMBER					DECEMBER					JANUARY				
	Obsn Hour Gp 01 to 08	09 to 16	17 to 24	Total Obsn	M C W B	Obsn Hour Gp 01 to 08	09 to 16	17 to 24	Total Obsn	M C W B	Obsn Hour Gp 01 to 08	09 to 16	17 to 24	Total Obsn	M C W B
100/104															
95/99															
90/94															
85/89															
80/84															
75/79															
70/74															
65/69		0		0	59										
60/64		0	0	0	54		0		0	53					
55/59	2	10	3	15	51	1	1	0	2	52					
50/54	11	26	17	54	48	2	4	2	8	47	1	1	2	4	48
45/49	37	54	46	137	44	11	18	11	40	44	6	11	7	24	43
40/44	60	64	64	188	40	25	39	35	99	40	25	34	27	86	39
35/39	75	54	67	196	36	64	65	65	194	36	59	63	62	184	35
30/34	35	23	34	92	31	61	53	55	169	31	52	55	56	163	31
25/29	16	6	8	30	27	31	30	35	96	26	39	36	38	113	26
20/24	3	1	1	5	22	26	20	20	66	21	26	20	23	69	21
15/19	1	0	1	2	18	14	13	16	43	17	19	16	16	51	17
10/14	0		0	0	11	8	4	6	18	12	12	8	12	32	12
5/9						3	1	2	6	8	6	2	3	11	7
0/4						1	0	0	1	2	3	1	1	5	2
-5/-1						0	0		0	-3	0		0	0	-2
-10/-6															

Tempera-ture Range	FEBRUARY					MARCH					APRIL					ANNUAL TOTAL				
	Obsn Hour Gp 01 to 08	09 to 16	17 to 24	Total Obsn	M C W B	Obsn Hour Gp 01 to 08	09 to 16	17 to 24	Total Obsn	M C W B	Obsn Hour Gp 01 to 08	09 to 16	17 to 24	Total Obsn	M C W B	Obsn Hour Gp 01 to 08	09 to 16	17 to 24	Total Obsn	M C W B
100/104																	0		0	68
95/99																	1	0	1	69
90/94																	7	1	8	70
85/89												0		0	62		18	4	22	67
80/84												2	0	2	61	1	53	16	70	65
75/79							0		0	56		1	0	1	59	4	119	45	168	63
70/74							0	0	0	55		8	2	10	57	26	221	114	361	60
65/69							1	0	1	52	0	12	6	18	55	87	279	200	566	58
60/64		0		0	51		7	1	8	50	2	22	13	37	52	251	335	331	917	56
55/59	0	2	1	3	50	0	15	4	19	48	9	38	27	74	49	411	317	372	1100	52
50/54	3	9	4	16	47	5	31	19	55	45	34	45	43	122	47	395	261	325	981	48
45/49	7	22	16	45	43	21	41	37	99	42	43	53	54	150	42	345	274	311	930	44
40/44	26	30	28	84	39	40	43	44	127	38	58	38	52	148	38	341	266	306	913	39
35/39	37	39	42	118	35	60	59	57	176	34	64	18	33	115	35	392	300	335	1027	35
30/34	51	50	50	151	30	60	36	57	153	30	25	2	10	37	31	290	220	263	773	31
25/29	36	34	39	109	26	46	13	24	83	26	4		0	4	27	173	119	145	437	26
20/24	24	17	22	63	21	12	1	3	16	21						91	59	69	219	21
15/19	18	11	12	41	17	3	0	0	3	17						55	40	45	140	17
10/14	13	5	6	24	12	1	0		1	13						34	17	24	75	12
5/9	6	2	3	11	7	0			0	7						15	5	8	28	7
0/4	2	1	2	5	2											6	2	3	11	2
-5/-1	1	0	0	1	-3											1	0	0	1	-3
-10/-6	1			1	-7											1			1	-7

WIESBADEN AB GERMANY

LAT 50 03N LONG 8 20E ELEV 460 FT

MEAN FREQUENCY OF OCCURRENCE OF DRY BULB TEMPERATURE (DEGREES F) WITH MEAN COINCIDENT WET BULB TEMPERATURE (DEGREES F) FOR EACH DRY BULB TEMPERATURE RANGE

Temperature Range	MAY Obsn Hour Gp 01 to 08	MAY 09 to 16	MAY 17 to 24	MAY Total Obsn	MAY MCWB	JUNE Obsn Hour Gp 01 to 08	JUNE 09 to 16	JUNE 17 to 24	JUNE Total Obsn	JUNE MCWB	JULY Obsn Hour Gp 01 to 08	JULY 09 to 16	JULY 17 to 24	JULY Total Obsn	JULY MCWB
95/99												1	1	2	71
90/94							0	0	0	69		3	1	4	70
85/89		0	0	0	69		3	2	5	66		9	5	14	68
80/84		2	1	3	65		13	7	20	65	0	18	11	29	67
75/79		12	6	18	62	0	31	17	48	63	2	36	22	60	64
70/74	0	25	14	39	59	3	45	29	77	61	10	47	36	93	62
65/69	3	38	28	69	57	24	54	51	129	59	31	56	52	139	60
60/64	22	57	50	129	54	55	51	59	165	56	64	54	62	180	57
55/59	51	61	61	173	51	77	32	49	158	53	86	22	43	151	54
50/54	77	39	54	170	48	59	9	22	90	49	42	2	13	57	50
45/49	57	12	26	95	44	18	1	4	23	45	11		2	13	45
40/44	28	2	5	35	40	4		0	4	40	1			1	41
35/39	8	0	2	10	35	0			0	37					
30/34	1	0		1	32										
25/29															

Temperature Range	AUGUST Obsn Hour Gp 01 to 08	AUGUST 09 to 16	AUGUST 17 to 24	AUGUST Total Obsn	AUGUST MCWB	SEPTEMBER Obsn Hour Gp 01 to 08	SEPTEMBER 09 to 16	SEPTEMBER 17 to 24	SEPTEMBER Total Obsn	SEPTEMBER MCWB	OCTOBER Obsn Hour Gp 01 to 08	OCTOBER 09 to 16	OCTOBER 17 to 24	OCTOBER Total Obsn	OCTOBER MCWB
95/99		0		0	68										
90/94		1	1	2	69										
85/89		4	2	6	68		0	0	0	65					
80/84		13	7	20	67		4	2	6	66					
75/79	0	31	18	49	64		11	5	16	63		1	0	1	63
70/74	4	51	34	89	62	0	32	15	47	61		3	1	4	61
65/69	30	70	62	162	60	4	52	36	92	59	0	14	4	18	58
60/64	74	53	67	194	57	33	68	62	163	56	4	37	23	64	56
55/59	82	23	43	148	54	73	51	63	187	53	29	53	43	125	53
50/54	46	2	14	62	50	74	20	44	138	49	52	66	71	189	48
45/49	11		0	11	45	40	3	12	55	45	73	47	60	180	44
40/44	1			1	42	14	0	1	15	41	54	22	34	110	40
35/39						1			1	37	26	4	9	39	36
30/34											9	1	2	12	32
25/29											1	0	0	1	27

WIESBADEN AB GERMANY

Temperature Range	NOVEMBER Obsn Hour Gp 01 to 08	NOVEMBER Obsn Hour Gp 09 to 16	NOVEMBER Obsn Hour Gp 17 to 24	NOVEMBER Total Obsn	NOVEMBER M C W B	DECEMBER Obsn Hour Gp 01 to 08	DECEMBER Obsn Hour Gp 09 to 16	DECEMBER Obsn Hour Gp 17 to 24	DECEMBER Total Obsn	DECEMBER M C W B
95/99										
90/94										
85/89										
80/84										
75/79										
70/74										
65/69		0		0	59					
60/64	0	2	1	3	55		0		0	58
55/59	4	9	7	20	51	1	2	1	4	53
50/54	14	29	15	58	48	4	7	6	17	48
45/49	40	59	53	152	44	13	22	16	51	43
40/44	65	63	69	197	40	34	45	44	123	39
35/39	59	48	51	158	35	61	59	65	185	35
30/34	45	27	35	107	31	63	57	57	177	31
25/29	11	4	7	22	26	37	32	33	102	26
20/24	1	0	0	1	21	18	14	16	48	21
15/19	0	0	0	0	16	12	8	8	28	16
10/14						4	1	2	7	12
5/9						0		0	0	7
0/4										
-5/-1										

Temperature Range	JANUARY Obsn Hour Gp 01 to 08	JANUARY Obsn Hour Gp 09 to 16	JANUARY Obsn Hour Gp 17 to 24	JANUARY Total Obsn	JANUARY M C W B	FEBRUARY Obsn Hour Gp 01 to 08	FEBRUARY Obsn Hour Gp 09 to 16	FEBRUARY Obsn Hour Gp 17 to 24	FEBRUARY Total Obsn	FEBRUARY M C W B
95/99										
90/94										
85/89										
80/84										
75/79										
70/74										
65/69										
60/64							1	0	1	54
55/59		0		0	50	0	4	2	6	51
50/54	2	4	2	8	47	4	9	8	21	47
45/49	10	19	16	45	43	14	31	23	68	43
40/44	30	38	34	102	39	36	48	48	132	39
35/39	57	62	66	185	35	64	61	61	186	34
30/34	66	57	58	181	30	49	42	50	141	30
25/29	33	33	32	98	25	36	19	21	76	25
20/24	25	23	22	70	21	12	7	6	25	21
15/19	15	9	12	36	16	5	2	3	10	16
10/14	7	2	3	12	12	3	1	1	5	11
5/9	2	1	2	5	7	2	0	0	2	8
0/4	0	0	0	0	3	0	0		0	4
-5/-1	0			0	-2					

Temperature Range	MARCH Obsn Hour Gp 01 to 08	MARCH Obsn Hour Gp 09 to 16	MARCH Obsn Hour Gp 17 to 24	MARCH Total Obsn	MARCH M C W B	APRIL Obsn Hour Gp 01 to 08	APRIL Obsn Hour Gp 09 to 16	APRIL Obsn Hour Gp 17 to 24	APRIL Total Obsn	APRIL M C W B
95/99										
90/94										
85/89							0		0	65
80/84							1	1	2	63
75/79		0		0	57		3	1	4	60
70/74		0	0	0	57		9	4	13	57
65/69		2	1	3	55	0	15	9	24	54
60/64		5	3	8	52	4	30	23	57	52
55/59	0	18	11	29	49	15	48	39	102	50
50/54	9	33	30	72	46	45	55	60	160	47
45/49	37	62	52	151	43	63	44	48	155	43
40/44	57	57	60	174	38	61	28	37	126	38
35/39	60	38	45	143	34	37	6	16	59	35
30/34	48	23	33	104	30	15	0	2	17	30
25/29	26	7	9	42	25	1			1	26
20/24	6	1	2	9	21					
15/19	3	0	1	4	16					
10/14	1	0		1	12					
5/9	0			0	9					
0/4										
-5/-1										

Temperature Range	ANNUAL TOTAL Obsn Hour Gp 01 to 08	ANNUAL TOTAL Obsn Hour Gp 09 to 16	ANNUAL TOTAL Obsn Hour Gp 17 to 24	ANNUAL TOTAL Total Obsn	ANNUAL TOTAL M C W B
95/99		1	1	2	71
90/94		4	2	6	69
85/89		16	9	25	68
80/84	0	51	29	80	66
75/79	2	125	69	196	64
70/74	17	212	133	362	61
65/69	92	301	243	636	59
60/64	256	358	350	964	56
55/59	418	323	362	1103	52
50/54	428	275	339	1042	48
45/49	387	300	312	999	44
40/44	385	303	332	1020	39
35/39	373	278	315	966	35
30/34	296	207	237	740	30
25/29	145	95	102	342	25
20/24	62	45	46	153	21
15/19	35	19	24	78	16
10/14	15	4	6	25	12
5/9	4	1	2	7	7
0/4	0	0	0	0	3
-5/-1	0			0	-2

ATHENS/HELLINIKON APRT GREECE

LAT 37 54N LONG 23 44E ELEV 33 FT

MEAN FREQUENCY OF OCCURRENCE OF DRY BULB TEMPERATURE (DEGREES F) WITH MEAN COINCIDENT WET BULB TEMPERATURE (DEGREES F) FOR EACH DRY BULB TEMPERATURE RANGE

Temperature Range	MAY Obsn Hour Gp 01 to 08	MAY 09 to 16	MAY 17 to 24	MAY Total Obsn	MAY MCWB	JUNE Obsn Hour Gp 01 to 08	JUNE 09 to 16	JUNE 17 to 24	JUNE Total Obsn	JUNE MCWB	JULY Obsn Hour Gp 01 to 08	JULY 09 to 16	JULY 17 to 24	JULY Total Obsn	JULY MCWB
100/104															
95/99							1		1	72		7	3	10	70
90/94							18	8	26	70	0	49	27	76	71
85/89		0	0	0	69	0	27	17	44	69	4	67	37	108	71
80/84		10	4	14	66	17	78	47	142	69	51	103	106	260	70
75/79	2	44	25	71	65	67	85	96	248	67	139	22	67	228	67
70/74	31	106	77	214	63	104	28	61	193	64	51	1	7	59	63
65/69	53	61	65	179	60	42	2	10	54	61	3			3	60
60/64	109	25	64	198	57	10	0	1	11	58					
55/59	49	2	14	65	53										
50/54	5		1	6	50										
45/49															

Temperature Range	AUGUST Obsn Hour Gp 01 to 08	AUGUST 09 to 16	AUGUST 17 to 24	AUGUST Total Obsn	AUGUST MCWB	SEPTEMBER Obsn Hour Gp 01 to 08	SEPTEMBER 09 to 16	SEPTEMBER 17 to 24	SEPTEMBER Total Obsn	SEPTEMBER MCWB	OCTOBER Obsn Hour Gp 01 to 08	OCTOBER 09 to 16	OCTOBER 17 to 24	OCTOBER Total Obsn	OCTOBER MCWB
100/104		1	0	1	75										
95/99		10	4	14	71		0		0	70					
90/94	0	59	26	85	71		4	2	6	71					
85/89	3	67	40	110	71		30	7	37	70		1	0	1	68
80/84	60	91	102	253	69	2	89	45	136	69		19	2	21	70
75/79	131	19	68	218	67	39	78	85	202	66	1	59	22	82	67
70/74	48	1	7	56	63	115	29	75	219	63	43	85	81	209	64
65/69	5		1	6	63	55	7	17	79	60	61	44	56	161	61
60/64	0			0	61	25	4	9	38	56	84	34	64	182	57
55/59						4		1	5	52	46	6	22	74	52
50/54											13	0	2	15	48
45/49											0			0	44

ATHENS/HELLINIKON APRT GREECE

Temperature Range	NOVEMBER Obsn Hour Gp 01 to 08	NOVEMBER 09 to 16	NOVEMBER 17 to 24	NOVEMBER Total Obsn	NOVEMBER MCWB	DECEMBER Obsn Hour Gp 01 to 08	DECEMBER 09 to 16	DECEMBER 17 to 24	DECEMBER Total Obsn	DECEMBER MCWB	JANUARY Obsn Hour Gp 01 to 08	JANUARY 09 to 16	JANUARY 17 to 24	JANUARY Total Obsn	JANUARY MCWB	FEBRUARY Obsn Hour Gp 01 to 08	FEBRUARY 09 to 16	FEBRUARY 17 to 24	FEBRUARY Total Obsn	FEBRUARY MCWB
100/104																				
95/99																				
90/94																				
85/89																				
80/84																				
75/79		8		8	66															
70/74	7	75	21	103	64		5	0	5	63		1		1	61					
65/69	25	66	63	154	62	4	27	9	40	61		3	0	3	60		4	0	4	58
60/64	84	59	97	240	58	42	71	57	170	58	5	39	13	57	57	4	43	19	66	56
55/59	82	21	36	139	54	50	59	65	174	53	35	68	67	170	52	30	62	57	149	52
50/54	26	8	16	49	47	75	49	61	185	48	71	70	70	211	48	61	60	71	192	47
45/49	14	4	7	25	42	51	32	47	130	42	84	44	62	190	43	76	38	50	164	42
40/44	3	0	1	4	38	23	4	9	36	39	22	11	15	48	38	35	12	19	66	38
35/39						4	1	0	5	36	19	9	16	44	34	14	5	7	26	34
30/34											12	5	5	22	30	4	1	1	6	32
25/29											1			1	25					

Temperature Range	MARCH Obsn Hour Gp 01 to 08	MARCH 09 to 16	MARCH 17 to 24	MARCH Total Obsn	MARCH MCWB	APRIL Obsn Hour Gp 01 to 08	APRIL 09 to 16	APRIL 17 to 24	APRIL Total Obsn	APRIL MCWB	ANNUAL TOTAL Obsn Hour Gp 01 to 08	ANNUAL TOTAL 09 to 16	ANNUAL TOTAL 17 to 24	ANNUAL TOTAL Total Obsn	ANNUAL TOTAL MCWB
100/104												1	0	1	75
95/99												18	7	25	71
90/94											0	130	63	193	71
85/89											7	192	101	300	70
80/84											130	390	306	826	69
75/79							3	0	3	59	379	318	363	1060	67
70/74		1		1	56		40	14	54	59	399	372	343	1114	63
65/69		19	5	24	57	4	66	35	105	58	252	299	261	812	60
60/64	9	80	51	140	56	58	94	106	258	56	430	449	481	1360	57
55/59	59	75	87	221	52	116	32	66	214	52	471	325	415	1211	52
50/54	93	54	70	217	47	48	5	16	69	48	391	246	307	944	48
45/49	65	18	30	113	43	14	0	3	17	43	304	136	199	639	42
40/44	18	1	5	24	38	0			0	39	101	28	49	178	38
35/39	5		1	6	35						42	15	24	81	35
30/34											16	6	6	28	30
25/29											*			*	25

IRAKLION AS/CRETE GREECE

LAT 35 20N LONG 25 11F ELEV 10[illegible] FT

MEAN FREQUENCY OF [illegible] DRY BULB TEMPERATURE (DEGREES F) WITH MEAN COINCIDENT WET BULB TEMPERATURE (DEGREES F) FOR EACH DRY BULB TEMPERATURE RANGE

Temperature Range	MAY Obsn Hour Gp 01 to 08	MAY 09 to 16	MAY 17 to 24	MAY Total Obsn	MAY MCWB	JUNE Obsn Hour Gp 01 to 08	JUNE 09 to 16	JUNE 17 to 24	JUNE Total Obsn	JUNE MCWB	JULY Obsn Hour Gp 01 to 08	JULY 09 to 16	JULY 17 to 24	JULY Total Obsn	JULY MCWB
100/104							2		2	68		1	0	1	70
95/99		0		0	64	0	5		5	67		3	1	4	67
90/94		3		3	65	3	10	1	14	66	1	5	1	7	71
85/89	1	6	2	9	64	4	17	9	30	66	3	17	6	26	71
80/84	4	16	6	26	64	11	55	25	91	67	20	116	47	183	70
75/79	11	52	22	85	64	52	111	84	247	66	83	103	132	318	68
70/74	32	79	54	165	62	72	36	86	194	63	102	3	59	164	64
65/69	48	76	74	198	60	55	4	25	84	61	34		2	36	62
60/64	87	14	69	170	57	38		9	47	57	6			6	59
55/59	56	2	20	78	53	4			4	55					
50/54	10		1	11	49										

Temperature Range	AUGUST Obsn Hour Gp 01 to 08	AUGUST 09 to 16	AUGUST 17 to 24	AUGUST Total Obsn	AUGUST MCWB	SEPTEMBER Obsn Hour Gp 01 to 08	SEPTEMBER 09 to 16	SEPTEMBER 17 to 24	SEPTEMBER Total Obsn	SEPTEMBER MCWB	OCTOBER Obsn Hour Gp 01 to 08	OCTOBER 09 to 16	OCTOBER 17 to 24	OCTOBER Total Obsn	OCTOBER MCWB
100/104		0		0	78										
95/99		1	1	2	70										
90/94	0	9	2	11	70	0	2	0	2	69		1		1	68
85/89	2	36	9	47	71	1	5	1	7	70		3	0	3	66
80/84	28	129	54	211	70	4	69	11	84	69		10	4	14	67
75/79	108	71	138	317	67	39	125	91	255	68	4	40	10	54	66
70/74	78	1	42	121	64	91	34	98	223	64	26	92	50	168	63
65/69	29	0	3	32	62	75	3	29	107	62	64	73	82	219	61
60/64	3		1	4	59	28	2	10	40	58	115	27	85	227	58
55/59						1			1	55	37	2	17	56	54
50/54											3			3	51

IRAKLION AS/CRETE GREECE

Temperature Range	NOVEMBER Obsn Hour Gp 01 to 08	NOVEMBER 09 to 16	NOVEMBER 17 to 24	NOVEMBER Total Obsn	NOVEMBER MCWB	DECEMBER Obsn Hour Gp 01 to 08	DECEMBER 09 to 16	DECEMBER 17 to 24	DECEMBER Total Obsn	DECEMBER MCWB	JANUARY Obsn Hour Gp 01 to 08	JANUARY 09 to 16	JANUARY 17 to 24	JANUARY Total Obsn	JANUARY MCWB
100/104															
95/99															
90/94															
85/89															
80/84		1	0	1	61										
75/79	0	11	1	12	63										
70/74	5	61	12	78	62	0	12	0	12	60		1	0	1	57
65/69	16	75	39	130	60	2	35	5	42	58	1	17	2	20	58
60/64	68	61	96	225	57	34	94	54	182	56	15	75	30	120	55
55/59	111	23	72	206	53	94	77	109	280	52	58	79	83	220	52
50/54	37	6	20	63	49	95	28	69	192	48	110	53	89	252	48
45/49	3	1	1	5	44	20	1	8	29	44	50	19	38	107	43
40/44						2	0	2	4	39	11	2	5	18	39
35/39						0	0		0	38	3	2	2	7	35
30/34													0	0	33

Temperature Range	FEBRUARY Obsn Hour Gp 01 to 08	FEBRUARY 09 to 16	FEBRUARY 17 to 24	FEBRUARY Total Obsn	FEBRUARY MCWB	MARCH Obsn Hour Gp 01 to 08	MARCH 09 to 16	MARCH 17 to 24	MARCH Total Obsn	MARCH MCWB	APRIL Obsn Hour Gp 01 to 08	APRIL 09 to 16	APRIL 17 to 24	APRIL Total Obsn	APRIL MCWB	ANNUAL TOTAL Obsn Hour Gp 01 to 08	ANNUAL TOTAL 09 to 16	ANNUAL TOTAL 17 to 24	ANNUAL TOTAL Total Obsn	ANNUAL TOTAL MCWB
100/104																	3	0	3	70
95/99												1		1	65	0	10	2	12	67
90/94												1		1	62	4	31	4	39	68
85/89												3	0	3	63	11	87	27	125	69
80/84							2		2	58	0	6	1	7	60	67	404	148	619	69
75/79		0		0	61	2	5	2	9	55	4	14	6	24	59	303	532	486	1321	67
70/74	0	8	1	9	58	1	12	5	18	55	6	28	11	45	58	413	367	418	1198	63
65/69	3	21	5	29	55	6	22	9	37	55	16	61	31	108	57	349	387	306	1042	60
60/64	13	82	33	128	54	14	82	36	132	55	51	78	77	206	55	472	515	500	1487	56
55/59	55	71	90	216	51	71	90	105	266	52	82	41	82	205	52	569	385	578	1532	52
50/54	100	32	69	201	48	110	29	72	211	48	66	7	28	101	48	531	155	348	1034	48
45/49	49	8	23	80	43	39	6	17	62	43	15		3	18	43	176	35	90	301	43
40/44	4	1	3	8	39	5	0	1	6	40						22	3	11	36	39
35/39						1			1	37						4	2	2	8	36
30/34																		0	0	33

AVIANO AB ITALY

LAT 46 02N LONG 12 36E ELEV 413 FT

MEAN FREQUENCY OF OCCURRENCE OF DRY BULB TEMPERATURE (DEGREES F) WITH MEAN COINCIDENT WET BULB TEMPERATURE (DEGREES F) FOR EACH DRY BULB TEMPERATURE RANGE

Temperature Range	MAY Obsn Hour Gp 01 to 08	MAY 09 to 16	MAY 17 to 24	MAY Total Obsn	MAY MCWB	JUNE Obsn Hour Gp 01 to 08	JUNE 09 to 16	JUNE 17 to 24	JUNE Total Obsn	JUNE MCWB
95/99										
90/94							0	0	0	72
85/89		0		0	69		8	2	10	71
80/84		5	1	6	67	0	35	11	46	69
75/79	0	30	9	39	64	6	60	27	93	66
70/74	4	60	24	88	61	24	66	50	140	64
65/69	18	68	47	133	59	63	43	67	173	62
60/64	54	51	71	176	56	80	21	53	154	59
55/59	86	27	60	173	53	48	5	24	77	55
50/54	58	6	28	92	49	16	1	6	23	50
45/49	19	1	6	26	44	2		1	3	45
40/44	6		2	8	40	0			0	43
35/39	2		0	2	34					
30/34	0			0	30					

Temperature Range	JULY Obsn Hour Gp 01 to 08	JULY 09 to 16	JULY 17 to 24	JULY Total Obsn	JULY MCWB	AUGUST Obsn Hour Gp 01 to 08	AUGUST 09 to 16	AUGUST 17 to 24	AUGUST Total Obsn	AUGUST MCWB
95/99		1	0	1	75		0		0	75
90/94		9	2	11	73		5	1	6	73
85/89	1	32	11	44	71	0	26	8	34	71
80/84	4	56	25	85	69	2	51	19	72	69
75/79	15	70	47	132	67	10	77	44	131	67
70/74	50	53	66	169	65	47	57	63	167	65
65/69	85	19	60	164	62	84	25	68	177	62
60/64	68	6	29	103	59	77	7	37	121	59
55/59	19	1	6	26	54	24	1	7	32	55
50/54	6	0	1	7	50	5		1	6	50
45/49	0			0	46	1			1	46
40/44										
35/39										
30/34										

Temperature Range	SEPTEMBER Obsn Hour Gp 01 to 08	SEPTEMBER 09 to 16	SEPTEMBER 17 to 24	SEPTEMBER Total Obsn	SEPTEMBER MCWB	OCTOBER Obsn Hour Gp 01 to 08	OCTOBER 09 to 16	OCTOBER 17 to 24	OCTOBER Total Obsn	OCTOBER MCWB
95/99										
90/94		0	0	0	67					
85/89		2	1	3	68					
80/84		17	3	20	67		1	0	1	66
75/79	0	53	13	66	66		6	1	7	63
70/74	6	77	37	120	63	0	32	4	36	61
65/69	43	60	68	171	61	4	55	17	76	59
60/64	84	27	72	183	58	26	76	46	148	56
55/59	63	4	34	101	54	49	52	62	163	53
50/54	32	0	11	43	49	57	22	57	136	49
45/49	10		1	11	45	54	3	42	99	44
40/44	1			1	41	42	1	16	59	40
35/39						13		3	16	35
30/34						3		0	3	31

AVIANO AB ITALY

Temperature Range	NOVEMBER Obsn Hour Gp 01 to 08	NOVEMBER Obsn Hour Gp 09 to 16	NOVEMBER Obsn Hour Gp 17 to 24	NOVEMBER Total Obsn	NOVEMBER MCWB	DECEMBER Obsn Hour Gp 01 to 08	DECEMBER Obsn Hour Gp 09 to 16	DECEMBER Obsn Hour Gp 17 to 24	DECEMBER Total Obsn	DECEMBER MCWB	JANUARY Obsn Hour Gp 01 to 08	JANUARY Obsn Hour Gp 09 to 16	JANUARY Obsn Hour Gp 17 to 24	JANUARY Total Obsn	JANUARY MCWB
95/99															
90/94															
85/89															
80/84															
75/79															
70/74		0		0	62										
65/69	0	1		1	59		0		0	47					
60/64	1	18	3	22	55		1		1	50		0		0	44
55/59	12	60	20	92	52	0	5	1	6	50		2	0	2	46
50/54	43	81	58	182	48	5	27	8	40	47	0	15	2	17	45
45/49	60	50	68	178	44	21	69	24	114	43	14	58	20	92	42
40/44	57	21	51	129	39	38	71	52	161	39	33	75	49	157	38
35/39	37	8	27	72	35	49	45	60	154	34	47	48	56	151	34
30/34	22	2	11	35	30	65	23	63	151	30	59	32	64	155	30
25/29	6	0	2	8	26	45	6	31	82	25	53	14	37	104	25
20/24	1		0	1	21	20	1	7	28	21	29	3	16	48	20
15/19						4	0	1	5	17	11	1	3	15	16
10/14						1		0	1	12	2	0	1	3	11
5/9											1			1	8

Temperature Range	FEBRUARY Obsn Hour Gp 01 to 08	FEBRUARY Obsn Hour Gp 09 to 16	FEBRUARY Obsn Hour Gp 17 to 24	FEBRUARY Total Obsn	FEBRUARY MCWB	MARCH Obsn Hour Gp 01 to 08	MARCH Obsn Hour Gp 09 to 16	MARCH Obsn Hour Gp 17 to 24	MARCH Total Obsn	MARCH MCWB
95/99										
90/94										
85/89										
80/84										
75/79										
70/74							1	0	1	57
65/69		1		1	61		5	2	7	55
60/64		3	0	3	52		14	4	18	52
55/59		9	2	11	48	0	45	13	58	49
50/54	0	31	8	39	46	16	67	48	131	47
45/49	14	57	33	104	43	53	59	68	180	43
40/44	38	60	56	154	39	65	37	55	157	39
35/39	51	38	58	147	34	54	14	35	103	34
30/34	54	19	37	110	30	41	4	17	62	29
25/29	38	5	22	65	25	14	1	5	20	25
20/24	21	1	9	31	20	4	0	1	5	20
15/19	7	0	1	8	16	1	0	0	1	15
10/14	0		0	0	14	0			0	10
5/9						0			0	8

Temperature Range	APRIL Obsn Hour Gp 01 to 08	APRIL Obsn Hour Gp 09 to 16	APRIL Obsn Hour Gp 17 to 24	APRIL Total Obsn	APRIL MCWB	ANNUAL TOTAL Obsn Hour Gp 01 to 08	ANNUAL TOTAL Obsn Hour Gp 09 to 16	ANNUAL TOTAL Obsn Hour Gp 17 to 24	ANNUAL TOTAL Total Obsn	ANNUAL TOTAL MCWB
95/99							1	0	1	75
90/94							14	3	17	73
85/89						1	68	22	91	71
80/84		0		0	59	6	165	59	230	69
75/79		5	1	6	60	31	301	142	474	66
70/74	0	15	4	19	59	131	361	248	740	64
65/69	1	33	13	47	56	298	310	342	950	61
60/64	6	47	27	80	54	396	271	342	1009	57
55/59	27	62	52	141	51	328	273	281	882	53
50/54	73	52	71	196	48	311	302	299	912	48
45/49	72	20	48	140	44	320	317	311	948	44
40/44	41	5	18	64	40	321	270	299	890	39
35/39	17	1	5	23	35	270	154	244	668	34
30/34	3	0	1	4	30	247	80	193	520	30
25/29	0			0	27	156	26	97	279	25
20/24						75	5	33	113	21
15/19						23	1	5	29	16
10/14						3	0	1	4	12
5/9						1			1	8

SIGONELLA NAF/SICILY ITALY

LAT 37 24N LONG 14 55E ELEV 72 FT

MEAN FREQUENCY OF OCCURRENCE OF DRY BULB TEMPERATURE (DEGREES F) WITH MEAN COINCIDENT WET BULB TEMPERATURE (DEGREES F) FOR EACH DRY BULB TEMPERATURE RANGE

Temperature Range	MAY Obsn Hour Gp 01 to 08	MAY Obsn Hour Gp 09 to 16	MAY Obsn Hour Gp 17 to 24	MAY Total Obsn	MAY MCWB	JUNE Obsn Hour Gp 01 to 08	JUNE Obsn Hour Gp 09 to 16	JUNE Obsn Hour Gp 17 to 24	JUNE Total Obsn	JUNE MCWB	JULY Obsn Hour Gp 01 to 08	JULY Obsn Hour Gp 09 to 16	JULY Obsn Hour Gp 17 to 24	JULY Total Obsn	JULY MCWB
115/119												0		0	75
110/114												0		0	75
105/109												0	0	0	73
100/104												6	0	6	72
95/99		0		0	67		2		2	69		16	1	17	72
90/94		3	0	3	66		17	1	18	70	0	61	5	66	71
85/89		10	1	11	66	1	57	6	64	69	3	102	22	127	71
80/84	0	32	2	34	65	5	78	21	104	68	15	53	51	119	69
75/79	2	77	10	89	63	14	58	38	110	66	29	8	75	112	68
70/74	9	78	28	115	62	30	22	61	113	64	57	1	69	127	65
65/69	22	33	56	111	60	56	6	69	131	62	102	0	22	124	62
60/64	47	10	74	131	58	79	1	38	118	59	38		2	40	59
55/59	71	4	56	131	55	47	0	6	53	55	4			4	55
50/54	66	0	20	86	51	8		0	8	51	0			0	52
45/49	27		3	30	46	1			1	47					
40/44	4		0	4	42										
35/39	0			0	36										

Temperature Range	AUGUST Obsn Hour Gp 01 to 08	AUGUST Obsn Hour Gp 09 to 16	AUGUST Obsn Hour Gp 17 to 24	AUGUST Total Obsn	AUGUST MCWB	SEPTEMBER Obsn Hour Gp 01 to 08	SEPTEMBER Obsn Hour Gp 09 to 16	SEPTEMBER Obsn Hour Gp 17 to 24	SEPTEMBER Total Obsn	SEPTEMBER MCWB	OCTOBER Obsn Hour Gp 01 to 08	OCTOBER Obsn Hour Gp 09 to 16	OCTOBER Obsn Hour Gp 17 to 24	OCTOBER Total Obsn	OCTOBER MCWB
115/119															
110/114															
105/109		2		2	74										
100/104		7	0	7	72		1		1	70					
95/99		24	2	26	72		3		3	70					
90/94	0	66	6	72	71		18	1	19	70		1		1	72
85/89	2	95	24	121	71		63	4	67	70		5	0	5	70
80/84	12	45	58	115	70	1	85	21	107	69		36	1	37	68
75/79	33	8	84	125	69	10	49	63	122	68	0	72	10	82	66
70/74	82	1	61	144	65	42	17	79	138	66	8	68	45	121	64
65/69	93	0	14	107	62	87	5	53	145	63	31	46	78	155	62
60/64	25		0	25	58	74	1	16	91	59	81	19	75	175	59
55/59	1			1	54	25		2	27	55	81	2	30	113	55
50/54						2		0	2	49	35		7	42	50
45/49											10		2	12	45
40/44											2		0	2	41
35/39															

SIGONELLA NAF/SICILY ITALY

Temperature Range	NOVEMBER Obsn Hour Gp 01 to 08	NOVEMBER 09 to 16	NOVEMBER 17 to 24	NOVEMBER Total Obsn	NOVEMBER MCWB	DECEMBER Obsn Hour Gp 01 to 08	DECEMBER 09 to 16	DECEMBER 17 to 24	DECEMBER Total Obsn	DECEMBER MCWB	JANUARY Obsn Hour Gp 01 to 08	JANUARY 09 to 16	JANUARY 17 to 24	JANUARY Total Obsn	JANUARY MCWB
115/119															
110/114															
105/109															
100/104															
95/99															
90/94															
85/89		0		0	68										
80/84		3		3	66										
75/79		20	0	20	65		0		0	60					
70/74	0	59	3	62	63		3		3	61		2		2	60
65/69	9	72	29	110	60		23	0	23	58		8	0	8	57
60/64	20	49	60	129	57	5	65	12	82	56		54	2	56	55
55/59	52	28	72	152	54	22	89	58	169	53	9	81	35	125	52
50/54	77	8	51	136	50	51	46	85	182	49	37	59	78	174	49
45/49	50	1	20	71	45	87	17	60	164	45	71	30	76	177	45
40/44	23		5	28	41	53	4	27	84	41	68	12	39	119	41
35/39	7		1	8	36	24	1	5	30	36	44	2	15	61	36
30/34	1			1	32	5	0	1	6	32	17	0	4	21	32
25/29						1			1	28	2		0	2	27
20/24											0			0	23

Temperature Range	FEBRUARY Obsn Hour Gp 01 to 08	FEBRUARY 09 to 16	FEBRUARY 17 to 24	FEBRUARY Total Obsn	FEBRUARY MCWB	MARCH Obsn Hour Gp 01 to 08	MARCH 09 to 16	MARCH 17 to 24	MARCH Total Obsn	MARCH MCWB	APRIL Obsn Hour Gp 01 to 08	APRIL 09 to 16	APRIL 17 to 24	APRIL Total Obsn	APRIL MCWB
115/119															
110/114															
105/109															
100/104															
95/99															
90/94															
85/89												1		1	67
80/84							1		1	65		4		4	64
75/79		0		0	61		3	0	3	62		18	1	19	62
70/74		5		5	61		13	1	14	60	0	42	3	45	60
65/69		19	1	20	58	0	49	4	53	57	2	78	13	93	58
60/64		61	6	67	55	1	81	18	100	55	12	66	43	121	56
55/59	10	59	40	109	52	21	65	61	147	53	46	25	81	152	54
50/54	34	47	66	147	49	57	29	80	166	49	62	4	63	129	50
45/49	50	26	60	136	44	67	7	55	129	45	65	1	27	93	46
40/44	66	5	38	109	40	57	1	22	80	41	42		7	49	41
35/39	42	1	12	55	36	33	0	7	40	36	10		1	11	37
30/34	19	0	2	21	32	10		1	11	32	2			2	33
25/29	2		0	2	26	1			1	27					
20/24	0			0	22										

Temperature Range	ANNUAL TOTAL Obsn Hour Gp 01 to 08	ANNUAL TOTAL 09 to 16	ANNUAL TOTAL 17 to 24	ANNUAL TOTAL Total Obsn	ANNUAL TOTAL MCWB
115/119		0		0	75
110/114		0		0	75
105/109		2	0	2	73
100/104		14	0	14	72
95/99		45	3	48	72
90/94	0	166	13	179	71
85/89	6	333	57	396	70
80/84	33	337	154	524	69
75/79	88	313	281	682	67
70/74	228	311	350	889	64
65/69	402	339	339	1080	61
60/64	382	407	346	1135	57
55/59	389	353	441	1183	53
50/54	429	193	450	1072	49
45/49	428	82	303	813	45
40/44	315	22	138	475	41
35/39	160	4	41	205	36
30/34	54	0	8	62	32
25/29	6		0	6	27
20/24	0			0	22

ROTA NAVAL STATION SPAIN

LAT 36 39N LONG 6 21W ELEV [illegible] FT

MEAN FREQUENCY OF OCCURRENCE OF DRY BULB TEMPERATURE (DEGREES F) WITH MEAN COINCIDENT WET BULB TEMPERATURE (DEGREES F) FOR EACH DRY BULB TEMPERATURE RANGE

Temperature Range	MAY Obsn Hour Gp 01 to 08	MAY 09 to 16	MAY 17 to 24	MAY Total Obsn	MAY MCWB	JUNE Obsn Hour Gp 01 to 08	JUNE 09 to 16	JUNE 17 to 24	JUNE Total Obsn	JUNE MCWB	JULY Obsn Hour Gp 01 to 08	JULY 09 to 16	JULY 17 to 24	JULY Total Obsn	JULY MCWB
105/109															
100/104												1	0	1	71
95/99		0		0	65		1		1	68		4	1	5	71
90/94		3	1	4	64		8	3	11	68		16	6	22	70
85/89		9	3	12	65		19	8	27	67	0	37	15	52	70
80/84		29	12	41	64	0	33	19	52	66	3	63	43	109	69
75/79	0	33	20	53	63	7	60	40	107	66	25	69	74	168	68
70/74	5	56	42	103	62	30	65	70	165	64	88	49	79	216	66
65/69	36	67	81	184	60	84	45	73	202	62	89	9	26	124	63
60/64	96	42	73	211	58	90	8	27	125	59	35	0	3	38	60
55/59	79	7	14	100	54	27	0	1	28	55	7		0	7	56
50/54	29	1	2	32	50	2			2	52	1			1	53
45/49	3	0		3	46										
40/44	0			0	44										

Temperature Range	AUGUST Obsn Hour Gp 01 to 08	AUGUST 09 to 16	AUGUST 17 to 24	AUGUST Total Obsn	AUGUST MCWB	SEPTEMBER Obsn Hour Gp 01 to 08	SEPTEMBER 09 to 16	SEPTEMBER 17 to 24	SEPTEMBER Total Obsn	SEPTEMBER MCWB	OCTOBER Obsn Hour Gp 01 to 08	OCTOBER 09 to 16	OCTOBER 17 to 24	OCTOBER Total Obsn	OCTOBER MCWB
105/109		0		0	73		0		0	75					
100/104		1	0	1	72		0		0	74					
95/99		4	1	5	70		2	0	2	71					
90/94		18	6	24	70		12	3	15	71		0		0	71
85/89		38	17	55	70		24	10	34	70		3	0	3	68
80/84	4	63	39	106	69	3	41	22	66	69		21	4	25	66
75/79	28	73	70	171	68	15	57	49	121	67		34	14	48	65
70/74	86	42	84	212	66	55	70	88	213	66	8	76	48	132	64
65/69	81	8	26	115	63	82	27	57	166	63	62	70	112	244	62
60/64	39	1	4	44	59	59	6	11	76	59	94	32	56	182	59
55/59	10		0	10	56	20	1	1	22	55	53	9	11	73	54
50/54	1			1	53	6			6	50	24	2	2	28	49
45/49						1			1	46	5	0	1	6	43
40/44											1		0	1	40

Temperature Range	NOVEMBER Obsn Hour Gp 01 to 08	09 to 16	17 to 24	Total Obsn	MCWB	DECEMBER Obsn Hour Gp 01 to 08	09 to 16	17 to 24	Total Obsn	MCWB	JANUARY Obsn Hour Gp 01 to 08	09 to 16	17 to 24	Total Obsn	MCWB
105/109															
100/104															
95/99															
90/94															
85/89															
80/84		0		0	61										
75/79		3	1	4	61										
70/74		13	3	16	61		0		0	57		0	0	0	58
65/69	7	54	27	88	61		8	2	10	58	0	7	3	10	57
60/64	47	82	89	218	57	14	59	36	109	57	14	65	36	115	57
55/59	63	50	77	190	54	42	76	77	195	53	54	80	88	222	54
50/54	70	26	33	129	50	52	52	73	177	49	58	47	77	182	50
45/49	39	9	9	57	46	66	29	38	133	45	58	28	31	117	45
40/44	13	3	2	18	41	48	17	20	85	41	43	14	10	67	41
35/39	1	0		1	38	22	7	2	31	36	19	6	2	27	36
30/34						3	1	0	4	31	2	1	0	3	31
25/29						0			0	26	0			0	28

Temperature Range	FEBRUARY Obsn Hour Gp 01 to 08	09 to 16	17 to 24	Total Obsn	MCWB	MARCH Obsn Hour Gp 01 to 08	09 to 16	17 to 24	Total Obsn	MCWB
105/109										
100/104										
95/99										
90/94										
85/89										
80/84										
75/79		1	0	1	61		4	1	5	59
70/74		3	2	5	59		12	6	18	58
65/69	0	14	6	20	57	2	36	19	57	57
60/64	9	69	41	119	56	17	87	72	176	56
55/59	51	74	91	216	53	74	69	101	244	53
50/54	62	35	61	158	49	77	27	39	143	49
45/49	58	18	20	96	45	52	10	10	72	45
40/44	34	8	3	45	41	24	2	1	27	41
35/39	9	2	0	11	36	2	0		2	36
30/34	1			1	32					
25/29										

Temperature Range	APRIL Obsn Hour Gp 01 to 08	09 to 16	17 to 24	Total Obsn	MCWB	ANNUAL TOTAL Obsn Hour Gp 01 to 08	09 to 16	17 to 24	Total Obsn	MCWB
105/109							0		0	73
100/104							2	0	2	72
95/99							11	2	13	70
90/94							57	19	76	70
85/89		1	0	1	66	0	131	53	184	69
80/84		5	2	7	63	10	255	141	406	68
75/79		12	5	17	61	75	346	274	695	66
70/74		34	17	51	59	272	420	439	1131	65
65/69	1	68	40	109	59	444	413	472	1329	61
60/64	41	77	104	222	57	555	528	552	1635	58
55/59	96	33	60	189	53	576	399	521	1496	54
50/54	74	10	11	95	50	456	200	298	954	49
45/49	27	1	1	29	45	309	95	110	514	45
40/44	2			2	42	165	44	36	245	41
35/39						53	15	4	72	36
30/34						6	2	0	8	31
25/29						0			0	26

TORREJON AB/MADRID SPAIN

LAT 40 29N LONG 3 27W ELEV 1991 FT

MEAN FREQUENCY OF OCCURRENCE OF DRY BULB TEMPERATURE (DEGREES F) WITH MEAN COINCIDENT WET BULB TEMPERATURE (DEGREES F) FOR EACH DRY BULB TEMPERATURE RANGE

Temperature Range	MAY Obsn Hour Gp 01 to 08	MAY 09 to 16	MAY 17 to 24	MAY Total Obsn	MAY MCWB	JUNE Obsn Hour Gp 01 to 08	JUNE 09 to 16	JUNE 17 to 24	JUNE Total Obsn	JUNE MCWB	JULY Obsn Hour Gp 01 to 08	JULY 09 to 16	JULY 17 to 24	JULY Total Obsn	JULY MCWB
105/109												0		0	67
100/104							0	0	0	66		2	1	3	66
95/99							5	2	7	65		16	7	23	65
90/94		1	0	1	63		12	6	18	64		41	25	66	64
85/89		8	3	11	62		28	15	43	63	0	63	38	101	63
80/84		18	9	27	61	0	38	23	61	62	2	61	47	110	61
75/79		30	15	45	59	4	46	33	83	60	17	41	48	106	60
70/74	2	46	27	75	57	16	43	38	97	58	47	19	43	109	58
65/69	8	50	39	97	55	34	36	40	110	56	70	4	25	99	56
60/64	25	48	48	121	53	57	23	40	120	55	67	1	12	80	53
55/59	57	30	52	139	51	63	8	28	99	52	34		2	36	49
50/54	72	14	37	123	48	43	2	12	57	48	11			11	46
45/49	52	3	16	71	44	19		3	22	44	0			0	47
40/44	25	0	3	28	39	3			3	40					
35/39	6		0	6	35	0			0	36					
30/34	1			1	31										
25/29	0			0	28										

Temperature Range	AUGUST Obsn Hour Gp 01 to 08	AUGUST 09 to 16	AUGUST 17 to 24	AUGUST Total Obsn	AUGUST MCWB	SEPTEMBER Obsn Hour Gp 01 to 08	SEPTEMBER 09 to 16	SEPTEMBER 17 to 24	SEPTEMBER Total Obsn	SEPTEMBER MCWB	OCTOBER Obsn Hour Gp 01 to 08	OCTOBER 09 to 16	OCTOBER 17 to 24	OCTOBER Total Obsn	OCTOBER MCWB
105/109															
100/104		1	0	1	66										
95/99		10	3	13	64		1	0	1	64					
90/94		36	18	54	64		10	3	13	63					
85/89	0	54	30	84	63		25	10	35	63		1		1	58
80/84	1	59	40	100	61		38	17	55	61		5	1	6	60
75/79	8	50	49	107	60	1	49	30	80	60		16	4	20	59
70/74	34	28	50	112	58	8	49	45	102	58		35	10	45	58
65/69	66	10	39	115	56	30	36	48	114	57	0	57	24	81	56
60/64	81	2	15	98	53	64	23	48	135	54	10	61	51	122	54
55/59	45		2	47	49	71	8	31	110	52	57	47	73	177	52
50/54	11		0	11	46	45	1	8	54	47	71	21	54	146	48
45/49	2			2	42	17		1	18	43	67	6	24	97	44
40/44						3			3	39	28	1	6	35	39
35/39						0			0	35	11	0	1	12	34
30/34											4		0	4	30
25/29											0			0	27

TORREJON AB/MADRID SPAIN

Temperature Range	NOVEMBER Obsn Hour Gp 01 to 08	NOVEMBER Obsn Hour Gp 09 to 16	NOVEMBER Obsn Hour Gp 17 to 24	NOVEMBER Total Obsn	NOVEMBER MCWB	DECEMBER Obsn Hour Gp 01 to 08	DECEMBER Obsn Hour Gp 09 to 16	DECEMBER Obsn Hour Gp 17 to 24	DECEMBER Total Obsn	DECEMBER MCWB
105/109										
100/104										
95/99										
90/94										
85/89										
80/84										
75/79		0		0	53					
70/74		2		2	52					
65/69		6	1	7	54					
60/64	0	18	5	23	52		2		2	50
55/59	5	42	15	62	50	0	15	1	16	49
50/54	26	78	52	156	47	8	50	21	79	47
45/49	56	57	75	188	44	32	69	53	154	43
40/44	58	26	55	139	39	52	57	69	178	39
35/39	50	8	24	82	35	53	35	52	140	35
30/34	30	2	11	43	31	49	15	34	98	31
25/29	14	0	2	16	27	35	4	15	54	26
20/24	1			1	23	17	1	2	20	22
15/19						1	0	1	2	17
10/14						1			1	12
5/9										
0/4										
-5/-1										

Temperature Range	JANUARY Obsn Hour Gp 01 to 08	JANUARY Obsn Hour Gp 09 to 16	JANUARY Obsn Hour Gp 17 to 24	JANUARY Total Obsn	JANUARY MCWB	FEBRUARY Obsn Hour Gp 01 to 08	FEBRUARY Obsn Hour Gp 09 to 16	FEBRUARY Obsn Hour Gp 17 to 24	FEBRUARY Total Obsn	FEBRUARY MCWB
105/109										
100/104										
95/99										
90/94										
85/89										
80/84										
75/79										
70/74							0	0	0	62
65/69		0		0	56		2	1	3	53
60/64		2	0	2	53		13	4	17	50
55/59	0	16	3	19	50	0	24	10	34	49
50/54	11	50	27	88	47	8	56	32	96	46
45/49	33	74	58	165	44	28	55	57	140	43
40/44	57	55	68	180	40	52	43	62	157	39
35/39	50	30	49	129	35	55	17	31	103	35
30/34	48	15	34	97	31	48	7	17	72	30
25/29	36	4	7	47	26	20	2	4	26	26
20/24	10	0	1	11	22	7	0	1	8	22
15/19	1	0		1	16	0	1	0	1	15
10/14	0	0	0	0	10	0	1	1	2	10
5/9	1	1	1	3	6	2	2	2	6	6
0/4	0	0	0	0	3	2	0	1	3	3
-5/-1	0			0	-1	1			1	-1

Temperature Range	MARCH Obsn Hour Gp 01 to 08	MARCH Obsn Hour Gp 09 to 16	MARCH Obsn Hour Gp 17 to 24	MARCH Total Obsn	MARCH MCWB	APRIL Obsn Hour Gp 01 to 08	APRIL Obsn Hour Gp 09 to 16	APRIL Obsn Hour Gp 17 to 24	APRIL Total Obsn	APRIL MCWB
105/109										
100/104										
95/99										
90/94										
85/89										
80/84							0	0	0	64
75/79		1		1	54		4	2	6	58
70/74		5	2	7	51		15	6	21	56
65/69		15	6	21	51		39	15	54	53
60/64	0	31	13	44	50	1	53	31	85	51
55/59	2	52	30	84	48	12	62	53	127	49
50/54	29	66	63	158	46	50	44	63	157	46
45/49	52	48	63	163	43	81	18	43	142	43
40/44	66	22	43	131	39	62	4	21	87	39
35/39	52	7	20	79	34	25	1	5	31	34
30/34	34	2	7	43	30	7		0	7	30
25/29	10	0	1	11	26	2			2	27
20/24	2			2	21					
15/19	0			0	15					
10/14										
5/9										
0/4										
-5/-1										

Temperature Range	ANNUAL TOTAL Obsn Hour Gp 01 to 08	ANNUAL TOTAL Obsn Hour Gp 09 to 16	ANNUAL TOTAL Obsn Hour Gp 17 to 24	ANNUAL TOTAL Total Obsn	ANNUAL TOTAL MCWB
105/109		0		0	67
100/104		3	1	4	66
95/99		32	12	44	65
90/94		100	52	152	64
85/89	0	179	96	275	63
80/84	3	219	137	359	61
75/79	30	237	181	448	60
70/74	107	242	221	570	58
65/69	208	255	238	701	56
60/64	305	277	267	849	53
55/59	346	304	300	950	51
50/54	385	382	369	1136	47
45/49	439	330	393	1162	43
40/44	406	208	327	941	39
35/39	302	98	182	582	35
30/34	221	41	103	365	30
25/29	117	10	29	156	26
20/24	37	1	4	42	22
15/19	2	1	1	4	16
10/14	1	1	1	3	10
5/9	3	3	3	9	6
0/4	2	0	1	3	3
-5/-1	1			1	1

BENTWATERS RAF STA UNITED KINGDOM

LAT 52 08N LONG 1 26E ELEV 85 FT

MEAN FREQUENCY OF OCCURRENCE OF DRY BULB TEMPERATURE (DEGREES F) WITH MEAN COINCIDENT WET BULB TEMPERATURE (DEGREES F) FOR EACH DRY BULB TEMPERATURE RANGE

Temperature Range	MAY Obsn Hour Gp 01 to 08	MAY Obsn Hour Gp 09 to 16	MAY Obsn Hour Gp 17 to 24	MAY Total Obsn	MAY MCWB	JUNE Obsn Hour Gp 01 to 08	JUNE Obsn Hour Gp 09 to 16	JUNE Obsn Hour Gp 17 to 24	JUNE Total Obsn	JUNE MCWB
85/89										
80/84							1	0	1	64
75/79		0		0	65		6	1	7	64
70/74		5	1	6	60	1	22	6	29	61
65/69	0	22	4	26	57	4	59	22	85	58
60/64	4	53	17	74	54	30	85	58	173	55
55/59	26	80	55	161	51	84	51	83	218	53
50/54	80	69	91	240	48	82	16	53	151	49
45/49	93	17	60	170	45	30	1	14	45	45
40/44	35	1	18	54	41	8		2	10	41
35/39	9	0	2	11	36	1		0	1	34
30/34	1		0	1	31					
25/29	0			0	27					

Temperature Range	JULY Obsn Hour Gp 01 to 08	JULY Obsn Hour Gp 09 to 16	JULY Obsn Hour Gp 17 to 24	JULY Total Obsn	JULY MCWB	AUGUST Obsn Hour Gp 01 to 08	AUGUST Obsn Hour Gp 09 to 16	AUGUST Obsn Hour Gp 17 to 24	AUGUST Total Obsn	AUGUST MCWB
85/89		0	0	0	71					
80/84		3	0	3	68		1	0	1	67
75/79	0	11	3	14	65		9	1	10	66
70/74	1	37	12	50	62	1	39	10	50	62
65/69	13	79	38	130	60	13	87	45	145	60
60/64	59	85	82	226	57	66	86	85	237	57
55/59	106	30	81	217	54	93	25	77	195	54
50/54	54	3	27	84	50	57	2	26	85	50
45/49	13		3	16	46	15		4	19	46
40/44	2		0	2	41	3		0	3	41
35/39						0			0	38
30/34										
25/29										

Temperature Range	SEPTEMBER Obsn Hour Gp 01 to 08	SEPTEMBER Obsn Hour Gp 09 to 16	SEPTEMBER Obsn Hour Gp 17 to 24	SEPTEMBER Total Obsn	SEPTEMBER MCWB	OCTOBER Obsn Hour Gp 01 to 08	OCTOBER Obsn Hour Gp 09 to 16	OCTOBER Obsn Hour Gp 17 to 24	OCTOBER Total Obsn	OCTOBER MCWB
85/89										
80/84		0		0	66					
75/79		3	0	3	65		0		0	62
70/74		14	2	16	62		2	0	2	62
65/69	2	58	14	74	59	0	15	1	16	60
60/64	36	101	63	200	57	11	53	24	88	57
55/59	83	55	94	232	54	49	84	64	197	54
50/54	72	9	50	131	50	75	59	78	212	49
45/49	36	1	14	51	45	58	28	51	137	45
40/44	10		2	12	42	38	7	24	69	41
35/39	1		0	1	37	14	1	6	21	36
30/34						3		0	3	32
25/29										

BENTWATERS RAF STA UNITED KINGDOM

Temperature Range	NOVEMBER					DECEMBER					JANUARY				
	Obsn Hour Gp			Total Obsn	M C W B	Obsn Hour Gp			Total Obsn	M C W B	Obsn Hour Gp			Total Obsn	M C W B
	01 to 08	09 to 16	17 to 24			01 to 08	09 to 16	17 to 24			01 to 08	09 to 16	17 to 24		
85/89															
80/84															
75/79															
70/74															
65/69		0		0	56										
60/64	0	3	0	3	56		0	0	0	58					
55/59	6	18	9	33	53	2	3	1	6	52		0		0	53
50/54	35	60	44	139	49	17	23	19	59	49	5	9	7	21	48
45/49	74	91	75	240	44	40	56	44	140	45	27	47	35	109	44
40/44	61	42	65	168	40	64	77	70	211	40	62	72	64	198	40
35/39	39	20	31	90	35	64	56	65	185	35	66	60	68	194	35
30/34	20	5	14	39	31	45	29	39	113	31	60	47	53	160	30
25/29	4	1	1	6	26	11	4	8	23	26	21	10	16	47	26
20/24	0		0	0	23	3	0	2	5	22	5	2	3	10	22
15/19						0			0	18	1	0	1	2	16
10/14											1	0	0	1	12
5/9											0			0	9

Temperature Range	FEBRUARY					MARCH					APRIL					ANNUAL TOTAL				
	Obsn Hour Gp			Total Obsn	M C W B	Obsn Hour Gp			Total Obsn	M C W B	Obsn Hour Gp			Total Obsn	M C W B	Obsn Hour Gp			Total Obsn	M C W B
	01 to 08	09 to 16	17 to 24			01 to 08	09 to 16	17 to 24			01 to 08	09 to 16	17 to 24			01 to 08	09 to 16	17 to 24		
85/89																	0	0	0	71
80/84																	5	0	5	67
75/79																0	29	5	34	65
70/74							0		0	54		1		1	58	3	120	31	154	62
65/69							2	0	2	54		2	0	2	57	32	324	124	480	59
60/64		0		0	55		2	1	3	51	0	11	2	13	53	206	479	332	1017	57
55/59		2	0	2	51	0	12	3	15	49	3	46	17	66	51	452	406	484	1342	53
50/54	4	13	7	24	48	3	42	19	64	46	29	67	49	145	47	513	372	470	1355	49
45/49	16	41	30	87	44	33	68	57	158	43	61	69	67	197	43	496	419	454	1369	44
40/44	52	59	56	167	40	84	68	75	227	39	80	36	67	183	40	499	362	443	1304	40
35/39	62	61	64	187	35	66	42	56	164	35	49	8	33	90	35	371	248	325	944	35
30/34	62	36	50	148	30	44	12	32	88	30	16	1	5	22	32	251	130	193	574	31
25/29	22	9	13	44	26	15	0	5	20	27	1		0	1	28	74	24	43	141	26
20/24	4	2	3	9	21	2	0	0	2	22						14	4	8	26	22
15/19	2	0	0	2	18	0			0	19						3	0	1	4	17
10/14																1	0	0	1	12
5/9																0			0	9

MILDENHALL RAF STA UNITED KINGDOM

LAT 52 22N LONG 0 29E ELEV 33 FT

MEAN FREQUENCY OF OCCURRENCE OF DRY BULB TEMPERATURE [illegible] WITH MEAN COINCIDENT WET BULB TEMPERATURE (DEGREES F) FOR EACH DRY BULB TEMPERATURE RANGE

Temperature Range	MAY Obsn Hour Gp 01 to 08	MAY 09 to 16	MAY 17 to 24	MAY Total Obsn	MAY MCWB	JUNE Obsn Hour Gp 01 to 08	JUNE 09 to 16	JUNE 17 to 24	JUNE Total Obsn	JUNE MCWB	JULY Obsn Hour Gp 01 to 08	JULY 09 to 16	JULY 17 to 24	JULY Total Obsn	JULY MCWB
90/94							0		0	75		0		0	67
85/89							1	0	1	71		2	1	3	69
80/84		0		0	67		6	1	7	65		6	2	8	68
75/79		4	1	5	63	0	15	5	20	63	0	18	8	26	64
70/74	0	14	4	18	59	1	36	14	51	60	2	41	21	64	62
65/69	0	30	9	39	56	4	57	34	95	58	11	72	43	126	59
60/64	7	53	29	89	54	24	67	57	148	56	54	81	76	211	57
55/59	25	70	50	145	51	76	41	68	185	53	100	26	74	200	54
50/54	65	58	74	197	48	81	15	45	141	50	63	2	21	86	50
45/49	89	18	59	166	44	42	1	13	56	46	17		3	20	46
40/44	44	1	18	63	40	9		2	11	41	2		0	2	42
35/39	13		4	17	36	2		0	2	36					
30/34	4		0	4	32	1			1	31					
25/29															

Temperature Range	AUGUST Obsn Hour Gp 01 to 08	AUGUST 09 to 16	AUGUST 17 to 24	AUGUST Total Obsn	AUGUST MCWB	SEPTEMBER Obsn Hour Gp 01 to 08	SEPTEMBER 09 to 16	SEPTEMBER 17 to 24	SEPTEMBER Total Obsn	SEPTEMBER MCWB	OCTOBER Obsn Hour Gp 01 to 08	OCTOBER 09 to 16	OCTOBER 17 to 24	OCTOBER Total Obsn	OCTOBER MCWB
90/94		0		0	71										
85/89		1	0	1	70										
80/84		4	1	5	67		1	0	1	67					
75/79		16	4	20	64		6	1	7	64		1	0	1	62
70/74	0	41	16	57	62		20	5	25	61		4	0	4	61
65/69	6	78	41	125	59	3	60	19	82	59	0	24	4	28	59
60/64	59	83	83	225	57	30	88	63	181	57	12	53	26	91	57
55/59	92	23	75	190	54	71	49	80	200	54	44	78	61	183	53
50/54	68	2	26	96	51	74	13	51	138	50	80	59	80	219	49
45/49	21		2	23	46	43	1	17	61	46	56	24	52	132	45
40/44	2			2	42	17		3	20	41	38	4	20	62	41
35/39						2		1	3	37	16	1	4	21	36
30/34						0			0	31	3		0	3	32
25/29						0			0	28					

MILDENHALL RAF STA UNITED KINGDOM

Temperature Range	NOVEMBER Obsn Hour Gp 01 to 08	09 to 16	17 to 24	Total Obsn	M C W B	DECEMBER Obsn Hour Gp 01 to 08	09 to 16	17 to 24	Total Obsn	M C W B	JANUARY Obsn Hour Gp 01 to 08	09 to 16	17 to 24	Total Obsn	M C W B
90/94															
85/89															
80/84															
75/79															
70/74															
65/69		0		0	58										
60/64	1	3	1	5	56										
55/59	5	16	10	31	53	2	3	2	7	53	1	2	2	5	52
50/54	27	56	36	119	49	15	23	17	55	49	12	25	15	52	49
45/49	67	81	66	214	45	38	50	38	126	44	36	46	40	122	44
40/44	62	55	70	187	40	55	71	63	189	40	46	57	52	155	40
35/39	42	21	38	101	36	64	58	62	184	35	57	57	63	177	35
30/34	26	7	15	48	31	44	32	46	122	31	57	44	50	151	31
25/29	8	1	3	12	27	18	8	14	40	26	24	13	17	54	26
20/24	2	0	1	3	23	10	2	4	16	22	9	3	7	19	22
15/19		0		0	19	2	0	1	3	17	3	1	3	7	17
10/14						0	0	0	0	13	1	0	1	2	12
5/9						0	0		0	9	1	0		1	8

Temperature Range	FEBRUARY Obsn Hour Gp 01 to 08	09 to 16	17 to 24	Total Obsn	M C W B	MARCH Obsn Hour Gp 01 to 08	09 to 16	17 to 24	Total Obsn	M C W B	APRIL Obsn Hour Gp 01 to 08	09 to 16	17 to 24	Total Obsn	M C W B	ANNUAL TOTAL Obsn Hour Gp 01 to 08	09 to 16	17 to 24	Total Obsn	M C W B
90/94																	0		0	70
85/89																	4	1	5	69
80/84																	17	4	21	67
75/79							0		0	57		0	0	0	63	0	60	19	79	64
70/74							0		0	54		1	0	1	58	3	157	60	220	61
65/69							2	0	2	53		6	2	8	55	24	329	152	505	59
60/64		1	0	1	53		4	1	5	51		23	5	28	52	187	456	341	984	56
55/59	0	6	1	7	51	0	23	6	29	50	4	50	24	78	50	420	387	453	1260	53
50/54	11	28	17	56	48	10	60	34	104	47	30	66	51	147	47	536	407	467	1410	49
45/49	21	46	35	102	44	39	63	61	163	43	56	62	65	183	43	525	392	451	1368	44
40/44	46	53	53	152	39	68	55	67	190	39	75	28	61	164	39	464	324	409	1197	40
35/39	60	55	59	174	35	69	30	48	147	35	49	4	27	80	35	374	226	306	906	35
30/34	57	28	43	128	31	38	8	24	70	30	22	1	4	27	31	252	120	182	554	31
25/29	19	6	11	36	26	18	2	6	26	26	4		0	4	27	91	30	51	172	26
20/24	6	1	3	10	22	5	0	0	5	22	0			0	23	32	6	15	53	22
15/19	2	0	1	3	16	0			0	18						7	1	5	13	17
10/14	1			1	13											2	0	1	3	12
5/9																1	0		1	8

NORTH AMERICA

ARGENTIA NAS/PLACENTIA NFLD CANADA

LAT 47 19N LONG 53 59W ELEV 51 FT

MEAN FREQUENCY OF OCCURRENCE OF DRY BULB TEMPERATURE (DEGREES F) WITH MEAN COINCIDENT WET BULB TEMPERATURE (DEGREES F) FOR EACH DRY BULB TEMPERATURE RANGE

Temperature Range	MAY Obsn Hour Gp 01 to 08	MAY 09 to 16	MAY 17 to 24	MAY Total Obsn	MAY MCWB	JUNE Obsn Hour Gp 01 to 08	JUNE 09 to 16	JUNE 17 to 24	JUNE Total Obsn	JUNE MCWB	JULY Obsn Hour Gp 01 to 08	JULY 09 to 16	JULY 17 to 24	JULY Total Obsn	JULY MCWB
75/79												0		0	68
70/74							0	0	0	60	0	3	1	4	66
65/69		1	0	1	60	0	2	1	3	60	5	21	10	36	63
60/64	0	1	1	2	59	1	8	4	13	57	27	68	47	142	59
55/59	3	9	2	14	54	8	30	14	52	54	91	106	111	308	55
50/54	7	22	11	40	49	52	90	75	217	50	103	47	70	220	51
45/49	22	55	37	114	44	93	80	92	265	45	22	3	10	35	47
40/44	72	102	97	271	40	70	28	47	145	41	0		0	0	43
35/39	110	54	87	251	36	16	2	7	25	37					
30/34	33	5	13	51	32	0			0	33					
25/29	0			0	26										

Temperature Range	AUGUST Obsn Hour Gp 01 to 08	AUGUST 09 to 16	AUGUST 17 to 24	AUGUST Total Obsn	AUGUST MCWB	SEPTEMBER Obsn Hour Gp 01 to 08	SEPTEMBER 09 to 16	SEPTEMBER 17 to 24	SEPTEMBER Total Obsn	SEPTEMBER MCWB	OCTOBER Obsn Hour Gp 01 to 08	OCTOBER 09 to 16	OCTOBER 17 to 24	OCTOBER Total Obsn	OCTOBER MCWB
75/79		1	0	1	66										
70/74	0	5	1	6	66	1	2	0	3	66	0	0	0	0	67
65/69	9	38	18	65	63	4	10	5	19	63	2	2	1	5	63
60/64	65	124	95	284	59	16	51	24	91	58	4	8	4	16	59
55/59	126	68	106	300	56	68	101	88	257	54	16	28	18	62	54
50/54	39	10	25	74	50	88	57	86	231	50	49	73	57	179	49
45/49	8	2	4	14	45	50	18	32	100	45	83	86	94	263	44
40/44	0			0	41	12	1	4	17	40	62	39	53	154	39
35/39						0			0	35	27	10	18	55	35
30/34											5	2	3	10	30
25/29											0	0		0	26

ARGENTIA NAS/PLACENTIA NFLD CANADA

Temperature Range	NOVEMBER Obsn Hour Gp 01 to 08	NOVEMBER Obsn Hour Gp 09 to 16	NOVEMBER Obsn Hour Gp 17 to 24	NOVEMBER Total Obsn	NOVEMBER MCWB	DECEMBER Obsn Hour Gp 01 to 08	DECEMBER Obsn Hour Gp 09 to 16	DECEMBER Obsn Hour Gp 17 to 24	DECEMBER Total Obsn	DECEMBER MCWB	JANUARY Obsn Hour Gp 01 to 08	JANUARY Obsn Hour Gp 09 to 16	JANUARY Obsn Hour Gp 17 to 24	JANUARY Total Obsn	JANUARY MCWB
75/79															
70/74		0		0	67										
65/69	0	0	0	0	62										
60/64	1	2	2	5	59	0	0		0	59					
55/59	8	11	8	27	55	3	3	2	8	55		0		0	53
50/54	22	21	19	62	51	8	6	8	22	50	1	2	1	4	49
45/49	39	49	43	131	45	9	14	9	32	45	5	6	6	17	45
40/44	55	64	60	179	40	29	33	32	94	40	9	11	11	31	41
35/39	66	62	69	197	35	54	65	63	182	35	49	50	47	146	35
30/34	35	25	32	92	30	71	64	65	200	30	63	69	65	197	30
25/29	13	5	5	23	25	42	40	45	127	26	52	52	53	157	25
20/24	1		1	2	21	22	15	17	54	21	30	30	34	94	20
15/19						7	6	6	19	16	24	19	20	63	16
10/14						3	1	2	6	11	11	6	7	24	11
5/9						0		1	1	7	3	2	3	8	7
0/4											1	1	0	2	2
-5/-1											0	0		0	-4

Temperature Range	FEBRUARY Obsn Hour Gp 01 to 08	FEBRUARY Obsn Hour Gp 09 to 16	FEBRUARY Obsn Hour Gp 17 to 24	FEBRUARY Total Obsn	FEBRUARY MCWB	MARCH Obsn Hour Gp 01 to 08	MARCH Obsn Hour Gp 09 to 16	MARCH Obsn Hour Gp 17 to 24	MARCH Total Obsn	MARCH MCWB	APRIL Obsn Hour Gp 01 to 08	APRIL Obsn Hour Gp 09 to 16	APRIL Obsn Hour Gp 17 to 24	APRIL Total Obsn	APRIL MCWB
75/79															
70/74															
65/69															
60/64		0		0	59										
55/59		0	0	0	55		1	0	1	52	0	1	0	1	52
50/54	1	3	1	5	49	1	2	1	4	49	2	5	3	10	49
45/49	7	8	7	22	45	2	5	2	9	45	7	16	8	31	44
40/44	11	12	12	35	41	8	19	11	38	40	17	45	25	87	40
35/39	24	30	28	82	35	38	60	49	147	35	75	107	96	278	35
30/34	54	62	59	175	31	89	87	98	274	31	102	54	92	248	31
25/29	49	48	52	149	26	62	49	55	166	26	27	10	13	50	26
20/24	32	29	29	90	21	28	17	24	69	21	8	1	3	12	21
15/19	23	20	21	64	16	15	7	6	28	16	2		0	2	17
10/14	14	8	11	33	11	5	1	1	7	12					
5/9	4	3	3	10	6	1	0	0	1	7					
0/4	4	1	1	6	2										
-5/-1	0			0	-3										

Temperature Range	ANNUAL TOTAL Obsn Hour Gp 01 to 08	ANNUAL TOTAL Obsn Hour Gp 09 to 16	ANNUAL TOTAL Obsn Hour Gp 17 to 24	ANNUAL TOTAL Total Obsn	ANNUAL TOTAL MCWB
75/79		1	0	1	67
70/74	1	10	2	13	66
65/69	20	74	35	129	63
60/64	114	262	177	553	59
55/59	323	358	349	1030	55
50/54	373	338	357	1068	50
45/49	347	342	344	1033	45
40/44	345	354	352	1051	40
35/39	459	440	464	1363	35
30/34	452	368	427	1247	31
25/29	245	204	223	672	26
20/24	121	92	108	321	21
15/19	71	52	53	176	16
10/14	33	16	21	70	11
5/9	8	5	7	20	7
0/4	5	2	1	8	2
-5/-1	0	0		0	-3

THULE AB GREENLAND

LAT 76 32N LONG 68 42W ELEV 253 FT

MEAN FREQUENCY OF OCCURRENCE OF DRY BULB TEMPERATURE (DEGREES F) WITH MEAN COINCIDENT WET BULB TEMPERATURE (DEGREES F) FOR EACH DRY BULB TEMPERATURE RANGE

Temperature Range	MAY Obsn Hour Gp 01 to 08	MAY 09 to 16	MAY 17 to 24	MAY Total Obsn	MAY MCWB	JUNE Obsn Hour Gp 01 to 08	JUNE 09 to 16	JUNE 17 to 24	JUNE Total Obsn	JUNE MCWB	JULY Obsn Hour Gp 01 to 08	JULY 09 to 16	JULY 17 to 24	JULY Total Obsn	JULY MCWB
60/64							0	0	0	51	0	0	0	0	50
55/59						0	1	1	2	48	1	3	1	5	46
50/54						3	6	4	13	42	10	17	14	41	44
45/49	0		0	0	38	10	12	10	32	39	33	40	37	110	41
40/44	2	4	2	8	35	19	29	27	75	36	59	73	65	197	38
35/39	6	12	7	25	32	54	67	58	179	33	82	74	79	235	35
30/34	23	41	35	99	29	87	88	94	269	30	57	38	48	143	31
25/29	45	58	55	158	25	55	33	41	129	26	7	2	4	13	28
20/24	58	61	62	181	20	10	4	5	19	21					
15/19	46	31	33	110	16	0			0	18					
10/14	24	22	22	68	11										
5/9	17	13	14	44	6										
0/4	15	5	11	31	1										
-5/-1	8	2	6	16	-3										
-10/-6	5	1	2	8	-7										
-15/-11	1		0	1	-13										
-20/-16	0		0	0	-17										
-25/-21															

Temperature Range	AUGUST Obsn Hour Gp 01 to 08	AUGUST 09 to 16	AUGUST 17 to 24	AUGUST Total Obsn	AUGUST MCWB	SEPTEMBER Obsn Hour Gp 01 to 08	SEPTEMBER 09 to 16	SEPTEMBER 17 to 24	SEPTEMBER Total Obsn	SEPTEMBER MCWB	OCTOBER Obsn Hour Gp 01 to 08	OCTOBER 09 to 16	OCTOBER 17 to 24	OCTOBER Total Obsn	OCTOBER MCWB
60/64															
55/59	0	1	0	1	45										
50/54	6	12	8	26	44										
45/49	25	41	30	96	41	1	2	0	3	38					
40/44	56	80	64	200	38	5	12	7	24	36	0			0	36
35/39	85	75	89	249	34	24	43	29	96	33	1	2	1	4	33
30/34	60	35	47	142	30	60	76	70	206	29	12	13	10	35	29
25/29	16	5	9	30	27	63	52	56	171	25	27	29	28	84	25
20/24	0			0	22	46	35	39	120	20	35	41	34	110	20
15/19						22	12	21	55	16	46	40	41	127	15
10/14						12	6	9	27	11	38	39	46	123	11
5/9						6	2	6	14	6	36	35	33	104	6
0/4						2	0	2	4	2	26	27	28	81	1
-5/-1						0	0		0	-3	17	15	18	50	-3
-10/-6											6	4	7	17	-8
-15/-11											2	1	2	5	-13
-20/-16											1	1	1	3	-18
-25/-21											1	0		1	-22

THULE AB GREENLAND

Temperature Range	NOVEMBER Obsn Hour Gp 01 to 08	09 to 16	17 to 24	Total Obsn	MCWB	DECEMBER Obsn Hour Gp 01 to 08	09 to 16	17 to 24	Total Obsn	MCWB
60/64										
55/59										
50/54										
45/49										
40/44	0			0	34					
35/39	0	0		0	32	0	0		0	29
30/34	3	3	3	9	29	1	1	1	3	28
25/29	5	4	5	14	24	1	1	2	4	24
20/24	10	11	11	32	19	3	3	3	9	19
15/19	18	18	18	54	15	6	6	7	19	15
10/14	37	31	31	99	11	10	11	14	35	11
5/9	34	36	35	105	6	19	18	17	54	6
0/4	36	36	33	105	1	23	23	20	66	1
-5/-1	28	30	30	88	-4	29	29	27	85	-4
-10/-6	26	28	31	85	-8	42	40	41	123	-9
-15/-11	23	25	24	72	-13	39	41	40	120	-13
-20/-16	15	14	14	43	-18	35	36	34	105	-18
-25/-21	4	4	4	12	-22	25	25	25	75	-23
-30/-26	1	1	1	3	-27	10	10	11	31	-28
-35/-31	0			0	-31	3	3	4	10	-32
-40/-36							0		0	
-45/-41										

Temperature Range	JANUARY Obsn Hour Gp 01 to 08	09 to 16	17 to 24	Total Obsn	MCWB	FEBRUARY Obsn Hour Gp 01 to 08	09 to 16	17 to 24	Total Obsn	MCWB
60/64										
55/59										
50/54										
45/49										
40/44							0	0	0	34
35/39	0	0	0	0	32	0	1	0	1	31
30/34	2	3	2	7	28	3	3	3	9	28
25/29	4	2	4	10	25	3	2	4	9	24
20/24	4	5	4	13	20	2	3	2	7	20
15/19	5	7	4	16	15	3	6	3	12	15
10/14	9	6	11	26	10	9	10	7	26	10
5/9	13	12	14	39	5	16	15	14	45	6
0/4	25	24	24	73	1	17	15	16	48	1
-5/-1	26	27	22	75	-4	24	19	27	70	-4
-10/-6	29	29	28	86	-9	25	26	25	76	-9
-15/-11	34	32	35	101	-14	28	30	27	85	-14
-20/-16	42	41	39	122	-18	32	33	32	97	-18
-25/-21	33	36	33	102	-23	30	33	30	93	-23
-30/-26	15	15	19	49	-28	20	18	19	57	-28
-35/-31	7	6	8	21	-33	10	10	10	30	-33
-40/-36	2	1	1	4		2	1	3	6	
-45/-41										

Temperature Range	MARCH Obsn Hour Gp 01 to 08	09 to 16	17 to 24	Total Obsn	MCWB	APRIL Obsn Hour Gp 01 to 08	09 to 16	17 to 24	Total Obsn	MCWB
60/64										
55/59										
50/54										
45/49										
40/44										
35/39						0	1	0	1	32
30/34	0	0	0	0	28	1	1	1	3	28
25/29	1	1	1	3	25	2	3	3	8	24
20/24	1	1	0	2	20	4	11	5	20	19
15/19	1	2	1	4	15	11	18	13	42	15
10/14	3	4	4	11	10	17	29	23	69	10
5/9	5	7	5	17	5	20	35	27	82	6
0/4	12	17	13	42	1	28	48	38	114	1
-5/-1	24	27	25	76	-4	40	48	44	132	-4
-10/-6	28	38	31	97	-9	50	29	40	119	-8
-15/-11	39	50	41	130	-14	36	8	27	71	-13
-20/-16	47	43	47	137	-18	16	6	11	33	-18
-25/-21	39	27	36	102	-23	8	2	7	17	-23
-30/-26	21	16	21	58	-28	5	1	2	8	-28
-35/-31	16	12	15	43	-33	1		0	1	-32
-40/-36	10	2	6	18						
-45/-41	1		0	1						

Temperature Range	ANNUAL TOTAL Obsn Hour Gp 01 to 08	09 to 16	17 to 24	Total Obsn	MCWB
60/64	0	0	0	0	51
55/59	1	5	2	8	46
50/54	19	35	26	80	43
45/49	69	95	77	241	41
40/44	141	198	165	504	38
35/39	252	275	263	790	34
30/34	309	302	314	925	30
25/29	229	192	212	633	25
20/24	173	175	165	513	20
15/19	158	140	141	439	15
10/14	159	158	167	484	11
5/9	166	173	165	504	6
0/4	184	195	185	564	1
-5/-1	196	197	199	592	-4
-10/-6	211	195	205	611	-9
-15/-11	202	187	196	585	-13
-20/-16	188	174	178	540	-18
-25/-21	140	127	135	402	-23
-30/-26	72	61	73	206	-28
-35/-31	37	31	37	105	-33
-40/-36	14	4	10	28	
-45/-41	1		0	1	

PACIFIC OCEAN

GUAM/ANDERSEN AFB MARIANA ISLANDS

LAT 13 35N LONG 144 55E ELEV 624 FT

MEAN FREQUENCY OF OCCURRENCE OF DRY BULB TEMPERATURE (DEGREES F) WITH MEAN COINCIDENT WET BULB TEMPERATURE (DEGREES F) FOR EACH DRY BULB TEMPERATURE RANGE

Tempera-ture Range	MAY Obsn Hour Gp 01 to 08	MAY 09 to 16	MAY 17 to 24	MAY Total Obsn	MAY MCWB	JUNE Obsn Hour Gp 01 to 08	JUNE 09 to 16	JUNE 17 to 24	JUNE Total Obsn	JUNE MCWB	JULY Obsn Hour Gp 01 to 08	JULY 09 to 16	JULY 17 to 24	JULY Total Obsn	JULY MCWB
90/94		0		0	78		0		0	79		0		0	79
85/89	0	30	1	31	77	0	43	3	46	78	0	37	3	40	78
80/84	43	196	90	329	76	63	171	129	363	76	59	175	121	355	77
75/79	199	21	155	375	74	174	25	107	306	75	180	34	122	336	75
70/74	5	1	2	8	72	3	1	1	5	72	8	2	2	12	72

Tempera-ture Range	AUGUST Obsn Hour Gp 01 to 08	AUGUST 09 to 16	AUGUST 17 to 24	AUGUST Total Obsn	AUGUST MCWB	SEPTEMBER Obsn Hour Gp 01 to 08	SEPTEMBER 09 to 16	SEPTEMBER 17 to 24	SEPTEMBER Total Obsn	SEPTEMBER MCWB	OCTOBER Obsn Hour Gp 01 to 08	OCTOBER 09 to 16	OCTOBER 17 to 24	OCTOBER Total Obsn	OCTOBER MCWB
90/94		0		0	77							0		0	79
85/89	0	37	2	39	78		23	0	23	78		27	0	27	78
80/84	61	172	125	358	77	42	172	94	308	77	56	177	109	342	77
75/79	174	33	116	323	75	188	42	140	370	75	181	41	136	358	75
70/74	13	5	5	23	72	11	4	6	21	72	11	2	3	16	72

											0		0	80																	0		0	78
	22	0	22	78		7	0	7	77		3		3	76		2		2	76		2		2	75		5		5	77	0	238	9	247	78
62	193	109	364	77	30	189	56	275	76	10	139	29	178	74	6	118	21	145	74	2	162	25	189	74	9	194	43	246	75	443	2058	951	3452	76
172	24	130	326	75	211	50	190	451	74	204	100	205	509	73	184	98	190	472	72	220	81	216	517	73	221	39	195	455	73	2308	588	1902	4798	74
6	I	I	8	72	7	2	2	11	71	33	5	14	52	71	34	6	13	53	71	26	3	7	36	71	10	2	3	15	71	167	34	59	260	71
					0			0	65	0		0	0	66						0		0	0	65						0		0	0	66

MIDWAY NAVSTA MIDWAY ISLAND

LAT 28 12N LONG 177 23W ELEV 12 FT

MEAN FREQUENCY OF OCCURRENCE OF DRY BULB TEMPERATURE (DEGREES F) WITH MEAN COINCIDENT WET BULB TEMPERATURE (DEGREES F) FOR EACH DRY BULB TEMPERATURE RANGE

Temperature Range	MAY Obsn Hour Gp 01 to 08	MAY 09 to 16	MAY 17 to 24	MAY Total Obsn	MAY MCWB	JUNE Obsn Hour Gp 01 to 08	JUNE 09 to 16	JUNE 17 to 24	JUNE Total Obsn	JUNE MCWB	JULY Obsn Hour Gp 01 to 08	JULY 09 to 16	JULY 17 to 24	JULY Total Obsn	JULY MCWB
85/89		0		0	74		2	0	2	77		1	0	1	74
80/84		9	1	10	72	6	65	20	91	74	5	143	38	186	74
75/79	11	69	30	110	70	91	132	126	349	72	190	96	186	472	72
70/74	99	119	115	333	67	117	36	81	234	68	52	7	24	83	70
65/69	113	46	84	243	63	25	5	12	42	63	1	0	0	1	68
60/64	25	5	17	47	58	1	0	1	2	61					
55/59	0			0	58										

Temperature Range	AUGUST Obsn Hour Gp 01 to 08	AUGUST 09 to 16	AUGUST 17 to 24	AUGUST Total Obsn	AUGUST MCWB	SEPTEMBER Obsn Hour Gp 01 to 08	SEPTEMBER 09 to 16	SEPTEMBER 17 to 24	SEPTEMBER Total Obsn	SEPTEMBER MCWB	OCTOBER Obsn Hour Gp 01 to 08	OCTOBER 09 to 16	OCTOBER 17 to 24	OCTOBER Total Obsn	OCTOBER MCWB
85/89		4	1	5	76		9	0	9	74		1		1	75
80/84	14	189	70	273	74	22	175	69	266	74	1	58	8	67	73
75/79	217	50	170	437	73	191	50	153	394	72	100	123	116	339	71
70/74	17	5	7	29	71	27	7	17	51	68	128	60	110	298	67
65/69	0	0	0	0	68	1	0	1	2	67	17	7	14	38	61
60/64											1	0	0	1	60
55/59															

85/89																															17	I	18	75
80/84		8	0	.8	73		0		0	68												0		0	70		0		0	73	48	647	206	90I	74
75/79	21	84	29	134	71	1	22	4	27	70		3	0	3	69	0.	3	0	3	68		9	2	II	69	0	17	3	20	68	822	658	819	2299	72
70/74	126	103	123	352	67	71	108	77	256	67	25	62	36	123	66	13	50	24	87	66	24	73	37	134	66	28	89	52	169	66	727	719	703	2149	67
65/69	80	4I	77	198	62	117	94	115	326	62	94	114	101	309	62	87	109	96	292	62	107	113	III	331	62	II4	I02	113	329	62	756	631	724	2111	62
60/64	12	4	I0	26	59	53	23	48	124	57	109	63	98	270	'57	100	58	88	246	57	97	50	86	233	57	91	30	69	190	58	489	233	417	II39	57
55/59	1	1	0	2	87	7	1	4	12	55	20	5	13	38	54	24	4	16	44	53	18	3	12	33	52	7	1	4	12	53	77	15	49	I4I	53
50/54							0		0	53	0	0	0	0	5i	0			0	51	1		0	1	49	0	0	0	0	50	1	0	0	I	50

CLARK AB PHILIPPINE ISLANDS

LAT 15 11N LONG 120 33E ELEV 478 FT

MEAN FREQUENCY OF OCCURRENCE OF DRY BULB TEMPERATURE (DEGREES F) WITH MEAN COINCIDENT WET BULB TEMPERATURE (MCWB) FOR EACH DRY BULB TEMPERATURE RANGE

Temperature Range	MAY Obsn Hour Gp 01 to 08	MAY 09 to 16	MAY 17 to 24	MAY Total Obsn	MAY MCWB	JUNE Obsn Hour Gp 01 to 08	JUNE 09 to 16	JUNE 17 to 24	JUNE Total Obsn	JUNE MCWB	JULY Obsn Hour Gp 01 to 08	JULY 09 to 16	JULY 17 to 24	JULY Total Obsn	JULY MCWB
95/99		16	1	17	75		2	0	2	77		0		0	81
90/94		97	21	118	76		45	4	49	78		18	2	20	78
85/89	9	93	45	147	76	5	96	25	126	77	2	95	16	113	77
80/84	77	29	101	207	74	36	64	74	174	76	21	90	61	172	76
75/79	148	12	73	233	73	167	29	123	319	74	171	40	145	356	74
70/74	14	2	7	23	71	32	4	13	49	72	54	5	24	83	72
65/69															

Temperature Range	AUGUST Obsn Hour Gp 01 to 08	AUGUST 09 to 16	AUGUST 17 to 24	AUGUST Total Obsn	AUGUST MCWB	SEPTEMBER Obsn Hour Gp 01 to 08	SEPTEMBER 09 to 16	SEPTEMBER 17 to 24	SEPTEMBER Total Obsn	SEPTEMBER MCWB	OCTOBER Obsn Hour Gp 01 to 08	OCTOBER 09 to 16	OCTOBER 17 to 24	OCTOBER Total Obsn	OCTOBER MCWB
95/99							0		0	81					
90/94		15	1	16	78		6	0	6	77		8		8	77
85/89	1	79	10	90	77	1	76	7	84	77	0	113	8	121	75
80/84	18	98	51	167	76	11	106	45	162	76	16	101	65	182	74
75/79	166	53	159	378	74	156	48	164	368	74	172	22	157	351	73
70/74	62	4	26	92	72	72	3	24	99	72	60	3	18	81	70
65/69	0			0	67						0			0	67

																0		0	73		3	0	3	74		8	0	8	74		29	I	30	75
	4		4	75		2		2	74		4		4	73		14	I	15	72		59	8	67	73		104	20	124	74		376	57	433	75
0	90	3	93	74		89	3	92	73		68	7	75	71		77	15	92	71	0	104	34	138	72	3	94	47	144	74	21	1074	220	1315	75
7	110	47	164	73	3	119	40	162	71	I	115	36	152	70	2	93	42	137	70	13	69	76	158	71	46	31	I00	177	73	251	1025	738	2014	73
133	32	152	317	71	90	35	I4I	266	70	45	52	112	209	69	44	36	96	176	69	128	12	105	245	70	162	3	70	235	71	1582	374	1497	3453	72
94	4	38	136	68	135	3	61	199	67	147	7	80	234	66	134	3	63	200	66	97	1	24	122	67	28	0	4	32	68	929	39	382	1350	68
6		I	7	64	20		3	23	63	52	0	13	65	62	42	0	8	50	62	10		1	II	63	1		0	I	63	131	0	26	157	63
					0			0	60	3		0	3	58	2		0	2	58	I		0	1	56	0			0	60	6		0	6	58
										0			0	54																0			0	54

CHAPTER 5

COOLING DEGREE DAY DATA FOR SITES IN THE UNITED STATES

State Station	Annual Cooling Degree Days
ALABAMA	
Alabama Ordnance Works	1886
Anniston Army Depot	1886
Birmingham MAP	1928
Brookley AFB/Mobile	2549
Craig AFB/Selma	2550
Florence	1834
Fort McClellan/Reilly AAF	1886
Fort Rucker/Cairns AAF	2386
Gadsden	1751
Gunter AFS	2489
Hall ANG Station	2386
Hunter Loop Comm Facility	2489
Huntsville	1808
Maxwell AFB/Montgomery	2489
Mobile/Bates Field	2577
Montgomery/Dannelly Field	2238
Muscle Shoals	1834
Redstone Arsenal	1808
Sheffield	1834
Tuscaloosa MAP	2138
ALASKA	
Anchorage IAP	0
Annette	14
Barrow	0
Bethel	0
Bettles	0
Big Delta/Allen AAF	34
Cold Bay AFS	0
Cordova	0
Eielson AFB/Fairbanks	30
Elmendorf AFB/Anchorage	8

State Station	Annual Cooling Degree Days
Fairbanks IAP	32
Gulkana	9
Homer	0
Juneau MAP	0
King Salmon	0
Kodiak	0
Kotzebue	0
McGrath MAP	14
Nenana	19
Nome MAP	0
Northway Aprt	19
St. Paul Island	0
Shemya AFB	0
Sitka	0
Tanana	20
Unalakleet	0
Yakutat	0
ARIZONA	
Davis-Monthan AFB/Tucson	2985
Flagstaff	140
Fort Huachuca/Libby AAF	1573
Gila Bend	3943
Holbrook	1091
Luke AFB/Glendale	3601
Navajo Army Depot	140
Phoenix/Sky Harbor IAP	3508
Tucson IAP	2896
Williams AFB/Chandler	3503
Winslow MAP	1203
Yuma MCAS/IAP	4195
Yuma Test Station	4261

State Station	Annual Cooling Degree Days
ARKANSAS	
Blytheville AFB	1789
El Dorado/Goodwin Field	2204
Fayetteville/Drake Field	1487
Fort Chaffee	2022
Fort Smith MAP	2022
Harrison	1447
Hot Springs	2205
Little Rock/Adams Field	1925
Little Rock AFB	2034
Pine Bluff Arsenal	2314
Texarkana/Webb Field MAP	2245
Walnut Ridge MAP	1938
CALIFORNIA	
Alameda NAS/Nimitz Field	189
Arcata	0
Bakersfield/Meadows Field	2179
Barstow-Daggett Aprt	2729
Beale AFB/Marysville	1525
Berkeley	86
Bishop	1037
Blue Canyon Aprt	302
Burbank	1179
Camp Parks Comm Annex	713
Camp Roberts	699
Castle AFB/Merced	1566
Centerville Beach	0
Chico MAP	1385
China Lake NAF/Armitage Fld	2549
Chula Vista	333
Compton	1085

State Station	Annual Cooli Degree Da
Concord NAD	7
Corona	11
Coronado	4
Costa Mesa ANG Station	6
Crows Landing	11
Cuddeback Dry Lake Range	18
Daggett	27
Dixon	9
Edwards AFB	18
El Centro NAF	43
El Toro MCAS/Santa Ana	8
Fallbrook Annex	9
Fort Baker	
Fort Barry	
Fort Irwin	22
Fort MacArthur	6
Fort Mason	
Fort Ord/Fritzsche AAF	
Fresno/Air Terminal	16
George AFB/Victorville	18
Hamilton AFB/San Rafael	2
Imperial Beach NF/Ream Fld	4
Klamath AFS	
Kramer	18
Lemoore NAS/Reeves Field	17
Letterman Army Hospital	
Livermore	7
Long Beach	6
Long Beach/Daugherty Field	9
Los Alamitos NAS	6
Los Angeles City Office	11

State Station	Annual Cooling Degree Days
CALIFORNIA (continued)	
Los Angeles IAP	615
March AFB/Riverside	1310
Mare Island NAVSHIPYD	244
Mather AFB/Sacramento	1303
McClellan AFB/Sacramento	1406
Miramir NAS/Mitscher Field	717
Moffett Field NAS	239
Mojave	1958
Montague/Siskiyou Co Aprt	562
Monterey FWC	32
Monterey/Presidio	32
Mt Laguna AFS	449
North Highlands ANGB	1406
Norton AFB/San Bernardino	1499
Oakland Army Base	128
Oakland IAP	128
Oakland Navy Hospital	420
Ontario IAP	1499
Palmdale	1724
Pasadena	1187
Pendleton MCB	717
Pendleton MCB Coast	584
Pillar Point AFS	5
Pt Arena AFS	0
Pt Arguello	0
Pt Mugu NAS/Port Hueneme	200
Pt Sur NF	32
Pamona	1109
Port Hueneme	200
Red Bluff MAP	1904
Red Mountain Flight Annex	2113
Riverbank AAP	1566
Sacramento	1159
Sacramento Army Depot	1159
San Bernardino	1557
San Bruno	108
San Clemente Is NALF	201
Sandberg	800
San Diego FWF	584
San Diego IAP	722
San Francisco IAP	108
San Francisco/Presidio	39
San Jose MAP	444
San Luis Obispo	246
San Nicolas Island	204
San Pedro	615
San Rafael	280
Santa Ana MCAS	972
Santa Barbara MAP	218
Santa Catalina	613
Santa Maria	84
Santa Rosa/Sonoma Co Aprt	315
Seal Beach NAD	615
Shafter AFS	2179
Sharpe Army Depot	1259
Skaggs Is NSGA	244
Stockton	1259
Sunnyvale	239

State Station	Annual Cooling Degree Days
CALIFORNIA (continued)	
Travis AFB/Fairfield	831
Treasure Is NS	189
Twentynine Palms MCB	2948
Two Rock Ranch Station	293
Vandenberg AFB/Lompoc	66
Van Nuys/Los Angeles	1179
West Coast Radio Station	781
COLORADO	
Buckley ANGB/Denver	582
Colorado Springs/Peterson	461
Denver/Stapleton IAP	625
Ent AFB/Colorado Springs	561
Fitzsimons AH/Denver	625
Fort Carson/Butts AAF	692
Grand Junction/Walker Field	1140
La Junta	998
Lamar	1199
Lowry AFB/Denver	625
Pueblo Army Depot	981
Pueblo Memorial Aprt	981
Rocky Mountain Arsenal	625
Trinidad	705
USAF Academy/Colorado Springs	100
CONNECTICUT	
Bradley IAP/Windsor Locks	584
Bridgeport	735
Groton	376
Hartford/Brainard Aprt	605
New Haven	573
Stamford	735

State Station	Annual Cool[illegible] Degree D[illegible]
Waterbury	[illegible]
DELAWARE	
Dover AFB	1[illegible]
Lewes	[illegible]
Wilmington	[illegible]
Wilmington Airport	[illegible]
DISTRICT OF COLUMBIA	
Army Map Service	1[illegible]
Bolling-Anacostia Mil Cmplx	1[illegible]
Fort McNair	1[illegible]
Walter Reed Army Medical Cen	1[illegible]
Washington National Aprt	1[illegible]
Washington Navy Yard	1[illegible]
FLORIDA	
Apalachicola	2[illegible]
Avon Park	3[illegible]
Big Coppitt Key	4[illegible]
Bowman Bayou	2[illegible]
Brandon	3[illegible]
Cape Canaveral AFS	2[illegible]
Clausen	2[illegible]
Cocoa Beach	3[illegible]
Daytona Beach	2[illegible]
Eglin AFB/Valparaiso	2[illegible]
Fort Lauderdale	3[illegible]
Fort Myers/Page Fld	3[illegible]
Gainesville MAP	2[illegible]
Homestead AFB	3[illegible]
Hurlburt Field/Eglin No 9	2[illegible]
Jacksonville AFS	3[illegible]

State Station	Annual Cooling Degree Days
FLORIDA (continued)	
Jacksonville/Cecil Fld NAS	[illegible]
Jacksonville IAP	2596
Jacksonville NAS/Towers Fld	3059
Jupiter	3786
Key West IAP	4888
Key West NAS	4663
Lakeland	3298
Lynn Haven	2778
Macdill AFB/Tampa	3493
Mayport NAVSTA	2683
McCoy AFB/Orlando	3354
Melbourne Beach	3265
Miami IAP	4038
Milton/Whiting Field NAS	2588
Orlando	3447
Panama City/Bay County	2778
Patrick AFB/Cocoa Beach	3405
Pensacola/Ellyson Field NAS	2562
Pensacola NAS/F Sherman Fld	2642
Pensacola/Saufley Field NAS	2562
Ponce de Leon	2919
Richmond AFS	3906
Rivera Beach	3786
St. Augustine	2794
St. Petersburg/Clearwater IAP	3410
Tallahassee MAP	2563
Tampa IAP	3366
Tyndall AFB/Panama City	2737
Valkaria	3352
Vero Beach	3512

State Station	Annual Cooling Degree Days
West Palm Beach	3786
GEORGIA	
Albany NAS/Turner AFB	2631
Athens MAP	1722
Atlanta Army Depot	1589
Atlanta/Hartsfield IAP	1589
Atlanta NAS/Dobbins AFB	1611
Augusta/Bush Field	1995
Augusta/Daniel Field	1995
Columbus Metro Aprt	2143
Dobbins AFB/Marietta	1611
Fort Benning/Lawson AAF	2203
Fort Gordon	1995
Fort McPherson/Atlanta	1589
Fort Stewart/Wright AAF	2414
Glynco NAS/Brunswick	2423
Hunter AAF/Savannah	2372
Macon/L B Wilson Aprt ANG	2294
McCollum Aprt ANG/Marietta	1611
McKinnon Aprt ANG/Brunswick	2774
Moody AFB/Valdosta	2716
Moultrie/Spence AF Aux Fld	2513
Robins AFB/Macon	2276
Rome/Russell Field	1615
Savannah AFS	2372
Savannah ANG Sta	2372
Savannah MAP ANG	2317
Statesboro Radar Bomb Site	2317
Turner AFB/Albany NAS	2631

State / Station	Annual Cooling Degree Days
HAWAII	
Barbers Point NAS	3929
Barking Sands	3497
Bellows AFB	3719
Ford Island	4221
Ft DeRussy	4221
Ft Ruger	3881
Ft Shafter	4221
Helemano	2807
Hickam AFB/Honolulu IAP	4221
Hilo	3066
Kaala AFS	24
Kaena Point	1850
Kahului	3732
Kaneohe Bay MCAS	4080
Kunia Comm Annex	2821
Lihue	3719
Palehua AF Solar Obsy	1925
Pearl Harbor	4221
Punamano AFS	3623
Schofield Barracks	2821
South Point AFS	2873
Tripler Army Hospital	4221
Wahiawa	2821
Wheeler AFB	2821
IDAHO	
Boise	714
Idaho Falls/Fanning Fld	286
Lewiston	657
Mountain Home AFB	907
Pocatello	437
Saylor Creek	513

State / Station	Annual Cooling Degree Days
Twin Falls	399
Wilder	568
ILLINOIS	
Chanute AFB	1052
Chicago/Midway Aprt	925
Chicago/O'Hare IAP	664
Danville/Vermilion Co	997
Decatur	1197
Forest Park NOP	925
Fort Sheridan/Haley AAF	826
Galesburg MAP	951
Glenview NAS	832
Granite City Army Depot	1640
Great Lakes NTC	826
Joliet MAP	933
Moline/Quad City Arpt	893
Peoria	968
Quincy MAP	1380
Rock Island Arsenal	1007
Savanna Army Depot	741
Scott AFB/Belleville	1421
Springfield/Capital	1116
INDIANA	
Anderson MAP	981
Bakalar AFB/Columbus	1017
Bloomington/Monroe County	1177
Camp Atterbury	1017
Crane	1302
Evansville/Dress Rgnl Aprt	1364
Fort Benjamin Harrison	974
Fort Wayne/Baer Fld	748

State Station	Annual Cooling Degree Days
INDIANA (continued)	
Gary MAP	859
Grissom AFB/Bunker Hill	837
Indiana AAF	1268
Indianapolis/Weir Cook MAP	974
Jefferson Proving Ground	1191
Newport AAP	1094
South Bend/St Joseph Aprt	695
Terre Haute/Hulman Fld	1110
IOWA	
Burlington MAP	994
Cedar Rapids MAP	812
Des Moines MAP	928
Dubuque MAP	606
Fort Dodge MAP	779
Iowa Army Ammunition Plant	994
Iowa City MAP	886
Mason City MAP	580
Sioux City MAP	932
Waterloo MAP	675
KANSAS	
Chanute	1595
Dodge City	1411
Forbes ANGB/Topeka	1430
Fort Leavenworth/Sherman AAF	1292
Fort Riley/Marshall AAF	1503
Goodland/Renner Fld	925
Hutchinson MAP	1626
Kansas City/Fairfax MAP	1420
Kansas Ordnance Plant	1808
McConnell AFB/Wichita	1687

State Station	Annual Cooling Degree Days
Olathe NAS	1370
Parsons/Tri City	1677
Salina MAP	1627
Schilling Manor	1627
Smoky Hill AF Range	1626
Sunflower Ordnance Works	1370
Topeka/Philip Billard	1361
Wichita	1673
KENTUCKY	
Ashland	1173
Blue Grass Army Depot	1197
Covington	1080
Fort Campbell/Campbell AAF	1472
Fort Knox/Godman AAF	1360
Lexington/Blue Grass Field	1197
Louisville/Standiford Field	1268
Owensboro	1444
Richmond	1197
LOUISIANA	
Alexandria/Esler Field	2193
Barksdale AFB/Shreveport	2451
Baton Rouge/Ryan Aprt	2585
Claibourne	2606
England AFB/Alexandria	2606
Fort Polk/Polk AAF	2666
Hammond ANG Comm Sta	2575
Lafayette	2632
Lake Charles AFS	2739
Lake Charles MAP	2739
Louisiana Ordnance Plant	2451
Monroe MAP	2367

State Station	Annual Cooling Degree Days
LOUISIANA (continued)	
New Orleans Army Terminal	2706
New Orleans/Moisant IAP	2706
New Orleans NAS	2703
Shreveport	2538
MAINE	
Augusta	271
Bangor IAP/Dow AFB	304
Bar Harbor	167
Brunswick NAS	308
Bucks Harbor AFS	121
Caribou MAP	128
Caswell AFS	152
Charleston AFS	93
Loring AFB	152
Millinocket	231
Portland	252
Searsport	200
Winter Harbor	167
MARYLAND	
Aberdeen PG/Phillips AAF	1076
Andrews AFB	1237
Annapolis USNA	1155
Bainbridge NTC	1076
Baltimore/Martin Aprt	1115
Baltimore/Washington IAP	1108
Bethesda NAVNATMEDCEN	1147
Cumberland MAP	828
Edgewood Arsenal	1115
Fort Detrick	948

State Station	Annual Co[illegible] Degree
Fort Holabird	
Fort Meade/Tipton AAF	
Fort Richie	
Frederick	
Hagerstown	
Indian Head NOS	
Patuxent River NAS	
White Oak NAVSURFWPNCEN	
MASSACHUSETTS	
Army Mat/Mech Res Cen	
Boston/Logan IAP	
Boston Navy Base	
Fall River	
Fort Devens/Devens AAF	
Hanscom AFB/Bedford	
Lawrence MAP	
Lynn	
Maynard	
Nantucket	
Natick Laboratories	
New Bedford MAP	
North Truro AFS	
Otis AFB/Falmouth	
Pittsfield MAP	
Quincy	
Salem	
South Weymouth NAS	
Springfield	
Wellesly ANG Station	
Westfield/Barnes MAP	
Westover AFB	

State Station	Annual Cooling Degree Days
MASSACHUSETTS (continued)	
Worcester	387
MICHIGAN	
Alpena/Phelps Collins Field	208
Ann Arbor	706
Battle Creek Aprt	628
Bayshore	349
Benton Harbor/Ross Field	638
Calumet AFS	105
Detroit Arsenal	743
Detroit/City Aprt	743
Empire AFS	302
Flint/Bishop Aprt	438
Grand Rapids/Kent County	575
Hancock/Houghton Co Mem	167
Houghton	167
Kincheloe AFB	173
K I Sawyer AFB	198
Lansing/Capital City Aprt	535
Michigan Army Missile Plant	743
Mount Clemens NAF	661
Muskegon/Muskegon Co Aprt	469
Port Austin AFS	366
Port Huron	605
Saginaw/Tri City Aprt	487
Sault Sainte Marie AFS	139
Selfridge ANGB/Mt Clemens	661
Traverse City Aprt	376
Wurtsmith AFB/Oscoda	363
Ypsilanti	726

State Station	Annual Cooling Degree Days
MINNESOTA	
Baudette AFS	254
Bemidji MAP	241
Duluth IAP	176
Finland AFS	148
International Falls IAP	176
Minneapolis-St. Paul IAP	527
Rochester MAP	474
Twin Cities Ordnance Plant	527
MISSISSIPPI	
Columbus AFB	2039
Gulfport	2682
Jackson/Allen Thompson Fld	2321
Keesler AFB/Biloxi	2793
Meridian/Key Field ANG	2231
Meridian NAS/McCain Fld	1935
MISSOURI	
Columbia Regional Aprt	1269
Fort Leonard Wood/Forney AAF	1314
Gateway AAP	1605
Hannibal	1138
Jefferson Barracks ANG	1640
Joplin MAP	1670
Kansas City MAP	1420
Lake City Arsenal	1261
Malden MAP	1780
Richards-Gebaur AFB/Grandview	1261
St. Joseph/Rosecrans Aprt	1334
St. Louis AFS	1475
St. Louis/Lambert IAP	1475
St. Louis Ordnance Depot	1640

State Station	Annual Cooling Degree Days
MISSOURI (continued)	
Springfield MAP	1382
Whiteman AFB/Knob Noster	1410
MONTANA	
Billings/Logan IAP	498
Butte	58
Cut Bank	140
Dillon	199
Glasgow AFB	404
Great Falls IAP	339
Havre AFS	304
Helena	256
Kalispell AFS	9
Lewistown	192
Malmstrom AFB	370
Miles City	752
Missoula	188
Opheim AFS	350
NEBRASKA	
Cornhusker AAP	1036
Grand Island	1036
Hastings MAP	1107
Lincoln MAP	1148
North Platte/Lee Bird Fld	802
Offutt AFB	1157
Omaha/Eppley Airfield	1173
Scottsbluff	666
NEVADA	
Bald Mountain	102
Beatty	826

State Station	Annual Cool Degree D
Carson City	
Cherry Creek	
Desert Rock Camp	1
Egan Range	
Elko MAP	
Ely	
Fallon AFS	
Fallon NAS/Van Voorhis Fld	
Goshute	
Hawthorne NAD	
Indian Springs AF Aux Fld	1
Las Vegas/McCarran IAP	2
Nellis AFB/Las Vegas	3
Reno IAP	[illegible]
Stead AFB/Reno	[illegible]
Tonopah AFS	[illegible]
Tonopah MAP	[illegible]
Winnemucca AFS	[illegible]
Winnemucca MAP	4
Worthington Mountain	3
NEW HAMPSHIRE	
Concord MAP	3
Grenier Fld/Manchester	3
Hanover	3
Manchester	3
NH Satellite Tracking	3
Pease AFB/Portsmouth	4
Portsmouth	2

State Station	Annual Cooling Degree Days
NEW JERSEY	
Atlantic City	864
Bayonne NSC	1024
Burlington Ordnance Plant	1181
Camden	1104
Clifton	958
Coyle ANG	983
Dover	504
Earle NAD	770
Elizabeth	953
Fort Dix	983
Fort Hancock	951
Fort Monmouth	770
Gibbsboro AFS	872
Jersey City	871
Lakehurst NAS	947
McGuire AFB	983
Newark IAP	1024
Perth Amboy	1024
Picatinny Arsenal	430
Trenton	968
NEW MEXICO	
Albuquerque IAP/Kirtland AFB	1394
Cannon AFB/Clovis	1297
Carlsbad	1993
Cloudcroft	36
Farmington MAP	749
Holloman AFB/Alamogordo	1870
Kirtland AFB/Albuquerque IAP	1394
Las Cruces	1585
Melrose Range	1230
Roswell	1560

State Station	Annual Cooling Degree Days
Sacramento Peak	122
Truth Or Consequences	1558
Tucumcari	1357
Walker AFB/Roswell	1500
White Sands Missile Range	2243
Wingate Army Depot	593
Zuni	473
NEW YORK	
Albany	574
Army Procurement Center	1048
Binghampton/Broome Co Aprt	369
Brooklyn Navy Shipyard	1048
Buffalo IAP	437
Camp Drum	452
Dunkirk MAP	373
Fort Hamilton	861
Fort Tilden	861
Fort Totten	1048
Fort Wadsworth	861
Freeport	861
Glen Falls/Warren Co Aprt	495
Griffiss AFB/Rome	472
Huntington	881
Ithaca/Tompkins Co Aprt	384
Jamestown/Chautauqua Co	470
Liverpool	551
Lockport AFS	493
Montauk AFS	359
New Rochelle	913
New York/JFK IAP	861
New York/La Guardia Aprt	1048

State Station	Annual Cooling Degree Days
NEW YORK (continued)	
New York NB	1048
Newburgh/Stewart Aprt	731
Niagara Falls IAP	549
Ogdensburg	417
Oswego	435
Plattsburg AFB	341
Poughkeepsie/Dutchess Co	809
Rochester/Monroe Co Aprt	531
Roslyn	881
Saint Albans NAVHOSP	861
Saratoga AFS	540
Schenectady	642
Seneca Army Depot	655
Suffolk Co/Westhampton Bch	547
Syracuse/Hancock IAP	591
Troy	574
Utica/Oneida Co Aprt	467
Watertown IAP	461
Watervliet Arsenal	654
Westchester Co/White Plains	810
West Point USMA	830
Whitestone	1048
Yonkers	913
Youngstown	549
NORTH CAROLINA	
Asheville MAP	872
Badin ANG	1596
Camp Lejeune MCS	1810
Cape Hatteras	1550
Charlotte/Douglas MAP	1596

State Station	Annual Coo Degree
Cherry Point MCAS	
Dare County	
Edenton Recovery Site	
Elizabeth City CGAS/MAP	
Fort Bragg/Simmons AAF	
Fort Fisher AFS	
Greensboro	
New River MCAS	
Pope AFB/Fayetteville	
Raleigh/Raleigh-Durham Aprt	
Roanoke Rapids AFS	
Seymour Johnson AFB	
Sunnypoint Mil Ocean Trml	
Wadesboro ANG	
Wilmington/New Hanover Co	
Winston-Salem	
NORTH DAKOTA	
Bismarck MAP	
Dickinson MAP	
Fargo/Hector Field	
Finley AFS	
Fortuna AFS	
Grand Forks AFB	
Minot AFB	
OHIO	
Akron/Akron-Canton Aprt	
Blue Ash ANGB/Cincinnati	[illegible]
Camp Perry ANG	
Chillicothe	[illegible]
Cincinnati Aprt/Covington	[illegible]

State Station	Annual Cooling Degree Days
OHIO (continued)	
Cleveland/Hopkins IAP	613
Clinton County AFB/Wilmington	908
Columbus IAP	809
Dayton MAP	936
Fort Hayes	809
Gentile AFS	1036
Lima/Allen Co Aprt	828
Lima Ordnance Mod Center	828
Lorain Co Reg Aprt	676
Mansfield/Lahm MAP	818
Newark	761
Portsmouth	1217
Ravenna AAP	577
Rickenbacker AFB/Columbus	933
Ridgewood AAP	1080
Springfield MAP	1009
Toledo/Toledo Express Aprt	685
Wright-Patterson AFB/Dayton	1036
Youngstown MAP	518
Zanesville MAP	754
OKLAHOMA	
Altus AFB	2347
Clinton-Sherman AFB	1904
Fort Sill/Post AAF	2217
McAlster NAD	2106
Norman	2067
Oklahoma City AFS	2068
Oklahoma City Aprt	1876
Stillwater/Searcy Field	1947
Tinker AFB/Oklahoma City	2068
Tulsa IAP	1949

State Station	Annual Cooling Degree Days
Vance AFB/Enid	2088
OREGON	
Astoria	13
Burns	289
Corvallis MAP	231
Eugene	239
Grants Pass	553
Keno AFS	50
Kingsley Field	228
Klamath Falls	228
Medford	562
Mt Hebo AFS	27
North Bend AFS	0
Pendleton	656
Portland IAP	300
Redmond	170
Salem/McNary Field	232
Umatilla Army Depot	738
PENNSYLVANIA	
Allentown	772
Altoona/Blair Co Aprt	617
Brookville	417
Carlisle Barracks	995
Columbia	1025
Erie IAP	373
Folsom	1104
Fort Indiantown Gap	945
Frankford Arsenal	1104
Harrisburg IAP/Olmsted	1025
Johnstown/Cambria Co Aprt	170

State Station	Annual Cooling Degree Days
PENNSYLVANIA (continued)	
Lancaster	826
Letterkenny Army Depot	793
Mechanicsburg	1025
New Castle	665
New Cumberland Chem Plant	1025
Philadelphia IAP	1104
Philipsburg	277
Pittsburg/Gtr Pittsburg IAP	647
Reading MAP	1066
Scranton AAP	630
State College ANG Station	583
Tobyhanna Army Depot	434
Valley Forge General Hosp	950
Wilkes-Barre-Scranton Aprt	608
Williamsport	698
Willow Grove NAS	946
RHODE ISLAND	
Davisville	690
Newport NB	690
North Kingston ANG Sta	690
North Smithfield ANG Sta	502
Providence/Theo T Green MAP	532
Quonset Point NAS	690
SOUTH CAROLINA	
Aiken AFS	2012
Beaufort MCAS	2294
Charleston AFB/MAP	2078
Charleston Army Depot	2078
Columbia	2087

State Station	Annual Cool Degree D
Donaldson AFB/Greenville	1
Florence MAP	1
Fort Jackson	2
Georgetown	2
Greenville-Spartanburg Aprt	1
McEntire ANGB/Columbia	1
Myrtle Beach AFB	1
North Charleston AFS	2
North Field	2
Parris Island MARCORPCRUITDEP	2
Pointsett	2
Shaw AFB/Sumter	2
Sumter	2
SOUTH DAKOTA	
Aberdeen MAP	
Ellsworth AFB/Rapid City	
Huron	
Pierre MAP	
Rapid City	
Sioux Falls/Foss Fld	
TENNESSEE	
Alcoa ANG Sta	1
Arnold Eng Dev Cen	1
Bristol/Tri City Aprt	1
Chattanooga/Lovell Field	1
Holston Ordnance Works	1
Kingsport	1
Knoxville/Alcoa ANG Sta	1
Memphis Army Depot	2
Memphis IAP	2
Memphis NAS/Millington	1

State Station	Annual Cooling Degree Days
TENNESSEE (continued)	
Milan Ordnance Plant	1637
Nashville	1694
Stewart AFB/Smyrna	1691
Tullahoma Aprt	1423
Tullahoma/Arnold AFS	1212
Volunteer Ordnance Works	1636
TEXAS	
Abilene MAP	2466
Aero Maintenance Center	3474
Amarillo	1433
Austin/Robert Mueller MAP	2908
Beaumont/Jefferson Co	2798
Beaumont Army Hospital	2098
Beeville/Chase Field NAS	3389
Bergstrom AFB/Austin	3078
Brooke Army Medical Center	2994
Brooks AFB	3339
Brownsville IAP	3874
Brownwood	2588
Camp Bullis	2270
Carswell AFB/Fort Worth	2858
Corpus Christi IAP	3474
Corpus Christi NAS	3687
Dallas/Love Field	2755
Dallas NAS/Hensley Field	2751
Del Rio IAP	3363
Dyess AFB/Abilene	2500
Eagle Pass AFS	3621
Ellington AFB/Houston	2937
El Paso IAP	2098

State Station	Annual Cooling Degree Days
Fort Bliss/Biggs AAF	2253
Fort Hood/Hood AAF	2792
Fort Hood/Robert Gray AAF	2792
Fort Sam Houston	2994
Fort Wolters	2440
Fort Worth IAP	2587
Galveston	3004
Garland ANG Station	2755
Goodfellow AFB/San Angelo	2702
Harlingen	3939
Hondo MAP	3009
Houston IAP	2889
Kelly AFB/San Antonio	3190
Kingsville NAS	3669
Lackland AFB	3190
Laredo IAP	4137
Laredo AFB	4137
Laughlin AFB	3281
Lone Star Ordnance Plant	2245
Longhorn Ordnance Works	2459
Lubbock	1647
Lufkin AFS	2592
Midland	2250
Nederland ANG Station	2798
Oilton Msl Tracking Site	4137
Orange	2739
Paris/Cox Field	2247
Perrin AFB/Sherman	2337
Port Arthur	2798
Randolph AFB/San Antonio	2995
Red River Army Depot	2245

State / Station	Annual Cooling Degree Days
TEXAS (continued)	
Reese AFB/Lubbock	1738
San Angelo/Mathis Field	2702
San Antonio IAP	2994
San Antonio AFS	2994
Sheppard AFB/Wichita Falls	2606
Tyler/Pounds Field	2388
Waco/James Connally Aprt	2878
Waco/Madison Cooper	2863
Webb AFB/Big Spring	2382
Wichita Falls MAP	2611
UTAH	
Bryce Canyon	41
Cedar City	615
Deseret Test Center	639
Dugway PG/Michales AAF	1088
Hill AFB/Ogden	920
Hill AF Range	1051
Ogden MAP	814
Provo	892
Salt Lake City IAP	927
Tooele Army Depot	859
Utah Army Depot	814
Wendover AF Range	1137
VERMONT	
Burlington IAP	396
St Albans AFS	280
VIRGINIA	
Arlington Hall	1415
Bedford AFS	194

State / Station	Annual Cooling Degree Days
Cameron Station	14
Camp A P Hill	1[illegible]
Camp Pickett/Blackstone AAF	1[illegible]
Cape Charles AFS	15
Charlottesville	12
Dahlgren NAVSURFWPNCEN	13
Dam Neck	14
Dulles IAP	9
Fort Belvoir/Davison AAF	1[illegible]
Fort Eustis/Felker AAF	15
Fort Lee	13
Fort Lee AFS	13
Fort Monroe	15
Fort Myer	14
Fort Story	14
Langley AFB/Hampton	15
Little Creek NAVPHIBASE	14
Lynchburg MAP	11
Manassas/Davis Field	11
Newport News/Patrick Henry	15
Norfolk	14
Norfolk NAS/Chambers Field	17
Oceana NAS	14
Portsmouth	14
Quantico MCAS	13
Radford Ordnance Works	7
Richmond/Byrd IAP	13
Richmond Quartermaster Depot	13
Roanoke/Woodrum Aprt	10
Staunton/Shenandoah Valley	10
Vint Hill Farms Station	9

State Station	Annual Cooling Degree Days
VIRGINIA (continued)	
Williamsburg	1345
Yorktown	1539
WASHINGTON	
Aberdeen	13
Bangor	89
Bellingham IAP	44
Blaine AFS	44
Bremerton NAVSHIPYD	89
Ephrata MAP	941
Everett	49
Fairchild AFB/Spokane	416
Fort Lawton	60
Fort Lewis/Gray AAF	110
Four Lake Comm Sta ANG	416
Keyport	89
Longview	135
Madigan Army Hospital	94
Makah AFS	0
Marietta	44
McChord AFB/Tacoma	94
Mica Peak AFS	109
Moses Lake/Grant Co	707
Olympia	101
Othello AFS	666
Paine AFB/Everett	60
Pasco/Tri-Cities Aprt	826
Seattle NSA	162
Seattle-Tacoma IAP	129
Spokane IAP	388
Tacoma	138
Tatoosh Island	0
Walla Walla Aprt	793
Whidbey Island/Ault Fld	6
Whidbey Is/Oak Harbor	24
Yakima Firing Center	479
Yakima MAP	479
WEST VIRGINIA	
Beckley/Raleigh Co Aprt	490
Charleston/Kanawha Aprt	1055
Elkins/Randolph Co Aprt	389
Fairmont	841
Huntington	1098
Martinsburg MAP	922
Parkersburg	1045
Wheeling/Ohio Co Aprt	647
WISCONSIN	
Antigo AFS	318
Badger Ordnance Works	631
Camp McCoy	573
Green Bay/Austin-Straubel	386
La Crosse MAP	695
Madison/Truax Field	460
Milwaukee/Gen Mitchell Fld	450
Oshkosh/Wittman Field	547
Volk Field ANG/Camp Douglas	708
WYOMING	
Casper IAP	458
Cheyenne MAP	327
F E Warren AFB/Cheyenne	327
Lander/Hunt Field	383
Rock Springs	227
Sheridan	446

CHAPTER 6

COOLING DEGREE DAY DATA FOR SITES OUTSIDE THE UNITED STATES

Area / Country / Station	Annual Cooling Degree Days
Africa	
Algeria	
Alger	1453
Ethiopia	
Addis Ababa	507
Kenya	
Mandera	7004
Libya	
Benghazi	2322
Wheelus AB	2167
Morocco	
Kenitra/Port Lyautey	1044
Rabat-Sale	781
Somalia	
Mogadiscio	5551
South Africa	
Pretoria	1543
Sudan	
Khartoum	7576
United Arab Republic/Egypt	
Alexandria/Nouzha	2243
Cairo IAP	3089
Asia	
Aden	
Aden IAP	6945

Area / Country / Station	Annual Cooling Degree Days
Afghanistan	
Kabul IAP	1171
China	
Peking	1486
Shanghai	1816
Hong Kong	
Hong Kong IAP	3266
India	
Bombay	5886
Calcutta	5811
Hyderabad	5317
Madras	6855
New Delhi	5230
Iran	
Abadan IAP	5641
Esfahan	2005
Kerman	1736
Tehran/Mehrabad IAP	2286
Israel	
Jerusalem	1415
Tel Aviv	1932
Japan	
Atsugi NAS	1278
Futema MCAS/Okinawa	3141
Itazuke Aux Airfield	1566
Iwakuni MCAS	1555
Kadena AB/Okinawa	3168
Misawa AB	520
Nagasaki	1773

Country / Station	Annual Cooling Degree Days
Japan (continued)	
Nagoya/Komaki AB	1552
Osaki IAP	1497
Sapporo	437
Sasebo NB	1788
Tokyo IAP	1371
Yokosuka FWC	1315
Yokota AB	1192
Jordan	
Amman	1838
Korea	
Kangnung	892
Kunsan AB	1274
Kwangju AB	1479
Mosulpo	1381
Osan AB	1183
Pusan IAP	1200
Seoul/Kimpo IAP	1063
Taegu	1475
Kuwait	
Kuwait IAP	5625
Lebanon	
Beirut IAP	2183
Pakistan	
Karachi Aprt	5150
Peshawar	4190
Saudi Arabia	
Dhahran AB	5906

Country / Station	Annual Cooling Degree Days
Taiwan	
Ching Chuan Kang AB	3055
Tainan AB	3926
Taipei IAP	3269
Thailand	
Bangkok/Don Muang IAP	6602
Chiangmai	4675
Korat	5876
Nakhon Phanom	5122
Ubon	5718
Udorn	5647
U-Tapao	6371
Turkey	
Ankara/Esenboga	765
Cigli AB/Izmir	1720
Diyarbakir AB	2223
Incirlik AB/Adana	2391
Istanbul/Yesilkoy	979
Malatya	1552
Vietnam	
Saigon/Tan Son Nhut	6564
<u>Atlantic Ocean</u>	
Azores	
Lajes Field	621
Bermuda	
Bermuda NAS/Kindley AFB	2631
Iceland	
Keflavik NAS	0

Area / Country / Station	Annual Cooling Degree Days
Australia	
New South Wales	
Sydney IAP	923
Northern Territory	
Darwin	5714
Queensland	
Townsville	4209
South Australia	
Adelaide	644
Woomera	2262
Western Australia	
Northwest Cape	3952
Perth IAP	1189
Caribbean Sea	
Bahama Islands	
Grand Bahama AAFB	3634
Cuba	
Guantanamo Bay NAS	5537
Puerto Rico	
Ramey AFB/Aquadilla	4709
Roosevelt Roads NAS	5576
San Juan/Isle Verde	4982
Central America	
Canal Zone	
Albrook AFB	6003

Area / Country / Station	Annual Cooling Degree Days
Europe	
Austria	
Innsbruck	313
Belgium	
Brussels IAP	146
Ostend	63
Denmark	
Copenhagen/Kastrup	90
Finland	
Helsinki/Seutula	130
France	
Bordeaux/Merignac	309
Lyon/Bron	351
Marseille/Marignane	899
Nantes	172
Paris/Orly	193
Germany	
Ansbach	168
Augsburg	237
Bad Tolz/Greiling AAF	104
Berlin/Tempelhof AB	235
Bitberg AB	93
Bremen	203
Bremerhaven	112
Coburg	212
Feucht AAF	218
Frankfort/Rhein Main AB	191

Area Country Station	Annual Cooling Degree Days
Germany (continued)	
Giebelstadt AAF	157
Grafenwohr AAF	88
Hahn AB/Hunsruck	71
Hanau AAF	256
Hannover	203
Heidelberg AAF	311
Illesheim AAF	221
Kitzingen AAF	301
Muenster	221
Munich	139
New Ulm	206
Nurnberg/Furth AAF	157
Ramstein AB/Landstuhl	107
Rhein Main AB	191
Sembach AB	113
Spangdahlem AB	94
Stuttgart/Echterdingen AB	154
Tempelhof AB/Berlin	235
Wiesbaden AB	219
Wurzburg	338
Zweibrucken AB	131
Greece	
Athens/Hellinikon Aprt	2002
Iraklion AS/Crete	1550
Souda Bay/Crete	1474
Hungary	
Budapest/Ferihegy	602

Area Country Station	Annual Cooling Degree Days
Ireland	
Dublin IAP	68
Shannon IAP	92
Italy	
Aviano AB	629
Brindisi	1103
Cagliari/Elmas/Sardinia	1177
Firenze	955
Livorno/Leghorn	1008
Milano/Linate	868
Monte Cimone	4
Monte Venda	546
Naples NAF	1024
Pisa/San Guisto	920
Rome/Ciampino	1116
Sigonella NAF/Sicily	1472
Venezia/Tessera	717
Verona/Villafranca	884
Netherlands	
Soesterberg AB	103
Norway	
Oslo/Fornebu	140
Poland	
Warsaw/Okecie	258
Portugal	
Lisbon/Portela	864
Spain	
Alicante/Santa Pola	1482

Area Country Station	Annual Cooling Degree Days
Spain (continued)	
Cordoba	2059
Madrid	1022
Menorca/Mahon	1137
Moron AB	1667
Rota Naval Station	1195
Torrejon AB/Madrid	889
Zaragoza AB	1049
Sweden	
Goteborg/Torslanda	64
Stockholm/Bromma	159
Switzerland	
Bern	240
Geneva/Cointrin	334
United Kingdom	
Aberdeen/Dyce Scotland	22
Alconbury RAF Sta	39
Bentwaters RAF Sta	30
Edinburgh/Scotland	34
Flyingdales	8
Greenham Common	30
Lakenheath RAF Sta	53
Leuchars/Scotland	10
Liverpool Aprt	54
London/Heathrow Aprt	92

Area Country Station	Annual Cooling Degree Days
Wethersfield RAF Sta	38
USSR	
Moscow/Sheremetievo	259
Yugoslavia	
Belgrade IAP	785
<u>Indian Ocean</u>	
Chagos Archipelago	
Diego Garcia NB	5854
<u>North America</u>	
Canada	
Argentia NAS/Placentia Nfld	7
Calgary Aprt Alta	105
Cambridge Bay Aprt NWT	0
Cape Dyer NWT	0
Cape Parry NWT	0
Churchill Man	0
Edmonton/Namao Aprt Alta	136
Fort Nelson BC	105
Fort Smith Aprt NWT	93
Frobisher Bay NWT	0
Gander IAP Nfld	74
Goose Bay AB Nfld	56
Grand Prairie Alta	83
Halifax IAP NS	80
Hall Beach NWT	0

Area Country Station	Annual Cooling Degree Days
Canada (continued)	
Ottawa IAP Ont	387
Port Hardy BC	0
Prince George BC	56
Resolute Aprt NWT	0
St. Johns/Torbay Aprt Nfld	14
Saskatoon Sask	256
Stephenville Aprt Nfld	25
The Pas Man	151
Toronto IAP Ont	445
Vancouver IAP BC	72
Whitehorse YT	16
Winnipeg IAP Man	339
Yarmouth NS	19
Greenland	
Easterly Ice Cap	0
Kulusak	0
Sondrestrom AB	0
Thule AB	0
Mexico	
Mexico City/Tacubaya	396
Pacific Ocean	
Carolina Islands	
Koror Is Aprt	6008
Ponape	5652
Truk	5888
Yap	5916
Johnston Island	
Johnston AFB	5086

Area Country Station	Annual Cooling Degree Days
Mariana Islands	
Guam/Agana NAS	5865
Guam/Andersen AFB	5398
Marshall Islands	
Eniwetok	6299
Kwajalein/Bucholz AAF	6164
Majuro	5904
Midway Island	
Midway Island NAVSTA	2752
New Zealand	
Christchurch	57
Mount John	0
Wellington Aprt	117
Philippine Islands	
Baguio	750
Clark AB	5762
Cubi Point NAS	6285
Sangley Pt FWC	6340
Subic Bay NB	6285
Wake Island	
Wake Island AFB	5455
South America	
Argentina	
Buenos Aires	1342
La Quiaca	0
Brazil	
Rio de Janeiro Aprt	4145

Area Country Station	Annual Cooling Degree Days
Chile	
Santiago/Pupahuel	572
Columbia	
Bogota/Eldorado	37
Equador	
Quito/Mariscal Sucre	76
French Guiana	
Cayenne	5156
Paraguay	
Asuncion/Stroessner	4095
Peru	
Lima/Callao	1592
Surinam	
Zanderij/Paramaribo	5542
Uruguay	
Montevideo/Carrasco	1047
Venezuela	
Caracas/La Carlota	2868

BY ORDER OF THE SECRETARIES OF THE AIR FORCE, THE ARMY, AND THE NAVY

OFFICIAL

JAMES J. SHEPARD, Colonel, USAF
Director of Administration

LEW ALLEN, JR., General, USAF
Chief of Staff

OFFICIAL

J. C. PENNINGTON
Brigadier General, United States Army
The Adjutant General

BERNARD W. ROGERS
General, United States Army
Chief of Staff

D. G. ISELIN
Rear Admiral, CEC, U. S. Navy
Commander, Naval Facilities
Engineering Command

SUMMARY OF CHANGES

The statistics in this revision are based on a 15-year period of record of hourly surface observations when available. Statistics included for the first time in this manual are as follows: Prevailing wind direction and mean wind speed coincident with the 97½% temperature, annual heating degree days, mean daily range of the dry bulb temperature and the prevailing wind direction coincident with the 2½% dry bulb temperature, and annual cooling degree days. In chapters 3 and 4 the three time periods have been started 1-hour earlier in order to better define time periods in which various facilities are used. A list of abbreviations used has been included. Coordinates and elevations for all sites are listed. The 10% values of summer dry and wet bulb temperatures have been deleted.

Distribution:

Air Force: F

Army: To be distributed in accordance with DA Form 12-34B, requirements for TM 5-800 series: Engineering and Design for Real Property Facilities.

Navy: (2 copies each unless otherwise specified)

SNDL 23A1 (COMNAVFORAZORES only); 24J1; 27G (SUPPFORANTARCTICA only); 39B; 39C1 (Twentieth only); 39E; 42A3; 45B; 51A; 51B1; 51B3; B1 (SECDEF only); B2 (JCS, NSA, DLA, and DNA only); B5 (USCG only); C4F9 (Annapolis only); C4F9 (Port Hueneme only (3 copies)); C4F9 (New London only 15 copies)); C4F36; C4J (SHAPE only); C4N (6th MARCORPS only); E3A (Washington and Oakland only); FA6 (Bermuda, Brunswick, Cecil Field, Key West, Jacksonville, Virginia Beach only); FA7 (Guantanamo, Keflavic, Mayport, Roosevelt Roads only); FA10; FA18; FA23 (Antigua, Barbados, Brawdy, Buxton, Eleuthera, Lewes, Turks Island only); FA25 (10 copies each); FA32; FB6; FB7 (Alameda, Barbers Point, Fallon, Lemoore, Oak Harbor, Miramar, North Island, Moffet Field only); FB10 (Adak and Midway only); FB21; FB26; FB31 (Subic Bay and Guam only); FB34 (Okinawa only); FB36 (Big Sur, Coos Head, Ferndale, and Pacific Beach only); FB41; FC3 (London only); FC4 (Sigonella only); FC5; FC7; FC12; FD2; FE2; FE4 (Edzell, Galeta Island, Homestead, Winter Harbor, Sabana Seca, and Sonoma only); FF1 (Washington only); FF4; FF6; FF19 (Brooklyn, Long Beach, New Orleans, and Seattle only); FF38; FG2 (Balboa, Diego Garcia, Harold Holt, Morocco, Nea Makri, Stockton, and Ponce only); FG3 (Cheltenham and East Machias only); FG6 (Wahiawa, and Norfolk only); FH3 (Beaufort only); FH6 (Bethesda Only); FH8 (Cairo Only); FH25 (Philadelphia, Portsmouth Va, Camp Lejeune, Oakland, Newport, Great Lakes, and Long Beach only); FKA6A1; FKA6A2; FKA6A3A; FKA6A3B; FKA6A9; FKA6A12; FKA6A15 (Code LA 151); FKA6A16; FKA6B1; FKM8; FKM9; FKM12; FKM13; FKM15 (Phildelphia 19111 only); FKN1 (North, Lant and Ches Only (25 copies each)); FKN1 (West only (115 copies)); FKN1 (South and Pac only (55 copies each)); FKN2 (Port Hueneme only (4 copies)); FKN3 (Less Bremerton) (15 copies each); FKN3 (Bremerton only 25 copies each); FKN5 (15 copies each); FKN8; FKN10; FKP1A; FKP1B (less Concord); FKP1B (Concord Only (3 copies)); FKP1E; FKP1J; FKP1M; FKP3A; FKP7 (5 copies each); FKP8; FKP11; FKQ3; FKR1A; FKR1B; FKR2A (Dallas only); FKR3A (3 copies each); FKR3H; FKR4B; FKR5; FR3; FR4; FR9 (San Francisco only); FT1; FT2; FT6 (less Kingsville); FT6 (Kingsville only 3 copies)); FT13; FT18; FT19 (San Diego only); FT22; FT27 (Idaho Falls only); FT28 (4 copies each); FT31; FT37; FT55; FT63; FT64;

FT73; FT74A (Colorado, MIT, Purdue, and Texas only); FT74B (California, Illinois, Rensselaer, Georgia Tech, and Tulane only); FT76 (3 copies each); FT78 (3 copies each); V1; V2; V3; V5 (Less Kaneohe Bay and Iwakuni) (6 copies each); V5 (Kaneohe Bay and Iwakuni (2 Copies)); V8; V12 (15 copies each); V14; V15; V16 (15 copies each); V17; V23 (Albany only).

Copy to: (1 copy each unless otherwise specified)

SNDL 21A; A2A (ONR only); A3; A4A; A5 (2 copies each); A6 (Code LFF,(2 copies)); FD1; FE1; FG1; FKA1A; FKA1B (2 copies each); FKA1C (Code (043) 20 copies each); FKA1F (2 copies); FKN2 (Port Hueneme (Code 156) only (2 copies)); FR1.

*U.S

Lightning Source UK Ltd.
Milton Keynes UK
UKHW011603120219
337178UK00008B/481/P

9 780260 314567